DICTIONARY OF
JEWISH
BIOGRAPHY

DICTIONARY OF JEWISH BIOGRAPHY

Geoffrey Wigoder

SIMON & SCHUSTER
A Paramount Communications Company

New York   London   Toronto   Sydney   Tokyo   Singapore

Academic Reference Division
Simon and Schuster
15 Columbus Circle, New York, NY 10023

A Paramount Communications Company

Library of Congress Cataloging-in-Publication Data

Wigoder, Geoffrey, 1922-
    Dictionary of Jewish biography / Geoffrey Wigoder.
        p.   cm.
    ISBN 0-13-210105-X
    1. Jews— Biography— Dictionaries.   I. Title.
DS115.W49   1991
920 0092924— dc20   90- 29276
    [B]   CIP

CONTRIBUTORS

Donna Abraham
Helene I, Avraham
Michael Ajzensdadt
Shlomo Carmel
Chrystaı Corcos
Elizabeth Eppler
Eda Flexer
Elaine Hoter
David Geffen
Judith Goldberg
Shlomo Ketko
Michael L. Klein-Katz
Tsipi Kuper-Blau
Julian Landau
Rachel Lev-Ari
Pesah Lichtenberg
Debbie Lipson
Sol Liptzin
Meron Medzini
Chanah Moshe
Arieh Newman
Yael Oberman
Avraham Oz

Judith Paull
Leon Paull
David Pileggi
Robert Rockaway
Victor Roth
Robert Rozette
Suzan Hersh Sachs
Denise Salama
Marc Elliott Shapiro
Jesse Silver
Gabriel Sivan
Channah Slutzkin
David Solomon
Dora Sowden
Julie Stahl
Sefton D. Temkin
Pascal Themanlys
Hillel Tryster
Bernard Wasserstein
Geoffrey Wigoder
Ora Wiskind
Danny Wool

Project Manager: Georgette Corcos
Production Manager: Rachel Gilon
Layout: Techiya Rosenthal
Illustration Research: Sharon Rothschild

FOREWORD

"Let us now praise famous men, and our fathers that begat us. The Lord created in them great glory, even his mighty power from the beginning. Such as did bear rule in their kingdoms, and were renowned for their power, giving counsel by their understanding, such as have brought tiding in prophecies: leaders of the people by their counsels, and by their understanding, men of learning for the people; wise were their words in their instruction; such as sought out musical tunes, and set forth verses in writing; rich men furnished with ability, living peaceably in their habitations; all these were honored in their generations and were a glory in their days." (*Ecclesiasticus*, 44:1-7)

These words, written two thousand years ago by Ben Sira, are an early expression of the Jewish admiration for its elite. For Jews, historical memory has always been crucial, and the memory of their great men and women has played a major role in Jewish education and consciousness.

The nature of the Jewish elite has changed through history. In Bible times, it comprised the pioneers of the Jewish people and its faith and practice: the patriarchs, Moses, the prophets, leaders of the nation, and kings and warriors such as David and Judah the Maccabee. By the end of the Second Temple period, the spotlight had been turned on outstanding rabbinical thinkers, and for the 1,700 years after the destruction of the Temple, the paragon was the man of Jewish learning. After the Jews emerged from the ghetto beginning with the Emancipation of the late eighteenth century, they entered the world of general culture. From a forced particularism in which they had concentrated almost exclusively on Jewish subjects, they now gloried in the opportunities opened before them and entered the broad scene of world culture. Soon there was not a branch of universal learning and human leadership to which they were not making a contribution. Their long tradition of learning and scholarship was now applied to the universal scene. A simple barometer of the resulting achievements is the disproportionately high number of Jewish Nobel Prize winners. With the emergence of modern Zionism and the establishment of the State of Israel, political and military leaders in a Jewish framework have reemerged as members of the elite, closing the circle since Bible times.

This volume was inspired, on the one hand, by the Jewish tradition of recalling its famous men and women, often as role models, and on the other, by the existence of dictionaries of national biography in various countries. Many of these dictionaries are national in scope and multivolume. *The Dictionary of Jewish Biography* is much more modest and popular in presentation, aiming to give more than the dry facts usually found in standard reference works. In the period between the two World Wars, a number of works were commissioned to describe the Jewish contribution to civilization. While containing excellent material, they were apologetically motivated to counter the then-current theories, propounded particularly by the Nazis, that the Jews were an "inferior race." Such nonsense is not heard these days and works on Jews can be written without need for the sort of inner censorship that once prevented describing weak as well as strong points of character and filtered out figures who were notorious or colorful rather than singularly praiseworthy.

One problem in any Jewish reference book is determining who is Jewish. In the modern world, Jewish identity is a complex matter and often not given to the easy solutions of pre-Emancipation times. In editing this volume we have followed the precedents of most standard Jewish reference works. First, we go by the traditional Jewish religious principle that a person born a Jew is always regarded as a Jew "no matter how much he sins." This applies even in the case of converts to other faiths or those who publicly disassociate themselves from Judaism or the Jewish people — although we note of course any such public act. We also accept as candidates for inclusion any person with either a Jewish mother or a Jewish father or who has converted to Judaism. Inevitably there are dubious borderline cases where a decision in either direction could prove controversial.

Also controversial is the selection of representative individuals. No hard-and-fast rules can be laid down and followed with ease. In any encyclopedia or Who's Who there must be some subjectivity as to who is included and who omitted. A line has to be drawn and there will always be figures who fall close to either side of it. Readers of this work, especially book reviewers, will at once ask why x is in and y is out. Decision, had to be made, and those figures considered but regretfully omitted could easily fill another volume — a possibility we entertain with enthusiasm. One rule that we were able to make and follow was the rule to exclude the living, for whom the criteria of inclusion are especially problematic. We are also aware that we may be criticized for the comparatively low proportion of women, but this reflects the realities of much of Jewish life. From Bible times to the nineteenth century, few women entered the Jewish elite. This can be explained and regretted but it must be accepted as a fact. In modern times, the situation has changed — as is reflected in our pages — but there is still a lack of proportion in much of the Jewish elite.

This dictionary contains a number of special features. One of these is the use of boxed inserts for quotations by or about the subject of the biography or for special anecdotes or piquant information. We have also sought originality in our selection of illustrations, avoiding the usual portraits that tend to be found in similar works of biography. We have looked instead for action pictures showing the subject at work or in an unusual environment or with friends. For some subjects — especially those whose contribution lay in the visual arts — we have selected a painting, sculpture, photograph, or cartoon. This, we hope, will add to the liveliness of the volume. The bibliographies at the ends of articles focus on books in English.

Finally, I wish to convey my thanks to the publishers, Charles E. Smith of Simon and Schuster and Shlomo S. Gafni of The Jerusalem Publishing House, for their understanding and cooperation. Appreciation is also due to Georgette Corcos, coordinator of the project, without whom the many challenges could not have been overcome.

Geoffrey Wigoder

"Read no history, only biography, for that is life without theory."

Disraeli

A

AARON (c. 13th cent. BCE) First Israelite high priest and founder of the priestly family, elder brother of Moses (q.v.) and a member of the tribe of Levi, which became consecrated to the service of the sanctuary, and later the Temple. When Moses - because of his stammer - was reluctant to accept the divine order to appear before Pharaoh and demand the release of the enslaved Israelites, God told him to take Aaron as his spokesman. The brothers acted together during the period of the ten plagues, although Moses was always the major figure. Aaron personally brought on three of the plagues, using the staff given by God to Moses. With the Exodus his role diminished, but when Moses was on Mount Sinai, the people became impatient and turned to Aaron with their request to make a golden calf for them to worship. Aaron gathered their golden ornaments and fashioned the idol. After Moses' descent, God wished to destroy Aaron, but he was saved at Moses' intercession (Deut. 9:20).

When the sanctuary was constructed, Moses appointed Aaron its high priest, whom he anointed and dressed in the special robes ordained for the office (Lev. 8-10). Of Aaron's four sons, who were also consecrated for the priesthood, two, Nadab and Abihu, met their death for offering "a strange fire." The other two, Eleazar and Ithamar, served faithfully, enabling the hereditary continuation of the priesthood, which has traditionally been maintained to the present (*kohen*, the Hebrew for priest, is in various forms still preserved in many Jewish names) among the descendants of Aaron.

Aaron and his sister Miriam were involved in a quarrel with Moses concerning Moses' wife. Aaron again escaped punishment but Miriam was struck with leprosy and only cured on Aaron's intervention. It was his incense offering on behalf of the Israelites who had sided with Korah in his revolt against Moses that led God to end the plague He had brought on the people as punishment (Num. 16-18). After this incident his priesthood was vindicated and reaffirmed when his staff blossomed with almonds.

Aaron was associated with Moses in striking the rock to produce water instead of addressing it as God had commanded (Num. 20), and both brothers were punished by dying before they entered the Promised Land. Aaron died in the wilderness on Mount Hor, at the age of 123, in the last year of the Israelites' wanderings. Before his death his high-priestly robes were transferred to Eleazar.

Aaron, the High Priest. From an anthology on texts on the Bible, religion, grammar, astrology. France, c. 1280.

AARON IN JEWISH TRADITION

In Jewish tradition Aaron symbolized peace, and Rabbi Hillel, also noted for his peacefulness, stated, "Be of the disciples of Aaron, one who loves peace and pursues it, who loves all men and brings them near to the Torah." (*Avot* 1:12)

ABRABANEL See Abravanel, Isaac

ABBA ARIKHA (Abba bar Aivu or Abba Arikha, i.e., Abba the Tall; known by the epithet Rav c. 175-247) Rabbi who helped to lay the foundations for rabbinic Judaism in Babylonia. Born to a distinguished Babylonian family, he went to Palestine to join his uncle, the noted scholar Rabbi Hiyya, and to study at the academy of Rabbi Judah ha-Nasi (q.v.), who ordained him to teach and to deliver legal decisions. He remained a considerable time in Palestine, achieving widespread recognition.

In 217 Rav returned to Babylonia and two years later founded his own academy in Sura, which for hundreds of years was to remain a great focus of rabbinic teaching and authority. He helped to raise the reputation of Babylonian scholarship, bringing it on a par with Palestinian, and students flocked to his academy in the hundreds. In Rav's time, the academy had 1,200 permanent students, and many others coming for short periods. Although he may not himself have stood at the head of the academy, he was its outstanding figure, his reputation enhanced by the tradition of his descent from the house of David and by his daughter's marriage into the family of the community's lay head, the exilarch.

SAYINGS OF ABBA ARIKHA

- God Himself prays, "May My mercy overcome My anger."
- When your mind is not at ease, do not pray.
- In the future world there will be no eating, drinking, propagation, business, jealousy, hatred or competition, but the righteous will sit with crowns on their heads enjoying the brilliance of the Divine Presence.
- What is improper in public, is forbidden in secret.
- Each individual will be called to account in the hereafter for every enjoyment he declined without sufficient cause.

He was closely associated with Samuel (q.v.) the head of the academy in the town of Nehardea; Samuel excelled in civil law, Rav in ritual law. Their discussions feature prominently throughout the Babylonian Talmud. Rav was a noted homilist and theological interpreter. He was responsible for a New Year prayer emphasizing creation, and composed the standard prayer for the New Moon. Rav regarded Torah study as the supreme duty of the Jew. Stressing ethical teachings, he stated that the advent of the Messiah depended on repentance and the performance of good deeds. However, he strongly opposed asceticism, stating, "Every individual will be made accountable in the world to come for every enjoyment in this world which he refused without adequate reason."
J. Neusner. *A History of the Jews of Babylonia*, 1966-1970, vol. 1 and 2.

ABBAYE (c. 280-338 CE) Babylonian rabbi, head of the academy at Pumbedita. An orphan from the day of his birth, he was educated by his uncle, Rabbah bar Nahmani, and later by Joseph bar Hiyya, who served in turn as head of the Pumbedita academy. Both helped to develop Abbaye's gift for logical analysis and his comprehensive knowledge of traditional sources. As a youth, he was obliged to finance his daytime study by working the land he owned at night; this gave him an understanding of the common people and sheds light on his belief that Torah study should be combined with productive labor.

Together with Rava (q.v.), his childhood companion and fellow student, Abbaye was the leading teacher of the age in Babylonia. After Joseph bar Hiyya's death (c. 323), Abbaye succeeded him in Pumbedita while Rava opened a new academy at Mahoza. The debates of these two men over points of Jewish law derived from the Mishnah, receive a good deal of space in the Talmud, and became virtually synonymous with Talmudic argumentation.

Through private tutorials and public instruction, Abbaye exerted a wide influence; he was a great upholder of rabbinic authority and declared

---

SAYINGS OF ABBAYE

- One should run to synagogue.
- Speak not one thing with your mouth and another with your heart.
- Your servant should be your equal. You should not eat white bread and he black bread; you should not drink old wine and he new wine; you should not sleep on a feather bed and he on straw.
- In prayer always associate yourself with the congregation and say "*Our* God, lead *us....*"

---

that those whom he taught should serve as moral (not merely intellectual) examples. Yet he could also be down-to-earth, quoting familiar proverbs, giving advice about the cure for some ailment, and (when the rabbinic law seemed doubtful) telling his students to "go and see what ordinary folk have to say about the matter."

An exemplary performer of good deeds, Abbaye figured in many popular tales crediting him with the receipt of heavenly communications and immunity from demonic powers. It was Abbaye who began the practice of observing a feast to mark the completed study of a Talmudic tractate, and it was he who fostered the idea of thirty-six "hidden saints" gaining merit in every generation and thus preserving the world from destruction.
J. Neusner, *A History of the Jews in Babylonia*, 1966-1970, vol. 4.

ABRAHAM BEN DAVID OF POSQUIÈRES

(known by the acronym *Ravad*; c. 1125–1198) Talmudic scholar in Provence, southern France. He was born in Narbonne, studied in Lunel, and lived for many years in Posquières, near Nîmes, where he established a Talmudic academy that attracted students from far and near. It is known that for a time (1172–1173), he had to flee Posquières because of the enmity of the local ruler, but he soon returned and resumed his activities. Abraham was the outstanding rabbinic authority of his time in western Europe and queries were referred to him for his ruling from many countries. He enjoyed considerable affluence (possibly through his dealings in textiles) and helped to maintain his academy and subsidize its students.

His literary activity was varied and included codification of rabbinic law, critiques of his predecessors, Talmudic commentaries, homiletics, and responses to legal queries. He was the first scholar to comment on legal literature other than the Talmud. Abraham was an outstanding critic of Moses Maimonides (q.v.), and immediately on the publication of the latter's code, *Mishneh Torah*, wrote a detailed criticism of it, also incorporating approbation for those sections with which he concurred. Among his objections were Maimonides' failure to indicate his sources and his pioneering formulation of dogmas of Judaism which Abraham felt to be contrary to Jewish tradition. He also wrote glosses on the codes of Isaac Alfasi (q.v.) and Zerahiah ben Isaac ha-Levi, and was known as *ba'al hassagot* ("Preeminent Critic"). Abraham feared that the appearance of codes would lead to the neglect of the Talmud, although he himself was the author of codifications that concentrated on practical issues. Not all his writings have been preserved, while some have survived by virtue of their having been incorporated in the works of later authorities.

I. Twersky, *Ravad of Posquières*, 1962.

ABRAHAM

(c. 19th cent. BCE) Biblical patriarch and traditional originator of monotheism. His original name was Abram ("the Father is exalted") but was changed by God to Abraham, interpreted as meaning "father of a multitude of nations" (Gen. 17:5).

He was born in Ur of the Chaldees in southern Mesopotamia and taken by his father, Terah, to Haran in northwestern Mesopotamia, where his father died. There God instructed him to leave his native land for a still undisclosed destination with the divine promise that he would become a great and blessed nation (Gen. 12:1–3). At age seventy-five, he took his wife Sarai (later renamed Sarah [q.v.]), his nephew Lot, and their entire household, and moved to the land of Canaan, which God informed him would be the land of his offspring. He lived a nomadic life, mainly in the southern part of the country (the Negeb), making covenants with the local kings, and expounding his monotheistic creed.

At one period when the land was struck by famine, Abraham and his family went to Egypt, where Abraham, fearing that he might be killed by the Egyptians because of Sarah's beauty, passed her off as his sister. Pharaoh took her to his palace and rewarded Abraham, but when he was afflicted by plagues, he discovered the true relationship and returned Sarah to Abraham.

Back in Canaan, a dispute between the followers of Abraham and Lot led to the two parting company, with Abraham remaining in the Negeb and Lot moving to the Dead Sea region. Subsequently, when four invading kings captured the area where Lot lived and took him captive, Abraham armed

ABRAHAM IN RABBINIC LORE

The rabbis told many stories about Abraham. According to one of the best-known, Abraham was left alone with the idols of his father, Terah. Taking an ax, he destroyed all of them except the largest, in whose hands he placed the ax. When his father saw the damage, he asked who was responsible, and Abraham told him that the remaining idol had shattered all the rest, adding, "If you don't believe me, ask him." His father said angrily: "You are telling lies. These are only wood and stone which I made myself," to which Abraham responded, "So how can you worship these idols who have no power to do anything?"

A similar story is told about Abraham destroying the idols of King Nimrod. Nimrod in his fury ordered Abraham's imprisonment and sentenced him to burn in a great furnace. He was delivered by the angel Gabriel and emerged alive. The princes of Nimrod in reaction acknowledged the One God of Abraham. Because of Abraham's proselytizing activity, he was seen in Jewish tradition as the father of all proselytes, and to this day all converts to Judaism are called "son [or daughter] of Abraham."

his servants, defeated the invaders, and rescued Lot. On his return from this expedition, he encountered Melchizedek, king of Salem (taken to be Jerusalem), whose offer of gifts Abraham magnanimously declined.

In a series of revelations, God promised to grant Abraham a multitude of progeny who would become a great nation. Abraham undertook to serve only the one true God. This was affirmed in a solemn covenant ceremony, and its sign was circumcision, which Abraham performed on himself and on all the male members of his household.

As Sarah remained childless, she gave Abraham her maidservant Hagar as wife and when Abraham was eighty-six, Hagar bore a son, Ishmael. Some thirteen years later, Abraham was visited by three weary travelers, whom he did not recognize at first as angels. His warm reception of these strangers made him a symbol of hospitality in Jewish tradition. They announced that he and Sarah (both of them now aged about a hundred) would have a son. They also informed Abraham of God's decision to destroy Sodom and Gomorrah for their wickedness. Abraham pleaded for them to spare the cities and was answered that God would relent if ten righteous men be found in the cities. Abraham was unsuccessful in this quest and the cities were destroyed by fire and brimstone.

In due course, Sarah bore a son, Isaac (q.v.). As she felt that Ishmael constituted a threat to her son's rightful inheritance, she insisted that Abraham expel Hagar and Ishmael into the wilderness. There an angel of God appeared and they were miraculously saved (Gen. 21).

Abraham's greatest trial came when he was commanded by God to sacrifice Isaac. Unhesitatingly, he obeyed, taking the young lad to a mountain in the land of Moriah. Only at the last moment, when the boy was already bound and Abraham's hand raised with the knife, did an angel intervene to stop him and explain that this was a divine test of his faith. This story was to be influential in Jewish theology as a prototype of complete faith and willingness for martyrdom. Some scholars have seen it as condemnation of the practice of child sacrifice prevalent in those days.

After the death of Sarah, Abraham purchased the cave of Machpelah in Hebron as a family burial plot. In his latter years he saw Isaac marry his kinswoman Rebekah (q.v.), brought by Abraham's servant from the city of Nahor so that Isaac would not take a Canaanite wife. He himself remarried, and had six children with his new wife Keturah. When Abraham died, according to the Bible at age 175, his two sons, Isaac and Ishmael, buried him in the cave of Machpelah.

J. Van Seters, *Abraham in History and Tradition*, 1975.

ABRAHAM, KARL (1877–1925) Psychoanalyst, born in Germany; he completed his medical studies in 1901. In 1905 he began work as a psychiatrist at the famed Burgholzi clinic in Zurich, where he came into contact with C. G. Jung and Eugen Bleuler. In 1907 he met Sigmund Freud (q.v.) and soon became a member of his inner circle. Abraham was the first German psychoanalyst and the founder of the German Psychoanalytic Society and Institute. He analyzed many of the leading early analysts — Theodor Reik (q.v.), Melanie Klein (q.v.), Sandor Rado, Helene Deutsch, and others.

He is remembered as a kind, even-tempered, and optimistic man, with a sharp, critical eye. His experience with severely ill, hospitalized psychiatric patients afforded him the opportunity to extend psychoanalytic theory to manic-depression and schizophrenia. He elaborated upon the phases of infant sexuality posited by Freud — oral, anal, and genital — and he hypothesized that fixations at early stages of development can produce severe psychiatric illness. A milestone in the child's development is the ability to experience ambivalence — a sense that the parent may contain both good and bad qualities. This was in effect an early recognition of the complexity of people and relationships.

In other writings, Abraham interpreted myths and fairy tales in a psychoanalytic light. In a trenchant analysis of war and totem festivals, he noted that in both community action provides sanction for what the individual would never be permitted to do alone.

Abraham's observations made while working with soldiers during World War I enriched the understanding of psychological reactions to the stress of war.

K. Abraham, *Selected Papers* (trans. D. Bryan and A. Strachey), 1953.

M. Grotjahn, "Karl Abraham," in *Psychoanalytic Pioneers* (eds. F. Alexander, S. Eisenstein, M. Grotjahn), 1966.

P. Roazen, *Freud and His Followers*, 1975.

ABRAHAMS, HAROLD MAURICE (1899–1978) British Olympic sprint champion. He followed two older brothers into athletics and Cambridge University. His brother Sidney had represented Great Britain in the 100 meters and the long jump in the 1906 and 1912 Olympic Games.

Between 1920 and 1923 Abrahams enjoyed an outstanding athletic career at Cambridge. He had eight victories over Oxford in three events. He was less successful in the 1920 Olympics in Antwerp, Belgium, where he failed to win a medal.

In 1924 he devoted himself to the Paris Olympic Games. His intensive training produced an English long jump record, and then an Olympic gold medal in the 100 meters and a silver medal as a member of the British 400-meter relay team.

The medal had a bearing on my career, of course. I was a celebrity. People knew me through my victory, but that was not the reason I tried to win. My brothers were both well-known athletes and, eventually, I wanted to show I could do better than they had. When I won, there wasn't any great surge of patriotism in me, though I was pleased for Britain. But another reason why I hardened myself to win was that there was a certain amount of anti-Semitism in those days. Certainly, now, I didn't run in the Olympics to win for all Jews. I ran for myself. But I felt I had become something of an outsider, you know. That may have helped.

Harold Abrahams, 1972

Abrahams recalled: "For months I trained as conscientiously as any runner of my generation. Though I had won all my races in England, I had no illusions about the strength of the opposition, particularly the four Americans, three of whom had been in the final of the 1920 Olympics. Truthfully, I did not think I had a chance of a gold medal, nor did anyone else."

The following year a leg injury ended his competitive career, but not his interest in sport. He became a laywer and was a member of the general committee of the British Amateur Athletic Association for fifty years and became its president, and was secretary, treasurer, and chairman of the British Amateur Athletic Board.

In 1936 Abrahams became a controversial figure when he refused to back attempts to boycott the Berlin Olympics. The *Jewish Chronicle* reported that Abrahams "expressed the view that as an individual he could better assist German Jewry through his contacts in the sporting world. He broadcast for the BBC from the Berlin Olympic stadium when the games opened in Hitler's presence."

The Marquess of Exeter, a good friend and a member of the International Olympic Committee, said of Abrahams, "He was a tremendous collector of statistics relating to the sport and produced a number of volumes on the Olympic and Commonwealth Games. He had a first-class brain and decisive views which he never hesitated to express strongly."

In 1981 a somewhat fictional version of incidents in his athletic career was made into the award-winning motion picture, *Chariots of Fire.*

ABRAVANEL, ISAAC BEN JUDAH (1437–1808)

Statesman, Bible commentator, and philosopher. His name is also spelled Abarbanel. He was descended from a family that had long lived in Seville, Spain, but that emigrated to Portugal after the 1391 massacres. His father was financial adviser to King Alfonso of Portugal, a position also attained by Isaac. Abravanel received a broad education not only in Jewish studies but also in classical and Christian literature. When Alfonso died in 1481 he was succeeded by John II, who broke the power of the nobles. After an unsuccessful revolt, in which Abravanel participated, he found refuge in Castile and was sentenced to death in absentia in Portugal. In Castile, Isaac Abravanel became a financial agent for Queen Isabella and even lent her a large sum of money to carry on her war against the last Spanish Muslim territory in Granada. After this ended in victory in 1492, Isabella and her husband, Ferdinand of Aragon, signed the decree expelling the Jews from Spain.

At this great crisis, Abravanel was the spokesman of the Spanish Jewish community, pleading for the revocation of the edict and diplomatically interceding with leading courtiers for their support. The plea was backed by the offer of a large sum of money. Abravanel appealed to the queen, stressing the eternity of the Jewish people, who had

outlived and would continue to outlive all its persecutors. Moreover, he pointed out that those who sought to destroy the Jews ended by destroying themselves. All arguments and inducements proved useless and the edict was enforced. Abravanel had to leave with his family, although he was allowed to take part of his fortune with him.

He sailed to Naples where again he became a courtier, this time at the court of King Ferdinand I of Naples. However, in 1495 he was on the move again, accompanying the king, who took refuge from the conquering French in Sicily. Abravanel's home was despoiled and his library destroyed. At the beginning of 1496 he moved to Monopoli, a port in southern Italy, where he devoted himself to his literary work. He stayed there for seven years before making his final move to Venice, where once again he was a diplomatic adviser to the ruler.

Abravanel was the author of lengthy commentaries on the Bible (except for the Hagiographa), which were largely philosophical. Instead of writing a verse-by-verse commentary as his predecessors had done, he divided the Bible into sections, providing each section with an introduction opening with six questions, which he proceeded to answer at length. His messianic views were influential, even after the Messiah failed to arrive in 1503 as he had predicted, and strengthened the faith of his despairing fellow exiles. His own political experience served him well in his explanations of politi-

Page from an illustrated Haggadah with a commentary by Isaac Abravanel. Central Europe, 1741.

cal events in the historical books of the Bible. His philosophy is not particularly original and he wanted to eradicate any opinions that could be harmful to faith. Nevertheless, he was respected as the last of the Jewish medieval philosophers and, in Latin translation, his Bible commentaries were extensively used by Christian scholars in the following centuries.

His son **Judah**, known as Leone Ebreo (c. 1460–c. 1523), was a distinguished Renaissance philosopher whose Latin work, *Dialoghi d'Amore*, sought to combine Judaism and Neo-Platonism, with love as the key to the universe and its goal a union with God.

B. Netanyahu, *Don Isaac Abravanel*, 1968.

ADLER, ALFRED (1870–1937) Psychiatrist; founder of the school of individual psychiatry. Although often neglected and occasionally maligned in the history and theory of psychology, he was a creative pioneer in examining interpersonal relationships, in social psychology and group psychotherapy, and in psychosomatic medicine.

Adler was born in a Vienna suburb, the sickly second son of a struggling grain merchant. He barely passed medical school in Vienna, and after a stint in a clinic and the army, opened his own practice there. At this time, he already showed a definite interest in social medicine, publishing a booklet in which he demonstrated that poor work conditions and economic straits, and not just biological factors, may precipitate disease.

In 1902, he met Sigmund Freud (q.v.) and became an early member of the inner circle with which Freud surrounded himself. During the next nine years, Adler contributed a great deal to the development of psychoanalytic thought. It was he who coined the term "inferiority complex." He spoke of organ inferiority, whereby a deficient part of a person's body may lead to feelings of inferiority and attempts to compensate by striving for superiority. This he believed could have far-reaching ramifications for personality and neurosis.

Disagreement on theoretical grounds, in which Adler diminished the role of sexual factors in neurosis, as well as personal competitiveness, led in 1911 to a rupture between Freud and Adler. Adler went on to establish "individual psychology." He emphasized the uniqueness and indivisibility of each human being. He stressed that the personality may be reflected in every action and in every memory. Indeed, one of his well-known innovations was to inquire after earliest memories, which, he believed, regularly revealed much about a personality.

Eventually he developed a psychology that encompassed all human behavior and psychopathology. He stressed the role of environment and society in neurosis. He believed that human behavior is derived from the individual's sense of community and from his own strivings for superiority. He maintained that each person is not simply a victim of unconscious conflicts, but a being who,

Alfred Adler bandaging the arm of a little girl, Sweden, 1934.

with sufficient courage, can discover the hidden goals which determine his behavior and the fictions which may mar his perspective of the world, and in this way change his lifestyle. Thus he believed psychotherapy can lead a patient from secluded self-preoccupation to productive functioning within the community.

His other important contributions include his attention to sibling position in forming character (creating for example, the responsibility-laden eldest, or the pampered youngest), and the concept of masculine protest, a reaction to the unjustified male domination of society. He also became an advocate of therapeutic education, counseling teachers and parents and setting up experimental schools. He was, however, always denied the university post he coveted.

An unassuming man who conducted his meetings in the coffee houses of Vienna, Adler was alienated from his Judaism. He did not want to be a member of a religion limited to one ethnic group. At the age of thirty-four, he had himself and his children baptized and became a Protestant. Late in life, in dialogues with a Lutheran minister, he attempted to reconcile psychology with religion and psychotherapy with salvation.

Foreseeing the Nazi menace, he relocated, in his last years, to the United States. He died of a heart attack during a lecture tour in Scotland.

F. Ellenberger, *The Discovery of the Unconscious*, 1970.

P. Roazen, *Freud and His Followers*, 1975.

S. T. Selesnick, "Alfred Adler," in *Psychoanalytic Pioneers*, eds. F. Alexander, S. Eisenstein, and M. Grotjahn, 1966.

ADLER, CYRUS (1863–1940) U.S. Jewish leader and scholar. Born in Van Buren, Arkansas, to the owner of a cotton plantation, Cyrus Adler was taken by his family to Philadelphia when he was four, after his father died. After graduating from the University of Pennsylvania (1883), he studied Assyriology and taught Semitics at Johns Hopkins University, Baltimore (1890). Adler visited the Far East as special commissioner of the World's Columbian Exposition and became librarian at the Smithsonian Institute in 1892. In the same year he founded the American Jewish Historical Society and served as its president for more than two decades, having played a part in the establishment of the Jewish Publication Society of America (1888), whose committees he chaired and whose Hebrew press he instituted. His commitment to Jewish scholarship was further expressed as editor of the first seven volumes of the *American Jewish Year Book* (1899–1905) and of a department of the *Jewish Encyclopedia* (1901–1906).

Adler played a central role in the early reorganization of New York's Conservative Jewish Theological Seminary of America at the beginning of the 20th century, chairing its board of trustees (1902–1905) with Solomon Schechter (q.v.) as its president. After assuming the presidency following Schechter's death (1915), he led the building campaign for new facilities. Concurrently, he took on the presidency of Dropsie College in Philadelphia, for which he edited the *Jewish Quarterly Review* (1910–1940), and, eventually the presidency of the United Synagogue of America, having been among its founders in 1913. An organizer of the American Jewish Committee, Adler was called to chair its executive (1915–1919), to represent it at the Paris Peace Conference, and to become its president at the beginning of the Great Depression (1929). Adler's frequent clashes with the American Zionist establishment did not prevent him from participating in the Jewish Agency for Palestine, which was founded in 1929.

Adler's rare talents of far-reaching vision and tireless, exacting administration combined with his scholarship both in Jewish and general (including governmental) areas of expertise served to make him a pivotal figure in bringing the needs of the American Jewish community to the attention of the philanthropists of his day. The organizational network that he helped to found continues to represent and shape American Jewry today.

C. Adler, *I Have Considered the Day*, 1941.

A. A. Neuman, *American Jewish Year Book, 1940–41*, Philadelphia, 1940.

H. Parzen, *Architect of Conservatism Judaism*, 1964.

ADLER, DANKMAR (1844–1900) U.S. architect and engineer, best known for collaborative work with his partner, Louis Sullivan. Adler was born in the town of Stadtlengsfeld, Germany. His father, Rabbi Liebman Adler, named him by compounding the German word for thanks, *dank*, with the Hebrew word for bitter, *mar*, for Adler's mother had died at his birth. At the age of ten, Adler emigrated with his father to America. They lived in Detroit, where Adler received a public school education and began his architectural career. He and

his father moved to Chicago in 1861, where Rabbi Adler headed Congregation Anshe Ma'ariv. Adler worked as a draftsman for Augustus Bauer until the start of the Civil War, when he fought in the Union army, participating in campaigns in Kentucky, Tennessee, and Georgia before finishing his commission as a draftsman in the Topographical Engineer's Office in Tennessee.

After the war, Adler worked for Bauer and then for O. S. Kinney; in 1871, he formed a partnership with Edward Burling. He and Burling designed over one hundred buildings in their first year together, their success due in part to repairing and replacing the damage caused by the Chicago fire.

Adler formed his own architectural firm in 1879 and completed his first important project, the Central Music Hall in Chicago, that same year. This project, which allowed him to make use of his knowledge of acoustics, led to other commissions for theaters, and to a position as acoustic consultant for Carnegie Hall (1889).

Louis Sullivan became Adler's partner in 1881. The two men complemented each other perfectly; Sullivan handled the creative design work, while Adler managed the engineering and administrative work. They became known for modern style buildings that were original in design. Frank Lloyd Wright trained in their office. Sullivan designed the bold unifying designs for buildings such as the Wainright in Saint Louis (1890–1891), and Adler devised the mechanical and structural means to make the designs work. Among their many successful commercial projects are the Auditorium Building (1887–1889), and the Stock Exchange Building in Chicago (1893–1894), and the Prudential (Guaranty) Building in Buffalo (1894–1895). Among their commissions were a number of synagogues in Chicago, including Zion Temple, Sinai Temple, and Adler's father's synagogue, Cingregation Anshe Ma'ariv.

Adler wrote many articles concerning the technical and legal aspects of architecture. He was politically active, fighting for the reform of building codes in Chicago and drafting proposals for state regulation of the architectural profession. Adler was also active in professional associations, serving as first treasurer of the Western Association of Architects in 1884 and as the organization's president the following year. He was treasurer of the newly formed Illinois Chapter of the American Institute of Architecture in 1890. The economic depression of 1893 took its toll on the architectural profession, causing Adler to leave Sullivan in 1895. He then worked as consulting architect and sales manager for an elevator company, but after six months returned to architecture. On his own, Adler never received another significant commission, but continued to design small projects and write articles and papers. His last architecural project was the Isaiah Temple in Chicago, completed one year before his death.

H. Morrison, *Louis Sullivan: Prophet of Modern Architecture*, 1952.

ADLER, JACOB P. (1855–1926) Yiddish actor. Born in Odessa, Adler left school early and entered the business world. His lack of education always plagued him but he had an excellent memory. He became an avid theatergoer, partial to serious, realistic plays, a taste that would become important in later years. When in 1879 Abraham Goldfaden (q.v.) brought his troupe to Odessa, Adler became friendly with the actors and joined them on the tour. For a brief time he headed his own company but when the tsar closed all Yiddish theaters in 1882, he went to London.

From 1882 to 1889 Adler worked in London and the United States. At first unsuccessful in London, he eventually became a star and a famous carouser, moving from cafe to cafe with a train of hangers-on whom he insulted in both Russian and Yiddish. The first time a New York theater sent him money to cross the Atlantic, he squandered it and was forced to stay behind. He used to swagger through London parks, looking like an Oriental prince in his black cloak. Englishwomen would follow him, hoping just once that he would look at them and smile. Adler had several wives before he married the actress Sara Heine-Hamovitch. He sired a family of Yiddish and American actors: Celia, Stella, Jack, Luther, and Frances. He is also said to have left a trail of illegitimate children from his many affairs.

In 1889, after four theatrical managers begged him to come to New York, he made his debut, billed as a combination of Salvini, Barrett, and Booth. Rather than appear in *Uriel Acosta*, a play befitting this billing, he chose instead *The Ragpickers*, a comedy. The audience, expecting a tragedy, did not laugh and in horror, the unhappy managers rushed before the curtain and told them that Adler was a bad actor and had deceived them. Adler later had his revenge when he became owner of the theater and dismissed the entire company.

Adler was far from an overnight success. He did not sing or dance well, a serious handicap in the Yiddish theater. While financially successful acting in melodramas and operettas with Boris Thomashevsky (q.v.) and David Kessler he was restless and yearned for higher artistic and moral ideals. On and off stage he created his public personality. But it was not until his meeting with Jacob Gordin (q.v.) that he found the "word" that satisfied his longing for art. Gordin gave Adler "realism," plays that dealt with the lives and problems of ordinary Jews; heads of households, matriarchs running businesses, disoriented immigrants, and families torn apart by generational clashes. Adler's first important role was Gordin's *Yiddish King Lear* in 1892. In 1894 he produced three of Gordin's plays. Throughout the 1890s he continued with translations of Shakespeare and continental writers and in 1901 performed a powerful Yiddish Shylock. Two years later he performed the same role on Broadway, with Adler speaking Yiddish and the other actors English.

While the sacred word for Adler was realism, his own acting style was by no standard realistic. He would begin with a character from ordinary Jewish life and magnify the role to heroic proportions. A Gordin character became Adler. He was over six feet tall, with a noble and expressive face. His nickname was *Nesher Ha-Godol* ("The Great Eagle"; Adler is the Yiddish word for eagle) for his piercing gaze, strong profile, and commanding stage presence. In later years he sported a mane of pure white hair. Sholem Asch (q.v.) said that Adler "looked like a lord and carried himself like a king." Isadora Duncan saw him as "a reincarnation of Greek beauty."

In 1902, after twenty years of stardom he fell sick. He had an announcement placed in the Yiddish press that he was dying and wished his admirers to come to his hospital bed so he could say farewell. On Saturday, the biggest matinee day for Yiddish theater, all the Yiddish theaters were empty. The thousands had come to his hospital window. Adler boasted that even from a hospital bed he could empty all the other shows on the Lower East Side.

When Adler died in 1926, he had carefully planned his funeral. His coffin was carried from Yiddish theater to Yiddish theater. He lay in a black mourning coat with Windsor tie and prayer-shawl. Thousands attended the funeral and when the first shovel of dirt hit the coffin, the crowd wailed, "The king is dead!"

ADLER, VICTOR (1852–1918) Creator of the Austrian Socialist party. He was born in Prague, but when he was four, his family moved to Vienna, where they prospered and were able to leave the Leopoldstadt ghetto for a fashionable part of the city. Although he received an elementary Jewish religious education, Adler soon assimilated into German culture.

He studied at medical school at the University of Vienna, receiving his degree in 1881. One of his contemporaries was Sigmund Freud (q.v.), with whom he once fought a duel. Adler too specialized in psychiatry at the university, but went on to devote his life to politics.

In 1878 he converted to Protestantism (although his wife remained Jewish) arguing that he was severing himself from Judaism to make it easier for his children and save them from embarrassment. Ironically his son Friedrich, who was baptized at the age of seven, married a Lithuanian Jewess who insisted on a religious wedding ceremony.

In the 1870s Adler supported Pan-Germanism. However, in 1885 when an anti-Jewish paragraph was introduced into its program, Adler was forced out of the movement. Even as a "new" Christian, Adler was not permitted to join "völkisch" clubs and various societies and associations. Socialist ideology appealed to many Germanized Jews, and in 1886 Adler joined the Austrian labor movement. In 1888–1889 he was responsible for the establishment of the United Austrian Social Democratic Party. Within the party, Adler showed remarkable

Statue of Victor Adler in Vienna.

talents for diplomacy in preserving the internal unity of the Austrian Socialists. Politically, perhaps his biggest success was when the imperial government in 1905 granted universal suffrage. He was a member of the Austrian Parliament from 1905 to 1918 and foreign minister in the Socialist government of 1918, but died shortly after his appointment, on November 11, 1918, the day before the Republic was proclaimed.

Adler was forever conscious of his Jewish origins. His opponents were forever pointing a finger at the Jewish leadership of the Socialist party. Adler however refused to take a clear stand on Jewish issues. In his need to be fair he denied both anti-Semitism and philo-Semitism in equal measure.

As an assimilated Austrian Marxist Adler refused to accept the specific problems of a Jewish proletariat and saw Zionism as futile, irrelevant and, unacceptable.

His son **Friedrich Adler** (1879–1960) was also a leader of the Austrian labor movement and the Socialist International. In 1916 he shot dead the Austrian premier, Count Sturgkh, to protest the war, but his death sentence was commuted and then quashed with the end of World War I. He was secretary of the Labor and Social International

---

- One must have Jews as comrades, but not too many.
- The last anti-Semite will disappear with the last Jew.
- I have no vocation for quiet academic work but I am a serviceable hawker of foreign ideas - we Jews seem predestined for peddling.
- The Jews' fear of the anti-Semites is only equaled by the anti-Semites' fear of the Jews.

Victor Adler

---

from 1923 to 1939. He found refuge in the United States during World War II but subsequently returned to Europe.

J. Braunthal *Victor und Friedrich Adler* (German), 1965.

R. S. Wistrich, *Revolutionary Jews from Marx to Trotsky*, 1976.

ADORNO, THEODOR WIESENGRUND (1903–1969) German philosopher, sociologist, and music critic. He was born in Germany, the son of a wine merchant whose family name was Wiesengrund. He adopted Adorno, his mother's maiden name, after being driven from Germany by the Nazis.

Adorno attended the liberal Johann Wolfgang Goethe University, where he studied philosophy, sociology, and music. After his graduation in 1924, he went to Vienna where he studied musical composition with Alban Berg and Eduard Steurman, and edited a musical journal. During this period of his life, Adorno was remembered by a colleague as a "shy, distraught, esoteric young man with a subtle charm."

In 1931 Adorno finished his dissertation on the Danish philosopher Søren Kierkegaard and became an assistant professor of philosophy at the University of Frankfurt. Two years later, when the Nazi party came to power, he lost his teaching position and fled to England. He taught at Merton College, Oxford University, for three years and then went to the United States. From 1938 to 1941 he served as musical director of the Princeton Radio Research Project and from 1941 to 1948 was codirector of the Research Project on Social Discrimination at the University of California at Berkeley.

Adorno's studies and writing focused on cultural problems, especially the role of the individual in society. He worried about the effacement of the individual in modern society and about the concern for complete objectivity in research. Adorno saw the "truth" as lying somewhere between concrete reality as society defined it and subjective experience. He fought to maintain subjectivity in the humanities and the social sciences.

Though influenced by Hegel and Marx (q.v.), he rejected authoritarianism, believing in the possibility of an egalitarian society. He tried to use Marxism to counter the rise of fascism in Germany, which he claimed was the logical outcome of capitalism. Later, he rejected the brutality of Stalinism in the Soviet Union. He believed that the events that took place at Auschwitz during the Holocaust typified the entire course of history and society and its "progress toward hell." Influenced by Freudian psychoanalysis he thought that society might have to go to complete ruin in order to fully recover.

During the 1940s Adorno worked with his fellow German refugee and long-time friend and associate, Max Horkheimer, in the development of these ideas and their contribution to the Frankfurt school of critical theory. Returning to Germany in 1953, he became a professor of sociology at the University of Frankfurt and eventually director of the Institute for Social Research there. His philosophy became popular with radical left-wing German students. When they turned to violence as a means to achieve their ends, Adorno spoke out against them saying, "When I made my theoretical model, I couldn't have guessed that people would want to realize it with Molotov cocktails." The students then turned against him, disrupting his lectures and eventually taking over the building that housed the Institute for Social Research. Final examinations at the institute had to be held under police surveillance. The ultimate humiliation was an "attack" by three female members of a militant action group during one of his lectures. The three rushed at him, baring their breasts and attacking him with flowers and erotic caresses. Three months later, on a vacation in Switzerland, Adorno succumbed to heart failure.

His major works include *Dialektik der Aufklärung* ("*Dialectic of Enlightenment*," 1947) written with Max Horkheimer; *Philosophie der neuen Musik* ("*Philosophy of Modern Music*," 1949); *The Authoritarian Personality* (1950), written with the Berkeley Public Opinion Study Group; and *Ästhetische Theorie* ("*Aesthetic Theory*," 1970).

H. Brunkhorst, *Theodor W. Adorno*, 1990.
R. Wiggershaus, *Theodor W. Adorno* (German), 1987.

ADRET, SOLOMON BEN ABRAHAM (known by the acronym *Rashba*, Rabbi Shelomo ben Adret; c. 1235–c. 1310) Rabbinic authority in Spain. He was born to a leading Jewish family of Aragon and spent his entire life in Barcelona, where he was a rabbi for forty years. He was recognized by the rulers of Aragon as the outstanding Jewish representative of the kingdom and, thanks to his learning and personality, was called the rabbi of Spain.

Adret was actively involved in the intellectual disputes of his day. One of these raged between Jewish advocates of the teaching of science and philosophy and those who sought to ban such studies. Those in southern France supporting the latter view had ruled that Jews could not pursue secular studies until they reached the age of thirty. After three years of correspondence, Adret issued his ruling. This reduced the minimum age for the study of physics and metaphysics to twenty-five and abolished the restriction altogether for astronomy and medicine. He also permitted Jews to read the works of Moses Maimonides (q.v.) and other Jewish philosophers whose writings had created a furor in many circles because of their rationalist tendencies.

Adret engaged in polemics with both Christianity and Islam. He attacked the book *Pugio fidei* ("Dagger of Faith") by the Spanish Dominican Raymund Martini, which sought to prove the truth of Christianity from Jewish sources. Adret in his reply stressed the eternity of the Torah and the value of the practical commandments. Adret not only argued with the Christians on paper but on at least one occasion participated in a public debate. He also wrote a refutation of the anti-Jewish works of the 11th century Spanish Moslem scholar, Ahmad ibn Hazm, in which he attacked the dogmas of Islam, especially the divine origin of the Koran.

He was famed throughout the Jewish world and questions on matters of Jewish law and learning were sent to him from many countries. His replies (*responsa*) were collected and thousands have survived. These are important not only for their religious decisions and the influence they exerted on later rabbis, but also for the light they shed on Jewish history of his period, including such subjects as the self-government of the communities and the workings of the various communal institutions. From them it is learned, for example, that when Maimonides' grandson David was falsely accused and arrested by the Egyptian sultan, Adret raised large sums of money from Spanish Jews to secure his release.

His works on rabbinic literature were classics, studied by later scholars, especially his code *Torat ha-Bayit* ("Law of the House"), which dealt with Jewish home life, notably the dietary laws and the rules about the ritual purity of women.

I. Epstein, *The Responsa of Rabbi Solomon ben Adreth of Barcelona*, 1925.
L. Jacobs, *Theology in the Responsa*, 1975, pp. 57–79.

AGNON, SHMUEL YOSEF (Czaczkos, Samuel Josef; 1888–1970) Hebrew writer and Nobel Prize winner. Born to a fur merchant in Buczacz, Galicia, he grew up in a home that was influenced by both Hasidic traditions and European culture. He learned *aggadot* (rabbinical legends) from his father while his mother told him German stories. He studied Talmud and German with private tutors, absorbed Hasidic literature in the synagogue, and read secular Hebrew and Yiddish writings by himself.

A precocious writer, he began to write at the age of eight and published his first poem at the age of fifteen. He was soon regularly publishing his Hebrew work in Cracow, and by the time he had left his home town at the age of nineteen, had published some seventy pieces in Hebrew and Yiddish. After leaving Buczacz, he never again wrote in Yiddish, but the town always remained an integral part of his consciousness. It became the prototype for the shteil (small Jewish town) in his writing. The shtetl, as he named it in one of his early works, was "The City of the Dead," a living corpse whose slow painful disintegration he felt compelled to write about.

He arrived in Eretz Israel in 1908. The move represented a total upheaval in his life. He went there alone, leaving his religion behind with his family. Although transplanted to the center of the revival of Hebrew literature, he was not at ease. He was no longer religious, yet he did not identify completely with the modernism of the pioneers, and actually felt more comfortable in the historical atmosphere of Jerusalem. He did not mix well either with the Russian Jews, who scorned him as a Galician, or with the new settlers, for whom labor was the highest value. He clearly felt otherwise and supported himself with such nonpioneering employment as giving private lessons, taking various clerical positions and occasional writing.

In 1908 he published the story "Agunot," from which he was to derive his pseudonym Agnon. "Agunot" is about separation: between lover and beloved; between man and his soul; between the Land of Israel and the Diaspora; and between religion and secular life. He felt such separations deeply and chose a name which reflected the paradoxes which were so important a source of literary inspiration for him.

In 1912, he returned to Germany and began a happier period of his life. He had the opportunity to associate with Jewish scholars and Zionist officials, to read German and French literature, and to increase his knowledge of Judaica. He also began to collect rare Hebrew books. Although initially he supported himself by tutoring and editing, he soon began receiving financial support, first from the publisher, Abraham Yosef Stybel, and then from a wealthy businessman, Salman Schocken, who supported him and published his works. These were productive years for his writing. He lived comfortably, untroubled by the inflationary forces at work in Europe and wrote a great deal. He joined a circle of Hebrew writers in Hamburg, and when his stories began to be translated into German, became well known among German Jews.

This period ended with the first of two fires that were to wreak havoc on his life. The first, in 1924, destroyed his home and most of his books and manuscripts. The second occurred in Jerusalem during the riots of 1929, and ruined many books and rare manuscripts. In one of his novels, *A Guest for the Night*, he reflected on the symbolic overtones of these two fires, comparing them to the two destructions of the Temple, and viewing his sojourn in Germany as a symbol of Jewish exile.

In 1924 Agnon returned to Eretz Israel and settled in Jerusalem. He had retained his bond to Jewish tradition and that bond lived on in his writing. He saw himself as the heir of the holy scribes insofar as he believed that modern Hebrew literature was a substitute for the sacred texts. But as a modern writer who could no longer participate in Jewish ritual; he had to reexpress his link with the tradition through secular fables that only hinted at the traditions he had forsaken. The Jewish factor in his writing was balanced by the influence of Western writers, among them Scandinavian authors, such as Knut Hamsen, and Flaubert.

His early works, usually set in Poland, were often positive characterizations of the lives of the pious. His later work, however, reflects a complicated negative relationship to the world, which is shaped by contradictory sources of inspiration: his hometown versus Israel, and Jewish tradition versus Western culture and modern Hebrew literature. His heroes are torn between the old world to which they are bound and the new which they admire. Often their stories end in catastrophe. His themes are decline of the old order, loss of innocence, ambivalence, and exile. He has been compared to Franz Kafka (q.v.), although he himself denied the similarity. His style is often surrealistic, introspective, and dreamlike. In *A Guest for the Night*, the narrator visits his home town in Galicia after a long absence and finds it desolate. Based on Agnon's own return to Buczacz in 1930, the novel paints a grotesque picture of a city with shattered inhabitants and empty synagogues, and reflects the spiritual desolation of the Jewish world.

During his lifetime he wrote four long novels (*The Bridal Canopy, A Guest for the Night, The Day before Yesterday,* and *Shirah*) and over two hundred stories. He received the Israel Prize in 1954 and 1958 and the Nobel Prize, the first given to a Hebrew writer, in 1966.

A. Band, *Nostalgia and Nighmare*, 1969.
B. Hochman, *The Fiction of S. Y. Agnon*, 1970.
G. Shaked, *Shmuel Yosef Agnon. A Revolutionary Traditionalist*, 1989.

Shmuel Yoseph Agnon receiving the Nobel Prize in Stockholm, 1966. On the left is King Gustav VI.

If the Temple still stood, I should take my place on the dais with my fellow poets and daily repeat the songs which the Levites used to chant in the Holy Temple. Now, when the Temple is still in ruins... [and] from all our goodly treasures which we had in ancient days nothing is left us but a scanty record, I am filled with sorrow, and this same sorrow causes my heart to tremble. Out of this same trembling I write my fables, like a man who has been exiled from his father's palace, who makes himself a little booth and sits there telling the glory of his forefather's house.

Shmuel Yosef Agnon

Ahad Ha-Am, second from the left, and Chaim Nachman Bialik, on the right. Tel Aviv, 1926.

AHAD HA-AM (pen name of Asher Hirsch Ginsberg; 1856–1927) Hebrew writer, leading Zionist thinker, and exponent of Jewish culture. Born in Skvira, a village outside Kiev, the Ukraine, into a wealthy merchant Hasidic family, he received a traditional Jewish education that he supplemented independently with the study of European languages and the writings of the Haskalah. The latter's prevailing influence fueled a rationalist nature that led to an eventual estrangement from his religious roots.

At age thirty, with a commercial position in Odessa, he found himself in the center of the early Zionist movement, Hovevei Zion (Love of Zion), and in contact with the foremost Hebrew authors of the day. As a member of the Hovevei Zion Committee under the chairmanship of Leon Pinsker, Ginsberg argued against the movement's policy to attract settlers to Palestine by appealing to their self-interest. He instead proposed an educational approach which would awaken within settlers a love of Zion and the Jewish cultural heritage and thus prepare them for a life of toil and tribulation in rebuilding the ancestral national homeland. His first published essay, "Lo Zeh ha-Derekh" ("This Is not the Way"), appeared in 1889 in the movement's *HaMelitz* under the pen name of Ahad Ha-Am ("One of the People") and catapulted him into immediate fame and intensive literary activity. Subsequently, he became the spiritual leader of the secret society of B'nei Moshe ("Sons of Moses") an elite group of "lovers of Zion" who for seven years worked together to open Hebrew libraries, set the stage for modern Hebrew schools, and establish the first elementary school where Hebrew was the language of instruction.

The conclusions of his first article were confirmed during two subsequent visits to Palestine in 1891 and 1893, after which he concentrated his efforts on defining with greater precision his philosophy of Judaism and Jewish nationalism. In 1895, he became the editor of *Ha-Shiloah*, a new Hebrew monthly, as business reverses forced him to seek an alternative career. Under his leadership, the periodical flourished, attaining a high standard of style and language.

In the wake of the First Zionist Congress (Basel, 1897), inaugurating the movement for political Zionism, Ahad Ha-Am's well articulated opposition found a response among the Eastern European Jewish intelligentsia. His suspicions of Theodor Herzl's (q.v.) diplomacy and assimilationist values, coupled with his dogged commitment to Jewish education as a prerequisite to settlement in the Land of Israel, led him to reject the Jewish state as the primary goal on the national agenda. Instead, he argued, a "national spiritual center" in Palestine could help in the overall program of revitalizing a Jewish moral consciousness among a people suffering from the debilitating effects of two millennia of homelessness. The moment should not call for a homeland as refuge, but a comprehensive answer to address both the ethical backwardness of the ghetto and the void in Jewish content of emancipated Jewry.

Ahad Ha-Am responded to the Kishinev pogroms (1903, 1905) with a call for Jewish self-defense, and to the Sixth Zionist Congress' Uganda Plan (1904) with the consistent and urgent cry for a return to Jewish values. In 1902 he left *Ha-Shiloah* to return to business and in 1908 he became manager of the London office of Wissotzky's tea firm, remaining active in public affairs and devoting time to what would become some of his best-known essays. He participated with Zionist leaders in London in the negotiations with the British government that led to the Balfour Declaration and voiced concern specifically about the national rights of Arabs in Palestine.

In 1922 Ahad Ha-Am settled in Tel Aviv where he completed *Al Parashat Derakhim* ("At the Crossroads"), a four-volume collection of essays started in 1895, prepared his letters for publication, and dictated some autobiographical reminiscences before his death. He left a lasting legacy to the staunch adherents of cultural Zionism in their struggle against the practical and political schools of Zionism, though the force of the latter ultimately won the dedication of most of the movement's leadership. Ahad Ha-Am is considered one of the foremost influential Jewish thinkers and writers of his time. His theoretical and political essays and articles continue to occupy the attention of students from across the Zionist spectrum in Israel and the Diaspora, exemplifying an outstanding achievement in the course of modern Hebrew literature.

N. Bentwich, *Ahad-Ha-Am and His Philosophy*, 1927.

L. Simon, *Ahad Ha-Am: Asher Ginzberg; a Biography*, 1960.

Now we stand before a new period of our national work in Palestine, and soon we may be faced by problems and possibilities of overwhelming magnitude. We do not know what the future has in store for us, but this we do know: that the brighter the prospects for the reestablishment of our National Home in Palestine, the more urgent is the need for laying the spiritual foundations of that home on a corresponding scale which can only be conceived in the form of a Hebrew University. By this I mean — and so, I am sure, do you — not a mere imitation of a European University with Hebrew as the dominant language, but a university which from the very beginning, will endeavor to become the true embodiment of the Hebrew spirit of old and to shake off the mental and moral servitude to which our people has been so long subjected in the Diaspora. Only so can we be justified in our ambitious hopes as to the future universal influence of the "Teaching" that "will go forth out of Zion."

Ahad Ha-Am to Chaim Weizmann on the occasion of the laying of the cornerstone of the Hebrew University of Jerusalem in 1918.

AKIVA (ben Joseph; mid-first cent. CE–c. 135) One of the key figures in the formative period of rabbinic Judaism. Akiva's early history is shrouded in legend. Traditionally the son of a proselyte, he was a poor and ignorant youth who earned his living as a shepherd for the rich landowner Ben Kalba Sabua. Akiva married his daughter, Rachel, who encouraged him to start studying when he was forty (he learned the alphabet together with his son) and even sold her hair to find money for food. His father-in-law was enraged that his daughter had married Akiva and refused to recognize their marriage. They lived in poverty but Rachel uncomplainingly looked after the children while he went away to study at the academies of famous rabbis. According to the story, he returned after twenty-four years, accompanied by thousands of disciples, to whom he proclaimed that he and they owed everything to Rachel.

Whatever the historical accuracy of these traditions, Akiva had, before the end of the century, become one of the outstanding rabbinic authorities and had established a distinguished academy at Benei Berak, which produced nearly all the leading rabbis of the next generation. By this time his father-in-law was reconciled and Akiva enjoyed wealth as well as wisdom. He was regarded as one of the heads of the Jewish community in Eretz Israel on whose behalf he traveled extensively including a mission to Rome in 95 CE to obtain from the Emperor Domitian the cancellation of anti-Jewish legislation.

In his time, Judaism was guided by a vast accumulation of oral traditions. These were collected, organized according to subject matter, and committed to writing by Akiva, thereby laying the foundation for the Mishnah, the authoritative code of Judah ha-Nasi (q.v.), which in turn was the basis of the Talmud. His innovativeness in the field of Jewish law led to the saying, "What was not revealed to Moses was discovered by Akiva." In particular he held that every word, letter, and mark in the Bible was sacred and possessed a meaning. (A legend related that Moses in heaven saw God making crowns for the letters of the Torah and asked for the reason. God replied, "A man called Akiva will arise who will deduce rules of Jewish law from every curve and crown on these letters.") Akiva derived laws from even the apparently most unimportant and redundant words of the Bible,

Rabbi Akiva, in a Haggadah. Spain, 14th century.

SAYINGS OF AKIVA

- Who is wealthy? The man with a virtuous wife.
- "Love your neighbor as yourself" is the great principle of the Torah.
- Whatever God does is for the best.
- Tradition is a protection ["fence"] for Torah; tithes are a protection for wealth; vows for abstinence; silence for wisdom.
- Before you taste anything, recite a benediction.
- He who sheds blood impairs the divine image.
- If a husband and wife are worthy, the Shekhinah [divine presence] abides with them; if they are not, fire consumes them.
- Everything is foreseen, yet freedom of choice is granted. The world is judged favorably, yet all depends on the preponderance of good deeds.
- Whoever neglects to visit a sick person is like one who sheds blood.
- More than the calf wants to suck, the cow wants to suckle [i.e., the teacher wants to teach even more than the pupil wants to learn].
- Beloved is man, for he was created in the image of God.
- Beware of unsolicited advice.
- The judge who passes sentence must fast on the day of execution.
- As a house implies a builder, a dress a weaver, a door a carpenter, so the world proclaims God, its Creator.
- Take your place a little below your rank until you are asked to move up; it is better to be told "come up higher" than "move down."

seeking to demonstrate how the written law — the Bible — contained the oral tradition. This approach was a matter of controversy with another great scholar, Rabbi Ishmael ben Elisha, who insisted that the Bible speaks in human language and should be understood through its plain meanings and not through the fanciful, homiletic approach expounded by Akiva. Akiva was also one of the pioneers of Jewish mysticism who - in the guarded words of the rabbis - "entered the heavenly garden and emerged unscathed."

After the Jerusalem Temple had been destroyed (70 CE) and Jewish independence lost, Akiva was convinced that national redemption would ensue. In the year 132, following measures by the Roman Emperor Hadrian that incensed the Jewish population, a revolt broke out under Simeon bar-Kokhba (q.v.) that achieved impressive initial successes. It is thought that Akiva was one of the religious forces behind the rebellion. Certainly he enthusiastically supported it and even hailed Bar-Kokhba as the potential messiah, proclaiming "A star has stepped out of Jacob" (hence the epithet "Bar-Kokhba." i.e., "son of a star," for the leader, whose real name was Bar Kosiba). After three years of bitter fighting, the rebellion was quelled by the Romans with much cruelty. Hadrian issued a series of edicts aiming at the elimination of Judaism, including a ban on study of the Torah, which was ignored by Akiva. Imprisoned by the Romans, he continued to teach his pupils in devious ways, even while in prison. Eventually Akiva, now in his nineties, was sentenced to be executed in Caesarea. The story goes that he insisted on reciting the Shema even while his persecutors were tearing his flesh with iron combs. He was asked how he could continue to pray while in agony and answered: "All my life, I have sought to serve God with all my heart, all my soul, and all my might [as is written in the Shema, cf. Deut. 6:5]. Now I realize the meaning of serving God 'with all my soul,' that is, even though he is taking away my life." The connection of the Shema with the great martyr led to its recitation being adopted as a final confession of faith for later Jewish martyrs and for Jews on their deathbeds. L. Finkelstein, Akiba: Scholar, Saint, and Martyr, 1962.

ALBO, JOSEPH (c. 1380–c. 1444) Religious philosopher in Spain. In 1414, the Church imposed on the Jews of Spain a public disputation which was held in Tortosa. The longest of the medieval disputations, this lasted until the following year and had the effect desired by the Church - the demoralization of large sections of Spanish Jewry. Albo was one of the twenty-two scholars appearing on the Jewish side and took a prominent and courageous part in the discussions. Afterwards he wrote a book Sefer ha-Ikkarim ("Book of Principles"), inspired by the various religious arguments of the period and seeking to refute those elements which had led to widespread apostasy among Spanish Jewry.

In particular he took issue with Moses Maimonides' (q.v.) formulation of thirteen principles of the Jewish faith. He felt these were too general and contained principles which were not unique to Judaism but could be accepted by Christianity and Islam. He was also not satisfied with his teacher Hasdai Crescas' (q.v.) formulation of six basic principles. He reduced the fundaments to three: (1) the existence of God; (2) divine revelation; (3) reward and punishment.

From these he derived a number of "roots" or doctrines, which are not fundamentals but have to be believed to attain the afterlife. These are: (1) God's unity; (2) God's incorporeality; (3) his independence of time; (4) his freedom from defects; (these four are derived from the fundamental principle of divine existence); (5) God's omniscience; (6) prophecy; (7) the authenticity of God's messengers (Adam, Noah, Abraham, Moses) (these three are derived from the fundamental principle of revelation); and (8) individual providence (derived from the fundamental principle of reward and punishment).

From these roots Albo further derives six

"branches," which are not fundamentals and one can even be a good Jew without accepting all of them: (1) God's creation of the world *ex nihilo* (out of nothing); (2) Moses as the greatest of the prophets; (3) the eternal validity of the Pentateuch; (4) the potential for human perfection by the observance of even a single commandment; (5) the resurrection of the dead; (6) and the coming of the Messiah.

The low priority given to the belief in the Messiah may have been a reaction to Christian teachings. He also attacked Christianity for contradicting the fundamental principles of the unity and incorporeality of God.

Over the subsequent centuries, Jews engaged in polemics with Christianity frequently had recourse to the writings of Albo.

I. Husik, *Sefer Ha-'Ikkarim: Book of Principles*, 5 vols., 1929.

ALEXANDER, SAMUEL (1859–1938) Philosopher. He was born in Sydney, Australia; his father was a saddler who, soon after Samuel's birth, moved to Melbourne. Alexander studied for two years at Melbourne University and then went to Oxford, where he graduated with many honors. In 1882, he was appointed a fellow of Lincoln College, Oxford — the first Jew to be awarded a fellowship to a college of Oxford or Cambridge. In 1887 he was awarded the Green Moral Philosophy Prize for his essay "Moral Order and Progress" (1889) in which he first propounded his views on evolutionary ethics.

In 1893, after studying experimental psychology in Germany for a year, he was appointed professor of philosophy at Manchester University (after three unsuccessful attempts at a professorship). He was greatly beloved by his students and friends, despite his increasing deafness, and eccentric behavior, which included wiping the blackboard with the sleeves of his raincoat. One of his close colleagues at the university was the young chemist, Chaim Weizmann (q.v.).

During World War I, Alexander gave the prestigious Gifford lectures at Glasgow University, and these lectures formed the basis of his most famous book, *Space, Time and Deity* (2 vols., 1920). He regarded metaphysics as the science which describes the levels of reality. Each level of reality is rooted in the one which precedes it and has a tendency towards the higher level. Matter emerges from a matrix of space and time, mind rises above matter, and another level of reality, deity, transcends mind. The advent of that highest level of reality is suggested by religious consciousness and the desire to contemplate the Divine.

After his retirement in 1924, he spent much time in the study of aesthetics, publishing *Beauty and Other Forms of Value* in 1933. The posthumous *Philosophical and Literary Pieces* (1939) reflects the wide range of his interests.

He received many honors, including the Order of Merit (1930), was president of the Aristotelian

Samuel Alexander. Sculpture by Sir Jacob Epstein.

We were practically next-door neighbors of Alexander. I had an enormous admiration for him. After a time, he began to take an interest in the affairs of his people and became, within his very modest means, a contributor to Zionist funds. He used to come now and then to Jewish meetings and lecture on Spinoza. He followed closely the development of the Hebrew University and sent us one of his best men, Professor Leon Roth, to occupy the chair of philosophy. I tried hard to get Alexander to go to Jerusalem himself but it could not be managed; in his later years he became rather deaf and had to be looked after.

He looked like some ancient Jewish prophet. He was very tall, had a vast beard and a magnificent dome of a forehead - and he went about in the shabbiest of clothes. He was shockingly absent minded. He was a rather odd sight when he mounted his bicycle and rode to or from the university - the more so as he would be riding on the sidewalk as often as on the road, to the delight of passersby, who all knew him well, and the great distress of the local police.

Chaim Weizmann on Samuel Alexander, in *Trial and Error.*

Society, and was a Fellow of the British Academy. His bust, by Jacob Epstein (q.v.), is exhibited in the arts building of Manchester University. He was a member of the Manchester Jewish Community and vice-president of the Friends of the Hebrew University.

B. D. Brettschneider, *Philosophy of Samuel Alexander*, 1964.

M. R. Konvits, *On the Nature of Value: The Philosophy of Samuel Alexander*, 1946.

J. Laird, Introduction to *Philosophical and Literary Pieces*, 1939.

ALEXANDER YANNAI See Yannai, Alexander

ALFASI, ISAAC BEN JACOB (known by the acronym *Rif*; 1013–c. 1103) Outstanding scholar and codifier of Jewish law in North Africa and Spain. Born near Constantine in Algeria, he studied in Kairouan, and settled in Fez (hence his name, Alfasi, i.e., a man of Fez). He lived and taught there until the age of seventy-five. Then, against a background of political intrigues, two enemies denounced him to the authorities (the charge is unknown), and he had to flee to Spain. In his time, the great centers of Talmud study in Babylonia were declining and North Africa had become the new focus. After a period in Cordoba, Alfasi established a talmudic academy at Lucena which played an important role in determining Spain as the next great center of rabbinic studies. Alfasi was regarded as the leading scholar of his generation and many disciples came to study with him, some of them in turn becoming renowned authorities.

His classic achievement is his *Sefer ha-Halakhot* ("Book of Laws"), which systematically organized the legal sections of the Talmud — civil, criminal, and religious law — excluding those areas not relevant in the Diaspora following the destruction of the Temple (such as sacrifices, dues to the priests, and laws of impurity connected to the Temple). The book keeps the original structure of the Talmud and does not attempt to organize a code, but it was so influential that similar earlier compilations were made obsolete and neglected. It was called the little Talmud and was studied even more than the Talmud itself, especially as, unlike the Talmud, it guided the student to clear conclusions. Later codifiers also used Alfasi as a basic source: Moses Maimonides (q.v.) said that only on ten basic issues did he disagree with Alfasi, while Joseph Caro (q. v.) founded his standard code, the *Shulhan Arukh*, on three sources, one of which was *Sefer ha-Halakhot* (which was also known as Alfas).

S. W. Baron, *A Social and Religious History of the Jews*, vol. 6, 1958.

AL-HARIZI, JUDAH BEN SOLOMON (1170–1235) Spanish Hebrew poet, translator, and writer on music. Probably born in Andalusia, he lived in Languedoc and visited Provence. He traveled extensively in the Near East, visiting Egypt, Palestine, Syria, and Iraq. These journeys enabled al-Harizi to find several patrons willing to subsidize translations of Jewish books from Arabic to Hebrew, in addition to placing him in the position to spread Spanish-Jewish culture to other areas of the world.

Writing at a time when Arabic was the main language of Jews writing in Spain, al-Harizi insisted on writing in Hebrew, thus striving to demonstrate the richness and harmony inherent in the Hebrew language. In his translation into Hebrew of the Arabic poet al-Hariri's satire *Maqamas*, al-Harizi succeeds in reproducing both the beauty of the language and the elaborateness of the style of the original Arabic in what appears as an original Hebrew composition. A devoted follower of Maimonides (q.v.), al-Harizi began a translation of his commentary to the Mishna into Hebrew (commissioned by the Jewish community of Marseilles), and completed a translation of *The Guide of the Perplexed*. Although Samuel ibn Tibbon's translation, considered to be a more accurate one, became the standard text in translation, al-Harizi's text was responsible for spreading Maimonides' ideas throughout the Christian world because it was used as a basis for translations into other languages.

Al-Harizi is best known for his rhymed prose, *Book of Tahkemoni*, a series of humorous episodes, witty verse, word games, and ingenious applications of traditional texts. The episodes are bound together by the presence of the hero and narrator, Heman the Ezrahite, who represents the author. In this work, al-Harizi provides a critical inquiry into the Jewish culture of his times as well as criticism of the literary achievements of other poets. In addition, his use of Hebrew in secular satire and in religious poetry constitutes an important contribution to the development of Hebrew as a poetic language. Al-Harizi also wrote on music, helping to introduce late Hellenic notions of the therapeutic powers of music into Jewish culture.

V. E. Reichert, *The Fourteenth Gate of Yehudah Al-Harizi's Tahkemoni*, 1963.

ALKALAI, JUDAH SOLOMON HAI (1798–1878) Sephardic rabbi, precursor of modern Zionism. Born in Sarajevo, capital of Bosnia, he studied in a Sephardic yeshiva (Talmudic college), where he imbibed his deep love for the land of Israel. After continuing his studies in Jerusalem, he was called, at the age of twenty-seven, to serve as chief Sephardic rabbi in Zemun, the then capital of Serbia, and was soon the driving spiritual force in the community. Not long before, the Greeks had won their independence, and nationalism was beginning to stir among other Balkan peoples; Alkalai applied the concept to the national freedom of his own people. In 1834 he published a book maintaining that the establishment of Jewish settlements in the Land of Israel was an essential prelude to the redemption of the Jewish people. He urged all Jews to dedicate one-tenth of their income to the support of those living in Jerusalem.

Profoundly influenced by the Damascus anti-Jewish blood libel of 1840, he became convinced that the Jews had to settle in the Holy Land for their own security and safety. Although these ideas were usually greeted with scorn and derision, he traveled widely to propagate them. He journeyed to Vienna, Berlin, Paris, and London, founding societies wherever possible, to further his goals. He believed that it would be possible to purchase the Land of Israel from its Ottoman rulers just as in biblical times Abraham bought the cave of Machpelah from Ephron the Hittite. Everywhere he taught that political Zionism was an integral part of the Jewish faith. He raised money to have his writings published; when this ran out, his wife sold her jewels to finance his books so that his ideas could reach the widest possible public.

In 1871 he went to Jerusalem and founded a society for the settlement of the land, with the support of the Sephardic community. He was called back to Europe as the position of Serbian Jewry had deteriorated and he beseeched the Turkish authorities to permit their emigration to the Land of Israel, but was refused. While in Europe he learned that the opposition of Jerusalem zealots had led to the failure of the society that he had established there.

In 1874 he left Europe for Jerusalem for the last time and continued to try to influence the Jews in Jerusalem. Alkalai predicted that the resettlement of Eretz Israel would strike a chord of unity in the hearts and minds of world Jewry and from this would emerge a world organization which would secure the support of European governments to help transfer large numbers of Jews to Israel, where land would be bought for the purpose. He advocated the creation of a national fund for the purchase of land and the floating of a national loan.

The grandfather of Theodor Herzl (q.v.) lived in Zemun and was well acquainted with Alkalai and his ideas. It is thought likely that he spoke of them to his grandson and perhaps in this way Alkalai influenced the father of the modern Zionist movement.

A. Hertzberg, *The Zionist Idea*, 1960.

ALROY, DAVID (12th cent.) Pseudomessiah in Kurdistan. The 12th century was a period of widespread messianic expectation among Jews in the wake of the tragedies they experienced in the course of the First Crusade. The best-known pseudomessiah of the time was born in Kurdistan. His name was Menahem ben Solomon, but he became famous as David Alroy (David has an obvious messianic significance, while Alroy is a corruption of his Arabic family name).

Little is known of his origins or his personal life. The messianic movement was originally created by his father, Solomon, who claimed to be the prophet Elijah and who notified various Jewish communities that Jewish exiles from all lands would soon be gathered in their own homeland under his leadership. Nothing further is known of this plan, but years later David Alroy collected a considerable armed Jewish force with which he intended to conquer the Holy Land. His impressive appearance, scholastic excellence (founded on studies in the Talmudic academies of Baghdad), his familiarity with Jewish mysticism, and his skill in sorcery, all combined to win him a large and devoted following. When he announced his intention to return to Jerusalem, he called on his adherents to fast and pray as an essential penitential preparation, and they obeyed without hesitation. In the words of the Spanish Jewish traveler, Benjamin of Tudela (q.v.): "He took it into his head to revolt against the king of Persia and to gather around him the Jews who lived in the mountain of Chaftan, in order to wage war against the Gentiles and to capture Jerusalem. He showed miraculous signs to the Jews and declared that God had sent him to capture Jerusalem and to lead them forth from among the nations, and they believed in him and proclaimed him the Messiah."

Alroy managed to take possession of his native town of Amadia, which was a strategically placed fortress. He dispatched messengers to many communities, including Baghdad, to prepare for his military advance. His messengers (or perhaps opponents masquerading as messengers) told the Jews of Baghdad to gather on their rooftops on a certain night in order to be flown miraculously to join the messiah. Many Baghdadi Jews obeyed and spent the night on their roofs. The official Jewish leadership condemned the movement and threatened its adherents with excommunication, while

Title page of the English version of one of Judah Alkalai's pamphlets advocating the return to Eretz Israel.

מבשר טוב

HARBINGER OF GOOD TIDINGS,

AN ADDRESS TO THE JEWISH NATION,

BY

RABBI JUDAH ELKALI.

ON THE PROPRIETY OF

ORGANIZING AN ASSOCIATION

TO PROMOTE THE

REGAINING OF THEIR FATHERLAND.

LONDON.
PUBLISHED BY S. SOLOMON, 37, DUKE STREET, ALDGATE.
5012.—1852.

[*Price Six Pence.*]

the local authorities began to take energetic measures against his influence. Alroy was captured and imprisoned for conspiracy and political agitation. Rumors of his magical escape from prison are in keeping with the miracles ascribed to the messiah.

Two different traditions account for his early death. One states that the authorities had him killed; the other that he was murdered by his father-in-law, who had been bribed by the Turkish authorities. The Jews of the region continued to revere his memory and were known as Menachemites. The Jews of Kurdistan to this day regard him as one of their heroes. When the Jews of Iraq went to Israel in 1950–1951 they called one of their settlements Kefar Alroy ("Alroy's Village").

In the 19th century his career fascinated Benjamin Disraeli (q.v.) who wrote the first modern Jewish historical novel, *The Wondrous Tale of Alroy*. He called it "the celebration of the gorgeous incident in that sacred and romantic people from whom I derive my blood and name."

AMATUS LUSITANUS (Juan Rodrigues de Castelo Branco; 1511–1568) Physician, medical researcher, and author. Born to Marrano parents in the town of Castelo Branco, Portugal, the young Juan learnt much of his Jewish heritage, including the Hebrew language from his outwardly practicing Christian parents. He went to Spain to study medicine at the University of Salamanca. About 1530, after receiving his medical degree, he returned to Portugal, but antagonism to and oppression of the Marranos made him flee to Antwerp three years later. There he practiced medicine for seven years. His many patients included the mayor and the Portuguese consul. In 1536 he published his first book, the *Index Dioscoridis*, a treatise on medicinal botany. Amatus achieved renown as a scientist and in 1540 the duke of Ferrara appointed him lecturer in medicine at the University of Ferrara. There, Amatus worked with other famous scientists of his day on studies in human dissection. His aim was to clarify human anatomy and investigate practical surgical techniques.

In 1547, while on his way to Ragusa (modern Dubrovnik) to take up a position as municipal physician, Amatus stayed at Ancona, where he was called upon to treat the sister of Pope Julius III. This incident led to a position as the physician of the Augustinian and Dominican friaries, where he was able to study the diseases of the friaries in detail. In Ancona he published his first *Centuria* (1549), a collection of one hundred case reports, with descriptions, commentary, anatomy and treatment considered in detail. He went on to publish many more *Centuria* during his medical career, and these established his reputation as a physician, researcher and anatomist in various fields including, internal medicine, dermatology, and mental disease.

Amatus was called to various cities and his reputation grew further after he treated the pope in 1550. In the revised 1553 edition of his book on

Amatus Lusitanus

Dioscorides, Amatus criticized the work of another contemporary botanist and Viennese court physician, Matthioli. This led to bitter antagonism between the two and when the new pope, Paul IV, published decrees against the Marranos in 1555, Amatus was persecuted largely at Matthioli's instigation. He lost his valuables and manuscripts and

---

EXCERPTS FROM AMATUS LUSITANUS' OATH

I swear by Almighty God and by his most holy Ten Commandments given on on Mount Sinai by the hand of Moses the lawgiver that I have never in my medical practice departed from what has been handed down to us in good faith; that I have never practiced deception; I have never overstated or made changes for the sake of gain; that I have ever striven that benefit might accrue to mankind; that I have praised no one nor censured any one to indulge private interests but only when truth demanded it. I have not desired for the remuneration of medical service and have treated many without accepting any fee, but with none the less care. I have given my services in equal manner to all — Jews, Christians, and Muslims. I have accorded the same care to the poor as to those of exalted rank. ...I have never revealed a secret. I have never given a fatal draft. No woman has ever brought about an abortion with my aid. I have done nothing that might be considered unbecoming an honorable and distinguished physician....

Salonica, 1559

fled to Ragusa for two years and then in 1558 moved to Salonika, where he practiced his Judaism freely and openly. There he had a large practice, mainly Jewish.

Amatus was responsible for much progress in the knowledge of anatomy, especially concerning the structure and function of the veins and the female breasts. He also described enlargement of the spleen in chronic malaria, treatments for esophageal structures (using enemas), and treatment for inflammation of the lactating breast and for gastric ulcers. About the latter, he quoted the opinions of Maimonides (q.v.) on the Jewish dietary laws.

Among his other published works was a medical oath in the name of "The Holy Ten Commandments which were delivered into the hands of Moses on Mount Sinai." This oath demonstrates Lusitanus's deep faith in Judaism, and its medical ethics as well its philanthropic and practical religious practices.

Amatus died in Salonika in a plague epidemic. H. Friedenwald, *The Jews and Medicine I*, 1967.

AMOS (8th cent. BCE) Biblical prophet. He was a herdsman and sycamore gatherer in Tekoa, traditionally in the kingdom of Judah, south of Bethlehem, but some scholars have suggested that Tekoa should be located in the northern kingdom of Israel, where he prophesied. All his recorded activities were in the northern sanctuaries of Bethel and (probably) Samaria. He lived in the reigns of Uzziah of Judah (c. 783–c. 742 BCE) and Jeroboam of Israel (c. 782–c. 743 BCE). Amos was the earliest of the literary prophets; his moral prophecies were uttered in his later years and reflect conditions in the last period of the rule of Jeroboam. Living in a period of prosperity, he was obviously closely acquainted with the life of the country's money- and property-grabbing elite, whose way of life he thunderously denounced, threatening dire calamities if they did not mend their ways. One of his warnings was the possibility of exile from the land (presumably based on his knowledge of the Assyrian policy of deporting subject nations) and he was the first of the ancient Israelites to raise such a possibility. When Jeroboam's priest, Amaziah, ordered him to leave the country and continue his mission in Judah where he could prophecy freely, Amos angrily replied that he was not a prophet by choice but a messenger of God who could not desist. His subsequent fate is not known.

Amos's warnings were directed not only to his fellow countrymen, but to pagan nations and to neighboring countries for the wrongs inflicted on Israel. God, he said, was responsible for the fate of all nations and in this way his message of social justice was of universal relevance. He foresaw the Day of the Lord when Israel would be saved and its enemies judged, but also warned that Israel itself would be judged and punishment would be inevitable, except for the righteous and the repentant. His wrath was primarily directed against the social and moral evils of society, such as the oppression of the poor, cheating in commerce, and the pampered life of luxury of the noble and wealthy. Amos spoke with contempt of rituals and sacrifices offered by those whose way of life is corrupt and stressed that sacrifice has no meaning unless linked to morality. He was a pioneer in emphasizing the supremacy of ethical and moral values by which Israel would be judged.

Amos's prophecies are contained in the biblical book of Amos, the first such collection in the Bible. A. J. Heschel, *The Prophets*, 1962, chap. 2.

ANAN BEN DAVID (8th cent.) Founder of a Jewish sect (the Ananites) that developed into the Karaite schism. Little is known of Anan's life. A Babylonian of aristocratic descent, he lived in an eastern country and returned to Babylonia where he studied under the outstanding rabbinical authority, Yehudai Gaon. At this time the lay leader of the Babylonian Jewish community was known as the exilarch (head of the exile community), an office greatly honored not only by the Jews but also by the caliph. Anan was the eldest son of the exilarch's brother and expected to succeed to the office. As a result he behaved haughtily and fearlessly, which alienated the leaders of the rabbinic academies. It was also suspected that some of his views were not orthodox. As a result, when the exilarch died, the academies did not follow precedent but passed him over for his younger brother. Various accounts, some of them legendary, seek to explain his subsequent rebellion, but the usually accepted story is that it was motivated by jealousy of his younger brother. For refusing to accept his brother's authority, he was jailed and, according to one account, was only saved from being put to death by following the advice of a Muslim legal scholar who was in the same prison. The Muslim suggested that if he said that he headed a breakaway group, he would be saved as the Muslim authorities were tolerant of sects.

Anan brought together various dissident Jewish fundamentalist groups who did not accept rabbinic authority and interpretation of the Bible. Anan's struggle was now transformed from the question of the exilarch to the validity of rabbinic law which he rejected.

Anan's book *Sefer ha-Mitzvot* ("Book of Commandments") provided the ideological basis of the Karaite schism. Only fragments survive but its general tenor is apparent. It addressed itself to the legal basis of Judaism and rejected the rabbinic tradition that an oral tradition had been given by God to Moses on Mount Sinai and preserved by successive generations until written down by Judah ha-Nasi (q.v.) in the Mishnah, in the early 3rd century CE. Anan held that the Bible was the exclusive authority, and this referred to the Prophets and Writings as well as the Pentateuch.

The Karaites grew rapidly in the ensuing centuries and at one time threatened the hegemony of rabbinic Judaism. The threat was contained lar-

gely due to the activities of Saadia Gaon (q.v.).
Small groups of Karaites, who still regard Anan as
the founder of their sect, continue to exist in Israel,
Egypt, Turkey, the United States, and the Soviet
Union.

The word *Karaite* comes from the Hebrew *kara*,
which is the root of *mikra* (scripture). The British
Chief Rabbi, Hermann Adler, at the beginning of
the 20th century divided the Jews into the "Karaites" and the "Don't Karaites."
L. Nemoy, *Karaite Anthology*, 1952.

ANIELEWICZ, MORDECAI   (1919 or 1920–1943)
Commander of the Warsaw Ghetto uprising.
Anielewicz was born in the slums of Warsaw.
While still a youth, he joined the Ha-Shomer ha-
Tsair Socialist Zionist movement and became one
of its leading figures. On September 7, 1939, less
than a week after the Germans invaded Poland,
Anielewicz, like many of the leaders of the Zionist
youth movements, fled Warsaw. He reached the
Soviet-occupied area of Poland and attempted to
go to Romania, hoping from there to find his way
to Palestine. Caught by the Soviet authorities, he
was jailed for a short time.

After his release, en route back to Warsaw,
Anielewicz visited a number of Jewish communities to gain an impression of their situation. After a
short stay in Warsaw, he went to Vilna, where
many Zionist youth had concentrated. There some
of them decided to return to German-occupied
Poland to lead the movement's activities surrepti-
tiously. Anielewicz volunteered to go back to
Poland.

In Warsaw he organized clandestine cells, held

*The memorial to Mordecai Anielewicz by the sculptor,
Natan Rapaport, at kibbutz Yad Mordekhai.*

seminars, and aided the development of an underground press, to which he contributed articles.
Upon receiving reports of the murder of Jews in the
German-occupied areas of the Soviet Union, in the
summer of 1941, Anielewicz pushed for the creation of an armed Jewish underground. The first
such organization, the Antifascist Bloc, was never
really established and, following a wave of arrests
of some of its Communist members, was dissolved.

Anielewicz went to Bedzin to help establish an
armed underground, shortly before the mass
deportations in Warsaw began in the summer of
1942. He returned to Warsaw to discover that only
about 60,000 Jews remained and that the new
armed underground organization, the Jewish
Fighting Organization, was still quite weak. He set
about restructuring and adding life to the organization, and in November 1942, became its
commander.

The first armed clashes between the Jews and the
Germans occurred during the deportation drive of
January 18, 1943. In a brief battle, in which many
Jewish fighters fell, Anielewicz was saved by his
men. The deportation ended rather quickly, and
the Jews of Warsaw believed it was Anielewicz's
fighters who caused the Germans to abandon their
operation. Anielewicz and the armed underground's
prestige rose to such a degree in the ghetto that they
became its de facto leaders. Now the Jews of Warsaw feverishly built bunkers and readied themselves for a armed resistance.

On the eve of Passover, April 19, 1943, the Germans began their final deportation drive in Warsaw. The armed underground reacted with all the
weapons it had managed to obtain. Anielewicz
commanded the fighting which at first took place
in the streets and then was confined to the bunkers.
With most of his staff, he entered a bunker on 18
Mila Street. On May 8, amid the burning ruins of
the ghetto, Anielewicz was killed when the bunker
fell to the Germans. He is considered one of the
outstanding heroes of the Holocaust. Kibbutz Yad
Mordecai in Israel was named for him.

ANIELEWICZ'S LAST LETTER,
APRIL 23, 1943

What happened is beyond our wildest dreams.
Twice the Germans fled from our ghetto. One
of our companies held out for forty minutes
and the other, for over six hours.... I have no
words to describe to you the conditions in
which the Jews are living. Only a few chosen
ones will hold out; all the rest will perish
sooner or later. The die is cast. In the bunkers
in which our comrades are hiding, no candle
can be lit for lack of air.... The main thing is:
My life's dream has come true; I have lived to
see Jewish resistance in the ghetto in all its
greatness and glory.

Y. Gutman, *The Jews of Warsaw, 1939–1943*, 1980.
B. Mark, *Uprising in the Warsaw Ghetto*, 1975.

ANTIN, MARY   (1881–1949) U.S. writer. Born in Plotzk, Russia, she suffered humiliation at the hands of other children until her father, who had sailed for the United States, sent for his family. Antin arrived in Boston, Massachusetts, at the age of thirteen. Her first poem, "Snow", was published in the *Boston Herald* when she was fifteen, and her first book, *From Plotzk to Boston* (originally written in Yiddish), when she was eighteen. It consisted of a series of letters to her uncle in Russia in which she recounted her experiences.

Antin studied at Teachers College, Columbia University, from 1901 to 1902, and Barnard College for the next two years. While still a student, she married a non-Jewish professor of geology.

She wrote *The Promised Land* before the age of thirty. First serialized in the *Atlantic Monthly*, it is a personal memoir, the story of a little girl who left the oppressive tsarist regime in Russia to start a new life with her family in America, the story of a voyage from a deep-rooted belief in Judaism to a denial of the existence of God and a rejection of the traditions and beliefs from her pre-American life. She justifies her writing an autobiography by pointing out that her life is illustrative of scores of unwritten lives. "I am only one of many whose fate it has been to live in a page of modern history. We are the strands of the cable that binds the Old World to the New." Explaining how the book had been written, she said, "In the fullness of time it wrote itself." Antin received many literary honors, but viewed herself as "an unwilling celebrity."

They Who Knock at Our Gates, Antin's third book, was less successful. Published in 1914, its thesis is "that what we get in the steerage is not the refuse, but the sinew and bone of all the nations." From then on, Antin's popularity declined. In 1920 her husband left her, and her few years of fame were followed by years of hardship. Over the following years she moved constantly, working as a social worker to support herself.
M. H. Wade, *Pilgrims of Today*, 1920.

I can never forget, for I bear the scars. But I want to forget — sometimes I long to forget. I think I have thoroughly assimilated my past — I have done its bidding — I want now to be of to-day. It is painful to be consciously of two worlds. The Wandering Jew in me seeks forgetfulness. I am not afraid to live on and on, if only I do not have to remember too much. A long past vividly remembered is like a heavy garment that clings to your limbs when you would run.

Mary Antin, Introduction to *The Promised Land*

ANTOKOLSKI, MARK MATVEYEVICH   (1843–1902) Russian sculptor, born in Vilna. During his childhood in the ghetto, Antokolski showed signs of talent in sculpture. After a short time in *hedar* (elementary Hebrew school), he concentrated on wood carving. Against the wishes of his parents, he went at age twenty-one to the Imperial Academy of Fine Arts in Saint Petersburg, where he won many prizes and established a reputation. The academy would not elect him a member, but offered him the title of honorary citizen, which he turned down. He studied in Berlin on a scholarship and upon his return to Russia won immediate fame with his statue of *Ivan the Terrible* (1871), which, with precise attention to detail, reveals the remorse of the tsar as he contemplates his awesome past. He was appointed to the Saint Petersburg Academy at the express order of Tsar Alexander II, who bought the statue and placed it in the Hermitage. He then received a fellowship to work in Italy, where he continued to develop a technique that was more European than Russian; although the realistic, humanist quality of his work was consistent with the Russian tradition of portrait sculpture. In Italy, he belonged to a group of young Russian artists who called themselves the Wanderers because it was their purpose to travel through Russia, bringing art to the people. In 1875 he returned to Saint Petersburg. In 1878 his preeminence in European sculpture was acknowledged when an international jury awarded him first prize for sculpture at the Paris Exposition.

Ivan the Terrible. Sculpture by Mark Antokolski

Antokolski worked in marble, bronze, and ivory. His work includes many statues on Russian themes: *Pushkin* (1875); *Peter the Great*; *Empress Marie Fedorovna*; and the Cossack hero *Yermak, Conqueror of Siberia*. His sculptures on Jewish themes include: *The Jewish Tailor* (1864); *The Talmudic Discussion* (1869); and *Descent of the Inquisition on a Jewish Family on the Feast of Passover* (1867). His interests were wide, ranging from a statue of *Socrates* (1876) to *The Kiss of Judas* (1866). Well known outside of Russia is his evocative ivory statue of *Mephistopheles* seated, like a wound-up spring waiting for the unwary.

During the surge of pogroms in the early 1880s, Antokolski was attacked as a Jew who had no right to portray Russian heroes. He moved to Paris, where he exhibited his marble statue of *Spinoza* (1882), which of all his many full-length portraits was his favorite.

M. Grunwald, *Mark Antokolski* (German), 1926.

ARENDT, HANNAH (1906–1975) Social and political theorist, editor, writer, and teacher. German-born, she left her highly assimilated family and upper-middle-class home in Hanover to study at universities in Heidelberg, Marburg, and Freiburg (1924–1929). In 1933, she fled from Nazism to Paris, where she worked with Youth Aliya, serving as its French director between 1935 and 1938 and accompanying groups of young Jewish refugees to Palestine. In 1940, a refugee herself, she was interned in the Gurs concentration camp in France but reached the United States in 1941, when President Franklin D. Roosevelt intervened on behalf of a hundred intellectuals and their families. Having proven herself a scholar of great ability and penetration with her essay, "From Dreyfus to France Today" (1942), she was chosen as the research director of the Conference on Jewish Relations' and editor in chief of Schocken Books. Later, she directed the Jewish Cultural Reconstruction (1948–1952) and taught at the University of Chicago and the New School for Social Research in New York.

Her critiques of modernity, read and misread by political scientists, philosophers, historical sociologists, liberals and conservatives alike, embrace both a commitment to the concept of private property and a sympathy for Third World revolution, a resolve to be an active participant in world politics and a penetrating cynicism about the role of the intelligentsia. More particularly, her *Origins of Totalitarianism* (1951) speaks of the Jewish experience as being central to an understanding of modern European history, asserting that anti-Semitism and other such dehumanizing and depoliticizing attitudes must be viewed as causes of totalitarianism and the decline of the nation state. Her report on the 1961 Adolf Eichmann trial, *Eichmann in Jerusalem: A Report on the Banality of Evil* (1963), made her a household name in Jewish circles. An acrimonious Jewish intellectual controversy erupted over this work. She was accused of blaming the European Jewish leadership for having failed to save its people from destruction through resistance, of minimizing Eichmann's crimes and claiming that each individual has a capacity for such evil as his, and of insisting that Israel had no right to try or execute the former Nazi war criminal. Gershom Scholem (q.v.) described the tone of her work as "heartless...sneering and malicious," a widely held opinion that contributed to her alienation, in part self-imposed, from the Jewish community.

To Scholem's accusation of her lack of *ahavat Yisrael* (love of the Jewish people), she reportedly replied, "You are quite right.... I have never in my life loved any people or collective.... Indeed I love 'only' my friends and the only kind of love I know of and believe in is the love of persons." Hans Morgenthau and others defended her publicly and her contacts with the Jewish community resumed slowly. She maintained an active membership on the board of directors of the Conference on Jewish Social Studies until shortly before her death, and was known to display a deep emotional attachment to Jews and Judaism while consistently maintaining a veneer of universalism and a profound concern for the future of modern democratic civilization.

R. H. Feldman, *The Jew as Pariah*, 1978.

M. A. Hill, *Hannah Arendt: The Recovery of the Public World*, 1979.

ARI See Luria, Isaac

ARLOSOROFF, CHAIM VICTOR (1899–1933) Labor Zionist politician and thinker, born in the Ukraine to a wealthy and educated family. After witnessing a pogrom, his family moved to Germany and he was educated in Berlin, receiving his doctorate there in 1923. As a student he was a cofounder of the German branch of the Zionist Socialist party Ha-Poel Ha-Tzair and became the editor of its monthly, *Die Arbeit*. He made his Zionist debut at a meeting in Carlsbad, where his knowledge of finances and economics shone. He was already seen as a brilliant mind, a rising star in

Chaim Arlosoroff (left) with Arthur Wauchope, the high commissioner in Palestine, 1931.

Socialist-Zionist politics. In 1924 he immigrated to Palestine.

A noted orator and writer, he believed in popular socialism, opposing Marxism and its doctrine of class warfare. He attempted to link his brand of pragmatic socialism with constructive Zionism and called for more settlement and the slow creation of a Jewish infrastructure in Palestine to enable the Jews to make a claim at a later date for a future Jewish state. He supported the conciliatory policies of collaborating with the British authorities pursued by Chaim Weizmann (q.v.). In the 1920s he fulfilled a number of speaking and fund-raising missions in Europe and the United States, where he impressed his audiences with his incisive presentations. Upon the foundation of the Labor Party, Mapai, he became one of its leaders and editor of its monthly.

In 1931 Arlosoroff was elected to the executive of the Jewish Agency, becoming the head of its political department in charge of foreign relations.

The Palestine Police Force Poster offering a reward for information concerning the murder of Arlosoroff.

That year he traveled to Britain to help convince Prime Minister Ramsay Macdonald to rescind the 1930 White Paper, the statement of policy that for the first time made Jewish immigration to Palestine conditional on the absorptive capacity of that country. The mission was successful.

The rise of Hitler and Nazism alarmed him and in the final year of his life he was engaged in a scheme that called for the transfer of German Jewish assets and property to Palestine. At the time he reached the conclusion that the Jewish state would eventually emerge as a result of an armed struggle and not through a peaceful takeover by the Jews.

In June 1933, he was murdered while walking with his wife on Tel Aviv beach. This occurred at a time of violent controversies between the Labor movement and their ideological opponents, the Zionist Revisionists. The two assassins were unidentified and there was widespread speculation that the motives were political. Two members of the Revisionist movement were arrested and charged with the crime. The defense claimed that the murder was the work of Arabs. At the trial one of the defendants was convicted and sentenced to death but the verdict was overruled by a higher court for lack of corroborative evidence. The mystery was never solved, but for many years gave rise to speculation and continuing suspicions between the left wing and the right wing of the Zionist movement. A committee of enquiry in 1982, headed by a Supreme Court judge, concluded that there was no fresh evidence to shed new light on the case.

A key theoretician of socialist Zionism, Arlosoroff wrote prolifically in Hebrew and German, on political and economic subjects. A collection of his writings was published posthumously in seven volumes and his private notes appeared in his *Jerusalem Diary* (1950).

S. Avineri, *Arlozoroff (1899–1933)*, 1988.

ARON, RAYMOND (1905–1983) French philosopher, sociologist, and writer. Aron was born into a Parisian intellectual middle-class family. In 1924 he entered the Ecole Normale Supérieure, where he achieved the first place in the *agrégation* examination in philosophy. From Paris he moved to Cologne, as assistant to Leo Spitzer, and there wrote his thesis on the limits of historical knowledge. This thesis contained the two main themes that were recurrent throughout his life work. The first was the denial of all transcendency in favor of empiricism. The second was the rejection of determinism (in history), preferring the idea of a fragmented historical rationality, combining necessity and chance.

Aron wrote on various subjects, such as international relations and the nature of modern industrial society, which he saw as the clash of competing political systems. He taught at various institutions and on the outbreak of World War II was professor of social philosophy at the University of Toulouse.

Aron described himself as a "de-judaized Jew."

His intellectual approach to Judaism was as a rationalist atheist. Judaism he saw as a moral relationship between the individual and the universal, and the State of Israel was for him merely an entity in international law. The analysis of the creation of the State of Israel was put in terms of 19th-century nationalism, of a people with the dichotomy of double nationality. Thus, after the Six-Day War (1967), and the capture of the West Bank and Gaza, Aron underwent a crisis of identification with Israel. His book *De Gaulle, Israel, and the Jews* (1968) condemned Charles de Gaulle's remarks about the Jews and Israel after the Six-Day War.

During his long career, Aron wrote numerous works on international relations, industrial society, Algerian independence (which he supported), and historical knowledge. He was one of the leading intellectual critics of the policies of President de Gaulle. He edited *La France Libre* in England from 1940 to 1944, and was a columnist for *Le Figaro* from 1947 and for *L'Express* from 1977. After the war, he continued to teach and was professor of sociology at the Sorbonne, 1955–1968. It was only in the final ten years of his life that Aron was fully accepted by French intellectual circles. His success was demonstrated in the publication of his memoirs in 1983 by his students and followers.

His works include *Peace and War* (1966), *The Great Debate: Theories of Nuclear Strategy* (1965), and the two-volume *Main Currents in Sociological Thought* (1965, 1968).

R. Colquohoun, *Raymond Aron*, 1986.

ASCH, SHOLEM (1880–1957) Yiddish dramatist and novelist. The son of a learned Kutno (Poland) family, Asch received a traditional Jewish education. At seventeen, he taught himself German well enough to read the classics, having come upon a copy of Moses Mendelssohn's German translation of the book of Psalms. His parents' concern that he was straying from the accepted path took him to a small village where he taught Torah to children and had his first studied glimpse into the local peasants' life. Before he was twenty, he moved to Wloclawek, where he served as a professional letter writer for the illiterate of the town. In 1900, he sought out I. L. Peretz (q.v.) in Warsaw with his first literary attempts and was advised to pursue a career in Yiddish writing. As a result, several of his works in Yiddish and Hebrew were published by 1903, all written in a tone of youthful sadness. In addition to Yiddish, Hebrew, Russian, Polish, and German literary influences, Asch's early works show signs of his friendships with A. Reisen and H. D. Nomberg, with whom he lived in Warsaw, "lodged in dark, damp holes, encountering the needy and the poverty-stricken." Fortunately his life changed upon meeting the Polish Jewish writer M. M. Shapiro, whose daughter, Mathilde, he later married.

From 1904, his prolific writings introduced a fresh appreciation of the passion and genuineness of village life to the Yiddish literary world. A

Sholem Asch (left), Isaac Leib Peretz and his son, and Hersh David Nomberg.

reputed playwright whose acclaimed plays such as *Got fun Nekomeh* ("God of Vengeance," 1907) were staged in Russia, Poland, and Germany, he soon set his sights upon new horizons with visits to Eretz Israel (1908) and the United States (1910). This period is characterized by concerns that transcend the confines of the village and touch upon worldwide Jewish problems, as with the novel *Mary* (1917) and its sequel *Der Weg tzu Zikh* ("The Way to Oneself").

Asch spent the war years from 1914 to 1917 in the United States, then returned to Poland and went on to France to write *Motke Ganev* ("Motke the Thief," 1917), *Onkl Mozes* (1918), the historical novel *Kiddush Ha-Shem* (1919), and *Di Kishufmakerhin fun Kastilien* ("The Witch of Castile," 1921). Each story is woven with contrasts and questions of faith and morality as Asch artfully juxtaposes the mundane with the sacred, the Sabbath with the workday, and the harsh external realities of Eastern European Jewish life with the individual Jew's will to overcome them.

Before returning to the United States, in 1938, he mastered the descriptive narrative and began to develop a recognized Aschian character as evidenced in *Di Muter* ("The Mother," 1919), *Toyt Urteyl* ("Death Sentence," 1924), and *Khaym Lederers Tsurikkumen* ("Chaim Lederer's Return," 1927). Zachary Mirkin, in particular, as the hero of Asch's *Farn Mabul* ("Before the Flood," a trilogy written between 1921 and 1931) typifies the author's own believing quest into the world of the ideal, while describing Jewish life in Saint Petersburg, Warsaw, and Moscow at the beginning of the 20th century. His topical choice of setting and subject were notable in *Baym Opgrunt* ("The Precipice," 1937), about pre-war inflationary Germany, and *Dos Gezang fun Tol* ("The Song of the Valley," 1939), set in the Palestine of the *halutzim* (pioneers).

Once in America, his vivid style made him a respected and beloved storyteller to English-speaking, as well as Yiddish-speaking, audiences. In contrast to a most encouraging reception by the general English press to his trilogy about the beginnings of Christianity (*The Nazarene, The Apostle*, and *Mary*, 1943–1949), vicious attacks from the Yiddish press, and particularly the leading daily, *Forward*, accused Asch of furthering the invasive work of Christian missionaries of the day, and he was especially condemned for publishing such works while the Holocaust was in progress. In spite of the ensuing alienation from Yiddish literature and from many of his Jewish social contacts, Asch went on to complete his American-Jewish narrative *Ist River* ("East River," 1946), his novel about Germany under the Nazis, *Der Brenendiker Dorn* ("The Burning Bush," 1946), *Moyshe* ("Moses," 1951), and his last work, based upon Isaiah, *The Prophet* (1955).

The blossoming of Sholem Asch from a village wordsmith to an internationally acclaimed novelist witnessed the introduction of Yiddish literature to a much wider reading public in Europe and America, bringing with it the beauty and grandeur of Jewish culture. His library and private art collection were distributed among Los Angeles, Yale University, and the museum in Bat Yam, Israel, that bears his name.

C. Madison, *Yiddish Literature*, 1968.

ASHER BEN YEHIEL (known by the acronym *Rosh*; c. 1250–1327) Codifier and communal leader in Germany and Spain. He studied in his native Germany; his teachers included his father and uncle, both distinguished scholars of the school of medieval pietists. After a time in France, he moved to Worms, where his teacher was Rabbi Meir of Rothenburg (q.v.). When Meir was imprisoned and held for ransom, Asher succeeded him as head of the Jewish community of Ashkenaz (France and Germany). He worked for the reconstruction of the German communities after massacres in 1298 and also for Meir's release, but when he realized that he himself was in danger of suffering a similar fate, he left Germany in 1303. In the following year he reached Spain, where he became rabbi of the prestigious community of Toledo. He arrived without means and died poor, living on a small salary. Although Spanish Jews were very different from those in Germany, Asher's learning and personality ensured that his authority was recognized throughout the country. Difficult legal queries were submitted to him from many quarters and his influential role was endorsed by the royal court.

Students flocked to his rabbinical academy from as far away as Russia.

He became involved in the controversy over the study of philosophy. He felt that the ban imposed by Solomon ben Abraham Adret (q.v.) on the pursuit of philosophy by students below the age of twenty-five did not go far enough and would have preferred an absolute ban on such education. He eventually endorsed Adret's ruling but insisted that this should not be taken as any sort of support for philosophy.

Asher contributed to every branch of rabbinic learning. Sometimes he opposed customs that he found prevalent in Spain because they had emerged from the Christian environment. These included the provision that women receive equal rights in inheritance, the grant to eldest sons of the entire inheritance, and the custom of forcing a husband to give a divorce if his wife said she did not wish him to continue to be her husband. Over 1,200 of his *responsa* (replies to legal queries) are known.

His legal works comprise commentaries on parts of the Mishnah and Talmud; discussions of problems in the Talmud; and a codification of Jewish law that abstracts the legal parts of the Talmud, adding the views of subsequent rabbinic scholars, for the first time combining the views of the German and Spanish rabbinical authorities. This work was to form the basis for the definitive code, the *Turim*, written by his son, Jacob ben Asher (q.v.). Y. F. Baer, *A History of the Jews in Christian Spain*, vol. 1, 1961.

ASHI (c. 335–c. 427) Babylonian rabbinic scholar and chief editor of the Babylonian Talmud. Ashi was born into a wealthy, scholarly family and studied with the great rabbis of his day. While still a young man, he was appointed to head the famed academy at Sura, which had been closed for a few decades, and he remained in that position for more than half a century. Under Ashi, Sura became the outstanding and authoritative center of Jewish learning. It was said that since the days of Judah ha-Nasi (q.v.) "never were erudition and social distinction so united in one person as in Ashi." He

Reconstruction (from Diaspora Museum) showing Rav Ashi (right) at the Sura Academy.

was recognized as the spokesman and spiritual leader of the community and even the chief lay leader, the exilarch, usually notably jealous of the religious leaders, bowed to his authority. Ashi not only restored the fame of the academy but reconstructed the building and its adjacent synagogue, personally supervising the work and partly financing it himself.

Twice a year, in the months of Adar and Elul, he conducted a study month to which Jews flocked from many countries to join the academy's scholars and pupils in the study of a tractate of the Mishnah. Over the long period of Ashi's direction, the entire Talmudic material was reviewed twice in this way.

Ashi commenced the monumental task of redacting the extensive traditions and discussions concerning the Mishnah which had emerged in the Babylonian academies over the two centuries since the Mishnah was redacted by Judah ha-Nasi. For over thirty years, he and his colleague, Ravina, were responsible for collecting and organizing the legislative discussions and decisions, the lore, legends and sayings that had accumulated. The work was finalized after his death by scholars from his academy following the guidelines and precedents that Ashi had laid down.

Among his sayings were: "The haughty will eventually be humbled"; "a scholar who is not as hard as iron is not a scholar"; and "witnesses were created only against liars."

J. Jacobowitz, *Aspects of the Economic and Social History of the Jews in Babylonia*, 1878.

ASHKENAZI, TZEVI HIRSCH (known as Hakham Tzevi, c. 1660-1718) Rabbi and halakhic authority. Born and raised in Hungary, where his family had sought refuge during the Cossack atrocities of 1648-1654, he grew up in a mixed Ashkenazi-Sephardi community that enjoyed the benefits of Turkish rule. Encouraged to familiarize himself with Sephardi practice, he continued his studies farther afield, mainly in Salonika (1676-1679), but fate dealt him a cruel blow when his wife and child were killed during the Hapsburg siege of Buda in 1686. He then fled to Sarajevo, where the Sephardim appointed him their *hakham* (rabbi), a title that he proudly retained with the adopted surname of Ashkenazi.

The Danish-ruled city of Altona, in northwest Germany, was his home from 1688 until 1709. There he remarried and consolidated his reputation as an eminent scholar in Jewish law, questions being submitted to him from many parts of Europe. One dealt with the Turkish false messiah, Shabbetai Tzevi (q.v.), and his secret adherents; another insinuated that David Nieto, the Sephardi chief rabbi of London, had preached in favor of Spinozism - a charge that Hakham Tzevi investigated and dismissed (1705).

Hakham Tzevi succeeded his father-in-law as rabbi of Altona-Hamburg-Wandsbeck Triple Community in 1707, but fell sick and resigned two

Silver seal of Tzevi Hirsch Ashkenazi.

years later when a controversy broke out over one of his more unusual decisions. In 1710 he was elected chief rabbi of the Ashkenazi Jews in Amsterdam and was welcomed by the local Sephardi magnates and lay leaders. His volume of rabbinic decisions published there in 1712, also drew many compliments from the Sephardi rabbinate, headed by Solomon Ayllon. The following year, however, communal harmony was shattered by the arrival of Nehemiah Hayon, a smooth-tongued follower of Shabbetai Tzevi who had just published a heretical kabbalistic work in Berlin. Hayon asked the Sephardi leaders to permit the sale and distribution of his "learned" book in Amsterdam, but they made this conditional on a rabbinic endorsement. Having reason to suspect their own chief rabbi's orthodoxy, these lay leaders decided to consult Hakham Tzevi as well as Solomon Ayllon. Without waiting for his Sephardi colleague's decision in the matter, Hakham Tzevi proceeded to condemn the book as a Shabbatean tract and to excommunicate its author. This high-handed step enraged Ayllon, who made his quarrel with Hakham Tzevi the pretext for a general campaign of incitement against the "Ashkenazi upstarts."

Rather than continue to endure the violent hostility of his opponents, Hakham Tzevi left Amsterdam in 1714 and accepted the Ashkenazic rabbinate of Lemberg in Poland, where he died a few months after assuming office, worn out and embittered by his experiences. His son, Jacob Emden (q.v.), remained a life-long enemy of the followers of Shabbetai Tzevi.

A. Predmesky, *Life and Work of Rabbi Ashkenazi*, 1946.

ASSER, TOBIAS MICHAEL CAREL (1838-1913) Dutch jurist, awarded the Nobel Peace Prize in 1911. Born in Amsterdam, Asser was appointed the Dutch representative on the International Commission on the Freedom of Navigation on the Rhine in 1860. In 1862 he became professor of commercial and private international law at the University of Amsterdam. At the same time he was a successful barrister. In 1868, together with others, he began the *Revue de droit international et de législation comparée*. Five years later he helped found the Institut de Droit international.

In 1891 he persuaded the government to convene The Hague Conference for the unification of private law, which later became a permanent institution and was responsible for the 1902–1905 Hague treaties on family law.

In 1893 he resigned from his professorship, retired from the practice of law, and became a member of the Dutch Privy Council. Asser was a delegate to the Hague Peace Conferences of 1899 and 1907 and helped organize the Hague Permanent Court of Arbitration, of which he was appointed a member in 1900 and where he arbitrated international problems such as the dispute between the United States and Russia over fishing rights in the Bering Straits.

He was active in the Jewish community of Amsterdam and wrote numerous books on law.

Statue of Asser Tobias.

AUER, LEOPOLD (1845–1930) Violinist and teacher. Born in Veszprem, Hungary, he studied at the Vienna Conservatory and then with Joseph Joachim at Hanover. He was a concertmaster at Düsseldorf from 1863 to 1865 and then at Hamburg for a year. In 1868 he was appointed professor of violin at the Imperial Conservatory, Saint Petersburg, where he succeeded Henryk Wieniawski (q.v.) and remained there until 1917. He was an occasional conductor and violin soloist at the court of the tsars and in 1894 was knighted by Nicholas II. One of his functions as court violinist was to play solos during the ballets at the imperial opera house.

Auer was noted for his interpretations of the classical concertos. Tschaikovsky wrote his violin concerto for Auer but was offended when Auer suggested revisions and changed the dedication to the violinist Adolf Brodsky. However in its final form it was influenced by Auer and became his favorite work. Also interested in chamber music, Auer founded a well-known quartet.

After the February 1917 revolution, he left Russia and went to New York where he devoted himself exclusively to teaching. Many distinguished violinists were his pupils at various times in his life, including Mischa Elman (q.v.), Jasha Heifetz (q.v.), and Efrem Zimbalist. His method of teaching included considerable time devoted by Auer to playing during lessons. He sought to bring out the special qualities of each student but at the same time insisted on a full understanding and respect for the violin, realizing its limitions while exploiting its potentialities.

He wrote a number of books including *Violin Playing as I Teach It* (1921) and *Violin Master Works and their Interpretation* (1925).
L. Auer, *My Long Life in Music*, 1923.

AUERBACH, BERTHOLD (1812–1882) German novelist. Born in Nordstetten, a village in Würtemberg, of a middle-class family, he began his studies at the Talmudic academy of Hechingen and continued at Karlsruhe and Stuttgart. His desire to enter upon a rabbinical career, however, waned during his years at several German universities as he came in contact with the philosophy of Spinoza (q.v.) and the radical theology of David Friedrich Strauss. His participation in an illegal student movement also made it impossible for him to take the examination for the rabbinate and even subjected him to two months imprisonment.

While in prison, he began a novel on Spinoza whose works he later translated from Latin. He attracted attention with a polemic pamphlet directed against the literary critic Wolfgang Menzel, who had instigated the banning by the German federal diet, in December 1835, of the past, present, and future works of Young Germany, a group of writers who made literature a vehicle for their radical ideas on politics, religion, and society. Although only two of these writers, Ludwig Borne and Heinrich Heine (q.v.), were of Jewish birth, Menzel, in his attack on the group, suggested that "Young Palestine" might be a more appropriate designation than "Young Germany."

Auerbach, in his pamphlet *Das Judentum und die neueste Literatur* ("Judaism and the New Literature," 1836), emphasized the injustice in Menzel's anti-Semitic charges of Jewish subversion of German literature. He pointed out that even Borne and Heine could not be labeled Jews since they had converted to Christianity, while also pleading with the Germans to abandon their demonic hatred of Jews.

Compared to Borne and Heine's venomous and satirical replies to Menzel, Auerbach's polemic was mild, even apologetic. He did not want to be tarred as a radical and thought of himself as a patriotic German of Mosaic persuasion. In his twenties, he wrote biographies of famous Jews, the best of which was on Gabriel Riesser, a champion of Jewish emancipation. He also wrote the novels *Spinoza* and *Dichter und Kaufmann* ("Poet and Merchant," 1939), whose hero was the minor Jewish-German poet Ephraim Moses Kuh. His lasting renown in German literature rests upon his more mature *Schwarzwälder Dorfgeschichten*, ("Village Tales of the Black Forest",) published in many volumes between 1843 and 1871. These ushered in the genre of village tales and dealt with the peasants of the Black Forest. They were based upon observations and memories from his formative years when he had lived among the peasants.

Auerbach joined his friend Gabriel Riesser in the struggle for Jewish rights in Germany, both before and after the revolution of 1848. Yet he opposed the views of his classmate Moses Hess (q.v.), who urged him to espouse the cause of Jewish national regeneration and the settlement of Jews in their ancient homeland, Eretz Israel. He held that to affirm the existence of a Jewish nationality would undo a century's struggle for Jewish emancipation and would play into the hands of anti-Semitic agitators. He claimed he was a German who had more in common with his fellow Germans than with Jews outside of Germany and differed from his church-attending neighbors only by his adherence to the Mosaic faith. He even suggested that it might be better to call his religion Mosaism rather than Judaism.

Despite his patriotic protestations, Auerbach had to conclude, during his last years, that the tide of anti-Semitism was rising and that for half a century he had lived and worked in vain for German-Jewish symbiosis.

S. Liptzin, *Germany's Stepchildren*, 1944.

AVICEBRON See Ibn Gabirol, Solomon

AZEFF, YEVNO FISHELEVICH (1869–1918) Russian revolutionary and agent provocateur. Yevno Azeff was born in the small town of Lyskovo in the Jewish Pale of Settlement. His father moved the family to Rostov, where Azeff attended school and became active in the budding socialist revolutionary movement. Upon graduation he gave lessons, was a reporter for a local newspaper, and worked as a clerk, but was not particularly successful in earning a living. His continued activities in the revolutionary movement came to the attention of the authorities, and Azeff was forced to flee to Germany.

Azeff settled at Karlsruhe where he studied engineering and continued his revolutionary activities. Although he left Russia with a considerable sum of money, he soon found it depleted. He wrote a letter to the Ochrana, the Russian secret police, offering to sell his services as an informer against his revolutionary comrades. He made contact with the Union of Social Revolutionaries Abroad, a presocialist party that provided him with letters of introduction to leaders of the socialist underground in Russia. In 1899 Azeff returned to Moscow where he found a position with a general electrical-supply company. At the same time, he became a prominent member of the Union of Social Revolutionaries underground.

Azeff was recognized as a leading advocate of terror as a means of liberating Russia. He often declared that "terror is the only way", but at the same time asked a friend in confidence, "Do you really believe in socialism? It's necessary for the youth and the workers but for you and me...." Despite his rejection of socialism, he quickly rose in the ranks of the newly-founded Social Revolutionary Party, and was appointed to the party's first triumvirate. As a party leader, the information he provided the Ochrana was invaluable, and on several occasions his loyalty to he party was questioned by his comrades. He was, nonetheless, appointed leader of the Battle Organization, the militant terrorist arm of the party.

Azeff was ideologically committed to neither police nor party. He was a mercenary, prepared to sell out to the highest bidder. He refused to give information compromising the party's leadership to the Ochrana when he realized that the 50,000 ruble award offered for that information would go to his superiors rather than to him. Furthermore, as head of the Battle Organization, he controlled the purse strings of that movement, allowing him greater financial independence than the Ochrana offered. He also felt betrayed by the police for their arrest of leading members of the party, an act that cast suspicion upon himself.

To clear himself from suspicion, Azeff took an active role in the planning and execution of the assassination of the Russian interior minister, Vyacheslav Plehve, the man responsible for the Kishinev pogrom of 1903, in which forty-five Jews were murdered and hundreds more brutally beaten. Although Azeff never identified with the Jewish nationalist movement, the horrors of the pogrom revived memories of his childhood. The successful assassination of Plehve brought Azeff's Battle Organization to the forefront of Russian revolutionary politics. Many leading party activists were arrested as a result of information provided by Azeff to the authorities, but he managed to convince the police that he knew nothing of the details of the plot, and was therefore unable to stop it. Azeff was also instrumental in the assassination of Grand Duke Sergei, uncle of the tsar and a leader of the reactionary party at court. Once again, he turned in his coconspirators while convincing the Ochrana of his inability to prevent the assassination.

After a shake-up in the police, Azeff plotted to blow up the dreaded Ochrana headquarters in Saint Petersburg. Although suspicions were again brewing about him, this daring suggestion strengthened his position as leader of the revolutionary terrorists. It was later suggested that he planned the act to destroy any documents connecting him to the Ochrana rather than in the interest of revolution. Nothing came of this plot, nor did anything come of his later plan to assassinate the tsar himself, although Azeff later confided to friends that he himself would have killed the tsar if possible.

The deteriorating situation in Russia saw the defection of several police officers to the Social Revolutionary Party. One such officer informed the party leadership that an informer had infiltrated the higher ranks of the party, however he only knew of him by the code name Raskin. A party historian determined that this informer was Azeff. Azeff surmised that he was under suspicion and fled to Paris. He was tried in absentia and sentenced to death.

Azeff moved to Germany and settled in Berlin with his mistress, Madame N., a Russian cabaret singer of German origin. The Germans imprisoned him during World War I because of his supposed revolutionary leanings. He was released from prison following the October revolution in Russia, but died soon after. Only Madame N. attended his funeral.

B. Nikolajewskii, *Aseff the Spy, Russian Terrorist and Police Stool*, 1934.

AZULAI, HAYIM JOSEPH DAVID (known by the acronym *Hida*; 1724–1806) Rabbinic scholar. A prolific author, he penned eighty-three books on a wide range of Judaic subjects, including Bible commentary, homiletics, Jewish law, Kabbalah, sermons, and bibliographies. Already in his first book, *Ha'lim Devar*, written at the age of fifteen, he demonstrated that many sages of Jewish law had made slips due to faulty knowledge of bibliography and chronology.

Azulai was born in Jerusalem, then under Ottoman rule, into a family of scholars. His father was considered to be one of the more notable rabbis of the Holy Land. He studied under several rabbis but did not spend much time engaged in his studies; due to his growing fame, he was summoned to public duty at a relatively young age.

During this period, much of the financial support for the minuscule and destitute Jewish community in Eretz Israel depended on enlisting the aid and contributions of well-to-do communities of the Diaspora. An indispensable means of gaining this support was performed by the *shaliah* (emissary), usually a Torah scholar of some eminence, who agreed to undertake a mission overseas that could last several years. During his travels, the *shaliah* would call on far-flung Jewish communities, from Morocco and Amsterdam to Warsaw and the West Indies. There he would take up appeals for funds on behalf of the scholars of the Holy Land and their families.

Azulai was twenty-nine when he made his first journey to Italy as a *shaliah*, and had still to publish any of his works. Yet he earned the acclaim of the Italian communities, especially those of Leghorn (Livorno) and Ancona. An affluent Leghorn Jew

even provided him with the money necessary for publishing his first book.

Wherever he went, Azulai made an impression on Jew and non-Jew alike by virtue of his profound and broad knowledge, power of oratory, and personal charm. He was respected by the leading scholars of his generation, and his books were well-received by members of the Sephardic and Ashkenazic communities alike.

Unlike preceding emissaries, Azulai did not perceive his function as one of a mere fund-raiser, but used his travels to inquire into and unearth ancient Jewish books and documents. He would study these texts in order to broaden his knowlege, at times copying sections into his notebook, and whenever possible, purchasing them outright. He was the first Jewish scholar to research the Hebrew manuscripts that laid buried within the *genizot* (archives of disused Jewish writings) of the French and Italian libraries.

Azulai always took along his ubiquitous notebooks when manuscript hunting. These served him as a means to record material he had uncovered, or to note new Torah interpretation that occurred to him while perusing the works of the ancient authorities. In addition, they served to record the gist of his own discourses as well as those of others, queries put to him on Jewish subjects, and his replies to them.

Signature of Hayim Joseph David Azulai.

In 1768, Azulai was a member of a delegation to Constantinople on behalf of the Jerusalem community, presenting their grievances against an oppressive official before the sultan. When the mission failed he did not return to Jerusalem, but went to Egypt, where he served as rabbi in the Cairo Jewish community for over four years. Due to the outbreak of a revolt and the ensuing famine, he returned to Eretz Israel and settled in Hebron. Four years later, he once more set out as an emissary on behalf of the Hebron community. Passing through Egypt and Tunisia, he made his way to Italy, France, and the Low Countries, finally making his home in Leghorn, for the next thirty-eight years until his death. In 1960, his remains were brought from Leghorn and reinterred in Jerusalem.

His writings include *Mazal Tov*, an account of his travels, and *Shem ha-Gedolim* with biographies of 1,300 scholars and a description of 2,200 works.
L. Jung, *Guardians of Our Heritage*, 1958.

B

BAAL SHEM TOV (known by the acronym, *Besht*; Israel ben Eliezer; c. 1700–1760) Charismatic founder of the Hasidic movement. He was born to poor and elderly parents in Okop, Podolia (now in the western Ukrainian S.S.R.), and was orphaned when a child. Most information concerning his youth is legendary, but he clearly sought solitude in the fields and woods of his surroundings. He earned his living as a teacher in elementary Hebrew schools and as a ritual slaughterer, and married at age eighteen. In his twenties, he withdrew with his wife into the Carpathian Mountains for a long period of seclusion while earning his living as a lime digger. During this time, he began to achieve a reputation as a wonder worker and healer and he was especially known as the Baal Shem Tov (Good Master of the Name [of God]), who not only healed by amulets and incantations but also was an outstanding spiritual figure.

About 1736 he settled in Medzibozh, Podolia, and for the rest of his life concentrated on his religious teachings. Admirers flocked from near and far and it is estimated that at his death he had over 10,000 followers. At this time, there were a number of similar figures, but he became the dominant personality and the others disappeared from the scene.

He was not a profound Talmudic scholar in rabbinics, his expertise laying in his knowledge of the Bible, rabbinic legend and folklore (*aggada*), and Jewish mysticism. He did not construct a systematic theology and code of practice but presented his teachings primarily in aphorisms, probably in Yiddish. He was very much influenced by the mystical thought of Isaac Luria (q.v.) and his school, but introduced many of his own innovations. To him, the great goal of religious life was spiritual communion with God, a cleaving (*devekut*) to the Divine, to be achieved not only in prayer but also in every aspect of daily life. Prayer must be uttered with complete devotion (*kavvana*); the study of Torah also brings man to the divine but this too must be undertaken with utter devotion, and not undertaken merely as an intellectual exercise. All man's deeds must be an expression of his worship of God — even in his eating and in conducting business. This teaching was attacked by his critics, the Mitnaggedim (literally, opponents) who saw it as threatening their own exclusive stress on Torah study.

The Baal Shem Tov also angered the Mitnaggedim by giving the emotional precedence over the rational, simple faith over study, joy over asceticism, and devotion over discipline. He believed that his own prayers opened the gates of heaven and that there were other righteous people in every generation with similar powers (giving rise to the Hasidic doctrine of the *tzaddik*, the righteous leader of the community with superhuman powers).

He spoke to his followers through stories, anecdotes, and parables and did not commit his teaching to writings (this was done by his disciples). He appealed especially to the unlearned who found a special appeal in his teachings that the way to God did not require great learning. His own folksy way of life attracted the masses — telling stories in the marketplace or smoking his pipe and dressing like the peasants with whom he chatted as they came for evening service. His criticism of ascetic practices and emphasis on joyful observance of the commandments also helped to win him his popular following. The rabbinical leaders attacked his behavior as "licentious", but this did not deter him from his way.

Innumerable legends spread about the Baal Shem Tov. It was said that he understood the language of birds and trees; that his body was entirely spiritual and that whenever food passed his lips, a fire came down from heaven and caused it to ascend; that he walked over the river Dniester on his girdle; that he brought the dead to life; that he knew every secret; that every Saturday afternoon he taught new meanings of the Torah to a heavenly academy; that he regularly communicated with the Messiah, who revealed to him that redemption would come when the whole world accepted the teachings of the Baal Shem Tov.

From the Baal Shem Tov's teachings grew the populist, renewal movement of Hasidism, which changed many of the traditional values and practices of Judaism. Instead of praying in synagogues, his followers worshiped in small, unassuming prayer rooms and their prayer was marked by ecstatic devotion. The Mitnaggedim were horrified

by this unconventionality, by the downgrading of the values of learning, and by the doctrine of the *tzaddik* as the intermediary between man and God and did all they could to crush the new movement, but it swept like wildfire through much of eastern Europe and still is a force within Judaism today.
D. Ben-Amos and J. R. Mintz, *In Praise of the Baal Shem Tov*, 1970.
S. Birnbaum, *The Life and Sayings of the Baal Shem*, 1933.
G. Scholem, *The Messianic Idea in Judaism*, 1972.

SAYINGS OF THE BAAL SHEM TOV

- In the struggle with evil, only faith matters.
- The important thing is not how many separate commandments we obey, but the spirit in which we obey them.
- Woe unto us! The world is full of radiant, wonderful and elevating secrets and it is only the small hand held up before our eyes which prevents us from seeing the light.
- There is no room for God in a person who is full of himself.
- If the vision of a beautiful woman, or of any lovely thing, comes suddenly to mind, let a man say to himself: The source of such beauty must be from the divine force which permeates the universe. So why be attracted by a part? Better be drawn after the All. Perception of beauty is an experience of the Eternal.
- If you seek to lead your neighbor in the right path, you must do so out of love.
- God hides himself behind many partitions and iron walls but all farseeing persons know that these belong to the inner being of God, for no place is without Him.
- All things above and below are a Unity.
- Pray for the suppression of evil but never for one's own material well-being, for a separating veil arises if one admits the material into the spiritual.
- If you wish to live long, don't become famous.
- As a man prays for himself, so must he pray for his enemy.
- A man must make the observance of three rules his aim in life: love of God, love of Israel, and love of Torah. With these, penance is unnecessary.
- If I love God, what need have I of the world to come?

BABEL, ISAAC EMMANUILOVICH (1894–1939?) Soviet author and prominent victim of Stalinism; one of the most accomplished short-story writers in Russian literature. Throughout his life, revolutionary ideals seem to have clashed with the moral values of his Jewish upbringing. Born in the

lively, cosmopolitan Black Sea port of Odessa, Isaac Babel received a traditional religious as well as a secular education. After completing his studies in Kiev, he managed to acquire forged papers enabling him to evade anti-Semitic police regulations and move to Petrograd, where his earliest stories appeared in Maxim Gorky's periodical *Letopis* (1916). Though modeled on the type of French *conte* written by Flaubert and Maupassant, they eventually displayed great individualism in their content and linguistic style.

Isaac Babel and his wife at the beach of Saint Idesbald, Belgium, summer 1928.

Like many other Jewish intellectuals of his time, Babel welcomed the downfall of tsarism in 1917 and fought on the Bolshevik side during the Russian Civil War. As a political commissar attached to Semyon Budyonny's First Cavalry Army, he may well have been the first Jew to ride with the dreaded Cossacks. From 1923, Babel devoted himself to writing plays, scripts for films that have apparently vanished, and narrative works. His true genius was revealed, however, in the two collections of short stories that brought him worldwide renown and that Ilya Ehrenburg (q.v.), a close friend, judged to be the *chef d'ouevre* of a "superlative craftsman." These were *Konarmiya* (1926), translated into English as *Red Cavalry* (1929), and *Odesskiye Rasskazy* ("Odessa Tales," 1927).

Drawing on his own experiences during the Polish campaign of 1920, Babel's *Red Cavalry* tales made skillful use of Russian and Ukrainian dialect to create an authentic atmosphere and convey both the heroism and the horrors of full-scale war. In one episode, "Gedali," the writer underlines the plight of simple Hasidic Jews who find themselves caught between the warring camps; while hopeful that the revolution will abolish injustice, they are already aware of its dire impact on their traditional life style. Equally vigorous and convincing are the "Odessa Tales," laced with Yiddish, in which Babel paints a broad canvas of urban Jewish society - from pious householders and traders like his own father to an underworld of gangsters headed by the archrogue Benya Krik. A memora-

ble story here, entitled "The History of My Dove-
cote," gives a small boy's account of the 1905
pogrom in Nikolayev, where the Babel family was
living at the time.

The left-wing Jewish idealists who figure in Babel's stories are mainly reflections of himself — "a guy
wearing specs" eager to be accepted by his comrades, but incapable of descending to their rough-
and-ready level, the Bolshevik son of a rabbi who
carries portraits of Lenin and Maimonides with
him into battle. Thus, while helping to build a new
world, he could not entirely shake off the old,
attending synagogue on the Day of Atonement and
observing the traditional Passover Seder.

After 1929, Babel fell foul of the Soviet literary
establishment and, while continuing to write, chose
to publish very little. The death of Maxim Gorky in
1936, as Stalin's purge of veteran communists was
gathering speed, robbed Babel of his most influential protector. Whatever the grounds for his arrest
by the NKVD in 1939, he vanished completely and
may well have been shot immediately, without the
brief reprieve of a Siberian labor camp. Babel's
name and best-known works were finally "rehabilitated," however, in the 1950s, after Stalin's death.
Many unpublished tales have been lost; some
printed earlier were reissued as *Collected Stories*
(1955); others, rescued from oblivion by Isaac
Babel's daughter, appeared in her biographical
volume, *The Lonely Years, 1925-1939*, published
outside of the USSR in 1964.

R. Hallett, *Isaac Babel*, 1973.

J. E. Falen, *Isaac Babel: Russian Master of the
Short Story*, 1974.

BACHER, WILHELM (1850-1913) Hungarian
orientalist, rabbinical and Semitic scholar. Born
Vilmos Bacher in Liptoszentmiklos, Hungary (now
in Czechoslovakia), he was interested in Jewish
scholarship from an early age and was educated in
Pressburg (now Bratislava, Czechoslovakia). From
1867 he attended the University of Budapest,
receiving his doctorate for a thesis on the 12th-
century Persian poet, Nizami. After being ordained
as a rabbi at the Breslau Rabbinical Seminary, he
was appointed rabbi of Szeged in 1876. The following year, the Budapest Rabbinical Seminary was
opened, and Bacher became one of its three profes-
sors and the only Hungarian Jewish scholar
appointed to it by the Hungarian government. He
taught biblical exegesis, homiletics, Midrash, and
Hebrew poetry and grammar. He continued lecturing until his death and for the last six years of his
life also served as rector.

His scholarly output was rich and varied, including 48 books and some 700 articles. He touched on
all aspects of Jewish studies, Bible and Talmud,
Semitic languages and lexicography, history and
thought, medieval poetry and grammar as well as
Judeo-Persian literature. His writings were clear
and straightforward, usually breaking new ground.
Under his guidance, the Budapest Rabbinical
Seminary became an important center for the

scientific study of Judaism (*Wissenschaft des Judentums*). For thirty years he was the central figure
in Jewish scholarly life in Hungary.

While a thorough scholar, he was also a believing Jew and his biblical scholarship was conservative. The text was sacrosanct and not to be
amended. Although familiar with the works of the
biblical critics, he did not present them to his students because he thought they lacked significance
and contradicted basic Jewish belief. Instead, he
emphasized traditional Jewish exegesis as a source
for the understanding of the Bible. To make these
works more available, he translated some from
Arabic to Hebrew.

In his Talmudic studies he made a special contribution to *aggada* (the nonlegal sections of the
Talmud). Before his time, few scholars had devoted
their attention to this subject. Thanks to Bacher, it
became a field of research and interest, and he laid
the foundation for the study of its historical development. He wrote on hundreds of early rabbis and
was one of the first scholars to devote special attention to the Palestinian (as opposed to the Babylonian) Talmud. He was the only Jewish scholar of
his generation to be an authority on Judeo-Persian
and was the first to study the poetry of the Yemenite Jews.

The lasting impact of his works is reflected in
their reprints in the 1960s and the 1970s and in the
translation of many of them into Hebrew in Israel.

BAECK, LEO (1873-1956) German rabbi,
communal leader, and Jewish theologian. He was
born to the local rabbi in Lissa, Posen (Poznan),
then part of Prussia. He studied at Breslau University and then in Berlin, where he received his rabbinical diploma (1897) from the Liberal rabbinical
seminary. After occupying pulpits in Oppeln (Upper
Silesia) and Düsseldorf, he returned to Berlin in

Leo Baeck (right) with Martin Buber.

1912 as rabbi and as lecturer in the Liberal seminary. During World War I he served as army chaplain on both the western and eastern fronts. After the war, he became chairman of the national association of German rabbis (1922) and president of the B'nai B'rith fraternal organization in Germany.

As early as 1897 he showed his readiness to stand up for unpopular principles when he refused to sign an anti-Zionist declaration supported by the majority of German rabbis. Baeck's leadership qualities, which included courage and integrity, were clearly demonstrated during the Nazi years, when he turned down many opportunities to emigrate in order to remain at the head of his community. When Hitler came to power in 1933, a small central committee (the Reichsvertretung der Juden in Deutschland) was established to represent German Jewry before the government and Baeck was appointed its chairman. Realizing and stating that the thousand-year history of German Jewry was reaching its end, he successfully united all its activities on a nationwide scale so as to ensure its maximum strength in face of the heavy blows rained on it. On two occasions he was arrested by the Gestapo but was released and resumed his position. Despite the personal danger, he remained at his post after the outbreak of World War II until the beginning of 1943 when he was deported by the Nazis to the ghetto at Theresienstadt. In that concentration camp, he was one of the leaders of the Jewish Council and, through his teaching and preaching, bolstered the morale of the inmates. Early in his life, his poor eyesight had accustomed him to lecturing and preaching without notes; now he taught without books. He even drafted a new work called *The People of Israel: The Meaning of Jewish Existence*. On one occasion the Germans decided to deport him to an extermination camp but a mix-up occurred and someone of a similar name was taken.

After liberation in 1945, Baeck moved to London and in his last years served as chairman of the World Union of Progressive Judaism, taught at the Hebrew Union College in Cincinnati, headed the Council of German Jews in England, and helped found the Leo Baeck Institute, the international research institute for the study of the Jews of Central Europe. Everywhere he was revered as a saintly symbol of spiritual resistance to the Holocaust suffering.

His best-known work was his *Essence of Judaism*, a polemical reaction to Adolf von Harnack's *Essence of Christianity*. He saw the core of Judaism as morality and firmly upheld its superiority over Christianity. A strong impact was made by his distinction between Judaism as a "classic religion," which makes ethical demands, and Christianity as a "romantic religion," which induces passivity because it is based on emotion in which faith and revelation are seen as the fulfillment of religion. Judaism is a religion of polarity between the mystery of the Divine and the commandment of the ethical imperative. In Judaism, man becomes free through the commandments; in Christianity, through grace.

A. H. Friedlander, *Leo Baeck, Teacher of Theresienstadt*, 1968.
L. Baker, *Days of Sorrow and Pain: Leo Baeck and the Berlin Jews*, 1978.

FROM THE WORKS OF LEO BAECK

- Through faith man experiences the meaning of the world; through action he is to give it a meaning.
- We are encompassed by questions to which only awe can respond.
- Religion may be the concern of a people but it must never become a concern of the state.
- Man's creed is that he believes in God and therefore in mankind, but not that he believes in a creed.
- Jewish piety and Jewish wisdom are found only where the soul is in the possession of the unity of devotion and deed.

BAGINSKY, ADOLF ARON (1843–1918) German founder of modern pediatrics. Born in Ratibor, Silesia, he studied medicine at the University of Berlin, graduating in 1866. In 1881 he joined the faculty and later became a professor of pediatrics at the university.

Baginsky concentrated mainly on infectious diseases in children and on the use of milk and general hygiene in infants. Together with Rudolf Virchow, in 1890, he founded the children's hospital, Kaiser und Kaiserin Friedrich Krankenhaus, and became its director.

In 1879 he founded and became editor of the journal *Archiv für Kinderheilkunde*. He also wrote widely on chemistry and physiology.

Baginsky was a brilliant teacher and author. His *Lehrbuch der Kinderheilkunde* ("Textbook of Pediatrics," 1882) became a classic that went into eight editions and was translated into many languages. Among his other publications were *Handbuch der Schulhygiene* ("Manual of School Hygiene," 1877) and *Praktische Beitrage zur Kinderheilkunde* ("Practical Contributions to Pediatrics," 1889–1884). He also wrote articles approving the hygienic aspects of the Bible.

He was active in the Berlin Jewish community and fought against anti-Semitism in Germany.

BAHYA IBN PAKUDA (11th cent.) Jewish moral philosopher living in Spain. Nothing is known of his life except that he was a religious judge who probably lived in Saragossa. His fame stems from his book, *Duties of the Heart*, written in Arabic and translated into Hebrew under the title *Hovot ha-Levavot*. This was the most popular Jewish ethical work of the Middle Ages.

Bahya was heir to the medieval Jewish philosophical synthesis of rabbinic Judaism with Islamic Neo-Platonism to which he added traditions from Arab mysticism, including a unique tendency among the Jewish philosophers toward ascetism. Despite these outside influences, Bahya remained completely within a Jewish framework.

He divides Jewish life into the observance of the practical commandments and the "duties of the heart," which are the obligations of man's inner spiritual life and are no less binding than the former. In this way, he sought to intensify the life of devotion and to direct the worshiper on the true path of divine worship. The duties of the heart, he held, had been neglected in Jewish circles; they demand intellectual preparation and not only Jewish tradition but philosophy must be employed to grasp them as a preliminary step to their observance. I. Husik, *A History of Medieval Jewish Philosophy*, 1916, pp. 80–105.

M. Manson (ed.), *The Book of Directions to the Duties of the Heart*, 1973.

The ten treatises of Bahya's book indicate the main lines of his thought.

1. *The unity of God*: Every believer must prove for himself the existence and unity of God.

2. *The examination of created things*: Divine wisdom is manifested through the complexity of the universe.

3. *The service of God*: The world to come is attained through both Torah and reason.

4. *Trust in God*: God is omnipresent and protects man from the dangers that surround him.

5. *Wholehearted devotion*: Man must consecrate his deeds to God alone.

6. *Humility*: Humility before God will be reflected in man's behavior toward other people.

7. *Repentance*: The return of man to the service of God after he has gone astray.

8. *Self-examination*: Everyone must constantly examine himself in accordance with his own abilities.

9. *Abstinence*: Moderate abstinence of the body is a step toward the well-being of the soul.

10. *The true love of God*: The supreme degree of spirituality.

BAKST, LEON (Lev Samuilovich Rosenberg; 1866–1924) Russian artist and stage designer. Born to an affluent commercial family who lived in Saint Petersburg, at the age of twelve he won an art prize at school and developed an interest in painting. His parents withdrew their opposition when the famous Jewish sculptor Mark Antokolski (q.v.) saw and praised his work, and at sixteen he became a stu

dent of the Académie des Beaux Arts. Although he was there for only eighteen months since he was criticized for his use of strong colors (for which he became noted in his stage designs), this experience proved valuable. There he made friendships that brought him into the circle of Sergey Diaghilev that met at the home of Alexandre Benois, who also later designed decor for the Diaghilev Ballets Russes.

Bakst became one of the contributors to *Mir Isskustva* ("World of Art"), founded and published by Diaghilev in Russia, and from 1909 was senior designer for the Diaghilev ballet company in Paris. His first stage decor, however, was for *The Fairy Doll* (1903) in Saint Petersburg. Among his designs in Paris were *Cléopâtre* (1909), choreographed by Michel Fokine, with Ida Rubinstein (q.v.) in the title role; *Sheherazade* (for which he suggested the theme), also choreographed by Fokine to music by Rimsky-Korsakov; and *Spectre de la rose*, choreographed by Vaslav Nijinsky to the music of Claude Debussy. His imaginative theatri-

Costume design by Leon Bakst for the ballet Sheherazade *1921.*

cal design both for scenery and costume was regarded as revolutionary and was greatly influential. He also established himself as a painter, mostly of portraits, including those of Isadora Duncan and of Diaghilev. A contemporary described Bakst as "a delightful person, full of imagination and often highly comical, sometimes without meaning it" and he was described as "a gay carefree man about town." When he fell in love with a Russian Orthodox woman, he converted to the Orthodox Church (having first tried other churches) in order to be able to marry her; when he quarreled with his wife and found that a law had been promulgated allowing Jews to revert to their faith, he was among the first to do so.

When Bakst was preparing the decor for *Cléopâtre*, he fell in love with Ida Rubinstein (one of the most beautiful women of her time); when she left the Diaghilev company to form her own, he made stage designs for her production of *The Martyrdom of St. Sebastian* (Debussy).

R. Lister, *The Moscovite Peacock: A Study of the Art of Leon Bakst*, 1954.

BALABAN, BARNEY   (1887–1983) U.S. motion picture executive. He was born to Russian immigrants in Chicago. His father was a grocer, and he himself worked at a cold storage company from the age of twelve, making his way up from messenger boy to chief clerk.

The credit for his entry into the movie business goes to his mother, who accompanied him to a film playing at a nickelodeon and marveled that people would pay for the film, even before they saw it. Recognizing the opportunity to make money, Balaban and his brother, A. J. Balaban, rented the theater and introduced attractions such as a violinist to attract customers, and an electric fan. Balaban himself worked as pianist and usher. The Circle Theater followed two years later, boasting seven hundred seats, an organ, an orchestra, ventilation, and a higher ticket price.

The Balaban and Katz company, founded in 1908, expanded. Soon they were buying interests in other theaters and offering facilities for seating large audiences, air conditioning, comfortable chairs, balconies, plush lobbies, and ushers, as well as long vaudeville programs before he films. When Paramount Pictures bought two-thirds of Balaban and Katz in 1926, they owned twenty-five theaters in the Midwest. The Balabans, in due recognition of their abilities, remained as managers at Paramount and in 1936 Barney was elected president of the company. During the war, he stated "We, the industry, recognize the need for informing people in foreign lands about the things that have made America a great country." He undertook that Paramount films would bring that message even to taking a loss in revenue, if necessary.

Always an astute businessman, Balaban foresaw correctly that the era of plush theaters and super-productions costing many millions of dollars would one day end, and in 1958 he sold the television rights to Paramount's early movies for fifty million dollars.

At his death he was still honorary chairman of Paramount Pictures.

C. Balaban, *Continuous Performance: The Story of A. J. Balaban*, 1942.

BALCON, MICHAEL   (1896–1977) British film producer, knighted 1948. Born and educated in Birmingham, he left a position in the rubber industry to join his friend Victor Saville (later to achieve fame as a producer and director) in film distribution. After entering production, Balcon and Saville, with their business partner, John Freedman, formed Gainsborough Pictures in 1924. While acting as head of production for Gainsborough, Balcon gave Alfred Hitchcock, until then an art director and screenwriter, the chance to direct.

In his later years, when he was regarded as the elder statesman of the British film industry, Balcon preached against dependence on American assistance. In his first efforts at production, however, he took care to bolster his chances of a wide audience by using popular American stars, such as Betty Compson and Mae Marsh. Clive Brook and Victor McLaglen were among the British stars discovered by Balcon at Gainsborough.

Balcon was director of production at Gaumont-British from 1931 to 1936, when a decision to cease production resulted in his dismissal. While at Gaumont-British, Balcon oversaw the making of films as varied as the musical *Evergreen*, the documentary *Man of Aran*, and the British version of Feuchtwanger's *Jew Suss*. A reunion with Hitchcock also produced the highly successful *The Man Who Knew Too Much*.

A brief period heading MGM's London office was followed by over two decades as head of production for Ealing Studios. The best-known of over a hundred films produced between 1939 and 1959 are a handful of comedies including *Kind Hearts and Coronets*, which is famous for Alec Guinness's multiple roles. The freedom he granted his creative staff built his reputation as "an artist's businessman." A later commentator succinctly summed up the situation at Ealing with the observation that "in the absence of money, they had to make do with talent."

After Ealing closed, Balcon became head of Bryanston Films, a consortium of sixteen independent producers, retaining this position until 1975. From 1964 to 1966 he was chairman of British Lion.

In keeping with the uncompromising Britishness of his Ealing productions, Balcon fought for the British cinema as a whole and strove to provide

---

BALCON ON THE SUCCESS OF THE EALING COMEDIES

The comedies were, if you like, a mild protest — but a protest about nothing more sinister than the regimentation of the times, after a period of war. I think we were going through a mildly euphoric period then — believing in ourselves and having some sense of, yes it sounds awful, national pride. And if I were to think and think I couldn't give you a deeper analysis.

opportunities for newcomers to the industry. In 1951, three years after being knighted, he became chairman of the British Film Institute Experimental Film Fund (later the BFI Production Board), a body offering grants to young independent filmmakers.

His daughter was the actress Jill Balcon and his grandson the Oscar-winning actor, Daniel Day-Lewis.

J. Fluegel (ed.), *Michael Balcon: The Pursuit of British Cinema*, 1984.

Michael Balcon Presents... A Lifetime of Films, 1969.

BALLIN, ALBERT (1857–1918) Hamburg shipping magnate and architect of imperial Germany's merchant marine. After building up the steamship company that his father, a Danish immigrant, had established, Ballin showed an unrivaled grasp of the new opportunities afforded by the trans-Atlantic passenger trade. Thanks to the modifications that he introduced, German ships were able to carry far more steerage passengers while improving both their speed and the level of service available to those in first and cabin class. From 1886, Ballin transformed the Hamburg-Amerika (Hapag) Line into Germany's foremost shipping concern, with a fleet of 400 vessels and an international reputation. It offered new standards of comfort and safety, as well as pleasure cruises in the winter season. Ballin was not merely a business wizard, but also a skilled negotiator who concluded the German-U.S. shipping agreement of 1912 and then tried to negotiate an Anglo-German naval agreement with the help of Sir Ernest Cassel (q.v.).

The West German stamp commemorating the centenary of Albert Ballin's birth.

No less a devoted Jew than a staunch German patriot, Ballin worshiped at the Bornplatz Synagogue of the Orthodox Deutsch-Israelitischer Synagogenverband in Hamburg. It was on his initiative that ships of the Hapag Line provided kosher dietary arrangements for the observant

Jewish passenger. Wilhelm II turned to him for economic advice and Ballin was often a guest on the kaiser's yacht. Unlike other "court Jews" admitted to the Imperial circle, however, Ballin never received a patent of nobility, despite his many services to the crown, because of his refusal to convert.

During World War I, Ballin organized the shipping of foodstuffs to Germany, circumventing the Allied naval blockade. Though distrusted by the kaiser's warmongering generals, he became one of the chief negotiators for an armistice and peace talks in 1918. The humiliation which he felt after Wilhelm's abandonment of the throne and flight to Holland drove Ballin to take his own life. Within the next twelve years, the Hapag company that he had made the symbol of German prestige became *judenrein*. On the centenary of his birth (August 15, 1957), a commemorative postage stamp honoring Albert Ballin was issued by the German Federal Republic.

L. Cecil, *Albert Ballin: Business and Politics in Imperial German 1888–1918*, 1967.

BALOGH, THOMAS (1905–1985) Hungarian-born economist in England who specialized in planning, development, and labor economics; made life peer, 1968. Balogh studied law and economics at the universities of Budapest and Berlin and subsequently was invited to the United States as a Rockefeller Fellow at Harvard University. During the 1930s he worked in France and Germany, eventually settling in England where he was appointed lecturer at University College, London (1934–1939). Balogh's career at Oxford began as a lecturer at Balliol College in 1939. In 1945 he was elected to a fellowship. While at Oxford he helped to establish the Institute of Statistics, which enabled refugee scholars to continue their work.

During World War II Balogh was chairman of the Mineral Development Committee. After the war he was appointed deputy chief of a United Nations mission to Hungary and soon after began to advise the governments of a number of underdeveloped countries, including India, Malta, and Jamaica. In the late 1950s he served as advisor to the U.N.'s Food and Agriculture Organization (FAO).

After the Labour party's victory in Parliament in 1964, Prime Minister Harold Wilson appointed Balogh adviser on economic affairs. Balogh believed that the Labour government would be committed to policies of faster growth in Britain. He supported increased government involvement in industry. Balogh remained loyal to Wilson even in the face of economic policies of which he did not approve. In 1968 he received a life peerage. His influence in the government led to the creation of the Department of Economic Affairs to handle the planning and expansion of Britain's economy. Balogh was also able to get economists placed in jobs, although it was said that he held most of the work done by economists in contempt. Still, he proclaimed the importance of professional training for economists and their usefulness to industry and government.

After the defeat of the Labour government in 1970, Balogh returned to Oxford and continued to teach and write. He retired in 1973, but the following year was called back into public service and was appointed minister of state at the Department of Energy. He played a key role in the creation of the British National Oil Corporation and served as its deputy chairman from 1976 to 1978. He strongly advocated government participation in extracting oil from the North Sea.

In 1979 Balogh received an honorary doctorate from the University of Budapest. His published works include *Dollar Crisis* (1949), *Unequal Partners* (1963), *Planning for Progress* (1963), and *Economics of Poverty* (1966).

BAMBERGER, SIMON   (1846–1926) U.S. mining and railroad pioneer; governor of Utah. Born in Germany, Simon Bamberger went to the United States in 1860 on the eve of the Civil War. Too young to be drafted, he worked for an older brother in Wilmington, Ohio. Subsequently, the brothers became clothing manufacturers in Saint Louis. While trying to catch up with a company debtor, Bamberger relocated to a railroad work camp in Wyoming, where he provided shacks and tents as housing for railroad workers.

In 1869 after spending some time in Ogden, Utah, he settled in Salt Lake City, where he was soon joined by his brothers. Since they were more interested in the business than he was, he gravitated to the gold fields, ultimately finding his fortune in the Centennial Eureka Mines. Later he also built a railroad line from the coalfields in southern Utah. Struggling for eighteen years against the interests of two existing railroads seeking to block a new competitor as well as the Union Pacific, whose lines he had to cross, he ultimately won out and the Bamberger Railroad, the only one ever named for a Jew in the United States, operated between Salt Lake City and Ogden. The line was opened in 1908 and electrified in 1912.

In 1869 he was a founder of the Liberal Party. Bamberger was elected as member of the Salt Lake City Board of Education in 1898, and distinguished himself by fighting to improve the conditions for teachers. For four years (1903–1907), he served in the State Senate of Utah. In 1916 he was elected governor of the state of Utah, the first Democrat and non-Mormon to hold the office. He served for four years and was noted for his pro-labor views. His administration improved public health facilities, upgraded teacher's salaries, introduced farming benefits, and legislated for the control and supervision of public utilities.

Committed to the small Jewish community in Utah, Bamberger was a founder and president of its first congregation, Bnai Israel in Salt Lake City. He aided in the efforts of the Jewish Agriculture Society to create a farming community in Utah for Jews from the east. He was also one of the founding members of the American Jewish Committee in 1906.

L. L. Watters, *Pioneer Jews of Utah*, 1952.

BARANY, ROBERT   (1876–1936) Otologist and Nobel Prize winner. Born in Vienna of Hungarian parents, he studied medicine at the University of Vienna, from which he graduated with a degree in medicine in 1900. During the next five years he engaged in medical research at hospitals in Frankfurt, Heidelberg, and Freiburg before returning to the University of Vienna as an assistant professor in otology. Here he researched the structure and function of the inner ear. In 1906 he announced his "caloric test" for distinguishing the functions of either labyrinth by separate use of cold and hot water to irrigate the external ear. He was the first to describe the condition which became known as otosclerosis (hardening of the ear) and created a practical operative procedure to relieve sufferers. He also devised a "pointing test" for the cerebellum and its relation to equilibrium disturbances. In 1914 he was awarded the Nobel Prize for medicine and physiology for "his work on the vestibular apparatus."

In World War I he served as a surgeon in the Austrian army. He was captured in 1915 by the Russians but was released in 1917 in view of his Nobel Prize. Because of his Jewish origin, he was never appointed to a full professorship in Austria and in 1917 went to the University of Uppsala in Sweden as a full professor, heading the ear, nose, and throat clinic.

Barany only began to take an interest in Jewish matters with the rise of Nazism. In his will he donated his valuable library to the National Library in Jerusalem. He was a member of many professional societies and contributed to medical journals. His books include *Die primäre Wundnaht bei Schussverletzungen des Gehirns* and *Die Radikaloperation des Ohres ohne Gehörengangplastik bei chronischen Mittelohreiterungen.*

BAR-GIORA, SIMON   (d. 71 CE) Jewish military leader. Together with John of Giscala (q.v.) he helped defend the city of Jerusalem against the Roman onslaught in the final year and a half of the Jewish Revolt (69–70 CE). Unlike John, Simon was a representative of the lower classes, with a decidedly social-revolutionary outlook, physically castigating the wealthy and granting many Jewish slaves their freedom. His name, Giora, implies that he was of proselyte stock and, according to the Jewish historian, Josephus (q.v.), came from the Hellenistic city of Gerasa in Transjordan.

As in the case of John of Giscala and other Jewish personalities of the period of the Great Revolt, the primary source of information on Shimon is Josephus. Josephus must be treated with the greatest caution in this respect however, since he was notoriously antipathetic to Simon, as he was to the other Jewish rebels.

Simon appeared in the fighting at the outset and toward the latter part of the revolt - more specifically in the year 66 CE, with the successful assault upon the Roman commander, Cestius Gallus, and from the spring of 69 to the destruction of the Temple in the summer of 70 CE.

Simon seems to have leaned more toward the extreme zealot Sicarii revolutionary party. Many Sicarii left the fortress of Masada to make common cause with Simon, who fought in the south, capturing Idumea and Hebron.

After entering Jerusalem in the spring of 69, Simon gained control of the Upper City and part of the Lower City. The remaining portion of the Lower City and the Temple Mount area was held by John of Giscala. Hostility and bitter clashes marred relations between the two groups. Eventually they made common cause to face the Roman general Titus and his legions, but the previous period of divisiveness had taken its toll and Jerusalem fell before the Roman onslaught in the summer of 70.

Both leaders fell into Roman hands. After the Temple was destroyed Simon hid in an underground passage; when he emerged among the Roman soldiers, dressed in white, with a purple mantle, they seized and bound him. Taken to Rome, he and John of Giscala were exhibited in the Roman victory parade, but only Simon was sentenced to execution, indicating that the Romans regarded him as their foremost opponent. Simon's courage, military leadership, and physical prowess were noted even by Josephus. Some fifteen thousand of the total of twenty-four thousand fighting men of all factions flocked to his banner. Equally apparent are his charisma and semimessianic aura, indicated by the fact that his followers are reported to have treated him with kingly respect.
M. Hengel, *The Zealots*, 1989.
Josephus, *Jewish War* 4.

BAR KOKHBA, SIMON (d. 135 CE) Leader of Jewish revolt against Rome in Judea, 132–135. There are few reliable sources about his life and most of what is known derives from Talmudic legends of his courage and heroism and from administrative and economic documents. The name Bar Kokhba (son of the star) probably alludes to the messianic hopes placed in him by Rabbi Akiva (q.v.); his real name appears to have been Ben or Bar Koseva, which appears on contemporary documents. After the defeat, his name was given a derogatory interpretation, son of a lie (derived from the Hebrew *kazav*, lie).

The revolt was provoked when the Roman Emperor Hadrian rebuilt Jerusalem as a Roman city, with a temple to Jupiter. This enraged the Jews who had dreamed of restoring their own temple there. He also restricted Torah study and Jewish religious observance, including a ban on circumcision. Within a short time, Bar Kokhba organized a revolt which covered the entire country and captured Jerusalem, minting coins which

he dated according to the year of "Jerusalem's liberation" or "Israel's redemption."

He had the reputation of being an autocratic and domineering ruler, requiring total obedience to his authority and total commitment to ending Roman rule of Judea and reestablishing the Temple. Legend relates that in order to join his army, men were required to cut off a finger and that the rabbis, disapproving of the practice, suggested that in its place the men be required to uproot a cedar root. Saint Jerome wrote that Bar Kohba used to keep fanning a lighted blade of straw in his mouth to give the impression that he was spewing out flames. From stories such as this emerges the picture of Bar Kokhba as a driven and uncompromising leader. He seems to have been arrogant and hot-tempered. Another legend relates that he relied more on his own power than that of God, and that when greeted with the greeting "God will help" on going into battle, responded "God will neither assist nor weaken." However, there is historical evidence that he was indeed a religious man. In recent years, signed letters from him have been found in the Judean desert, addressed to one of his commanders, reminding him to separate the tithe and to provide Sabbath accommodation for visitors.

After their initial setbacks, the Romans organized a large army of some 35,000 men that slowly retook the territory lost to Bar Kokhba, including Jerusalem. The cruel war, which lasted three and a half years and was supported by the Jews in the Diaspora, approached its end with Bar Kokhba

A coin of Bar Kokhba struck over a Roman coin.

besieged in Bethar, in the Judean Hills. When this fortress finally fell, Bar Kokhba was killed, traditionally on the Ninth of Av (anniversary of the destruction of the two temples) in 135. There were said to have been 585,000 Jewish casualties, apart from those who died of disease and hunger.

The aftermath of the war saw cruel repressions by Hadrian that desolated Judea, turned Jerusalem into a heathen town, and imposed severe restrictions on the practice of Judaism. Bar Kokhba was retained in Jewish memory as a great folk hero, but as the Roman repression made it unsafe to commit to writing details of his revolt, information about him is sketchy. The popular semifestival of Lag ba'Omer seems to commemorate the revolt but the exact connection is unknown.

Y. Yadin, *Bar-Kokhba*, 1971.

BARNA, VICTOR "VIKI" (1911–1972) Hungarian world table tennis champion. He was the best of an outstanding group of Hungarian Jewish players who dominated the sport in the 1920s and 1930s.

Barna played his first game of table tennis in 1924 at a bar mitzvah party in Budapest. A fellow Hungarian, Sandor Glancz, recalled that he and Barna toured the world giving exhibitions and that "Barna was a champion on and off the table, and because of him the game enjoyed its highest popularity."

"I remember him as a scrawny little kid," Glancz said. "he developed into the greatest player of all time. He had every stroke in the book and

Victor Barna, table tennis champion, in action.

knew how to use them. He was fast and intelligent and he could make a losing game turn into a winning one by changing his game completely. Of course, his famous backhand flip will always be remembered. Because of him the Hungarians controlled the game of table tennis for ten years."

Between 1929 and 1939 Barna used his extraordinary talent to win five singles, eight doubles, and two mixed doubles world titles and helped Hungary win the Swaythling Cup, the world team championship, seven times.

Barna suffered a broken playing arm in 1935 in an automobile accident and never won a world singles title again. Out of competition for a year after doctors told him he would never play again, he underwent an operation that enabled him to resume his career in 1936. The following year Barna moved to England and became a British citizen.

During World War II Barna's younger brother was murdered by Hungarian fascists. Speaking of this tragedy, Barna said, "Imagine, he won the Hungarian title, he followed in my footsteps, he had a great future in table tennis, and they killed him. I wish the people could have saved him, and not my trophies." He went on to explain how his neighbors had hidden his valuable collection during the Nazi takeover and had returned it to him after the war ended.

Barna quit competitive table tennis in the 1950s and became an executive in a sporting goods company.

"Victor brought table tennis to a disbelieving world," the president of the International Table Tennis Federation said, "and never after him was there a person who did not say 'Victor Barna' when ping pong really became translated into table tennis."

BARNATO, BARNEY (1852–1897) South African mining magnate. He was born Barnett Isaacs in London, where his father had a prosperous business in the famous East End open market along Petticoat Lane. His mother was related to the distinguished lawyer, Sir George Jessel (q.v.). Barney was sent to the Jews' Free School, the best Jewish school in London, but showed little inclination learning. His childhood was dominated by two loves — boxing and the theater. He appeared with his brother Henry in the music halls a comedian conjurors known as the Barnato Brothers and the name stuck.

In 1873 he went to the South African diamond center of Kimberley during the diamond rush, but when he arrived the industry was experiencing a slump. Work was hard to find and Barnalo got a job with the local circus by challenging a fierce, mustachioed boxer to a fight. Despite his physical disadvantage he knocked out his opponent. He then went through his London stage repertoire ending by standing on his hands and reciting Hamlet's soliloquy "To be or not to be" (Shakespeare and fancy waistcoats were his abiding passions). However, his job with the circus ended quickly when he told a joke about diamonds — they were no laughing matter and the audience walked out.

He soon became involved in Kimberley's social life and for a time ran a theatrical company. Then he began to work in the diamond industry and gradually learned its many facets. Together with his brother, he was able to buy diamond claims at a time when many thought the supply of diamonds was coming to an end. Barnato believed, contrary to the popular view, that deep digging would reveal more diamonds and eventually was proved right. His four claims in the center of a great mine brought him a fortune. Seven years after his arrival in South Africa, he and his brother founded the Barnato Mining Company, which soon rivaled the greatest company, Cecil Rhodes' De Beers. The two engaged in keen competition until 1888, when Barnato entered into a profitable amalgamation with De Beers.

He next turned to finance and became a member of the Johannesburg Stock Exchange. He was highly successful in the new Rand gold mines, doing much to promote the development of the new town of Johannesburg. He was elected to the legislative assembly and his speeches, characterized by a cockney wit and common sense, were popular, even with his opponents. In 1895 his commercial skills saved the Rand from a serious economic depression. However, the greater his success, the more he became depressed. Finally, while on a sea voyage to England, he jumped overboard while in a state of frenzy, and drowned.

S. Jackson, *The Great Barnato*, 1970.
R. Lewinsohn, *Barney Barnato*, 1937.

BARNATO'S WIT

During a debate in the South African parliament, Barnato told a story to show the absurdity of the Cape liquor laws, which prohibited the sale of liquor on Sundays unless accompanied by a substantial meal. He related that one Sunday when he was hot and thirsty he had entered a respectable hotel for a drink. The landlord placed before him a bottle of beer and a leg of pork, the only food available. Barnato asked the House: "What was I supposed to do? If I ate the pork, I broke the law of Moses. If I drank the beer without eating, I broke the law of the land. Between the Chief Rabbi and the Chief Justice, I was in a very awkward situation."

BARON, SALO WITTMAYER (1895–1989) Jewish historian. He was born in Tarnow, Galicia, where his father was a banker and communal leader. He had both a traditional and secular education and received doctorates from the University

Salo W. Baron at the Eichmann trial, 1961.

of Vienna in philosophy (1917), political science (1922), and law (1923). In 1920 Salo Baron was ordained as a rabbi at the Jewish Theological Seminary in Vienna. He taught history at the Jewish Teachers College in Vienna until 1926, when he moved to New York. He was on the staff of the Jewish Institute of Religion until 1930 when he was appointed professor of Jewish literature and institutions at Columbia University. He was the first member of an American history faculty to teach Jewish studies, created the Center of Israel and Jewish Studies in 1950, and made a unique contribution to Jewish social studies. He retired from the professorship in 1963 but remained director of the Center until 1968. On his retirement Columbia University created a new chair in Jewish history, named in his honor.

Throughout his long life, Baron played an active role in numerous organizations in the American Jewish community, and was president of the American Academy for Jewish Research, the American Jewish Historical Society, and the Conference on Jewish Social Studies. In 1947 he founded the Jewish Cultural Reconstruction, which set out to identify and reclaim libraries and cultural treasures despoiled by the Nazis. He appeared at the Eichmann trial in 1961 as the first witness for the prosecution, describing the significance of the annihilation of European Jewry against the background of the contemporary history of the Jewish people prior to the Holocaust.

Baron was a prolific writer and editor, and his bibliography contains 500 items. Although he was first and foremost a historian of the modern era, he undertook a number of comprehensive works, which brought out his immensely wideranging knowledge and erudition. Foremost among these are *A Social and Religious History of the Jews* (originally three volumes in 1937, but expanded to eighteen volumes by the time of his death; the series extended to the mid-17th century) and the three-volume *Jewish Community* (1942).

Baron's conception of Jewish history was comprehensive, examining not only the external forces but also the inner life of the Jews. He sought to understand the creative elements within Jewry, for example the Jewish community and its organization, within a broader historical context from which Jews derive forces and to which they also contribute. He was scathingly critical of an earlier school of historiography which he termed "the lachrymose conception" according to which "they beat us and they beat us some more." This, he was convinced, was a distortion, as was the earlier historians' concentration on outstanding individuals, notably the scholars, and their ignorance of the ordinary men of all kinds who combined to constitute Jewish society down the ages.

S. Lieberman, ed., *S. W. Baron – Jubilee Volume on the Occasion of his Eightieth Birthday*, 1974.

BARUCH, BERNARD MANNES (1870–1965)

U.S. stock analyst and statesman. He was born in Camden, South Carolina, to a German Jewish immigrant physician and an American-born mother. After the family moved to New York, he graduated from New York City College (1889) and worked as an office boy and then on Wall Street. In the 1890s he began to play the stock market, becoming a multi-millionaire within a decade. In 1912 Baruch turned to politics, contributed generously to Woodrow Wilson's first presidential campaign and, from early 1915, was a leading Democratic advocate of American military and industrial preparation for war. In March 1918, Wilson appointed him chairman of the War Industries Board, which was in charge of mobilizing America's industrial resources for the war effort. After the armistice, Baruch was an economic adviser to President Wilson at the Paris Peace Conference and helped to frame the economic clauses of the Peace Treaty; he described his role in *Making of the Reparations and Economic Sections of the Peace Treaty* (1920).

After 1919, Baruch filled the role of commentator on current events and unofficial economic adviser to presidents. Throughout, he continued to be involved in Democratic party affairs and helped finance its campaigns. He was a friend and adviser to President Franklin D. Roosevelt and his wife, Eleanor. As Hitler grew stronger, Baruch advised America to prepare in good time and was in close touch with his friend, Winston Churchill. During World War II he chaired the Rubber Survey Committee (1942) and was adviser to the war mobilization director, James Byrnes (1943). In 1944 he was a member of a committee that studied postwar adjustment problems. He was also the author of the first official U.S. policy proposal on the control of atomic energy submitted to the United Nations on June 14, 1946; however, the proposal was never adopted. In 1946 he was appointed a member of the American delegation to the United Nations Atomic Energy Commission.

Baruch was not a totally committed Jew: his children were reared in his wife's Episcopalian faith and he claimed to be first an American and then a Jew. He took an increasing interest in the plight of the Jews during World War II, giving sums for relief of Jewish refugees and proposing that they be settled in Uganda. At first he opposed the establishment of the State of Israel, but rallied to the Zionist cause during the debate at the United Nations in 1947. In later years, however, he never actively supported it.

A colorful figure, Baruch won popular recognition as an elder statesman. He often held his meetings on and dispensed his advice from a park bench. He published the first part of his autobiography, *My Own Story*, at the age of eighty-seven and the second part, *The Public Years*, three years later.

M. L. Coit, *Mr. Baruch*, 1957.
C. Field, *Bernard Baruch, Park Bench Statesman*, 1944.
M. W. Rosenblum, *Peace through Strength: Bernard Mannes Baruch and a Blueprint for Security*, 1953.
J. A. Schwartz, *The Speculator: Bernard Baruch in Washington, 1917–1965*, 1981.
H. I. Shumway, *Bernard Mannes Baruch, Financial Genius, Statesman and Advisor to Presidents*, 1946.
W. L. White, *Bernard Baruch, Portrait of a Citizen*, 1950.

- Vote for the man who promises least; he will be the least disappointing.
- I will never be an old man. To me, old age is always fifteen years older than I am.
- An elder statesman is someone old enough to know his own mind and keep quiet about it.
- [On being asked on a radio program what book he would choose if shipwrecked on a desert island] A practical guide to boat building.

Bernard Baruch

BARUCH BEN JEHIEL OF MEDZIBEZH

(1757–1810) Hasidic rabbi in the Ukraine. The grandson of the Baal Shem Tov (q.v), founder of Hasidism, Baruch was a vain and ambitious leader who inherited few of his grandfather's good qualities. Believing that a *tzaddik* (a Hasidic leader) earned his position by virtue of birth and divine appointment, he assumed that his distinguished ancestry gave him special rights in Medzibezh. He also claimed that as a *tzaddik*'s powers are divinely endowed and not given by man, he need not be judged by the same standards as his subjects, that is, he is as justified in serving God by indulgence in material pleasures as by devotion to prayer and a holy ascetic life. He himself chose the former. He held court in an autocratic and luxurious manner, but demanded severe asceticism from his followers, as well as expecting them to comply fully with the custom of giving gifts to the rabbi.

Baruch of Medzibezh aroused the opposition of his fellow Hasidic leaders, of whom he was equally contemptuous. After officiating as rabbi in Tulchin from 1780 to 1788, he was compelled to return to Medzibezh because of opposition from the *tzaddikim*. In 1808 he held a meeting with Shneur Zalman of Lyady (q.v.), with whom he had a particularly vehement quarrel over the latter's rationalization of Hasidism.

Notwithstanding his demands on the Hasidim, and his own unconstrained lifestyle, he was admired by his followers. He wrote *Amarot Tehorot* (1865), *Degel Mahaneh Ephraim* (1850), and *Buzina di-Nehora* (1880).

M. Buber, *Tales of the Hasidim*, vol. 1, 1947.
J. S. Minkin, *The Romance of Hasidism*, 1935.

BAUER, OTTO (1881–1938) Austrian Socialist leader; leading theoretician of the Austrian Democratic Party in the interwar period. Bauer was born in Vienna, the son of a wealthy textile industrialist. Like many Jewish intellectuals of his time, he joined the socialist movement. His parents were assimilated into German culture and there is no evidence that Bauer received any Jewish or religious education or indeed had any knowledge of Judaism.

Bauer's interests were broad, including sociology, history, philosophy, literature, anthropology, psychology and Marxist politics. When only ten years old, he wrote a play describing the fall of Napoleon.

After obtaining his law degree from the University of Vienna, he cofounded the monthly *Der Kampf* ("The Struggle"). This journal became a forum for socialist discussion. As a leader of the neo-Marxian school in Vienna and secretary to the Socialist faction in the Austrian Parliament, Bauer presented a reassessment of the "national" question. A nation, he claimed in his classic work, *Die Nationalitätenfrage und die Sozialdemokratie* ("The Nationalities Question and Social Democracy," 1907), was "the totality of men united through a community of fate into a community of character."

> Judaism has always reached the summit of its achievement wherever Jewish natural talents and European cultural tradition have met and crossfertilized each other.
>
> Fascist dictatorship destroys the results of the political emancipation of the individual, in order to prevent the social emancipation of the masses.
>
> **Otto Bauer, 1936**

However, Bauer did not regard the Jews as a nationality. He advocated assimilation and tried to prove that the Jews had no future as a nation; he was therefore critical of Zionism.

During World War I he fought in the Austrian army and was a prisoner-of-war in Russia. In November 1918, following the collapse of the Austro-Hungarian Empire, Bauer became the first foreign minister of the Austrian Republic. Ironically in this capacity he strove for an *Anschluss* (unification) with Germany and worked to keep the Sudeten Germans inside of Austria. He resigned in July 1919 but remained a dominant force in his party. When Engelbert Dollfuss's regime came to power in 1934, Bauer took a leading part in the uprising of the workers in Vienna. He was forced to find refuge in Czechoslovakia and then Paris.

Seeing the deteriorating situation in Austria and the anti-Jewish decrees, Bauer abandoned his earlier views on the inevitability of assimilation. In his final article before his death in 1938, Bauer appealed to world conscience to save the 300,000 Jews in Austria from Nazi aggression.

Bauer was an outstanding figure within the Socialist International; a prolific writer of socialist problems, opposing communism but representing the Marxist left wing.

O. Leichter, *Otto Bauer Tragödie oder Triumph?* 1970.
R. S. Wistrich, *Revolutionary Jews from Marx to Trotsky*, 1976.

BAUM, VICKI (née Hedwig Baum; 1888–1960) U.S. author. Born in Vienna, she was educated at a music school and made her first appearance as a harpist at the age of eleven. She played in various theater orchestras in Vienna for the next several years. At the age of eighteen she married a writer, but they soon separated and she moved to Germany, where she continued playing the harp and taught music. She met the conductor Richard Lert while playing for the Darmstadt orchestra, but when she married him in 1916, she gave up her musical career.

Always a compulsive writer, she published her first story under a pseudonym when she was fourteen. Her first book, *Falling Star*, was published only after a friend accidentally discovered her manuscripts in 1920.

In 1921 she began working as an editor for the Ullstein publishing house. Some of her novels were later serialized in illustrated weeklies also published by Ullstein. In 1928, she published *Helen Willfür*; this was followed in 1929 by *Menschen in Hotel* (English translation, Grand Hotel), which made her internationally famous.

Grand Hotel was staged as a play, first in Berlin and then all over Europe and the United States, published as a novel in English, and made into a successful film in the United States starring Greta Garbo. She visited New York in 1931, planning to stay for two weeks and see the play, but instead decided to remain, bring her family over, and settle in California. In 1938 she became an American citizen. She continued to write in German but with the advent of the Nazi regime in 1933, her works were banned in Germany and began to be published in Amsterdam. Altogether she published twenty-five novels.

She is praised particularly for her intense emotional portrayals, which made her characters larger than life, and for her vibrant style, which presented a kaleidoscopic view of their interrelated lives.
V. Baum, *Autobiography*, 1962.

BEACONSFIELD, EARL OF See Disraeli, Benjamin

BEARSTED, VISCOUNT See Samuel, Marcus

BEER, WILHELM (1797–1850) German astronomer. Born in Berlin to a banker, he and his brothers received a modern and liberal education. One of his brothers, Giacomo Meyerbeer (q.v.), became a noted composer. The other, Michael Beer, was a poet. Wilhelm, at the age of sixteen, volunteered for the military and served in the campaigns of 1813 and 1815 against Napoleon. Shortly afterward he left the army and joined his father's banking house, succeeding him in 1826.

Beer pursued astronomy as a hobby and together with his friend, Johann Heinrich von Mädler, built a private observatory in the garden of his villa. They observed Mars during the oppositions of 1828, 1832, 1835, and 1837 and published their results. Beer's name was used for one of the markings of the planet.

One of his more important contributions to astronomy was a map of the moon he compiled with Mädler from 1834 to 1836 Beer's map was a great improvement on any that had been done previously and entailed years of painstaking measurements. The first such map constructed

Diagram of the moon, showing areas named after Jews, including Wilhelm Beer. From the Jewish Chronicle, *London, July 1969.*

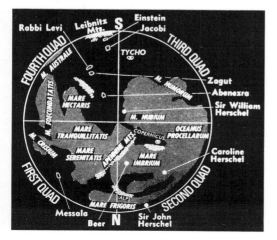

with quadrants, it was a meter in diameter and was a standard work until 1878.

When Mädler was invited to head an observatory at the University of Darport, Beer drifted away from astronomy and became involved in politics. In 1845 he was elected to the Prussian Chamber of Deputies and subsequently published his political ideas in several pamphlets. A mountain on the moon is named for him.

BEER-HOFMANN, RICHARD (1866–1945) Austrian dramatist. Born in Vienna, he was the son of Hermann Beer, a young, affluent lawyer. His mother died in childbirth and, until age fourteen, he lived in the home of her sister, who was married to Alois Hofman, a textile manufacturer of Brünn (now Brno), Moravia. This childless couple adopted him; hence his hyphenated name. When his foster parents moved to Vienna, he continued his education there and graduated from the University of Vienna as a doctor of jurisprudence but never practiced law.

As a dandy and aesthete of the *fin-de-siècle*, he was associated with the literary groups of Jungwien, whose most prominent members were Arthur Schnitzler (q.v.) and Hugo von Hofmannsthal. Young Theodor Herzl (q.v.), a feuilletonist and dramatist, was on the periphery of this group; from 1896, he tried to convert its Jewish members to his Zionist vision but failed.

Beer-Hofmann's first book, *Novellen* ("Novellas," 1893), betrayed the influence of Maupassant in subject matter and of Flaubert in style. More important was his *Schlaflied für Miriam* ("Lullaby for Miriam," 1897), a philosophic lullaby designed to be chanted by a father at the cradle of his child. Its stanzas touch on birth, death, and loneliness, and end with the affirmation that deep within us flows the heritage of our fathers, full of unrest and pride. This ending is the first expression of the poet's roots in his people.

The same conclusion occurs in his novel *Der Tod Georgs* ("George's Death," 1901). The hero, a tired and melancholy aesthete, is aroused by the death of his friend Georg to realize the meaninglessness of his own existence. He breaks with aestheticism and accepts his Jewishness with its burdens and blessings.

Thereafter Beer-Hofmann became the poetic spokesman of his Jewish heritage. His first drama, *Der Graf von Charolais* ("The Count of Charolias," 1904), won wide acclaim. Beer-Hofmann then began his biblical trilogy centering on David, in whom he saw the symbolic personification of the Jewish soul. The play *Jaakobs Traum* ("Jacob's Dream," 1918) served as prologue to the trilogy. It was staged not only in the German original in Vienna and Berlin but also in a Hebrew version in Moscow, Tel-Aviv, and New York. It depicts the struggle between the brothers Jacob and Edom (Esau), and climaxes in Jacob's vision during the night at Beth-El when he made his covenant with God. The most memorable performance took place in Berlin in 1935 when Nazi stormtroopers were stationed at the theater entrance to prevent so-called Aryans from entering.

Der junge David ("Young David", 1933) could not be staged because of the Nazi rise to power. It depicts the struggle between David and Saul and culminates in David's coronation. He accepts for his people the burden and the blessing which his ancestor Jacob had earlier accepted. He does not want to fashion another superpower comparable to Egypt or Babylon but rather seeks a peaceful breathing spell for his people so that he can implant in them the seed of a more moral faith. Through the mouth of David, the dramatist voices his opposition to the ultranationalism then rampant in Central Europe. He believes in a nationalism that aspires to supranationalism and world unity.

In 1936 Beer-Hofmann visited Palestine and was impressed by the idealism of its pioneers. When the Nazis overran Vienna, he was forced into exile. En route to New York in 1939, his wife Paula, died in Zurich. Broken-hearted, he gave up further work on his trilogy and devoted his last years to record his memories of her. These appeared posthumously in *Paula* (1949). On American soil he found hospitality, understanding, and a circle of devoted friends. His collected poems were published in the slender volume *Verse* (1941).

Shortly after his death, the Burgtheater in liberated Vienna could again stage *Jaakobs Traum*. In 1963, his *Gesammelte Werke* ("Complete Works") appeared with an eloquent introduction by Martin Buber.

E. N. Elstun, *Richard Beer-Hofmann, His Life and Work*, 1983.
S. Liptzin, *Richard Beer-Hofmann*, 1936.

BEER-HOFMANN AND HERZL

After Herzl failed to win Beer-Hofmann over to the Zionist vision, he exploded: "You are ashamed of the Yellow Badge!" The poet remained calm and merely asked: "What are the names of your children?" "Pauline, Hans, and Trude, as you well know," answered Herzl. Beer-Hofmann then countered: "Mine are Miriam, Naema, and Gabriel and my wife Paula has also taken on the biblical name Ruth." The next day Herzl sent a copy of his feuilletons to the poet with the dedication, "To the Jew, Richard Beer-Hofmann."

BEHRMAN, SAMUEL NATHANIEL (1893–1973) U.S. playwright. A writer of "comedies of manners," he was praised for his urbane dialogue and incisive characterization as he explored social, political, and moral issues while exposing the inconsistencies of human behavior.

He spent his childhood "immersed in assorted literature' and developed an early interest in the

theater, writing a vaudeville skit, in which he cast himself, at the age of twenty. In 1916 he graduated with a B.A. in theater from Harvard, and then unable to find work as a playwright in New York, studied at Columbia University for an M.A. in English, which he received in 1918.

For nine years he lived from hand to mouth, writing book reviews for the *New York Times,* contributing short stories and articles to various magazines and collaborating on two unsuccessful plays, *Bedside Manners* (1923) and *The Man Who Forgot* (1926).

He had accepted a position as an instructor in a small college, a job that promised security but made him miserable about leaving the world of theater, when a friend advised him to tear up the railway ticket to the obscure college town and begin his next play. He took the advice and wrote *The Second Man* (1927), a high comedy about a writer who forsakes love for wealth, astonishing audiences and critics with his mature talent. Succeeding plays, including *Serena Blandish* (1929), *Brief Moment* (1931), and *Biography* (1932), continued to focus on the romantic interests of the upper-class liberal who is being challenged by an intolerant radical character, while an impartial third party stands by, enjoying the mental stimulation yielded by their dispute.

Toward the 1930s more serious themes began to enter his work. *Meteor* (1929) about a Wall Street egotist's lust for power, indicated the inception of this less lighthearted trend. In *Rain from Heaven* (1934), the issue was fascism; in *End of Summer*, it was the illegitimacy of inherited and accumulated wealth. As the detachment of comedy gave way to the seriousness needed for tackling weightier issues, he was often accused of being didactic, biased, and unfocused. *No Time for Comedy* (1939) about a comedy writer who cannot reconcile his own taste for comedy with society's wish for more serious drama, is a partially autobiographical play that reflects his creative state of mind during this phase of his career. Despite the mixed reactions to his work, however, some of his later plays, among them *I Know My Love* (1948) and *Fanny* (1954) were long-run successes on Broadway.

In the 1950s he became preoccupied with writing prose: essays for the *New Yorker*; a biography of the art dealer Joseph Duveen (q.v.); an account of his American Jewish youth in Worcester, Mass. (which was also the basis for a well-received play); and one novel, *The Burning Glass* (1968). He also worked alone, and in collaboration, on many film scripts. His last work *People in a Diary: A Memoir* (1972) reviews his life and work in the theater.
K. Reed, *S. N. Behrman*, 1975

BEILIS, MENACHEM MENDEL (1874–1934) Victim of blood libel in tsarist Russia. A brick factory superintendent in Kiev, Ukraine, he became the defendant in the case that became known worldwide as the Beilis trial. It began when the body of a thirteen-year-old boy was discovered in a

The Beilis family in 1914.

cave on the outskirts of Kiev in the year 1911. This served to spark off the most sensational blood libel accusation of the 20th century. The entire weight of a corrupt and decadent empire, its departments of police and justice, plus a virulently anti-Semitic press, church, and various ultra-nationalistic groups, were all brought to bear on Menachem Beilis, accused of using the boy's blood for the baking of unleavened bread for Passover. By clear inference, all other Jews stood accused as well.

Beilis himself was a family man of few pretensions. The most powerful motive that could be adduced by the prosecution for placing him in the defendant's dock was the claim that Judaism enjoined its adherents to practice ritual murder, and the fact that Menachem Beilis was the only Jew residing in the vicinity where the body had been found. He was subject to a long period of torture and cross-examination in the vain hope of extorting a confession.

After being incarcerated for two years, Beilis was finally bought to trial. By now, the government's plan had misfired completely. Public opinion, both throughout the nation and the world, had rallied behind Beilis and condemned the case as a tragic mockery of justice. At the trial itself, witness after witness pointed an accusing finger, not at Beilis, but at Vera Tchebiriak, mother of a friend of the dead boy, and a person of unsavory repute. Intended to be a witness for the prosecution, her testimony did not bear up to cross-examination, and she proved to be her own worst enemy. In addition, so-called "theological evidence" produced by a Father Pranaitis to demonstrate that the Jewish religion itself prescribed ritual murder was demolished by the defense, who produced a serious scholar to testify. The same fate befell another expert, who suggested that the murder bore all the signs of a religious crime of vengeance.

The result was by now predictable. After a trial that lasted thirty-four days, the jury handed in a verdict of not guilty.

Menachem Mendel Beilis walked out of courtroom a free man amid an outburst of spontaneous rejoicing. Later in life, after an unsuccessful attempt to settle in Palestine, he moved to the United States where he wrote his memoirs, *Die Geschichte fun Meine Leiden* ("The Story of My Life," New York, 1925).

Beilis's story inspired Bernard Malamud's novel *The Fixer*, which was also a noteworthy film.
M. Samuel, *Blood Accusation: The Strange History of the Beilis Case*, 1966.

BEIT, ALFRED (1853–1906) German-British financier instrumental in the development of the diamond and gold industries in South Africa and in the foundation of Rhodesia. Born to a Portuguese Jewish family of gold and silver refiners that settled in Hamburg in the 16th century, his parents were both baptized a year after their marriage and brought up their children as Lutherans. The Beit family established copper and metallurgical smelting companies and were the owners of shipyards in Hamburg, but Alfred's father, an importer of silk goods from France, was considered the "poor relation."

A quiet and self-effacing boy, Alfred Beit was educated at a private school in Hamburg, and at the age of seventeen was sent to work with a firm of wool importers and diamonds from South Africa. In 1871 he went to Holland to learn diamond cutting and in 1875 joined a relative's firm in South Africa as a diamond buyer. At first Beit went from dig to dig buying rough stones, but once he had become popular with the miners he set up office in a corrugated iron shanty and they brought their discoveries to him. He soon revealed his integrity, his instantaneous grasp of complicated detail, and his power of rapid calculation and range of financial imagination.

In 1890 he established the firm of Wernher, Beit and Company, which, in addition to the Kimberley diamond mines, developed the Witwatersrand goldfields, meeting with success through the evolution of deep-level mining. Beit soon became chairman of a number of gold-mining companies. He also set up and controlled the Pretoria Waterworks, the Pretoria Electric Lighting Company, and the National Bank of South Africa.

Alfred Beit's meeting with Cecil Rhodes in 1879 was the beginning of a long friendship leading to his loyal support of Rhodes's political, financial, and educational schemes. Beit gave financial backing to the British South Africa Company when it was established in 1889 and became a director of the Chartered Company. He was a director of the De Beers Consolidated Mining Company, founded together with Rhodes. Beit wholeheartedly supported Rhodes's aims and was involved with Rhodes in a conspiracy to overthrow the government of Transvaal that culminated in the 1895 Jameson raid. As a result, he was forced, together with Rhodes, to resign from the board of the Chartered Company. He never appeared in public, but the parliamentary committee of inquiry called him one of the "promoters and moving spirits" of the raid.

After the death of Rhodes in 1902, Beit devoted himself to opening up Rhodesia, and especially to Rhodes's scheme of a Cape-to-Cairo railway. That same year he was reelected to the board of the

Chartered Company and in 1904 became its vice president.

During his last years, despite his failing health, Beit visited Germany and France, being received by the heads of state. Under the guidance of the curator of the Kaiser Friedrich Museum in Berlin, Wilhelm Bode, he began to collect works of art, placing them in his London home. He endowed a chair of colonial history at Oxford University and also provided for assistant lecturers and an annual prize for an essay on imperial citizenship. Beit died a bachelor, on his estate in Hertfordshire, England.

In his will, Alfred Beit created the Railway Trust Fund, with the purpose of developing communications in Rhodesia and adjacent lands. As a result, five major bridges were built between 1929 and 1949, the first being the Beit Bridge across the Limpopo River uniting South Africa and Rhodesia (now Zimbabwe). A bronze plaque of Alfred Beit was placed on a tower on the center pier of this bridge and a nearby town is called Beitbridge. The trustees formed a company in 1933 to develop civil aviation in Rhodesia and after World War II it became Central African Airways. Beit also specified that moneys should be provided for educational purposes, and scholarships were set up to enable promising pupils to have a university education.

A. Beit and J. G. Lockhart, *The Will and the Way, 1906–1956, An Account of Alfred Beit and the Trust Which He Founded,* 1957.

G. S. Fort, *Alfred Beit,* 1931.

BELASCO, DAVID (1859–1931) American theatrical producer and playwright. Born to a family of Portuguese origin (original name Velasco), his father was an actor in London pantomimes. Little is known of his private life and many of the facts are contradictory. At an early age the family moved to Vancouver, Canada. They were very poor and Belasco ran away from home several times. He was placed under the tutelage of a Father McGuire and in later years he claimed that his affectation of austere dress combined with a clerical collar was a homage to this man. This, along with his personal manner, earned him the name the bishop of Broadway.

He began his theatrical career as a child actor, probably in 1864, acting with Charles Kean in *Richard III.* He later performed in stock companies and mining camps and was secretary to the playwright Dion Boucicault. He claimed to have written his first play at the age of twelve.

The 1870s found him in San Francisco working as an actor-manager and play adapter. In 1879 he toured in *Hearts of Oak* with James A. Herne and in 1880 moved to New York, where he was associated with a number of theaters as stage manager. After a brief stay in San Francisco he returned to New York permanently in 1886. In 1890 he leased a theater and became an independent producer; in 1906 he built his own theater, including a laboratory for testing of lighting and scenic effects.

Belasco claimed to have been connected with the production of 374 plays during his theatrical career, most written and/or adapted by himself. Among the most notable are: *The Heart of Maryland* (1895), *Madame Butterfly* (1900), *The Girl of the Golden West* (1900), *Du Barry* (1901), *The Music Master* (1904), and *Lulu Belle* (1926). His meticulously arranged stage effects and the performances of his well-disciplined actors turned many of these claptrap plays into resounding successes. He brought new standards of production to the American stage.

He was obsessed with external realism. One play recreated a Child's Restaurant, complete with steaming cups of coffee. For *Du Barry* (1901) he sent to Paris for the fittings. For *The Return of Peter Grimm* (1911) he purchased old Dutch furniture two years before the play was produced. In *The Easiest Way* he tried to reproduce a cheap theatrical boarding house in New York. Unable to meet his expectations, he visited a cheap theatrical boarding house and bought the entire interior of its most dilapidated room: patched furniture, threadbare carpet, tarnished gas fixtures, and broken cupboards, doors, and window casings.

• Lights are to drama what music is to the lyrics of a song. No other factor that enters into the production of a play is so effective in conveying its moods and feeling. They are essential to every work of dramatic art as blood is to life.

• Everything must be real. I have seen plays in which thrones creaked on which monarchs sat, and palace walls flapped when persons touched them. Nothing so destructive to illusion or so ludicrous can happen on my stage.

• The secret is that it is much easier to appeal to the hearts of audiences through their senses than through their intellects. People go to the play to have their emotions stirred. When they respond they become a part of the play itself. We on the stage instantly feel this subtle influence, so they really give us more than we give them.

David Belasco

Many critics felt the realism of his settings masked a lack of artistic seriousness. They deplored his theatricalism, his lack of taste and artistic judgment, and his failure to encourage the better dramatists. Others hailed him as the Stanislavsky of the New York stage.

Off stage, he had a favorite trick for getting his own way. He would throw a temper tantrum and stamp on his watch. He kept a stock of cheap watches especially for this purpose.

He reached the height of his popularity in the first two decades of the 20th century and while he continued to produce plays until 1928, his popularity waned after World War I. The Stuyvesant Theater, which he built on Broadway in 1907, was later called the Belasco Theater.

D. Belasco, *The Theater through Its Stage Door*, 1919.

BEN-GURION, DAVID (1886–1973) Israeli statesman and first prime minister of the State of Israel. Born in Plonsk, Russia, he received a traditional Jewish education and acquired Zionism from his father. As a boy he organized the Ezra Society to promote the study of Hebrew and Zionist ideology. Between 1904 and 1906 he worked as a teacher in Warsaw and became involved in Labor Zionist politics, attending the first conference of the Labor Zionist movement, Poale Zion, in Poland in 1905. He was also involved with Jewish self-defense during the 1903 pogroms and from then on recognized the need for Jewish power. In 1906 he took a decisive step when he immigrated to Eretz Israel in the wave of immigration of the Second Aliya, from whose ranks came the founding fathers of modern Israel. He worked at first as an agricultural laborer in Galilee, but continued his political activity, being one of the founders of Poale Zion in Eretz Israel (1907). The party stressed the need for Jewish labor, Jewish defense, the creation of a just, equal, and progressive society, and the revival of Hebrew and Jewish culture. It shunned the Marxist ideology of class struggle and revolution, adapting its line to the realities of the country at the end of the Ottoman period.

After the 1908 Young Turks revolution in Turkey, Ben-Gurion prepared himself to take part as a representative of the Jewish community of Palestine in the Turkish parliament. For that purpose he enrolled at Istanbul University to study law and spent two semesters there, but the outbreak of World War I cut short his studies. He returned to Palestine but a few months later was expelled by the Turkish government for subversive Zionist activities. He went first to Alexandria and then to the United States (May 1915). He made his living by writing and by political and organizational work through the pioneering Zionist Ha-Halutz movement. He advocated the establishment of a Jewish legion in the British army to help liberate Palestine from the Turks and joined the legion when it was formed in 1918, arriving in Palestine in June in British army uniform.

Even before his release from the army, he brought about the unification of the Labor movement in Palestine by establishing the Ahdut ha-Avodah party. In 1920 he was one of the founders of the Histadrut, the General Federation of Trade Unions, heading it as secretary general from 1921 to 1935. From then until his retirement in 1963, he was the leading figure in the Jewish community, participating in all Zionist congresses, as a member of the elected assembly and as a leader of his party. A short visit to the Soviet Union in 1923 taught him the value of the organization in political life as well

French president Charles de Gaulle and David Ben-Gurion, 1960.

as the need for the Labor movement to acquire an economic power base. This he achieved in the Histadrut, with its manifold activities, agricultural settlements, and industries. In 1930 he achieved another dream, by further uniting the Labor party with the creation of Mapai, the dominant party in the Jewish community and Israel from its establishment until 1977.

His Zionist Socialism called for the gradual creation in Palestine of the economic, industrial, agricultural, educational, military, and cultural infrastructure on which the future Jewish state would be built, led by the Labor movement. He called for national control over natural resources and public utilities, stressed socialist education, and advocated massive immigration. In the 1930s he met with a number of leading Palestinian Arabs but failed to reach any significant agreement with them. Although he opposed the Revisionist Zionists' ideology, he entered into an agreement with Vladimir Jabotinsky (q.v.), seeking coexistence in Palestine, but a majority of the Histadrut members failed to ratify the agreement. While calling for the creation of a strong Jewish defense force, he also realized the need to maintain working relations with the British government as long as the Jewish community was small and relatively weak vis-à-vis the Arabs.

Elected to the Zionist executive in 1934, he became, the following year, the chairman of the Jewish Agency, the international representative arm of the World Zionist Organization, and headed that body until 1948. Together with Chaim Weizmann (q.v.) and Moshe Sharett (q.v.) he led the struggle for the creation of a Jewish state. In 1937 he supported the partition plan of the British Royal Commission arguing that even a sliver of Jewish sovereignty would help to rescue the growing number of refugees fleeing from Nazi Germany. In 1939 he participated in the Round Table conference in London. When the conference failed, the British government issued the May 1939 white paper limiting Jewish immigration to Palestine and all but banning the sale of land to Jews there, thus dooming its Jews to the mercy of the Arabs. When World War II broke out, Ben-Gurion coined the phrase, "We shall fight the white paper as though there was no war, and we shall fight the Nazis as though there was no white paper." During the war he was involved in political and diplomatic work in London, New York, and Washington, and attended the Biltmore Conference, which called for the creation of a Jewish commonwealth after the war. In 1945 he visited the Holocaust survivors in camps in Germany and became convinced of the absolute necessity of the immediate establishment of the Jewish state.

He pushed for an activist anti-British policy of resistance and for illegal immigration to Palestine in the face of British restrictions. In 1946 he took over the defense portfolio of the Jewish Agency and began to prepare the underground army, the Haganah, for the coming inevitable struggle for independence, acquiring heavy weapons in Europe and the United States.

In March 1948 he was named chairman of the People's Executive and in this capacity he proclaimed the independence of the State of Israel on May 14, becoming its first prime minister and defense minister. He was the key figure in the military and political moves during the War of Independence. His visionary and determined leadership was fundamental in bringing about an Israeli military victory and the firm foundation of the country's independence. He guided the country for the next fifteen year (with a two-year respite), in which Israel received and absorbed over a million immigrants, forging its diplomatic position in the world, entrenching its economy, and expanding its settlement and trade.

Ben-Gurion stressed the concept of *mamlakhtiyut* (statism), which called for the state to take over institutions and functions which had been the responsibility of political parties in the prestate era. He created a unified Israel Defense Force subservient to the civilian authorities, banning all private armies. He established a state school system, a state labor exchange, a social security system, and a nonpolitical civil service. He fought for a democratic constitution and for a reform in the country's electoral system but failed to achieve either.

In foreign policy he espoused strong ties with the West, which was a source of arms and economic aid. He pushed for the signing of an agreement with West Germany for reparations and later forged close military ties with France. Between late 1953 and early 1955 he was in retirement in the Negev kibbutz Sde Boker, where he had made his home in a symbolic gesture to attract settlers to the south of the country. Recalled to office in view of the deteriorating military situation, he began to plan a military campaign against Egypt. He led Israel into the October 1956 Sinai campaign, together with Britain and France. In a swift military campaign Israel occupied Sinai but was forced to withdraw under Soviet and American pressure. Nevertheless the campaign gave Israel a decade of relative tranquility, and a stronger and more confident army and country, making it a factor to be reckoned with in the Middle East. It failed however to break Arab hostility.

Domestic politics marred Ben-Gurion's final days in office. He sought to bypass the second echelon of Mapai leaders and choose his successor from among the native-born third generation leaders whose interests lay more in performance than in ideology. The veterans, headed by Golda Meir (q.v.), Levi Eshkol (q.v.), Pinhas Sapir, and Zalman Aranne, rebelled against what they considered his dictates. When he insisted that a security misjudgment in Egypt in 1954 be investigated by a judiciary commission, they opposed him. They objected to his ideas on electoral reforms, fearing that the party would lose its power. There was also opposition to his German policy. He resigned in June 1963, feeling that his colleagues had betrayed him. Two years later he split Mapai when he created the breakaway Rafi party. The party won ten seats in the 1965 Knesset elections and after the Six-Day War returned to Mapai but without Ben-Gurion. He advocated withdrawal from all the

---

BEN-GURION ADDRESSING THE KNESSET (JULY 3, 1950)

The motives at work in the Jewish immigration to the Land of Israel in all generations, including our own, have been many and varied. Longings for redemption, ancient memories, religious feelings, love of homeland, and, above all, distress — economic, political and spiritual distress. With the foundation of the state, a new factor has been added whose strength will continually increase: the power of appeal and attraction embedded in the State of Israel. The pace and scope of the return of the exiles will in no small measure depend on our ability to augment this appeal and turn the State of Israel into the center for the realization of the longings of the nation and for the satisfaction of its material and spiritual needs.

territories taken in that war, except Jerusalem and the Golan Heights, in return for real peace.

He was buried in Sde Boker, where his grave, with its impressive desert vista, attracts many visitors. More than any other leader, he made the greatest impact on the State of Israel. Through his vision, prickly tenacity, leadership, and organizational skill, he was able to mobilize the resources of world Jewry and the Jewish community of Palestine to wage the War of Independence and place Israel on the world map. Golda Meir called him "the greatest Jew in our generation."

A. Avi-Hai, *Ben-Gurion: A State Builder*, 1974.
M. Bar-Zohar, *Ben-Gurion, A Biography*, 1978.
S. Tevet, *Ben-Gurion: The Burning Ground*, 1987.

BEN-HAIM, PAUL (1897–1984) Israeli composer. Born Paul Frankenburger in Munich, he studied piano, composition, and conducting at the Munich Academy of Arts between 1915 and 1920. He then served as assistant conductor under Bruno Walter (q.v.) and Hans Knappertsbusch, and in 1924 took a post at Augsburg as a conductor. In 1931 he returned to Munich with the aim of making his name as a composer, but with the advent of Nazism he emigrated to Palestine, where he settled in Tel Aviv, taking the name Ben-Haim.

He worked as a piano accompanist and teacher until he was in a position to support himself as a composer and teacher of composition. Eventually he established himself as the leading Israeli composer. After 1940 Ben-Haim sought to create a national movement to "synthesize" the eastern and western musical traditions. Together with a group of young Israeli composers who formed the Eastern Mediterranean School of Composition, he was influenced by Middle Eastern folk songs and synagogue cantillation and the rhythms of dances, in particular, the hora.

Ben-Haim was a late Romantic, and much of his music shows strong influences of Claude Débussy and Maurice Ravel. He was a fine orchestrator and craftsman, and his *First Symphony* (1940) shows affinities with Jean Sibelius and Sir William Walton.

His vocal music is notable for its lyricism, generally stemming from oriental influences. His long friendship with the Yemenite singer Bracha Tzfira played a large role in the development of his style of melodic writing, as can be seen in his *Three Songs without Words*. Other vocal works include *Six Love Songs in Ladino*, *A Star Fell Down* (op. 69), and *Elehay Tzidki*.

The first of Ben-Haim's piano works written in Israel were the *Canzonette* and *Toccata*, forming the Piano Suite (1945). Within this composition the connections between different musics is increasingly apparent. In 1954 Ben-Haim wrote a piano sonata that showed baroque tendencies. It reflects the eclecticism of his style, chromatically motivated through-out in character and typically vocal in style, to the extent of being declamatory. The use of trills (rapidly repeated notes) adds a distinctly oriental flavor.

Other works also employ the florid melodies and intricate rhythms of the east combined with a lyricism often rising to dramatic heights, creating a combination of the desert, the exuberance of Israeli youth and deep meditational feeling. These works include *Hymn from the Desert* (based on a hymn discovered in the Dead Sea Scrolls; 1962); *Evocation*, for violin and orchestra (1942); and symphonic movements, *Sweet Psalmist of Israel*, for which Ben-Haim was awarded the 1957 Israel Prize.

J. Hirshberg, *Paul Ben-Haim: His Life and Works*, 1990.
P. Gradenwitz, *Music and Musicians in Israel*, 1959.

BENJAMIN OF TUDELA (12th cent.) Spanish traveler. Nothing is known of him apart fom the account of his travels to the Middle East. Apparently he set out in 1159 (some think 1167) and returned in 1172, after which he wrote the account of his journeys. He came from Tudela in Navarre, Spain, but the object of his journey is unknown. He was presumably a merchant, but nothing clear emerges from his book. It contains a unique picture of Jewish life in many countries in his time, with communal, economic, and literary details that make the work a primary source of information for non-Jewish as well as Jewish life. Written clearly, concisely, and observantly it was quoted approvingly by the English historian, Edward Gibbon.

Leaving Spain, Benjamin went first to Provence, visiting all its major cities and writing about its distinguished scholars. He sailed from Marseilles to Genoa, making his way down Italy to Rome, describing its beauty and its antiquities. From there he traveled to southern Italy, telling of the great medical university of Salerno and the petroleum wells near Sorrento. He sailed to Corfu and then to Constantinople, about which he writes at length ("a busy city to which merchants come by sea or land, and there is none like it in the world, except Baghdad"). He moved on to the Aegean islands and the Syrian coast where he noted the Jewish glassblowers, the cultivation of the mastic tree, which exudes a resin used in medicine, the waterworks of Antioch, and the Shiite sect of assassins, explaining that the word originated from "hashish," which they used as an opiate.

He visited every important city in Palestine, mentioning some of their Latin and French names, gave locations for the graves of famous rabbis, and providing a detailed account of the holy places. His account of the Druze sect is the first to be found in non-Arabic literature. This was the time of the Crusades and he encountered only a few Jews in Jerusalem, earning their living as dyers and living under the shadow of the Tower of David.

He writes extensively of Damascus, but his longest account is of Baghdad, of the court of the caliph, of the great Jewish academies, and the splendor of the exilarch (the head of the Jewish community) and the honor accorded to him.

Benjamin then gives information on communities throughout Asia, but the likelihood is that he did not visit them but relied on hearsay. He next visited Egypt and returned home via Sicily and Italy.

The book is written in rabbinic Hebrew in a simple style. The contents are largely objective, with hardly any personal material. It was translated into various European languages, first into Latin. Its reliability was confirmed by later travelers. Among Jews *The Travels of Benjamin of Tudela* was popular reading and went through many editions.

E. N. Adler, *Jewish Travellers*, 1930.

BENJAMIN OF TUDELA DESCRIBES THE JEWISH EXILARCH IN BAGHDAD

Every fifth day, when he goes to pay a visit to the great Caliph, horsemen — gentile and Jewish — escort him and heralds proclaim in advance "Make way before our Lord, the son of David, as is due to him." He is mounted on a horse and attired in robes of silk and embroidery with a large turban on his head, and from the turban is suspended a long white cloth adorned with a chain upon which the cipher of Mohammed is engraved. Then he appears before the Caliph and kisses his hand and the Caliph rises and places him upon a throne which Mohammed had ordered to be made for him, and all the Mohammedan princes who attend the court of the Caliph rise before him.

BENJAMIN, JUDAH PHILIP (1811–1884) U.S. statesman and lawyer. Benjamin was born a British subject at Saint Croix in the Virgin Islands. His family moved in 1813 first to Wilmington, North Carolina, and then to Charleston, where he grew up, already displaying the intellectual prowess that was to mark his career. He attended Yale University for two years but left without receiving a degree. In 1828 he moved to New Orleans "with no assets other than his wit, charm, omnivorous mind, and boundless energy with which he would find his place in the sun."

Benjamin clerked in a law firm in New Orleans and also supported himself by tutoring in English. One of his students was the Creole belle Natalie St. Martin, a Catholic, whom he married. She brought a dowry of $3,000 and two slaves, but the young couple lived with their in-laws for several years. They were married in church, even though he had not converted; the wedding record identifies him as Philip Benjamin. Admitted to the Louisiana bar in 1832, he became one of the leading lawyers in the state in the next decade and published a major legal work on contracts that was a standard text for many years. In 1849 he was admitted to practice before the Supreme Court of the United States; in 1853, he turned down a nomination to the Supreme Court.

Trouble with his eyesight led him to retire for a while from his law practice and to devote his energies to a Louisiana sugarcane plantation with 140 slaves, where he made an original contribution to the process of sugar refining. However, when called upon to pay a note for $60,000, that he had guaranteed for a friend, he had to return to law.

Entering politics, he was elected U.S. senator from Louisiana in 1852 and served until his state seceded from the Union in 1861. He made a deep impression with his speeches on the legal basis for slavery and the constitutional grounds of states' rights. In the Senate he struck up a close friendship with Jefferson Davis, a senator from Mississippi. Benjamin's Senate speeches are still considered among the best ever given in that legislative institution.

In March 1861 Jefferson Davis, now President of the Confederate States of America, which had seceded from the Union, appointed Benjamin attorney general of the new Confederate government. Subsequently, he was appointed secretary of war. The shortages and reverses suffered by the Confederacy led to growing criticism of "the Jew whom the President retained at his council" and to anti-Semitic barbs at "Judas Iscariot Benjamin." He had to leave the post, but Davis appointed him secretary of state. Although he came under a continuing barrage of anti-Semitism, Benjamin held his own, maneuvering the Confederacy through many diplomatic channels, trying to obtain recognition from France and England for the secessionist government.

After the Confederate surrender at Appomattox in April 1865, Benjamin, like other Confederate leaders, went into exile. A hunted fugitive, he escaped from Florida in a tiny boat, making his way to Nassau and then to England.

Reestablishing himself as an attorney, Benjamin became one of the leading legal minds in England. He published books on aspects of English law that became the quoted sources in the field. He enjoyed great success and commanded high fees. On his retirement, he was toasted at a farewell banquet attended by the lord chancellor and the lord chief justice as "the only man who has held conspicuous leadership at the bars of two countries." After living apart from his wife and daughter for many years since they maintained a home in Paris, he rejoined them after his retirement in 1882. Benjamin, who had no contact with Judaism, was buried in a Catholic cemetery in Paris.

E. N. Evans, *Judah P. Benjamin: The Jewish Confederate*, 1988.

BENJAMIN, WALTER (1892–1940) German philosopher and literary critic. Born to an upper-middle-class Jewish family in Berlin, and raised in a controlled and protected environment, he attended the elite preparatory school, Haubinda, where one of his teachers was Gustav Wyneken, a radical

Walter Benjamin.

reformer in education. Under Wyneken's influence, he joined and became active in a German youth movement. He spent some time in Freiburg and Paris and returned to Berlin, where he was elected president of the Berlin student organization, Free Students.

On the first day of World War I he joined his friends in volunteering for service in the Prussian army. Soon, however, he became disenchanted by the youth movement's acceptance of the war and in 1915 wrote a letter to Wyneken breaking off his relationship with the movement. He managed to avoid his own induction by drinking so much coffee before the physical examination that he appeared pale and trembling and was rejected on medical grounds. On the whole, thereafter, he tended to avoid politics and to retreat into the world of the intellect, concentrating on philosophy, literature, and linguistics, rather than on social issues.

In October 1915 he went to Munich, where he met Gershom Scholem (q.v.), who was to become a close friend. In 1917, he moved to Bern, Switzerland, to study philosophy, literature, and aesthetics. He returned to Berlin in 1920 and remained there until 1933, working as a critic, translator, and reviewer for various magazines.

In 1924, on a vacation trip to Capri, he met and became involved with a Latvian actress, Asja Lacis, whose radical communism inspired a similar interest in him, although he never committed himself to the Communist party. He later toyed with the idea of immigration to Palestine and accepted a fellowship obtained with Gershom Scholem's help,

to study Hebrew prior to accepting a teaching job in Jerusalem. In 1930, however, he wrote to his old friend, explaining that he intended to stay in Germany. When the Nazis came to power three years later, he moved to France where he continued to write occasional reviews while trying to avoid the attention of Nazi authorities, and attempting to obtain a visa to leave Europe. In September 1940, having obtained a visa for the United States, he crossed the French-Spanish border with a group of fellow refugees. They were threatened by a border official on the Spanish side that they would be returned to the French the next day and handed over to the Gestapo. Benjamin took his life with an overdose of morphine; the other refugees were promptly allowed into Spain.

Benjamin is considered one of the most important German critics between the two wars. In his latter years, he tended toward Marxism and was close to Bertolt Brecht. A prolific writer of essays, articles, and reviews, he wrote only a few books (one of them a seminal study on the origin of German drama), though various posthumous collections of his work appeared, including one by Gershom Scholem with Theodor Adorno (q.v.), (1966). His work can be loosely grouped into autobiographical, metaphysical, and leftist writing as well as translations from French to German.

G. Scholem, *Walter Benjamin: The Story of a Friendship*, 1981.
R. Wolin, *Walter Benjamin: An Aesthetic of Redemption*, 1982.

BENNY, JACK (1894–1974) U.S. radio, TV, and film comedian who made a trademark of his meanness and "slow burn." He was born Benjamin Kublesky in Waukegan, Illinois, his father operated first a saloon and later a dry-goods store; as a boy, he helped out in the store. Benny studied violin and entered vaudeville at seventeen, using his violin as a stage prop. This unpromising career was interrupted by World War I and during his service in the U.S. Navy, his comic talent came to light. Upon his return to civilian life, he reentered vaudeville.

He made his first film appearance in 1929, but gained stardom on radio and later repeated his success on television. Among his best films were *Charley's Aunt* and *George Washington*; in *To Be or Not to Be*, Benny played the role of the head of a Polish theater troupe who becomes involved in espionage during World War II.

Benny's radio program began in 1932 on NBC. From 1934 to 1936 the program led the popularity polls and after that it was seldom out of the top ten. Benny continued on radio until 1955, switching to CBS in 1948. His television program, "The Jack Benny Show," began as an occasional special in 1950 and continued as a biweekly and then weekly until 1965. He won Emmys in 1957 and 1958.

Benny created a continuing-sketch comedy in which he represented himself as an aging and pompous bachelor who was also a miser and a self-deprecating violin player. For his more than forty years on radio and television, he surrounded himself with the same troupe of supporting players: his wife, Mary Livingstone (married 1927); Eddie "Rochester" Anderson as a black valet; announcer Don Wilson; band leader Phil Harris; and comedian Mel Blanc (known also as the voice of Bugs Bunny). He was neither a joke teller nor a slapstick comedian. His created character was the source of his humor and the butt of insults, made even funnier by the Benny catalog of stock mannerisms and responses that became comedy motifs to be savored week after week: a martyrlike stare with chin resting on hand, three fingers on the cheek, facial expressions of disbelief or frustration, and the utterances "Well!," "Hmmm," and "Now cut that out!" and the perfectly time pause.

Benny's shows were filled with familiar trappings: an antiquated Maxwell car and the violin on which Benny regularly turned in an inept performance of "Love in Bloom." His annual celebration of his thirty-ninth birthday became famous and he maintained a mock feud with fellow comedian Fred Allen.

From 1965 he limited himself to a few specials a year, and his final show, "Jack Benny's Second Farewell," was broadcast in 1974.

I. A. Fein, *Jack Benny, an Intimate Biography*, 1976.

Jack Benny.

THE HUMOR OF JACK BENNY

- A cannibal is a man who goes into a restaurant and orders the waiter.
- Hold-up Man: "Your money or your life!"

Benny: "I'm thinking it over!"

- Give me my golfclubs, fresh air and a beautiful partner and you can keep my golf clubs and the fresh air.

BEN-YEHUDA, ELIEZER (1858–1922) Pioneer of the modern Hebrew-language revival. Born in Lithuania, Eliezer Perlman was sent to a yeshiva (Talmudic academy), but soon left to study privately with a rabbi. This rabbi introduced the boy to a Hebrew translation of *Robinson Crusoe* and from that moment Ben-Yehuda became fanatical in his belief that the Hebrew tongue should be not only a language of prayer but also a secular language. When his family heard of the boy's new interests, they brought him home; when he was caught reading secular books, he was turned out. He was taken in by an "enlightened" Jewish family called Yones, whose eldest daughter, Deborah, taught Perlman French, German, and Russian. He left them to study at a high school and then went to Paris to study medicine because he hoped that this would bring him into contact with people who could help him fulfill his dream: to live in a Jewish homeland in the Land of Israel where Hebrew would be the spoken vernacular.

In his first published article, in a Viennese Hebrew journal, Ben-Yehuda (who had now Hebraized his name) appealed for settlement in the Land of Israel. Health problems sent him for a time to Algiers, where the climate helped his condition, but he was to suffer from tuberculosis for the rest of his life. On his return to Paris, he found that his appeal in the Viennese journal had been widely reprinted and had evoked considerable reaction -most of it negative.

He then started sending articles to the Jerusalem Hebrew journal *Havatzelet*, expressing his ideas that Hebrew had to be modernized to be used as a language that unified the Jews. Realizing that he might be regarded as a hypocrite for remaining in Paris while advocating Jewish resettlement in Eretz Israel, he decided to move there. En route he reencountered and married Deborah Yones, and the couple arrived in Jaffa in 1881. They settled in Jerusalem, where Ben-Yehuda worked as associate editor of *Havatzelet*.

Ben-Yehuda's insistence on speaking Hebrew brought him many enemies, especially among the Orthodox, who regarded Hebrew as a holy tongue not to be desecrated by everyday use. Sometimes he was attacked with stones as he traveled around Jerusalem, but his home was a Hebrew-speaking home, with Ben-Yehuda insisting on a Sephardic pronunciation, which he felt was the closest to the Hebrew of the Bible. His children were brought up speaking Hebrew, which made it very difficult for them as they had no playmates with whom they could talk.

Ben-Yehuda started to teach Hebrew at a new school under French Jewish auspices, but he lost his job on the journal because his views were too radical for its editor. He then founded his own weekly, *Ha-Tzevi*, the first modern, European-style journal in the country.

In 1891, his wife died, leaving him with five children, three of whom died within the following three months. Subsequently, Eliezer married his

Eliezer Ben-Yehuda.

wife's sister, Hemda, who was to help him actively in his work and publications. In 1890 he founded the Hebrew Language Committee, which determined standards for the use of Hebrew and developed, in the State of Israel, into the Academy of the Hebrew Language. On one occasion, the Ottoman authorities objected to an article in Ben-Yehuda's journal (which, in fact, had been written by his father-in-law) and imprisoned him for a time, took away his newspaper license for a year, and forbade him to leave the country (as a result he missed the first Zionist Congress). By 1897, the use of Hebrew had begun to spread throughout the country, partly thanks to the support of the new settlers who had arrived from Eastern Europe. Books and plays began to appear, and Ben-Yehuda started to devote himself to what was to become his greatest monument, his Hebrew dictionary. He maintained that as the Jews had produced a vast literature down the centuries, old words could usually be used to express everyday language. He set out to trace lost Hebrew words and, when these were not forthcoming for what he wanted to express, he coined new words, sometimes borrowing from cognate Semitic languages. He introduced his new words through his newspaper and encouraged his family to use them wherever possible so as to encourage their dissemination. Most of his suggestions passed into common parlance.

Ben-Yehuda put the old and the new words into a dictionary that included translations into French, German, and English for purposes of definition, with references to many Hebrew sources and to a multitude of other languages. It was also a thesaurus with a list of connected words appearing after each entry. And also showed the changes undergone by each word throughout its history. By 1914 he had completed half of his dictionary, but when Turkey entered World War I, he had to leave the country and moved to the United States. On his return after the war, he was greeted by the British governor of Jerusalem with the Hebrew words "Shalom aleikhem." Ben-Yehuda said he had never dreamed that he would be greeted in Hebrew by a British governor. Under British rule, Hebrew became one of the country's three official languages and Hebrew teachers in the Diaspora found themselves in great demand. Ben-Yehuda lived to see the results of a census in which a majority of the country's Jews gave Hebrew as their mother-tongue.

He left his dictionary unfinished at his death. His widow and son looked after its completion, and the last of the seventeen volumes appeared in 1959.
R. St. John, *The Tongue of the Prophets*, 1952.

BEN-ZVI, YITZHAK (1884–1963) Second president of the State of Israel. Born in Poltava in the Ukraine, he had a traditional Jewish upbringing. He studied in Kiev, but his schooling was interrupted by pogroms. He became active in Jewish self-defense and in organizing the Poale Zion socialist party with its founder Ber Borochov (q.v.). In 1906 he escaped from the Poltava police, who accused him of illegal Zionist activities: the following year he immigrated to Eretz Israel, where he forged a life-long friendship and collaboration with David Ben-Gurion (q.v.). Together they established the Eretz Israel branch of Poale Zion, which stood for a fusion of democratic-socialism and Zionism, calling for the revival of Hebrew, return to the soil, Jewish labor, and self-defense. Before World War I he was one of the founders of Ha-Shomer (the Watchman Defense association, which was the forerunner of Jewish self-defense in the country) and the print workers union and served as delegate to various Zionist and socialist gatherings. In 1914 his law studies in Istanbul were abruptly terminated by the war. A year later he and Ben-Gurion were expelled from Palestine by the Turkish authorities. They proceeded to the United States and engaged in Zionist socialist work. In 1917 they joined the Jewish Legion, returning with it to Palestine a year later as part of the British Army.

In the 1920s Ben-Zvi was one of the founders of the Histadrut Trades Union Federation and the Ahdut ha-Avodah labor party and became a senior official in both. In 1927 he was elected member of the Jerusalem municipal council. From 1931 to 1944 he served as chairman of the National Council of Palestinian Jewry (Va'ad Le'umi), which looked after the affairs of the country's Jewish community in the spheres of health, welfare, education, religious matters, and local authorities, and became its president in 1945. During Israel's war of independence, he was one of the leaders of the beleaguered Jewish communtiy of Jerusalem. His son Eli fell in battle.

President Yitzhak Ben-Zvi.

Elected to Israel's parliament, the Knesset, in 1949 and 1951, he was nominated to be Israel's president following the death of Chaim Weizmann (q.v.), and was elected to the office three times, an unprecedented feat, thanks to his enormous popularity. He served from 1953 to 1963 and died shortly after the beginning of his third term. A modest man, he sought to bring the exalted office of the president closer to the people of Israel, who were then being welded into a nation as large numbers of immigrants streamed into the country. He instituted an open-house policy, inviting the public to the presidential residence on holidays. He paid special attention to Israel's minorities and advocated the rights of the small Samaritan community, on whom he wrote a standard work. A noted scholar and researcher, his field of study was the history of the Holy Land and the special character of various Jewish communities in the Diaspora. He was a prolific writer who authored books and articles in these areas, including *The Exiled and the Redeemed* (Philadelphia, 1957) and encouraged research and publications, founding the Ben-Zvi Institute for the Study of Middle Eastern Jewish Communities. He rose above the daily political tumult, able to find that which united and bridged over differences.

His wife **Rachel Yanait Ben-Zvi** (1886–1979), was also an outstanding leader of the Labor movement and a pioneer of Jewish self-defense. She founded various educational establishments including an agricultural school for girls in Jerusalem. Her memoirs, *Coming Home*, appeared in 1963.

Yad Ben-Zvi, *Izhak Ben-Zvi in Memoriam, 1884–1963*, 1965.

D. A. Wertheim, *Izhak Ben-Zvi, Second President of Israel*, 1963.

BERENSON, BERNARD (1865–1959) U.S. art historian and connoisseur. His method of identifying an artist by examining his work not only in the context of his own progress as a painter, but in the context of his period and place, had a major effect on art history.

Berenson was born in Vilna (now Vilnius), Lithuania. His father changed his name from Valvrojenski to Berenson when he emigrated to Boston in 1875. During World War I, Bernard Berenson worked for the U.S. Intelligence Service in Paris and dropped the German spelling of his first name. Bernhard (as he was called in his youth) Berenson received a good secular education, studying at Boston University and Harvard. After graduating, he went to Europe, traveling in France, Italy, and England for several years, supported by allowances from friends, viewing pictures in museums, private collections, and churches.

In 1894, Berenson's *The Venetian Painters of the Renaissance* was published, the first of a torrent of books and articles that he would write during his long and productive career, among them such classics as *The Florentine Painters of the Renaissance* (1896), *The Drawings of the Florentine Painters* (1903), *Italian Painters of the Renaissance* (1906), *Aesthetics and History* (1948), and *Rumor and Reflection* (1952).

Visiting London in 1895, Berenson went to an exhibition of Venetian painters at the New Gallery. He found, and wrote, that only one of the thirty-three paintings attributed to Titian was really a Titian original, and insisted that only fifteen of the other eighty-seven paintings in the show were correctly attributed. The London art establishment reacted vehemently and never forgave him.

By this time, Berenson was already advising wealthy Americans who wanted to collect European art. Later, he worked with the British art dealer Joseph Duveen (q.v.), an association profitable for both.

It was Berenson's wish that as many as possible of the great European works of art should find their way into American collections. He not only recommended superior paintings to American purchasers, but was not above helping to smuggle them out of Italy.

He made his home in I Tatti, a villa near Settignano, Italy, where he accumulated a library of over 40,000 books. There, he wrote and entertained friends and what he called enemy-friends, including famous people in literature, the arts, and the sciences, politicians and statesmen, princes, and presidents. He bequeathed I Tatti to Harvard University.

Berenson accumulated many honors. He was a member of the American Academy of Arts and Sciences and the academies of Belgium and Norway. The city of Florence made him an honorary citizen. On his ninetieth birthday, he received a medal of honor from the Italian government for his immense contributions to the study of Italian art. Although as a youth he had become an Episcopalian and later a Catholic, Berenson felt that he owed to his early studies of Hebrew scriptures and literature his intense interest in origins and his quick indignation at injustice. A section of his *Aesthetics and History* is devoted to refuting the antihumanist and racist theories of Strzygowski, whose doctrines spread throughout Europe and America long before the appearance of Nazism.

Berenson was criticized for saying that Jews, like Arabs, "have displayed little or no talent for the visual arts," although, "to the Jews belonged the splendor and rapture of the word." In the ancient world, he said, "the Jews alone retained a scheme, simple, clear, and plausible, which would appeal to the perplexed, the disintegrated, the despairing. The world has not got over it yet, so little in fact, that today [1938], three empires are attacking it openly or furtively, brutally or sneakingly".

Berenson listed the sources of art connoisseurship as documents, tradition, and the works of art themselves, but warned that documents must be evaluated carefully in the context of the customs and economics of the period, and the personality and the financial situation of the artists. Tradition, he warns, has a habit of turning into myth as time passes, and must be, if not taken with a grain of salt, at least carefully checked. An art that exists only as tradition, with no examples or masterpieces still existing, is dead art. The works of art themselves are the only reliable materials for the art historian, but even then, "connoisseurship is a guess."

B. Berenson, *Sketch for a Self-portrait*, 1949.
N. Mariano (ed.) *Sunset and Twilight: From the Diaries of 1947–1958*, 1964.
E. Samuels, *Bernard Berenson: The Making of a Connoisseur*, 1979.

Bernard Berenson.

BERGELSON, DAVID (1884–1952) Yiddish writer. Born in Russia to a prosperous lumber and grain merchant, he was orphaned in his early teens and was subsequently raised by his elder brothers.

The first of his works to attract literary notice was his novelette *Railroad Station*, published in 1909, which brought him renown in Yiddish literary circles. It was followed in 1913 by *After All*, a novel about the slow death of the Jewish middle class; its heroine is a young woman who vaguely but futilely dreams of freeing herself from her banal existence.

In 1921 he moved to Berlin, where he began to write for the New York *Jewish Daily Forward*. In 1926 he began the journal *In Shpan*, which held that Yiddish literature should be directed to the Jewish working class. He supported the ideals of post-revolutionary Russia and his endorsement of Soviet ideology manifested itself in, among other things, work for the New York communist Yiddish paper, *Morning Freiheit*. His later writing also focused more on revolutionary themes than on the issue of social decay, which had featured in his earlier work.

In 1929 he visited the United States, and after traveling in Europe, settled in Moscow in 1934. During the 1930s his major works included a collection of short stories called *Biro-Bidjaner* (1934) and two longer novels, *Penek* and *Dnieper*, which chronicled the difficulty of adjusting to the new order in Russia. During World War II he continued to write short stories, but in 1948 he suddenly disappeared from view. It was later learned that along with other Yiddish writers he had been arrested and imprisoned without trial, and had been shot on his sixty-eighth birthday.

A product of both Russian and Yiddish literary influences, his style is one of impressionism and understatement. A prevalent theme, particularly in his earlier writing, is the slow death of the Jewish middle class, and it is on this theme that he seems to have been at his best. His last novel, *Two Worlds*, was published in Moscow in 1948.
S. Liptzin, *A History of Yiddish Literature*, 1972.

BERGNER, ELISABETH (1897–1986) Stage and screen actress. Born in Drohobycz, Galicia, she received her dramatic training at the Vienna Conservatory and made her stage debut in 1919 in Zurich. After a number of small parts, she was cast for the role of Ophelia in Alexander Moissi's production of *Hamlet* and followed this success with Rosalind in a production of *As You Like It* that brought her back to Vienna. She was often cast in roles requiring male attire; with her slight build and elfin features the effect was never unbecoming. Along with Rosalind in *As You Like It*, Shaw's *Saint Joan* became a staple of her repertoire.

In Berlin, she was directed by Max Reinhardt in Shakespeare at the Deutsches Volkstheater and in 1928 undertook a memorable tour of Holland, Denmark, Sweden, Germany, and Austria, playing in works by Shakespeare, Ibsen, and others.

From 1923 onwards she appeared in films, mostly directed by Paul Czinner, whom she married in 1933. These included the screen version of Arthur Schnitzler's *Fraulein Else*, a role much associated with her. She emigrated with her husband to Britain in 1933, making her London stage debut in Margaret Kennedy's *Escape Me Never*. For the film version, directed by Czinner two years later, she was nominated for an Academy Award. Her first British film was *Catherine the Great*, which became the first film suppressed in Nazi Germany because of Jewish participation. Bergner had made no secret of her feelings toward the Nazi regime and was the subject of an attack in the *Völkischer Beobachter* by Alfred Rosenberg. In 1936 Czinner directed her in a film version of *As You Like It* opposite Laurence Olivier.

In 1936, she starred in Sir James Barrie's last play, *The Boy David*, which had been written specially for her but which was not successful. However, on Barrie's death, a few months later, she was one of the beneficiaries in his will, for having given "the best performance ever given in any play of mine." Bergner spent most of the war in America, where she made only one film, but enjoyed a long run in *The Two Mrs. Carrolls* on the New York stage. In the late 1940s she took her first steps in the new medium of television and toured extensively, including an appearance in the new State of Israel in 1949.

Apart from sporadic film appearances, her remaining work was done in the theater, with appearances in West Germany, Austria, Britain and Australia during the 1950s. She was widowed in 1972 and two years before her death was one of six émigré actors feted at the thirty-third Berlin Film Festival.

E. Bergner, *Bewundert viel und gescholten...: Unordentliche Erinnerungen*, 1978.

> Somebody asked me, if I could share what I thought on 30 January 1933 [the day Hitler became chancellor of Germany]. So I said: How should I know what I thought on 30 January 1933. What happened then? I had no idea what he was talking about. It was as if you were to ask me: what did you think last week on Thursday? I had no idea. — I was already in England then. Really a godsend, that I was there already. What did I think? I thought: this is nonsense. I really believed that, for a long time. Until I saw, it remains nonsense, but it becomes more and more tragic.
>
> **Elisabeth Bergner, 1982**

BERGSON, HENRI LOUIS (1859—1941) French philosopher and Nobel Prize winner. He was born in Paris. His Polish father, scion of a Hasidic family, was a pianist and composer, who had been a

Henri Bergson. Medal by H. Kautsch, 1913.

pupil of Chopin; his mother was English. Bergson went to school in Paris and then taught high school at Angers and Clermont-Ferrand. In 1889 he returned to Paris where he published his doctoral thesis, *Time and Free Will: An Essay on the Immediate Data of Consciousness* (1889; English translation, 1911), and lectured at the Ecole Normale Supérieure. In 1900 he was appointed professor at the Collège de France, where the elite flocked to hear his lectures. Greatly admired for his literary style, he was elected a member of the Académie Française in 1914 and was awarded the Nobel Prize for literature in 1928.

Bergson's *Matter and Memory* (1896; English translation, 1911) was written after a long period in which he made an intensive study of memory. He rejected the then-prevalent theory of a psychophysical parallelism between mind and body, claiming that memory is independent of the body, which it only utilizes for its own ends. The work won widespread acclaim. "Bergsonism" became very much in vogue, with many commentaries being written on his work and his theories proved widely influential, for example on the work of his wife's cousin, Marcel Proust (q.v.).

His doctrine of creative evolution also received literary echoes, notably in the writings of George Bernard Shaw, who was impressed with Bergson's conviction of the unlimited potential for the progress of mankind. It was presented in his best-known work, *Creative Evolution* (1907; English translation, 1911), based on his process philosophy. This was rooted in evolutionary theory, maintaining that the process of evolution embodies the endurance of the vital impulse (*élan vital*) with conciousness and matter as manifestations of this central impulse. The world contains two opposing tendencies — the *élan vital* and the resistance of the material world to that force.

Duration is lived time, which is not the divided and measurable time of science, and which constituted innermost reality. Philosophy is the return to the immediate data of intuition, which makes scientific methods more flexible and brings them closer to reality. Only the privileged few are granted this intuition, and here Bergson had much admiration for the great mystics, given expression in his last major work, *The Two Sources of Morality and Religion* (1932; English translation, 1935); in which he discerns the two sources of morality, one based in intelligence, the other in intuition.

One of his works that aroused great interest was *Laughter: An Essay on the Meaning of the Comic* (1900; English translation, 1911), which suggests that comedy expresses a lack of adaptability to society. An individual out of touch with his fellows is comic, and the function of laughter is to bring him to a state of reality within a societal framework.

Bergson was always remote from Judaism. In his later years he was attracted to Catholicism, which he regarded as the fulfillment of Judaism. However, he was deterred from taking the formal step of conversion by the widespread prevalence of anti-Semitism. "I want to be among those who will be persecuted," he said.

During the German occupation of France in

World War II, he refused the offer of the Vichy Government to be exempted from the anti-Jewish laws and to be treated as some sort of "honorary Aryan." He returned all the medals he had received

from the French government. Despite his ill-health (from which he had suffered for many years), he insisted on going out and standing in line to be registered as a Jew, an exertion that aggravated his sickness and hastened his death.

I. W. Alexander, *Bergson, Philosopher of Reflection*, 1957.

L. Kolakowski, *Bergson*, 1985.

H. A. Larrabee (ed.), *Selections from Bergson*, 1949.

B. Scharfstein, *Roots of Bergson's Philosophy*, 1943.

BERKMAN, ALEXANDER (1870–1936) U.S. anarchist. Born in Vilna (Vilnius), then in Russia, Alexander Berkman emigrated to the United States in 1888. He became a member of the Pioneers of Freedom, one of the first Jewish anarchist groups founded by Russian immigrants, and later joined the German anarchist movement. Together with Emma Goldman (q.v.), he led the anarchist movement in America.

In 1892 in Homestead, Pennsylvania, Berkman shot and attempted to kill the director of the steelworks as a protest against the treatment of the workers during a strike. Although he only wounded the director, he was sentenced to twenty-two years imprisonment, and was released after fourteen years. He renewed his association with Emma Goldman and, during World War I, was convicted for engaging in propaganda against conscription and obstructing the draft. He was again sent to prison and upon his release in 1919, was deported to the USSR.

Berkman could not reconcile Bolshevik philosophy with his libertarian principles and was disappointed with the Bolshevik regime that he found in the USSR. In 1922 he left the Soviet Union for Germany, and in 1925 moved to France.

Berkman's publications included *Prison Memoirs of an Anarchist* (1970), *The Kronstadt Rebellion* (1922), *The Bolshevik Myth* (1925), *The Anti-Climax* (1925), and *Now and After, the ABC of Communist Anarchism* (1929). In 1936, he committed suicide in Nice.

R. Drinnon, *Rebel in Paradise*, 1961.

BERLIN, IRVING (Israel Baline; 1888–1989) U.S. songwriter. The son of a cantor and kosher butcher, Berlin was born in Temun, Ṣiberia, and went to the United States with his family, who fled the pogroms, when he was six. At eight, following his father's death, he began helping to support his family, progressing from selling newspapers to singing while he waited on tables at Chinatown's Pelham Café. It was on the piano there that he first taught himself to play — on the black keys only, the basis of his hit "Always"; in more successful days he would work on an instrument especially built to change whatever music he played into the only key he had mastered, F sharp. It was also for the Pelham that he first wrote lyrics, and an error on the sheet music gave him a new name, Irving Berlin. His cakewalks and rags soon brought him a reputation.

- There are general problems that interest everyone and must be dealt with in language comprehensible to everybody. The solution to these problems is frequently subordinated to those questions which interest only the scholars. These may be dealt with in technical terms.
- Action is what matters. We are present where we act.
- What is found in the effect was already in the cause.
- Obedience to duty implies resistance to self.
- The mystics bear witness that God needs us.
- There is no state of mind, however simple, which does not change every minute.

Henri Bergson

Irving Berlin.

Berlin found himself capable of writing music as well as lyrics and in 1911 he became a household name when "Alexander's Ragtime Band" swept the country. Serious ballads began to join the novelty songs in his repertoire after his bride, Dorothy Goetz, died of typhoid shortly after their wedding in 1914, he graduated from individual hits to complete stage scores, and by 1921 he was writing them for his own theater, the Music Box, as well as acting as his own publisher.

With the inclusion of his "Blue Skies" in the historic part-talkie *The Jazz Singer*, Berlin's songs became as important for the screen as they had become for the stage. He wrote three film scores for Fred Astaire and Ginger Rogers and two for the team of Astaire and Bing Crosby. The first of the latter, *Holiday Inn*, contained his greatest song success, "White Christmas." Another hit was *Easter Parade*. During both world wars, he was responsible for fund-raising soldier shows (including *This Is the Army*) and the song "America," originally written for the first of these, gained the status of unofficial American anthem. Immediately after World War II, he produced his most renowned work for the stage, *Annie Get Your Gun*. Its star, Ethel Merman, also starred in Berlin's last major success, *Call Me Madam*, in 1950. In 1955 he received the congressional gold medal for his patriotic songs and widespread celebrations marked his one hundredth birthday in 1988.

L. Bergreen, *As Thousands Cheer: The Life of Irving Berlin*, 1990.
C. Brahms and N. Sherrin, *Song by Song*, 1984.
D. Ewen, *The Story of Irving Berlin*, 1950.
M. Freedland, *Irving Berlin*, 1974.

SOME OF IRVING BERLIN'S HITS

"Alexander's Ragtime Band"
"Always"
"What'll I Do"
"White Christmas"
"Easter Parade"
"Oh How I Hate To Get Up in the Morning"
"Blue Sky"
"This Is the Army"
"There's No Business Like Show Business"
"Anything You Can Do I Can Do Better"
"Over There"
"A Pretty Girl Is Like a Melody"
"All Alone"
"The Song Is Ended"
"Puttin' On the Ritz"
"Soft Lights and Sweet Music"
"I've Got My Love to Keep Me Warm"
"Cheek to Cheek"
"The Girl in the Magazine Cover"
"Lets' Face the Music and Dance"
"Top Hat"
"Isn't This a Lovely Day"
"Change Partners"

"Irving Berlin has no place in American music. He is American music."

Jerome Kern

BERNHARDT, SARAH (1844–1923) French actress. Born Sarah Henriette Rosine Bernard, she was the illegitimate daughter of Judith van Hard, who came from a Dutch Jewish family and who had a reputation both as a courtesan and music teacher, and Edouard Bernard, French student of law. As the child's presence interfered with her mother's way of life, she was placed in a convent and baptized, but was always conscious and proud of her Jewish origin. She thought of becoming a nun, but one of her mother's lovers, the half-brother of Napoleon III, felt that she had a vocation as an actress and arranged for her to attend the government-sponsored acting academy. Her teachers were not particularly impressed with her ability and the feeling was largely reciprocated.

She began her career at the Comédie-Française in 1862 in the title role of Racine's *Iphigénie en Aulide*, but attracted little attention and was dismissed from the company after slapping the face of another actress. A period of self-doubt followed. At this time, she bore a son to Henri, prince de Ligne. In 1866, she joined the Odéon theater and there achieved her first triumphs, notably in Coppée's *Le Passant*, her first male part, which received a command performance before Napoleon III. She organized a military hospital in the theater during the siege of Paris in 1870. Subsequently she appeared in *Ruy Blas*, by Victor Hugo, who called her "golden-voiced" and "the divine Sarah."

She returned to the Comédie-Française in 1872 and had further successes, including Voltaire's *Zaire*, Racine's *Phèdre* and *Andromaque*, and Hugo's *Hernani*. Her temperament led her to leave the Comédie-Française in 1880, by which time she had become an international star, and she then toured Europe's capitals, the United States, Australia, and South America. Her greatest successes were in *La dame aux camélias* by André Dumas fils and Edmond Rostand's *L'aiglon*, in which she played Napoleon's son. The dramatist Victorien Sardou wrote a series of plays especially for her. She founded her own theater company, which became the Théâtre Sarah Bernhardt in 1899 and which she directed until her death. One of her popular roles there was Hamlet.

In 1905, while playing Sardou's *Tosca* in Latin America, she jumped off a cliff in the last act and hurt her knee. The injury was neglected and ten years later, the leg had to be amputated. Nevertheless she continued acting in plays specially written for her, often playing her roles while lying on a sofa. For eighteen months, she was carried around the World War I fronts, appearing before the French troops. She made a number of films, the best-known being *Queen Elizabeth* (1912), an exaggerated performance conveying only a slight idea of her powers. Her last movie, *La voyante*, was filmed in her own home in Paris. She also wrote a novel, *Petite idol*, a book on acting, and an autobiography, *Ma double vie* (1907).

J. Richardson, *Sarah Bernhardt*, 1959.
C. O. Skinner, *Madame Sarah*, 1967.
L. Verneuil, *The Fabulous Life of Sarah Bernhardt*, 1942.

Sarah Bernhardt.

BERNSTEIN, EDUARD (1850–1932) German Social Democratic propagandist and political theorist. Born in Berlin, one of fifteen children of a railroad engineer, Bernstein first worked as a junior employee of the S. & L. Rothschild Bank in Berlin. He was moved politically toward social democracy by the events of the time, particularly the economic crisis of the early 1870s, which reinforced his belief in the fragility of capitalism, and the speeches of German radical and socialist leaders following the 1870 Franco-Prussian war. In 1872 he joined the Marxist wing of the labor movement.

Bernstein formulated the basis of a democratic socialism that suited the changing conditions of capitalist society. He was the first German socialist to challenge the fundamental economic assumptions on which Marx's model of revolution was based, and he questioned the concentration on the final goal of socialism at the expense of the means and the method by which it was achieved.

Bernstein left Germany following the enactment of Bismarck's antisocialist laws and made his base in Switzerland, where he became editor in 1881 of *Der Sozialdemokrat*, which was the official organ of the underground exiled Socialist party (SPD). The paper was published in Zurich and smuggled into Germany.

At the request of Bismarck, Bernstein was expelled from Switzerland in 1888. He moved to London where he continued the publication of the periodical until 1890. In this period he was much influenced by the Fabian Society in England which advocated a gradualist development of socialism. Here he published his main work, *Evolutionary Socialism* (1899; English translation, 1909).

In 1901 Bernstein returned to Germany to become the theoretician of the revisionist school of the reformist labor movement. He rejected Marx's theory of an imminent collapse of capitalist society, pointing out that the middle class was not declining, the peasants were not sinking, crises were not growing larger, and mass misery was not increasing. He argued that the prospects for lasting success lay in steady advancement rather than mass upheaval.

In 1902, Bernstein was elected a member of the Reichstag, sitting until 1906 and again from 1912 to 1918. During World War I he sided with the Independent Socialists protesting against war and militarism. From 1920 to 1928 he sat in Parliament as a Social Democrat.

Although not a practicing Jew, Bernstein felt growing concern for the fate of Jews who were persecuted. Many Zionists, for example Zalman Shazar (q.v.) and Chaim Weizmann (q.v.) tried converting Bernstein to Zionism, which he opposed before World War I. He modified his views to support the concept of national autonomy for Jews in individual European countries and thought Jewish nationalism reconcilable with modern democratic ideas of self-determination. In his last years he became more supportive of Zionism.

Bernstein was worried about the growth in anti-Semitism in Germany even before his return in 1901. He became alarmed by Hitlerism and the rise of the right-wing National Socialist party but was powerless to prevent its advance. He died in 1932 six weeks before Hitler's accession to power. His memoirs, *My Years of Exile*, appeared in 1921.

P. Gay, *The Dilemma of Democratic Socialism: Eduard Bernstein's Challenge to Marx*, 1952.
R. S. Wistrich, *Revolutionary Jews from Marx to Trotsky*, 1976.

BERNSTEIN, JULIUS (1839–1917) Experimental neurophysiologist and genius, who used physical-chemical theories to develop a membrane theory of nervous conduction. Born in Berlin, he was the son of Aron Bernstein, a noted political and scientific writer and a founder of Reform Judaism in Berlin. He studied medicine in Breslau and Berlin and graduated from Berlin University in 1862. From 1864 he was an assistant in Heidelberg and in 1871 became associate professor in physiology at the University of Halle, being promoted to full professor the following year.

Bernstein conducted classical research on the physiology of muscle and nerve tissue, blood circulation, the heart, respiration, and the special senses. He published papers on toxicology, the problems of educating medical students, physics, and mathematics. In his studies he used photography to measure the latent period of muscle stimulation. He also investigated galvanic neuromuscular stimulation, introduced the differential rheotome in 1890, and applied the laws of physical chemistry to the study of muscular physiology and the thermodynamics of muscular contraction (1902–1908).

His publications include: *Researches on the Processes of Irritation of the Nervous and Muscular Systems* (1871); *The Mechanical Theory of Life, Its Basis and Success* (1890); *A Textbook of Physiology of the Animal Organism* (1894; 3rd edition, 1909); *The Preliminary Education of Medical Students* (1899); *The Vigor of Motion in the Living Substance* (1902); and *Electrobiology* (1912).

BERNSTEIN, LEONARD (1918–1990) U.S. composer and conductor. He was born in Lawrence, Massachusetts, to immigrants from the Ukraine. His father ran a beauty-supply business, which he wished his son to enter, and he long opposed a musical career. Bernstein attended the Boston Latin School, Harvard University, and the Curtis Institute in Philadelphia, where he was a pupil of Fritz Reiner. His talents attracted the attention of the conductors Artur Rodzinski and Serge Koussevitzky (q.v.), who helped him with his career.

Bernstein burst onto the musical scene in 1943 when, at a few hours notice, he substituted for the ailing Bruno Walter (q.v.) in conducting the New York Symphony Orchestra. His debut was so sensational that it made the front page of the *New*

Leonard Bernstein conducting the Israel Philharmonic Orchestra, Tel Aviv, 1957.

York Times. In the next two years he published his *Jeremiah Symphony*, wrote the successful *Fancy Free* ballet (choreographed by Jerome Robbins) and a hit Broadway show, *On the Town.* In 1945 he was appointed conductor of the New York Symphony; in 1957 its coprincipal director (it had by then merged with the New York Philharmonic Orchestra); and in 1958 its music director. Bernstein was the first American-born conductor of a major U.S. orchestra and his relationship with the New York Philharmonic marked a golden age. With the Philharmonic he produced recordings that sold millions of copies.

As a conductor Bernstein was uninhibited and emotional. After he conducted a performance of Igor Stravinsky's *Symphony of Psalms* in the presence of the composer, Stravinsky had only a single comment: "Wow!" Bernstein was responsible for creating an upsurge of interest in the works of Gustav Mahler (q.v.), but his repertoire was eclectic, ranging from classical to jazz. A popular guest conductor, he was associated especially with the Vienna Philharmonic and the Israel Philharmonic. He first conducted in Israel in 1947, returned the following year to conduct concerts near the front line during the War of Independence, and remained closely associated with it until his death. He took the orchestra on a world tour in 1986 for its fiftieth anniversary, for which he wrote his *Jubilee Games.*

Bernstein was also a superb teacher, as exemplified by his "Omnibus Concerts," "Young People's Concerts," and television lectures in the 1950s and 1960s, in which he and the New York Philharmonic brought classical music into millions of homes. The televised lecture series made Bernstein a household name and demonstrated that he was as brilliant in verbalizing as in composing.

Bernstein's large-scale compositions, often inspired by Jewish themes, included his *Second Symphony* (*The Age of Anxiety*), *Third Symphony* (*Kaddish*), *Chichester Psalms* (Hebrew settings written for Chichester Cathedral), and a mass in memory of President John F. Kennedy (which included some Hebrew substitutions for the traditional Latin text). However, his most popular and influential compositions were his stage works, the musical *Wonderful Town*, the operetta *Candide*, and especially *West Side Story*. Based on the Romeo and Juliet theme and telling the story of rival gangs in New York, *West Side Story* was acclaimed as a masterpiece, played and revived the world over; it was made into a highly successful film.

Bernstein was an extrovert and a showman, with a feeling for the occasion. After the 1967 Six-Day War, he conducted the Israel Philharmonic in a concert on Mount Scopus, now reunited with Jewish Jerusalem. In 1988 he conducted Mahler's *Resurrection Symphony* in a vast open-air concert in Jerusalem to mark the fortieth anniversary of the foundation of the State of Israel. One of his last performances was in the summer of 1990 when he conducted the Berlin Philharmonic on the site of the destroyed Berlin wall in a performance of Beethoven's *Ninth Symphony*, substituting in the choral finale the word *Freiheit* ("freedom") for *Freude* ("joy"). He was always active in liberal causes, being labeled by the novelist Tom Wolfe "radical chic."

On his death, the London *Times* wrote, "He was the most spectacularly versatile of all American musicians of the 20th century. Exuberantly gifted, he possessed an uncanny touch of success with all kinds of music and all manner of musicians," while *Time* called him "the Brightest and the Best" and *Newsweek* "the greatest figure in the history of American musicians."

BESHT See Baal Shem Tov

BETTELHEIM, BRUNO (1903–1990) Psychiatrist; best known for his pioneering work with emotionally disturbed and autistic children. Bettelheim, born in Austria to a middle-class Viennese family, was early influenced by Sigmund Freud's (q.v.) work in psychoanalytic theory. His interest began when a girl he liked was impressed by an older boy who knew about Freud's ideas. Bettelheim determined to study the subject by himself and became so entranced that he later reported walking down the street where Freud lived "only because Freud lived there." He continued studying

psychology and became particularly interested in autistic children, who suffer from a little-understood disease that causes them to withdraw into their own worlds, communicating little, if at all, with others. Believing that autistic children could be reached, he took an afflicted child into his own home in 1932, in search of successful therapy. The experiment was abruptly ended in 1938, shortly after Bettelheim received his doctorate from the University of Vienna, because of the occupation of Austria by the Nazis. Bettelheim was arrested and taken to Dachau, and later transferred to Buchenwald.

After spending over a year in the camps, Bettelheim was released due to intervention by Eleanor Roosevelt and New York Governor Herbert Lehman (q.v.). He arrived in the United States in 1939 and began working as a research associate in the Progressive Education Association at the University of Chicago. Four years later, he attracted considerable attention when he published an article entitled "Individual and Mass Behavior in Extreme Situations," which recalled his experiences in the concentration camps. In 1944 he was appointed assistant professor of psychology and head of the Sonia Shankman Orthogenic School, a residential treatment center for emotionally disturbed children. Bettelheim turned the center into a total "therapeutic milieu," administering therapy as an all-day experience in a completely supportive environment rather than at isolated treatment hours. The children in his center lived in plush surroundings and ate from china plates. The doors of the school were locked to the outside, but always open from the inside. Although his claim of an 85 percent cure rate, defined as a full return to participation in life, has been challenged, there is no doubt that he set new standards in the treatment of severely emotionally disturbed and autistic children.

Bettelheim related the extreme distress he and other victims suffered in Nazi concentration camps to the pain suffered by emotionally disturbed children. His views on the Holocaust, however, were considered controversial. Bettelheim held Jews partially responsible for their own fate at the hands of the Nazis because of what he called "ghetto thinking." He said Diaspora Jews had long been trained into a docility and compliance, which usually allowed them to survive in alien cultures. The Jews who marched "like lemmings" to the death camps were permitting themselves to be punished, not for what they did but for who they were, and this, Bettelheim concluded, meant that they were already "dead by [their] own decision." Later in a 1976 article, "Surviving," he wrote that those who survived the death camps were able to do so because they believed in some cultural or religious ideal that helped them transcend themselves.

In his first book, *Love Is Not Enough* (1950), Bettelheim discussed his method of treatment and the causes he believed were responsible for creating disturbed children. Although in his early writings he blamed "schizophrenic mothers" for autistic children, he later revised his views in *A Good Enough Parent* (1987). In this work he concluded that children were innately good and parents innately good enough. His other major works include *The Uses of Enchantment* (1976), about the role of fairy tales in childhood; *Children of the Dream* (1967), which discusses communal child rearing on Israeli kibbutzim; and *The Informed Heart* (1960), about human behavior under severe stress.

Bettelheim was living in a nursing home when he took his own life on March 13, 1990, on the fifty-second anniversary of the date the German army had invaded Austria.

B. Bettelheim, *Recollections and Reflections*, 1990.

BIALIK, CHAIM NACHMAN (1873–1934) Hebrew author, father of modern Hebrew poetry. Born in a Ukrainian village, in his poetry he fondly recalls his childhood as a lost paradise of fields and woods. His happiness ended abruptly at the age of seven when his father died and he was sent to Zhitomir to be raised by his grandfather, whose stern Orthodox upbringing he found unbearably stifling. At the age of fifteen, he entered the yeshiva (Talmudic academy) of Volozhin in Lithuania, hoping to find some way of mediating for himself between the Jewish Enlightenment and Orthodoxy. While there, he began to write Hebrew poetry and prose. He also came under the influence of Ahad Ha'Am (q.v.), the spokesman of Jewish national revival, and joined a clandestine Zionist society. Although he was a good student, he found the yeshiva atmosphere too confining and left for the great cultural center of Odessa, where he began to gain recognition as a Hebrew poet.

He returned for a period to Zhitomir, where he worked as a timber merchant for his father-in-law, and during this time wrote profusely. Four years later, he returned to Odessa to teach in the Hebrew

Chaim Nachman Bialik (standing, second from the left), with friends. Jaffa, 1909.

school and lived there for the next twenty years, writing essays, stories, and poems, and editing and publishing Hebrew literary journals. A great part of his poetry was written during this period.

With the rise of Zionism and the revival of Hebrew, he came to be known as the poet-prophet of Jewish nationalism. His influence was immense. He inspired Zionists and revolutionaries in Russia, pioneers in Palestine, and thousands of school-children who studied his poetry wherever modern Hebrew was taught.

During the years preceding World War I, he stopped writing poetry for a period that has come to be known as the silence, and which is a subject of endless speculation. During that time he became preoccupied with the concept of *kinus*, the collection of diverse elements of Jewish culture from the Diaspora.

After three years in Berlin, Bialik settled in Palestine in 1924. He became a national figure and was so busy in his public functions that his literary activity declined. He established the *Oneg Shabbat* Saturday afternoon cultural gatherings. He was chairman of the Hebrew Language Council and became active in the collection and editing of the great Hebrew poets of Spain and the legends of the rabbinic tradition (*aggada*), and he participated in the establishment of the Dvir publishing house and the Hebrew University. He was regarded, somewhat to his own embarrassment, as the great poet of Jewish nationalism and was widely honored. One anecdote tells of two children who spotted him in a barbershop in Tel Aviv. One said, "There's Bialik!" "Don't be silly," his friend replied. "Bialik is a street name."

He was one of the greatest masters of Hebrew in modern times and wrote essays as well as poetry. His poetry (written according to the Ashkenazi pronunciation) ranges from nationalist poems which deal with the crisis of faith, the nationalist revival, the tension between his love of Jewish life and his scorn for all that was stifling in that life, to the

The Bible is always with me, I do not dip pen in ink without looking at it.
● Reading a poem in translation is like kissing a woman through a veil.
● Each people has as much heaven over its head as it has land under its feet.

● Say this when you mourn for me:
There was a man — and look, he is no more.
He died before his time.
The music of his life suddenly stopped.
A pity! There was another song in him.
Now it is lost
forever.

From Bialik's "After My Death"

private poems filled with images of childhood grief lost, love and yearning for the innocence and security of childhood. He scorned Jewish apathy and many of his poems criticized his fellow Diaspora Jews for their humble acceptance of the negative aspects of their existence. Most notable was *In the City of Slaughter*, written after the 1903 pogrom in Kishinev, in which he both expressed his sorrow and attacked the cowardly, parasitical survivors. This poem was a major stimulus to the Jewish self-defense movement. Many other such "poems of wrath" followed between the years 1903 and 1906.

He was often sent abroad as an emissary of the Zionist organization. His death of a heart attack in Vienna, at the height of his fame, was seen as a national tragedy. His home in Tel Aviv is now the Bialik Museum.

D. Aberbach, *Bialik*, 1988.
R. Nevo (transl.), *Chaim Nachman Bialik: Selected Poems*, 1981.
L. V. Snowman (ed.), *Chaim Nachman Bialik: Poems from the Hebrew*, 1924.

BLEICHRÖDER, GERSON VON (1822–1893) Banker to German Chancellor Otto von Bismarck. His father Samuel ran an exchange office and an agency for the redemption of lottery tickets, eventually becoming a merchant banker. Born in Berlin, Gerson entered his father's business in 1839, became a partner in 1847, and succeeded his father as head of the firm in 1855. Exploiting the ties his father had made with the Rothschilds (q.v.), he formed syndicates with other banks to establish investment companies. He became involved in the metallurgical industry and in railroads, being appointed official banker to the Cologne-Minden and Rhenish railroads. In 1859 Bleichröder became the cofounder of a syndicate to finance Prussian mobilization during the Franco-Austrian war.

Bleichröder's relationship with Bismarck, which was to last over a period of nearly thirty years, began when the latter made Bleichröder his personal banker. The association was strengthened when Bismarck was elected premier in 1862, Bleichröder becoming his confidant and financial adviser. The Bleichröders came to be regarded as the greatest banking house in Berlin. Bleichröder enjoyed the high esteem of the College of Elders of Berlin Merchants and of King William, who repeatedly requested his advice on financial matters. Throughout the Franco-Prussian War, Bleichröder used his connections with bankers in France (especially the house of Rothschild) to act as a go-between and carried out missions of the greatest secrecy. He also acted as paymaster for the 300,000 French soldiers imprisoned in Germany. In 1870 the king appointed him treasurer of the Wilhelm-Stiftung fund for aid to wounded or sick soldiers. At the end of the war in 1871, Bleichröder joined Bismarck in Versailles to help arrange payment of France's indemnity. Bleichröder undertook the reorganization of the Silesian coal complex, and developed interests in the mining industry.

He had investments in nearly every country in Europe and elsewhere, enabling him to play a significant role in German foreign affairs. He was involved in the expansion of German colonization. In 1880 he formed the Deutsche Seehandels-Gesellschaft to provide the capital needed to save the South Sea plantations in Samoa, and in 1884 headed the New Guinea Consortium, which established a company protectorate in that country. The following year he set up the Deutsche Kolonial-Gesellschaft für Südwestafrika to support the German possessions in Africa. In 1888 he played a leading role in the supervision of Turkey's finances, a pioneering role in Germany's interests in the Middle East. He organized loans to Mexico, Greece, and Russia and was a member of the consortiums that founded the Deutsch-Asiatische Bank to provide banking services in China and the Banca Commerciale Italiano in Milan.

Despite the fact that in all these ventures Bleichröder worked hand in hand with Bismarck, the latter made no mention of him in his memoirs. It is only in recent years, with the discovery of Bleichröder's private archives in New York after World War II, containing thousands of letters between these men, that efforts have been made to portray his major role during the Bismarck era.

Gerson von Bleichröder was awarded numerous decorations throughout his life. In 1872 he was raised to the hereditary nobility by King William and was appointed British consul general in Berlin.

Bleichröder was proud of his Jewish background. From the 1860s he was an active member of the Berlin Jewish community and contributed generously to Jewish causes. He took up the cause of Romanian Jewry and successfully attained Bismarck's support in the struggle to protect them from oppression and discrimination. He orchestrated the lobbying by international Jewry at the Congress of Berlin (1878), where a resolution was passed demanding that Romania extend equal rights to the Jews. The Jews of Jassy wrote a poem likening him to Moses, which he begged them not to publish.

Bleichröder's philanthropy encompassed numerous organizations, but his greatest was undoubtedly his contribution to research in tuberculosis by Robert Koch, the discoverer of the tuberculosis bacillus, and the donation, anonymously, of one million marks for the construction of a hospital for Koch's patients.

C. Iancu, *Bleichröder et Crémieux. Le combat pour l'émancipation des Juifs de Roumanie devant le Congrès de Berlin. Correspondance inédite (1881–1880)*, 1987.
F. Stern, *Gold and Iron: Bismarck, Bleichröder and the Building of the German Empire*, 1977.

BLIOKH, IVAN See Bloch, Ivan

BLITZSTEIN, MARC (1905–1964) U.S. composer. Born in Philadelphia into a fairly well-to-do family, he took piano and organ lessons from an early age, then went on to study composition at the Curtis Institute in Philadelphia and piano in New York. At fifteen he was a soloist with the Philadelphia Orchestra.

In 1926 he went to Europe to further his musical studies. He studied composition with Nadia Boulanger at the Boulangerie in Paris and with Arnold Schönberg (q.v.) in Berlin. After his return to the United States, he devoted himself almost entirely to composing works of "social consciousness" of the genre produced in German by Bertolt Brecht and Kurt Weill, whose *Threepenny Opera* he adapted and translated into English with enormous success.

Blitzstein was a stimulating teacher, lecturer, and critic. He sparkled as a satirist and was a talented and witty commentator on political and social issues. Through his music he would often give vent to his proletarian sympathies and democratic ideals. He disowned almost all his early works, which tended to be so "abstract" as to be discordant and violent. His operas, which he called "plays in music," were conceived for small, cabaret-type theaters. The first of these was *The Cradle Will Rock* (1936), a satire with tragic undertones, followed by *No for an Answer*, a short satirical tragedy.

Blitzstein adopted the structure of the commercial musical, complete with dialogue, set numbers, and various blends of drama and music. He even introduced certain cinematic techniques; in this he anticipated Gian Carlo Menotti, yet was subtler and more expressive. In the words of W. Mellers, he created "a kind of 'American recitative' in which ... he reveals the roots of some features of jazz in the American dialect ... this vocal line provides a link between musically accompanied speech and song ... He combined Menotti's stage sense with Gershwin's instinctive musicianship." He wrote his own libretti.

Regina, a musical revue based on Lillian Hellman's drama, *The Little Foxes*, was expanded into a full-scale opera. First performed in Boston in 1949, it enjoyed great success.

Apart from numerous other musical plays, his oeuvre includes: a ballet suite; an opera-ballet; an oratorio, *The Condemned*; *Percussion Music for Piano* and other piano pieces; numerous orchestral works, including *Freedom*, a symphonic poem; a string quartet; and compositions for various vocal and instrumental combinations, among them *Cantata (This Is the Garden)* for chorus and orchestra, which was performed by the Interracial Fellowship Chorus in New York in 1957. He also wrote film music and incidental music for several Shakespearean and other plays.

Blitzstein had unswerving confidence in himself as a theater composer. He said: "Music in the theater is a powerful, an almost immorally potent weapon." He died at Fort-de-France, Martinique, of a brain injury sustained during a political dispute in a bar.

W. Mellers, *Music in a New Found Land*, 1964.

BLOCH, ERNEST (1880–1959) American composer and teacher. Born in Geneva, Switzerland, Bloch studied the violin and composition in his hometown and continued his studies in Brussels and Frankfurt. After spending some time in Munich and Paris, Bloch returned to Geneva where he entered his father's clock business. Musical engagements as a conductor followed in Neuchâtel and Lausanne. Bloch also lectured on aesthetics at the Geneva Conservatory.

In 1916 he welcomed the opportunity to travel to the United States and leave war-torn Europe behind. But his tour with dancer Maud Allan was far from successful, and he soon returned home. He returned to America a year later, and taught at the David Mannes School of Music in New York. It was during this time that Bloch established his reputation as a Jewish composer.

In 1920 Bloch became the first director of the Cleveland Institute of Music, a position he held for five years. During his tenure Bloch suggested a number of radical reforms that were not acceptable to his colleagues. He proposed, for example, that the students' live musical experience should replace the traditional examinations and textbooks. From 1925 to 1930 he headed the San Francisco Conservatory. In 1927 he was awarded the first prize in a contest sponsored by the magazine *Musical America* for his epic rhapsody, *America*. The composer had hoped that the concluding choral outburst, which presented America as the ideal of humanity, might become a national hymn. But he was disappointed when it was soon forgotten.

Bloch returned to Europe, where he spent most of the 1930s, but returned to the United States in 1940 to escape anti-Semitism in Europe and in order to avoid losing his American citizenship. He settled at Agate Beach, Oregon, in 1941 and taught at the University of California, Berkeley, until his retirement in 1952.

Although Bloch started composing highly romantic works during his student days in Geneva, he is above all known as a Jewish composer. Bloch's Jewish compositions can be divided into two groups. His Jewish cycle comprises seven works written between 1911 and 1918, and it was through these works that the composer's search for musical identity was fulfilled. Although there is little direct quotation from Hebrew material, except for verses from the Song of Songs in the *Israel Symphony*, the works are Jewish in character. In *Schelomo*, a suite for cello and orchestra which is one of the composer's most popular works, the sounds of the shofar may be detected. The musical quality of the Jewish chant in the synagogue is found in many of his works of this period.

After neglecting the world of Jewish music for about five years, Bloch returned to Jewish compositions in 1923, and wrote several more in the course of the following twenty-eight years. They include three Jewish poems for orchestra, *Baal Shem* and *Abodah* for violin and piano, and *From Jewish Life* for cello and piano.

Above all stands *Avodath Hakodesh* ("Sacred Service"), one of the few works that have ever set an entire Jewish prayer service to music.

Writing between 1930 and 1933 on commission from the Temple Emmanuel congregation in San Francisco, Bloch a masterpiece based upon the text of the American *Union Prayer Book for Jewish Worship*. It is set for a cantor (usually a baritone), a mixed chorus and a large orchestra. At times a narrator is included. Bloch's other works include *Concerto Grosso*, a piano quintet, and five string quartets which project a powerful impact and intensity.

Bloch was an advocate of music and art and once said that when art, "becomes an expression of a philosophy of life, it is no longer a luxury. It is a storm that carries one away, unites all men in a unit of solidarity, shakes them to the bottom of their souls, waking them to the greatest problems of their common destiny." The composer also said that he aspired "to write Jewish music not for the sake of self-advertisement, but because it is the only way in which I can produce music of vitality.... It is the Jewish soul that interests me, the complex, glowing, agitated soul that I feel vibrating through the Bible."

In 1968, nine years after his death, his children's efforts led to the inception of the Ernest Bloch Society in the United States. In 1990 the first Bloch Festival was presented in Newport, Oregon, featuring concerts, lectures, panels, and a composers' symposium.

W. M. Jones, *The Music of Ernest Bloch*, 1963.

D. Z. Kushner, *Ernest Bloch and His Symphonic Works*, 1967.

R. Strassburg, *Ernest Bloch; Voice in the Wilderness: A Biographical Study*, 1977.

**Bloch, on writing *Avodath Hakodesh*
in the Swiss village Roveredo-Capriasca,
high above Lugano**

I have now memorized entirely the whole Service in Hebrew and I know its significance word by word. What is more important, I have absorbed it to the point that it has become mine, and as if it were the very expression of my soul. It has become the very text I was after since the age of ten - a dream of stars, of forces. I declaim out loud, amidst the rocks and forests in the great silence. It has become a "private affair" between God and me.... I am battling against notes, sounds, rhythms, to extirpate out of my soul all the unexpressed music which has been latent for centuries, which was awaiting this marvellous text. Though intensely Jewish in its roots, this message seems to me above all a gift of Israel to the whole of mankind.

BLOCH, ERNST (1885–1977) German Marxist-humanist philosopher, known for his philosophy of hope (*Philosophie der Hoffnung*). Born in the Rhineland city of Ludwigshafen, he studied physics, philology, and philosophy before beginning a teaching career at the University of Leipzig in 1918. He became a refugee in 1933, fleeing to Switzerland before emigrating to the United States in 1938, where two volumes of his three-volume *Das Prinzip Hoffnung* ("The Hope Principle," 1954–1959) were completed. After World War II, he was welcomed back to the University of Leipzig to teach philosophy and was awarded East Germany's Nationalpreis in 1955. His criticism of Marxism as providing a partial view of reality led to concerted antagonism from the Communist party, which suppressed the philosophical journal he edited, *Deutsche Zeitschrift für Philosophie*, prohibited him from publishing, and publicly condemned him as a revisionist in 1957. Consequently, he defected to West Germany during a visit in 1960 and became a visiting professor at the University of Tübingen.

Bloch's creative principle of hope was rooted in the idea that being is ultimately becoming, that true reality is yet to unfold, and that the future of humankind must be our primary concern. His social philosophy of "humanity in action" demanded a commitment to changing our lives and our world toward the ideal of perfect freedom. Although he was highly critical of Theodor Herzl's (q.v.) Zionism and any attempt to define Judaism in territorial terms, he outspokenly advocated Israel's right to exist at a symposium held at Frankfurt University in 1967.

S. Unseld (ed.), *Ernst Bloch zu Ehren*, 1965.

BLOCH, FELIX (1905–1983) Swiss-American physicist and Nobel Prize winner best known for his discovery of nuclear induction — the physical principle that led to the development of the powerful analytical technique of nuclear magnetic resonance spectroscopy.

Bloch was born in Zurich, Switzerland. In accordance with the wishes of his father, a wholesale grain merchant, he enrolled in 1924 at the Swiss Federal Institute of Technology to study engineering, but soon transferred to the institute's physics division, where he came under the influence of Erwin Schrödinger. Schrödinger, along with Niels Bohr (q.v.), Max Born (q.v.), Werner Heisenberg, and others, was at that time formulating quantum mechanics — the fundamental principles underpinning almost all of modern physics. Although Bloch arrived just a few years too late to contribute to the formulation of quantum mechanics, his life's work was to lie in its direct application. Thus his Ph.D. thesis (with Heisenberg in Leipzig) developed the analogue in the case of a crystalline solid to the electron structure of the atom. This paved the way for an understanding of electrical conduction in metals, semiconductors, and insulators, and even today Bloch states and Bloch functions are familiar concepts to any physics undergraduate.

Upon Hitler's ascent to power in the spring of 1933, Bloch left Germany and was later invited to a position at Stanford University, which, like other centers of learning, was eager to avail itself of the talent to be found among the European refugees arriving in the United States. There, Bloch conceived of a method for detecting the magnetic moment of the recently discovered neutron (i.e., that it behaves like a small magnet) and, together with L. W. Alvarez, made the first accurate measurement of its value.

During World War II Bloch was engaged in the early stages of the Manhattan Project to manufacture the atomic bomb and, later, in the development of methods of countering radar detection of airplanes. The enormous refinements in radio techniques that were made during the war years suggested to him a new and more precise method of measuring the neutron magnetic moment. His idea, based on rigorous theoretical analysis and borne out in practice at Stanford in 1945, was that a neutron or nucleus with nonzero magnetic moment, when subject to a magnetic field, would absorb radio waves of a frequency determined by the value of its magnetic moment — a process later termed magnetic induction. The corollary to this is that if the magnetic moment of a particular nucleus is known, its presence within a material sample can be detected. This new technique of materials assessment was christened nuclear magnetic resonance (NMR) spectroscopy. It is a prime example of how basic scientific research, seemingly specialized and without immediate practical application, can produce in the long term a tool of great practical utility. NMR spectroscopy revolutionized chemistry and biochemistry and contributed to clinical medicine by offering a noninvasive diagnostic method, safer than X-ray tomography and in certain respects superior to it.

Nuclear induction was, in fact, discovered concurrently and independently at Harvard and Stanford, and Felix Bloch was awarded the 1952 Nobel Prize in physics jointly with its codiscoverer, Edward Purcell.

In 1954, Bloch was appointed first director general of the European Commission of Nuclear Research (CERN) in Geneva.

T. Wasson (ed.), *Nobel Prize Winners*, 1987.

BLOCH, IVAN (1836–1901) Russian pacifist, financier, and writer. Born in Radom, Poland, Bloch (also spelled Bliokh) became a successful banker and was involved in the construction and operation of the Russian railway system. He amassed so large a fortune that he became known as the Polish Rothschild.

Bloch was also internationally famous as a pacifist, and in 1898 published in Russian a study of war ("The War of the Future in Its Technical, Economic and Political Significance"). The six-volume endeavor was said to have helped convince Tsar Nicholas II to convene the 1899 Hague Peace Conference. With volumes on weaponry and

munitions, strategy and tactics in land warfare, war at sea, economic dislocation and material losses, and the problem of casualties, the study covered all aspects of modern-day war with the assistance of illustrations, statistics, graphs, maps, and diagrams. Its conclusion was that war between modern armies could only end in stalemate, and would be fought at the cost of tremendous financial expenditures and damage to the economy. Therefore, he concluded, international arbitration was the only solution. His critics, however, maintained that his analysis of war and his thesis that war was not feasible as an instrument of policy took into account only material forces without consideration for moral and human factors that would help determine an outcome.

Although Bloch himself converted to Calvinism, he was preoccupied with the fate of Russian Jewry and actively campaigned on their behalf. He fought against anti-Semitic discrimination and published *A Comparison of the Material and Moral Welfare of the Western, Great Russian, and Polish Provinces* (1901), which pointed to the contributions of the Russian Jews to the economy of their country. The five-volume book was confiscated and burned after publication, but a few copies rescued from the flames were later summarized by A. P. Subbotin and published under another title in Russian ("The Jewish Question in Its Right Light") in 1903.

Bloch was a friend of Theodor Herzl (q.v.) whom he had met at the Hague Peace Conference of 1899 and he helped Herzl in his efforts to meet prominent Russian authorities. He was also involved in the Jewish Colonization Association in Russia.

Shortly before his death he established the International Museum of War and Peace in Lucerne, Switzerland.

R. Chickering, *Imperial Germany and a World without War*, 1975.

BLOCH, MARC (1886–1944) French historian. Born in Lyons, Bloch received his education at the Ecole Normale Supérieure in Paris. After his graduation in 1908, he studied in Germany at Leipzig and Berlin for a year, returning to France to work in Paris, where he began an intensive study of French medieval society.

An ardent French nationalist and patriot, Bloch served in the French army during the two world wars. Though not required to serve due to his age, he enlisted at the start of World War II in 1939, serving as a fuel supply officer until the defeat of his country. Between the wars he managed to influence a generation of French historical scholarship through his teaching and the journal he founded with Lucien Febre, *Annales d'Histoire Economique et Sociale*.

Bloch held chairs at Strasbourg University and at the Sorbonne. His books on French medieval society, including *French Rural History* and *Feudal Society*, are admired for the bold breadth of their coverage and their insights. He also wrote about his own profession in *The Historian's Craft*. He held that the chief task of the historian was to pose important questions, and not to simply collect and present data.

In his final book, *L'étrange défaite* ("Strange Defeat," 1949) published posthumously in 1946, Bloch discussed his relationship with Judaism. He stated, "By birth I am a Jew, though not by religion, for I have never professed any creed, whether Hebrew or Christian. I feel neither pride nor shame in my origins.... I am at pains never to stress my heredity save when I find myself in the presence of an anti-Semite.... France will remain the one country with which my deepest emotions are inextricably bound up. I was born in France. I have drunk the waters of her culture. I have made her past my own.... I breathe freely only in her climate, and I have done my best with others, to defend her interests."

After the defeat of France, Bloch taught in Vichy France for three years and then joined the French resistance. His fellow resistance fighters valued his bravery, intelligence, and skill in deciphering secret codes and hand-delivering messages under cover. In 1944 the Nazis arrested, tortured, and executed this gentle man who until his dying day professed a belief in humanity. It is said that he died standing before a firing squad with the words "Vive La France!" on his lips.

M. Bloch, *Strange Defeat*, 1949.
C. Fink, *A Life in History*, 1990.

BLOOM, SOL (1870–1949) U.S. congressman and businessman. His career is a classic story of a rise from rags to riches. Bloom, the son of poor Orthodox Polish immigrants, was born in Pekin, Illinois. In 1875, his family moved to San Francisco where he attended public school for exactly one day. Lacking the money to buy books, he was given texts stamped with a phrase that made it clear that the books were being loaned. Refusing to take charity, Bloom proudly left school and received lessons in Hebrew and English from his mother.

To contribute to his family's income, Bloom sold newspapers and flowers by the age of six, and began operating a treadle in a brush factory when he was seven. He was an energetic and intelligent youth, and the owner of the factory noticed his talent with numbers and promoted him to bookkeeper at age thirteen. A few years later, Bloom began to work in San Francisco theaters performing a number of jobs, including usher, concession salesman, and occasionally performer. Quick to seize an opportunity, Bloom, while working as hat checker, became an expert in encouraging patrons of the theater to leave him large tips. He found if he chewed garlic cloves a few minutes before the end of the show, patrons who came to retrieve their hats would hurry away from the station booth gasping for air - often leaving their change behind! While Bloom worked in the theater he developed an eye and an ear for talent, which later allowed him to become a successful impresario. In addition to his work in the theater, Bloom developed a retail business with his brother, and became involved in party politics in San Francisco. By the time he was nineteen, entrepreneur Bloom had made enough money in various enterprises to support his family and retire.

Sol Bloom, however, was not about to retire. At twenty-one he was given a position as manager of the Midway Plaisance at the World's Columbian Exposition in Chicago in 1893. To that world's fair, Bloom brought exotic performers from all over the world, including an Algerian group he had discovered on his trip to the international exposition in Paris in 1889. After his success at the world's fair he opened a music publishing business.

In 1903 Bloom moved to New York City, where he entered the real estate and construction industries. By 1920 he retired from business and began a career in politics. He was elected to the House of Representatives as a Democrat in 1923, and served there until his death. As a member of the Committee on Industrial Arts and Expositions, Bloom organized celebrations throughout the nation for the two-hundredth anniversary of the birth of George Washington in 1932. He was a staunch supporter of New Deal legislation in the 1930s and as chairman of the Foreign Affairs Committee throughout the crucial years from 1939 to 1947, he guided through Congress such key measures as the draft bill and the lend-lease provision.

When World War II broke out, Bloom unsuccessfully tried to persuade his fellow lawmakers to increase the number of Jewish refugees from Europe that were allowed entrance to the United States. He argued the fairness of the Displaced Persons Act of 1948, which admitted to the United States persons who had entered western Europe before December 1945. Bloom held that the act discriminated against Jews, many of whom had left Poland in 1946. Bloom became an ardent supporter of Palestine as a homeland for victims of the Holocaust.

A supporter of the United Nations, he was chosen by President Franklin D. Roosevelt to serve as a delegate to the San Francisco Conference in 1945. There he worked for the passage of Article 80, which promised to protect the rights of Jews in Palestine. Later he supported the U.N. resolution calling for the partition of Palestine into separate Arab and Jewish states.

Bloom served as a delegate in London to the second meeting of the United Nations. In 1947 he served on the delegation committee to the Rio de Janeiro Conference. That year the Democrats lost control of the House and the chairmanship of the Foreign Affairs Committee went to a Republican. Nevertheless, Bloom worked with the new chairman to approve funding for the Truman doctrine and the Marshall plan. The following year the Democrats regained control of the House and the seventy-eight-year-old Bloom became chairman again for the last time before his death.

S. Bloom, *The Autobiography of Sol Bloom*, 1948.

BLOOMINGDALE FAMILY Department store owners in New York City. Benjamin Bloomingdale emigrated to New York from Bavaria in 1837 and became, among other things, a traveling merchant.

His eldest son, **Lyman Gustavus Bloomingdale** (1841–1905), after serving in the Kansas Volunteers during the Civil War, entered the hoopskirt business with his father. In 1872 he opened a drygoods store on New York's Third Avenue with his brother Joseph, and in 1886 they founded Bloomingdale Brothers Department Store, which became a landmark. An active Jewish philanthropist and patron of the arts, he contributed to the Metropolitan Museum of Art and helped found the Country Sanitarium for Consumptives in Bedford, New York, and Montefiore Hospital. **Joseph Bloomingdale** (1842–1904), who retired from the family business in 1896, was founder and first president of the Hebrew Technical Institute as well as one of the founders of Barnard College and a trustee of the Young Men's Hebrew Association. **Emanuel Watson Bloomingdale** (1852–1928) a third brother, studied law at Columbia University and was an attorney as well as working with the family department store from 1883 to 1905. Active in politics, he supported the Republican party; he was a member of the New York State Bridge and Tunnel Commission and president of the board of managers at the House of Refuge in New York.

Samuel J. Bloomingdale (1873–1968) Lyman's son, after studying architecture at Columbia University, managed the store from 1895, and was president from 1905 to 1930. He was a trustee of Montefiore Hospital, and of the Federation of Jewish Philanthropies, and a member of the Metropolitan Museum of Art and the American Jewish Committee. **Hiram C. Bloomingdale** (1876–1953), Lyman's younger brother was vice-president of the business, with a particular interest in high-standard advertising.

BLUM, LEON (1872–1950) First Jewish and first socialist prime minister of France. Born in Paris of an old Alsatian family, he was prodigiously gifted from youth. After brilliant studies at the law faculty in Paris, he earned a reputation as a poet and author, publishing *En lisant: Réflexions critiques, Au théâtre* (4 vols.; 1905–1911), *Marriage* (1907), and a work on Stendhal (1914). In his essay on marriage, Blum daringly recommended that young girls should enjoy as much freedom as young men and advocated trial marriages. (When he became prime minister, his friends urged him to refuse permission to reprint this book because it was too controversial, but Blum answered that his ideas had not changed and that he saw no reason to oppose a new printing).

From 1896 to 1919, he served in the government as a legal advisor in the council of state, and rose to become master of requests. The Dreyfus (q.v.) affair and his friendship with the socialist leader, Jean Jaurès, drew him to politics and the Socialist party. He became a deputy (member) in parliament

Léon Blum.

for the Socialist party in 1919 and after the Communists split off from the party, he applied himself to reorganizing the Socialist movement so successfully that he soon became one of its leaders. In 1921, he founded the Socialist daily, *Le Populaire*. Although his party made gains in the 1932 election, Blum refused to cooperate with the Radical Socialists.

When the 1934 Paris riots that broke out in the wake of the Stavisky affair, revealed a serious threat of fascism in France, Blum took the lead in regrouping the leftist factions and established the Popular Front of Socialists, Radical Socialists, and Communists. It obtained the majority in parliament in June 1936 and Blum became prime minister. Confronted by strong opposition and many social problems, Blum's government worked quickly at making good on its promises by introducing daring reforms such as forty-hour work week, paid vacations, and nationalization of war industries and of the Bank of France, all within a few weeks of taking office.

Blum was aware of the problems facing national defense in the light of German rearmament. When Great Britain refused to help the republicans in the Spanish Civil War, the French government adopted a similar policy of nonintervention, which was criticized by the left. Blum tended toward conciliation by nature. He was no great orator and convinced his audiences with purely logical arguments. Thus in June 1937, defeated in parliament after a right-wing campaign tinged with anti-Semitism, Blum resigned. He served as vice-premier in the subsequent Popular Front government and was premier for nine months again in March 1938. He refused office, however, in the Daladier government and approved the Munich agreement.

In 1938 Blum founded the Socialist Committee for Palestine. He accepted Chaim Weizmann's invitation to participate in the first meeting of the enlarged Jewish Agency in Zurich in 1929. He was not a religious man, but he met with his brothers each year at the synagogue for a commemoration service on the anniversary of the death of their parents.

At the beginning of the German occupation of France in 1946, the Vichy government had Blum arrested and accused him of having supported the war. In 1942 he was brought to trial at Riom and conducted a brilliant defence which led the Germans to suspend his trial. At the trial, he noted that at the beginning of his political career he had been accused of being a pacifist, but that because he had tried to maintain the military capacity of France, he was now being accused of being an advocate of war:

"If, in September 1936, I entered into direct and personal negotiations with a representative of Hitler, this was because one of the major points of the conversation was that Germany agreed to negotiate on arms limitations. Dr. Schacht came to see me, in the name of the Reich and I told him, 'I am a Marxist, and I am Jew, and that is why I am even more than anxious that our conversation be followed up.' With regard to armaments, I only had the interest of my country in mind. I fulfilled my duty as a Frenchman... By a cruel irony it is our loyalty which has become treason. Yet this loyalty is not spent; it still endures. And France will reap the benefit of it in the future, in which we place our hope and for which this trial, directed against the Republic, shall help to prepare."

Blum remained in prison and was then sent to a concentration camp in Germany from which he was freed by the American army in 1945. Upon his return to France, he resumed his political activities

---

The men of Vichy failed to break Léon Blum's spirit. After months of imprisonment he never wavered in his faith in the victory of civilization over barbarism or in his hope in the final victory of socialism. The last message I received from him just before he was taken to Germany breathed the same unconquerable spirit. There was no word of his personal sufferings and danger. His whole thoughts were devoted to plans for the future of the world when victory should have been won and civilization saved. His enemies may enslave his body, they cannot subdue his soul.

Clement Attlee on Léon Blum, 1943.

---

and negotiated a financial agreement between France and the United States. In December 1946, he formed a Socialist government that lasted only one month, and was again deputy prime minister in 1948.

He is regarded as one of the great figures of French and international Socialism. He intervened several times in favor of the establishment of the State of Israel and to prevent the cessation of illegal immigration to Palestine. In Israel, a kibbutz, Kfar Blum, has been named after him.

J. Colton, *Léon Blum: Humanist in Politics*, 1974.
L. E. Dalby, *Léon Blum: Evolution of a Socialist*, 1963.

BOAS, FRANZ (1858–1942) Father of American anthropology and descriptive linguistics. Born in Minden, Westphalia, son of a merchant, he began his career as a student of physics and geography in the universities of Heidelberg, Bonn, and Kiel, where he received his doctorate. A field trip to study the Eskimos in Baffin Island (1883–1884) to further his geographical studies led him to specialize in the anthropology of North America. After a short teaching period at Berlin University and an assistantship at the Royal Ethnographic Museum, Berlin, he settled in the United States (1887). He was appointed to the staff of *Science* and accepted a position at Clark University (1888–1892). In 1899 he was appointed professor of anthropology at Columbia and in 1901 curator of the American Museum of Natural History. From 1908 to 1925 he edited the *Journal of American Folklore* and in 1917 founded the *International Journal of American Linguistics*.

His chief contribution to anthropology and linguistics was his painstaking method of description of the culture and language of unfamiliar societies, uncontaminated by the ideological and scientific preconceptions of the researcher. His two main works, both published in 1911, were *The Handbook of American Indian Languages* and *The Mind of Primitive Man*, later burned by the Nazis. They underline the impact of environmental and historical happenings on cultural phenomena against the background of the fundamental sameness of the mental processes in all races. He was an advocate of relativism, emphasizing the endless diversity of languages and pointing out that sophisticated and delicate modes of expression were to be found in both so-called primitive and advanced societies. For decades all the great American linguists learned their subject from Boas at first- or second-hand. His biometric techniques for comparing the measurements of parents and children challenged the current dogma that held that the physical type of any organism was hereditarily determined. His investigation of children in the Hebrew Orphan Home demonstrated the advantage of a home environment over an institutional one, considerably influencing orphan administration.

Later in life he lent the full force of his scientific authority to the campaign against Nazi racism. On

March 27, 1933, he published an open letter to Hindenburg protesting his acceptance of Hitler. Also in that year he published the article "Aryans and Non-Aryans," which perhaps achieved the widest circulation of any of his writings. The German version was distributed by the anti-Nazi underground. His death occurred suddenly in 1942 during a luncheon he gave in honor of a colleague, a refugee from Nazi persecution, while he was speaking of the need to expose the scientifically false and immoral philosophy of racism.
M. J. Herskovits, *Franz Boas*, 1953.

> It is somewhat difficult for us to recognize that the value we attribute to our civilization is due to the fact that we participate in this civilization.
>
> **Franz Boas**

BOHR, NIELS HENRIK DAVID (1885–1962) Danish physicist and epistemologist; a guiding spirit and major contributor to the development of modern physics. Bohr was born to a non-Jewish father, a distinguished physiologist; his mother was a daughter of the prominent Jewish financier, politician, and philanthropist, D. B. Adler.

At school he was a less brilliant pupil than his younger brother Harald, who was to become an eminent mathematician. However, at the University of Copenhagen he stood out as unusually perceptive. His first research project won him a gold medal from the Royal Danish Academy of Sciences.

In 1911 Bohr received his doctorate for a thesis on the electron theory of metals. He then traveled to England and joined Ernest Rutherford in Manchester, who had recently discovered the atomic nucleus.

Bohr eagerly took up Rutherford's nuclear model and soon recognized its far-reaching implications for an understanding of observed patterns of radioactive decay, and for the existence of a theoretical basis to the then only empirical periodic table of elements. Almost everyone, including Rutherford himself, remained insensible to the logical cogency of Bohr's arguments, but Bohr went on to develop a theory of the arrangement of the atom's orbiting electrons which provided a more complete model of the structure of the atom and an explanation for the observed atomic spectra. Bohr's work on atomic structure won him the Nobel Prize in physics (1922).

In 1916 Bohr returned to Denmark to assume the directorship of the newly created Institute for Theoretical Physics, a position he held until his death. The isolation in which Bohr had hitherto found himself gave way to lively collaboration, and the institute developed into a center of thought, discussion, and progress.

Bohr was painfully aware that his whole theory of atomic structure rested on certain rather arbitrary assumptions and knew that it would take nothing less than a revolution in physics to explain them. The revolution he had foreseen came about in 1925 with the birth of quantum theory - a theoretical framework for the description of the behavior of small particles. Bohr himself laid a cornerstone of the new physics with his complementarity principle, which he explained metaphorically: "One

Niels Bohr, during a lecture at the University of Copenhagen.

cannot simultaneously view both sides of the same quantum-mechanical coin and thus must renounce a certain amount of the reality normally lent to its classical counterpart. A quantum-mechanical coin can thus best be visualized as having only one side, which is part head and part tail. Whether the side resolves itself into a head or a tail at the instant of observation is a matter of pure chance."

This was a decisive break with classical thinking. That Albert Einstein (q.v.) could not make a similar break remained a matter of surprise and regret to Bohr. Although their mutual esteem and affection never diminished, the debate between these two great men raged throughout the next thirty years. Only very recently was Bohr's standpoint vindicated.

By the middle 1930s the main interest had shifted in Copenhagen, as elsewhere, to nuclear physics. Again Bohr was to make an essential contribution: his liquid-drop model of the nucleus played a major role in the understanding of nuclear fission.

In 1943 Bohr was dragged into the turmoil of the war (his Jewish ancestry and anti-Nazi views were

well-known) and escaped to England. There he was suddenly confronted, to his surprise and dismay, with the advanced stage of a project he had hitherto deemed beyond the realm of technical accomplishment — the manufacture of the atom bomb.

Although Bohr did participate in discussions of physical problems relating to its development, his main concern was to foster awareness among physicists and politicians of the political and human implications of this new source of power. It is a striking example of his optimism that, besides its obvious dangers, he also stressed its potential advantages: the existence of a weapon equally accessible and equally threatening to all nations. However, his political efforts to promote an open-world policy, although carried out at the highest levels, did not meet with success.

In the post-war years he became a leading figure in the development of nuclear research and in 1957 was awarded the first U.S. Atoms for Peace Award. More than ever, he became a public figure and honors were conferred on him from all quarters.

BY AND ABOUT NIELS BOHR

- That the insecure and contradictory foundation [of physics in the years between 1910 and 1920] was sufficient to enable a man of Bohr's unique instinct and tact to discover the major laws of the spectral lines and of the electron shells of the atoms together with their significance of chemistry appeared to me like a miracle — and appears to me as a miracle even today. This is the highest form of musicality in the sphere of thought.
- He utters his opinions like one perpetually groping and never like one who believes [himself] to be in the possession of definite truth. He is truly a man of genius.

Albert Einstein

- Never express yourself more clearly than you think.

N. Bohr

- It was quite a shock for Bohr ... he did not see the solution at once. During the whole evening he was extremely unhappy, going from one to the other and trying to persuade them that it couldn't be true, that it would be the end of physics if Einstein were right; but he couldn't produce any refutation. I shall never forget the vision of the two antagonists leaving the club: Einstein a tall majestic figure, walking quietly, with a somewhat ironical smile, and Bohr trotting near him, very excited.... The next morning came Bohr's triumph.

L. Rosenfeld

BORN, MAX (1882–1970) German physicist, teacher, humanitarian, and Nobel Prize winner; best known as one of the pioneers of quantum mechanics — the physical theory that predicts the behavior of small bodies and their composites, such as atoms.

He was born in Breslau, Germany (now Wroclaw, Poland). His father, professor of anatomy at the local university, advised his son "never to specialize." Max Born was to remain true to this ideal in that, throughout his life, he maintained an active interest in art, philosophy, and literature.

He was educated at the universities of Breslau, Heidelberg, Zurich, and Göttingen and, after receiving his Ph.D. from Göttingen in 1907, took up teaching positions in Berlin and Frankfurt-am-Main. In 1921 he was appointed professor of theoretical physics at Göttingen, one of the foremost schools of theoretical physics of that era, where much of the new theory of quantum mechanics was to be worked out. By the time that quantum mechanics was formulated, in 1927, Born was already a renowned physicist and teacher who had published more than one hundred research papers and had written six books. But although he himself made major contributions to the understanding of quantum mechanics, its mathematical formulation was thrashed out mainly by much younger men, notably his pupils, Werner Heisenberg and Pascual Jordan. Born is generally credited as the first to recognize the probability interpretation of quantum mechanics in 1926 and, in recognition of this, was awarded the Nobel Prize in physics of 1954 (jointly with Walther Bothe). The essence of probability is, in Born's own words, that "the motion of particles follows probability laws but the probability itself propagates according to the laws of causality." The introduction of probability as an inherent feature of physics (rather than simply as an expression of a lack of concern with details) signaled a profound break with classical thinking and one with which Albert Einstein (q.v.) could never come to terms. There followed a prolific correspondence between the two men (which has since been published). In one letter, dated shortly after Born's first publications on the probability interpretation, Einstein made his famous observation: "Quantum mechanics is very impressive. But an inner voice tells me that it is not yet the real thing. The theory produces a good deal but hardly brings us closer to the secrets of the Old One. I am at all events convinced that *He* does not play dice."

Born was chagrined that his papers on the probability concept were not at first adequately acknowledged. However, in Copenhagen (the other leading center of theoretical physics between the world wars), Niels Bohr (q.v.) considered it an obvious development of formalism, saying, "We had never dreamt that it could be otherwise," illustrating how the probability interpretation is a prime example of an idea that is initially perceived only by a tremendous leap of the imagination but in retrospect is so obvious.

Although Born had dissociated himself from the Jewish community, he was automatically dismissed from Göttingen when the Nazis came to power as a practitioner of what Hitler termed "Jewish physics." After taking refuge in Britain he continued to teach for many more years at the universities of Cambridge and Edinburgh. During this time he produced a flood of books and essays which aimed to unravel the complex new physics to an uncomprehending public.

Following his retirement to Heidelberg in 1953, he became increasingly concerned about the ethical issues that arose out of scientific progress. He believed that no scientist could remain morally neutral with respect to the consequences of his work, no matter how basic his research or how ivoried his tower. Appalled by the spiraling number of military applications of the science that he had

---

- Our hope [for the future] is based on the union of two spiritual powers: the moral awareness of the unacceptability of a war degenerated to mass murder and the rational knowledge of the incompatibility of technological warfare with the survival of the human race.
- Intellect distinguishes between possible and impossible; reason distinguishes between the sensible and senseless: Even the possible can be senseless.
- Physics, as we know it, will be over in six months. [A prediction made in the heady days after the formulation of quantum mechanics and before the existence of particles other than the electron and proton was suspected].

Max Born

---

helped create, he felt a crushing responsibility and devoted his final years to writing and speaking about the "social, economic and political consequences of science, primarily the atom bomb, but also other pathological symptoms of our scientific age, like rocket research, space travel, overpopulation, and so on." He described the space program as a manifestation of "the crippled value system of the modern technological age."

Born was one of the few leading atomic physicists of the day who had the moral resolution to refuse all involvement with the development of the atom bomb.

M. Born, *My Life: Recollection's of a Nobel Laureate*, 1978.
M. Born, *My Life and My Views*, 1968.

BOROCHOV, BER (1888–1917) Socialist Zionist, also known as Dov Borochov, who synthesized Zionism and Marxism. Born in Zolotonosha, Ukraine, Ber Borochov grew up in Poltava, site of many anti-Jewish pogroms. The Ukrainian city was also an intellectual hub, a center of dissident activity in the 1880s, and the heart of the Zionist movement.

Borochov graduated from one of Poltava's secondary schools in 1900, but was denied access to university because he was Jewish. In the same year he followed in the footsteps of Marxist mentors by joining the Social-Democratic party. His interest, however, in creating a Jewish homeland and addressing Jewish issues alienated him from the party, which sought to erase nationalism. Because of his beliefs he was ousted in 1901.

Borochov immediately formed the Zionist Socialist Workers Union at Yekaterinoslav. The organization helped set up Jewish self-defense groups and advanced the concerns of Jewish laborers.

Like most Jewish activists of the day, Borochov felt the disparity between Marxism and Zionism. The writings of Karl Marx (q.v.) seemed to point the way to a more just society, yet the age-old quest for a Jewish homeland stirred in Borochov's heart.

He therefore tried to combine Zionist nationalism with the atheistic antinationalism of Marx. At first, his theory extended only to the Jewish worker; he said that the laborer could only be fulfilled in a land of his own. There, he said, the worker could truly express himself in socialism. Once the worker was free from fear of persecution and the bondage of being a minority, he would flourish. Later, however, Borochov's theory embraced not only the Jewish worker, but all Jews in the world, whom he believed should live in their own land in Palestine.

In 1905, Borochov joined the Poalei Zion party. As a Zionist, he not only supported the idea of a Jewish homeland but believed it should be in the land of Palestine. His interest in Marxism however, never matched his sense of Jewishness and espousal of Zionism. Indeed so strong was his identification with Jewishness that it led him to become a scholar of the Yiddish language.

Dov Ber Borochov.

After being arrested in 1906 and escaping in 1907, Borochov left the Ukraine and traveled throughout Europe. He cofounded the World Confederation of Poalei Zion (Zionist Workers), but spent his time in Europe both working with Zionist Socialist pursuits and following his scholarly ambitions. To form a foundation for the study of the Yiddish language, he sought out every article written about the Yiddish language through the centuries. The resulting bibliography, *The Library of the Jewish Philologist*, included 499 works, spanned 400 years and dated as far back as 1514. This bibliography became the springboard for the modern study of the Yiddish language.

With the outbreak of World War I, Borochov was forced to leave Austria and traveled to the United States, where he broadened his theory of a Jewish homeland to include all Jews and not just the common man. At the start of the Russian Revolution, however, Borochov felt it his duty to return home. En route, he stopped in Stockholm to attend an international conference of the Socialist Commission of Neutral Countries as a Poalei Zion delegate.

Upon arriving back in Russia, Borochov was immediately caught up in political activities. He toured and lectured day and night, but the strenuous schedule proved too much for him; he caught pneumonia and died.

In order to honor Borochov's contribution to Zionism, his remains were reinterred in Israel at the Kinneret cemetery in 1963.

Borochov's firm belief in the equality of people and in socialism remains part of Israeli politics to this day. The leftist, Socialist party, Mapam, is based on Borochov's brand of socialism.

I. Gershon, *The Founding Fathers of Israel*, 1980.
M. N. Penkower, *The Emergence of Zionist Thought*, 1968.

BRANDEIS, LOUIS DEMBITZ (1856–1941) U.S. jurist and Zionist; the first Jew to be appointed to the U.S. Supreme Court. Born in Louisville, Kentucky, he was the son of immigrants from Prague; his mother was descended from supporters of the pseudo-messiah, Jacob Frank (q.v.). After a brilliant career at Harvard Law School, he became a successful lawyer in Boston, known as the people's attorney. Brandeis distinguished himself for investigating insurance practices and in 1907 established savings bank insurance in Massachusetts (later copied in other states), which put life insurance within the reach of the workers. He defended statutes prescribing maximum working hours, opposed transport monopolies, and in general was seen as a defender of the rights of consumers and labor unions. His legal approach, known as the Brandeis brief, introduced economic, sociological, and statistical data as well as historical background.

By 1914, he was one of America's best-known lawyers. Mooted for a cabinet position, he was turned down, largely because the financial community feared his progressive ideas. In that year, he wrote *Other People's Money and How the Bankers Use It*, showing how the investment bankers controlled industry.

Vested interests and anti-Semites protested his nomination by President Wilson to the Supreme Court in 1916 but were unable to block the confirmation. On the Supreme Court bench, he was an outstanding advocate of judicial and liberalism and, together with Justice Oliver Wendell Holmes, wrote many dissenting opinions on matters of social and economic policy. Under Franklin D. Roosevelt's presidency, he was one of the few justices to uphold most of the New Deal. Brandeis often adopted a didactic approach and was regarded as a great teacher. To some, he was even of a prophetic nature and Roosevelt called him Isaiah.

In the earlier part of his life, he had no Jewish affiliation. He found his identification with Judaism in its emphasis on justice. This accorded with the Reform Judaism of his day, with its exclusive concentration on ethical values and its belief in a universalistic Jewish mission. His first association with the Jewish masses came in 1910 when he arbitrated the garment workers' strike in New York and was impressed by the Jewish working classes and their moral standards.

Shortly before World War I, he was attracted to Zionism and in 1914 became chairman of the Provisional Committee for General Zionist Affairs in the United States, which meant the leadership of U.S. Zionism. He rejected accusations of dual loyalty and advocated what came to be known as cultural pluralism. His friendship with Woodrow Wilson helped to win the President's support for

Justice Louis D. Brandeis with Nathan Straus (on the left), and Rabbi Stephen S. Wise (on the right).

- The greatest menace to freedom is an inert people.
- Order cannot be secured merely through fear of punishment; it is hazardous to discourage thought, hope and imagination; fear breeds repression; repression breeds hate; hate menaces stable government.
- My sympathies are with those Jews who are working for a revival of a Jewish state in Palestine. My sympathy with the Zionist movement rests primarily upon the noble idealism which underlies it and the conviction that a great people, stirred by enthusiams for such an ideal, must bear an important part in the betterment of the world. [1910]
- Every American Jew who aids in advancing the Jewish settlement in Palestine, though he feels that neither he nor his descendants will ever live there, will be a better man and a better American for doing so.

Louis D. Brandeis

the Balfour Declaration. After World War I, he became Honorary President of the World Zionist Organization. However, a rift developed between Brandeis and his American followers, on the one hand, and Chaim Weizmann (q.v.) and the East European Zionists on the other. Brandeis was strongly criticial of the handling of Zionist funds and also felt that the Zionist Movement should concentrate on practical problems of assisting the Jewish community in Palestine, which should be left to handle the political aspects on its own. The clash became so serious that Brandeis and his followers withdrew from the Zionist Movement. but continued to support Zionist development through the establishment of the Palestine Economic Corporation to encourage investment in Palestine. Brandeis remained committed to Zionist development to which he left large sums in his will.

Brandeis University in Waltham, Massachusetts, is named in his honor.

R. Burt, *Two Jewish Justices; Outcasts in the Promised Land,* 1989.
A. T. Mason, *Brandeis: A Free Man's Life,* 1946.
E. Rabinowitz, *Justice Louis D. Brandeis: The Zionist Chapter of His Life,* 1968.
P. Strum, *Louis D. Brandeis: Justice for the People,* 1984.

BRANDES, CARL EDVARD (1847–1931) Danish writer and left-wing politician; brother of Georg Brandes (q.v.). Originally studying oriental languages at the University of Copenhagen, he specialized in Persian and Sanskrit, publishing translations from Sanskrit. He later turned to literature and politics. As well as criticism of modern Danish and foreign drama, he wrote his own plays and even tried his hand at acting.

Together with his brother he put out the literary perodical, *Det 19. Aahundrede*. He also worked as a journalist for and was influential the Radical party. When the party split away from the left Reform in 1884, he founded and solely edited the opposition paper, *Politiken*. Aside from belonging to the Chamber of Deputies twice, from 1889 to 1894, and from 1906 to 1927, he was minister of finance in 1909—1910 and 1913—1920.

BRANDES, GEORG (1842–1927) Danish literary critic and writer, who had an enormous influence on Danish culture but was never fully accepted by the Danes and never felt at home in Denmark.

Born Morris Cohen into an assimilated family in Copenhagen, he was himself ambivalent about his Jewish identity. He studied literature and philosophy at the University of Copenhagen and, influenced by the writings of Kierkegaard, John Stuart Mill, and Taine, introduced the concept of realism to Danish literature. In a series of public lectures inaugurated in 1871, and later published as *Main Currents in Nineteenth-Century Literature*, he criticized the abstract idealism of 19th-century Danish writing and demanded that literature deal with real problems and modern issues. He was a friend of Ibsen and saw themselves as allies in the struggle against cultural provincialism.

His unconventional views branded him as a radical and "an atheist Jew" among conservative Danish circles and he was accordingly denied a professorship at the University of Copenhagen. Disappointed, in 1877, he left Denmark for Berlin and lived there until 1882, where, developing the conviction that individuals were more important than ideas, he began to write about personalities such as Benjamin Disraeli (q.v.), John Stuart Mill, and Gustave Flaubert. In the interim, Denmark had become open to more liberal ideas and on his return in 1882, he was accepted there with greater enthusiasm.

In the 1880s he became familiar with Nietzsche's writings and published a seminal article on the hitherto unknown German philosopher. His subsequent writing reflected a philosophy of hero worship which manifested itself in works on great figures such as Shakespeare, Goethe, Voltaire, Julius Caesar, and Michelangelo.

In 1902, he finally received the previously coveted position as professor of aesthetics at Copenhagen. One of his latest works was *Jesus, a Myth* (1925; English translation, 1927), in which he attempted to refute the historical basis of Christianity. His collected appeared in Danish and in German.

J. Moritzen, *Georg Brandes in Life and Letters*, 1922.

B. Nolin, *George Brandes*, 1976.

BREUER, JOSEPH (1842–1925) Austrian physician and physiologist whom Freud (q.v.) called the originator of psychoanalysis (although he later changed his mind). His father was a Hasidic leader, who played an important role in his son's development. Breuer studied medicine in his native Vienna, receiving the degree of M.D. in 1863. From 1867 to 1875 he was an assistant at Oppotzer's Clinic and from 1875 began to teach medicine at the University of Vienna. For over fifty years he was one of the most prominent internists in Vienna, and many of the most important men of science were among the patients in his large private practice.

In addition to his clinical work Breuer was also involved in neurological, respiratory, and otic research. In 1868 he reported his discovery, together with Ewald Hering, of vagus nerve control of respiratory movements (the Hering-Breuer reflex). In 1874 he published another article demonstrating the otic labyrinth as the organ of equilibrium and motion sensation. In 1894 he was elected a member of the Viennese Academy of Science in recognition of his work as both physician and researcher.

Breuer's most famous work, first published in 1880, was on the use of catharsis under hypnosis in the treatment of hysteria. His most famous case was that of Anna O. (see Bertha Pappenheim). He demonstrated that his patient's neurotic symptoms, which were induced by unconscious processes, improved and even disappeared after "purging" her mind and bringing to consciousness, her past experiences. This provided Sigmund Freud, with a basis for his theory of psychoanalysis and led to years of cooperation between Freud and Breuer that lasted until 1900. Freud often solicited Breuer's advice on personal, professional, and Jewish matters. Together they published a paper "On the Physical Mechanism of Hysterical Phenomena" in 1893 and a book, *Studies in Hysteria* (1895), which described Breuer's treatment of hysteria.

At that time Breuer wrote, "Freud's intellect is soaring at its highest. I gaze after him as a hen at a hawk." Subsequently the two men disagreed on theories of therapy and they ceased to work together.

Breuer was a man of magnetic personality, vision, culture, creativity, and striking intelligence. He was very active in the Jewish community in Vienna. In 1894, annoyed at the reaction of Jewish students to anti-Semitism, he wrote to the Jewish fraternity, Kadima, "Our epidermis has become too sensitive. I wish that we Jews had a consciousness of our own value which would make us quiet and half-indifferent to the judgment of others rather than this unwavering, easily insulted, hypersensitive *point d'honneur* which is a product of assimilation."

BRICE, FANNY (1891–1951) U.S. entertainer. Born Fannie Borach on the Lower East Side of New York, she grew up in the seething cauldron of immigrant society. Her ability to mimic different accents and intonations was one of the key aspects of her career on the vaudeville stage, in the movies, and especially on radio. In 1910, Florenz Ziegfeld heard her singing in a burlesque show and made her a regular performer in the *Ziegfeld Follies*. She appeared in musical shows in the 1920s and 1930s; her best-known songs included "Second-Hand Rose" and "My Man." Brice gained nationwide fame through a character whom she originally created for one of her musical comedy acts; as Baby Snooks, a naughty, big-mouthed brat, Brice was known far and wide to musical comedy audiences and then to radio audiences from 1938 almost until her death.

Her three husbands included a noted gangster, Nicky Arstein, and a producer, Billy Rose (q.v.). In the 1960s a play about Brice's life, *Funny Girl*, introduced the new musical singing talent, Barbra Streisand. The play (1964) and subsequent movie (1968), together with the sequel, *Funny Lady* (1975), brought to life the career of Brice and helped to endear her to another generation of musical comedy lovers.

B. Grossman, *Funny Woman: The Life and Times of Fanny Brice.* 1991.

N. Katkov, *The Fabulous Fanny, the Story of Fanny Brice*, 1953.

BRISCOE, ROBERT (1894–1969) Irish businessman and nationalist who became first Jewish mayor of Dublin. He was born in Dublin; his father was an immigrant from Lithuania and his mother from Germany. Briscoe received his education in Ireland and England. He was sent by his father to Germany, where he studied electrical engineering and business while working for an import-export company. Briscoe was enjoying the beginnings of a successful career when World War I broke out. As he attempted to join his parents who were vacationing in Austria, he was captured by the Austrian authorities and jailed for a brief period. In a prisoner-exchange arrangement, he and his parents were allowed to return to British-ruled Ireland, on condition that Briscoe abstain from fighting with the British. Briscoe, an Irish nationalist, had no trouble agreeing to this condition.

Upon the family's return to Dublin, Briscoe's father decided that his son's future would be more secure in the United States. Briscoe arrived in New York City in 1914 and quickly achieved success as a partner in a Christmas light manufacturing firm. Upon hearing about the Easter rising of 1916 and subsequent events, Briscoe returned to his homeland to fight for the independence of Ireland. He became part of the Irish Republican movement, joining the Sinn Fein and the Irish Republican Army (IRA).

Briscoe earned the nickname of "Captain Swift" for deftness at handling his assignments. On one of

Robert Briscoe receiving the mayoral chain from the outgoing lord mayor of Dublin in June 1961.

his missions he was accompanied by his wife and infant daughter. While the British officials thoroughly searched Briscoe and his wife, the secret dispatches they were transporting remained safe in their daughter's diaper. During the war he smuggled shiploads of arms to Ireland under the noses of the British. The British issued a circular about him, warning that he was "unlike most Irish rebels" in that he had "a gentlemanly appearance, which makes him most elusive."

The first stage of the revolution for Irish independence ended with the signing of the Articles of Agreement (1921). The following year, disagreements over the treaty led to civil war. Briscoe, siding with the opposition to the treaty, joined with Eamon de Valera, leader of the Irish revolutionary movement, and others to continue the fight. During the struggle, Briscoe traveled to New York City with his family to raise support for the Irish nationalists. In 1923 the struggle ended in another compromise, and Briscoe returned to Ireland.

Back in Ireland, Briscoe took control of his family's import business in Dublin. He joined de Valera's newly formed Fianna Fail Party, and in 1927 won a seat in the Dail Eireann, the Irish parliament. He retained his seat for thirty-eight years. At the same time, he maintained his business interests, and at one stage directed a packing house that produced kosher meat.

In 1956 Briscoe was appointed lord mayor of Dublin, the first Jew to receive that honor. In his acceptance speech he said, "It is a magnificent gesture that in Catholic Ireland it is possible to elect to this important office a man of a different faith, particularly my own, which proves that in this Catholic Ireland tolerance exists. I hope it will go forth from this chamber to the world that in a free Catholic Ireland there would be no intolerance." As lord mayor that year, Briscoe traveled to New York City to be the guest of honor in the annual Saint Patrick's Day parade. It was related that one onlooker, upon learning that he was seeing the Jewish mayor of Dublin, commented, "Only in America could this happen." He took with him a liberal collection of green yarmulkes for distribution and told audiences he was "an Irish Jew — one of the lepre-cohens." He also toured the United States to solicit support for the State of Israel.

Briscoe, always proud of his Jewish heritage, became an enthusiastic supporter of Zionism in the wake of the rise of Nazism in the 1930s and as a result of his meeting with Vladimir Jabotinsky (q.v.). Jabotinsky visited Ireland to learn about the tactics used by the IRA in its struggle against the British. Before the end of World War II, Briscoe was helping Jews escape from Europe to Palestine. He traveled to the United States to try to convince the government to put pressure on Britain to create a Jewish state. His new family crest, a blue Star of David draped with a red band bearing the Irish words for freedom, equality, and fraternity, proclaimed his pride in being both a Jew and an Irishman. By the time of his death he had won another term for mayor in 1961. Later, his son Benjamin followed his father both as a member of the Dail and as lord mayor of Dublin.

R. Briscoe, *For the Life of Me*, 1958.

BROD, MAX (1884–1968) German novelist, essayist, musician, and Zionist. Born in Prague, he studied law at its German university. After receiving his doctorate, he entered government service although his main interests were literature, music, and Zionism. From 1924 until the Nazi occupation of Czechoslovakia in 1939, he was associated with *Prager Tagblatt* as literary and music critic. Thereafter he lived in the Tel Aviv area and was drama adviser of the Habimah, the foremost Hebrew theater.

Brod's literary career began in 1906 with lyrics and narratives. His early tales were generally centered in Prague, often in a Jewish milieu, and incorporated erotic scenes. With his trilogy, *Tycho Brahes Weg zu Gott* ("Tycho Brahe's Way to God," 1916), *Reubeni Fürst der Juden* (Reuben, "Prince of the Jews," 1925), and *Galilei in Gefangenschaft* ("Galileo in Confinement," 1947), he rose to fame as the creator of more serious historical novels. Unforgettable is Brod's portrait of Danish astronomer Tycho Brahe, who toward the end of his life recognized the more correct astronomical conclusions of young Johannes Kepler and had the courage to plead for their acceptance by Emperor Rudolph II, even though they contradicted his own.

Brod's greater fame stemmed from his close friendship with Franz Kafka (q.v.), whose genius he was the first to recognize. Kafka, aware of approaching death, designated Brod as his literary executor, with instructions to destroy his unpublished manuscripts, but Brod disobeyed the instructions and devoted himself to publishing, editing, interpreting, and, in a series of studies extending over four decades, calling attention to his friend's life and works.

Brod's interest in music led him to write and to translate libretti, to further the popularity of the Czech composer of operas, Leos Janáček, and to publish a study on Gustav Mahler (q.v.) (1961) as well as a booklet, *Die Musik Israels* ("The Music of Israel," 1951), in which he tried to define the specific character of Jewish music from the biblical cantillations and the folksongs to the modern composers of the Diaspora and the newest developments in the Jewish State. He was also a composer, whose works included *Requiem Hebraicum*.

Brod's devotion to Zionism and national humanism went back to 1913, when Prague was still part of the Austro-Hungarian Empire. By 1918 the empire was tottering. The Jews of Prague were caught between the claims of the German and Czech nationalities. Brod, who was becoming active in Jewish affairs, called upon his coreligionists to keep aloof from both and to give priority to Jewish national interests. He championed Zionism as the most dynamic expression of the Jewish people. For him, Zionism was more than merely a political movement. It was the way of life of all those Jews who accepted Jewish nationalism, whether in Palestine or in the Diaspora. If, however, the interest of humanity at large conflicted with specific Jewish interest, then national feeling must yield to the higher category of true humanity.

In the two volumes of *Heidentum, Christentum, Judentum* ("Heathenism, Christianity, Judaism," 1921), Brod documented his religious faith. He hoped that a world that had experimented with heathenism and with Christianity, and which had failed to achieve a healthy relationship between individuals and peoples, would turn to the Jewish

Max Brod reading a script to two Habimah Theater directors, Baruch Chemerinsky (center) and Zvi Friedland, c. 1939

pioneers in the Holy Land for guidance on the formation of a more moral society.

In the 1920s and 1930s, Brod gathered about him a circle of Jewish intellectuals whose uniqueness he delineated in *Der Prager Kreis* ("The Prague Circle," 1966) and in his autobiography *Streitbares Leben* ("Life of Struggle," 1960).

L. Kahn, *Mirrors of the Jewish Mind*, 1968.
M. Pazi (ed.), *Max Brod*, 1987.

BRONFMAN, SAMUEL (1891–1971) Canadian liquor and oil magnate. Born in Brandon, Manitoba, to a family from Bessarabia who had brought their rabbi with them, he worked with his father peddling firewood and frozen whitefish. His schooling ended at the age of fifteen. After an apprenticeship with Distillers Trust in Scotland, he joined his elder brothers in the hotel business and in his early twenties took charge of a hotel in Winnipeg, Manitoba. When prohibition was introduced in Manitoba in 1916, the Bronfman family entered the liquor trade and Sam developed the mail-order side of the business. Prohibited by legislation passed in 1918 from manufacturing liquors, the Bronfmans obtained a license to sell drugs and liquors for medicinal purposes, and Sam established connections with American bootleggers, who transported their liquor by car, air, and sea. By 1929, with Sam virtually running the family business after joining Distillers Corporation–Seagram Ltd., the Bronfman concern had become one of the world's largest distilleries.

When prohibition ended in 1933 Bronfman settled into the life of a Montreal millionaire and did his utmost to gain the respect of the community. He moved into the lucrative U.S. liquor market, producing quality blended whiskies in keeping with his definition, "distilling is a science; blending is an art." Joseph E. Seagram & Sons Inc. became a multinational corporation with headquarters in New York, operating in over 120 countries with sales of over a billion dollars. During the early 1950s, Bronfman took Seagram's into the petroleum business and in 1963 acquired Texas Pacific Oil Company, one of the largest independent oil companies in the United States. In 1951 he set up Cemp Investment Ltd., which grew into one of the western world's most impressive private investment instruments. Bronfman's own version of the history of Seagram's, *From Little Acorns*, was published in 1970.

Traditionally Jewish, Samuel Bronfman gave generously to Jewish charities and endowed academic chairs, art collections and business fellowships. The Samuel Bronfman Building at McGill University in Montreal (of which he was a governor) houses the faculties of management and languages. He was made a Companion of the Order of Canada (1967) and Knight of Grace of the Order of Saint John of Jerusalem (1969).

He also served as chairman of Montreal's Federation of Jewish Philanthropies (1934–1950), and at the outbreak of World War II he set up the Canadian Jewish Congress Refugee Committee which was instrumental in persuading the Canadian government to allow 1,200 Jewish "orphans" (and their parents) from Europe to enter the country. He was president of the Canadian Jewish Congress from 1938 to 1961, during which time he was the most dominant power in Canadian Jewry, strongly supporting Israel throughout. The Canadian Jewish Congress offices are situated in the Samuel Bronfman House, built in Montreal in 1968.

S. Bronfman, *From Little Acorns* (published with the 1970 Seagram's annual report).
P. C. Newman, *King of the Castle. The Making of a Dynasty: Seagram's and the Bronfman Empire*, 1979.

BRUCE, LENNY (1925–1966) U.S. entertainer. Lenny Bruce has been praised as "the most radically relevant of all contemporary social satirists" and denounced as "obscene." As a comedian during the late 1950s and early 1960s, he shocked his audiences by satirizing subjects considered sacred by most people, such as religion, incest, and the Holocaust.

Lenny Bruce, born Leonard Alfred Schneider, grew up on Long Island, New York. His parents divorced when he was five, and thereafter he was shuttled between his father, a shoe salesman, and his mother, an occasional performer in local night clubs. Bruce's biographer, Albert Goldman, reports that although Bruce's parents made no attempt to teach him the practices or principles of the Jewish religion, he thoroughly identified himself as a Jew. When he was embroiled in court battles over the decency of his comedy act, Bruce held that the judge did not understand his comedy because the judge could not "appreciate the values that motivated him as a Jew."

Under age, Bruce enlisted in the U.S. Navy at sixteen, participating in World War II landings at Anzio and Salerno, Italy. After three years in the service, he was discharged and spent the next few years studying drama in Los Angeles and trying to find work. His first break came in 1949 when his impersonations won him first place on "Arthur Godfrey's Talent Scouts." Bruc then took his act on the road.

At first, Bruce's material was considered "clean" and fairly standard for the small nightclubs and striptease clubs in which he worked. It was in California that Bruce began to draw the attention of audiences and critics. His routine became increasingly wild and "hipper" as he added the type of material for which he is known. A record of his performance, called "Sick Humor," was nominated for a Grammy Award in 1959.

At the height of his career, Bruce performed in theaters all over the United States, including Carnegie Hall in New York City. However, his fall came quickly. In 1961 and again in 1962, he faced narcotics and obscenity charges. Bruce went to trial, often insisting on defending himself before the court. He began studying law by night and appearing in court by day. He seemed obsessed with having justice served, but at the same time his ineptness probably contributed to his ultimate convictions. From 1964 on, he was legally banned from stages in New York and no one wanted to book his act elsewhere. The trials left him unemployed and financially drained; he declared bankruptcy in 1965.

The final blow came in 1966, when Bruce received notice that his home was being forfeited to a bank. Utterly devastated, he seems to have begun to construct some kind of legal defense for himself and began to type the following, "Conspiracy to interfere with the Fourth Amendment const...." Later that day, he was found dead on his bathroom floor with a needle protruding from his arm.

J. Cohen, *The Essential Lenny Bruce*, 1972.

A. H. Goldman, *Ladies and Gentlemen — Lenny Bruce!*, 1974.

- Every day people are straying away from the church and going back to God.
- My mother-in-law broke up my marriage. My wife came home from work one day and found me in bed with her.

Lenny Bruce

BRUCKNER, FERDINAND (1891—1958) Austrian playwright. He was born in Vienna as Theodor Tagger to an Austrian merchant and his French wife and raised in Graz. His studies, which included German literature, music, medicine, and law, took him to Vienna, Paris, and Berlin, where under his given name, he founded in 1923 the Berlin Renaissance Theater, which he directed until 1927. Under his original name he had already translated Pascal and the book of Psalms, edited a bimonthly journal to which the young Gottfried Benn, Alfed Döblin, and Franz Werfel contributed, published his expressionist poetry, and was to publish the short play *Te Deum* (1929).

In 1926, however, Hamburg applauded a successful new play, *Krankheit der Jugend* ("Pains of Youth"), which painted a cynical picture of the life of disillusioned, morally confused, and corrupt postwar medical students and their girlfriends, indulging in sexual perversions, suicide, and murder. The play was written under the pseudonym Ferdinand Bruckner, his true identity remaining unknown for several years. Tagger himself turned the play down at his Berlin Renaissance Theater for being too permissive and risqué, and it had to wait for his successor to receive its Berlin premiere. The mysterious Bruckner went on to produce another box-office hit: *Die Verbrecher* ("The Criminals," 1928), a simultaneous portrayal of an entire, lowly residence block, containing several human stories culminating in a miscarriage of justice. It was forcefully directed in 1929 by Max Reinhardt

(q.v.). This was followed by *Die Kreatur* ("The Creature," 1929), a marriage play in the vein of Strindberg. Only with the huge success of the historical drama *Elizabeth of England*, in 1930, which used the same impressive technique of multiple settings as *Die Verbrecher* to present the historical material concerning Elizabeth, Essex, and Philip of Spain in modern psychological and political terms, was it publicly disclosed that the mysterious Ferdinand Brucker was none other than Tagger himself, who had turned down his own play. No satifactory reason has been given so far for his hide-and-seek practice.

While adapting and modernizing Shakespeare's *Timon of Athens* and Heinrich von Kleist's *Die Marquise von O*, the contemporary menace in Germany emerged to the foreground in his forceful anti-racist drama *Die Rassen* ("The Races," 1933), depicting an academic community succumbing to racial and anti-Semitic laws. With the rise of the Nazi regime he went into exile and spent seventeen years in America, writing scripts for Hollywood as well as historical and poetic drama, such as *Napoleon I* (1936), *Heroische Komödie* ("Heroic Comedy," 1938) about Madame de Staël, and the panoramic, two-part *Simon Bolivar* (1945). He returned to Germany in 1951 and resettled in Berlin, where he worked as a dramaturge and resumed his playwriting. His later dramatic work includes verse plays hiding classical themes behind modern plots, such as *Der Tod einer Puppe* ("The Death of a Doll," 1956) and *Der Kampf mit dem Engel* ("The Struggle with the Angel," 1957).

Much of Bruckner's drama is about the battle of the sexes. In the juxtaposition of the male and female worlds, the females turn out to be the more thoroughly genuine explorers of life, while most males are careless egocentrics. Bruckner's interests range from psychopathology and legal injustice to modern reading of historical characters, his plots always stressing his concern with ethical and moral problems.

Of more than fifteen plays the most widely translated and produced was *Elizabeth of England* (1931); among the others translated were *Pains of Youth*, (1989) and *The Races* (1944).

H. Friedman and O. Mann, *Deutsche Literatur im 20. Jahrhundert*, 1961.

E. Rieder Laska, *Ferdinand Bruckner*, 1961.

BUBER, MARTIN (1878–1965) Theologian, philosopher, and educator, noted for his philosophy of dialogue. Born in Vienna, he was brought up by his grandfather Solomon Buber, a distinguished rabbinic scholar. He went to school at Lemberg (Lvov) and to university in Vienna. At twenty, he was attracted to the recently founded Zionist movement, advocating a cultural Zionism and, at the invitation of Theodor Herzl (q.v.), took over the editorship of *Die Welt*, the official Zionist journal, which he edited from 1901 to 1904. He maintained that full Jewish creativity and spirituality could only be achieved with the return of most

Jews to their ancient homeland. In 1901 he was one of the leaders of the Democratic faction of the World Zionist Movement, which advocated Zionist cultural activities, preparations for the establishment of a Jewish university, and the separation of Zionism and religion. In 1904 he became interested in Hasidism and devoted the next five years to its study. He began to write on its religious message, from which he chose selectively, developing an existential Jewish philosophy that became known as Neo-Hasidism. Buber rejected those aspects that he saw as superstition and bigotry, and concentrated on its anecdotes and myths which he saw as teaching true religiosity. He identified Hasidism's major counsels of perfection as cleaving to God (*devekut*), humility, holy intention, worship, enthusiasm, and joy. Buber's writings, including his retelling of the tales of the Hasidic masters, brought Hasidism to the attention of the western world.

Settling in Berlin, he founded in 1916 the monthly *Der Jude*, which became one of the most influential organs of Jewish thought in Central Europe. He also began to publish his main philosophical works, notably *Ich und Du* ("I and Thou," 1923), in which he described two basic relationships: I–Thou, which is the relation between one person and another, implying mutuality and involving meeting and direct encounter, and I–It, which lacks these characteristics and is the relation of an individual to a thing or a subject to an object. While there is always the danger of the Thou deteriorating into an It, the one unchangeable and eternal Thou is God, who is present in every dialogue. Buber was a noted educator and put his theories in a pedagogical framework, maintaining that the I–Thou dialogue is the true teacher-student relationship.

Buber worked closely with Franz Rosenzweig (q.v.) and in 1925 the first volumes of their widely acclaimed German translation of the Bible appeared. This recaptured the original meanings and rhythms of the Hebrew text. The bulk of the work was completed by Buber after Rosenzweig's death. Buber's works on the Bible, such as *Moses* and *Kingship of God* sought to reach the living situations of the Bible and derive theological conclusions.

From 1923 Buber taught at the University of Frankfurt but had to resign his chair after the Nazis came to power in 1933. He then founded and directed the Central Office for Jewish Adult Education, since Jews had been forbidden to attend German educational institutions. He lectured extensively throughout Germany and attracted a wide following, especially among the youth. However, in 1938 the Nazi authorities forbade him to continue teaching and he decided to emigrate to Jerusalem. He joined the Hebrew University but because of his critical approach he was appointed not to teach Bible, as he had wished, but to the chair of social philosophy. He became deeply involved in adult education in the Jewish community and was a revered figure in many institutions,

Martin Buber.

being the first president of the Israel Academy of Sciences and Humanities (1960–1962) and a founder of the Mosad Bialik publishing house. Politically, he was a central figure in movements advocating Jewish-Arab rapprochement and, before 1948, supported the establishment of a binational state. He was also deeply involved with the kibbutz movement, which he saw as an experiment in utopian socialism that had not failed.

Buber applied the concept of dialogue to the Jewish-Christian relationship and pioneered the new thinking that was to develop after World War II. He felt that we can acknowledge as a mystery that which someone else confesses as the reality of faith, even if it appears to contradict our own knowledge. This implies the recognition by the Jews of the reality of Christianity as a path to God and a similar recognition by Christianity of Judaism. It also involves a rejection of the Christian claim of a monopoly on the path to salvation. While stressing the wide gap between the two faiths, he saw Jesus as a great religious figure whom he called "my brother." He stressed the role of Jewish peoplehood in the Jewish religion, seeing this as part of the Jewish theological mainstream and one of the chief factors distinguishing Judaism from Christianity.

Buber's philosophy of dialogue has been influential in 20th-century thought, perhaps even more in Christian than in Jewish theological circles.

M. Friedman, *Martin Buber, The Life of Dialogue*, 1976.
M. Friedman, *Martin Buber's Life and Work* (3 vols.), 1981–1983.
G. Shaeder, *The Hebrew Humanism of Martin Buber*, 1973.
P. Vermes, *Buber*, 1988.

- The God of history and the God of nature cannot be separated and the land of Israel is a token of their unity.
- There is no opposition between the truth of God and the salvation of Israel.
- The yearning of Judaism for God is the yearning to prepare a resting place for Him in genuine community. Judaism's understanding of Israel is that genuine community will spring from that people. Its messianic expectation is the expectation of genuine community fully realized.
- To him who knows how to read the legend, it conveys more truth than the chronicle.
- The Jew carries the burden of an unredeemed world. He cannot concede that redemption is an accomplished fact for he knows it is not so.

Martin Buber

BUCHALTER, LOUIS "LEPKE" (1897–1944) U.S. labor racketeer, criminal syndicate leader, and murderer. Born in New York City to hard-working immigrant parents, he was the only one of eleven children to embark on a life in crime. His nickname, Lepke, derived from Lepkeleh, an affectionate Yiddish diminutive used by his mother, which meant Little Louis. Buchalter's small stature, conservative dress, and soft-spoken demeanor belied the fact that he was the greatest exponent of violence in the rackets. As one Buchalter associate put it, "Lep loves to hurt people."

Buchalter began his career in crime as part of a neighborhood juvenile gang that rolled drunks, picked pockets, and robbed from pushcarts. In the early 1920s, when most mobsters sought to make their fortune in bootlegging, he chose to go into labor racketeering. At his peak, he commanded an army of gangsters who, through terror and violence, controlled unions in the New York garment and food industries and extorted millions of dollars from legitimate businesses. The gang's weapons were acid, bludgeons, blackjacks, knives, fire, ice picks, and pistols.

A close associate of Meyer Lansky (q.v.), Frank Costello, and Joe Adonis, Buchalter became part of the leadership that formed the national crime syndicate. The founders recognized the need for an enforcement arm within the organization and he was put in charge of what the press dubbed Murder, Inc. Under Buchalter, this group carried out hundreds of killings.

As the money poured in, Buchalter adopted the life style of a multimillionaire. He lived in a luxurious apartment in mid-Manhattan and maintained chauffeur-driven cars for trips to race tracks and night clubs. All this ended in 1941, when he was indicted and convicted for the killing of a garment trucker whom he had driven out of business. Lepke was executed in the electric chair of Sing Sing Prison, the only national crime boss to die in that way.
B. B. Turkus and S. Feder, *Murder, Inc.*, 1951.

BURNS, ARTHUR FRANK (1904–1987) U.S. economist. Born in Stanislau, Austria, Burns earned a Ph.D. in economics at Columbia University in 1934. Serving as economic adviser to four U.S. presidents: Eisenhower, Nixon, Carter, Ford, and Carter, he played an important role in shaping American economic policy.

While completing his doctorate on production trends in the United States, Burns taught economics at Rutgers University (1927–1944). From 1930 he was associated with the National Bureau of Economic Research, serving as its director of research (1945–1953) and its president (1957–1967). From 1947 he taught at Columbia University, becoming a professor of economics there in 1959.

In 1953 Burns became chairman of President Dwight D. Eisenhower's Council of Economic Advisers, a position he held until 1956. In 1969 he became economic adviser to President Richard M. Nixon, and in later years he advised Gerald Ford and Jimmy Carter. From 1970 to 1978 he was also chairman of the Federal Reserve Board.

Burns followed a pragmatic policy of tightening the money supply when inflation increased, and increasing the money supply when inflation decreased. In 1974, when in response to double-digit inflation, he raised the interest rates, he was partially blamed for the recession that followed.

In 1980 he actively participated in the founding of the Committee to Fight Inflation. From 1981 to 1985 he was United States ambassador to West Germany.

He wrote *Economic Research and the Keynesian Thinking of Our Times* (1946), *Measuring Business Cycles* (coauthored with W. C. Mitchell, 1946), *Frontiers of Economic Knowledge* (1954), and *Prosperity without Inflation* (1957).
J. Davis, *The New Economics and the Old Economists*, 1971.

C

CAHAN, ABRAHAM (1860–1951) American journalist, editor, and author. Born in of Podbere-zye near Vilna (now Vilnius, Lithuania), then part of Russia, Cahan studied at the Teachers' Institute in Vilna and taught at a government school in that city. He had originally planned to train for the rabbinate, but contact with left-wing students converted him to socialism. In 1881 his revolutionary activities forced him to flee Russia. Arriving penniless in New York in 1882, he found a job in a cigar factory. Within a few months he had learned English and began his journalistic career. He met the socialist leader Morris Hillquist (q.v.), and the two founded the New York *Arbeiter Zeitung*, a Yiddish daily newspaper dedicated to socialist ideas, to introducing the Jewish immigrants to their new country, and to ways of improving their living and working conditions. His weekly column, *Sedre*, started by discussing the weekly Bible reading but soon digressed to discussing socialist matters. At the same time he edited the *Naye Zeit* and the *Zukunft*.

In 1897 he helped found the *Jewish Daily Forward*, and for a brief period served as its editor. However, Cahan soon broke with the radical socialists at the Yiddish daily and left the *Forward*, turning to the English-language press. For the next five years he wrote stories of Jewish life, feature articles and literary criticism for the *New York Sun*, the *New York Evening Post*, the *New York World*, and other papers.

In 1896 he published his first novel, *Yekl, A Tale of the New York Ghetto*, which was hailed as contributing more to the understanding of his people than any previously written book.

Cahan rejoined the *Forward* in 1902. He remained its editor for almost half a century until his death in 1951. He changed the paper's format, turning it into the most influential Jewish daily in the United States and a powerful voice for the Jewish labor movement committed to democratic socialism, trade unionism, and the elimination of sweatshops. He emphasized American customs and manners, theater, arts, and literature, as well as politics. Cahan and the *Forward* chronicled the age of Jewish immigration to America, counseled and consoled the new immigrants, gave lessons in English and educated its readers. Despite its wealth and popularity in its heyday, the *Forward* maintained an unparalleled loyalty to the needs of its readers. The newspaper reached its peak in the 1920s, when the circulation of its local and regional editions as far west as Chicago reached some 200,000. But its readership declined steadily following Louis Marshall's (q.v.) intervention to save it from being closed by the U.S. government for its pro-German leanings during World War I. Cahan was a founder of the Social Democratic party in 1897, and from 1902 supported the Socialist Party.

Cahan vigorously attacked Soviet totalitarianism and although he did not consider himself a Zionist, took a sympathetic view of Zionism following his visit to Palestine in 1925. In 1933 he became the first Socialist Party member to support Franklin D. Roosevelt and, as a result, was threatened with expulsion from the party.

Among Cahan's other books were *Imported Bridegroom* (1898), *The White Terror and the Red* (1905), written under the impact of the Kishniev pogrom, his famous *The Rise of David Levinsky* (1917), and a five-volume Yiddish autobiography, *Blatter von mein Leiben* (1926–1931). Almost the entire final volume of these memoirs is devoted to the case of the lynching of Leo Frank, which greatly affected him.

A. Cahan, *The Education of Abraham Cahan*, 1969.
R. Sanders, *Downtown Jew*, 1969.

CANTOR, EDDIE (1892–1964) U.S. entertainer. Born Isidor Iskowitch on the East Side of New York, Cantor won his first music contest in 1907 and then started to tour with a comedy blackface act. After traveling around the United States with the act, he eventually made it onto the major vaudeville circuits and was booked for lengthy runs at the major American music houses. His first real claim to fame was top billing in the *Ziegfeld Follies* of 1917, 1918, and 1919. Starting in 1923 he starred in the musical *Kid Boots*, which ran for several years. Known for his banjo eyes and for his big song hit "Makin' Whoopee," Cantor made the transition into movies easily. Some of his known films were *The Kid from Spain*, *Roman Scandals*, and *Ali Baba Goes to Town*.

Eddie Cantor and his family

A warmhearted individual, Cantor felt that he had to help those in need. Just prior to World War II, he led a number of drives to save Jewish children who were being separated from their families and taken to Palestine and the United States. His work to assist the Youth Aliyah programs was monumental. He also was asked by President Franklin Delano Roosevelt to raise money for the campaign against polio. It has been claimed that Cantor coined the name March of Dimes for the countrywide campaign.

In the early years of television, Cantor became one of its outstanding performers with his singing and comedy routines. A deeply attentive family man, Cantor frequently brought his beloved wife Ida on television and boasted about his daughters. In 1964 President Lyndon Johnson awarded him a presidential medal for his services to the United States and humanity.

A great supporter of Israel, Cantor was particularly active in Israel Bond campaigns. His visit to the country in 1951 included performances for Israel army troops throughout the country.
E. Cantor, *As I Remember Them*, 1963.

CAPA, ROBERT (1913–1954) U.S. combat photographer. Born Andrei Friedmann in Budapest, he worked as a darkroom assistant and freelance photographer in Paris, until Stefan Lorant, the editor of the London magazine *Picture Post*, launched his career as a photo journalist by assigning him to cover the Spanish Civil War. Capa proved to be an excellent combat photographer who combined a good eye with reckless daring, taking intimate war pictures at the very center of the war itself.

His career as a photojournalist was marked by his coverage of a succession of wars. He swam ashore with the first American troops in Normandy, photographing them at close range, and captured the 1948 Israel War of Independence at first hand. He was killed when he stepped on a land mine while covering the war in Indochina.

His work was distinguished by an ability to get close to and capture action. His photographs told stories; their subjects were completely unaware of the photographer at work, capturing the smallest nuances of violence and fatigue.

After World War II, he participated in the founding of the international photographic agency Magnum Photos. After his death, his work at the agency was continued by his brother, Cornell, also a noted photographer.

CARDOZO, BENJAMIN NATHAN (1870—1938) Lawyer and justice of the U.S. Supreme court. He was born in New York, where his family, descendants of prominent Sephardi Jews, had settled prior to the American Revolution. His father was a justice in New York State supreme court. Benjamin's childhood was molded by tutors who came to the Cardozo home to instruct the children. Throughout his life he was most devoted to his family and especially to his older sister, Nel, who brought him up after both parents died when he was quite young. He never married and lived with Nel until her death. Cardozo was deeply affected by the disgrace involved when his father — who had Tammany Hall connections—had to resign from the supreme court in 1872 under threat of impeachmant. He studied at Columbia Law School, and upon graduation in 1891, was admitted to the New York State bar, where he practiced law until elected as a reform candidate to the supreme court of New York State in 1913. He served as associate judge of the Court of Appeals (New York State's highest court) for fourteen years, was chief judge of the Court of Appeals from 1927, and was appointed to the U.S. Supreme Court in 1932.

Benjamin Cardozo has been ranked as one of the ten foremost judges in American judicial history. His skill and learning helped to make the New York Court of Appeals the leading state court in the nation. He made a lasting contribution in the U.S. Supreme Court because of his ability to join legal rule and social need. Cardozo was a defender of New Deal social legislation. He has been described as a charming, lovable man with a highly sensitive nature and a scholar with a brilliant mind. At thirty-three he published his first book, *The Jurisdiction of the Court of Appeals of the State of*

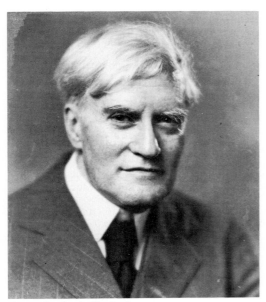

Justice Benjamin N. Cardozo.

New York, considered to be the authoritative work on the subject. This was followed by *The Nature of the Judicial Process* (1921), a collection of the Storrs Lectures at Yale University, and *The Growth of Law* (1924), another series of lectures discussing constructive legal philosophy, methods of judging, and the functions and ends of law. *Paradoxes of Legal Science* (1928) is a collection of lectures delivered at Columbia University. His last book was *Law and Literature* (1931) containing essays and addresses. His *Selected Writings* (ed. M. E. Hall) appeared in 1947.

Cardozo was an active member of the Spanish and Portuguese Synagogue in New York. He took a great interest in Jewish education and was involved in the activities of the Jewish Educational Association. He ardently believed in Americanism and remained aloof from Zionism in its early stages, but events in Europe during the 1930s led him to see the value of Palestine as a haven for the oppressed of his people.

M. J. Aronson, *Cardozo's Doctrine of Sociological Jurisprudence*, 1938.
G. S. Hellman, *Benjamin Cardozo; American Judge (1870–1938)*, 1940.
B. H. Levy, *Cardozo and Frontiers of Legal Thinking*, 1938.
J. P. Pollard, *Mr. Justice Cardozo; A Liberal Mind in Action*, 1935.

CARO, HEINRICH (1834–1910) German chemist. He was born in Posen, Prussia (later Poznan, Poland), the son of a successful grain merchant. In 1842 he moved to Berlin and received vocational training as a dyer at the Gewerbeinstitut. From 1852 to 1855, he was a lecturer at the University of Berlin.

In 1855 Caro was hired as a colorist in a calico dyeing-printing firm in Mülheim-an-der-Ruhr, where he worked on the use of natural and secret recipes for dyes. The year following Sir William Perkin's discovery of mauve analine dye, Caro was sent to England to study new techniques. After his return to Germany, he became so enthusiastic over developments in the dye industry that he resigned from the firm in Mülheim and in 1859 went back to England to work as an analytical chemist for Roberts, Dale and Co., Manchester, where he became a partner. There he discovered more efficient methods of producing mauve analine dye and gained important technical experience as an industrial organic chemist. While in England he began his own lines of research and discovered many more dyestuffs, including Induline (a diazo compound), Bismarck brown, and Martin's (Manchester) yellow. In addition he worked for ten years on the triphenylmethane structure of rosanaline dyes. While in England he maintained contact with his contemporaries in Germany and returned there in 1866. Initially he worked in R. W. Bunsen's laboratory in Heidelberg, but from 1868 he developed and organized Badische Analin und Soda-Fabrik (later a principal constituent of I. G. Farbenindustrie), Mannheim, and was its director from 1869 to 1889. This was the first true industrial research organization in Europe.

In 1869 Caro discovered a cheap method of producing alazarin. In 1874 he developed a process of converting Baeyer's fluorescein to eosin, a red fluorescent dye used in medicine, and in collaboration with Baeyer and other researchers, discovered methylene blue, chrysoidine, orange, fast red, naphthol yellow, persulphuric acid ("Caro's acid"), and indigo.

In 1883 Caro became the leading spokesman of the German chemical industry and was especially involved in the protection of patents in the chemical industry. Besides his own discoveries he often helped his colleagues with their researches.

Most of Caro's published work was in the form of patents of individual articles. His correspondence with Baeyer, Liebermann, and others is collected in the Deutsche Museum in Munich.

CARO (or KARO), JOSEPH (1488–1575) Codifier of rabbinic law and mystic. He belonged to a family of distinguished scholars in Spain; it is uncertain whether he was born before or after his family left Spain and went to Portugal, from where they soon moved to Turkey. His father died when he was young and his main teacher was his uncle, Isaac Caro. Many Jews expelled from Spain and Portugal in the 1490s settled in the Ottoman Empire, which became a leading center of Jewish learning. Caro himself lived in Turkey for forty years, in Salonika, and mostly in Adrianople and Nikopol. He was a leading figure in both rabbinical academies and in kabbalistic circles. In 1536 Caro moved to Safed in the Holy Land where he became head of the local rabbinical court and of an impor-

Title page of the Shulhan Arukh, *Joseph Caro's most famous work. Amsterdam, 1698.*

tant academy. Safed at the time was an outstanding center of Jewish learning and mysticism and one of Caro's students and colleagues was the kabbalist Moses Cordovero (q.v.).

While living in Nikopol, Caro began work on his monumental codification of Jewish law, *Bet Yoseph* ("House of Joseph"), which he completed two decades later when he was in Safed. This is a massive comprehensive work following the four-part division of Jewish law that had been adopted in the *Turim* of Jacob ben Asher (q.v.). Over the previous centuries numerous attempts had been made to codify Jewish law and the profusion of authorities had become bewildering. Caro therefore sought to lay down one code that would be universally acceptable and would establish religious norms in Judaism. He compared the great codes of Isaac Alfasi (q.v.), Moses Maimonides (q.v.), and Asher ben Yehiel (q.v.) and, in the event of a disagreement among the three, he accepted the majority view. He also collected and studied the writings of many rabbinic authorities, Ashkenazic and Sephardic, tracing each law from its Talmudic source throughout rabbinic discussion down the ages and deriving what he saw to be the authoritative decision. While *Bet Yoseph* was widely studied, even more influential was the *Shulhan Arukh* ("The Table Is Prepared"), Caro's own digest of *Bet Yoseph*, originally prepared for young students. This became the recognized guide to Jewish reli-

gious practice and the most popular book of Jewish law ever produced, opening rabbinic law not only to the scholar but to the average Jew. At first, its appeal was limited because it restricted itself to Sephardi custom and practice but with the supplement of the *Mappah* of Moses Isserles (q.v.), adding Ashkenazi aspects, the *Shulhan Arukh* became and has remained the standard code for the entire Jewish world.

Caro was already in his lifetime recognized as an outstanding kabbalist, especially in Sephardi circles. He believed that he was visited each night by a supernatural spirit who revealed to him divine mysteries and instructions on ascetic conduct as well as inspiring his everyday life and his studies. Caro called this manifestation his *maggid* (literally, narrator), whom he defined as the personification of the Mishnah. Communication was through automatic writing contained in his mystical diary published as *Maggid Mesharim* ("Narrator of Righteousness").

R. J. Z. Werblowsky, *Joseph Karo: Lawyer and Mystic*, 1980.

CARO, NIKODEM (1871–1935) German chemist. Born in Lodz, Poland, he studied chemistry at Berlin University and received doctorates in engineering and agriculture. He set up his own laboratory for industrial chemistry and later became a consultant to the chemical industry and director of the Bavarian firm Stickstoffwerke A.G.

Nikodem Caro's main areas of research involved the catalytic oxidation of ammonia, calcium carbide and acetylene, the partial condensation of gases, and the gasification and gas production of turf. He developed the cyanamide process for nitrogen fixation.

Together with Adolf Frank, Caro discovered the fixation of nitrogen by its reaction with calcium carbide to form calcium cyanamide, an important fertilizer. The Caro method of assaying calcium carbide became the official German standard and much of the manufacture of cyanamide is produced in Frank-Caro ovens.

Caro took out many patents and published *Handbuch Für Acetylen* in 1904. He was a member of the Leningrad Academy.

CASSEL, ERNEST (1852–1921) British financier and philanthropist, baronet. He was a descendant of Joseph Cassel, a court Jew of the Prince Elector of Cologne from 1668 whose son was purveyor to the court. Ernest was the youngest of three children born to Jacob Cassel, who had a small banking business in Cologne. He was an excellent pupil but left school at the age of fourteen and began working as a bank clerk. In 1869, aged sixteen, Cassel traveled to Liverpool, where he found a position as clerk with a firm of grain merchants. The following year he was employed by the Anglo-Egyptian Bank in its Paris branch, but was forced to leave on the outbreak of the Franco-Prussian War. He returned to England, where he joined the

London financial house of Bischoffheim and Goldschmidt. Cassel was sent to Constantinople to look into the affairs of a Jewish firm in financial difficulties. After solving this problem and another in connection with Nicaragua, Cassel was promoted and in 1874 was appointed manager of the firm.

One of his early successes in connection with the Erie Railroad in the United States brought Cassel into contact with the American Jewish financier Jacob Schiff (q.v.), with whom he developed a close friendship. In 1884 Cassel established his own banking business, gaining success in disentangling the affairs of the New York, Pennsylvania, and Ohio Railway and in negotiating loans for the Mexican government. In 1878 he acquired the rights in Sweden for the Thomas Process for making basic steel from phosphorus ore and he bought a substantial interest in Swedish mines, steel mills, and railway companies.

In 1878 Cassel married Annette Maxwell and on the day of his marriage became a British subject. Three years later his wife died, and he acceded to her last wish to accept her creed as a Catholic so as not to be separated in the hereafter. This fact was known to few people during his lifetime and was revealed only at his funeral.

A caricature of Sir Ernest Cassel, entitled Egyptian Finance, by Spy, from Vanity Fair, *1899.*

By 1896 Cassel had become one of the wealthiest and most powerful financiers in the City of London, with a reputation for integrity and sound judgment. He was instrumental in the purchase of Vickers Sons & Co., which became Britain's largest munitions manufacturer. He also played a leading role in financing of the Electric Traction Company and the Central London Railways. Cassel was involved in the arrangement of the finances of the Mexican Central Railway and the issue of government loans in Mexico, China, and Uruguay. Toward the end of the century, Cassel acquired shares in the Anglo-Austrian Bank and was concerned with the creation of the State Bank of Morocco in 1906 and the National Bank of Turkey in 1909. His interests also extended to Egypt, where he was involved in the construction of the Aswan Dam and the creation of the National Bank of Egypt. From 1914 Cassel was financial adviser to the khedive of Egypt. He was made a baronet for these services.

Cassel's public benefactions included hospitals and medical research, education, and numerous other fields. During World War I he was attacked by anti-German extremists in Britain, but even so he assisted the British government to solve its financial problems.

Sir Ernest was an epicure and had impeccable taste in art. He was described by Margot Asquith as "a man of natural authority ... dignified, autocratic and wise, with a power of loving those he cared for." He acted as artistic mentor to Jacob Schiff and helped him assemble a collection of 19th- century French paintings and Oriental jades. Cassel had access to the highest levels of British financial and political power. He had the ear of King Edward VII, to whom he acted as financial adviser. His intimate relation with the king earned him the nickname of Windsor Cassel. His granddaughter, Edwina (1901–1960) married Earl Mountbatten of Burma.

B. Connel, *Manifest Destiny*, 1953.

R. Vansittart, *The Misty Procession*, 1938.

CASSIN, RENÉ SAMUEL (1887–1976) French jurist and statesman; Nobel Prize winner. He was born in Bayonne to a distinguished Jewish family; his father came from Alsace and his mother was descended from refugees from the expulsion from Spain. He studied literature and law in Aix-en-Provence and Paris, was called to the bar in 1909, receiving his doctorate of law in 1914. He served in the infantry in World War I, during which he was severely wounded and was awarded the croix de guerre and the médaille militaire. He began his academic career at the University of Lille (1920) and then was appointed professor of law at the University of Paris (1929), where he taught until 1960. He also taught at the Academy of International Law at The Hague and the Institut Universitaire des Hautes Etudes Internationales in Geneva.

From 1924 Cassin was a member of the French delegation at the League of Nations and later

René S. Cassin

represented France at the United Nations and UNESCO, of which he was one of the founders. During World War II he drew up the agreements between Winston Churchill and Charles de Gaulle defining the status of the Free French Forces. He held the post of national commissioner for justice and education in the French government-in-exile (1941–1943). From 1946 he was a member and then president of the UN Commission on Human Rights, where together with Eleanor Roosevelt he initiated the Universal Declaration of Human Rights adopted in 1948.

Cassin held numerous government and international posts, among them vice-president of the French conseil d'état (1944–1960), president of the Ecole Nationale d'Administration and the Cour Suprême d'Arbitrage (1945–1960), member of the conseil constitutionnel (1960), and president of the European Court of Human Rights. In 1968 Cassin was awarded the Nobel Peace Prize for his activities in the area of human rights; he devoted the prize money to the establishment of the Human Rights Institute in Strasbourg. He was also awarded the Goethe Prize in 1973.

Cassin was proud of his Jewish heritage, but was not active in Jewish affairs until he was appointed by de Gaulle in 1943 to deal with the institutions of the Alliance Israélite Universelle throughout the world. As president he was instrumental in developing its educational and cultural activities in France, North Africa, Asia, and Israel. In October 1987, his remains were transferred to the Panthéon in Paris.

CASSIRER, ERNST (1874–1945) Philosopher. Born in Breslau (now Wroctaw, Poland) to a suc-

cessful merchant, he received his doctorate from the University of Marburg. He changed his major two times — from jurisprudence to German literature to philosophy — and moved back and forth between universities in Leipzig, Heidelberg, and Berlin, before deciding upon Marburg, where he felt he would finally find the mentor he had sought, in the Neo-Kantian philosopher Hermann Cohen (q.v.).

In 1903 he took up a teaching position at the University of Berlin that he was to hold for the next thirteen years. In Berlin, exposed to the intellectual and cultural life of a city in which many members of his own family were prominent, he began to develop his philosophy. His first book was *Leibniz' System* (1902), which was followed in 1904 by an edition of Leibniz's writings. At this time he became interested in the question of knowledge, and his next work was a four-volume book on the problem of knowledge in philosophy and science in the modern age. In this work he aimed to understand the concept of knowledge as it evolved historically. Later he was to develop the concept that the history of ideas is a continuous process in which ideas are constantly being carried to new conclusions and giving birth to new thoughts.

In his *Substance and Function* (1910), he developed the theory, already hinted at in the earlier works, that in the study of mathematics, physics and chemistry, the concept of substance should be replaced by that of function, that is, that science as the study of things should be replaced by science as the study of functional relations between phenomena.

In 1919, he was offered chairs at the universities of Frankfurt and Hamburg, and, accepting Hamburg's offer, he left Berlin. One of the attractions of Hamburg, for him, was the Warburg Library, which held a collection of books remarkably close to his own areas of interest.

During his stay in Hamburg he developed his theories of symbolic form and myth, upon which he expounded in various works written during this period, among them *Language and Myth*, which was translated into English. He moved away from the attribution of a privileged position to mathematics and science in the understanding of concepts, while developing the thesis that language, mythology, and science are all different symbolic expressions for understanding the world.

In 1929, after having again turned down the chair of philosophy at the University of Frankfurt, he was elected rector of the University of Hamburg, a position which he held until November 1930. The upward trend in his career in Germany ended, however, with Hitler's rise to power in 1933. Fearing the consequences of Nazi rule, he left Germany with his family. Not lacking offers to teach, he spent two years at Oxford, from 1933 to 1935, and then moved on to Sweden, where he taught for six years. As a Swedish citizen, however, he had to retire at the age of sixty-five, and in order to continue teaching he decided to emigrate to the

United States. On the perilous wartime trip across the Atlantic, he spent many hours talking with the linguist Roman Jakobson (q.v.), who had an influence on his work.

In the United States he taught at Yale, from 1941 to 1944, and then at Columbia, until his death. His other well-known works include *Essays on Man* (1944) and *The Philosophy of Symbolic Form* (1953–1965).

C. H. Hamburg, *Symbol and Reality: Studies in the Philosophy of Ernst Cassirer*, 1956.

J. M. Krois, *Cassirer: Symbolic Forms and History*, 1987.

CELAN, PAUL (1920—1970) Poet, noted for his contribution to German lyrical poetry. His verse reflects his tragic experience as an eastern European Jew during the Holocaust. He was born Paul Antschel in Czernowitz, Romania, to orthodox parents. At age eighteen he spent a year in France studying medicine and in 1940 studied Romance philology in Romania. When Romania came under Nazi control in World War II, both of his parents were murdered, while he survived by working in forced-labor camps in Romania. His poetry expresses deep anguish over his personal loss and the loss of millions.

From 1945 to 1947 Celan worked in Bucharest as a translator and publisher's reader. During this period he began to use the name Celan, which some believe he derived from the word *celandine*, an herb used for curing weak sight. He moved to Vienna in 1948 and there published seventeen of his poems in a literary journal. Later that year, he published his first collection of poems, *Der Sand aus den Urnen* ("The Sand from the Urns"). He was outraged over errors in his first volume and refused to have it reprinted. After six months in Vienna, he moved to Paris, where he remained for the rest of his life, eventually becoming a French citizen. He received a degree in German literature in 1950 and found work translating French, Italian, English, and Russian poetry and classics into German. Later, he taught German at the Ecole Normale Supérieure.

Celan wrote his poetry in German and worked in the German language, although he had never lived in Germany. Some found this peculiar since it was the language of his former oppressors. Yet, though familiar with a number of languages, he considered German his mother tongue and claimed that "only in one's mother tongue can one express one's own truth. In a foreign language the poet lies." It was also the language spoken by his own mother, to whom he had been deeply attached and to whom he made frequent references in his poems. Nevertheless, use of the German language seemed to cause some conflict for Celan as expressed in "Black Flakes," an early poem: "And can you still bear, mother, as formerly, alas, at home, the soft, the German, the painful rhyme?"

Celan's poems are emotionally charged and difficult to interpret. Influenced by French surrealism and the tragedy of the Holocaust, he often wrote in a cryptic style in which words have double and triple meanings; a boat might mean a coffin, a thrown stone might mean a star, and rain could be a sign of God's grace. He also used etymological dictionaries, the Bible, and other works of literature to develop his carefully constructed verses.

In 1952 Celan published his second collection of works, *Mohn und Gedachtnis* ("Poppy and Memory"), winning recognition and an invitation to the Gruppe 47, an informal group of young writers. Despite his successes, however, he never achieved financial solvency and also seemed to have been a victim of mental illness. He was subject to attacks of paranoia during which he saw signs of anti-Semitism and Nazism all around him. He never spoke about his experiences during the war, but the imagery of his verse suggests that he was tortured by them. Judaism is also a frequent theme in his poetry and a friend relates that Celan "had a passionately affirmative relationship with Judaism until his death." Another friend said, "His relation to Judaism was personal, individual and highly complex. He often said that although his father was orthodox he had to struggle for his own relation to Judaism." One of his volumes entitled *Die Niemandsrose* ("The No-Man's Rose"), published in 1963, is a collection of kabbalistic poems. In 1969 he visited Israel.

POEMS OF PAUL CELAN

Grapegrowers dig
for the dark-houred clock
depth by depth,

you read,

the invisible one
he orders the winds
behind their borders,

you read,

the open ones carry
the stones behind their eye,
it recognizes you
on the Sabbath.

From "Einmal" (Once)

Once
I heard him,
he was washing the world,
unseen, nightlong,
real.
One and infinity.
dying,
were I'ing.
Light was.
Salvation.

In 1958 Celan received the literature prize of the city of Bremen, and two years later was awarded the Georg Buchner prize for his poetry. Toward the end of his life, his poems reflected a deepening isolation and anguish. In April 1970, his body was found in the Seine River, victim of suicide.

Three volumes of his work were published posthumously: *Lichtzwang* ("Light-Force," 1970); *Schneepart* ("Snow-Part," 1971) and *Zeitgehoft* ("The Farmstead of Time," 1976). English translations of many of his poems are to be found in *Speech - Grille and Selected Poems*, (1971). J. Glenn, *Paul Celan*, 1973.

CELLER, EMANUEL (1888–1981) One of the longest serving U.S. congressmen. Born in Brooklyn, New York, Emanuel Celler got his first look at politics as a child, listening to a speech by William Jennings Bryan from his fathers' shoulders.

Educated as a lawyer at Columbia Law School, Celler began his political career in 1922, when he was asked to run as the Democratic candidate for the tenth congressional district. His campaign plan was simple but effective. He went from house to house and street to street. Sometimes he set off firecrackers in the street, and after a crowd gathered, began his rally. His efforts proved successful and he was elected as the first Democrat from the Brooklyn district.

In his first term of office he became involved in the issue of immigration to the United States and fought for the repeal of bigoted aspects of the Immigration Act of 1924, which limited the immigration of certain peoples because of their ethnic origins.

Celler was a liberal, supporting President Franklin D. Roosevelt's New Deal and President Harry S. Truman's Fair Deal, which were designed to get the country back on its feet after the Depression.

After World War II, he championed the cause of political Zionism and urged the U.S. government to take a pro-Zionist stance.

During his time in Washington, Celler saw the country through many crises and in 1948, a senior congressman, he was elected head of the House Judiciary Committee. In that position he was able to propose antitrust laws and legislation allowing more immigration.

Although Celler's political career took him to Washington, his heart always remained in Brooklyn. He returned to his constituency on weekends,

---

Emanuel Celler on how to be successful in Washington

One must have the friendliness of a child, the enthusiasm of a teenager, the assurance of a college boy, the diplomacy of a wayward husband, the curiosity of a cat, and the good humor of an idiot.

---

and that faithfulness earned him twenty-four re-elections to the U.S. House of Representatives.

In 1972, after fifty years as a congressman, Celler was defeated in a Democratic primary. He returned to Brooklyn to continue in a law practice he had successfully maintained while in political office. He continued to practice law almost until his death at age ninety-two.

CHAGALL, MARC (1887—1985) Painter. He was born in Vitebsk, Russia, and scenes of his native town and of the village of Lyozno where he used to visit his grandfather, were depicted in scenes, of his childhood — the family and their friends, the homes, the life of the Jewish community and its spire, the life of the Jewish community and its officials, the landscapes and the skyscapes, were to crowd his paintings, seemingly out of time and space in a dreamlike world of fairy-tale imagination.

Although in a spiritual sense he never left Vitebsk, he needed broader horizons and moved to Saint Petersburg to study at the School for the Imperial Society for the Encouragement of the Arts. He lived in poverty and, as a Jew, was forced to dwell outside the city. For a time he studied with the famous Leon Bakst (q.v.), the designer for the Diaghilev Ballet.

Thanks to assistance from a patron, he was able to move to Paris in 1910, and soon found his place in what was then the artistic capital of the world. Many of his paintings at this time continued to be based on his life in Russia. His colors were exuberant (Bakst who visited him said "Now, your colors sing"). Many of his works show the influence of Cubism and Fauvism although he could never be pigeonholed as belonging to a particular school.

In 1914 Der Sturm gallery in Berlin held a one-man exhibition of his works. Chagall visited Berlin, where there were over 200 of his pictures that he was destined never to retrieve. He went on to Vitebsk, where he was caught by the outbreak of World War I. There he married Bella Rosenfeld, and began a joyous series of pictures featuring Bella, as well as for further paintings of Vitebsk scenes. Often two lovers, representing himself and Bella, wafted aloft above the roofs of the houses. For a time he was drafted into military service and stationed in Saint Petersburg.

After the Revolution of 1917 he was appointed commissar of fine arts in Vitebsk and director of the Vitebsk Art Academy. He also started a museum. In the first official exhibition of the new government, two rooms were reserved for Chagall's work and the state purchased twelve of his paintings. However, he was soon disillusioned with the official attitude to art and one day, returning from Moscow, found that he had been displaced as director and his Free Academy had been turned into a Supremacist school. He and his family moved to Moscow and never returned to Vitebsk.

He was invited to design the sets and costumes for the new State Jewish Theater. On the theater's long wall, he painted a mural, *Introduction to the*

Marc Chagall in his Paris studio with his wife Bella and his daughter Ida, 1927.

Jewish Theater, his largest work, showing Jewish actors, dancers, and musicians. In his designs, he had a particular affinity for the works of Sholem Aleichem (q.v.). He also taught in a settlement for war orphans. It was at this period that he began to write his autobiography, published as *My Life*.

In 1922 he left Russia for Berlin, where he studied etching with Hermann Struck, but was unable to settle down because of the difficult economic situation. Paris beckoned and he returned there. The paintings he had left were gone, but he set about reconstructing his old works as well as painting new ones. He worked on etchings for Gogol's *Dead Souls*, La Fontaine's *Fables*, circus scenes, and pictures influenced by the light and colors of southern France.

In 1931 he visited Palestine with his family for the opening of the new Tel Aviv Museum and toured Egypt and Syria. The results of this journey were 105 biblical etchings, which have been called some of the finest masterpieces of the art of etching. He was profoundly affected by the anti-Semitic developments of the 1930s. In 1937 the Nazis exhibited some of his paintings as "degenerate art." A famous picture of this period is *White Crucifixion*, in which the Christ figure obviously symbolizes the tragedy of the Jewish people.

After the fall of France in 1940, it was not safe for Chagall to remain there, and the following year he arrived in New York. Americans were charmed with Chagall's work. His distortions and defiance of the laws of gravity — in both senses of the word — his unique blend of sophisticated techniques, his lively colors, and his evocation of folk art were irresistible. When asked why he painted a calf in a cow's head and why a milkmaid's head floated above her body in his *Country Life in Russia*, Chagall answered: "In the first instance, I had to fill an empty place. In the second, I had to create one." However, the terrible events in Europe during those years were reflected in a new gloominess in his canvases. This was heightened when his wife died in 1944. For nine months he was unable to work until he illustrated *Burning Lights*, a book she had written, and worked on the sets, scenery, and costumes for Igor Stravinsky's *Firebird* for the Ballet Theater.

In 1947, he again returned to France, and represented France in the Venice Biennale, receiving a prize for the graphic arts. He lived first in Paris, then at Saint-Jean-Cap-Ferrat, eventually establishing his home at Vence, near Nice. He was honored with several important exhibitions including a retrospective at the New York Museum of Modern Art and the opening show of the National Museum of Modern Art in Paris.

Chagall began at this stage to turn to new media and to experiment. He did major work in stained glass, designing the Twelve Tribes of Israel for Hadassah Hospital, Jerusalem, the Peace Window for the U.N. Secretariat, New York, and windows for the Vatican and for the cathedral of Metz. Although the designs were rendered by skilled craftsmen, Chagall worked closely with them and always did the grisaille. He designed three Gobelin tapestries for the Israeli Knesset (parliament) and a mosaic floor for its state reception hall. He also worked in sculpture and ceramics. He painted the ceiling of the Paris Opera and two large murals for New York's Lincoln Center. The National Museum of the Biblical Message of Marc Chagall opened in Nice in 1973, with many of his works — paintings, stained-glass windows, and a mosaic — on biblical themes. For his ninetieth birthday in 1977, he was given an exhibition at the Louvre, the first ever for a living artist, and received the grand cross of the Legion of Honor. In 1981, after sixty years' absence, he was able to visit Moscow for an exhibition of his work at the Tretiakov Gallery. After his death, the Pushkin Museum held an exhibition of 250 of his works.

Although critics have criticized his art for its facility, it has retained its almost magical popularity. In a period when art was becoming increasingly obscure, the public appreciated the art of Chagall, which did not challenge them, and were happy to participate in the world he created. He is renowned as a particularly Jewish artist but his appeal was universal.

J. Cassou, *Chagall,* 1965.
R. McMullen, *The World of Marc Chagall,* 1968.
F. Meyer, *Marc Chagall,* 1964.

CHAIN, ERNST BORIS (1906–1979) Biochemist and Nobel Prize winner for his work on penicillin, knighted in 1969. He was born in Berlin to Russian-German parents. His grandfather was an Orthodox Jew and a tailor who spent most of his spare time studying Jewish literature. His father emigrated from Russia at the end of the 19th century and became a successful chemical engineer in Berlin; his mother was a relative of a leading Bavarian politician. His parents instilled in him the conviction that the only worthwhile occupation in life was the pursuit of intellectual activities and that any career that was not a university career was unthinkable.

As a youth he loved music, especially the piano, at which he was highly proficient, to the extent that he even considered making it his career. He was, however, persuaded by a cousin to forego music for a scientific career, and, during his studies in the chemistry department of the Pathological Institute in Berlin, was impressed by the biological approach to chemistry. He received his Ph.D. from the Pathological Institute in 1927 and worked on the optical specifity of esterases in enzymes. In 1929 Alexander Fleming, in England, announced his discovery of penicillin. This event, together with Hitler's rise to power, prompted Chain to leave Germany for England and he went to work with Howard Florey in Oxford.

At first he worked on a substance, lysosyme, which he discovered to be an enzyme, but he later turned his attention to the industrial development of penicillin. This goal became especially important during World War II, during which Chain was involved in a serious ethical argument as to whether the enemy should be allowed knowledge of penicillin development for humanitarian reasons. His superior, Florey, was persuaded to withhold the information demanded by the Red Cross in Switzerland and traveled to the United States to investigate the possibilities of developing penicillin commercially in collaboration with the Americans. Chain was not informed of this decision until hours before Florey left. This event initiated a long period of ill-feeling and disagreement between Chain and Florey that was resolved only when, in 1948, Chain took up a post in Rome, Italy, where he created the first International Center for Antibiotic Research.

Chain was a committed Jew and was active in the Jewish communities in which he moved. He was an ardent Zionist and in 1946–1947 Chaim Weizmann (q.v.) approached him to take up a senior position in Palestine at the Weizmann Institute in Rehovot. Chain gave this proposal serious consideration but eventually rejected the offer, giving preference to Italy, since he did not believe that the newly formed State of Israel could or would have the means to become a major producer of penicillin. He visited Israel frequently as a member of the Board of Governors of the Weizmann Institute.

For his work in the development of commercial penicillin Chain was awarded the Nobel Prize in 1945 together with Fleming and Florey. After the war Chain became a leading figure in the development of "tailor-made" penicillins against organisms resistant to the original penicillin preparations. This he achieved during the 1950s by changing the "side-chain" structure of the basic penicillin molecule. While in Italy he worked in collaboration with the Beecham Company in England on the development of oral and other penicillins. This eventually led to a legal wrangle with the Italian government in which his Italian co-workers were charged and convicted of criminal activities for receiving foreign monies. As a result Chain returned to England in 1964 and became head of the biochemistry department of Imperial College, London. For his work in developing antibiotics he received honors and was knighted in 1969.

Chain described himself as a "temperamental Continental" who influenced the role that the British government was to play in medical research, developing the relationship between industry and the universities. He also became involved in the ethical problems which arose as human beings began to take more control over matters of life and death.

CITROËN, ANDRÉ GUSTAVE (1878—1935) French engineer and industrialist. As a young man Citroën studied engineering at the Ecole Polytechnique in his native Paris. In 1908 he was given the responsibility of reviving the failing Mors automobile company. He was able to increase the yearly output nearly tenfold.

Citroën's spectacular success prompted the French government to entrust him with a large part of munitions production at the beginning of World War I. During the war he established the great arms factory on the quai de Javel and produced millions of shells.

After the war, Citroën converted his munitions plant into an assembly line for the production of automobiles. His main objective was to mass produce an affordable, small automobile — the famous little Citroën, which sold for 17,700 francs. His success in popularizing the horseless carriage in France earned him the nickname of the French Henry Ford. Of the 1,800,000 automobiles in France the year before his death (1934), one-third were Citroëns.

In 1922, Citroën sponsored the Citroën Central African automobile crossing — the first automobile trek across the Sahara desert. The significance of the journey was threefold. First, it showed that it was possible to establish rapid and permanent communications between Algeria and western Africa. Second, it established outposts along the great routes linking the African colonies. Finally, it opened the door to the use of the automobile as a vehicle for exploration throughout the world.

Also to Citroën's credit were the first traffic-light system in Paris and the use of the Eiffel Tower for advertising by means of an electric marquee. He also presented Paris, with the fooldlighting for the Arch of Triumph and the Place de la Concorde.

In spite of all his successes, Citroën's dreams proved too grand for the economy during the Depression. He continued to aim for expansion in the production of his car but by 1934 was forced to turn over the majority of stock in his company to his biggest creditor, Pierre Michelin, head of the Michelin Tire Company.

Although the company recovered somewhat the following year, Citroën himself did not. His failure, one of the largest commercial disasters in French history until that time, left him broken and disillusioned.

COHEN, BENJAMIN VICTOR (1894–1983) Lawyer and U.S. government official; a member of Franklin D. Roosevelt's "brain trust," he was responsible for drafting much of the New Deal legislation. Cohen was born in Muncie, Indiana, the son of Polish immigrants. A brilliant student, he graduated from the University of Chicago in 1914 and earned his law degree there the following year. By 1916 he had received his doctorate in law from Harvard University, where he came under the influence of Felix Frankfurter (q.v.) and Louis D. Brandeis (q.v.), future U.S. Supreme Court justices.

During World War I Cohen worked as an attorney for the U.S. Shipping Board. After the war he was sent to London by Brandeis to represent the American Zionists at the Paris Peace Conference and to work with Chaim Weizmann (q.v.) on the Palestine issue. Cohen was committed to the creation of a Jewish national home, and worked with the League of Nations toward that goal.

Upon his return to the United States, Cohen settled in New York City and opened a successful law practice specializing in corporation reorganization. He also gave legal advice to the Amalgamated Clothing Workers Union and the National Consumers' League.

At the urging of Frankfurter, Cohen went to Washington, D.C., in 1933, and along with other legal and scholarly minds joined President Roosevelt's group of elite advisers, who became known as the "brain trust." He began as general counsel to the Public Works Administration, but eventually joined forces with Thomas G. Corcoran to write some of the Roosevelt administration's most significant pieces of legislation during the Great Depression, among them the Securities and Exchange Act, the Public Utilities Holding Company Act, the Tennessee Valley Authority Act, and the Fair Labor Standards Act. Cohen, by nature a quiet, shy man, not only framed the bold legislation, but successfully defended most of it before the Supreme Court.

Cohen and his fellow workers would hold all-night sessions to draft legislation and prepare for its defense. One of his colleagues recounts that Cohen was known to slip out of these meetings on occasion to catch the late show at the nearest movie theater. Exhausted, he would invariably soon fall asleep.

Cohen was a key draftsman of the lend-lease legislation (1941) through which the United States. gave Britain and other allied nations arms and ammunition. In 1941 he was sent to London as economic counselor to the U.S., embassy and participated in the negotiations for this deal. When he returned to the United States, Cohen became counsel to James Byrnes in the offices of economic stabilization and war mobilization. When Byrnes became secretary of state in 1945, he appointed Cohen counselor to the State Department.

Cohen retired in 1947, the last of Roosevelt's inner circle to leave the government. His retirement was short-lived: the following year President Harry S. Truman drafted him as a member of the U.S. delegation to the United Nations General Assembly. He served in this capacity until 1952, when he was named to represent the United States on the U.N. Disarmament Commission. Even into John F. Kennedy's administration Cohen continued to be active in government service, taking a position as a special assistant on disarmament. He never really did retire, continuing to operate his own practice until the 1970s and to advise those government officials and friends who came to see him. His colleague Joseph L. Rauh, Jr., said Cohen was "the greatest public interest lawyer who ever lived. He thought not in terms of himself or of politics, but of what was best for the most."

Cohen's partner, Corcoran, called him "the high priest... the saint."

E. W. Schoenebaum (ed.), *Political Profiles: The Truman Years*, 1978.

COHEN, ELI (1924–1965) Israeli spy who managed to infiltrate the Syrian leadership and transmit to Israel a wealth of secret information regarding Syrian defense, weapons, etc., helping Israel to defeat the Syrian forces within a matter of hours in the 1967 Six-Day War.

His father was a shopkeeper from North Syria, but Cohen was born in Alexandria, Egypt. He was an outstanding pupil both at the lycée (high school) and at the Midrasha (the Institute of Higher Hebraic Studies). As a youth he considered himself a patriotic Egyptian as well as a Jew, and in his free time worked for the Nationalist Movement for a free Egypt, participating in anti-British street demonstrations. His hobbies as a youth — photography and collecting pictures of weapons — were to be very useful in the future.

Cohen began to study applied electricity at Farouk University in Alexandria, but with the establishment of the State of Israel and the growth of anti-Semitism, and he and other Jewish students were forced to leave the university. He then devoted himself to underground Zionist activities and was recruited to a ring of young Egyptian Jews in what became known as the Lavon affair. Cohen was sent to Tel Aviv for three months basic intelligence training. The group was ordered to sabotage public buildings in Alexandria, the idea being to damage American and British property in order to create tension. Fortunately for Cohen, no arrested members of the ring mentioned his name, and after

Eli Cohen.

four months of imprisonment due to implication from various documents, he was released. He was arrested again after the 1956 Suez operation and interned by the Egyptian government on the ship *Marianis Rosso*, which contained a miniature torture chamber. He was then released and expelled from Egypt.

Arriving in Israel in 1957, he first worked as a translator at the Ministry of Defense and later, after an initial refusal, he joined the Mossad.

Sent to Syria to infiltrate the higher ranks there and send information to Israel, he was given a new identity, Kamel Amin Tabet. In order to establish his cover he was sent to Buenos Aires where, posing as a successful businessman wanting to return to his fatherland in Syria, he was accepted in Syrian society. He made useful contacts including Amin al-Hafez, the military attaché who was to become chief of staff and president of Syria. After several months he left Argentina with letters of recommendation to people of importance in Damascus.

During his three years in Syria, his cover was so good that two weeks before his capture his name was put forward by members of the National Revolutionary Council for the post of minister of information in the upcoming cabinet realignment, and several influential officers suggested he be appointed deputy minister of defense.

Cohen convinced those around him that he was a committed Marxist and member of the Arab socialist Baath Party, and he rose quickly in the party. He was also known and respected as a businessman and exporter. Thus he was able to learn about the political scene in Syria and to relay information, pictures, and microfilm invaluable to Israel's defense.

He often claimed to his Arab friends that he was skeptical about the readiness of Syria's armed forces. As a result, he was invited to inspect the lines along the border with Israel on a number of occasions. The Mossad received sketches of bunkers and precise coordinates of artillery emplacement (hidden in the backgammon boards that he exported to Europe). He was also able to reveal information about the new MiG 21 fighter planes supplied by the Soviet Union. One of his missions was to obtain information about the Syrian scheme for diverting the waters of the Jordan, which would have endangered Israeli irrigation and its main water supply. Feigning interest in buying land in the area, he was able to "acquire" a map with the intended project delineated. The project was consequently blown up by the Israeli air force.

In January 1965, while sending a message to Israel, he was apprehended by new tracking equipment that detected his illicit transmitter. The photography laboratory, microfilm, soap filled with plastique, a second transmitter, and a tape recorder built into the wall of the green guest room, were all discovered in the search of his apartment.

Initially the Syrians thought he was an Arab but when questioned in depth on Muslim customs, it became apparent that he was not. He underwent third-degree torture methods under which he admitted, "I am an Israeli operative employed by the Mossad. My name is Eliahu ben Shaul Cohen, and I live with my wife and three children in Bat Yam, near Tel Aviv. All I will add is that I have operated in the best interest of my country." He was condemned to death by a Syrian military court. Despite worldwide appeals for clemency (from the pope, President Charles de Gaulle, etc.), he was publicly hanged in Damascus. Many attempts have been made to have his body returned to Israel but the Syrians have refused. An attempt made by agents to retrieve his body was aborted when the group was pursued by border guards and forced to leave the body behind.

A. Aldouby and J. Ballinger, *The Shattered Silence*, 1971.

Ben Dan (Ben Porat and Dan Yeshayu), *The Spy from Israel*, 1969.

E. Ben Hanan, *Our Man in Damascus: Elie Cohen*, 1969.

COHEN, HENRY (1900—1977) British physician, created Baron Cohen of Birkenhead. Born in Birkenhead, near Liverpool, England, he graduated from the University of Liverpool medical school. At the age of thirty-four he became a professor of medicine, at Liverpool medical school and divided his time between this part-time appointment and his large private practice. In 1943 he was appointed a member of the council of the Royal College of Physicians and presided over many important national committees.

Cohen was one of the architects of the British National Health Service (1949). He was appointed chairman of the Central Health Services Council and knighted in recognition of his services to British medicine. In 1952 he became president of the British Medical Association and later of the Royal Society of Medicine and the General Medical Council. In 1956 he became a life peer, the first English provincial physician to receive this honor. In his maiden speech in the House of Lords he spoke on the subject of vivisection and defended Jewish dietary methods of slaughter as humane against anti-Semitic attempts to have Jewish ritual slaughter banned in England.

From 1950, Cohen took an active interest in the history of medicine, serving as president of the British Society for the History of Medicine and as chairman of the History of Medicine panel of the Wellcome Trust.

Cohen was short of stature, soft spoken, and rarely raised his voice above a whisper in normal conversation. He was a great orator with a ready wit and much in demand as an after-dinner speaker. He was also a superb organizer with a keen legal mind, which served him well as a mediator, innovator, and judge while active on the General Medical Council.

Many anecdotes about their famous professor circulated among students at the medical school. One concerned a senior assistant with whom he had disagreed over a point in treatment. Exasperated by his assistant's assertions he was heard to say "Who do you think you are? God Almighty?" to which the subordinate replied, "No, sir, only his second-in-command!"

Lord Cohen retired from the professorship in 1965 but continued his communal work until his death.

COHEN, HERMANN (1842–1918) Philosopher of religion, founder of the Marburg school of Neo-Kantian philosophy. His father was a cantor and Hebrew teacher in the small German town of Koswig (Anhalt), and Cohen received a comprehensive Jewish education in addition to his general studies. He went to Breslau (now Wroctaw, Poland) to attend the rabbinical seminary and the university but soon dropped the former to concentrate on general philosophy. He continued at the University of Berlin, where he fell under the influence of Kant. His thesis on Kant's theory of experience made an immediate impact and he was invited to teach at the University of Marburg, being appointed a full professor of philosophy within three years. In Marburg, he married the daughter of the famous composer of Jewish cantorial music, Louis Lewandowski (q.v.); she perished in the Holocaust in the Theresienstadt concentration camp. Cohen taught in Marburg until 1912 and was an outstanding figure in European intellectual life. He founded a group of philosophers known as the Marburg school of Neo-Kantianism which advocated a radical idealism rooted in reason.

His Judaism initially was identified with liberal Christianity and he said to a colleague, "What you call Christianity, I call prophetic Judaism." However, in 1879 he was stung by a pamphlet by Heinrich von Treitschke, *Ein Wort über unser Judentum* ("A Word on Our Judaism") which called Judaism the national religion of an alien tribe. The following year, Cohen published a response, *Ein Bekenntnis zur Judenfrage* ("The Jewish Question: A Confession"). It advocated a policy of assimilation and was sharply condemned by the German Jewish establishment. However, it marked the beginning of his renewed interest in and study of Judaism. From the 1890s, this developed from an objective approach to a warm commitment. Cohen also spoke out on Jewish matters and appeared as an expert witness in a trial in which the Marburg Jewish community accused a public school teacher of slandering Judaism. Cohen published his testimony as *Die Nachstenliebe im Talmud* ("Brotherly Love in the Talmud"), in which he sought to reconcile Judaism's universalism with its particularism. The supreme message of Judaism, to him, was the prophetical concept of God as morality. He even saw the acquittal of Captain Alfred Dreyfus (q.v.) in 1899 as an act of redemption, writing: "Dreyfus has suffered for the Redeemer of Israel."

After his retirement from the university in 1912, he moved to Berlin, where he became deeply involved in Jewish thought, writing his *Die Reli-*

gion der Vernunft aus den Quellen des Judentums ("Religion of Reason from the Sources of Judaism"), accord to which the historical role of the Jewish people is to disseminate ethical monotheism throughout the world (he rejected Zionism as contradicting this mission). While Judaism is a religion of reason, it is a faith interpenetrated by ethics. The major ethical concepts were created by the Hebrew prophets who enabled religion to disentangled from myths. The Messiah should be seen as the triumph of good and the achievement of the human drive to perfection.

Cohen's work influenced subsequent Jewish thinkers including Franz Rosenzweig (q.v.), Martin Buber (q.v.), and Joseph Ber Soloveichik. His belief that man shares the task of creation through his correlation with God foreshadowed the philosophy of dialogue.

S. H. Bergman, *Faith and Reason*, 1961, pp. 27–54.
E. Jospe (ed.), *Religion and Hope; Selections from the Jewish Writings of Hermann Cohen*, 1971.
S. Kaplan (ed.), *Religion of Reason out of the Sources of Judaism*, 1972.
N. Rotenstreich, *Jewish Philosophy in Modern Times*, 1968, pp. 52–105.

The Essence of Judaism According to Hermann Cohen (1910)

1. It emphasizes God's uniqueness and absolute difference from all creatures (which excludes pantheism).
2. Man confronts God directly and without any intermediary.
3. There is an indissoluble relationship between knowledge and belief. Study is a sacred duty and there is no conflict between faith and knowledge.
4. The Sabbath is central.
5. It emphasizes freedom and the individual's moral responsibility, and rejects original sin.
6. History has a direction and a goal: the unity of man in messianic times.

COHEN, MORRIS ABRAHAM ("Two-Gun Cohen"; 1887–1970) General and gunrunner in the Chinese army. Morris (Moishe) Abraham Cohen was born to Orthodox Polish immigrants in the East End of London. The young Cohen attended the Jews' Free School, but because of his habitual fighting and petty thievery he was sent to a reform school at the age of ten. Upon his release, his parents sent him to Canada in the hope of keeping the teenager from a life of crime.

In Saskatchewan he tried his hand at ranching, peddling, and liquor smuggling. But Cohen soon achieved fame throughout western Canada as a crack shot and a gambler. Always armed, Cohen once shot and wounded two cowboys after they

called him a "dirty Jew." Later when he served in China, correspondents named him Two-Gun because of the pistol braces he regularly wore. Cohen used his gambling sense to make a small fortune in real estate speculation in Edmonton, Alberta. In his business contacts Cohen befriended the city's Chinese community. Learning their language, he devoted himself to working for Chinese rights during a period of intense anti-Asian sentiment. Cohen met Sun Yat-sen in 1910, when the Chinese revolutionary was in Canada to raise support for his party, the Kuomintang. He acted as Sun's personal bodyguard and was later appointed secretary of the Kuomintang in western Canada.

At the outbreak of the World War I, Cohen enlisted in the Irish Guards, in which he headed a Chinese labor battalion in France. After the war Sun summoned Cohen to China and gave him command of the presidential bodyguard. On several occasions Cohen reportedly saved Sun from an assassin's bullet. Two-Gun was also put to work purchasing arms and recruiting officers for Sun's army as well as organizing banking and customs services. Chiang Kai-shek, who succeeded Sun upon his death in 1925, promoted Cohen to the rank of general. With no formal military training, he was given the monumental task of arming and training Chiang's forces. The 19th Route Army, one of the most successful Chinese military forces to confront the Japanese, was assembled by Cohen.

Cohen is also remembered for saving Madam Sun's life in Hong Kong. He was captured by the invading Japanese in 1941. During twenty-one months of internment he was brutally tortured and sentenced to death in 1944, and only narrowly escaped a Japanese firing squad. After the war Cohen attempted to reconcile the communists with their rivals on Taiwan. Although his efforts were futile, he was one of the few people to find a warm welcome in both Peking and Taipei. He returned to England and spent his last years in Manchester. Unlike most of China's generals and warlords whom he knew so well, Two-Gun Cohen died peacefully

The sharp-shooting general always let it be known that he was a proud and loyal Jew. He took an active role in B'nai B'rith in China and Canada and always explained his support for China by arguing that the Chinese were the only people who had never persecuted the Jews. He was also a supporter of Zionism and appeared on Zionist platforms during the struggle for the State of Israel.
C. Drage, *The Life and Times of General Two-Gun Cohen*, 1954.

COHEN, MORRIS RAPHAEL (1880–1947) U.S. philosopher. Morris Cohen was born in the Belorussian city of Minsk. His family moved to the United States in 1892 and settled in New York City. Cohen received his B.A. from the City College of New York in 1900; he continued his studies, first at Columbia University (M.A., 1902), and then at Harvard (Ph.D., 1906), where he was assistant to such leading philosophers as William James, Josiah Royce, George Santayana, and Hugo Munsterberg.

After a brief stint in the New York public school system, Cohen began to teach mathematics and philosophy at City College in 1902. He received full professorship in 1912 and continued teaching there until 1938. Between the years 1938 and 1942, he taught at the University of Chicago. He was an outstanding leader and a favorite guest lecturer at numerous universities, notably Johns Hopkins, Columbia, and Yale.

Although Cohen was a socialist in his youth, he was highly critical in his later life of most philosophical systems. He developed a philosophy of his own in which he combined elements of pragmatism with logical positivism and linguistic analysis. This philosophy had important ramifications for the legal system. As a specialist in legal philosophy, Cohen, raised awareness in America of the importance of a philosophy of law underlying any legal system. He claimed that law was not an imposition of random will but the result of continuing development based in philosophy.

Cohen was active in the intellectual life of America for many years. In 1913 he organized the Conference of Legal and Social Philosophy, and he headed the American Philosophical Organization in 1929. He was also active in Jewish issues, chairing the Conference on Jewish Relations (1933–1941) and founding the journal *Jewish Social Studies* in 1939. A collection of essays, *Reflections of a Wandering Jew* (1950), and an autobiography, *A Dreamer's Journey* (1949), were published posthumously.

Cohen was a prolific author. He was editor of the *Modern Legal Law Review* and wrote numerous books on legal philosophy, history, and ethics. Among his works are: *Reason and Nature* (1931), *Law and the Social Order* (1933), *Introduction to Logic and Scientific Method* (1934 with Ernest Nagel), *Faith of a Liberal* (1946), and *The Meaning of Human History* (1946).

A Tribute to Professor Morris Raphael Cohen: Teacher and Philosopher, 1928.

L. C. Rosenfield (Cohen), *A Portrait of a Philosopher: Morris R. Cohen in Life and Letters*, 1962.

COHN, EDWIN JOSEPH (1892—1953) U.S. scientist. Born in New York, he studied biochemistry and was appointed professor of biochemistry at Harvard University in 1935, becoming head of the department in 1938. His research concerned mainly the liver, plasma proteins, and tissue proteins. In 1928 he developed a fractionation method by which he was able to produce the first liver extract ("Cohn fraction") active against pernicious anemia.

Cohn also published numerous articles and papers concerning the physiology of spermatozoa; the chemistry of sea water; the physical chemistry of amino acids, proteins, peptides and phospholipids; the separation of gamma-globulin, thrombin protein-rich solutions.

He discovered a new method for the production of blood plasma and pioneered in the utilization of blood derivatives in the treatment of diseases. His two major works were *Proteins, Amino-Acids, and Peptides as Ions and Dipolar Ions* (1943) and *Research in the Medical Sciences* (1946). In 1948 he was awarded the U.S. governments' Medal of Merit.

COHN, FERDINAND JULIUS (1828–1898) German botanist and bacteriologist whose efforts in developing bacteriology as a separate science earned him the title "father of modern bacteriology." He was born in Breslau (now Wroctaw, Poland), where his father was the Austro-Hungarian consul. His childhood was troubled by poor health and weak hearing. He studied at Breslau University, acquiring both a classical and scientific education and was awarded his Ph.D. in 1848 from the University of Berlin because Breslau would not accept Jews as doctoral candidates. His liberal views almost led to his arrest in Berlin in the aftermath of the 1848 revolution.

In 1850 he became a lecturer in botany at Breslau University and by 1857 had become the first Prussian Jew to achieve the rank of professor, but had to wait twenty years before being granted the laboratory space he required.

Cohn was the first to establish that bacteria is a form of plant life. He developed methods for producing, separating, and growing pure bacteriological cultures on solid media, using potato peels, meat, and hard-boiled eggs, instead of the hitherto popular fluid media. He also developed methodological tools for bacteriological assessment.

In 1854 he published the first monograph on bacteriology, *Über die Entwicklung mikroskopische Algen und Pilze* ("On the Evolution of Microscopic Algae and Fungi") and in 1874 produced the first major classification of bacteria into species and genera, showing that bacteria with similar morphologies could have different physiological properties.

Together with another scientist he succeeded in proving the specificity of various bacterial pigments. He also described the sexual process in algae, the existence of heat-resistant bacterial spores, heat production in plants, and fermentation by bacteria. He actively encouraged his students to develop this branch of science; among his students was Robert Koch, who later became the foremost German bacteriologist of his age.

In 1888 Cohn founded the Institute of Plant Physiology and the Botanical Museum at Breslau University. He was also the founder and editor of the journal *Beiträge zur Biologie der Planzen* ("The Journal of Botany"), in which he published articles by himself and Koch which launched bacteriology. In addition he founded the German Society of Botany.

After his death, the Breslau city council erected a statue of him to perpetuate the memory of the "father of modern bacteriology."

W. Balloch, *The History of Bacteriology*, 1938.

H. A. Lechevalier and M. Solotorovsky, *Three Centuries of Microbiology*, 1965.
P. Cohn, *Ferdinand Cohn, Blätter der Erinnerung*, 1901 (Germ.)

COHN, HARRY (1891–1958) U.S. film executive. Born in New York to immigrant parents, Cohn left school at fourteen and, after a series of odd jobs, formed a vaudeville partnership with pianist Harry Rubinstein (later the songwriter, Harry Ruby). When the act broke up, Cohn worked for a time as a streetcar conductor and then returned to show business as a song plugger.

In 1918 he joined his brother Jack at Carl laemmle's [q.v.] Universal Studios, as Laemmle's secretary. In 1920 the brothers, along with another Laemmle employee, Joe Brandt, broke away to form their own company, named CBC (Cohn-Brandt-Cohn). Columbia Pictures become the company's new name in 1924, after the partners had wearied of being referred to as "Corned Beef and Cabbage."

Unlike most of his fellow moguls, who were well entrenched as bosses of major studios by the early 1920s, Cohn was in charge of an enterprise that was considered "poverty row" until the mid thirties. Under his guidance (Brandt departed in 1931, leaving Jack to run the New York office) Columbia enjoyed slow but steady growth and was relatively unharmed by the economic depression. Cohn's biggest asset was director Frank Capra, who joined Columbia in 1927. The enormous success of his film, *It Happened One Night*, in 1934, made Columbia a force in the industry and it was Capra who directed all but two of the films that brought the studio Oscars in the 1930s.

Cohn was no remote administrator and brought his often abrasive personality to bear on all aspects of the running of his studio. Many of his personal interventions were unfortunate (he told Humphrey Bogart that his talents lay in the theater, not the cinema). An early admirer of Mussolini, Cohn saw to it that his own word was law, even in the private lives of Columbia stars such as Rita Hayworth, Kim Novak, William Holden, and Glenn Ford. It was Cohn's personal passion for the singer Al Jolson (q.v.) that led him to produce *The Jolson Story* after the idea had been rejected by other studios, and the film and its sequel proved Columbia's biggest money-makers of the 1940s. As the old studio system faded, Cohn still prospered with hits on the scale of *From Here To Eternity, On the Waterfront*, and *The Bridge on the River Kwai*, in part because of his willingness to pioneer in the production and sale of films for television. After Harry Cohn's death, two years after that of Jack Cohen, Columbia went into the red for the first time in its history. When an acquaintance expressed suprise at seeing so many people at Cohn's funeral, Ben Hecht (q.v.) commented "They want to be sure he's dead."
R. Larkin, *Hail Columbia*, 1975.
R. Thomas, *King Cohn*, 1967.

COPLAND, AARON (1900–1990) U.S. composer. He was born in Brooklyn to a Russian-Jewish family, in which there was little music except for his older sister, who was an amateur pianist and with whom he began his musical training. When he was sixteen he decided to be a composer and after graduating from high school studied harmony, counterpoint, and sonata form. One of his teachers was Rubin Goldmark, but Copland became dissatisfied with Goldmark's Germanic bias and saved money to go to France. Here he remained for three years and studied with the influential teacher Nadia Boulanger.

Returning to New York in 1924, he began his composing career. At Boulanger's suggestion, Serge Koussevitsky (q.v.) put Copland's *Organ Symphony* on the program of the Boston Symphony Orchestra with Boulanger at the organ. Its dissonances and aggression created a scandal. Copland incorporated jazz elements into his *Music for Theater* (1925) and *Piano Concerto* (1927), but in the early 1930s his work was modernist and austere, as in the *Short Symphony* (1933) and the *Statements for Orchestra* (1934). During this time, he worked tirelessly for American music, organizing, with Robert Sessions, concerts of new American music and helping to found the American Composers' Alliance. However, he felt he was only reaching an élite and missing out on the wider music public. He now wrote a series of explicitly American pieces which became enormously popular. They included the ballet scores *Billy the Kid* (1938) and *Rodeo* (1942), concert pieces like *El Salón México* (1937) and *Lincoln Portrait* (1942), and his most popular work *Appalachian Spring* (1944), originally a dance score commissioned by Martha Graham, for which he was awarded a Pulitzer Prize. He quoted cowboy songs in *Billy the Kid* and constructed the last part of *Appalachian Spring* around the Shaker hymn "Simple Gifts." He composed music for films including *Of Mice and Men, Our Town*, and *The Heiress*.

Copland was a leading figure on the musical scene — president of the American Composers' Alliance from 1937 to 1945, a director of the League of Composers, a member of the faculty of the Berkshire Musical Center at Tanglewood, Massachusetts, concert organizer, organizer of new music, and guide to a whole new generation of composers. Leonard Bernstein (q.v.) said of him that "he was the leader to whom all young composers brought their compositions." At the same time he was an outspoken supporter of liberal and leftist causes.

In the 1950s he adopted the twelve-tone system and once again found his work appealing to only a limited public. After 1970 he stopped composing and concentrated on conducting and lecturing. As a conductor his brisk beat and lack of affectation endeared him to the players. In 1964 he was awarded the medal of freedom by the U.S. government.

As early as in 1932 he had been called "dean of

American composers" although, in his modesty, he disliked the appellation. At his death, the *New York Times* characterized him as "America's best-known composer of classical music and a gentle yet impassioned champion of American music in every style."

His writings include *What to Listen for in Music* (1957), *Copland on Music* (1960), and *The New Music: 1900–1960*, 1968.

A. V. Berger, *Aaron Copland*, 1953.
A. Dobrin, *Aaron Copland, his Life and Tiem*, 1967.
J. F. Smith, *Aaron Copland, his Work and Contribution to American Music*, 1955.

When asked how a Brooklyn Jewish boy could write *Rodeo*, Copland said, "I preferred to imagine being on a horse without actually getting on one."

"Copland was like a colt — all legs, head, and body, cantering past on long, uncertain stilts — the colt of American brass and momentum, all that's swift and daring, aggressive and unconstrained in our life."

Paul Rosenfeld on Aaron Copland

CORDOVERO, MOSES (1522–1570) Mystic and moralist. His entire activity was centered in the town of Safed in Eretz Israel, the great kabbalistic focus of the 16th century, which may have been his birthplace. He studied rabbinics with Joseph Caro (q.v.) and the Kabbalah with his brother-in-law, the distinguished Solomon Alkabets. Before long, Cordovero was recognized as the outstanding teacher of mysticism in Safed and the next generation of scholars were nearly all his students including, for a time, Isaac Luria (q.v.). Like his teacher, Joseph Caro, he experienced supernatural manifestations. While he and Alkabets were visiting the graves of Talmudic rabbis in the Galilean hills, they would be overcome and utter automatic speeches, which were the source of their understanding of the mysteries of the Kabbalah.

He wrote prolifically. His best-known kabbalistic work, *Pardes Rimmonim* ("Pomegranate Orchard") was completed when he was twenty-seven. This is a systematic exposition and synthesis of kabbalistic thought from the classic *Zohar* (13th century) to his own time. He deals with the fundamental problem of creation, seeing God as First Cause from whom emanate ten *sefirot* ("radiances") seen as vessels, which make possible the multifaceted functioning of a single Godhead. Nothing exists outside of God but while God is all reality, not all reality is in God.

Cordovero wrote *Tomer Devorah* ("Deborah's Palm Tree"), an ethical work in a mystical spirit, which was for long one of the most influential Jewish ethical works. Its guide to proper behavior is rooted in the relation between the individual and the ten *sefirot*.

L. Fine, *Safed Spirituality*, 1984.
L. Jacobs, *The Palm Tree of Deborah*, 1974.

COSTA URIEL DA (Acosta; 1585—1640) Freethinker in Amsterdam. He was born as Gabrel da Costa in Oporto to a Marrano family. His father was a devout Catholic who taught his son equestarianism. In Coimbra Da Costa was apprenticed in the legal profession, and then became a minor church official. However, his studies of Jesuit teachings had raised grave doubts in his mind and, under the impact of the study of the Bible, he became strongly attracted to Judaism and the Jewish people. But, without the possibility of first-hand acquaintance of Jews, he constructed his own romanticized version of Judaism. He converted his family (his father had died) and in 1617 they decided to flee in order to live as Jews openly and to avoid the prying of the Inquisition. The family sailed to Amsterdam, where he and his four brothers had themselves circumcised and openly identified themselves as Jews.

However, Da Costa was soon disillusioned when he discovered that official Judaism was very different in practice from the concept he had imagined. He found the ritual burdensome and rigid and was soon openly criticizing the "pride and arrogance" of the Amsterdam rabbis, calling them "the Pharisees of the Amsterdam synagogue." Moreover he prepared a book, *An Examination of the Pharisaic Traditions Compared with the Written Laws*, doubting the doctrines of the immortality of the soul (which he regarded as non biblical) and of reward and punishment. The elders of the community saw this not only as a heretical threat to their faith but as endangering their own recently won status in Christian society. In 1624, Da Costa was excommunicated, arrested, briefly imprisoned, and fined, and his book was burned.

For fourteen years, he was boycotted and lived a life of isolation; even children in the street called him "Renegade! Heretic!" However, he did not want to live cut off indefinitely and eventually he decided to take nominal steps ("I will be an ape among apes") to rejoin the community. But the reconciliation did not last long and Da Costa was soon again expressing unorthodox views. "I doubted whether Moses' law was in reality God's law and decided it was of human origin," he wrote, and embraced a natural law, calling himself a deist. He rejected established religion and ceased Jewish practices. The community's anger was again roused when he tried to dissuade two Christians, an Italian and a Spaniard, who had come to Amsterdam to adopt Judaism, from converting. He gave them a frightening picture of Judaism and warned them against putting the yoke of rabbinic Judaism around their necks. When they reported his remarks, he was again excommunicated and remained in almost complete isolation for a further seven years. Again Da Costa could suffer it no longer and applied to rejoin the community. The price was a public penance, a humiliating ceremony held in Amsterdam's Portuguese Synagogue. Hundreds gathered to hear his recantation in which — clothed in sackcloth — he declared he deserved a thousand deaths, after which he was subjected to thirty-nine lashes of the whip. Finally he had to prostrate himself on the threshold of the building as the departing throng spat at him and trampled him. Completely devastated by the experience, he went home, wrote a few pages of autobiography, and then took two pistols, fired first at a passing relative (whom he missed) and then shot himself.

Da Costa had some influence on Benedict Spinoza (q.v.; there is a tradition that the two were related) who was to be likewise excommunicated, and two centuries later was seen as a great hero by freethinking Jews, who celebrated his story in literature and music.

L. W. Schwartz, *Memoirs of My People*,

CRÉMIEUX, ISAAC ADOLPHE (1796–1880) French statesman and Jewish communal leader. Born in Nîmes to an assimilated family originating from the the town of Crémieux in southeast France, he was one of the first Jewish pupils to be admitted to the Lycée Impérial in Paris. Crémieux gained his law degree at the University of Aix-en-Provence and upon being admitted to the bar at Nîmes in 1817, refused to take the *more judaico* oath required of Jews in lawsuits with non-Jews, which had an explicit character of a curse. After defending other Jews who also refused to take the oath, he successfully fought for its abolition in 1827. He soon attained national fame when he defended a group of young republicans against the reactionary Bourbon régime, as well as Protestants, whose rights were restricted. He was active in the Freemasons and in liberal organizations. In 1830 Crémieux moved to Paris and, as a member of the Central Consistory, supported King Louis Philippe. In 1842 he entered the Chamber of Deputies as a member of the opposition, where he distinguished himself as a brilliant orator and in 1843 was appointed president.

Crémieux was active in the 1848 revolution and was one of the officials who accompanied the king and queen to the hall where they submitted their resignation. He held the post of minister of justice in the provisional government, and was instrumental in abolishing capital punishment for political offenses, in passing a law against slavery in the French colonies, and in introducing the system of trial by jury in France. In 1869 he returned to parliament on the Republican ticket, and in 1870 was appointed minister of justice. Crémieux was elected a member of the National Assembly in 1871, and in 1875 was appointed a life senator.

Despite his assimilated background (his wife had his children baptized unbeknown to him), Crémieux waged a constant battle to improve the lot of the Jews in France and fought against the oppression of Jews everywhere. In 1831 he obtained

Isaac A Crémieux.

regular government funding for the salaries of rabbis and elected functionaries in Jewish communities; in 1835 he contested the Basel canton's attempt to expel French Jews from its territory, as a result of which France broke off diplomatic relations with Basel. In 1840 he accompanied Moses Montefiore to Egypt with a delegation that secured the acquittal and release of Jews arrested as a result of the Damascus blood libel and succeeded in persuading the sultan to issue an order against such libels. In 1858 Crémieux became involved in the Mortara case in Bologna, in which a Jewish child was kidnapped by the Catholic church and baptized against the will of its parents. Crémieux spoke out vehemently against the pope (Pius IX) who justified the action.

In 1864 Crémieux became president of the Alliance Israélite Universelle, the French Jewish organization that established Jewish schools in Mediterranean countries with the support of French Jewry and set out to help oppressed Jewish communities in Morocco, Rumania, and Russia. In 1870 he signed, as minister of justice, the Décret Crémieux (Crémieux decree) by which the Jews of Algeria were granted French citizenship. In the 1860s he became interested in the return of Jews to Zion and helped Charles Netter to establish the Mikveh Israel Agricultural School near Jaffa in 1870, as well as other schools in the main towns of Eretz Israel. His writings include *Liberté! Plaidoyers et discours politiques* (1869); *Gouvernement de la défense nationale* (1871); and *Discours et lettres* (1883).

S. V. Pozner, *Adolphe Crémieux*, 2 vols., 1933–1934.

CRESCAS, HASDAI (1340–c. 1410) Spanish community leader and Jewish philosopher. He came from a distinguished family of scholars and merchants of Barcelona, where he was born and taught. When he was twenty-seven, he was imprisoned together with his teacher, Rabbi Nissim Gerondi, and other colleagues on a false charge of desecrating the host, but they remained steadfast and were eventually vindicated and released. Most of his colleagues then moved away from the city, leaving Crescas as the outstanding scholar in Barcelona. He was soon regarded as a leader of all Spanish Jewry and frequently intervened at court on behalf of his fellow-Jews. He received the title of member of the royal household and was granted extensive juridical authority, including the power to enforce excommunication. In 1389 he moved to Saragossa, where he served as rabbi. The following year, he was appointed by the queen of Aragon as judge of cases of Jewish informers throughout the kingdom, with authority to impose even capital punishment. This was a unique example of the appointment of a Jewish official with nationwide jurisdiction. In the document of his appointment he was described as superior to all other Jews of the kingdom "not only in knowledge of the Mosaic law but in his power of reasoning."

In 1391, thousands of Spanish Jews were killed in mob massacres, and one of the victims in Barcelona was Crescas's only son. A letter from the queen asking the authorities to protect members of the Crescas family arrived too late. Hasdai Crescas himself became the focus of all attempts to rescue and restore the broken Jewish communities. The king and queen, who were interested in the rehabilitation of the Jewish communities, backed him in his work, which he executed with energy, dedication, and wisdom. He issued a series of regulations that, although modified by the queen, set the tone for the restructuring of Jewish life.

Crescas' major philosophical work is *Or Adonai* ("Light of the Lord"), a critique of Aristotelianism especially as represented in Jewish thought by Moses Maimonides (q.v.). His aim was to replace external influences by internal Jewish sources and understandings. He starts with the three roots of the Torah: (1) God's existence, (2) God's unity, and (3) God's incorporeality.

Then follow six fundamental dogmas: (1) God's omniscience, (2) His providence, (3) His omnipotence, (4) prophecy, (5) human choice, and (6) the purposefulness of the Law.

To these he adds beliefs which are obligatory but not fundamental, the denial of which would not constitute heresy: God's creation of the world *ex nihilo*; the immortality of the soul; reward and punishment (corporeal and spiritual); resurrection of the dead (for the elect); the eternity of the Torah; the superiority of Moses over other prophets; the high priest's oracular powers based on the Urim and Thummin; the coming of the Messiah; the efficacy of prayer and of repentance; and the special nature of the Jewish holidays.

Crescas also wrote a polemical anti-Christian work in Catalan.

Y. F. Baer, *A History of the Jews in Christian Spain*, Vol. 2, 1966.

> Rabbi Hasdai Crescas was the greatest philosopher of his day, even among the Christian and Muslim scholars, not to mention among the Jewish ones.... And he was the greatest of the king's advisers, for the king would not do anything, great or small, without consulting him.
>
> **Rabbi Joseph Yabetz**

CZERNIAKOW, ADAM (1880–1942) Chairman of the Warsaw Jewish Community Council during World War II. Shortly after World War I Czerniakow cast off the assimilationist attitude of his family and became involved in Jewish life. A chemical engineer by profession, he dedicated himself to promoting the interests of Jewish craftsmen and taught in Warsaw's Jewish vocational school network. From 1927 until 1934 he was a member of the Warsaw city council and before World War II was elected to the executive council of the Warsaw Jewish community.

On September 23, 1939, the mayor of Warsaw, Stefan Starzynski, appointed Czerniakow head of the Jewish Community Council. Early in October the Nazis named him head of the Judenrat (Jewish council). In many quarters, the Jewish council was severely criticized for its activities and some groups in the ghetto tried to oust Czerniakow. Historians have shown that Czerniakow strove to run the ghetto with as little outside interference as possible, thus making it possible for illegal underground economic activities, like food smuggling, to be carried out. Czerniakow himself was in close contact with the German authorities in Warsaw. He tried unsuccessfully to arouse their concern for the ghetto population and felt he had built a working relationship with the ghetto commissar, Heinz Auerswald.

On the eve of the great deportation from the ghetto, which began on July 22, 1942, Czerniakow asked Auerswald if a deportation was about to take place and was told no such thing was in the offing. On the following day, when he discovered the truth, Czerniakow committed suicide, rather than collaborate with the Germans in the deportation drive. According to one account his suicide note said: "They are demanding that I kill the children of my people with my own hands. There is nothing for me to do but to die."

From September 6, 1939, until the day of his suicide, Czerniakow kept a diary of events in Warsaw. His writings are of inestimable value in understanding not only his activities and those of the Jewish council, but also the general situation in the Warsaw ghetto.

Y. Gutman, *The Jews of Warsaw, 1939–1943*, 1980.

D

DA COSTA, URIEL See Costa, Uriel da

DA GAMA, GASPARD, See Gama, Gaspard da

DAMROSCH Family of musicians.

Damrosch, Leopold (1832–1885) Conductor, violinist, and composer. Born in Posen, Prussia (now Poznan, Poland), he exhibited musical talent at an early age but in obedience to his parents, studied medicine, graduating as a doctor in 1854. He then devoted himself to music, to the disgust of his parents who promptly ceased to give him any assistance. He lived miserably, working as a violinist in small towns and spas. Subsequently he began to conduct at small theaters, before being admitted as a violinist to the court orchestra at Weimar, under Franz Liszt. The two men became friends and Liszt dedicated one of his compositions to Damrosch. In 1858 he was appointed conductor of the Breslau Philharmonic Concerts and also founded the Orchestral Society and Choral Union in Breslau. His enthusiasm for the new German music created difficulties for him in Breslau, however, and he gladly accepted, in 1871, an invitation to become conductor of the Arion Male Choral Union in New York.

Damrocsh played an important role in New York musical life. In 1873 he fcunded the Oratorio Society and in 1878, the New York Symphony Society. He conducted New York's first great musical festival, with over 1,200 singers and 250 instrumentalists. Shortly before his sudden death he conducted a brilliant season of German opera at the Metropolitan.

Damrosch composed many works including seven cantatas, a symphony, music for Schiller's play *Joan of Arc*, songs, works for violin, and "biblical idylls."

Damrosch, Walter Johannes (1862–1950) German-American conductor, educator, and composer; son of Leopold Damrosch (q.v.). Born in Breslau (now Wroclaw, Poland), he studied harmony, piano, and conducting with his father as well as other eminent teachers both in Germany and New York, to which his family moved in 1871. In 1881 he was conductor of the Newark, New Jersey, Harmonic Society and in 1885 succeeded his father both at the New York Oratorio Society (until 1898) and the New York Symphony Society (until 1903). He was also assistant to his father and to Anton Seidl as conductor of German opera at the Metropolitan Opera in New York (1885–1891).

In 1894 Damrosch organized the Damrosch Opera Company, which he directed for five seasons, presenting German singers of German repertoire in major cities across the United States. In 1902 he became the conductor of the New York Philharmonic Society, and a year later he returned to the now reorganized New York Symphony Society as its regular conductor, staying with the ensemble until 1927, and taking it on a European tour in 1920. Damrosch later organized, at the request of General John Jo Pershing, the American Expeditionary Force bands, and in 1918 founded schools for bandmasters in Chaumont, France.

In 1925 Damrosch conducted the New York Symphony Society Orchestra in the first network broadcast over the newly organized NBC and a year later was appointed musical adviser for the network, a position he held for twenty years. During this time he also conducted the NBC Symphony Orchestra in a series of weekly music-appreciation hours heard in schools and colleges all over North America. Harold C. Schonberg, the doyen of music critics, dismissed this pioneering experience completely: "It is estimated that every Friday morning as many as six million impressionable school children were forced to listen to his broadcast in the name of culture. Many alive still remember his hearty, unctuous salutation: "My dear children..." Damrosch conceived the idea of implanting great melodies in his youngsters' heads by writing words to the tunes and having the children sing along. Goodness knows how many potential music lovers were permanently maimed by this procedure. To this day there are those who cannnot listen to the Schubert *Unfinished* without hearing the words: 'This is/the symphonee/that Schubert wrote and ne-ver/finished.'"

Damrosch led the American premieres of many staples of the repertoire, like the Third and Fourth symphonies of Brahms or the Fourth and Sixth symphonies of Tchaikovsky. In 1938 he received the gold medal of the National Institute of Arts and Letters.

Damrosch composed several operas, including *The Scarlet Letter, Cyrano de Bergerac,* and *The Man without a Country.* He also composed incidental music for the theater and many songs.

W. Damrosch, *My Musical Life,* 1923.

DANIEL, YULI MARKOVICH (1925–1988)

Russian poet, translator, and satirical short-story writer who published under the pseudonym Nikolai Arzhak. He was the son of the prominent Yiddish writer Mark Daniel, who fought in the Russian Revolution and passionately championed the ideal of freedom for the common man. In his writings, the common man was invariably his hero. This endeared him to the first generation after the revolution.

Yuli Daniel grew up with this same commitment to his country and revolutionary ideas. At age eighteen he fought in World War II, until he was critically wounded and disabled. In 1946, he had sufficiently recovered to continue his education at Kharkov University and the Moscow Province Teachers' Training College. He graduated in 1951 and began his teaching career.

Late in the 1950s, he forsook teaching literature and turned to his first love — writing. He began to develop as a poet in his own right and at the same time successfully translated poetry from Ukrainian, Armenia, the Balkan languages, and Yiddish, becoming known as one of the foremost poetic translators in the country.

However, his favorable position lasted only about eight years. It ended abruptly in 1965 when Daniel and his good friend Andrei Sinyavsky were arrested for allegedly publishing seditious works. Until that time Daniel was virtually unknown outside his own country. He had smuggled three short stories and a short novel out of the country for publication. "Hands," "Atonement," and "The Man from Minap" as well as his most famous work, *This Is Moscow Speaking,* were published under the pseudonym Nikolai Arzhak. Although the works had already appeared, it was the trial itself that had made Daniel and Sinyavsky internationally famous.

The two authors' writings were alleged to be anti-Soviet, aimed at subverting the regime. The trial was unusual in that it marked the first time artists were tried for their actual works as opposed to other political or "subversive" deeds. During the hearing, which lasted four days, the authors were accused of being the incarnate version of the characters they had created.

That may have been true in part in the case of Daniel's *This Is Moscow Speaking,* where the novel's hero, like Daniel himself, is a war veteran. However, the prosecution gave the piece a different meaning from the one Daniel intended.

This Is Moscow Speaking depicts a day which the Kremlin declares a "Public Murder Day." On the specified day all citizens over the age of sixteen have the right to murder any other citizen, with the exception of certain categories such as police and army. Before the said day, the hero ponders the hate in his own heart and who would be worthy of revenge. But into his musings crash the memories of death around him on the battlefield and these ideas jolt him back to reality. The murder day in general is a fiasco, with very few people actually being killed.

Daniel maintained that his tale was opposed to murder and to state terror, but the prosecution claimed it advocated murder. In the end, Daniel was sentenced to five years in prison, receiving a lighter sentence than Sinyavsky, who received a seven-year sentence.

Daniel served his term in a labor camp and Vladimir prison, one of the worst in the Soviet Union. He was released after serving exactly five years. He left prison with a broken spirit. He was refused permission to return to Moscow to live, a banishment he accepted. He settled ninety miles outside of the capital and became a petty clerk, writing poetry and translating.

M. Dalton, *Andrei Siniavskii and Julii Daniel: Two Soviet "Heretical" Writers,* 1973.

M. Hayward (trans. & ed.), *On Trial: The Soviet State versus "Abram Tertz" and "Nikolai Arzhak,"* 1966.

DA PONTE, LORENZO (1749–1838)

Italian poet, librettist, and adventurer. Originally named Emanuele Conegliano, he was descended from a prominent Jewish family long resident in Ceneda (Vittorio Veneto). His parents, Geremia and Rachele Conegliano, abandoned Judaism in 1763, changed their names, and had their son trained for the Roman Catholic priesthood. At the age of twenty-six, however, Lorenzo (an ordained teacher of rhetoric) sought a more adventurous life in Venice. There he turned to writing, made friends with the notorious Giacomo Casanova, and became involved in scandalous love affairs. Public opinion was further outraged by his satirical verse, and in 1779 he was expelled from Venice. Three years later, he established himself in Vienna and, thanks to the patronage of Emperor Joseph II, embarked on a new career as the imperial opera's Italian librettist.

In this role Da Ponte displayed a genuine talent for witty and sparkling dialogue, the essence of comic opera. Those who made use of his librettos included Antonio Salieri as well as two foreign composers, Stephen Storace (*Gli equivoci,* 1786) and Vicente Martin y Soler (*Una cosa rara,* 1786). It is because of his fruitful association with Wolfgang Amadeus Mozart, however, that Da Ponte has a lasting claim to fame. Mozart chose librettos by Da Ponte for his cantata *Davidde penitente* (1785) and for three celebrated operas: *Le Nozze di Figaro* (1786), *Don Giovanni* (1787), and *Cosi fan tutte* (1790). The first, inspired by Beaumarchais' play *Le mariage de Figaro* (1784), and the last were both premiered in Vienna. *Don Giovanni,* based partly on the text of an earlier work by Gazzaniga, softened the impact of the Don Juan theme and was first staged in Prague. These tales of jealousy, seduction and fickle love must have gained much from the librettist's own Casanova-like escapades.

Following the death of Joseph II in 1790, Da Ponte's appointment was terminated and he left Vienna. Though still nominally a priest in holy orders, he is asid to have gone through a form of Jewish marriage in Trieste before settling in London (1793). He first resumed his career at the Theater Royal, Drury Lane, but then tried his luck as a bookseller, ran up debts, and in 1805 sought refuge from his creditors by emigrating to the United States. Over the next twenty years, Da Ponte entangled himself in various other disastrous enterprises, finally achieving respectability at the age of seventy-six. He arranged the first American performance of *Don Giovanni* (1825) and thereafter served as professor of Italian language and literature at Columbia College, also helping to establish the New York Opera House in 1833. His entertaining, if highly colored, memoirs appeared in a four-volume revised edition (New York, 1823–1827) and were later published in English (London and Philadelphia, 1929).

A. Fitzlyon, *The Libertine Librettist*, 1955.

J. L. Russo, *Lorenzo da Ponte: Poet and Adventurer*, 1922.

DASSAULT, MARCEL (Marcel Bloch; 1892–1986) French aircraft designer and manufacturer. Born in Paris, where his father was a physician, he was very close to his two brothers – one of whom became a general in the French army and a member of the Academy of Sciences and the other a distinguished surgeon who perished in the Holocaust. Even as a schoolchild, Dassault was fascinated with airplanes and studied electricity. After graduation he worked in a car factory, where he acquired an appreciation for factory organization and teamwork. He subsequently enrolled in an aeronautical school.

When World War I broke out, Dassault was chosen to design planes and was responsible for building propellers, one of which, the Guynemer, was so successful that it is commemorated in a monument in the Place des Invalides. His work on propellers meant that he received information on all types of planes and his knowledge of French planes was unrivaled. With two colleagues, he constructed the fighter plane SEA 4, which was so successful that a thousand were ordered. Before they came off the assembly line, however, the war ended and the order was cancelled. Dassault was told to use the factory he had built to produce doors, windows, and wheelbarrows. Throughout the 1920s he concentrated on general construction.

In 1930, the French government, realizing that the French airplane industry was lagging behind that of other European countries, commissioned a three-motor plane for the postal services from Dassault. Dassault designed an all-metal plane, but no planes were ordered. Nonetheless he used the knowledge he had acquired to build a first-aid plane which did prove successful. He then built a two-motor plane, the 220, for Air France, which went into operation in 1938. Plans for various other planes were ended by World War II and the fall of France.

During the war, Dassault was arrested as a Jew and deported to the Buchenwald concentration camp. A group of French deportees in a position of relative power secretly assisted other Frenchmen and saved Dassault from deportation to one of the major death camps. In the last days before liberation, he contracted diphtheria. When repatriated from Buchenwald, he flew for the first and only time!

After six months of treatment for post-diphtheric paralysis of the legs, Dassault became head of an aircraft factory and began building a new plane, the Dassault 315, participating in every stage of its creation. The plane was judged outstanding in its category and three-hundred were ordered. His Mystère IV was the first European plane to break the sound barrier. It was followed by the Super-Mystère B2, the Mirage III; the F1, and finally the Mirage G, all of which received international acclaim. Dassault himself considered his greatest successes to have been the civilian plane, the Mystere 20, and the Mirage G, sixty of which were delivered to Israel, making a major contribution to the Israeli victory in the 1967 Six-Day War. The Société des Avions Marcel Dassault became the outstanding French exporting company, numbering Pan Am among its prime customers.

In 1951, Dassault entered politics, running as deputy and senator, and proposing a law which would enable people of low income to own their own homes. He also founded the journal *Jours de France*, which concentrated on "good news."

M. Dassault, *Le talisman*, 1970.

DAVID (c. 1037–c. 967 BCE) Second and greatest king of Israel. Born in Bethlehem. The youngest son of Jesse of the tribe of Judah and great-grandson of Boaz and Ruth (q.v.), he grew up as a shepherd and a skilled musician. While still tending the sheep, he was anointed by the prophet Samuel (q.v.) as the future successor to King Saul (q.v.). He was taken to Saul's court to play to the king, who was passing through one of his fits of depression. At first the king took to David and made him one of his courtiers. He was regarded by the people as a warrior hero after he had killed the Philistine giant, Goliath, in single combat, and became an armor bearer of Saul and later one of his commanders. He married the king's daughter Michal and his friendship with Saul's son and heir Jonathan remains proverbial. However, repeated attempts by the mentally disturbed king on David's life led him to flee and take refuge among the Philistines. Now, he lived as an outlaw, but received religious legitimacy when he was joined by Abiathar, sole survivor of Saul's massacre of the priests of Nob. David took service with Achish, king of Gath, receiving in return Zik-

David playing the harp, depicted on the mosaic floor of the 6th-century synagogue at Gaza.

lag in southern Judah. He was not averse to joining the Philistines in their attack on Saul but they remained suspicious of him and sent him away from the battlefield. In the ensuing battle and Philistine victory, Saul and Jonathan were killed. On hearing this David uttered his famous lament: "How are the mighty fallen!... Tell it not in Gath, publish it not in the streets of Ashkelon... Saul and Jonathan, beloved and lovely, in life and death they were not divided; they were swifter than eagles, stronger than lions" (2 Sam. 1).

David returned to Judah and settled in Hebron, the ritual and tribal capital, where he was crowned king and remained for over seven years. He defeated an attempt to crown Saul's son Ishbosheth in his stead, and in a series of battles, succeeded in eliminating the Philistine menace. He also, by a stratagem, captured the enclave city of Jebus, which had defied the Israelites since time of Joshua, and made it his capital, Jerusalem, because of its central and strategic location and its independence of any of the tribes. He brought the ark of the covenant to Jerusalem, making the city the focus of the cult. Although he obtained a site for building a temple, he was divinely informed that this task was not for him but for his son (2 Sam. 7).

David built an empire in stages. After defeating the Philistines, he undertook campaigns against other hostile neighbors, including the Moabites, the Edomites, and the Ammonites. During the Ammonite war David committed adultery with Bathsheba and engineered her husband's death so that he could marry her. For this he was severely rebuked by Nathan the prophet, and punished by the death of their first offspring and by the divine decree that the sword would never depart from his house. Finally, he defeated the Arameans, captured Damascus and extended his rule as far as the river Euphrates.

David was an accomplished administrator. He laid the foundations for the division of the country into districts; the establishment of a competent officialdom; the reorganization of the army; and the setting up of a systematic priesthood in which the chief priests served as royal officials. However, rivalries continued between the northern and southern parts of the kingdom and several crises occurred. The most serious was the rebellion led by David's son Absalom, put down only with great difficulty. It ended with the death of Absalom whom David mourned in another famous lament: "O my son, Absalom... Would I had died instead of you, O Absalom, my son, my son" (2 Sam. 18). In David's old age, he was confronted with a struggle for the succession between his son Adonijah, next in line for the throne, and Solomon (q.v.), his son by Bathsheba. Court maneuvers by Bathsheba and Nathan the prophet ensured the succession to Solomon.

The personality of David made a deep and lasting impression on the Jewish people, later transmitted to the Christian and the Muslim traditions. He was admired for his courage, energy, wisdom, and deep trust in God. According to tradition he was the "sweet singer of Israel" to whom the book of Psalms was attributed. The kings of Judah were descended from him (the house of David) and so traditionally would the Messiah, who would restore the kingdom of the house of David, symbol of the link between God and the Jewish people.

David was buried in the City of David in Jerusalem but the site is unknown. Since the Middle Ages, a grave in Jerusalem has been venerated as David's tomb, but the identification is the result of a misunderstanding.

Bright, J. *A History of Israel*, 3d ed., 1981.

DAVIDSON, JO (1883–1952) U.S. sculptor. Born in New York, he attended art classes at Yale and at the Art Students League. It was at the School of Fine Arts in New Haven that he discovered his penchant for sculpture.

He served an apprenticeship with the sculptor Herman MacNeill, but left when he felt he was learning nothing. In 1905 he received his first commission, and his statuette of *David* was exhibited in the Art Students League annual exhibition in 1906. The following year he went to Paris where he enrolled in the Ecole des Beaux-Arts, but after a few weeks decided to work on his own.

He had a talent for sculpting portrait heads, and soon began receiving commissions. In 1909 his bronze statuette, *La terre*, was accepted for the Salon. In 1910 a one-man show of his work was exhibited in New York and was represented in the famous Armory Show of 1913.

During World War I, Davidson served alongside the soldiers as an artist-correspondent. He visited the White House to do his first portrait of a United States president, Woodrow Wilson. Later he sculpted Franklin Delano Roosevelt and Dwight D. Eisenhower.

At the end of the war, he made busts of the leading statesmen and generals, including General John J. Pershing and Marshal Ferdinand Foch. Among his many sensitive portraits were those of Albert Einstein (q.v.), Tomáš Masaryk, Bernard Baruch (q.v.), the great Hindu poet Rabindranath Tagore, and Golda Meir (q.v.).

He was commissioned by John D. Rockefeller, Jr., to carve a large marble bust of his father, to be placed in the Standard Oil Company Building in New York, and by George Doran to sculpt a series of writers — James Joyce, Arthur Conan Doyle, Arnold Bennett, and others. He also did a figure portrait of Gertrude Stein (q.v.), who read her manuscripts aloud to him during her sittings.

In 1940 he completed a bronze statue of Walt Whitman, which he had been working on for fourteen years; it stands in Bear Mountain State Park in New York. A bronze statue of Will Rogers is in the Statuary Hall of the U.S. Capitol in Washington, D.C. (a second casting is in the Will Rogers Memorial in Claremont, Oklahoma).

When, after World War II, statesmen from around the world gathered in San Francisco for the meeting that led to the creation of the United Nations, Davidson planned to sculpt the delegates, but his work was interrupted by a heart-attack. When he recovered, he went to his home in France, where he worked on memorials to the town of Lidice — totally destroyed by the Nazis — and to the Jews who perished in the Holocaust.

In America, the Academy of Arts and Letters held a large retrospective of Davidson's work. For the Benefit of the United Nations Children's Appeal, he displayed six hundred sculptures in an exhibition at Rockefeller Center.

Davidson said that it took two to make a successful portrait bust, and that most important was a rapport between the sculptor and the sitter. He never posed his models, but conversed with them while he worked. These lively conversations gave him the insight into their personalities which is the hallmark of his portraits.

Although many of his contemporaries experimented with cubist, abstract or nonobjective forms in sculpture, Davidson continued to work in his personal, naturalist style. He worked in marble and stone, but his favorite medium was clay, because of its responsiveness to the touch of his hands. The necessity for working quickly on his portraits resulted in a simplification of forms. Mahatma Gandhi, observing the bust of himself that Davidson had just completed, commented: "You make heroes out of mud".

J. Davidson, *Between Sittings*, 1951.

DAVIS, EDWARD (1816–1841) Australian bushranger (highwayman). Born in London, in 1832 he was sentenced by an English court to deportation for seven years to Australia for stealing a shopkeeper's wooden till containing five shillings in copper. In Australia he was confined but escaped and was recaptured three times, for which his sentence was increased by four years. After his fourth escape he took refuge in the bush and emerged as leader of a gang of bushrangers, convict slaves like himself who had deserted the farms of their masters. He became widely known as Teddy the Jewboy and his gang was called the Jewboy gang. An outstanding rider, Davis and the gang worked on horseback. For two years they ranged over northern New South Wales, imposing a reign of terror, raiding towns and villages, and holding up and robbing travelers.

He differed, however, from other gang leaders of his time, in that he robbed the rich and helped the poor, for which he earned a reputation as Australia's Robin Hood. He even rounded up a party of police who were searching for him, took their cattle and money, and rode away in triumph — in the best tradition of the hero fo Sherwood Forest. Davis and his men considered themselves "chevaliers of the road." They were gallant to women and distributed part of their booty among convict servants, who, like the common people, revered him and made him a legendary figure.

One account in a contemporary paper reports that the gang waylaid a doctor but upon discovering his identity, returned to him everything they had taken. The doctor said he had been treated in a most gentlemanly way and never spent a happier night in his life. They insisted that he make himself at home, fed him lavishly, cleared a sofa for him to lie on, and covered him with their greatcoats "the pockets of which were stuffed with ball cartridge and buckshot." He reported, "Their attire was rather gaudy as they wore broad rimmed hats, turned up in front with an abundance of braid, pink ribbons, satin neck cloths, splendid brooches, rings, and watches. One of them (a Jew I believe) wore five rings. They used neither violence nor uncivil language. They then went off to rob people on the highway."

For two years the gang scrupulously avoided murder but eventually one of their members, John Shea, killed a storekeeper. This spurred the authorities to an intense search and in 1840, after a gun battle, Davis and his men were captured. At the trial in Sydney the Jewish community engaged a lawyer to defend Davis, but it was to no avail as Davis, Shea, and four others were sentenced to death. Davis was the first Jew to be hanged in Sydney. Dressed in a black suit, he went penitently to his death, accompanied by the *hazan* from the Sydney synagogue. His body was saved from the common criminal grave and buried in the Jewish cemetery.

His brother, John, who had also been deported to Australia, served his sentence, joined the police, and at the time of Edward's execution was chief constable of Penrith. Because of the notoriety of the case he had to resign. He eventually founded a leading Tasmanian paper and became a member of the Tasmanian House of Assembly. John's son became Sir John George Davis, speaker of the Tasmanian House of Assembly.

DAYAN, MOSHE (1915–1981) Israeli soldier, diplomat, and politician. Born on a farm in Moshav Nahalal in the Jezreel Valley, he graduated from a teachers' seminar there and settled as a farmer in Nahalal. He joined the underground army, the Haganah, at an early age and rose in its ranks, In 1939 the British mandatory authorities jailed him in an Acre prison together with forty-two others for illegal possession of arms. As the German army approached Egypt, the British army decided to evict the Vichy regime from Syria and Lebanon. Dayan and his comrades were released and in June 1941, serving as a scout in southern Lebanon for the British troops, he was shot by a sniper and lost an eye. His eye patch became his symbol. Upon recovery and until 1948 he was on the permanent staff of the Haganah.

During Israel's War of Independence he won the appreciation of David Ben-Gurion (q.v.). Dayan commanded the eighty-ninth battalion, which captured Lod (Lydda) and Ramleh, and later fought in the Negev. In September 1948 he was appointed commander of Israeli forces in Jerusalem and for the next two years was involved in secret negotiations with King Abdullah of Jordan that yielded the Israel-Jordan armistice agreement and a draft of the Israel-Jordan nonaggression pact. His rise in the army was meteoric; in 1950–1951 he was commander of the southern command and in 1952–1953 chief of military operations.

In November 1953, he became Israel's fourth chief of staff and revitalized the army, overseeing a massive rearmament effort with French-made weapons. He raised the morale of the troops, creating special strike units and the paratroopers. He believed in a policy of retaliation against Arab incursions. At Ben-Gurion's orders, the army

Defense Minister Moshe Dayan (center), Commander in Chief Ytzhak Rabin (right), and Commander of the Central Area Forces Uzi Narkiss, enter the Old City of Jerusalem, June 7, 1967.

began to plan the Sinai campaign against Egypt, which Dayan led in October 1956. In a hundred hours Israel captured most of the Sinai peninsula and held it until March 1957, withdrawing in return for understandings with the United States on freedom of navigation and security.

Dayan retired from the army in 1958, studied briefly at the Hebrew University, and became active in the young generation circle of Mapai, the Israel Labor party. In 1959 he was elected to Israel's parliament, the Knesset, and remained a member until 1981. He joined Ben-Gurion's last cabinet as minister of agriculture serving until 1964. When RAFI, Ben-Gurion's breakaway party, was formed in 1965 he joined it. During those years he traveled extensively, including a well-publicized trip to Vietnam for an American newspaper. On the eve of the 1967 Six-Day War, the seemingly faltering leadership of Prime Minister and Defense Minister Levi Eshkol (q.v.) led to a growing public clamor to appoint Dayan defense minister. This was vehemently opposed by the Mapai veterans led by Golda Meir (q.v.), but they failed and on June 1, 1967, Dayan joined the newly formed government of national unity as defense minister. He did not make any major changes in the existing war plans, but provided leadership during the fighting and was seen as the hero of the war.

After the war, as minister of defense responsible for the territories occupied by Israel in the war, he instituted benevolent and liberal occupation policies with "open bridges" for trade and travel across the Jordan River and the economic integration of the territories with Israel. He was the major political figure in the government of Golda Meir (1969–1974), initiating ideas for a partial settlement with Egypt and the reopening of the Suez Canal. He was deeply involved in all the diplomatic moves at the time, mainly after the end of the War of Attrition (1968–1970).

In the summer of 1973 he warned that war with Egypt could be imminent, but did not insist on a full alert and frontline readiness. In the Yom Kippur War, he felt that Israel should withdraw to a line thirty kilometers from the Suez Canal. He was blamed for the initial unpreparedness at the time of the Egyptian-Syrian attack and at the end of the war there was a public demand for his resignation, although a commission of inquiry exonerated him (and the entire political echelon) from sins of omission on the eve of the war. However, his image was tarnished.

When Golda Meir resigned in April 1974, he was not included in the cabinet of Yitzhak Rabin. Dayan remained in the Knesset, wrote his memoirs, and traveled. In the 1977 elections Labor was defeated, and Dayan, although elected on the Labor ticket, accepted an invitation by Menachem Begin to leave the opposition and join his cabinet as foreign minister. In that capacity he played a key role in making the initial breakthrough to Egypt that led to the visit of Anwar Sadat to Jerusalem, the Camp David agreement, and the Israel-Egypt peace treaty signed in March 1979. His fertile and imaginatve mind was instrumental in overcoming many hurdles and he was a major architect of the peace treaty with Egypt. He resigned in October 1979 when he realized that Begin had little intention of implementing Palestinian autonomy as prescribed by the Camp David agreement. An attempt to establish his own party for the July 1981 elections proved a failure when only two members were elected. Dayan is remembered as a dashing, flamboyant, original, and highly controversial personality in modern Israel.

M. Dayan, *Story of My Life*, 1976.
Y. Dayan, *My Father, His Daughter*, 1985.
S. Tevet, *Moshe Dayan*, 1972.

DEBORAH (c. 12th cent. BCE) Judge and prophet in ancient Israel. She was the wife of Lappidoth, of whom nothing is known, and judged the people under a palmtree between Ramah and Bethel, north of Jerusalem. In her time, the Israelites were sorely oppressed by Jabin, the Canaanite king who ruled in Hazor. To lead their war of liberation, she selected Barak and ordered him to fight Jabin's general, Sisera. Barak refused to go to battle without her and the two gathered together a strong coalition of northern and central tribes at Mount Tabor. Sisera prepared to fight them with nine hundred iron chariots (Israel having none) and all his army. The time of battle was determined by Deborah, who promised her troops victory in the name of God. She ordered Barak to exploit the fortuitous flooding of the valley of the Kishon Brook, where Sisera's chariots sank in the mud and were disabled and his army was wiped out. Sisera himself fled the field of battle and took refuge in the tent of Jael, wife of Heber the Kenite, who killed him in his sleep. The victory marked the decline of the Canaanite kingdom and ushered in a forty-year period of tranquillity for Israel.

Two accounts are contained in the Bible of these events - one in prose (Jud. 4) and the other in verse ("The Song of Deborah," Jud. 5). The latter is one of the earliest examples of poetry in the Bible and is a triumphant song of victory written with intense personal emotion. It praises God, who brought "the stars in their courses" to combat Sisera, for the great victory. It applauds those tribes that participated in the battle and derides those who absented themselves. It also lavishes blessings on Jael and ends with a call for the destruction of all God's enemies.

Deborah played an unusually prominent role for a woman of the period. She was the only female biblical judge and was a charismatic figure.
R. G. Boling, *Judges* (Anchor Bible), 1975.

DE HAAN, ISRAEL See Haan, Israel de

DE LEON, DANIEL (1852–1914) U.S. socialist leader. De Leon was born in the Carribean island of Curaçao, which was first colonized by the Dutch and had a long-established Jewish community. His father, Salomon, was a surgeon with the Dutch colonial army and a prominent colonial government official. In appreciation for his heroic stance in both treating the sailors of a typhus-infested ship and protecting the population, Salomon was made a knight of the Order of Saint Danneborg by the Danish government. He died when Daniel De Leon was twelve years old, and was the first person to be buried in the new Jewish cemetery of Curaçao. De Leon was always reluctant to admit his Jewish origins in the midst of a widespread anti-Semitism among his opponents.

Having been brought up in Curaçao, where slavery was the main source of income until it was abolished in 1863 (when De Leon was eleven), De Leon, even as a child, was acutely aware of the social injustices surrounding him. It was said that when news came of the escape of one of their slaves, his family members reacted with shock at the slave's ingratitude, whereas Daniel demanded "But did anyone ever offer to give him his liberty?"

Upon the death of his father, De Leon went to Europe to continue his education. He received the degree of Bachelor of Philosophy from the University of Leyden and, upon going to the United States in 1872, had a distinguished career at the Columbia Law School; he was awarded a prize for constitutional law by the expresident of Yale and also obtained the prize for interntional law. He was lecturer at Columbia on Latin American diplomacy (1883–1889).

While still at Columbia, he was drawn to the labor movement. He joined the Knights of Labor in 1888 during a period of intense strikes and struggles in labor organization, and emerged as the strong leader the labor movement needed. His active involvement in the labor movement was not looked upon very favorably by the Columbia University administration. After not being appointed to a promised professorship, De Leon left Columbia and dedicated himself to the labor movement. In 1890, he became a member of the Socialist Labor party, upon which he had a dominating influence for the following two decades in his various capacities as nationwide public speaker and, especially, through his editorship of its newspaper, The *Weekly People* (later, *Daily People*). As editor of the journal from 1892 until his death, he stamped his personality on the party. He also ran for public office as socialist candidate on several occasions; in 1891 he ran for the governorship of New York State. He wanted to create a labor movement that would include unskilled workers and would constitute a political revolutionary force. To this end he founded, in 1895, the Socialist Trade and Labor Alliance as an alternative to the established unions. However, his inflexibility and doctrinaire Marxism brought him to loggerheads with many other leaders. In 1895, a group of leading Jewish socialists left the party in reaction to his policies and in 1899 Morris Hillquit (q.v.) and his colleagues withdrew in protest against his radicalism. De Leon has been blamed for his attempts to establish an authoritarian rule over his party through personal invective, the expulsion of opponents, and control of the press.

In 1905, he organized the Workers' International Industrial Union, to challenge the "capitalist" unions. When he and his followers were expelled in 1908 by extremists he organized the rival Workers' International Industrial Union, but it did not flourish.

De Leon was one of the chief advocates of socialism in the United States, seeking to put an end to the capitalist system, but his uncompromising positions served to fragment the movement. He wrote a considerable body of polemic literature.

S. Coleman, *Daniel De Leon*, 1990.
A. Peterson, *Daniel De Leon*, 2 vols. 1941–1953.
C. Reeve, *The Life and Times of Daniel De Leon*, 1972.

DE SILVA FRANCISCO MOLDANO See Silva, Francisco Moldano de

DEUTSCHER, ISAAC (1907–1967) Marxist historian and political scientist. He was brought up in Cracow, Poland, in an Orthodox Jewish household. He earned a name for himself as a child genius and was famed for his great knowledge of the Talmud. Against his own wishes, his father sent him to the Hasidic rabbi of Ger to study. He was ordained as a rabbi by virtue of his brilliant speech on the occasion of his bar mitzvah.

However, he had already begun to question some of the religious tenets of his forefathers. Of his bar mitzvah ceremony he recalled, "I was putting on an act and I was pleased with the theatrical side of my performance." His rebellion began one year later with a symbolic act of protest. Accompanied by a friend, he ate a ham sandwich with butter at the graveside of a rabbi on the Day of Atonement. He recalled, "I half hoped and half feared that something terrible would happen... but nothing did." At the meal marking the end of that day of repentence and fast, he felt remorse at having deceived his parents, but not at having deceived God.

His first poems, published in Polish literary periodicals when he was sixteen years old, still had strong Jewish ties. He left Cracow for Warsaw at age eighteen, making a gradual transition from poetry to literary criticism, philosophy, and finally Marxism and his ultimate rejection of Judaism.

In 1927 he joined the banned Polish Communist party, soon becoming the chief editor of the clandestine Communist press.

In 1932 he was expelled from the Communist party, ostensibly for "exaggerating the threat of Nazism and spreading panic in the Communist ranks." This was due to his having formed, upon his return from the Soviet Union, an anti-Stalinist splinter group within the Polish Communist party. His publication of an article entitled "The Danger of Barbarism over Europe" led to his expulsion.

He traveled to the Soviet Union in 1934, rejecting a number of academic positions that had been offered to him.

In 1939 Deutscher became the London correspondent for a Polish Jewish newspaper. When the war broke out he was forced to find a way of earning a living in England. He devoted himself to learning English with the same zeal he had applied as a child to his Talmudic studies. His first article in English appeared in *The Economist*; this marked the beginning of his career in English-language journalism. He joined the Polish army in Scotland in 1940, but during a large part of his service he was considered a "subversive element" due to his protests against anti-Semitism in the army.

In 1942 he became *The Economist*'s expert on Soviet affairs and its chief European correspondent. At the same time he wrote for *The Observer* under the pseudonym "Peregrine."

Deutscher's first book on Soviet affairs, *Stalin: A Political Biography* (1949), was widely translated. It was followed by a trilogy on Trotsky, (q.v.) *The Prophet Armed* (1954), *The Prophet Unarmed* (1959), and *The Prophet Outcast* (1963). Much of the material for his trilogy was gleaned from the closed section of Harvard University's Trotsky archives, which is to remain closed until the end of the twentieth century, and to which he obtained access by special permission of Trotsky's widow.

He called himself a "non-Jewish Jew," and his autobiography, published posthumously, bears that title.

He was opposed to any form of nationalism, viewing it as an historically retrogressive movement. His attitude toward Zionism was no different, although he conceded that "if, instead of arguing against Zionism in the 1920s and 1930s, I had urged European Jews to go to Palestine, I might have helped to save some of the lives that were later extinguished in Hitler's gas chambers."

Deutscher died in Rome before he was able to fulfill his ambition to write a biography of Lenin.

I. Deutscher, *The Non-Jewish Jew*, 1968.

DHU NUWAS, YUSUF (c. 490–525 CE) South Arabian king and proselyte; last ruler of independent Himyar (Sabea). Before ascending the throne in 517 CE, he was converted to Judaism by rabbinical emissaries from Tiberias (with whom he remained in contact), yet there is no mention of him in ancient Jewish sources. Christian works, however, notably the Syrian *Book of the Himyarites* and *History of the Nestorians*, give his name as Masruq. South Arabian inscriptions discovered in the early 1950s call him ·As'ar or Yath'ar; and in Arabic literature he was known as Dhu Nuwas. He presumably added Yusuf (Joseph) to his original name at the time of his conversion. The Himyarite kingdom, approximating in its boundaries to present-day Yemen, had an old, established Jewish community of merchants and farmers who dreaded the Byzantine Empire's expansion into Sabea. Their fear of Christian intolerance was matched by native Himyarite suspicion of the Christian minority, which did in fact serve as a fifth column anticipating the arrival of Ethiopian invaders from the opposite shore of the Red Sea.

It was probably in response to the Jewish king's enthronement that Christian rebels seized Zafar, the Himyarite capital, in 517. After mustering an army, Dhu Nuwas inflicted a costly defeat on the rebels, taking thousands of prisoners and destroying their church. When Ethiopian troops landed in the following year, Dhu Nuwas scored another major victory. Flushed with success, he now saw himself as the great champion of Arabian Jewry; and it has even been suggested that his ultimate purpose was the creation of a new Jewish empire stretching from Eretz Israel to Himyar, in the belief that an imminent war between Persia and Byzantium would make this plan feasible.

A renewed Christian revolt, in the northern Himyarite center of Najran (c. 523), led to many Jewish casualties. When the rebels spurned his peace terms, Dhu Nuwas swore vengeance, besieged the town, and executed several hundred of the vanquished traitors. His repressive measures, together with an inflated account of the slain, provoked a stormy reaction throughout eastern Christendom. With Byzantine supporet, a full-scale Ethiopian invasion of Himyar was launched in 525. This time, unfortunately, Dhui Nuwas could neither win foreign aid nor rely on all of his own troops, and had to take the field with a much smaller army. The decisive battle was fought near Zabid, close to the Red Sea, where the Himyarites were routed and their king almost certainly perished. An Arab tradition asserts, however, that Dhu Nuwas avoided such dishonor by riding his horse over a cliff and plunging to his death in the waves below. Legends woven around this heroic figure and his tragic end may have influenced later Jewish folklore about the Ten Lost Tribes.

H. Z. Hirschberg, *Yisra'el be-Arav* (Hebrew), pp. 76–111; 1946.

DIMANSTEIN, SIMON (1886–1937) Russian communist. Dimanstein was born in the Belorussian town of Vitebsk to a devoutly religious family. He studied in a Hasidic yeshiva (Talmudic academy) and received ordination from Rabbi Haim Ozer Grodzensky, a leading Talmudist of the day. At the same time he studied Russian and became active in the revolutionary movement. In 1904 he joined the Bolsheviks of Vilna, but was soon arrested for distributing propaganda to Jewish workers. He managed to escape, first to Minsk and then to Riga, but was arrested again in 1908 and sentenced to six years' hard labor in Siberia. He escaped again in 1913 and made his way to France, where he spent several years in exile.

Returning to Russia following the 1917 revolution, Dimanstein was appointed minister of labor in Lithuania. In 1918 he helped establish the Yevsektsiya, the Jewish wing of the Communist party and became commissar of Jewish affairs. He also edited its Yiddish journal, *Der Emes*, noted for its antireligious, anti-Zionist, and anti-Bundist stance.

During the civil war, Dimanstein, an expert on minority nationalities, held various positions in different provinces; he was labor commissar for Lithuania and headed the regional government in Belorussia. In Turkestan he was commissar of education, while in the Ukraine he headed the political education department. Although the positions were often nominally minor, in the turmoil sweeping the country at the time, Dimanstein's status was far greater than his titles suggested, and on several occasions he found himself the acting head of the region. Following Lenin's victory, he was appointed director of the Institute for National Minorities. Dimanstein believed that the situation of the Jews in Russia would improve following the revolution. He attempted to bring the message of communism to the Jewish masses by translating Lenin into Yiddish. Rabidly anti-Zionist, he supported a territorial solution for the Jewish problem and was a founder of Birobidzhan, the semiautonomous Jewish republic on the Sino-Russian border, seeing it as protection against outside intervention in Soviet affairs in the Far East.

As an expert on minority issues, Dimanstein cooperated closely with Stalin in the early days of the revolution, even serving as his assistant. Following Stalin's rise to power, however, his influence decreased. He dropped from sight during the great purge of 1936 and is believed to have been executed in 1937.

DISRAELI, BENJAMIN, EARL OF BEACONS-FIELD

(1804–1881) British statesman and novelist. Born in London, he traced his origins to a family of Jews expelled from Spain in the 15th century which found asylum in the Venetian republic. His grandfather, Benjamin, settled in England in 1748 and traded in corals. His father Isaac, who wrote books on the history of literature, was a skeptic who loathed Jewish ritual. His mother, Maria Besevi, came from an Ashkenazic family that immigrated to England from Verona, Italy, in 1762. Benjamin's father objected to his son's attending classes in Christian religion at school, and employed a Hebrew teacher to instruct Benjamin during these classes. However, after quarreling with the Bevis Marks Synagogue, he had his son baptized at the age of thirteen. Benjamin hated sports, but took secret boxing lessons to defend himself against bullies who harassed him, calling him a Jew and a foreigner. As a youth he was already very handsome, and his grandiloquent manner of speaking was exaggerated by an ostentatious taste in clothes — velvet jackets, outsize cravats, frills and ruffs, gaudy trousers, and colored stockings.

Disraeli's formal schooling ended at age seventeen, when he was employed in a solicitor's office. He speculated unsuccessfully in South American mining shares and got deeply into debt. He began to write satirical novels on English political society that met with a certain amount of success. The first, *Vivian Grey* (1826), was published anonymously, but after a bout of bad health he decided to go on tour and in 1830 set out on a sixteen-month tour of the Mediterranean. His eccentric behavior and dandified appearance created a sensation wherever he appeared. In Malta he wore an Andalusian costume and left the island dressed as a Greek pirate, complete with red shirt and immense silver buttons, sky-blue trousers, red cap, and slippers, with pistols and daggers in his sash. In Turkey he wore green embroidered pantaloons with a fringed shawl around his waist.

This tour helped determine Disraeli's attitude toward Syria, Cyprus and Palestine. He spent a week in Jerusalem, a visit which spurred his concept of the renaissance of Palestine by the Jewish people, expressed in his novel *The Wondrous Tale of David Alroy* (1833), based on the exploits of a medieval Jewish hero. *Contarini Fleming* (1832) contains many autobiographical references and discusses the difference between the northern (Scandinavian) and southern (Italian) temperaments.

Disraeli was attracted to politics, but his early attempts to be elected as an independent radical and later as a Tory failed. His political manifestos written during this period, *A Vindication of the English Constitution* (1835) (an outline of his political credo) and *The Letters of Runnymede* (1836) (a bitter attack on the Whig leadership), were well received. In 1837 he was elected to Parliament as Conservative member for Maidstone in Kent, and his maiden speech was met with hooting and laughter at his appearance — his hair set in black ringlets and wearing a bottle-green coat and white waistcoat hung with gold chains. In desperation he exclaimed, "Though I sit down now, the time will come when you *will* hear me!"

In 1838 he married Mary Anne, widow of his fellow member of parliament, Wyndham Lewis, whose affluence relieved his financial problems. During his period as a backbencher Disraeli continued writing, and his novels were treatises on political and religious matters in literary form. These included *Coningsby, or The Younger Generation* (1844), a best-seller, which in addition to presenting the views of the "Young England" parliamentary group he had formed in 1841, served as a platform for his views on racism and a description of the situation of the Jews. *Sybil, or The Two Nations* (1845), based on an investigation of working-class conditions in the north, described the chasm between rich and poor and denounced the horrors of the factory system. The last of the trilogy was *Tancred, or The New Crusade* (1847), the story of a young English aristocrat who travels to Jerusalem to seek spiritual guidance and inspi-

A collection from Punch *of caricatures of Benjamin Disraeli ranging over a period of forty years. In inset is a photograph of the earl of Beaconsfield in 1872 when he became prime minister.*

ration as an antidote to European materialism. In his biography of Lord George Bentinck (1852), Disraeli explained his theory of the superiority of the Semitic race and the spirituality of the Jew which was embodied in the Church.

In 1850, Disraeli — widely known as "Dizzy" — became the leader of the Conservative opposition, but in 1852 he was appointed chancellor of the exchequer in Lord Derby's government, a position he held again in 1858 and in 1865. It was during the latter period of office that Disraeli succeeded in having a Reform Bill passed by the House of Commons enfranchising borough householders and thus doubling the electorate. In 1868 he replaced Lord Derby as prime minister, only to have his short-lived government brought down by W. E. Gladstone.

Plagued by gout and asthma, Disraeli became increasingly gloomy and introspective, obsessed with religion — all expressed in his novel *Lothair*, a satire on English society and the Catholic Church.

Disraeli developed a close relationship with Queen Victoria, becoming her confidant and counselor. She showered him with gifts and had her own doctor tend his ailments. When between 1874 and 1880, he once again headed a Conservative government, the queen strongly supported him. He proudly presented her with the controlling shares in the Suez Canal Company, which he had purchased with finance provided by the Rothschilds (q.v.). This was followed by the passage in parliament of a bill conferring upon Victoria the title of Empress of India. Disraeli was awarded the title of Earl of Beaconsfield as a reward for his services.

In the course of his premiership, important social legislation was passed in parliament under Disraeli's direction. These included acts providing for slum clearance, improvement in public health, and improvement of working conditions in factories. In foreign policy, too, he succeeded in opening the route to India and obtaining a foothold in Egypt. From 1876 to 1878 his premiership was dominated by the Eastern Question — Russian oppression against Turkey and its attempts to reach the Mediterranean. At the Congress of Berlin, Disraeli supported the Turks against the Russians, and he signed a secret defense agreement with Turkey, under which Cyprus was ceded to Britain.

In 1880 Disraeli was forced to resign because of riots and bloodshed in the colonies, as well as agricultural distress and industrial depression. In poor health, he succeeded in completing his last novel, *Endymion*, in which he surveyed his early career.

Disraeli constituted a foreign element in British political life; his political ambitions were viewed with suspicion and he was incessantly attacked as being a "clandestine Jew." Yet he had little real knowledge of the Jewish people, often making unfounded statements. He fought for equal rights for Jews everywhere, and believed in the return of the Jews to Palestine.

THE WIT AND WISDOM OF DISRAELI

- Every man has the right to be conceited until he is successful.
- As a general rule, nobody has money who ought to have it.
- Next to knowing when to seize an opportunity, the next important thing in life is to know when to forgo an advantage.
- No government can be long secure without a formidable opposition.
- Youth is a blunder; manhood a struggle; old age a regret.
- [Gladstone] is a sophistical rhetorician inebriated with the exuberance of his own verbosity.
- Read no history — only biography, for that is life without theory.
- When a man falls into his anecdotage, it is a sign for him to retire from the world.
- The Privileged and the People form Two Nations.
- There should be moderation even in excess.
- Nature has given us two ears but only one mouth.
- An agreeable person is a person who agrees with me.

When the Irish leader, Daniel O'Connell, referred disparagingly in Parliament to Disraeli's Jewish ancestry, Disraeli retorted, "Yes, I am a Jew. And when the ancestors of the right honorable gentleman were living as savages in an unknown island, mine were priests in the Temple of Solomon."

More books and research works have been published on Disraeli in England, the United States, and Europe than on any other British political figure in the 19th century.

R. Blake, *Disraeli*, 1967.
P. Bloomfeld, *Disraeli*, 1961.
R. W. Davis, *Disraeli*, 1976.

DOV BER OF MEZHIRICH (c. 1704–1772) Hasidic leader, who succeeded the Baal Shem Tov (q.v.). He was born in the village of Lukach in Volhynia. His father was too poor to provide for his son's education, but the local rabbi was impressed with the boy's gifts and took him into his academy. The boy's learning was so great that he soon outgrew the local academy and was sent to the yeshiva at Lvov, where he studied for a number of years. Dov Ber became a teacher in a small village and, influenced by the surroundings of nature, immersed himself in mystical studies. He also began a program of self-mortification, sometimes fasting for several days. He took up the life of an itinerant preacher (*maggid* in Hebrew), and was noted for his oratory and imaginative use of parables. Dov Ber came to be known as Ha-Maggid (i.e., *the* preacher, par excellence).

His penances and fastings affected his health and seeking a cure, he was advised to turn to the charismatic Baal Shem Tov who had a reputation for working wonders. On hearing Dov Ber expound a kabbalistic passage, Baal Shem Tov told him, "Your interpretations are accurate — but they lack soul." Dov Ber remained as a devoted disciple and he claimed that the Baal Shem Tov, "revealed to me the language of the birds and the trees, the secrets of the saints and of holy incantations; he showed me the writing of angels and explained the significance of the letters of the alphabet." Before long it was obvious that he would be the successor of the Baal Shem Tov whose life was coming to an end. After his death, Dov Ber was accepted as the leader of Hasidism which he organized into a movement. Because he did not want to remain in the Baal Shem Tov's town of Medzibozh and made his home and center in the village of Mezhirich.

Unlike the Baal Shem Tov and his own earlier practice, he no longer wandered, sending out traveling teachers who imparted Hasidic teachings. Many disciples gathered around Dov Ber; reportedly he had over three-hundred close followers but only thirty-nine are known by name. Some of them became great Hasidic masters in their own right. Many left their homes to spend all their time with the great preacher. Thousands flocked to Mezhirich to listen to his expositions; in view of his continuing poor health, he received his followers only on the Sabbath and during the rest of the week remained secluded with his disciples.

In his later years, some of his teachings proved controversial. There were those who detected elements of pantheism while others criticized his neglect of traditional rabbinic scholarship and his adoption of a Sephardi version of the prayers.

Dov Ber himself left no writings, but his doctrines were gathered and committed to writing by his disciples. He was famous for his table teachings, infused with mystical doctrines. In particular he emphasized the attainment of ecstatic joy and the transcendence of everyday concerns by cleaving to the Divine. God fills all space and man is called on to penetrate the material cloak to find the underlying spiritual content. The highest degree of spiritual perfection can only be attained by the *tzaddik*, the righteous Hasidic leader who mediates between man and God.

Dov Ber's talents as thinker, teacher, and organizer were responsible for the establishment of Hasidism as a movement. After his death, it branched out in various directions and only the Baal Shem Tov and Dov Ber in their lifetimes enjoyed complete authority over the movement as a whole.

J. G. Weiss, *The Great Maggid's Theory of Contemplative Magic*, 1960.

DREYFUS, ALFRED (1859–1935) French army officer accused of treason in the Dreyfus affair, which divided France and aroused deep feeling throughout the world, pitting nationalists and anti-Semites against liberals and intellectuals. His father was a wealthy, assimilated manufacturer from Mulhouse, Alsace, who moved to Paris out of French patriotism when Alsace came under German rule as a result of the Franco-Prussian War. Alfred Dreyfus studied at the Ecole Polytechnique and entered the army as an engineer with the rank of lieutenant. He overcame anti-Semitic pressures to be appointed a captain on the general staff, and was its only Jewish member. A quiet and loyal soldier, devoted to his family and remote from anything Jewish, he was amazed by the tragedy that overwhelmed him.

In 1894, a French intelligence agent discovered a suspicious paper in the wastebasket of the German military attaché. It contained an undertaking, written in French, to deliver a secret French artillery manual to the Germans. The experts could not identify the handwriting but one of the intelligence heads, Major Hubert Joseph Henry, persuaded his superiors that Dreyfus, a Jewish "outsider" in the military establishment, was the most likely culprit. He was thrown into solitary confinement and accused of treason before a military court-martial. Henry told the tribunal that he had secret information inculpating the accused that he could not divulge. The court-martial at first found it difficult to reach a verdict but by this time a public clamor, headed by the Catholic, royalist, and anti-Semitic press, and proclaiming an international Jewish conspiracy, demanded a conviction. Accordingly the court found Dreyfus guilty and sentenced him to expulsion from the army and life imprisonment in exile. At the beginning of 1895 he was degraded at a public ceremony, surrounded by a vast mob shouting anti-Jewish slogans, at which his sword was broken in two by his superior officer. Dreyfus continued to affirm his innocence. He was transported in chains to a prison on Devil's Island, off the coast of Guyana, South America.

His family and many liberals in France con-

Saying of Dov Ber of Mezhirch

Learn the ten principles of service from a little child and a thief.

From the child, learn: To be merry for no particular reason; never to be idle; and when you need something, demand it vigorously.

The thief can show you seven things: Do your service by night; what you do not finish one night, conclude the next; love those who work with you; risk your life for slight gains; what you take should be so worthless that you are willing to surrender it for a pittance; do not be put off by blows and hardships; enjoy your occupation to the extent that you would not change it for another.

tinued to claim that he had been framed and received unexpected confirmation in 1896, when the same French intelligence agent discovered a fresh piece of paper promising the delivery of military secrets to Germany in the same handwriting as before. This was traced to another officer, Count Ferdinand Esterhazy. When Henry was informed of this, he responded that the army could not admit a mistake without impugning its reputation. Lieutenant Colonel Georges Picquart, head of intelligence, was on the verge of making further investigations when, in order to forestall the findings, Henry forged a letter from the Italian attaché to prove Dreyfus's guilt. Picquart was transferred to Africa but before leaving, told the story to his attorney, who passed it on to the vice-president of the Senate, Auguste Scheurer-Kestner, who publicly accused Esterhazy and proclaimed Dreyfus's innocence. He began a campaign for a retrial at the same time that Dreyfus's brother obtained a copy of the original document and passed it to an expert who identified the handwriting as that of Esterhazy. The army had to bring Esterhazy to trial by court-martial, where the proof was bolstered by evidence of his lavish way of life which left him in constant need of money, and by a diary entry which noted his hatred of France. The general staff and the government, however, would not admit any miscarriage of justice and Esterhazy was acquitted while Picquart was thrown into prison.

The Dreyfus affair had by now rent French society into two. Two days after Esterhazy's acquittal the famous novelist Emile Zola published an open letter entitled "J'Accuse" ("I Accuse") in the newspaper *L'Aurore*. Two hundred thousand copies of the issue were sold and a wide public read Zola's attack on the general staff. Zola himself was

Captain Alfred Dreyfus sentenced to life imprisonment at a closed trial in Paris, 1894.

brought to trial on a charge of libel, found guilty, and had to flee to England.

The uproar in French society reached a climax in the summer of 1898 forcing the new war minister to reopen the case. The dossier was reexamined and immediately it was apparent that the charges were based on forgery. Henry was jailed, and the same night, committed suicide. Although even then a sizable segment of French public opinion refused to accept the turn of events (and even established a Henry memorial fund), the court of appeal had to order a new trial which was held in an atmosphere of countrywide tension. All this time, Dreyfus was unaware of the furor that had been raging. Now he was brought back to France for the second trial. During this trial the anti-Semitic outbursts of the royalist press did not abate, but the evidence presented described Henry's and Esterhazy's guilt. Nevertheless, the verdict was again "guilty," but because of "extenuating circumstances" the sentence was reduced to ten years imprisonment. The new president of France, Emile Loubet, a liberal who was scandalized by the verdict, granted Dreyfus a pardon a few days later.

It took another seven years before Dreyfus was finally exonerated by the court of appeal. By that time, a Radical government was in power which, alarmed by the part played by the Catholic church in helping to direct the anti-Dreyfus campaign, had legislated the separation of church and state, the most dramatic consequence of the affair.

Following his exoneration, Dreyfus himself was reinstated in the army with the rank of major. He retired a year later but rejoined the army in World War I, was promoted to lieutenant colonel in 1916, and was awarded the Legion of Honor. After the war he lived in Paris in retirement until his death.
J. D. Bredin, *The Affair: The Case of Alfred Dreyfus*, 1986.
N. Halasz, *Captain Dreyfus: The Story of a Mass Hysteria*, 1957.
B. Schechter, *The Dreyfus Affair: A National Scandal*, 1965.

DREYFUSS, BARNEY (1865–1932) U.S. baseball executive, creator of the modern World Series. Born in Freiburg, Germany, he emigrated to the United States in 1881 and settled in Paducah, Kentucky. He worked in a whiskey distillery and joined the local baseball club.

His interest in baseball heightened in 1888 when he and the distillery moved to Louisville, Kentucky. He became a stockholder in the Louisville Colonels of the National League and by 1899 was the club's president.

With the close of the 1899 season Dreyfuss was out of a job. The National League announced that four of its twelve teams would be eliminated, one of them being Louisville. Determined to remain in major-league baseball, Dreyfuss quickly acquired an interest in the Pittsburgh Pirates. His new club was placed second in the 1900 championship race. The following year Dreyfuss took over as president and the Pirates won three consecutive pennants.

In 1903 Dreyfuss proposed to the owner of the American League's leading Boston team that the clubs meet in a best-of-nine series in the fall. The two shook hands on it. The meeting had taken place despite a simmering feud between the owners of the established National League, and their three-year-old rival, the American League. The teams played and Boston won, five games to three. This interleague contest evolved into the modern World Series.

An oddity of the first series was that the losers earned more money than the winners. Boston players received 75 percent of the proceeds, the rest going to the team owner, while Dreyfuss turned over all of the Pirates' share of the proceeds to his players.

In 1909 Dreyfuss built Forbes Field, a modern stadium, and the team responded by winning its first World Series. For a club with limited resources, Pittsburgh enjoyed an outstanding record of success during the Dreyfuss era. Between 1900 and 1931 the Pirates won two World Series (1909, 1925) and six pennants, and were out of the first division only six times.

Off the playing field Pittsburgh was a one-man operation. Dreyfuss did everything. He was an outstanding appraiser of baseball talent and was constantly on the lookout for good young players. Many of those he discovered are in the Baseball Hall of Fame.

He helped establish the office of the commissioner of baseball, and was a long-time member of the schedule committee. In 1929 he became the National League's first vice-president.

DUBINSKY, DAVID (1892–1982) U.S. labor leader. Born in Brest-Litovsk, then Russia, Dubinsky grew up in Lodz, a predominantly industrial, slum-ridden city in Poland, where he became acutely aware of the exploitation of works in the industrial community. His father was the owner of a small basement bakery. David attended school for three full terms (considered fortunate in his poverty-ridden Jewish neighborhood) until the age of eleven when, like his eight elder brothers before him, David began to work as a baker. He learned the trade so quickly that within three years he was considered a master baker.

The Lodz bakers' conditions were difficult. Thus, when the possibility of having a bakers' union within the newly created General Jewish Workers' Union began to spread among Jewish laboring masses, the young Dubinsky quickly embraced the idea. He not only joined the bakers' union but also became its secretary since he was one of the few bakers who could read and write both Polish and Yiddish. Following their first strike when bakers' wages were increased, the organizers of the union, including Dubinsky, were arrested. This event marked the beginning of a long career of political involvement.

In 1911, after having been in and out of several Polish and Russian political jails, Dubinsky — a nineteen-year-old escapee from banishment to Siberia — arrived in New York. After only ten weeks in the United States, he became involved in the public outcry that followed the Triangle Shirtwaist Company fire. He began working as a cloak cutter, a craft of substantial skill rated highly in the Jewish working community and one of the best paid of all garment crafts. Six months after arriving in New York, Dubinsky received a membership card in the Cutters' Union of the International Ladies Garment Workers Union. He soon overcame the language barrier and rose very rapidly to a position of leadership within the ILGWU; in a period of a few years he went from union member to being a member of Local 10's executive board to being elected to the ILGWU's general executive board. In 1932, Dubinsky reluctantly accepted the presidency of the union, which was much divided internally in the midst of a national economic crisis, facing bankruptcy along with an increasing loss of power among the garment workers.

The new president and four other executives pledged all their personal assets as security for a loan to commence the union's first organizing drive during President Franklin D. Roosevelt's New Deal. By the time Dubinsky left his position as president in 1966, the ILGWU had not merely overcome its financial difficulties but had become a flourishing welfare organization that was to set the pattern for labor in general. The ILGWU was a pioneer in pensions, welfare, and paid vacations, among other workers' benefits. Its membership having grown twentyfold, the ILGWU became a stabilizing force in a very volatile industry. In addition to his accomplishments with the ILGWU, Dubinsky also played an important role in unifying the American Federation of Labor and the Congress of International Organizations in 1955. His fight against corruption among union leaders helped to precipitate the antiracket code accepted by the AFL-CIO in 1957.

M. D. Danish, *The World of David Dubinsky*, 1957. D. Dubinsky and A. H. Raskin, *David Dubinsky: A Life With Labor*, 1977.

DUBNOW, SIMON (1860–1941) Jewish historian and political ideologist. Born in Belorussia, Dubnow received a traditional Jewish education. By the age of eleven he became disillusioned with religion, and travelled to Dvinsk, Vilna, and Saint Petersburg to seek secular knowledge. Having obtained a resident's permit by bribing a clerk and enlisting as a laborer, Dubnow was free to study at the Imperial Public Library in Saint Petersburg, where he prepared for university. His attempts to enter Saint Petersburg University ended with his failure to pass the mathematics and writing exams.

Dubnow's life work was the study of Jewish history and its sociological interpretations. In his *Introduction to Jewish Philosophy* he advanced the thesis that Jewish history is a pattern of autonomous centers of Jewish national creation and hegemony. At all times one community has been more independent and creative than the others and this center has exercised a hegemony over the others, as in the case of Babylonia in the early Middle Ages. Jewish nationality is the highest type of cultural-historical or spiritual nation. The teachings of Judaism approximate the culture of humanity.

In 1890, Dubnow moved to Odessa, then the great center of Jewish literature. There he began to gather materials for his studies. From 1898 he wrote a series of works on Jewish history, believing that through the study of history, he could find a solution to the future of the Jewish people. He rebelled against Jewish historiography based primarily on martyrdom and literature, and pioneered in introducing the social sciences into the study of Jewish history. He considered the Jews a European people, whose homeland is the entire world. Accordingly he rejected Zionism, which he called a pseudo-messianic venture, and advocated in its stead, his own plan of Diaspora nationalism which he named autonomism.

Related to these beliefs was his attitude to religion, which he considered a necessary discipline, imposed upon the nation when it stood alienated from the other cultures of the world (Christianity and Islam). In the age of emancipation, however, he believed that religion was no longer necessary. His *History of Hasidism* praised East European Jewry for its preservation of tradition, but warned that the Jews should cooperate with the other nations of the world by adopting a secular culture.

In 1903 Dubnow moved to Vilna and in 1906, to Saint Petersburg, to occupy a chair for Jewish history in a progressive university. The first volume of his great ten-volume history of the Jews appeared in 1910. In 1922 he left Russia for Berlin.

With the rise of Hitler in 1933, Dubnow was offered refuge by friends in Switzerland, America, and Israel. The first he disliked, the second was too far for him and his wife (both in their seventies), and Israel he refused, saying that he saw a danger to Judaism in the emptying of the Diaspora. He settled in Riga. After Riga's capture by the Germans, his work was confiscated, and he could only continue writing by engraving upon copper containers. In 1941 the eighty-one-year-old Dubnow was rounded up by the Nazis with the other Jews of Riga. Sick and feverish, he did not move quickly enough and a drunken Latvian guard shot him on the spot. He was buried in a mass grave in the Riga Jewish cemetery. It was related that his last words were "Brothers, don't forget! Recount what you hear and see — record it all."

S. Dubnow, *Nationalism and History*, 1961.
A. S. Steinberg, *Simon Dubnow: The Man and His Work*, 1963.

DURKHEIM, EMILE (1858–1917) French social scientist credited with founding modern sociology. Durkheim's most important work includes the

Emile Durkheim

development of a framework for sociological method in *Les règles de la méthod sociologique* ("The Rules of Sociological Method," 1895). He also published works on social phenomena, such as *De la division du travail social* ("The Division of Labor in Society," 1903) and *Le suicide* ("Suicide," 1897). Another major contribution was in the improvement of education in France, as exemplified in the posthumously published series of lectures, *L'évolution pédagogique en France* ("Pedagogical evolution in France," 1938). He worked tirelessly in an effort to establish sociology as a positive social science that would promote solidarity among people and help them to realize a unified purpose as a part of society.

He was born in Epinal, France, to an Orthodox family. It was assumed that Durkheim would become a rabbi in the tradition of his family. However, as a youth he turned away from Judaism and became an agnostic. He entered the Ecole Normale Supérieure in 1879 and began studying toward a teacher's degree in philosophy. Always a serious student, Durkheim was critical of most of his teachers at the Ecole. He complained that they were shallow, due to their concern with "surface polish" and rhetoric in their students' work, rather than with substantive research and scientific progress.

Years later, when Durkheim taught the first university-sanctioned sociology course, he said in his first lecture: "We live in a country that recognizes no master other than [public] opinion. That this master may not become an unintelligent despot, it is necessary for us to enlighten it; and how, if not by science?"

Durkheim became a teacher of philosophy in 1882. For the next five years he worked in several provincial high schools near Paris, taking a leave of absence in the academic year of 1885–1886 to study the state of social science in France and Germany. His research in Germany yielded two surveys detailing the state of philosophy and the science of ethics in that country, winning him a reputation as a serious thinker.

In 1887 Durkheim was offered a position as lecturer (and later professor, holding the first chair in social science in Europe) at the University of Bordeaux in sociology and education. He began to organize *L'Année Sociologique* and published the first 563-page volume in 1898. The *Année* represented the current research and theory in sociology and the related social sciences.

Durkheim was called to the Sorbonne in 1902 to teach sociology and education, and he remained there for the rest of his life. In addition to teaching, he pursued research in the science of moral phenomena and religion in search of a secular, scientific, rational basis for a system of ethics. The last major work published in his lifetime was *Formes élémentaires de la vie religieuse* ("The Elementary Forms of Religious Life," 1915).

Durkheim maintained that sociology was a system or method for investigating social phenomena, and that sociologists could benefit from the information gathered by the related social sciences: history, geography, or psychology, for example. He believed that successful sociological research depended on team work in which all members of the team were committed to objectivity in their research, and could therefore keep subjective influences in check.

Upon the outbreak of World War I, Durkheim felt a duty to volunteer his services as a sociologist to his country, and became secretary of the Committee for the Publication of Studies and Documents on the War. His only son was killed in the war in 1916. Durkheim's grief may have hastened his own death a year later.

S. Fenton, *Durkheim and Modern Sociology*, 1984.
A. Giddens, *Emile Durkheim*, 1979.

DUVEEN, JOSEPH (1869–1939) Art dealer, created Lord Duveen of Millbank. Born in Hull, he inherited his love for art from various members of his family, among them his father, who sold delft, furniture and objects of art. From childhood Joseph, the eldest of a family of eight boys and four girls, helped in his parent's store but he soon decided that dealing in paintings and sculptures would be more lucrative than selling porcelains, furniture, tapestries, and silver. He began to learn about the field by courting experts, the first of whom was Wilhelm von Bode, director of the Kaiser Friedrich Museum in Berlin, and later the American Jewish expert on Italian painting, Bernard Berenson (q.v.). Under Bode's guidance Duveen began investing in art and in 1901 paid over fourteen thousand pounds sterling for a paint-

ing, the highest price ever paid until then for a picture sold at a British auction. He followed a policy of buying full collections rather than individual pictures and sculptures, thus enabling him to fix the price of individual items for resale. He acquired the Rodolphe Kann Collection in Paris for five million dollars and another Paris collection for three million dollars. Duveen now possessed the greatest number of works of art any art dealer ever owned, and he sailed for New York.

Once settled in the United States, Duveen set himself a twofold mission: to teach millionaire American collectors to appreciate the great works of art and to teach them that they could get those works of art only through him. To this end he preached his dictum, "When you pay high for the priceless, you're getting it cheap."

During his five decades of selling in the United States, he transformed American taste in art. He not only educated the small group of collectors who were his clients, but encouraged the public to visit the museums to which he brought the finest works of the world's masters of painting.

In the course of time, Duveen established galleries in New York, Paris, and London and divided his time among them. In New York, at the corner of Fifth Avenue and Fifty-sixth Street, he built a five-story, thirty-room reproduction of the Ministry of Marine building in Paris, which served as his gallery in America. His accommodations at other points of his annual itinerary was always transformed into a small-scale art gallery, and employing his infallible taste for decoration, he arranged the paintings, sculptures, and objets d'art he brought with him so that his clients and friends could visit him in the proper setting, and possibly take home some of the items. He kept his current favorite picture beside him on an easel whenever he dined in his suite and took it to his bedroom when he retired.

Among the numerous personalities Duveen introduced to the world of art was Ramsay Macdonald, who, when he became prime minister of England in 1929, appointed Duveen to the board of the National Gallery in London. The appointment was revoked in 1937 by Neville Chamberlain, who claimed that a person who sold art should not be party to the purchase of art on behalf of the public.

Joseph Duveen was knighted in 1919, made a baronet in 1927, and elevated to the peerage in 1933, taking his title from the district of Millbank in London where the Tate Gallery is situated. During the last years of his life, painfully suffering from cancer, he devoted his energies to persuading the renowned American art collector and later secretary of the treasury, Andrew Mellon, to endow the National Gallery of Art in Washington.

Duveen Pictures in Public Collections of America, A Catalogue Raisonné with Three Hundred Illustrations of Paintings by the Great Masters, Which Passed through the House of Duveen, 1941.
S. N. Behrman, *Duveen*, 1972.

E

EHRENBURG, ILYA GRIGORYEVICH (1891–1967) Russian author and journalist; one of the most noted and influential Jewish figures in Soviet literature. Although his home background in Kiev was wealthy and assimilated, Ehrenburg became a teenage revolutionary, flirted briefly with communism (1905–1909), and waged an unrelenting lifelong battle against Russian anti-Semitism. He spent many years in voluntary exile in France (1908–1917, 1921–1936, 1939–1940), then became the Soviet Union's leading anti-Nazi propagandist and, after obediently toeing the Stalinist cold war line, reemerged at last as the champion of intellectual freedom. These well-timed reversals helped Ehrenburg survive when many others in the USSR perished, but they tarnished his reputation.

A prolific and much translated writer, Ehrenburg also gained renown as a war correspondent on the western front (1915–1917), during the Spanish Civil War (for *Izvestia*), and after Hitler's invasion of Russia in June 1941 (for *Pravda* and *Red Star*). His diatribes against the "fascists" had not endeared him to some politicians in the West, but they condemned him to silence while the Russo-German pact remained in force. With Stalin and the Kremlin hierarchy dumbfounded by the "treacherous" Nazi attack, it was the voice of Ilya Ehrenburg that aroused sympathy for beleaguered Russia in distant lands and galvanized the will to fight back among soldiers and civilians alike in an initially tottering USSR. Almost until the end of the Great Patriotic War, when Stalin began to play down the anti-German line, Ehrenburg's published evidence of Nazi atrocities and his daily calls for retribution made him a folk hero to millions as the Red Army rolled from the Ukraine to Berlin.

In his first novel, *The Extraordinary Adventures of Julio Jurenito* (1922), Ehrenburg lampooned western civilization in a witty manner reminiscent of Voltaire and Anatole France. *The Stormy Life of Lazik Roytshvants* (1929), with its tale of a Jewish *luftmensch* wh is pursued by injustice and racial discrimination from the civil war down to his miserable end in Palestine, could obviously appear only outside the USSR. Though inferior to earlier works of reportage, *The Fall of Paris* won the Stalin Prize for its author in 1942, a year before he

received the highest Soviet decoration, the Order of Lenin. Some guarded criticism of the war effort in 1941 as well as a dutiful attack on "western imperialism," characterize *The Storm* (1948), which also included a full account of the mass murder of Jews at Babi Yar outside Ehrenburg's native Kiev during the Nazi occupation.

Portrait of Ilya Ehrenburg by Picasso.

On the eve of World War II, Ehrenburg had managed to avoid the fate of his "dearest and most loyal friend," Isaac Babel (q.v.), and other Jewish intellectuals who vanished in Stalin's purges. After the war, he seemed to bear a charmed life — obligingly conducting anti-Western propaganda, warning Soviet Jews (in a notorious *Pravda* article of September 21, 1948) that they must have no ties with the State of Israel, and deliberately covering up Stalin's vicious anti-cosmopolitan (i.e., anti-Jewish) campaign in 1952–1953, an ominous build-up to the so-called doctors' plot. Throughout those last years of the Soviet dictator's terror, Ehrenburg remained out of reach while his old comrades of the wartime Jewish Anti-Fascist Committee, headed by Solomon Mikhoels (q.v.), were arrested and liquidated. In one case only, when danger threatened, was it necessary to invoke Stalin's personal intervention.

From the Khrushchev era onward, Ilya Ehrenburg tried to explain and justify his postwar subservience to authority. He now emerged as the great advocate of liberalization, championing dissident writers, portraying the atmosphere after Stalin's death in *The Thaw* (1954), and completing a volume of memoirs entitled *People, Years, Life* (1961), which ran to six volumes in English (London, 1961–1966). Uniquely important as a document of modern Soviet cultural history, this work again set him at odds with the all-powerful establishment under Leonid Brezhnev. Yet the only Jewish issue that continued to preoccupy Ehrenburg was the negative blight of anti-Semitism. Ironically, *The Black Book* of Nazi crimes against Soviet Jewry, compiled with Vasili Grossman in 1943–1944 but later suppressed when Stalin launched his anticosmopolitan witch-hunt, appeared in Israel years after Ehrenburg's own death, as *Chornaya Kniga* (Jerusalem, 1980).

Anatol Goldberg, *Ilya Ehrenburg: Writing, Politics, and the Art of Survival*, with an introduction, postscript and additional material by Erik de Mauny, 1984.

EHRLICH, PAUL (1845–1915) German medical scientist and Nobel Prize winner. He was born in Strehlen (then Germany, now Strzelin, Poland) to an affluent family. After studying in various German universities, he graduated in 1878 and became an assistant at Berlin University. His entire career was characterized by a fight for the promotion of medical science, coupled with a deep rooted optimism, always aimed at perfection and evermore difficult targets, and an unshakable faith in progress.

In his early scientific career, Ehrlich specialized in the histological structure of cells and in hematology. He developed staining methods for bacteria and methods for staining dead, and later live, cell specimens, including the bacterium that caused tuberculosis. He also discovered the diazo reaction for identifying aromatic compounds in the urine of typhoid fever sufferers. His paper "The Requirement of the Organism for Oxygen" determined that the consumption of oxygen varied according to the type of tissue and these variations affected cell processes. His main interest was in the field of immunology, concentrating on different methods of immunization, setting standards for therapeutic sera and their long-term preservation.

During his researches, he worked with Robert Koch on the cause of tuberculosis. While researching the tubercle bacillus, he contracted the disease and went to Egypt for two years, where he was cured. On his return to Berlin in 1889, he was appointed a professor. The following year he

Paul Ehrlich (center) with a group of scientists at his institute in Frankfurt.

helped in developing the first diphtheria antitoxin in cooperation with Emil von Behring, who had created the antitoxin; only by utilizing Ehrlich's technique of using the blood of live horses, however, did the serum reach its maximum effectiveness.

In 1896, Ehrlich became director of the Royal Institute for Serum Research in Berlin, which three years later was transferred to Frankfurt-am-Main as the Royal Prussian Institute for Experimental Therapy (later amalgamated with the George Speier Institute for Chemotherapeutic Research). In 1904 he was appointed honorary professor at the University of Göttingen and in 1908 received a Nobel Prize for medicine and physiology for his work on immunity.

By now he recognized that serum therapy had its limitations and realized the specifity of cells to certain dyes; he began his search for chemical substances that would selectively kill bacteria and other microorganisms without harming their host cells. His researches pioneered modern chemotherapy. He concentrated on the organism that caused the widespread scourge of syphilis. With ample funding and an excellent staff, he persevered until he discovered what was first called substance 606, later known as salvarsan (and later neosalvarsan), which proved successful in the treatment of syphilis. Ehrlich called it a magic bullet (and a 1940 Hollywood movie biography, in which Edward G. Robinson (q.v.) played Ehrlich, was called *Dr. Ehrlich's Magic Bullet*). The manufacturer with whom he had cooperated released large quantities, without charge, to doctors in many parts of the world. In some cases, there were deleterious side effects, which led competitiors to attack Ehrlich. He eventually brought a lawsuit against the more slanderous allegations and on of the most extreme detractors was sentenced to prison.

Ehrlich himself was showered with honors. In 1914, he became a professor at Frankfurt University, was decorated with many royal orders, and was appointed real privy counsel to the German government with the title of Excellency. The institute he founded in Frankfurt still bears his name. Personally, he was noted as kind and considerate, and for his sense of humor and absentmindedness, especially when it came to returning books. He enjoyed reading, animals, and cigar smoking. Academically, he preferred research to lecturing. His style of writing was informal and he disliked publicity. Although he was not involved in religion or politics, he was interested in Jewish affairs and was a member of the Supporters of Zion (*Lema'an Zion*) movement. On his death, the London *Times* commented "The whole world is in his debt."

F. Himmelweit (ed.), *The Collected Papers of Paul Ehrlich*, 1956–1957.

S. Munther, *Paul Ehrlich, Founder of Chemotherapy*, 1966.

EINSTEIN, ALBERT (1879–1955) Mathematical physicist, humanist, and Nobel Prize winner. Einstein made major contributions to the development of modern physics and is most widely known for evolving the theory of relativity. He was born in Ulm, Germany, but grew up in Munich, where his father and uncle had set up a small electrochemical plant. His scientific interests were awakened early, but at school, under the rigors of the harsh and unimaginative German educational system, he showed little aptitude other than in mathematics and music. (He later became an accomplished violinist and found in his music a source of solace and strength.)

Einstein left school at the age of fifteen but after a year of meandering in Italy was persuaded to equip himself for a profession and eventually completed his secondary education in Aarau, Switzerland. Qualified for little else, he went on to study physics and mathematics at the polytechnic in Zurich, with a view toward teaching. However, the double handicap of his Jewishness and lack of Swiss citizenship excluded him from a regular teaching position and, in 1901, he accepted a junior appointment at the patent office in Bern.

It was during the seven years that he spent as a patent examiner that Einstein laid the foundations for large parts of 20th-century physics. The year 1905 was his *annus mirabilis* for it saw his publication of three important discoveries: a mathematical analysis of Brownian motion; an explanation of the photoelectric effect in terms of light as a shower of particles, or energy quanta, rather than as the continuous flux that it had hitherto been considered (which helped pave the way for television); and an exposition of the special theory of relativity, including the now famous equation $E=mc^2$.

The special theory of relativity deals with the motion of bodies moving feely on the two basic assumptions that nothing travels faster than light and nothing can be said to be at rest, unless it is with respect to something else. It differs from classical mechanics only for motion approaching the

Albert Einstein and his wife with Hopi Indians at the Grand Canyon, Arizona, 1931.

Page of Einstein's manuscript "Elementary Derivation of Mass and Energy," 1946.

speed of light and explains how, in such circumstances, time and position, and mass and energy are but different aspects of each other.

It was followed, in 1916, by the general theory of relativity, a generalization of the special theory to include bodies moving under the influence of gravity. Although the general theory can be neatly summarized in a single equation, $R^{mw} - g^{mw}R/2 = -KT^{mw}$, a proper understanding of it has defied all but a small handful of scientists. At first, its very inaccessibility rendered it contentious and it was a considerable relief to the Nobel committee in Stockholm when they were finally able to sidestep the issue by awarding his prize for "his services to theoretical physics and especially his discovery of the law of the photoelectric effect." The particle-like nature of radiation (and, correspondingly, the wavelike nature of matter, deduced by Einstein in 1924) was to become a basic premise in the construction of quantum mechanics. Its significance was not at first fully appreciated, and not before 1922 was it deemed worthy of the Nobel Prize for physics.

Einstein was offered, and accepted, a succession of academic appointments culminating, in 1914, in the directorship of the Kaiser Wilhelm Institute for Physics in Berlin. During World War I his scientific work was at its peak but in other ways his life did not go well. He would not join in the widespread support given to the German cause by German intellectuals and did what he could to preserve a rational, international spirit and to urge the immediate end of the war. His feeling of isolation was deepened by the end of his marriage to Meleva Maric and separation from his two sons. His subsequent marriage to his cousin Elsa, a widow with two daughters was, in many respects, one of convenience.

International fame came to Einstein in 1919, when the Royal Society of London announced that its scientific expedition to Principe Island, in the Gulf of Guinea, had photographed the solar eclipse on May 29 of that year and completed calculations that verified that the precise angle of deviation of light passing near the sun was that predicted by the general theory of relativity. His name and the term relativity became household words. The publicity that ensued changed Einstein's life. He was now able to put the weight of his name behind causes in which he believed. The two movements he backed most forcefully in the 1920s were pacifism and Zionism, particularly the creation of the Hebrew University in Jerusalem. In 1921 he went to the United States with Chaim Weizmann (q.v.) on a Zionist fund-raising tour and was received everywhere with acclamation and honor. In 1923 he gave the inaugural lecture at the not-yet-opened Hebrew University, prefacing his address on relativity with a few sentences in Hebrew paying tribute to the Hebraic spirit. As a memorial of his visit he presented the National Library at the university with the manuscript of his first treatise on relativity. (In the 1930s, he fell out

AN EINSTEIN SAMPLER

• Equations are more important to me than politics, because politics are for the present, but an equation is something for eternity.
• I was originally supposed to become an engineer. But I found the idea intolerable of having to apply the inventive faculty to matters that make everyday life even more elaborate — and all just for dreary money-making.
• I cannot conceive of a personal god who would directly influence the actions of individuals, or would directly sit in judgment on creatures of his own creation. I cannot do this in spite of the fact that mechanistic causality has, to a certain extent, been placed in doubt by modern science.
• My religiosity consists in a humble admiration of the infinitely superior spirit that reveals itself in the little that, with our weak and transitory understanding, we can comprehend of reality. Morality is of the highest importance — but for us not for God.
• God does not play dice with the world.
• The value of Judaism lies exclusively in its ethical and spiritual content and in the corresponding qualities of individual Jews. For this reason, from olden times till now, study has rightly been the sacred endeavor of the capable ones among us. That is not to say, however, that we should earn our livelihood by intellectual work as is, unfortunately, too often the case among us.
[In 1919 after his theory had been vindicated]
• Today when I am a hero I am described in Germany as a German scientist and in England as a Swiss Jew. Had I not been vindicated I would have been a Swiss Jew to the Germans and a German scientist for the English.
• Falling in love is not at all the most stupid thing that people do — but gravitation cannot be held responsible for it.
• Nationalism is an infantile sickness. It is the measles of the human race.
• It never occurred to me that every casual remark of mine would be snatched up and recorded. Otherwise I would have crept further into my shell.

with the university authorities after severely criticizing the direction that the university had taken, but eventually there was a reconciliation and he bequeathed his papers to the university library.) He also took an active part in the work of the League of Nations' Committee on Intellectual Cooperation.

Soon after the end of World War I, Einstein and relativity became targets of the anti-Semitic extreme right wing. He was viciously attacked in speeches and articles and his life was threatened. Despite this treatment Einstein remained in Berlin until Hitler came to power in 1933. He then promptly resigned his position and joined the Institute for Advanced Study at Princeton, where he remained for the remaining years of his life.

During the 1930s Einstein renounced his former pacifist stand, since he was now convinced that the menace to civilization embodied in Hitler's regime could be put down only by force. In 1939, at the request of Leo Szilard, Edward Teller, and Eugene Wigner, he wrote a letter to President Franklin D. Roosevelt pointing out the dangerous military potentiality offered by nuclear fission, which Germany might well exploit. This letter helped to initiate the American efforts that eventually produced the nuclear reactor and the fission bomb, but Einstein neither participated in nor knew details of their development. After the bomb was used and the war had ended, Einstein devoted his energies to advocating a world government and permanently abolishing war. He also spoke out against repression, urging intellectuals to stake their careers, if necessary, on the preservation of freedom of expression.

Einstein received a variety of honors in his lifetime. After Chaim Weizmann's death in 1952, David Ben-Gurion (q.v.) offered to propose Einstein's nomination as president of the State of Israel, but Einstein did not accept. When Einstein died in 1955, there lay on his desk the incomplete draft of a statement written in honor of Israel's seventh Independence Day. It proclaimed that "what I seek to accomplish is simply to serve, with my feeble capacity, truth and justice, at the risk of pleasing no one."

B. Hoffman and H. Dukas, *Albert Einstein: Creator and Rebel*, 1972.
P. Michelmore, *Einstein: Profile of the Man*, 1962.
P. A. Schilpp, *Albert Einstein: Philosopher-Scientist*, 1973.
K. Seelig, *Albert Einstein: A Biography*, 1956.
A. Vallentin, *Einstein: A Biography*, 1954.

EISENSTEIN, SERGEI MIKHAILOVICH

(1898–1948) Russian film director. Born in Riga, Latvia, the son of a Jewish father and a non-Jewish mother, Eisenstein studied architecture at the Petrograd Institute of Civil Engineering. When the Russian revolution began in 1917, he joined the Red Army, eventually pursuing his artistic bent by becoming a poster artist on one of the so-called agit-trains that brought newsreels, expressly edited to arouse revolutionary fervor, to the Russian provinces.

In 1920 Eisenstein joined the Moscow Proletkult Theater as a set designer. He participated in a directing workshop under the guidance of Vsevolod Meyerhold, whose ideas were to influence him heavily. During this period, he also became acquainted with the work of FEX (Factory of the Eccentric Actor), which in addition to amalgamating different kinds of performing styles, also made use of distinctly cinematic elements.

The result of Eisenstein's exposure to such concepts was his "montage of attractions," demonstrated in his first production for the Proletkult, *Even a Wise Man Stumbles*. The atmosphere was circuslike and the attractions included firecrackers exploding underneath the seats of the audience and a short film parodying the Kino-Pravda newsreel. In 1924 he directed his first feature film, *Strike*, also under the aegis of the Proletkult. In this tale of a strike, the breaking of which culminates in the slaughter of the strikers, Eisenstein deliberately eliminated the idea of an individual hero, concentrating instead on the masses.

Eisenstein's next film, *Battleship Potemkin*, acclaimed as one of the greatest works in cinema history, was originally intended as a historical survey of the events of the failed 1905 rebellion, but the impressive marble staircase in Odessa, leading to the harbor, made him decide to concentrate instead on a single incident: the mutiny aboard the *Potemkin*. The film's most famous scene, taking place on the steps, has as its central action the massacre by tsarist troops of a crowd that has gathered in sympathy with the mutineers.

When *Potemkin* was released, Eisenstein's detractors within the Communist party leveled against him charges of "formalism," which implied a preoccupation with artistic form at the expense of propaganda. *Potemkin*'s enormous success, however, especially outside the Soviet Union, prevented any steps from being taken against Eisenstein at that point. None of his subsequent projects was to be so free of interference.

October was the official film made to celebrate the tenth anniversary of the revolution. While

Sergei Eisenstein (top) directing.

Eisenstein was making the film, Leon Trotsky (q.v.) was expelled from the Politburo and exiled by Stalin, and his decisive role in the events of 1917 was therefore ordered cut from the film. The mutilated film was not understood by the public and this failure made Eisenstein more vulnerable to his establishment opponents. His next film, originally called *The General Line*, was one of his most beautiful and dealt with agriculture under Soviet rule.

In 1929 the Soviet authorities capitalized on Eisenstein's worldwide fame by sending him on a tour abroad. The writer Upton Sinclair helped finance a Mexican production for Eisenstein. To have been called *Que Viva Mexico*, the project was halted shortly before the end of shooting because of budgetary excesses. The footage that had been shot subsequently appeared in a number of different versions, none edited by Eisenstein.

His classic, *Alexander Nevsky* (1938), with music by Prokofiev, was renowned for its battle sequence on ice. The clear equation of the 13th-century Teutonic villains with the contemporary Teutons massing at Russia's borders caused the film to be withdrawn, when the Soviet-Nazi nonaggression pact was signed in 1939; with the 1941 German attack on the Soviet Union, however, the film was once again considered patriotic. During the war, Eisenstein joined other Jewish intellectuals and artists to proclaim their pride in being Jews and to protest to the world against acts being committed against all racial minorities in Europe, especially the Jewish people.

His last work, *Ivan the Terrible*, was to have been a trilogy, but the second part, completed in 1946 and containing Eisenstein's only work in color, was withheld by Stalin, who was overly sensitive to the title character's despotism. After suffering a heart attack, Eisenstein continued to plan the third part of his epic, but died before he could begin production. The second part was not viewed until ten years after his death.

Y. Barna, *Eisenstein*, 1973.
S. M. Eisenstein, *The Film Sense*, 1942.
M. Seton, *Sergei M. Eisenstein, A Biography*, 1952.

EISENSTEIN IN AN ADDRESS TO WORLD JEWRY, NOVEMBER 1941

As a Russian representative of the Soviet intelligentsia, and working as I do in the sphere of Russian cinematography and Russian art, the very principle of racial hatred is foreign and loathsome to me... the time has come to fight. In this sacred struggle, the Soviet Union is uniting all peoples who, with sword in hand, are ready to rise for the right to call themselves Czechs, Poles, Dutchmen, Belgians, Russians, or Jews.

EISNER, KURT (1867–1919) German journalist and statesman. His father was a Berlin merchant with a lucrative business in military accessories and decorations. He attended school with the sons of officers and businessmen in Berlin and went on to university, but broke off his studies in 1889 without taking his degree.

His parents had hoped he would enter the now faltering family business, but he chose instead to begin working as a news agency reporter. Two years later he obtained a position with a newspaper in Frankfurt. His new job coincided with an upsurge of the Social Democrats to whom Eisner, a rebel since his school days, was drawn. It also sparked in him an interest in philosophy and he published his first work, a book about Nietzsche. He had mixed feelings about Nietzsche, but concurred with his criticisms of elitist German institutions, among them universities, which he himself once described as "penitentiaries for future bureaucrats."

In 1892, his work took him to Marburg, where he studied with Hermann Cohen (q.v.) and began to develop a personal philosophy that combined Kant with socialism. His journalism gave him opportunity to use his caustic wit to good effect in criticizing the current political trends. On one occasion, however, a criticism of the kaiser entitled "Ceasar Mania" landed him in prison for nine months. Although his jail term disqualified him for the position he had been offered at Marburg University, his notoriety led to his appointment as editor of the Social Democrats' newspaper, *Vorwarts*. Interparty disputes, and his own propensity to alienate every faction of the party led to his dismissal in 1907, at which time he left Prussia for Bavaria. He worked for a time in Nuremburg, then moved to Munich, where he continued to work as a journalist. When, in August 1914, he used his column to criticize German aggression, he again lost his job. He became known as somewhat of an eccentric who wandered around Munich with a knapsack of books or provisions on his back.

In 1916, he founded, at a tavern in Munich, a weekly discussion group with an antiwar slant. Although the authorities took little notice of this activity, he soon had audiences of some one hundred listeners. At least part of the attraction was evidently his own outlandish appearance, a deliberately effected look of etherealism. In 1917 he joined the Independent Social Democratic party and became its leader.

In 1918, he was arrested as a leader in the antiwar strikes and imprisoned for eight and a half months without trial or charge. Upon his release he immediately became involved in the bloodless revolution which overthrew the Bavarian monarchy, proclaimed the Bavarian Republic, and demanded peace. Eisner became the first prime minister and foreign minister. He tried to effect internal security, unity among the Socialist factions in Bavaria, and economic and social reforms. In February 1919, he was murdered by a half-Jewish revolutionary student while on his way to the Bavarian parliament to present his resignation. His collected works were published in 1919.

R. Grunberger, *Red Rising in Bavaria*, 1973.

A. Mitchell, *Revolution in Bavaria 1918–19*, 1965.

ELEAZAR BEN JUDAH OF WORMS (also known as Eleazar Rokeah; c. 1165–c. 1230) Kabbalist, religious scholar, and poet; the last major figure in the school of medieval German Jewish pietists (the Hasidim of Ashkenaz). He belonged to a distinguished family of scholars and his main teacher was Judah ben Samuel he-Hasid (q.v.). He was born in Mainz, from which he had to flee as a result of Christian attacks, and settled in Worms, where he lived most of his life. After the Crusaders in the Holy Land lost Jerusalem to Saladin, Jews were attacked by Christians in Europe. In 1196 two Crusaders burst into Eleazar's home in Worms, killing his wife and two daughters before his eyes, seriously injuring Eleazar and mortally wounding his son. Eleazar mourned his wife and children for the rest of his life and wrote a moving elegy for them. From 1201 he served as rabbi in Worms and was one of the leading figures in Rhineland Jewry.

Through is many writings, he introduced the mysticism of teh Ashkenazic pietists to a broad circle. His major mystical composition, *Sodei Razayya* (Secrets of Secrets) was strongly influenced by German kabbalists. He explained the secrets of existence through wordplay and letter combinations. God must be sought through the pious life, involving saintliness and humility, sincere prayer, and a truly ethical life.

He also wrote a code of religious law, *Sefer ha-Roke'ah* (the word *Roke'ah* means chemist, but the numerical value of its Hebrew letters is the same as that for Eleazar). This expounds the influence of the Kabbalah on everyday religious life, to which he appended two chapters on ethics. He also wrote the first Jewish commentary in the Middle Ages expounding the liturgy, especially from a mystical point of view.

ELEAZAR BEN JAIR (1st cent. CE) One of the three main military leaders during the period of the great revolt against Rome in the Land of Israel. He is mentioned for his capture of the Dead Sea fortress of Masada in the year 66 and later, during Masada's very last days, its fall to the Roman forces (73/74).

Eleazar was a member of a family of freedom fighters that had its origins well over a century earlier with Hezekiah the Galilean, who rallied around him Jews opposed to the Herodian family because of its subservience to Rome.

In the year 74 (or possibly 73), after a prolonged siege, the Masada bastion fell to the Romans, but the defenders were never captured alive; preferring mass suicide to torture and death at Roman hands. A total of 960 men, women and children, led by Eleazar ben Jair, died by their own hands, while making certain to leave their food stores intact to make it clear that it was not the fear of starvation that drove them to their last defiant act. Ten of the defenders were chosen by lot to do away with all the rest and ultimately themselves. A remarkable find at Masada of shards with names on them, by the Hebrew University archeologist Yigael Yadin (q.v.) in the 1960s, and in particular a shard with the name "Ben Jair," appear to be striking corroboration of the historical account found in Josephus (q.v.).

Josephus relates that two women of the group who, together with five children, concealed themselves in the fortress's subterranean aqueduct and later gave themselves up to the Roman legionnaires. The final act of suicide, according to the survivors, occurred after Eleazar had exhorted the defenders to kill themselves, stressing the importance to die nobly as free Jews. Josephus concludes: "The Romans encountering the mass of slain, instead of exulting as over enemies, admired the nobility of their resolve and the contempt of death they displayed in carrying out their act."

Y. Yadin, *Masada, Herod's Fortress and the Zealots' Last Stand*, 1973.

SAYINGS OF ELEAZAR BEN JUDAH OF WORMS

- Envy a man nothing — except his virtue.
- The most beautiful thing a man can do is forgive.
- All blessings begin "Blessed be Thou," as though the person making the blessing was addressing a close friend.
- Accept your afflictions with love and joy.
- No monument sheds such glory as an untarnished name.

Conclusion of Eleazar ben Jair's speech before the Masada mass suicide

Our hands are still at liberty and have a sword in them: let them be subservient to us in our glorious design: let us die before we become slaves under our enemies, and let us go out of the world, together with our children and our wives, in a state of freedom....Let us make haste and instead of affording the Romans so much pleasure as they hope for in getting us under their power, let us leave them an example which shall at once cause their astonishment at our death and their admiration of our resolution.

ELIEZER BEN HYRCANUS (c. 40–before 120 CE) Rabbi; sometimes called Eliezer the Great; in Talmudic literature he is most often referred to as Rabbi Eliezer. A native Jerusalemite, he first showed signs of genius after becoming a student in his twenties. According to his teacher, Johanan ben Zakkai (q.v.), Eliezer then outshone all other pupils in memorizing traditional sources like "a plastered well that retains every single drop." Together with Joshua ben Hananyah, he was responsible for Rabbi Johanan's escape (in a coffin) from Jerusalem when the Roman siege was at its height, after which the Roman general Vespasian gave permission for the Sanhedrin's reestablishment at Yavne. Eliezer became one of Yavne's foremost sages after the destruction of the Temple in 70 CE, undertook various overseas missions, and once accompanied Rabbi Johanan on a journey to Rome (c. 95 CE). He founded an academy of his own at Lydda, where the most famous students were Rabbi Akiva (q.v.) and Aquila the Proselyte, who produced a Greek version of the Bible for Diaspora Jews.

A dynamic but inflexible personality, Eliezer ben Hyrcanus seems to have followed the school of Shammai (q.v.) in his legal conservatism and anti-Roman outlook. While ready to accept genuine proselytes, he distanced himself from heathen, advocated minimal social contact with them, and believed that his wrongful arrrest on one occasion was the punishment ordained for his thoughtless approval of a Judeo-Christian teaching. When Eliezer defied a majority vote by the Sanhedrin on a legal issue (c. 97 CE), his brother-in-law, the Patriarch Rabban Gamaliel II (q.v.), proclaimed a ban excluding him from the company and deliberations of fellow sages. This unusually severe decree embittered Eliezer until his dying day.

Not only did the sages mourn Eliezer's passing, but they also rescinded the ban and reaffirmed many of his decision which became authoritative legal rulings. Eliezer's great prestige and contribution to rabbinic lawmaking are widely demonstrated by the recurrence of his name in the Mishnah, numerous debates in the Talmud arising from his legal opinions, the support given to him by a heavenly voice (*Bat Kol*) in his fateful controversy with Rabban Gamaliel and the other sages, and, centuries later, the ascription to him of the midrashic work *Pirke de-Rabbi Eliezer* (Chapter of Rabbi Eliezer). One of his memorable injunctions was to "repent one day before your death," in other words, as a daily routine. "Know before whom you stand!" another celebrated aphorism, is a text often displayed on the reader's platform or lectern in synagogues.

Y. Gilat, *Rabbi Eliezer ben Hyrcanus: A Scholar Outcast*, 1984.
J. Neusner, *Eliezer Ben Hyrcanus: The Tradition and the Man*, 1973.

ELIJAH (first half of 9th cent. BCE) Israelite prophet who, in later Jewish tradition, was regarded as the precursor of the Messiah. He prophesied in the northern kingdom of Israel during the reigns of Ahab, Ahaziah, and Jehoram.

Elijah was a Tishbite from the region of Gilead in Transjordan and is depicted as a lonely figure with no settled home, roaming through the kingdom, suddenly appearing and then disappearing. He belonged to the company of prophets in Judah and Israel who were fighting for the pure worship of God and who bitterly opposed all manifestations of polytheism and idolatry. His zeal brought him into constant conflict with the establishment, especially the royal house.

The Messiah on a donkey entering Jerusalem, preceded by Elijah. From the Venice Haggadah, *18th century.*

King Ahab continued the policy of his father, Omri, which involved a close alliance with Tyre. Ahab himself was married to a Tyrian princess, Jezebel of Sidon, who introduced Tyrian Baal worship to Israel. While Ahab remained faithful to his people's religion, he tolerated the paganism brought in by his wife, which attracted many of the people. Elijah first clashed with Ahab when he foretold a two-year drought as punishment for the widespread Baal worship. He had to flee for his life, but returned to challenge the 850 prophets of Baal to a famous confrontation on Mount Carmel. The efforts of the Baal prophets went unanswered and Elijah mocked them while accusing the people of "hopping between two opinions," i.e., between God and Baal. In answer to Elijah's prayer, God sent fire from heaven to consume Elijah's sacrifice and the wonder-struck people cried out in one voice "The Lord is God." This was followed by a massacre of the false prophets. However, when Jezebel learned of the events, Elijah had to flee from her anger and journeyed to the distant desert. He eventually reached Mount Horeb, the mount of God (identified with Mount Sinai) where he experienced a divine revelation parallel to that of Moses; but God came, not in thunder and lightning, but in a "still small voice" (1 Kings 19:12). While on the mountain, he was commanded to anoint Hazael as king of Aram, Jehu as king of Israel, and to appoint Elisha (q.v.) as his own successor. He succeeded only in the last mission; the first two were accomplished by Elisha.

Elijah fought for social justice. After his return to Samaria, he found that Jezebel had engineered the execution of the innocent Naboth on a false charge so that Ahab could obtain possession of his vineyard. The prophet confronted the king with the words, "Would you murder and also take possession?" (1 Kings 2:19) This issue damaged the royal image among the people and Elijah forecast the end of the dynasty. His last recorded prophetic act was his rebuke to Ahab's successor, the ailing Ahaziah, for consulting Baal-zebub, god of Ekron, concerning his recovery instead of the God of Israel. Elijah correctly foretold Ahaziah's early death.

When the time came for Elijah to die, he appointed his disciple Elisha as his successor. Then "As they kept on walking and talking, a fiery chariot with fiery horses suddenly appeared and separated one from the other; and Elijah went up to heaven in a whirlwind" (2 Kings 2:11).

Elijah's powerful personality, the miracles ascribed to him, and the manner of his death soon made him a legendary figure. in biblical times the prophet Malachi said, "Behold, I will send the prophet Elijah to you before the coming of the awesome, fearful day of the Lord. He shall reconcile parents with their children and children with their parents" (2 Kings 3:23–24). Elijah assumed an important role in Jewish eschatology and was identified as the herald and even the partner of the Messiah. He is also an outstanding figure in Jewish folklore, who reappears in disguise to rescue the righteous in their hour of need and to see that justice is done. He also comes to synagogues to complete the prayer quorum of ten. In Jewish law, insoluble problems were put aside "until the Tishbite comes." During the Passover Seder service a cup of wine is placed on the table for him and the door is kept open to welcome Elijah in the confidence that he would be arriving to announce the imminence of the messianic age. He is also associated with the circumcision ceremony, where a special seat is provided for him. At the end of the Sabbath, a popular hymn *Eliahu ha-Navi* (Elijah the prophet) is sung to pray for his arrival, expressing the longing for redemption. Elijah also plays a prominent role in Christian and Muslim legend.

The main biblical account of his life is to be found in 1 Kings 17–2 Kings 2.
J. A. Montgomery, *A Critical and Exegetical Commentary on the Book of Kings*, 1951.

ELIJAH BEN SOLOMON ZALMAN OF VILNA (the Vilna Gaon; 1720–1797) Rabbinic authority who made a deep impression on Jewish life in eastern Europe at the beginning of the modern period. He was born in Selets, near Grodno, to a family of Talmudic scholars. A child prodigy, by the age of six he was studying the Bible and the Talmud on his own, and giving learned discourses at the Great Synagogue in Vilna (now Vilnius, Lithuania), the famous center of Jewish learning. As he grew older, he intensified his studies and mastered all branches of rabbinic knowledge. Unusual for Talmudic sages of the time, he was also versed in secular subjects, including philosophy, history, astronomy, mathematics, and

anatomy, which he studied in order to illumine his knowledge of all aspects of Judaism. Elijah became recognized as an authority throughout Ashkenazic Jewry, who referred to him simply as the Gaon (the genius).

For the first half of his life he lived austerely as a recluse. At the age of twenty, he left his wife and home in Vilna and spent eight years in Jewish communities in Poland and Germany, and then returned to Vilna, where he spent the rest of his life, except for an unsuccessful attempt to travel to the Holy Land. A special house of study was built for him where he spent his days, but he refused any public office and devoted himself to scholarship. His Talmudic expertise covered not 'only the Babylonian Talmud but also the Jerusalem Talmud, which was exceptional at that period. His approach was critical, intellectual, and single-minded — he was said to have slept only two hours each night and to have forbidden any conversation not devoted to the Torah. His teaching was logical and he opposed the hairsplitting casuistry that characterized much Talmudic study. The Gaon paid special attention to the various manuscripts of the Talmud in order to arrive at correct readings. He also became more involved in community affairs and was the effective head of the community of Lithuania and indeed of Russian Jewry. When he was forty he began to lecture to a group of disciples who spread his teachings throughout the rabbinical academies of Lithuania.

Elijah ben Solomon Zalman, the Gaon of Vilna.

He found his type of Judaism challenged by two main developments — Haskalah (Enlightment) and the Hasidic (pietist) movement. He rejected the priority of rationalism that characterized Haskalah, insisting on the primacy of Torah and halakhah. His bitterest fights were with the Hasidim, whose emotional, intuitive, and often anti-intellectual form of Judaism contradicted the traditional emphasis on learning. Hasidism was sweeping large areas of eastern Europe, even reaching Lithuania, and Elijah took the lead in combatting its spread. He was appalled by the apparent levity of the Hasidism in their attitude to the Torah and concerned that it might develop into a pseudo-messianic movement that would be as disastrous as that of Shabbetai Tzevi (q.v.). Convinced that the Hasidism were distorting Judaism, he issued repeated excommunications of the new sect and when a group of Hasidic leaders approached his place of study in Vilna in an attempt to meet with him, he refused to see them and they were turned away. Under Elijah's guidance, Vilna became the center of anti-Hasidic activities, and most Lithuanian Jews *Mitnaggedim* (opponents) of Hasidism.

Although Elijah's approach was rational and intellectual, he was also a student of Jewish mysticism. However, he separated his mystical visions from his scholarly and legal writings. Some of his disciples became the great personalities of the succeeding generation and the inspirers of the famous Lithuanian yeshivot (rabbinical academies), such as Hayyim of Volozhin.

His disciples posthumously published his writings, because Elijah refrained from publishing his works in his lifetime. The seventy works he left included commentaries on most of the Bible, the Mishnah, both Talmuds, and the *Shulhan Arukh* code, writings on the mystical classics, and works on mathematics, astronomy, biblical geography, and Hebrew grammar.

L. Jung (ed.), *Jewish Leaders*, 1953.
L. Ginzberg, *Students, Scholars, and Saints*, 1958.

SAYINGS OF THE VILNA GAON

- It is impossible to understand the fundamentals of creation, how all segments are closely tied and wonderfully arranged, unless we infer the unity of the Creator and of reality.
- The commandments are interwoven and supplement each other as they are one commandment, one single truth.
- Desires must be purified and idealized, not eradicated.
- Life is a series of vexations and pains, and sleepless nights are the common lot.
- It is better to pray at home, for in the synagogue it is impossible to escape envy and hearing idle talk.
- Like rain, the Torah nourishes useful plants and poisonous weeds.
- The tongue's sin weighs as much as all other sins together.
- Only things acquired by hard labor and great struggle are of any value.

ELISHA (9th cent. BCE) Israelite prophet. He came from Gilead in Transjordan, and prophesied in the northern kingdom of Israel during the reigns of kings Jehoram, Jehu, Jehoahaz, and Jehoash. He was the outstanding disciple and successor of the prophet Elijah (q.v.). The Bible relates that when Elijah was on Mount Horeb he was commanded, in a vision, to anoint Elisha as a prophet. Elijah followed the divine command by laying his mantle on Elisha, who at the time was working as a farmer tending his father's land. Elisha served as Elijah's attendant until the latter's miraculous ascent to heaven, at which time he received Elijah's mantle and commenced his own work.

Many miracles were ascribed to him over a career that lasted six decades. These included dividing the river Jordan so that he could cross it; replenishing a poor widow's cruse of oil; restoring the life of an apparently dead child; and curing the Aramean army captain, Naaman, of leprosy (Naaman, in gratitude, undertook to worship the Israelite God exclusively).

Unlike Elijah, who was a recluse, living much of his life in the desert, Elisha was a city dweller, appearing frequently in public in the main Israelite religious centers. He lived with a group called the sons of the prophets, who were probably his disciples. His main work was political. He successfully completed Elijah's struggle against the Baal worship introduced by the House of Ahab. He provided water to a parched army, and helped to defeat the Moabites and avert a Syrian victory over the Israelites. The divine command to Elijah to anoint Jehu as king of Israel and Hazael as ruler of Aram were in fact accomplished by Elisha. On his deathbed he foretold Joash's defeat of the Syrians.

Although the stories seem to incorporate legendary elements, it is evident that Elisha made a deep impression on his contemporaries and was a man of great courage and deep convictions. The Bible stresses his moral demands and his total domination of the spiritual life of the people in his time.

His story is told in 1 Kings 19–2 Kings 13.
J. Blenkinsopp, *A History of Prophecy in Israel*, 1983.

ELISHA BEN AVUYAH (c. 70–c. 145 CE) Palestinian rabbi who in later life gained notoriety as an apostate. His outstanding and devoted pupil was Rabbi Meir (q.v.). Nowhere in the Mishnah or Talmud does the title of Rabbi precede Elisha's name; rather than implying that he never received ordination, this may point to its withdrawal by the sages once he turned heretic. Most of the biographical data available in rabbinic sources emphasize Elisha's loss of faith and its causes and effects. The process began with his involvement in mystical speculation: together with three fellow sages (Ben Azzai, Ben Zoma, and Rabbi Akiva q.v.), he "entered the *pardes* [orchard of mysteries] where he destroyed the shoots," that is, suffered a crisis of belief that led him to reject traditional norms. This experience may have coincided with the anti-Jewish persecutions instigated by the Emperor Hadrian, which gave rise to the ill-fated Bar Kokhba (q.v.) revolt against Rome (132–135). According to the Talmud, Elisha ben Avuyah reacted to the suffering of innocent Jews by mocking the notion of Divine Providence and denying the concept of reward and punishment. Various traditions maintain that his negation of Torah precepts served to justify a wholesale attack on the Jewish heritage. Apart from belittling teachers and students, he publicly flouted Sabbath laws, compelled others to do so, and gave himself up to sensual pleasures. Abhorred as a Roman collaborator, Elisha was dubbed *Aher* (other person), whose name should be suppressed.

With astonishing broad-mindedness, Meir honored and stood by his old teacher. Meir's endeavor to make him repent evidently succeeded when Elisha was on his deathbed. It was probably thanks to his eminent disciple that some of Elisha ben Avuyah's sayings are preserved.

The medieval philosopher Judah Halevi (q.v.) attributed the fate of Elisha to his repudiation of religious observance: "These actions [he said] are merely instruments for attaining spiritual rank. That rank I have attained and so I have no need of religious ceremonies." Enlightenment writers of the 19th century, drawn to the figure of *Aher*, often made him an ancient Jewish prototype of Faust. Modern scholars have occasionally sought an explanation for his abandonment of Judaism in Gnostic and other alien beliefs. Elisha ben Avuyah's life formed the subject of Milton Steinberg's novel *As a Driven Leaf* (1939).

W. S. Green, *To See Ourselves as Others See Us*, 1985.

ELMAN, MISCHA (1891–1967) Violinist. He was born in Talnoye, Ukraine; his family came from the city of Berdichev, where his grandfather was a violinist of distinction and his father, a Hebrew scholar, helped his son achieve the career he himself had never dared take up.

When Elman was six years old, his father took him to study the violin in Odessa. The young prodigy progressed in a remarkable way and at the age of eleven, the famous violinist and teacher Leopold Auer (q.v.) heard Elman and observed: "Look at this tiny atom! Inside it is the most extraordinary force. At his age, had I played as he does, I should now be ten Auers, not one." Auer immediately accepted Elman as a student in the Saint Petersburg conservatory. Two years later Elman made his debut in Saint Petersburg. This was followed by a successful tour of Germany, which included a sensational debut in Berlin on October 14, 1904. The music critics in town commented on the sheer perfection of the artist's performance, the mature virtuosity of his technique; his great rounded tones so full of musical life; and his remarkable grasp of musical organization.

Elman made his English debut in 1905. The critic of *The Strad* wrote that "from the moment he stepped onto the platform until he had played his last encore at 11.20 P.M. (and even then the public seemed to want some more) his success in this country was an assured thing. He tackled the terrific difficulties of Tchaikovsky's D Major Concerto as though they were a mere bagatelle — this little fellow literally "waltzed around it", made light of its technical pitfalls, and gave a rendering of it so thoroughly in accord with the spirit in which it was written that the audience literally rose to him." That same year in London Elman also performed the premiere of Aleksandr Glazunov's violin concerto. Although the composer had dedicated the work to Auer, Glazunov was so entranced by Elman's playing that Auer withdrew from the premiere, allowing his pupil the honors.

Elman made his American debut in New York in 1908 and in 1911 he settled in the United States. He performed with all the major orchestras in the world and was known above all for his rich and expressive tone and interpretation of romantic music, especially the concerti of Tchaikovsky, Felix Mendelssohn (q.v.), and Henryk Wieniawski (q.v.). In 1926 he founded the Elman String Quartet. During 1936–1937 Elman presented a series of five concerts in New York's Carnegie Hall entitled "The Development of Violin Literature," in which he performed over fifteen violin concerti. In 1944 Elman performed the premiere of a violin concerto by Bohuslav Martinu, which was written especially for him.

Donald Brooks summed up Elman's musicality: "The outstanding feature of his playing is not the technical mastery of his instrument nor yet the satisfying breadth of tone, but that spiritual Hebraic quality that artists of Jewish ancestry seem to be able to put into music of a somber mood."

Elman made many recordings and over two million of his records were sold in his lifetime. He published some arrangements for the violin and also composed a few short pieces for the instrument.

M. Campbell, *The Great Violinists*, 1981.
S. Elman, *Memoirs of Mischa Elman's Father*, 1933.

EMDEN, JACOB (1697–1776) German rabbi, scholar of Jewish law, controversialist, and son of Hakham Tsevi Ashkenazi (q.v.). One of the most versatile, well-informed and pugnacious Jewish writers of the 18th century, he was born in Altona but acquired his surname from the town where he officiated as a rabbi (1728–1733), although he preferred the Hebrew acronym Yavets (i.e., Ya'akov Ben Tsevi). The communal disputes in which he was involved, and the vicissitudes of his own family life (Emden lost two wives in succession and several children), made him a harsh critic of German Jewish society. The violent campaign launched against his father in Amsterdam (1713–1714), and his own discovery of heretical imposters (1732), turned Emden into an unrelenting opponent of Shabbateanism, the pseudo-messianic movement founded by Shabbetai Tsevi (q.v.), which he regarded as traditional Judaism's mortal enemy.

After returning to his native Altona in 1733, Jacob Emden abandoned the rabbinate and engaged in various business schemes with the hope of achieving financial independence. He was disdainful of Jonathan Eybeschutz (q.v.), rabbi of the Altona-Hamburg-Wandsbeck Triple Community, whose post he may have considered rightfully his. From 1744, Emden ran a printing press and published dozens of works reflecting his own scholarly interests and outspoken attitudes. Within the framework of his books, he discussed an astonishing range of topics from medicine and sex to geography and Confucianism. Among his publications were over 350 *responsa*; commentaries on the Bible, Mishnah, and Talmud; grammatical and ethical treatises; anti-Shabbatean polemics; and an annotated prayer book known as *Siddur Beit Ya'akov* (1745–1758) which adopted Hakham Tsevi's unbiased approach to Sephardic tradition.

In 1751, Emden was shown an amulet designed to guard expectant mothers from the evil eye, deciphered the text, and judged it to be the work of a secret Shabbatean. This amulet was one of several prepared by Eybeschutz. Ignoring the dreadful implications, Emden steadfastly maintained his adverse judgment, which was upheld by most of the German rabbinate. Violent scenes took place in synagogue and at the stock exchange; the conflict made headlines in the general press and split Jewish opinion from Holland to Lithuania. Eybeschutz found new supporters outside Germany and remained in office until his death (1764), but Emden continued the battle with a scholarly critique of the Zohar — written to undermine Shabbatean claims — which appeared four years later.

Much valuable information about the social and religious history of his time is contained in *Megillat Sefer* (1896), Emden's autobiography. Recent investigation points to the accuracy of Emden's charge that the venerated Jonathan Eybeschutz was a crypto-Shabbatean. There can be little doubt, however, that the war between these two men (anticipating an even more violent conflict over Hasidism at the end of the 18th century) helped to weaken rabbinic authority on the threshold of the modern age.

M. J. Cohen, *Jacob Emden: A Man of Controversy*, 1937.

J. J. Schacter, *Rabbi Jacob Emden: Life and Major Works*, 1990.

EMIN PASHA (Eduard Schnitzer; 1840–1892) German-born administrator and explorer, a native of Oppeln in Prussian Silesia. At the age of two he was baptized in a Protestant church, since his assimilated Jewish parents believed that this step would further his career. As a child, he liked to travel. After training as a physician, he practiced medicine in Albania, adopting Turkish ways and styling himself Mehemed Emin Effendi. In 1875, however, the lure of Africa drew him to Khartoum, where his medical work favorably impressed the British general Charles George Gordon, who secured him an appointment in the Equatorial province of southern Sudan, which Emin zealously explored. Once Gordon had become governor-general of the Sudan in 1878, he arranged for Emin to succeed him as Equatoria's Anglo-Egyptian governor. Emin, later known as Emin Pasha, conducted a sound and effective administration; together with Gordon, he devoted much time and effort to combating and eradicating the Arab trade in African slaves. As a doctor and linguist, he also became an expert on the peoples and natural history of central Africa.

The fall of Khartoum, in which General Gordon met his death in 1885, left Emin Pasha isolated and exposed to attack by the Mahdi's dervish rebels. Although British and German attempts to rescue him failed, Emin held out for two more years and was the object of various relief expeditions until H. M. Stanley's arrival in 1888. With much reluctance, he then accompanied the British explorer to safety in Zanzibar. His next assignment, for the German colonial authorities in Tanganyika, was to explore and claim new territory in the Lake Victoria region of east Africa in 1890. This expedition he rigorously pursued, despite German efforts to recall him after a boundary agreement had been reached with the British. While on his return journey, in late October of 1892, Emin was murdered by vengeful Arab slave traders. Emin Pasha Gulf, the southwestern bay of Lake Victoria (now in Tanzania), was named in the explorer's memory.

G. Schweitzer, *Emin Pasha: His Life and Work*, 1898.

H. M. Stanley, *In Darkest Africa*, ed. J. S. Keltie, 1890 (reprinted 1969).

A. F. A. Symons, *Emin, Governor of Equatoria*, 1928.

EPSTEIN, JACOB (1880–1959) Artist, Knighted in 1954. Epstein was born in New York's Lower East Side to Polish Jewish parents. At an early age he started sketching the people among whom he lived: immigrants from all over the world; Jews garbed in the traditional attire of the Old World ghettoes, and people from nearby Chinatown. When his family moved to another neighborhood, he remained on Hester Street, where he rented an attic. He worked in a foundry during the day and in the evening studied at the Art Students League with the sculptor George Gray Barnard. He sold many of his drawings of the colorful people of the Lower East Side and was asked by Hutchins Hapgood to illustrate his book, *The Spirit of the Ghetto*, for which he earned enough money to pay the fare to Paris. He went to Paris in 1902, and, on his second day there, attending the funeral procession of Emile Zola, who had been active in the defense of Alfred Dreyfus (q.v.), he witnessed the attempts of anti-Semites to disrupt the funeral.

In Paris, Epstein studied at the Ecole des Beaux Arts and at the Académie Julien. In 1905, he moved to London, becoming a British citizen two years later. His first important commission was for

Jacob Epstein at work.

the British Medical Association Building, for which he carved eighteen figures. When the first four were unveiled in 1908, they were attacked as obscene.

When he completed a powerful demon-angel for the tomb of Oscar Wilde, he displayed it to great crowds in his studio on the Chelsea Embankment. Yet when the monument was placed at the Père Lachaise cemetery in Paris (1912) it was condemned as indecent and covered by a tarpaulin, which was not removed until 1914. In Paris Epstein met Picasso, Brancusi, and Modigliani, and was introduced to African sculpture. In 1913 he exhibited drawings in a show called "English Post-Impressionists, Cubists, and Others." His work was classed with the Cubists.

Epstein was in great demand as a portrait sculptor, and had many famous sitters. This aspect of his work was widely acclaimed and provided him with financial security. The subjects of his portraits range from children to strong personalities, such as George Bernard Shaw, Chaim Weizmann (q.v.), Yehudi Menuhin, and others. His famous portrait of Albert Einstein (q.v.) is unfinished, for during the sitting Einstein left suddenly for the United States. One of his most sensitive portraits is that of

---

The whole integrity of art lies in its tradition. Tradition does not mean surrender of originality. On the contrary, all great innovators in art were in the great tradition, you cannot quote one exception, however much they may have been considered rebels by their contemporaries.

Jacob Epstein

---

his friend, the British Hebrew poet Moshe Oved, whose work, *The Book of Affinity*, was illustrated with seven watercolors by Epstein.

During World War I, Epstein served with the Artists Rifles, after being turned down for the War Artists program. In 1924 he received a commission for the W. H. Hudson Memorial, a bas-relief, in Hyde Park. The president of the Royal Academy demanded its removal, and hoodlums splashed paint on it. In 1929, he was asked to carve two groups above the entrance of the new head offices of the underground railway in Westminster, London, and chose the subjects *Night* and *Day*. These two sculptures also met with public censure and *Day* was attacked with tar and feathers. He did not receive another public commission until 1951, when he did *Youth Advancing* for the Festival of Britain.

In 1942, a retrospective exhibition of his work was held, and ten years later another retrospective, at the Tate Gallery, drew about ten thousand visitors a week.

Epstein received many honors for his work, which culminated with his knighthood in 1954. His monumental works reflect his passionate concern for humanity as well as a profound understanding of the possibilities and limitations of his material. His works were always designed to make the most of their surroundings. His conceptions were forceful and original. His religious work was noble, austere, and intense. Although definitely of his time, Epstein's work was rooted in sculptural tradition reaching back to Egyptian, Polynesian, and African sources. His other sculptures included *Ecce Homo* (1935) *Adam, Genesis, Lazarus* (1948), *Madonna and Child* (1953), *Christ in Majesty* and *St. Michael and the Devil*, the last for the rebuilt Coventry Cathedral.

Epstein wrote *The Sculptor Speaks* with A. Haskell in 1931 and *Let There Be Sculpture* (1940).
R. Black, *The Art of Jacob Epstein*, 1942.
R. Buckle, *Jacob Epstein, Sculptor*, 1963.

ESHKOL, LEVI (1895–1969) Prime minister of Israel. Born Levi Shkolnick in Oratova, Russia, he studied traditional Jewish subjects in Vilna (present-day Vilnius, Lithuania). Having joined a Zionist youth movement as a teenager, he imigrated to Eretz Israel in 1914 and became an agricultural worker, before serving in World War I in the Jewish Legion which he described as "a collection of Palestine pioneers and London tailors." In 1920 he was one of the founders of Kibbutz Degania B and became active in the self-defense force (Haganah), the Labor Federation (Histadrut) in arms acquisition, and in the development of water resources. One of the leaders of the Mapai Labor party, he served as the powerful secretary of the Tel Aviv Workers' Council from 1944 to 1948. He was known as a person who got things done calmly and with good humor, a person who was able to bridge differences and reduce personal tensions and conflicts. His reputation as a mediator was such that a joke went around that once when asked "Tea or coffee?" he replied, "Half and half."

During Israel's War of Independence he served as deputy defense minister under David Ben-Gurion (q.v.). His expertise in finances (he was the Haganah's treasurer) led to an eleven-year stint as minister of finance (1952–1963), in which capacity he oversaw the absorption and integration of almost a million immigrants, the creation of hundreds of settlements, and the establishment of Israel's industrial and agricultural infrastructure.

Chosen by Ben-Gurion to succeed him as prime minister in 1963, he also took over the defense portfolio and played a key role in preparing the Israel army for a future war. His policies were moderate and conciliatory. He stressed deterrence, close relations with the United States, and growing economic ties with Europe (he negotiated the early stages of Israel's involvement with the European Economic Community). At home his style of leadership was seen as hesitant and uncertain. The attacks on him from the Ben-Gurion camp intensified, leading to a split in the ruling Mapai party in 1965. As the situation along the borders deteriorated from 1964, Eshkol was unable to stem raids from across the border, giving rise to accusation of faltering leadership. The few retaliatory operations he authorized led to tension with the United States.

On the eve of the 1967 Six-Day War the public demanded that he resign altogether or at least give up the defense ministry in favor of Moshe Dayan (q.v.), the hero of the 1956 war. Under mounting pressure from within Mapai, he yielded to the demands and acquiesced to the creation of a government of national unity with Dayan in charge of defense.

Few Israelis credited Eshkol with the stunning victory of the Six-Day War; the credit went to Dayan and the army generals. Eshkol's final two years were bitter. He realized that an addition of a million Arabs in the territories was placing Israel under an intolerable moral, financial, economic, security, and demographic burden. But as long as the Arab states clung to the doctrine of no peace, no recognition, and no negotiations with Israel, he reluctantly agreed to preserve the new status quo created by the war. His last major act was to preside over the unification of the Labor Party when rival factions ceased their independent existence. Underrated during his life, since his death many Israelis have come to view him as one of their most successful leaders.

S. Perla, *Levi Eschkol, Unifier of a Nation*, 1970.
T. Prittie, *The Man and the Nation*, 1969.

ESTHER Consort of the Persian ruler Ahasuerus (Xerxes) and heroine of the bibical book named for her. Of remarkable beauty, she was selected by Ahasuerus to replace his rejected queen, Vashti, in his palace in Shushan (i.e., Susa). When the king's vizier, Haman, sought to destroy all the Jews in the kingdom, Esther's uncle, Mordecai, enlisted her in a scheme to foil Haman's plan. She had not made her origin known but Mordecai warned her that her fate would be no different from that of the other Jews. Esther invited the king and Haman to a banquet at which she requested that the king deliver her people and herself from the ordained destruction. In response to the king's question as to who had plotted such a deed, she accused Haman. Ahasuerus left the feast in anger and when he returned, Haman was lying on Esther's couch, leading the king to suspect that he was about to ravish the queen. He immediately ordered Haman's execution on the gallows that Haman had prepared for Mordecai. At Esther's request, the king also quashed Haman's anti-Jewish orders and gave all Haman's property to Esther.

Esther and Mordecai ordained the anniversary of this deliverance as the feast of Purim. The previous day is observed as the Fast of Esther in

U.S. President Lyndon Johnson and Prime Minister Levi Eshkol in Texas.

> Esther was a captive in a strange land and yet she, a weak, trembling girl, was the savior, the benefactor of thousands: and her name has come down through a thousand ages, wreathed with the admiring love of that very people whose ancestors she saved.
> **Grace Aguilar in *The Women of Israel*, 1872.**

Illuminated Scroll of Esther. Ferrara, 1616.

Jewish tradition, but this was a much later institution and is not connected with Esther's request that the Jews of Shushan observe a fast while she prepared to appear before Ahasuerus to plead for her people. On the annual Purim festival, the scroll of Esther is read in the synagogues and the children dress up, many of the girls as Queen Esther, one of the best-loved women in Jewish history. The story of Esther has received no confirmation from other sources and scholars are divided concerning its historicity. Esther's Hebrew name was Hadassah (myrtle); the rabbis explained that just as the myrtle spreads fragrance, so Esther spread good deeds throughout the land.
C. A. Moore, *Esther* (Anchor Bible), 1971.

EYBESCHUTZ, JONATHAN (1690–1764) Talmudic scholar and kabbalist; from 1750 chief rabbi of the Altona-Hamburg-Wandsbeck Triple Community. Although born in Cracow, Poland, he took his surname from the Moravian town (Eibenschitz or Invancice) where his father held office as rabbi. An infant prodigy, Eybeschutz was destined to become a celebrated Talmudist. Thanks to his teaching ability, scholarship, and brilliant preaching, he gained thousands of admirers; only a few of the many books that he wrote, chiefly on Talmudic law and lore, however, appeared in his lifetime.

During the first half of the 18th century, there were still many Jews who retained an undercover allegiance to the heretical false messiah, Shabbetai Tzevi (q.v.). As a student in Prostejov, Eybeschutz was first influenced by the local Shabbatean "prophet" and, even after his move to Prague

(1715), where he became head of the rabbinic academy and a member of the rabbinical court, his crypto-Shabbateanism seems to have persisted. On the one hand, Chief Rabbi David Oppenheim was infuriated by his subordinate's attempt to publish an "expurgated" edition of the Talmud, while Eybeschutz was also rumored to be the true author of a scandalously heretical kabbalistic work. On the other hand, Eybeschutz had acquired such prestige as a Talmudist that no one dared to accuse him of heterodoxy, not least in view of the fact that the Prague rabbinate's anti-Shabbatean ban (September 1725) bore his signature.

Ruled out as Oppenheim's successor, Eybeschutz left Prague to serve as a rabbi of Metz (1741–1750) before attaining his final post with the Triple Community. There, he encountered a resentful heresy-hunter, Jacob Emden (q.v.), who may have had the new chief rabbi on his list of Shabbatean suspects. An unforseen development played into Emden's hands. At the request of pregnant women, Eybeschutz had distributed amulets to ward off the evil eye; after deciphering their kabbalistic formulas early in 1751, Emden pronounced them, and their author, to be unmistakably Shabbatean. Eybeschutz promptly denied the charge of heresy, and the ensuing conflict spread far and wide.

Whereas many opponents of Eybeschutz in the German rabbinate sided with Emden, the lay leaders of the Triple Community, as well as leading Polish, Bohemian, and Moravian rabbis, gave their support to the apparent victim of Emden's witch-hunt. Violent confrontations were reported in the German press, both Hamburg's senate and the Danish authorities in Altona were forced to intervene, and Eybeschutz had his status as chief rabbi reconfirmed. He then launched a belated counter-attack, publishing messages of support from rabbinical authorities together with an unconvincing explanation of the kabbalistic formulas that he had written. Most Orthodox Jews who stood by him were presumably unaware that some Christians, as well as crypto-Shabbateans in Central Europe, believed Eybeschutz to be one of their own.

Except for periodical rejoinders by Emden, it seemed that Eybeschutz was a wronged man, entitled to spend his last years in tranquillity. As far as the eminent Talmudist's Shabbatean sympathies are concerned, modern scholarly opinion remains divided. Some insist on his complete innocence of the charge, others maintain that he severed his links with the underground movement in Prague (c. 1725); still others contend that Eybeschutz was an artful dissembler whom Emden quite rightly unmasked. Those in the last group point out that Eybeschutz was denied the chief rabbinate of Prague (1736) because of the controversy surrounding him; that he refused to explain himself before an assembly of rabbis when the amulets dispute still raged; that his own son and grandchildren proved to be followers of the Shabbatean heresiarch, Jacob Frank (q.v.); and that there is an undeniably striking resemblance between the heretical work ascribed to him and the only kabbalistic book by him to be published (*Shem Olạm*, 1891).

In the collected sermons published some years after his death, Jonathan Eybeschutz assailed materialism, praying by heart, the tendency of colleagues to preach only on safe topics, and other human failings.

J. Cohen, *Jacob Emden: A Man of Controversy*, 1937.

EZEKIEL (6th cent. BCE) Biblical prophet who prophesied during the Babylonian exile. He is the third of the major prophets, whose book is incorporated in the Prophets section of the Bible.

He belonged to a family of priests from the elite of the kingdom of Judah. Before being carried off by Nebuchadnezzar to Babylonia in 597 BCE or shortly thereafter, he officiated in the Jerusalem Temple. In exile he lived in or near Tel Abib, a settlement of Jews near the Chebar canal. There he experienced his first vision — of the throne-chariot of God — and began his prophetic activities among the exiles.

He prophesied for twenty-two years. Until 586, when Jerusalem and its Temple were destroyed by Nebuchadnezzar, he was a prophet of reproof, castigating the Judeans for their evil ways and foretelling the fall of Jerusalem. After the fall, however, his mood changed completely, becoming one of consolation and hope, anticipating the restoration of his people with a new heart and with the divine guarantee of eternal happiness. This is most dramatically expressed in his vision of the dry bones (Ez. 37), symbolizing the resurrection of the moribund people of Israel.

During the period before the exile, he reproved the people for the sins that warranted the punishment of exile and warned them of even more complete destruction and harsher conditions if they failed to repent. Like Jeremiah, he attacked the popular belief that the Temple would protect the people from harm and he also refuted the false prophets who raised vain hopes. Only repentance and rightful conduct, he insisted, could save the people from certain destruction. He reinforced his message with a series of symbolic acts such as eating a scroll inscribed with lamentations and words of woe, baking loaves of barley on human excrement to represent the unclean food Israel would have to eat in exile, and shaving his head and beard. His oracles of doom also encompassed foreign nations, who were denounced for their anti-Judean policies, especially after 586.

The last part (chap. 33ff.) of the book of Ezekiel contains oracles of consolation and restoration. Ezekiel forecasts the return of the exiles to their land, the rebuilding of the country and the Temple, and a wonderful future for the revived people. In his vision, the exiles of all twelve tribes — both those of the northern kingdom who had been exiled by the Assyrians and those of Judah exiled by the Babylonians — would be reunited in the restored Israel under a ruler of the house of David and would never again be separated or removed from their land. He laid down a plan for the division of the people into tribes, the leadership of the country, and the rebuilding of the Temple, and set out details of the procedure of worship and of the commandments incumbent on the ruler, the priests, and all the people.

Ezekiel's prophecies had a strong impact on later Judaism, although the rabbis were troubled by certain divergences from traditional views and only accepted the book of Ezekiel as canonical after long debates. The vision of the throne-chariot influenced Jewish and Christian mystics, with a special branch of Jewish mysticism being devoted to the subject.

According to a Jewish tradition, Ezekiel was buried in Babylonia, and his grave is identified between the Euphrates and the Chebar canal.

S. B. Freehof, *The Book of Ezekiel*, 1978.

THE VALLEY OF THE DRY BONES

The hand of the Lord came upon me and brought me out in the Spirit of the Lord, and set me down in the midst of the valley; and it *was* full of bones.

Then He caused me to pass by them all around, and behold, *there were* very many in the open valley; and indeed *they were* very dry.

And He said to me, "Son of man, can these bones live?" so I answered, "O Lord God, You know."

Again He said to me, "Prophesy to these bones, and say to them, 'O dry bones, hear the word of the Lord!

'Thus says the Lord God to these bones: "Surely I will cause breath to enter into you, and you shall live.

"I will put sinews on you and bring flesh upon you, cover you with skin and put breath in you; and you shall live. Then you shall know that I *am* the Lord."

Ezekiel 37:1–6

EZRA (5th or 4th cent. BCE) Priest and scribe who led a group of exiles from Babylonia to Jerusalem, where he reconstituted the religious life of the community. A descendant of the last high priest before the destruction of the First Temple, he was "a skilled scribe in the law of Moses" in Babylonia, that is, he made copies of the Pentateuch. In the seventh year of the rule of King Artaxerxes of the Persian dynasty that ruled the region, Ezra received permission from the king to lead a large group of 1,754 families of Jews to Jerualem to join those already settled there. The king was in all probability Artaxerxes I, in which case Ezra would have gone to Jerusalem in 458 BCE; however, many scholars have suggested that it was Artaxerxes II, in which case Ezra would have gone in 397. Ezra was moved in his decision by reports of the absence of spiritual leaders in the Jerusalem community, the lax religious life, and the unsatisfactory situation in the Temple. Before setting out, he received broad authority from the king, with many rights, including permission to receive gifts for the Temple, to exempt Temple officials from paying tax, to teach the Torah, and to appoint judges. He selected compatible priests, Levites, and teachers to join him. He did not ask Artaxerxes for military protection for the four-month journey as he had told the king that the returning Judeans relied solely on God to guarantee their safety.

Once in Jerusalem, he instituted a number of religious reforms, based on the Torah, which were to mold the future of Judaism. When he realized the extent of mixed marriages contracted by the Jews of Judah with women from other peoples, he convened a mass assembly in which the populace voluntarily agreed to dissolve alliances with foreign wives and repudiate children of such marriages (his success could not have been complete because he later had to fight this practice again).

His other major action was the reading of the Torah to a mass assembly at the New Year festival. This met with a popular response in which the people confessed their sins, made a covenant to observe the Torah, reiterated their opposition to mixed marriages, and undertook not to work on the Sabbath and to support the Temple. This great demonstration seems to have been inspired by and followed immediately upon Nehemiah's (q.v.) completion of the wall of Jerusalem.

The last act of Ezra mentioned in the Bible was his participation in the dedication of the wall. His memoirs end after recording about one year of active leadership. Nevertheless, he made a great impression on the Jewish people and was highly respected in rabbinic tradition. He was seen as the father of the oral law and an essential link in the chain of tradition. It was believed that he founded the Great Assembly (or its precursor), which was the key legislative institution for most of the Second Temple period. According to the rabbis he ordained ten crucial decrees including the regular reading of the Torah and the change from the ancient Hebrew script to the square script that is still standard, and it was held that he participated in the final codification of the Pentateuch. Indeed he was esteemed so highly that it was said, "If God had not given the Law through Moses, he would have given it through Ezra."

His story is contained in Ezra 7–10 and Nehemiah 8–9. No mention is made of his death. Josephus records the tradition that he was buried in Jerusalem, but another tradition locates his grave near the banks of the River Tigris in Babylonia (modern Iraq).

J. M. Myers, *Ezra-Nehemiah* (Anchor Bible), 1965.
C. C. Torrey, *Ezra Studies*, 1910.

F

FAJANS, KASIMIR (1887-1975) Physical chemist. Born in Warsaw, he received his doctorate in chemistry from the University of Leipzig. He took up postgraduate positions at the University of Heidelberg (1909) and later at the universities of Zurich, Switzerland, and Manchester, England, where he worked with Ernest Rutherford.

From 1911 to 1917 he was at the Technische Hochschule in Karlsruhe, Germany, for two years as assistant and then as a lecturer in physical chemistry. In 1917 he took up a position at the University of Munich, where he stayed until 1935 and was professor of physical chemistry from 1923. From 1932 1935 he was also director of the Institute for Physical Chemistry in Munich, with the support of the Rockefeller Foundation.

With the rise of Nazi power in Germany, Fajans emigrated to the United States and in 1936 joined the faculty of the University of Michigan as professor of chemistry, a position from which he retired in 1957.

Fajans's work, while he was still in Germany, involved the study of the chemical forces and optical properties of natural substances, radioactive elements, transformations, and isotopes. Together with Otto Gohring, he discovered brevium (since 1918, called protactinium, element 91; also called uranium X2).

Fajans was an active educator and author. He established the laws of radioactive displacement and adsorption indicators, and was the initiator of the concept of heat of hydration of gaseous ions; he also developed the quanticle theory of electronic molecular structure and chemical binding.

His numerous publications include *Radioaktivät und neueste Entwicklung der Lehre von chemischen Elementen* (1919; five editions); *Physikallsch-chemisches Praktikum*, (with J. Weust 1929; two editions); *Radioelements and Isotopes* (1931), and *Quanticle Theory of Chemical Binding* (1961). He also edited various scientific journals and textbooks.

Fajans was a member of many scientific societies and was fellow of the American Physical Society and chairman of the American Chemistry Society (1947). He received many awards and medals for chemistry both in Europe and America and in 1956 the Kasimir Fajans Award for Chemistry was established at the University of Michigan.

FERBER, EDNA (1987–1968) Novelist and playwright. Born in Kalamazoo, Michigan, she developed a love of America that shone through all her writings. Her only distinctly pleasant memories of Ottumwa, Iowa, the miserable coal-mining town of her childhood, were of the stock theater companies that passed through the town.

Immediately following her graduation from high school, upon learning that the family could not afford to send her to study elocution (she had previously won the state prize for public speaking), Ferber began working as a reporter for the *Appleton Crescent*. Lauded for her work there, she soon moved on to the *Milwaukee Journal*. An illness requiring a lengthy convalescence forced her back to her family home in Appleton. There, as she began to recover, she bought a used typewriter and started her career as a writer of fiction.

One of her earliest fictional creations was Emma McChesney, an independent woman who supported her family as a traveling saleslady, as featured in a series of stories. Yet there seems to have been no conscious feminist drives prompting her creative effort. After seeing just one McChesney story, *American Magazine* requested the series.

Ferber moved to New York City, where she met other writers, artists, and famous individuals from various fields. She covered the national Democratic and Republican conventions of 1912 and sold the drama rights for the McChesney stories.

This spate of successful writing — followed by a grand tour of Europe — set the pattern for the rest of her life. She returned to Europe several times and twice visited Israel. But these locations never formed the landscape of her fiction. Only her American travels appeared as the background — sometimes the center — of her works.

Show Boat, turned into an outstanding musical by Jerome Kern (q.v.) and Oscar Hammerstein and presented by Florenz Ziegfield in 1927 — was based on a "floating palace" she had gone to see off the coast of North Carolina. "I never have been on the Mississippi or in the deep South..." she said of her research for *Show Boat*. Yet clearly, the North Carolina trip, and all her reading about show boats (she spent many hours in winter in the New York Public Library) prepared her imagination for writing.

Giant, which became a 1952 James Dean movie,

had been researched in a similar fashion — a trip to Texas and Oklahoma, interviewing a number of people there, and background reading. Other of her works, such as *So Big*, the 1925 Pulitzer Prize winner, about a middle-aged woman and her son who were truck farmers on the outskirts of Chicago, were drawn from memory and imagination, with little or no special investigation. *Ice Palace* resulted from a trip to Alaska undertaken as one of her vacation trips, in between stints of writing.

In her travels and imaginative writings she covered the broad United States. "I found creative satisfaction in writing only about the people and the land I knew and, in a measure, understood," she said. She never married and referred to her books as "my children." These children rarely gave evidence of Ferber's Jewish identity, but never hid it either. It was just that the "American" factor was uppermost in her life as in her works.

Edna Ferber's other novels were *Dawn O'Hara* (1911), about a newspaperwoman in Milwaukee, *The Girls* (1921), *Cimarron* (1929), a historical romance of the Oklahoma land rush, *Come and Get It* (1935), and *Saratoga Trunk* (1941), set in New York in the 1890s. Among the plays she wrote with George S. Kaufman (q.v.) were *The Royal Family* (1927), *Dinner at Eight* (1932), and *Stage Door* (1936).

E. Ferber, *A Peculiar Treasure*, 1947.
E. Ferber, *A Kind of Magic*, 1963.

FERENCZI, SANDOR (Fraenkel; 1873–1933) Hungarian psychoanalyst and psychiatrist. Educated at the universities of Budapest and Vienna, he served for a time as an army doctor. His primary interest was hypnosis. He began practicing psychiatry and neurology in Budapest in 1900. He first met Sigmund Freud (q.v.) in 1908 and became a close friend and correspondent; they exchanged over one thousand letters. As a senior member of Freud's group, he went to the United States with Freud in 1909 and became a central figure of the psychoanalytic movement, lectured on the subject, and was an outstanding therapist. In 1913, he founded the Hungarian Psychoanalytical Society. His pioneer works on psychosexual disturbances and on active and passive homosexuality and its relation to paranoia were published in 1908 and 1911 respectively. From 1909 to 1914 he was an active supporter of the Galileo Circle, a group composed mainly of radical Jewish intellectuals, who later formed the Radical party of Hungary. In 1913 he published *Entwicklungsstufen des Wircklichkeitssinnes* ("Stages of Development in the Perception of Reality"), a classic in the field based on his observation and analysis of children, which describes the child's view of his own omnipotence and sense of reality.

Ferenczi expanded and checked Freud's findings and developed new methods of analysis. The theoretical work *Versuch einer Genitaltheorie* (1924; published in English in 1938 under the title *Thalassa: A Theory of Genitality*) explains bioanalysis, the method he invented that relates sexual drives to the wish to return to the womb. He also pioneered techniques of active therapy, first described in 1921 and reviewed in 1925 in *Kontraindicationen der aktiven psychoanalitischen Technik* ("Contraindications of Active Psychoanalytical Techniques"). *Further Contributions to the Theory and Technique of Psychoanalysis* (1926) comprises elaboration and systematization of his technique and clinical essays including those on hysteria and tics.

Ferenczi was the first to stress the paramount importance of loving physical contact with the mother for the development of the child and the dangers inherent in too-active stimulation of the infant by adults. In his latter years, there was a growing distance between him and Freud, whose sharp criticism of Ferenczi's theories and technique, along with his own failure to produce the expected results, caused Ferenczi to revise some of his theories by 1931. Nevertheless, his ideas on the early development of the child's personality and the hidden functions of the ego have influenced analysts, prompted discussion, and resulted in new theories. Ferenczi was appointed a professor at the University of Budapest in 1918 but because of his Jewish origin his chair was abolished after the fall of the proletarian dictatorship in 1919.

I. De Forest, *The Heaven of Love*, 1954.
S. Ferenczi, *Selected Papers*, 1950–1955.

FEUCHTWANGER, LION (1884–1958) German novelist, one of the most prolific and successful writers of his generation. Born in Munich, the son of a well-to-do Orthodox Jewish manufacturer, he wrote his doctoral thesis on Henrich Heine's [q.v.] unfinished romance, *The Rabbi of Bacharach*, which he also endeavored to complete. Feuchtwanger's military service during World War I transformed him into a pacifist and Social Democrat, but his Jewish loyalties never waned. At the outset of his career, he wrote dramas (a few in collaboration with Bertolt Brecht), but it was as an exponent of the historical novel that he revealed his true genius and achieved worldwide renown. *The Ugly Duchess* (1923), set in medieval Tyrol, first demonstrated his skilfull intermingling of Jewish and German themes, his concern for historical accuracy, and his brilliant portrayal of character.

With *Jud Suss* ("Jew Suss," 1925; retitled *Power* in the United States), Feuchtwanger became an international celebrity. This gripping evocation of Joseph Suss Oppenheimer, the 18th-century court Jew and financier whose execution was contrived by jealous opponents, enjoyed a phenomenal success. In its many editions and translations it sold millions of copies, also inspiring a British motion picture directed by Lothar Mendes (1934). Later, Veit Harlan's German screen version (1939) became one of the most notorious examples of Nazi race propaganda. The Nazis had good reason to dread Feuchtwanger's influence on public opinion. He had made them an object of derision in *Success* (1930), while Hitler's rise to power supplied back-

Lion Feuchtwanger.

ground for *Die Geschwister Oppenheim* (1933), a German Jewish family saga which, under its English title (*The Oppermanns*), reemerged half a century later as a television film series.

The Nazi takeover in Germany occurred while Feuchtwanger was on a lecture tour of the United States. Hearing that his books had been burnt and that he had been deprived of his citizenship, he abandoned all thoughts of returning to his native land, and spent the next seven years (1933–1940) as an exile in France. There he continued to write books until his dramatic escape from a Vichy detention camp and subsequent flight to the United States. His experiences provided material for *The Devil in France* (1941) and two other novels.

Until the end of his life, Feuchtwanger remained in California, where he published many more bestsellers and completed the Josephus trilogy first begun in pre-Hitler Germany: *Der jüdische Krieg* (*Josephus*, 1932); *Die Sohne* (*The Jew of Rome*, 1935); and *The Day Will Come* (1945). This historical work traced the dramatic story of the Jewish 1st century historian, Josephus (q.v.). Some of his later themes were borrowed from American history (as in *Proud Destiny*, 1947–1948), from medieval legend (*Spanische Ballad*, or *Raquel the Jewess of Toledo*, 1955), and in one case from the Bible (*Jephthah and His Daughter*, 1957).

FEUERMANN, EMANUEL (1902—1942) Cellist.
Born in Kolomea, Galicia, to a musical family, Feuermann began his musical education by observing his older brother, Sigmund, practice the violin with his father. As a child he was taken to Vienna, where he first studied the cello with his father. He made his recital debut there at the age of ten and played in many recitals with his brother, organized by his proud and busy father. His official debut with the Vienna Philharmonic came in 1914, playing the Haydn Cello Concerto under Felix Weingartner.

In 1917 Feuermann moved to Leipzig to continue his studies with Julius Klengel. At the age of sixteen Feuermann was appointed to the faculty of the Gurzenich Conservatory in Cologne, where he was the first cellist in the orchestra as well as a member of the Bram Eldering Quartet. He made regular guest appearances in Riga, Warsaw, and Prague. A typical review from the time praises his "unlimited technique... the intensity of his timbre... in turn warmly dreaming and ecstatically temperamental." Feuerman began recording in 1925 and eventually made some eighty records.

In 1929 Feuermann was appointed professor at the Hochschule für Musik in Berlin, but was forced to leave Germany when the Nazis came to power. During 1934–1935 Feuermann embarked on a world tour during which he made his American debut with the Chicago Symphony. A *New York Times* review from 1935 suggested that "difficulties do not exist for Mr. Feuermann, even difficulties that would give celebrated virtuosi pause. It would be hard to imagine a cleaner or more substantial technique, which can place every resource of the instrument at the interpreter's command. And there is, more than technique. There is big tone, finely sustained in singing passages, and warm. There is palpable sincerity, earnestness, musicianship attained as the result of exacting study."

FEUERMANN ON TALENT

What is talent? Desire to make sounds? Desire to create something beautiful? Vanity? A longing for something inexpressible? The fingers? The powers of concentration? Talent is composed of many talents and is dependent on fate. One likes serious music, another likes lighter music; one likes classical, the other modern. Speaking of the purely physical aspects, one may have a better left hand, the other a better right; one may have faster fingers, yet many have difficulties with trills; staccatos are also accomplished differently by each player. The greater the talent the greater the number of these qualififcations the performer will be able to accumulate. Even perfect pitch does not predestine one for music. The really important factors are a feeling for form, perseverance and patience, thoroughness and lust for discovery.

Feuermann appeared as soloist with most of the leading American orchestras and performed chamber music, initially with Artur Schnabel (q.v.) and Bronislaw Huberman (q.v.) and then with Arthur Rubinstein (q.v.) and Jascha Heifetz (q.v.), before his premature death.

S. W. Itzkoff, *Emanuel Feuermann, Virtuoso: A Biography*, 1979.

FEYNMAN, RICHARD PHILLIPS (1918—1988) U.S. physicist, who shared the Nobel Prize for physics in 1965 for the formulation of a new theory on quantum electrodynamics. Born in New York City, his penchant for working out problems earned him a neighborhood reputation as a ten-year-old genius who could "fix radios by thinking."

He earned his B.S. at Massachusetts Institute of Technology in 1939 and his doctorate at Princeton University in 1942. While writing his thesis, Feynman was recruited to the secret team at Princeton working to create an atom bomb. In 1943 he was sent to Los Alamos, New Mexico, where he worked on the atom bomb project until 1945. He was the bane of the military censors and security officials, repeatedly getting into trouble when letters arrived from his wife with codes for Feynman to decipher as a challenge. He and his wife devised intricate ways of frustrating censorship, including exchanging letters cut up into jigsaw puzzles.

After the war he was appointed associate professor of theoretical physics at Cornell University, where he completed the work that was to win him the Nobel Prize. Feynman reached a formulation of a revised theory of quantum electrodynamics independently, but at the same time as Sin-Itero Tomonaga of Tokyo University and Julian Schwinger of Harvard University. Feynman started

---

FEYNMAN THE SAFECRACKER

To demonstrate that the security in the Los Alamos atomic bomb plant was deficient, whenever Feynman required a report, he would enter the official's office, crack open the lock on the filing cabinet and remove the report. Later he would return it to the astonished official, saying, "Thanks for your report."

The highlight of his safecracking "career" was his success in cracking the combination on nine filing cabinets which contained all the secrets to the atomic bomb. These included the plutonium production schedules, the purification processes, the amount of material required, how the bomb works — "the whole schmeer!," as Feynman wrote in his autobiography.

After removing the document he wanted, he took a red pencil and wrote, "I borrowed document no. LA4312 - Feynman the safecracker," leaving the note on top of the papers in the filing cabinet.

---

from scratch, rather than revising the old theories. A close associate at Cornell University said of him: "He tried to rediscover the whole of physics by himself. Somewhat to his disappointment, what he discovered was in agreement with what other people had done." Feynman himself attached little importance to awards and honors, and said of the Nobel Prize, "I won the prize for shoving a great problem under the carpet."

Feynman's theory viewed physical events in terms of interactions of particles, instead of the traditional wave theory, and he formulated diagrams to describe these interactions, now known as Feynman graphs.

From 1950 until his death he was a professor at the California Institute of Technology. During this time, he carried out major research on a theory of weak interations, on liquid helium, and on the scattering of electrons at high energy. Feynman received the Einstein Award in 1954, the Oersted Medal in 1972, and the Niels Bohr International Gold Medal in 1973. His publications include *Lectures in Physics* (3 vols., 1963–1965).

Although he generally avoided sitting on committees, he was a member of the presidential commission investigating the explosion of the space shuttle *Challenger* in 1986. Calling for a glass of ice water, Feynman performed a dramatic and simple experiment before the commission, taking a piece of the O-ring material used to seal the joints between the rocket's sections and immersing it in the water. He demonstrated that the cooled material did not spring back to its original shape after being squeezed, and concluded that the disaster could have been avoided if the space agency had considered this property.

Feynman summed up his philosophy in these words: "I don't feel frightened by not knowing. I can live with doubt and uncertainty. I think it's much more interesting to live not knowing than to have answers which might be wrong."

R. P. Feynman, *Surely You're Joking, Mr. Feynman*, 1985.

Physics Today, February 1989. Special issue in memory of Feynman.

FLEG, EDMOND (originally Flegenheimer; 1874–1963) French writer. He was born in Geneva into a family attached to Jewish tradition, but while young his ties to his Jewish origins grew tenuous. Nonetheless the Alfred Dreyfus (q.v.) affair, which unfolded while he was a student in Paris, and later the early Zionist congresses, as well as his friendship with the British writer, Israel Zangwill,(q.v.), all fostered in him a strong Jewish and Zionist orientation, and many of his writings were, in some way, answers to the questions he began to ask himself at that time.

In Paris he was a successful playwright, theater critic, poet, and essayist. Apart from original plays, he translated Goethe's *Julius Caesar* into French. He increasingly turned, however, to Jewish subjects, while his poetry and thought were inspired by the Jewish mission, messianic inspiration, and the future of humanity. His plays also adopted Jewish motifs, such as his *Le Juif du Pape* about the meetings between the messianic kabbalist, Solomon Molcho (q.v.) and Pope Clement VII.

Apart from the period of World War I, when he served in the French Foreign Legion, Fleg wrote a series of works of Jewish interest, which proved highly influential among French Jewry and challenged its youth to think of their faith and spirituality. He translated Shalom Aleichem (q.v.) and the Passover Haggadah, and produced a monumental summary of Jewish thought in *L'anthologie juive* (which appeared in English in 1925). One of his major works of poetry was the verse cycle *Ecoute Israël*, which covered all Jewish history from the creation to the establishment of the State of Israel.

Fleg was a devout Zionist and in 1927 published *Ma Palestine*. However, to the young Jews leaving for Eretz Israel he said regretfully, "I will never be able to tear myself away from the quays of the Seine." During World War II, he left Paris for the south of France but refused an opportunity to find refuge in Switzerland. Years later, at a ceremony planting a forest in his honor in Israel, one of his assistants said, "You were always our spiritual leader but during the war, when you refused to leave us, you became, in scouting terms — our chief."

Edmond Fleg. Bust by Chana Orloff, 1921

FLEG'S CREED

I am a Jew because, born of Israel and having lost her, I have felt her live again in me, more living than myself.

I am a Jew because, born of Israel and having regained her, I wish her to live after me, more living than in myself.

I am a Jew because the faith of Israel demands of me no abdication of the mind.

I am a Jew because the faith of Israel requires of me all the devotion of my heart.

I am a Jew because in every place where suffering weeps, the Jew weeps.

I am a Jew because at every time when despair cries out, the Jew hopes.

I am a Jew because the word of Israel is the oldest and the newest.

I am a Jew because the promise of Israel is the universal promise.

I am a Jew because, for Israel, the world is not yet completed: men are completing it.

I am a Jew because, for Israel, Man is not created: men are creating him.

I am a Jew because, above the nations and Israel, Israel places man and his unity.

I am a Jew because, above man, image of the divine Unity, Israel places the divine unity, and its divinity.

FLEISCHER, MAX (1885–1972) Producer of animated cartoons; creator of Popeye. Born in Austria, he was taken to the United States at the age of five and educated at various schools in New York. Working as a cartoonist for the Brooklyn *Daily Eagle* and as art editor of *Popular Science Monthly*, he became interested in animated cartoons. In Los Angeles, in 1917, developing a technique for animating cartoons, he produced the first animated feature. The film, which had required a year's preparation, lasted less than a minute.

In 1919, he founded the Fleischer Studios, with himself as artistic and technical director and his brother, Dave, as producer. Within the next two decades, the studio became a major enterprise, grossing millions of dollars from the production of animated cartoons for Paramount Pictures. Among his most famous characters were Ko-Ko the Clown, from *Out of the Inkwell*, Betty Boop, and Popeye, whom he brought to the screen from paper comics. Betty Boop had a short career as her behavior was criticized for being "immoral," but Popeye and his girlfriend, Olive Oyl, became national institutions.

As an innovator in the field of animated cartoons, Fleicher took out over two dozen patents for various technical production inventions. Most famous was the rotoscope, a tool that brought verisimilitude to animation and became indispensable to cartoonists.

Although he also produced educational films for the armed forces, as well as several scientific features, he is best known for revolutionizing the world of cartoons and making animated pictures a substantial part of the movie industry.

FLEISCHMANN, GISI (1897–1944) Leader of the Slovak Jewish underground Working Group (Pracovna Skupina) during the Holocaust. She was the head of WIZO (Women's International Zionist Organization) in Slovakia before the war. When the Jewish Center, the Slovak Jewish council, was established in 1940, she became the head of its emigration department. At the time of the deportations from Slovakia, in March 1942, she was one of the founders of the Committee of Six, which was the precursor to the Working Group.

During the period of the deportations, the Working Group tried to end the flow of transports to the east. They attempted to convince members of the Slovak government, Slovak church leaders, and the Vatican to intervene on behalf of the Jews. They succeeded in establishing three work camps in Slovakia, where most of the inmates were safeguarded from deportation. They also made contact with Dieter Wisliceny, Adolf Eichmann's representative in Slovakia, and began negotiations with him for the cessation of the deportations. Fleischmann played a central role in all these activities, especially in the negotiations. Soon after the Working Group paid Wisliceny the required sum (50,000 dollars), the deportations ended. She, along with Rabbi Michael Dov Weismandel, and the other leaders of the Working Group, believed that the payment had led to the end of the deportations. They embarked on expanded negotiations with Wisliceny to end the deportations of Jews from throughout Nazi-dominated Europe to Poland. These discussions came to be known as the Europa Plan.

Fleischmann played a pivotal role in the Europa Plan. With Weismandel, she corresponded with representatives of Jewish organizations in Switzerland, Istanbul, and Hungary, in an attempt to raise the 200,000 dollars down payment demanded by the Nazis. She was arrested several times for her other rescue activities. The most serious charge against her was that she had given a bribe to the wife of a chairman of a government office, Dr. Koso, in order to stop the deportations. Although imprisoned, she was released through Wisliceny's intervention.

During the suppression of the Slovak National Uprising in 1944, a Gestapo officer burst into her office and arrested her. Alois Brunner, who was responsible for the renewed deportations, told her that if she would divulge the whereabouts of Jews in hiding she would be released. Fleischmann refused. She was sent to Auschwitz, with the express order that she be killed, and she was gassed on arrival.

J. Campion, *In the Lion's Mouth: Gisi Fleischmann and the Jewish Fight for Survival*, 1987.
Y. O. Neumann, *Gisi Fleischmann: The Story of a Heroic Woman*, 1970.

FLEXNER, ABRAHAM (1866–1959) U.S. educator who played an important part in introducing modern scientific and medical education to the United States. He was born in Louisville, Kentucky; his parents "remained to the end of their lives pious Hebrews, attending the synagogue regularly and observing religious feasts." He grew up in the years just after the Civil War and experienced the poverty and hardships resulting from the panic of 1873.

Flexner developed an interest in the study of Greek and this formed the background of his college education. Throughout his life, this intellectual pursuit provided "a flowing spring of interest and enlightenment." When he was seventeen, his older brother, Jacob, funded his education at Johns Hopkins University in Baltimore. Following his graduation, Abraham taught in the Louisville High School and then founded an innovative college preparatory school in which no examinations were required and no records were maintained. In 1905 he went to Harvard University to continue his studies in psychology, philosophy, and science, dealing particularly with educational problems. The following year he spent studying at the University of Berlin.

Following these additional years of study, in 1908, Flexner published a review of higher education, *The American College: A Criticism*. This led to a commission from the Carnegie Endowment for the Advancement of Teaching to survey medical schools throughout the United States. This study appeared in 1910 under the title *Medical Education in the United States and Canada* (known as the Flexner Report) and examined 155 medical colleges. His report, which rated each college, helped to initiate a basic reform in all areas of medical education in the United States. He also published *Medical Education in Europe* (1912) and *Prostitution in Europe* (1914). In 1912 he was invited to join the Rockefeller Foundation's General Education Board, the first of the great American foundations devoted strictly to education. He was on the staff for seventeen years, prepared a number of educational surveys under its aegis, and was responsible for allocating large sums of money to medical education. His last major project was founding and organizing the Institute for Advanced Study at Princeton University. He served as director, 1930–1939, and among those he attracted to the Institute was Albert Einstein (q.v.).
A. Flexner, *Abraham Flexner: An Autobiography*, 1960.

FORD, ALEKSANDER (1908–1980) Polish film director. A native of Lodz, Ford was educated in art history at Warsaw University and made his first short films as the Polish cinema's silent era drew to an end. His first feature film, *Mascot*, was made in 1930 and did little to advance his career. At this time he became a cofounder of the Society of the Devotees of the Artistic Film, better known as START. Ford and friends, such as the director

Wanda Jakubowska and the film historian Jerzy Toeplitz, aimed to raise the artistic and technical level of Polish cinema while also winning for it wider official recognition. The group lasted until 1935, its achievements more theoretical than practical.

In 1932 Ford's *The Street Legion*, a realistic drama set in the streets of Warsaw, was a popular success. He traveled to Palestine a year later to make *Sabra*, featuring the stars of the Habima Theater in a plot that dealt with a dispute over water between Zionist settlers and local Arabs. Back in Poland in 1937, Ford helped found a group similar to START, the Cooperative of Film Authors. From 1939, he was in the Soviet Union, where he produced films for the Red Army, becoming head of the film group of the First Polish Division in 1943. His position was further consolidated in 1945, when, with the nationalization of the Polish film industry, he became head of Film Polski.

The postwar period saw some of Ford's best work: *Border Street*, dealing with the Warsaw ghetto revolt, *The Young Chopin, Five Boys from Barska Street*, and the epic *Knights of the Teutonic Order*. During these years Ford also served as head of the Lodz film school, which he had helped to found, and as director of the film production group Studio. In the late 1960s political pressure forced Ford from his position and in 1970 he emigrated to Israel. Unable to adapt to the Israeli filmmaking climate, he made only two more films, one about Janusz Korczak (q.v.), the other an adaptation of Aleksandr Solzhenitsyn's *The First Circle*, before his death in Los Angeles.
G. Moskowitz, "The Uneasy East: Aleksander Ford" in *Sight and Sound*, Winter 1957/58.

FORTAS, ABE (1910–1982) Lawyer, civil libertarian, New Deal activist, and justice of the U.S. Supreme Court. Son of an Orthodox Jewish cabinetmaker who immigrated to the United States from Britain, Fortas was born in Memphis, Tennessee. He worked his way through Southwestern College as a clerk in a shoe store and a violin player in a jazz band. At Yale University, he was editor of the law journal and graduated first in his law school class in 1933. Fortas remained at Yale for four years after graduation as an assistant professor under William O. Douglas and also served as consultant to the Agricultural Adjustment Administration and the Securities and Exchange Commission (SEC).

In 1937 he left Yale for a full-time appointment at the SEC, and from 1939 to 1941 served as general counsel to the Public Works Administration (PWA). In 1941 he entered the Department of the Interior and became its undersecretary one year later. He was adviser to the U.S. delegation to the organizational meeting of the United Nations in San Francisco in 1945 and to the first U.N. General Assembly session in London in 1946. Later that year, he resigned from government service in order to establish the private law firm of Arnold, Fortas, and Porter in Washington, D.C., which soon became one of the most successful and prestigious firms in the city.

Fortas was both a noted corporate counsel and a civil libertarian, defending victims of Senator Joseph McCarthy such as Owen Lattimore. In 1963 he successfully argued the case of Gideon v. Wainwright before the Supreme Court, winning a landmark decision which gave poor criminal defendants the right to free legal counsel.

In 1948 Fortas represented Lyndon B. Johnson against a challenge to the latter's senatorial nomination and subsequently became his close friend and adviser. In 1965, as president, Johnson chose Fortas as his first appointee to the Supreme Court. For the next four years, Fortas, allied with Justice William O. Douglas, his former professor, sided with the court's liberal majority in numerous decisions against censorship, racial discrimination, restrictions on the rights of political dissenters, and violations of church-state separation.

When Johnson nominated Fortas to succeed retiring Chief Justice Earl Warren in 1968, a strong conservative coalition of Republican and Southern Democrat opponents, as well as charges of "cronyism" and the improper acceptance of fees, led to a filibuster in the Senate. As a result, his name was withdrawn and Fortas became the first nominee to the post of Chief Justice since 1795 to fail to receive Senate approval.

A year later, the revelation in *Life* magazine that Fortas had agreed to accept an annual fee from the family foundation of Louis E. Wolfson, who was subsequently convicted of securities violations, raised a storm of public protest and the possibility of impeachment. Consequently Fortas resigned from the court, the first justice ever to do so under the pressure of public criticism.

Following his resignation, Fortas practiced law in Washington, D.C., until his death.
L. Kalman, *Abe Fortas*, 1990.
R. Shogan, *A Question of Judgment: The Fortas Case and the Struggle for the Supreme Court*, 1977.

FOX, WILLIAM (1879–1952) U.S. film executive. Of German Jewish stock, Fox (then named Fried) was brought to the United States from Hungary before his first birthday. At eleven years of age he left school to help support his family. He worked in a variety of jobs, eventually putting his hard-earned savings into a business of his own, the Knickerbocker Cloth Examining and Shrinking Company. Attracted by the lucrative potential of the early motion pictures, Fox bought a penny arcade and by 1904 had opened his first nickelodeon in New York. Within a short time he owned a chain of cinemas, and, seeing the greater profits being made by his suppliers, founded the Greater New York Film Rental Company.

Fox was one of the most successful of the independent film distributors who fought the monopolistic practices of the Motion Picture Patents Company, which had a virtual stranglehold on the infant film industry untill 1912. He reacted to the attempt to buy him out for 75,000 dollars by asking for ten times the amount and then by initiating a 6,000,000 dollars lawsuit for violation of the Sherman Antitrust Act. Following his legal victory, he entered the field of film production in 1914. His new enterprise, the Box Office Attractions Film Rental Company, was soon better known under its new name, the Fox Film Corporation.

In 1916, Fox followed the westward trend of the American film industry and opened a studio in Hollywood. Among the stars he claimed as his own in the years he headed the studio were Theda Bara and Tom Mix. In the twenties, he imported the prestigious German director F. W. Murnau and helped develop homegrown talents like John Ford and Howard Hawks.

On the technical front, he was responsible for having the first Hollywood studio to adopt a sound-on-film system; in June 1927, nearly four months before the premiere of the so-called first talkie, Warner Brothers' *The Jazz Singer*, the Fox Movietone newsreel allowed Americans to hear as well as see triumphant aviator Charles Lindbergh. The Grandeur 70 mm widescreen process was another, less successful, innovation he attempted to introduce.

Fox's ambitions for monopoly of the market were, if anything, greater than those of the pioneer producers he had bested in court in 1912. In 1929, having acquired many film theaters, including the world's largest, the Roxy, and the rights to American and foreign sound-on-film systems, he bought a controlling interest in Loew's Inc., the parent company of MGM.

On the brink of becoming the most powerful of the movie moguls, several adverse events befell him in fairly rapid succession. MGM's Louis B. Mayer (q.v.), endangered by the takeover, used his influence with the Hoover administration to have the Justice Department raise the antitrust issue, forcing Fox to relinquish his control of Loew's. Fox himself was incapacitated for several months as the result of a serious automobile accident. His recovery coincided with the collapse of the stock market. The price of Fox shares fell from 119 dollars to one dollar. The enemies he had made during his rise to power were many and in 1930 he was ousted from his own company. Following this, various legal proceedings were instituted against him and in 1936, the year after Darryl F. Zanuck's [q.v.] 20th Century Productions had merged with the Fox Film Corporation, William Fox was declared bankrupt. In 1941 he was convicted of an attempt to bribe a judge at his bankruptcy hearing and he later spent six months in prison. A return to filmmaking never materialized, but those patents remaining to him after the protracted litigation left him well provided for in his last years.

T. Ramsaye, *A Million and One Nights: A History of the Motion Picture*, 1926.
U. Sinclair, *Upton Sinclair Presents William Fox*, 1933.

FRANK, ANNE (1929–1945) Dutch victim of the Holocaust and author of a diary. Anne Frank and her family left Germany for Amsterdam soon after the Nazis seized power in 1933. Like many Dutch Jews they went into hiding during the German occupation of the Netherlands. From the summer of 1940 onward, Anne's father, Otto Frank, began preparing for the eventuality of hiding. On July 5, 1942, Anne's sixteen-year-old sister Margot received a letter from the Central Office for Jewish Emigration, ordering her to appear for forced labor. The next day the family moved into the vacant annex of Otto's office, with the knowledge and help of four of his employees: Victor Kugler, Johannes Kleiman, Elli Voskuijl, and Miep Gies. A week later they were joined by the family of Otto Frank's partner, Hermann van Pels. On November 16, 1942, an eighth person came to hide in the annex, the dentist Fritz Pfeffer. The small space was very crowded, and food and clothing were difficult to obtain. Otto's employees, however, managed to supply the needs of their charges.

On August 4, 1944, the SD (the security and intelligence service of the SS, the Nazi elite) in Amsterdam was informed that Jews were hiding in the annex at Prinsengracht 263 and the eight Jews were found and arrested. Kleiman and Kugler were also arrested and interned in the Netherlands. The eight Jews were sent to the Westerbork camp, and from there the Franks were sent to Auschwitz on the last transport to leave the Dutch camp. Anne's mother Edith died in Auschwitz, and Anne and her sister were sent to Bergen-Belsen at the end of October 1944. Both died in March 1945 of typhus. Otto Frank survived Auschwitz and was liberated by the Soviets on January 27, 1945.

Anne had been given a diary for her thirteenth

Page from Anne Frank's diary, October 1942.

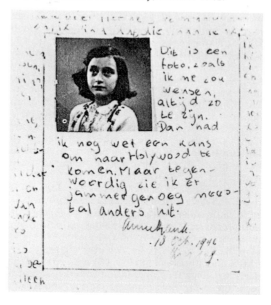

FROM ANNE FRANK'S DIARY

We have been pointedly reminded that we are in hiding, that we are Jews in chains.... We Jews mustn't show our feelings, must be brave and strong, must accept all inconveniences and not grumble.... Some time this terrible war will be over. Surely the time will come when we are people again, and not just Jews. Who has inflicted this upon us? Who has made us Jews different from all other people? Who has allowed us to suffer so terribly till now? It is God that has made us as we are, but it will be God, too, who will raise us up again. If we bear all this suffering and if there are still Jews left, when it is over, then Jews, instead of being doomed, will be held up as an example. Who knows, it might even be our religion from which the world and all peoples learn good, and for that reason and that reason only do we have to suffer now. We can never become just Netherlanders, or just English, or representatives of any country for that matter, we will always remain Jews, but we want to, too. During that night I really felt that I had to die... but now, now I've been saved again, now my first wish after the war is that I may become Dutch!

I don't believe that the big men, the politicians and the capitalists alone are guilty of the war. Oh, no, the little man is just as keen.... There is an urge and rage in the people to destroy, to kill, to murder, and until all mankind, without exception, undergoes a great change, wars will be waged.

April 11, 1944

birthday, on June 12, 1944, and immediately began making entries addressed to her imaginary friend Kitty. In the annex she continued to write. She wrote of her own development, her family relationships, the experience of hiding, the events around her, and her reactions to them. The diary also describes the efforts made by those who hid the Franks to provide for them and protect them. In addition to the diary Anne wrote stories and a "Book of Beautiful Phrases," full of quotations she liked. After the eight Jews had been arrested, Miep Gies took the diary and other papers she found in the annex. When Otto Frank returned from Auschwitz, she returned them to him.

In 1947 the diary, under the title *The Annex*, was first published. It has since appeared in over fifty editions, in numerous languages, in roughly twenty million copies. A stage version based on the diary premiered on Broadway on October 5, 1955, and won the Pulitzer Prize for best play of the year. A film version followed in 1959. For many people the diary is their first confrontation with the Nazi persecution of the Jews, and throughout the world,

Anne Frank has become a symbol of the millions of victims of the Holocaust. The diary has served as a source of inspiration for artists, musicians, and choreographers, the world over.

In 1960 the annex on Prinsengracht 263 was made into a museum about the struggle against anti-Semitism and racism. The Anne Frank Foundation maintains a documentation center, produces teaching aids, and organizes traveling exhibits. The original diary is on loan to the house from the Anne Frank Foundation, and is on display there. A book of Anne's stories, *Tales From the Secret Annex* (English edition, 1950), was also published. A. Frank, *The Diary of Anne Frank: The Limited Edition*, 1989.

E. Schnabel, *Anne Frank: A Portrait in Courage*, 1959 (published in Britain as *The Footsteps of Anne Frank*).

FRANK, JACOB (1726–1791) Pseudo-Messiah. Born in Podolia, he was a dealer and trader with no special learning, but while in Turkey he came into contact with the Donmeh, the group that continued to believe in the messiahship of Shabbetai Tzevi (q.v.). He began to study the mystical classic, the Zohar, and became convinced that he should return to Poland to lead the secret believers in Shabbetai Tzevi there, who at the time were oppressed and disorganized. A charismatic figure, he began to regard himself as a reincarnation of Shabbetai Tzevi and, like him, apparently converted to Islam for a time. However, he developed a simpler theology, with a trinitarian basis that paralleled Christianity (God, the Messiah, and the *Shekhinah*, a female hypostasis of God).

He acquired a following, especially in Galicia, Hungary, and the Ukraine, and the rabbis excommunicated him in 1756 for his heretical teachings, antinomianism, and transgression of the commandments (including the sexual restrictions). The rabbis denounced the group to the Catholic authorities as a new religion, which was forbidden by canon law, while the Frankists for their part put themselves under the protection of the Catholic bishop of Kamienic-Podolski. Hoping that the sectarians could be converted to Christianity, the bishop ordered a public disputation at which the rabbis would have to defend the Talmud. In the seven-day disputation, the Frankists presented the nine principles of their faith, including the threefold face of God, his corporeal manifestation, and the falsity of the Talmud. The bishop decreed in favor of the Frankists and ordered the burning of thousands of copies of the Talmud in the Kamienic-Podolski marketplace. When, the bishop died suddenly and the rabbis renewed their attacks on the Frankists, they received protection from the king, Augustus III (1758). Frank declared himself a living embodiment of God's power and said that he and his adherents were destined to adopt Christianity as a guide. The Frankists also revived the anti-Jewish blood libel.

At a second disputation held in 1759, the Frankists were outwitted, but in its wake they accepted Christianity and Frank himself was baptized in Warsaw cathedral with the king as his godfather. The Polish clergy remained skeptical, however, in their attitude to the sect and Frank's doctrines and manner of living aroused their suspicions. He was arrested and examined by an ecclesiastical court that exiled him to the fortress of Czestochowa, where he remained for thirteen years. During this time, he maintained his relations with his followers, who now saw him as a martyr, the suffering Messiah. Many settled in the town and continued to gain inspiration from his teaching.

His imprisonment ended with the first partition of Poland when he was released by the commander of the Russian troops who occupied the town in 1772. He and his followers moved to Brünn (Brno) in Moravia and he again won favor at court. His past, however, caught up with him and he moved to Offenbach in Germany, where the sect was reestablished under the "Holy Lord," who now called himself Baron von Frank.

Even after his death, the sect continued to exist under the leadership of Frank's daughter, Eve, who was seen as the queen and high priestess, and continued to practice its secret rites, allegedly including ritual orgies. Eventually it disintegrated. Many of its former adherents married into the Polish aristocracy and were absorbed into Polish society. Descendants of the Frankists included the Polish poet Adam Mickiewicz and the U.S. Supreme Court justice Louis D. Brandeis (q.v.).

G. Scholem, *Kabbalah*, 1974.

FRANKFURTER, FELIX (1882–1965) U.S. Supreme Court justice. Born in Vienna, Frankfurter moved to the United States with his parents when he was twelve and settled on the Lower East Side of New York. He graduated from City College of New York in 1902 and with highest honors from Harvard Law School in 1906. After a few months in private practice, Frankfurter became an associate of Henry L. Stimson, whom he served from 1906 to 1909 as assistant U.S. Attorney for the Southern District of New York, to which Stimson had been appointed by President Theodore Roosevelt. Later he became personal assistant to Stimson when Stimson served as secretary of war from 1911 to 1913. During this period he began a two-decade long friendship with Supreme Court Justice Oliver Wendell Holmes, with whom he shared a passionate belief in judicial restraint.

In 1914 Frankfurter was appointed professor at Harvard Law School, a position that he held for twenty-five years, until his appointment to the Supreme Court. During World War I he was legal adviser on industrial problems to Secretary of War Newton Baker, first secretary and then counsel of the President's Mediation Commission, and chairman of the War Labor Policies Board in 1918. These positions brought him into the forefront of the labor struggles of that period. These included the conviction of Tom Mooney in 1916 for a bomb-

ing in San Francisco and the 1917 deportation from Arizona of striking copper miners for alleged membership in the radical Industrial Workers of the World (IWW; "Wobblies"). In both cases Frankfurter ruled in favor of the unions, earning a reputation as an extreme liberal.

This reputation was strengthened by Frankfurter's fight for a new trial for Sacco and Vanzetti (1927), his role as one of the founders of the American Civil Liberties Union (ACLU) in 1920 and the *New Republic* magazine, as well as the fact that he served as legal adviser to the National Association for the Advancement of Colored People (NAACP) and counsel to the National Consumers' League.

During World War I Frankfurter was drawn increasingly into Zionist affairs by Louis D. Brandeis (q.v.), who had accepted the chairmanship of the Provisional Committee for General Zionist Affairs (PZC). Even after Brandeis was appointed to the Supreme Court in 1916 he maintained his active Zionist role and, together with Frankfurter, helped secure the support of President Woodrow Wilson for the Balfour Declaration and "the aspirations and historic claims of the Jewish people with regard to Palestine."

Frankfurter and Brandeis advocated the convening of an American Jewish Congress to elect the Jewish representatives to the Peace Conference in Paris; in 1919 Frankfurter joined the American Zionist delegation. Serving as President Wilson's legal adviser and helping to draft the International Labor Office program, Frankfurter actively worked on the draft of the Palestine mandate. On March 1, 1919, Emir Feisal, son of Sherrif Hussein, wrote to Frankfurter confirming the agreement he had signed two months earlier with Chaim Weizmann (q.v.), insisting that "we Arabs... look with deepest sympathy on the Zionist movement."

In 1921 Frankfurter joined the Brandeis group in withdrawing from the mainstream of Zionist activity over the issue of fiscal autonomy for the American Zionists. He nevertheless remained friends with Weizmann, and continued to support Zionist aims.

In the late 1920s and early 1930s Frankfurter served as adviser to New York governors Alfred E. Smith and Franklin D. Roosevelt. He continued to advise Roosevelt on New Deal legislation when the latter was elected president in 1932, and in January 1939 Roosevelt appointed Frankfurter to the U.S. Supreme Court. Frankfurter served as a justice until 1962, when a stroke forced him to retire.

Frankfurter's philosophy of judicial restraint gave greater weight to federal or state legislative action than to individual rights or the victims of legal injustice. In *Wolf* v. *Colorado* (1949), for example, he insisted that the evidence illegally seized did not have to be excluded by the court, and in *Baker* v. *Carr* (1962) he unsuccessfully argued that inequitable legislative representation is a "political controversy" not subject to judicial review. Thus, Frankfurter's pre-court liberal reputation gave way to a conservative label at a time when the liberal philosophy called for an active judicial process.

In July 1963 President John F. Kennedy awarded Frankfurter the medal of freedom.

Among the books that Frankfurter wrote were *The Business of the Supreme Court* (1927), *Mr. Justice Holmes and the Supreme Court* (1938), *Law and Politics* (1939), *The Case of Sacco and Vanzetti* (1954), *Of Law and Men* (1956), and *Felix Frankfurter Reminisces* (an oral history, 1960).

L. Baker, *Felix Frankfurter*, 1969.
P. B. Kirkland, *Felix Frankfurter on the Supreme Court*, 1970.
W. Mendelson, *Felix Frankfurter* (2 vols.), 1964.H. S. Thomas, *Felix Frankfurter: Scholar on the Bench*, 1960.

FRANKLIN, ROSALIND ELISE (1920–1958) British chemist whose research contributed to the discovery of the structure of the DNA molecule. Franklin was born to a leading English-Jewish family. Raised in an unusually egalitarian atmosphere, she enjoyed the same advantages as her brothers, including a good education. When her father suggested she become involved in charitable works, she informed him of her wish to become a scientist. In 1938 she entered Newnham College, Cambridge, where she studied physical chemistry.

Franklin proved to be a gifted scientist and a determined personality. Once, she knelt accidentally on a sewing needle and walked to a hospital to have it removed; the astonished doctor was amazed that she could have walked with a needle angled across her knee joint. She applied the same resolve to her studies. During her college years, World War II often disrupted classes and students were forced to work independently much of the time. Franklin throve in this atmosphere, working long hours in the laboratory and developing work habits that would serve her well in the future.

Upon graduation in 1941, she accepted a research scholarship from Newnham College. She studied gas-phase chromatography until 1942, when she was hired by the British Coal Utilization Research Association in London. With the association she worked on the physical structure of coals and carbonized coals. Her writings on coal were considered fundamental to the field for many years. An Oxford professor later remarked that her research "brought order into a field which had previously been in chaos."

In 1947 she accepted an offer from the Laboratoire Central des Services Chimiques de l'Etat in Paris. There she learned X-ray diffraction techniques and used the method to study carbons and structural changes accompanying graphitization. She also worked on the crystallography of coal and graphite, laying the foundation for what was later called carbon-fiber technology.

After three years in Paris, Franklin responded to an offer from John Randall's Medical Research Council unit at King's College, London. Randall offered her the opportunity to set up a new X-ray diffraction laboratory and to apply the technique to the study of dioxyribonucleic acid (DNA). Using her X-ray diffraction photographs, she found two forms of DNA: form A, a crystalline form, and form B, a wet form. Franklin began to study the A form using the Patterson synthesis, a complex mathematical technique. At first she was convinced that the A form did not have a helical structure, hypothesizing a figure-eight structure. Upon further investigation, she realized that the A and B forms had to be double helixes — two coaxial helical chains running in opposite directions. Franklin also correctly postulated that the main sugar phosphate chain of nucleic acid lay on the outside of the spiral. Years later, a colleague studying her laboratory notes realized that she was two steps away from deciphering the entire DNA structure.

In spite of her successes, she was unhappy at King's College. Female scientists seemed to be less accepted and she put up with daily annoyances like being excluded from joining her fellow scientists in the all-male dining room. In 1953 she moved to Birkbeck College, London, where she remained until her death. At Birkbeck she pursued pioneering research on tobacco mosaic virus (TMV). Using her expertise in X-ray diffraction, she discovered the infective element of the virus particle, which turned out to be its ribose nucleic acid (RNA). Her model of the TMV molecule was the first of its kind and was the central feature of the virus exhibit at the Brussels World Fair.

In 1956, at the height of her career, her doctor detected cancer and though she had several operations, the disease proved fatal. Franklin told few people of her illness and continued her work at Birkbeck, and the rest of her life, as usual.

In her last years, against the wishes of her colleagues, she began to study poliomyletis, a dangerously infective virus. Upon her death, the head of the laboratory at Birkbeck wrote of her, "As a scientist Miss Franklin was distinguished by extreme clarity and perfection in everything she undertook. Her photographs are among the most beautiful X-ray photographs of any substance ever taken. She was an admirable director of a research team and inspired those who worked with her to reach the same high standards."
A. Sayles, *Rosalind Franklin and DNA*, 1975.

FREUD, ANNA (1895—1982) Psychoanalyst. She was the youngest child of Sigmund Freud (q.v.), and the only one to follow in his footsteps as a psychoanalyst. She started her career as an elementary school teacher, but with time, began gravitating toward the Vienna Psychoanalytic Society and soon became a member. From the start, she worked mainly with children and adolescents.

Though writing extensively in the field and founding the prestigious annual, *The Psychoanalytic Study of the Child*, which she edited until her death, her most noted work was *The Ego and the Mechanism of Defense* (1937). This book marks a shift in the focus within psychoanalysis from the stress upon unconscious conflicts to a study of the ego or "seat of observation," which mediates between instinctual drives and reality. Anna Freud elaborated upon the different defense mechanisms, such as repression, projection, and sublimation, whereby the ego wards off anxiety and enables a person to function.

Anna Freud provided much insight into child psychoanalysis. She founded, in 1943, the famed Hampstead Clinics in Great Britain, whose original aim was to investigate the effect of war upon children, particularly those separated from their parents by the cruel "experiments of nature" presented by the war. In subsequent work at this clinic, she pioneered a diagnostic system that stressed the level of psychological development and organization rather than merely symptoms.

Anna Freud never married. She devoted herself to caring for her father, especially during the last years of his life, when he struggled with cancer. In 1938, she even convinced the Gestapo to take her in for interrogation and to spare her elderly father the ordeal. The closeness of the two, emotionally and intellectually, is evidenced by Anna's having been psychoanalyzed by her father — an aberrant situation in a field that places a premium upon the therapist's strict neutrality and that posits the sexual longing of a child for the parent of the opposite sex.

Although Anna Freud lacked formal psychiatric training, she became a force in the field, and was considered, by many, her father's successor. Tensions with the rival school of Melanie Klein (q.v.) in Great Britain, where the Freuds moved after the Nazi *Anschluss* of Austria, hardly diminished her stature. A survey late in her career among American psychiatrists and psychoanalysts rated her as the foremost practitioner of her day. A summary of her theories is contained in her *Normality and Pathology in Childhood* (1968).

Anna Freud's connection to Judaism was apparently quite peripheral. Nevertheless her pride in her ethnic background may be surmised from a remark she made at a Jerusalem conference honoring her father: "[Psychoanalysis has] been criticized for its methods being imprecise, its findings not open to proof by experiment, for being unscientific, even for being a 'Jewish science.' However the other derogatory comments may be evaluated, it is, I believe, the last-mentioned connotation which, under present circumstances, can serve as a title of honor."
E. Pumpian-Mindlin, *Pschoanalytic Pioneers* (eds. F. Alexander, S. Eisenstein, M. Grotjahn), 1966.
P. Roazen, *Freud and His Followers*, 1975.

FREUD, SIGMUND (1856–1939) Founder of psychoanalysis. He was the eldest of seven children born to a merchant in Moravia. His family moved to Vienna when Freud was four. He received some religious instruction, and developed a keen sensitivity to anti-Semitism that was to play a role in some of his later struggles. Though he was to be distinguished for the high literary style of his German, even receiving the coveted Goethe Prize for German literature, his mother, who lived until 1930, could speak only Yiddish fluently.

Freud completed medical school at the University of Vienna, where he concentrated on neuroanatomical research. He subsequently joined the Vienna General Hospital. Ambitious for a successful academic career, he initially tried to make his mark by experimenting with cocaine, then a new drug, as a treatment for depression and fatigue. The side effects, particularly addiction, as well as the controversy which his researches stirred up led him to abandon these efforts.

At the age of twenty-nine he traveled to Paris to study with the famed French neurologist, Jean-Martin Charcot. Once there, he observed the use of hypnosis in the treatment of hysterical disorders. This was the turning point in his career, which sent him in search of the hidden factors in abnormal human behavior.

During the following ten years, Freud married Martha Bernays, his fiancée of four years and granddaughter of Rabbi Isaac Bernays of Hamburg, the first to formulate a modern Jewish Orthodoxy, fathered six children, and developed his private practice in Vienna, specializing in nervous disorders. During this period too, Freud undertook to decipher the peculiar neurotic and hysterical symptoms which his patients presented to him. He became disillusioned with the temporary effects of hypnosis, and sought other tech-

Sigmund Freud.

niques, eventually developing what remains even today the basic technique of psychoanalysis: free association, whereby the patient relaxes and relates whatever comes to mind. Thus hints of unconscious material emerge in the stream of the patient's spoken thoughts. Freud himself, to better understand his patients, embarked at this time upon a painstaking self-analysis, delving into his own deepest forgotten childhood memories in a quest for self-understanding. While observers before him had spoken of a realm of the human mind of which we are not aware, he was the first to develop a systematic exposition of the unconscious. This marked the beginning of psychoanalysis.

This period of research and introspection culminated in the publication in 1900 of *The Interpretation of Dreams*. Dreams, Freud said, are the "royal road to the unconscious." Through wily distortions introduced by an internal "dream censor" unfettered by any of the accepted rules of logic, the dreamer is presented with disguised images of his own long-submerged infantile yearnings, often of a sexual nature — yearnings too forbidden to be allowed more direct expression. A neurosis may result if these repressed desires become too powerful to remain buried in the unconscious, yet too anxiety-provoking to be acknowledged. The result is a distorted, compromised outlet in the form of a neurotic symptom.

A fuel that powers the person in normality and pathology is a raw form of sexual drive or instinct, biological in origin, that we are aware of as libido. For the newborn, this may take the form of oral gratification derived by suckling at the mother's breast; later, the site of pleasure can be anal, as the baby learns to control his bowel movements; afterwards, the genital area will gain primacy — all this by the age of four or five. During the last stage, the child fantasizes about replacing the parent of his or her sex as a partner for the other parent. How the child copes with this first and deepest love, and with the inevitable and necessary disappointment that ensues, will leave its mark on all subsequent personality development. This drama was dubbed "the Oedipus complex" by Freud.

Freud turned to the outside world to disseminate his teachings. Despite early difficulties in gaining acceptance by academic medicine, he drew about him a circle of some of the most remarkable and creative minds in Europe and, later, America. Some of his followers remained loyal adherents — Karl Abraham (q.v.), Sandor Ferenczi (q.v.), and Ernest Jones — while others eventually broke away and came to be regarded as heretics — Carl G. Jung, Alfred Adler (q.v.), and Otto Rank (q.v.). Freud, a gifted speaker and writer with rare persuasive skills, was authoritarian in cultivating the movement and could be zealously intolerant of divergent opinions. Yet it was clear that Freud's struggles, far from efforts at self-aggrandizement, were driven by his sense of mission to expose the repressed and to advance man's understanding of himself.

Throughout his life he continued to develop and revise his theories. He was close to age seventy when, to account for certain clinical facts, he formulated a tripartite model of the psyche: the id, a seething cauldron of desire with which we are born; a superego, bearer of conscience but itself capable of aggression in the form of self flagellation (taken to the extreme in some instances of suicide); and the ego, which, consciously or not, attempts to mediate between the id and superego, and between our inner needs and outer reality. This naturally led to a greater emphasis upon the elucidation of the psychological defense mechanisms, whereby the ego copes with various competing demands of id, superego, and reality, while trying to hold anxiety at a minimum.

In his later years, Freud abandoned the exclusivity of the libido as the primal determinant of human behavior, and, influenced by the carnage of World War I and perhaps by his own cancer, he speculated that within us all resides also a death instinct seeking to destroy and to revert to a state of nonbeing.

Freud did not limit his research to individual patients, but sought to extend his findings to culture and the arts. He psychoanalyzed, as it were, a childhood memory of Leonardo da Vinci. He speculated, sometimes fancifully, about the origins of society in a primordal horde lorded over by a dominant male figure ultimately deposed by his sons. And in *Civilization and Its Discontents*, he wrote that the strictures that civilization placed upon the instinctual drives of its members as the price for advancement may produce insolvable conflicts and guilt-ridden neuroses.

Religion was also scrutinized by Freud. An avowed atheist, he considered religion to be little more than neurosis on a mass scale, a reversion to infantile wishes to overcome helplessness by connecting with an omnipotent father-figure-in-the-sky. He expounded upon these ideas in books such as *Moses and Monotheism*, his final publication (1938), in which he also attempted to interpret the historical Moses, a figure with whom he was obsessed in the last years of his life.

At a time when many of his Jewish colleagues were opting for baptism in order to gain acceptance in Gentile society, Freud was unswerving in his affirmation that he was a Jew; he even attended many meetings of the local B'nai B'rith lodge, occasionally lecturing there. He possessed a wide repetoire of Jewish jokes and anecdotes that he would employ as justified by the circumstances. Most of his collaborators were Jewish, so much so that when the non-Jewish Jung joined the fold, Freud jumped at the opportunity to have a prominent Gentile among his followers and thus to evade the accusation that psychoanalysis was a peculiarly Jewish psychology. Although not a Zionist, Freud held an honorary position with the Hebrew University of Jerusalem. When asked what was Jewish in his teachings, Freud responded "not very much, but probably the main thing."

An inveterate cigar smoker, Freud suffered the last sixteen years of his life from a malignant cancer of the jaw to which, after thirty-three operations and a prosthesis which hampered his ability to speak, he finally succumbed. Despite his illness, and the pessimistic cast of thought it occasionally engendered, Freud remained active as a therapist and as an innovative theoretician until his final months. His occasionally sardonic humor was not diminished by adversity. When, a little more than a year before his death, the Nazis, new rulers in Austria, required Freud to sign a statement avowing that he had been well treated by the authorities, before he was permitted to leave the country, Freud complied and added after his signature, "I can heartily recommend the Gestapo to anyone." Freud moved to London, where he died three weeks after the outbreak of World War II.

H. F. Ellenberger, *The Discovery of the Unconscious*, 1970.

S. Freud, *The Standard Edition of the Complete Psychological Works of Sigmund Freud*, J. Strachey, ed., 1953–1974, 24 volumes.

P. Gay, *Freud, Atheism and the Making of Psychoanalysis*, 1987.

E. Jones, *The Life and Works of Sigmund Freud*, 1957, 3 volumes.

P. Roazen, *Freud and His Followers*, 1975.

E. Roith, *The Riddle of Freud: Jewish Influences on his Theory of Female Sexuality*, 1987.

FRIED, ALFRED HERMANN (1864—1921) Austrian pacifist, winner of the Nobel Peace Prize. Born in Vienna, he worked briefly as a diplomat, but soon turned to book dealing and publishing, establishing a publishing house in Berlin. He began devoting himself to the cause of peace in 1891. He founded the German League for Peace, which was the focus of Germany pacifism up to World War I. He edited journals, such as *Die Waffen Nieder* ("Lay Down Your Arms"), from 1899 called *Friedenswarte* ("The Peacekeeper"), and wrote books, pamphlets and newspaper articles on peace. Among his other activities for peace were membership in the International Institute for Peace, and holding the positions of secretary for central Europe of the International Institute for Peace and general secretary of the Union Internationale de la Presse pour la Paix. He also founded peace societies in Germany and Austria.

He received the Nobel Peace Prize in 1911 jointly with Tobias Asser (q.v.). During World War I, he tended prisoners of war in Switzerland and wrote *Kriegstagebuch* ("My War Diary," 1918–1920). He remained in Switzerland because he had been accused of high treason for his pacifist activities in Austria, but returned to Vienna after the collapse of the Dual Monarchy. He advocated a European union of states after the war and the foundation of international judicial organizations.

His writings include *Friedenskatechismus* (1895), *The Press as an Instrument of Peace* (1911), *War Obviated* (1915), *The Restoration of Europe* (1916), and *My War Diary* (4 vols., 1918–1920).

R. Goldscheid, *Alfred Fried* (German), 1922.

FRIEDELL, EGON (1878–1938) Austrian playwright, cabaret director and actor, journalist and cultural historian. He was born in Vienna as Egon Friedmann, the third child of a prominent silk manufacturer. His mother deserted the family when Egon was eighteen months old. His father died when he was thirteen, and he was raised by an aunt.

Little is known of his early childhood. He was expelled from school at the age of fifteen due to misdemeanors, and was considered a poor student in most of the succession of schools he attended. He subsequently studied at the universities of Berlin and Heidelberg.

Friedell converted to Protestantism in 1897, and changed his name the same year in order to avoid confusion with his older brother, who was also a novelist and playwright. He joined the Viennese bourgeois circle of the Bohemian poet Peter Altenberg, a group consisting of poets, actors, journalists, and dancers, and became himself a central figure in Viennese cabaret society.

His own career as a cabaret performer began in 1901, as he starred in one-act parodies, monologues, and anecdotes, directed the Cabaret Fledermaus, and acted in his own plays.

When World War I broke out, Friedell, who was in Berlin at the time, was rejected for army service due to obesity. He returned to Vienna in 1915, giving lectures, which consisted of tirades against the "enemies." He believed that the war was "the agency of Germany's spiritual liberation" and that the "world's barbarians" (the Russians, French, and British) were conspiring to separate the German and Austrian peoples.

Friedell next turned to writing, an endeavor that led to his financial ruin. His work reflected his anti-Semitic and anti-liberal views; in 1920 he wrote the play *Judastragödie* (which premiered in 1923) about Judas's betrayal of Christ. He is also well known for his extensive works of cultural history: the three-volume *Kulturgeschichte der Neuzeit* (1927–1932; English translation, *A Cultural History of the Modern Age*, 1931–1932) and the two-volume *Kulturgeschichte des Altertums* (1936–1949). Friedell tried to make a deal with the Nazis to get his works published, using a friend's connections with officials from the German Interior and Propaganda ministries, however, by 1936 he realized the futility of such efforts. By 1937 his works were banned in Germany.

In 1938, when a number of SA men knocked on his door looking for the "Jude Friedell," he committed suicide by jumping out of the window to his death.

In the 1950s, his former secretary, Walther Schneider, published eight collections of his letters, essays, and aphorisms. In 1959, interest in Friedell revived when *Kulturgeschichte der Neuzeit* was republished, becoming a best-seller for a while.

G. M. Patterson, *The Misunderstood Clown*, 1979.
P. G. Marshall, *The Misunderstood Clown: Egon Friedell and his Vienna*, 1979.
W. Schneider, *Friedell-Brevier* (German), 1947.

FROMM, ERICH

FROMM, ERICH (1900–1980) Social psychologist. Descended from a rabbinic family, he grew up studying Judaism with noted scholars. Although he would soon repudiate organized religion, his professed atheism always remained tinged with more than a little mysticism.

In his twenties, after studying sociology and psychology at Heidelberg and receiving his Ph.D., he trained at the Berlin Psychoanalytic Institute. His orthodox Freudianism, however, soon went the way of his orthodox Judaism, although he was certainly more conscious of his continued reliance on the former in the course of his subsequent research.

Fromm shifted his focus from the individual to society. As early as 1929, he initiated a study of German society which attempted to ascertain the possibility of German support for Hitler (the results were inconclusive). He emigrated to the United States in 1934 and taught at various universities and institutions including Bennington College (1941–1950), the National University of Mexico (1951–1961) and simultaneously at Michigan State University (1957–1961), and at New York University from 1961. In the United States he began to apply the concept of neurosis not only to

> ### FROM ERICH FROMM
>
> ● The Jewish tradition itself was one of reason and intellectual discipline, and besides that, a somewhat despised minority had a strong emotional interest to defeat the powers of darkness, of irrationality, of superstition, which blocked the road to its own emancipation and progress.
>
> ● The Bible is an extraordinary book, expressing many norms and principles that have maintained their validity throughout thousands of years. It... has proclaimed a vision for men that is still valid and awaiting realization.

individuals, but to society as well, which, he believed, thwarts man's innate potential for growth.

Fromm, calling himself a dialectic humanist, developed a far-reaching synthesis of the teachings of Sigmund Freud (q.v.) and Karl Marx (q.v.). He believed that man is fundamentally good, though certain societal conditions are required to permit him to realize his potential. He developed his theories in a series of books written in a lucid style free of arcane jargon, which made them accessible to the lay public as well as to his colleagues.

In *Escape from Freedom* (1941), he examined how totalitarianism exploits the sense of aloneness which freedom engenders. *Man for Himself* (1949) draws from the rabbinic dictum "If I am not for me, then who is for me?" in order to develop a humanistic ethic. *The Sane Society* (1955) attacks the problem of alienation in culture. In *The Art of Loving* (1956), which has been termed a modern midrash, Fromm sometimes waxes mystical in analyzing the complexity of mature love and human bonds. Fromm also turned to the Hebrew Bible, extracting from its pages his interpretation of humanism and morality, presented in *You Shall Be as Gods* (1966).

Fromm was married three times. His first wife, Frieda Fromm-Reichman, was noted in her own right as a pioneer in the psychoanalytic treatment of schizophrenia.

R. I. Evans, *Dialogue with Erich Fromm*, 1966.
J. S. Glenn, *Erich Fromm: a Protestant Critique*, 1966.
C. S. Hall, *Theories of Personality*, 1978.
D. Hausdorff, *Erich Fromm*, 1972.

FUNK, CASIMIR (1884–1967) U.S. biochemist who discovered vitamins. He was born in Warsaw, where his father was a physician specializing in dermatology. As a boy he suffered from a congenital dislocation of one of his hips which, despite care by the most famous orthopedic doctors of his day, remained unsuccessfully treated and left him with a permanent disability. As a result of prolonged treatment in Germany when he was a young boy, he learned German as well as his native Polish. At the age of sixteen, he was sent to study biology in Switzerland. He was awarded his Ph.D. in 1904, at the age of twenty.

From Switzerland he went to the Pasteur Institute in Paris where he began his long career in biology and biochemistry, concentrating on protein chemistry and metabolism and the cause of gout. From 1906 to 1910 he was in Berlin and then went to the Lister Institute in London (1910–1915), which was devoted to preventive medicine. There he began his work on beriberi, a sickness found to occur only in populations feeding on polished rice.

Funk realized that the cause of beriberi was not a protein deficiency but a "something" that was absent only to polished rice eaters and not to those eating unpolished rice. He developed a fractionation method that, by a process of elimination, led to the discovery of thiamine (later called vitamin B_1) as the cure for beriberi.

Funk postulated three other substances, one against pellagra (later found to be niacin), another against scurvy (vitamin C), and the last against rickets (vitamin D). He called these substances *vitamines*, believing them to be life (*vita*)-supporting "amines" (nitrogenous protein precursors). He was later shown to be only partially correct since not all *vitamine* substances contain nitrogen. There was considerable early opposition to accepting the term *vitamine* but it later received wide acceptance when changed to *vitamin*.

Funk firmly established that not all diseases were caused by pathogenic organisms, but that some were due to the absence of food factors that were required only in minute amounts yet were nevertheless essential to health. He later showed that this was because they contributed to the structure of enzyme catalysts which are themselves normally present only in small amounts in the body metabolism.

While working in London, Funk received the highly coveted D.Sc. from the University of London, but being an alien, was forced to travel to America at the outbreak of World War I. There he began working at the Harriman Research Laboratory in 1915, researching female and male sex hormones, pituitary hormones, and the hormonal factors concerned with diabetes mellitus; he also succeeding in producing a synthetic adrenaline. In 1920, he was naturalized as a U.S. citizen. In 1926–1927 he purified the digestive enzymes trypsin and pepsin (rennin) as well as the hormone insulin.

Casimir Funk was a shy person, hesitant with strangers, but a man of definite opinions.

B. Harrow, *Casimir Funk: Pioneer in Vitamins and Hormones*, 1955.

G

GABIROL, SOLOMON IBN See Ibn Gabirol, Solomon

GABOR, DENNIS (1900–1979) Physicist and electrical engineer who received the Nobel Prize in physics in 1971 for the invention of holography. Born in Hungary, he was educated in Budapest and Berlin. Gabor taught at the University of Berlin-Charlottenburg until 1926, when he left to carry out research for German industrialist concerns: at first in a research association for high-voltage equipment and later in an engineering firm. He left Germany in 1934 to escape the Nazi regime and settled in Britain, eventually becoming a naturalized British subject.

Gabor first conceived of the idea of holography, a photographic technique creating a three-dimensional image out of a flat photographic print, in 1947, long before the invention of the laser, which would make holography possible. He originally envisioned the technique as a means of improving the resolution of electron microscopes. Although the original application has not proved feasible, holography is now widely used as a method for optical image formation and has many applications in medicine, cartography, communication, and computer technology. His invention was far ahead of its time. After his death, a close associate of Gabor said that in the 1960s, "the discovery of holography would probably have been inevitable" due to the invention of lasers, but in the 1940s "no one else was even dreaming of such things." Instead of using regular photographic lenses, holography employs two light beams that interfere with each other, creating an "interference pattern" from which an image is reconstructed. Gabor experimented with the light of a mercury arc.

In 1956 he was elected a fellow of the Royal Society, and in 1958 he became professor of applied electron physics at the Imperial College of Science and Technology, University of London. He was a consultant for the CBS Technology Center in Connecticut. Gabor also worked on oscilloscopes, television, and physical optics.

From the early 1970s, Gabor was active in the campaign for Soviet Jewry and was instrumental in obtaining emigration permits for a number of Soviet Jewish scientists.

GAMA, GASPAR DA (original name unknown; c. 1440–c. 1510). Traveler. He was born in Posen, Poland, but fled with his parents in 1450, when the family was given the choice of baptism or expulsion. They made their way to Jerusalem and then to Alexandria. When the boy grew up, he traveled extensively in pursuit of commercial contacts, dealing especially in jewels. In India he became a Muslim and entered the service of the ruler of Bijapur, who put him in charge of commercial affairs in the Goa region. When the Portuguese explorer, Vasco da Gama, reached the coast of India, a boat came alongside carrying this man, dressed in linen, a turban on his head and a sword at his waist. He introduced himself as a former Christian, now a Muslim, who had been sent by the local ruler to welcome the Portuguese and offer them ships and supplies. Da Gama grew suspicious of his unease and the contradictions in his remarks. Indian sailors who were asked about the man said he was in the service of pirates who were preparing to attack the Portuguese. Under torture, the man admitted he was indeed a spy.

A few days later, da Gama sailed away, taking the man with him. On the journey to Portugal, he forced him to become baptized and gave him his own surname. And so the Polish Jew arrived in Portugal as Gaspar da Gama (also known as Gaspar of India and sometimes as Gaspar the Jew).

Vasco da Gama was received by King Manuel of Portugal, who asked to meet Gaspar and wrote in a letter: "Our men brought back five or six Indians from Calicut, including a Jew who has converted to Christianity and who is a merchant and dealer in precious stones." Manuel was fascinated by Gaspar, granting him many favors and gifts, including clothes from his own wardrobe, horses from the royal stables, and servants from among the Christian converts brought from India. Gaspar was made a knight of the king's household and allowed to import merchandise from India duty-free. The king was impressed by Gaspar's wide linguistic skills and his knowledge of Asian lands, which he saw as helpful in furthering his plans to incorporate India into the Portuguese empire.

Over the next decade Gaspar da Gama accompanied three Portuguese expeditions to India. The first of these established a major trading post in

Cochin and was greatly helped by da Gama's connections (his wife was a Jewish Cochini). The third expedition set sail in 1505 and on this occasion he remained for almost five years in India. Gaspar's letters to King Manuel describe his tasks in India. As translator, he dealt with the local population and arranged for food and other supplies. He acted as general political and commercial adviser and negotiated with the local Muslim traders, succeeding, for example, in getting them to lower the exorbitant price they were asking for pepper. He helped the Portuguese in their purchases of precious stones, while his geographical knowledge proved invaluable in the Portuguese wars with the Indians. He returned to Portugal in 1509, but after 1510 no more is heard of him. His Cochini wife remained in India and refused all entreaties that she too be baptized. She was a pious, learned, and deeply conscious Jew who was prominent in community affairs.

GAMALIEL I THE ELDER   (c. 10 BCE–c. 65 CE) Pharisee president (*nasi*) of the Sanhedrin in Jerusalem and early rabbinical authority; grandson of Hillel the Elder (q.v.). The first sage to be given the title of *Rabban* (our master), he was active throughout the last decades of the Second Temple and died a few years before its destruction. As one who enjoyed supreme religious authority, Gamaliel I maintained regular contact with Jewish communities in Palestine and in the Diaspora, dictating numerous letters (three of which are quoted in the Talmud) on matters such as the proclamation of a new moon or the approach of a leap year. Following his grandfather's example, he also enacted various ordinances to protect divorcees and enable

Rabban Gamaliel and his disciples. From a 14th century Spanish Haggadah.

widows whose husbands' deaths could not be proved by the statutory two witnesses to remarry after a single witness had provided evidence. This liberal and humane interpretation of Halakhah (Jewish law) was further visible in Gamaliel's care to prevent miscarriage of justice and in his positive attitude toward Gentiles.

He had close ties with the Judean royal family, and King Agrippa I relied on him for expert legal advice. According to New Testament sources, Gamaliel was an honored and popular "doctor of the law" who intervened on behalf of Peter and his companions when they were arraigned before the Sanhedrin; Paul, the erstwhile Pharisee, also took pride in the fact that he had studied under Gamaliel (Acts 5:34–40, 22:3). "When Rabban Gamliel died," said the rabbis, "the glory of the Torah ceased, along with purity and saintliness." He was the founder of a dynasty that included his immediate successors, R. Simeon ben Gamaliel (q.v.) and Gamaliel II of Yavneh (q.v.), and his great-great-grandson Judah ha-Nasi (q.v.).
L. W. Schwarz, ed., *A Golden Treasury of Jewish Literature*, 1937.
E. E. Urbach, *The Sages*, 1969.

GAMALIEL II OF YAVNEH   (c. 45–c. 115 CE) Palestinian rabbi, head of the Yavneh academy, and president (*nasi*, or patriarch) of the Sanhedrin located there. In contradistinction to Gamaliel I, (q.v.), his grandfather, he was usually known by the honorific title of Rabban Gamaliel of Yavneh. Assuming office in succession to Johanan ben Zakkai (q.v.) around 80 CE, Gamaliel consolidated the work of religious and national reconstruction that Johanan had undertaken a decade earlier after the Romans laid waste the Temple. His principal aim and major achievement was to make Yavneh not only a focus of Jewish scholarship, but a great fortress of Jewish leadership as well — one to which the nation could look for guidance and inspiration after the rallying point of the Temple had vanished.

This ambitious program involved the setting of new standards of conduct for admission to the academy, ending the old strife between the schools of Hillel (q.v.) and Shammai (q.v.), establishing a coherent policy toward the outside world, and centralizing Jewish authority in the sages (with Gamaliel himself at their head). It was this very insistence on unquestioned authority, however, that brought Rabban Gamaliel into conflict with other leading scholars, notably his own brother-in-law, Eliezer ben Hyrcanus (q.v.), and Joshua ben hananiah. As a result of the culminating humiliation suffered by Joshua over the date on which he calculated that the Day of Atonement would fall, Gamaliel was deposed and temporarily replaced by Eleazar ben Azariah (c. 90 CE). His true nature soon became evident when a reconciliation brought the expatriarch and his offended colleague together once again; the sages promptly restored him to office, nominating Eleazar as vice-president of the Sanhedrin.

Though somewhat high-handed and domineering in public life, Gamaliel was a modest, saintly, and kind-hearted individual whose consideration for others extended not only to pupils and the Jewish community at large but also to well-intentioned Gentiles and his own faithful, pious slave, Tabi. While under suspension, he continued to discharge his ordinary duties with a good grace, believing that every step had been taken "not for his own honor, nor for that of his house, but for the honor of God alone, so that factions might not grow apace in Israel." At his bidding, therefore, a nineteenth benediction was added to the *Amidah* prayer, designed to exclude Judeo-Christians and other heretical elements from synagogue worship. At the same time, righteous proselytes were mentioned favorably in a separate *Amidah* blessing; and the delegation of leading sages, headed by Rabban Gamaliel, that journeyed to Rome (c. 95 CE) apparently aimed to avert a decree outlawing conversion to Judaism, after the Emperor Domitian's own cousin, Flavius Clemens, had embraced the Jewish faith.

One of the foremost teachers of his generation, renowned for his authoritative judgment and for his broad cultural interests, Gamaliel attained vast prestige as the official spokesman and representative of his people. He was responsible for many enactments that had far-reaching impact on Jewish life: determining the biblical canon; perpetuating remembrance of the Temple in various laws and customs; reformulating the Passover seder ritual; giving a set form to the *Amidah* prayer, the recitation of which became a daily obligation; and, through his personal example, doing away with elaborate burial rites so as to avoid social distinctions. Above all, he promoted a unification of Jewish legal, theological, and ethical traditions that served as the basis for his grandson Judah ha-Nasi's (q.v.) later achievement in the Mishnah.

A.Y. Bitterman, *Rabban Gamaliel of Yavneh: His Teachings and Role in the Development of Talmudic Law*, 1974.

S. Kanter, *Rabban Gamaliel II; The Legal Tradition*, 1980.

GANCE, ABEL (1889–1981) French film director. Born in Paris, Gance's ambitions lay in the direction of literature and theater. While a stage actor and dramatist (his play *La Victoire de Samothrace* was to have been produced with Sarah Bernhardt [q.v.] but for the outbreak of World War I), he was already writing and directing films for extra cash. In his 1915 film *La folie du Docteur Tube* he used distorting mirrors to present images from the perspective of a madman; all his life he would continue to seek such innovations. *Mater Dolorosa*, in 1917, firmly established him as a bankable director. Toward the end of the war he directed *J'accuse*, a powerful antiwar drama in which he utilized real soldiers, most of whom were

Abel Gance in the role of Saint-Just in Napoleon.

killed in battle days later, in a sequence in which the dead rise from the battlefield to question the value of their sacrifice.

In 1921 he made *La roue*, a tragic romance triangle featuring new concepts in editing regarded by many as representing a turning point in film art. After an interlude directing a short comedy for Max Linder, Gance embarked upon his most ambitious project, for which he is still best known. *Napoléon* brought together all the dazzling technique he had developed with the addition of Polyvision, and a triple-screen system that allowed him to give his five-hour epic a hitherto unimaginable sweep.

Much of Gance's promise was unrealized in the sound era. *Un grand amour de Beethoven* was one of his better efforts during a period that saw him remaking his silent successes as talkies, often utilizing the old footage. In the 1950s he unveiled a color version of Polyvision as Magirama. Well into his eighties he was still tinkering with his obsession, combining new material with his silent and sound *Napoléon*s to produce *Bonaparte et la Révolution*. His last years enabled him to bask in the adulation of a new public that had thrilled to film historian Kevin Brownlow's restoration of the silent *Napoléon*, complete with triple-screen effects and a newly composed orchestral score.

K. Brownlow, *Napoleon: Abel Gance's Classic Film*, 1983.

N. King, *Abel Gance*, 1985.

S. P. Kramer and J. M. Welsh, *Abel Gance*, 1978.

GARY, ROMAIN (originally Kacev; 1914–1980) French writer and diplomat. Gary declared himself to be of mixed parentage: "part Cossack and Tartar, part Jew." Born in Vilna, he moved with his family to Poland in 1921 and then to Nice, France, in 1926. His mother had a strong personality and a shaping influence on his life. His father, who was deported to Germany during World War II, he called "the man who gave me his name." His mother's constant refrain, "You will be a hero, d'Annunzio, French ambassador" exasperated him, but most of her fantasies about her son were fulfilled. He was a fighter pilot during World War II, French consul in Los Angeles (1956-1960), and at the same time an author of repute. He joined Charles de Gaulle and the Free French Forces in London and took part in many air raids until the liberation of France. He wrote his first novel, *A European Education* (1945; English translation, 1945, 1960), in London. It reflected the sorrows of war and was a great success. *Lady L* (1958) and *The Ski Bum* (1965) also appeared in English.

For his book *The Roots of Heaven* (1956; English translation, 1958), which reflects his concern for wildlife preservation, he was awarded the Prix Goncourt in France. There he also published *Promise at Dawn* (1960; English translation, 1961) in which he describes his mother's character and the air raids for which he received the Croix de la Libération from de Gaulle.

He was deeply shaken by a trip to Warsaw which made him sharply aware of his Jewish heritage and the problems and feelings aroused in him by the Holocaust. Following this he wrote *The Dance of Genghis Cohn* (1967; English translation, 1969), the story of a Jewish comedian whose ghost returns to haunt his Nazi killer.

In the later years of his life the autobiographical aspect of his work was more predominant than the fictional. He also wrote two books under the pen name Emil Ajar. His identity, which he had meant to keep secret, was revealed when he was awarded a second Prix Goncourt for one of them, *La vie devant soi* (1975). These two books (the other was *L'angoisse du roi Salomon*) had deep Jewish content. Several of his works were made into successful films in which, as in his written work, humor mingles with a secret sadness. He himself directed his wife, Jean Seberg, in the film *Les oiseaux vont mourir au Pérou* (1968). Gary committed suicide after the death of Jean Seberg.

> ...The Nazis stamped the yellow star on the Jewish dreamers to punish these usurers who have continuously endowed society with treasures of imagination, music, philosophy, and religion and demand in return an exorbitant interest in currency of progress, revolutions, and universal love.
>
> **Romain Gary,** *Europa*

GEIGER, ABRAHAM (1810-1874) German Jewish scholar and ideologist of Reform Judaism. Born in Frankfurt to a distinguished family, he received an excellent education, both rabbinical and secular, obtaining a doctorate from Bonn University for a thesis on what Mohammed took from Judaism. From 1832 to 1838 he was rabbi in Wiesbaden, where he achieved a reputation by his liberal reforms and objections to traditional rabbinic practices, which he saw as having lost their validity and lacking esthetic form. In 1837 he called a conference of Reform rabbis in Wiesbaden to discuss synagogue reform. Believing that the scientific study of Judaism (*Wissenschaft des Judentums*) was required to effect both political and religious changes, he founded the journal *Wissenschaftliche Zeitschrift für jüdische Theologie*.

In 1838 he was invited to Breslau as *dayyan* (religious judge) and assistant rabbi, but his inauguration was deferred for two years due to the objections of the Orthodox rabbi, Solomon Tiktin. Eventually he was empowered to introduce reforms and remained in Breslau until 1863. The Reform rabbinical conference of 1846 was held in Breslau and Geiger was a moving spirit.

During this period, he was not only a leader of the Reform movement but wrote major works of Jewish scholarship. He helped to inspire the foundation of the Breslau Theological Seminary, but was disappointed when the less Reform-minded Zacharias Frankel (q.v.) was appointed its first head. In 1863 he moved to Frankfurt to serve as rabbi there and from 1870 was in Berlin as Reform rabbi and as head of the newly established Liberal rabbinical seminary (the Hochschule für die Wissenschaft des Judentums), which he directed until his death.

Geiger criticized traditional Judaism as archaic and for its national character as expressed in many laws and rituals. In 1854 he published a prayer book that omitted any reference to angels, the resurrection of the dead, the chosenness of the Jewish people, the restoration of the Temple and the sacrificial system, and the return to Zion. The innovations he introduced included choral singing, the confirmation ceremony, and sermons in the vernacular. In later life, his views became less extreme and, for example, he reinstated second days of festivals, which he had previously rejected. His public views were also more moderate than his private opinions; he never publicly advocated the abolition of the dietary laws or circumcision, although privately he accepted neither. Judaism, he held, must divest itself of its particularism and become a universalistic faith, a religion of humanity. At the same time as much tradition as possible should be retained for the sake of continuity.

His scholarly work was extensive and he mastered all aspects of Jewish studies. Seeking to integrate Judaism into Western culture, he applied modern scientific approaches to many branches of scholarship. Among the fields in which he made especially significant contributions were Jewish relations to Christianity and Islam, Bible, rabbinical law, Jewish history, religion, and literature.

J. J. Petuchowski (ed.), *New Perspectives on Abraham Geiger*, 1975.
M. Winer, *Abraham Geiger and Liberal Judaism*, 1962.

ABRAHAM GEIGER ON THE STATUS OF WOMEN IN JUDAISM

From now on let there be no distinction between duties for men and women, unless flowing from the natural laws, governing the sexes; no assumption of the spiritual minority of woman, as though she were incapable of grasping the deep things in religion; no institution of the public service, either in form or content, which shuts the doors of the temple in the face of women; no degradation of woman in the form of the marriage service, and no application of fetters which may destroy woman's happiness. Then will the Jewish girl and the Jewish woman, conscious of the significance of our faith, become fervently attached to it, and our whole religious life will profit from the beneficial influence which feminine hearts will bestow on it.

GERCHUNOFF, ALBERTO (1884–1950) Argentinian author, Zionist, political thinker. He was born in the Ukrainian province of Kamenets-Podolski in the small town of Proskurov. The family moved to Tulchin, where his father ran a small business. The Gerchunoff home was a meeting place for influential townspeople and Jewish thinkers who were attracted not only to Gregory Gerchunoff's charm as a conversationalist and a talented storyteller, but also to his vast knowledge of Judaism. It was here that the young Gerchunoff first learned about Baron de Hirsch's (q.v.) settlements in Argentina.

Moved by Hirsch's dream, the Gerchunoff family decided to emigrate to Argentina, and in 1890 embarked on what was to be a long and fascinating journey to Buenos Aires. The family was taken to Moisesville, one of the first Hirsch settlements. There, the Jewish Colonization Association provided them with fifty hectares of land, along with tools and seeds, with which they were to create a home out of the desolate area of the Argentinian province of Santa Fe. The JCA ensured a Jewish education for all, so that Alberto Gerchunoff attended the settlement school during the mornings and Hebrew school in the afternoons. Due to the hardships of rural life, to the hostility of their neighbors, and to the death of Gregory Gerchunoff, the family moved to Entre Rios. While Gerchunoff's older brother decided to become a farmer, a Jewish gaucho, in Entre Rios, the rest of the family moved to Buenos Aires. It was in Entre Rios that the richness of the colloquial Spanish, reminiscent of an archaic 16th-century Spanish, aroused Gerchunoff's interest in the Spanish language.

Upon arriving in Buenos Aires, Gerchunoff worked as a street vendor and construction worker in the busy suburbs of the Argentinian capital. As a student, he began attending meetings of the Socialist party, where he met and became close friends with influential intellectual figures such as Leopoldo Lugones, Payro, and later Ruben Dario. Although financial difficulties forced him to leave his university studies, Gerchunoff persisted in his desire to write, and by 1901 was writing for several city newspapers. He later worked as editor and director of *La Nacion* and *El Mundo* and published several books on the life of the Jewish gauchos, among other topics. In 1931 he was invited to become a member of the first Argentinian Academy of Language, an honor he refused in protest against the military takeover of the government.

With the outbreak of World War I, Gerchunoff dedicated himself fully to the Jewish cause. As a journalist in the 1930s, he was active in anti-Nazi publications. Following World War II, he became an active Zionist and in 1947, traveled throughout South America to solicit contributions for the foundation of the Jewish state.

He is considered an important figure in Argentinian literature of the modernist period. Among his works are: *El cafe de los inmortales, Nuestro Señor Don Quijote, El nuevo regimen, Vida nuestra, Cuentos de Ayer, El cristianismo. precristiano, La jofaina maravillosa, Las imagenes del pais*. He gained popularity for his book *Los gauchos judios* (1910; made into a film in 1975), based on the experiences of the Jewish settlers in Entre Rios in the early 20th century. He received several literature prizes including the third Argentinian national prize for literature in 1927.

M. E. Gover de Nasatsky, *Bibliografia de Alberto Gerchunoff*, 1976.
M. Kantor, *Sobre la obra y el anecdotario de Alberto Gerchunoff*, 1960.
B. Marqui Stambler, *Vida y Obra de Alberto Gerchunoff*, 1985.

Often, towards sunset, after a day of profound identification with the universal Christian life of the metropolis and the country, I feel a morbid need for the ghetto. That is when I submerge myself in the cafe of Corrientes, where amid the turmoil of tea cups and neighborhood quarrels, I contemplate the animated movement of this strange and fabulous world. The mysterious attraction of Jewishness is satisfied in me as if I would be returning from a trip to Warsaw, to Bucharest, to Odessa.

Alberto Gerchunoff

GERO, ERNO (1898–1980) Hungarian communist leader. Born in Budapest, he joined the Communist party in 1918 and was active in the revolution led by Bela Kun (q.v.) the following year. When that failed he escaped to Germany but later returned clandestinely to Hungary, where he edited a communist underground newspaper. Gero lived for a time in Soviet Russia and was in Spain during the Civil War, apparently guiding the Catalan communists. He returned to Hungary in 1944 with the Russian army and was soon occupying leading positions. As minister of transport, he directed the rebuilding of the ruined country and its industry and was responsible for the reconstruction of the bridges over the Danube. Gero was then successively minister of finance (charged with implementing the five-year economic plan) and, from 1950 minister of state and minister of foreign trade. From 1956 to 1966 he was deputy prime minister and a member of the Politburo, a key personality in governing Hungary. In 1956, when Matyas Rakosi (q.v.) fell victim to the anti-Stalinist movement in Moscow, Gero was appointed first secretary of the Communist party. His rule was short and unpopular; he introduced harsh measures to try to counter the revolution, but was swept aside during the heady ten days of liberation from Russian domination. He appealed in vain to the Russian army to save him but was deposed and fled the country, reportedly in one of the Russian tanks he had summoned to restore the communist autocracy.

Prevented from returning to Hungary, Gero then lived for a number of years in the USSR, but was allowed to return in 1962, although he was expelled from the Communist party. Thereafter, he remained quietly in retirement.

GERSHOM BEN JUDAH (known as Rabbenu Gershom, our master, Gershom, and as *Me'or ha-Golah*, Luminary of the Diaspora; c. 965–1028). One of the first great German rabbinical authorities and Jewish spiritual leader. Little information is known of his life. He may have been born in Metz but was chiefly associated with Mainz. Those of his liturgical poems that have been preserved reflect the troubled experiences of Rhineland Jewry of his day and he wrote, "From day to day my suffering increases, the next day is harder than the one that passed." One of his poems refers to the persecution and expulsion of the Jews from Mainz in 1012. The apostasy of his only son may have been connected with this expulsion. Gershom's Talmudic academy in Mainz attracted students from many countries and he was one of the first rabbinic scholars to bring the scholarship of the great rabbinic academies of Eretz Israel and Babylonia to western Europe. He made important contributions to establishing the text of the Talmud, which previously was known in northern Europe only in a very unsatisfactory version. He copied out the entire Mishnah and Talmud, basing himself on the best manuscripts he could find throughout the Jewish world. He also copied out an entire Bible,

> Rabbenu Gershom has enlightened the eyes of the Exile for all live by his instruction. All the Jews of these [European] countries call themselves disciples of his disciples.
>
> **Rashi**

containing the traditional marks and accents (the Masora). He did not write any large work. The only original work known by him is a lost compilation on the laws of forbidden meat (*tereifot*).

Gershom is best remembered for a series of ordinances that were of great influence on medieval Jewry. It is not certain whether all of these enactments were issued by Gershom himself (some may have been inserted in his name to give them authority). These ordinances helped to adapt rabbinic law to European conditions and became accepted as normative. Some of them deal with communal issues such as the ruling that the authority of the majority of the community must be accepted by the minority. Others dealt with individual behavior including the ban on reading another person's correspondence or on reminding a penitent apostate of his former lapse from Judaism. Best-known is his ban on polygamy, which was binding on all Ashkenazic communities and was eventually accepted also in many non-Ashkenazic communities. He also abolished a man's right to divorce his wife against her will.

His *responsa* (answers to legal and ritual problems submitted to him from many localities) were also regarded as authoritative. Many of these deal with business questions, relaxing prohibitive laws concerning business relations with non-Jews.

A. Marx, *Essays in Jewish Biography*, 1947, pp. 39–60.

GERSHWIN, GEORGE (1898–1937) U.S. composer. The son of Russian immigrant parents, Gershwin was born Jacob Gershovitz in Brooklyn. A piano purchased for the musical education of his older brother, Ira (1896–1983) swiftly became George's domain and three years later he was studying with Charles Hambitzer, a musician who was to heavily influence the young Gershwin. Composition increasingly preoccupied him (he first had a song published in 1916) and by 1919, when he applied to Irving Berlin (q.v.) for the position of musical secretary, he was sufficiently accomplished to be told by the senior songwriter that he would be better off working for himself. In that year Gershwin enjoyed his first hit song, "Swanee", sung by Al Jolson (q.v.). Over the next few years he gained a name as an outstanding composer of songs for musical comedy, some of the lyrics being written by Ira. His music was characterized by its pronounced rhythms, catchy melodies, and lively wit which pioneered a new era in American popular music.

In 1924, for a concert entitled "Experiment in

George Gershwin at work.

Some of the Best-Known Songs of George and Ira Gershwin

"But Not For Me"
"Embraceable You"
"A Foggy Day"
"Fascinating Rhythm"
"I Got Rhythm"
"It Ain't Necessarily So"
"Somebody Loves Me"
"Someone to Watch Over Me"
"I's Wonderful"
"They Can't Take That Away from Me"

"Let's Call the Whole Thing Off"
"Our Love Is Here to Stay"
"The Man I Love"
"Love Walked In"
"Oh Lady Be Good"
"Nice Work If You Can Get It"
"Strike up the Band"
"Summertime"
"They All Laughed"

Modern Music" that was being given by "King of Jazz" bandleader, Paul Whiteman, Gershwin produced "Rhapsody in Blue." This was not Gershwin's first attempt to introduce elements of popular music into a classical form — it had notably been preceded by the opera *Blue Monday* in 1922 — but it did prove a milestone in the wider acceptance of such experiments. Gershwin followed up with his Concerto in F in 1925 and the tone-poem *An American in Paris* in 1928. Throughout the 1920s he maintained his success in musical comedy, now working exclusively with Ira. Particularly popular were two shows the brothers wrote for Fred and Adele Astaire, *Lady be Good* (1924) and *Funny Face* (1927).

The Gershwins' 1931 Broadway show *Of Thee I Sing* became the first musical to win the Pulitzer Prize, while their first original film score, *Delicious*, gave birth to the Second Rhapsody. George's most ambitious work, the folk opera *Porgy and Bess* (1935), was not widely hailed in his lifetime as the classic it has since become. His last music was written in Hollywood. He wrote the scores for two films with Fred Astaire before dying of a brain tumor while at work on songs for the film *Goldwyn Follies*.

A. Kendall, *George Gershwin*, 1987.
R. Kimball and A. Simon, *The Gershwins*, 1973.
C. Schwartz, *Gershwin: His Life and Music*, 1973.

GERSONIDES, See Levi ben Gershom

GERTLER, MARK (1891–1939) English artist. Although born in London, his early childhood was spent in Poland, where his father left the family while seeking a livelihood in the United States. His mother worked in a Jewish restaurant, feeding her five children on the daily leftovers. After five years, the family was reunited in England, where they lived at first in one room, all seven of them sleeping on the floor. Tuberculosis was rampant in Whitechapel, where they lived, and Mark's health was affected. There, he also had the first attack of a serious depression that was to plague him all his life.

From 1907 he studied art in the evenings and worked in a stained glass factory until the Jewish Educational Aid Society paid for his studies at the Slade School of Art, where he won many scholarships and prizes. A portrait of his mother, painted in 1911, is now in the Tate Gallery. He also painted many pictures of his Jewish neighbors in Whitechapel.

Gertler was elected a member of the New England Art Club, and in 1914 was included in the Whitechapel Gallery's exhibition, "Twentieth Century Art." He made many friends among artists and writers, among them D. H. Lawrence, Lytton Strachey, and Gilbert Cannan, whose book, *Mendel*, published in 1916, was based on Gertler's life.

In 1916 he painted *Merry-Go-Round*, considered the most outstanding World War I painting by a noncombatant. It showed women and men, mostly soldiers, painted in a stylized manner that suggests puppets, riding on a carousel. Lawrence wrote to Gertler that this was "...the best *modern* picture I have seen; I think it great and true. But it is horrible and terrifying."

Gertler was one of the leading British painters of the 1920s, but during this period he was confined to tuberculosis sanatoriums on several occasions, and his bouts of severe depression became more frequent. He fell in love and lived with Dora Carrington, who subsequently left him and went to live with Strachey as his housekeeper. Meeting them in the street, Gertler attacked Strachey in a fit of jealous fury.

In the 1930s, he suffered a number of setbacks, including unsuccessful exhibitions. In 1936, during a three-month stay at a sanatorium he made an unsuccessful suicide attempt, but eventually, in 1939, killed himself.

Gertler developed a robust style that was influenced by the French Post-Impressionists, particularly Derain. He painted many landscapes, still lifes, and voluptuous and sensual nudes, by the British public attributed to of his Polish-Jewish background. His goal was to paint "the beauty that trembles on the edge of ugliness..." to paint a picture "in which I hope to express all the sorrow of Life...."

J. Woodeson, *Mark Gertler*, 1972.

GIMBEL FAMILY   U.S. merchants and philanthropists. **Adam Gimbel** (1817–1896), born in Bavaria, went to the United States in 1835 and worked for several years as a peddler, making his way north from New Orleans. After seven years of peddling along the Mississippi River, he established a small general store in Vincennes, Indiana, in 1842, introducing novel ideas such as advertising with handbills, a refund policy for dissatisfied customers, and equally good service for all his customers. By stocking a wide variety of goods under one roof, he also created one of the first department stores. The business lasted for over forty years and grew to include four shops by the time he sold it to join his sons' business.

Jacob Gimbel (1851–1922) and his brother **Isaac Gimbel** (1857–1931) opened a department store in Milwaukee in the 1880s, after failing in a similar venture in Danville, Illinois. With their success in Milwaukee, they decided to open another store in Philadelphia in 1894. In 1910 the New York branch was opened and began purchasing other firms, among them Saks and Company in 1923. The Saks subsidiary later opened stores on Fifth Avenue, in New York, and Beverly Hills, California. The brothers also took over the Kaufman and Baer Company in Pittsburgh in 1926.

Charles Gimbel (1861–1932), and **Ellis A. Gimbel** (1865–1950), also sons of Adam Gimbel, headed the Philadelphia store. **Bernard F. Gimbel** (1855–1966), son of Isaac Gimbel, was president of the firm in 1927, and was also active in the New York City world fairs of 1939 and 1964–1965. By 1961, the chain boasted fifty-three stores. In 1973 the company was absorbed by Brown and Williamson Tobacco Corp. It went out of business in the 1980s.

GINZBERG, LOUIS   (1873–1953) Talmudic and rabbinical scholar. His mother was the granddaughter of the brother of Elijah ben Solomon Zalman, the Vilna Gaon (q.v.), a fact that was to have a profound effect on his upbringing. When Ginzberg was seven years old his family moved from Kovno, Lithuania, to Klin, near Moscow, and his formal education was begun with a private tutor. He then studied at the yeshivot (Talmudic academies) of Telz and Slobodka, which at the time were the centers of the *Musar* (moralist) movement. He completed his preuniversity studies

in Frankfurt and then studied semitics, Assyriology, and philosophy at the universities of Berlin and Strasbourg and was awarded his Ph.D. degree, for a thesis on biblical legends, that are preserved in the church fathers, at Heidelberg Univerity. In 1894 he was ordained as a rabbi.

Ginzberg had a wonderful sense of humor, loved to play pranks, and was a great storyteller. He had a phenomenal memory, made few notes, and only committed to writing whatever he wished to publish. He wrote: "In my *Legends of the Jews*, I have 36,000 references, all of which I kept in my head. I did not gain very much by this, since I might easily have written them down, but if one has a good memory one hates to bother, and secondly, my handwriting is so bad that I wouldn't have been able to read it."

In 1899 Ginzberg immigrated to the United States to accept an appointment at the Hebrew Union College, Cincinnati, but on his arrival found that it had been canceled when the college discovered that he advocated biblical criticism. He found employment as editor of the rabbinic section of the *Jewish Encyclopedia*, for which he wrote over four hundred articles.

He was also instrumental in determining the direction that Conservative Judaism took in the United States. From 1902 until his death he served as professor of Talmud at the Conservative movement's Jewish Theological Seminary in New York; during this period the seminary ordained about 650 rabbis, all of whom had studied with him.

In 1920 Ginzberg founded the American Academy of Jewish Research and was its first and long-time president. Its major activity was stimulating the publication of research in Jewish scholarship in America and abroad.

He also researched fragments from the Cairo *Genizah* and his introductions and commentaries to the various texts have become classics in the study of Talmudic and rabbinical literature. His major work was *The Legends of the Jews*, published in seven volumes (1908–1938), containing legends, maxims, and parables from the midrashic literature presented as a narrative tale about biblical figures and events. The work analyzes the evolution of Jewish legends from rabbinical texts, the apocryphal books, Hellenistic literature, early Christian texts, the Kabbalah and other texts, and compares them with legends of other cultures. The first two volumes were translated from the German manuscript by Henrietta Szold (q.v.), the secretary of the Jewish Publication Society of America, which published the work. During this period a close friendship developed between Ginzberg and Henrietta Szold, who was also his tutor in English and at the same time a student of the young professor at the seminary. At the age of 43, she fell in love for the first time, believing it to be mutual. However, when visiting Europe in 1908, he became engaged to another woman and Henrietta Szold was heartbroken.

A shortened version of *Legends* was published in

1956 as *Legends of the Bible*. Ginzberg's *Students, Scholars and Saints* (1928) contains portraits of great Jewish leaders such as the Vilna Gaon, Israel Salanter, Zachariah Frankel, and Solomon Schechter. His numerous works deal with the origins of *halakhah* (Jewish law) and *aggadah* (Talmudic lore) and the literature of the Geonim, the heads of the Babylonian Academies. He also wrote histories of Jewish communities, for example, *Petersburg 1789-1950* (1950) and *Virgina 1685-1900* (1969). The first three volumes of his *Commentary on the Palestinian Talmud* (1941) were published when he was nearly seventy, and although he worked on a further two volumes, he did not succeed in publishing them. The first item in the bibliography of Ginzberg's works is a short piece on Zionism published in a Dutch journal in 1898.

He was elected to the Seventh Zionist Congress at Basel in 1905, but decided not to attend since he did not represent any constituent body. He maintained a deep and continuing interest in the problems of Zionist ideology and the attitudes and reactions of various sectors of the American community to the rebuilding of the Holy Land. However, he never played an active role in the Zionist movement. As president of the American Academy of Jewish Research he was involved, in an advisory capacity, in the establishment of the Institute of Jewish Studies at the Hebrew University of Jerusalem. In 1928-1929 he served as visiting professor at the Hebrew University, inaugurating the Department of Halakhah. During this period he developed a close friendship with the poet Chaim Nachman Bialik (q.v.). In 1933-1934 Ginzberg was a member of an American Survey Committee, charged with making recommendations aimed at improving the organization of the Hebrew University. The Louis Ginzberg Chair of Talmud was established at the Hebrew University in honor of his eightieth birthday.

B. Cohen, *Bibliography of the Writings of Professor Louis Ginzberg*, compiled on the occasion of his sixtieth birthday, 1933. Updated in 1945.
E. Ginzberg, *Keeper of the Law: Louis Ginzberg*, 1966.

My first memory is when I was between three and four when I got an apple from my mother. I was a little boy, so I bit into it without saying a *beroche* (blessing). My mother rebuked me, since the saying of the *beroche* is taught to children at the very beginning of their Jewish education. She said, "The [Vilna] Gaon would have said it." I asked her how she knew, and she said, "You silly boy. The Gaon would have said it even when he suckled." In our family what the Gaon would have done was thrown at our heads every other minute.

**From *Keeper of the Law: Louis Ginzberg*,
by Eli Ginzberg**

GLASER, EDUARD (1855-1908) German explorer and Arabist. Glaser was born in Deutsch-Rust, Bohemia. At the University of Prague he studied mathematics and astronomy, and studied Arabic privately. Although he was to make a career for himself in Arabic studies, he held a position as an assistant at the observatory of Vienna before becoming an explorer in southern Arabia. He made four trips to Arabia. On the first (1883-1884), he crossed southern Arabia in various directions. The second was in 1885-1886, and on the third (1887-1888) he managed to reach Marib (the ancient Saba), and copied about one thousand previously undiscovered Sabean and Himyaritic inscriptions. His last journey (1892-1894) took him from Aden to the interior and he mapped the country from Hadramaut to Mecca, collecting inscriptions and manuscripts. He also identified many sites in Yemen and made studies of various Arabic dialects and the Sabean language.

In his writings, which include *Skizze der Geschichte und Geographie Arabiens* (1889), *Abessenier in Arabien und Afrika* (1895), and *Punt und die südarabishcen Reiche* (1899), he wrote about the history of Arabia.

After his death his ethnographic collection was distributed among various museums and his library went to Dropsie College in Philadelphia.

GLÜCKEL OF HAMELN (1646-1724) Memoirist; chronicler of life in central Europe. Born in Hamburg, Germany, she moved with her family to nearby Altona, then under Danish rule, when she was two years old and the Jews were expelled from Hamburg. Some ten years later, when Altona was overrun by Swedes, Glückel's father was the first Jew permitted resettlement in Hamburg.

Glückel celebrated her engagement to Chayim Hameln, whom she had never met, at the age of twelve. She married him at the age of fourteen — and the union was apparently a highly successful one. When, after thirty years and twelve children, her husband died, she wrote: "I truly believe I shall never cease from mourning my dear friend."

"In my great grief and for my heart's ease, I begin this book the year of Creation 5451 [1690-1691] — God soon rejoice and send us His redeemer!" is how Glückel opens her memoirs. She explicitly states two reasons for writing: "I began writing it, dear children, upon the death of your good father, in the hope of distracting my soul from the burdens laid upon it," and goes on to define her deep sense of loss and resultant insomnia. Later, in spelling out details of her early childhood, she adds, "I am writing down these many details, dear children mine, so you may know from what sort of people you have sprung." She denies any intention of moralizing for her children, but in fact cannot resist a good allegory or edifying tale, whether from contemporary, classical Greek, or Talmudic sources.

The value of her work lies in the picture of Jewish life three hundred years ago evoked by this

FROM GLÜCKEL'S MEMOIRS

Before I was twelve years old I was betrothed and the betrothal lasted two years. My wedding was celebrated in Hameln. My parents, accompanied by a party of twenty people, drove there with me. When we reached Hanover we wrote to Hameln for carriages to be sent to us. My mother imagined it to be a town like Hamburg and that, at the very least, a carriage would be sent for the bride and her parents. On the third day three or four farm wagons arrived, driven by such old horses that looked as if they themselves should have been given a lift in the wagons. My mother was greatly offended but as she could not change it, entrusting ourselves to the God of Israel, we seated ourselves in the carts and arrived in Hameln....

About the time we came to Hamburg, I became pregnant, and my mother was in the same condition. I was happy when the All Highest presented me with a beautiful healthy baby. My mother expected her child about the same time but was pleased that I had mine first and that she could attend me and the child the first few days. Eight days later she also gave birth to a daughter so there was no envy or reproach between us. We lay in one room, beside each other, and had no peace from people who came running to see the wonder of mother and daughter lying in childbed together.

witness of no mean descriptive skill. One of Glückel's earliest memories is of the survivors of the 1648–1649 Chmielnicki massacres who sought refuge in her father's house. She records memories of life in a town where Jews have "no right of residence," of the gates of the Jewish section, of the dangers of travel between communities and of the dread of plague. Shabbetai Tzevi (q.v.) was no remote figure to her — he was the precursor of the Messiah whose call her in-laws awaited momentarily. They had their belongings packed in barrels, ready for the voyage to the Holy Land.

On positive features of her childhood, Glückel asserts, "My father gave his children, girls and boys, a secular as well as a religious education." Indeed, Glückel's descriptions call into question the assumption of the inferior status of traditional Jewish women of the past. An assertive woman herself, she shared fully in her husband's business enterprises, which were significant. Thus she obtained the background and confidence to manage on her own business after his death.

A sense of family life both rich and warm is confirmed in her writing. Glückel's memoirs are punctuated by the round of the holiday cycles and advent of the Sabbath. Her maternal duties began at the age of fifteen or sixteen, with the birth of her first child. By the time the children reached twelve or thirteen years of age, she began arranging for their marriages.

Marrying her children off well was the focus of her life. The intricacies of finding and securing the right match for each of them required all her care. Supporting the young couple in the earliest stages of their marriage added to the economic burdens she assumed with barely a complaint.

When it came to a second marriage for herself, however, she was less successful. The last two segments of the memoirs were penned after the bankruptcy and subsequent death of her second husband, with whom she had experienced a not so benign relationship.

Glückel's memoirs were passed down through the generations of her family. (Heinrich Heine [q.v.] was one of her many descendants, Bertha Pappenheim [q.v.] another.) On the basis of a copy of her manuscript prepared by her son, Rabbi Moses Hameln of Baiersdorf, the memoirs were first published in their original Judeo-German in 1896.

The Life of Glückel of Hameln Written by Herself, trans. B. Z. Abraham, 1962.

The Memoirs of Glückel of Hameln, trans. M. Lowenthal, introduction by R. S. Rosen, 1977.

GOLDBERG, ARTHUR JOSEPH (1908–1990) U.S. jurist and statesman who served as U.S. Secretary of Labor, Supreme Court Justice, and ambassador to the United Nations. Born on Chicago's east side, he was the eighth son and eleventh child of poor Russian immigrants. At the age of twelve, he was an errand boy delivering boots and shoes. He worked his way through school and graduated first in his law class at Northwestern University, being called to the Illinois bar in 1929. He specialized in labor law, in which he soon achieved renown. During World War II he headed the labor division of the U.S. Office of Strategic Services (OSS), with the rank of major. As a lawyer, his reputation was as a champion of human rights and an arbitrator who excelled in devising formulas which safeguarded the interests of both sides in industrial disputes. The Republican senator Barry Goldwater said of him "He is the only labor leader I can talk to without getting angry."

In 1948 he was appointed general counsel both of the United Steelworkers of America and of the Council of Industrial Organization (CIO). He played a central part in negotiating the merger between the CIO and the American Federation of Labor (AFL) and in drafting anticorruption rules that contributed to breaking the communist hold on certain unions.

With this background he was President John F. Kennedy's natural choice for secretary of labor at the beginning of 1961. As secretary, he worked to raise the minimum wage and to increase unemployment benefits. He was praised for not allowing his former interests to influence his new policies. In the summer of 1962 Kennedy appointed him an associate justice of the Supreme Court, where he was part of the liberal majority that expanded constitutional rights, including the rights of privacy. He wrote several historic decisions including the right of every accused prisoner to be advised by a lawyer during police interrogation.

In 1965 he was persuaded by President Lyndon B. Johnson to leave the Supreme Court in order to succeed Adlai Stevenson as U.S. representative to the United Nations. He was intensely active during the critical period preceding, during, and following the 1967 Arab-Israel war. During the six days of the war, he called for a cease fire without Israeli withdrawal, was involved in negotiations to end the war, and subsequently helped to draft Security Council Resolution 242, which was to set the tone of Arab-Israel relations for many years to come. The Arabs accused him of swinging U.S. policy in a pro-Israel direction. Goldberg had also to deal with the Rhodesian crisis and the question of admitting Communist China to the United Nations. He also looked for ways to end involvement in Vietnam and hoped to apply his negotiating skills to this end. He was disappointed, however, at not being given a larger role and when he resigned in 1968, he cited Vietnam as one of his greatest frustrations.

He resumed his legal practice, but entered politics to take charge of Hubert Humphrey's presidential campaign in New York, one of the states carried by Humphrey. In April 1970, Goldberg was nominated Democratic candidate for the governorship of New York State, opposing Nelson Rockefeller. His defeat was partially due to his failure to win the endorsement of a New York trade union for which he had once done so much.

Public service came for the last time when he was roving ambassador for President Jimmy Carter (1977–1978), his main assignment being to head the U.S. delegation to the first review conference of the Helsinki European Security and Cooperation accords. There he was responsible for putting human rights issues, especially the situation of Soviet Jews under Leonid Brezhnev, at the top of the agenda of the thirty-five nation gathering, and he repeatedly took the Soviets to task for their shortcomings on this issue.

Throughout his career he was active in Jewish and Zionist affairs. He was president (1968–1969) and then honorary president of the American Jewish Committee, chairman of the board of overseers of the Jewish Theological Seminary (1963–1969), honorary chairman of the American Friends of the Hebrew University, and president of the International Association of Jewish Lawyers.
D. P. Moynihan (ed.), *The Defenses of Freedom: The Public Papers of Arthur J. Goldberg*, 1966.

GOLDBERG, LEA (1911–1970) Hebrew poet and critic. Born in East Prussia, she spent her early childhood in Russia, returning after the revolution with her family to their home in Kovno, Lithuania.

She was a precocious child who began to produce poetry at an early age. Some of her teachers report that to entertain herself during the dull and lengthy task of lacing her high shoes, the little girl used to compose poems out loud. She studied at the Hebrew Gymnasium (high school) of Kovno and at the universities of Berlin and Bonn, receiving her doctorate in Semitic languages.

In 1935, she went to Palestine, where she joined Abraham Shlonsky's literary group, Yachdav, and began to publish her poetry in its literary forum. Shlonsky became her friend and colleague, in a friendship which was to last long after their political and literary interests took them in different directions.

Goldberg worked as a teacher of drama and as a literary critic for various newspapers. She wrote poetry, prose, drama, and literary criticism, and translated many classics into Hebrew, among them Shakespeare's *As You Like It* and Tolstoy's *War and Peace*. She was well loved as a writer for children with whom she had a wonderful rapport, both in writing and in person. She was most famous, however, for her poetry which is characterized by conversational style, simple though symbolic language, and almost complete disassociation from ideological or Jewish themes. She preferred traditional verse forms, concrete imagery, and familiar but refreshing language to write about universal matters such as childhood, nature, love, aging, and death. Her best known poems include *Songs of the Stream*, in which natural symbols represent the poet's aesthetic concerns, and *After Twenty Years*, about an encounter between two estranged lovers.

An invitation in 1952 to head the Department of Comparative Literature at the Hebrew University of Jerusalem paid tribute to her versatility as a writer, poet, and critic. She held the post until her death.
R. F. Mintz (ed.), *Modern Hebrew Poetry*, 1968.

Cool in its dream, I kissed the stone:
It is the quiet, I am the song,
It is the riddle, I make it known,
From one eternity we were both hewn.
    I kissed the stone, its lonely flesh.
I am the betrayer, it is vowed faithfulness.
It is the constant, mystery of creation.
I am change, its revelation.
    I know I touched a heart grown mute.
It is the world and I the poet.

From "The Stream Sings to the Stone"
Songs of the Stream
by Lea Goldberg

GOLDBERG, RUBE (Reuben Lucius; 1883–1970) U.S. cartoonist. Born in San Francisco, he and his siblings were reared, after the early death of their mother, by their highly disciplined father. As

FOOLISH QUESTIONS – NO. 1,407.

FOOLISH QUESTIONS – NO. 19.

Two of Rube Goldberg's Foolish Questions.

a reaction to his father's flamboyant nature and his older brother's strong sense of self-confidence, Rube grew up shy. His fascination for cartoons manifested itself early. When he was eleven, he paid for professional drawing lessons from a man who painted billboards, Charles Beall. Beall also emphasized discipline, but he immediately recognized Goldberg's inborn talent. By the time Goldberg was twelve, he had won his first art prize.

His father had no appreciation for Rube's burgeoning talent, and although he gave up on the idea of sending his son to a military academy, he did coerce him into studying mining engineering at the University of California, Berkeley. While a sophomore, Goldberg studied art under William Morris Hunt, from whom he acquired the philosophy that "humor comes from everyday situations because nothing is as funny as real life." Upon graduating, he worked at mapping sewer pipes and water chains for one of San Francisco's sewer experts. After only six months, he quit and, despite his father's admonitions, took on a very low-paying position with the *San Francisco Chronicle* art department, beginning, like most early cartoonists, with the sports page. He left the *Chronicle* for the *Bulletin,* but the possibility of greater prospects in New York challenged him to overcome his father's apprehensions and leave the relative security of his position in San Francisco.

In New York, after many rejections, he got a position with the *Evening Mail* in 1906, and his career as a cartoonist received a great boost. In the following years he created *Boob McNutt, Professor Lucifer Gorgenzola Butts, Fifty-Fifty, Life's Little Jokes, Ike and Mike, Foolish Questions,* and his great, hilarious *Inventions.* During his lifetime he created over 50,000 cartoons, including one *Invention* a week for twenty years.

Goldberg's cartoons were based on his perceptions of the foibles of humanity. His special sense of the comic depicted situations in which technological advances invented for the well-being of mankind backfired into uncontrollable monstrosities (e.g., *Another Triumph for Science,* or *Our Lives Are All More of Less Run by Machinery*).

His cartoon heroes were often featured with cigars; he himself smoked five cigars a day for sixty-five years, claiming they were his "incense-and-myrrh." After he married, the women in his cartoons evolved from overweight, big-mouthed caricatures to sensible individuals.

Over his objections, he became increasingly known as the philosopher-humorist. He tried his hand at writing, but his books did not exhibit the same genius as his drawings. He also took part in vaudeville acts, in which his humor proved successful. In 1916 he tried his hand at movies, producing *The Boob Weekly, The Fatal Pie,* and others. However, a seven-and-a-half-minute reel required 1,500 drawings which made it impossible for Rube to maintain his hectic output at the *Evening Mail,* so he dropped movies. Despite the admiration and recognition he received, he sent for his father every year when it came to renegotiating his salary. His esteem for his father is reflected in his cartoon *Father Was Right.*

After a dry spell between 1928 and 1934, Goldberg regained his creative momentum and joined the *New York Sun* as political cartoonist in 1938, winning the Pulitzer Prize for his drawing "Peace Today" in 1947, which warned against the danger of atomic weapons. He helped establish the annual award of the National Cartoonists' Society, named in his honor the Reuben.

At the age of eighty he decided to move from newspaper work to sculpture, and devoted the rest of his life to making small sculptures that showed the same humorous wisdom as his drawings. Three exhibitions of his bronzes were held at the Hammer Galleries while he was still alive, and Hammer continued to exhibit his work posthumously.

In 1970 the Smithsonian Institute's Museum of Science and Technology held a large retrospective of Goldberg's work. The artist, aged eighty-seven, attended the opening reception. He died two weeks later.

C. Kinnaird, *Rube Goldberg vs the Machine Age,* 1973.

P. C. Marzio, *Rube Goldberg: His Life and Work,* 1973.

GOLDFADEN, ABRAHAM (1840–1908) Pioneer of the Yiddish theater; author, composer, director, and producer. Born in Alt-Konstantin, Volhynia (then part of Russia), he received both a traditional religious and a secular Russian education. At the rabbinial academy of Zhitomir, he came under the influence of Abraham Baer Gottlober, a Hebrew and Yiddish writer, who stimulated him to write in both languages and to compose songs for musical evenings. After graduating from the Zhitomir academy, he unsuccessfully tried to make a living as teacher, tradesman, and journalist. In the course of his wanderings and temporary sojourn in Odessa and Lemberg, he came in contact with the popular Broder Singers in the Rumanian town of Jassy. He was fascinated by their songs and dramatic monologues, impersonating various Jewish types and callings, which they acted out in wine cellars and restaurant gardens. By then, he himself had already written and published poetic booklets, whose lyrics were becoming known to folksingers, and in Jassy he heard his own songs sung and acted out in costume, to the hilarious applause of large audiences.

It occurred to him that their dramatic effect would be intensified if the songs were combined with prose dialogues between two actors and woven into an interesting plot or humorous situation. In October 1876, the first performances authored and directed by Goldfaden, took place in a wine cellar in Jassy and their success spurred him on to project an entire series of comedies with more than two actors. These additional actors were recruited from itinerant singers and cantors' assistants, whom he trained for the stage. One of his daring innovations was to have the feminine roles played by women and not by men in disguise. Thus the Yiddish theater was born.

The Goldfaden troupe traveled throughout eastern Europe and soon found imitators. The various troupes flourished and increased from year to year until 1883, when catastrophe struck. The Russian government, fearing the possible revolutionary impact of this influential medium for stirring up the emotions of the masses, banned all Yiddish performances. The actors and theatrical entrepreneurs dispersed across Europe and to the United States. Goldfaden also moved on to London, Paris, and New York. His American experiences, from 1887 to 1889, were not happy and his theatrical ventures there were unsuccessful. He did not return to the United States until 1903 and spent his last years in New York.

Goldfaden contributed sixty plays to the Yiddish theater. Despite the absence of any training in musical composition, he enriched the Yiddish musical repertoire with many catchy tunes, dance melodies, patriotic hymns, and festive choruses. His early comedies included *Shmendrik*, whose title-hero has become the proverbial gullible, good-natured schlemiel; *Die beede Kuni-Lemel*, which is still played on Yiddish and Hebrew stages and became an Israeli film; and *Kabzenson et Hungerman*, which owes its plot to Moliere. These come-

Abraham Goldfaden appearing in one of his plays.

dies not only entertained but also offered moral enlightenment, castigating the excrescences and superstitions of the shtetl, to which medievalism still clung. However, when pogroms swept over these shtetls in the 1880s, Goldfaden wrote more serious dramas that warned against excessive enlightenment and hasty rejection of ancestral traditions. Instead of Jewish assimilation to foreign ways, his plays advocated Jewish national resurgence and the realization of Zionist hopes. The musical comedy *Shulamis* and the tragedy *Bar Kochba* were most popular. The songs of *Shulamis* (notably his adaptation of *Rozhinkes mit Mandlen*) are still sung and its scenes of love and laughter conjured up the legendary events of ancient Judea and aroused longing in the hearts of denizens of the Pale for a return to freedom from oppression and the rebirth of independence in the ancestral land. *Bar Kochba* depicts the last, desperate revolt of the Jews against the Romans and emphasizes Jewish heroism and self-sacrifice.

Ben Ami, Goldfaden's last play, called for Jewish national redemption in answer to Russian pogroms. Its plot is based on George Eliot's *Daniel Deronda*. Its aristocratic hero, on discovering his Jewish origin and witnessing a pogrom in Odessa, leaves the bloodstained Russian soil for a new life in Eretz Israel, where he will train Jewish youth to till the soil of the Holy Land and work for Jewish national regeneration.

The Goldfaden tradition continued to dominate Yiddish theater for generations because his texts, melodies, philosophy, and morality were in harmony with the spirit of Yiddish audiences.

S. Liptzin, *The Flowering of Yiddish Literature*, 1963.

A. A. Roback, *The Story of Yiddish Literature*, 1940.

GOLDMAN, EMMA (1869–1940) U.S. anarchist. Born in Kovno (Kaunsas), Lithuania, she became conversant with revolutionary ideas in Saint Petersburg before going to the United States in 1886. She worked initially in a clothing factory in Rochester, N.Y., and at a corset factory in New Haven, Conn. In 1887, the trial and execution of four anarchists accused of exploding a bomb that killed seven policemen in Chicago's Haymarket Square motivated her to join the anarchist movement herself.

On moving to New York City in 1889 she met Alexander Berkman (q.v.), who became her sometime lover and lifelong companion. During the Homestead Strike in 1892 guards of the Carnegie Steel Company shot several steel strikers. Goldman and Berkman felt that the company president,

---

From the Emma Goldman Obituary, Circulated by Associated Press, May 14, 1940

Emma Goldman, apostle of philosophic anarchism and of "voluntary communism," was born in Russia, spent 33 years of her life in the U.S. fighting for her ideals, for which she suffered imprisonment, and was an incorrigible revolutionist to the end.

She was deported from the U.S. in 1919 for obstructing conscription, fled in 1921 from Soviet Russia, where she had hoped to find the realization of her social dreams but found only disillusionmment, and saw her ideals defeated again in the civil war in Spain, in which she took an active part. In the social history of the United States she wrote a chapter all her own, and in the history of the worldwide revolutionary movement of her time she made a place for herself beside that of her teacher, Peter Kropotkin.

After fighting for a generation against what she considered the ills of the social system in the U.S., she opposed Lenin and Trotsky because she believed them guilty of betraying the socialist ideal by establishing what she denounced as the new despotism. Her experience in Russia confirmed her in her belief that all government was wrong, and that the new society for which she stood could be established only on the basis of anarchism, through the free cooperation of the masses.

Henry Clay Frick, was responsible for the strikers' death and plotted to kill him. After his attempt on Frick's life failed, Berkman was imprisoned for fourteen years. Goldman led the anarchist cause during these years. A spellbinding orator, she delivered lectures in German, Russian, Yiddish, and English. In 1893 she herself was imprisoned for seven months. In 1901 she was even accused of inspiring Leon Czolgosz to shoot President William McKinley. In many American Jewish communities during the week between the attack on McKinley and his death, there were open accusations of the Jewish role in this assassination, because of Goldman.

Her best-known publication was a monthly magazine that she founded in 1906 entitled *Mother Earth*. It appeared for eleven years, being coedited by her and Berkman after he was released from prison. An early feminist, she also traveled throughout the United States lecturing on behalf of birth control and women's rights. She noted that "everything within a woman that craves assertion and activity should reach its fullest expression." In 1916 she was imprisoned for violating laws that prohibited the distribution of birth control information.

In 1917, during World War I, she and Berkman were jailed for two years for opposing the draft. As a result of the Red Scare in the United States that which followed the Bolshevik Revolution, they were deported to Russia in 1919. In her work, *My Disillusionment in Russia*, (1924), she described their unhappiness with the new Russian government. Two years after their arrival they left as exiles without a country. Goldman later married a Welsh anarchist and ultimately settled in the south of France where she wrote her autobiography, *Living My Life* (1931). She died in Canada and was buried in Chicago near the graves of the anarchists of the Haymarket riot.

R. Drinnon, *Rebel in Paradise*, 1961.

GOLDMANN, NAHUM (1895–1982) Zionist leader. Born in Visznevo, Lithuania, he was taken as a child to Germany, first to Königsberg (now Kaliningrad, USSR) and then to Frankfurt-am-Main where his father taught Hebrew at a Jewish teachers' training college and edited a weekly Jewish journal. Goldmann was nurtured in Zionism and delivered his first public Zionist address, "Hellenism and Judaism," before he was fourteen. At the Orthodox Jewish school he attended, he propounded Zionist ideas and sold the *shekel* (the membership fee of the Zionist Organization) to his fellow students, arousing the wrath of the passionately anti-Zionist school authorities. By the age of seventeen, he was well versed in European literature, spoke fluent French and Hebrew, and soon learned English as well. He read two or three books a day, both fiction and nonfiction.

At age sixteen, he attended the Eleventh Zionist Congress in Basel, to which his father was a delegate. In 1912 he entered the law faculty of Heidelberg University, obtaining a doctorate in law, to which he later added another in philosophy. He studied philosophy under Heinrich Rickert and Karl Jaspers, sociology under Max Weber, and literature under Friedrich Gundolf. In 1913, he spent five months in Palestine, and published in 1914 his impressions under the title *Erez Israel -Reisebriefe aus Palästina*.

At the outbreak of World War I, the Goldmanns, although fervent German patriots, were still Russian citizens, and Goldmann, an enemy alien, was barred from Heidelberg University and rejected as a volunteer by the army. He began to write articles for the *Frankfurter Zeitung*, on the strength of which he was invited to join the propaganda division of the German Foreign Ministry, where he was assigned first to the news division and then to Jewish affairs. In the immediate post-war years, he worked as a freelance journalist and in 1923 established the Eshkol publishing house, and with his lifelong friend, Jacob Klatzkin, started the German-language *Encyclopaedia Judaica* project. Eventually, the Nazis stopped the work, which remained a ten-volume skeleton until many years later when he revived the idea in the form of the English-language *Encyclopaedia Judaica*, published in 1972.

Between 1925 and 1933, while working at the German Foreign Ministry, Goldmann began to engage seriously in Zionist political work. He represented the Radical party at Zionist congresses and was elected to the Zionist General Council. At this time, he also began to take an interest in Zionist foreign policy, in which from the start, he was nonconformist.

In 1934 he was appointed representative of the Jewish Agency for Palestine accredited to the Mandates Commission of the League of Nations. He worked hard to establish the World Jewish Congress (WJC) and was elected chairman of its executive at its 1936 founding assembly. In addition to the fight against Nazism, his Zionist work, and activity in relation to Palestine, he became increasingly involved with the German refugee problem and later also with Austrian and Czechoslovak refugees. In the face of serious opposition within the Zionist movement, he negotiated the *Haavarah* agreement, by which German Jews emigrating to Palestine, were able to transfer their assets upon payment of a capital sum.

When the 1939 Zionist Congress in Zurich broke up on the eve of World War II, Goldmann realizing that little more could be achieved in Geneva, moved to Paris, where he headed the WJC Executive. At the fall of France in 1940, he went to the United States, where he took a prominent part in wartime Jewish and Zionist activities. From May 1943, he served as head of the Jewish Agency's Washington political office. With his friend Stephen Wise (q.v.), he led the WJC and came into conflict with Abba Hillel Silver (q.v.), who demanded that all political work in Washington be directed by the American Zionist Executive Council, while Goldmann insisted on total independence for the Jewish Agency office. Throughout the war, he was in constant touch with the WJC's Geneva and London offices, getting almost daily reports on the ongoing destruction of European Jewry and trying desperately to get help. In later years, he admitted that it had been the greatest failure of the Jewish leadership of his generation that more European Jews had not been rescued. In 1946–1947, he played a leading role in Zionist diplomacy, and after Stephen Wise's death in 1949, he was elected president of the WJC, thus becoming the recognized representative of Diaspora Jewry. Later he was also elected chairman of the Jewish Agency and president of the World Zionist Organization (1956–1968).

Of all his achievements, probably the most important was to bring about the Luxembourg agreements between the Federal German Republic on the one hand and the State of Israel and the Conference of Jewish Material Claims against Germany on the other. The idea that Germany should pay moral and material reparations to the Jewish people had been raised within the leadership of the WJC as far back as 1942, but it only became reality when after Goldmann's first secret meeting with the German chancellor, Konrad Adenauer, the latter made a historic statement to the German Parliament (September 27, 1951). Goldmann created the Claims Conference for the purpose of negotiations on behalf of Diaspora Jewry, and later also the Conference on Material Claims against Austria and the Memorial Foundation for Jewish Culture, presiding over all three. In negotiating with the Germans, he had the full support of David Ben-Gurion (q.v.), but there were so many opponents to the negotiations, that for the only time in his long life, Goldmann had to have a bodyguard. Earlier, he had also established and presided over the Conference of Presidents of Major American Jewish Organizations (Presidents' Conference), initially to ensure that American Jewry spoke with one voice during the Palestine debate before the establishment of the State of Israel.

Goldmann was the first to place the problem of Soviet Jewry on the international and Jewish agenda; he organized the unified Jewish representation at the Vatican in connection with the Second Vatican Council and initiated contacts between the WJC and Third World states. Under his leadership, the WJC maintained contacts with all those countries that, after the 1967 Six Day War and the 1973 Yom Kippur War, severed relations with Israel. With the exception of the Soviet Union, which would not invite him in his capacity as president of the WJC, he traveled to meet with leading heads of state and politicians.

In his later years, he became increasingly critical of Israeli policies vis-à-vis its Arab neighbors and Palestinians, and often came into sharp conflict with the mainstream of Israel's foreign policy. He propounded the utopian idea of Israel's neutrality, guaranteed by the great powers and by the Arabs, and of a Middle Eastern economic community in which a neutral Israel would play a leading role. At the same time, he expected that the idea of the centrality of Israel for world Jewry should mean not only financial support by the Diaspora but that Israel should become Jewry's spiritual center, whose influence upon the Diaspora would assure its survival. His views aroused widespread criticism in the Jewish world, especially in Israel. At one time he established his home in Jerusalem but then moved to Geneva. In 1977, he relinquished the presidency of the WJC. He published two versions of his autobiography, in English and then in German, as well as several volumes of essays and numerous articles.

One of Goldmann's qualities was his ability to compromise, to relieve tension during debates with a bon mot or a Jewish joke drawn from his inexhaustible treasury, using these anecdotes, both in public addresses and in private conversations even with the most powerful personalities he met. A powerful orator, and an astute, but charming and witty negotiator, he was nonconformist to the end.
J. Draenger, *Nachum Goldmann*, (German, 2 vols.), 1959.
N. Goldmann, *Autobiography*, 1969.

GOLDMARK, KARL (1830–1915) Hungarian composer, music teacher, and critic. His father, Ruben, was cantor at the Keszthely (Hungary) synagogue; Karl was one of twelve children. He had scant general education and no musical training until age eleven. When he was twelve, means were found to send him to study the violin twice a week with a teacher in Sopron. In 1844 he went to Vienna to study music. Three years later, he qualified for entrance to the polytechnic for regular studies and to the conservatory. With the outbreak of the revolution of 1848, the polytechnic and the conservatory closed for the duration. Goldmark's brother Joseph joined the rebels and had to flee for his life to America. Goldmark himself was briefly caught up in the fighting and found himself stranded during a lull in the war at Gyoer, a hotbed of the revolution. When the theater of the nearby town of Sopron visited, he found a job as a violinist in the orchestra. Once again unlucky, he was caught by the victorious Austrians and sentenced to death as a revolutionary. His desperate protests that he was just an innocent fiddler in the local theater were not accepted. However, this time he was lucky; the two men assigned to execute him were actors in civilian life and instead of shooting him, smuggled him out of town.

After the debacle of 1849, he returned to Vienna but was too poor to continue his studies. Instead, he gave music lessons, studied the scores of classic composers, and began composing himself. In 1858, he returned to Budapest and for a year and a half taught himself counterpoint, canons, and fugues. From 1860, he again lived in Vienna, taught the piano, and started to compose in earnest. When J.

Hellmesberger the elder, founder of Vienna's most famous chamber group, rejected his Quartet in B-Flat, Goldmark hired the group to play it at an all-Goldmark concert. The evening was such a success that Hellmesberger added the quartet to his own repertoire and afterwards played every new chamber work by Goldmark.

Goldmark first used Oriental and Jewish melodies in his successful *Overture Sakuntala* (1865). His first grand opera, *The Queen of Sheba* (op. 27) premiered at the Vienna Court Opera in 1875, with Hermann von Mosenthal's text. It was immediately acclaimed and Goldmark had forty curtain calls. The next year he wrote the symphony *Rustic Wedding*, followed by the Violin concerto in A Minor (op. 28) and the operas *Merlin* (based on the Arthurian legend), *The Cricket on the Hearth* (from a story by Dickens), *A Winter's Tale* (based on Shakespeare), and *The Prisoner of War*. Between the operas, he produced distinguished orchestral and chamber works.

Of unprepossessing appearance, Goldmark was a very likeable person. In the great controversy between Brahms and Wagner, which resulted in bitterly opposing factions among their followers, Goldmark alone managed to retain the friendship of both; Brahms remained his friend even after Goldmark had published a piece in praise of Wagner.

At the age of eighty-one, Goldmark wrote a short autobiography in German, which appeared in his niece's English translation in 1927, entitled *Notes from the Life of a Viennese Composer*.

GOLDSCHMIDT, VICTOR MORITZ (1888–1947) Norwegian mineralogist and geochemist. He was born in Zurich, Switzerland, where his father, Professor Heinrich Jacob Goldschmidt, was a distinguished physical chemist. Victor was educated in Heidelberg and at the University of Christiania (now Oslo,) where he studied chemistry, geology, and mineralogy. In 1905 he became a Norwegian citizen.

Goldschmidt received his doctorate in 1911 for his thesis on the factors governing mineral associations in contact metapmorphic rocks from samples collected in southern Norway. He was an instructor at the University of Christiania for two years before being appointed, at the age of twenty-six, professor and director of the Mineralogical Institute, in 1914.

As a result of his researches Goldschmidt established the mineralogical phase rule, namely that the maximum number of crystallogical phases that can coexist in rocks in stable equilibrium is equal to the number of components. In 1912 he undertook petrological studies in regional metamorphism as the first stage of his scientific career. His reports *Geologisch-petrographische Studien*, were published in five volumes between 1912 and 1921.

Goldschmidt became one of the foremost mineralogists and crystallographers of his generation and was the acknowledged founder of the science of geochemistry. In 1917 he was appointed chairman of the Norwegian government Commission for Raw Materials and director of the Raw Materials Laboratory, where he devoted himself to the practical utilization of science for the benefit of society. In the second phase of his career he carried out investigations into the factors governing the distribution of chemical species in nature.

The basis of the geochemical investigations undertaken in his Oslo laboratory consisted of the use of recently developed X-ray crystallography techniques. On the basis of this work he established the crystalline structure of over 200 compounds of 75 chemical elements and from these studies he derived the basic laws of geochemical distribution.

He prepared the first tables of atomic and ionic radii and of the substitution of elements in crystals. He established patterns of elemental behavior and showed that complex formulas of minerals like tourmaline were due to the maintenance of charge neutrality for positive and negative ions. He related hardness of crystals to structure, ionic changes, and interatomic distances. A monograph on the subject, *Geochemische Verteilungsgestze der Elements I–IV* was published in nine parts between 1923 and 1938.

In 1929 Goldschmidt was appointed professor at the University of Göttingen's Faculty of Natural Sciences and was made head of the Mineralogical Institute. Here he built a model of the earth, predicting the structural distribution of different elements in the earth's crust and atmosphere and classifying the natures and distributions of the various elements concerned.

In 1935 he resigned his chair in Göttingen as a result of Nazi policies and returned to a similar position in Oslo where he continued his studies of cosmic and terrestrial chemical distribution and isotopic geology. In the practical sphere he concentrated on the use and development of olivine rock in industrial refractories, the production of aluminum from silicates, the formation of mineral pigments, and the use of biotite as a fertilizer.

In 1937 he became chairman of the Norwegian Friends of the Hebrew University of Jerusalem.

During the World War II, after the Nazi invasion of Norway in 1940, he was hounded by the Germans and twice arrested, but in 1942 succeeded in escaping to Sweden and from there to England. He joined the staff of the Macaulay Institute of Soil Research in Aberdeen, and then the Rothamsted Experimental Station at Harpenden, where he continued his work on atomic energy. After the war he returned to Oslo.

GOLDSMID, English family descended from **Aaron Goldsmid** (born in Amsterdam, d. 1782), who settled in London during the 1740s and founded the firm of Aaron Goldsmid and Son.

Benjamin (1755–1808) and **Abraham Goldsmid** (1756–1810) prospered as bill brokers, and by the outbreak of the Napoleonic wars (they helped raise loans favorable to the government), were already rich men with large estates. As bankers they served as a link between the emerging country banks and the financial center in London.

In 1795 Abraham and Benjamin provided a large part of the monies raised by Prime Minister William Pitt for the war against France and underwrote still more. They took on a fourteen million pounds sterling loan, but the losses incurred by the change of the British military fortunes proved too much for Benjamin, who after a period of depression committed suicide. A short while later, Abraham undertook a loan of a similar size for the firm of Barings, but when Sir Francis Baring died suddenly, the stock collapsed. The East India Company, which had placed exchequer bills with the Goldsmids for negotiation, became alarmed and demanded the return of their money. On September 28, 1810, Abraham was discovered dead with a pistol in his hand.

Abraham had moved in the highest social circles and was an intimate friend of Horatio Nelson, who stayed with him in his Surrey home the night before leaving for the Battle of Trafalgar. He was also on friendly terms with the sons of George III, which helped to break down social prejudices against Jews in England and furthered the struggle for emancipation. Although Abraham held offices in the Great Synagogue, he worshiped in a private synagogue on the grounds of his estate and set aside a section of his grounds to grow wheat for the chief rabbi's Passover matzoth (unleavened bread). He was well known for his philanthropy and was associated with the establishment of Jews' Hospital and the Royal Naval Asylum.

Sir Isaac Lyon Goldsmid (1778–1859), son of Aaron's second son **Asher Goldsmid**, one of the founders of Mocatta & Goldsmid, bullion brokers to the Bank of England, made a fortune mainly by financing the construction of railroads in England. The firm of Mocatta & Goldsmid still preserves a letter of application from Isaac Goldsmid to the East India Company for the function of bullion broker.

Isaac played a prominent role in the struggle for Jewish emancipation in England and was one of the founders of the nonsectarian University College, London, and are of the founders of the Reform Synagogue movement in England.

In 1841, he was made a baronet, being one of the first professing Jews to receive an English hereditary title. In 1846 he was created baron de Palmeira by the king of Portugal for his services in settling an intricate monetary dispute between Portugal and Brazil.

Isaac's wife, Isabel, and his daughter, Anna Maria, were pioneers of the movement for higher education for women in England.

Sir Francis Henry Goldsmid (1808–1878), eldest son of Isaac Lyon, was the first Jew in England to be admitted to the bar. He was a Liberal member of Parliament from 1860 until his death and took an active part in his father's campaign for emancipation, publishing *Remarks on the Civil Disabilities of* the Jews (1839) and *A Reply to the Arguments against the Removal of the Remaining Disabilities of the Jews* (1848).

Sir Julian Goldsmid (1838–1896), son of **Frederick David Goldsmid** (1812–1866), was for many years a Liberal member of Parliament and a deputy speaker. He was the chairman of the Reform Synagogue, and vice president and later president of the Anglo-Jewish Association.

S. Aris, *Jews in Business*, (1970).

GOLDSMID, ALBERT EDWARD WILLIAMSON (1846–1904) British military officer and ardent early Zionist, a leader of the British Hovevei Zion (Lovers of Zion) movement. Born in Poona, India, he was raised as a Christian and only discovered his Jewish roots after he grew up. He returned to the Jewish faith, assuming the name of Michael, at the age of twenty-four. He viewed himself as a model for Daniel Deronda, George Eliot's characterization of an assimilated Jew who rediscovered his roots.

Goldsmid enlisted in the British Army in 1866, and was transferred with his regiment to India. He was appointed deputy assistant adjutant-general in 1889, was promoted to colonel in 1894, and gained distinction during the Boer War as a staff officer. He retired from the army in 1903.

Goldsmid was a firm believer in the Jewish settlement of Palestine and in the revival of Hebrew as a living language.

In 1892 he took a year's leave of absence from the British War Office in order to administer baron de Hirsch's (q.v.) Jewish settlement project in Argentina. He viewed the settlements as a temporary solution to alleviate the Jews' plight and an opportunity to spread Hovevei Zion ideals and Jewish nationalism. In an interview on the eve of his departure, Goldsmid declared, "The Jewish question will never be solved until a Jewish state guaranteed by the Powers is established in the Land of Israel." During his stay in Argentina, large tracts of land were parceled out in Santa Fe and Entre Rios, and approximately seven hundred families were settled in four settlements, the majority untrained in agriculture.

When he returned to England a year later, Goldsmid was elected president of the English Hovevei Zion movement. He was active in the Jewish community, helping to found the Maccabeans and the Jewish Lads' Brigade in 1895.

Theodor Herzl (q.v.) made his acquaintance during a visit to England, and the two became friends, depite differences of opinion. Goldsmid considered himself a national, religious Zionist, and he viewed Hovevei Zion as the natural Zionist organization, opposing the foundation of a new Zionist organization based in Vienna. Herzl attempted to win Goldsmid over, and relations between the two became strained. Goldsmid's refusal to attend the First Zionist Congress in Basel in 1897 led to a rift in the London Hovevei Zion leadership, and the congress's great success undermined his leadership even further, beginning the movement's decline.

Goldsmid remained in contact with Herzl, finally collaborating with him after the latter had won over the London Rothschilds for Zionism. Herzl enlisted Goldsmid as the secretary of the expedition that left for El Arish in the Sinai peninsula in 1903 to study settlement possibilities. The weeks of negotiations in Cairo brought Herzl and Goldsmid into close contact. In May Goldsmid cabled Herzl, who had returned to Vienna, to inform him that negotiations had failed.

J. Fraenkel, *Herzl Yearbook*, vol. 1, 1958.

GOLDWYN, SAMUEL (c. 1879—1974) U.S. film executive. Relatively few facts concerning Goldwyn's early life are universally agreed upon, but there seems little doubt he was born Shmuel Gelbfisz in Warsaw into a large, impoverished family. In 1895 he left Warsaw seeking a brighter future. Traveling via Germany, Great Britain, and Canada, he arrived in the United States four years later. Goldwyn, by then known as Goldfish, worked his way up through the glove business until he had become one of its most successful salesmen. The prospect of potentially greater wealth lured Goldwyn and his brother-in-law, Jesse Lasky (q.v.), to set up a film company bearing Lasky's name in 1910. The company and its star director, Cecil B. DeMille, were successfully launched with *The Squaw Man* in 1913.

In 1916 the Lasky Company merged with that of Adolph Zukor (q.v.), and became known by the name Paramount. That same year due to friction with Zukor, Goldwyn departed and founded Goldwyn Pictures with the brothers Edgar and Archibald Selwyn. Goldwyn's association with the company, whose name he adopted, lasted until he was ousted in 1922. For the rest of his career he remained an independent producer, releasing his product during most of the twenties and thirties through United Artists and subsequently through RKO.

Goldwyn saw to it that his name on a film meant quality to audiences. Prestigious actors like Gary Cooper, Ronald Colman, and David Niven spent significant parts of their careers under contract to Goldwyn, as did the comics Eddie Cantor (q.v.) and Danny Kaye (q.v.). Apart from the films these stars made for him, Goldwyn was also responsible for such diverse entertainments as *Stella Dallas, The Best Years of Our Lives, Guys and Dolls, The Little Foxes,* and *Porgy and Bess.* He was proud of the choruses of beautiful, long-legged girls, known as the Goldwyn Girls, that appeared in his musicals. Goldwyn's eccentricities gained him much personal publicity. F. Scott Fitzgerald said, "You always knew where you were with Goldwyn — nowhere." During the production of *Dead End* he paid daily visits to the realistic slum set and always collected the rubbish carefully arranged there by his art director. He had a genius for publicity. His manglings of the English language (some of them invented) became famous as "Goldwynisms." Three years before his death he was awarded the Medal of Freedom by President Richard M. Nixon.

A. S. Berg, *Goldwyn*, 1989.
C. Easton, *The Search for Sam Goldwyn*, 1975.
S. Goldwyn, *Behind the Screen*, 1923.

GOLDWYNISMS

- Gentlemen, kindly include me out.
- We are dealing in facts,not realities.
- Anyone who goes to a psychiatrist should have his head examined.
- This atom bomb is dynamite.
- I'll give you a definite maybe.
- I'm so happy, I could dance a jigsaw.
- Why did you call your baby 'John'? Today every Tom, Dick and Harry is called John.
- A verbal agreement isn't worth the paper it's written on.

GOLDZIHER, IGNAZ (Itzhak Yehuda; 1850–1921) Hungarian Orientalist, a founder of modern Islamic scholarship. Born in Székesfehérvár, where his father, a merchant, settled in 1842, he was brought up in strict Orthodox tradition. At the age of five, he was well versed in the Bible, and at the age of eight began Talmudic studies. For the first five years of high school, he was a pupil at the local Cistercian school. In 1862 he published his first booklet, *Sihat Itzhak*, a critical analysis of liturgical poetry (*piyut*), and, at his bar mitzvah, delivered an hour-long sermon from the pulpit of the synagogue.

When his father's business did not prosper, the family moved to Budapest in 1865, and Goldziher completed his high school studies at the Calvinist school. At university he studied Arabic, Turkish, and Persian. From early youth until his death, he adhered to a strict schedule, working until 2:00 a.m. and rising at 6:00 a.m. In 1869, at the recommendation of Baron J. Eötvös, he was granted a state scholarship. In his letter of recommendation, Eötvös, then minister of education, wrote: "If I am not mistaken — though with my experience of a number of budding scholars, I stopped being optimistic — we can expect that Goldziher will one day become an eminent lecturer in Semitic languages."

In 1869, Goldziher began studying Judeo-Arabic literature in Berlin. He moved to Leipzig, where he was a pupil of the ephoch's great Arabist, H. L. Fleischer, and obtained a Ph.D with a philological thesis on the medieval Jewish Bible exegetes and authors of dictionaries who wrote in Arabic. The happiest time of his youth was 1873–1874, when, with a Hungarian state scholarship, he journeyed to Damascus, Jerusalem, and Cairo. His command of Arabic, Turkish, and Persian, and deep knowledge of Muslim religious and secular literature, assured him entry into the highest echelons of spiritual and political society. The Jews of Damascus suspected him of being either a convert or missionary because of his great knowledge of Talmud and Islam. He even fell in love with his Muslim host's sister who could recite from memory Arabic poetry and the song of Deborah in Hebrew. In Cairo, he was the first European to enter the Azhar Seminary, whose principal, the convert son of a rabbi, became suspicious of this Hungarian Jew. In Cairo, he learned much about Islam and Muslim-folklore. Wishing to experience Islam, he entered the mosque dressed as a Muslim and joined the worshiping multitudes.

On his return home, he found that a Christian theologian had been appointed to the chair promised him by the previous minister of education. This caused him great disappointment although, since 1872, he had been an assistant professor (*Dozent*). He became full professor only in 1904.

From 1874 to 1904 the ailing and poverty-stricken Goldziher earned his living as secretary of the Jewish community in Pest. Frustrated, he saw these years as time wasted and recalled them with great bitterness in his *Diary*. He despised the wealthy, uneducated, honorary officers, who he felt treated him as a slave. This was in fact not so, for there is ample evidence of the high regard in which his superiors held him. His relationship with the rabbinical seminary was similar. Having participated in the preparations for its establishment in 1877, he became a member of the governing board but could not be appointed a teacher for lack of a rabbinical diploma. However from 1899 he was invited to lecture on Jewish religious philosophy.

Goldziher traveled extensively, mainly to international congresses on Oriental studies and religious history. It was at such a congress in Stockholm (1899) that King Oscar II presented him with a gold medal. He was a guest of some forty academies and learned societies and a member of eight. The universities of Cambridge and Aberdeen honored him with doctorates and numerous universities offered him positions. He refused all these offers out of his deep loyalty to Judaism and to his family, and his fervent Hungarian patriotism. From 1876, he was a corresponding member, and from 1892 a member, of the Hungarian Academy of Sciences and from 1905 chairman of its First Department (philosophy). He resigned from this office in 1919 after L. Loczy's anti-Semitic attack, refuted in a memorable address in which he declared his great Jewish pride.

Of his two sons, the elder, Miksa Adolf (1880–1900), committed suicide and the younger, Karl (1881–1955), became a noted professor of mathematics. Karl's marriage to the Egyptologist, Maria Freudenberg, in 1913, caused a great change in the bitter sixty-three year old scholar. He himself literally fell in love with her, felt rejuvenated, and worked with increased vigor. In 1918, Maria victim to Spanish influenza; he was shattered and began to go into a decline. He continued with his scholarly work, but became increasingly alienated from the world. He drew some satisfacion from the fact that he was elected dean of the philosophical faculty of Budapest University and often refers in his *Diary* to the pride he felt when, in his Hungarian national costume and cocked hat, he was driven in his carriage through the streets of the ghetto where he lived, with a hussar sitting next to the coachman.

Goldziher's paramount importance in the scholarly world lay in his being the first to systematically explore the legal, religious, philosophical, cultural, and historical aspects of Islam. His chief interest lay in uncovering its inner forces and the influence of outside forces upon its development. He found that the inner forces created the *Koran* and the *Sunna*, of which the tenets of *Hadith* take the traditional chain back to an associate of Muhammad. The principal result of his critical researches was the assertion that these traditions had nothing to do with Muhammad himself, that is, that they were the deliberate creations of *Koran* exegetes, religious practices, political groupings, dynasties, and pretenders.

H. Loewe, *Ignaz Goldziher* (German), 1929.

GOMPERS, SAMUEL (1850–1924) U.S. labor leader; a major influence on the formation of the American labor movement. Born to a working-class family in London, after a few years of elementary education he became an apprentice shoemaker at six pence a day, and then an apprentice cigar maker (his father's trade). In 1863, he immigrated with his family to the United States, where they settled on the Lower East Side of New York City.

President Woodrow Wilson and Samuel Gompers in 1916.

There, Gompers joined the local branch of the Cigar Makers' National Union. During the 1870s he was very active in the union and became one of its leaders. In 1886 he played a central role in establishing the American Federation of Labor, of which he was president from its inception until 1924 (excluding 1895). From 1894 until his death he edited its journal.

Practical and tough-minded, Gompers was a powerful personality who dominated any meeting in which he participated. He was noted for his opposition to revolutionary trade unionism. Rejecting the concept of class struggle, he opposed socialism, believing that the advancement of the worker is best achieved within the capitalist system through the power of collective barganing and direct negotiations with employers. He advocated binding written contracts. He was so completely opposed to the politicization of the labor movement that when, in 1896, William Jennings Bryan, seeking the support of organized labor in his bid for the presidency, promised to offer Gompers a position in his cabinet, Gompers refused, stating that "under no circumstances" would he accept political office. Nevertheless, he did support the Democrats in 1908 because their platform included an anti-injunction plank. During World War I, Gompers was instrumental in mobilizing support for the war effort among American labor. President Woodrow Wilson appointed him to the Commission for International Labor Legislation intended to formulate better labor laws.

Gompers became the universally acknowledged spokesman of organized labor, following the slogan "reward your friends and punish your enemies." Although himself of immigrant origin, he suppported limiting immigration in order to protect the position of existing workers in America.

S. Gompers, *Seventy Years of Life and Labor*, 2 vols, 1967.

R. H. Harvey, *Samuel Gompers*, 1935.

S. B. Kaufman, *Samuel Gompers and the Origin of the American Federation of Labor, 1848–1896*, 1973.

B. Mandel, *Samuel Gompers*, 1963.

F. C. Thorne, *Samuel Gompers, American Statesman*, 1969.

GOODMAN, BENNY (1909–1986) U.S. clarinetist and band leader. The tall, apple-cheeked band leader was known as the King of Swing for inaugurating a new era of popular music with a rhythmic and driving beat. Benjamin David Goodman was born in Chicago to a large family that struggled to get by on a tailor's salary of twenty dollars a week. When Benny was ten, he borrowed a clarinet and took music lessons at the local synagogue; by the time he was fourteen, he was earning more than twice as much money as his father for playing four nights a week with a neighborhood band.

Goodman studied at the Lewis Institute in Chicago, and at the age of sixteen joined the Pollack band in California. He played with several popular

Benny Goodman, the King of Swing, in the 1950s.

bands as well as working as a freelance musician before forming his own twelve-piece band in 1933. Ironically, until a crucial summer night in 1935, Goodman's band was not a success. It is said that on that August 21, 1935, when the band first performed musical arrangements by Fletcher Henderson at the Palomar Ballroom in Los Angeles, the crowds went wild and swing was born. Suddenly, the band was a hit and Goodman became the King of Swing.

Inventive at jazz arrangements, ingenious at improvisation, demanding the utmost from his band and himself, and playing a blend of jazz and contemporary popular music that the public wanted to hear, Goodman led a preeminent ensemble. He was also noted for being the first major band leader in the 1930s to put black and white musicians together on stage. His trio with Teddy Wilson on piano and Gene Krupa on drums founded in 1935

ABOUT BENNY GOODMAN

"Working with Benny Goodman wasn't a job, it was an experience."

Frank Sinatra

"He was the world's greatest artist on the clarinet, and his orchestra was one of the best of all time."

Steve Allen

"All the time I was with 'Good' he was never satisfied. With him, perfection was just around the corner. I figure Benny will die in bed with that damn clarinet."

Jess Stacy, his pianist

(which in 1936 became a quartet with Lionel Hampton on vibes) was one of the outstanding jazz ensembles of all time. His band played at hotels, night clubs, theaters, and ballrooms. On January 16, 1938, they first brought jazz to Carnegie Hall in a historic concert.

The Benny Goodman band also featured in movies such as *Big Broadcast of 1937* (1936), *Hollywood Hotel* (1938), *Stage Door Canteen* (1943), and *Sweet and Lowdown* (1944). The band, which launched other stars, such as Peggy Lee and Harry James (q.v.), to fame, continued to play until 1950. In 1966, they reunited briefly on a trip to bring jazz to the USSR Meanwhile, in 1938, Goodman had begun a second career as a classical clarinet player, playing Mozart, and commissioning works by Bela Bartok and Aaron Copland (q.v.). He was said to have been the most recorded solo instrumentalist in history.

D. R. Connor, *BG–Off the Record*, 1958.
B. Goodman, *The Kingdom of Swing*, 1961.
P. Maffei, *Benny Goodman*, 1961.

GOODMAN, PERCIVAL (1904–1989) U.S. architect. Born in New York, he studied there and in France, and later became a professor of architecture at Columbia University. Aside from being a talented architect, he was also a city planner and a designer of furniture for mass production.

Coming to the building of synagogues out of a belief in Jewish kinship, rather than faith, he sought to express the human element of the congregation rather than the overwhelming aspect of divinity in his designs. Thus his buildings are modest and intimate. Their emphasis on lightness and portability attempts to evoke the nomadic element of the Jewish people, while their size and style and the use of such materials as wood, weaving, mosaic, and stained glass, generate a feeling of warmth.

Unlike many of his contemporaries, for whom art was only a tool of architecture, he believed that art must be permitted an independent role in the synagogue. He maintained that the artist can express aspects of tradition that the building alone cannot convey. Setting a trend for modern synagogue architecture, he tended to dedicate specific space to artistic objects, rather than integrating objects of art into his architecture. In this respect he was also a catalyst for the development of the field of synagogue art.

Notwithstanding his nonreligious background, he designed numerous synagogues, among them Shaarey Zedek in Southfield, Michigan, B'nai Israel in Millburn, New Jersey, Temple Beth El in Springfield, Massachusetts, and Beth El in Rochester, New York.

A. Kampf, *Contemporary Synagogue Art*, 1966.
R. Wischniter, *Synagogue Architecture in the United States*, 1955.

GORDIN, JACOB (1853–1909) Yiddish playwright. Born in the Ukraine, and son of an adherent of the enlightenment movement Gordin wrote and spoke Russian more comfortably than Yiddish. Throughout his career, the quality of his Yiddish was serviceable. Although self-educated, during his teens, Gordin wrote articles in Russian for the left-wing newspapers and worked for underground causes such as the independence of the Ukraine from the rest of Russia, but not for the civil rights of Jews. He blamed the Jews for the 1881 pogrom, claiming they had failed to be "Russian" and to live by farming. He himself worked for several years as a farm laborer, believing that the soil was the only answer for humanity. In 1891 he went to America with the group *Am Olam* (Eternal People), to establish a utopian socialist farming commune.

The commune failed, and Gordin, with a wife and eight children to support, went to work for a radical Yiddish newspaper. Among his early efforts was a sketch of Jewish life with much dialogue. Zelig Molgulesco, a member of Jacob Adler's (q.v.) company, had the sketch dramatized and a meeting was arranged with Adler and other actors. Gordin was astonished by the actors. He expected boors who wiped their noses on their shirt sleeves. Instead met elegant gentlemen in top hats and silk shirts who seemed sensitive and spoke intelligently.

Here the facts vary. In one version Adler, impressed by Gordin's obvious intellect and fluent Russian, commissioned him to write a play. In another, his new friends invited him to attend his first Yiddish play. In horror he swore to write a whole new type of Yiddish drama. And thus *Siberia*, the first "realistic" Yiddish drama, was born.

Siberia told of the ordeal of a Russian Jew who as a youth had been sentenced to Siberia, escaped, assumed a new identity, became wealthy, and who was betrayed to the police by a business rival. The actors disliked the play, finding it dry. Gordin attempted to oversee the rehearsals in order to prevent the actors from embroidering his lines, or adding melodramatic situations, songs, and comic bits. Still, the opening night audience found Gordin's brand of realism uncomfortable. It was not until Adler stepped on stage before the third act and admonished the audience for its inability to understand a masterpiece, that the play was accepted.

For the next two decades Gordin was a central presence in Yiddish theater. He replaced the flowery Germanisms of early works with simple, clear Yiddish, declaring that Yiddish was a language, not just a jargon. He brought the common man to the center of the Yiddish stage, enforced a strict moralism, and translated from Hugo, Ibsen, Gogol, and Shakespeare. He was responsible for the tendency of Yiddish writers and audiences to use "realism" as a term of automatic approval. He made the intellectual elite feel that a theater in the Yiddish language could be their concern and pride. Most of all he brought a firm discipline to the stage, insisting upon strict adherence to scripts and a decent system of rehearsals.

Several of Gordin's plays became standard in Yiddish repertoire, notably, *The Jewish King Lear; God, Man, and Devil*; and *Mirele Efros* (first called *The Jewish Queen Lear*). Jacob Adler and David Kessler became known as Gordin actors. Under Gordin's influence, the Yiddish theater acquired serious actors such as Bertha Kalish, Sara Adler, and Esther Rachel Kaminska. By the time of his death other serious Yiddish dramatists and actors had begun to produce work in the realistic vein. Gordin's most creative years, around the turn of the century, are known as the golden age of American Yiddish theater or the Gordin era.

GORDON, AARON DAVID (1856–1922) Ideologist of Labor Zionism. He was born in Troyanov in the Ukraine, where his religious parents brought him up in a rural environment, ensuring that he received both a traditional and secular education. Gordon worked as a clerk on the farming estates of Baron Horace Günzberg (q.v.), a distant relation. He was respected for his honesty but found the job routine and not compatible with his nature. Five of his seven children died in infancy, which added to his general depression. Gordon found an outlet for his talents in his contacts with young people, whose education and welfare he helped to foster within the Jewish community.

The 1881 pogroms brought him to a Zionist outlook and he joined a branch of the Lovers of Zion movement. Gradually Gordon became attracted to the idea of working as a laborer in Eretz Israel. However, it took him many years to achieve this objective in view of his family obligations. Eventually, after the death of his parents and the financial independence of his children, he was able to take the step and at the age of forty-eight arrived in Jaffa. At first this frail and untrained intellectual could not obtain work on a farm as he so ardently desired. Gordon refused an administrative post and eventually started to work in an orange grove, followed by night labor in a wine cellar. "Labor tires the body but it gives so much to the soul," he wrote to his wife who had remained in Russia.

The following years were difficult. Gordon had bouts of malaria, periods of unemployment, and even hunger. When his daughter arrived in 1908 she found her father almost unrecognizable with his white hair and shabby clothes. However, she was impressed by his "animated expression and shining eyes." The following year his wife joined him and the family made their home in a sparsely furnished room in the settlement of Ein Ganim. Shortly afterward, his wife died.

Gordon's high moral standards became legendary. He objected to help from Zionists abroad as charity. Serving as a guard, he carried a whistle but refused a gun. He rejected any compensation for the essays he was publishing, on the grounds that creative writing should be a by-product of manual labor. Gordon was unusual in the pioneer settlements for his Orthodox lifestyle and his putting on *tefillin* (phylacteries) and praying each morning.

In 1919 Gordon was invited to live in the communal settlement of Deganya, where he shared a room with three other pioneers. Like the settlement members, he participated in all the regular tasks. When he got word of his son's death, he got up from his place in the dining room without a sound and went out to find solace in his work in the fields.

In his last years, his bearded figure was revered by the Jewish youth of Eretz Israel, who flocked to hear him expound his views. Influenced by the writings of Tolstoy, Henry George, and Thoreau, Gordon stressed the concept of purity of labor as a cosmic force which should be inherent to human nature. Work redeems the individual, he argued and the same applies to nations. The Jews will not be able to lay a claim to the new land unless they redeem it with the sweat of their brow. He championed the concept of "Jewish Labor" and claimed that part of the plight of the Jewish people in the Diaspora was in their removal from productive work. Being a socialist he opposed the exploitation of the many by the few, calling for the nationalization of the means of production and of the land. His influence was exercised because he not only preached, but also practiced the ideas which he propagated. He shunned politics and saw himself as an educator and a guide to an entire generation of young Jews who devoted themselves to building their old-new land. Gordon was one of the first Zionist thinkers to relate fundamentally to the Arab population in Eretz Israel. "Our attitude to them must be one of humanity," he wrote, "of moral courage which remains on the highest plane, even if the behavior of the other side is not all that is desired. Indeed their hostility is all the more reason for our humanity."

S. Avineri, *The Makings of Modern Zionism: The Intellectual Origins of the Jewish State*, 1981.
A. Gal, *Socialist Zionism: Theories and Issues in Contemporary Jewish Nationalism*, 1973.

GORDON, GEORGE (1751–1793) English nobleman and statesman, convert to Judaism. Born in London, son of Cosmo George, third duke of Gordon, Lord George Gordon served in the army and the navy, gaining an officer's commission in 1772. He entered Parliament in 1774, representing a family borough, but no particular party. An impassioned Protestant, in 1779 he became President of the United Protestant League and in 1780 fought in parliament for the repeal of the 1778 act by which Catholic disabilities in England had been removed, and even led a march to Parliament House to present the "No-Popery" petition. The crowd of about 50,000 was roused to a pitch of great excitement when he informed them that the petition would probably not be accepted. When the petition was rejected by Parliament, riots ensued ("the Gordon riots"), lasting several days. Criminals broke out of prison, shops and houses were plundered; 300 people were killed, 192 were convicted of crimes, and 25 were executed. Gordon was tried for treason and inciting to revolt, but was acquitted. His character and appearance at the time has been recorded by many authors. Edmund Burke described him as a Don Quixote, Horace Walpole called him "The Lunatic Apostle," and Dickens wrote in *Barnaby Rudge* "his face was suggestive of an air of indefinable uneasiness."

Gordon's popularity did not wane after the trial. In 1781 he was nominated as candidate for the City of London, but declined, devoting himself to the cause of stemming the progress made by Roman Catholicism. He came to loggerheads with the established church and in 1786 was excommunicated by the archbishop of Canterbury.

In 1787, Gordon was charged with having written and published a pamphlet about a request by prisoners to prevent their banishment to Botany Bay, Australia. His criticism of the government was considered libelous and he was arrested. He was also charged with publishing a libelous article on the moral and political conduct of the queen of France. He was found guilty on both counts. He fled to Holland, but when he found he was unable to remain there he returned to England and retired to Birmingham.

Lord Gordon expressed his interest in Judaism and attraction to the Jewish people in a number of letters which he wrote to the heads of the Spanish and Portuguese as well as the German and Dutch communities in London. The Hebrew quotations in the letters prove that he had some knowledge of Jewish sources. In 1786 he decided to become a Jew. Although his application for conversion was rejected by the Chief Rabbi, he was circumcised in 1787 and took the name Israel bar Abraham. He grew a beard and dressed in the fashion of Orthodox Jews.

In January, 1788, he was imprisoned in the notorious Newgate jail, and lodged with the common prisoners in damp, cold conditions. He continued to write pamphlets and letters to people of note and submitted articles to newspapers on political and social developments. In time, he was able to better his prison conditions, thanks to help from his friends. The Christian theologian John Wesley, who paid him a visit, reported that his quarters were "more like the study of a recluse in a private house than a prison." His fame attracted many visitors and he commented "I am become one of the shows of London." Poorer Jews were said to have regarded him as "a second Moses who would lead them back to the promised land." Even the royal princes, sons of George III, came to see him and join his lavish meals. Once every two weeks he gave a formal dinner party, followed by music and dancing. When he had spare time, he played the violin or played ball with other prisoners, to whom he frequently extended generosity and financial help.

Throughout his imprisonment in Newgate he meticulously practiced the precepts of Judaism. Every morning he donned his phylacteries (*tefillin*) and prayer shawl (*tallit*) and prayed. Every Satur-

A CONTEMPORARY BALLAD (excerpts)

Ye Jews, Turks and Christians, I pray now
draw near,
When a comical ditty you quickly will hear,
Concerning Lord George who for Protestant
laws,
His life said he'd lose in so glorious a cause....

To a Jew he turned, with a beard long as a
goat,
The Mosaical law he has now   . by rote.
What a glorious defender ot . rotestant laws!
With pork or fat bacon I'd well rub his jaws.

So we wish them much joy of this new convert
Jew,
Tho' my tale is odd, yet I'm sure it is true,
So farewell my Lord since to Newgate you're
taken,
You may find it hard to save your own bacon.

SAYINGS OF
JUDAH LEIB GORDON

● I maintain that every Jew of our time who
has the ability to do something and the opportunity of doing it on behalf of his people,
morally, intellectually, or economically, and
does not do it is guilty of the crime of treason.
● Can we deny that Judaism, in its present
state, is opposed to all culture?... I realize now
that Jewish persecution is worse than Gentile
persecution.
● A successful settlement in Eretz Israel, a
family of Jews engaged in agriculture, may be
the beginning of a national resurrection. But I
do not believe in such a possibility. I will not
call upon my brethren to give up the Enlightenment [Haskalah], return again to the ghettos or teach their children jargon [i.e., Yid-
dish]. But before we go to Palestine, we must
prepare ourselves in a way to redeem our
minds before we redeem our bodies.

day he was joined by nine Polish Jews to make a
prayer quorum (*minyan*). His impressive beard
reached down to his waist, the delight of contemporary portrait painters who frequently came to
the jail to paint his striking likeness.

After five years in prison he was due to be
released but was unable to find guarantors and was
returned to his cell. Within a few months, he died
of jail fever. The Jewish community refused, or did
not dare, to bury him; his own relations interred
him in a Protestant churchyard in Hampstead,
London, and the site of his grave was soon
forgotten.

P. Colson, *The Strange History of Lord George
Gordon*, 1937.
C. Hibbert, *King Mob: the Story of Lord George
Gordon and the London Riots of 1780*, 1958.
C. Roth, *Essays and Portraits in Anglo-Jewish His-
tory*, 1962.
I. Solomons, *Lord George Gordon's Conversion to
Judaism*, 1914.

GORDON, JUDAH LEIB (Leon; 1831–1892)
Hebrew poet, writer, and critic. One of the most
prominent Hebrew writers of the 19th century,
Gordon sought, through his works, to awaken the
entire Jewish nation. In verse, satirical feuilletons,
and polemic essays, he vehemently supported the
movement of national revival, the renaissance of
the Hebrew language, and deliverance from what
he called the "yoke of ignorance" imposed by rabbinic tradition.

Gordon was born in Vilna (now Vilnius,
Lithuania); his education combined thorough Judaic
studies and European culture and languages (Russian, German, Polish, French, and English). From
1853 he taught in government Jewish schools. The

subject of his first epic poem, *Ahavat David u-
Mikhal* (1857) was the love between David and
Michal, daughter of Saul. This and subsequent
works of Gordon's romantic period, with their
biblical themes and diction, were infused with the
spirit of the Jewish Enlightenment (Haskalah).

Drawing on vast stores of Talmudic knowledge,
Gordon's chosen mission throughout his poetic
works, was to call attention to the misery of Jewish
life in Russia of his day. The cycle of poems *Korot
Yameinu* (History of our times), describes with
pathos and realism the plight of women and other
groups victimized by archaic rabbinic law and
demands religious reforms from within traditional
Judaism.

In 1872 Gordon was called to Saint Petersburg
to take the office of secretary of the Jewish community and of the Society for the Promotion of
Culture among the Jews. During this period he
continued writing and editing prolifically.
Denounced to the government as a nihilist in 1879,
he and his wife were banished to Petrozavodsk, in
northern Russia. After one hundred days of exile,
the charges of anti-tsarist activity were proven false
and Gordon returned to Saint Petersburg. But the
indifference of the Jewish community to his fate
and its passivity during his arrest cast Gordon into
despair. As the younger generation of Jewish
"enlightened" became increasingly assimilated,
abandoning Jewish values along with the Hebrew
language, he realized the impossibility of his
former conviction that one could be "a Jew at
home and a man in the street." The undercurrent
of his despair is audible in his poem *"Le-mi ani
amel"*(For whom do I labor?).

All dreams of Russian emancipation were crushed
with the pogroms of 1881. The two great advocates

of the new Zionist movement, Perez Smolenskin (q.v.) and M. L. Lilienblum, mandated extreme rejection of European culture and national rebirth in Israel. In opposition, Gordon believed that "our redemption can come about only after our spiritual deliverance," and favored emigration to western countries, particularly the United States.

Indisputably a prime force in the Haskalah, Gordon's social commentary as well as the new style he forged in Hebrew verse were influential in the history of Hebrew literature.

J. S. Raisin, *The Haskalah Movement in Russia*, 1913.
A. B. Rhine, *Leon Gordon: An Appreciation*, 1910.
S. Spiegel, *Hebrew Reborn*, 1930.

GOREN, CHARLES (1901–1991) Contract bridge authority. Born in a poor Philadelphia, Pennsylvania, neighborhood to a family of Russian immigrants, he studied in Canada at McGill University, Montreal, and returned to Philadelphia to practice law. He became fascinated by the game of bridge and was technical assistant to Milton Work, the outstanding authority on auction bridge, at a time when auction bridge was giving way to contract bridge. Goren made a name as a player and teacher of contract bridge. Eventually he held virtually every record of note in tournament play. From 1933 he won many major titles, including thirty-one national championships, the Spingold Knockout Teams championship in 1944 and 1945; from 1944 to 1962 he stood at the top of the career master-point rankings. He was awarded the McKenney trophy for the top masterpoint winner in a year on eight occasions. He was the only bridge player to win every major bridge championship in the United States.

Goren stressed adaptability and natural tactics rather than systems and artificial conventions and his methods are standard throughout the United States. Goren became a world champion in Bermuda in 1950 as a member of the American team in the first of the Bermuda Bowl series.

In 1933 he succeeded Ely Culbertson as bridge columnist for the *Chicago Tribune* and the *New York Daily News*. He also contributed regularly to *Sports Illustrated*. He wrote voluminously on the subject, publishing some forty books that sold over ten million copies and were translated into many languages. His *Contract Bridge Complete* (1942) was a classic work and his *Point-Count Bidding* (1949) helped to revolutionize bridge by advocating the point-count system, which displaced the previous honor-trick valuation favored by Culbertson. Goren also starred in the first successful television bridge program, which ran from 1959 to 1964 and was called "Championship Bridge with Charles Goren." By the 1950s, Goren was known as Mr. Bridge and was featured on a *Time* magazine cover.

GRAETZ, HEINRICH (1817–1891) The outstanding Jewish historian of the 19th century. The son of a butcher, he was born in Xions, Posen (Poznan), and spent his early years there, in Zerkow and in Wolstein (Wolsztyn). He then went to Oldenburg to study with Samson Raphael Hirsch (q.v.), from whom, however, he soon diverged as he adopted a rationalistic-scientific approach to Judaism. He received his doctorate from the University of Jena for a thesis on Judaism and Gnosticism. At this time he intended to become a rabbi, but his lack of ability in public speaking turned his career toward teaching — from 1845–1848 he was principal of the Orthodox school of the Breslau community and from 1850–1852 taught at Lundenburg.

A turning-point in his career came with an invitation from the Berlin community to give a course of lectures on Jewish history. He was then appointed to teach the subject at the recently founded Jewish Theological Seminary in Breslau. This allowed him to devote much time to his scholarly activities, notably the writing of his classic, *History of the Jews*.

He attained an international reputation and in 1869, the University of Breslau appointed him honorary professor.

He continued to publish volumes of his history, but left the first two volumes, on the biblical period, until he could visit Eretz Israel, which he did in 1872. While there, he also helped to establish an orphanage in Jerusalem. In Europe he was in contact with some of the outstanding thinkers of his time. While on holiday in Carlsbad he met Karl Marx (q.v.), who, on his return to London, sent Graetz a copy of his *Das Kapital*; in return Graetz sent Marx his book on Ecclesiastes, one of his series of biblical studies. He adopted a traditional attitude to the Pentateuch, insisting on its unity and preexilic origin, but was radical in his treatment of the Prophets and Writings, propounding the theory of the two Hoseas and three Zechariahs and dating the book of Ecclesiastes to the period of Herod.

Graetz's history was received critically in Jewish circles while an attack by the German nationalistic historian, Heinrich von Treitschke, evoked sharp controversy. Treitschke, who was strongly anti-Semitic, accused Graetz of being anti-Christian and of opposing Jewish integration into the German nation. Graetz responded to the attacks, but considerable sections of German Jewry, especially the assimilationists, were also critical of his views. Indeed when a commission was appointed by the Union of Jewish Communities to publish the sources for a history of German Jewry, Graetz was not invited to join. Elsewhere in the Jewish world, however, his work was recognized and he received many honors on his seventieth birthday.

History of the Jews, both in its original eleven-volume edition and in a three-volume abridgment, became a Jewish classic. It was a monumental achievement, combining scholarship and style, although its biases, including critiques of Orthodoxy and Reform and disdain for mysticism and

Hasidism, left it open to criticism from many quarters. Christian historians reacted negatively to his bitter account of the Christian treatment of the Jews through the ages. Nevertheless, the book has remained popular and it is probably the only work of 19th-century Jewish scholarship still read and appreciated, not only by scholars but by a wide public.

S. W. Baron, *History and Jewish Historians*, 1964
P. Bloch, *Heinrich Graetz*, 1898.
L. Kochan, *The Jew and his History*, 1977.

GRATZ, REBECCA (1781–1869) Founder of the first Jewish benevolent organization in the United States and of Sunday schools for Jewish children. She was born into a German Jewish family of some prominence in the newly established United States of America. Her father, Michael Gratz, and his brother Bernard, confirmed patriots during the Revolutionary War, had successfully expanded their fur trade and export business. In so doing, they had traveled throughout Pennsylvania and beyond, while making their homes in Philadelphia.

Rebecca was the seventh of ten surviving children. Following her parents' relatively early deaths, she looked after the household, which included several unmarried brothers and later the nine children of her sister Rachel, who died quite young. Reportedly Rebecca herself rejected a Christian suitor because of the divergence in their religions and chose to remain single.

A close friend of hers had become engaged to Washington Irving. Intrigued by this fine Jewish woman (portraits by the colonial artist, Thomas

Rebecca Gratz. Portrait by Thomas Sully.

Sully, draw out her loveliness) he described Rebecca to Sir Walter Scott. Following the publication of *Ivanhoe*, Scott sent a note to Irving saying, "How do you like your Rebecca? Does the Rebecca I have pictured compare well with the pattern given?"

In 1819 Gratz founded the Female Hebrew Benevolent Society, the first nonsynagogal Jewish charitable organization in America, and possibly the first Jewish organization anywhere, specifically for women. She divided Philadelphia into districts and established committees to cover each district, setting out to discover applicants and administer to their relief. It was not Gratz's debut into community or organizational life. In 1801 she had become the secretary of the Female Association for the Relief of Women and Children in Reduced Cirumstances, and it is likely that she borrowed ideas and structure for the later Female Hebrew Benevolent Society from this early women's group. In 1815 she was a charter member of the Philadelphia Orphan Society, and in 1819 she became its secretary.

The Female Hebrew Benevolent Society distributed food and clothing to the needy. Later, two offshoots of this organization developed: the Sewing Society and the Fuel Society. In 1838 Gratz and the women of congregation Mikveh Israel established the first Hebrew Sunday school in the United States, which served as a model for all others that followed. It was a community school attached to no congregation, free and open to all, especially girls. Prayer hymns composed by Gratz together with a reading from the Scripture and its interpretation formed the curriculum (the only text on Bible history had been produced by Christian Sunday schools, so Gratz pasted little bits of paper over objectionable passages); a moral attitude was transmitted, along with a sense of Jewish identity. Gratz remained its president and superintendent, teaching every Sunday until 1864, her eighty-fourth year, and calling it "the crowning happiness of my days."

In 1855 her concern for Jewish children took another turn; largely through her efforts the Jewish Foster Home and Orphan Asylum was founded. She had written an appeal for its founding in *The Occident*, a magazine for American Jews, signing her statement, "A Daughter of Israel."

Her niece wrote of her, "My aunt was an old maid, at least in the common acceptance of the term. True she never married, but she was a mother to the orphan and the destitute, to the friendless and oppressed, to those in poverty and want, and to the sinner and contrite."

R. G. Osterweis, *A Study in Charm*, 1935.
D. Philipson (ed.), *Letters of Rebecca Gratz*, 1894.

GREENBERG, HENRY BENJAMIN ("Hank"; 1911–1986) U.S. baseball star; the first Jewish player elected to the Baseball Hall of Fame (1956). Born in New York City to immigrant parents, he grew up in the Bronx where he excelled in high school sports.

A year after the big (six feet, four inches, 215

Hank Greenberg.

pounds) first baseman joined the Detroit Tigers, the team won its first American League championship in twenty-five years, with Greenberg leading the team in home runs and runs-batted-in.

Earlier, with the season nearing its end, Greenberg had faced a difficult decision. Would he play ball, or would he absent himself on the Jewish high holidays? He played on Rosh Hashanah, but not on Yom Kippur. A Detroit newspaper carried a headline in Hebrew on Yom Kippur that read, "Happy New Year, Hank!"

In 1935 the Tigers won again as league champions and Greenberg won the most valuable player award. A fractured wrist forced him to miss most of the 1936 season, but the next year he returned with a near record of 183 runs batted in. It was the third best effort of all time and only one run short of the American League record. The 1938 attack on Babe Ruth's home run record missed its goal by two, but his total of 58 tied the best home run mark by a right-handed hitter. Shifted to the outfield in 1940, he won his second Most Valuable Player Award and the Tigers won another pennant.

Between 1941 and 1945 Greenberg served as a World War II captain in the U.S. Army Air Corps in India and China. He returned to the Tigers' outfield in July 1945. He homered in his first game, and on the final day of the season won the pennant for Detroit with a ninth inning grand-slam home run. He played with the Tigers again in 1946. The following year he was traded to the Pittsburgh Pirates, where he ended his playing career.

During Greenberg's stay with the Tigers the team won four pennants and two World Series. His career statistics show a .313 batting average, 331 home runs and 1,276 runs batted in, in 1,394 games. He was a four-time champion in home runs and runs batted in.

Greenberg served as a vice-president and general manager for the Cleveland Indians and the Chicago White Sox between 1948 and 1963. He left baseball of Wall Street.

His son Stephen, a lawyer and former first baseman with Yale University and the minor leagues, became the deputy commissioner of baseball in 1989.

GROSSMAN, VASILI SEMYONOVICH (1905–1964) Russian author and journalist. The son of an engineer, he grew up in the religiously traditional and largely Yiddish-speaking milieu of Berdichev, to which he formed a lifelong attachment. Having graduated from Moscow University, he first worked as a chemical engineer in the coal-mining Donbas region of the Ukraine and later in Moscow from 1932 to 1934, but finally chose to become a writer. *Stepan Kolchugin* (1937–1940), a three-volume novel set in prerevolutionary Russia, was his major achievement before the appearance of *Narod bessmerten* ("The People Is Immortal," 1942), Grossman's most famous work and the first outstanding novel of World War II published in the Soviet Union. A *Red Star* war correspondent, like Ilya Ehrenburg (q.v.), he quickly grasped the extent and significance of the Holocaust, his close relatives being annihilated with the rest of Berdichev Jewry in 1941. It was this specific aspect of the Nazi invasion that Grossman felt bound to emphasize whenever he dealt with the Great Patriotic War.

Some months before his cooption into the government-inspired Jewish Anti-Fascist Committee (April 1944), Grossman had begun collaborating with Ehrenburg and others in a full-scale attempt to document all available evidence of Nazi crimes against Soviet Jewry. The material for this *Black Book* comprised eyewitness testimony, letters and diaries, first-hand published reports (including Ehrenburg's), and documents provided by the Soviet State Committee on Nazi Atrocities. As the war drew to a close in spring 1945, however, Ehrenburg's violently anti-German line no longer suited the Kremlin, and he was replaced as chairman of the editorial committee by Grossman, who finished the *Black Book* a year later. In his preface he not only stressed the fact that Jews had been the main target of Nazi viciousness, but also underscored Jewish resistance (moral and physical) as well as the role of anti-Semitic collaborators in German-occupied territory. Such declarations were likewise no longer in tune with official Soviet policy: though already serialized in the Yiddish weekly *Eynikayt* and translated overseas into English (New York, 1946) and Romanian (Bucharest, 1947), the original *Black Book* was deliberately held up in the press until November 1948, when the text vanished and many members of the Jewish

Anti-Fascist Committee died in Stalin's "anticosmopolitan" campaign.

Grossman, like Ehrenburg, managed to survive, but he had fallen into permanent disfavor with the Soviet establishment. Having suppressed one volume on the Holocaust, champions of the new party line were not inclined to tolerate another work in the same vein disguised as fiction. *Za pravoye delo* ("For the Just Cause," 1952), complementing Grossman's wartime novel of a decade earlier, portrayed the battle of Stalingrad, but no complete version ever appeared. It met with fierce ideological criticism on two accounts: for "underrating Communist motivation" in the victorious Red Army, and for "overestimating" the Jewish tragedy in World War II. Grossman's last work could thus only be published in a censored and mutilated definitive edition (1954). Years after his death, a Russian-language restoration of the ill-starred *Black Book* finally appeared in Jerusalem (*Chornaya kniga*, 1980).

GRUENBAUM, YITZHAK (1879–1970) Polish Jewish leader and Zionist. Born in Warsaw, he grew up in Plonsk and while still in high school joined the Zionist movement. He began to study medicine but turned to law in 1904. From an early age, he contributed articles to the Jewish press and before long was editing newspapers in Hebrew, Yiddish, and Polish. From 1905 onward, he was a delegate to Zionist congresses, and at the Helsingfors conference of Russian Zionists in 1906 was a leading advocate of struggling to achieve Jewish political rights in the Diaspora (*Gegenwartsarbeit*). In 1908 he was appointed general secretary of the Central Committee of Russian Zionists in Vilna. In 1914 Gruenbaum was editing a Warsaw Yiddish weekly but with the outbreak of war, moved to Saint Petersburg (Petrograd). Returning to Warsaw in 1918, he resumed his editorship of the Yiddish weekly and for a time edited the Hebrew daily *Ha-Tzefira*. In Zionism, he was prominent in the General Zionist Movement and advocated the secularization of Jewish life.

From 1919 to 1930 Gruenbaum was a member of the Polish parliament (the Sejm), where he fought for the rights of national minorities in general and the Jews in particular. He was a member of the committee that drafted the Polish constitution and initiated and organized a "national minorities' bloc" which scored a significant electoral success in 1922. Throughout the 1920s he was one of the outstanding leaders of Polish Jewry and a dominant figure in the parliamentary representation of Polish minorities. For a number of years he was also president of the Polish Zionist organization. One of his great interests was the promotion of Hebrew language and culture in Poland, and toward this aim he became one of the organizers of the Tarbut movement. He strongly opposed Chaim Weizmann (q.v.), who he believed put too much emphasis on Palestine. Gruenbaum felt that the primary objective of the world Zionist movement should be the welfare of the Jews in the Diaspora. When he challenged Weizmann in 1925, Weizmann retorted "I am a Jewish statesman and you are an assimilatory Jew."

In 1932 Gruenbaum moved to Paris. The following year he was elected to the Zionist executive and settled in Palestine. From 1933 to 1935 he headed the immigration department of the Jewish Agency and from 1935 to 1948, its labor department. During World War II he worked hard to assist Polish Jewry, heading the Jewish Agency's rescue committee. However, he was criticized for long refusing to believe the reports of mass extermination and later, for despairing of rescue possibilities and recommending concentrating on the rehabilitation of survivors. He engaged in widespread fund-raising and correspondence to get as many Jews as possible out of Europe into safe havens wherever possible. During this difficult period, Gruenbaum had to face criticism on the rescue committee's lack of achievement and tension with the religious Zionist parties. He was under additional strain in the knowledge that his son was being held in a concentration camp. (After the war his son was charged with having been a *kapo* — a Nazi-appointed head of a camp work gang — but was acquitted of the charge. Later, he was killed fighting in Israel's 1948 War of Independence.)

After the war, Gruenbaum was one of the Jewish Agency leaders arrested and interned by the British in 1946 in retaliation for the agency's hostile underground activities. After his release, he worked for cooperation between the Jewish Agency's underground force, the Hagana, and the dissident Irgun.

In 1948, Gruenbaum was a signatory of Israel's Declaration of Independence (although he could not take part in the official ceremony in Tel Aviv as he was stranded in besieged Jerusalem). He was appointed minister of interior in Israel's provisional government (1948–1949) and was responsible for organizing the country's first elections. In these elections, in 1949, he submitted his own party list but received no seats. He continued for a time to serve on the Jewish Agency Executive and remained active in Zionist affairs. Later, he retired to spend most of his time in literary, journalistic, and scholarly pursuits, including a history of Zionism and the editorship of the *Encyclopedia of the Diaspora*. He was a member of Kibbutz Gan Shemuel and his views grew increasingly leftist as he moved away from rightist General Zionism and joined the Marxist Mapam party.
R. Prister, *Without Compromise: Yitzhak Gruenbaum, Zionist Leader and Polish Patriot* (Hebrew), 1987.

GRUENING, ERNST (1887—1974) U.S. journalist, governor of Alaska, U.S. senator. Born in New York City to a family of German extraction, he studied medicine at Harvard University, graduating in 1907. Based on his experience as a reporter during medical school, he decided to become a journalist. He worked for the Boston *American* as a reporter; for the Boston *Traveller* as copy reader, city editor, and managing editor; for the *New York Tribune* as managing editor (1916–1920); and as managing editor of *The Nation* (1920–1923).

During World War I he served as an artillery officer and worked for the bureau of imports for the War Trade Board. In 1924 he was national publicity director in the presidential campaign of Senator Robert M. La Folette, Sr. After spending two years in Mexico, he founded the Portland, Maine, *Evening News* in 1927. In his position as editor, which he held for five years, he campaigned against giving control of Maine water resources to a power company, as well as initiating many state reforms.

He was particularly active in opposing U.S. exploitation of Latin America. As editor of *The Nation*, a post to which he returned in 1933, he uncovered details of the U.S. occupation of Haiti and Santo Domingo, as well as doing extensive research on the Cuban sugar industry. He also served as general adviser to the U.S. delegation to the seventh Pan-American Conference at Montevideo.

In 1934 he became editor of the New York *Evening Post*, but left the same year when he was appointed director of the federal Division of Territories and Island Possessions. This position, which he held until 1939, included supervision over Alaska, Hawaii, Puerto Rico, and the Virgin Islands. In Puerto Rico, where he was also relief and reconstruction administrator from 1935 to 1937, he was responsible for a longterm reconstruction program. In 1939 he was appointed governor of Alaska and remained in that position until 1953. He advocated Alaskan statehood and, after Alaska became a state, was elected a U.S. senator in 1958. He was reelected in 1962, but lost his third campaign in 1968, his advanced age and his position on Vietnam contributing to his defeat. He published *Mexico and Its Heritage* (1928), *Public Pays and Still Pays* (1931, 1964), *State of Alaska* (1954), and *Vietnam Folly* (1968).

GUGGENHEIM   American family of industrialists and philanthropists. They made the largest fortune ever amassed by a Jewish family in the United States, and the largest family fortune ever accumulated from mining and metallurgy. The family also had one of the largest private collections of modern art in the world, eventually housed in the Guggenheim Museum in New York. The Guggenheims have dispensed millions of dollars to charities and have endowed laboratories, university institutes, museums, hospitals, and numerous foundations.

The American branch of the Guggenheim family originated in 1848 when **Simon Meyer Guggenheim** (1792–1869) emigrated from Lengnau, Switzerland. He began to work with his eldest son **Meyer** (1828–1905) as a traveling salesman. Meyer branched out and became a manufacturer of polish, a shop

owner, spice merchant, and importer of fine lace and embroidery from Switzerland. In 1877 he established the firm of M. Guggenheim's Sons in Philadelphia, and was soon on his way to being a millionaire. A shrewd businessman, he purchased an interest in the Leadville mines in Colorado in 1881, and in 1888 moved his headquarters to New York, establishing, together with his seven sons, the Guggenheim Exploration Company (Guggenex) to search for profitable mines throughout the world. In 1901 the Guggenheims bought the American Smelting and Refining Company, thus laying the foundation for the family enterprises in lead, silver and copper mines and smelters in the United States, Mexico, and other countries. This became one of the greatest industrial empires of modern times.

When Meyer retired, **Daniel** (1856–1930), his second son, expanded and modernized the family business, became president of the American Smelting and Refining Company and purchased copper, tin, gold, and diamond mines in North and South America as well as Africa. He endowed the Daniel and Florence Guggenheim Foundation for the Promotion of Aeronautics, which today is devoted to aerospace science.

Meyer's third son, **Murry** (1858–1939) played an active role in the management of Guggenheim Brothers and American Smelting. His philanthropic activities included the establishment of the Murry and Leonie Guggenheim Foundation which opened a free dental clinic in New York and is devoted to the promotion of dental science.

Solomon Robert (1861–1949), Meyer's fourth son, developed the family mining interests in Mexico and Chile. He was a benefactor of many philanthropies including the Mount Sinai and Montefiore Hospitals, and endowed the Solomon R. Guggenheim Foundation which encourages art and art education, and operates the Guggenheim Museum in New York.

Simon (1867–1941), sixth son of Meyer, ran the family mining interests in Colorado and represented the State of Colorado in the U.S. Senate from

Meyer Guggenheim, seated center, and his seven sons.

1907 to 1913. In 1925 he established the John Simon Guggenheim Memorial Foundation to provide fellowships to scholars, scientists, artists, writers, composers, and historians of music.

Peggy (1898—1979), second daughter of Meyer's fifth son **Benjamin Guggenheim** (1865—1912), made a major impact on modern art in Europe and the United States. Her father was drowned on the *Titanic*, and although hers was the least wealthy branch of the family, Peggy invested her inheritance in what became the largest private collection of modern art in the world, housed in the Palazzo Venier dei Leoni in Venice. During the 1920s and 1930s, Peggy lived in Europe and opened the Guggenheim Jeune Gallery in London, exhibiting the works of Europe's leading avant-garde artists. When the Nazis invaded France, she shipped her art collection to New York where she opened the Art of This Century Gallery. In 1946 Peggy returned to Europe and opened her art museum in Venice, the responsibility for which was taken over after her death by the Guggenheim Museum in New York and was declared as a national monument by the Italian government.

Peggy wrote two volumes of autobiography, *Out of This Century* and *Confessions of an Art Addict*.
J.H. Davis, *The Guggenheims: An American Epic 1848-1988*, 1988.
E. P. Hoyt, *The Guggenheims and the American Dream*, 1967.
M. Lomask, *Seed Money; The Guggenheim Story*, 1964.
H. O'Connor, the Guggenheims: *The Making of an American Dynasty*, 1937.

GUGLIELMO EBREO (William the Jew, also known as Guglielmo da Pesaro; 15th cent.) Dancer and dance teacher in Italy. He may have been born in Spain, probably before 1440, but was associated with Pesaro. Little is known of his life. He studied with Domenico da Piacenza, founder of a new school of dancing, whose mastery he acknowledged in his treatise on dance (1463), and many of whose dances he incorporated in his own work. The two men collaborated in creating and organizing the wedding festivities of Costanzo Sforza and Camilla d'Aragona in Pesaro (1475). The Jews of Pesaro participated in the occasion, passing the bridal pair with great pomp, bearing a wooden elephant on which sat the queen of Sheba on a golden throne. When she reached the bride and groom, the queen of Sheba delivered an address in Hebrew and presented the couple with the Jewish community's wedding gift. She was followed by a character who gave a further address beseeching the favor of the rulers for the Jewish community, and then came 120 young people doing special dances choreographed by Guglielmo.

It is possible that Guglielmo later converted to Christianity. He traveled extensively, teaching "social dances" and arranging festive dances in many cities, including Milan, Mantua, Urbino, Bologna, Naples, and Venice. A miniature in the

Guglielmo da Pesaro with dance students, depicted in his Treatise on the Art of Dancing, *c. 1463.*

The glance of a lady who is dancing should not be proud or wilful, darting here and there, as is often the case. Let her usually keep her eyes directed downward; not — as some do — with her head sunk on her bosom, but straight and in a line with the body.... And at the end of the dance when her partner leaves her, she should face him squarely and, with a sweet look, return his curtsy with a respectful curtsy of her own.

From Guglielmo de Pesaro's treatise on dance

National Library in Paris, showing a man and two women dancing elegantly to the accompaniment of a harp, is believed to depict Guglielmo and two of his pupils. It seems that in his later years he was sent to the court in Naples to teach the fashionable Milanese dance, *ballo lombardo*, and to the court of Ferrara where, in 1481, he taught ballet to the future Isabella d'Este.

In his treatise, *Trattato del'arte de ballo* (Treatise on the art of dancing), he lists the essentials of dance: *misura* (musicality and keeping time to the music), *memoria* (remembering the sequence of steps), *patire del terrano* (judging the extent of the space), *aiere* (control of body movement), *maniere* (style and coordination of foot and direction — technique), and *movemento* (moving with grace). He describes numerous dances and gives one of the most complete descriptions of the dances of the Italian renaissance. He was said, by a contemporary, to have "excelled all men in dance."

GÜNZBURG Family Russian bankers, philanthropists, and advocates of Jewish rights. Believed to have originated in a small Bavarian town in the vicinity of Ulm-on-the-Danube, the Günzburgs, escaping the German persecution of Jews, moved to Poland during the 17th century. The Günzburg name appears repeatedly among distinguished rabbis and Jewish scholars of Germany and Poland. By the 18th century, the Günzburgs moved to Russia, where **Naphtali-Herz Günzburg**, breaking with the family tradition, chose a career in commerce. His generosity and dedication to the Jewish people in Russia was to be carried on by his descendants.

His grandson, **Yevsel Günzburg** (1812–1878), became a spokesman of the Jews in the commercial concessions offered by the government of Nicolas I (r. 1825–1855). This role put him in close contact with highly influential officials and allowed him to be active in the pursuit of Jewish rights in Russia. In 1859, he founded the Günzburg Banking House, which quickly became one of the most important banking centers of Saint Petersburg and an instrument in the establishment of solid ties between Russia and western Europe. It is no coincidence that the creation of the Günzburg bank came soon after, and was made possible by the promulgation of a law that, for the first time in Russian history allowed a certain group of Jews to live outside of the area to which Jews were confined (the Pale of Settlement). Günzburg was influential in the passing of this law which authorized those Jews who owned solid commercial enterprises to live in the provinces. In 1874 Yevsel Günzburg was granted the title of baron, and the Günzburg name was inscribed among those of the Russian nobility.

The Günzburg family also had a Paris home which was a rich center of intellectual activity and a meeting place for well-known writers, artists, thinkers, and politicians of the time. Among them was Ivan Turgenev, who became a close friend of the family. Baron Yevsel Günzburg ensured an extensive Jewish education for his children during their stay in Paris.

Yevsel's son, Baron **Horace Günzburg** (1833–1909), continued his father's devotion to the Jewish cause in Russia. He was nominated consul-general in Russia by the archduke of Hesse-Darmstadt, the only Jew to hold such a position under the Russian government. He built up the bank founded by his father into one of Russia's leading financial institutions. He was appointed an alderman in Saint Petersburg, a position not usually held by Jews, and dedicated his life to the struggle for better conditions for Russian Jews. Partly due to his energetic intervention, indiscriminate arrests of Jews living outside the Pale were suspended. With the increasingly anti-Semitic attitude of the government of Alexander II (r. 1855–1881), Horace Günzburg assumed the role of the leader of the "Jewish Politic" and advocated an organized defense of Jewish rights in Russia. In 1879, in response to grave accusations of the ritual murder of a Christian boy in Kutais, Günzburg organized the defense of the Jews of the town. The Jews of Kutais were acquitted and the verdict concluded that no ritual deaths can be inspired by the Jewish religion. During the reign of Alexander III (r. 1881–1897) when the Russian Jews were assailed by pogroms, Günzburg organized the Committee for the Aid to Pogrom Victims and personally sought funds to assist the afflicted.

Horace Günzburg had succeeded his father as head of the Saint Petersburg Jewish community and he was followed by his son Baron **David Günzburg** (1857–1910). David Günzburg was an orientalist of renown, who published many works and studies, especially on Jewish and Arabic literature. His library, one of the world's greatest Judaica collections, is now housed in the Lenin State Library, Moscow. He was an editor of the Russian Jewish encyclopedia, and in 1908 established a Jewish Academy in Saint Petersburg.

H. Sliosberg, *Baron Horace O. de Guinzbourg: Sa vie et son oeuvre* (Russian), 1933.

H

HAAN, JACOB ISRAEL DE (1881—1924) Dutch poet, journalist, and ultra-Orthodox leader in Palestine, whose last years gave rise to a storm of controversy. The son of a poor cantor, he turned his back on Judaism, flirted with Christianity, and joined the Socialist movement. By the outbreak of World War I, however, he had reverted to an Orthodox life style and become a militant Zionist. In 1919, he left Holland for Palestine, abandoning the non-Jewish wife whose support had enabled him to obtain a law doctorate. Apparently chagrined by his lukewarm reception in Jerusalem, he soon made another about-face, turning from the religious Zionist Mizrachi to the ultra-Orthodox Agudat Israel party, and conducting violently anti-Zionist propaganda. This new attitude was reflected in articles written for the Dutch and British press, in the Agudat alliance with Arab nationalists, and in the memoranda that he sent both to the League of Nations and to the British mandate government.

Jacob Israel de Hann.

As a literary figure, De Haan established his reputation with *Het Joodsche Lied* ("The Jewish Song," 1915–1921), two volumes of poetry on religious and mystical themes, followed by travel sketches and reportages entitled *Palestine and Jerusalem* (1921). When his first book, an autobiographical novelette (1904) had appeared, however, his undisguised homosexuality caused a public scandal in the Netherlands. References to it are scattered throughout his Dutch works, notably in the erotic and somewhat blasphemous poems of his quatrains (*Kwatrijnen*, 1924), to which ultra-Orthodox Palestinian Jews had no access. It therefore seems probable that De Haan's Arab lovers exploited or blackmailed him for their own political ends, and that he was incapable of desisting from his anti-Zionist activities, however many warnings he received from Zionist leaders in Palestine. After heading one Agudat delegation that went to Amman and planning another such visit to London, this outwardly pious Jew found himself a hated outcast among his own people. He was shot to death in Jerusalem, presumably by agents of the Jewish defense organization, the Haganah, and, despite police investigations together with the offer of a large reward, his killers were never apprehended.

The victim of his own tormenting inner conflicts, a man forced to lead a double life, De Haan inspired a novel by Arnold Zweig (q.v.).
Jaap Meijer, *De zoon von een gazzen: Het leven van Jacob Israel de Haan*, 1967.

HABER, FRITZ (1868–1934) German physical chemist and Nobel Prize winner. He was born in Breslau, Silesia (now Wroclaw, Poland), the son of a local alderman and successful chemical and dye merchant. After receiving a classical education, he began a career in industry and business but in 1893 enrolled at the Technische Hochschule in Karlsruhe and later at the University of Berlin, to study chemistry. He received his Ph.D. and in 1906 was appointed professor of physical and electrochemistry at Karlsruhe. Between 1911 and 1933 he was the first director of the Kaiser Wilhelm Institute for Physical Chemistry in Berlin.

Haber's scientific work involved the study of carbon bonding, which led to a chemical law that bears his name. In 1904 he developed the Haber process for the industrial development of ammonia from atmospheric nitrogen and hydrogen. In 1909 he produced a glass electrode for the measurement of acidity of a solution. He also researched thermodynamic gas reactions.

During World War I the Kaiser Wilhelm Institute was turned over to the war effort and in 1915 Haber was responsible for the German development and direction of the development and use of chlorine and mustard gases. Although during the war the Haber process was important for the production of the nitrates needed in explosives, after the war it became important in the development of fixed nitrogen for fertilizers.

In 1918, Haber, together with Bosch, received the Nobel Prize for chemistry for the synthesis of ammonia from its elements.

In the 1920s Haber was the leading chemist in Germany, which had become the world center of physical chemistry. He was elected chairman of the German Chemical Society and created the Verband deutscher chemische Vereine. He also established the Japan Institute in Tokyo and Berlin to promote mutual understanding between the two countries. His publications included *The Theoretical Basis of Technical Electrochemistry* (1892), and *Thermodynamics of Technical Gas Reactions* (1905).

HABER AND WEIZMANN

In his *Trial and Error*, Chaim Weizmann relates how he initially resented Haber because of his conversion to Christianity and attempt in 1921 to dissuade Einstein from joining Weizmann on a Zionist mission. When Haber had to leave Berlin in 1933 he went for a time to London where Weizmann tried to help him and suggested he move to Palestine. In the course of that year, the Zionist Congress was being held in Prague and Weizmann refused to attend for political reasons. While dining with Haber, urgent telephone calls came requesting him to come to Prague. Haber reacted by saying to Weizmann:

Dr. Weizmann, I was one of the mightiest men in Germany. I was more than a great army commander, more than a captain of industry. I was the founder of industries: my work was essential for the economic and military expansion of Germany. All doors were open to me. But the position which I occupied then, glamorous as it may have seemed, is as nothing compared with yours. You are not creating out of plenty — you are creating out of nothing in a land that lacks everything. And you are, I think, succeeding. At the end of my life I find myself a bankrupt. When I am gone and forgotten your work will stand, a shining monument in the long history of our people. Do not ignore the call — go to Prague.

After World War I, Haber had returned to and reconstituted the Kaiser Wilhelm Institute. A great German patriot when Germany was faced with paying reparations, he tried to extract gold from seawater. He rejected his Jewish origins and left the faith, an action which saved him from direct Nazi oppression, but when, in 1933, the Nazis demanded the dismissal of all Jews on his staff at the institute, he refused and resigned as director. In 1933 he fled to a sanatorium in Switzerland because of progressive ill health and died in Basle.

In 1952 a memorial plaque was erected to his memory at the Kaiser Wilhelm Institute.

M. Goran, *The Story of Fritz Haber*, 1967.

HADAMARD, JACQUES SALOMON (1865–1963) French mathematician; the first to receive the prestigious Feltrinelli Prize for Mathematics. Born in Versailles, he was licensed as a scientist in 1892 by the Ecole Normale Supérieure (the teachers' training college) in Paris, and received his Ph.D. in sciences from the University of Paris in 1892.

He worked there as a lecturer from 1895 until 1901, when he became an associate professor. In 1909 he became a professor at the Collège de France in Paris, where he continued to work until his retirement. From 1912 he was also at the Ecole Polytechnique. In 1912 he joined the French Academy of Sciences, and later became dean of that institute. From 1920 to 1935 he also taught at the Ecole Centrale des Arts et Manufactures.

Hadamard was active in the struggle for human rights, serving as a member of the central committee of the Ligue des Droits de l'Homme for sixty years. He was a brother-in-law of Alfred Dreyfus (q.v.) and was actively involved in his defense. He sat on the administrative board of the Hebrew University of Jerusalem and on the French-Palestine Committee, and was active in the attempt to help German Jewry in the 1930s.

In 1941 he escaped from France, living first in the United States, and later settling in England, where he carried out research for the Royal Air Force during wartime.

Hadamard is renowned for his research in diverse fields of mathematics, particularly in number theory (he proved the prime number theorem), differential geometry, functional analysis, and calculus of variations. His work on the partial differential equations of mathematical physics was of especial importance. His book *Lessons on the Calculus of Variations* (French, 1910) was basic to the subject. He coined the term *functional*. Another of his major works was his *Essay on the Psychology of Invention in the Mathematical Field* (1945).

HAFETZ HAYYIM (Israel Meir Ha-Kohen Kagan; 1838–1933) Rabbinical scholar. He was born in Zhetel, Poland, where his father, a teacher, died when he was ten. His mother moved to Vilna, where Israel Meir continued his education. After his marriage at the age of seventeen, he settled in Radun, a muddy village between Grodno and

Vilna, where he lived the rest of his life and which became famous by virtue of his presence there. He refused to enter the rabbinate and earned his living through a small grocery store run by his wife for which he did the bookkeeping. However, business competition was too strong and he turned to teaching and Talmud instruction. In 1869 he founded a yeshiva that became one of the most renowned centers of Talmudic study. The student body increased steadily and in 1904 the school acquired its own building. Israel Meir worked hard at raising funds to support this institution, he himself lived very simply. When one of the Rothschilds [q.v.] sent him three hundred francs for a set of his books, Israel Meir deducted the actual cost of thirty francs and returned the remainder to Rothschild, suggesting he send it as a contribution to the yeshiva, which Rothschild did — with a considerable addition.

Israel Meir became universally known as the Hafetz Hayyim (literally, "He who wants to live") after his first book of that name (published anonymously in 1873) devoted to the laws of slander, and gossip and talebearing, to which he wrote a complementary volume *Shemirat ha-Lashon* ("Guarding the Tongue"), on the importance of righteous speech. His *Ahavat Hésed* ("Loving Kindness") expounded the legal and moral aspects of love and kindness, advocating a society that would ensure the rights of both labor and capital. His *Mahaneh Yehuda* ("Camp of Judah") offered guidance to Jewish soldiers away from home in alien environments. With the mass emigration of the 1880s many Jews left eastern Europe and found themselves in distant lands; for them he wrote *Nidehai Yisrael* ("The Dispersed of Israel"), emphasizing among other things, the importance of continuing to observe the Sabbath.

Hafetz Hayyim's major work is the six-volume comprehensive commentary on part of Joseph Caro's [q.v.] code, *Shulhan Arukh*, which he called *Mishna Berura* ("Lucid Learning," 1884–1907). The most important section is devoted to everyday life and the treatise gained widespread acceptance as a practical guide. He was the author of books on family life, especially directed to women to maintain the laws of ritual purity, and also published the five-volume *Likutei Halakhot* ("Collections of Laws") concerning the Temple service that he felt to be topical in view of his belief in the imminent arrival of the Messiah and rebuilding of the Temple.

He was active in eastern European religious leadership and was involved in the organization of the ultra-Orthodox movement, Agudat Israel, and revered as its spiritual mentor. In the last decade of his life he wished to move to the Holy Land and a house was prepared for him, but the pleas of his followers in Poland persuaded him to remain. He helped to found the Va'ad ha-Yeshivot ("Council of Talmudic Academies") which sustained the yeshivot of eastern Europe. After his death, many yeshivot and religious institutions were named for him.

M. Weinbach, *Who Wants to Live*, 1980.
M. Weinbach, *Give Us Life*, 1969.
M. M. Yosher, *Saint and Sage*, 1937.

HAFFKINE, WALDEMAR MORDECHAI (1860–1930) Bacteriologist. He was born Vladimir Aronovitch Chavkin in Odessa, Russia; his mother died when he was a young boy and he had a lonely childhood. At age twelve he was sent to high school in Berdyansk where he excelled in sports and natural sciences.

In 1879 he moved to the faculty of natural sciences of the University of Novorossik (now the University of Odessa) where he studied physics, mathematics, and zoology.

While at university Haffkine came under the influence of Elie Metchnikoff (q.v.), the microbiologist and future Nobel Prize winner. At the same time, in an effort to combat open anti-Semitism he became active in the Jewish self-defense league. As a result, he ws arrested by the Russian authorities but was released following Metchnikoff's intervention.

Haffkine received his diploma in natural sciences in 1883, and although at the time there was great emigration from Russia to the United States, he chose to remain in Odessa with Metchnikoff. From 1883 to 1888 he worked on the staff of the Zoological Museum of Odessa and became involved in original research into the fundamental phenomena of organic life. He could have received a teaching position if he accepted baptism, but refused. However, it became apparent that he could not progress in Russia as a result of anti-Jewish government edicts. Metchnikoff emigrated to France to join the Pasteur Institute in Paris, while Haffkine moved to Switzerland, where he worked as an assistant in physiology at the medical school in Geneva for a year until he was able to become a laboratory assistant and librarian at the Pasteur Institute.

While at the Institute, Haffkine began to study the protozoon, paramecium, and published a paper entitled "A Contribution to the Study of Immunity" (1890). He also turned his attention to studies of typhoid fever and cholera and the development of an inoculation serum against the cholera vibrio (which had been discovered by Robert Koch at the institute in 1883). Promotion in 1892 enabled him to further his research into an attenuated cholera inoculation and that same year he injected himself with his preparation to prove it was harmless to humans.

Following Haffkine's success, the former viceroy of India, Lord Dufferin and Ava, then British ambassador to France, persuaded him to make India the testing ground for his cholera inoculations rather than Siam (Thailand) as he had intended. Haffkine began his work in India in 1893. Despite initial tribal opposition, his success with those who agreed to be inoculated was so remarkable that, following an outbreak of plague in 1896, he was sent to Bombay by the government to develop a suitable vaccine. Within three months he developed the appropriate vaccine and his fame became worldwide. Queen Victoria honored him with the Order of the Indian Empire in 1897 and two years later he became a British subject.

Haffkine's treatment of another outbreak of plague in 1902 was marred by nineteen deaths from tetanus contracted from a contaminated bottle of serum. Despite the thousands who benefited from his vaccine, his opponents used these deaths as an excuse to attack him and his methods. Haffkine was forced to leave India pending an official inquiry and was exonerated from all blame concerning the preparation of the contaminated serum only in 1907. He returned to India to continue his inoculation program and research and, whereas initially he had been opposed by the skeptical Indian tribesmen for using his revolutionary inoculations, now he was criticized for not producing enough.

In 1915, at the age of fifty-five, Haffkine retired. He settled in Paris, becoming deeply involved in Jewish religious and Zionist affairs and in the minority rights of Jews in eastern Europe.

In 1925 the Plague Research Laboratory in Bombay was named the Haffkine Institute in his honor.

Haffkine had been an observant Jew for most of his life and in 1929, shortly before his death, he created the Haffkine Foundation in Lausanne, setting aside much of his amassed wealth to foster Jewish education in eastern Europe.
S. A. Waksman, *The Brilliant and Tragic Life of Waldemar Haffkine, Bacteriologist*, 1964.

HAI GAON (939–1038) Last outstanding head of the Babylonian Jewish academy and authority on religious law. He assisted his distinguished father, Sherira ben Hanina (q.v.) who was *gaon* (head) of the great Talmudic academy of Pumbedita (situated at that time in Baghdad), in teaching and administering the academy. After Sherira retired in 998, he was succeeded as *gaon* by Hai, who was the most prominent personality in the Jewish world of his time. Scholars came to study with him from many parts of the Jewish world, including Byzantium and western Europe. Although Babylonian Jewry had started to decline, Hai, like his father, maintained Babylon's great prestige as a center of learning and authoritative legal rulings.

Hai is best known for his *responsa* (replies to problems of Jewish law). About a thousand of these are extant, about a third of all the known responsa of the gaonic period. Even other great rabbinic authorities appealed to him for final decisions and some queries came from as far away as Spain and Ethiopia. He based his rulings on the Talmud, the views of his predecessors, and customary practices. His replies are written in the same language as the queries — Hebrew, Aramaic, or Arabic. He also wrote monographs on civil and religious law, in which he organized the scattered Talmudic discussions into topical units. These

---

SAYINGS OF HAI

- God performs signs and wonders through the righteous even as he did formerly for the prophets.
- Coming close to a king is like coming close to a lion. Others will be afraid of you, but your fear too will be great.
- Never do business with your relatives.
- Life is a terrible disease, curable only by death.
- Let your tongue be imprisoned in your mouth.

---

were written in Arabic and subsequently translated into Hebrew. Only parts of his commentary on Talmudic tractates have survived. He was also the author of a short work on the messianic redemption, and wrote liturgical poems. Hai continued to write and teach until his one hundredth year.
S. W. Baron, *A Social and Religious History of the Jews*, 1952–1980, Vols. 5–8.

HALEVI, JUDAH See Judah Halevi

HALPRIN, ROSE (1896–1978) U.S. Zionist leader. Born in New York to a Zionist family, she was taught Hebrew as a child and became fluent in French, German, and Yiddish. She attended the Teachers' Institute of the Jewish Theological Seminary of America and studied at Hunter College and Columbia University.

Halprin assisted Henrietta Szold (q.v.) in rescuing Jewish children from Europe in the 1930s and helping them to reach Palestine and settle there. She was active in Zionist work, serving twice as president of the Hadassah Women's Organization, from 1932 to 1934 and from 1947 to 1952. From 1934 she spent five years in Jerusalem, representing American Hadassah during the construction of the hospital complex on Mount Scopus. In 1942 she became treasurer of the American Zionist Emergency Council and was its vice-president between 1945 and 1947. When Mount Scopus was cut off from west Jerusalem in 1948, Halprin was active in finding temporary accommodation for the hospital and medical school and was involved in its relocation to the new complex in Ein Karem.

Halprin served from 1946 on the Jewish Agency executive for over twenty years, and was a representative of the American section in the 1947 negotiations at the United Nations for the resolution for the establishment of the State of Israel. From 1949 to 1954, she chaired an interorganizational finance committee which sought to raise funds to help Israel meet its needs during the years of mass immigration. She was acting chairperson of the American Section of the Jewish Agency from 1955 and chairperson between 1960 and 1968. She was also cochairperson of the World Confederation of General Zionists.

HA-NASI, JUDAH, See Judah ha-Nasi

HART, MOSS (1904–1961) American playwright and director. He was born and grew up in poverty on the Lower East Side of New York. His early theatrical training was as assistant to the producer-impresario Augustus Pitou. He worked as a producer in Jewish clubs and in summers was entertainment director in the borscht circuit (the Jewish hotels in the Catskills). His first attempts at play writing were failures, but collaboration with George S. Kaufman (q.v.) established his career.

The first work of the two wits was *Once in a Lifetime* (1930), a satire on Hollywood. Hart then turned to musicals, writing librettos and sketches, for example with Irving Berlin (q.v.) in *Face the Music* (1932) and with Cole Porter in *Jubilee* (1935). He then teamed up again with Kaufman for a series of hits, including *Merrily We Roll Along* (1934), which describes the career of a disillusioned playwright; the Pulitzer Prize-winning *You Can't Take It With You* (1936), which was also a successful film directed by Frank Capra; *I'd Rather Be Right* (1937), for which George M. Cohan came out of retirement to play the central figure, based on President Franklin D. Roosevelt; *The Man Who Came to Dinner* (1939), whose main character was a takeoff on Alexander Woollcott (also made into a film); and *George Washington Slept Here* (1940), a satire of city people who try to restore a dilapidated country house.

Hart then wrote the book for the musical *Lady in the Dark* (1941), with music by Kurt Weill (q.v.) and lyrics by Ira Gershwin (q.v.), which sought to psychoanalyze a woman editor. He wrote a number of other dramas including *Light Up the Sky* (1948), about a tryout for a play, and his last stage work, *The Climate of Eden* (1952), an adaptation of a novel whose central figures are a missionary and his daughter confronted by a deranged man in British Guiana. So many of his works are collaborations that it is difficult to assess his individual talent, but those he wrote on his own are characterized by their literate dialogue and character studies.

Hart had another career as director and producer, staging some of Broadway's greatest hits, including *My Fair Lady* (for which he was awarded a Tony in 1956) and *Camelot*. He was also a film writer; among his best-known work was *Gentleman's Agreement* (1947) exposing anti-Jewish discrimination and prejudice. He was married to the actress Kitty Carlisle.

M. Hart, *Act One*, 1959.
S. Meredith, *George S. Kaufman and the Algonquin Round Table*, 1977.

HATAM SOFER, See Sofer, Moshe

HAYS, ARTHUR GARFIELD (1881– 1954) Lawyer and noted civil libertarian. Born in Rochester, New York, Hays was educated at Columbia University where he received his B.A. degree in 1902 and his law degree in 1905.

Hays established a lucrative legal practice, representing numerous corporate institutions, public figures, and wealthy individuals. During the first years of World War I, he lived in London where he represented American shipping interests.

Devoted to the cause of civil liberty, Hays served as general counsel of the American Civil Liberties Union (ACLU) from 1912 and was associated with that pioneer organization all his life. He was defense counsel in most of the celebrated civil liberties cases of his time. These included the 1925 Scopes "monkey trial" in Tennessee (with Clarence Darrow), the Sweet housing segregation case in Detroit in 1926 (also with Darrow); the obscenity trial of H. L. Mencken and the *American Mercury* magazine in Boston in 1926; the Sacco and Vanzetti anarchist case in Boston in 1927; the case of communists accused of burning the Reichstag in Berlin in 1933; and the Scottsboro case in Alabama in 1931.

Hays was also active in politics, first as a supporter of Theodore Roosevelt, then as a founder of the Farmer-Labor party in 1919, and as New York State chairman of the Progressive (La Follette) party in 1924.

He was the author of *Let Freedom Ring* (1928), *Trial by Prejudice* (1933), and *Democracy Works* (1939).
A. G. Hays, *City Lawyer*, 1942.

HAZON ISH, See Karelitz, Avraham

HECHT, BEN (1893–1964) U.S. playwright, screen-writer, and novelist. The son of immigrants from Minsk, Russia, he was born in New York and grew up in Racine, Wisconsin. Four crates of books given to him by his father on his bar mitzvah turned him into an avid reader. At age sixteen, he drifted into journalism in Chicago and from 1918 to 1920 was a foreign correspondent in Germany. Returning to Chicago, he founded and edited the *Chicago Literary Times* from 1923 to 1925. It was at this time that Ezra Pound wrote, "Why should I come back to that God-forsaken desert; there is only one intelligent man in the whole United States to talk to — Ben Hecht."

In the 1920s Hecht wrote several of his eleven novels. His early depiction of Jews, as in *A Jew in Love* (1930), is unsympathetic. He had his first real success in Hollywood. Lured to Paramount by his friend Herman J. Mankiewicz, Hecht, partly out of frustration at the limitations placed on sympathetic characters in the films of his time, wrote a script peopled exclusively by villains. The result was *Underworld* (1927), reputedly the first real gangster film, for which Hecht received an Academy Award at the very first Oscar ceremony (he used the statuette as a doorstop). In all he was to work on 150 films, many of them uncredited, earning, in his words, "tremendous sums of money for work that required no more effort than a game of pinochle." He was the first Hollywood writer to earn a thousand dollars a day. He wrote another seminal gangster film, *Scarface*, was a coauthor of the Marx Brothers' [q.v.] *Monkey Business*, and among the other classics on which he worked were *Stagecoach, Gone with the Wind, Wuthering Heights*, and three Hitchcock movies, *Spellbound, Notorious*, and *Rope*. He became one of the few writers in Hollywood to be granted complete control of his work from conception to shooting to final cutting. It was said that he created a new and exciting language for the screen, as Hemingway was doing for the novel.

Hecht also gained fame as a playwright, making a big impact with *The Front Page*, written with another ex-newspaperman, Charles MacArthur, with whom he also wrote *Twentieth Century*.

The rise of Nazism affected him deeply and he devoted himself increasingly to Jewish activism. His "Remember Us," first staged as a pageant in Madison Square Gardens and then published in the *American Mercury* was the first article in a major American journal to call attention to the Nazi genocide of the Jews. A delegation from Palestine persuaded him to head the League for a Free Palestine, the American propaganda and fund raising arm of the Irgun, the Jewish underground in Palestine. Hecht became similarly involved in the Hebrew Committee of National Liberation, which had similar aims. He wrote a pageant called *A Flag is Born*, performed 120 times in New York, which raised a million dollars, used to buy a former German cruise boat. It was renamed the *Ben Hecht* and sailed to Palestine with Jewish refugees but was stopped by the British and the refugees transferred to internment in Cyprus. In 1947 he placed a full-page advertisement in fifteen American newspapers praising the Jewish underground for its attacks on the British in Palestine, writing: "Every time you blow up a British arsenal, or wreck a British jail, or send a British railroad train sky high, or let go with your bombs and guns at the British invaders of your homeland, the Jews of America make a little holiday in their hearts." One consequence of this was a British boycott of all films with his name and a resultant slump in his career. In 1954 he published an autobiography, *A Child of Our Century*, and in 1961 wrote *Perfidy*, attacking the Zionist establishment, especially David Ben-Gurion (q.v.).

A Treasury of Ben Hecht, 1959.

D. Fetherling, *The Five Lives of Ben Hecht*, 1977.

W. MacAdams, *Ben Hecht: The Man behind the Legend*, 1990.

HEIFETZ, JASCHA (1901–1987) Russian-born American violinist, one of the greatest modern masters of the violin. Born in Vilna (now Vilnius, Lithuania), he began studying the violin with his father at the age of three. At the age of six he mastered the Mendelssohn violin concerto and a year later began performing in public. At nine he was accepted as a student at the Saint Petersburg conservatory. At ten he started touring Russia and at eleven he began performing all over Europe,

with an important Berlin debut in 1912. Even before he made his American debut (in 1917 in New York's Carnegie Hall) the American public had got word of the extraordinary prodigy. The *Musical Courier* reported on a musician who at the age of eleven was "already beyond the pale of criticism.... a great artist in every respect."

After the 1917 Russian Revolution, the Heifetz family traveled from Vilna across Siberia to Japan, where they boarded a steamship to San Francisco. A few days after his successful American debut, Heifetz gave a second concert in the same hall with the New York Symphony Orchestra. One musician who had heard all the great violinists of his time commented on Heifetz's "elegance, grace and resourcefulness... the polish of his style and the destination and yet breadth of his conception."

American tours followed and Heifetz began performing and recording all over the world. His London debut (1920) was followed by tours of Australia (1921), the Orient (1923), Palestine (1926), and South America. Two years after his New York debut Heifetz was already netting 2,250 dollars per concert, which made him the highest paid violinist of his time.

In 1953 he played, in Israel, a work by Richard Strauss, whose compositions were not played in Israel because of the composer's Nazi connections. An irate young Israeli attacked Heifetz in protest with an iron bar outside the King David Hotel in Jerusalem and injured his arm, fortunately not seriously.

Very little is known about Heifetz's private life. His public behavior, however, was often eccentric. At one time, when he gave a party for one of his students, Heifetz invited the guests for 4 P.M. He opened his door promptly at the precise hour and closed it one minute later. Those who were late were not allowed in.

From time to time Heifetz disappeared from the concert platform for long periods. The first of these many breaks lasted twenty months, beginning in 1947. By that time he had played one hundred thousand hours and traveled two million miles. Once Heifetz stopped playing he became a recluse and refused any interviews. He summed up his autobiography thus: "I played the violin at three and gave my first concert at seven. I have been playing ever since."

Heifetz was the elegant gentleman of the violin. His playing delighted music lovers all over the world. In his farewell tour of Israel, with cellist Gregor Piatigorsky in the late 1960s, Heifetz was still the perfectly astute performer on the stage. Playing his violin with a frozen face he delivered the haunting sounds the audience came to hear. It was magical music, but very cold. One critic described Heifetz's technique: "His tone is of a noble substance and is of magical beauty, and there is not the smallest flaw in his technical equipment." His large discography is testament to his flawless technique.

When, in 1977, Herbert R. Axelrod edited and

published an "unauthorized pictorial biography" of Heifetz, the violinist filed a lawsuit for 7.5 million dollars against both the publisher and the compiler for the invasion of his privacy.
H. C. Schönberg, *The Virtuosi*, 1988.

HEIJERMANS, HERMAN (also Heyermans; 1864–1924) Dutch playwright, journalist and novelist. Born in Rotterdam, he abandoned commerce for journalism, was founder-editor of *De Jonge Gids* (1897—1901), and subsequently coeditor of *De Nieuwe Tijd*. From 1912 he edited another paper in Amsterdam. It is, however, as the leading Dutch naturalist playwright of his time that Heijermans is now chiefly remembered. A socialist, whose forte was the portrayal of working-class life, he owed his success to a combination of masterly stage technique, humor and dialect. *Op hoop van zegen* ("The Good Hope," 1900), which dramatized the wretched existence of Dutch fishermen, is regarded as his best play and was adapted to the movie screen. Other dramas, such as *Het zevende gebod* ("The Seventh Commandment," 1903) aroused public indignation because of the author's antireligious views and belief in free love.

Typical of their day were the works that Heijermans wrote on Jewish themes. While *Ahasverus* (1893), one of his first plays, dealt with Russian Jewish suffering in the contemporary pogroms, *Ghetto* (1899), and the novel *Diamandstad* (1904) contrasted the Amsterdam Jewish quarter's narrow-mindedness with the tolerance of Christian Netherlanders. This biting criticism on the part of a left-wing Jewish secularist gave way to a more sympathetic approach in the 660 tales or sketches of Dutch family life which Heijermans published, under the pen name of Samuel Falkland, in *De Telegraaf* and *Het Algemeen Handelsblad*. First serialized in those Amsterdam dailies (1896–1915), his tales were later collected in book form. To mark the centenary of his birth, a complete edition of Heijermans's plays was issued in 1965.
S. L. Flaxman, *Herman Heijermans and His Dramas*, 1954.
H. Yoder van Neek, *Dramatizations of Social Change: Herman Heijerman's Plays*, 1978.

HEINE, HEINRICH (1797–1856) German poet and essayist; one of the world's outstanding lyric poets. As a teenager in his native Düsseldorf, Heine experienced the benefits of French rule, which accorded civic rights to the Jews and made him a fervent admirer of Napoleon. His ambiguous religious outlook and sense of Jewish identity were, however, partly influenced by his mother Betty, a freethinking Voltairean. After the downfall of Napoleon, political reaction in Germany thwarted his ambitions and he also experienced various personal disappointments, all of which helped to inject a bitter, sardonic note into his writing.

These troubles began with a commercial venture, financed by Heine's wealthy uncle (Salomon

Heinrich Heine and his wife, in Paris. Painting by Ernst Ketz, 1851.

Heine), a Hamburg banker, which proved unsuccessful after only two years; and with short-lived romances involving Salomon's daughters, Amalie and Theresa. It was nevertheless thanks to his uncle that Heine then found it possible to study law at the universities of Bonn, Berlin, and Göttingen, to frequent Berlin's prestigious literary salons, and to play an active role in the Verein für Kultur und Wissenschaft der Juden, a young Jewish intellectual circle headed by the scholarly Leopold Zunz (q.v.). While in Berlin, he came under the philosophical influence of Hegel and published his first volumes of poetry.

Unlike most of his associates, Heine displayed a romantic feeling for Jewish history and nationhood, which found expression in several ways: an unusual regard for the old-fashioned traditionalists whom he encountered during a visit to Poland (1822); siding with the Neo-Orthodox voice in their opposition to the Hamburg Reform *Tempelgemeinde* (1823); and the interest aroused in him by the U.S. proto-Zionist ("Ararat") scheme of Mordecai M. Noah (q.v.). From the letters he wrote to close friends throughout the 1820s, it is also clear that Heine scorned "enlightened" German Jewish assimilationists, mocked those who converted to the dominant faith, and never lost his fondness for Jewish cookery; he had already started work on *Der Rabbi von Bacherach*, a prose epic of Jewish life in the Middle Ages.

To obtain his doctorate and further his career, however, "yesterday's hero" became "today's scoundrel" (as Heine phrased it in a bitter poem) when he followed other renegades to the Lutheran font in June 1825, an act that his mother had apparently encouraged. "The baptismal certificate is an admission ticket to European culture," Heine would later quip, but in this case it brought no civil service or academic rewards. Worse still, Jews and Christians alike derided him as a turncoat and opportunist, with the result that Heine lived to regret his formal conversion.

Having no other prospects, he then turned to literature, the only field in which he could hope to earn a livelihood. Heine's *Buch der Lieder* (1827), a 19th-century best-seller, established his reputation in Germany and, through translations into other languages, gained him a substantial readership abroad. It included poems and ballads such as "The Two Grenadiers," "On Wings of Song," "Almansor" and, most famous of all, "Die Lorelei." In the four-volume prose work entitled *Reisebilder* (Pictures of travel, 1826–1831), Heine satirized the bourgeoisie, Jewish parvenus, and the clerico political establishment; though widely acclaimed and successful, it outraged both Prussia's governing elite and the anti-Semites. Now threatened with an official ban, he took advantage of the liberal July Revolution in France and from 1831 spent most of his later years as an exile in Paris.

There, Heine published many more works in verse and prose, enhancing his reputation (as

---

QUOTATIONS FROM HEINE

● Since the Exodus, Freedom has always spoken with a Hebrew accent.
● A book, like a child, needs time to be born. Books written quickly — within a few weeks — make me suspicious of the author. A respectable woman does not bring a child into the world before the ninth month.
● My ancestors did not belong to the hunters so much as to the hunted, and the very notion of attacking the descendants of those who were our comrades in misery goes against the grain.
● The Jews trudged around with the Bible all through the Middle Ages, as with a portable fatherland.
● Experience is a good school, but the fees are high.
● It is extremely difficult for a Jew to be converted, for how can he bring himself to believe in the divinity of another Jew?
● Were not ancestral pride foolishly inconsistent in a champion of the Revolution and its democratic principles, the writer would be proud that his ancestors belonged to the noble house of Israel, that he is a descendant of those martyrs who gave the world a God and a morality, and who have fought and suffered on all the battlefields of human thought.
● *Dieu me pardonnera, c'est son métier* (God will pardon me: that is his business).

---

leader of the radical Young Germany school) with another lyrical volume, *Neue Gedichte* (1844), the satirical *Atta Troll* (1847), critical essays on the theater, and masterly *feuilletons* which appeared in both France and Germany, and on the strength of which, he served as a cultural mediator between the two nations. At the same time, Heine had begun to reassess his own position as a "baptized but unconverted Jew." When the unfinished *Rabbi von Bacherach* rolled off the press in 1840, evidence of French government connivance in the Damascus blood libel affair had little effect on public opinion. To Heine, however, it was unthinkable that a ritual murder charge against Syrian Jews could be accepted by so-called liberals in France; he even denounced the "trembling Israelites" of French Jewry who at first remained silent, and he began signing his German *feuilletons* with a Magen David (shield of David) in place of his name.

Since 1825, Heine had given his allegiance to various causes of a left-wing nature, most recently to the socialist ideology of his fellow exile, Karl Marx (q.v.). The disastrous failure of the 1848 revolution in Germany, which coincided with the onset of Heine's paralysis, brought all these utopian expectations to an abrupt end. On his "mattress grave," where he continued to write and receive visitors, Heine now saw himself as a "poor, deathly-sick Jew." Rereading the Hebrew Bible, he extolled its humanitarian outlook, marveled at the genius of "our teacher, Moses," and insisted that he had not returned to Judaism "because I never left it." *Romanzero* (1851), a verse collection of this period, included three *Hebräische Melodien*, which took their inspiration from a newly published work by Rabbi Michael Sachs on the Jewish religious poetry of medieval Spain, as well as from Byron. Upon his death, in accordance with his instructions, he was buried in the non-Jewish cemetery of Montmartre, but without Christian rites.

Heine's writings have exerted a vast influence on Western literature, music and thought. His unsparing attacks on "Teutomania," philistinism, religious bigotry and antidemocratic government infuriated reactionaries, yet both Metternich and Bismarck were among his admirers while Richard Wagner did not hesitate to borrow the themes of two operas, *Tannhäuser* and *The Flying Dutchman*, from Heine's verse. It is estimated that around 6,000 musical settings of his poems were written by great composers such as Schumann, Schubert, Liszt, and Mendelssohn. When Goebbels condemned a host of works to the flames in 1933, Heine's naturally headed the list, although a vain attempt was made to pass off his "Lorelei" as an anonymous folksong. "Where men burn books, they will also burn people," Heine once declared — a prophecy fulfilled by the Nazis.

No amount of prejudice, not even the rejection of a proposal that Düsseldorf's university be renamed in Heine's honor (1972), has dimmed his international fame. Translated into many languages, Heine's works appear in new German critical editions; and other postwar developments include the founding of a Heine Institute in Düsseldorf (1970), a biennial prize, and the unveiling of Heine monuments.

H. Bieber, *Heinrich Heine: Confessio Judaica*, 1925; revised English edition by Moses Hadas, *Heinrich Heine, A Biographical Anthology*, 1956.
S. S. Prawer, *Heine, the Tragic Satirist*, 1961.
R. Robertson, *Heine*, 1988.
J. L. Sammons, *Heinrich Heine: A Modern Biography*, 1979.

HELENA (1st cent. CE) Queen of Adiabene; convert to Judaism. She was the wife of the ruler of a vassal kingdom in the domain of ancient Parthia (northeast of Babylonia). Sometime in the early 1st century CE, she converted to Judaism together with her sons, Monobaz and Izates, and was probably followed by other members of the family and perhaps others of her court. The conversion was influenced by two itinerant Jewish merchants, Eleazar and Hananiah. This was a period when Jews were actively engaged in propagating the Jewish faith, and the two travelers may have been engaged in a missionary venture. Preceding the conversion was an interesting conflict of opinion between the two Jews, for and against the requirement of circumcision for male converts.

The new royal proselytes immediately immersed themselves in activity on behalf of the Jewish people. Queen Helena herself, and members of her family, made their first pilgrimage to the Temple in Jerusalem, and the queen added to its luster by contributing various objects, including a golden candlestick and vessel handles of gold. In the year 46 she came to the aid of the famine-stricken Jews of the Holy Land. She lived the last part of her life in Jerusalem, where she built herself a palace. The Jewish sages tell of her twenty-one years of Nazirite chastity following her conversion. A revealing illustration of the Adiabene proselytes' total involvement in Jewish affairs is provided in yet another Talmud passage in which Izates's successor, also named Monobaz, is chided for the large sums he squandered on various Jewish charities. His reply: "My fathers stored up below [i.e., earthly possessions], and I am storing above [in heaven, i.e., things of the spirit]."

Helena figures prominently as an object lesson in many discussions of a legal nature in Talmudic literature. Some of these, such as the description of the huge *sukkah* (tabernacle) she provided for the town of Lydda, again attest to her generous philanthropies. A striking example of the results of the step initiated by the former pagan queen was the prominent participation of members of her family in the Jewish revolt against Rome, which erupted in the year 66 CE.

Modern day Jerusalem contains the archaeological remains of the royal proselyte family's mausoleum, known as the Tomb of the Kings.

Josephus, *Jewish Antiquities*, 20:17ff.
P. Kahle, *The Cairo Geniza* (2nd ed.), 1959.

HELLMAN, LILLIAN (1905–1984) U.S. playwright. As a child she spent her time moving back and forth between New York and her native New Orleans. She claimed in her memoirs that the constant moving was responsible for her failures in school and college.

Hellman began her literary career working as a manuscript reader for a publisher and was then a theatrical play reader and a film scenario reader before beginning to produce her own plays in the 1930s. Her first play, *The Children's Hour*, about a schoolgirl's malicious accusations of lesbianism against her teachers, was an instant success. She continued to write plays on strong and provocative themes such as race, greed, hypocrisy, and sex, notably *The Little Foxes*, a portrait of the American South. Another play that attracted much interest was the anti-Nazi drama, *Watch on the Rhine*, which was partially based on her own experiences in Spain during the Spanish Civil War. Many of her plays were adapted for the screen.

She also wrote three books of memoirs, which are full of the names of the now famous authors with whom she associated, among them F. Scott Fitzgerald and Ernest Hemingway. One of the memoirs, *Pentimento*, was made into the film *Julia*.

The themes of her literature were often public issues, such as agitation, fascism, appeasement, and isolationism, although private themes surfaced too, for example, middle age, in *The Autumn Garden*, and the pretences of family love, in *Toys in the Attic*. Her gifts included a talent for dialogue and for stage technique, and an ability to handle powerful themes.

Hellman was a woman of strong personal opinions who was blacklisted for leftist sympathies throughout the 1950s. Her rocky personal life reflected her strong character, and after a first unsuccessful marriage, she intermittently carried on a relationship with the detective story writer

LILLIAN HELLMAN TO THE HOUSE COMMITTEE ON UN-AMERICAN ACTIVITIES, MAY, 1952.

I am not willing, now or in the future, to bring bad trouble to people who, in my past association with them, were completely innocent of any talk or any action that was disloyal or subversive. I do not like subversion or disloyalty in any form and if I had ever seen any I would have considered it my duty to have reported it to the proper authorities. But to hurt innocent people whom I knew many years ago in order to save myself, is, to me, inhuman and indecent and dishonorable. I cannot and will not cut my conscience to fit this year's fashions....

Dashiell Hammet, who was also her very strict coach and mentor.

L. Hellman, *Pentimento*, 1973.

L. Hellman, *Scoundrel Time*, 1976.

L. Hellman, *An Unfinished Woman*, 1969.

HELTAI, JENÖ (originally Herzl; 1871–1957) Hungarian writer, poet, and journalist. Born in Budapest, he was a cousin of Theordor Herzl (q.v.), with whom he kept up a correspondence. He interrupted his law studies at Budapest University and turned to journalism, joining the daily *Magyar Hirlap*. His first volume of poetry, *Modern Songs* (1892), caused a minor scandal and was declared immoral. He offended the prudery of contemporary society with his light, tongue-in-cheek verses, whose single theme was carnal love. The frivolity of the tone was unusual, in the style of the French chanson and novel, in the sense that he presented the new type of young urban man and woman. The old type of patriarchal upper middle-class ideal was replaced by the irresponsible, irreverent, but likeable bohemian who ironically shrugged off the vicissitues of daily life.

Heltai spent several years in Vienna, Paris, London, Berlin, and Constantinople and translated plays and novels from English, French, and German. In recognition of his excellent translations from French literature, he was admitted to the Legion of Honor (1927). For a time he was president of the Hungarian PEN club.

From 1900 he became increasingly involved with the theater and directed several leading Budapest theaters. In 1916, he became president of the Association of Hungarian Playwrights.

As a journalist, he contributed to *The Week, Pesti Hirlap, Magyar Hirlap,* and *Pesti Napló*. He was editor in chief of the Athenaeum Publishing Company.

Heltai's short stories and novels are set in the same congenial atomosphere as his poetry. They are peopled by such easy-going characters as *Jaguar* (1914), a struggling reporter, or the hero of another novel modeled on Ferenc Molnar (q.v.) in *The Last of the Bohemians* (1911). His "serious" novel *House of Dreams* (1929) was an ambitious attempt to portray post-war Budapest and shows the influence of Freud.

Heltai was a very successful playwright. In his writings for the theater he retained the basic recipe: a touch of sentimentality mixed with a large dose of cynicism. In *The Tuenderlaki Girls* (1914), he relates the fate of three sisters of an upper-class family, "two of whom are respectable; the third falls into disgrace," for which she is despised, but it is this youngest daughter who sacrifices her reputation to secure the happy marriage of her sisters. Heltai wrote several plays in verse, in which he revived the comedies of past epochs in his own romantic-ironical style; particularly successful was *The Silent Knight* (1936; English translation, 1937). A number of his plys and novels were translated into German, English, French, and Hebrew.

Heltai converted to Christianity in 1919 but returned to the Jewish fold when the Jewish law of 1938 was promulgated. He participated in the activities of the OMIKE (National Hungarian Jewish Cultural Association), which from 1939 until the Nazi invasion of 1944 maintained a theater that became the home of Jewish actors, musicians, and other artists prevented from appearing elsewhere. He was awarded the prestigious Kossuth Prize of the Hungarian state shortly before his death.

HEROD ANTIPAS (21 BCE–39 CE) Tetrarch of Galilee; son of King Herod (q.v.) of Judea. Upon his father's death in 4 BCE, he became ruler (tetrarch) of most of Galilee and parts of Transjordan. Like his father he was a builder and restorer of cities, though not nearly on his father's vast scale. The most famous of these cities was Tiberias, which he built in honor of the Roman emperor Tiberius. It soon came to be the capital of Galilee.

In another respect, however, Antipas digressed from his father's general practice of showing respect for his Jewish subjects' feelings. The founding of Tiberias was a violation of Jewish law because its location on a former burial site made it ritually impure for Jewish habitation for a certain period. Antipas disregarded this sacrilegious aspect and went ahead with his project. On the other hand, he lodged a complaint with Tiberius against Pontius Pilate, the Roman governor (procurator) of Judea, for the latter's callous attempt to flout Jewish feelings by installing an offensive votive shield in Herod Antipas' Jerusalem palace. The emperor ordered the shield removed. Herod Antipas, like his father, was also careful to issue coinage with symbols would not offend his Jewish subjects' religious susceptibilities.

An episode described by both Josephus (q.v.) and the New Testament is Antipas' execution of John the Baptist. In Josephus' view, John's death was caused by the political fears his activities aroused in the tetrarch, while in the Christian version the execution was a gift to the tetrarch's stepdaughter (called Salome by Josephus). The New Testament story claims that John objected to the ruler's violation of Jewish law by his second marriage to his sister-in-law Herodias and was jailed for his presumptuousness. While in prison, the account continues, a gala banquet took place in honor of Antipas' birthday. His stepdaughter's dancing so delighted him that he promised to fulfill her every wish. At her mother's urging she asked for John's head as a gift and this wish was granted her.

It was the tetrarch's highly ambitious wife who brought about her husband's downfall. She kept encouraging him to press for the royal title. The emperor Gaius Caligula, annoyed by this unseemly request, ordered him banished from the country in the year 39 CE. His wife loyally accompanied him into exile.

H. Hoehner, *Herod Antipas*, 1972.

S. Perowne, *The Later Herods*, 1958.

HEROD THE GREAT (73–4 BCE) King of Judea, 37–4 BCE. Herod was descended from Idumean (Edomite) stock, a people whose mass conversion to Judaism took place in the 2nd century BCE. Herod's grandfather and father, both called Antipater, were high-ranking officials, his grandfather having apparently served as governor of Idumea (Edom).

The highly ambitious Antipater inculcated in his offspring a remorseless drive toward authority and high position and the need to serve Rome unquestioningly. These lessons were learned well by Herod in particular. His early days as Roman governor of Galilee were marked by his suppression of the nascent anti-Roman Jewish freedom movement. Hezekiah, the most distinguished of its leaders, was summarily executed together with large numbers of the Jewish rebels.

The stringent requirements of Jewish law as regards capital punishment were flagrantly flouted by Herod, and the consequent Jewish outcry led to charges against him on two occasions. He was finally let off without trial through the intervention of the Roman governor of Syria, but not before a distinguished Pharisee sage, Samaias (perhaps Shammai [q.v.]), had castigated the assembled Jewish judges for fearing to bring Herod to trial. This man, he said, would yet visit his wrath upon them.

Herodian rule was marked by bitterness, conflict, and violence from the very outset. Although officially appointed king of Judea in the year 40 BCE through the courtesy of his carefully cultivated (and massively bribed) friend Mark Antony, it took Herod three years and Roman military intervention before he could finally remove the threat posed by Mattathias Antigonus, the last of his Hasmonean opponents, beloved of the mass of the people. In general, it was Herod's keen sense of maneuver in the dangerous shoals of Roman politics that not only helped him survive, but eventually earned for him rule over almost the entire Land of Israel.

Years of rage ensued, including the destruction of the closest members of his own family — wife, mother-in-law, sons, many other close relations, and others too numerous to mention. The Roman emperor Augustus, no squeamish character himself, reportedly remarked of Herod's execution of his sons, "I'd rather be Herod's pig than his son."

Herod was one of the greatest builders of antiquity. He constructed or enhanced entire cities, such as the port town of Caesarea and Sebaste in Samaria, and restored or constructed hippodromes and buildings in the Land of Israel and beyond. His masterpiece, certainly in Jewish eyes, was the magnificently embellished Temple in Jerusalem, of which the rabbis stated, "He who has not seen Herod's house [i.e., the Temple] has never beheld a beautiful building in his life."

By the same token he made efforts not to flout Jewish tradition publicly, avoiding offensive representations on his coinage and insisting that members of his family marry Jews or spouses converted to Judaism. His assistance in times of famine was notable. The Jews of the Diaspora were equally indebted to him for his intercession with the authorities in cases of anti-Jewish manifestations. Yet Herod engaged in the practice, unforgivable in Jewish eyes, of appointing and demoting high priests at will, and commenced and concluded his reign with the execution of many respected sages.

The countryside was infested by informers and fear was rampant throughout his lengthy reign. The mention of his "massacre of the innocents" in the New Testament, though possibly anachronistic (he died in 4 BCE), is undoubtedly a throwback to his harsh legacy. The Talmud frequently hurls at him the contemptuous epithet of slave as it recalls his murder of the sages.

M. Grant, *Herod the Great*, 1971.
A. H. M. Jones, *The Herods of Judea*, 1960.
S. Perowne, *The Life and Times of Herod the Great*, 1956.

HERZL, THEODOR (Benjamin Zeev; 1860–1904) Founder of political Zionism, playwright, journalist. He was born in Budapest to a well-to-do merchant, who was a typical, assimilated, middle-class Jew. In his early years, Herzl went to a Jewish school and at the age of ten was sent to a secondary school, where the emphasis was on the sciences, for which he had little taste. He soon transferred to the Lutheran High School, one of Hungary's most eminent schools, where there were many other Jewish boys. His bar mitzvah was celebrated at the famous Dohany Street Synagogue, next door to his birthplace. His first newspaper article appeared anonymously because he was still at school. When,

First page of Theodor Herzl's Altneuland.

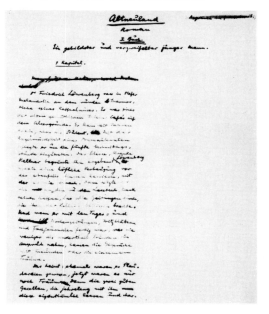

during his last school year, his only sister Pauline died at the age of eighteen, his mother became so melancholy that his father decided to move the family to Vienna. There he enrolled at the law faculty of the university and joined the Albia student fraternity, which he left when it passed a resolution not to admit any more Jews.

Having obtained a doctorate in law in 1884, he joined the practice of a judge as an unpaid clerk. This took him to Salzburg, where he started writing plays. In 1885 the *Wiener Allgemeine Zeitung* accepted his first feuilleton and, at the end of that year, he went to Berlin, where he had a job with the *Berliner Tagblatt*. In 1887 his first collection of humoristic pieces, *Das Buch der Narrheit*, was published in Leipzig and his play *Seine Hoheit* was presented in Berlin in 1888. Another play, the *Die Wildleibe*, written with Hugo Wittmann, was produced, without the authors' names, at the Burgtheater. They also put on his play *Der Fluechling*, while Herzl became theater critic of the *Wiener Allgemeine Zeitung*. In 1891, another play, written in collaboration with Wittmann, *Die Dame in Schwarz*, was produced at the Burgtheater and he was appointed Paris correspondent of the prestigious Vienna daily, *Neue Freie Presse*.

Although aware of the existence of anti-Semitism, until 1894 his reaction was rather superficial. At one time, he even suggested that the solution to the Jewish question was that all Jews should convert to Christianity. When in Paris, he covered the Dreyfus (q.v.) affair, which sharpened his awareness of anti-Semitism and helped to set him on the road to Zionism. Suddenly inspired, he prepared a proposal for a political solution and he turned to the Jewish philanthropist Baron de Hirsch (q.v.), but the two men did not find a common language.

This was the turning point; Herzl started what he later called his Zionist Diary, in which he elaborated a blueprint for the establishment of a Jewish state and before long, in July 1895, in Paris, wrote "in a white heat" *Der Judenstaat* ("The Jewish State"). In September, he returned to Vienna, was appointed to the editorial staff of the *Neue Freie Presse*, and in November once again in Paris, discussed his ideas with the thinker Max Nordau (q.v.), who enthusiastically endorsed them. Nordau introduced Herzl to the English writer, Israel Zangwill (q.v.), who, in turn, arranged for an invitation for Herzl to address the Maccabean Club in London, whose members gave him their full support. The small booklet *Der Judenstaat* was published in February 1896 and almost overnight, Herzl was surrounded by enthusiastic supporters, including many Jewish students. It was at this point that he was approached by William Hechler, chaplain to the British Embassy in Vienna, who offered his assistance. Through Hechler, Herzl was introduced to the grand duke of Baden, a relative of the kaiser. Since, from the start, it was Herzl's contention that a Jewish state could only be achieved through the guarantee of the powers, he set out on a course to win the benevolent sponsor-

Photomontage of Herzl meeting with Kaiser Wilhelm II in Palestine 1898.

ship of the German kaiser, the Russian tsar, and the Turkish sultan, with a view to obtaining what he called the Charter.

While his public popularity grew, his private life became unhappy, his marriage suffering from his devotion to his domineering mother. In June 1896, Herzl was received by the grand vizier in Constantinople and visited Bulgaria and England, where he was acclaimed by the Jews of Whitechapel. In Paris, he met Baron Edmond de Rothschild (q.v.) who, to Herzl's suprise, disapproved of the idea of a Jewish state. Herzl was to learn that the notion of Jewish peoplehood did not appeal to most of the contemporary Jewish lay and spiritual leadership.

This became eminently clear during the year of preparation for the First Zionist Congress. The somewhat naive, romantic Herzl felt sure that all Jews would jump at the possibility of ending the powerless state of the Diaspora, and persisted with his visionary beliefs in the face of strong opposition and sharp criticism, and even ridicule.

He devoted his great administrative talent to organizing the First Zionist Congress in Basel in August, 1897. This proved a resounding success, establishing the World Zionist Organization. At its conclusion, Herzl wrote in his Diary. "At Basle I created the Jewish State. If I were to say this out loud everybody would laugh at me. In five years,

בנימין זאב הרצל

תר״ך - תש״ך

Theodor Herzl

1860 - 1960

Herzl centenary stamp issued by the Israel Post Office, 1960.

perhaps, but certainly in fifty everybody will agree.'' (Almost exactly fifty years later the United Nations decided on the establishment of a Jewish state.)

By the time the first congress had convened, Herzl had gathered around himself a group of staunch supporters from both eastern and western Europe, and even from the United States. He launched the movement's journal, *Die Welt*, and laid down its organizational structure. The first congress approved the constitution and discussed the establishment of the organization's financial instrument, the bank. After the second congress (August 1898), Herzl made his only journey to Eretz Israel and had a number of inconclusive

meetings with the kaiser. The Jewish Colonial Trust was incorporated in London in 1899 as the financial arm of the World Zionist Organization and began to sell its shares. In Holland Herzl met the grand duke of Hesse, the tsar's brother-in-law, who promised to explain Zionism to the tsar. Soon after the Third Zionist Congress (1899), Herzl wrote his first letter to the tsar, once again through the intermediary of the grand duke of Baden. Following a serious illness in 1900, he presided over the Fourth Zionist Congress in London. In 1901, Herzl was received in Constantinople by the Sultan Abdul Hamid II and offered to pay the Turkish debt in exchange for a declaration of support for Jewish settlement in Palestine. His offer was rejected, but he received a Turkish decoration.

In January 1902, Herzl received the sultan's offer of a ''Charter'' — but in Mesopotamia, Syria, or Anatolia and not in Palestine — which he refused. He made another offer to the Sultan of 1,600,000 pounds sterling for a charter, which was rejected. In October his utopian novel, *Altneuland*, was published; this envisioned a Jewish state in Palestine and the ideal society that would be created here. Later that year, he met the British Colonial Secretary Joseph Chamberlain, who made the offer of El Arish in Africa for Jewish settlement, subject to the approval of Lord Cromer, the British representative in Egypt. At Herzl's instigation, the Zionist Organization sent an expedition to El Arish in January 1903, and the plan gathered momentum as it gained the support of Lord Rothschild. However, Lord Cromer remained cool and Lord Lansdowne, the foreign secretary, and Chamberlain proposed instead a settlement area in Uganda (now in Kenya). When Herzl showed inclination to accept this offer, the seeds of the greatest controversy of his career were sown. In the wake of the Kishinev and other pogroms, Herzl wrote to the Russian minister of the interior, Vyacheslav Plehve, who received him in August. He also met the tsar's minister of finance, Sergey Witte, who, although hostile to Zionist aspirations, authorized the establishment of the Russian branch of the Jewish Colonial Trust and the sale of shares in Russia. During his visit, Herzl was gratified by the tremendous reception accorded him by the Jews of Vilna.

The Sixth Zionist Congress in August 1903 was a watershed; it almost split the Zionist movement over the Uganda issue. In the end, the ''Zionists of Zion'' won, and in a dramatic statement to the Congress, Herzl vowed to fight for the establishment of a Jewish national home in Eretz Israel.

The following January, Herzl had an audience with the king of Italy, who showed sympathy for the Zionist idea, and with Pope Pius X, who completely rejected it. By May, Herzl was totally exhausted and in June went to take a rest at Edlach (Austria) where he died on July 3, 1904. His Vienna funeral has been described as one accorded only to heads of state. A real state funeral took place in the newly established State of Israel in August 1949, when his remains were brought to Jerusalem and reinterred on Mount Herzl in Jerusalem.

A. Bein, *Theodor Herzl*, 1942.

A. Elon, *Herzl*, 1975.

E. Pawel, *The Labyrinth of Exile: A Life of Theodore Herzl*, 1989.

FROM HERZL'S DIARIES

- What I need now is the condensation of my vaporous organization — the liquefaction of that mass of hot air called the Zionist Movement.
- First and foremost I have learned to know Jews — and that was sometimes even a pleasure.
- In the Tuileries before Gambetta's statue: I hope the Jews will put up a more artistic one of me.
- The "Jewish Mission" is spoken about by all those who are doing well in their present places of residence — but they are the only ones.
- On being called to the reading of the law on the Sabbath following the first Congress: The few Hebrew words of the *brokhe* caused me more anxiety than my opening and closing addresses and the whole direction of the Congress.
- If we ever get Jerusalem and I am still able to do anything actively at that time, I would begin by cleaning it up.
- Diplomacy is the art of dealing with robbers.

HERZOG, ISAAC HA-LEVI (1888–1959) Rabbinic scholar and second Ashkenazi Chief Rabbi of modern Israel. Born in Lomza, Poland, he later lived in Leeds, England, and Paris, France, where his father served in rabbinical positions. He pursued rabbinical studies on his own, and by the age of sixteen had completed study of the entire Talmud. Herzog also devoted himself to secular studies, and received a doctorate in literature from London University for his thesis on "The Dyeing of Purple in Ancient Israel." He served as rabbi in Belfast (1916—1919) and in Dublin, the capital of Ireland (1919—1936). He was appointed Chief Rabbi of the Irish Free State, and forged excellent relations with its politcal and ecclesiastical leaders.

In 1936, Herzog was elected to succeed Abraham Isaac Kook (q.v.) as Ashkenazi Chief Rabbi of Palestine. Settling in Jerusalem in 1937, Herzog was soon caught up with the difficult problems that beset the country's Jewish community. He made numerous journeys to Europe both during and after the Holocaust to return Jewish children who had been placed for safekeeping in Christian homes and institutions to their people.

Herzog worked incessantly to guide the Orthodox community after the establishment of the State of Israel in 1948. He had to deal with a host of halakhic problems which had been purely academic since the fall of the Second Commonwealth. Among these was the observance of the Sabbath and dietary laws within the framework of a modern state and society. Above all, he struggled to secure recognition for halakhic standards in the spheres of marital and personal status.

Endowed with a brilliant analytical mind and a phenomenal memory, Herzot was recognized as one of the leading rabbinical scholars of his time. He published the first two volumes of his planned five-volume work, *Main Institutions of Jewish Law* (1936, 1939). Three volumes of his extensive responsa, entitled *Hekhal Yitshak*, appeared posthumously (1960–1972). These are a valuable source of rabbinic guidance for contemporary issues.

HESCHEL, ABRAHAM JOSHUA (1909–1972) Jewish scholar, existentialist philosopher, and theologian. He was born in Warsaw to a distinguished Hasidic family. His studies were in Talmud and mysticism. He moved to Berlin for a modern education, attending the Institute (Hochschule) for Jewish Studies and studying philosophy at the university. He taught Talmud at the institute and in 1937, succeeded Martin Buber (q.v.) in the Central Organization for Jewish Adult Education. In October 1938 he was expelled from Germany together with all other Polish Jews who did not hold German citizenship. After teaching for a time in Warsaw, he left Poland on the eve of the war and, after a few months in England, reached the United States, in 1940, to join the faculty of Hebrew Union College in Cincinnati. He remained there for five years and then moved to New York, where, until his death, he was professor of ethics and mysticism at Jewish Theological Seminary.

In the last decades of his life, he was deeply involved in various public issues which gave him a high profile and evoked great admiration, especially among the younger generation. Active in interfaith understanding, he visited Rome during the Second Vatican Council for meetings with Cardinal Agostino Bea, in connection with the formulation of the document of Catholic relations with the Jews. His social-ethical teachings found practical expression in his involvement with the civil rights movement. He marched with Martin Luther King, Jr., and participated in protest marches and demonstrations to secure equal rights for U.S. blacks and to end the U.S. military intervention in Vietnam. He was also a leading figure in the campaign to enable Soviet Jews to emigrate.

His books cover many aspects of Jewish thought. He sought to create a synthesis welding traditional piety and learning with the rational thought and scholarship of western Jewry. He believed that the essence of Judaism lies in the collective memory of the Jewish people, with the Bible as the source of certainty. This relates not only to man's search for God but also to God's search for man, as reflected in his book titles *Man's Quest for God* and *God in*

Search of Man. He was deeply influenced by western thought, especially Neo-Kantianism, but insisted that Jewish thought cannot be simply fitted into philosophical categories and that God is more than a postulate of reason. Judaism, he believed, teaches a living relationship between man and God and true Jewish observance is expressed when God's concern for His creatures evokes, in man, a response of love and devotion. The experience of wonder is crucial to true religious expression, leading to an awareness of the grandeur of God.

Heschel stressed the holiness of time in Jewish thought and practice. Judaism, he noted, has not created holy places, and unlike modern technological civilizations does not emphasize space, but hallows times, notably the Sabbath and festivals.

His writings are aphoristic, poetic, and sensitive. His theological works include *Man Is Not Alone* and *Who Is Man?* (a defense of human dignity). *The Prophets* (based on his doctoral thesis) seeks to analyze the prophetic consciousness. *The Sabbath* is a paean to the Sabbath day, while *The Earth Is the Lord's* is a poignant evocation of the lost world of east European Jewry. The broadness of his interests is illustrated by his two books on great Jewish thinkers: the rationalist *Maimonides* and his last work on the Hasidic teacher, Menahem Mendel of Kotsk.

In his teaching, writing, and lecturing, Heschel proved a strong influence on modern Jewish thought, especially in the United States where he left a deep impression on both Jews and non-Jews.
M. Friedman, *Abraham Joshua Heschel and Elie Wiesel*, 1987.
J. C. Merkle, *The Genesis of Faith: The Depth Theology of Abraham Joshua Heschel*, 1985.
F. A. Rothschild *Between God and Man: An Interpretation of Judaism from the Writings of Abraham J. Heschel*, 1976.

HESS, MOSES (1812–1875) German socialist, forerunner of Zionism, who provided a sociophilosophical basis for Jewish nationalism. Born in Bonn, he received an Orthodox upbringing at the home of his grandfather, since his parents had moved to Cologne, where his father established a sugar refinery. At the age of fourteen, when Hess's mother died, his father brought him to Cologne to train him for a business career. The lad proved to be unsuitable for business, however, preferring to immerse himself in messianic visions and philosophical books, especially those of Spinoza (q.v.) and Hegel. He was self-taught, except for a few terms at the University of Bonn, from 1837 to 1839.

At age twenty-five, Hess published his first book, *The Sacred History of Mankind by a Young Disciple of Spinoza* (1837). He clothed his philosophic views in Christian symbols, grouping his division of human history under the headings God the Father, God the Son, God the Holy Ghost. In his second book, *The Europlan Triarchy* (1841), he advocated the reconstruction of the social and political order into a European federation on a socialistic basis under the leadership of the three powerful states, Prussia, France, and England. In such a united Europe, Jews would be permitted to make their patriotic contribution. He pleaded for their right to marry Christians so as to facilitate the process of merging both groups in a higher synthesis. He himself practiced what he preached and married a Christian prostitute, which he saw as an attempt to redress social injustice.

As a native of the Rhineland, he participated in the Battle of the Poets, begun in 1840 and fought over whether the Rhineland rightfully belonged to the Germans or the French. The battle of words was initiated on the German side by Nicholas Becker and on the French side by Alfred de Musset and Alphonse de Lamartine. Other poets joined in the fray, which culminated in Nikolaus Becker's ultrapatriotic German hymn, *Die Wacht am Rhein.* Hess composed a melody to Becker's poem and sent it to him. It was returned with the comment, "You are a Jew."

Hess received similar rebuffs on other occasions in his wooing of Germany. Karl Marx (q.v.) and Friedrich Engels's *Communist Manifesto* ridiculed Hess's humanitarian socialism, despite Hess's help to Engels in editing a left-wing monthly. Eventually Hess realized that his nationality was indeed Jewish nationality rather than German, a conclusion he embodied in his *Rome and Jerusalem* (1862), a pioneering classic of Zionism. In the 1840s and 1850s, however, his main contributions were to socialist theory. He collaborated and differed with Karl Marx and other radicals. In the columns of the first socialist daily, *Rheinische Zeitung*, which he help to found and edit, he gave expression to his political views. His Jewish origins were not overlooked, either by friends or opponents; he was even dubbed "the communist Rabbi Moses." Without abandoning his faith in socialism, his thinking gradually began to concentrate on the Jewish question.

In *Rome and Jerusalem*, he confessed that he had long been estranged from the Jewish people, but that he had come to realize that they could never be an organic part of other peoples, since Jews were a separate nationality, linked by unbreakable bonds to their ancestral heritage and to the Holy Land that first fashioned them. As a nation, Jews had once made important contributions to humanity. They could do so again if they were reconstituted as a nation on their ancient soil. There the vision of Jewish sages and prophets of transforming the individualistic, capitalistic system into a socialistic, messianic system could be realized by the founding of Jewish cooperative communities. Preparations for the resumption of a normal Jewish national existence had to be made by agitating for national alertness, by gathering financial resources for the moment when a favorable opportunity would present itself, and by establishing a network of Jewish settlements north of the projected Suez Canal and throughout the area between the Mediterranean and the Jordan. His book had no immediate repercussions, but forty years after it was written Theodor Herzl (q.v.) read it and noted in his diary, "What a noble exalted spirit. Everything that we tried is already in this book."

Hess's last years were concentrated on socialist activity, and he cooperated closely with Ferdinand Lassalle (q.v.). He lived mostly in Paris and at his request was buried in a Jewish cemetery near Cologne. His remains were transferred with great honor to Israel, in 1961, and buried next to the Sea of Galilee.

I. Berlin, *The Life and Opinion of Moses Hess*, 1957
J. Weiss, *Moses Hess, Utopian Socialist*, 1960.
M. Schulman, *Moses Hess, Prophet of Zionism*, 1963.

HESS, MYRA (1890–1965) British pianist. Of German Jewish ancestry, Dame Julia Myra Hess was born in a traditional Jewish home in a genteel part of London. She showed uncommon musicality from an early age and attended the Guildhall School of Music, where, at the age of twelve, she won a scholarship to the Royal Academy of Music. There, she studied exclusively with Tobias Matthay, who was to be her mentor and a major influence on her until his death in 1945. He devised a triangular apparatus to increase her span, and his theories on touch helped her form her style, which combined a masterful technique with lightness.

She made her debut at seventeen in the Beethoven G Major Concerto under Thomas Beecham at Queen's Hall, London. The following year she gave an all-Beethoven recital, which was fairly well received. Recognition, however, was slow. Depressed, she toyed with the idea of mutilating her hands so that she would never again be able to play.

She suffered the constraints of Jewish Orthodoxy until the age of twenty and finally left home in 1914 after a disagreement with her father. Yet even after embracing Christianity some years later, she remained proud of her Jewish roots, attributing her self-discipline to her strict Jewish upbringing.

Throughout her career she devoted part of her time to teaching and delighted in furthering young talent. Her only serious love affair was with the talented violinst, Aldo Antonietti. In 1907 she accompanied him on a highly acclaimed recital tour of Holland. Their romance was short-lived, however, since Hess was not prepared to sacrifice her career for family life. There were many other suitors, among them Mischa Elman and Benno Moisewitsch, both of whom proposed marriage, but she was steadfast in renouncing further intimate relationships so as to devote herself to music.

In 1912 she appeared with the Amsterdam Concertgebouw, already one of the finest orchestras, under Willem Mengelberg. Reviews were ecstatic, comparing her sensitive, poetic playing of the Schumann A Minor Concerto to that of the venerated Clara Schumann. In Europe she was an immediate box-office draw long before she was fully recognized in her native England. She also established an immediate rapport with American audiences. For four decades, from 1922 onward, she made repeated coast-to-coast tours into the United States and Canada. Even during the depression, when most audiences dwindled, hers grew.

During World War II, she conceived, directed, and often appeared in the Myra Hess midday concerts held in London's National Gallery, denuded of the art treasures that had been removed for safe keeping. Since the regular concert halls were closed, her concerts filled a profound need for music lovers from all walks of life. Almost 1,700 concerts were held, even during periods of bombing. Myra Hess was credited with helping to keep up the morale of the war-ravaged capital. She endeared herself to audiences by asking if they were all "comfy" and suggesting that they "have a good cough and get it over."

In 1941 she was made a Dame Commander of the British Empire "for her lasting services to British music and to world musical achievement." In the same year she received the Royal Philharmonic Society's gold medal.

Her vintage years were highlighted by the Casals summer festivals at Perpignan (1951) and Prades (1952), and she collaborated with Pablo Casals, Isaac Stern, and Joseph Szigeti (q.v.) in chamber ensembles.

Myra Hess's transcriptions of baroque music for two and four hands, notably the chorale from J.S. Bach's Cantata no. 147, "Jesu, Joy of Man's Desiring," became inextricably associated with her.
Marion C. McKenna, *Myra Hess: A Portrait*, 1976.

HEVESY, GEORGE JOSEPH VON (1885–1966) Chemist and Nobel Prize winner. He was educated at Budapest and Freiburg universities obtaining his Ph.D. in 1908. Beginning his research at Zurich University as assistant professor (1909–1911), he worked with Fritz Haber (q.v.) at Karlsruhe University and in 1911 was granted a fellowship at Manchester University in the Rutherford Institute, where he worked on isotopes until 1913. His fundamental work, *Radioactive Indication or Labeling*, was written in Manchester and published in 1913. This paper is regarded as the basis for all methods using radioactive isotopes for labeling, whether applied in biology, metallurgy, medicine, or analytical chemistry. However, its significance was realized only after the production of synthetic radioactive isotopes on an industrial scale. It was for this achievement that he was awarded the Nobel Prize in chemistry, in 1943. He also worked for a while with F. Paneth, at the Radium Institute in Vienna, where he came to the conclusion that radioactive radium D cannot be isolated chemically from radium G and lead but can be applied to the tracing of lead.

Returning to Budapest in 1913, he served in the army during World War I, and until 1920, worked on the perfection of metallurgical, chemical, and biological application of his methods. In the academic year 1918–1919, he was professor of physical chemistry at Budapest University, but was dismissed from his post by the Horthy regime because he was a Jew. He emigrated to Denmark where he continued his researches at the Niels Bohr (q.v.) Institute for Theoretical Physics in Copenhagen. It was there, in 1922, that he discovered an elusive chemical element of the periodic system. Assuming, on the basis of Bohr's atomic theory that the as yet unknown 72nd element would not be found among the rare-earth metals but rather in the titanium group near to zirconium, with the assistance of D. Coster and by means of X-ray spectroscopy, he demonstrated its presence in zirconium minerals containing ores. They called the new element hafnium, after Copenhagen's Latin name.

In subsequent research, Hevesy applied the labeling technique in medicine, particularly in tumor examinations. In 1926, he accepted a chair at Freiburg University. There, he invented two important testing methods: the techniques of X-ray fluorescence and of isotope dilution. In 1935, he studied phosphorous metabolism in bones, blood, and malignant growths by application of the phosphorous-32 isotope that he discovered along with the kalium-41 isotope. On the basis of his research, he concluded that the elements of the living organism are in a dynamic state and are gradually exchanged in the course of biochemical processes taking place within them.

When the Nazis came to power in Germany, Hevesy moved to Copenhagen and after the occupation in 1943 fled to Stockholm, where he became a professor of organic chemistry. While in Copenhagen, he elaborated the extremely important method of neutron activation analysis, which is still the most sensitive technique for testing high-purity materials and is indispensable in engineering, where increasingly pure substances are required.

For his achievements in radioactivity research, he was awarded the Faraday, Copley, and Bohr medals, the Fermi Prize, and the second Atoms for Peace Award (1959).
The Collected Papers of George Hevesy, 1962.

HEZEKIAH   (reigned c. 727–c. 698 BCE) King of Judah. When he was twenty-five he succeeded his father, Ahaz, and reigned for twenty-nine years. The kingdom had been through a difficult period during Ahaz's reign when the northern kingdom of Israel had rebelled against Assyria as a result of which its territory had been truncated and an Assyrian province established in part of the kingdom. Judah itself was firmly under Assyrian hegemony.

In the first years of his reign, Hezekiah was careful not to be drawn into revolts against Assyria and so did not suffer when the northern kingdom was completely conquered by Assyria and its inhabitants exiled (722–721 BCE). He also kept out of a subsequent rebellion led by the king of Hamath against the Assyrian ruler, Sargon, preferring to pay tribute to Assyria.

With the strengthening of the power of Egypt, elements arose in Judah advocating an alliance with Egypt in order to throw off the Assyrian yoke. Nevertheless Hezekiah refrained from joining the revolt of the Philistine cities, which was put down by Sargon in 711. Ashdod was made an Assyrian city and Hezekiah continued to pay tribute. One of his chief advisers was the prophet Isaiah (q.v.), who warned him against relying on Egypt. By now Judah was the only kingdom in the region that had not been conquered by Assyria and Hezekiah was able to strengthen the kingdom.

In 705 Sargon died and was succeeded by Sennacherib. This was the signal for the revolt of many provinces in the Assyrian Empire, supported by the Egyptians, and this time Hezekiah participated, apparently conquering the Gaza area. He was encouraged by the Babylonian king, Merodach-Baladan, who was challenging Assyria, but again Isaiah opposed the revolt. In 703 Sennacherib began to take action to put down the rebellion and started by ejecting Merodach-Baladan from Babylon. He then turned his attention to the Mediterranean area, subduing the Phoenician cities, defeating an Egyptian army, and advancing down to defeat the Philistine cities. He then entered Judah, conquering forty-six cities from Hezekiah (701). His siege and conquest of Lachish is graphically documented on his monuments (now in the British Museum). He then laid siege to Jerusalem, where Isaiah encouraged Hezekiah not to surrender. Just when the fate of the city seemed desperate, a calamity befell the Assyrian camp (apparently a plague) and Sennacherib abandoned the siege and hurried back to Assyria. However, Judah did not regain its independence and Hezekiah continued to pay tribute.

Internally, Hezekiah is praised in the Bible for his devotion to God. He purified the cult of idolatrous elements, smashing idols and destroying high places, and upgraded the status of the Temple. He conducted an outstanding Passover celebration (probably after 721) to stress the role of Jerusalem as the ritual center for those remaining in the former northern kingdom of Israel. He took a number of steps to try to induce these survivors to acknowledge that he was the rightful heir to the kingdom of Israel. He repaired the walls of Jerusalem and organized a professional army. In order to enable Jerusalem to withstand a siege he built a tunnel from the Gihon spring outside the walls that brought water to the pool of Siloam in the city (the tunnel still exists). He developed the country's economy and agriculture and the initial long, quiet period of his reign provided the atmosphere for fruitful literary activity. The sources emphasize his righteousness and he remained close to Isaiah throughout. Indeed during the Sennacherib campaign, when he fell ill, Isaiah worked miracles, and prophesied his recovery and his deliverance from the Assyrians (Is. 38).
M. Cogan and H. Tadmor, *II Kings* (Anchor Bible), 1988.

HIDA, See Azulai, Hayim Joseph David

HILDESHEIMER, EZRIEL (ISRAEL) (1820–1899)

Rabbi, scholar, educator, and leader of Orthodox Jewry in Germany. A scion of a traditional rabbinic family, he was born in Halberstadt, and had both a secular and religious education, being ordained as rabbi in 1842. He studied philosophy and Semitic languages at the universities of Berlin and Halle, becoming one of the few Orthodox rabbis to receive a secular doctorate (a study of the Septuagint, the first Greek translation of the Bible) up to that time (1846). In 1851 he was appointed rabbi of the Austro-Hungarian community of Eisenstadt and established the first yeshiva (Talmudic academy) in the Western world to include both secular and traditional religious instruction in its curriculum. All subjects were taught in German and Hungarian, not Yiddish. Hildesheimer's belief that it was necessary to create a modern variety of Orthodox Judaism which took into account the political, religious, and cultural changes that were transforming central and western European Jewish life, following the philosophy of Samson Raphael Hirsch (q.v.), *Torah im derekh eretz* (traditional Jewish study combined with Western culture). The majority of Orthodox Hungarian rabbis pronounced a ban of excommunication on him for his innovations. When he came under fire at the Congress of Hungarian Jewry convened in December 1868 to discuss the establishment of a rabbinical seminary for the whole of Hungary, he broke away from the main Orthodox stream and formed the Cultural Orthodox group.

In 1869 Hildesheimer moved to Berlin to take up the post of rabbi of the Adass Jisroel community, the largest in Germany, where he established a modern Orthodox elementary religious school for boys and girls. In 1873 he founded the Berlin *Rabbinerseminar*, the first Orthodox rabbinical seminary to be established in Germany. The scientific study of Judaism (*Wissenschafts des Judentums*) was combined with an allegiance to the principle that Torah, both written and oral, was the divine revelation.

Hildesheimer led the struggle against the Reform movement and especially against its main proponent in Berlin, Abraham Geiger (q.v.). He assisted the organization for refugees from pogroms in Russia and helped collect funds to build a hostel for pilgrims and the poor in the Old City of Jerusalem. In 1872 he founded the Association for Settlement in Eretz Israel, the aims of which were to provide support for the Jewish community in the Holy Land, build hostels in Jerusalem, and obtain legacies for this purpose. Despite these and other activities in behalf of Eretz Israel, he saw the rebuilding of the Land of Israel in religious terms and refused to participate in Hovevei Zion, a conference convened by the early Zionist movement at Kattowitz, because the majority of the participants were nonreligious.

By the end of his career in Germany, Hildesheimer had attained a position of stature and respect in both the German and the European Jewish communities and he was called upon to adjudicate disputes within the community and to represent the community in relations and dealing with the secular authorities in various lands. His students were constantly sought by communities throughout Europe and by 1884 he did not have enough graduates of his seminary to fill requests for rabbis.

Hildesheimer wrote several books and articles in the accepted German academic style, and in 1870 established the German Jewish weekly *Die Jüdische Presse* to enable him to disseminate his views to the German-reading public. It included Hebrew and Yiddish sections and ceased publication in 1923. His works in Hebrew and German dealt with rabbinical subjects, a description of the Herodian Temple, commentaries on manuscripts in the Vatican, an article on the blessing of the new moon, and *responsa* on numerous subjects. His collected essays were published in German *Gesammelte Aufsätze* (Frankfurt, 1923) and his responsa in Hebrew, *The Responsa of Rabbi Esriel* (1969 and 1976).

D. H. Ellenson, "Continuity and Innovation: Esriel Hildesheimer and the Creation of Modern Orthodoxy", doctoral dissertation, 1982.

HILLEL (late first cent. BCE–early first cent. CE)

Pharisee leader and outstanding sage of the later Second Temple period. Biographical information about him is scarce. He was born and began his education in Babylonia but continued in Jerusalem, where he was a student of the leading Pharisee teachers, Shemaiah and Avtalyon. Stories are told of his poverty and the menial tasks he undertook to support his family. Almost nothing is known of his career until he emerged as one of the most noted scholars in Jerusalem. He was appointed *nasi* (prince, president), one of the heads of the Sanhedrin, and was reputed to be a descendant of the house of David.

He is especially remembered as founder of a school that rivaled the school of his colleague, Shammai (q.v.); over three hundred controversies are recorded between the two schools. Hillel's legal interpretations usually tended to the lenient, Shammai's to the rigid. The differences reflect social divisions; Hillel and his followers were identified with the poorer classes, Shammai, with the more affluent. Hillel spoke for the common people and made progressive decisions; Shammai was conservative and reflected the views of the establishment. Thus, Shammai wanted to limit entrance to the schools to the more aristocratic, better-off students, whereas Hillel insisted they be open to all, irrespective of background. Eventually Hillel's rulings were, with a few exceptions, recognized as authoritative; in the words of the Talmud (*Eruvin* 13b), "The words of both scholars are the words of the living God, but the legal decisions follow the school of Hillel, because they were gentle and modest and studied not only their own views but those of the other school and even quoted their opponents' before their own views."

Several authoritative enactments of a social

One of Hillel's sayings: "If I am not for myself, who is for me?" illustrated by Ben Shahn.

nature were attributed to Hillel. One was the introduction of the *prosbul*. This was a document designed to prevent hardship to the poor in anticipation of a sabbatical year when all loans were cancelled. Creditors were reluctant to give loans when such a year approached but Hillel devised a formula, essentially a legal fiction, that solved the problem for the poor.

Hillel was regarded as a paragon of many virtues, among them patience, modesty, charity, and conciliation. A famous story tells of a potential proselyte who demanded that while he stood on one leg, Hillel should teach him Judaism. Instead of responding angrily, Hillel replied: "What is hateful to you, do not do to others. This is all the law; the rest is commentary. Now go and study."

Hillel was the first scholar to formulate hermeneutic rules for the elucidation of the Bible. He formulated seven basic principles, expanded by his successors to thirteen and then to thirty-two rules, which provided directives for the derivation of legal rulings from the biblical text and which formed the frame for the oral law.

Learning, he taught, was the great ideal. He set high standards for his pupils and insisted that Torah must be studied for its own sake and not for

SAYINGS OF HILLEL

- On divine justice:
  Hillel saw a skull floating on the face of the water and said to it, "Because you have drowned others, they have drowned you; but those that drowned you will eventually be drowned themselves."
- Be a disciple of Aaron, loving peace and pursuing peace, loving your fellow-man and attracting him to the study of the Torah.
- Once when Hillel was leaving his disciples, they asked him where he was going. He replied, "To perform a pious deed." When they asked him what that may be, he answered that he was going to take a bath. When they asked whether he considered that a pious deed, he answered, "Yes; if in the theaters and circuses the images of the king must be kept clean by the person responsible for them, how much more so is it the duty of a human being to take care of the body, since mankind has been created in the divine image."
- He who seeks fame loses his name; knowledge that does not grow will decrease; one who does not study deserves to die; one who uses the crown of the Torah for material gain will perish.
- The more Torah, the more life;
  the more study, the more wisdom;
  the more counsel, the more discernment;
  the more charity, the more peace.
- Do not withdraw from the community, do not be sure of yourself until the day you die, do not judge your fellowman until you have stood in his place, and never say "I will study when I have time" — you may never have time.
- If I am not [concerned] for myself, who will be for me? But if I am for myself alone, what good am I? And if now is not the time to act, when will be?
- And others said of Hillel:
  In ancient days, when the Torah was forgotten from Israel, Ezra came from Babylon and reestablished it. Then it was again forgotten until Hillel came from Babylonia and reestablished it.
- It was said of Hillel that he had learned all the words of the Sages; that he had studied all types of speech, even the speech of mountains, hills, and valleys, of trees and plants, of beasts and animals, stories of spirits, folktales, and parables — everything he had learned.

any ulterior motive. Whatever privations had to be endured because of this study would be compensated for by God. Only through learning could an individual achieve the highest status, that of the *hasid*, the pious. The curriculum to be studied consisted of both the written law and the oral law, and Hillel was the first to insist that both, emanating from Sinai, enjoyed equal divine origin. It was thanks to the work of Hillel that Judaism could be reconstructed after the destruction of the Temple in 70 CE, under the guidance and inspiration of his pupil Johanan ben Zakkai (q.v.).

It was Hillel who molded the formation of rabbinic Judaism, which was to be the normative religion of the Jewish people. This postulated that while the source of Judaism is the divine revelation at Sinai, its development and application is by the human scholar. Ethically, in relations with one's fellow, the Jew must be guided not only by considerations of justice but by mercy and conciliation, with special consideration for the poor and underprivileged. Hillel's ideals inspired subsequent generations of Jews and also influenced the thoughts of the founders of Christianity a generation or two later. The admiration he inspired is reflected in the recognition of his descendants as hereditary leaders of the Jweish community in Eretz Israel down to the fifth century.

N. N. Glatzer, *Hillel the Elder: The Emergence of Classical Judaism,* 1956.
J. Neusner, *The Rabbinic Traditions about the Pharisees before 70,* 3 vols., 1971.

HILLMAN, SIDNEY (1887–1946) U.S. labor leader. Born in the Lithuanian village of Zagare, Simcha Hillman was the second of seven children in a family of long-established rabbis. His grandfather, Rabbi Mordecai Hillman, was the governing figure of the village and an important influence in Sidney Hillman's life. His parents resolved that it was Sidney who would carry on the family tradition and study to be a rabbi. In 1901, at the age of fourteen, he was sent to the Kovno (Kaunas) yeshiva, a distinguished center of Jewish studies.

At Kovno, Hillman was suddenly exposed to a range of fresh ideas and new possibilities. He began secretly to take Russian lessons from an assimilated Jewish friend, Zacharias Matis. One year later he left the rabbinical college to pursue his nonreligious studies. He found a job with his friend's father, who encouraged him in his desire to learn. The Matises were Jewish activists and their home was often the meeting place of the local leaders of the Jewish underground labor movement. Thus, Hillman's youth was marked by years of intense discussions with his friend and other young intellectuals who frequented the Matis home. By the age of sixteen, Hillman was actively taking part in the outlawed Jewish labor movement. In 1904 there was an open demonstration for the first time in Kovno. Hillman led a small group of workers, was arrested, and jailed for several months.

In 1906 Hillman left Russia for England, but soon set sail for the United States. After a brief stay in New York, he joined Matis in Chicago. He began working at Sears, Roebuck and Company, where he became acutely aware of the unfair conditions of the American worker.

In 1909 he was working in a Chicago clothing factory and in 1910 was one of the leaders of a strike that spread from the plant to embrace all the city's 35,000 garment workers. During the following years he was a union organizer, helping to establish the Amalgamated Clothing Workers of America and getting the city's garment industry to accept the principle of union organization. He sought to ensure what he called "industrial democracy" and "law and order" in the women's garment trade based on harmony between labor and management.

In 1914 he moved to New York, where he worked for the Cloakmakers Joint Board in the women's garment industry. He was also elected president of the Amalgamated Clothing Workers of America, which in 1915 was accepted as the chief bargaining representative of New York garment workers. His trade union was a model in the field of social security and arbitration and he introduced novel practices, such as cooperative housing. He aimed for widespread reforms, hopefully by negotiations, otherwise by strikes. In 1918 he won the forty-four-hour week and in 1920 unemployment insurance.

In 1935 Hillman helped to found the Congress of Industrial Organizations (CIO), a new body for the steel, automobile, rubber, shipyard, and radio workers.

During his last years, he concentrated on making the democratic system work. It was Hillman who, according to President Franklin D. Roosevelt, in the face of a persistent minority resistance in Congress, helped to win the passage of the minimum wage law of 1938, now considered a basic reform of the New Deal era. His friendship with Roosevelt enabled him to be a moving force behind many New Deal measures. In 1940 he was labor member of the National Advisory Committee and during World War II was Roosevelt's chief labor adviser. He helped to found the American Labor party, serving as its chairman (1944–1945). After the war, he was involved in the international labor movement, helping to create the World Federation of Trade Unions of which he was vice-president.

A supporter of Zionism and the labor movement in Palestine and later Israel, he was a non-Zionist member of the Jewish Agency when it was established in 1929.
M. Josephson, *Sidney Hillman: Statesman of American Labor,* 1952.
G. Soule, *Sidney Hillman: Labor Stateman,* 1939.

HILLQUIT, MORRIS (1869–1933) U.S. socialist. He was born Moishe Hillkowitz in Riga; his father was a factory owner who enrolled his son in a non-Jewish secular school. At age fifteen, Hillquit already saw himself as a socialist, following many other secular Jewish students of the time. With the decline in his father's fortunes, the family emigrated to the United States in 1886. Settling in New York, Hillquit was drawn to East Side Jewish radical circles and on his eighteenth birthday joined the Socialist Labor party, soon becoming one of its active crusaders against anarchism. He also participated in antireligious demonstrations, including a Yom Kippur ball marked by feasting and smoking. Like other cosmopolitans he saw no future in preserving a unique Jewish way of life. Nevertheless he worked as a Yiddish journalist and organizer as an official of the United Hebrew Trades of Jewish Labor.

In 1891 he entered New York University Law School, suporting himself by tutoring students in Latin and teaching English to immigrants. He now disapproved of ethnically oriented socialism, which brought him into conflict with other Jewish socialists. After graduation, he and his brother opened a successful law practice, often representing unions. In 1899 he was one of the leaders of the right-wing opposition faction of constitutional socialists, which split from the Socialist Labor party in protest against the radical leadership of Daniel De Leon (q.v.). This led in 1900 to the foundation of the Social Democratic party, which in turn evolved into the Socialist party, in which Hillquit was the outstanding ideologist and tactician. Hillquit was now a major figure in the socialist movement, in which he took a centrist position between the revolutionary left and the reformist right. From 1901 to 1906 he served as New York representative on the party's national committee. On several occasions he ran for Congress but was never elected. Hillquit remained the leading polemicist in the party against the left wing and emerged as the champion of a gradualist, lawful socialist position.

After World War I broke out in 1914, he used his energies to keep the party intact and to launch an aggressive antiwar crusade. He published a peace platform that blamed the war on European capitalists and imperialists and sought to keep the United States out of the war. Running for Congress in a New York district he was only narrowly defeated. He was now more prepared to cooperate with other antiwar organizations and was a founder of the People's Council for Democracy and Peace. In 1917 he ran for mayor of New York and attracted a broad coalition of support in his unsuccessful bid, in which he received 22 percent of the votes.

After the war, he played a prominent role in expelling the left wing from his party, seeking to emphasize its firm American roots. The war period saw him draw closer to the Jews; he championed the Jewish worker in the United States and in Europe and became the lawyer for major Jewish unions in New York. He became a hero to Jewish workers when, in 1915, he successfully defended seven Jewish officials of the Cloakmaker's Union charged with murdering a strikebreaker. He was also prominent in the International Ladies Garment Workers Union, for which he was counsel. However, in the 1920s he rarely championed Jewish causes and his image as a Jewish leader faded.

He represented American socialists in the Socialist and Labor Internationals. From 1920 he campaigned against American communists, regarding them as a harmful alien import. Until the 1930s he dominated his party's international relations and in 1929 was elected chairman of the national party. At this time he took a more cautious attitude, seeking to soften socialism so as to make it more palatable to the American people. His model was now the British Labor party, which was achieving electoral success in Britain. His views roused the ire of Lenin, who called him a social traitor and excluded him from membership in the Communist International. Hillquit continued to anger the left-wingers with his cautious attitude to strikes, his agreement to government-dictated arbitration agreements, and his indifference to democratic reform within the unions. He continued to run for Congress and again in 1932 ran for mayor of New York, but soon afterwards succumbed to tuberculosis, from which he had long suffered.

He wrote *From Marx to Lenin* (1921), a critique of the non-Marxist aspects of Bolshevism, and his autobiography, *Loose Leaves from a Busy Life* (1934).

N. F. Pratt, *Morris Hillquit*, 1979.

HIRSCH, MAURICE DE (Baron de Hirsch; 1831–1896) Financier and philanthropist who planned and organized a large-scale emigration and resettlement of eastern European Jews in the New World. He came from a distinguished family of Jewish landowners and bankers. His grandfather, Jacob von Hirsch, the first Jewish landowner in Bavaria, was ennobled in appreciation of his contribution in the Napoleonic Wars. His father, a banker with the Bavarian court, was

Baron Maurice de Hirsch in Turkish costume, Turkey, 1875.

honored with the title of baron in 1869. Hirsch, who was born in Munich, received a solid Jewish education thanks to his mother, who came from Frankfurt, the center of Jewish Orthodoxy in Germany. Having received a traditional Jewish upbringing and schooling in Brussels, in 1851 Maurice de Hirsch joined the Bischoffsheim and Goldschmidt banking institution, in which he was to play a prominent role. In 1855 he married Clara Bischoffsheim (1833–1899), daughter of the head of the firm. She was to share his interest in philanthropic activities and was a source of much encouragement to him.

He was successful in several business enterprises in copper and sugar and established a Belgian bank, but he demonstrated his brilliance primarily in the construction of railroads. In 1869 he obtained a concession from the Ottoman authorities for a rail link between Turkey and western Europe. The Oriental Railway was a risky venture, and Hirsch had to spend a considerable time in Constantinople dealing with Turkish bureaucracy — not least by dispensing baksheesh. The result was successful and profitable, producing much of Hirsch's fortune, estimated at $100 million in 1890. The project proved a visionary enterprise, highly important in important in the economic development of Europe, and Hirsch became known as *Turkenhirsch* ("Turkish Hirsch").

Hirsch moved from Brussels to Paris, received French citizenship (in addition to his Bavarian, Belgian, and Moravian nationalities), and bought for his home the former palace of Empress Eugenie. He also owned a chain of estates from England to Moravia. His hobby was horse racing and he moved among European nobility, including King Edward VII of Britain, Prince Rudolf of Austria, the king of Bulgaria, and the president of France.

Despite his Orthodox upbringing his religious links were slim. He became involved in Jewish philanthropy in the 1860s, when he helped to finance the educational activities of the French organization, Alliance Israélite Universelle. After the pogroms of the early 1880s, he offered the Russian government a large sum of money for the educational and vocational training of Russian Jews, but when Hirsch refused to allow them carte blanche in expending the funds, the offer fell through.

When his only son, Lucien, died in 1887, he declared, "My son I may have lost but not my heir; humanity is my heir." He looked for a Jewish homeland, and rejected Palestine because of the weakness of the Turks and the proximity of the Russians. He acquired large tracts of land in Latin America, particularly in Argentina, dreaming of settling Russia's three million Jews there and turning them into landowning farmers. He felt that the solution to the problems of the Jews was a return to the soil. He took care that his philanthropic activities would provide not merely charity, but economic rehabilitation. In fact, thousands of Jews were settled on the lands of his Jewish Colonization Association (ICA), but most of them left after a few years. However, those that remained kept the project going. It is still in existence today, but those Jews still on the Hirsch lands in Argentina are generally in managerial positions. Hirsch also established a program (the Baron de Hirsch Fund) for settling immigrants in the United States. His scale of philanthropy was unequaled by any other individual in his day, and it is estimated that he devoted over 500 million francs to philanthropy. In 1895, when Theodor Herzl (q.v.) first became enthused with his concept of a "Jewish State," the first person to whom he turned was Baron de Hirsch. The meeting was a fiasco, but Herzl continued to write to him, and on hearing of his death shortly afterwards wrote in his diary, "His death is a loss to the Jewish cause. Among the rich Jews, he was the only one ready to do something for the poor."

After Hirsch's death, his wife continued his philanthropic work.

A. Allfrey, *Edward VII and his Jewish Court*, 1990. K. Grunwald, *Turkenhirsch: A Study of Baron Maurice de Hirsch, Entrepeneur and Philanthropist*, 1966.

From Maurice de Hirsch's *My Views on Philanthropy*

It is my utmost conviction that I must consider myself as only the temporary administrator of the wealth I have amassed, and that it is my duty to contribute in my way to the relief of the suffering of those who are pressed by fate. I contend most decidedly against the old system of alms-giving, which only makes so many more beggars; and I consider it the greatest problem in philanthropy to make human beings who are capable of work out of individuals who would otherwise become paupers, and in this way to create useful members of society.

HIRSCH, SAMSON RAPHAEL (1808–1888) Jewish religious thinker in Germany; founder of Neo-Orthodoxy. Born in Hamburg, he studied for a year (1829) at the University of Bonn, where he established a close friendship with Abraham Geiger (q.v.) who was later to become one of his main ideological opponents. From 1830 he was chief rabbi of Oldenburg and while there wrote his classic works, *Nineteen Letters on Judaism*, in which he first expounded his theological system, Neo-Orthodoxy, and *Horeb: Essays on the Duties of the Jewish People in the Diaspora*, on Jewish law and revelation.

In 1841 Hirsch became rabbi of Aurich and Osnabrück in Hanover and in 1846 chief rabbi of Moravia. Despite his Orthodoxy, his modern innovations, including support for Jewish political emancipation, adoption of clerical garb, and stress on studying the Bible (instead of the traditional Orthodox exclusive concentration on the Talmud), caused a rift with the extreme Orthodox community in Moravia, and he moved to Frankfurt. There he organized an autonomous Orthodox community, separate from the Reform community that dominated the Frankfurt Jewish community (like most others in Germany). This community became the model for other separatist Orthodox communities throughout Germany and in 1876, Hirsch was a leading figure in obtaining Prussian legislation that permitted Jews to secede from the existing state-recognized communities and so gave legal recognition to the Orthodox separate communities.

Hirsch adopted as his motto a phrase from the Mishnah tractate *Avot* (2:2): *Torah im Derekh Eretz*. In its original context, this phrase advocated a combination of Torah study with a worldly occupation; to Hirsch, however, it meant the combination of traditional Jewish study with modern secular culture. This came to characterize what became known as Neo-Orthodoxy or modern Orthodoxy.

Judaism to Hirsch is a historic phenomenon that must be understood according to its own source — the Torah. Nothing matters outside the Torah, which is not intended to prove philosophical truths but rather to lay down the law to be observed. From the Torah is to be learned the true nature of man. The commandments bring the Jew to the highest stage of perfection, of which the ideal type is the *Yisraelmensch*, that is, the law-observing Jew. The laws he divided into six categories: doctrines (the historically revealed principles of Jewish faith), principles of justice governing conduct toward one's fellowman, statutes (laws whose motivation is not readily seen but which bring justice to all creation), symbolic observances that ennoble the life of man, and worship in all its forms.

The Torah, he claimed was given in the desert to show that nationhood does not depend on nation or soil. The Land of Israel had "seduced the Jewish people from its allegiance to God." Judaism is nothing more than a religious sect. Israel had a spiritual mission until humanity as a whole would turn to God. At the same time he wrote, "The Jewish people, although it carries the Torah throughout the Diaspora, will only find its table and lamp in the Holy Land."

Hirsch created a network of schools in the Neo-Orthodox spirit, combining religious and secular studies. He translated the Pentateuch, Psalms, and prayer book into German, adding commentaries which proved very influential.

M. Breuer, *The "Torah-Im-Derekh Eretz" of Samson Raphael Hirsch*, 1970.
I. Grunfeld (ed. and trans.), *Judaism Eternal: Selected Essays from the Writings of Rabbi Samson Raphael Hirsch*, 2 vols., 1956.
N. H. Rosenbloom, *Tradition in an Age of Reform: The Religious Philosophy of Samson Raphael Hirsch*, 1976.

SAYINGS OF SAMSON RAPHAEL HIRSCH

- We live in a divine world.
- If you are truly a Jew, you will be respected because of it, not in spite of it.
- A life of isolation, devoted only to prayer and meditation, is not Jewish.
- Israel's mission is to teach the nations of the world that God is the source of all blessing.
- Join a community — only in this way can your work be made universal and eternal.
- The highest ideal of Judaism is the universal brotherhood of man.

HISDAI IBN SHAPRUT (also Hasdai; c. 915–c. 970) Statesman, physician, and community leader in Muslim Spain. His father, the wealthy Isaac ibn Shaprut, had moved from Jaen to Cordoba, where Hisdai was born. During the reign of Abdar-Rahman III (912–961), who adopted the title of caliph in 939, Cordoba was not only the Umayyad empire's capital but also (with some 500,000 inhabitants) the most populous city in Europe. After studying medicine, Hisdai became physician to the caliph, a post that he retained under his successor, Hakam II (961–976). The tolerant Abdar-Rahman had sufficient confidence in his Jewish doctor to make him an adviser on foreign affairs as well as director of customs and overseas trade.

Thanks to his medical research, Hisdai reputedly discovered an antidote to certain poisons, and there were times when his diplomatic and medical tasks overlapped. After a Byzantine delegation visiting Cordoba had presented the caliph with a rare Greek pharmaceutical manuscript (c. 948), Hisdai led the team of scholars that quickly translated it into Arabic. Hisdai was also entrusted with diplomatic missions. He conducted negotiations with envoys of the Holy Roman Emperor, Otto I (953), but achieved his greatest triumph in Navarre, while treating the deposed King Sancho of Leon for obesity (958). Not only did Hisdai cure his patient, but he also helped restore him to the throne by inducing Sancho and his grandmother, the queen of Navarre, to sign a peace treaty with Abdar-Rahman in Cordoba.

As the foremost Jewish notable in Muslim Spain, Hisdai ibn Shaprut used his wealth and prestige to safeguard Jewish interests and to inaugurate a golden age of Jewish learning. A scholar in his own right, he financed the purchase or copying of Hebrew manuscripts, fostered the writing of secular Hebrew poetry, and extended his patronage to learned Jews. Hisdai likewise took the initiative of appointing Moses ben Hanokh the Babylonian as Cordoba's chief rabbi and head of a new Talmudic college there. This step, virtually severing the old ties with the Babylonian academies, made Spanish Jewry an independent cultural community.

Tales of a warlike Jewish kingdom in Asia had long intrigued the medieval West. Through his diplomatic contacts, Hisdai managed to verify these reports of a Khazar buffer state near the Caspian Sea and then earned a special place in history by the story of the letters he dispatched (c. 958) to Khaqan Joseph, the last ruler of Khazaria. Joseph's detailed reply explained how King Bulan and many of his people had come to embrace Judaism — a theme which Judah Halevi (q.v.) would later take up in his philosophical *Kuzari* — and also described the Khazar kingom's situation only a decade before its power was shattered by Russian invaders (in 969). This correspondence had an enormous psychological impact on Jews at a time when they were damned by Christendom as a "perfidious" and stateless nation. However, since the original Hebrew letters have not been preserved, their authenticity is now a matter of scholarly conjecture and debate.

E. Ashtor, *The Jews of Moslem Spain* (2 vols.), 1973, vol. 1.
D. M. Dunlop, *The History of the Jewish Khazars*, 1954.

HOOK, SIDNEY (1902–1989) U.S. social and political philosopher and educator. Born and educated in Brooklyn, N.Y., he studied at City College and with John Dewey at Columbia, graduating with a doctorate in 1927. That year he began teaching at New York University and from 1931 also at the New School for Social Research. After his retirement in 1972, he became senior research fellow at the Hoover Institution at Stanford University.

He was recognized internationally as an outstanding American intellectual and was a leading representative of the pragmatic tradition in American thought, applying pragmatic intelligence to ethical, social, and political issues and applying historical theory to American philosophy. This involved the experimental testing of his ideas by observing their results in behavior.

He was often called a neoconservative thinker — a conservative committed to democratic socialism. His early reading of Karl Marx (q.v.) led him to try to reinterpret Marx in pragmatic terms. Indeed he was one of the first scholars in the United States to subject Marx's thought to serious scholarship. Hook was a strong opponent of Stalinism and, criticizing totalitarian expressions of Marxism, was politically active in stemming the influence of communism in America. He was passionately committed to democracy, which he saw as based in the ethical principle of equality, and opposed all forms of authoritarianism and absolutism.

As an educator, he regarded the object of learning as the development of a critical intelligence. He rejected attempts to introduce external political criteria, such as admission quotas, in institutions of higher learning and insisted on academic freedom.

Hook has been described as a secular humanist. He was critical of religion, feeling that evidence for the existence of God is inadequate. He therefore objected to the effort to use theological premises to derive ethical conclusions.

He was the chief organizer of a number of activities among intellectuals, including the Committee for Cultural Freedom. He also organized the Conference on Methods in Philosophy and Science, the Conference on Scientific Spirit and Democractic Faith, and University Centers for Rational Alternatives. He was president of the American Philosophical Society (1959).

Hook was a prolific writer and editor of thirty-five works, including *Pragmatism and the Tragic Sense of Life* (1974), *John Dewey, an Intellectual Portrait* (1939), *Heresy, Yes — Conspiracy, No* (1953), *Common Sense and the Fifth Amendment* (1957), and his autobiography, *Out of Step* (1987).
J. D. Crowley, *Knowledge and Freedom in Sidney Hook*, 1966.
P. Kurtz, *Sidney Hook and the Contemporary World*, 1968.
P. Kurtz, *Sidney Hook*, 1983.

HORE-BELISHA, LESLIE, LORD (1898–1957) British politician. Of Spanish origin, the Belisha family had resided in England for 150 years when Leslie's father, a Royal Fusilier, died suddenly while preparing to go on parade. Leslie was then only nine months old. His mother subsequently married Adair Hore, a distinguished non-Jewish civil servant, whose surname he added to his own.

Hore-Belisha took up law and at Oxford exercised a passion for oratory by walking up and down the corridors of his house declaiming Burke's speeches, which he had learnt by heart. Prior to World War I, he studied at the Sorbonne, Heidelberg, and Oxford. During the war he served in the army in France and Greece, went on missions to Cyprus and Egypt, and was mentioned in dispatches, but was later sent home because of malaria. He then resumed his studies at Oxford where he was elected president of the student union.

Shortly after Hore-Belisha was called to the bar in 1922, he fought the election to Parliament on the Liberal ticket for the district of Devonport. He hired an old stage coach, harnessed four bay horses to it, and drove through the constituency, stopping at corners to address the crowds who came out at the sound of the coaching horn. He lost to the incumbent Conservative candidate, but defeated him in the 1923 general election. In addition to politics he wrote the "Londoner's Diary" column for the *Evening Standard* and later wrote for the *Daily Express* and the *Sunday Express*. He also wrote as "The Man with the Lamp" in the *Saturday Review* and regularly contributed to the *Spectator* as well as to other magazines and journals in Britain and America.

In 1931 Hore-Belisha was appointed parliamentary secretary to the Board of Trade, and a year later became financial secretary in the Treasury, as assistant to Neville Chamberlain, upon whose recommendation he was made minister of transport in 1934. He launched an attack on road accidents, introducing a new highway code, driving tests, and silent zones where the sounding of horns was prohibited between 11.30 P.M. and 7.00 A.M. His best-known innovation was the use of illuminated beacons at pedestrian crossings. Known as Belisha beacons, they were the subject of jest on the stage and radio, and were sold in miniature as cigarette holders and pencils.

He was made privy councillor in 1935, given a seat in the Cabinet in 1936, and appointed by Neville Chamberlain as secretary of state for war in 1937. During the two years and seven months he held this office, Hore-Belisha introduced sweeping reforms in the conditions under which soldiers served and extended the period of service, enabling soldiers to qualify for a pension. He also raised the recruiting age for all combatant ranks from twenty-five to thirty, and introduced sweeping changes in training, equipment, and tactics. Tank units and other mechanized formations were also created.

All these reforms were immensely popular with the troops but were met with constant opposition from the army officer corps, especially when younger men were appointed to senior positions over the heads of older officers. They objected violently to Hore-Belisha's attempts to democratize the army with the new system of commissioning officers directly from the ranks. Anti-Semitism also played a role in the opposition he encountered among the military establishment.

When World War II broke out, Hore-Belisha had already prepared the territorial army and had introduced partial conscription. Many of the senior officers who had been by-passed through the promotion of younger men were given positions of responsibility and were now able to settle the score. The hostile atmosphere at army headquarters and complaints of civil interference in military matters, led Chamberlain to propose to Hore-Belisha a transfer to the Board of Trade. He refused and resigned from the government in January 1940.

Hore-Belisha remained in Parliament, constantly advocating the need to harness the country's resources for the military forces. In 1945 he was appointed minister of national insurance in Churchill's short-lived caretaker government. He introduced legislation on family allowances and workman's compensation for industrial injuries, but lost his seat in the 1945 general elections. In 1947 he was elected to the Westminster City Council and was raised to the peerage in 1954.

For many years he was an elder of London's Spanish and Portuguese synagogue.

R. J. Minney (ed.), *The Private Papers of Hore-Belisha*, 1960.

HOROWITZ, VLADIMIR (1904–1989) Pianist.
Born in Kiev (some sources say Berdichev, Ukraine), the son of an electrical engineer, he studied privately with his mother and well-known teachers, and at the Kiev conservatory. He graduated at the

age of seventeen and made his debut at Kharkov, where his fees were paid in food and clothing. He gave a series of performances in Russian cities that became legendary. In Leningrad he appeared in twenty-three concerts without repeating a single work — a repertoire of over two hundred pieces. He enjoyed similar successes in various European capitals. In 1928 he first appeared in New York, playing Tchaikovsky's First Piano Concerto conducted by Sir Thomas Beecham. Pianist and conductor had different views on the interpretation but in the last movement Horowitz took the initiative and finished seconds ahead of the orchestra. In the words of the *New York Times*, "the piano smoked at the keys."

He remained in New York and played the Beethoven concertos under Toscanini, whose daughter, Wanda, he married. In 1936 he made the first of his many retirements from the concert stage, this time for three years. He withdrew again in 1953 for twelve years but continued to make recordings. His return, at a Carnegie Hall concert in 1965, was a sensation but he again retired in 1970, giving only rare performances. In 1978 he appeared with an orchestra for the first time in twenty-five years.

Poor health was one reason given for his long silences; this was attributed at least partly to nervous causes, i.e., strain brought on by his own and the public's high expectations. Stories were told of certain eccentricities: on the day of a performance he would eat only white Dover sole and gave all his recitals at 4 P.M. That year he also appeared at the White House for President Jimmy Carter, where he was called "a national treasure," and he played for President Ronald Reagan in 1986. It was also in 1986 that he returned for the first time in sixty years to the Soviet Union, where he was warmly received.

Opinions were sharply divided on his playing. Some thought him the greatest pianist of the century; others complained of his subjective interpretations, sometimes labeling them distortions. His admirers spoke of his remarkable speed, cool accuracy, unrivaled technique, and ruthless standards. He excelled in the romantics such as Liszt, Chopin, Tchaikovsky, Rachmaninoff, and Prokofiev and made an important contribution to promoting the works of Scriabin. Although he initially wished to become a composer, none of his original work was published apart from some virtuoso transcriptions.

Horowitz was buried in Milan in the Toscanini family tomb. Before his funeral, his body lay in state at the La Scala opera house as thousands filed past and loudspeakers played a selection of his recordings.

HOSEA (8th cent. BCE) Israelite prophet; one of the twelve minor prophets included in the Prophet section of the Bible. He prophesied in the northern kingdom of Israel during the reigns of kings Jeroboam II and Menahem. The only information on his life emerges in the early part of the book, in which he is commanded to marry a harlot to symbolize Israel's unfaithfulness to God. He there-

upon marries Gomer and fathers three children. She is unfaithful and the prophet divorces her, but later they are reconciled and remarried.

It is not clear whether the story of the Hosea-Gomer relationship actually happened or was intended to convey symbolically the relations between God and Israel. As such, the symbolism would suggest that even though Israel's love is deflected to the pagan god Baal this defection is only temporary. God continues to love Israel and will reaccept her when Israel returns, as she surely must.

God is seen as being angered by Israel's sins, which include both ethical misbehavior and exaggerated reliance on the cult and on military strength. Immoral acts are not mitigated but are compounded by recourse to ritual deeds in the belief that these will serve as expiation even without a change of heart. In particular, God is infuriated by Israel's apostasy — worship of other gods and acceptance of other religious rites, such as idol worship and adoption of divination. Even the country's foreign alliances are a form of rejection of their reliance on the true God.

Significantly, however the door of mercy is not closed and the call for repentance brings a message of hope, for Hosea's concept of divine forgiveness is a significant innovation in the Israelite conception of the Divine.

F. I. Anderson and D. N. Freedman, *Hosea* (Anchor Bible), 1980.
A. J. Heschel, *The Prophets*, 1962, pp. 39–60.

HOUDINI, HARRY (1874–1926) U.S. magician and escapologist. Originally named Ehrich Weiss, he was only a few weeks old when his parents emigrated to the United States from their native Budapest. He grew up in Appleton, Wisconsin, where his father became the rabbi of a small Orthodox congregation. To earn much-needed cash, he started work as a boy trapeze artist (1882) and eventually his family joined him in New York. There he had begun performing as an illusionist under the stage name of Houdini, which reminded audiences of the great French magician, Jean-Eugène Robert-Houdin (1805–1871). After marrying Beatrice Rahner in 1894, Houdini trained her as his stage assistant and they appeared together in

dime museums, circuses, and vaudeville, where he made a specialty of baffling escapes from every type of restraint. During his early career, for a mere twenty dollars, he offered to explain these "tricks" to four separate New York dailies, but they showed no interest; later, when Houdini gained renown, he refused to divulge his secrets and they went with him to the grave. He once attributed his success to his great strength and to his being bowlegged.

A dramatic turning point came in 1900, when Houdini (beginning his four-year tour of Europe) packed London's Alhambra Theater night after night following a well-publicized demonstration of his abilities at Scotland Yard. Another exploit, involving an "escape-proof" police van in Russia (1903), also boosted Houdini's fame. Now hailed as "The World's Greatest Magician," he became the highest-paid celebrity in the field of entertainment. Crowds flocked to see him walk through a wall, escape from a water torture cell, or make an elephant disappear from the stage of New York's Hippodrome (1918). One characteristically dangerous feat was escaping from a straitjacket in which he had been hung upside down, twenty-five meters in the air; another was emerging in less than two minutes from a weighted packing case in which he had been manacled and lowered into the sea. Houdini went on to found the London Magicians' Club and the Society of American Magicians; to thrill moviegoers in a number of silent pictures; and, as a pioneer aeronaut, to make the first sustained flight over Australia (1910).

While relying on mechanical knowledge and

Houdini, magician and escapist.

sensational effects, Houdini kept himself at the peak of physical fitness in order to show that Jews were capable of muscular (as well as intellectual) achievement. He debunked his one-time idol in *The Unmasking of Robert-Houdin* (1908) and then devoted much effort to the exposure of fake mediums and mind readers. In order to brand such charlatans and forewarn gullible members of the public, Houdini offered a substantial reward to anyone demonstrating "supernatural phenomena" which he could not reproduce. He also published two detailed accounts of his investigations: *Miracle Mongers and Their Methods* (1920) and *A Magician among the Spirits* (1924). Within the American Jewish community, he helped to organize the Rabbis' Sons Theatrical Benevolent Association.

Houdini died of peritonitis resulting from a stomach injury, and bequeathed his rare collection of books (on magic, spiritualism, etc.) to the U.S. Library of Congress. A volume entitled *Houdini's Magic* (1932) was later compiled from his notebooks. The Paramount motion picture *Houdini*, starring Tony Curtis, was released in 1953.

M. Christopher, *Houdini: The Untold Story*, 1969.
W. B. Gibson, *Houdini's Escapes*, 1930.
W. L. Gresham, *Houdini: The Man Who Walked through Walls*, 1960.

HOWARD, LESLIE (1893–1943) British stage and screen actor. Son of a Hungarian father, Howard was born Leslie Howard Stainer in South London. While excelling in amateur dramatics at school, he was a poor student and until the out-

Leslie Howard with Wendy Hiller in Pygmalion.

break of World War I worked as a bank clerk, a job he obtained through his stockbroker father. Obtaining a commission in the Twentieth Hussars, he married the daughter of a regular army officer shortly before being sent to France. In 1917 he was invalided out of the army, having suffered severe shell shock on the western front.

After his recovery, he decided to attempt a stage career. Parts in touring companies soon led to his first London appearance in *The Freaks*. Howard's roles increased in importance and in 1920 he accepted an offer to appear in New York for the American impresario Gilbert Miller. The play in question, *Just Suppose*, was a success and marked the beginning of a profitable decade for Howard, who supplemented his Broadway stardom with forays across the Atlantic to London's West End. Major plays of this period in which he starred included *Aren't We All, Outward Bound, Her Cardboard Lover*, and *Berkeley Square*.

Quite early in his British career, Howard had had his first film experience when he founded Minerva Films with Adrian Brunel. Howard appeared in a few films but it was not until 1930 that his screen career truly began. The 1930s were as rich in film parts for Howard as the 1920s had been for him on stage. In his Hollywood films, he came to epitomize not only the essence of Britishness, but also an infinitely rarer commodity, a screen hero whose intellect matched his charm and good looks. He starred in *Of Human Bondage*, which brought Bette Davis to prominence, and in Ingrid Bergman's first American film, *Intermezzo*. When his Broadway hit, *The Petrified Forest*, was to be filmed, Howard directly assisted in the birth of a new star by agreeing to make an appearance in the movie on the condition that Humphrey Bogart was retained to recreate his stage role as a gangster.

Howard's British films were no less illustrious, including the enormously popular, *The Scarlet Pimpernel* and *Pygmalion*. None of his other films could compare with *Gone With the Wind*, the last of his American films to be released, in which he played Ashley Wilkes. After 1939, all Howard's film work was done in Britain and connected to the war effort. Particularly notable was *Pimpernel Smith*, a contemporary updating of *The Scarlet Pimpernel*, with the Nazis as the new villains, which

Howard directed and produced in addition to playing a starring role.

During the war, Howard was intensely involved in the propaganda campaign on behalf of the Allies and in 1943 agreed to go on a lecture tour of Spain and Portugal under the auspices of the British Council. It was while returning from Lisbon that his plane, a clearly marked civilian aircraft, was shot down by German fighters. Among the theories advanced to explain this exceptional attack on a commercial flight is one that holds that the Nazis thought Winston Churchill was on board.

R. Howard, *In Search of My Father: A Portrait of Leslie Howard*, 1981.

L. R. Howard, *A Quite Remarkable Father*, 1959.

HUBERMAN, BRONISLAW (1882–1947) Polish violinist. Born in Czestochowa, Poland, he began studying the violin at a very early age at the Warsaw Conservatory, as a result of an unusual ocurrence. In 1887 the shah of Persia came to Warsaw and heard a pianist prodigy. The enthusiastic shah awarded the young musician many prizes and a lifetime allowance. This incident ignited the imagination of many Jewish families and children were at once sent to study the piano. In 1892 Huberman's father took him to Berlin to study with Joseph Joachim (q.v.), but as the eminent violinist would not teach child prodigies he referred Huberman to his assistant. In Berlin the young violinist also studied, secretly, with Charles Grigorovich. Later in life Huberman confessed that Grigorovich "taught me everything that could be learned from a teacher." However, Huberman never graduated from any musical institution. He used to say that the audience is the best teacher and that the concert stage the best school.

By the age of eleven Huberman had already performed in Amsterdam, Brussels, and a year later in London and Paris. When he was fourteen, he played Brahms's Violin Concerto in Vienna. The composer was in the audience and was very satisfied with the performance, giving Huberman a photograph signed, "from your grateful listener." Huberman toured the United States in 1896–1897, retired for four years from the concert stage, and then reappeared with many more successful concerts all over the world. He gave a series of fourteen concerts in Paris (1920), ten in Vienna (1924–1925), eight in Berlin (1926), and toured the United States again in 1937.

When the Nazis came to power in 1933 Huberman canceled all his engagements in Germany. Huberman was a consistant anticommunist and an avid socialist. One of his Vienna concerts took place after the Austrian chancellor, Engelbert Dollfuss established a fascist government and gave orders to shoot those who would resisted the new regime. Huberman declared that all receipts from one of his recitals would be given to families of the dead working-class victims. The press did not carry the announcement, but Huberman repeated it during the performance.

Bronislaw Huberman. Lithograph by Eugene Spiro.

It was on Huberman's initiative that a new Palestine Symphony Orchestra was established, composed of Jewish musicians who had lost their positions in Europe after the rise of the Nazis. He started organizing the new orchestra in 1934, when he informed Meir Dizengoff, the first mayor of Tel Aviv, that the receipts from his most recent recital would be dedicated to the new orchestra. Huberman did not wish to organize a mere musical ensemble in Palestine. He wanted to inaugurate one of the best orchestras of the time.

Huberman auditioned potential members for the Palestine Symphony in Zurich and Vienna, Budapest and Warsaw. He gave fundraising speeches wherever he performed and slowly but surely the dream became a reality. Under the baton of Arturo Toscanini, the Palestine Symphony, which later became the Israel Philharmonic Orchestra, gave its first concert on December 26, 1936, in Tel Aviv. The excitement in the country was so great that one woman who gave birth to twins on that day named them Tosca and Nini.

Huberman himself did not perform with the new orchestra in its first season. He planned to do so in its second season but suffered a hand injury in a plane crash. His doctors decreed that he would never perform again, but the violinist persisted and returned to the platform. At the age of sixty-three, Huberman performed Brahms's concerto for the last time in Lucerne in a concert that was broadcast throughout Europe.

After his death his library and papers were transferred to the Central Music Library in Tel Aviv, where the street on which the home of the Israel Philharmonic is located is named after him. On the centenary of his birth, the greatest violinists of the generation — Isaac Stern, Ida Handel, Ivri Gitlis, Itzhak Perlman, Pinchas Zukerman, Henryk Szeryng, and Shlomo Mintz — went to Huberman Street and celebrated a Huberman Festival with the Israel Philharmonic, under its conductor, Zubin Mehta.

Huberman's violin playing was always controversial. While some musicians, like Toscanini, Bruno Walter (q.v.), and Artur Schnabel (q.v.) for example, admired his work, others, especially violinists, were far from admiring his playing. Carl Flesch criticized Huberman as "the most remarkable representative of unbridled individualism."
I. Ibbeken (ed.), *The Listener Speaks: 55 Years of Letters from the Audience to Bronislaw Huberman*, 1961.
I. Ibbeken and T. Avni (eds.), *An Orchestra Is Born: A Monument to B. Huberman*, 1969.

HUROK, SOL (1888–1974) U.S. impresario. A native of the Russian town of Pogar, Hurok arrived in the United States in 1906 with three rubles in his pockets. While working in a variety of jobs he began to give expression to his artistic bent by organizing concerts for labor organizations. An important breakthrough in this career came when he arranged for noted violinist, Efrem Zimbalist, to play at a benefit performance for the Socialist party. In 1914 he became a naturalized American citizen, and two years later, had already come into his own as an impresario, regularly presenting famous artists at New York's Hippodrome.

Though the performers Hurok presented during his six decades of entrepreneurial activity included many of America's finest artists, he became most well known as an importer of the best foreign talent. He was responsible for the visit of the Habimah Theater in 1926 and of the Moscow Art Players in 1935, and many subsequent tours by performers such as the Sadlers' Wells Ballet, the D'Oyly Carte Opera Company, and the Bolshoi and Kirov ballets. Among the individuals who appeared under the legend "S. Hurok Presents," the most prominent were Isadora Duncan, Anna Pavlova, Feodor Chaliapin, and, in later years, Isaac Stern, Maria Callas, and Rudolf Nureyev. Not only was he noted for his lavish treatment of the established stars he brought over; he also went out to discover his own great names, most notably

If you love the things you do you don't age, you always remain young. Age is for the calendar. I hope to live to see the day when we have music on the moon.
Sol Hurok

the contralto Marian Anderson. Hurok exported well too, giving many foreign audiences the chance to see American artists.

In 1953 Hurok's personal fame inspired a Hollywood film, *Tonight We Sing*, which purported to tell his story. Proud of an unblemished success record, Hurok originated the oft-quoted saying "When people don't want to come, nothing will stop them." Although he never ceased his activities, Hurok sold his company in 1969. In 1972 the Jewish Defense League was linked to the firebombing of his offices in Manhattan, an attack in which a secretary was killed. The apparent motive was to protest against Hurok's cultural ties with the Soviet Union at a time of restricted Jewish emigration from that country.
S. Hurok (with R. Goode), *Impresario*, 1946.

HUSSERL, EDMUND GUSTAV ALBRECHT (1859–1938) German philosopher. Husserl is acclaimed as a "giant of our century," a thinker who "casts a long shadow." Recognized as the father of phenomenology, he inspired various schools of close disciplines. First active in Germany, and guiding such brilliant thinkers as Max Scheler and Martin Heidegger, Husserl's philosophy was rediscovered after World War II in France, and his thought was especially formative in the works of Jean-Paul Sartre, Maurice Merleau-Ponty, and Paul Ricoeur. In a third phase of influence, philosophical phenomenology crossed the

Edmund Husserl.

Atlantic, and by the 1960s had been established as a tradition.

Husserl was born in Prossnitz, Moravia (then part of Austria), and studied mathematics, physics, and astronomy in universities in Leipzig, Berlin, and Vienna. As a young adult, like many other German and Austrian Jewish academicians of his time, Husserl converted to Protestantism. In Vienna, under the influence of Franz Brentano, he became increasingly interested in philosophy. He taught first at the University of Halle (1887–1901), and later at the universities of Göttingen and Freiburg (1906–1916) until his retirement in 1929.

The decisive concept in Husserl's contribution to modern philosophy is *world*, with its later variant *lifeworld*. His position of ontological neutrality, beyond idealism and realism, marks a turning point in the age-old debate of the distinction between appearance and reality. Other themes and concerns central in his thought are: the problem of conceptual relativism, the relationship of phenomenology to history, and the concept of intentionality. Phenomenology, which may be characterized as the "logic" of consciousness, has permeated diverse fields, such as the social sciences, literary theory and criticism, religion, art, and education.

Shortly after Husserl's death, his voluminous manuscripts were secreted out of Nazi Germany. During the occupation of Belgium, while in hiding, a few scholars of Jewish origin transcribed these works; after the war they would become the core of the Archives-Husserl at the University of Louvain. Hesserl's writings and university lectures have been published by the archives in eleven volumes of the series *Husserliana* (1950–1966).

D. Carr, *Interpreting Husserl: Criticism and Comparative Study*, 1987.

J. J. Kockelmans, *A First Introduction to Husserl's Phenomenology*, 1967.

P. Ricoeur, *Husserl: An Analysis of His Phenomenology*, 1967.

HYRCANUS, See John Hyrcanus

I

IBN DAUD, ABRAHAM (also known by the acronym *Ravad*; c. 1110–1180) Spanish Jewish historian and philosopher. Little is known of his life. He was born in one of the larger Spanish communities and at some time settled in Toledo. While his mother tongue was Arabic, he was deeply versed in all fields of Jewish learning, as well as in Moslem and Christian culture. In his later years, he wrote four books: *Sefer Kabbalah* ("The Book of Tradition"), one of the outstanding Jewish historical works of the Middle Ages; a philosophical work, *Emunah Ramah* ("Exalted Faith"); a work on astronomy; and a polemic against the Karaites, of which the latter two were lost. It is thought that he met his death as a martyr.

His historical book seeks to trace the uninterrupted development of rabbinic Judaism from the time of Moses to te author's own time, that is, the "train of tradition." He endeavors to show that one generation of scholars immediately succeeded another without examining whether the new generation fully accepted the teachings of their predecessors. By showing the continuity of rabbinic tradition he wanted to rebut the Karaite contention that rabbinic tradition was a late fabrication. He also wished to show that the rabbis of Spain, especially Andalusia, represented the incarnation of the ideal type of rabbi and had been singled out to herald the new redemption. The book is an important source of Jewish history.

As a philosopher, he tried to harmonize Judaism and Aristotelianism and has been described as the first Jewish Aristotelian philosopher. *Emunah Ramah* starts with an exposition of physics and metaphysics which are seen as essential prerequisites to the study of philosophy (combating the view of many contemporary rabbis that the study of science is harmful to Judaism). True philosophy is seen as being completely in accord with Jewish religious tradition, and the truths which science aims for with such difficulty, are viewed as nothing more than the ancient Jewish heritage.

I. Husik, *A History of Medieval Jewish Philosophy*, 1944, pp. 197–235.
A. Ibn Daud, *Sefer ha-Qabbalah, The Book of Tradition*, 1967.

IBN EZRA, ABRAHAM (c. 1092–1167) Bible commentator, poet, grammarian, and scientific writer. Born in Tudela, Spain, while still a youth he won a reputation as a Hebrew poet and a scholar in various branches of learning. Nevertheless, he experienced much suffering and poverty, provoking him to write, "Were I to deal in candles, the sun would never set. Were I to trade in shrouds, men would live forever."

He was a wandering scholar who never settled in any place for long. Initially, he traveled from place to place in Spain but at the age of about fifty he began to wander to other countries. It has been suggested that his first such journey, to the Middle East (Egypt, Eretz Israel, and Mesopotamia), was connected with the conversion of his son, Isaac, to Islam and his attempts to win him back. Returning to Spain he briefly found a benefactor but after the latter's death, set forth again. He lived in Rome for a time (1140–1145), receiving honor and recognition from the Jews of the city. While there his literary activity included commentaries on Job and Ecclesiastes, books of grammar, and poetry. He then spent a few years in other Italian cities including Verona (1147–1148), before moving to France where he lived for ten years, again in several cities.

FROM THE WRITINGS OF
ABRAHAM IBN EZRA

- Desire blinds the wise.
- The evil of the eye grows from the evil of the heart.
- Many man who do not fear God wrap themselves in a prayer shawl.
- Man was not brought into this world to enjoy himself.
- Reason is the angel that mediates between God and man.
- A little sin becomes a big sin when committed by a big man.
- Fruits take after their roots.
- Wisdom engenders humility.

From 1158 to 1160 he was in England. He then returned to France and Spain, dying at Calahorra, on the borders of Navarre and Aragon.

Ibn Ezra was a prolific writer and according to one tradition was the author of 108 books, although far fewer are extant. The best known is his Bible commentary, which reveals his independent and critical mind. His style is succinct and aims at expounding the simple, literal meaning, rejecting the prolix exegetical approach of some of his predecessors. Notwithstanding his respect for tradition, he made a number of daring observations that led some modern critics to acclaim him as the forerunner of biblical criticism. For example, he hinted that the last verses of Deuteronomy were written by Joshua, not Moses, and indicated that Isaiah 40–66 was not by the same person as Isaiah 1–39, but was written by a prophet in the Babylonian exile. He probably wrote a commentary on the complete Bible, only parts of which have survived.

His philosophic views were mainly derived from his Bible commentary. His philosophy was in the Neo-Platonic tradition and of limited originality. He divided the universe into three worlds. The highest, eternal world is that of separate intelligences or angels; the intermediate world, also eternal, comprises the nine spheres, the seven planets, and the fixed stars; and the lowest is composed of the four elements and their mixtures, of which man is the noblest. The universe was created in time by God, acting through his angels. After death, the reward of the righteous is his reabsorption into the world soul. Man's most important activity is knowledge of God.

His commentary often devotes itself to philological and grammatical problems, reflecting his important contributions to Hebrew grammar. He was a distinguished poet, whose verse spanned a wide variety — sacred poems, poems of friendship, love, and wine, and didactic poems on science. He even wrote a long poem on chess, describing all the rules of the game. A master of the Hebrew language, some of his poems are constructed ingeniously and can be read in two directions or are based on alliteration. His sacred poems express his deep religious soul and he was also the author of a long philosophical poem.

In addition, this versatile scholar wrote scientific treatises, including a work on the calendar, books on astronomy and astrology including a work on the astrolabe, and several books on mathematics and geometry. He was one of the first medieval Jewish scholars to write on these subjects in Hebrew rather than Arabic.

M. Waxman, *A History of Jewish Literature*, vol. I, 1960.

IBN EZRA, MOSES (c. 1055–after 1135) Spanish Hebrew poet. He was born in Granada, to a prominent and cultured family. His father held an honored position, his three brothers were noted scholars, and he himself received a sound Jewish

and Arabic education. He encouraged and befriended Judah Ha-Levi (q.v.), whom he invited to Granada. In 1090, however Granada came under the rule of the fanatic Moslem Almoravids and the Jewish community was destroyed. Moses managed to reach Christian Spain, but never returned to Granada, to which he was deeply attached. For most of his life, he was a wanderer in Spain, not succeeding in settling in a permanent home and often having difficulties in finding patrons to support his literary activities.

Apparently, his early life was overshadowed by a tragic love affair. He fell deeply in love with his niece (a relationship permitted by Jewish law) but his father interfered and she had to marry his younger brother. The wounds of this affair are reflected in his poetry as are some of his other sorrows: he felt that his brothers had not supported him in times of need and also had complaints about his children's behavior.

One of the great masters of Hebrew poetry, over 300 of his secular poems and some 220 religious poems are known. Much of his poetry is gloomy and morose, but at times he wrote about the joy of life, for example: "A beautiful woman, a cup of wine, a lovely garden, the song of a bird, the murmur of a brook are the cure of the lover, the joy of the lonely, the wealth of the poor, and the medicine for the sick." His poems take up themes of love, wine, and nature, as well as celebrating his many friendships.

The best-known of his secular works is his *Sefer ha-Anak* ("Necklace"), which contains 1,210 verse couplets; the lines in each end in homonyms. He also wrote a work in Arabic on rhetoric and poetics, which is a valuable source on the Hebrew poetry of medieval Spain and discusses a variety of other subjects, such as whether it is possible to compose poetry in a dream and whether the poetic gift of the Arabs was due to the climate of Arabia.

His greatest contribution lies in his religious verse, especially in his penitential poems (*selihot*). As an individual he is contrite, seeking forgiveness from God, if not for evil deeds, then for wrongful thoughts. He expresses the sadness of the Jewish people in exile, calling on man to examine his ways, and recognize the emptiness of life and its pleasures. Many of these poems found their way into the Sephardic prayer book. He also wrote, a poetic paraphrase of the book of Jonah, which was incorporated in the prayer rite of the Jews of Avignon.

Moses also wrote a philosophic work called *Arugat ha-Bosem* "Bed of Spices", dealing with the familiar subjects of medieval philosophy: the relationship between God and the universe, creation, and the nature of the soul and the intellect.

H. Brody and S. De Solis Cohen, *Selected Poems of Moses Ibn Ezra*, 1934.

IBN GABIROL, SOLOMON (c. 1020–c. 1057) Poet and philosopher in Spain, known in Latin sources as Avicebron, Avencebrol, and Avicembron. Ibn Gabirol's life was short and tragic. Born in Malaga, he was apparently orphaned at an early age and left without any family. In addition, from his youth he suffered from a malignant sickness.

Already as a boy he was an accomplished poet. He moved to Saragossa, which was noted for its learning; there he achieved a literary reputation by the age of sixteen and found a patron, who, however, was killed in an uprising. All these bitter experiences only enhanced his morose disposition and he lived a lonely life, dying in Valencia.

Ibn Gabirol is one of the greatest of medieval Hebrew poets and hundreds of his poems, sacred and secular, are known. The latter include poems on love, wine, and nature as well as didactic poems, elegies on his departed friends, and poems of friendship. He also wrote national verse in which he deplored the situation of the Jewish people in their exile and expressed his longing for redemption and the advent of the Messiah. However, he is best known for his sacred poetry, as he created a body of verse outstanding in its religious feeling and command of the Hebrew language. Many of these works entered the liturgy of Jewish communities, Sephardic and Ashkenazic alike. They are suffused with his love of the Divine and sometimes express a mystic longing to merge into God. His outstanding poetic composition is the long work, *Keter Malkhut* ("Royal Crown"), an ode to the Almighty, which is both a philosophical meditation and a prayer. It is divided into four sections: the first two are devoted to the names of God, the third is devoted to the nature of the universe, and the fourth is a prayer.

His major philosophical work is *Mekor Hayyim* ("Fountain of Life"). Written in Arabic (the original text has disappeared), it maintains that all things have matter and form, which are united in the universe by God's will. It presents a general system which is largely, but not entirely, neo-Platonic. Unlike other medieval works by Jewish thinkers, this book is devoid of biblical or Jewish references. It survived in its Latin translation, *Fons Vitae*, and was presumed to have been written by an Arab philosopher called Avicebron. As such, it exerted considerable influence on Christian thinkers of the 13th century. Only in the 19th century did the French scholar, Salomon Munk, discover a Hebrew translation and identified Avicebron with Ibn Gabirol.

Ibn Gabirol also wrote an ethical work, *On the Improvement of the Moral Quantities*. This was translated into Hebrew from the original Arabic and was popular in Jewish circles. The work relates personal characteristics and virtues to the five senses and describes what benefits and what harms the human soul.

I. Davidson (ed.), *Selected Religious Poems of Solomon Ibn Gabirol*, 1973.
I. Husik, *A History of Medieval Jewish Philosophy*, 1944, pp. 59–79.
B. Lewis, *Keter Malkhut: The Kingly Crown*, 1961.
R. Lowe, *Ibn Gabirol*, 1989.
S. S. Wise, *The Improvement of the Moral Qualities*, 1902.

IDELSOHN, ABRAHAM ZVI (1882–1938)

Musicologist. Originally from Latvia, Idelsohn began his studies in cantoral music (*hazzanut*) at Leipzig. He moved, for some to to the Stern Conservatory in Berlin and returned to the conservatory in Leipzig.

From 1903 to 1905, he was cantor at Regensburg, and then after a year in Johannesburg, went to Jerusalem, where he worked from 1906 to 1921. There he began his research into music preserved through the oral tradition by various Jewish communities.

In Jerusalem, Idelsohn also taught music and composed as well as lecturing at the Hebrew Teachers' College. In 1909 he received a research grant from the Academy of Science in Vienna, together with the gift of a phonograph; this enabled him to become a pioneer in the use of phonographic recordings to aid musicological fieldwork and research.

In 1910 Idelsohn founded the first Institute of Hebrew Music, and in 1914 he published the first of ten volumes of his *Thesaurus of Hebrew-Oriental Melodies*. This initial volume was devoted to the Yemenite Jewish tradition. The thesaurus itself was completed in 1932, and provided the musical world with the first in-depth studies and reports on the music of the Near Eastern Jews.

During World War I Idelsohn worked in Gaza as a bandmaster in the Turkish army; after the war, in 1919, he resumed his work in Jerusalem. He settled in Cincinnati in 1922 and in 1924 was appointed professor of Jewish Music at Hebrew Union College. Through his efforts this college became the major center for research in Jewish music in the United States.

Ibn Gabirol's "Shahar Avakkeshka"

At the dawn I seek Thee,
  Refuge, Rock sublime;
Set my prayer before Thee in the morning,
  And my prayer at eventime.

I before Thy greatness
  Stand and am afraid:
All my secret thoughts Thine eye beholdeth
  Deep within my bosom laid.

And, withal, what is it
  Heart and tongue can do?
What is this my strength, and what is even
  This, the spirit in me, too?

But, indeed, man's singing
  May seem good to Thee;
So I praise Thee, singing, while there dwelleth
  Yet the breath of God in me.

(Translated by Nina Salaman)

From 1930 his health began to deteriorate and he became physically incapacitated. In 1937 he joined his family in Johannesburg, dying the following year.

Idelsohn is remembered for many important ethnomusicological innovations, including the discovery that the musical heritage of the Near Eastern Jews possesses considerable originality. His wide knowledge of Jewish music, from the European Ashkenazic to the eastern Sephardic traditions, created the possibility of comparative ethnomusicological research. Idelsohn treated the "oral" traditions of development as seriously as the "written" traditions. In his studies of Near Eastern Maqany systems he pioneered research into aspects common to both Jewish and Christian liturgical music traditions. His writings include *Jewish Music in Its Historical Development* (1929). This classic work presents the result of the author's research in the field of Jewish music over a quarter of a century. His other works include *Sepher ha-Shirim* ("Hebrew Songs, 1922), *Tzelile ha-Aretz* ("Love and Folk Songs," 1922), *Jewish Song Book for the Synagogue* (1928), *The Kol Nidre Tune* (1931—1932), *Jewish Liturgy and Its Development* (1932), and *Parallels between the Old French and the Jewish Song* (1933).

I. Adler, B. Bayer, and E. Schleifer, *The A. Z. Idelsohn Memorial Volume: Yuval 5, 1986.*
A. Holde. *Jews in Music*, 1959.

ISAAC (c. 18th cent. BCE) Second of the three patriarchs of Israel. At his birth his father Abraham (q.v.) was one hundred years old and his mother Sarah (q.v.) ninety. When divine messengers foretold that Sarah would give birth at that age, she laughed, and thus the name Isaac was derived from the Hebrew verb *to laugh*. Abraham, who had previously despaired of having a child with Sarah, had fathered a son, Ishmael, with his wife's handmaid, Hagar. After the birth of Isaac, Sarah was jealous of any claims Ishmael may have had on the birthright and insisted on the expulsion of Ishmael and Hagar from the household. In later life, it is related that the two half-brothers came together to bury their father.

The sacrifice of Isaac. From a 6th century mosaic pavement in the synagogue of Beth Alpha in the Jezreel Valley.

The most traumatic event of Isaac's youth occurred when God ordered Abraham to sacrifice him (Genesis 19). It is generally thought that this occurred when Isaac was a youngster, but the rabbis reckoned that he was already thirty-seven at the time. Abraham took Isaac, as commanded, to the top of Mount Moriah and bound him to an altar in preparation for the sacrifice. Only at the last moment, when the knife was raised for the killing, did an angel stay his hand and explain that God had not intended the death of Isaac but was testing Abraham's faith. It has been suggested that the story was intended to warn against the custom of child sacrifice, which was common at the time.

After the death of Sarah (brought on, according to the rabbis, by the near sacrifice of her son), Abraham sent his servant to his relations in Mesopotamia to bring back a wife for his son from among his family, so that he would not intermarry with the daughters of the Canaanites. The bride was Isaac's cousin, Rebekah (q.v.). After a prolonged period of childlessness, she gave birth to twins, Esau and Jacob (q.v.).

Isaac lived with his family in southern Canaan where he was a successful farmer and cattleraiser. Indeed, so successful was he as an agriculturist that at one time his Canaanite neighbors sent him away out of envy. He became involved in a conflict with Philistines over the wells that had been dug by Abraham and by himself. Eventually, like his father, he concluded a treaty with the ruler of Gerar (Genesis 26).

In his old age, he lost his eyesight and this enabled his younger son, Jacob, conspiring with Rebekah, to deceive him into giving to Jacob the birthright which should have gone to the elder twin, Esau. Jacob had to flee to Mesopotamia to escape Esau's wrath.

Isaac lived to the age of 180 and was buried by his two sons, now reconciled, in the cave of Machpelah, the family tomb in Hebron.
N. Sarna, *Understanding Genesis*, 1966.

ISAAC, JULES (1877–1964) French historian. He was born into an assimilated family in Rennes. As a historian he was most active in writing history textbooks that were used in French schools until World War II. Among his better known works were studies of the origins of World War I, of popular prejudices, and of the suicidal trend of scientific progress. Isaac eventually rose to the rank of chief inspector of history education at the Ministry of Education in Paris.

His professional career as a historian was abruptly ended by the Nazi occupation of France. His wife and daughter were deported to the death camps. Prior to their departure, his wife succeeded in sending clandestinely a note to her husband, saying, "Save yourself for your work; the world is waiting for it."

In hiding during the war, Isaac devoted himself to studying the problem of anti-Semitism, which he believed, was rooted in the Christian teaching of contempt for the Jews and Judaism. After the war he also formulated an eighteen-point plan for the purification of Christian teaching regarding Jews. He played a major role at the 1947 Christian-Jewish Conference at Seeligsberg, Switzerland, during which the Christian participants published a ten-point plan that became the basis for subsequent dialogue between the two faiths. Isaac was invited to an audience by Pope Pius XII and told him that Nazi anti-Semitism was a secular radicalization of the anti-Jewish impulses of historic Christianity. The pope was moved to delete an anti-Jewish phrase from the Good Friday liturgy. Isaac also played an important role in persuading Pope John XXIII to propose that the Second Vatican Council (1962–1965) pass a declaration on Judaism that reworked the traditional accusation that the Jews of all time had been guilty of deicide, and opened a new era in Catholic-Jewish relations.

Isaac wrote *Jesus and Israel* (French, 1959; English, 1971); *La genèse de l'antisémitisme* (1956); and, at the age of eighty-five, *The Teaching of Contempt* (1964).

ISAACS, ISAAC ALFRED

ISAACS, ISAAC ALFRED (1855–1948) Australian statesman and governor-general of Australia, knighted 1928. Born in Melbourne, he was first educated by his parents and then in the local schools. He was a good pupil, but his inquiring mind took him off to the mining camps, where he learned to speak the languages of the gold diggers. His mother was an ambitious and dominating woman who had a strong influence over Isaacs throughout his life. From 1870 to 1875 he worked as a teacher in local schools, and then studied law at Melbourne University, graduating in 1883. In the course of his studies, he developed an amazing memory skill: he was able to quote from memory not only the general nature of documents, case law, legal theories, and judgments, but also their details. In 1882 he began practice at the Victoria bar and built up what became one of the most extensive private legal practices in the state. During his years at the bar, Isaac was an active freemason, and in 1889–1890 was the first grand registrar of the United Lodge of Victoria.

From 1892 to 1901 Isaacs served as a member of the Victorian legislative assembly; from 1893 he held the post of solicitor-general and from 1894 the post of attorney-general. He was active in support of social legislation, the control of gambling, and women's suffrage. He advocated the federation of the states of Australia and was a member of the commission that framed the commonwealth constitution (1897–1898). In 1901 he was elected to the first federal Australian parliament, was involved in the organization of the federal judicature, and in 1906 was appointed a justice of the federal high court, in which he served until appointed chief justice of Australia in 1930. In 1931 he was the first Australian-born person to be appointed governor-general of the Dominion of Australia and held the post until 1936.

After he retired in 1937, Isaacs wrote pamphlets and scholarly articles on biblical and religious subjects, and he published a series of articles on Jewish ethics prior to the Christian era. He wrote a weekly column for the New South Wales *Hebrew Standard* and for other Jewish and non-Jewish newspapers and periodicals.

Throughout his long public career, Isaacs showed kindness and friendliness to people in diverse walks of life. However, he was a determined, ambitious, and unrelenting man, which made him a controversial figure. He had a tendency to verbosity and his speeches were replete with references based on his wide reading in science, religion, and literature.

Isaacs was secretary of the Melbourne Jewish Young Men's Russian Relief Fund and was instrumental in founding the United Jewish Education Board, holding the post of president for a short time. However, from the mid-1890s he had little official connection with Jewish religious or other community organizations. Although he did not attend synagogue regularly, he was acutely aware of his Jewishness. Isaacs was deeply interested in Jewish religious doctrine and writings, and studied and wrote on such matters extensively. In public life he was very sensitive to anti-Semitic attacks and responded to them angrily.

Although his opposition to Zionism began in the 1920s, since he saw Zionism as posing complications of dual loyalty, only after his retirement did

Sir Isaac Isaacs as governor of Australia. Painting by John Langstaff, 1936. (In Parliament House, Canberra).

he speak out against political Zionism, calling the public protest made in 1941 against the British White Paper policy in Palestine as "un-Australian." In 1943 he published a series of articles in the *Hebrew Standard* denouncing political Zionism, claiming that Jewish nationalism had no validity since Jews were Jewish by religion only, and were citizens and nationals of Australia and other countries. He called those who opposed this view no less than traitors. However, the majority of the Jewish community vehemently objected to Isaacs using his standing in the non-Jewish community to express a minority opinion.

Z. Cowen, *Isaac Isaacs*, 1967.

M. Gordon, *Sir Isaac Isaacs, A Life of Service*, 1963.

ISAACS, NATHANIEL (1808–c. 1860) South African explorer; a founder of Natal. Born in England, at age fourteen he was sent to Saint Helena to work for his uncle, but soon took an opportunity to sail to the Cape of Good Hope. When the commander of the boat heard that a friend of his was lost in East Africa, Isaacs, then sixteen years old, agreed to help him search for the missing man. In 1825, their brig arrived in Port Natal but was totally wrecked; the surviving Europeans, among them Isaacs, had no way of leaving. They began to build a ship, which took three years to complete. Meanwhile Isaacs determined to make the best of the situation by cultivating the soil and instructing some of the natives in the vicinity.

The Europeans decided to explore the interior and reached the notorious Zulu king, Tchaka, who received them civilly. Isaacs, however, was shocked by the ghastly methods of torture commonly used at the court. Tchaka had only to nod his head and executioners would seize a score of people and kill them on the spot. The Europeans for their part were at Tchaka's mercy and any unfavorable whim could mean their end. Tchaka decided that his reputation would be boosted if the white men were to assist him in his wars. The Europeans gave Isaacs the responsibility of dissuading Tchaka from this plan, which he did by presenting the king with the white men's tent. Tchaka was so delighted that he excused the white men from fighting, confident that the tent would strike fear into the heart of his enemies.

Isaacs had to attend the royal kraal regularly and continued to witness massacres. At first the Europeans were protected and even favored, but relations became tense when two of the Europeans' servants committed a brutal crime against the wife of a Zulu chief. As punishment, Tchaka threatened to kill all the white men and only agreed to spare them on condition that Isaacs lead a war party against his enemies, the Swazis. Isaacs had to agree, and, thanks to his European weapons, scored a victory, although he himself was seriously wounded. His reputation, however, was established while Tchaka gave him a new name, Tamboosa (brave warrior), and made him a Natal chief.

He was granted a large area of land and extensive rights of trading with the Zulus.

He continued to live in Natal under Tchaka's successor and assassin, Dingaan. He ranged through Dingaan's lands, bartering brass armlets, beads of ivory, hippopotamus teeth, and cattle. He proposed the planting of sugar in Natal when he noticed the presence of a wild variety in its interior. For seven years he did his utmost to extend commerce with the British and was among the founders of Durban. He urged the British authorities to establish trade relations with Natal and pressed the British government to annex the territory. He trained the Zulus in agriculture and cattle raising. All this he achieved before the age of twenty-four, when he left Natal, never to return.

The British annexed Natal in 1843, but by then Isaacs was a trader in Sierra Leone. His book *Travels and Adventures in Eastern Africa* was published in 1836 and became a standard work for matters related to the tribes of southeastern Africa, especially the Zulus. In the words of a historian of Natal, "Isaacs was hardy, bold, keen in perception, resourceful in action. He came to Natal a mere boy, he departed a stripling — but he left a vivid impress on its nascent years."

H. G. Mackeurton, *The Cradle Days of Natal*, 1930.

ISAACS, RUFUS DANIEL, First Marquess of Reading (1860—1935) British lawyer and statesman. Son of a London fruit merchant, he was a rebellious child and at the age of sixteen spent a year at sea as a ship's boy. The family had lived for several generations in England; his great-uncle was the boxer, Daniel Mendoza (q.v.) and his uncle was lord mayor of London. At the age of nineteen he went into the stock market, but a few years later was suspended following his failure to meet his financial obligations. He then studied law and became a barrister in 1887. His forensic talents were spectacular and he enjoyed great success as leading counsel in many famous cases. Isaacs represented the crown in two sensational cases: the Seddon murder trial (where his cross-examination was crucial in obtaining a conviction) and the Archer-Shee ("Winslow Boy") case. He became very wealthy and received numerous honors, being elected to Parliament in 1904 as a Liberal Imperialist. In 1910 he was appointed attorney-general and also knighted. His career stagnated briefly because of his involvement in the Marconi scandal, in which he and other ministers were accused of benefiting from a government contract with the Marconi Company. Three months after a select committee cleared the ministers of the charges, Isaacs was made lord chief justice, the first (and so far, the only) Jew to hold the post. He was raised to the peerage, taking the title of Lord Reading.

During World War I he was sent by the British government to the United States where he negotiated a 500 million dollar war loan and was the key link between British Prime Minister David Lloyd George and President Woodrow Wilson (through his contacts with Colonel Edward House). He was special ambassador to Washington, convincing the American government to make a full commitment to the war. He also played a role in the postwar peace negotiations.

In 1920 he was appointed viceroy of India. There he tried to organize a roundtable conference and was willing to make concessions to the nationalists, but the conference never materialized. He temporarily reduced Gandhi's influence and blocked the noncooperation movement, leading to a period of peace and stability. His liberal sympathies and wide perceptions were appreciated by the various groups in India. On his return to England in 1926, he was made a marquess — the first commoner to rise to that rank since the Duke of Wellington. He then held various company directorships but was called back to public service as foreign secretary in the 1931 national government of Stanley Baldwin, but held office for only ten weeks.

Although always an open Jew, Isaacs had no religious identity and his reactions to Zionism were guarded. However, he did say in 1915, "the Jews ought to have a place of their own and a government of their own. They ought not to be fighting for their separate interests in the life of foreign nations."

N. B. Birkett, *Six Great Advocates*, 1962.

L. Broad, *Advocates of the Golden Age: Their Lives and Cases*, 1958.

H. M. Hyde, *Lord Reading: The Life of Rufus Isaacs, First Marquis of Reading*, 1968.

ISAIAH (late 8th cent. BCE) One of the major prophets of ancient Israel, whose prophecies are to be found in the biblical book of Isaiah. Modern scholarship maintains that only the first thirty-nine chapters of the book are to be attributed to Isaiah, son of Amoz, who lived in Judah in the reign of four kings: Uzziah, Jotham, Ahaz, and Hezekiah. The rest of the book (chaps. 40–66), it is held, was written by another prophet (whom the scholars call Deutero-Isaiah, i.e., Second Isaiah) during the Babylonian exile in the 6th century BCE. Some even identify a third author (Trito-Isaiah) as the author of the last eleven chapters (56–66) because the subject matter of this section appears to refer to the period of the prophets of Malachi and Zechariah after the return to Zion from the Babylonian exile.

Various theories have been propounded concerning Isaiah's origin. It has been suggested that his background was aristocratic, priestly, or prophetic. His wife was also a prophet and they had two children who were given symbolic names: Shear-Jashub ("a remnant shall return," implying that part of Judah would survive the expected onslaught of Syria and the northern kingdom) and Maher-Shalal-Hash-Baz ("the spoil speeds, the prey hastens," perhaps foretelling the defeat of Syria and the northern kingdom by the Assyrians).

A crucial event in his life was his first vision and call to prophecy. Here Isaiah "saw" God and accepted the mission to bring the divine message to the people of Israel, despite his own sense of inadequacy and realization of the opposition he was bound to encounter. He was appalled at the social and moral situation in the country, with its underprivileged being oppressed by a strong establishment and corrupt rulers, and the general decadence of the rich for whom he foretold a grisly fate when the Day of the Lord would arrive. His sympathies were with the poor and deprived, the defenseless, the widows, and the orphans who were at the mercy of depraved overlords. He proclaimed that God demands morality of his people and that it is an essential element in their covenant. The utterly unjust society in which his countrymen existed could only end in God cancelling the covenant. God would never be satisfied with the perfunctory performance of cult and ritual unless it was accompanied by an upright heart and a moral life. While God would save his people from peril if their behavior was righteous, he would not hesitate to chastise them for their immorality. At one time, Isaiah saw Assyria as the instrument of God's wrath, but then he attacked the Assyrian ruler for his pretentiousness in believing that his conquests had been achieved by himself and not by God. Indeed, in the reign of Ahaz, Isaiah confronted the king and demanded that he oppose the invading Assyrians as the danger to the country lay not in the external threat but in the internal wickedness and absence of trust in God.

In 701 BCE, when Jerusalem was under siege from the Assyrian king, Sennacherib, Isaiah stood out in his opposition to the generals who wished to seek help from Egypt. Calling Egypt a broken reed, Isaiah proclaimed that effective support can only come from God and that only a return to morality

---

FROM THE BOOK OF ISAIAH

- The ox knows its owner, the ass its master's crib (1:3).
- They shall beat their swords into plowshares, their spears into pruning hooks: Nation shall not take up sword against nations: They shall never again know war (2:4).
- The wolf shall dwell with the lamb and the leopard shall lie down with the kid (11:6).
- Eat and drink for tomorrow we die (22:13).
- The arid desert shall be glad, the wilderness shall rejoice and blossom like a rose (35:1).
- "Comfort ye, comfort ye, my people," says your God.
- "Speak tenderly to Jerusalem and declare to her that her term of service is over" (40:1–2).
- Grass withers, flowers fade — but the word of our God is always fulfilled (40:8).
- Thus said the Lord: "The heaven is my throne, and the earth my footstool" (66:1).

could save the people and the country. It was only God, not humans, who could rout the proud Assyrians.

Isaiah was not, however, a prophet solely of gloom and despair. He preached that the country would be saved by a return to a rightful way of life. Even in the event of a calamity, a remnant would survive and form the basis for a new beginning. His great vision of the ultimate reign of God, when the lion shall lie down with the lamb and the sword be beaten into a plowshare, became a universal expression of the dream for a world of perfect peace under the reign of God.

According to a late Jewish tradition, Isaiah was put to death in the reign of King Manasseh (698–642 BCE). In any case, there is no evidence that he continued to be active after Sennacherib raised the siege of Jerusalem in 701 BCE.

The second part of the book of Isaiah presupposes the fall of Jerusalem, which occurred in 586 BCE, and the exile to Babylonia. All indications are that it was written in Babylonia, which, it forecasts, would be conquered by the Persian ruler, Cyrus (mentioned by name), as a result of which the exiles would be redeemed. The traditional interpretation, recognizing the contrast in background and date, held that under the influence of prophecy, Isaiah was able to foresee events that would occur more than a century later.

The mood of the second part of the book contrasts sharply with the first part. Here, the prophet offers consolation, hope and reconciliation. The people have been punished for their sins and God is going to give them a new start. An important motif is the suffering servant, the servant of God who will proclaim truth and justice to the world. The passage has given rise to much argument: is the servant an individual or a collective? For Jews, the servant referred to Israel as a whole, the prophet, or a messiah; Christians identified the servant with Jesus.

The book ends on a note of triumphant hope. The exiles will be delivered, the Temple rebuilt, and in the glorious future, idolaters will be destroyed, and all nations will worship the one God.

S. H. Blank, *Prophetic Faith in Isaiah*, 1958.
S. B. Freehof, *The Book of Isaiah*, 1972.
A. J. Heschel, *The Prophets*, 1962.
J. L. McKenzie, *Second Isaiah*, 1968.

ISAK, ARON (also Isaac; 1730–1816) Founder of the Swedish Jewish community. Born in Germany, he began to earn his living as a peddler but taught himself seal-engraving, at which he proved talented and successful. During the Seven Years' War he learned from Swedish soldiers that no one in their country was practicing the craft and after the war, when his own business took a turn for the worse, he decided to try his luck in Sweden. No Jew had ever lived in the country and it took courage to go to a hostile environment as a pioneer.

Isak received letters of recommendation to the king of Sweden and a passport to visit the country and arrived in Stockholm in 1774. He first visited the lord mayor of Stockholm, to whom he had an introduction and who told him, "This is an extremely difficult matter. A Jew has never lived in Sweden. My friends recommend you highly but it is not in my power to grant your wish." He advised him, nonetheless, to persevere and promised that he would personally deliver Isak's petition for right of residence to the king. The king in turn forwarded the application to his council who replied, "We cannot permit you to practice your religion in this country, much less to engage in business." The lord mayor then suggested that Isak appeal and he was summoned to the town hall by the magistrates. Isak describes the scene in his memoirs (which he wrote in Yiddish): One of the magistrates addressed me in German saying "My dear Herr Aron, you have petitioned the king for the right to live here. We have all seen your recommendations. You have been praised as a man of character and an excellent craftsman. The king himself favors your remaining, especially as there is no other seal engraver in the kingdom. But your adherence to the Jewish religion is an insurmountable obstacle. Let me quote from our laws: 'If a Jew comes to our shores on a ship that requires repairs, that ship shall have precedence over all the others so that the Jew may leave as soon as possible. If a Jew becomes ill while the ship he is traveling on is in port, a doctor shall be sent to cure him as quickly as possible so that he can leave the realm quickly. A Jew may neither buy nor sell in our kingdom.' No Jew has lived in our kingdom since the beginning of time. But as it is the king's wish, we have decided to allow you to remain here. You cannot do this as a Jew because that would be against our laws; but if you accept Christianity you will have immediate citizenship and exemption from taxes for ten years. Think this over and let us have your decision within a week."

Isak replied immediately, "I do not need to think that over. I would not change my religion for all the gold in the world. I did not come here to trade in religion. How could I deny a faith through which I hope to gain salvation?"

The magistrate remarked, "We know nothing of the Jewish religion and its doctrine of salvation."

Isak responded, "I am not a learned man and this is not the place to expound religious doctrine. But I can tell you that the fundamental doctrine of Judaism is to fear God and love one's neighbors — and this I will do as long as I live."

The magistrates' decision was negative and Isak was on the verge of returning to Germany. He paid a last visit to the lord mayor, who was also chairman of the magistrates. The lord mayor told him that they had had no alternative in making their decision but added, "Why don't you institute a suit against me?" He directed Aron on how to make a legal protest to the king, who subsequently overruled the ban. When Isak at last received permission to live in Sweden from the king he hurried to thank the lord mayor whose reaction was, "I've done the Devil's work and prefer not to hear of it."

Isak brought his brother and partner to Stockholm and their business flourished. Following this precedent, other Jews began to settle in Stockholm and Isak headed its community for many years.
L. W. Schwartz, *Memoirs of My People*, 1963, pp. 166–181.

ISRAEL BEN ELIEZER See Baal Shem Tov

ISRAEL MEIR HA-KOHEN KAGAN, See Hafetz Hayyim

ISRAËLS, JOZEF (1824–1911) Dutch artist. Born in Gröningen, Holland, Israëls was both ardently Duthc and genuinely Jewish. In his childhood he learned Hebrew and Jewish wisdom and lore, and throughout his long life, his studio was always closed on the Sabbath.

As a child, Israëls attended art classes after school. When he was sixteen, he went to Amsterdam to study with Jan Adam Kruseman, a celebrated painter of historical pictures, and in 1841 he was admitted to the Academy of Fine Arts. He went to Paris in 1845, where he studied with Paul Delaroche and Horace Vernet. Back in Holland, he lived in Amsterdam and painted historical and biblical subjects. In 1855, however, after a severe illness, he visited the seashore to recuperate. In the fishing village of, Zandvoort, Israëls lived among the villagers and painted them at their everyday activities. The seashore changed his palette. His colors became light and brighter. The strong line of his earlier work was softened by the light. He was an impressionist a quarter of a century before the first impressionist exhibition in Paris.

Because of this break with contemporary style and subject matter, he found himself the leader of the Hague school, artists who painted life and landscape. He himself had moved to The Hague in 1871. His painting *The Shipwrecked Mariner* was exhibited in London and Paris; this marked the beginning of his popularity outside Holland, which quickly reached the United States. Art lovers and collectors were attracted by his sympathy for his subjects and his pictures which were felt to have "soul."

When Israëls was seventy-four, he went on a journey to Spain, Morocco, and Italy. His book *Spain*, a collection of notes and sketches, tells the story of the trip. Visiting the Jewish section of Tangier, he entered a dark room where a man asked him, in Hebrew, what he wanted. In Hebrew, Israëls greeted the man, and said he was a Jew from Holland. The man had never heard of Holland but he invited Israëls to enter the room There the artist found an old scribe, writing on parchment. When Israëls returned to Holland, he made a painting of this scene called *Torah Scribe*.

In 1910, Israëls's dealer, Goupil (Boussod, Valadon & Cie), held a retrospective exhibition to celebrate their fifty-year association. They had handled hundreds of his works, and were familiar with every aspect of his development.

When he died the following year, all Holland mourned. He was buried in the old Jewish cemetery in Scheveningen. The queen sent a representative to his funeral; streets and squares were named after him; and Groningen, his native city, erected a monument in his memory, depicting the fishermen that he had loved to paint.

Israëls's proficient work, whether oils, watercolors, or etchings, included many portraits. He made several sketches of the sitter and then painted the portrait from the sketches. Many of his paintings depicted Jewish subjects. One of the best known, *Son of the Ancient People*, is painted in drab colors and shows a sad Jewish man sitting in front of his drab store. Israëls's palette, though, was both rich and subtle. He worked with tones, gradations, and light that shimmers and vibrates. Although he himself always stressed the formal basis of his work — structure, the composition, and line — it is the artist's warmth, empathy, and humanism that is the hallmark of his work.

His son, Isaac Israëls (1865–1934), was also a distinguished painter. Influenced by the impressionists, many of his works reflect contemporary social life.
Boussod, Valadon & Cie, *Half a Century with Jozeph Israels*, 1910.
M. Eisler, *Jozef Israels*, 1924.
J.E. Pythian, *Jozef Israels*, 1912.

ISSERLES, MOSES (known by the acronym *Rema*; c. 1525–1572) Rabbi, scholar of religious law, and codifier in Poland. His father, Israel, was a wealthy leader of the Cracow community who, in 1553, received royal dispensation to build a synagogue in memory of his wife, which stands to this day under the name of the Rema Synagogue. It contains the pew where Moses prayed and in its adjoining graveyard are buried Moses and members of the Isserles family.

From a young age, Moses was an outstanding authority, thanks to his prodigious learning, wealth, and social position. The rabbinic academy that he established in Cracow was esteemed throughout Europe. He himself studied in Lublin and then returned to Cracow as its chief rabbi, a post he held until his death.

He first achieved a scholarly reputation through his responsa (replies to queries on matters of rabbinic law) and his decisions were accepted as authoritative. He was noted for his leniency on issues involving economic or social hardship, especially for the underprivileged.

He wrote commentaries and notes on the Bible and rabbinic literature, but is especially remembered for his supplements to the work of his contemporary Joseph Caro (q.v.). When Caro published his comprehensive work on Jewish law, *Beit Yoseph*, Isserles wrote *Darkhei Moshe* ("The Ways of Moses"), which was both a commentary and critique of Caro's work, stressing the intrinsic importance of local custom in the development of Jewish law and adding the views and practices of

Ashkenazic (Central European) rabbis and communities, which had been neglected by Caro who was writing out of the Sephardic (Spanish) tradition. Ten years later, Caro produced his *Shulhan Arukh* ("Prepared Table"), an abridgement of *Beit Yoseph*. Isserles feared that it would become universally accepted in Ashkenazic circles, and that they would forget their own traditions. He therefore wrote his *Mappah* (literally tablecloth, i.e., to cover the *Shulhan Arukh*), a supplement of Ashkenazic thought and practices. The combined work then became the standard guide to the practice of Judaism throughout the Jewish world, and has never been superseded in Orthodox circles. Apart from his writings on Jewish law, Isserles wrote on philosophy, mysticism, and the natural sciences. In *Torat ha-Olah* ("Law of the Offering"), concerned with the commandments related to the Temple, he combined philosophy and mysticism but stressed the primacy of religious law over both.

I. Twersky in J. Goldin (ed.), *The Jewish Expression*, 1976.

J

JABOTINSKY, VLADIMIR (Ze'ev; 1880–1940) Zionist leader; founder and head of the Revisionist movement in Zionism; author. Born in Odessa, he received a Jewish and general education and at a young age mastered Hebrew. He was early attracted to journalism and literature. Upon completing his high school education, he traveled to Bern and later to Rome, where he studied law and served as correspondent for Odessa newspapers. Upon his return to Russia in 1901, he embarked on a journalistic career and began to take part in local Zionist activity. At an early age he made his mark on Russian Zionism through the force of his personality, his literary and oratorical skills, and his ideology, which called for the need to educate Jews in

Vladimir (Ze'ev) Jabotinsky.

their traditional heritage and values, revive the Hebrew language and Jewish culture, and awaken in Jews pride in their nationhood.

When World War I broke out he covered the front line for the liberal Moscow newpaper, *Russkiya Vedomosti*. In 1915 he reached Egypt and began to advocate, together with Joseph Trumpeldor (q.v.), the creation of a Jewish army that would fight with the Allies against the Turks and help liberate Palestine. Later he continued this campaign in England and in Russia. His efforts were crowned with success when Britain set up the 38th Royal Fusilliers Battalion, in which Jabotinsky served as an officer in Palestine in 1918. He remained there and while still in uniform took part in local politics and served as the commander of the Jerusalem defense during the April 1920 Arab riots. For this he was tried and sentenced to fifteen years of hard labor. Released after a few weeks in Acre prison, he went to London and participated in the July 1920 Zionist conference. He was one of the founders of Keren Hayesod, the fund-raising arm of the World Zionist Organization. A year later he was elected member of the Zionist Executive and engaged in Zionist work in England and in Palestine. He resigned from this post early in 1923, in protest over what he considered the openly pro-British policy pursued by Chaim Weizmann (q.v.), president of the World Zionist Organization. Two years later, in Berlin, he established the Revisionist movement.

His brand of Zionism stressed political work and action designed to lead to the early establishment of a Jewish state on both banks of the river Jordan. He opposed the 1922 partition of Palestine that led to the creation of Transjordan. He called upon the Zionists to issue a clear-cut definition of their goals, and demanded unrestricted mass immigration to Palestine instead of the gradualist policy accepted by the official Zionist leadership. At the time he also began to develop his ideas about the need to build a Jewish fighting force for any eventuality. He emphasized the need to build paramilitary organizations to mobilize the masses. He opposed the Marxist idea of class warfare and thought that Palestine should be built through the efforts of private capital and private enterprise, thereby clashing with the dominant Labor movement in Palestine.

As president of the Revisionist and of the Betar (Revisionist youth) movements, he traveled around the world, but his largest following was among Polish Jewry, whose impending destruction he foretold long before the Holocaust. The gap between Jabotinsky and the official Jewish leadership in Palestine grew. He was barred by the British mandatory government from living in Palestine, especially after he advocated a policy of active defense and retaliation against Arab terrorists following the 1929 riots. In 1934 he entered into an agreement with David Ben-Gurion (q.v.) to ease the tensions between the Revisionist and the Labor movements in Palestine, but a majority of the Labor membership refused to ratify the agreement. A year later he seceded from the World Zionist Organization, which he accused of ineptitude and of abandoning the political vision of Theodor Herzl (q.v.). He established and headed the New Zionist Organization, the main preoccupation of which in the late 1930s was to evacuate as many Jews as possible from eastern Europe to Palestine, through illegal immigration if need be. During the 1936–1939 Arab rebellion in Palestine, he called for an end to the policy of self-restraint practiced by the official Jewish underground, Haganah, and was instrumental in establishing the activist Palestine underground, the Irgun Tzevai Leumi (Etzel), which he directed from overseas. That body began a series of retaliatory actions against Arabs and the British in Palestine. In 1937 he appeared before a British royal commission and spoke against the proposed scheme to partition Palestine on ideological grounds and because he felt that the proposed size of the Jewish area would not be large enough for the 1.5 million Jews evacuated from eastern Europe. On the eve of World War II, Jabotinsky was living in Paris; he later moved to London. He wanted to pressure the Polish and Romanian governments into pushing Britain to revise its immigration policies, but the effort was unsuccessful. His last effort was to bring about the creation, once again, of a Jewish army within the framework of the British army to fight the Nazis.

He died near New York and was buried there. According to his wishes, his remains were reinterred by the government of Israel in a state ceremony, in 1964, on Mount Herzl in Jerusalem.

Jabotinsky was one of the most prominent of Zionist leaders. A charismatic personality, fluent in seven languages, and a master orator and writer, he charmed the masses and world leaders, but during his lifetime was not among the major decision makers in the Zionist movement. After World War II, the Labor leaders of the Yishuv adopted aspects of his strategy when they created Israel through an armed struggle, first against the British mandate and then against the invading Arab forces. His disciples came to power in Israel only in 1977, when Menachem Begin became prime minister.

He was a prolific author in Hebrew, Russian,

> The first aim of Zionism is the creation of a Jewish majority on both sides of the Jordan River. This is not the ultimate goal of the Zionist movement, which aspires to more far-reaching ideals, such as the solution of the question of Jewish suffering throughout the entire world and the creation of a new Jewish culture. The precondition of these noble aims, however, is a country in which the Jews constitute a majority. It is only after this majority is attained that Palestine can undergo a normal political development on the basis of democratic, parliamentary principles without thereby endangering the Jewish national character of the country.
>
> **Vladimir Jabotinsky in 1926**

and English. His best-known work was the biblical novel, *Samson the Nazirite* (1926) written in Russian (and used as the basis for the Hollywood film, *Samson and Delilah*). He translated Poe's "The Raven" and Dante's *Inferno* into Hebrew and the poems of Chaim Bialik (q.v.) into Russian.

J. B. Schechtman, *Jabotinsky: Rebel and Statesman*, 1956.

J. B. Schechtman, *Jabotinsky: Fighter and Prophet*, 1961.

JACOB   (c. 18th cent. BCE) He was born to Isaac (q.v.) and Rebekah (q.v.) and was the younger twin of Esau. His story is told in the book of Genesis. According to popular etymology, he was born holding Esau's heel, hence the name Jacob, derived from the Hebrew word for "heel." However, before the birth it was predicted to Rebekah that the younger son would rule the elder, and indeed the relationship of the siblings was characterized by a strong rivalry, perhaps reflecting the sociological tensions between the hunter (Esau) and the husbandman (Jacob).

On one occasion when Esau returned from the hunt, weary and hungry, he requested a meal from Jacob (a dish of lentils, better known from the heading to Genesis 25 in the Genevan Bible as "a mess of pottage"). Jacob's condition for feeding his brother was that Esau grant him the birthright, to which Esau agreed. Later Jacob obtained the blessing his father had intended for the firstborn through a deceit concocted with his mother, who favored her younger son. Isaac had gone blind and could not distinguish between the twins. At his mother's bidding, Jacob covered his hands and neck with goat skins and Isaac, on touching him, accepted that he was the hairy Esau. Despite his suspicion ("The voice is the voice of Jacob but the hands are the hands of Esau"), he gave Jacob the blessing of the firstborn. When Esau discovered the deception, he plotted to kill Jacob, who fled for his life to his mother's family in Paddan-Aram, Mesopotamia. En route, he had a dream vision at

children, eponymous ancestors of the Twelve Tribers. According to Genesis Jacob died at the age of 147 and his body was taken by his children for burial in the family grave in Hebron in the cave of Machpelah. N. Sarna, *Understanding Genesis*, 1966.

JACOB BEN ASHER (c. 1270–1340) Rabbinic codifier and Bible commentator in Spain. He studied in his native Germany with his father, Asher ben Yehiel (q.v.), with whom he moved to Toledo, Spain, in 1303. In order not to be distracted from his studies, he refused any rabbinical office and at times lived in great poverty. His education was almost entirely rabbinic and he had little secular learning.

His first significant work was an abridgment of his father's commentary on the Talmud, citing its decisions but omitting the discussions. Like his

---

THE FOUR PARTS OF THE *TUR*

1. *Orah Hayyim* ("The Path of Life," see Ps. 16:11) on the laws of Jewish religious conduct from waking up in the morning until going to sleep at night — blessings, prayers, and synagogue ritual; observance of the Sabbath, festivals, and fast days.

2. *Yoreh De'ah* ("The Teaching of Knowledge," see Isa. 28:9) on forbidden and permitted things (*issur ve-hetter*), including dietary laws, family purity, oaths, charging interest, and mourning.

3. *Even ha-Ezer* ("The Stone of Help," see I Sam. 5:1) on laws concerning women, notably marriage and divorce.

4. *Hoshen Mishpat* ("The Breastplate of Judgment," see Ex. 28:15) on civil jurisprudence and legal procedure.

---

father, he was devoted to the upgrading of Talmudic studies in Spain and to the coordination of the rabbinic traditions of Spain and Germany.

His greatest work was the *Arba'ah Turim* ("Four Rows," referring to the rows of precious stones, which served as oracles, on the breastplate of the high priest; cf. Exodus 28:17). From this book, he was widely known as *Ba'al ha-Turim* ("author of the Turim"). The quadrapartite division of the book became the basis for the *Shulhan Arukh* of Joseph Caro (q.v.) and through Caro they were accepted as the standard divisions of Jewish legal codification. The *Tur*, as the work was popularly known, owed much to the *Mishneh Torah*, the codification of Moses Maimonides (q.v.), but unlike his predecessor, Jacob summarized the diverse viewpoints of previous authorities, usually ending the discussion with the views of his father. Like his father, he omitted all laws that were related to the Temple or relevant only when living in the Land of Israel. Much of the material reflects the author's

---

THE CHILDREN OF JACOB

From his wife, Leah: Reuben, Simeon, Levi, Judah, Issachar, Zebulun; Dinah
From his wife, Rachel: Joseph, Benjamin
From his concubine, Bilhah: Dan, Naphthali
From his concubine, Zilpah: Gad, Asher

Bethel in which he saw angels ascending and descending a ladder to heaven. At the top was God, who promised Jacob and his numerous progeny divine protection and possession of the Land of Canaan.

In Paddan-Aram, Jacob worked for his mother's brother, Laban, whose daughters, Leah (q.v.) and Rachel (q.v.), he married in return for fourteen years' work in minding Laban's sheep. Susequently he used a stratagem to acquire for himself a large part of Laban's flocks. Relations between the two became strained and Jacob decided to return to Canaan. On the way, at the ford of the Jabbok River, he encountered a mysterious being, traditionally thought to be an angel, with whom he wrestled through the night. Before leaving at daybreak, Jacob was told that his name had been changed to Israel (from the Hebrew word "to strive") "for you have striven with God and with men and have prevailed." The Bible, however, continues to use the name Jacob.

Jacob was informed that his brother, Esau, was approaching with a large troop of men. He feared that Esau still sought to kill him, but the encounter proved to be a reconciliation. He then settled in Shechem, but after the rape of his daughter, Dinah, by Shechem, his sons sacked the town and he moved to Bethel. His partiality to his son, Joseph (q.v.), provoked his other sons into selling Joseph into slavery in Egypt, where Joseph became the country's vizier. When famine affected Canaan, Jacob and his other sons moved to Egypt, where Joseph settled them in the territory of Goshen. During his last illness Jacob blessed Joseph and his sons, Ephraim and Manasseh, and then his other

Jacob's dream. From an 18th-century bookbinding.

own single-minded piety. The language is clear and the style simple, which contributed to the work's great popularity throughout the Jewish world.

Jacob ben Asher was also the author of a Bible commentary strongly influenced by Nahmanides (q.v.), although he omitted the latter's mystical explanations and concentrated on literal meaning. Each section opens with a preface in which Jacob's explanations lean heavily on wordplay and numerology as well as the orthography of the traditional text. These prefaces were widely appreciated and were reprinted in many editions of the Hebrew Bible.

M. Waxman, *A History of Jewish Literature*, vol. 2, 1960.

JACOBI, KARL GUSTAV JACOB (1804–1851)
German mathematician who made fundamental contributions to the fields of mathematical analysis, number theory, geometry, and mechanics, and who, with the Norwegian Niels Henrik Abel, created the theory of elliptic functions.

The name of Jacobi crops up frequently in the sciences, though not always in reference to the same man. In the mid-19th century there was a prominent German physicist, then working in Saint Petersburg, named Moritz Hermann Jacobi (1801–1874), who had a comparatively obscure younger brother, Karl Gustav Jacobi. But while Moritz's chief fame, as founder of the fashionable quackery of galvanoplastics, was only transitory, Karl achieved an enduring reputation, and influenced most branches of mathematics, as well as mechanics and the future science of quantum mechanics.

The Jacobi brothers were the eldest of the four children of a prosperous banker in Potsdam. From the first, Karl Gustav Jacobi gave evidence of what the rector of his gymnasium termed "a universal mind"; however, it was to mathematics that he was most strongly drawn. After a protracted tussle, in which Karl rebelled at learning mathematics by heart and rule, his teacher left him to work on his own. This early self-instruction molded his genius into the form that was later to generate his masterpiece, the theory of elliptic functions, which has been said to be to 19th-century mathematical analysis what Columbus's discovery of America was to 15th-century geography. His formalistic, as opposed to idealistic, approach made Jacobi the natural successor to Euler, the master of ingenious devices; for sheer manipulative ability in tangled algebra, Euler and Jacobi have had no rival.

Both Karl and his brother Moritz converted to Christianity so as to be eligible for salaried academic tenures. Karl was for eighteen years a professor at the University of Königsberg, until diabetes forced him to move to the gentler climate of Berlin. However, an unfortunate political imprudency soon cost him his secure status at the University of Berlin and, having lost his inherited fortune in a bankruptcy some years previously, he was forced to move to Gotha. It was only when he was on the verge of accepting a professorship in Vienna, in 1849, that the Prussian government, realizing the damage to its credibility that Jacobi's departure would engender, reinstated him on his original terms at Berlin.

Jacobi's tireless activity throughout his lifetime produced impressive results in both mathematical research and academic instruction and generated a revival of interest in mathematics within German academic circles. His innovative teaching methods involved lecturing on his own latest discoveries in order to imbue mathematics with the life that had been so conspicuously absent from the education offered to his own generation of students.

Jacobi did not suffer an early death from overwork, as some of his friends had predicted, but from smallpox in his forty-seventh year.

L. Konigsberger, *Karl Gustav Jacob Jacobi* (German), 1904.

JAKOBSON, ROMAN (1896–1982)
Philologist and linguistic literary theoretician; one of the founders of structuralism. Born and raised in Moscow, he recalled being captivated, as a boy of ten, by the task of compiling long lists that illustrated the different meanings of grammatical cases. The small boy who loved grammar grew up to be an eminent scholar in the fields of linguistics and Slavic studies, and made notable contributions in phonology, literature, anthropology, communication sciences, and art history.

Jakobson studied first at Moscow University and then at Prague University, where he obtained his Ph.D. At the age of nineteen, with six other students, he founded the Moscow Linguistic Circle to study linguistics, poetics, metrics, and folklore. The circle has been grouped, in the history of literary criticism, under the heading of Russian Formalism, a school that rejected biographical or cultural interpretations of literary works and insisted on concentrating instead on the literary devices used in the text itself. Although Jakobson himself later rejected various aspects of Russian formalism, some of his basic ideas took root there.

In Prague he was a founder of the Cercle Linguistique de Prague, which established the Prague school of structural linguistics, studying primarily phonology, morphology, poetics, and the history of Slavic language and literature. Jakobson understood structuralism as a general science for the systematization of all other systems and believed that all languages have a similar fundamental structure. Departing from the classic structuralist approach of the Swiss linguist Ferdinand de Saussure, Jakobson proposed that the method for studying the function of speech sounds could be applied both synchronically (i.e., to language as it exists) and diachronically (i.e., to language as it develops and changes), unlike Saussure, who believed that the principles of each methodology were distinct and mutually exclusive.

In the 1930s Jakobson taught at Masaryk University in Brno, Czechoslovakia, as a professor of

Russian philology from 1933, and of Czech literature from 1937. He fled the Nazis in 1939, moving from the University of Copenhagen, to Oslo, and Uppsala (Sweden). During these years in flight, he began his studies on childhood and aphasia. In 1941 he emigrated to the United States. He was a professor at Columbia University from 1946 to 1949 and at Harvard from 1949 to 1967, where he taught his future colleague and the founder of transformational grammar, Noam Chomsky. Jakobson received a lifetime position at the Massachusetts Institute of Technology in 1967. During his years in the United States he met the anthropologist Claude Lévi-Strauss who said that Jakobson was a scholar who "has not only raised the same problems [as Lévi-Strauss] but has already solved them well."

Fluent in six languages, and able to read twenty-five, Jakobson wrote some six hundred papers, including "Child Language, Aphasia, and Phonological Universals" (1941) and "Preliminaries to Speech Analysis" (1952). Various collections of his work have appeared in several langauges, among them *Selected Writings* (1971–1982). He had just completed *Dialogues* (1983) at the time of his death.

D. Armstrong and C. H. van Schooneveld, (eds.) *Roman Jakobson — Echoes of His Scholarship*, 1977.

E. Holenstein, *Roman Jakobson's Approach to Language*, 1976.

JAMES, HARRY (1916–1983) U.S. trumpet player and band leader. A flamboyant and exciting trumpet player, who played popular hits for over forty years, James seemed destined for performing from birth. His father was a circus director and trumpet player, while his mother was a trapeze artist who continued performing until one month before Harry James was born.

Harry learned to play the drums at the age of four. When he was eight, he began to learn to play the trumpet; at the age of nine he was playing in his father's band; at ten he was playing solos, and two years later he was leading his own circus band.

James traveled with the circus as a contortionist for several years, and then settled with his family in Texas. He had played with various local bands and been turned down for a place with Lawrence Welk when he caught the attention of Ben Pollak, formerly of Benny Goodman's [q.v.] band. After playing with Pollack's orchestra for two years, he was invited to join Goodman's group, where, with Ziggy Elman and Chris Griffen, he played in the "powerhouse trio," one of the most famous big band trumpet sections in jazz history. Two years later, in 1939, he formed his own band. He invited an unknown young vocalist named Frank Sinatra to join, but the soon-to-be-famous singer shortly left James for more lucrative positions.

As a musician James was most popular not only for his skill as a jazz trumpeter, but also for emotional renditions of romantic ballads such as "You

Made Me Love You," which left the critics lukewarm, but drove his listeners wild with excitement. Inspired by his success with this first ballad, James introduced others and became an overnight sensation. Before long he was appearing on radio programs and making records that sold millions. His popularity increased even further when he married famous actress and pin-up girl, Betty Grable. During their marriage, he himself made appearances in films such as *Do You Love Me* and *Springtime in the Rockies.*

Although the big-band era came to an end in the late 1940s, James was one of the last band leaders to keep a band. He settled in the later part of his life in Nevada, where he also became interested in racing and baseball. He last performed on the trumpet just a few weeks before his death.

JAVITS, JACOB KOPPEL (1904–1986) U.S. Republican Senator and attorney. Born on Manhattan's Lower East Side, which he called "the right place for a New York politician of my generation," Javits came from the intersection of Orchard and Stanton Streets, a particularly bustling Jewish market area, with small shops, clothing stalls, pushcarts, and crowded tenement buildings. His father, like many other Jewish immigrants, began working in the garment industry on the Lower East Side until he became the janitor of several tenement buildings.

Born in one of these buildings, Javits was to spend the first and most influential thirteen years of his life in this corner of the immigrant ghetto. It was here that he discovered his talent for persuasion as he helped his mother hawk used kitchenware. Critical of his father, who passed favors for the Democratic Tammany Hall, Javits developed a distaste for petty corruption and this aversion was to be at the core of his commitment to public service. Even as a young child, he was acutely aware of the diverse ethnic groups surrounding his Jewish part of the ghetto: Italians, Irish, Germans lived to the west, and Jews from Russia, Austria-Hungary, Poland, and the Baltic countries to the east, all struggling to become American.

Having started to work as a young child, Javits sold lithographic supplies by day in order to finance his studies at Columbia University by night. Upon obtaining a law degree from New York University, he went into partnership with his brother and made a reputation as a trial lawyer. During World War II he served with the U.S. Army, leaving with the rank of lieutenant colonel. He was drawn to politics by the New York mayor, Fiorello La Guardia (q.v.). He was first elected to the Senate in 1956, after having served in the House of Representatives for eight years (1946–1954) and as attorney general for New York State. His massive influence on voters was remakable and he won as a Republican candidate when New York had been voting consistently for the Democrats.

However, he was, not immediately accepted in the inner circles of Senate power. He was an outsider partly due to his reputation as a maverick who, as a Liberal Republican, often held Democratic views, and partly due to his different background and social habits. Unlike most senators, Javits was known for his unfailing attendance at Senate committee meetings, where he would readily plunge into every available political debate of the postwar era. In a national poll of 1980, he was ranked the third most persuasive debator and the fourth most respected senator. He was reelected to the Senate eight times, serving for twenty-four years. In his autobiography he emphasizes the stimulating "ebb and flow of debate" and the "philosophical tensions" inherent in the work of the senator — a job consisting of "balancing lofty principles against sectional or selfish interests, welding together antagonistic human and economic and ideological forces into the coherent schemes of governance that we call laws."

In the hope of preventing future Vietnams, Javits was instrumental in the drafting the War Powers Resolution of 1973 and in its passage over President Richard M. Nixon's veto. This was the first time in over two hundred years of American history that an attempt was made to draw the line between the presidential and congressional powers, thus limiting the president's power as commander-in-chief. In 1974 Javits helped create the Pension Reform Act as well as the National Endowment for the Arts. He was a leading proponent of civil rights, foreign affairs, and progressive labor legislation. As an active supporter of Israel, he was of great influence in galvanizing public opinion and in working toward a harmonious relationship between the United States and Israel. From 1969 he was a member of the Senate Foreign Relations Committee. Afflicted with a paralyzing nerve disorder toward the end of his life, Javits continued to demonstrate the phenomenal drive and energy that characterized him throughout his lifetime. He kept up with a busy schedule of speeches and continued to be active in important issues such as rights for the terminally ill.

He was the author of several books, among which are *Discrimination in the U.S.A.*, *Order of Battle*, and *Who Makes War?*

J. K. Javits, and K. Steinberg, *Autobiography of a Public Man*, 1981.

JEREMIAH (7th–6th cent. BCE) Second of the three major biblical prophets. He was born at Anathoth, near Jerusalem, to a priestly family. He moved to Jerusalem, where his long career coincided with the decline and end of the Assyrian Empire and the rise of Babylonia. More is known of his personal life than of that of other prophets. He never married, as a sign that children would not survive (Jer. 16:1–4), and he did not participate in mourning or festive occasions as an indication that in the calamitous future, none would remain to mourn or rejoice (Jer. 16:5–8). His prophecies aroused bitter hostility and there were plots to kill him; he was confined to the stocks in the Temple

for predicting the destruction of Jerusalem and he was tried for blasphemy.

Jeremiah first prophesied in 626 BCE, during the reign of King Josiah, initially speaking out against apostasy and idolatry. He was shocked by the sinfulness of the citizens of Jerusalem and fearlessly spoke out against it. He gave a sermon in the Temple stressing the contradiction between the behavior of the populace and the ideals conveyed by the Temple, and foretold that if they did not repent, the Temple would be destroyed. On occasion, he made his point by symbolic actions, such as wearing a yoke to indicate the captivity which would be the lot of the people. The priests, as well as the people, were infuriated by his teachings and sought his death. As a precaution, in the year 605 he dictated his teachings to his scribe and amanuensis, Baruch, for the latter to read in public in the Temple. When these were read to the king, Jehoiakim, he had them destroyed column by column. He wished, also, to kill the prophet, but Jeremiah escaped and, foretelling that the king would have the burial of an ass, proceeded to dictate an expanded version of his words.

Jeremiah's political views were particularly unpopular. After the first exile to Babylonia in 597, he consistently preached submission to Babylonia, advising those who had been carried off to Babylonia to make the most of their exile and to continue to observe their religion, as God was present in all lands and could be worshiped far from the cultic center in Jerusalem. He regarded the Babylonian ruler, Nebuchadnezzar, as a divine instrument who was executing the will of God. Eventually the Babylonians, for their part, would receive due punishment, but meanwhile they were to be endured. When King Zedekiah decided to resort to arms in a desperate attempt to fight the Babylonians, Jeremiah openly opposed him, warning that the move was destined to be futile and would bring disaster. He was thrown into a damp cistern with the hope that he would starve to death, but was rescued by an Ethiopian eunuch.

After Nebuchadnezzar captured Jerusalem, destroyed the Temple, and exiled the aristocracy, Jeremiah remained in Judah, enjoying the respect of the conquerors because of his known pro-Babylonian orientation. He urged those who remained to live in peace, but, after the murder of the Babylonian-appointed governor, Gedaliah, the community, fearing vengeance, turned to Jeremiah and asked him for divine guidance on whether they should remain or flee for their lives to Egypt. When Jeremiah advised them to stay, his decision was rejected and the people fled to Egypt, forcibly taking Jeremiah and Baruch along with them. Jeremiah is last heard of in Egypt, still condemning manifestations of idolatry and still proclaiming the future victory of the Babylonians, this time against the Egyptians.

It was traditionally thought, though probably erroneously, that Jeremiah was the author of the book of Lamentations and for this reason he

FROM THE BOOK OF JEREMIAH

- Saying "Peace, peace" — when there is no peace (6:14).
- Is there no balm in Gilead? Is there no physician there? (8:22).
- Thus says the Lord: "Let not the wise man glory in his wisdom, let not the mighty man glory in his might, let not the rich man glory in his riches; but let him who glories, glory in this, that he understands and knows me, that I am the Lord who practice steadfast love, justice and righteousness in the earth" (9:23-24).
- Can the Ethiopian change his skin or the leopard his spots? Then also you can do who are accustomed to do evil (13:23).
- Fear not, O Jacob my servant, says the Lord, nor be dismayed O Israel; for lo I will save you from afar, and your offspring from the land of their captivity. Jacob shall return and have quiet and ease, and none shall make him afraid (30:10).
- In those days they shall no longer say "The fathers have eaten sour grapes and the children's teeth are set on edge" but every one shall die for his own sin; each man who eats sour grapes, his teeth shall be set on edge (31:29-30).

Sir George Jessel. Caricature by Spy.

received the reputation of a mournful prophet (cf. the English word "jeremiad"). Yet an examination of the book of Jeremiah shows that his basic message is one of hope. Although condemning the national guilt of his contemporaries, he maintains his faith in God's power and will to save. He is sure that the worship of God will survive and that eventually the Jews will return to their land, purified and devoted to God. This restoration will encompass not only those exiled in his time but the earlier exile of the ten tribes of the Northern Kingdom. He foresees a new covenant being made between God and Israel, and the Law henceforth being written not merely on tablets of stone, but on the heart of every Jew. Jeremiah also stresses the primacy of the ethical law, without which ritual has no meaning, as well as the eternal nature of Israel and its relationship to God.

J. Bright, *Jeremiah*, 1965.
A. J. Heschel, *The Prophets*, 1962.

JESSEL, GEORGE (1824–1883) British jurist, knighted 1872. Born in London, the son of a diamond merchant, he was educated at a Jewish school and studied philosophy and mathematics as well as botany at the University of London. He then studied law, and in 1847 began to practice at Lincoln's Inn, soon becoming eminent as a chancery lawyer. In 1865 he was made a queen's counsel.

In 1868 Jessel entered Parliament as the Liberal member for Dover and in 1871 was appointed solicitor general in Gladstone's administration, the first Jew to become a minister of the crown. In 1873 Jessel was appointed master of the rolls, a post which gave him precedence after the lord chief justice, becoming the first Jew to wear the judicial ermine in England. He became president of the chancery division of the court of appeal, and was a member of the committee of judges making rules and procedures for the high court of justice and the court of appeal. From 1873 to 1883 he was head of the Patent Office.

Jessel was averse to writing, and during the years on the bench his powerful memory enabled him to dispense with notes and he usually delivered his judgment immediately at the end of a case. He advocated remodeling the bankruptcy law and criticized the English legal system, claiming that it should be based on Roman law.

He was active in the management of the University of London, of which he was vice-chancellor from 1880 until his death. He was a member of the royal commission which led to the Medical Act of 1886, the vice-president of the council of legal education and a fellow of the Royal Society.

Sir George was a good Hebrew scholar and his activities on behalf of the Jewish community included membership of the council of Jews' College from its inception in 1855 until 1863 and helping to draft its constitution. He was also a vice-president of the Anglo-Jewish Association.

A. P. Peters, *Decisions of Sir George Jessel*, 1883.

JOACHIM, JOSEPH (1831–1907) Austro-Hungarian violinist, composer, teacher, and conductor. He was born in Kitsee (now Kopcseny), and when he was two years old his family moved to Pest, where the young boy began to study the violin. At the age of eight Joachim gave his first public performance as a violinist. Two years later he was sent to study at the Vienna Conservatory. In 1843 Joachim performed in Leipzig, where the composer Felix Mendelssohn (q.v.) accompanied him on the piano. Mendelssohn declared that Joachim needed no more violin tuition, although he could benefit from advice and criticism. Playing duos with Mendelssohn provided the young violinist with many musical insights. Mendelssohn said of him "of all the young talents that are now going into the world, I know none that is to be compared with this violinist. It is not only the excellence of his performances, but the absolute certainty of his becoming a leading artist."

Joachim's first major post was as concertmaster at Weimar, where Liszt was conducting (1850). Joachim became an integral part of the local musical scene, and in 1851 inaugurated a series of chamber music soirees. The following year Joachim was appointed violinist to King George V in Hanover, and took the opportunity to disassociate himself from Liszt, who had never really favored the young violinist. When Joachim heard Liszt conduct some of the violinist's own compositions, he commented, "A more vulgar misuse of sacred forms, a more repulsive coquetting with the noblest of feelings for the sake of effect, has never been attempted. I shall never want to meet Liszt again, because I should want to tell him that instead of taking him for a mighty errant spirit striving to return to God, I have suddenly realized that he is a cunning contriver of effects, who has miscalculated."

These are the words of a musician who firmly believed that music should be played for the sake of the music itself and those who composed it, and not as a vehicle to display virtuosity. Although Joachim could have become a virtuoso violinist, he opted to devote his career to the cause of what he considered to be the best music. It was Joachim who established the violin recital as known today, and he who made chamber music a popular art form throughout Europe and especially in England, where his annual concerts were eagerly awaited.

In 1863 Joachim married the singer Amalie Weiss. They had six children, but their marriage was far from harmonious. Weiss always insisted on being the center of attention and also suffered from long periods of ill health. Joachim was never happy with her, and in 1881 accused his wife of having an affair, implying that their sixth child was illegitimate. Weiss was found innocent in a court case, but her husband filed a divorce suit.

In Hanover Joachim developed a close friendship with Clara and Robert Schumann, as well as with the composer Johannes Brahms, who praised the performances of his early chamber composi-

JOACHIM PROTESTS ANTI-SEMITISM

Joachim, like many Jewish musicians at the time, was baptized in order to secure a post at court. But he never denied his ancestry. and when he encountered anti-Semitism in Hanover he felt compelled to resign. This happened when a Jewish member of the orchestra, a Mr. Grun, was denied promotion because he was a Jew. Joachim wrote the following letter on behalf of the musician:

"If Herr Grun, in spite of his excellent services and fidelity to duty, acknowledged by all his superiors, and after years of patient waiting, is not to be promoted after I have called attention to the matter, *because he is a Jew*, and if, for this reason, the promises made to me on behalf of a higher authority are not fulfilled, then according to my idea of honor and duty, I shall have no alternative but to justify myself by retiring from my appointment at the same time as Herr Grun. If I remained in my present position after the rejection of Herr Grun I should never be able to get over the purely personal feelings that because I had become a member of the Christian church I had gained worldly advantage and had obtained a privileged position in the Royal Hanoverian Orchestra, while others of my race were forced into humiliating situations."

tions by Joachim's own quartet. Brahms wrote to Clara Schumann in 1856, "There is more in Joachim than in all of us young people put together." However, this friendship cooled when Brahms sided with Amalie Weiss in Joachim's divorce suit.

Joachim was a conductor and a composer, but his fame came from his teaching and above all his violin playing. He was, in the words of Arnold Schönberg (q.v.), "the person who changed the position of the violinist from entertainer to artist." J. A. Fuller Maitland, *Joseph Joachim*, 1905.

JOFFE, ABRAHAM FEODOROVICH (1880–1960) Russian physicist. Born in Romny, Ukraine, Joffe, whose work contributed to the launching of his country's Sputnik, was among the pioneers of physics in the USSR and was instrumental in the establishment of sixteen important research centers throughout the Soviet Union. Specializing in semiconductors, Joffe was appointed professor extraordinary of physics at the Polytechnic Institute in 1913, and was made a full professor in 1915, receiving the prize of the Academy of Sciences. In 1918 he created the Physical-Technical Institute of Leningrad, which played an exceptional role in the development of physics. As the director of this institution for over thirty years, Joffe took part in the development of physics all over the USSR. He was responsible for an extensive network of physical-technical institutes and laboratories that served as a scientific basis for industrial growth. After the Bolshevik revolution, he became a member of the Central Committee of the Soviet Communist Party and of the Soviet Academy of Sciences, providing the initiative for founding the Physio-Technical Institute of the Academy of Sciences in 1951. He also contributed to the organization of physical-technical institutes in Kharkov, Dnepropetrovsk, Tomsk, and Sverdlovsk, and carefully chose the scientists who formed the nuclei of these scientific bodies.

Joffe's remarkable personality, his immense scientific prestige and wide erudition, his unquenchable passion for science, his ability to inspire his students, and his rare modesty and affability, won him the admiration of scientists in the Soviet Union and around the world. During a visit to Berlin in 1921, Joffe met Albert Einstein (q.v.), with whom he also discussed the issue of Zionism. Joffe argued for assimilation as a solution to the Jewish problem.

Joffe's scientific work was concentrated in three fields: the mechanical properties of crystals, the electrical properties of dielectric crystals, and semiconductors. Among his works, the most widely read are *Physics of Semi Conductors* (Russian, 1957; English translation, 1960), which was translated into several languages, and *Basic Concepts of Modern Physics* (Russian, 1949).

Joffe won the Stalin Prize for his work in 1942 and was named Hero of Socialist Labor in 1955. In addition, he was awarded two orders of Lenin along with the Sickle and Hammer medal.

JOFFE, ADOLF ABRAMOVICH (1883–1927)

Diplomat of the early years of Soviet Russia. Joffe was born in Simferopol, and originally joined the Mensheviks. He was befriended by Leon Trotsky (q.v.) when they were both living in Vienna. He helped Trotsky edit the Viennese *Pravda*, and organized the smuggling of the paper into Russia. Joffe was arrested and imprisoned by the tsarist authorities in 1912; he was released following the February 1917 revolution, and in July 1917 joined the Bolsheviks.

After the Bolshevik revolution in October, he led the Soviet delegation to the peace talks with Germany in Brest-Litovsk, but was soon replaced by Trotsky, since Joffe favored continuing the war.

In April 1918 Joffe was appointed Soviet ambassador in Berlin, at which time he worked with German Socialists and revolutionaries to prepare for revolution in that country. He later admitted that his efforts "accomplished little or nothing of permanent value, for we were too weak to provoke a revolution." He was expelled from Germany in November 1918. In 1920 he led the Russian delegation to the peace talks with Poland.

In late 1922 he traveled to the Far East to strengthen Soviet influence in that region of the world. In China he sought to assure the nationalists that the Bolsheviks were not interested in promoting Chinese communism, something of which Moscow was ashamed in later years.

Joffe continued to be closely allied to Trotsky, and was part of the opposition to Stalin and the ruling triumvirate after Lenin's death. He was ambassador in Vienna (1923–1924) and Tokyo (1924–1925). By early 1927 he was gravely ill, but was refused permission to travel abroad for medical treatment — even at his own expense. Stalin subjected him to increasing harassment, and he shot himself in the Kremlin as a protest against the expulsion of Trotsky and Zinoviev (q.v.) from the party.

His farewell letter to Trotsky is unique as a human and political document and a statement of revolutionary morality: "All my life I have been convinced that the revolutionary politician should know when to make his exit and that he should make it in time... when he becomes aware that he can no longer be useful to the cause he has served.... Human life has sense only in so far as it is spent in the service of the infinite — and for us mankind is the infinite." He went on to say that perhaps his suicide would help arouse the party to the condition it had reached, one in which it was unable to react in any way to the "monstrosity" of Trotsky's expulsion from it.

Joffe's funeral was attended by thousands, even though it had not been announced, and was Trotsky's last public appearance in Russia.

Joffe's second wife, Maria Joffe whom he married in 1918, worked as an editor and secretary for Bolshevik publications and publishing houses. In 1929 she protested Trotsky's expulsion from the Communist party at a general editorial meeting. She was arrested, exiled, and later sent to a labor camp. She was only rehabilitated and allowed to return to Moscow after the twenty-second party congress in 1957. She then learned that the couple's son, born in 1919, had died in 1937. She emigrated to Israel in 1975 and wrote a book about her experiences, published in English as *One Long Night*.

JOHANAN BEN ZAKKAI (1st cent. CE) Sage

and Jewish leader in the period immediately following the destruction of the Second Temple. Few details are known of his life, and those that exist combine fact with legend. He seems to have studied in Jerusalem, but it is related that for eighteen years he was in the town of Arav in Lower Galilee. To his chagrin, during all that time, he was only twice asked for his views on matters of Jewish law, causing him to condemn the attitude of the Galileans to the Torah. He then moved to Jerusalem, where he taught and, as a prominent Pharisee, took part in controversies with the Sadducees. He was involved in abolishing the ordeal of the wife suspected of adultery (Num. 5) and perhaps also in discontinuing the ritual of beheading a heifer in cases of unsolved murders (Deut. 21). His life centered on teaching and he held that "a Jew was born to study Torah." He had many disciples and was

SAYINGS OF JOHANAN BEN ZAKKAI

• If you have a sapling in your hand and people say to you "Behold, there is the Messiah," go on with your planting and only then go out and receive him.
• Israel, you are a lucky people. When you obey God's will, no nation can rule over you. But when you do not obey His will, then you are at the mercy of every people, however lowborn.
• A fait accompli is not open to discussion.
• He who is learned and pious is like an artist with his tools ready to hand.
• If you have learned much Torah do not boast of it, because it was for that purpose that you were created.

one of the first rabbis to introduce mystical lore into his teachings. Deeply involved in the Temple ritual, he was responsible for seeing that its conduct did not conflict with pharisaic teaching. Inside the Temple, he devoted much time to expounding the Law to the pilgrims who flocked to Jerusalem.

When the Romans besieged Jerusalem, although Johanan avoided involvement in the internecine strife that split the Jews in the city, he was convinced of the ultimate victory of the Romans and took steps to leave the beleaguered town. The story of his escape is told in forms but the classic version relates that he was concealed in a coffin, carried out by his disciples, and subsequently appeared in the camp of the Roman general, Vespasian. He accurately foretold that Vespasian would soon be chosen emperor and in return received permission to settle in the small coastal town of Yavneh (Jamnia) where he would be permitted to teach and establish a house of prayer.

Whatever the background, his move to Yavneh and his activities there proved a revolutionary step in Jewish history. When the Temple was destroyed in 70 CE, the future of Judaism itself was threatened. Johanan's foundation, however, of a new center of authority made possible the continuity and transition of Judiasm to a new stage in which the synagogue, not the Temple, became the exclusive focus of Jewish public ritual. It also ensured that the festivals previously linked exclusively with the Temple would still be observed. In Yavneh, Johanan established a new seat for the Sanhedrin to continue to direct Jewish religious life, and, among other things, determining the date of the new moon on which a unified religious calendar depended. As head of the religious court, he was responsible for crucial decisions and was recognized as the leader of the people at that critical time. Under his guidance, the authority of the Pharisees was paramount and the former central role of the priests diminished. He also helped to create a

theology to replace the sacrificial system, teaching it had been replaced by acts of charity. Traditionally his last words to his disciples, before his death (c. 80) were "May you fear God as much as you fear man."

J. Neusner, *Development of a Legend: Studies on the Traditions Concerning Yohanan Ben Zakkai*, 1970. J. Neusner, *A Life of Yohanan ben Zakkai*, 1970.

JOHN HYRCANUS I (died 104 BCE) Hasmonean ethnarch in Judea between 135–134 and 104 BCE. The son of Simon the Hasmonean (q.v.), he came to power in a Jewish state that had known independence only seven years. He was a true scion of the Hasmonean family, who not only firmly consolidated his predecessors' gains but even expanded them.

During his father's rule, he was active in the country's military and administrative policies. He foiled his brother-in-law, Ptolemy, who killed his father and his two brothers, from killing him and seizing power. He was a high priest like his father and uncle, Jonathan, before him. The initial stages of his leadership were a time of trepidation. Antiochus VII (Sidetes), the last powerful ruler of the Seleucid dynasty in Syria, after seeking John's assistance in obtaining the Seleucid throne, turned upon him and for a short while it appeared as though Jewish independence was in jeopardy. Antiochus even laid siege to Jerusalem, but was eventually repelled. Hasmonean forces even joined the pagan ruler on a campaign (during which, at one point, the entire Seleucid army was held up for several days as the Jewish contingent celebrated the holiday of Pentecost!).

Hyrcanus took immediate advantage of Antiochus's disappearance from the scene in 129 and commenced his consolidation and further expansion southward, northward, and eastward. Idumea (home of the biblical Edomites) came under Jewish dominion, with the Edomite population accepting conversion, and placing themselves thenceforth squarely in the Jewish camp. To the north, the capital of the hostile Samaritans, Shechem, and eventually also the town of Samaria, were demolished by John's armies. In addition to this expansion into Lower Galilee, areas across the Jordan also fell into Jewish hands. John renewed the friendship treaty with Rome initiated by Judah Maccabee (q.v.). He elicited several additional important declarations of support from Rome for the territorial integrity of the Hasmonean domain, and a declaration of friendship from Pergamum in Asia Minor.

One unfortunate development marred Hyrcanus' years — the Pharisee-Sadducee schism. The Talmud and other ancient rabbinical sources display an ambivalent attitude toward John. Despite the accusation that he turned Sadducee toward the end, the Talmud credits him with important religious decisions. He may have been the first of the Hasmonean dynasty to strike coins of his own, a sign of independence in the ancient world.

His reign, says Josephus (q.v.), the ancient Jewish historian, was a happy one, an indubitable indication of economic well-being. Certainly in the demographic-territorial domain he vastly outshone his forebears.

S. Zeitlin, *The Rise and Fall of the Judaean State*, vol. 1, 1962.

JOHN OF GISCALA (died after 71 CE) One of the two main leaders of the Great Revolt against Rome (68–70 CE). Together with Simeon bar Giora (q.v.), John (Yohanan of Gush Halav as he is known in Hebrew) managed to hold the far greater and more powerful Roman forces at bay in beleaguered Jerusalem.

Information on John comes almost entirely from a hostile source — the historian Josephus (q.v.). He first mentions John in the town of Gush Halav (Giscala) in Upper Galilee, climbing the economic ladder to wealth as an oil merchant. Josephus was sent to the scene to organize the resistance to Rome and before long he and John disagreed as to the best ways of preparing Galilean Jewry for the clash with Rome. John at this very early stage (late 66 or early 67 CE) already had misgivings about Josephus's actual enthusiasm for the battle. His suspicions were shortly to be confirmed.

Sometime in late 67 John fled from Giscala together with his men and made his way to Jerusalem. Josephus states that John infused hope and courage in the city's inhabitants. Gradually, John strengthened his ties with the Zealot party, among whom were members of the highest priestly echelons.

John, the one-time moderate who, while in Galilee, had taken up arms only against the pagan non-Roman attackers of his hometown, now became the uncompromising leader of the war against the Romans. Eventually, though too late, he joined forces with the other outstanding leader of the anti-Roman fighters, Simeon bar Giora, with John defending the Lower City, including the Temple Mount area, and Simeon the Upper City. The long months of bitter infighting between the two, however, took their toll. Jerusalem fell and John was captured, taken to Rome, and sentenced to life imprisonment.

JOLSON, AL (1886–1950) Entertainer. Born Asa Yoelson in Srednik, Lithuania, he rose to international acclaim as a star of stage, screen, and radio. Jolson and his family emigrated to America when he was still a young boy. His father, the cantor and rabbi Moses Yoelson, tried to groom both his sons for careers in the synagogue, giving them voice lessons as soon as they could talk. However, Jolson and his brother Harry were drawn to the theater and began their careers performing in the streets of their hometown, Washington, D.C. In their teens, the boys ran away to New York numerous times to try their luck in show business. Al was luckier, or more talented, than

Harry and made his first stage appearance in 1899 in Israel Zangwill's play, *Children of the Ghetto*.

Jolson went on to work the vaudeville circuit, working up acts with his brother and other performers. It was during these years that he adopted the "blackface" minstrel act for which he became known. It was when he was working solo in San Francisco, after the 1906 earthquake, that Jolson's career began to take off. He relished the adoration he received from the San Francisco audience, and it was there that he came up with one of his trademark lines, "All right, all right, folks, you ain't heard nothing yet."

Jolson continued to tour the country until 1911, when he got a spot on the opening night bill of the new Winter Garden Theater in New York. He electrified audiences night after night, transforming every Broadway show in which he performed into an Al Jolson show. He would stop performances in midact and ask the audience whom they had come to see. They always responded with wild shouts of requests for him, after which he would perform solo for hours, varying his routines from show to show.

Jolson worked almost unceasingly after he became a hit on Broadway. He began a recording career, met with presidents, and later starred on radio, but he was never happier than when in front of a live audience. He was addicted to the devotion and applause and would jump off the stage and sing in the aisles to be closer to his public. Jolson's obsession with his work, no doubt, led to his status as superstar, but it also destroyed three of his four marriages and eventually harmed his health.

Jolson's career was at its height in 1927 when Warner Bros. asked him to appear in *The Jazz Singer*, the first full-length talking picture. The film, which told a story similar to Jolson's own life story, made a profit of over three million dollars. Jolson's next talkie was *The Singing Fool*, in which he sang the ever-popular "Sonny Boy." These talking pictures were big hits and ultimately revolutionized the movie industry.

On the set of The Jazz Singer *in 1927: From left to right, Darryl Zanuck; Jack Warner; Al Jolson; and Warner Oland.*

Jolson was a man of "firsts:" first talking movie, first radio program whose format used monologue and song, and first performer to go overseas with the United Service Organization (USO). Jolson called the White House himself and asked to be sent overseas to entertain and lift the morale of the troops. It was at a time when his popularity was on the wane, and the shows during World War II were just what he needed to boost his image.

After the war two films, *The Jolson Story* and *Jolson Sings Again*, immortalized the self-proclaimed "World's Greatest Entertainer" on screen. Larry Parks played Jolson but the songs were dubbed by Jolson himself. In 1950 Jolson performed what were to be his last shows for the troops in the Korean War. His health was beginning to fail when he began the tour, and when he returned to the United States, he suffered a fatal heart attack. His will left nine-tenths of his three million-dollar estate to be divided equally among Jewish, Catholic, and Protestant organizations.
M. Freedland, *Al Jolson*, 1972.

JOSELEWICZ, BEREK (c. 1768–1809) Polish patriot. A native of Kretinga in western Lithuania, he originally worked in commerce and entered the service of Vilna's prince-bishop. While on a business trip to Paris in 1789, Joselewicz was drawn to the new ideals of the French Revolution; these made him a natural ally of the Polish liberals, who favored Jewish emancipation, and of their leader, General Tadeusz Kosciuszko. Under the menace of a third and final partition of their country, the Poles decided to take up arms against their chief oppressors, Catherine the Great of Russia and Frederick William II of Prussia. Some Jews, aware of Kosciuszko's libertarianism, joined the insurrection that he launched in March 1794.

Following the expulsion of Warsaw's Russian garrison, Kosciuszko took the momentous step of granting Joselewicz permission to organize a separate Jewish cavalry regiment. Not only did the Polish commander welcome this proposal, but he also made a contribution toward the costs involved and appointed Joselewicz colonel of the "Jewish Legion." In an appeal for volunteers, printed in Yiddish (October 1, 1794), Joselewicz urged his fellow Jews to "be like lions and leopards so that, with God's help, we may drive the enemy from our land." Mostly poor youths with no military experience, the five hundred idealistic Jews who answered his call brought their own horses and had the rest of their equipment supplied by Warsaw's Jewish community. Ordered to defend the largely Jewish suburb of Praga, Joselewicz and his men held their ground when seasoned Russian troops under the redoubtable Count Alexander Suvorov began attacking this forward position on November 4. A local rabbi permitted fighting to continue on the Sabbath and, when kosher food no longer reached them, the pious Jews fought on with empty stomachs. Only Joselewicz himself and twenty other legionaries survived the battle, hewing their way

through the Russian lines. Praga's civilian population was then massacred by Suvorov's infuriated Cossacks.

Despite its failure, the Polish uprising headed by Kosciuszko saved revolutionary France by diverting Prussian troops eastward. Joselewicz later joined Napoleon's Polish Legion, became a French dragoon officer, and then commanded two of Prince Jozef Poniatowski's cavalry squadrons during the 1809 Austrian campaign. He received both French and Polish decorations for valor. His death in action, while leading a charge against Austrian hussars at the battle of Kotsk (May 5, 1809), made him a national hero and one of the legendary figures of Polish Jewry. Military prowess was also displayed by his son **Jozeph Berkowicz**(1789–1846), a former Polish legionary who was twice decorated for valor during Napoleon's Russian campaign of 1812. He joined the abortive Polish uprising of 1830–1831, renewing his father's call for Jewish participation and organizing a militia of 850 pious "beardlings" to fight alongside the Polish insurgents. Berkowicz emigrated to France but finally settled in Liverpool, England, where his novel, *Stanislaus, or the Polish Lancer in the Suite of Napoleon* (1846), was completed shortly before he died.
N. Ausubel, ed., *A Treasury of Jewish Folklore*, 1948.

JOSEPH (c. 17th cent. BCE) Eleventh son of the patriarch Jacob (q.v.) and the elder of his two sons by his favorite wife, Rachel (q.v.). His story is related in Genesis 37–50.

The favoritism he enjoyed from Jacob aroused the envy of his older brothers. Their jealousy was aggravated by his apparent arrogance in relating dreams portending his aggrandisement at their expense. They plotted to kill him but were convinced by one of the brothers, Judah, to sell him instead as a slave. After concealing him in a pit, they sold him to a passing caravan of merchants who were en route to Egypt. The brothers kept Joseph's striped garment (translated in the King James version as the "coat of many colors"), which they soaked in the blood of an animal and presented to their father as proof that he had been killed by a wild beast.

In Egypt, Joseph was sold to Potiphar, a high official of the royal court. He rejected the advances of Potiphar's wife, who sought to seduce him and who, in her anger at his refusal, accused him to her husband of trying to rape her. Joseph was imprisoned and in prison made the acquaintance of the royal butler and baker. He won a reputation by his accurate interpretation of their dreams. When the Egyptian Pharaoh experienced dreams that could not be explained Joseph was sent for and interpreted them as foretelling the advent of seven years of plenty for the kingdom, to be followed by a similar period of famine. These proved accurate and Joseph was appointed vizier, in which capacity he spent his initial years stockpiling grain in anticipation of the lean years to come. He married an

Egyptian women, Asenath, who bore him two children, Ephraim and Manasseh.

When the famine materialized, it also affected the land of Canaan, home of Joseph's family. Hearing that food was available in Egypt, Joseph's brothers journeyed to Egypt where they were spotted by Joseph, whom they did not recognize. He accused them of spying and put them in prison. After three days, he released them all except Simeon, who was held as a hostage to ensure their return, this time together with Benjamin (Joseph's full brother) whom they had prudently left behind. Despite Jacob's misgivings, they returned to Egypt together with Benjamin. At first Joseph played a trick on them, making it seem that Benjamin had stolen Joseph's silver goblet, but when he revealed his identity there was an emotional reunion. He forgave them their misdeed, interpreting it as an act of divine providence, and after telling them to return to Canaan and bring their father, Jacob, back to Egypt he settled the family in the province of Gosh, where they received land and grazing rights. This was the beginning of the Israelite settlement in Egypt which, traditionally, was to last for four centuries.

Before his death, Jacob blessed Joseph's two sons, Ephraim and Manasseh, and from each of them was descended one of the twelve tribes. When Jacob died, Joseph returned with all his brothers and household to Canaan to bury his father in the cave of Machpelah, in accordance with Jacob's dying wish. When Joseph died, aged one hundred, he too made his family swear that his remains would be buried in Canaan. His body was embalmed and when the Israelites left Egypt under Moses, they carried Jacob's body to Canaan and buried him near Shechem in the field of Jacob.
N. M. Sarna, *Understanding Genesis*, 1966.

JOSEPHUS, FLAVIUS (c. 38 CE–after 100 CE)
Jewish historian. Josephus was a paradoxical and controversial figure who loved his people, but betrayed them; who was hated by his fellow Jews, yet devoted himself to writing in their defense; who wrote copious histories that were full of inaccuracies, but was a literary master. His biography is complicated by the fact that all that is known about him came from his own pen, and that pen was unreliable. Yet, with a lifetime spanning the years prior to the revolt of the Jews against Rome, the period of the war itself, and the period just after the war, he is considered the most important source of the history of the Jewish people during the crucial 1st century CE. Although the validity of his histories is often suspect, and he is accused of distortion for personal purposes, his graphic representations and his skill as a writer, as well as the fact that his works are the only surviving sources for the period, contribute to his importance.

He was born Joseph ben Mattathias in Jerusalem, into a distinguished family of priests, which he claimed was related, on the maternal side, to the Hasmonean dynasty. He describes himself as a child prodigy so famous for his knowledge of the Torah that high priests and other important men would consult him on matters of religion and law. At age sixteen, he committed himself to studying the three main Jewish schools — Pharisees, Sadducees, and Essenes — in order to choose the one most appropriate for himself. Not satisfied with what he had learned, he decided to join a desert hermit, with whom he spent a period of three years living an ascetic life in the wilderness, wearing clothing made of reeds, and eating wild herbs. After this period of hermitage, he decided to join the Pharisees.

When he was twenty-six he was sent to Rome as member of a delegation that sought the release of certain priests who had been imprisoned and sent to the capital for trial by Emperor Nero. According to his autobiography, en route, his ship sank in the middle of the Adriatic Sea, but miraculously, he and some eighty others were rescued. Arriving safely in Rome, he obtained the release of the priests. His success was due, at least in part, to his having befriended the mistress and future wife of the emperor.

When the Jewish War broke out in 66 CE, he was given a key military appointment as commander of Galilee, where he was to prepare and command the defense against the expected Roman counterattack. What actually happened during those years is unclear, despite his copious writing on the subject, for the version he presented in his history, *The Jewish War*, differs greatly from his portrayal of the same events in his autobiography, *The Life*.

According to the former, he served as a brave champion of the Jewish cause and a formidable adversary of the Romans, but ultimately had to bow to necessity and surrender to the enemy. The pompous vanity of his accounts in *The Jewish War*, disappears in *The Life*, in which he portrays himself as a reluctant participant in the revolt, who did his best to dampen the war fervor and to seek peace, but to no avail.

In any case, he was not a successful military man, and the cities that he was supposed to have fortified were isolated and could not resist the Roman armies. However, he himself was a born survivor, and when the city of Jotapata fell, he fled with forty men to a cave. There each man swore to slay his neighbor rather than be taken by the enemy. Josephus managed to arrange the lots so that he was one of the last two men alive, and then persuaded his companion to surrender with him to the Romans.

He was being held prisoner by the Romans and awaiting possible execution when news of Nero's death spread, alongside rumors of Vespasian's aspirations to the emperor's throne. Josephus, making it known that he had the qualities of a diviner, uttered a prophecy that Vespasian would become the next Roman emperor. This was soon confirmed by Vespasian's election to the position. Josephus was rewarded for his prophecy with his life and freedom and subsequently accompanied Titus, the commander of the Roman army, to Jerusalem, where he attempted to prevail upon the rebels, his former fellows, to surrender. He was regarded with contempt by many Jews and Romans alike, by the former for being a traitor, and by the latter because they suspected him of spying. After the war, he settled in Rome, where he was permitted to reside in Vespasian's former villa, and never again returned to his home in Palestine.

He wrote three major works: *The Jewish War*, *Jewish Antiquities*, and *Against Apion*, to which his autobiographical work, *The Life*, was an appendix.

The Jewish War portrayed the background, outbreak, progression, conclusion and aftermath of the Jewish revolt against the Romans. It is assumed that Vespasian asked him to write *The Jewish War* because he believed that such a book would serve as a warning to other enemies of Rome, and Josephus was not in a position to refuse. In the introduction he declared that as an eyewitness reporter, and as a native of Jerusalem who had himself fought against the Romans as long as resistance was possible, he described the war without bias. The accuracy of this claim is belied by various distortions such as whitewashing of the actions of the Roman armies, in order to pacify his patron; deliberate downplaying of the Jewish role in the revolt, in order to redeem the Jewish nation as a whole in the eyes of the Romans; and a tendency to refrain from reporting what was unflattering to himself.

The second work, *Jewish Antiquities*, was a history of the Jewish people, written in the hope of educating non-Jews about Judaism. He believed that if the Gentiles could only learn to understand the Jews, their hatred of his people would disappear. In the *Antiquities*, he set out to prove that the Jewish nation was indeed an ancient one, retelling the stories of the Bible, and even embellishing them with midrash and haggada, but always with a Hellenistic touch.

The Life was written in response to an accusation of misconduct and betrayal on his part in Galilee, before the arrival of the Roman army, while *Against Apion* was a defense against anti-Semitic arguments, which consisted partly of a refutal of anti-Semitic claims and partly of affirmation of the ethical superiority of Judaism.

H. St. J. Thackeray, *Josephus: The Man and the Historian*, 1968.

A. Wasserstein, *Flavius Josephus*, 1974.

JOSHUA (c. 12th cent. BCE) Successor of Moses (q.v.) and leader of the Children of Israel in their conquest of Canaan. His original name was Hoshea and he was the son of Nun of the tribe of Ephraim. Already in the early stages of the wanderings in the desert, Moses appointed him field commander to lead the Israelites in their successful battle against the Amalekites at Rephidim (Exod. 17:8-13). He was still a young man when he accompanied Moses on the first part of his ascent of Mount Sinai and when the Tent of Meeting was constructed, he was in charge of its security. As Moses' spiritual disciple, he zealously defended his master's prerogatives. When Moses sent twelve spies, one from each tribe, to survey the land of Canaan, only Joshua (together with Caleb) brought back a favorable report, contrary to the defeatism of the others, and recommended a direct assault to capture Canaan. For this service, he and Caleb were the only Israelites who had left Egypt who were privileged to enter the Promised Land.

On God's instruction, Moses lay his hands on Joshua, whom he designated as his successor and gave him the responsibility — along with Eliezer the priest and an official from each tribe — of dividing up the land of Canaan among the tribes.

With the death of Moses, Joshua took over the leadership. Subsequent events are detailed in the Bible in the book of Joshua. The conquest of Canaan was achieved despite the military advantages of the Canaanites, who had experienced armies, chariots, fortified cities, and a cohesive system of alliances. Joshua succeeded by waging a "holy war" in the name of God and demanding obedience to the word of God.

After a miraculous crossing of the river Jordan, Joshua ordered the circumcision of all males — a rite neglected in the wilderness. Jericho was conquered after its walls fell down, and before long the city of Ai was destroyed. Joshua made use of military intelligence and other ruses, such as the spies he sent into Jericho (Jos. 2) and capture by ambush, as in the case of Ai (Jos. 8).

When he reached Mount Ebal he built an altar (apparently identified in a recent excavation) where he pronounced the blessings and curses as laid down by Moses (Jos. 8:30-35). He went on to make a covenant with the cities of Gibeon; score a victory over a coalition of five Amorite rulers; and defeat an alliance of northern monarchs led by the king of Hazor. After subduing most of the land (he was unsuccessful along the Mediterranean coast), he announced the allotment of territories to the various tribes. He also determined cities of refuge and forty-eight cities allocated to the Levites who had no tribal territory of their own. After his fare-

I have no intention of rivaling those who extol the Roman power by exaggerating the deeds of my compatriots. I shall faithfully recount the actions of both combatants; but in my reflections on the events I cannot conceal my private sentiments, nor refuse to give my personal sympathies scope to bewail my country's misfortunes.... For of all the cities under Roman rule it was the lot of ours to attain to the highest felicity and to fall to the lowest depths of calamity. Indeed in my opinion, the misfortunes of all nations since the world began fall short of those of the Jews.

Josephus, *Jewish War*, 1.9-1.12

The battle for Jericho from Joshua Roll. *Tenth-century illuminated manuscript.*

well address, in which he exhorted the tribes to be ruled by God alone, Joshua died at the age of 110 and was buried in his own allotted territory.
R. G. Boling, *Joshua* (Anchor Bible), 1982.

JOSIAH (7th cent. BCE) King of Judah, ruled 640–609 BCE. He succeeded to the throne at the age of eight on the assassination of his father, Amon. After a half century when the rulers of Judah condoned gross idolatry, Josiah was to provide pious leadership and reformation.

During his early years, the country remained a vassal of Assyria, but after 633 BCE the Assyrian Empire began to disintegrate, and like other states on the periphery, Judah regained its independence. In the course of his reign, Josiah was able to extend his kingdom to the Plain of Jezreel, to Galilee, and to the Philistine cities on the coast; to found new cities such as En Gedi; and to develop Jerusalem.

He is best remembered for his religious activities. When he was still only sixteen he rejected the idolatrous practices of his immediate ancestors and turned to the worship of God. At age eighteen, he began his reformation, no longer fearing objections from Assyria when he uprooted pagan practices. He undertook a basic overhaul of the Temple during which a book of the Law was discovered, which was read aloud to the king, who was deeply disturbed that the law was not being observed according to the precepts laid out in the book. Scholars have tended to identify this book with Deuteronomy, but are divided as to whether the book had been written long before and forgotten or whether it was an original composition from Josiah's time. The king now gathered the people in the Temple and the book was read to them. A solemn covenant with God was proclaimed that was accepted by all the people, who undertook to obey the Law. Josiah now abolished all idolatry in Jerusalem and the cities of Judah, destroyed the long-standing altar at Bethel as well as the high places of Samaria, and centralized the cult in Jerusalem, as instructed in Deuternomy. He also abolished child sacrifice, sacred prostitution, and other heathen practices. He concluded this activity with a great celebration of the festival of Passover, which had fallen into neglect.

In 612 the Assyrian Empire collapsed with the fall of Nineveh, and Babylonia now became an outstanding power under Nabopolassar, challenging the might of Egypt. Here Josiah made a fatal mistake. When the Assyrians were crumbling, Neco king of Egypt sent an army through Palestine to try and support them. Josiah had no interest in their preservation and rushed his army to Megiddo to stop the Egyptians. In the ensuing battle he was routed and fatally injured. His death was deeply mourned in Judah. Jeremiah (q.v.) lamented his passing and the author of the books of Kings commented, "Before him there was no king like him nor did any like him arise after him." (2 Kings 23:25)
M. Cogan and H. Tadmor, *2 Kings* (Anchor Bible), 1988.

JUDAH BEN SAMUEL HE-HASID OF REGENSBURG (died 1217) The main thinker of the medieval school of German Jewish pietists (*Hasidei Ashkenaz*). The other two men who fashioned this school were his father, Samuel he-Hasid and his relative, Eleazar ben Judah of Worms (q.v.). Judah's influence was strong and a contemporary said of him, "He would have been a prophet had he lived in the time of the prophets."

Many legends were told of him, but little is known of an life, partly because of his extreme humility which discouraged others from citing his name. He lived for many years in the Rhineland, probably in Speyer, but spent his later years in Regensburg, where he founded a yeshiva (Talmudic academy).

Because he maintained that an author should not acknowledge the authorship of his works, it is difficult to determine which of the writings of the German pietists should be attributed to him. They seem to have included a number of works that were lost or have been preserved only in manuscript or in citations. He was, however, the main author of

FROM JUDAH BEN SAMUEL'S BOOK OF THE PIOUS

- Do not enter into a learned discussion with your guests unless you are assured of their ability, so as not to put them to shame.
- One who causes grievance to another man is as though he has caused grievance to the whole world, for man is a microcosm.
- In speaking with a friend say "You and I," not "I and you."
- Better make friends with an ignorant man who is liberal with his money and of a pleasant nature than with a scholar who is mean and irascible.
- Never insult your servants and do not stint in praising them, for the worst quality is ingratitude. Indeed do not even be ungrateful to animals, for riders who stick their spurs in horses will be punished.
- If you have to hire a workman for a specialized job and one candidate can do only that job and the other can also do others, hire the former.
- A good man will not sell an animal to a cruel man.
- If you are proved right, you gain little, but if you are proved wrong, you gain much — you learn the truth.

the greatest work of his school, *Sefer Hasidim* ("The Book of the Pious"), which also includes sections written by others, notably his father and Eleazar ben Judah of Worms. The final compilation was probably made by Judah's disciples after his death. This was the most important manual of piety and ethics of its time. It is practical in its emphasis, covering virtually all aspects of everyday life, including man's relationship with God (prayer, Sabbath observance, penitence, etc.), business conduct, family life, attitudes to servants and to non-Jews, kindness to animals, rules for education, and even details of table manners and personal conduct. The fundamentals of conduct cited as are piety, humility, and fear of God. The book also includes much superstition, with legends of wizards, witches, demons and vampires, considerably influenced by German non-Jewish traditions. It includes many stories, some telling of the bravery of Jewish martyrs when attacked by the Crusaders. Despite the hostility of the environment, however, the book teaches a universal love of all men.

S. G. Kramer, *God and Man in the Sefer Hasidim*, 1966.

JUDAH HALEVI (c. 1075–1141) Poet and religious thinker in Spain. Born to a wealthy family in either Toledo or Tudela, he spent in his youth in various parts of Spain, receiving a rabbinical and secular education. He studied rabbinics, Hebrew and Arabic, medicine and philosophy. He worked as a doctor in Toledo but the difficult position of Jews under Christian rule induced him to move to Cordova in Muslim Spain where he continued his medical practice, and enjoyed success, fame, and affluence. However, when already in his sixties, he was driven by his longing for the Holy Land to leave his home and family and set out for Jerusalem. He firmly believed that a full Jewish life could not be lived outside the Land of Israel and was determined to settle there. Reaching Egypt, however, he became involved in various activities, remained for a considerable time, and died and was buried there without achieving his dream of seeing the Land of Israel. A popular legend, widely retold through the ages, relates that he arrived in Jerusalem where he was struck down and killed by an Arab horseman; this, however, has been disproved by recently discovered documents throwing light on his visit to Egypt and his death there.

Judah Halevi and Solomon Ibn Gabirol (q.v.), were the great Jewish poets of the Middle Ages. Halevi's poetry can be divided into secular, religious, and national poems. His early verse was largely secular, reflecting a cheerful outlook, and dealing with love and friendship, wine and nature, marriage and mourning, riddles, and praises and eulogies of patrons. His love songs betray his keen feeling for beauty, both human and in nature. Even in old age, when in Egypt, he wrote a poem praising the beauty of the land, but added:

"But fairer than all to me is yon gentle maiden.
Ah, time's swift flight I would gladly stay,
Regretting that my hair is gray."

However, as the years passed and the situation of Spanish Jewry, caught in the middle of the Muslim-Christian conflict, deteriorated, he became concerned with the Jewish plight, and paid far less attention to the pleasures of life. He was seized by a religious spirit and a love of God, thoughts of whom fill his poems. He also turned to messianism, and through the book of Daniel, tried to calculate the expected date of the arrival of the Messiah. Most especially, he was deeply conscious of the fate of the Jews and the tragedy of their exile from their homeland. His series of Songs of Zion (or Zionides), expressing the tragedy of Jewish homelessness and the love of Zion, became part of the beloved Jewish heritage of communities all over the world.

He wrote considerable religious poetry including *piyyutim*, poems that entered the liturgy; lamentations, both on the destroyed homeland and on individuals; and penitential prayers.

His famous prose work (written in Arabic) is *Sefer ha-Kuzari* ("The Book of the Khazars"). This is based on the story of the conversion to Judaism of the Khazars, a tribe in the lower Volga region. According to a tradition, this occurred after a public disputation before the Khazar king and nobles with the participation of Jewish, Christian and Muslim spokesmen. Judah Halevi wrote his book

FROM THE WRITINGS OF
JUDAH HALEVI

- My heart is in the East,
But I am in the furthermost West,
How then can I taste what I eat,
And how can food be sweet to me?
- Oh Lord, where shall I find Thee?
Hidden and exalted is Thy place;
And where shall I not find Thee?
Full of Thy glory is the infinite Space.
- Israel is the heart of mankind.
- For your songs, O God, my soul is as a
harp.
- [On Jerusalem]
Beautiful of elevation, joy of the world; city of
the great King;
For you my soul is longing,
O that I might fly to you on eagles' wings.
- The service of God spells freedom.

in the form of a dialogue based on this dispute.
Although the book has a philosophical intent,
Halevi was strongly critical of rationalist thought
and philosophy, teaching that Judaism propounds
a higher truth, based solely on biblical revelation.
Only religious faith brings man closer to God, and
Judaism is superior to the other faiths because it is
the original source from which the others derive.
The Jewish people, then, is the heart of spirituality
in the world, which imposes on the Jews special

Letter written by Judah Halevi in Arabic.

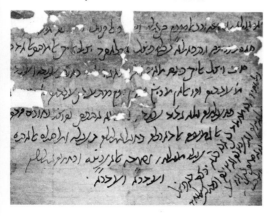

obligations. Their sufferings are to be seen as purification in anticipation of their return to their land.
Kuzari was one of the most popular of Jewish
theological books.

I. Heinemann, *Jehuda Halevi*, 1960.
M. Waxman, *A History of Jewish Literature*, vol. 1,
chaps. 9 and 11, 1960.

JUDAH HA-NASI   (i.e., Judah the Patriarch; late
2nd–early 3rd cent. CE) Leader of the Jewish
community of Eretz Israel and compiler of the
Mishnah, the basic codification of the oral law. He
was the son of the scholar-leader Simeon ben
Gamaliel (q.v.) whom he succeeded in the patriar-
chate at the crucial period following the unsuccessful revolt of Bar Kokhba (q.v.) against the Romans.
His leadership was unchallenged and his scholarship was such that he was usually known simply as
Rabbi (the teacher, par excellence). In his private
life, he was so pious and observant that he was also
called *Rabbenu ha-Kadosh* (our holy teacher).

The office of patriarch was reconstituted by the
Romans after the end of the revolt and Judah was
recognized as the Jewish leader not only by the
Jews in Eretz Israel and by the Romans but by the
Jewish communities in the Diaspora. He held
office for fifty years, living for most of the time in
Galilee. He established his academy at Bet Shearim
(not far from modern Haifa) but, for health reasons, spent his last seventeen years at Sepphoris.

His authority as patriarch and as head of the
Sanhedrin was virtually unlimited. He was responsible for the appointment of all judges and teachers
and devoted himself to the religious and economic
reconstruction of Jewish life after the tragic period
through which it had passed. He interpreted the
agricultural aspects of Jewish law so as not to cause
hardship to the agrarian population. He himself
was very wealthy, owning large tracts of land on
which he developed agriculture and raised cattle,
and being involved, as well, in wool and linen
manufacture, and exporting and importing on his
own boats. He was also noted for his generosity
and in times of famine opened his private store-
houses to the public.

His learning was so highly valued that it was said
"from the time of Moses to the time of Rabbi,
Torah and greatness were never so concentrated in
the one person." Although Aramaic was the country's spoken language, he insisted on speaking only
Hebrew with his family and friends. With Roman
officials, he spoke Greek.

Many stories were told of his friendship with the
Roman ruler "Antoninus." They appear to be
legends and it is unlikely that he had personal
contact with any emperor, but they reflect his close
links with the Roman authorities, and his own
quasi-royal status, and were perhaps even intended
to show that the Jewish leader was on a par with
the Roman emperor.

His greatest achievement was the Mishnah. For
centuries the oral law, traditionally emanating
from Sinai, had been handed down by word of

ON JUDAH HA-NASI

All of the seven qualities which the sages attributed to the righteous — handsomeness, strength, riches, wisdom, longevity, honor, and children — were all established in Judah Ha-Nasi and his sons.

(Avot 6:9)

SAYINGS OF JUDAH HA-NASI

● What is the virtuous path which a man should follow? Whatever brings honor to his Maker and honor from his fellowman.
● Be as punctilious in observing a light as a weighty commandment, for you do not know their relative reward.
● Contemplate three things and you will avoid transgressions: above you [in Heaven] is an eye that sees, an ear that hears, and all your deeds are faithfully recorded.
● Fulfill God's precepts joyfully, just as Israel accepted the Torah at Sinai with joy.
● I have learned much from my teachers, more from my colleagues, but most from my pupils.
● Do not be deceived by the outward appearance of age or youth; a new pitcher might be full of good, old wine while an old one might be empty altogether.
● A man should revere his father and mother as he reveres God, for all three are partners in him.

---

mouth, but in the generation preceding Judah, a number of collections of these statutes had been committed to writing. Judah examined and classified the material and organized it under six headings:
1. *Zer'aim* (seeds): primarily the agricultural laws but also dealing with prayers and blessings.
2. *Mo'ed* (appointed time): the laws of the Sabbath, feasts, and fastdays.
3. *Nashim* (women): the laws of marriage, divorce, and vows.
4. *Nezikin* (damages): civil and criminal law.
5. *Kodashim* (holy things): the laws of sacrifices and consecrated objects.
6. *Tohorot* (cleanliness): the laws of ritual purity and impurity.

The Mishnah was immediately accepted as authoritative and formed the basis for the Talmud, which is based on discussions of each verse of the Mishnah. It was a crucial link in the transition of Judaism from a religion focused on the Temple to one centered on Jewish law (halakhah).

Judah was bedridden for his last years. Before he died he told his disciples that throughout his life he had devoted all his strength to Torah but had never received any material benefit through it. He was buried in Bet Shearim, where his tomb became a site of Jewish pilgrimage.

A. Buechler, *Studies in Jewish History*, 1956.
J. Neusner, *A History of the Jews of Babylon*, Vol. 2, 1966.
J. Neusner, *Judaism, The Evidence of the Mishnah*, 1981.

JUDAH LOEW BEN BEZALEL (also known as Der Hohe Rabbi Loew and, from the acronym of his name, as *Maharal*; c. 1520–1609) Rabbinic scholar, mystic, and philosopher in Prague. He studied in rabbinical academies in Poland and for twenty years (until 1573) was rabbi in Nikolsburg, eventually becoming chief rabbi of Moravia. Subsequently he moved to Prague where he founded a yeshiva (Talmudic academy) which he headed for eleven years. From 1584 he was rabbi in Posen; returned to Prague for four years; went back to Posen as chief rabbi of Posen and of all Greater Poland, and finally returned to Prague in 1598, spending there his last eleven years as its chief rabbi. Wherever he served he introduced widespread reforms in community organization and Jewish education. As a pedagogue, he believed in adapting the curriculum to the age of the student and not attempting to set targets beyond their abilities. In this approach he relied on the belief of the early rabbis that a child should start the study of Bible at the age of five, the Mishnah at ten, and the Talmud at fifteen. In this way, he restored the Mishnah (see Judah ha-Nasi), which had tended to be neglected, to a major role in the educational curriculum. He also stressed the importance of studying Hebrew language and grammar. In Talmudic learning, he opposed the prevalent emphasis on casuistic argumentation (*pilpul*) and advocated a more literal approach. Although he himself was a distinguished mathematician, he opposed the introduction of secular subjects to Jewish education.

In his community reforms, he founded many societies, as the cells of the overall community, and developed the role of the rabbi as a focus of learning and spirituality rather than as a "political" figure.

Judah Loew was the author of commentaries and works of religious law, ethics, and homiletics with deep philosophical content. He based his beliefs on Jewish thought, especially mystical concepts. Philosophy, he held, could only provide a confirmation of what the Jew already knew through his tradition. Basic to his thought was the notion that opposites such as male and female, God and the world, complement each other. It is the Torah that mediates between God and the world. The Jew must therefore study and practice the Torah as his contribution to the world's ultimate fulfillment. The role of the Jewish people in this process is crucial and the return of the Jews to their own land is an essential precondition to mankind's eventual redemption.

Judah Loew's association with mysticism led to his identification in Jewish and Czech legend as the creator of the golem.

B. Z. Bokser, *From the World of Kabbalah: The*

RABBI JUDAH LOEW AND THE GOLEM OF PRAGUE

Like other peoples, Jews were intrigued with the possibility of creating a human being artificially. Ancient Talmudic literature used the term *golem* for a lump of clay mysteriously brought to life by the magical use of the secret name of God. Often the golem was the servant of his rabbinical creator. Sometimes it developed dangerous natural powers and its master had to return it to dust.

The most famous of these legends relates to Rabbi Judah Loew, who was concerned with saving the Jews of Prague from a blood libel. When they were threatened by a frenzied crowd and the situation became critical, Judah Loew called on Heaven to show how he could save his people. The answer came back: "Create a golem out of clay and it will destroy the enemies of the Jews."

The rabbi, with two of his disciples, went secretly to the river bank where they made the figure of a huge man out of the clay of the bank. They circled it seven times, reciting incantations and biblical verses, until it came to life. They dressed it in appropriate clothes for a *shammash* (synagogue sexton) and told it to guard the Prague ghetto. On one occasion when a Gentile butcher tried to hide the body of a dead child in the Jewish quarter so as to accuse the Jews of ritual murder, he was captured in the act by the golem who took him to the town hall where justice was executed.

There are differing versions as to the end of the golem. One says that it began to develop powers of its own and ran amok, endangering the lives of those it was supposed to protect and the rabbi was forced to destroy it (this is the end of most literary works, plays, and films based on the story). A less dramatic account is that after many years passed with no blood libels being raised, Judah Loew decided that the golem was no longer needed and took it to the attic of the synagogue where he returned it to a shapeless mass, wrapped it in a prayer shawl, and forbade his congregants ever to enter the attic. To this day, there are those who believe that the remains of the golem are to be found in the attic of Prague's famous Altneushul synagogue, awaiting either a new threat to the Jewish people or the advent of the Messiah.

Philosophy of Rabbi Judah Loew of Prague, 1954.
B. L. Sherwin, *Mystical Theology: The Life and Works of Judah Loew of Prague*, 1982.
F. Thieberger, *The Great Rabbi Loew of Prague*, 1954.

JUDAH MACCABEE   (died 160 BCE) Leader of the revolt of the Hasmonean (Maccabee) family. Judah the Maccabee (the significance of the name is disputed) was appointed by his dying father, Mattathias, of priestly stock, to continue the revolt against the anti-Jewish decrees and persecutions of the Syrian Greek monarch of the Seleucid house, Antiochus IV (Epiphanes). The rebellion, whose initial guiding figure was Mattathias, broke out in the village of Modiin in 167 BCE. Soon thereafter Judah assumed the leadership and, together with his four brothers, embarked upon a series of military campaigns to break the back of the Seleucid forces.

Making brilliant use of night attacks Judah at first engaged in guerrilla tactics to throw the enemy off balance and rout him. The first three campaigns against the experienced Macedonian commanders were an unqualified success. Southern Samaria and the Judean hill country (Beit Horon and Emmaus) were the scenes of the first three encounters. The campaign (in 165 BCE) at Emmaus, in the northwest of Judea, was an especially professional operation, as it entailed the simultaneous outmaneuvering of several enemy generals and their forces, which were dispersed across a broad area.

Desperate attempts were made simultaneously by the regime to quash the rebellion and to mollify the Jews by rescinding the harsh decrees against them. This did not prevent Judah's seizure of Jerusalem in 164 and the rededication of the Jewish Temple, which had been polluted by pagan worship before the uprising. A noteworthy and generally underplayed feature of Judah's generalship took place at about this time. Endangered and often battered Jewish enclaves in predominantly Gentile territories in Galilee, Transjordan, and even the pagan coast, were rescued and brought to safety in Judea. It was becoming increasingly clear that Judah was expanding his aims to include the extension of Jewish hegemony wherever possible throughout the Land of Israel.

Matters nevertheless did not go smoothly during these three years, especially after Lysias, the Seleucid vice-regent, had assumed personal charge of the military campaigns. Particularly successful was Lysias' strategy in engaging the Jewish forces in the southern Beit Zur sector, where the Jews suffered their first serious reversals.

The Jewish assimilationist-Hellenizer Menelaus, a vehement opponent of the rebels, had by now been removed from the scene, but he was followed shortly by Alcimus the pro-Seleucid high priest. He too was eventually overcome. Another attempt was made by the Syrian regime to stop Judah, but he won one of his most brilliant battles at Adasa, north of Jerusalem, over the enemy general Nicanor, a victory celebrated for generations thereafter as the Day of Nicanor.

Judah was also astute in the political arena. In 161, apparently not long after his victory over Nicanor, he concluded a friendship pact with the already powerful Rome. The treaty was to stand for some sixty years at least. The following year, Judah fell in battle at Elasa and his forces were routed. However, this was to prove but a temporary setback.

Judah Maccabee's military and political genius and gret personal charisma had laid the groundwork for the tremendous achievements of the Hasmonean dynasty.

B. Bar-Kochva, *Judas Maccabaeus*, 1989.
E. Bickerman, *The Maccabees*, 1948.
A. Tcherikover, *Hellenistic Civilization and the Jews*, 1959.

K

KADOORIE FAMILY Family of philanthropists and of communal leaders of Iraqi origin who made a considerable fortune in the Far East in banking, transportation, and construction. Their activities contributed to the growth and development of Shanghai and Hong Kong. Sir **Ellis Kadoorie** (1865–1922) was born in Baghdad and educated at the Alliance Israelite Universelle school. In 1880 he moved to Bombay, where he was employed as a clerk in the offices of the Sassoon family, and later set up business enterprises in Hong Kong and China. His philanthropic activities included the building of synagogues, a Jewish recreation club in Hong Kong (1909), and the establishment of educational and welfare institutions throughout Asia and the Middle East. He also endowed a chair in physics at Hong Kong University. Ellis Kadoorie was knighted in 1917. The Kadoorie Agricultural College was established in Palestine in 1931 with funds provided from his estate.

Sir **Elly Kadoorie** (1867–1944) was involved in the philanthropic activities of his brother Ellis. He became an active Zionist and in 1900 was elected president of the Palestine Foundation Fund in Shanghai. He contributed generously to the construction of the Hebrew University of Jerusalem. His philanthropic undertakings included the establishment of a school in Baghdad in honor of his wife Laura (1911); a girls' sewing school named after her (1922); an ophthalmic hospital named after his mother Rima (1924); and schools in Kirkuk (1934). He was knighted in 1926. During World War II Sir Elly helped rescue Jewish refugee children from Germany; he was imprisoned by the Japanese and all his possessions were seized.

KAFKA, FRANZ (1883–1924) Czech writer, posthumously recognized as one of the major figures of modern European literature. Born to a middle-class family in Prague, he was a lonely child and his relationship with his authoritarian father profoundly affected him. He studied at a German high school, where he began to write, but burned his compositions. At university, he tried a number of subjects but eventually became a doctor of law. After graduation he found a job with an insurance company, where the long hours left him no time for

Kafka and his fiancée, Felice Bauer, 1917.

writing. He then transferred to another company, where he worked assiduously and efficiently until he eventually had to resign owing to ill-health. Hours here were shorter and he had more time to devote to his writing, which reflects the bureaucratic world in which he often found himself. He tended to sleep in the afternoons and write at night, often arriving exhausted at the office in the morning.

He had a clique of friends, many of them among the Jewish intellectuals and writers of Prague. He also had a number of intensive relationships with women. From 1917 Kafka was ill with tuberculosis and thereafter much of his life was spent in sanatoriums. In his last year, he spent a period in Berlin, but returned to his hometown, dying in a nearby sanatorium; he was buried in the family tomb in the Prague Jewish cemetery.

In his last years, he had returned to an interest in

Judaism and even contemplated emigrating to Palestine. Only a few of his works were published during his lifetime and he left instructions to his friend and literary executor, Max Brod (q.v.), to destroy the remainder (which included his great novels). Brod disobeyed his instructions and the publication of the books brought Kafka international fame.

Best known are his novels *The Trial, The Castle,* and *America,* all written in German. Their dream-like quality, with its own inner logic, conveys a world of frustration and nightmarish hopelessness which brought the word *Kafkaesque* into the English language. Kafka was widely read, and many influences have been discerned in his work — including Jewish mysticism — but the style and atmosphere are completely original, with apparently everyday realities cloaking an expression of human alienation in modern society. It was symbolic that three of his sisters met their deaths in Nazi concentration camps.

H. Politzer, *Kafka: Parable and Paradox,* 1962.
R. Robertson, *Kafka: Judaism, Politics, and Literature,* 1985.

Page of an exercise book used by Franz Kafka when he began to study Hebrew.

Not one calm second is granted to the Western Jew. Everything has to be earned, not only the present and the future but also the past — something after all which perhaps every human being has inherited — this too must be earned; it is perhaps the hardest work.

Franz Kafka

KAHANE, MEIR (1932–1990) Rabbi and Jewish activist, founder of the Jewish Defense League (JDL) and Kach movement. Born in Brooklyn as Martin David Kahane, he was the son of a rabbi. A member of the Revisionist Zionist youth movement, Betar, as a teenager, he first got into trouble with the police at the age of fifteen when he smashed the windows of the car carrying visiting British Foreign Secretary Ernest Bevin, in protest against British Mandate policy on Jewish immigration to Palestine. He estimated that he spent a total of three years in U.S. prisons as the result of his various acts.

Kahana was ordained as an Orthodox rabbi and obtained a law degree from New York University. He served for a time as a synagogue rabbi in Queens and as editor of the Brooklyn-based *Jewish Press.*

During the 1960s he founded the Jewish Defense League in New York; it avowed the use of violence, including bombings, adopting the motto "Never Again" — no repeat of the Holocaust. Its activities included self-defense operations in urban areas (especially Brooklyn) where Jews felt threatened and the harassment of Soviet activities in New York as a protest against the Soviet anti-Jewish policy. Kahane claimed to have been an FBI undercover agent during the 1960s, using the name Michael King.

He moved to Israel in 1971, feeling that only in Israel can one live a full Jewish life and avoid assimilating the non-Jewish values found in all other environments. In 1976 he founded a movement, Kach, the main thrust of which was the removal of the Arabs from Israel. Standing for the Knesset (parliament), he eventually obtained a seat in 1981. His four years there were stormy and his behavior led to a number of suspensions. During this period the Knesset passed a resolution barring parties with a racist policy from standing for election; Kahane's party was subsequently disqualified. Kahane himself was condemned by almost the entire gamut of organized Jewry.

Kahane was assassinated in New York at a gathering of his supporters by an Egyptian-born, naturalized American.

Kahane wrote *The Jewish Stake in Vietnam* (under the name Michael King and coauthored with Joseph Thurber, 1967); *Never Again* (1970); *Letters from Prisons* (1974); and *They Must Go* (1980).

KAHINA, DAHYA AL- (7th cent.) Berber warrior queen in the Aurès mountains of southeast Algeria, at the time of the Arab conquest of North Africa. The real name of the Kahina, as she came to be known, was Dahya or Damya al-Kahina (The Prophetess), so called by the Arabs, who believed she could predict the future. She belonged to the tribe of the Jarawa, whose members were converts to Judaism.

At the time of Caliph Abd al-Malik (685–705), the Arabs were advancing in their conquest westward through North Africa. The caliph's army, led by his general Hasan ibn- Nu'man, captured Carthage and marched west to impose Islam on the free Berber tribes. Led by their queen, the tribes resisted fiercely on the slopes of the Aurès, using a powerful army of camelry. Hasan was defeated (688) and the Kahina took many prisoners, whom she released, with the exception of one youth, Khalid ibn Yazid. The Kahina adopted Khalid and treated him like her two other sons.

The defeated general, Hasan, retreated and settled at Barca to await the caliph's instructions. Five years later, Abd al-Malik sent reinforcements and orders to attack the Kahina.

In the meantime, the Kahina had devastated the fertile coastal region and cities to discourage the Arabs whom she thought coveted the riches of the country. Her policy created internal dissension that undermined her popularity among the people. Furthermore, Hasan received information from Khalid, her adopted son, who had become a double agent. Before the battle took place, the Kahina foresaw that she would be killed and the Berbers defeated. She said she had seen her head cut off and brought to her enemies. She made Khalid return to the Arabs and take along her two sons to save them. She herself resisted the conquerors to the end and was killed in battle in 695 at a place later called Kahina's Well.

The Kahina ruled with an iron hand for thirty-five years and blocked the Muslim invasion of North Africa for several years, leading her own tribe and other tribes of the region in battle. After her death the Arabs were able to complete the conquest of all North Africa to the Atlantic and Islamize the Berber tribes, then invading Spain with Berber troops.

According to one tradition, her sons, following her dying instructions, surrendered, were converted to Islam, and were given a military command, helping in the subsequent conquest and Islamization of the region.
H. Z. Hirschberg, *A History of the Jews of North Africa*, vol. 1, 1974.

KAHN, LOUIS ISADORE (1901–1974) U.S. architect and educator, credited with developing an influential philosophy of architecture that explores the nature of building materials, the role of servant and served space, and the use of design to achieve perfect form through ordered architectural methods.

Born in Osel (now Saaremaa), Estonia, Kahn emigrated to the United States with his family in 1905, and they settled in Philadelphia. They lived in poverty, sometimes relying on the money Kahn earned playing piano in silent-movie theaters. Kahn, musically and artistically gifted, won a scholarship to study art. Influenced, however, by an architectural-history class taken in his final year of high school, he determined to study architecture instead.

He earned a degree in architecture from the University of Pennsylvania in 1924 and worked in several architectural offices after graduation. During the depression he organized an architectural research group in Philadelphia and headed housing studies in the city planning commission for the Works Progress Administration. In 1937 he opened a private practice.

Kahn taught architecture at Yale University from 1947 to 1957. While there he designed his first important project, the Yale University Art Gallery (1951–1953). From 1957 until 1974 he taught at the University of Pennsylvania, where he was recognized as the intellectual and spiritual leader of the school of architecture. During this time, he designed the Richards Medical Research Building at the university (1957–64). This project most fully exemplified the principles of Kahn's philosophy and was the subject of an exhibition at New York's Museum of Modern Art in 1960.

His other significant commissions included the laboratory building for the Salk Institute in La Jolla, California (1959–1965), the national capital of Bangladesh in Dacca (1962–1974), the Olivetti-Underwood Corp. factory in Harrisburg, Pennsylvania (1969), and the library of the Phillips Exeter Academy in New Hampshire (1967–1972). Throughout his career he designed synagogues and community centers, including Ahavath Israel Synagogue in Philadelphia (1935–1939), the bathhouse and master plan for the Jewish Community Center in Trenton, New Jersey (1954–1959), and Temple Beth-El Synagogue in Chappaqua, New York (1966–1972).

In recognition for his contributions to the architectural community, Kahn received the gold medal of the American Institute of Architects (1970) and the royal gold medal for architecture of the Royal Institute of British Architects (1972).
J. Lobell, *Between Silence and Light: Spirit in the Architecture of Louis I. Kahn*, 1979.

KALISCHER, TZEVI HIRSCH (1795–1874) Rabbi and precursor of Zionism. Born in Lissa, a Polish town newly acquired by Prussia, he studied there, completed his rabbinic training under the distinguished Akiva Eger in Posen, and gained a knowledge of Jewish and general philosophy. From 1824, Kalischer lived in Thorn, choosing to serve as an unpaid communal rabbi. He wrote rabbinic and philosophical works, together with *Derishat Tziyyon* ("Seeking Zion," 1862), the volume that brought him worldwide renown.

Like Judah Solomon Hai Alkalai (q.v.), Kalischer was one of the very few Orthodox rabbis in 19th-century Europe whose belief in a messianic redemption did not exclude human effort to organize the Jewish people's return to Zion. He faced particular opposition in the west, from assimilationists and leaders of Reform Judaism whose struggle for emancipation made them indifferent or even hostile to any rebuilding of the ancient homeland, as well as from Orthodox traditionalists who regarded Kalischer's initiative as tantamount to blasphemy. Capable of outmaneuvering his opponents in theological debate, he pointed to revolutionary events taking place in Europe and the Middle East, alongside various notorious anti-Jewish episodes. If other oppressed nations were ready to fight and make sacrifices for their homeland, why must the Jews lag behind in the hope of some divine intervention?

Rabbi Tzevi Hirsch Kalischer

As early as 1836, Kalischer tried to interest Amschel Rothschild (q.v.) in his proposals, but the only Jew of means and influence to respond positively at that time was Moses Montefiore (q.v.). Convinced that "there is no greater service for the pious Jew to engage in than rebuilding the desolate Holy Land," Kalischer finally arranged a conference of his supporters at Thorn (1860), where a short-lived German Palestine Colonization Society was established. Its one major achievement, two years later, was sponsoring the publication of Kalischer's book, *Derishat Tziyyon*. A systematic program of land purchase, immigration, and settlement was contained in this "Zionist" blueprint, which laid emphasis on agricultural work and training, the need for Jewish police or self-defense units to guard the new settlements, and economic development to replace the existing charitable allocations from Diaspora Jewry. All of this "practical work," Kalischer believed, would hasten the Messiah's advent and the ultimate ingathering of the exiles. His underlying messianism accounts for the proposal that sacrifices be reinstituted in Jerusalem, even before the Temple's restoration, and that a wholesale renewal of biblical agricultural laws should accompany the "main objective" of land settlement in Palestine.

Despite hostile criticism in German and Palestinian Orthodox circles, the book was given an enthusiastic reception by various European Jewish intellectuals, including Moses Hess (q.v.), who quoted it in his own volume, *Rome and Jerusalem*, published later the same year. The most important outcome of Kalischer's scheme, however, was the founding of an agricultural school, called Mikveh Israel, under the auspices of the French Jewish organization, Alliance Israelite Universelle, in 1870. There, a few miles from Jaffa, young Jewish pioneers would learn the scientific farming methods that Kalischer had planned for his new settlement. Funds which he and his colleagues had raised were then transferred to Mikveh Israel, and it was only declining health that prevented him from taking up Netter's offer of a post as the new school's religious adviser in 1872.

A. Hertzberg, *The Zionist Idea*, 1960.

J. E. Myers, *Seeking Zion: The Messianic Ideology of Z. H. Kalischer*, 1985.

KALLEN, HORACE MEYER (1882–1974) American educator, philosopher, writer, and activist. Kallen was born into a rabbinic family from the Silesian town of Berenstadt. When he was five years old, his family emigrated to the United States. Having graduated from Harvard University in 1903, Kallen taught English at Princeton University (1903–1905) before returning to Harvard for his doctorate in philosophy. In 1908 he began to teach philosophy at Harvard as well as at Clark College, and subsequently spent seven years at the University of Wisconsin on both the philosophy and psychology faculties from 1911 to 1918. During this time he published *William James and Henri Bergson* (1914) and *The Book of Job as a Greek Tragedy* (1918). After World War I, *The Structure of Peace* and *The League of Nations, Today and Tomorrow* earned him the status of close associate to Colonel Edward M. House, then adviser to President Woodrow Wilson at the Versailles Peace Conference. He was one of the founders of the New School for Social Research, New York, in 1919, where he taught for thirty-three years, serving as the dean of the graduate faculty of political and social science from 1944 to 1946, and research professor 1952 to 1965. At the age of eighty-three he accepted a teaching position at Long Island University.

His activism in Jewish affairs found expression through the American Jewish Congress, the American Association for Jewish Education, and YIVO Institute for Jewish Research. Dedicated to the preservation of civil liberties and minority rights, Kallen sat on a number of governmental committees and organizations, including the Presidential Commission on Higher Education, the New York City Commission on Intergroup Relations, the International League for the Rights of Man, and the Society for the Scientific Study of Religion.

As a social philosopher, Kallen is best known for his theory of cultural pluralism (expounded in

Individualism: An American Way of Life (1933), and *The Education of Free Men* (1949) and his advocacy of consumers' cooperatives as an antidote to business exploitation (*The Decline and Rise of the Consumer*, 1936). Kallen believed that Jews and other ethnic groups should maintain a proud and knowledgable loyalty to their native heritage and in this way uniquely contribute to the rich variety that is American culture, where all differences should be welcomed. Consistent in his indebtedness to the values of Judaism (as expounded in *Judaism at Bay*, (1932), and *Of Them Which Say They Are Jews* (1954), edited by J. Pilch, he argued for over half a century in favor of a Jewish homeland in Eretz Israel (see *Zionism and World Politics*, 1921, and *Utopians at Bay*, 1958).

S. Hook and M. R. Konvitz, eds., *Freedom and Experience: Essays Presented to Horace M. Kallen*, 1947.

S. Ratner, ed., *Vision and Action: Essays in Honor of Horace Kallen on his 70th Birthday*, 1953.

KALLIR, ELEAZAR (also Kalir or ha-Kallir; c. 570–c. 630) Foremost liturgical poet (*paytan*) of the gaonic era whose works served as a model for later generations. His life and career are shrouded in mystery, all efforts to disentangle fact from legend having so far proved unavailing. The likelihood is, however, that Kallir was active shortly before the Muslim conquest of Eretz Israel (636 CE), that he studied under Yannai (another famous *paytan*), and that he distinguished himself as a synagogue cantor and writer of liturgical poems in Tiberias. According to a medieval legend, Yannai was so jealous of his former pupil's reputation that he ultimately had him killed by means of a deadly scorpion placed in one of Kallir's shoes, although there is no authentication of this story.

Stylistically, Kallir's hymns and prayers are notable for their use of alphabetical acrostics (sometimes reversed) and occasional display of internal rhyme. Here and there, the poet's signature replaces the Hebrew alphabet in the initial letters of successive lines. Another hallmark of Kallir's verse is the weaving together of biblical citations and midrashic themes or references; this feature, combined with his penchant for neologisms, often renders the text incomprehensible without explanatory notes, as medieval commentators soon observed. Furthermore, Kallir's language (basically an archaic Palestinian Hebrew) and his allusions to kabbalistic literature encouraged many to believe that he was actually a more ancient Eleazar, son of Rabbi Simeon bar Yohai (q.v.), who lived in Roman times!

Well over two hundred of Kallir's hymns are extant, most having been incorporated in the liturgy and prayer books of various rites at some early date, although it is the Ashkenazic (and Hasidic) ritual that now chiefly preserves them. Until modern times, Ashkenazim recited a large number of these poems (*piyyutim*) on holidays and fast days. The tendency nowadays, however, is to skip many in public worship or to relegate the more obscure compositions to an appendix. Those still generally recited, include a sequence of elegies for the Ninth of Av fast; the *hoshana* poems chanted congregationally on Sukkot; the prayer for dew recited by the cantor on Passover; and its counterpart, the prayer for rain, on Shemini Atzeret.

B. Halper, *Post-Biblical Hebrew Literature*, 1921.

KAMENEV, LEV BORISOVICH (originally Rosenfeld; 1883–1936) Russian revolutionary and Soviet leader. Lev Rosenfeld was born in Moscow to a Jewish father and a Russian mother. He studied law at the University of Moscow, where he joined the Social Democratic party. Following his arrest for antigovernment agitation, he fled to Paris in 1902 and became a confidante of Lenin. Nonetheless, he soon returned to Russia and joined the Bolshevik faction.

Rosenfeld moved to the Georgian city of Tiflis, where he headed the revolutionary movement. In Tiflis he assumed the Russian name Kamenev, meaning "Man of Stone." Although he was a man of little personal ambition, he was well connected to other leading revolutionaries; his wife, Olga Bronstein, was Lev D. Trotsky's [q.v.] sister. In Tiflis, he befriended Stalin and possibly introduced him to Lenin.

In 1908 Kamenev moved to Switzerland. There, as coeditor with Lenin of *Proletarii* and *Socialdemokrat*, two important party papers, he was first noted for his lucid and expressive writing. Although Lenin sent him back to Saint Petersburg in 1914 to oversee the progress of the Bolshevik faction in the Duma (Russian parliament), his reputation as a writer preceded him and Trotsky called on him to edit his own party newspaper, *Pravda*.

Upon the outbreak of World War I, Kamenev opposed Lenin's policy supporting Russia's defeat as a means of hastening the revolution. Despite this nationalist stance, for which he was later suspected of being an agent of the Okhrana (the Russian secret police), he was exiled to Siberia for the course of the war, only returning to Petrograd during the general amnest granted by the provisional government following the February revolution. In the capital, he renewed his ties with Stalin, with whom he directed the revolt.

Kamenev was generally noted for taking a cautious approach to the revolution. With Grigori Y. Zinoviev (q.v.), he opposed Lenin's plans for a coup d'etat to replace the provisional government, supporting instead the establishment of a wide coalition of all socialist parties. Lenin was so enraged by this that he demanded Kamenev's and Zinoviev's expulsion from the party. Trotsky, in his *History of the Russian Revolution*, later commented on Kamenev's moderation: "Kamenev grasped better than most Bolsheviks the general ideas of Lenin, but he grasped them in order to give them the mildest possible interpretation in practice."

The years 1920 to 1925 mark the pinnacle of Kamenev's power. After mending his breach with

Lenin, he was appointed chairman of the Moscow Soviet, deputy chairman of the Council of Peoples' Commissariats, and editor of *Pravda*. Following Lenin's death, Kamenev, together with Stalin and Zinoviev, formed a triumvirate that governed Russia. The main rival to the triumvirate's power was Trotsky, whom they opposed wholeheartedly. Only after discovering Stalin's true intentions of becoming dictator of the Soviet Union did Kamenev and Zinoviev join Trotsky in opposing Stalin. Stalin attempted to rid himself of Kamenev, first by sending him as ambassador to Fascist Italy in 1926, and then, in 1927, by having him expelled from the party and exiled to the Urals.

Although Kamenev recanted his Trotskyite views, Stalin continued to view him as a threat. He was again expelled from the party in 1932 and again he recanted. Stalin used the 1934 assassination of Politburo member Sergey M. Kirov as grounds for the great purges of 1936. Kamenev was sentenced to death in a show trial in which he "admitted" participating in a Trotskyite plot to assassinate all members of the ruling Politburo. Some have suggested that Stalin's motives in ridding himself of Kamenev were primarily anti-Semitic. Stalin himself denied this, saying, "We are fighting Trotsky, Zinoviev, and Kamenev, not because they are Jews but because they are Oppositionists."

N. Leven, *Jews in the Soviet Union from 1917*, 1980.
L. Rapaport, *Stalin's War against the Jews*, 1990.
L. Shapiro, *The Communist Party of the Soviet Union*, 1970.
J. Wieczynski, *Modern Encyclopedia of Russian and Soviet History*, 1984.

KAPLAN, MORDECAI MENAHEM (1881–1983)

U.S. religious thinker, founder of the Reconstructionist Movement. Born in Vilna, Lithuania, at age seven he was taken to New York by his father, Rabbi Israel Kaplan who served in the New York rabbinical court. He attended a yeshiva, a public school, the Jewish Theological Seminary, New York City College, and Columbia University, where he studied philosophy and sociology. His first appointment was to the Orthodox Kehilath Jeshurun congregation in 1903. He was not happy in the rabbinate and in 1909 moved to the Jewish Theological Seminary as principal of its recently created Teachers' Institute, which he directed until the 1940s. He was also prominent in the New York community, especially in the attempt by Judah L. Magnes to establish a New York *kehilla* (organized community). He became increasingly radical in his views, vehemently rejecting Orthodoxy and Reform, and feeling that Conservative Judaism required a new direction. In 1915 Kaplan became rabbi of a new synagogue in New York, the Jewish Center, and his concept of a combination of worship and leisure activities inspired the influential Jewish Center movement throughout the United States. He also was the first to institute bat mitzvah confirmation ceremonies for girls (initially for his daughter), corresponding to a boy's bar mitzvah.

In 1922, he founded the Society for the Advancement of Judaism out of which grew the Reconstructionist Movement, based on his teachings. He did not see it as a separate Jewish denomination but as a means to influence the existing ones, and it had a considerable impact in Conservative and Reform circles. Kaplan was critical of the traditional liturgy and published a series of prayer books that he felt were more suited to the modern Jew. The Union of Orthodox Rabbis burned his prayer book during an excommunication ceremony against Kaplan in New York. Kaplan continued to teach in the seminary's Rabbinical School until 1963. When the Reconstructionist Rabbinical College was established in Philadelphia in 1968 with Kaplan's son-in-law, Ira Eisenstein, as its president, Kaplan taught there. In his nineties, he moved to Jerusalem, but returned to the United States when he was ninety-eight to spend his last years there.

Kaplan's first and most influential book, *Judaism as a Civilization*, was published in 1934, followed by many other works containing his teachings, including *The Future of the American Jew*, *The Religion of Ethical Nationhood*, and *The Greater Judaism in the Making*.

He culled critically from the traditional (which he differentiated from Orthodox), Reform, Conservative, and Zionist traditions. He saw Judaism as an evolving religious civilization threatened by modern naturalism, which challenged supernatural faith, as well as what he saw as the outmoded belief that salvation would be achieved in the hereafter. Zionism he saw as the only trend capable of saving the historic nationhood of the Jews; it had adjusted itself to the modern situation far more successfully than the theological movements but had failed to provide a way of life for Jews in the Diaspora. His own program synthesized elements from all four trends: "From Reform, the capacity to treat Jewish religion as an evolving historical process; from Conservatism, the identification of the Jewish people as a permanent reality; from Orthodoxy, the acceptance of Torah as the Magna Carta of the Jewish religion and as a

---

- The foremost problem in Jewish religion is how to get the Jews to take the Bible seriously without taking it literally.
- To interpret the Torah properly we must remember that the whole of it is more than the sum of its parts.
- The ancient authorities are entitled to a vote — but not to a veto.
- The cure for anxiety about the future is not nostalgia for the past.
- People whose religion begins and ends with worship and ritual practices are like soldiers forever maneuvering but never getting into action.

Mordecai Kaplan

covenant with the homeland; and from Zionism the concept of Judaism as an all-embracing civilization rooted in the Land of Israel." Judaism, he taught, had to be reconstructed and adapted to the modern world. The ultimate purpose of life is salvation and he defined God as that power which makes for salvation.

I. Eisenstein in S. Noveck (ed.), *Great Jewish Thinkers of the Twentieth Century*,1963.

E. S. Goldsmith and M. Scult (eds.), *Dynamic Judaism: The Essential Writings of Mordecai M. Kaplan*, 1985.

R. Libowitz, *Mordecai Kaplan and the Development of Reconstructionism*, 1984.

KARELITZ, AVRAHAM YESHAYAHU (known by the title of his work, *Hazon Ish*; 1878–1953) Rabbinic authority. Born in Kossovo in the Russian province of Grodno, and educated by his father from the Talmud, Karelitz was well versed in natural sciences which he studied for the sake of the light they throw on Jewish law and practice. He lived in various centers of study (Kedainiai, Minsk, and Stolbtsy during World War I) and in 1920 settled in Vilna (Vilnius). He had already in 1911 published his first work on the *Shulhan Arukh*, the definitive code of Joseph Caro (q.v), under the name of *Hazon Ish* ("Vision of Man," the work Ish being an acronym of his first names). He wrote another twenty-three works on Jewish law, all under the same title. Karelitz held no official position, but his halakhic authority was universally recognized. he was consulted on legal, moral, public, and personal problems and was deeply respected for his saintly and a scetic mode of life.

In 1923 he moved to Palestine, settling in Benei Berak; because of his presence, the town's reputation as a center of Orthodoxy grew. Thousands visited his modest dwelling to obtain his legal decisions and views. He paid particular attention to the neglected agricultural laws of the Bible. Among his initiatives were the devising of milking machines for use on the Sabbath and permission to use hydroponics to raise produce in the sabbatical year. On one well-publicized occasion, he was visited by Prime Minister David Ben-Gurion (q.v.), who came to consult him on the issue of conscripting Talmudic students into the army.

L. Jung, *Men of the Spirit*, 1964.

KARMAN, THEODORE VON (1881–1963) Aeronautical research engineer; pioneer in the use of mathematics and sciences for aeronautics and astronautics. Born in Budapest, he was descended from Judah Loew ben Bezalel (q.v.). As a child he studied at the model high school that his father had founded. He showed a keen talent for mathematics, but was steered toward engineering by his father. He studied at the Royal Polytechnic University in Budapest and taught there between 1903 and 1906, then continued to the University of Göttingen, where he completed a doctorate while assisting in research on dirigibles.

In 1912 Karman became director of the University of Aachen, a position he retained until 1930. During World War I, he served in the Austria-Hungarian aviation corps. He was active in promoting international scientific cooperation and was appointed honorary president of the International Union of Theoretical and Applied Mechanics, which was founded in 1946.

Karman traveled widely as a visiting professor to Japan, China, India, Belgium, and England and received many academic honors. He first visited the United States in 1926 and four years later he accepted an invitation to direct the Guggenheim Aeronautical Laboratory at the California Institute of Technology. Karman participated in the founding of the U.S. Institute of Aeronautical Sciences and during his years there made major contributions to aerodynamics and hydrodynamics, vibration phenomena, and fluid mechanics. He developed fourteen prototypes for rockets and rocket engines later used in supersonic flight. During World War II he coordinated jet-propulsion research.

He continued to work for international scientific cooperation, helping to establish the International Council of the Aeronautical Sciences in 1956, and the International Academy of Astronautics in 1960. The academy sponsored the First International Symposium on the Basic Environmental Problems of Man in Space, the first international exchange of information on space.

A theory of turbulence and turbulent friction was named after Karman, as were several laboratories around the United States and a crater on the moon. In English he published *General Aero-Dynamic Theory* (1924) and *Mathematical Methods in Engineering* (1940).

Shortly before Karman's death President John F. Kennedy awarded him the first national medal of science.

D. S. Halacy Jr., *Father of Supersonic Flight: Theodore von Karman*, 1965.

T. von Karman and L. Edson, *The Wind and Beyond*, 1967.

KARO, JOSEPH See Caro, Joseph

KASZTNER, RESZO (Rudolf or Israel; 1906–1957) A leader of the Budapest Relief and Rescue Committee during the Holocaust. Born in Cluj, Transylvania, Kasztner became a journalist, lawyer, and Labor Zionist activist. After Hungary annexed northern Transylvania in 1940, he moved to Budapest. Towards the end of 1941 he tried to form a committee that included Jews and Hungarian liberals to help Jewish refugees in Hungary. The attempt did not succeed, but as a result several Jewish activists, among them Joel Brand, gathered around Kasztner, forming the Relief and Rescue Committee. The committee was officially recognized as an arm of the Jerusalem-based Jewish Agency rescue committee in early 1943.

From 1942 until the German occupation of

Hungary in March 1944, Kasztner and his committee not only tried to ameliorate the plight of the Jews of Budapest, but also helped bring refugees from Hungary's border to the capital. Beginning in February 1943, and gaining momentum in the fall of that year, Kasztner's committee, Zionist Youth, and the Slovak Jewish underground, sent agents to Poland to seek out Jews and bring them to safety in Hungary by way of Slovakia. Over one thousand Polish Jews were brought to Hungary by these rescuers.

Following the German occupation of Hungary in 1944, Kasztner became involved in negotiations with the SS for the rescue of Hungarian Jewry and eventually other Jews in Europe as well. First making contact with Eichmann's representative, Dieter Wisliceny, who had conducted negotiations in Slovakia, Kasztner later negotiated with Adolf Eichmann himself and with Kurt Becher, a representative of SS chief Heinrich Himmler. The first stage of negotiations led to the Joel Brand mission, in which Eichmann sent Brand to Turkey to inform the leaders of the mythical "world Jewry" that the SS was willing to exchange the lives of Hungarian Jewry for ten thousand trucks and other nonmilitary supplies. Owing to the reticence of the Allies, Eichmann's proposal was not taken up and Brand was not allowed to return to Hungary with a counteroffer. Subsequent negotiations took place between Kasztner and Becher, as a result of which a group of 1,685 Jews was permitted to leave Hungary, ostensibly for Spain. They were not sent to Spain, but to the Bergen-Belsen camp, from which they eventually reached safety in Switzerland. Kasztner managed to convince Becher to take steps to protect Budapest Jewry at the end of 1944, to hand over several concentration camps to the Allies without harming their occupants, and to allow a transport of Jews hiding in Bratislava to go to Switzerland.

After the war, Kasztner testified in favor of Becher and several of his subordinates. In the early 1950s, he was living in Israel, where he edited the Hungarian language newspaper, *Uj Kelet*, when he was accused of having agreed to the Bergen-Belsen transport, which included some three hundred people from his hometown, in exchange for acquiescing to the deportation of 437,000 Hungarian Jews. When an Israeli journalist, Malkiel Grunwald, said as much in an article, Kasztner sued him for libel. The case riveted the attention of the Israel public, for in effect Kasztner himself was put on trial. Judge Benjamin Halevy concluded that the specific claims of Grunwald were not true, and that during the period of the Holocaust, Kasztner had "sold his soul to the devil." In the ensuing uproar, while the Israeli supreme court was clearing his name, Kasztner was murdered. Although most historians do not doubt Kasztner's motives, in the minds of many Israelis, he remains a controversial figure.

KATZENELSON, YITZHAK (1886–1944) Yiddish and Hebrew poet and dramatist. He was born in Karelitz in the Minsk district of Belorussia, the descendant of a dynasty of rabbis and Hebrew scholars. Through his father, a rabbi and noted Hebrew author, he acquired a love and knowledge of the Jewish people and their language and literature. He soon showed an aptitude for literature and drama, writing his first play, *Dreyfus and Esterhazy*, at the age of twelve, and producing it with the help of a company of youngsters in his backyard. He also helped to teach in his father's modernized religious school in Sgierzh near Lodz.

Following an assistantship in a manufacturing business and an apprenticeship in his uncle's weaving shop, Katzenelson became a teacher, founding and heading a secular Hebrew school in Lodz. He was now writing poetry, prose, and drama in Yiddish and Hebrew. He pioneered a Hebrew theater, and established a dramatic society, staging plays on biblical themes especially for children, acted by the pupils under his direction. He wrote textbooks on the Hebrew language and literature for juniors and seniors and translated into Hebrew works of other writers, such as Heinrich Heine (q.v.). In 1910 he assembled his poems into two volumes named *Dimdumim* ("Twilight").

Katzenelson traveled through Europe, America, and Palestine in 1925 and 1934. He was very moved by the resurgence of Jewish life and culture in Palestine and dreamed of settling there one day. Ideologically, Katzenelson was linked to the Jewish labor movements, having close ties with some of its leaders.

Following the outbreak of World War II, when the Germans captured Lodz, Katzenelson went into hiding. He eventually agreed to escape to Warsaw. There, he and his family suffered hunger, cramped conditions, and the growing threat of impending destruction. His creative forces, which had been paralyzed by the outbreak of war, were rejuvenated in May–June 1940, when a Jewish underground was formed. It bore the name Dror (Freedom) and published some of Katzenelson's poems in its newssheet. Katzenelson taught young teachers to educate children whose parents had died or disappeared. He himself taught Hebrew and the Bible in the Dror high school. From this time on, Katzenelson wrote only in Yiddish so that the masses could be informed and influenced and find an expression of their agony.

The most productive of the ghetto writers, Katzenelson wrote plays in Yiddish to provide subjects for reading during the evenings. Unable in his plays to express directly his emotional response to the plight of the Jews, Katzenelson wrote symbolically on biblical themes, while his poems, which more overtly reflected the bitter reality, were published under different pen names. Perhaps because of the atrocities committed there, the Warsaw ghetto marked the most productive period of Katzenelson's creative powers. The only Jewish book published by Jews in Nazi-occupied Poland was Katzenelson's play *Job*.

When the Germans began mass extermination of the Jews, his wife and two younger sons were among those deported from Warsaw. Katzenelson was shattered. He now identified fully with the resistance movement, stating that "when the last remaining Jew has killed even one murderer, he has redeemed his people! Even a murdered nation can be saved!" His surviving son was a member of a fighting unit in the Warsaw revolt.

Together with other refugees, Katzenelson and his son escaped to the "Aryan" side of Warsaw, where they hid in a bunker for several weeks. He came out of his hiding place on receiving a certificate of foreign nationality, and with Honduras passports they were transported to the internment camp of Vittel in France on May 22, 1943. Although his living conditions were bearable, Katzenelson's distress at the annihilation of his people impeded his creative flow which in turn brought remorse at being lax and allowing the words that should reflect the destruction of the Jews to go unuttered. He fought his wish to die by seeing in his survival the vocation of being the voice of those already departed and dead, and accordingly began to write: "No! No! it must be recorded. The whole world must know what happened. A whole nation has been murdered in broad daylight before the very eyes of the world yet no one has ventured to utter a word! Not a single drop of our blood must go forfeit. The whole story must be told." Once he began writing his Vittel diary, he stopped only to teach the only three children of his "hotel" Hebrew and the Bible and to write stories and poems for them.

In 1944 Katzenelson, along with his son, was deported to Drancy — a concentration camp for French Jews. Upon his arrival there, Katzenelson began teaching Hebrew to the children. Shortly after, the Germans declared that all Polish Jews possessing South American passports were stateless and consequently were to be sent in cattle trucks to the furnaces of Auschwitz, and there Katzenelson and his son perished.

His famous poem "The Song of the Murdered Jewish Nation," one of the outstanding literary works of the Holocaust, was hidden in bottles buried in the grounds of Vittel, while his Vittel diary was smuggled out sewn into the garments of the launderess, who then hid them in tins in her mother's home.

KATZNELSON, BERL (1887–1944) Socialist Zionist.

Known as the soul and compass of the labor movement in Palestine, he became the outstanding ideologist and teacher to the generation of pioneers that built the foundation for what was to become the State of Israel.

He was born in Bobruisk (Belorussia) to a wealthy and educated family. Self-taught, he was soon at home with the writings of the Russian Socialists. The Russian revolution of 1905 made a deep impression on him and led him to study deeper the meaning of socialism and look for a way to fuse it with Zionism. Katznelson belonged to a number of Zionist-Socialist groups but decided to immigrate to Eretz Israel in view of what he considered the sterility of the arguments in these Socialist circles and their negative attitude toward the Jewish national renaissance and the need to settle the Jewish homeland.

Arriving in Eretz Israel in 1909, he immersed himself in physical labor in various Galilee settlements and began his political involvement alongside David Ben-Gurion (q.v.) and Yitzhak Ben-Zvi (q.v.). Katznelson preached the concept of "conquest of labor," that is, the importance of Jewish labor as the basis for Jewish society, and the need for Jewish farmers to employ Jewish laborers. He joined the communal settlement of Kinneret in 1911, and soon after became a founder and spokesman of the Galilee Agricultural Workers. From 1912 he began to plan the creation of a workers' trade union that would look after the special interests of the workers and help implement the Zionist ideology of creating an infrastructure for a future Jewish state. After a brief service in the Jewish Legion of the Allied armies in 1918 he helped to found the Histadrut (Trade Union Federation) in Haifa in 1920. By then he realized that unity of the labor movement in Palestine would make it a leading force in the Jewish community. At the same time he became one of the leaders of Ahdut Ha-Avodah labor party.

The Histadrut became his major arena of activity. In 1925 Katzelson became the editor-in-chief of its daily newspaper, *Davar*, and later founded a publishing company called Am Oved. He demanded that the Histadrut expand its operations to encompass cultural, educational, and even financial activities, in addition to serving as a pure trade union. In the process, he argued that it was inevitable that the labor movement must take control of the fate of the Jewish community and lead it gradually toward independence. He was very much concerned with the rise of right-wing nationalism in the form of the Revisionists under Vladimir Jabotinsky (q.v.) and challenged their ideology, saying that their irresponsible acts could endanger the future of the Jews in the country. He sought to cement the ties between the Jews in Palestine and the masses of Jews in the Diaspora, but was only partly successful. The Revisionists were able to capture the majority of Polish Jewry with their ideology of nationalism and direct action.

Katznelson prophesied the coming destruction of European Jewry but split from the leadership of his party when he opposed the British proposal in 1937 to partition Palestine, arguing that the Zionist movement must insist on the whole country. By nature and upbringing a liberal-humanist, he wanted to impart these traits to the generation of young workers growing up in Palestine. This he did through a series of seminars, lectures, and writings, becoming the teacher of many young men and women working their way up the ranks of the Histadrut and the Haganah underground organization.

His final years were marked by growing illness and sadness over the split in his party (Mapai) between the activists and the more moderate. The Holocaust proved to him that the only place for Jews is in their ancient homeland and that Eretz Israel must be made secure to absorb the survivors. His death came as a shock to the legion of his admirers and David Ben-Gurion cried: "The light of the movement has gone out." Katznelson's teachings were published in twelve volumes of his writings and letters.

A. Schapira, *Berl: The Biography of a Socialist-Zionist*, 1985.

KAUFMAN, GEORGE SIMON (1889–1961) U.S. playwright, director and journalist. Born in Pittsburgh, Pennsylvania, to parents of German origin, Kaufman started his career as a journalist and columnist, moved to New York, worked for the *New York Tribune* and for thirteen years held a post in the drama department of the *New York Times*. He left this job only in 1930, after he was already well established for some time as a famous and successful playwright on Broadway.

Most of Kaufman's plays were written in collaboration. The first of his many hits on Broadway was *Dulcy* (1921), written in collaboration with Marc Connelly. With Connelly he also wrote, among others, *Merton of the Movies* (1922), *Helen of Troy, New York* (1923), and *Beggar on Horseback* (1924). His most successful collaboration was with Moss Hart (q.v.), with whom he wrote, among others, *Once in a Lifetime* (1930), *Merrily We Roll Along* (1934), *You Can't Take It With You* (1936), *The American Way* (1939), a patriotic play, *The Man Who Came to Dinner* (1939), and *George Washington Slept Here* (1940).

Among his other collaborators were Edna Ferber (q.v.), with whom he wrote *Minick* (1924), *The Royal Family* (1927), *Dinner at Eight* (1932), *Stage Door* (1936), and others; Morrie Ryskind, who first assisted him with his solo play *The Cocoanuts* (1925), and then collaborated with him on *Animal Crackers* (1928) and the script of a *A Night at the Opera* (1935) — all to become successful features of the Marx Brothers (q.v.) — *Strike Up the Band* (1930) and the book for the Pulitzer Prize winning musical *Of Thee I Sing* (1931), the music and lyrics of which were written by the brothers George and Ira Gershwin (q.v.); Dorothy Parker (q.v.) (*Business Is Business*, 1925); Ring Lardner (*June Moon*, 1929); Alexander Woollcott (*The Channel Road*, 1929, *The Dark Tower*, 1933); Howard Dietz (*The Band Wagon*, 1931); Katharine Dayton (*First Lady*, 1935, a satire about Washington society); Howard Teichmann (*The Solid Gold Cadillac*, 1953, about a little old lady stockholder who takes over a large corporation). By himself Kaufman wrote only a few one-acters and two full-length plays: *The Cocoanuts* and *The Butter and Egg Man* (1925).

In his collaborations, Kaufman was always the dominant partner. Robert Benchley said once, "Every playwright has to collaborate on at least one play with George S. Kaufman or lose his licence." One of his later collaborators was the actress Leueen MacGrath, whom he married in 1949. Their greatest hit (together with Abe Burrows) was *Silk Stockings* (1955), a musical adaptation of Greta Garbo's film *Ninotchka*. Kaufman and MacGrath divorced in 1957 but remained friendly, and in his last year, when his health failed him, she turned down job offers to stay by him.

Kaufman also directed plays by others (such as MacArthur and Hecht's *The Front Page*, 1928, and *Guys and Dolls*, 1950), and did a lot of "play-doctoring." His notable touch were his funny wise-cracks and precise verbal humor, which remain his distinctive achievement in lifting conventional Broadway hits into the level of fine period pieces.

B. Atkinson, introduction to Kaufman and Hart's *Six Plays*, 1942.

S. Meredith, *George S. Kaufman and the Algonquin Round Table*, 1977.

KAUFMANN, DAVID (1852–1899) Theologian and historian. Born in Moravia, he was educated at local schools and attended the Breslau Jewish Theological Seminary, where he was ordained. He also attended the University of Leipzig, obtaining a Ph.D. in 1874 for his dissertation on the philosophy of religion of Saadiah Gaon (q.v.). Kaufmann was already recognized during his student days as a brilliant scholar and upon his ordination was invited to the chair of philosophy of religion and Jewish history at the newly established Rabbinical Seminary of Budapest, where he remained for the rest of his short life.

Kaufmann was one of the most prolific masters of the science of Judaism and joint editor of the outstanding journal of Jewish scholarship *Monatschrift für Geschichte und Wissenschaft des Judentums* (1897–1899). He was a great collector of books and manuscripts, being able to accumulate the collection because of his marriage to an heiress. After his death, his family donated this unique library to the Hungarian Academy of Sciences. Some items from the Kaufmann Collection have become known worldwide. The first was a facsimile edition of a beautifully illuminated late 14th-century *Haggadah* from Spain, known as the *Kaufmann Haggadah* (1954). Selected pages from Moses Maimonides' [q.v.] *Mishneh Torah*, the four-volume Codex Maimonides, were published in 1980. A third manuscript, an illuminated 18th-century *Scroll of Esther*, has also been reproduced in facsimile in its original scroll form.

He was known as a great fighter against manifestations of anti-Semitism affecting the Jewish community and the Jewish faith. He strongly opposed and disproved the theses of the German orientalist Paul Lagarde and the anti-Semitic preachings of the German court cleric Adolph Stoecker in two booklets.

Many of Kaufmann's scholarly writings dealt with medieval Jewish philosophy and philosophers, including Judah Halevi (q.v.) and Bahya Ibn Pakuda (q.v.). One of his works dealt with physiology and psychology in Jewish and Arabic sources in the Middle Ages. He also wrote historical works (e.g., on the expulsion of the Jews from Vienna and Lower Austria) and genealogical studies, on the Wertheimer and Bacharach families among others.

KAYE, DANNY

KAYE, DANNY (1913–1987) U.S. stage and screen comedian. Born David Daniel Kaminsky to Russian immigrant parents in Brooklyn, Kaye gained his first professional experience as an entertainer in the borscht belt resorts of the Catskill Mountains. While still in his early twenties, he embarked on a tour that took him to the Far East, but he was still an unknown when he made his first short film appearance in 1937. *The Straw Hat Revue* on Broadway (1939) brought him some attention and he shot to overnight stardom in *Lady in the Dark* (1941). It was in this show that he sang the song "Tschaikowsky," the most memorable example of his capacity for tongue-twisting, in which he managed to pronounce the names of fifty Russian composers in thirty-nine seconds.

Following another successful Broadway appearance in Cole Porter's *Let's Face It*, Kaye accepted an offer to star in films for producer Sam Goldwyn (q.v.). His first films, *Up in Arms* and *Wonder Man*, were instant hits and later successes included *The Secret Life of Walter Mitty* and *Hans Christian Anderson*. In many of the comedy films he made for Goldwyn, and later for Paramount, Kaye played double roles that enabled him to show off his talent for mimicry. At the end of the 1940s, he conquered London with his concerts at the London Palladium.

After the mid-fifties, Kaye largely abandoned films to tour the world on behalf of the United Nations International Children's Emergency Fund (UNICEF). In 1963 he began to host his own musical variety show on television; it ran for four seasons. In 1967 he broke all engagements to entertain

Danny Kaye with Israeli soldiers during the Yom Kippur War, Israel, 1973.

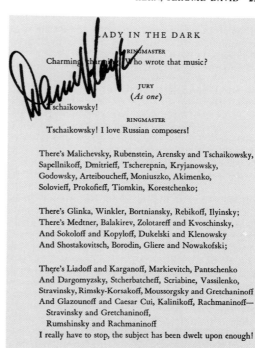

Danny Kaye's autograph on his show-stopping song in Lady in the Dark.

Israeli troops during the Six-Day War. It was not his first visit to Israel and he was to continue to appear there frequently.

In later concert tours Kaye indulged his passion for conducting; other fields in which he was a talented amateur included medicine, flying, and gourmet cooking. His last Broadway role was as Noah in Richard Rodgers' musical *Two By Two*. In 1981 he gave a rare serious performance as a Holocaust survivor in the TV movie, *Skokie*. Blood transfusions he received during heart surgery in 1983 led to hepatitis, of which he died in 1987.
M. Freedland, *The Secret Life of Danny Kaye*, 1986.
K. Singer, *The Danny Kaye Saga*, 1957.

KERN, JEROME DAVID

KERN, JEROME DAVID (1885–1945) U.S. composer. Born in New York to parents of German stock, Kern showed an early musical ability that was encouraged by his mother. His father, a successful businessman who entertained notions of young Jerome following in his footsteps, conceded defeat after only a brief experience of his son's business acumen. Following publication of his first song in 1902, Kern was sent to Europe to imbibe its musical atmosphere. On his return in 1905 he worked as a song plugger for several firms and wrote his first song hit, *How'd You Like to Spoon* *with Me?* In 1905 he returned to England (he had become an extreme Anglophile), but he was brought back to America by impresario Charles Frohman.

Until the outbreak of World War I, many of Kern's songs were written to be interpolated into the New York productions of London shows. In 1914 another great hit, *They Didn't Believe Me*, made Kern a force to be reckoned with and the following year saw the first of what became known as the Princess Theater shows. These were a series of lightweight, tuneful and witty musicals that Kern wrote with Guy Bolton and P. G. Wodehouse to great popular acclaim. During the 1920s he began his collaboration with lyricists Oscar Hammerstein II and Otto Harbach and his hit shows *Sally* and *Sunny* (both starring Marilyn Miller) were topped in 1927 by his most ambitious work, *Show Boat*.

Along with his undeniably important role in the fusing together of the various styles that created the American musical, *Show Boat* guaranteed Kern a place of honor in the history of musical theater. It dispensed with many trite conventions of the form and integrated its songs into the plot in a fashion hitherto unattempted. Further stage successes such as *Music in the Air* and *Roberta* followed and while in Hollywood, Kern produced a number of fine scores, notably *Swing Time* and *Cover Girl*. After World War II, during which he and Hammerstein won the Oscar for best song for their heartfelt *The Last Time I Saw Paris*, Kern was preparing to work on a musical about Annie Oakley when he died of a stroke. He participated in over a hundred stage and screen productions and composed over a thousand songs.

G. Bordman, *Jerome Kern: His Life and His Music*, 1980.

M. Freeland, *Jerome Kern: A Biography*, 1978.

SOME OF JEROME KERN'S FAMOUS SONGS

"Smoke Gets in Your Eyes"
"'Ol Man River"
"All the Things You Are"
"The Way You Look Tonight" (Academy Award)
"The Last Time I Saw Paris" (Academy Award)
"Long Ago and Far Away"
"They Didn't Believe Me"
"Can't Help Loving Dat Man"
"The Touch of Your Hand"
"Make Believe"
"I Won't Dance"
"Lovely to Look At"
"A Fine Romance"
"Look for the Silver Lining"
"Dearly Beloved"
"Who?"
"Why Do I Love You?"
"Yesterdays"

KESSEL, JOSEPH (1898–1979) French author, journalist, and script writer; member of the French Academy. Born to Russian parents in one of the Jewish agricultural settlements in Argentina, his parents took him back to Russia as an infant, and later settled in Paris when he was ten years old.

Although he trained as an actor at the Conservatoire Dramatique and acted for a brief period in the Odéon Theater, he embarked upon a career in journalism at an early age, beginning to write for the *Journal des Débats* at the age of sixteen.

He volunteered for service when World War I broke out, and served as a pilot and officer in the air force, receiving the Croix de Guerre and other military honors. After the war he wrote his first novel, *L'equipage* ("The Crew"), based upon his wartime experiences. The novel, published in 1922, became a best-seller in France. Another book, published the same year, was *La steppe rouge*, a collection of travel sketches.

He continued to write, becoming one of the most popular French authors between the two world wars. He published fifty novels and ten short stories in his lifetime, in addition to serving as a correspondent for a number of papers, including *France-Soir* and *Le Figaro*. Many of his books were adapted to the movie screen. In 1927 he received the grand prix du roman of the Académie Française for his novel *Les coeurs purs* ("The Pure Hearts").

In 1939–1940 he worked as a war correspondent. When France was occupied by the Germans he escaped to London, where he served as an aide to General Charles de Gaulle, and as a captain in the Free French air force squadron. He flew on many special missions into France, receiving the Croix de Guerre after the war, as well as being admitted to the Légion d'Honneur, the highest French distinctions, and receiving military decorations from Britain and the United States.

Among his best-known novels are *Belle de jour*, which was later adapted as a movie by Luis Buñuel, and *Le lion* ("The Lion"), which became a best-seller in the United States. He wrote extensively about aviation, including a novel, *Le bataillon du ciel* (1947).

Although he was not involved in Jewish life, he wrote a number of books on Zionism and Jewish-related topics, including *Terre d'amour* (1927) and *Terre de feu* (1948) on the State of Israel, which were later combined into one volume, and *Les mains du miracle* on Himmler's physiotherapist, Felix Kersten, who saved the lives of many Jews during the war. In 1964, upon election to the Académie Française, he stressed his pride in his Judaism in his first address.

KIMHI, DAVID (known by the acronym Radak; c. 1160–c. 1235). Bible commentator and Hebrew grammarian. He came from a distinguished family of scholars of Spanish origin who lived in Provence in southern France. His father, Joseph (1105–1170) was a Bible commentator, translator from Arabic to Hebrew, grammarian, and anti-Christian pole-micist. His elder brother, Moses (died c. 1190) was also a Bible commentator and grammarian. David Kimhi was born and lived in Narbonne. His grammatical works include *Sefer ha-Shorashim* ("Book of Roots"), which gives all forms of the Hebrew verbs and their derivatives, and *Mikhlol* ("Compendium"), a lucid Hebrew grammar compiling and systematizing earlier works on the subject and the first such book written in Hebrew. These contributions led to a greater scientific study of the Hebrew language.

He is best known for his Bible commentary, covering Genesis, the prophetical books, Psalms, and Chronicles. Kimhi took great efforts to establish the most accurate texts and traveled considerably to consult available Bible manuscripts. He was influenced by the commentary of Abraham Ibn Ezra (q.v.) and the writings of his father and brother. The result is a clear exposition, based largely on the literal meaning, and often involving grammatical analysis and insight. He sometimes makes references to contemporary events, such as the Crusades, and occasionally engages in anti-Christian polemics, especially attacking christological interpretations, which led to the censorship of certain passages. Nevertheless, his commentary, in its Latin translation, was very popular and influential in christian circles and its mark can be found, for example, in the King James (Authorized) Version of the Bible.

In his day, a bitter controversy was raging between traditionalist and rationalist circles over the philosophical writings of Moses Maimonides (q.v.). Kimhi was a leading figure in the rationalist camp, supporting Maimonides, and traveled to Spain to defend Maimonides' works.

His Bible commentary was incorporated in standard editions of the Hebrew Bible. Its indispensability is illustrated in the popular adaptation of the rabbinical saying, "If there is no flour (*kemah*, i.e., food), there is no Torah" into "If there is no Kimhi, there is no Torah."

W. Chomsky, *David Kimhi's Hebrew Grammar*, 1952.

F. Talmage, *David Kimhi, The Man and His Commentaries*, 1975.

KISCH, EGON ERWIN (1885–1948) Journalist and writer. Born in Prague to a linen merchant, he studied in the German university of Prague. From 1906 to 1913, he was the crime reporter of the Prague journal *Bohemia* and wrote about the Prague underworld in his *Prague Streets and Nights* (1912). At this time he moved in circles with the city's literary figures, both the German writers, such as Rilke, Franz Kafka (q.v.), and Max Brod (q.v.), and Czech authors, such as Jaroslav Hašek. He then spent a short stint in Berlin, where he began to write as a political journalist in the *Berliner Tageblatt* (uncovering the famous Redl spy case) and worked as dramaturgist at the Kunstler Theater. He served in the Austro-Hungarian army

Egon Erwin Kisch

in World War I in Serbia and was later press officer at army headquarters in Vienna.

A cofounder of the International Federation of Socialist Revolutionaries, he led the communist Red Guard in Vienna in 1918, for which he was imprisoned and expelled from Austria. He returned to Berlin and during the following decade became one of the best known publicists in the socialist world. Kisch traveled extensively (Europe and Africa, 1922–1924; the Soviet Union 1925–1926; the United States (visited illegally) 1928–1929; China, 1932), each journey being the subject of a descriptive book, with political and social analyses.

After the 1933 Reichstag fire, he was arrested and then freed on the intervention of the Czech government, and deported to Czechoslovakia. He then moved to Paris. In 1934 he arrived in Australia but was refused admission as an "undesirable alien," whereupon he jumped overboard into the sea at Perth, was arrested, sent to prison for six months and deported. In 1937–1938 he fought in the Spanish Civil War, but when World War II broke out he moved first to the United States and settled in Mexico, where he worked on the *Freies Deutschland* newspaper. After the war he returned to Prague, where he was honorary president of the Jewish community.

Apart from his travel books, he wrote extensively on Prague, including stories of Prague, Jewish life (*Tales from Seven Ghettos*, 1948) and an autobiographical work (*Sensation Fair*, 1941). His collected works were issued in 1960. He was highly respected throughout post-World War II eastern Europe and under the East German Communist regime one of the most prominent cafés on East Berlin's Unter den Linden was the Egon Erwin Kisch Café.

D. Schlenstedt, *Life and Works of Egon Erwin Kisch* (German), 1968.

E. Utitz, *Egon Erwin Kisch* (German), 1956.

KISLING, MOÏSE (1891–1953) French painter. He was born in Cracow, Poland, and at age fifteen studied at the Academy of Fine Arts there. Before the age of twenty he went to Paris, where he met many Jewish artists and writers, among them the writer Sholem Asch (q.v.), who was impressed by his work. After Asch returned to the Ukraine, Kisling began to receive a monthly stipend from a mysterious benefactor, who wrote that "Sholem Asch had suggested it." In 1912 Kisling's work was accepted for the Salon d'Automne, and he often exhibited subsequently in the salons d'Automne, salons des Indépendents, and the salons des Tuileries. In World War I he served in the Foreign Legion and was badly wounded.

A convivial personality, his studio was often full of friends, including American visitors. For a time he shared his studio with his close friend, Amedeo Modigliani (q.v.).

His work won wide acclaim in 1921, when he had his first one-man show, followed by many successful exhibitions in France, elsewhere in Europe and the United States.

Kisling was on the list of Jewish painters condemned by the Nazi regime. At the outbreak of World War II, he volunteered for the French army and, having become a French citizen in 1919, served in the Eleventh Regiment of the Army Service Corps. Demobilized in 1940 and with the Gestapo at his heels, he fled to Portugal and then to New York.

Kisling worked industriously. He exhibited at the Whitney Museum, went to Hollywood, where he painted several movie stars, and returned to New York, where he had a studio on Central Park South. As in Paris, his studio was always open to friends.

In America, Kisling worked for the Four Arts Association, collecting art supplies and other necessities for the families of artists living in France. After the war he returned to France with these materials, which he distributed to those who needed them. He found that his studio had been vandalized during the war, and built a new one near his home in Sanary-sur-Mer.

Kisling was considered one of the outstanding painters of the School of Paris. His paintings show strength, charm, and sensibility. His colors were beautiful and he has been described as an "opulent lover of color." His still lifes, particularly his paintings of flowers, are beautifully composed in brilliant colors.

Though his work sometimes showed the influence of cubism (he worked for a time at the Bateau-Lavoir and was a friend of Pablo Picasso and Georges Braque), it is severely classical and intensely individual.

His stylized portraits, are mostly of young women, graceful and tender. His nudes are painted with bold sensuality. Waldemar George saw them as having "the sweet perfume of Asia... Ispahan, Baghdad and Jerusalem."

A. Salman, *Kisling*, 1928.

G. Charensol, *Moïse Kisling* (French), 1948.

KISS, JÓZSEF (1843–1921) Hungarian poet and editor. His father owned a general store in a poor Hungarian village where Kiss was born. Until age thirteen, he had an exclusively traditional Jewish education and started high school when he was fourteen. He had to give up his studies when his father could no longer pay for them and from the age of seventeen he eked out a living as a teacher, wandering from village to village, teaching children of well-to-do farmers and Jews. In 1868 he arrived in Pest, where he published his first slim volume of poetry, *Jewish Songs*. This was the time of Jewish emancipation in Hungary and he wrote on an optimistic note: "Your day has dawned, Jew. You, too, have a fatherland now."

Kiss became the first Jew to write poetry in the Hungarian language, adopting the characteristics of the classics of Hungarian poetry, Sándor Petoefi and János Arány, whose ballads were written in a Hungarian folkloristic style and whose heroes spoke the language of the peasants. Most of Kiss's heroes and heroines were Jews, but they all spoke in the style and rhythms of the Hungarian folk song. In fact, there was something artificial about his "Magyarizing" style, which has long since been discredited.

Kiss's importance as a poet was gradually recognized by even the most prestigious literary societies. From 1870 to 1873, he edited the weekly, *Kepes Vilag* ("The World in Pictures"), and during an illness in 1874 wrote his first novel, *Mysteries of Budapest*, a crime story, under the pseudonym Rudolf Szentesi. His first period as a poet ended in 1876, when due to dire financial circumstances he was constrained to accept a poor, badly-paid job as notary of the Jewish community of Temesvár (now Timisoara, Romania).

In 1882, he returned to Budapest and held a clerical post at the French-Hungarian Insurance Society. The visit to Budapest by the Viennese actor Josef Lewinsky led to a favorable change in his fortunes when Lewinsky, who recited Petoefi's poems in German translation, included in his program a poem by Kiss that won general acclaim.

Kiss's return to the capital, in 1882, coincided with the notorious Tiszaeszlar blood-libel case, which moved him to write the gripping poem

"Against the Tide," and later, in the face of growing anti-Semitism, another great poem, "The New Ahasuerus".

Kiss's best poems testified to his unbending loyalty to Judaism and the Jewish tradition, as in the monumental ballad *Jehovah*, the hero of which is the biblical Job. In 1888 he published a collection of Jewish religious verse, *Holy Days*, which was commissioned by the Jewish community of Pest in 1882 on the recommendation of the community's then secretary, Ignaz Goldziher (q.v.). The community delegated Goldziher and Rabbi Samuel Kohn to be the arbiters of the poems' suitability. While stressing the poetry's artistic merit, they made suggestions for amendments of various theological, liturgical, and philological aspects. Kiss was offended and asked for the return of the manuscript, which he then published as a separate volume.

When French-Hungarian Insurance Society went bankrupt in 1889, Kiss was once again without a job. By this time, he had to provide for his five children. His friends, having failed to find him another job, lent him enough capital to start a new literary weekly, *The Week*, which appeared from 1890 to 1924. Kiss was by now aware of the doubtful value of assimilation as an alternative to a traditional Jewish life style; from this point on he wrote less in the Hungarian national style and devoted his energies to editing his weekly. *The Week* became established as a leading literary journal whose contributors included the best contemporary writers and poets. The journal was without fixed political viewpoints, accepting articles from writers who were convinced socialists and from conservative writers. The paper had a slightly elitist, somewhat ironical style and opposed the literary establishment.

Kiss's marriage to his cousin was not a happy one and when, in the mid-1880s, he made the acquaintance of a divorcée who had written him fan letters, he found a new muse. This rather platonic romance resulted in some of his best love poems ("The Naomi Cycle").

Of Kiss's five children, one died in 1936 and the other four were all victims of the Nazi deportations. Kiss's belated recognition by the Hungarian state came only after World War II, when a street was named for him in Budapest. After the 1956 uprising, a plaque was placed on his birthplace and a statue of him was erected there in 1967.
M. Smith, ed., *Kiss Jozsef koltemenyei*, 1954 (with an English introduction and several poems in English translation).

KLEIN, ABRAHAM MOSES| (1909–1972)
Canadian author. Born in Montreal to recently arrived Russian Jewish immigrants, A. M. Klein was one of Canada's foremost poets.

His four books of poetry, *Hath Not a Jew*, *The Hitleriad*, *Poems*, and *The Rocking Chair*, as well as his novel, *The Second Scroll*, his essays, and his posthumous collection of poetry reflect the dualities in Klein as an individual and as a literary figure.

The first duality is connected with Canada's character as a bilingual and bicultural nation. Although he was born and educated in an English-speaking environment, Klein spent the bulk of his professional life as a lawyer in the French-speaking climate of the Province of Quebec.

The second duality concerns Klein's identity as a Canadian and as a Jew. On the one hand, he was a major figure in Canadian letters and was appointed a visiting lecturer in English at McGill University

---

FROM THE POETRY OF A. M. KLEIN

In the following poem, Klein argues that the Zionist enterprise in mandatory Palestine calls for the creation of a new orientation for Jewish poetry (and, by inference, Jewish identity in the contemporary world) — a turning away from an overriding concentration on the suffering of Diaspora existence and, an emphasis on Jewish national rebirth in the ancestral homeland. The time for mourning over the loss of that homeland is over, for the dawn of a new era in Jewish history is fast approaching.

"To the Jewish Poet"

You cherished them as ancient gems, those tears
Of Jeremiah; through that night for you
These only shone; these jewels of the Jew
With which he graced his sorrow all the years.
But now forget them! Spurn them! The dawn nears!
The Dawn arises, tinted white and blue,
Upon a land, lean to the parvenu —
Make fat that land with sweat, and not with tears...
Do purge your voice; suppress the groan; abate
The weepings; cleanse the whimper; choke the whine...
You make grimaces, cast complaints on fate,
And speak about a cup of bitter wine?
That cup has now a crack, a crack as great
As the whole length and breadth of Palestine.

In the following excerpt Klein comments sardonically on assimilation:

From "Hath not a Jew"

Now we will suffer loss of memory;
We will forget the tongue our mothers knew;
We will munch ham, and guzzle milk thereto,
And this on hallowed fastdays, purposely...
To Gentile parties we will proudly go;
And Christians, anecdoting us, will say:
"Mr. and Mrs. Klein — the Jews, you know"

Montreal. His involvement in Canadian life extended to the political sphere as well: in 1949 he ran for Parliament as a candidate for the socialist CCF party. On the other hand, Klein was very much a Jewish poet. Many of his subjects are biblical figures. Klein's poem "Five Characters" describes the five major figures of the Purim narrative, while one of his ballads, "Legend of Lebanon," can be seen as a Wordsworth-like narrative poem on a biblical theme. His poems contain references to various aspects of Jewish tradition and culture, while his two books published during the period of the Holocaust — *Hath Not a Jew* and *The Hitleriad* — can be regarded as Klein's contribution to the struggle against anti-Semitism and Nazism. A symbolic novel that chronicles some of the major events of contemporary Jewish history, notably the creation of the State of Israel, *The Second Scroll* is Klein's modern-day appendix to the scroll of the law, the Pentateuch, and is thus similarly arranged into five books, bearing the same titles as those of the Pentateuch.

U. Caplan, *Like One That Dreamed: A Portrait of A. M. Klein*, 1982.

G. K. Fischer, *In Search of Jerusalem: Religion and Ethics in the Writings of A. M. Klein*, 1975.

S. J. Spiro, *Tapestry for Designs: Judaic Allusions in "The Second Scroll" and the Collected Poems of A. M. Klein*, 1984.

M. Waddington (Comp.), *The Collected Poems of A. M. Klein*, 1974.

KLEIN, MELANIE (1882–1960) Psychoanalyst. She was born in Vienna. At age fourteen, she decided to follow in her father's footsteps and study medicine, but with her engagement, at seventeen, her plans changed, and she studied art and history at the University of Vienna though she never completed her degree.

After moving to Budapest, she chanced upon the works of Sigmund Freud (q.v.), and was immediately drawn to psychoanalysis. After being analyzed by Sandor Ferenczi (q.v.), she relocated to Berlin (with her three children but without her husband; they later divorced), and finally, in 1926, she accepted the invitation of Ernest Jones and settled in London, where her technical and theoretical creativity flourished.

While Freud had woven complex theories about the first years of life, he had himself virtually no direct contact with children. Klein, rather than reconstructing childhood psychological biographies from analyses of adults, devoted herself to working with children, sometimes younger than three years old. She discovered early that the play of children is not an aimless activity, but the fruit of a rich fantasy life for which all the tools of psychoanalysis can be utilized. Much of what Freud postulated as occurring in the oedipal stage of childhood — ages three to five — Klein advanced to the first year of life.

Klein was keenly aware of the obstacles, theoretical, technical, and methodological, in attempting to penetrate the psyche of infants. To meet the challenge, she brought to bear an acute intuitive sense in extrapolating from adult and child psychoanalysis. Her language in describing the primitive inner life of infants is accordingly quite fantastic. A Kleinian baby lives in a world populated by good and bad breasts, imagines numerous penises to be incorporated in the mother's vagina, and desires to scoop out the mother's breast and to destroy its contents. These unusual and striking images can daunt the uninitiated and have even deterred many psychoanalysts from accepting her ideas. Nevertheless, her work altered the theory of psychoanalysis.

Klein's focus was not only upon innate drives and inner conflicts, which from the outset had marked psychoanalytic thinking. She also stressed the emotional ties with the outside world, consisting at first primarily of the mother. She was a founder of the object relations school of psychoanalysis.

Klein posited a paranoid-schizoid position, according to which, in the course of the normal development of a baby in the first half year of life, images of mother as good (helping, satisfying) and bad (frustrating, threatening) are kept separate. This is followed by the depressive position, the second half of the first year, during which the baby gradually discovers that mother is one. Having achieved integration of mother, loss becomes a possibility; for the first time, the infant may experience anxiety, guilt, and sadness.

In the politicized atmosphere of British psychoanalysis, Klein came into occasionally acrimonious conflict with Anna Freud (q.v.) over issues of technique and theory. In some of these conflicts, Klein's daughter, Melitta Schmideberg, also an analyst, took sides against her mother.

J. A. Lindon, "Melanie Klein," in *Psychoanalytic Pioneers*, eds. F. Alexander, S. Gisenstein, and M. Grotjahn, 1966.

H. Segal, *Introduction to the Work of Melanie Klein*, 2nd ed., 1974.

P. Roazen, *Freud and His Followers*, 1975.

KLEMPERER, OTTO (1885–1973) Conductor and composer. Born in Breslau, Klemperer received his first music lessons from his mother and continued studying piano, music theory, composition, and conducting in Frankfurt and Berlin. At the age of twenty-one Klemperer replaced a colleague at the last minute to conduct the famous Max Reinhardt (q.v.) production of Offenbach's *Orpheus in the Underworld* in Berlin. Later, Klemperer became chorus master and then conductor at the German theater in Prague. He also assisted Gustav Mahler (q.v.), whom he had met earlier in his career, preparing the world premiere of his Eighth Symphony, the "Symphony of a Thousand," in Berlin.

In 1917 Klemperer was hired for his first major permanent position as music director of the Cologne Opera. Subsequently Klemperer led the opera company in Wiesbaden and then the Kroll Opera in Berlin, a theater devoted to producing new works and a cultural institution that represented the new Weimar Republic. In all these theaters Klemperer presented many German premieres, including works by Igor Stravinsky, Kurt Weill (q.v.) and Arnold Schoenberg (q.v.). At this time he was considered one of the leading German conductors of his generation. In 1923 he refused the position of music director of the Berlin Staatsoper because he felt he would not have sufficient artistic independence.

In 1933 Klemperer's physical troubles began. During a rehearsal in Leipzig the conductor leaned back and went through the rail on the podium, landing on the base of his skull. Later that year, after the Nazis came to power, he was forced to leave Germany and emigrated to the United States, where he became the music director of the Los Angeles Philharmonic. In 1939 Klemperer had to undergo an operation for a brain tumor that left him partially paralyzed and for some years he could not conduct. Stories followed, some of which alleging that the maestro had a nervous breakdown and that he had escaped from an asylum. When these stories did not cease, Klemperer put a lot of money into staging a concert in Carnegie Hall, showing the world that he was still the same musician. Somehow he survived and eventually became the director of the Budapest Opera (1947–1950). Klemperer left Hungary when the communist regime's restrictive musical politics started to affect his work. Klemperer's health was deteriorating and the conductor often lost the memory of his own identity, and was even found wandering in the streets. In 1954 Klemperer began conducting and recording with the Philharmonia Orchestra of London, becoming the orchestra's principal conductor a year later.

Then aged seventy, a new chapter in Klemperer's life began. The conductor had his second bloom. A review of a 1961 Klemperer concert attests to both his ill health and musical prowess: "In an age of well-tailored virtuoso conductors, he stands out like a Michelangelo sculpture among Dresden figurines. He makes his way slowly to the podium, dragging his mighty body, cane in hand. On the podium is a large chair on which he sits after a curt nod to the audience. He does not use a baton and the score is open before him. Generally he beats time with his fists, a minuscule beat for so tremendous a man. Often no beat is visible at all. . . . His conducting retains its intense drive and vitality. Never has he had much charm. He is always ultra-serious, pursuing his ends in a straight, uncompromising line. In the big pieces of the repertoire there is nobody exactly like him. Nobody can so convey the size and grandeur of Beethoven, Brahms, Mahler, Bruckner. In a way he is a transfigured Kapellmeister — a non-virtuoso conductor who may even have something of the pedant in him, but whose vision and conception happen to be so big that he and his music emerge monument-size."

In 1970 Klemperer conducted in Jerusalem and accepted Israeli citizenship. Two years later he retired and resided in Zurich, Switzerland.

Although known above all as a stern conductor, Klemperer was also a composer in the romantic style. He composed an opera, *Das Ziel*, six symphonies, nine string quartets, and about one hundred art songs.

P. Heyworth, ed., *Conversations with Klemperer*, 1973.

KOESTLER, ARTHUR (1905–1983) Author and journalist. He was born in Budapest, where his grandfather had fled from Russia during the Crimean War. Most of his childhood years were spent living with his family in boarding houses in Budapest and Vienna, tended by a succession of governesses. With his father he maintained a civilized, reserved relationship. He recalled that his formative years were dominated by guilt, fear, and loneliness, factors he believed contributed to his "subsequent preoccupation with physical violence, terror, and torture."

He became attracted to communism at the age of fourteen when the Communist party rose to power in Budapest in 1919. In his autobiography, *Arrow in the Blue*, published in 1952, he wrote: "[Communism] had the sound of a good, just, and hopeful word."

Between 1922 and 1926, he studied technical engineering at the University of Vienna, but dropped out on an impulse before graduation, after having devoted most of his academic years to Zionist Revisionist politics and to the self-taught study of psychology and psychiatry.

In 1926 he boarded a ship to Palestine. After a futile attempt at settling in the Jezreel Valley, he endured a year of poverty and semistarvation while establishing and running, single-handed, a political press agency in Haifa. The agency closed down a few months later, and after a succession of short-lived jobs in Palestine, he spent a brief spell in Berlin, working for the Revisionist party. He was cynical about the ideals motivating the kibbutz society, and his experiences in Palestine formed the basis of his novel, *Thieves in the Night* (1946).

The turning point of his career came in 1927 when he received a post as the Middle East correspondent of the Ullstein newspaper chain, for which he worked in Jerusalem and later in Paris until 1930. Losing interest in Zionism, he spent the next three years as scientific editor of the *Vossische Zeitung* in Berlin and foreign editor of the *B.Z. am Mittag*. During 1931, he was the only member of the press on board the Graf Zeppelin polar expedition.

His sympathies increasingly turned toward Marxism with the "beginning of the age of barbarism in Europe," as he states in his autobiography, and he visited Russia during 1932 and 1933. However, he abandoned the party in 1938, following Stalin's purges. His novel *Darkness at Noon* (1941), in which a Bolshevik under inhuman psychological pressures admits to crimes he did not commit and denounces totalitarian judicial practices, was very influential. *The God that Failed* (1949) also describes his disillusionment with communism.

In 1936 Koestler became the war correspondent of the London-based *News Chronicle*. Sent to cover the Spanish Civil War, he was captured by the Nationalists and sentenced to death. The sentence was commuted to a prison sentence following the international protest that ensued, and he spent one hundred days in Franco's jails, describing his agonizing experience in *Spanish Testament* (1937).

In 1939–1940 he was interned in a French detention camp, after which he volunteered for the French Foreign Legion. He escaped to Britain when France fell and served in the British Pioneer Corps.

In 1945 he returned to Palestine as a special correspondent for the *Times of London* and served as a special correspondent for the *Manchester Guardian*, the *New York Herald Tribune*, and *Le Figaro* in 1948. His book *Promise and Fulfillment: Palestine 1917–1949* (1949) is a survey of the British Mandate period and the emergence of the State of Israel. Koestler himself, however, opted for assimilation, the only alternative he believed was open to Diaspora Jews who did not want to immigrate to Israel.

His book *The Yogi and the Commissar* (1945) contains essays on political subjects. From the late 1950s he turned to philosophical analyses of art, society, science, and religion, such as *The Lotus and the Robot* (1960), which examines the contemporary significance of Yoga and Zen Buddhism, and *The Act of Creation* (1964) on the creative process. His *Thirteenth Tribe* (1967) endeavors to show that the bulk of European Jewry is descended from the Khazars, an Indo-European people who settled in southern Russia.

On March 3, 1983, Arthur Koestler was found dead in his apartment together with his third wife, Cynthia, in an apparent suicide pact. He had been suffering from leukemia and Parkinson's disease. He left 600,000 dollars to promote university study of psychic phenomena.

ARTHUR KOESTLER ON HIS FAMILY

Over thirty years before his death from an overdose of tranquilizers, Koestler wrote in *Arrow in the Blue*, the first volume of his autobiography:

"The family tree of the Koestlers starts with my grandfather Leopold and ends with — me."

"With the present writer's death, which according to a Gypsy prediciton will be unexpected and violent, the Koestler, or Kostler, or Kestler, or Kesztler saga will come to a fitting end."

J. A. Atkins, *Arthur Koestler*, 1956.

H. Harris, *Astride Two Cultures; Koestler at Seventy*, 1976.

H. Levine, *Arthur Koestler*, 1984.

KOHLER, KAUFMANN (1843–1926) Scholar and leader of Reform Judaism in the United States. Born in Fürth, Bavaria, to Orthodox Jewish parents (his mother was descended from a long line of rabbis), he had his early education at the school attached to the Jewish orphanage, of which his father was the director. Between the ages of ten and twenty, his formal studies were in rabbinics; he received instruction in secular subjects from private tutors. In 1862 he entered the high school in Frankfurt and continued his rabbinical studies under Samson Raphael Hirsch (q.v.).

Kohler associated himself with the Kuenen-Wellhausen school of critical interpretation of the Bible, and in 1867 received a doctorate at the University of Erlangen for his thesis on the blessing of Jacob. One of the earliest essays by a Jew in the field of higher biblical criticism, it was met with consternation and was even banned by some teachers because of its radical character. When the young rabbi realized that he had no future in the Orthodox rabbinate in Germany, he embarked on an academic career and studied Oriental philology at the University of Leipzig. He began to take an interest in Reform Judaism, finding its reconciliation of viewpoints on historical, linguistics, and ethnological knowledge with traditional Jewish knowledge more to his satisfaction. In 1869, he was appointed rabbi of Congregation Bet-El in Detroit and immediately began to express his ideas on the significance and purpose of Reform Judaism. In 1871 Kohler became rabbi of Sinai Temple in Chicago, where, in view of the decline in synagogue attendance on the Sabbath, he introduced Sunday services. Many of his sermons, delivered during this period in both German and English, on topics such as Judaism and modern science, the adaptation of old doctrines and practices to modern life, and other relevant issues, appeared in Jewish journals. In 1876 he published a history of biblical times under the title *A Jewish Reader for Sabbath Schools*; in 1899 he issued a *Guide for Instruction in Judaism*.

In 1879 Kohler became rabbi of Temple Beth El in New York, succeeding his father-in-law, David Einhorn. Kohler convened the Rabbinical Conference in Pittsburgh (1885), and the declaration of principles called The Pittsburgh Platform adopted there constituted the basis of Reform Judaism in America. He was elected president of the Central Conference of American Rabbis and took a leading part in the preparation of the Union Prayer Book.

In 1903 Kohler was elected president of the Hebrew Union College, Cincinnati. He amplified and improved its course of studies, raised its academic standards, and succeeded in attracting leading scholars to its staff.

His publications include *Backward and Forward*, a compilation of his sermons in defense of the Reform movement and over eight hundred articles on biblical exegesis and Jewish philosophy. His best-known work is *Jewish Theology, Systematically and Historically Considered*, written in German in 1910; an English version was published in 1918. In it he defines the general concept of theology and of Judaism and sets out to determine the essence and basic beliefs of Judaism. Kohler was the editor of the philosophy and theology sections of the *Jewish Encyclopedia* (1901–1906), for which he wrote three hundred entries. He also acted as one of the editors of the English Bible issued by the Jewish Publication Society in 1917.

When he retired in 1921 as president emeritus of the Hebrew Union College, Kohler returned to New York and wrote books and articles for scholarly periodicals. Above all he devoted himself to his major historical study, *The Origins of the Synagogue and the Church*, published posthumously in 1929.

J. L. Blau, in K. Kohler, ed., *Jewish Theology*, 1968.
R. J. Marx, *Kaufmann Kohler as Reformer*, 1951.

KOHN, HANS (1891–1971) U.S. historian and political scientist. Born and educated in Prague, Kohn studied at the University of Prague, where he came under the influence of Kant and Nietzsche. He was an active member of Bar Kochba, a Zionist student group. After earning his doctorate in jurisprudence in 1914, he joined the Czech regiment of the Austro-Hungarian army. Captured by Russian forces, he was detained in camps in Samarkand and Siberia and there learned to speak Russian. He returned to Prague and in 1921 went to London where he joined the Independent Labour party led by Ramsay MacDonald, taking an active part in its affairs. He served as secretary to the Jewish delegation at the Paris Peace Conference, and from 1921 to 1925 was employed by the Keren Hayesod, the fund-raising arm of the World Zionist Organization. In 1928 he published *A History of Nationalism in the East*.

From 1925 to 1929 Kohn lived in Jerusalem, where he wrote books on the Middle East and served as correspondent for the *Frankfurter Zeitung* and the *Neue Züricher Zeitung*. He returned to Europe and in 1933 moved to the United States, where he joined the faculty of Smith College, lecturing on modern European history and the intellectual history of modern Europe. In 1949 he was appointed professor of history at City College of New York, where he remained on the faculty until his retirement in 1962.

Kohn's main work was *The Idea of Nationalism* (1944), a study of the development of nationalism and universalism from ancient times to 1789. This was followed by *The Age of Nationalism* (1962) and *Prelude to Nation States* (1967). He was also the author of works on Martin Buber (q.v.), Heinrich Heine (q.v.), and Zionist ideology and politics, as well as the editor of Ahad Ha-Am's [q.v.] *National-*ism and the Jewish Ethic*. He also translated into German Joseph Klausner's *History of Modern Hebrew Literature*. His autobiography *Living in a Modern World* (1954) contains a list of his publications.

In his writings and lectures, Kohn sought to mobilize world opinion against totalitarianism and during World War II he equated fascism with communism, telling his students that both Hitler and Stalin were gangsters. He was also an outspoken critic of American military involvement in Korea and expressed his doubts about the wisdom of rearming West Germany.

At first Kohn supported the idea of cultural Zionism but he became disenchanted with it in 1929, when he realized that the Arabs were not included in the plans for the Jewish homeland in Palestine.
Orbis, vol. 10 (Winter 1967). Special issue devoted to Hans Kohn.

KOOK, ABRAHAM ISAAC (1865—1935) Known widely as *Rav* ("Rabbi" Kook). Religious thinker; first Chief Rabbi of Palestine. Born in Grieve, a small town in north Russia, he was an exceptional student and known as a child prodigy. He studied in the famous yeshiva (Talmudic academy) of Volozhin, Lithuania, and then served as rabbi to communities in Lithuania and Latvia until moving to Eretz Israel in 1904 to become rabbi of Jaffa and the new Zionist settlements. In 1909 he was faced with the problem of the sabbatical year during which biblical law enjoined that the land be left fallow. In contrast to his colleagues, he issued a lenient ruling which enabled the land to be sold nominally to a non-Jew and cultivation to continue. This decision has been regarded as operative ever since.

In 1914 he went to Europe to participate in a rabbinical conference. Because of the outbreak of war the conference did not take place, but Rav

Rabbi Abraham Isaac Kook, (right) with the Sephardi Chief Rabbi, Yaakov Meir 1933.

Kook could not return. He lived first in Switzerland and from 1916 was rabbi of London's Mahzikei Hadas congregation. While in London he was active in the negotiations leading to the Balfour Declaration. In 1919 he returned to Palestine as chief Ashkenazic rabbi for Jerusalem, where he founded a rabbinic academy Merkaz ha-Rav ("The Center of the Rabbi") at which he taught his students his ideals of Jewish religious nationalism. In 1921, with the establishment by the British of a chief rabbinate for Palestine, Kook became the country's first Ashkenazic chief rabbi, a post he held until his death. He guided this new institution, seeing it as a key element in Jewish self-government, which he hoped could eventually lead to the reconstitution of a Sanhedrin. His views were bitterly opposed by the more extreme Orthodox, who refused to accept his authority and who established their own central rabbinical body. He frequently criticized the British administration, especially after the Arab riots in 1929 in which the Jews of the largely Orthodox community of Hebron were massacred.

He was outstanding in his knowledge of the Torah and his writings and for his devotion to the Jewish people and the Land of Israel. The Jews, he maintained, have a special gift for holiness, a gift that is fully realizable only in the Land of Israel, which is metaphysically different from the rest of the world, and so the return to Zion is a sacred phenomenon. Kook was the outstanding leader and thinker of the religious Zionist movement, at a time when the great majority of Orthodox Jewry opposed Zionism for refusing to wait for divine redemption and intervention to return the Jews to their land. For Kook, however, Zionism was holy, despite its shortcomings, such as its separation of nationalism from religion.

He endeared himself to the nonreligious elements in Eretz Israel by his sympathy and support for the secular sector, particularly in the agricultural settlements. He regarded all those who immigrated to the Land of Israel and participated in its building to be inspired by holy sparks, as they were laying the foundations for messianic redemption — whatever their personal beliefs.

His philosophy is not presented systematically, but has to be taken from his many writings, some of which remain unpublished. He was influenced by the Kabbalah and his ideas often are drawn from the mystical tradition. He maintained that everything emanates from God and depends on him for its existence; the world and God are therefore indissolubly united. The basic unity of all existence can be comprehended through a mystical understanding. His thinking brought together many strands of Jewish thought — traditional rabbinic knowledge, mysticism, modern secular sciences, and Zionism.

J. Agus, *High Priest of Rebirth: The Life, Times and Thought of Abraham Isaac Kuk*, 1972.

KORCZAK, JANUSZ (Henryk Goldszmit; 1879–1942) Polish educator, physician, author, and Holocaust hero. Born in Warsaw to a prosperous family that had been assimilated to Polish culture for several generations, he studied medicine at Warsaw University, where he began writing and was involved in liberal and social activities. As a physician he endeavored to assist the needy, and in 1904 was drafted into the Russian army to serve as a doctor in the Far East. His semiautobiographical *Child of the Drawing Room* won him acclaim and comparison with Charles Dickens. After his discharge from the army he specialized in psychiatry and visited hospitals and institutions in Berlin, London, and Paris. He abandoned hospital work, however, "to become a sculptor of the child's soul," devoting his life to homeless, unwanted, and unfortunate children.

In Warsaw he became a pediatrician, treated underprivileged children free of charge, worked in children's summer camps, and wrote children's books. In 1912 he was appointed director of a new Jewish orphanage in the city. His treatment of children was revolutionary, as he defended their rights, encouraged self-government and the active participation of the children in the problems of the establishment, and sought to comprehend and respect the emotional life of each of his charges, insisting on their autonomous individuality. Once, lecturing at the Warsaw children's hospital on "The Heart of the Child," he brought a small boy on to the rostrum, took off the child's shirt, placed him behind a fluoroscope and turned off the overhead light. Everyone could see the boy's heart beating rapidly on the screen. Korczak told his students, "Don't ever forget this sight. Always remember what a child's frightened heart looks like."

He was again drafted into the Russan army dur-

SAYINGS OF RAV KOOK

- There is nothing old under the sun.
- Nothing in the universe is absolutely secular.
- Israel's exodus from Egypt will always remain the springtime of the world.
- Piety should on no account push aside the natural sense of morality for it would then no longer remain pure piety.
- Even as there are laws of poetry, there is poetry in law.
- The doctrine of evolution concurs with the cosmic secrets of the Kabbalah more than any other philosophic doctrine.
- The world unites and reconciles all contradictions: all souls and all spirits, all events and all things, all desires, drives and enthusiams; everything is part of a larger order and kingdom. God is King.

ing World War I and while in service wrote *How to Love a Child*. After the war he continued to direct the Jewish orphanage and also ran a second orphanage for Polish non-Jewish children. In the 1920s he taught, established a Jewish children's newspaper, became a popular radio broadcaster under the name of "Old Doc," and published educational books (including *The Child's Right to Respect*) and children's books, of which *King Matthew the First* became a classic and was translated into many languages.

The 1930s were problematic years as anti-Semitic forces grew strong in Poland. Korczak became interested in Zionism, visited Palestine twice, and was deeply impressed by what he saw there, especially the educational system of the kibbutz movement. He even contemplated moving there, but could not bring himself to leave Warsaw. Three conflicts haunted him throughout his life: fear of inherited mental illness (his father had been a manic depressive); fear of possible homosexuality (leading him to a disciplined celibacy); and the conflict between being a Polish Jew and a Polish national.

Janusz Korczak with children in his orphanage.

After war broke out in 1939, he concentrated on his work with Jewish children. In defiance of German regulations, he refused to wear the distinctive Jewish badge and was imprisoned for a time. In 1940 his orphanage was moved to the Warsaw ghetto, where he concentrated on obtaining basic provisions and keeping his charges alive. He continued to maintain his old standards, insisting on cleanliness, maintaining close relations between the staff and the children, and organizing literary evenings. Non-Jewish friends offered him the opportunity to move out of the ghetto but he refused to leave. During this period he kept a diary, one of the most moving documents of the ghetto.

Eventually, during the mass deportations of summer 1942, Korczak, his staff, and the children, were ordered to go to the gathering point for deportation. He insisted on going along with his two hundred charges. Many witnessed that last march of the neatly dressed children and their beloved doctor who carried as many of the small ones as he could, lifting now one, and then another. When a child suddenly remembered, "I left my doll behind," Korczak reassured her, "They will send it

Message given by Korczak to graduates of the orphanage on leaving

We have not given you God because you must search for him and find him within yourself.

We give you no country, because you must make your own choice, the choice of heart and reason.

We give you no love of man, because there is no love without forgiveness. You must search for it through hard work.

We do give you one thing, however. We give you a longing for a better life, based on truth and justice, which you are destined to build for yourself.

We hope that it will be this longing that will lead you to God, to your Country, and to Love.

From his ghetto diary

The physical immortality of man lies in his children. His spiritual existence lies in radiating the idea of brotherhood, not only his brotherhood with men, but with the stars and God in search of the magic fact — eternity.

A man thinks of, and looks upon, death as the end of everything. But in fact it is only a continuation of life in a different form. If you don't believe in soul, you must admit that your body wll continue to live as green grass or a little cloud. You are, after all, dust and water.

to us later." He had told them they were going on a long excursion to the country but well knew the real destination. When some of the older children also realized they were going to die and clung to him hysterically, he tried to comfort them. Realizing that the death of this famous educator could prove an embarrassment, the Germans made him a last-minute offer of life and freedom. He refused without hesitation and mounted the train with his wards. The train was bound for the death camp of Treblinka and nothing further is known of their last journey.

B. J. Lifton, *The King of Children: A Biography of Janusz Korczak*, 1988.

H. Olczak, *Mister Doctor*, 1965.

KORDA, ALEXANDER (Sandor Laszlo Korda; 1982—1956). Film producer and director; knighted in 1942. Born in Hungary, he attended high school in the provinces and then the Royal University in Budapest. He started a journalistic career in Budapest, taking an early interest in motion pictures. He turned a small building near the city into his first studio and began to produce films. He was in Paris in 1911 and 1912, studying filmmaking and working as a contributor to a Hungarian trade journal, and also writing film notices and theoretical articles. Korda founded and edited three Hungarian trade journals: *Pest Movie* (1912–1913), *The Movie* (1913), and *Film Week* (1915–1918). He directed his first Hungarian film in 1915 and another eight in the summer of 1916, all in the framework of the company of the noted Hungarian theater director Jenoe Janovics in Kolozsvár (Cluj). He bought the company in 1918, took it to Budapest and established with this company Corvin Films, of which he became both manager and director, producing films based on works of Hungarian literature. In 1919 Korda participated in the proletarian dictatorship of Bela Kun (q.v.) as one of the heads of the motion picture organization, for which he was arrested when the regime fell.

Upon his release in November 1919, Korda emigrated to Vienna and, after some time in Berlin (where he made films for UFA Studios) and Paris, he went to Hollywood and finally settled in London, where he founded London Films Limited, one of the most important British film companies. Korda knew all the intricacies of the industry, had considerable talent, excellent taste, and great charm. In all, he produced 141 films but only directed eight of the movies made by Corvin Films. When, with the rise of Hitler many film directors, writers, and actors fled to England, he stood by them and employed many of them. He gave jobs to so many Hungarians that it has been said that there was a notice at his Piccadilly office: "It's not enough to be Hungarian, you also need some talent." His first wife, Antonia Farkas, became known as the actress Maria Korda. His second wife was the American film star, Merle Oberon. His two brothers, Zoltan and Vincent, were his closest collaborators.

The most famous films Korda directed included

Alexander Korda.

The Private Life of Henry VIII (1933) and *Rembrandt* (1936), both with Charles Laughton, and *Lady Hamilton*, with Vivien Leigh and Laurence Olivier (1941). Among his best productions were *The Scarlet Pimpernel* (1935), *Rembrandt* (1936), *The Thief of Baghdad* (1940), and *The Jungle Book* (1942).

M. Korda, *Charmed Lives*, 1979.

K. Kulik, *Alexander Korda: The Man Who Could Work Miracles*, 1975.

P. Tabori, *Alexander Korda*, 1959.

KOUSSEVITZKY, SERGE (1874—1951) Conductor. Born in Tver, (now Kalinin), Russia, into a musical family, Koussevitzky learned to play the trumpet and performed, with his three brothers, in a small wind ensemble, playing at balls, weddings and village fairs. At the age of fourteen Koussevitzky moved to Moscow where he was baptized, as Jews were not allowed to live in the city. He was then permitted to study the double bass at the Musico-Dramatic Institute in Moscow. He chose this instrument not because he had any special affinity to it, but because there were open scholarships only for the horn, trombone, and the double bass. In 1894 he joined the orchestra of the Bolshoi Opera, where in 1901 he became principal double bass player. Soon he became a renowned double bass soloist, an instrument of very low visibility at the time.

In 1901 Koussevitzky gave his first public concert in Moscow, performing an adaptation of the Handel cello concerto. In 1903 he gave a double bass recital in Berlin. He composed a few pieces for his instrument in order to widen the relative limited repertoire, and premiered his own double bass concerto, which he wrote with the help of Reinhold Glière, in 1905 in Moscow.

Soon after, he resigned from his position at the Bolshoi orchestra and explained, in an open letter to the Russian *Musical Gazette*, that economic and artistic difficulties in the orchestra had led to his decision. He left Russia and settled in Germany, where he continued to perform on the double bass and began his conducting career, making his debut in 1908 with the Berlin Philharmonic.

In 1909 Koussevitzky established a publishing house, Editions Russes de Musique, and signed contracts with famous composers. In the same year he organized his own symphony orchestra in Moscow, performing many premieres by Russian composers. He took his orchestra on several tours to cities along the Volga, on a special chartered steamboat. After the 1917 revolution Koussevitzky became the director of the State Symphony Orchestra, a post that he held for three years.

In 1920 Koussevitzky left Russia, and traveled to Berlin and Rome before settling in Paris, where he continued to conduct many works by Russian and French composers. In 1924 he was engaged as the permanent conductor of the Boston Symphony, a position he held for twenty-five years. In Boston Koussevitzky continued with his ongoing crusade, championing new music. He encouraged American composers to write especially for the Boston

Symphony and premiered works by Aaron Copland (q.v.), Samuel Barber, William Schuman, and many others. In the 1950s, after he left Boston, Koussevitzky began conducting regularly all over the world, from Rio de Janeiro to Jerusalem, as well as in Europe.

Koussevitzky established the Berkshire Music Center at Tanglewood, Massachusetts, which eventually became the summer home of the Boston Symphony and is still one of the most prestigious summer festivals in North America.

M. A. DeWolfe Howe, *Serge Koussevitzky, The Boston Symphony Orchestra, 1881–1931*, 1931.

H. Leichtentritt, *Serge Koussevitzky, the Boston Symphony Orchestra and the New American Music*, 1946.

A. Lourié, *S. Koussevitzky and his Epoch*, 1931.

KOVNER, ABBA (1918–1988) Armed resistance leader and Hebrew poet. Kovner was born in Sevastopol and in his youth joined the left-wing Zionist youth movement Ha-Shomer ha-Tsair. He was in Vilna when the Germans entered on June 24, 1941, and with other members of the movement, hid in a convent at the edge of the city. On New Year's Eve, 1941, he spoke out at a meeting of Zionist Youth in the convent. He asserted that Hitler wanted to kill all the Jews, and that the Jews could not allow themselves to "go like sheep to the slaughter," but must offer armed resistance. As a result of the meeting in the convent, the United Partisan Organization was founded three weeks later. Kovner became one of its leaders, and, after the arrest and suicide of its commander, Yitzhak Wittenberg, in the summer of 1943, Kovner took his place.

When the Nazis began to round up Vilna Jews for Estonian work camps, the organization launched its revolt, believing that the liquidation of the ghetto had begun. Without community support, however, the revolt floundered, and most of the fighters made their way to the Rudninkai Forest. There they formed the Revenge partisan unit, with Kovner at its helm.

When the Rudninkai area was liberated, Kovner became involved in setting up the Beriha movement, which sought to take Jews clandestinely out of eastern Europe to central Europe and from there to Palestine. He also was a leader of the Organization of Eastern European Survivors, which tried to unify the remaining Jews in response to the dangers which were still imminent. Among other things, the organization carried out revenge operations against former Nazis and their collaborators.

Kovner went to Palestine toward the end of 1945 to enlist help for his operations in Europe. While making his way back to Europe, he was arrested by the British and returned to Palestine. Released in 1946, he and his wife, also a resistance leader, joined Kibbutz Ein ha-Horesh. Kovner took part in the Israeli War of Independence in 1948 and then settled down to a career in writing poetry and prose. His symbolist poetry dealt mainly with the

---

In his day Koussevitzky was one of the big three American conductors, the others being Toscanini and Stokowski. Of the three, Koussevitzky was by far the most important to the cause of American music, for in him the composer had a spokesman and an exponent. In addition, Koussevitzky's taste was catholic enough to include the most significant works of the modern European school, with the exception of twelve-tone music (but nobody at that time paid much attention to the dodecaphonic school; that was to be a postwar phenomenon). A glamorous, egocentric figure, Koussevitzky managed to make every concert an experience, partly through his own overwhelming personality, partly through the great orchestra he had built. Music in Boston revolved around him. He was the star and he hated to share the spotlight. Not only did the Boston Symphony have very few guest conductors during Koussevitzky's tenure; it also had fewer soloists than any comparable orchestra the world over. Those years in Boston from 1924 to 1949 did represent what the Russians used to call a cult of personality. But what a personality!

Harold C. Schoenberg, *The Great Conductors.*

Abba Kovner giving evidence at the Eichmann trial.

Holocaust and the State of Israel. In 1970 he received the Israel Prize for Literature. He was also a founder of the Moreshet Holocaust Institute and the Diaspora Museum in Tel Aviv.
Y. Arad, *Ghetto in Flames*, 1980.

KRAUS, KARL (1874–1936) Austrian satirist and poet. He was born in a provincial Bohemian town to prosperous, assimilated Jewish parents. His family moved to Vienna when he was three years old, and he spent the rest of his life there. He began studying law at the University of Vienna, but left after finding that his interests lay mainly in writing and acting.

He began writing professionally at age eighteen. At first he wrote reviews of books and plays for various German and Austrian newspapers. His name appeared in the "Who's Who" of Viennese artists and writers in 1893, when he was still only nineteen. He rejected a position offered to him in the influential daily, *Neue Freie Presse*, in 1899, choosing instead to found his own satirical magazine, *Die Fackel* ("The Torch"), which he edited until his death.

He was concerned primarily with exposing local conditions in Austria, which he perceived as corrupt. He devoted himself to *Die Fackel*, at first with the contributions of other writers, but soon writing the entire magazine himself. Each new issue of the satirical magazine was awaited eagerly by the same public that Kraus attacked vehemently in print.

He was a fierce defender of the purity of the German language, and a venomous critic of liberalism, attacking what he viewd as permissiveness and hypocrisy. The press, which he considered one of the main corruptors of the language, was one of the chief victims of his pen. The *Neue Freie Presse*, a favorite target, led a counterattack of the Austrian and German press by ignoring him and refraining from mentioning his name.

Kraus saw compromise as his greatest enemy, and he judged everything in terms of the ideal. He was a conservative moralist who yearned for more discipline, and believed that the atmosphere of liberalism prevailing in Austria would lead to the decline of humanity and despiritualization of man. His aim was to improve society through the purification of its language, and to that aim he devoted his life.

Few of Kraus's writings have been translated. One critic, Thomas Szasz, asserts that this is due not merely to the difficulties in translating his German, but to the fact that "his writings run against the grain of our contemporary intellectual mores even more than they did against his."

Kraus converted to Roman Catholicism in 1921, after having officially left the Jewish faith four years earlier. He believed that Jews and the Jewish press were responsible for anti-Semitism, and he treated Zionism disparagingly. He was generally considered anti-Semitic himself, a charge he attempted to refute a number of times, with little success. Szasz believes Kraus's attitude toward Jews "depended more on their linguistic than on their religious behavior."

Although the bulk of his writings were essays for *Die Fackel*, he also wrote plays and lyric poetry. One play was a diatribe on the ruin of civilization in World War I, and a nine-volume collection of his poetry appeared under the name *Worte in Versen*. Some of the essays that appeared in *Die Fackel* were later collected and published, including a six-volume collection of essays written between 1908 and 1937, and a four-volume collection of works from 1909 to 1927.

One of Kraus's most memorable statements appeared in the 1934 issue of *Die Fackel*: "When it comes to Hitler, I just can't think of anything to say." Critics are divided on whether he foresaw the danger of Nazism. Some viewed this statement as evidence that Kraus was finally condescending to make his first compromise, others asserting that this was a prime example of his bitter irony.

Kraus was hit by a cyclist in February 1935, and suffered a heart attack as a result of the accident. He died a few months later, together with *Die Fackel.*
F. Field, *The Last Days of Mankind: Karl Kraus and his Vienna,* 1967.
E. Heller, *The Disinherited Mind,* 1952.
T. S. Szasz, *Karl Kraus and the Soul Doctors,* 1976.

KREBS, HANS ADOLF (1900–1981) Biochemist, Nobel Prize winner; knighted in 1958. He was born in Hildesheim, Germany, where his father was an ear, nose, and throat surgeon. He studied at several universities in Germany before graduating, with the degree of M.D. from the University of Hamburg in 1925. From 1926 to 1930 he was assistant to Otto Warburg at the Kaiser Wilhelm Institute, where Warburg was engaged in biochemical and metabolic research. In 1932 he published his discovery of the ornithine cycle for urea synthesis in the mammalian liver, just a short while before Hitler came to power. Krebs fled to England from the Nazis in 1933 and worked for a short time in Cambridge as a Rockefeller research student. From 1934 to 1935 he was a demonstrator in biochemistry at Cambridge before taking up a post as lecturer in pharmacology at Sheffield University in 1935.

In 1939 he became a naturalized British citizen just a few days after the outbreak of World War II, thus being spared the indignity of internment as a German alien.

A Sheffield University he continued the research into metabolic pathways that he had begun with

---

FROM KREBS'S AUTOBIOGRAPHY

On the Nobel Prize: "It is like having been stamped with a hallmark, a label of quality. Complete strangers ask for your comments and advice on all sorts of odd problems, assuming that Nobel laureates can answer any question."
On his escape from Germany: "By good fortune I published my work on the ornithine cycle just a few months before Hitler came into power. Had I worked too leisurely or too often postponed work till the next day, life might have run a different course.... I set out expecting nothing special from life — as I had been brought up to do — except to survive by my own efforts, but because I have had more than my share of luck and a lucky constellation of genes, life has felt special indeed."

Warburg, eventually completing the description of the tricarboxylic cycle (later known as the Krebs cycle) as an important step in the oxidation of foodstuffs. In 1945 he was appointed professor and became director of research into cell metabolism.

For his contribution to the discovery of the Krebs cycle he was awarded the 1953 Nobel Prize for medicine and physiology, together with his friend and former German colleague, Fritz Lipman (who discovered the role of coenzyme A in cell metabolism), "for their work on the citric acid cycle in carbohydrate metabolism."

In 1954 Krebs was offered the Whitley Chair of biochemistry at Oxford University, where he remained until his official retirement in 1967.

Among Krebs's other achievements were discoveries in glutamine synthesis, purine synthesis in birds, mechanisms involved in metabolic regulation, and the discovery of damino oxidase.

Krebs received international recognition for his work and numerous honors, including a British knighthood, fellowship in the Royal Society of London, and twenty-one honorary doctorates, including one from the Hebrew University in Jerusalem. Krebs was also the recipient of the gold medal of the Royal Society of Medicine and the medal of the American College of Physicians, Boston.
H. Krebs (with A. Martin), *Hans Krebs: Reminiscences and Reflections,* 1981.

KREISER, JACOB GRIGORYEVICH (1905–1969) Soviet general and World War II hero. Jacob Kreiser was the son of a Cantonist (Jewish soldier in the military service, who was coerced to convert to Christianity). He began his own military career at an early age and quickly rose in the ranks of the Soviet army, becoming a general at thirty-one. Upon the outbreak of World War II, he was commander of the Moscow Proletarian Infantry Division. The heroic defense provided by Kreiser's unit to the approaches of Moscow earned him the military honor hero of the Soviet Union.

Kreiser later served in various other important positions in the course of the war. In 1941 he was appointed commander of the Third Army, which fought on the Kalinin and Yelets fronts. He was moved to the Second Army and then to the Fifty-First, which fought the Germans in the western Ukraine and liberated Crimea. The fact that Crimea had been liberated by a Jewish officer refocused attention on an earlier Soviet plan to establish a Jewish autonomous republic in that territory to replace the failed Birobidzhan oblast. Although Jews constituted only 6 percent of the total population, they were primarily involved in agriculture, and, furthermore, the local Muslim Tatars had collaborated with the Nazis, creating an impetus for their own relocation. The Jewish Anti-Fascist Committee, of which Kreiser was a prominent member, endorsed the idea, although nothing came of it. Kreiser served in a series of campaigns in which the Baltic states were liberated. Toward the end of the war he was promoted to colonel-general; he ended the war whit the rank of general of the army.

Kreiser's status as a war hero earned him fame and status in the Soviet Union. Stalin once denied charges of anti-Semitism by stating that his best friend was the Jew, Jacob Kreiser. Upon the fabrication of the spurious doctors' plot to kill Stalin, however, the Russian dictator turned against Kreiser. Kreiser was one of only a handful of Jews who refused to sign a proposed open letter in *Pravda* disclaiming the existence of anti-Semitism in the Soviet Union and claiming that the doctors' plot was the result of an American and Zionist conspiracy. Kreiser was stripped of his command, but this was restored following Stalin's death shortly after.

Kreiser was appointed deputy to the Supreme Soviet in 1962. He maintained his command in the army, serving as commander of the sensitive Far East region, centered in Vladivostok, until his death.

B. Pinkus, *Jews of the Soviet Union*, 1988.

L. Rapaport, *Stalin's War against the Jews*, 1990.

KREISKY, BRUNO (1911–1990) Chancellor of Austria. His parents moved from Bohemia to Vienna, where he was born. His father was a wealthy textile merchant. From an early age Bruno was active in the Socialist party. When it was outlawed in 1934, he joined the underground, was arrested in 1935 and sentenced to sixteen months imprisonment for "high treason," but released a few weeks later. In 1938 he graduated in law from the University of Vienna, but was again arrested after the Anschluss. Instead of being sent to a concentration camp he was ordered to leave Austria and moved to Sweden, where he worked as a foreign correspondent. After the war he remained for a few years in Stockholm, as a member of the staff of the Austrian embassy.

In 1951 he returned to Austria where he was appointed deputy chief of cabinet in the office of the federal president. By 1953 he was undersecretary of state in the Foreign Ministry, and played a key role in 1955 in persuading Nikita Khruschev to accept a state treaty for Austria, which gave the country its independence in return for a commitment to maintain "permanent neutrality." In 1956 he was elected to the Austrian parliament and in 1959 was foreign minister in a coalition cabinet.

From 1967 he was chairman of the Socialist party and leader of the opposition.

He was elected chancellor in a minority government in 1970. The following year he called new elections and was elected with a majority, which increased in elections in 1975 and 1979. Internationally he followed a policy of active neutrality that gave his country an influence in international affairs out of all proportion to its size (he came to be known as "Kaiser Bruno"). His term of office marked the rehabilitation of Austria after half a century of lost world wars and a decade of four-power occupation, and his foreign policy put Austria in a key position between East and West and between North and South.

Kreisky played an important role in shaping Europe's postwar recovery and in determining East-West detente as an objective in the search for international peace. He was also one of the first to insist on the importance of the rich nations' aiding the Third World. Internally he guided his country to a period of prosperity, despite world economic crises. Inflation and unemployment were kept low; wages and prices were restrained; social reforms were vigorously pursued; and the country's stability was often cited as a success story. Kreisky's style was sometimes criticized as personal and arrogant, but he deeply respected democratic principles and was widely admired in Austria.

He described himself as an agnostic whose connection with the Jewish people was only "a community of fate." It was his intervention in Middle East politics that brought him into conflict with world Jewry and the State of Israel. In 1973, on the eve of the Yom Kippur War, his apparent surrender to Palestinian terrorists who had hijacked a train of Soviet Jewish emigrants and demanded the halt of Jewish immigration to Israel via Vienna, brought Israeli Prime Minister Golda Meir (q.v.) rushing to Vienna. The two personalities clashed and while Meir subsequently called Kreisky a "self-hating Jew," immigration did in fact continue. In 1980 Kreisky was the first Western leader to receive Yassir Arafat, chairman of the Palestine Liberation Organization (PLO), and to grant the movement de facto diplomatic recognition. He then persuaded the Socialist International to be less one-sided in its support for Israel. This policy was sharply criticized by both the State of Israel and much of world Jewry. At the same time, he told the PLO leaders to cease their attempts to delegitimize the State of Israel and to recognize its existence as a fact. He was also active on a number of occasions in behind-the-scenes negotiations to obtain the release of Israeli hostages and prisoners in the hands of Palestinian terrorist groups.

Kreisky regarded Austria's rejection of nuclear energy in 1978, against his advice, as a personal defeat. In the 1983 elections, the Socialist party failed to win an overall majority. Rather than put together a coalition, Kreisky resigned as prime minister and subsequently as head of the Socialist party.

KROCHMAL, NACHMAN (1785–1840) East European Enlightenment (*Haskala*) philosopher and historian; also known by his Hebrew acronym, *RaNak* (Rabbi Nachman Krochmal). Born to a wealthy merchant in Brody, Galicia (then part of the Austro-Hapsburg Empire), Krochmial received a traditional Talmud-centered education. Encouraged by his father's connections to the west European Enlightenment of Moses Mendelssohn (q.v.), he taught himself Latin, Arabic, French, and German, languages that opened doors to a broad range of medieval and modern philosophical literature. After his marriage at the age of fourteen, he moved with his wife to the home of the bride's parents in Zolkiew near Lvov, where Krochmal remained most of his life. He earned a reputation as a brilliant thinker and conversationalist, rejected an offer of a rabbinical post in Berlin, and attracted many leaders of the Enlightenment to his home. He returned to Brody when his wife died in 1826 and in 1838 moved to his daughter's home in Tarnopol.

Influenced by his studies of Maimonides (q.v.) and Ibn Ezra (q.v.), Krochmal adopted the approach of the German idealist school of philosophy in his scientific analysis of historic Judaism. His thought was clearly informed by the works of Kant, Fichte, Schelling, and Hegel. As one of the dynamic forces shaping Galicia's Enlightenment movement and in stark contrast to the prevailing Hasidic influence, Krochmal advocated the reform of Jewish education and the introduction of studies in the natural sciences and modern European languages, and insisted that Hebrew literature be subjected to the standards, genres and ideas of modern European literature.

His *Moreh Nevukhei ha-Zeman* ("A Guide for the Perplexed of the Time," 1851), written in Hebrew and named after the famous work of Maimonides, was edited and published posthumously by the distinguished scholar Leopold Zunz (q.v.). It records his understanding of the relationship of philosophy and religion, the importance of biblical monotheism for modern philosophy, the contrast of Jewish historical development with other nations, and the evolution of the halakhah (legal aspects) and aggadah (nonlegal aspects) in rabbinic literature. Krochmal posited the God of Judiasm in Hegelian terms as an absolute Being whose spirit is unqualified cognition. As such, God is perceived only implicitly through the imagery of religion, leaving the task of an explicit understanding of the divine to philosophical reason.

History, according to Krochmal, like every other aspect of civilization, is primarily defined by a transcendent quality. A nation's spiritual principle forms the foundation of its existence, its particular character being determined by the extent to which it dedicates itself to this principle. Following the historical philosophies of Vico and Herder, Krochmal attempted to prove empirically how the Jewish national spirit is like that of other nations, in that it follows the evolutionary three-phase cycle of growth, maturity, and death. The Jewish nation

The tombstone of Nachman Krochmal at Tarnopol, Poland.

is unique, however, in that it eternally renews itself, avoiding eventual extinction by an undying devotion to its singular, infinite, and immutable God, who restores the spiritual strength of Jewish culture in times of stagnation and decline. In Krochmal's view, the Jewish people had already survived three distinct cycles of national historical existence: the first from Abraham (q.v.) to the destruction of the First Temple, the second from the rebuilding of the Second Temple to the Bar Kokhba (q.v.) revolt, and the third beginning at the time of the Mishnah's codification, maturing with the development of early medieval Jewish philosophy, and declining in the late Middle Ages. Without specific reference, Krochmal probably envisioned the dawn of a fourth cyclical renaissance in the Enlightenment movement.

J. Guttmann, *Philosophies of Judaism*, 1964.
N. Rotenstreich, *Jewish Philosophy in Modern Times*, 1968.
S. Schechter, *Studies in Judaism*, 1958.

KUN, BELA (1886–1939) Hungarian communist leader. Born in a small Transylvanian town, the son of a storekeeper, he was educated at Kolozsvar (Cluj). he joined the Hungarian Social Democratic party in 1902, working first as a journalist and then as a clerk, and later manager, with the Kolozsvar

Workers' Insurance Fund. He was discharged from this job for misconduct. Kun joined the army in 1914 and was captured by the Russians in 1916. In Russia, he encountered Bolsheviks and helped them organize the revolutionary movement among prisoners of war in the Tomsk camp. Having joined the Bolshevik party before the October revolution, he met Lenin at Saint Petersburg (Petrograd) in 1917. From March 1918, Kun was leader of the Hungarian group in the Russian Communist party and edited its newspaper. From May, he was chairman of the International Federation of Socialist POWs, participated in the victory over the Moscow counter-revolutionaries, fought on the Perm front, and organized the international units of the Red Army. In November 1918 Kun returned to Hungary, founded the Hungarian Communist party and its organ *Voeroes Ujsag* ("Red Newspaper"), and wrote pamphlets. His fiery speeches led to his arrest and he was badly beaten by the police in February 1919. However, he continued to direct the preparations for the proletarian revolution from jail, and elaborated a scheme to unite the Social Democratic and Communist parties. He was liberated from prison on 21 March 1919, the day the Hungarian Soviet Republic was proclaimed and was immediately appointed Commissar for foreign and military affairs, that is, virtual leader of the government.

Calling his regime the dictatorship of the proletariat, Kun nationalized banks, large businesses, and estates. Ruthlessly suppressing opposition, he eliminated moderate elements in the government and exploited the wave of popular nationalism that had swept the country. He promised to obtain Soviet help in fighting the Romanians and created a Red Army that reconquered territory that had been lost to the Czechs and Romanians, and overran Slovakia. However, the reaction to his regime came quickly. The Soviet help failed to arrive. The peasants were alienated by the decision that private estates should be nationalized rather than distributed among them. Food distribution broke down. And after initial successes, the army refused to fight leading to its defeat at the hands of the Romanians. Within a few months the proletarian dictatorship fell and Kun emigrated to Austria, where he was taken into custody and held for a short time in an insane asylum. He then went to the Soviet Union, where he was elected an executive member at the Third Congress of the Communist International, serving from 1921 to 1936. Kun played a leading role in the reorganization of the Hungarian Communist party. In connection with this work, he returned to Vienna illegally in 1928, was discovered, jailed, and then sent back to Russia. He was also active in strengthening several other Communist parties. One of Kun's greatest errors was that he failed to recognize the menace of rising fascism for the Communist parties and the changes this circumstance brought about. He was arrested in 1937, during the Stalinist purges, accused of Trotskyism and was executed.

At the end of World War II when Hungary came into the Soviet orbit, and Stalinists surviving in Russia returned to organize the Communist party, Kun's name and the 1919 proletarian dictatorship became taboo. It was only after the 1956 revolution that he was rehabilitated; his collected writings and speeches were first published in Hungary in 1958.
O. Jaszi, *Revolution and Counter-Revolution in Hungary*, 1924.
R. L. Toker, *Bela Kun and the Hungarian Soviet Republic*, 1967.

KUZNETS, SIMON (1901–1985) Economist and third recipient of the Nobel Prize in economics. Kuznets was noted for his pioneering work in national accounting, which led to the development of the means to calculate the gross national product. The methodology he used in his studies brought the discipline of economics closer to a positive, quantitative science and he is considered one of the founders of an empirical science of economics and of quantitative economic history.

He was born in Pinsk, then part of Russia; Kuznets's family moved to Kharkov during World War I. His father, a fur dealer, emigrated to the United States when Simon was six. Kuznets studied economics in high school and went on to the University of Kharkov. He worked in the Division of Statistics of the Central Soviet of Trade, but in 1922 moved to the United States with his brother because, as he put it, of "the usual economic problems." Once in New York City, Kuznets was accepted by Columbia University with advanced standing and by 1926 had finished his doctorate. His dissertation on retail business cycles captured the attention of the Washington-based National Bureau of Economic Research and it invited him to join its staff.

It was with the National Bureau that Kuznets did his most important work on national incomes in the United States. During the depression, Congress needed information about the economy on which to base its policy and legislation. The National Bureau was given the task of gathering and analyzing data on U.S. incomes and Kuznets headed much of this effort. He defined national product and national income and studied these two concepts within the American economic structure. His quantitatively based data were extremely useful. Kuznets utilized his theory to project national income back to 1919 and in 1941 he published the two-volume *National Income and Its Composition, 1919–38*. This work was an important source for the research of English economist John Maynard Keynes.

Throughout his career, Kuznets accepted appointments at several prestigious universities. From 1930 to 1954 he was a professor at the University of Pennsylvania. During World War II he was associate director of the Bureau of Planning and Statistics of the War Production Board. He taught at Johns Hopkins University from 1954 to 1960, and at Harvard from 1961 to 1971.

Kuznets's research aimed to answer broad, all-encompassing economic questions. He believed strongly in the value of team research and long-term studies. Toward those goals he helped to found the Conference on Research in National Income and Wealth and the International Association for Research in Income and Wealth. His research on the economies of the United States and other nations led him to conclude tentatively that countries in the early stages of development experience a period of increasing inequality across socioeconomic boundaries, but later tend to move toward equality as development proceeds. This idea became known as the Kuznets curve. His work revealed twenty-year cycles, dubbed Kuznets cycles, in many aspects of the economy, including population growth, migration, domestic investment, and international capital flows.

In addition to studies of national economies, Kuznets made contributions to the research of business cycles, secular movements in production and prices, seasonal variations in industry and trade, professional incomes, income distribution, and the economic status of minority groups. He served as president to the American Economics Association and the American Statistical Association. His published works include *Quantitative Aspects of Economic Growth of Nations* (1956—1961), *Modern Economic Growth: Rate Structure and Spread* (1966), and *Economic Growth of Nations: Total Output and Production Structure* (1971).

Kuznets was awarded the Nobel Prize in 1971, and cited for his "empirically founded interpretation of economic growth which has led to new and deepened insight into the economic and social structure."

M. Abramovitz, "Simon Kuznets," in *Journal of Economic History* 46 (March 1986).

L

LAEMMLE, CARL (1867–1939) U.S. film executive. Born in Laupheim, Germany, Laemmle followed one of his brothers to the United States at age seventeen. He progressed from bookkeeper to store manager in a clothing company and was almost forty years old before conceiving of a more lucrative future in the infant film industry. In 1909, three years after opening his first nickelodeon, he emerged as the most prominent partner of the newly formed Motion Picture Patents Company that aspired to a total monopoly of all aspects of motion pictures. Producing films through his Independent Motion Picture Company (IMP), he initiated the star system when he won the "Biograph Girl," Florence Lawrence, away from her home studio. In 1912 the Universal Film Company was formed as the result of a merger between IMP and a number of other firms.

The conservative Laemmle resisted the transition to longer films than the one and two-reelers that had already proven themselves with audiences. *Traffic in Souls*, a ten-reeler dealing with white slavery, was made behind Laemmle's back and became Universal's biggest early hit. Two years later, in 1915, Laemmle opened his 230-acre Universal City studio in Hollywood. His brilliant former secretary, Irving Thalberg, became the studio's general manager; he was twenty-one, and he proved to be the only person capable of controlling the excesses of director Erich von Stroheim (q.v.).

Laemmle's son, Carl Jr., was put in charge of the studio as a twenty-first birthday present from his father. With *Dracula* and *Frankenstein* he continued the horror-film tradition established a few years earlier by Thalberg's production of *The Hunchback of Notre-Dame*. Following the 1930 Oscar-winning *All Quiet on the Western Front*, there was talk of Laemmle receiving the Nobel Prize for peace.

"Uncle Carl" was notorious for his nepotism. One nephew to whom he gave a start was William Wyler, soon to become a top director. Many blamed Carl Jr.'s extravagance for Universal's financial difficulties, which in 1936 forced Laemmle to sell out his interest in the studio he had founded. The new regime at Universal found some

Carl Laemmle.

seventy relatives and friends of Laemmle on the payroll, some already deceased.

J. Drinkwater, *The Life and Adventures of Carl Laemmle*, 1931.

M. G. Fitzgerald, *Big U: Universal in the Silent Days*, 1977.

LAFER, HORACIO (1893–1965) Brazilian politician and industrialist. Born in São Paulo, he studied economics, philosophy, and law before going on to a career in industry and politics.

Lafer worked with the Jewish-owned Klabin firm, which developed the cellulose and paper industry in Brazil. According to Lafer's account, President Gétulio Vargas accomplished the feat of getting industry off the ground in his agrarian and unindustrialized country by giving Wolff Klabin, who was reluctant to become involved, eight days in which to present a plan for paper production.

Aside from his involvement in the paper and pulp industry, Lafer also founded the Brazilian National Economic Development Bank and served as governor of the World Bank.

In 1928 Lafer became the Brazilian delegate to the League of Nations, and in 1934 was elected to the federal chamber of deputies, where he served for almost thirty years. He was appointed minister of finance in 1951 in President Vargas's government.

When a drought hit northeastern Brazil in 1951, Lafer engineered a plan to solve the problem of agricultural credit shortages, thus also initiating overall economic reform in the region. Upon visiting the northeast he stated that the Brazilian preoccupation with engineering and hydraulic works had overshadowed the economic aspect of the problem, and he suggested the establishment of a credit institution for the northeast. He drafted a law to create the Bank of the Northeast, which was to put major emphasis on the financing of agriculture. Although his efforts had been intended primarily to combat the shortage of agricultural credit, the bank's powers were eventually broadened to make it an important organ of overall regional development in the northeast.

As minister of finance, Lafer was also responsible for Brazil's new development policy. Under his five-year plan, known as the Lafer plan, a billion dollars were to be invested in basic industries, transportation, and power. Lafer encountered problems in the administration of his economic policies; whereas he favored stabilization of the economy, he was thwarted by the manager of the Bank of Brazil, who favored the allocation of easy credit. From 1959 to 1961 Lafer was the foreign minister in President Juscelino Kubitschek's government.

Throughout his career he was active on behalf of the Jewish community of Brazil, helping to ease the government's attitude toward Jewish immigration and toward the State of Israel, and campaigning against Nazi propaganda.

He published *Contemporary Philosophic Tendencies* (1929) and *Credit and the National Banking System* (1948).

E. N. Baklanoff (ed.), *The Shaping of Modern Brazil*, 1969.
R. S. Robock, *Brazil's Developing Northeast: A Study of Regional Planning and Foreign Aid*, 1963.

LA GUARDIA, FIORELLO HENRY (1882–1947) U.S. Congressman and mayor of New York. He was born in New York City to a Jewish mother, Irene Luzzato Coen, and a father born in Foggia, Italy, who emigrated to the United States. Since his father was a musician, serving as bandmaster in the U.S. infantry, La Guardia spent his childhood at army camps, and was educated in Prescott, Arizona. Soon after his father's discharge due to ill health the family went to Budapest, where at the age of nineteen La Guardia obtained employment in the U.S. consulate and was appointed interpreter in Trieste. While serving as consul at Fiume (then a Hungarian seaport), La Guardia set up the first American medical inspection center for immigrants. On his return to the United States he was employed as interpreter at the Ellis Island immigrant reception center, at the same time attending law school at night. In 1912 he opened his own law office, often providing legal advice and appearing in court without fee on behalf of the poor and new immigrants.

La Guardia first won public attention when he became involved in the 1912 New York garment workers' strike, and as their recognized leader was chosen as one of the arbitrators to settle the strike. In 1915 he was appointed New York State deputy attorney general, becoming involved in a number of major cases in which he was defeated by the local power barons. After a whirlwind campaign he was elected to Congress in 1916 on the Republican ticket, taking leave in 1917 to enlist in the armed forces. He was commissioned in the Army Air Service with the rank of captain, and was posted to Italy to train American flyers in the U.S. Aviation Instruction Center at Foggia, where in addition to his combat duties (for which he received the Italian war cross) he addressed mass meetings of Italians throughout the country in an effort to raise their morale. For these services the Italian government made him a Commendatore (knight commander) of the Crown of Italy.

In 1919 La Guardia — widely known as "Little Flower" due to his first name — was elected president of the New York Board of Aldermen, and in 1922 began his association with William Randolph Hearst, writing a series of articles in the *Evening Journal* advocating the establishment of a social welfare state. He was returned to Congress once more in 1922 and again in 1924, and was associated with some of the most progressive legislation in Congress.

After failing to be reelected in 1932, La Guardia successfully ran for mayor of New York City, routing Tammany influence from City Hall in his determination to give the city an honest, nonpartisan administration. He brought in experts to head municipal departments, set out to eliminate graft, and rid the city payroll of unneeded employees. During his three consecutive terms as mayor (he was reelected in 1937 and 1941), La Guardia led a successful campaign for a new city charter and the adoption of proportional representation method of electing members of the city council. He ran a drive for slum clearance and low-cost housing, improved the efficiency of the police and fire departments, carried out a drive against the connection of criminals and racketeers with politicians and policemen, and conducted a war against gambling rackets and slot machines. During his second term, his major achievement was the purchase by the city and merging of the local bus companies.

In the late 1930s La Guardia publicly spoke out against Hitler and Mussolini, and by the time the United States entered the war he had organized civilian defense in New York. He was then appointed by Eleanor Roosevelt as director of the Office of Civilian Defense, but was forced to give up the position when it proved too much for him. When the German consulate in New York asked for police protection, La Guardia sent an exclusively Jewish unit to ensure their security. Toward the end of his third term as mayor, La Guardia's administration came under constant fire and was even criticized by grand juries for a "most unusual and extremely deplorable state of lawlessness" in Brooklyn and for failing to provide adequate police protection for the residents of the borough. After the death of President Franklin D. Roosevelt, he no longer had the support of the White House, and at the end of 1945 left City Hall. He began a series of radio broadcasts, commenting on local affairs as well as on the national scene. He endeared himself to many by reading the comics on the radio during a newspaper strike.

La Guardia's last public position was director general of UNRRA (United Nations Relief and Rehabilitation Administration). During his nine-month administration, he spearheaded an international drive to provide food for starving countries. In 1947 he was presented with the One World Award for press and radio. La Guardia was eulogized in the United Nations Assembly as "a great friend of the underprivileged, a great promoter of peace, the real representative of the idea of one world and of the idea of the United Nations."

T. Kessner, *Fiorello H. La Guardia and the Making of Modern New York*, 1989.

L. M. Limpus and B. W. Leyson, *This Man La Guardia*, 1938.

A. Mann, *La Guardia, A Fighter against His Times, 1882–1933*, 1969.

LAND, EDWIN HERBERT (1909–1991) Inventor of instant photography. He was born in Bridgeport, Connecticut, where his father ran a scrap-iron business. When he was a seventeen-year-old freshman at Harvard, he was walking down Broadway and noted the glare from competing theater and billboard lights, wondering how it could be eliminated. He applied himself to the challenge single-mindedly (he never finished his course at Harvard) and when he was twenty he was able to launch his polarizing filter. The resulting polarizer he called Polaroid J sheet and in 1932 he cofounded Land-Wheelwright Laboratories, Boston, where he developed and began to use many types of Polaroid. In 1937 he founded Polaroid Corporation in Cambridge, Massachusetts. His many discoveries in the optical field included instant X-ray photographs and sunglasses that reduced glare. During World War II, he applied polarizing principles to antiaircraft–gun sights and night adaptation goggles. The camera in the U2 spy plane also utilized his patents.

In 1941 he developed a three-dimensional motion-picture process based on polarized light. About the same time he began to work on the possibility of instant photography and in 1948 the Polaroid system was put on the market. The system was clumsy at first, but Land worked on refining it and in 1970 the SX-70 system produced the first pocket-sized instant cameras capable of delivering dry color photos. In 1977 he introduced Polavision, which produced almost instant movies.

From his experiments in color vision, he reached the conclusion that the actual color perceived by the eye results from the comparison of at least three separate images formed by independent mechanisms in the eye.

In the course of his career, Land acquired over five hundred patents in light and plastics. Despite his lack of an academic degree, he was appointed to professorships at Harvard and the Massachusetts Institute of Technology. He built up the Polaroid Company to become one of the giants of U.S. industry; in 1970 its sales reached half a billion dollars. Land's own fortune was estimated at 500 million to 1 billion dollars, but he lived modestly and avoided publicity about his private life.

LANDAU, EZEKIEL (known as *Noda bi-Yehuda*, after his major work; 1713–1793) Community leader and rabbinical authority. He was born in Opatow, Poland, to a distinguished family of scholarly leaders descended from Rashi (q.v.). A brilliant student from his youth, he specialized in Talmud and rabbinic law. When he was thirteen he went to Brody, a great center of scholarship, and by the early age of twenty was appointed one of the city's rabbinic judges. Ten years later, he became rabbi of Jampol, and ten years after that, rabbi of Prague and the region where he remained for the rest of his life. He had the title of Chief Rabbi of the Austrian Empire and was recognized throughout the Jewish world as its leading authority. He founded a Talmudic academy that drew thousands of students from many countries, attracted by his reputation, personality, and his dialectic method of studying the Talmud. Each morning he taught Talmud and rabbinic codes; in the afternoon he presided at court sessions and participated in community administration; and in

---

FROM THE WRITINGS OF EZEKIEL LANDAU

My father raised me in an atmosphere of learning. He possessed scholarship and prestige. People would solicit his advice and favor. I am honored because of him. People have sought my instruction from my early youth. There is no special wisdom in me; there are far greater scholars living in obscurity, of whom no one makes inquiries, while I rise to find hundreds of people knocking on my door. God was indeed wonderful to me all these years because of the merit of my father.

Rabbi Ezekiel Landau.

the evening wrote his works and attended to his vast correspondence. His way of life was ascetic — for example, in the nine days up to the Ninth of Ab (a period of mourning for the destruction of the Temples) he ate only dry bread sprinkled with ashes. He was implacably opposed to the messianic movements of Shabbetai Tzevi (q.v.) and Jacob Frank (q.v.) and was similarly critical of Enlightenment tendencies, as expressed, for example, in the German Bible translation of Moses Mendelssohn (q.v.), which introduced a new attitude that he felt threatened traditional Jewish life. He was not, however, opposed to the acquisition of secular knowledge, with which he himself was familiar, and he encouraged his sons to follow his example.

When Prague was besieged in the Seven Years' War (1756–1764), he mobilized Jewish support for the government and as a result changed the attitude of the authorities from distrust to confidence in their Jewish subjects. When Empress Maria Theresa visited Prague at the end of the war, she accepted Landau's blessings at an official reception. He used his close relationship with the authorities to benefit the Jewish community.

Noda bi-Yehuda was the outstanding book of responsa (rabbinical replies to questions of Jewish law) of the eighteenth century. Landau's unrivaled reputation and position, his erudition and powers of analysis, all contributed to its widespread acceptance. His stature enabled him to make lenient decisions on matters of Jewish law, but some of these were revoked by stricter rabbis after Lan-

dau's death. He issued various sumptuary laws, that is, regulations restricting ostentatious behavior within the community. His other works included commentaries on parts of the Talmud, corrections of mistakes in texts of the codes, and ethical sermons.

S. Wind in *Jewish Leaders*, ed. L. Jung, 1953.

LANDAU, LEV DAVIDOVICH (1908–1968) Russian theoretical physicist and Nobel Prize winner. He was born in Baku (now Azerbaijan S.S.R.) on the Caspian Sea; his father was a successful engineer and his mother a doctor and teacher. By his own admission, by the age of nine he was investigating problems with which he was confronted and obstinately maintaining any conclusion he reached. From an early age, he developed an irrepressible urge to classify everything, and this urge would later characterize his research in physics. At thirteen he graduated from high school and attended the Baku Technical School and university, before studying at the physics department of the University of Leningrad, the major institute of physics in the USSR. At the age of nineteen, he became a graduate student at the Leningrad Physico-Technical Institute. That same year he also advanced a concept for energy called density matrix, which was used in quantum mechanics. In 1929 he was sent to Europe where he studied with Niels Bohr (q.v.) in Copenhagen.

Landau often lamented that he had been born several years too late to participate in the pioneering work in quantum mechanics, and at a colloquium on theoretical physics in Berlin in 1929, remarked, "All the nice girls have been snapped up and married, and all the nice problems have been solved. I don't really like any of those that are left." He found, nonetheless, that there were still plenty of interesting problems to solve in quantum mechanics and published papers on relativistic quantum theory and the diamagnetism of metals. He also studied low-temperature physics and later formulated mathematical equations explaining phenomena in that field. From 1932 he worked at the Ukrainian Physico-Technical Institute at Kharkov on the scattering of light by light, and on the absorption of sound by solids.

In 1937 Landau was invited to head the theoretical division of the Institute of Physical Problems, which was being established in Moscow by the USSR Academy of Sciences. There he studied the thermal conductivity of liquid helium. The openness of his criticism made him enemies in high places and in 1938, during the Stalin oppression, he was imprisoned on allegations of spying for Germany.

From the Soviet Union, Landau received the Order of Lenin, the Lenin Prize, and the Stalin Prize. Internationally, he was also awarded numerous marks of recognition, culminating in the Nobel Prize in 1962, for his theories on condensed matter, particularly liquid helium.

In January 1962, a traffic accident left the bril-

Lev Landau (with his wife) receiving the Nobel Prize from the Swedish ambassador in Moscow, 1962.

liant scientist almost completely incapacitated. He was declared clinically dead, but even after regaining his faculties was unable to resume his scientific pursuits. Six years later, he died.

T. der Haar (ed.), *Collected Papers of L. D. Landau*, 1965.

A. Dorozynski, *The Man They Wouldn't Let Die*, 1966.

A. Livanov, *Landau: A Great Physicist and Teacher*, 1978.

LANDAUER, GUSTAV (1870–1919) German socialist-anarchist, philosopher, essayist. Born in Karlsruhe to a prosperous family, he was educated in literature, philosophy, and social sciences at several universities in Germany and Switzerland. While still a student at Berlin, he participated in radical and socialist activities.

At age twenty-one, he edited and wrote for *Der Sozialist*, a journal which advocated a change in the political system and a reorganization of society more extreme than was advocated by the Social Democratic party and closer to anarchist thinking. Soon the mild-mannered, soft-spoken Landauer emerged as the chief theoretician of a utopian anarchist philosophy. In 1893 and 1899 he was imprisoned for propagating subversive causes. In his thirties, he matured as a writer and translator. He popularized the works of Peter Kropotkin, whose anarchist views resembled his own. He gave a modern rendering of the medieval German mystic Meister Eckhart. From English, he translated Shaw, Wilde, Whitman, and Tagore. He collaborated with Fritz Mauthner in the critique of language as an inadequate expression of thought and joined with Martin Buber (q.v.) in efforts to forestall a possible world conflict. However, World War I erupted before a conference they planned could take place. Drawn to the theater as an artistic

medium of communal expression, he lectured to receptive audiences on Shakespeare, lectures which were collected posthumously in two volumes (1923). Though not a Zionist, he advocated the establishment of workers' communes, such as later found realization in socialist kibbutzim in Palestine.

During the revolutionary upheavals that rocked Central Europe after the War, a Bavarian soviet republic came into existence for a few months. Its leader, Kurt Eisner (q.v.), invited Landauer to join the government as minister of public relations. After the collapse of the Communist regime following the assassination of Eisner, he was captured and shortly thereafter taken from prison by reactionary officers, brutally tortured, and trampled to death by their iron-shod boots. His last words to his killers are reported to have been: "To think that you are human!"

Landauer's affirmation of Jewishness made him a lifelong target for anti-Semites, despite his greater emphasis on his German roots and the utopian vision of a world brotherhood of peoples. This affirmation best came to the fore in his essay "Sind das Ketzerquedanken?" ("Are These the Ideas of a Heretic?"; 1913). He faulted the Zionists for negating the Diaspora and for concentrating all their efforts on Palestine, then an impoverished Turkish province. In accordance with his utopian philosophy, he forsaw in the not-too-distant future the transformation of existing states, based on oppression, exploitation, and violence, into juster and freer governmental structures that would liberate the creative energies now dormant in many groups. Jews, united by fate, history, and common ideals, regardless of whether they were in possession of territory, would be afforded an opportunity to place their national contributions at the service of the world at large, alongside other national groups, large and small. The Jews would be redeemed when mankind was redeemed.

R. L. S. Hyman, *Gustav Landauer; Philosopher of Utopia*, 1973.

E. Lunn, *Prophet of Community; The Romantic Socialism of Gustav Landauer*, 1977.

LANDOWSKA, WANDA (1879–1959) Harpsichord virtuoso. Born in Warsaw to a cultured family, Landowska was to become known as "the high priestess of the harpsichord" and an authority on 17th- and 18th-century music.

From the age of four, when she began to learn to play the piano, she showed a marked preference, amounting to a passion, for the baroque masters. Her early teachers, recognizing her genius, sent her to study with the renowned Chopin interpreter, Michalowski, at the Warsaw Conservatory. There the only Bach works on the curriculum were transcriptions by Liszt and other romantics, but Landowska always insisted on playing some Bach in addition to the set pieces.

She went to Berlin in 1895 to study counterpoint and composition. Much drawn to vocal music at the time, she composed many lieder. Her other compositions included *Hebrew Poem for Orchestra*; *Serenade for Strings*; numerous works for piano and for harpsichord; cadenzas for Mozart and Haydn concertos; and various transcriptions and arrangements of folk songs.

In 1900 she eloped with Henry Lew to Paris. Besides being an actor and a journalist, he was an eminent ethnologist, specializing in Hebrew folklore, and they collaborated on a book, *Musique ancienne* (1909).

From 1909 she devoted herself to the revival of the harpsichord. She was virtually alone in the belief that the modern piano is unsuited to the music of Bach and his contemporaries. Her husband helped her in her research and in her campaign to "reconstitute a harpsichord approaching as closely as possible those of the middle 18th century." She also had the backing of friends such as Albert Schweitzer, Paul Dukas, and Gabriel Fauré, although they were distressed that such a gifted pianist considered abandoning the piano for what they considered to be an old "tin-pan" instrument. It was not until 1912 that she was actually able to present the first of her fine Pleyel models, built to her specifications, at the Bach Festival in Breslau.

She first played the harpsichord in public in 1903. In 1913 she was appointed to head a harpsichord class at the Berlin Hochschule für Musik. She was also twice invited to stay with the Tolstoys at Yasnaya Polnaya, where she played the harpsichord to the great writer. Being a lover of old music, he became an ardent supporter of her cause.

The Lews were confined to Germany as aliens throughout World War I (1914–1918), though Landowska was permitted to continue teaching. Her husband was killed in a car accident soon after the war. Landowska left for Switzerland, then settled in Paris, resuming her concert tours and teaching.

She toured America for the first time and made her first recordings in 1923. She made extensive

Wanda Landowska.

- There's no such thing as "ancient music" — simply "music," that of today, yesterday, and forever.
- A successful miniature is better than a bad fresco. But the one needs to be studied at close range, the other looked at from a distance.
- A true artist always compares what he does with what he intended to do.

Wanda Landowska

ABOUT WANDA LANDOWSKA

Exceptional instruments demand exceptional performers; and in the end they always obtain them.

B. Gavoty

tours of Europe, Asia, Africa, and both Americas. In 1925 she founded her School for Ancient Music at the picturesque Saint-Leu-la-Forêt near Paris, and had a concert hall built in the garden. Pupils and music lovers flocked there from its inception until the outbreak of World War II. It was not until 1933 that she felt ready to give her first complete performance of Bach's *Goldberg Variations*. She confided to her audience that she had been practicing them for forty-five years.

Landowska inspired several composers to write for the harpsichord. In 1926 she commissioned Manuel de Falla to compose a concerto, and Francis Poulenc dedicated to her his *Concert champêtre*, which she premiered in Paris.

When the Germans marched on Paris in 1940, Landowska had to abandon her school, with its library and its museum housing her unique collection of musical instruments, which was subsequently looted by the invading army. She took refuge at Banyuls-sur-Mer in the eastern Pyrenees, and after a concert tour of Switzerland, she sailed for the United States in 1941, arriving there on December 7, 1941. For a time she lived in New York, and then settled permanently in Lakeville, Connecticut, where she continued to teach, compose, make recordings, and write prolifically on music.

B. Gavoty, *Wanda Landowska*, 1957.
D. Restout, *Landowska on Music*, 1969.

LANDSTEINER, KARL (1868–1943) Biochemist and winner of the 1930 Nobel Prize for physiology and medicine. Born in Vienna to the newspaper publisher Leopold Landsteiner, Karl received his medical degree from the University of Vienna in 1891. He spent the next five years studying chemistry in Wurzburg, Munich, and Zurich and working in laboratories and hospitals in Vienna and Berlin. In 1896 Landsteiner returned to Vienna to work in the department of hygiene at the University of Vienna. It was there that he first became interested in immunology and began his first studies of anti-body action in blood. He worked with A. Weich-selbaum (who discovered the bacteria causing meningitis and pneumonia) in the department of pathological anatomy. During his ten years there he performed over 3,600 post-mortem exami-nations.

His most famous discovery was first disclosed in a footnote in an article he wrote in 1900. Land-steiner noted that the interagglutination that occurs between serum and blood cells of different people is a physiological phenomenon. In an article the following year, he described three blood types, A, B, and C, grouped according to their clotting fac-tors. Later he changed type C to O and discovered a fourth blood type, AB. His discovery of an easy way to distinguish blood types led to safe blood transfusions and operations, and, when a way to preserve blood was discovered in 1914, to modern blood banks. Landsteiner believed that blood types could be used to identify people the same way fingerprints did. His investigation into serological identification led to the discovery of the M, N, and P factors in 1927. These factors along with the hereditary nature of blood were eventually used to help determine paternity cases.

Landsteiner left the university in 1908 for the Wilhelmina Hospital in Vienna, where he worked on poliomyelitis. His research formed the founda-tion for the discovery of the polio vaccine by Jonas Salk in 1954. After World War I Landsteiner moved to Holland to become a pathologist at the R.K. Ziekenhuis. In 1923 he joined the Rockefeller Institute of Medical Research, New York City, where he remained until his death. In 1930 he was awarded the Nobel Prize for his discovery of human blood groups. He traveled to Sweden to receive the prize with Sinclair Lewis, that year's winner of the Nobel Prize for literature. At a dinner reception Landsteiner, a shy, quiet man, said he would let "the master of words" speak in his behalf. Lewis then proclaimed, "You may call me a master of words, but what is he? He has been in a thousand cases the master of death."

Landsteiner's other work includes the develop-ment of a test for the diagnosis of paroxysmal cold hemoglobinuria (Donath-Landsteiner test) and the introduction of dark-field illumination for demonstrating spirochetes in syphilitic lesions. In collaboration with C. P. Miller, Landsteiner pub-lished a series of articles in 1925, "Serologic Stu-dies on the Blood of Primates," which supports the theory that man, ape, and monkey descended from a common stock.

Upon his retirement Landsteiner was appointed an emeritus member of the Rockefeller Institute. A dedicated scientist, he continued working at the laboratory. In 1940 he and Alexander Weiner found the rhesus (Rh) factor in human blood. The Rh factor was found to be linked to jaundice in newborn babies and was especially dangerous in cases in which the mother had a negative R factor and her baby had a positive Rh factor.

Landsteiner was working in his laboratory when he suffered a fatal heart attack. He died a Roman Catholic. In his lifetime he published over three hundred papers, in addition to his classic text *The Specificity of Serological Reactions* (1936). Upon his death the *New York Times* published an editor-ial saying, "He had the imagination, the original-ity, the outlook that always distinguished great research."

P. Mazumdar, *Karl Landsteiner and the Problem of Species*, 1976.
G. R. Simms, *The Scientific Work of Karl Land-steiner*, 1963.
P. Speiser and F. Smekal, *Karl Landsteiner*, 1975.

LANG, FRITZ (1890–1976) Film director. Born in Vienna, Lang was the son of a Jewish mother and a non-Jewish father. Expected by his father to follow him as an architect, Lang submitted to a little study before running away to become a painter. After a period spent traveling, he settled in Paris, returning to Austria when World War I broke out. Wounded in action three times, he was approached by the director of a Red Cross play and became a leading man. An introduction to the producer Erich Pommer brought him into the film industry as a script reader. Reading led to writing and, in 1919, to directing. Lang's first films were made as expres-sionism began to dominate the German cinema; with his artist's eye to aid him, he soon rose to prominence. Films like *Dr. Mabuse the Gambler*, and its sequel, *The Testament of Dr. Mabuse, Die Nibelungen*, and *Metropolis* made Lang an impor-tant name in films of crime, historical spectacle, and science fiction. He married the novelist Thea von Harbouv, who wrote the scripts for all his films from 1920 until 1932, when Lang left her because she was a member of the Nazi party.

An extremely impressive sound-film debut, *M*,

In '32, someone came to me and said, "Look, Mr. Lang, we have made so much money with *Mabuse*...." I said, "Yes, much more than I did...." He said, "Can't you give us another *Mabuse*?" So I started thinking about it and I said, "All right, what shall I do? This guy is insane and in an asylum — I can-not make him healthy again. It is impossible."

So I invented the next Mabuse — *The Tes-tament of Dr. Mabuse* — and then I said, "Now I am finished. Now I am killing him." I had been able to put into the mouth of an insane criminal all the Nazi slogans. When the picture was finished, some henchmen of Dr. Goebbels came to the office and threatened to forbid it. I was very short with them and said, "If you think you can forbid a picture of Fritz Lang in Germany, go ahead." They did so.

Fritz Lang, 1962

Fritz Lang with Brigitte Bardot.

was followed by the sequel to *Dr. Mabuse*, which was banned by the Nazis. On the strength of his earlier films, Lang was offered directorship of the film industry of the Third Reich by Joseph Goebbels, but fearing that his Jewish origin would be discovered, he fled to France the same day. In Paris he made one film, an adaptation of Ferenc Molnár's (q.v.) *Liliom*, before being brought to Hollywood by David Selznick (q.v.). Lang's first American film, *Fury*, was a success, but his status was less than it had been in the German film industry and he was not always creatively independent. During the war he made a number of anti-Nazi films, among them *Man Hunt* and *Hangmen Also Die*, as well as some westerns.

Since Lang was a leader of German expressionist cinema, it was not surprising that he mastered one of its spiritual descendants, the film noir. Films like *The Woman in the Window, Scarlet Street, Clash by Night*, and *While the City Sleeps* kept him popular with American audiences, but by the end of the 1950s he had wearied of Hollywood. He returned to Germany, where he remade one of his early silent epics, *Das Indische Grabmal*, and concluded his directorial career with another sequel to *Dr. Mabuse*. After he ceased directing, he made one memorable return to acting playing himself in Jean-Luc Godard's *Le mépris*.

P. Bogdanovitch, *Fritz Lang in America*, 1967.
L. Eisner, *Fritz Lang*, 1976.
P. M. Jensen, *The Cinema of Fritz Lang*, 1969.

LANSKY, MEYER (1902–1983) Financial manipulator and kingpin of U.S. organized crime. Born Maier Suchowljansky in Grodno, Poland, he came to the United States with his parents in 1911.

Lansky always called himself a gambler, but to law enforcement officials he was a major leader of organized crime in the United States. Lansky applied his financial and organizational acumen to bootlegging in the Prohibition era, to gambling in Cuba, the Bahamas, and the United States, and to underworld penetration of legitimate businesses. An agent of the Federal Bureau of Investigation once said of Lansky with grudging respect and admiration, "He would have been chairman of the board of General Motors if he'd gone into legitimate business." And in a moment of triumph, Lansky once boasted to an underworld associate that "we're bigger than U.S. Steel."

Lansky grew up poor on New York City's Lower East Side and never went beyond the eighth grade in school. As a youth, he became friends with Charles "Lucky" Luciano and Benjamin "Bugsy" Siegel (q.v.), who later became his criminal partners. During Prohibition, he and Siegel formed their own gang, the Bugs and Meyer Mob, which engaged in bootlegging, and hired themselves out as gunmen for other bootleggers. After the repeal of Prohibition in 1933, Lansky and Frank Costello opened illegal gambling casinos in upstate New York, New Orleans, and southern Florida. In 1934 Lansky helped found a national crime syndicate, which brought underworld gangs into a loosely organized national federation.

The expansion of organized crime in the United States after World War II was huge and Lansky was among its top investors. In 1970 the U.S. government charged him with income-tax evasion and he fled to Israel. After a two-year legal battle, he was deported. He stood trial in the United States and was acquitted of all charges. Despite all the publicity during the last decade of his life, Lansky remained the most shadowy of the organized crime leaders.

D. Eisenberg, U. Dann, and E. Landau, *Meyer Lansky: Mogul of the Mob*, 1979.

LASKER, EDUARD (originally Isaac; 1829–1884) Liberal German politician. Dissatisfied with his country's political system he sought to make changes that would strengthen the parliamentary powers in Germany. Although he received much support from the masses, his ideas were not always welcomed by the political establishment.

Lasker was born in Posen to a merchant family. He studied law and mathematics at the university of Breslau. During that time he also participated in the revolution of 1848, fighting against imperial troops.

After graduating from the university in 1853, Lasker traveled to England to study the British system of parliamentary government. His studies in England led to his enthusiasm for the parliamentary system. He returned to Germany in 1856 and became an associate judge in Berlin, waiting for the opportunity to implement his ideas.

In 1865 Lasker was elected to the Prussian parliament representing the Progressive party. However, two years later he broke from the party and founded the National Liberal party. He headed the Liberal party in the Reichstag after the formation of the German Empire in 1871.

Initially, Lasker was a friend of Otto Bismarck, aiding him in establishing Prussian leadership in Germany. He also contributed heavily to the passage of laws that were the foundation of the new German Empire. These included taxation laws, the codification of criminal law, and the revamping of the judicial system.

However, Lasker fell out of favor with Bismarck. His decline began in 1873 after he uncovered a financial scandal which caused the demise of one of Bismarck's closest associates. When Lasker died Bismarck refused to accept a message of condolence from the U.S. House of Representatives on behalf of the Reichstag. Bismarck claimed if he accepted the message it would be tantamount to criticizing German policy.

Lasker was visiting the United States when he died. He had traveled there in order to visit his brother and to study the republican form of government.

Born to Orthodox Jewish parents, Lasker maintained his commitment to Judaism and his Jewish roots throughout his life and was a champion of Jewish civil rights. he initiated a measure, passed by the Prussian parliament, which enabled ultra-Orthodox Jewish congregations to form independent communities.

One of the things that impressed Lasker on his trip to the United States before his death was the generosity of the American Jews, even though he felt they had greatly assimilated. In his last speech, given at Mount Sinai Hospital in New York, he said: "During my whole journey through America, the benevolent institutions of the Jews have made an especially acute and satisfactory impression on me. And the careful conservation of this holy duty induces me somewhat to overlook the fact that I have seen otherwise very little attempt among the Jews of America to preserve the traditions of the olden times.... I can recall nothing of all that I have seen in my journey in America which has had so refreshing and inspiring an effect upon me, as these evidences that the Jews, who are freer here than in any other land, devote themselves with all the more energy and devotion to the development of benevolence, and thus testify to the vast power for good which lies inherent in the Jewish race wherever they may be domiciled."

LASKER, EMANUEL (1868–1941) Chess master. Born in Berlin to a German cantor, he learned chess from his brother at the age of twelve. Although he studied mathematics at university, he found himself playing chess for a living because it was difficult for a Jew to get a position at a German university. At the age of twenty he had earned the title of chess master and entered an international competition in Amsterdam, where he played a brilliant game against J. H. Bauer. Tournaments that

followed in England found him easily defeating the leading British players.

In 1893 he won the New York Tourney and set a world record with thirteen straight wins. In 1894 he played for the world championship against William Steinitz (q.v.), who had held the world title for twenty-seven years, and defeated him then and again in 1896–1897. He defended the world title several times, until he lost it to the Cuban player José Capablanca in 1921, although he later defeated Capablanca at tournaments in New York and Moscow.

Though an extremely skilled and crafty player, Lasker advocated a philosophy of justice in chess that held that he had no right to win a game if his opponent had not made mistakes or broken rules. He managed to win, notwithstanding these ethics, by steering his opponents into complicated games in which it was difficult not to err.

In the early 1900s Lasker settled in New York City, where he began to publish *Lasker's Chess Magazine* and edited a chess column for the *New York Evening Post*. Although lacking the eccentricities that characterized other chess champions, he was known for never wearing a watch, claiming that he did not want to be enslaved by time.

An excellent mathematician, Lasker taught advanced mathematics at several universities and wrote many articles on various philosophical and social issues. He was insistent about being adequately paid for his chess matches, yet, during the German inflation of 1923 the nest egg he had set aside for himself when playing against Capablanca was completely dissipated.

Among his publications were *Common Sense in Chess* (1896), *Lasker's Manual of Chess* (1927), and *The Community of the Future*.
A. Cockburn, *Idle Passions: Chess and the Dance of Death*, 1974.
J. Gilchrist (ed.), *The Games of Emanuel Lasker, Chess Champion*, (2 vols.), 1955–1958.

LASKER-SCHÜLER, ELSE (1869–1945) German poet. Born in Elberfeld, Else Schüler was the daughter of prominent German Jews. Her first husband was Berthold Lasker. Her second husband, Herwarth Walden, was the editor of an important journal of German expressionism, *Der Sturm*.

A well-known figure in German literary circles and in the bohemia of Berlin and a dedicated proponent of German expressionism, Lasker-Schüler included many Jewish elements in her poetry. Several of her poems deal with biblical figures, presented in her own unique interpretation. She was particularly fascinated by the miracle-working rabbis of Europe. Although she wrote both prose and poetry, she is best known for her poetic output, especially her *Hebräische Balläden* ("Hebrew Ballads," 1913).

She was a noted eccentric who called herself "Prince Yussuf of Thebes" and "Princess Tino of Baghdad." In 1933, after Hitler came to power, she

Else Lasker-Schuler.

emigrated to Switzerland. In 1939, after having made two visits to Palestine (1933 and 1937), she decided to make her home in Jerusalem, where her eccentricity intensified. A final volume of her poetry. *Mein blaues Klavier*, was published three years prior to her death.

Her collected works in three volumes appeared between 1959 and 1962. Else Lasker-Schüler's best-known poetry collections are *Styx* ("The River of Death," 1902), *Der siebente Tag*, ("The Seventh Day," 1905), and *Hebräische Balladen*. Some of the books appeared with her own grotesque illustrations.

M. Kupper, *Else Lasker-Schüler* (German), 1966. M. Schmid (ed.), *Lasker-Schüler; A Memorial Volume* (German), 1966. J. P. Wallmann, *Else Lasker-Schüler* (German), 1966.

**FROM ELSE LASKER-SCHÜLER'S
"LORD, LISTEN"**

Where must I end? Lord, in the stars
I looked, and in the moon and the valleys of
Thy fruit.
The red wine is already tasteless in the grape
And everywhere, in every core, there's bitterness.

LASKIN, BORA (1912–1984) Canadian scholar and Supreme Court chief justice. Born in Fort William, Ontario, Laskin studied at the University of Toronto, Osgoode Hall law school, and Harvard University. He taught law at the University of Toronto for more than twenty years, first as a lecturer from 1940 to 1943, then as assistant professor from 1943 to 1945 and then, after a four-year period as lecturer at Osgoode, as professor of law from 1949 to 1965.

In 1965 Laskin was appointed justice of the Ontario Court of Appeals. Five years later he became the first Jewish judge of the Supreme Court of Canada. He was also the first purely academic lawyer and the youngest man appointed to the highest bench. In 1973 he was named chief justice. Laskin also served as chancellor of Lakeside University in Thunder Bay, as president of the Association of Canadian Law Teachers from 1953 to 1954, as president of the Canadian Association of University Teachers from 1964 to 1965, and as chairman of the Legal Committee of the Canadian Jewish Congress and the Toronto Friends of the Hebrew University.

An expert on constitutional and labor law, his books include *Canadian Constitutional Law* (3rd ed. 1966), *Cases and Notes on Land Law* (1958), and *British Tradition in Canadian Law* (1969). Laskin had a great influence on Canadian law students. He held five honorary degrees and was a judicial activist, committed to federalism.

LASKI, HAROLD JOSEPH (1893–1950) British political scientist and left-wing Socialist. Born in Manchester to Nathan Laski, a wealthy cottonshipping merchant and Jewish community leader, he was brought up in an Orthodox household and was taught Hebrew at an early age. After studying eugenics at University College, London, he published an article on the subject in the *Westminster Review*. He went to Oxford, where he gained firstclass honors in modern history. He then worked as a headline-writer on the Labor newspaper *Daily Herald*. At the outbreak of World War I, he was rejected as medically unfit for military service and taught history, first at McGill University, Montreal (1914–1916), and then at Harvard (1916–1920). Laski's stay in the United States came to an end in 1920 soon after he was attacked in the press and by members of the faculty for having spoken publicly on behalf of the police during the Boston police strike.

Laski became a lecturer in politics at the London School of Economics, where he developed a style of delivery that left a lasting impression on all who heard him.

In 1926 he was appointed to the chair of political science and over the years earned the profound respect of his numerous students, many of whom went on to hold leading academic, political, legal, and commercial posts throughout the world.

Laski was active in politics, in the belief that in order to teach the subject it was essential to have practice as well as theory. In 1932, at the time of the split within the Labor party, he joined the newly-formed Social League. In 1934 he was elected as Labor party representative on the Fulham council and served as alderman until 1945. He declined many offers to stand for election to Parliament and refused to accept an appointment to the House of Lords, advocating the abolition of the second house. In 1937 Laski signed the "Unity Manifesto" published by the Independent Labor party, the Communist party, and the Social League. In that year he was elected to the Labor party national executive, a post he retained until he retired in 1949.

During the depression of the 1930s, Laski traveled around the country addressing mass meetings, condemning the government for its indifference to the plight of the three million unemployed. He served on the board of Stafford Cripps's left-wing periodical, *The Tribune*. In 1941 Laski was appointed secretary of the Labor party's Central Committee on Reconstruction Problems and was involved in the preparation of policy papers that ultimately formed the basis for the party's 1945 election program, when he was serving as chairman of the Labor party. In the campaign he was singled out for special attack by the Conservative leader, Winston Churchill.

Laski's fascination with the United States drew him back year after year for lecture tours. He was on personal terms with distinguished American political figures including Franklin D. Roosevelt and John Kennedy (his student at LSE in 1935–1936). In 1947 he was invited to become the first president of the newly established Brandeis University, but refused, explaining that it was politically important for him to remain in England. In 1949 Laski gave a series of lectures later published as *Trade Unions in the New Society*. Two of his books on America are *The American Presidency* (1940), dedicated to President Roosevelt, and *The American Democracy* (1948).

Laski's interest in India began in 1931 when he was closely associated with the work of the Round Table Conference in London attended by Gandhi and Nehru. He often addressed the India League and openly expressed his support for Indian independence, which was acknowledged by the opening in 1954 of the Harold Laski Institute of Political Science in Ahmadabad, Gujarat state, India.

Laski was never involved in the Zionist movement and it was only after the news of the Holocaust reached England that he accepted an invitation to attend a Poale Zion executive meeting, at which he expressed his support of free immigration into Palestine. He openly clashed with Ernest Bevin over the foreign secretary's pro-Arab policy and attempts to curtail immigration of Jewish survivors of the Holocaust.

All Laski's numerous books, pamphlets, and articles were produced in minuscule handwriting and only on rare occasions did he make corrections. He wrote sitting in a easy chair on a large wooden board across his knees. His works include *The Problem of Sovereignty* (1917), *Authority in the Modern State* (1919), *The Foundations of Sovereignty* (1921), and *A Grammar of Politics* (1925). The latter received international recognition as a university textbook and was translated into several languages. Other works were *The State in Theory and Practice* (1935), *Parliamentary Government in England* (1938) and two books on the theme of the socialist revolution by consent in the West — *Reflections on the Revolution of Our Time* (1943) and *Faith, Reason, and Civilization* (1944). The twenty-year correspondence between Laski and U.S. Supreme Court Justice Oliver Wendell Holmes was published in two volumes in 1953. *Dilemma of Our Times*, expressing his disillusionment with the Soviet system appeared in 1952.

H. Deane, *The Political Ideas of Harold Laski*, 1972.

G. Eastwood, *Harold Laski*, 1977.

K. Martin, *Harold Laski, 1893–1950: A Biographical Memoir*, 1953.

LASKY, JESSE L. (1880–1958) U.S. film producer. Born in San Francisco to the children of German immigrants, Lasky appeared on the vaudeville stage from childhood. He was later joined in the act by his sister Blanche, who, like Jesse, played the cornet. At Blanche's urging, he relinquished performing for the more financially rewarding roles of booking agent and producer.

Blanche's husband, the glove salesman Samuel Goldfish (later Goldwyn [q.v.]), tried to persuade Lasky to enter motion-picture production with him. Lasky, however, wanted no part of the film business until he was made a lucrative offer for the use of his name, well-known in the theater, as the trademark of a film company. Realizing the potential of movies, Lasky, with his brother-in-law and a dramatically inclined friend, Cecil B. DeMille, formed the Jesse L. Lasky Feature Play Company in 1913. The company's first film, *The Squaw Man*, was a tremendous success. In 1916 Lasky merged his firm with that of Adolph Zukor (q.v.). The result of the merger, the Famous Players-Lasky Corporation, became more widely known by the name of Paramount, the distributor in which it owned a controlling interest. As vice-president in charge of production, Lasky ruled over the West Coast operations of Paramount for over fifteen years. Mary Pickford, Rudolph Valentino, Gloria Swanson, Ernst Lubitsch (q.v.), Josef von Sternberg (q.v.), the Marx Brothers (q.v.), Maurice Chevalier, Bing Crosby, and Cary Grant, to name but a few, were among the talents that graced the Paramount lot during Lasky's period.

In the early 1930s Lasky lost his executive post at Paramount, which was then struggling through the depression. He continued his career as a producer at a number of studios. He also produced for radio and had a short-lived partnership with Mary Pickford. Few of his post-Paramount films were notable, the most successful being *Sergeant York* in

1941, although *The Power and the Glory* and *The Gay Desperado* have increased in critical stature over the years. Constantly seeking to make a comeback, and in debt to the Internal Revenue Service, Lasky had returned to Paramount and was preparing a new film with Goldwyn and DeMille at the time of his sudden death. Lasky's son, Jesse Lasky Jr., was a screenwriter who also worked with DeMille.

J. L. Lasky and D. Weldon, *I Blow My Own Horn*, 1957.

J. L. Lasky Jr., *Whatever Happened To Hollywood?*, 1975.

LASSALLE, FERDINAND (1825–1864) German socialist and founder of the German labor movement. He was born in Breslau, Germany (today Wroclaw, Poland). His father was a wealthy silk merchant and town councilor who embraced the German Enlightenment. As a youngster Lassalle was precocious and undisciplined and was expelled from the Breslau classical high school for forging a signature on a school report. He dreamed of becoming a leader and wanted to head the Jews and avenge the Damascus blood libel of 1840, writing "I could... risk my life to deliver the Jews from their present crushing condition. I would not even shrink from the scaffold could I but once make of them a respected people."

Ferdinand Lassalle, "fighter against capitalism." Caricature.

After attending a trade school in Leipzig, he returned to Breslau in 1841 and prepared himself for university. There, the philosophy of Hegel influenced him profoundly and led eventually to his complete severance from Judaism. Lassalle studied philosophy, history, philology, and archeology at the University of Breslau, where he became involved in Jacobin-democratic propaganda, based on an "activated" but orthodox Hegelianism. In order to widen his horizons and perhaps to avoid expulsion for his political activities, he continued his education in Berlin, where he planned an academic career.

It was during this time, while on a study visit to France, that Lassalle met the German poet and essayist Heinrich Heine (q.v.); the two formed a close friendship. In 1846 he became friendly with the unhappily married Countess Sophie von Hatzfeldt, who had been unable to obtain a divorce from her husband although he had badly mistreated her in many ways. Seeing the case as one of gross social injustice, Lassalle decided to champion her cause. Although not a lawyer, he conducted thirty-five lawsuits on her behalf over a period of eight years. His flamboyant and theatrical personality brought him widespread publicity and fame. In 1854 the countess obtained a divorce, and rewarded Lassalle with a considerable annual income.

Moving to Düsseldorf, Lassalle participated in the revolution of 1848, when the liberal middle class tried to attain a constitutional monarchy that would grant such basic civil rights as freedom of assembly and freedom of the press. Lassalle was imprisoned for six months for inciting violence when he urged the militia to open revolt in November 1848. His defense against his arrest was printed as a pamphlet under the title of *Meine Assisen-Rede* (1849) and served to add to his fame and influence. During this period he established contact with Karl Marx (q.v.) and Friedrich Engels. Initially Marx and Lassalle cooperated but, although they continued to correspond, they gradually became estranged when Lassalle proclaimed that the revolutionary phase of socialism had ended and only a legal and evolutionary approach could now succeed. Engels disliked Lassalle and made him the object of anti-Semitic attacks.

Lassalle's standing as a scholar, poet, jurist, and journalist grew with the publication of his work on the Greek philosopher Heraclitus and his dramatic epic, *Franz von Sickingen* (1858), which assigns to personality a role in determining the course of history.

Lassalle was now a celebrity in the Berlin salons. Otto von Bismarck was attracted to Lassalle, admiring his charismatic personality and paternalist notions of democracy. Lassalle was aware of the importance of a sense of style in politics and exploited this to attract large audiences. He turned to the workingmen's associations, where he expounded his ideas for integrating the workers into a powerful, united Germany. He organized a suffrage army through which the workers could agitate for universal suffrage. When the ADAV (Allgemeiner deutscher Arbeiterverein, or General German Workers' Association), the first workers' political party in Germany, was founded in 1863, Lassalle was elected its first president.

Lassalle was ambitious. He had promised his fiancée that one day he would enter Berlin as president of the German Republic in a chariot drawn by six white horses. He was also authoritarian; the ADAV was a tool by which he propagated his political ideas and it was controlled by an absolute ruler: Lassalle. He succeeded in arousing the political awareness of the German workers, eliciting the enthusiasm of the masses who idolized him.

In 1864 he became engaged to Helene von Donniges in Switzerland. Lassalle foolishly challenged Helene's father and her former fiancée to a duel, ostensibly because her family did not approve of him. The latter accepted the challenge and shot Lassalle fatally in the abdomen. He was buried in the Breslau Jewish cemetery.

Lassalle left behind the legacy of a romantic

> "There are two classes of men I cannot bear: journalists and Jews — and unfortunately I belong to both."
>
> **Ferdinand Lassalle**

**Engel's letter to Marx
on September 4, 1864, following the news
of Lasalle's death in a duel**

What an extraordinary way to die. This would-be Don Juan really falls in love with the daughter of a Bavarian ambassador and wants to marry her. Then comes up against a rejected suitor of the lady — who incidentally is a swindler from Rumania — and gets himself shot dead by his rival. This could only happen to Lassalle, with his unique character, part Jew, part cavalier, part clown, part sentimentalist. How could a politician of his caliber let himself be shot dead by a Rumanian adventurer?

**Bismarck to the Reichstag on
September 16, 1878**

[Lassalle was] one of the most intellectual and gifted men with whom I have ever met, a man who was ambitious on a grand scale, but by no means a Republican: He had very decided national and monarchical sympathies; the idea which he strove to realize was the German Empire, and in that, we had a point of contact.

personality (his last love affair was the inspiration of George Meredith's novel *The Tragic Comedians*). His work and efforts in the workers' movement led to the formation after his death of the German Socialist Democratic party.

D. Footman, *The Primrose Path: A Life of Ferdinand Lassalle*, 1946.

R. S. Wistrich, *Revolutionary Jews from Marx to Trotsky*, 1976.

LAUTERPACHT, HERSCH (1897–1960) British international lawyer and jurist, knighted in 1965. Born in Galicia, Lauterpacht studied in Lvov, Vienna, and London. In 1927 he was appointed assistant lecturer at the London School of Economics and, in 1932, reader in public international law at the University of London. He held the post of professor at The Hague Academy of International Law. From 1938 to 1955 he was Whewell professor of international law at the University of Cambridge. In 1955 he became a barrister and judge of the International Court of Justice, The Hague, a position he held until his death.

Lauterpacht served as a member of the British War Crimes Executive (1945–1946) and the United Nations International Law Commission (1951–1955). He was president of the French-Swedish and the Norwegian-Portuguese Conciliation Commissions from 1951, and a member of the Permanent Court of Arbitration.

Among his books were *The Function of Law in the International Community* (1933), *Recognition in International Law* (1947), *International Law and Human Rights* (1950), and *The Development of International Law by the International Court* (1958). He edited *Oppenheim's International Law* from 1935 to 1955, the *British Year Book of International Law* from 1944 to 1955, and the *International Law Reports*. After World War II he published *An International Bill of the Rights of Man*, in which he pleaded for an international bill with constitutional embodiments of the principle.

He was a Zionist and active in Jewish affairs, and served as the first president of the World Union of Jewish Students on its formation after World War I.

Lord McNair, *Hersch Lauterpacht, 1897–1960*, 1967.

LAZARE, BERNARD (1865—1903) French writer and activist on behalf of the innocence of Alfred Dreyfus (q.v.). Born in Nîmes, Lazare came from an assimilated French-Jewish family of Sephardic origin. He moved in 1886 to Paris, where he studied at the Sorbonne.

Lazare soon became part of Parisian literary life and by the early 1890s was already a leading literary critic of the symbolist movement, expressing his belief that literature should be a tool of social justice. He also published volumes of symbolist poetry. His convictions led him to the anarchist and socialist movements in the framework of which he wrote articles in a number of periodicals.

These later formed the basis of his book *Anti-Semitism: Its History and Causes* (in French, 1894: English translation, 1903) in which he suggested that anti-Semitism could be of some use in bringing about the advent of socialism by teaching hatred of Jewish capitalism. This he claimed would inevitably turn into hatred of all forms of capitalism. He differentiated between *Juifs* and *Israélites*. The *Juifs* were the "foreign Jews," a cosmopolitan herd, who would contaminate everyone and everything with which they came into contact. The Israélites, on the other hand, were upright, decent people, assimilated into French society. In many ways, Lazare's work supported and strengthened the idea of the arch-anti-Semite, Edouard Drumont, and his writings were eagerly and approvingly quoted in anti-Semitic literature.

The Dreyfus (q.v.) affair was a turning point in his life. It forced him to reexamine his view of the Jewish problem and to revise his ideas. He severed his relations with Drumont by the standard procedure at the time, a duel, in which neither was injured. Lazare ironically was to become the bitterest enemy of the anti-Semites. he had come to the realization that even the most assimilated French Israélite was hated because he was Jewish and that anti-Semitism was growing from day to day. He published an anti-Drumont booklet, *Antisé-mitisme et révolution* in 1895 and wrote extensively in the press attacking anti-Semitism.

When Dreyfus was sentenced, Lazare did not at first doubt his guilt, but he was shaken by the way the trial was exploited to whip up anti-Semitism, even against the assimilated Jews. He claimed that Drumont and his supporters threatened the basic rights of man by seeking to deprive Jews from their freedom and to restore the medieval ghetto.

By 1895, when Dreyfus's brother turned to Lazare for support, Lazare was already beginning to doubt the justice of the verdict. He found the relevant documents, reexamined the testimony, and by consulting handwriting experts was able to prove that evidence had been forged and that Dreyfus was the victim of a conspiracy. Lazare published several booklets on the case in an attempt to demonstrate Dreyfus's innocence. He realized that the case was not only a legal injustice but a conspiracy against the republic.

Now realizing that assimilation, like emancipation, could not solve the Jewish problem, Lazare, in 1897 adopted a nationalistic position and in 1898 founded a Zionist journal. He participated in the Second Zionist Congress. Later he was to become disillusioned by Theodor Herzl's (q.v.) autocratic behavior and emphasis on diplomacy. Lazare's fellow French Jews were embarrassed by his campaign against anti-Semitism. They preferred passivity and relied on French liberal principles to protect them. Eventually Lazare was ostracized by the French Jewish community.

Lazare continued to fight for Jewish emancipation and traveled extensively in the Balkans and eastern Europe.

> This spurious doctrine [assimilation] far from ensuring the security and prosperity of the Jews, has undermined the foundations of their existance.
>
> It has left them powerless and incapable of self-defense as soon as they become the focal point of Gentile hatred. Assimilation has corrupted French Jewry, destroying the natural sentiment of solidarity with their less fortunate brethren... eroding traditional virtues and substituting the modern vices of mercenary egoism and callous indifference
>
> **Bernard Lazare**

CHARLES PÉGUY ON BERNARD LAZARE

> He had a heart which bled in Rumania and in Hungary, everywhere the Jew is persecuted, which is, in a certain sense, everywhere.

Lazare was a close friend of the Catholic poet and mystic, Charles Péguy who published some of his work. He credited Lazare in his essays as having taken a leading role in the Dreyfus affair. "In this great crisis he wrote the prophet of both Israel and the world was Bernard Lazare."

His last years were spent in poverty and loneliness. In his writings he attacked the rich Jews as responsible for holding back Jewish national emancipation.

R. S. Wistrich, *Revolutionary Jews from Marx to Trotsky*, 1976.

LAZARUS, EMMA (1849–1887) American poet. Born in New York City, she was the daughter of a well-to-do family of mixed Sephardic and Ashkenazic origin. Receiving a private education she showed her poetic ability in her first book of verse, *Poems and Translations*, published when she was seventeen. It brought her to the attention of Ralph Waldo Emerson, with whom she had an extended correspondence. Her second book of verse, *Admetus and Other Poems*, (1871), contained one poem on a Jewish theme, "In the Jewish Synagogue at Newport." This poem was reprinted in the *American Hebrew* newspaper, which subsequently carried her translations of Solomon Ibn Gabirol (q.v.) and Judah Halevi (q.v.). In the late 1870s she began to feel more a part of the Jewish community, and Rabbi Gustav Gottheil of Temple Emanu-El persuaded her to translate and write poetry for a new prayer book which he was preparing. William James once wrote to Lazarus, "The power of playing with thought and language... ought to be the overflowing of a life rich in other ways." What became the "overflowing" in Lazarus's life were her experiences with the Jewish refugees streaming to New York from eastern Europe. The anguish of her people brought Lazarus into the mainstream of efforts to aid the homeless Jews.

The Statue of liberty on the base of which is inscribed Emma Lazarus' "The New Colosus:"

Not like the Brazen Giant of Greek fame,
With conquering limbs astride from land to
land;
Here at our sea-washed sunset gates shall
stand
A mighty woman with a torch, whose flame
Is the imprisoned lightning, and her name
Mother of Exiles. From her beacon-hand
Glows world-wide welcome; her mild eyes
command
The air-bridged harbor that twin cities frame.
"Keep ancient lands, your storied pomp!"
Cries she
With silent lips, "Give me your tired, your
poor,
Your huddled masses yearning to breathe
free.
The wretched refuse of your teeming shore.
Send these, the homeless, tempest-tost to me.
I lift my lamp beside the Golden Door!"

save for my own people." Out of this concern grew her book of essays, *Songs of a Semite*.

The indelible mark she left on Jewish and general history came through a sonnet she penned for the new Statue of Liberty to be placed in New York Harbor. In 1883 efforts were being made to construct a pedestal for the statue, a gift of the French people, which was to reach the United States in 1885. An auction was planned to sell manuscripts by Longfellow, Walt Whitman, Bret Harte, and Mark Twain. Lazarus was also asked to contribute. Although at first hesitant, she penned a sonnet entitled "The New Colossus." When the poet James Russell Lowell read her verses, he wrote "I liked your sonnet about the Statue better than I liked the Statue itself. But your sonnet gives its subject a raison d'être which it needed as much as it needed a pedestal."
H. E. Jacob, *The World of emma Lazarus*, 1949.

LEAH (c. 18th cent. BCE) Wife of Jacob (q.v.); matriarch of the Jewish people. She was the elder and less attractive daughter of Abraham's nephew, Laban, living in Mesopotamia. When Jacob arrived from Canaan, he fell in love with her younger sister, Rachel (q.v.), whose hand he requested from Laban. Laban consented to the match in return for seven years' service by Jacob, but when the time came for the marriage, Laban by a ruse, substituted Leah. Jacob had to promise to work for another seven years in order to marry Rachel.

Leah, who suffered from weak eyes, was "unloved" (Gen. 29:30–31) and had to struggle for her husband's affections. However, unlike her sister, she was immediately fertile and bore four sons: Reuben, Simeon, Levi, and Judah. When she ceased bearing, she gave Jacob her maidservant Zilpah as concubine and Zilpah bore two sons, Gad and Asher. After getting the right from Rachel to again sleep with Jacob (in return for mandrakes gathered by Reuben), Leah gave birth to two more sons, Issachar and Zebulun, as well as Jacob's only daughter, Dinah.

Despite the friction between the two wives, Leah and Rachel were united on Jacob's side in his quarrel with Laban and they are mentioned together on a number of occasions. Leah died before Jacob went to Egypt, where he spent his latter years, and she was buried in the cave of Machpelah in Hebron. The two central institutions of the early Israelites — the priesthood and the monarch — were entrusted to her descendants, from the tribes of Levi and Judah respectively.
N. M. Sarna, *Understanding Genesis*, 1966.

LEESER, ISAAC (1806–1868) American rabbi, author, translator, editor, and publisher. Born in Neuenkirchen, Westphalia, Germany, he received a traditional religious and secular education. In 1824 he immigrated to the United States and settled in Richmond, Virginia, where he worked in his uncle's business and taught religion to youth. In 1829 he was appointed *hazzan* (reader) of the

Lazarus threw herself into all types of relief and rehabilitation work, and with her words inspired others to come forward and assist. She used her own money to help the immigrants, paying regular visits to Ward's Island, where they were housed, to help guide their first steps in their new homeland. As she wrote, "I am all Israel's now. Till this cloud pass — I have no thought, no passion, no desire,

Sephardic Congregation Mikveh Israel, Philadelphia. This was the beginning of his intensive pioneering activity both within his own community and the American Jewish community at large.

Isaac Leeser was the first American Jewish religious leader to deliver sermons in English (previously they had been delivered in German), which were eventually published in ten volumes (*Discourses on the Jewish Religion, 1867*). His major contribution to the development of the Jewish education system in the United States began when he advocated the introduction of a public school system in which formal religion would have no part. This was to counteract the danger of missionary activity in the Christian schools attended by the majority of Jewish children. Supplementary religious education would be provided after the public school classes and, to this end, Leeser supported the creation of Talmud Torah schools under synagogue auspices. He himself wrote an introduction to the Jewish religion, *Catechism for Younger Children* (1839), as well as a manual for home and school. He was also active in the field of adult education. In 1847 he published his program for the establishment of a school for the training of rabbis, who would be taught general sciences and Jewish studies and which should be given proper academic standing. It was only in the last year of his life (1867) that this vision became a reality with the establishment of the Maimonides College in Philadelphia. He was its first provost and professor of homiletics, belles lettres, and comparative theology.

Leeser was one of the first to act for the establishment of a Jewish hospital in Philadelphia to counteract missionary activity in general hospitals. He was also instrumental in the founding of the first Jewish orphanage in the United States, the Jewish Foster Home of Philadelphia. On his initiative the United Jewish Charities was organized in Philadelphia to provide aid for new immigrants arriving in the country from Europe.

In 1843 he founded and edited the monthly *Occident and Jewish Advocate* to provide news of events in the Jewish world and wrote many of its articles. In 1845 he published a plan, "Cheap Religious Publications," for the provision of good Jewish books to be printed in English in the United States. This resulted in the foundation in 1845 of the Jewish Publication Society in Philadelphia (the forerunner of the present JPS, established in 1888). He also printed Hebrew books locally, creating the Hebrew type and teaching the printers the Hebrew alphabet. He frequently set the Hebrew type himself.

When Leeser received information of attempts of missionaries to convert the few Jews remaining in China, his proposal that representatives be sent to "Judaize" the Jewish Chinese resulted in the creation of the Hebrew Foreign Mission Society in 1853. The organization did not last long due to lack of contact with overseas communities.

Probably Isaac Leeser's greatest contribution to the development of the Jewish community in the United States was his leadership of the school of thought (the historical school) which emphasized that traditional faith and Jewish communal existence must be based on the new conditions of modern society. This was the forerunner of Conservative Judaism. He sought to bring the native American Sephardic community closer to the immigrant Ashkenazic settlers and to bring together the dissident forces in the community by means of a program of religious union.

In 1850 Leeser resigned his position with the Mikveh Israel Congregation to devote himself to his literary work, especially to his major undertaking, the first English translation of the entire Bible by an American Jew, called the *Leeser Bible* (1853), on which he worked over a period of seventeen years and published at his own expense.

In 1857 Leeser became minister of Congregation Beth-El-Emeth, Philadelphia.

Leeser's works include translations of the Sephardic (1837) and Ashkenazic (1848) prayer books; *Ruhama: Devotional Exercises for the Use of the Daughters of Israel*, an English text supplementary to the Hebrew prayer book especially for women; and *The Inquisition and Judaism* (1860).

M. Davis, *Emergence of Conservative Judaism*, 1963.

L. Jung (ed.), *Guardians of Our Heritage*, 1958.

J. R. Marcus, *Memoirs of American Jews, 1775–1865*, 1955.

LEHMAN, HERBERT HENRY (1878–1963) U.S. politician, banker, and philanthropist. He was born in East New York to a family whose father, a partner in the investment bank, Lehman Brothers, had arrived in the United States from Bavaria in 1849 and whose mother became an ardent advocate of women's suffrage. Herbert Lehman was educated at a Jewish boys' school and then went on to Williams College. In 1899 he worked as a cotton-goods salesman and spent his evenings supervising a club for boys at the Henry Street Settlement, coaching basketball and debating teams.

In 1908 he entered the firm of Lehman Brothers as a partner, and in 1910 he married Edith Louise Altschul, daughter of a San Francisco banker. They adopted three children; their son Peter was killed in action over Britain in 1944 after having flown fifty-seven missions.

At the outbreak of World War I Lehman worked for several months in the office of Franklin D. Roosevelt, then assistant secretary of the navy. Lehman obtained a commission as captain in the U.S. Army, attaining rank of colonel by the end of the war, with responsibility for procurement and transportation on the general staff. He was awarded the distinguished service medal.

Lehman's interest in politics began in 1910 as a delegate to the Democratic party convention. In 1926 Governor Alfred E. Smith appointed him chairman of the finance, budget, and revenue committee and in this capacity he wrote a comprehensive report on the finances of New York City. In 1926 Lehman managed Governor Smith's election campaign and in 1928 was himself elected lieutenant governor to F. D. Roosevelt, giving up his position in Lehman Brothers. In 1930 he was reelected, again with Roosevelt. He assisted Governor Roosevelt with financial and budgetary problems, improving the scope and caliber of the state's administration agencies and social services, particularly in the area of hospital and prison reform, and in dealing with labor crises.

In 1932, when Governor Roosevelt was elected president, Lehman was elected governor of New York State, the first of five terms — more than any other person in New York's history. In his nine election campaigns he experienced only one defeat — for the Senate in 1946. As governor he introduced a comprehensive program of liberal legislation. He obtained enactment of statutes concerning labor relations, minimum wages, unemployment insurance, low-cost housing, and improvement of public utilities. His program of liberal legislation became known as the Little New Deal.

In 1942 Lehman resigned as governor and was drafted by President Roosevelt to become director of the Office of Foreign Relief and Rehabilitation which in 1943 merged with the United Nations Relief and Rehabilitation Administration, responsible for rebuilding a Europe devastated by the war. In 1946 he resigned from this position and became involved in dealing with the plight of Jewish refugees and the situation in Palestine. He was not formally a Zionist and was then opposed to the idea of a Jewish state, but publicly advocated free Jewish immigration into Palestine. After the establishment of the State of Israel, Lehman became a staunch supporter and in 1958 chaired the committee to celebrate Israel's tenth anniversary.

Herbert Lehman was elected to the Senate in 1949 and was one of the principal supporters of Truman's Fair Deal Program. He was an outspoken critic of Senator Joseph McCarthy's anti-communist witch-hunt and they clashed violently on the Senate floor. The Lehman-Tobey bill to relax the restrictions on immigration stipulated by the Walter-McCarran immigration bill was not successful. Lehman did not run for election to the Senate in 1956.

Herbert Lehman was a prominent member of the Jewish community and carried on the family tradition of welfare work. Already in 1914 he helped to found the American Jewish Joint Distribution Committee and after the war chaired its Reconstruction Committee. He was an active fund-raiser for the Federation of Jewish Philanthropies, the United Jewish Appeal, and many other causes, and he helped in the organization of the Palestine Loan Bank and the Palestine Economic Corporation. He was particularly interested in supporting organizations dealing with child welfare. In 1960 he and his wife gave half a million dollars for the establishment of a children's zoo in New York's Central Park to mark the occasion of their golden wedding anniversary. He was a champion of black rights and persistently advocated civil rights in the Senate.

Herbert Lehman died as he was about to leave for the White House to receive the presidential medal of freedom, the highest peacetime award made to a civilian. The citation stated that as "citizen and statesman he used compassion as the tools of government and has made politics the highest form of public service."

J. Bellush, *Selected Case Studies of the Legislative Leadership of Governor Herbert H. Lehman*, 1959. A. Nevins, *Herbert H. Lehman and His Era*, 1963.

LEIBOWITZ, SAMUEL S. (1893–1978) American lawyer and judge. Born in Jassy, Romania, Samuel Lebeau was taken to the United States in 1897 by his parents, who were seeking to escape anti-Semitism and who changed their name to Leibowitz. He was brought up in Brooklyn, New York, and worked his way through Cornell University Law School, from which he graduated in 1915. Upon admission to the bar in 1917 he took a position in a civil law firm because that was the "correct" job for a Cornell graduate according to the dean of the law school.

Leibowitz, however, wished to practice criminal law and volunteered his services to indigent defendants. He successfully defended numerous men and women accused of criminal actions by careful study that revealed the flaws in the prosecutor's case, destroyed the circumstantial evidence against the defendant, and persuaded the jury to free his client.

By 1929, Leibowitz, who had opened his own office ten years earlier, was considered "the most spectacular criminal lawyer in New York City" and was famous for his flamboyancy. Among his clients was underworld leader Al Capone, whom Leibowitz freed four times on writs of habeas corpus. From 1933 to 1937 he served, without fee, as chief defense counsel for the nine black defendants in the Scottsboro case who were sentenced to death in Alabama for assaulting two white women. Leibowitz's efforts resulted in a Supreme Court decision in 1935 that banned the exclusion of blacks from juries in the South. In a period of over twenty years, up to 1940, Leibowitz defended some 140 persons accused of murder. Only one was executed.

In 1940, Leibowitz was elected judge in Kings County Court in Brooklyn. He served in that post until 1961. During his tenure, he was presiding judge at the Brooklyn grand jury investigations of graft in the New York City Police Department and of racketeering on the Brooklyn waterfront. From 1961 to 1969 he served as a New York supreme court justice; he imposed severe sentences on criminals and fought corruption. He was active in Jewish affairs, as president of the United Organization for Israel Pioneers, and in 1948 organized the first visit of an Israeli soccer team to New York.

Q. Reynolds, *Courtroom*, 1950.

LEONARD, BENNY (Benjamin Leiner; 1896–1947) U.S. world boxing champion. Born in New York, he entered the prize ring in 1911, changing his name because he knew that his immigrant parents would have strong objections to the boxing profession.

By the time Leonard defeated Freddy Welsh of Wales for the world lightweight championship in 1917, in New York City, he was considered a master boxer. The outstanding trainer Ray Arcel, who had watched him destroy Welsh in 1917 and was still active in the 1980s, called him the greatest fighter that ever lived.

The Ring magazine said of him, "Through long years of practice he mastered a style of boxing of singular beauty and difficulty. He would rock rhythmically in and out of hitting range with a coordinated grace which was ballet-like in execution.... He was highly intelligent and perfected moves which have not been duplicated since. On top of this he was a tremendous puncher with either hand."

A younger brother, Joe Leonard, when asked to comment on stories that his brother never had his hair mussed up in the ring, or that he was a mama's boy, recalled, that "Benny was a little vain about his pompadour and if anybody knocked it askew, he made him pay for it. Benny was a sweetheart; he was gentle, yet he could kill you. He was very attached to my mother. When he quit boxing in

Benny Leonard.

1925 it was for her." Leonard retired as an undefeated lightweight champion.

Hit hard by the stock market crash in 1929, the thirty-five-year-old Leonard returned to the ring two years later. His comeback as a welterweight ended in 1932 when Jimmy McLarnin knocked him out in the sixth round at New York's Madison Square Garden. His final ring record showed 209 bouts, 68 knockouts, and only 5 losses. Three of the losses occurred in the first three years of his career, and another was on a foul.

Leonard served in both world wars, in the army in World War I, and as a lieutenant-commander in the U.S. Maritime Service in World War II. While working as a New York referee in 1947, he suffered a heart attack and died in the ring.

Following his death, Jewish publications noted, "He was an observing Jew. He never fought on Jewish holidays. He was aware of his Judaism, and after his fighting days were over, he worked hard for Jewish organizations, particularly the Zionist Organization. When Benny Leonard reached the heights in boxing he aided not only himself, but the entire American Jewish community."

N. Fleischer, *Leonard the Magnificent*, 1947.

LEONE EBREO, See Abravanel,

LEROY, MERVYN (1900–1987) U.S. film producer and director. Born in San Francisco, LeRoy performed on the vaudeville stage from the age of twelve. His first screen appearances came when he was still in his early teens, but it was not until 1919 that he asked his cousin Jesse Lasky (q.v.), then a senior executive at Paramount, for a job behind the scenes. Although he soon realized that directing was what he really wanted to do, he did not achieve his ambition for eight years, whiling away the time working in the costume department and the film laboratory and as assistant cameraman, actor, and gagman. His directorial career began at First National and continued at Warner Brothers.

For most of the 1930s, LeRoy was one of Warner Brothers. most reliable directors, his name being associated with their best efforts in the gangster and musical genres (*Little Caesar, I Am a Fugitive from a Chain Gang, Gold Diggers of 1933*). Shortly before moving to Metro-Goldyn-Mayer (MGM) in 1938, he added producing to his activities, and it was as a producer that he made his first films at his new studio; they included *The Wizard of Oz*. He adapted easily to the glossier MGM style of filmmaking and his later films were as characteristic of MGM as his earlier vehicles had been of Warners.

A period of lavish, high-budget films that included *Little Women* and *Quo Vadis?* ended in the mid 1950s when a dispute with MGM head, Dore Schary, resulted in LeRoy's return to Warner Brothers. Many of his last films were based on adaptations of stage successes, among them *Mister Roberts* and the musical *Gypsy*. In the mid 1970s, a decade after he had ceased to be active in films, he was awarded the Irving Thalberg Memorial award

Mervyn Leroy (right) with French actor Fernand Gravet.

by the Academy of Motion Picture Arts and Sciences. Though never an Oscar winner for his directing and producing, he was the recipient of a special award in 1945 for *The House I Live In*, a short film preaching tolerance.

M. LeRoy and A. Canfield, *It Takes More than Talent*, 1953.

LEVI, CARLO (1902–1975) Italian writer, painter, politician, and antifacist. He was born in Turin, where he completed medical school, but he never practiced as a doctor. Instead, he embarked on a variety of other, more radical careers.

Levi was one of the founders of an underground antifascist movement, Justice and Liberty. He was arrested three times for his political activities. The second time, at the outbreak of the Abyssinian War (1935), he was sent into internal exile in Lucania. Later he wrote his best-known book, *Christo si e fermato a Eboli* (1945; *Christ Stopped at Eboli*, 1948), about his experiences there. The book, which describes life deep in the heart of southern Italy, where he lived for a year under police surveillance, shocked the world and Italians alike with its view of the primitive lifestyle of the people. Its title came from the local saying, "We're not Christians.... Christ stopped short of here, at Eboli." Levi added, "Christian, in their way of speaking, means human being, and this almost proverbial phrase... may be no more than the expression of a hopeless inferiority."

The *New York Times* reviewer, Paolo Milano, called the book "a diary, an album of sketches, a novelette, a sociological study, and a political essay." "It has", he wrote, "more than a trait of each genre; yet it remains as hard to classify as every beautiful book, or as the man who wrote this one."

Levi was indeed hard to classify. After he left southern Italy, he moved to France to join the Resistance. He returned, however, to his native Italy during World War II and was once again arrested on political charges.

During the postwar years, Levi wrote several other books, among them *Of Fear and Freedom* (1950), *Words Are Stones* (1956), and *The Linden Trees* (1962). He also continued his left-wing political activity and served in the Italian senate as a communist from 1963 to 1972.

As a painter, Levi was influenced by French masters, but later developed his own style. Near the end of his life, his paintings fetched a high price.

H. S. Hughes, *Prisoners of Hope: The Silver Age of Italian Jews*, 1983.

C. L. Ragglianti, *Carlo Levi* (Italian), 1948.

LEVI, HERMANN (1839–1900) German conductor. The son of a rabbi, Levi was born at Giessen in Upper Hesse. He studied music with Vincenz Lachner at Mannheim from the age of thirteen, then continued his studies at the Leipzig Conservatory until 1858. He held various conducting posts, including Saarbrücken, the German Opera in Rotterdam, and Karlsruhe. His most important appointment was as Hofkapellmeister (general music director) at the Court Theater of Munich.

He was acclaimed as one of the foremost conductors of his time, to be ranked with Hans Richter, Felix Josef Mottl, and Anton Seidl among the most prominent of the first generation of Bayreuth conductors. His innovative translations of Mozart's operas (*Le nozze di Figaro*, *Don Giovanni*, and *Cosi fan tutte*) were huge successes.

He counted Clara Schumann and Johannes Brahms among his friends, and produced Robert Schumann's *Genoveva*. His correspondence with Brahms was published in Berlin in 1912. His reflections on Goethe's works (*Gedenken aus Goethes Werken*), published posthumously, ran into several editions.

In 1869, Levi won Richard Wagner's recognition with performances of *Rienzi* and *Die Meistersinger*. Cosima, Wagner's second wife (and daughter of Liszt), regarded Levi as "a most excellent person with real delicacy of feeling," while for Wagner himself, he was "the ideal *Parsifal* conductor." There were, however, some almost insurmountable obstacles to be overcome. Wagner had tried in vain to persuade Levi to embrace Christianity. That a Jew should conduct *Parsifal*, which depicts the central Christian mystery, was inconceivable. An anonymous letter charging this, and also denouncing Levi as Cosima's lover, impelled him to resign. King Ludwig II of Bavaria intervened in the impasse, paving the way for a reconciliation between the two men. Levi conducted the première of *Parsifal* at Bayreuth on July 26, 1882, to Wagner's complete satisfaction.

In her capacity as art director of the festival plays, Cosima replaced Levi with Mottl in 1888, but he was reinstated the following year and presided over performances of *Parsifal* until 1884. He retired in 1896.

Levi was unofficial musical adviser to the synagogue in Munich. He composed works of Jewish interest; among them a setting of the Sabbath *Ve-Shomru* prayer and a composition for the dedication of the Mannheim synagogue.

There was a spirituality in Levi's interpretations that inspired admiration. His conducting style, which combined a masterly technique with economy of gesture, was to influence the coming generation of conductors, particularly Felix Weingartner.
A. Holde, *Jews in Music from the Age of Enlightenment to the Present*, 1970.
J. Katz, *The Darker Side of Richard Wagner's Anti-Semitism*, 1986.

LEVI, PRIMO (1919–1987) Italian author and survivor of Auschwitz whose fictional and autobiographical treatment of his experiences made an outstanding contribution to modern Italian and world literature. Born in Turin, the son of a civil engineer, member of the small acculturated Jewish community, Levi experienced little or no Jewish practice in the home. "My Hebrew," he related, "is the bar mitzvah Hebrew of the religious majority that one learns at thirteen and forgets before eighteen." Levi graduated with distinction in chemistry from the University of Turin in 1941 at a period when Jews could not be employed and were excluded from academic life. Nevertheless he was able to work in his field with the help of a colleague who ignored the racial laws. In 1943 he joined the Italian anti-Fascist partisans, was captured, and deported to Auschwitz. Toward the end of his ten-month incarceration and at death's door, he was "selected" to work as an industrial chemist in a laboratory connected with the production of synthetic rubber for the German war effort. This saved him from the fate of most of his countrymen. (Only 24 of the 650 Italian Jews deported with him survived.) In 1945 he was liberated and returned to Turin to work once again in his field, where he became an authority on ceramic wire coating.

Levi declared: "When I came home I couldn't help writing about Auschwitz. It was a double obligation. I felt a duty to bear witness to what I had seen; I was deeply depressed and I felt that by speaking or writing about it I could relieve myself of this burden." The result was his masterpiece, *If This Is a Man* (1945). His second book, *The Truce* (1963), described his attempt to reach home in a memorable odyssey through postwar Europe. *The Periodic Table* appeared in 1975, a "micro-history" employing Dimitry Mendeleyev's periodic table of chemical elements to literary ends. Each of the elements suggests some episode or character from the author's past. Cerium, for instance, represents the obsessional hunger in the camps; vanadium, an exchange of letters with a former German laboratory overseer whose signature he recognized in his postwar correspondence as an industrial chemist. *The Wrench* (1979) is a series of tales told by a rigger about bridges that collapsed and jobs that succeeded against all odds. *If Not Now, When*

I do not know, and it does not much interest me to know, whether in my depths there lurks a murderer, but I do know that I was a guiltless victim and I was not a murderer; I know that the murderers existed, not only in Germany, and still exist, retired or on active duty, and that to confuse them with their victims is a moral disease or an aesthetic affection or a sinister sign of complicity; above all, it is a precious service rendered to the negators of truth.

It is no longer a man who, having lost all restraint, shares his bed with a corpse. Whoever waits for his neighbor to die in order to take his bread, is though blameless — further removed from the model of thinking man than the most vicious sadist.

(1984) is a novel about a band of Jewish partisans. Levi's last book *The Drowned and the Saved* (1986) is a collection of essays analyzing different aspects of life in the camps. One essay deals with the sense of shame felt by the survivors, another with the phenomenon of the collaborators, particularly with those assigned to deal with the corpses.

Levi's writings are distinguished for their compassionate and detached understanding, even when describing the most horrific of crimes he witnessed, constantly reminding his readers that the unimaginable can happen again if we are not eternally vigilant. Above all he scorned the easy answer and half-truth. To his German translator he wrote: "I am alive and I would like to understand you in order to judge you." One of his German readers wrote to him to say that his work had awakened some resonance in her country. Levi wryly noted that it had indeed but only "among the Germans who least needed to read it: I received penitent letters from the innocent but not the guilty."

An agnostic and apostle of absolute personal truthfulness, Levi resisted the temptation to pray in the face of imminent death while waiting to file past the dreaded selection commission: "A prayer under these conditions would have been blasphemous, laden with the greatest impiety of which a nonbeliever is capable."

Levi's suicide — he threw himself down the stairs of the apartment building in which he had been born and spent the greater part of his life — confounded his closest friends. But it was evidently triggered by a severe attack of depression, for which he was undergoing treatment.
P. Bailey, introduction to P. Levi, *The Drowned and the Saved*, 1988.
H. S. Hughes, *Prisoners of Hope*, 1983.
P. Levi, *Tullio Regge Conversations*, 1989.
A Rudolf, *At An Uncertain Hour*, 1990.

LEVI BEN GERSHOM (known also as Gersonides or by the acronym *Ralbag*; 1288–1344) Philosopher, mathematician, astronomer, and rabbinic scholar in southern France. He was born in Bagnols and lived in Orange and Avignon, but little is known of his life. He was friendly with leading Christians and taught astronomy at the papal university and medical school. More than half of his major work, *The Wars of the Lord*, is devoted to astronomy and, as soon as the book was published, Pope Clement VI had the astronomical section translated into Latin. In his book, Levi describes an improved quadrant which he had invented, more easy to handle than the clumsy instruments previously used. The famous astronomer Regiomontanus was so impressed that he followed Levi's instructions to build an instrument which he called Jacob's staff. This was utilized by all the great explorers, including Columbus, for their calculations and remained in nautical use for three hundred years. He also devised a camera obscura for astronomical observation and put forward an original explanation for the movement of the stars. He wrote a treatise on a cure for gout and an exposition of parts of Euclid's *Elements*.

Levi commented on most books of the Bible. His explanations contained both grammatical and lexicographical interpretations as well as summaries of the philosophical and ethical aspects. In seeking to reconcile the Pentateuch with the philosophy of his day, he often resorted to symbolism and allegory.

His *Wars of the Lord* was meant to fill in lacunae left by earlier thinkers, notably Moses Maimonides (q.v.). Its six philosophical sections deal with the soul (psychology), prophecy, God's knowledge, divine providence, the nature of the heavens (cosmology), and the eternity of matter. Some of his ideas, notably on divine knowledge, were regarded as heretical and led some Jewish thinkers to ban his works for study (they called his book "The Wars against The Lord"). Spinoza (q.v.) was among those he influenced. According to Levi, the world was not created out of nothing but was formed from eternal matter. A strong believer in astrology, he held that whatever happens on earth depends on the celestial spheres.

J. D. Bleich, *Providence in the Philosophy of Gersonides*, 1973.

N. M. Samuelson, *Gersonides' The War of the Lord, Treatise Three*, 1977.

J. J. Staub, *The Creation of the World according to Gersonides*, 1982.

LEVI-CIVITA, TULLIO (1873–1941) Italian mathematician and mathematical physicist, best known for his discovery of the absolute differential calculus and his extension of the concept of parallelism to "curved" spaces.

Levi-Civita was born in Padua to Giacomo Levi-Civita, an eminent lawyer who was later appointed to the Italian senate. In 1890 Tullio Levi-Civita enrolled in the faculty of mathematics at the University of Padua where, as student, instructor, and eventually, professor, he passed the most fruitful years of his scientific career. There, he came under the influence of Gregorio Ricci-Curbastro ("Ricci"), whose absolute differential geometry Tullio applied (c. 1900) to the development of an absolute differential calculus (what is now called tensor calculus). This is, in reality, an extension of the ordinary laws of mathematics and physics to "curved" spaces — spaces outside of our normal range of perception in which rulers bend and twist and shrink and stretch depending on where they are and how they are moving. A fundamental problem in such spaces is how a ruler would move if left to its own devices; analogous to how a free particle would move in ordinary space. Levi-Civita himself supplied the solution with his enunciation, in 1917, of the concept of parallelism.

At the time of his development of the absolute differential calculus, curved spaces were merely a mathematical curiosity, but some years later it became apparent that in the vicinity of very massive objects, such as stars, space is in fact curved. Levi-Civita's formalism thus became an essential ingredient for Albert Einstein (q.v.) in his development of the general theory of relativity.

In 1918 Levi-Civita was offered the chair of mathematics at the University of Rome, where he remained until his career was prematurely terminated in 1938, with the passage of fascist racial laws against Jews. Because of ill health he was unable to accept offers of appointments outside Italy where he remained until his death.

Levi-Civita was a many-sided scientist and did outstanding work also in hydryodynamics (his favorite field) and celestial mechanics (the three-body problem) as well as solving a variety of mathematical problems suggested by atomic physics. He was widely honored and respected for his character, his broad outlook on science, and his natural aptitude as teacher and inspirer of subsequent generations of mathematicians.

LEVI ISAAC OF BERDICHEV (c.1740–1810) Hasidic rabbi. Born into a noted family of rabbis in Hoshakov, Galicia, he married a wealthy wife and devoted himself to rabbinic scholarship. However, he was won over to Hasidism and became a close disciple of Dov Ber of Mezhirich (q.v.) and the leading exponent of his teachings. He was appointed rabbi in Zhelechow, Poland, and Pinsk, Belorussia, but in each case was hounded out of his pulpit by opponents of Hasidism. His house was broken into and his possessions rifled, he was evicted from his home and dismissed from his jobs until he suffered a nervous breakdown. Fortunately, he found peace in the community of Berdichev in the Ukraine where he served for the last twenty-five years of his life.

Levi Isaac was one of the best-loved figures in popular imagination and was seen as the defender of the Jewish people before the bar of heaven. Innumerable stories tell of him pleading with God

SAYINGS OF LEVI ISAAC OF BERDICHEV

● O Lord! I do not wish to know why I suffer but only whether it is for Your sake.
● Lord, if You ever issue a harsh decree against the Jews, we Tzaddikim [Hasidic leaders] will not fulfill Your commands.
● Here in Exile, God Himself is also in Exile
● Seeing a youth smoking on the Sabbath, Levi Isaac asked him whether he realized what he was doing, and the young man replied "Yes, I am sinning knowingly." The Rabbi looked to heaven and said "God, see the holiness of Your people who would rather admit that they sin than tell a lie."
● Whether a man really loves God can be determined by his love for his fellow men.

From his song to God:
You! You! You!
Sky is You! Earth is You!
You above! You below!
In every trend, at every end,
Only You, You again, always You!
You! You! You!

for the people of Israel. It was said that one day he saw a coachman oiling his coach while saying his prayers, leading Levi Isaac to cry aloud "Lord of the universe, see how much your people love and serve you. Even when oiling cartwheels, they pray and serve you. And yet you dare to complain against Israel." In one famous story, he even summoned God to a religious court to account for the sufferings of the Jewish people, challenging him "You are always making demands on your people. Why not help them in their troubles?" At the same time, he rebuked Jews for their wrongdoing. From a rooftop he shouted down to the marketplace, "You people are forgetting to fear God."

His major work was the two-part *Kedushat Levi* ("The Holiness of Levi"), a commentary on the Torah and rabbinic legends. He emphasized humility, which is a religious value that does not consist in ignoring one's own merits and achievements but in realizing how petty they — and indeed all humankind — are before the overwhelming presence of the Divine. According to Levi Isaac, God, the Torah, and the Jewish people formed a mysterious trinity for whom the ultimate deliverance will come on the day of the Messiah. Throughout his life, he awaited the arrival of the Messiah, who would take the Jews back to the land of their forefathers. Convinced of the inherent goodness of man, he regarded every Jew as holy and blameless, and destined on the day of the Messiah also to be omniscient. "All the worlds above and below, God created only for the sake of Israel" was one of his favorite sayings.

The Hasidim of the Ukraine called him "the Defender of Israel" referring both to his disputations with God and his deep devotion to the welfare of every Jew on earth. Discovering the terrible conditions of girls working in the factories for baking *matzot* (unleavened bread), he rebuked his congregation: "The enemies of the Jews accuse us of baking *matzot* with the blood of Christians. They are wrong. We are baking them with the blood of Jews."

S. H. Dresner, *Levi Yitzhaq of Berditchev: Portrait of a Hasidic Master*, 1974.

LEVY, MOSES ELIAS (1782–1854) Pioneer in Florida who undertook to settle the territory even before it came under American sovereignty. He was the father of David Levy-Yulee (see Yulee) the first senator from Florida.

He was born in Mogador, Morocco, to a family of businessmen of Portuguese descent, some of whom held high positions at the Sultan's court. His father, Elias Levy, was a vizier of the Sultan but had the bad luck of discovering a plot fomented by the crown prince to dethrone his father. The Sultan had his son imprisoned but died soon after and Elijah Levy found himself in a difficult situation. To avoid being sentenced to death by the new ruler, the former crown prince, he converted to Islam. But to be on the safe side, fled o England in 1799 with his son Moses and died there a Jew, a few months later.

Moses E. Levy found work on a sailing ship traveling to the West Indies. He disembarked on the island of Saint Thomas in the Caribbean and quickly succeeded in the lumber business. His activities took him to Havana in Cuba where he became an army purveyor in 1816. At the time Florida was governed out of Havana by a Spanish intendant. In 1819 Moses Levy purchased vast plots of land in Florida and acquired more land there later. He invested much money, with the aim of exploiting the land. Since Levy was strongly opposed to slavery, he sailed to England to find Jewish and Christian settlers, but without much success. While in England he spoke in various forums against slavery and even published a pamphlet to that effect which caused quite a sensation. He also made himself known as a speaker and wrote articles on Jewish subjects (occasioning the publication of a book by T. Thrush, late captain in the Royal Navy, *Letters to the Jews with a Copy of a Speech Said to Have Been Delivered by Mr Levy of Florida*, 1829).

Levy tried to further his project in Charleston, Philadelphia and among the immigrants in New York, where he planned the establishment of a Hebrew agricultural school in 1821. But once again he failed and had no choice but to utilize slaves to further his project of colonization.

He settled in Saint Augustine in 1921 and was an energetic and able colonizer. He imported seeds from Cuba and it is even said that he was the first planter to bring sugarcane into the United States.

Unfortunately, his Florida dream did not materialized. By 1840 he possessed a large estate but was plagued with financial difficulties and involved in many lawsuits. Many of his farms were burned by the Indians during the Seminole wars, others by the Confederate troops in the hope that the Indians would not be tempted to return there. Finally, he succeeded in getting out of his legal entanglements and took an active part in the politics of Florida, particularly in educaton, and wrote some articles in the daily press under the pen name "Youlee." Youlee, taken from the first words in Hebrew of Psalm 86:9, had been the name his father had added to his name.

Moses Levy was "a man universally respected in Saint Augustine. His probity, large intelligence, and benevolence were recognized. "He was just and generous," wrote a prominent attorney of Saint Augustine.

LEVY, URIAH PHILIPS (1792–1862) American naval officer. Born to a Sephardic family in Philadelphia, Levy, by the age of fourteen, had decided on joining the navy. Throughout his career he was fully conscious of his Jewish origins, both as a proud Jew and as a subject of anti-Semitism. He first sailed at age ten as a cabin boy. When he was fourteen he was apprenticed to a shipmaster for four years, went to navigational school in Philadelphia, and was later press-ganged into service on a British ship bound for Jamaica. During this voyage Levy astounded the British captain by refusing to swear allegiance to the king, on the grounds that he was an American and a Jew and could not swear on their testament, especially without his head covered.

After his release from British service, Levy purchased a third share in a schooner, and in 1811 became the first Jewish sea captain, with a mezuzah on his cabin door. During the War of 1812 Levy volunteered for service, but he was captured by the British, and spent most of the war in Dartmoor Prison, being released at the war's end in a prisoner exchange.

As a Jew in the navy, Levy became subject to much antagonism from officers, especially after he was challenged to a duel by an officer. Levy refused to shoot his challenger, who did not succeed in hitting him. Finally when one bullet nicked Levy's ear he shot the officer in the chest, killing him instantly. In 1817 Levy became the first Jewish officer in the U.S. Navy. He subsequently had to face a series of six court-martials, in which he was found guilty on a multiplicity of charges. Tired of fighting the anti-Semitic hierarchy, Levy took leave a of absence from the navy and moved to New York, where he became rich by investing in property. Finally in 1855, a congressional Act to promote efficiency in the navy, led to an inquiry into Levy's capabilities as an officer. Levy claimed in the inquiry that he had been the victim of anti-Semitism, and he was backed by character witnesses of the highest social standing in America.

Commodore Uriah Phillips Levy.

Levy was acquitted and returned to active service. In 1860 he became the commodore (the highest possible rank) of the entire Mediterranean fleet.

One of Levy's most significant achievements was the reform of disciplinary measures used in the navy. Sickened by the practices of flogging and other forms of corporal punishment, Levy adopted his own methods. For example, theft and drunkardness were punished by hanging signs on the offending sailor, saying "thief" or "drunkard."

A STATEMENT MADE BY LEVY IN HIS OWN DEFENSE AT THE THIRD COURT MARTIAL

I beg to make the most solemn appeal to the pure and heavenly spirit of universal toleration that pervades the constitution of the United States, in the presence of this court... whoever may be the party arraigned, be he Jew or Gentile, Christian or pagan, shall he not have the justice done to him which forms the essential principle of the best maxim in all their code, "do unto others as ye would have them do unto you."

Levy also pursued his campaign against corporal punishment in the American press, decrying the antiquated measures employed by the navy. Finally, under the instigation of Senator J. P. Hale, in 1850 Congress abolished the use of flogging in the navy, and over the next few years a series of naval disciplinary reforms were instituted. By the time of Levy's death, he had become known as the "father of the law for the abolition of the practice of corporal punishment in the U.S. Navy."
S. Birmingham, *The Grandees*, 1972.
D. Fitzpatrick and S. Saphire, *Navy Maverick: Uriah Philips Levy*, 1963.

LÉVY-BRUHL, LUCIEN (1857–1939) French philosopher, psychologist, and ethnologist. After graduating from high school in his native Paris, he hesitated between studying philosophy or becoming an orchestral conductor. In fact, throughout his life he exhibited an avid interest in music. Nonetheless, he decided to study philosophy, graduating in 1879 from the Ecole Normale Supérieure.

Lévy-Bruhl taught at Poitiers and Amiens before being appointed professor of higher rhetoric at the Lycée Louis-Le-Grand, and a lecturer at the Ecole Normale Supérieure. The following year, he moved to the Sorbonne. Concurrently he lectured at the Ecole Libre des Sciences politiques.

Lévy-Bruhl's views, as expounded in his books on preliterate culture and the nature of primitive mentality, evolved from the concept that the primitive's thought was indifferent to the laws of logic and therefore mystical, to the contradictory idea that prelogical and preliterate societies did possess logic to the extent required by the practical demands of the natural environment. Among his books, *Ethics and Moral Science* is a study of moral systems in which he acknowledges that an absolute ethic is impossible because of the incommensurability of thought systems of different cultures; this book earned him the chair of history of modern philosophy at the Sorbonne in 1904.

Despite his reputation at the university and his works which gained renown, he was a modest man. In World War I, a former pupil of his — Albert Thomas, minister for munitions — asked him to become an attaché in his bureau and Lévy-Bruhl served voluntarily in that capacity from 1915 to 1919. In 1917 he took over the administration of the *Revue Philosophique* and in the same year, became a member of the *Académie des Sciences morales et politiques* within the Institut de France. From 1919 on, Lévy-Bruhl's reputation spread beyond France. In 1925 he established the Institut d'Ethnologie. Wishing to devote himself entirely to research into the primitive mentality, he resigned his chair at the Sorbonne and retired in 1927.

Responding to many invitations, he lectured all over the world, while keeping up his research and extensive writing on the topic of primitive mentality. His works included studies of the myths of the Australian aborigines and the Papuans.
J. Cazeneuve, *Lucien Lévy-Bruhl*, 1972.

LEWANDOWSKI, LOUIS (1821–1894) German composer and conductor of cantorial music (*hazzanut*). He was born in Wreschen near Posen to a poor family. As a child he already showed a bent for religious music. During the High Holy Days, his father was the cantor in the local synagogue and he brought his five sons to help him with the service.

After his mother's death, Louis Lewandowski went to Berlin where he studed violin and piano. At the age of twelve he joined the Berlin Synagogue as a singer, under the instruction of the local cantor, Ascher Lion.

Lewandowski became the first Jewish student at the Berlin Academy of Arts. During that time he was awarded prizes for two of his compositions, a cantata and a symphony. He himself conducted their premiere.

Lewandowski became the music director of the Old Synagogue in the Heidereutergasse in Berlin in 1840. In 1886 he moved to the New Synagogue in the city, in Oranienburgerstrasse. Lewandowski compiled the Jewish service music for use by the Berlin Jewish community. He tended to reduce the exotic and asymmetrical pattern of the Jewish cantilena to simple song meters that came from German romantic music. These melodies contributed to the popularity of Lewandowski's service music. He published *Kol Rinnoh utefilloh* and *Todo v'Zimroh*.
A. M. Rothmuller, *The Music of the Jews*, 1954.
A. Z. Idelsohn, *Jewish Music in Its Historical Development*, 1948.

> The most outstanding talent in Lewandowski was his tasteful and skillful re-shaping in modern forms of old material. His recitatives and solos for the Synagogue song have the wonderful quality of being suitable for and easily rendered by any voice of fair quality. His recitatives and solos, even the traditional tunes, are not merely well preserved, but they are creations moten anew. His greatest strength in that branch is the cantabile, in the region between tune and recitative, in the free-flowing Jewish solo singing, in minor. he created and developed a noble warm breathing style of Jewish melody, purged of the tangled fungous growth of sentimentality.
>
> **A. Z. Idelsohn**

LEWIN, KURT ZADEK (1890–1947) Psychologist. A pioneer in group dynamics, Lewin introduced field theory and was one of the first to write, in his field, on the nature of causation. Born in the tiny village of Mogilno, Germany, he grew up in his family's home above the general store owned by his father. He did not excel during his elementary school years and was known primarily for occasional temper tantrums, for which his family nicknamed him the Furious Herring. It was not until the last two years of high school that his keen intelligence was suspected.

He entered the University of Freiburg in 1909, planning to study medicine, but soon transferred to biology. His stay at Freiburg was short and he moved to the University of Munich, again for only a brief period, finally settling at the University of Berlin, where he developed his interests in philosophy and psychology and began working at the university's Psychological Institute.

At the Psychological Institute he became interested in the theories of the Gestalt school of psychology, although later he was to abandon it for his own theories on group dynamics. Despite a successful career at the institute, he left Berlin in 1933, because of Nazism, and accepted an invitation to teach at Cornell University. During his two years there he concentrated on studies of the effect of social pressure on the eating habits of children in the Cornell Nursery School. *A Dynamic Theory of Personality*, a collection of his most important translated articles, appeared in 1935. *Principles of Topological Psychology*, written in German, never appeared in Lewin's mother tongue, but was published in English in 1936. Lewin had tried to develop a systematic theory of psychology, describing behavior by a mathematical description. The book, devoted primarily to the foundations of topological and vector psychology, and using mathematical models that were unfamiliar to American psychologists, did not at first receive wide attention. Lewin, meanwhile, was deeply involved in his project for a psychological institute at the Hebrew University. This plan failed for lack of funding.

When his term at Cornell came to an end, Lewin moved to the University of Iowa as professor of child psychology. There he was to settle for the next nine years into his pioneering work in the theory and practice of behavioral psychology.

In 1939 Lewin also became involved in action research in industry. He had always been interested in the role of work in man's life. When a newly opened manufacturing plant in a rural community in Virginia began to experience problems training its staff, Lewin came to its assistance. The plant, because of unemployment, was hiring only local and therefore inexperienced workers and finding that its production levels were not up to standard. Lewin suggested initially lowering the standards, so that they would not seem completely unattainable to the workers, interacting with workers in groups rather than as individuals, and introducing at least a small number of experienced workers into the plant, to make production levels seem more achievable, and thus raise self-confidence among workers. Lewin's suggestions were productive, and his association with the plant lasted eight years.

Toward the end of his period at Iowa, Lewin became restless with seeking explanations of behavior and sought to begin researching methods for changing and improving behavior. He was convinced that it was possible to build up a body of knowledge and construct a general theory that would apply to any group. He saw group behavior as a function of both the single person and the social situation. Thus he sought to found an autonomous institute loosely attached to some university, in which he could continue his projects of action research and group dynamics. He began to raise funds for his project and in 1944, was invited to set up the Research Center for Group Dynamics at the Massachusetts Institute of Technology (MIT). The center was to focus on six areas: group productivity; communication and the spread of influence; social perception; intergroup relations; group membership and individual adjustment; and training of leaders and the improvement of group functioning.

Lewin's psychological interests were not separated from his feelings on Jewish issues. He saw Zionism as a sociological necessity and believed that Jews need their own country in order to live normal lives. He spent time studying problems of Jewish maladjustment and self-acceptance as members of a minority group. Always associated with Jewish educational work, he believed that the early development of a sense of belonging in the Jewish community was essential to the happiness of Jewish children. His search for funds for the institute at MIT had put him in contact with the American Jewish Congress, and he launched its Commission on Community Interrelations. Toward the end of his life, he also became involved in an attempt to establish the International Jewish Research Foundation — intended to aid in the psychological rehabilitation of former inmates of displaced-persons camps following World War II.

Lewin wrote many books, including *Field The-*

> The psychologist finds himself in the midst of a rich and vast land full of strange happenings: there are men killing themselves; a child playing; a child forming his lips trying to say his first word; a person who, having fallen in love and being caught in an unhappy situation, is not willing or not able to find a way out; there is the mystical state called hypnosis, where the will of one person seems to govern another person; there is the reaching out for higher and more difficult goals; loyalty to a group; dreaming; planning; exploring the world; and so on without end. It is an immense continent full of fascination and power and full of stretches of land where no one ever has set foot.
>
> Psychology is out to conquer this continent, to find out where its treasures are hidden, to investigate its danger spots, to master is vast forces, and to utilize its energies.
>
> **Kurt Z. Lewin**

ory in *Social Science* (1951), numerous papers, and seventy experimental studies.

A. J. Marrow, *The Practical Theorist: The Life and Works of Kurt Lewin*, 1969.

LIBERMAN, YEVSEY GRIGORYEVICH

LIBERMAN, YEVSEY GRIGORYEVICH (1897–1983) Soviet economist and statistician. In the 1960s he suggested a program for economic reform in the Soviet Union, which included using profit as a means of measuring success in an industry and offering bonuses to factories whose output was profitable beyond expectation. Though his ideas received worldwide attention for their innovation and were to some extent tested in the Soviet Union, they failed to be fully instituted and were eventually rejected by party bureaucrats.

Born in Volyn in the Ukraine, he was educated at Kiev University and Kharkov Engineering Economics Institute. After his graduation in 1933 he worked as an engineer in factories. With over fifteen years of experience behind him, he was appointed chair of economic and organization of machine building industry at the Kharkov Institute in 1947, where he remained until his retirement. Liberman earned his doctorate in economic science in 1957, and that same year published an article entitled "The Planning of Profit in Industry."

Liberman's ideas on making the economy of the Soviet Union more productive and efficient were noticed by mathematician and economist Vasily Nemchinov. Nemchinov convinced Soviet Premier Nikita S. Khrushchev to allow Liberman to air his views on the economy, and in 1962 an article appeared in *Pravda* under the title "Plan, Profit, and Bonus." Liberman suggested moving away from central planning by giving factory management more responsibility for economic planning. The role of central planners would be limited to setting objectives for production volume and delivery schedules, leaving the rest to local management. Liberman's other ideas included using profit, rather than output, as a measurement of successful management, using supply and demand to establish prices, and establishing direct links between state businesses and regions.

Although he did not challenge the fundamental Marxist idea of public ownership of the means of production, party bureaucrats objected to Liberman's plan because it appeared to incorporate many elements from Western capitalism. In fact, the Western press labeled his ideas "Libermanism" and was quick to publicize elements of his plan that it felt were direct adaptations of capitalism. Liberman objected to the press labeling his ideas as such, stating: "The importunate attempt by bourgeois commentators to put my name in the headlines makes one laugh rather than be indignant. It is due only to ignorance that all the titanic research and the entire generalization of practical experience is reduced to the invention of an individual scientist." He heartily defended the role of profit in a socialist economy explaining: "Where does profit go in the USSR? By no means does it go into the

pockets of managers and other industrial executives. The bulk of it is used for expanding socialist production and cultural services for the population."

Liberman's ideas obtained a favorable response from the Soviet public, and he reported receiving thousands of letters in support of his proposed reforms. His ideas were tested in many factories over the next few years. Though somewhat successful, Liberman himself reported that the old way of doing things through central bureaucracy was deeply entrenched and had "proved more persistent than had been expected." He saw an "inertia of thought, views, and ideas" when it came to making innovations. Government agencies resisted change in order to maintain their power, and factory management was continually bogged down in a mire of conflicting orders.

Officially retired in 1963, Liberman continued to teach and develop his ideas at the University of Kharkov. By the end of the 1960s, his ideas were largely abandoned and though he continued to write, he lived the rest of his life in relative obscurity from the world community. In 1965 he and the Nobel Prize-winning physicist Lev Landau (q.v.) wrote a letter to the *New York Times* denying the existence of anti-Semitism in the USSR and castigating those who unnecessarily interfered in the lives of Soviet Jews. The letter was considered propaganda by most Westerners who were involved in this cause. Yevsey Liberman's passing in 1983 was noted by only one publication in the USSR, *Eko*, a Siberian journal. The exact date and place of death were not noted in the obituary, but ironically it was stated that Liberman was a "great Soviet scientist" whose ideas reflected "the collective wisdom of the party."

LICHINE, DAVID (1910–1972) Dancer and choreographer. Born David Lichtenstein in Rostov-on-Don, Russia, he was taken as a boy to Paris, where he attended the Russian high school. He began dancing at an early age, studying with two celebrated Russian émigrés: Lubov Egorova, a prima ballerina in the Diaghilev company, and Bronislava Nijinska, the sister of the famous Vaslav Nijinsky.

Lichine made his debut as a dancer with the company of Ida Rubenstein (q.v.). For a year he was a member of Anna Pavlova's company; in 1932 he joined Colonel de Basil's Ballets Russes de Monte Carlo and began choreographing extensively. He remained with this company as a principal dancer, appearing in many leading roles, such as George Balanchine's *Le bourgeois gentilhomme* (music by Richard Strauss) and Leonide Massine's *Jeux d'enfants* (music by Geoges Bizet). Lichine choreographed some of his own best works, including *Graduation Ball* (music by Johann Strauss, arranged by Antol Dorati), which is still performed by ballet companies all over the world.

In 1941 he and his wife, the ballerina Tatiana Riabouchinska, went to the United States, where they joined the American Ballet Theater as guest artists. In later years Lichine danced again for the ABT, mostly in his own ballets. For the ABT he also completed Fokine's unfinished work *Helen of Troy* (music by Jacques Offenbach [q.v.]). He created dances for musicals on Broadway such as *Beat the Band* and *Rhapsody* and for films (his *Graduation Ball* was filmed in Mexico in 1961).

In 1947 the Lichines moved to South America where they both danced and he choreographed for the Teatro Colon in Buenos Aires. The following year, back in Europe, he created two works for the Ballets des Champs Elysées: *La création* (a ballet without music) and *La rencontre* (music by Henri Sauguet), about the Oedipus story.

Returning to the United States in 1952, Lichine and his wife opened a school and ran a company in Los Angeles until his death. Lichine was noted for his immense charm as well as his great skill, and for his exceptional expressiveness in comic as in serious roles.

F. Gadan-Pamard and R. Maillard (eds.), *Dictionary of Modern Ballet*, 1959.

LIEBERMANN, MAX (1847–1935) German artist. Born in Berlin to a well-to-do family, he studied art with Karl Steffeck at age fifteen, but his father later sent him to university to study philosophy. However, by 1868 he was at the Art Academy in Weimar, studying with Ferdinand Pauwels and Charles Verlat. In 1871 he made his first trip to Holland, where he spent many summers, and became acquainted with the work of The Hague School, notably Jozef Israels (q.v.) and Anton Mauve.

His first large painting, *Women Plucking Geese* (1872), created a stir in Berlin. The critics were outraged by the "ugliness" of the subject and the somberness of the background. Nevertheless, the painting was sold. Lieberman went to Paris in 1873, where he stayed for five years. There he was impressed by the work of Gustave Courbet, and by the Barbizon painters, J.-F. Millet, Camille Corot, and Charles-François Daubigny. His next painting, of peasants cleaning vegetables, was well-received in Paris, and he decided to remain there, although he continued his visits to Holland and painted some of his most important pictures on Dutch subjects. In 1876 he exhibited *Workers in a Turnip Field* at the Paris Salon, and painted *The Synagogue in Amsterdam*.

Liebermann went to Venice and Berlin in 1878, but settled in Munich. His large painting of *Christ in the Temple*, which he painted in Venice using an Italian boy as a model, brought accusations of blasphemy. After that he avoided religious subjects.

Liebermann returned to Berlin in 1884, and soon became a leading figure in the Berlin art world. He was a founding member of the "Group of XI," who proclaimed their independence of the Berlin art establishment, the painters of historical and sentimental pictures. The XI later developed into the Berlin Secession movement, which was founded

Max Liebermann in his study.

in 1898, the year after Liebermann had a one-man show at the Berlin Academy and became a professor there — and the year he became a member of the academy. Nevertheless, he was president of the Berlin Secession for more than ten years.

During World War I, he ceased his visits to Holland and painted scenes of Berlin and Wiesbaden. In 1920 he began his long service as president of the Berlin Academy, which held a retrospective in his honor on his eightieth birthday.

Liebermann was one of the leading German impressionists. Like the Dutch impressionists, he often painted people at their everyday tasks, and explored the effect of changing sunlight on colors and shadows. He was not receptive to the French Impressionists' experiments with divided colors, although his palette-knife painting techniques and his brighter palette were influenced by their work. His great strengh lay in the daring structure of his compositions, and in his firm, clear drawing. Though his favorite subjects included working people and the poor, he was in great demand as a portraitist among the German elite and intelligentsia.

He was one of Germany's outstanding and most respected painters when, in 1933, the Nazis included his work in their first exhibition of "degenerate" art. They forced him out of his position as president of the academy and stripped him of all his honors, but because of the veneration with which the German public regarded him, they limited their persecution to removing his works from all museums and public collections, and forbidding him to paint. He died in 1935. Eight years later his widow committed suicide when notified by the Nazis that she was to be deported.

K. Scheffler, *Max Liebermann*, (German), 1953.
F. Stultmann, *Max Liebermann*, (German), 1961.

LILIENTHAL, DAVID (1899–1981) U.S. attorney, chairman of Tennessee Valley Authority. Born in Morton, Illinois, Lilienthal became a lawyer in 1923. Throughout his career his major imperatives were the conservation of human and natural resources. The former concern was reflected in his activity on behalf of labor; as a young lawyer he assisted in the drafting of prolabor legislation. Until 1931, he served as a utilities lawyer in Chicago, where he was counsel to the city in litigation over a telephone rates controversy in which 20 million dollars was eventually awarded to Chicago telephone users.

In 1931, when he was appointed to the Wisconsin Public Service Commission, one of Lilienthal's major concerns was the co trol by giant corporations of the nation's natural resources and of the utilities which made them available for public consumption. In 1933 President Franklin D. Roosevelt appointed him director of the Tennessee Valley Authority (the U.S. government agency responsible for developing the Tennessee River basin), and in 1941 he became its chairman. During his term of office, he was active against the monopolistic power companies and on behalf of the needs of local communities.

In 1946 Lilienthal became chairman of the Atomic Energy Commission. In that capacity he authored the Lilienthal plan which proposed international control of atomic energy as a solution to the nuclear arms race.

His doubts about American production of the hydrogen bomb spurred controversy that convinced him to leave public life. His commitment to the conservation and proper utilization of natural resources remained strong, and in 1955 he formed the Development and Resources Corporation, dedicated to the utilization of resources and the development of programs for dams, irrigation, electricity, and flood control in underdeveloped countries.

Lilienthal's books included *TVA: Democracy on the March* (1958); *This I Do Believe* (1949), *Big Business: A New Era* (1953), *Change Hope and the Bomb* (1963), and *Atomic Energy, A New Start* (1980).
J. Daniels, *Southerner Discovers the South*, 1938.
D. E. Lilienthal, *Journals of David E. Lilienthal*, 5 vols., 1964–1971.
W. Whitman, *David Lilienthal: Public Servant in a Power Age*, 1948.

LINDER, MAX   (1882–1925) French film comedian. Born Gabriel Leuvielle near Bordeaux to parents who had abandoned the stage for the vineyard, he determined to be an actor at an early age. After winning prizes at the Bordeaux Conservatoire, he spent three years with a Bordeaux repertory company, the Théâtre des Arts. Arriving in Paris, Linder played small parts on the legitimate stage as well as entertaining in nightclubs. From 1905 onwards he augmented these nocturnal performances with work before the cameras at the Pathé studios during the day, using the name Max Linder in order not to jeopardize his standing in the theater. In 1907 Pathé's star comedian, André Deed, left the company and Linder was given the opportunity to star in his own series of comedies.

Of the many and varied characterizations attempted by Linder in his search for a suitable screen persona, one emerged that was to make him famous worldwide. Almost always topped by a high silk hat, the figure adopted by Linder was that of a well-dressed, dapper gentleman with a neat moustache who could be counted on to wring disaster from everyday social predicaments. The popularity of Linder's films was phenomenal, and several hundred were produced before the outbreak of World War I. At the height of his prewar fame, Linder, who by then usually also directed his own films, made personal appearances throughout Europe.

Linder, whose health was frail, volunteered for the French army when war broke out. He was wounded in action twice and subsequently suffered a nervous breakdown. While recuperating from an ill-advised stint as an air force pilot, he accepted an offer from the American studio Essanay to replace Charles Chaplin. Linder's first American sojourn was unsuccessful, but he returned (at Chaplin's urging) in 1919 and formed his own production company. Of his American feature films, only the first, *Seven Years Bad Luck*, was profitable, and Linder returned to Europe. Increasing depression culminated in the double suicide of Linder and his wife in Paris in 1925. Their daughter, Maud, barely four months old at the time of her parents' death, has since been active in reviving, restoring and gaining recognition for her father's work.
W. Kerr, *The Silent Clowns*, 1975.

THE GENIUS OF MAX LINDER

He was brilliant and unpredictable, and ad libbed frequently. He never did the act the same way twice. Linder was one of the truly great comedians of our time. His pantomime and appeal were eloquent. He had an inspired comedy sense, and he also had an analytical, ingenious mind.

Except for Chaplin, I have never known another comedian who had such an objective view of his art. Linder was sensitive and responsive to any audience, and could talk audience psychology with the intellectual perception of a professor. On stage he would introduce a new bit suddenly and without previous thought, and later he would give a profound and apposite reason for having done what had come spontaneously.

Film composer Dimitri Tiomkin, Linder's accompanist at his 1914 personal appearance in Saint Petersburg, speaking in November 1951.

LIPCHITZ, JACQUES (1891–1973) Born in Druskieniki, Lithuania, he went to school in Bialystok and Vilna, where he became interested in sculpture. When he was eighteen, he went to Paris to study. At the Académie Julien, he learned a method of working that he used all his life. He usually began by making drawings, and then a small sketch in clay. He would then make a larger sketch, adding details and changes; then another, larger, sketch, and so on until he reached the size he wanted and the details satisfied him. Since the clay deteriorated and could not be fired because of the armatures, they were cast in plaster, and the finished work in bronze.

He had a wide circle of friends, including Fernand Léger, John Metzinger, André Derain, Pablo Picasso, and Diego Rivera. In 1914 Rivera gathered a group of friends to vacation in Majorca, but while they were there, World War I broke out. Since Lipchitz was not called up for service — he did not become a French citizen until 1925 — he and Rivera went to Madrid. Rivera was a cubist at that period, and Lipchitz was receptive to the cubist influence. After Lipchitz returned to Paris in 1915, he signed a contract with Leonce Rosenberg, the outstanding dealer of cubist works, to make a series of stone figures.

In 1922 Lipchitz met Albert Barnes, a wealthy American collector, who showed Lipchitz architect's drawings of the building he was constructing in Merion, Pennsylvania, to house his collection. He commissioned Lipchitz to make a series of stone lintels for the building. Lipchitz made them full size, and exhibited them in Paris before sending them to America. At this time Lipchitz bought land in Boulogne-sur-Seine and built a house and studio designed for him by Le Corbusier.

Lipchitz began to work on what he called transparents. He started by cutting a hole in one of his sculptures. Thus, he said, the empty space and the light function as part of the sculpture. He made a Pierrot out of planes of cardboard, with the light dramatizing the planes seen through the large cutout. To have this small piece, five inches high, cast in bronze, Lipchitz made it over in wax. For over five years he worked on his transparents.

In 1927 he was commissioned to make a garden sculpture for Vicomte Charles de Noailles. The result was *Joy of Life*, a transparent seven feet tall, a dancing figure holding a musical instrument. Lipchitz placed it on a tall pedestal in which was a motor to make it turn slowly.

Striving for a more emotional content in his work, Lipchitz began to introduce more organic forms in such works as *Return of the Prodigal Son* (1931) and *David and Goliath* (1933) on which he carved a swastika on the fallen Goliath. Commissioned by the Popular Front government of Léon Blum (q.v.) to make a sculpture for the Paris world's fair of 1937, he made a gigantic *Prometheus* wearing a Phrygian cap of liberty, his chains broken, struggling with the eagle. It was awarded a gold medal, and after the fair closed, it was moved to a site on the Champs Elysées; it was later destroyed for its antifascist message.

When the Nazi armies approached Paris, Lipchitz fled to the south of France and then to New York in June 1941. After the war, he found that the work he had left in his studio had been preserved, and he had it shipped to New York. In 1952, Lipchitz's studio in New York was completely destroyed by fire, and much of the work he had done there was ruined. Funds for a new studio were collected by a committee with the aid of the Museum of Modern Art, which Lipchitz's repaid with sculpture. In 1954 the Museum of Modern Art held a retrospective of Lipchitz' work.

Lipchitz put together several of his chisels and had them cast. He made twenty-six *Variations on a Chisel*. He made a series of small sculptures of "found" objects — anything that took his fancy — which he had cast in bronze. He showed them in 1959 in an exhibition called *À la limite du possible*. That year, in Great Britain, the Arts Council arranged a Lipchitz exhibition at the Tate Gallery.

When the State of Israel was established in 1948, he had made a triumphant sculpture, *The Miracles*, based on Jewish themes. In 1961 Lipchitz visited Israel and said he was fulfilling a dream of longstanding by bequeathing to the still-to-be-built Israel Museum three hundred of his plasters.

From 1962, Lipchitz lived part of the year in Italy, near Lucca. The works from Lipchitz's studio in France, shipped to New York and cast in bronze, were shown at the Otto Gerson Gallery in 1963. Among his commissions at this period, are *Sieur du Luth* for the Tweed Museum of Art in Duluth, Minnesota; *Bellerophon Taming Pegasus* for the Columbia University Law School, New York; *Government of the People* for the Municipal Plaza, Philadelphia; and *Our Tree of Life* for Mount Scopus, Jerusalem, commissioned by Hadassah in 1967, the last depicting the Jewish patriarchs and the generations descending from them.

For his eightieth birthday, the Metropolitan Museum in New York had a large retrospective of his work. Lipchitz went to Israel to celebrate his birthday. The opening show at the Tel Aviv Museum included a large exhibition of his sculpture and drawings. He donated a set of 157 bronzes of his Paris work to the Israel Museum in Jerusalem, where a Lipchitz Gallery was constructed, and his brother Reuben donated 130 maquettes.

Lipchitz died in Capri, Italy, and was buried in Jerusalem.

The Jacques Lipchitz Foundation donated sculptures to the Musée National d'Art Moderne (Paris); the Kroller-Muller Museum, Otterlo, Holland; the University of Arizona Museum of Art, Tucson; and the Tate Gallery.

Lipchitz felt that art was a human language and that reality was the raw material of the artist. Though his early cubist work liberated him from a strict dependence on nature, he saw nature not only as the source of the content but of the form of the work of art. It is the necessity of the sculpture that determines the form, and each work has its own necessities.

The artist's forms arise, he said, "from a restless equilibrium between realism and abstraction, rationality and inspiration, order and chaos." Volume and space were the concerns of the sculptor.

B. Van Bork, *Jacques Lipchitz: The Artist at Work*, 1966.

D. F. Jenkins and D. Pullen, *The Lipchitz Gift: Models for Sculpture*, 1986.

J. Lipchitz with H. H. Arnason, *My Life in Sculpture*, 1972.

I. Patai, *Encounters: The Life of Jacques Lipchitz*, 1961.

D. A. Stott, *Jacques Lipchitz and Cubism*, 1970.

LIPKIN, ISRAEL BEN ZE'EV See Salanter, Israel

LIPPMANN, WALTER (1889–1974) U.S. journalist and political analyst. The only child of a wealthy Jewish family, Lippmann was born in New York and graduated in 1910 from Harvard, where he associated with philosophers George Santayana and William James. He began his journalistic career as editor of Lincoln Steffens's *Everybody's Magazine* in 1911, published his first book, *A Preface to Politics*, in 1913, and a year later helped to found the liberal weekly *New Republic*, becoming its associate editor.

In 1917 Lippmann served as an assistant to the secretary of war and was a captain in military intelligence during World War I. He influenced President Woodrow Wilson, both personally and through his articles, helping to formulate Wilson's Fourteen Points for the postwar settlement and the concept of the League of Nations. He was briefly assistant secretary of war and attended the Versailles peace conference in 1919.

Lippmann joined the editorial staff of the reformist *New York World* in 1921, becoming its editor in 1929 and serving in that post until it ceased publication in 1931. That year he began his column "Today and Tomorrow" in the *New York Herald Tribune*. The column was eventually syndicated internationally in some 250 newspapers and Lippmann was awarded the Pulitzer Prize for it in 1958 and 1962.

Lippmann's political philosophy gradually moved from socialism to liberalism to neoconservatism. He advocated an internationalist foreign policy and warned against developments in modern society, such as the speed of communications, which might hinder the "liberal democracy" he supported.

Lippmann's carefully researched (usually by frequent travels abroad), clear, and broad articles and books had a marked influence on American foreign and domestic policy. He retired in 1967.

M. W. Childs and J. B. Reston (eds.) *Walter Lippmann and his Times*, 1959.

B. F. Wright, *Five Public Philosophies of Walter Lippmann*, 1973.

LISSITZKY, EL (ELIEZER) MARKOWICH (1890–1941) Russian painter, typographer and designer. He was born in Smolensk to parents who were hatters. From an early age he was determined to be an artist, but after passing the entrance examination to the Saint Petersburg Art Academy he was rejected because the Jewish quota had been filled. In 1909 he went to Darmstadt, Germany, to study architecture, although his passion remained freehand drawing. When war broke out in 1914 he had to return to Russia. For the next five years, the major influence in his life was Marc Chagall (q.v.), who introduced him to "Jewish art." After the 1917 revolution, anti-Jewish restrictions were cancelled and a Jewish artistic renaissance ensued. Much of Lissitzky's work at this time consisted of gouaches and peasant woodcuts for Jewish books (including children's books). He was also a propagandist for the Red Army and designed the very first Soviet flag, which was paraded in the 1918 May Day procession. His first outstanding poster depicted red triangles and white circles on a black and white ground with the message "Beat the Whites with the Red wedge."

He identified with the new Russian government, which gave him the freedom to experiment, providing him with a steady income, and for the rest of his life was responsible for architecture, design and exhibition arrangement on its behalf. One of his last works was a poster bearing the legend "Give more tanks" across a collage of proud Russian workers and munitions.

When Chagall was appointed commissioner of artistic affairs in Vitebsk, he engaged Lissitzky as an instructor in 1919. There he met the painter Kasimir Malevich, whose totally abstract art was known as suprematist art. Lissitzky was intrigued and, abandoning "Jewish art," embraced suprematism. He called his new paintings collectively "Proun" but never explained the meaning of the word (some suggest that it is an abbreviation of the Latin *pro uno vis*, "all for one purpose"). Lissitzky was also a leading figure in the related constructivist movement, which sought to integrate aesthetic concepts with Marxism. By now he was recognized as one of the great Russian artists and a pioneer of nonrepresentational art. He could easily switch from architectural art to commercial art, three-dimensional constructs, and even photography, and he exerted a strong influence in mass communications through his work in typography and advertising exhibition design.

From 1925 to 1928 he lived in Hanover, Germany. There in the Landesmuseum he designed a Room of Abstracts, which was destroyed by the Nazis in 1936 as "decadent Jewish art."

Back in Russia he founded progressive art journals and wrote *Russia: The Reconstruction of Architecture in the Soviet Union* (1930). Throughout the 1930s he continued to put his talents at the disposal of Stalin's propaganda machine.

His enormous output has a unity, and he wrote: "Every piece of work I did was an invitation not to

make eyes at it but to take it as a spur to action, to urge our feelings to follow the broad aim of forming a classless society."
S. Lissitzky-Küppers, *El Lissitzky: Life and Letters*, 1968.
F. Lubbers, *El Lissitzsky: 1890–1941*, 1991.

LITVINOV, MAXIM (1876–1951) Russian revolutionary and Soviet diplomat. He was born Meir Moiseevich Wallach in Bialystok, where he had his early schooling. Attracted to socialist ideas from his teens, he joined the Russian Social Democratic party in 1898. He was arrested in 1901 and exiled. In 1902 he escaped to Switzerland, where he first met Lenin and fell under his spell. The following year he infiltrated back to Russia and took part in the 1905 revolution. After its failure he spent the next twelve years in exile in France and Britain, working closely with Lenin. A few days after the 1917 Bolshevik revolution he was appointed the Soviet agent in Britain, but was arrested by the British for propaganda activities and exchanged for the leader of the British expedition to Russia, Robert Bruce Lockhart.

By 1921 Litvinov had become deputy foreign minister of the Soviet Union under Georgi V. Chicherin. A year later he took part in the Rapallo Conference, which culminated with the signing of the German-Soviet treaty, ending the Soviet Union's isolation from Europe. During the 1920s he participated in many international conferences and was active in disarmament negotiations. His policy was to ensure the growth of the Soviet Union and to remove threats of war. From 1928 to 1930 he was acting foreign minister and from 1930 to 1939 he served as foreign minister.

After Russia entered the League of Nations in 1934, his chubby figure became well known in the halls of the League in Geneva, where he pleaded the cause of collective security (saying "peace is indivisible") and world disarmament. In 1933 he headed the Soviet delegation that negotiated with President Franklin D. Roosevelt the resumption of diplomatic relations with the United States. A fervent anti-Nazi, he urged the League of Nations to plan collective resistance against Nazi Germany. He resigned shortly before the signing of the 1939 German-Soviet nonaggression pact and was replaced by Vyacheslav M. Molotov. After the outbreak of World War II he returned to duty and, when Germany invaded Russia in June 1941, he was appointed ambassador to the United States. His excellent command of the English language and his vast diplomatic experience made him a popular figure in Washington, where he served until 1943. He was appointed deputy commissar of foreign affairs, but retired later that year. He supported the creation of the United Nations as a central instrument for preserving peace.

While he never hid his Jewish ancestry, Litvinov opposed Zionism. His wife, Ivy, was the niece of Sir Sidney Low (Loewe), a leading English historian and imperialist, and sister of Edith Eder, a leader of WIZO (Women's International Zionist Organization).

D. G. Bishop, *Roosevelt-Litvinov Agreements*, 1965.
G. Craig, *The Diplomat, 1919–1939*, 1953.
A. U. Pope, *Maxim Litvinov*, 1943.

LOEWI, OTTO (1873–1961) German physician and pharmacologist, and Nobel Prize winner. Born in Frankfurt, he graduated from Strasbourg University in 1896. Early in his career he became interested in biochemistry and began his scientific work at the pharmacological institute in Marburg. From 1906 to 1909 he was associate professor of pharmacology in Vienna, and from 1909 to 1938, professor of pharmacology in Graz. His studies concerned metabolism; the vegetative nervous system; renal (kidney) function; the action of cations; the effects of digitalis; and diabetes mellitus.

From 1900 he contributed to the understanding of synthesis of animal body proteins. Loewi discovered that nitrogen balance was due to amino-acid hydrolysis. In 1902 he began working on the formation of sugar from protein and the influence of pilocarpin and atropin on the circulation and the salivary glands. He demonstrated the effect of cocaine on sensitivity to adrenaline.

Physiologico-pharmacological research on the stimulation and retardation of the vagus nerve to the heart led to his description of the humoral transmission of nerves and its effect on the nerves to the heart. Loewi proved that acetylcholine or adrenaline was liberated from the nerve endings by a nerve impulse traveling along its fibers and that it was the presence of these chemicals that produced a reaction in the target organs. This achievement earned Lowei the Nobel Prize for physiology and medicine in 1936 (together with Sir Henry Dale) "for the fundamental discovery of the chemical transmission of nerve impulses."

Loewi also wrote papers on the liver in diabetes mellitus and the effects of insulin and developed the Loewi test for pancreatic insufficiency.

In 1938 he was arrested by the Nazis, imprisoned for two months, stripped of all his possessions, and then allowed to leave Germany. He spent a year in Brussels before arriving in Oxford, England, where he spent another year, finally emigrating to the United States in 1940, where he remained for the rest of his life. From 1940 he was professor of pharmacology at the New York College of Medicine.

Loewi was described as a man with a keen sense of humor and in 1946 Frederick Yonkman of Columbia University paid the following tribute to him: "This unusual man of science, driven from his native Austria by Nazi madness, was deprived of all his tangible possessions and not even permitted to use his Nobel Prize money. This exceptional individual was not soured by these harrowing experiences but rather he was stimulated by adversity to new heights of achievement."

LOMBROSO, CESARE (1836–1909) Italian criminologist, considered the founding father of the modern school of criminology. Lombroso came from a family of rabbis and Hebrew scholars. His parents belonged to the Jewish aristocracy of Cheri and Verona and, Lombroso was born in Verona at a time when his family enjoyed its highest economic standing. In fact, he was born and lived for the first years of his life at the Palazzo del Greco in Verona. Growing up in a period of political unrest that led to the unification of Italy, Lombroso was an acute observer of his changing environment. By the age of fifteen, he had already published two essays on Roman history. He went on to study literature, linguistics, and archaeology, devoting particular attention to Hebrew, Arabic, and Chinese. Pursuing his interest in medicine, Lombroso obtained his doctorate from the University of Turin and studied at the universities of Padua, Paris, and Vienna. During his studies, Lombroso became increasingly interested in the study of insanity.

During the 1859 war against Austria he served as a physician in the army, and published two papers on amputation which earned him the only official award he ever received, the Riberi Prize. Upon being refused permission to visit the Pavia asylum to study mental disorders more closely, Lombroso decided to leave the army. He was then offered the professorship of psychiatry and medical jurisprudence at Turin, a position he accepted on condition that he be given a laboratory to continue his anthropological collections. At this laboratory, he conducted extensive post mortem studies on criminals in search of morphological markers for criminality. Studying the shape of the skull as an indicator of abnormality, Lombroso amassed a collection of skulls of criminals that is considered to be the largest and most inclusive of its kind. During the twenty years that he held the professorship at Turin, Lombroso developed ideas on crime that caused an uproar in the scientific community.

Originally arousing violent opposition, Lombroso's ideas on the causes of criminal behavior came to change the whole focus of the study of crime from that of the criminal act to that of the criminal. Stressing inborn, biological factors, Lombroso held that criminals are born with a criminal instinct. They belong to a degenerate class of human beings that is characterized by certain anatomical features and represents a regression to a primitive form of the human species. The criminal falls into several categories of abnormal types that can be either defective or excessive; the atavism of this biological regression results in the development of criminals or idiots, while the evolution allows for artists and poets. Lombroso advocated the rehabilitation of certain types of criminals for whom education would create a safe outlet for their criminal instinct, so that they would be able to fit into society with a minimal chance of breaking the law. He favored severe limitations on the application of the death penalty. Lombroso's ideas on crime and its humane treatment were incorporated in the 1931 Italian penal code and, more impor-

tantly, marked the beginning of a new scientific discipline — criminology.

Lombroso, however, did not limit his studies to causes and effects of crime. He was interested in all aspects of mental phenomena. Soon after the publication of his controversial theory of criminality in *The Criminal Man* (1876), Lombroso published *The Man of Genius* (1891), in which he sought to prove the existence of a connection between a certain type of genius and epilepsy. So insistent was he on proving this notion, that some of his critics were inclined to place Lombroso himself in this category of geniuses.

In 1906 the Sixth International Congress of Anthropologists, in appreciation of his contributions to science and medicine, presented Lombroso with a testimonial in London. Upon returning to what he considered a hostile and ungrateful Italian scientific community, Lombroso was much moved by the homage prepared for him by the Italian Congress of Criminal Anthropology. Collegues, students, friends, admirers, even distant childhood friends appeared to pay him tribute.

An early supporter of Zionism, he was a friend of Max Nordau (q.v.) and published a work on anti-Semitism as an atavistic manifestation (1894).
H. G. Kurella, *Cesare Lombroso: A Modern Man of Science*, 1911.
H. Mannheim, *Pioneers in Criminology*, 1960.

LORRE, PETER (Ladislav Lowenstein; 1904– 1964) Actor. Born in Rozsahegy, Hungary, Lorre moved to Austria with his family as a child. In 1921, eager for a theatrical career, he left home, but had to struggle until 1924, when he first obtained a walk-on part in a play. In the interim, he had worked in a bank, established an amateur dramatic group, and studied psychiatry under both Alfred Adler (q.v.) and Sigmund Freud (q.v.). In 1929, having performed in Vienna, Breslau, and Zurich, Lorre first made his mark in Berlin in *Die Pioniere von Ingolstadt*. In *Frühlings Erwachen* by Frank

Peter Lorre (right) and Humphrey Bogart in Casablanca.

Wedekind, his role as a student who commits suicide because of his sexual problems was noted by film director Fritz Lang (q.v.). Lang cast Lorre as the child-murderer in his first sound film, *M*, which earned Lorre international stardom upon its release.

After *M*, Lorre continued to work on the Berlin stage and in films until the rise of Nazism sent him back to Austria. Finding little work there or, subsequently, in Paris, Lorre went to England, where Alfred Hitchcock cast him as the villain in *The Man Who Knew Too Much*. Taking a Hollywood offer, Lorre made a great impression in his first American film, *Mad Love*, for which he emphasized his bulging eyes and prominent lips by shaving his head. Under contract to Fox in the late 1930s, he starred in a series of films as a Japanese detective, Mr. Moto. In 1942 he appeared with Humphrey Bogart and Sydney Greenstreet in *The Maltese Falcon* at Warner Brothers; both actors shared the screen with him again in several subsequent films.

After the war, with successes such as *Casablanca*, *Arsenic and Old Lace*, and *The Beast with Five Fingers* behind him, Lorre returned to Germany for his sole venture into film direction, *Der Verlorene*. Working as coscreenwriter of the film, he starred in it as a Nazi scientist unable to control his homicidal tendencies. A serious illness in the early 1950s resulted in a considerable increase in Lorre's weight and many of his last film were comedies in which he parodied the kind of role for which he had become famous.

C. T. Beck, *Heroes of the Horrors*, 1975.

T. Sennett, *Masters of Menace: Greenstreet and Lorre*, 1979.

LUBETKIN, ZIVIA (1914–1976) Founder of the Zydoswka Organizacja Bojowa (ZOB, "Jewish Fighting Organization") in World War II. A native of Beten, Poland, Lubetkin became active in a Zionist youth movement. At the outbreak of World War II, she was in eastern Poland but fled to Warsaw as soon as she could. She became a founding member of the Antifacist Bloc, the first partially successful attempt to set up an armed underground in Warsaw.

In July 1942, when the deportations from Warsaw were proceeding at an intensive pace, she helped found the ZOB. She became a member of the Jewish National Committee and the Coordinating Committee — the political arm of the ZOB — and the coordinating committee between the ZOB and the Jewish Socialist Bund. Lubetkin fought in the short January 1943 uprising in the Warsaw ghetto and again in the revolt that broke out on April 19, 1943. On May 10 she escaped by way of the sewers and remained in hiding until the Red Army took Warsaw, only emerging to take part in the Polish Warsaw uprising.

After the war she became active in survivor circles and the Beriha, an organization devoted to bringing Jews from Europe to Palestine. She reached Palestine herself in 1946 and helped found the Ghetto Fighters' Kibbutz and its museum. She

Zivia Lubetkin.

married another former underground leader, Yitzhak Zuckerman (q.v.).

Z. Lubetkin, *In Days of Destruction and Revolt*, 1980.

LUBITSCH, ERNST (1892–1947) Film director and producer. Born to a Berlin tailor, Lubitsch was stagestruck from early youth. While acting as his father's bookkeeper, he apprenticed himself to comedian Victor Arnold, who later introduced him to the director Max Reinhardt (q.v.). Accepted by the latter in 1911, Lubitsch's greatest success while with Reinhardt was as the hunchback clown in *Sumurun* (the film version of which Lubitsch was later to star in and direct in 1920). By 1913 he had become a film comedian, playing a Jewish character known as Meyer in a long-running series. He directed his first comedies the following year, and in 1918 turned to serious historical epics. While comedies of the 1920s, such as *Kolheissels Tochter*, were enormously popular in Germany, it was his more serious films with Emil Jannings and Pola Negri (*Carmen, Madame Dubarry*, and *Anne Boleyn*) that brought him worldwide fame. It was this fame that led Mary Pickford to bring him to the United States in 1923 to direct her in *Rosita*.

Shortly after arriving in America, Lubitsch hit upon the type of witty social comedy for which he is best remembered. The "Lubitsch touch," a little twist given to an often slightly risqué but familiar situation, was already an expression in currency in the late 1920s. Lubitsch's touch was effective on a number of fronts; both critically and commercially

NO MORE LUBITSCH FILMS

After Lubitsch's funeral, his friends Billy Wilder and William Wyler were walking sadly to their car. Finally, to break the silence, Wilder said, "No more Lubitsch." Wyler answered, "Worse than that — no more Lubitsch films."

his rate of success was consistently high.

The greatest part of Lubitsch's American career was spent at Paramount, where he also spent a year in the mid-1930s as head of production. The undeniable attraction of his own name on a film was usually combined with that of high-powered stars: the team of Jeanette MacDonald and Maurice Chevalier that he created, Marlene Dietrich, and one memorable comedy, *Ninotchka*, starring Greta Garbo. Other well-known films included *The Love Parade, Trouble in Paradise*, and *The Merry Widow*. During the war he attacked Nazism with laughter in *To Be Or Not To Be*, but his subsequent productions were attended by poor health. In 1947, while filming *That Lady in Ermine*, his first musical in over a decade, Lubitsch died of a heart attack.

W. Paul, *Ernst Lubitsch's American Comedy*, 1983.
A. Poague, *The Cinema of Ernst Lubitsch*, 1978.
G. Weinberg, *The Lubitsch Touch*, 1968.

LUDWIG, EMIL (1881–1948) German biographer and writer. Born Emil Cohn in Breslau (Wroclaw), the son of a famous Jewish ophthalmologist, he was baptized and raised as a Christian. His parents changed their surname to Ludwig in order to prevent anti-Semitic discrimination. However, he became involved in Judaism, and finally renounced Christianity following the murder of the Jewish German statesman Walther Rathenau (q.v.) in 1922.

Ludwig left Germany in 1907, and became a Swiss citizen with the rise of Nazism. He lived in Ascona, in the Italian part of Switzerland. After Hitler's rise to power, he was declared an enemy of the Nazi state and his books were burned.

Ludwig wrote extensively from the age of twenty-five, after a brief career as a lawyer. He first wrote plays and poems, only later turning to other genres, including political essays and the novel. He also wrote historical and geographical studies — one of his famous studies is *The Nile* (1937). However, he became most famous for his colorful biographies and character sketches, which involved a deep understanding of the social and historical conditions in which his subjects lived.

Ludwig's first biography was a three-volume study of *Goethe* (1920), followed shortly after by a biography of *Bismarck*. The dramatized version of

this work was banned in Berlin, but an appeal to the courts led to a repeal of the ban, and the play ran for over 1,000 performances.

His biographies cover a vast range of personages, including Jesus Christ, Beethoven, Franklin D. Roosevelt, Abraham Lincoln, Napoleon, Kaiser Wilhelm II, Michelangelo, Cleopatra, Stalin, and Sigmund Freud (q.v.).

He often worked on two or three books simultaneously. At the time of his death he had been researching King David, and writing biographies of Alexander and Karl Wilhel von Humboldt.
N. Hansen, *Der Fall Emil Ludwig*, 1930.

LUKÁCS, GEORG (1885–1971) Hungarian Marxist philosopher and aesthetician. He was born into a middle-class family, his father, a bank director, being ennobled in 1899, when he converted to Christianity. As a teenager he began to write poems and plays but destroyed the latter when he was eighteen. From 1902 he studied law and political science at Budapest University, obtaining an LL.D. in 1906 at Kolozsvár (now Cluj-Napoca, Romania). In 1904 he was a founder of the Thalia Society, an avant-garde theater for which he translated several plays, including Ibsen's *Wild Duck*, and also participated in the group's management. In 1906 he began studying in Berlin, and in 1909 received a Ph.D. for his dissertation, *The Form of Drama*, an enlarged edition of which, *History of the Development of Modern Drama*, was published in 1911.

Following a series of personal tragedies, he moved to Heidelberg, where he came under the influence of Max Weber and his circle. His interests at this time centered on problems of the philosophy of history and ethics, about which he wrote in the introduction to his *Die Theorie des Romans* "Theory of the Novel," (1914). Lukács did not share his German philosopher colleagues' enthusiasm for World War I and published his objections in an article, "German Intellectuals and the War." From 1917, he frequently returned to Budapest and formed the Sunday Circle, in which he met his friends to debate problems of philosophy, history, and religion. Members of the circle founded the Free School of Liberal Arts, where Lukács taught ethics.

His rejection of the prevalent social order brought him to Marxism. When, as a consequence of the victorious revolution of 1918, the hitherto theoretical philosophical-ethical questions became practical, he joined the Communist party and edited its organ, *The Red Newspaper*. In the proletarian dictatorship of Bela Kun, he was deputy commissar for education and from June 1919 commissar for education and culture. After Kun's fall, he remained in Budapest with the task of organizing the illegal Communist party, but eventually had to flee to Vienna. In 1920–1921, he was a member of the Hungarian Communist party's provisional central committee and wrote numerous articles on theoretical problems of communism for *Kommunismus*, the organ of the Communist International. Lukács kept in touch with the Communist underground in Hungary and participated in the Third Congress of the International in Moscow. On his return to Vienna, he published a book of essays, which Lenin criticized for their Hegelian idealism. In February 1924 he wrote a long essay on Lenin, who had died in January, in which he analyzed the "correlation of Lenin's thoughts" and revised his own earlier "messianistic Marxism."

For the next few years, his attention was directed to the history of Marxist ideology and of the workers' movement in essays on Moses Hess (q.v.) and Ferdinand Lassalle (q.v.). In 1928 the Hungarian party's central committee directed him to prepare the platform for the party's upcoming second congress. Under his party nom de guerre, Blum, he prepared the theses in which, basing himself on the program of the Communist International's sixth congress, he argued that the immediate strategic goal of the Hungarian party was not a dictatorship of the proletariat but the "democratic dictatorship of workers and peasants." When the central committee rejected his draft theses, Lukacs withdrew his draft and at the request of the central committee exercised public self-criticism. In fall 1929 he spent three months illegally in Budapest, directing the party's day-to-day work. When the Austrian authorities refused to renew his permit to stay in Austria, he moved to Moscow, where he became a member of the Marx-Engels-Lenin Institute. He worked with D. Ryazov on the philological reconstruction of the manuscript of Marx's economic-philosophical essays written in 1844. In 1931, he traveled to Berlin on behalf of the International Association of Revolutionary Writers, to represent the line of socialist realism in opposition to the proletarian avant-garde in the Association of German Proletarian-Revolutionary Writers.

Returning to Moscow in 1933, his articles were regularly published in the new Soviet journal, *Literary Criticism*. Together with M. Lifshitz, he set out to collect and interpret the comments of Marx and Engels on aesthetics with a view to reconstructing Marxist aesthetics as an integral part of Marxist philosophy. From 1935 to 1939 he was a member of the Philosophical Institute of the Soviet Acadamy of Sciences, working on his monograph, *The Young Hegel* (1948). His book, *The Historical Novel*, first appeared in Russian. In 1939, he formulated his political standpoint in the essay "People's Tribune or Bureaucrat," a veiled critique of the cult of personality. In 1938, under the popular front program of the Communist International, the Hungarian language periodical *New Voice* was launched. Lukács and J. Revai (a future leading ideologist of the Stalinist Community party in Hungary), became its leading contributors, and from that time Lukács again focused his attention on events in Hungary.

Having survived the Stalin purges and World War II, he returned to Hungary in 1945. Until 1949, he was professor of aesthetics and philosophy of culture at Budapest University, from 1948 a member of the Hungarian Academy of Sciences; and in 1949–1958 a member of its presidium. From 1946, he was one of the editors of the social-science journal, *Forum*, and a member of the editorial board of *Social Review*. In his articles and lectures on the cultural policy of the Hungarian Communist party, he presented the Marxist viewpoint, while in contemporary ideological discussions he held that the progressive democratic traditions of Hungarian literature should become the norm. As a critic of bourgeois philosophy, he violently attacked the existentialists.

What is now known as the Lukács controversy erupted in 1949 over his theory of democracy, which clearly opposed the prevalent cult of the personality. His views were deemed right-wing deviation. In the end, he published yet another self-criticism, "Conclusions of a Literary Debate," in *Social Review*. He was also castigated for failing to study Soviet literature and socialist realism. As a result, he published an essay on Soviet writers. During the ensuing years, he was engaged in theoretical research on reactionary irrationalism (*The Forced Abdication of Reason*, 1954).

After the October 1956 uprising, he was minister of education in Imre Nagy's government and participated in the formation of the Hungarian Socialist Workers' party as a member of its executive, but voted against secession from the Warsaw Pact. On 4 November he fled to the Yugoslav embassy, from which he was taken to Romania. There he wrote the first part of his Marxist aesthetics, in which he opposed political control of artists. He was allowed to return to Budapest in April 1957 but stopped participating in public life. He continued his research and writing, finishing the manuscript of the elaboration of Marxist ethics shortly before his death. In 1967, he again returned to public life, his party membership was restored, and in fall 1970 he started his autobiography, of which only a forty-page outline was published (*Gelebtes Leben*). On his seventieth birthday he was presented the Goethe Prize of the city of Frankfurt. His essays *History and Class Consciousness*, a sharp critique of communism as it developed in Russia, were published in 1971 and aroused yet another controversy. He wrote studies of Goethe (1947), Hegel (1948), Lenin (1970), and Solzhenitsyn (1970).

E. Bahr and R. G. Kunzer, *Georg Lukács*, 1970.

G. Lichtheim, *Lukács*, 1970.

LURIA, ISAAC (known as the *Ari*, an acronym of the Hebrew for "the Divine Rabbi Isaac"; 1534–1572) Kabbalist who founded a school of Jewish mysticism known as the Lurianic Kabbalah. He was born in Jerusalem, where his father had moved from Germany or Poland (hence, he was known as Isaac Ashkenazi). After his father's death, his mother moved to Cairo, where Luria was raised in the home of his uncle, an affluent tax collector. He studied with eminent rabbis and became involved in the study of kabbalistic literature.

Luria earned his livelihood as a merchant. Few specific details are known of his life, although he became the subject of many legends. About 1570 he moved to Safed in Galilee, where he continued his mystical studies with Moses Cordovero (q.v.). He himself soon became the center of a group of students, his chief disciple being Hayim Vital (q.v.). Deeply revered and possessing strong charisma, he soon had the reputation of a saint enjoying divine inspiration, and it was even believed that he understood the language of animals. In the vicinity of Safed, he "identified" many graves as those of the Talmudic rabbis and these became an object of pilgrimage that has continued to this day. He used to go with his disciples on Friday afternoons and prostrate himself on these graves to unite with the souls of the dead. After only two years in Safed, he died in a plague epidemic.

Luria wrote almost nothing, explaining that when he held a pen, visions appeared before him like a great river and he could not channel this river through a mere pen. Both he and Vital tried to keep his teachings a secret, but his disciples took notes. These were collected by Vital, but two of Luria's students refused to hand them over, although these too were eventually published. According to legend, those in Vital's keeping were stolen from his possession while he was ill, copied, and distributed. Whatever the source, Luria's ideas became widely known and influential from the latter part of the sixteenth century.

Luria modified earlier Jewish mystical teaching (see Moses de Leon) and stressed the striving of the soul for redemption, which would be attained through mystical devotion involving prayer, observance of the commandments, ascetic practices, and good deeds. Every individual had a part to play in the messianic drama and every action had national and messianic significance. He introduced three basic concepts: "contraction," that is, God contracted within himself, thus creating space for creation; "breaking of the vessels," a cosmic catastrophe in which destruction replaced creation; and "mending" (Hebrew, *tikkun*), the process whereby the divine sparks scattered in the catastrophe could be recovered and divine light restored to the Godhead. Human beings, by correct practices, contribute to this mending process, while God's own people serves as a special instrument.

Luria's teaching spread rapidly throughout the Jewish world in the seventeenth century. It brought a new messianic hope and was a major factor in the popular acclaim for the pseudomessiah, Shabbetai Tzevi (q.v.). The Hasidic movement was also strongly influenced by Lurianic Kabbalah and adopted the special liturgy that developed from his doctrines.

L. Fine, *Safed Spirituality*, 1984.
G. Scholem, *Major Trends in Jewish Mysticism*, 1961.
G. Scholem, *Sabbatai Sevi*, 1937.

LUXEMBURG, ROSA (1871–1919) Left-wing revolutionary and coleader of the Spartacus League,

later the German Communist party. She was born into a family of bourgeois merchants in Zamość, eastern Poland. Although physically handicapped and barely five feet tall, she possessed enormous physical energy and a combative and fiery nature. She joined the Polish revolutionary movement while still at school in Warsaw and went on to study history and political science at the University of Zurich. At the university she was active in a clandestine socialist movement of Polish exiles, and was a cofounder of the Social Democratic party of Poland and Lithuania. She became a German citizen in 1898 and worked as a journalist for several German socialist journals and newspapers.

Luxemburg knew Lenin, but their relationship was stormy. She rejected his willingness to perceive nationalism as an emotional reality and a potential force for revolution in a pamphlet, "The Crisis in Social Democracy" published in 1916. Nevertheless, she was an admirer of Lenin and once commented to a colleague, "Have a good look at that man; that's Lenin. Observe his obstinate, self-willed skull."

Luxemburg was a participant in the 1905–1906 revolution in Warsaw and was briefly imprisoned. She managed to escape and resumed her political and revolutionary activities in Berlin. In 1914, together with Karl Liebknecht and Franz Mehring, she founded the Spartakusbund ("Spartacus League"), which opposed World War I. The Spartacists followed the teachings of Marx (q.v.) and Engels, and the only possible benefit to derive from the war, in their opinion, was to further their revolutionary aims, or to achieve, in Luxemburg's phrase, "a great united German republic."

Luxemburg spent most of the war in prison and was only released in 1918 when revolution had broken out in Germany. In the latter part of that year, she and Liebknecht transformed the Spartacus League into the German Communist party. Liebknecht started to plan a Spartacist putsch in Berlin, although this move was opposed by Luxemburg.

On November 11, 1918, the war ended, to be replaced with a very real threat of separatism and revolution within conquered Germany. Friedrich Ebert, a leader of the Social Democrat party became the last chancellor of the German Empire. At the same time, Liebknecht tried to proclaim a German soviet republic. As anarchy threatened to overwhelm Germany and its democratic institutions, Ebert and his fellow Social Democrats concentrated their fire on the Spartacists.

The armistice in fact spelled the death knell of the Spartacist League. Rosa Luxemburg had intended to forge a link with the Independent Socialists, an eventuality that would have seriously damaged the ambitions of Ebert and the Social Democrats. The Frei Korps, an organization of alienated and out-of-work army officers (who became the forerunners of the Nazis), were only too willing to be turned loose against workers and

Rosa Luxemburg addressing a gathering.

liberals. On January 16, 1919, columns of Frei Korps officers entered Berlin, where they brutally broke up the Spartacist ranks. Rosa Luxemburg was beaten unconscious when she was dragged from the Hotel Eden where she was being interrogated. She was shot in the head and her body was thrown into a canal. Liebknecht was taken by car and on the way to the Moabit Prison his captors shot him in cold blood.

Rosa Luxemburg's thinking embodied the concept of supranationalism: she developed a universal socialist philosophy that transcended and was intended to replace national boundaries. She saw the defeat of capitalism as an inevitable and essential target in the economic struggle of the proletariat and developed her economic theories in several articles and especially in her book, *The Accumulation of Capital* (1915).

Perhaps her major intellectual contribution to the theory of class struggle was the thesis that in an age of international imperialism locked in a struggle to the death with international socialism, the historical significance and importance of nations was bound to disappear. At the same time, she showed great sensitivity to the needs of a strong and meaningful democratic system, as can be seen from the following prophetic words written in 1918 in a comment on the Bolshevik revolution: "With the repression of political life in the land as a whole, life in the Soviets must also become more and more crippled. Without general elections, without unrestricted freedom of the press and assembly, without a free struggle of opinion, life

dies out in every public institution, becomes a mere semblance of life in which only the bureaucracy remains as the active element."
P. Frölich, *Rosa Luxemburg*, 1972.
P. Nettl, *Rosa Luxemburg*, 1966.
M. A. Waters (ed.), *Rosa Luxemburg Speaks*, 1970.

LUZZATTI, LUIGI (1841–1927) Italian prime minister and economist. Luigi Luzzatti was born into a prominent Venetian Jewish family. Raised an Orthodox Jew, he drifted away from his strict upbringing. He dedicated his time and energy to tackling social and economic issues, in order to better the conditions of the poor.

In 1863 Luzzatti received his degree in jurisprudence, but never practiced law. Instead, he preferred the science of economics and became a professor of economics and constitutional law. His passion for economics finally earned him acclaim as one of the greatest financiers and economists in Europe.

Luzzati's first achievement was the establishment of a mutual aid society for gondoliers in Venice. However, the organization was not approved by the Austrian authorities and, in 1863, Luzzatti was expelled from the city as a revolutionary.

After his expulsion Luzzatti went from city to city studying the situation of the working class and looked for opportunities to start mutual benefit societies. He believed that these societies would assemble all men together as brothers. The societies, as he saw them would, "assure you a subsidy in case of illness, a pension fund provides for your old age, workmen's associations enable you to acquire your own homes, cooperative warehouses provide food and other necessaries at a low price."

Another scheme in which Luzzatti participated was the establishment of a people's bank. The first one, comprising 180 small farmers, became a model for other banking institutions.

Luzzatti was called to Florence by the minister of agriculture, industry, and commerce to be his general secretary in 1869. However, he was not confirmed to the post until 1871 because he was too young to be elected to Parliament. Shortly after his thirtieth birthday he was confirmed by Parliament and officially began his political career as a parliamentarian. He served almost continuously for the next fifty years as a right-wing politician in the Chamber of Deputies. He spent his last year in politics in the Senate.

Luzzatti's years in government were turbulent times in Italy. He saw the country's transition from Italian union to fascism under Benito Mussolini.

In 1891–1892, Luzzatti served in the cabinet as treasury minister. He held the post three other times (1896–1898, 1903–1906, and for a few months in 1920) in different governments. He was responsible for twenty-four commercial treaties, including the 1898 agreement which put an end to the tariff war between France and Italy.

Luzzatti joined the Sonnino cabinet in 1910 as the minister of agriculture, industry, and commerce. Together the two men managed to reduce the treasury deficit and secure conversion of public debts, thus saving Italy from bankruptcy.

In 1910 Sonnino (whose father was Jewish) resigned and Luzzatti took over as prime minister and interior minister. Though his time as prime minister was short-lived, Luzzatti did manage to enact important legislation such as laws against pornography, white-slave traffic and cruelty to animals. The next year he was ousted by socialist and left-wing leaders.

During his many years in parliament, Luzzatti was also credited with initiating the law for compulsory accident insurance and many regulations regarding emigration. His contributions to the country were recognized in 1906, when he was given the honorary post of minister of state.

From 1906 until his death, during periods when he was not in the parliament, he resumed lecturing in constitutional law. He was also a well-respected economic adviser, receiving inquiries from political leaders throughout Europe.

While he had drifted away from the practice of his religion, Luzzatti always maintained a deep respect for Judaism. He was outspoken for the cause of European Jewry, demanding civil rights on behalf of Romanian Jews. He also supported Zionist activities in Palestine, especially the agricultural settlements.

Luzzatti's support of oppressed groups also extended to the other religions, namely the Christian Armenians. Late in his life he wrote, "I am a theist without a particular church, and I defend all who are persecuted for their faith."
C. L. Villari, "Luigi Luzzatti," in *Twelve Jews*, 1934.

LUZZATTO, MOSES HAYYIM (known as Ramhal; 1707–1747) Mystic, poet, and moralist in Italy. Born in Padua into a wealthy and scholarly family, at an early age he was acclaimed for his broad learning in both Jewish and Italian culture, as well as in general sciences and languages. By the time he was fifteen he ceased formal education and established a mystical group in his home. When he was twenty, he experienced visions of a heavenly mentor who "revealed" to him celestial secrets that he wrote down; most of these works were lost. He conveyed these doctrines to his circle of intimates to whom he indicated that he might be the Messiah, seeing himself as a reincarnation of Moses. He also indulged in "practical Kabbalah" (magical practices) to attain supernatural powers. When this became known to the local rabbis, they were alarmed, especially as the memory of the bitter experience of the pseudomessianic movement led by Shabbetai Tzevi (q.v.) was still strong. Under these pressures Luzzatto agreed in 1730 to conceal his esoteric writings and not to convey his kabbalistic views to others. However, he continued to be persecuted and left Italy for Amsterdam, where he earned a living as a diamond polisher. Here too the local rabbis opposed him and put his writings under a ban. He refrained from public expression of his views but he enjoyed a measure of tranquility and was able to write his ethical work *Mesillat Yesharim* ("Path of the Upright"). In 1743 he moved to Eretz Israel, probably out of messianic motivations. He settled in Safed, where his wife and son died in a plague. He moved to Acre, where he himself died a year later.

In retrospect, he is seen as one of the fathers of modern Hebrew literature. He formulated a new theory of Hebrew versification, preferring the neoclassical Italian style to the medieval, and his verse greatly influenced subsequent Hebrew poetry. His chief literary activity was the composition of three plays: *The Story of Samson*, in which his deep identification with the hero may stem from messianic reasons; *Tower of Strength*, influenced by contemporary Italian pastoral drama, which some see as a kabbalistic allegory; and *Praise to the Righteous*, which reflects his own experiences as a persecuted victim. These dramas are secular works, with a biblical Hebrew style. He also wrote on philosophy, logic, rhetoric, polemics, and Talmudic dialectics.

Path of the Upright became one of the most popular of all Jewish ethical works. It expounds ascending grades of ethical conduct and was studied for moral and religious self-discipline.
S. Ginzburg, *The Life and Works of Moses Chaim Luzzatto*, 1931.
M. Waxman, *History of Jewish Literature*, vol. 3, 1960.

M

MACK, JULIAN (1866–1943) U.S. jurist, communal leader, and Zionist. Born in San Francisco, he obtained his LL.B. at Harvard and pursued graduate studies at Harvard, Berlin, and Leipzig before opening a law practice in Chicago. He was professor of law at Northwestern University from 1895 to 1902 and then at the University of Chicago from 1902 to 1911. From 1903 to 1911 he was a judge of the circuit court of Cook County, Illinois, and in 1913 was appointed a United States circuit court judge. He fought for a progressive approach to juvenile delinquency and was active in the efforts to establish and then to expand a juvenile court system in the United States. In 1908 he chaired a White House conference on children.

Mack was prominent in Jewish affairs and in 1906 was one of the fifty founding members of the American Jewish Committee. At the end of World War I he played an important role in persuading that non-Zionist body to support the Balfour Declaration. He himself was drawn to Zionism by his belief in American cultural pluralism, seeing it as a social movement and as part of the historical evolution of the American (not so much the Jewish) people. In December 1916 he stated: "This country has large numbers of nationalities fusing together into a new nation, the American nation, of which we are part. Each strain that goes to make up the American nation will be preserved as part of their American nationality."

From 1918 to 1921 Mack was president of the Zionist Organization of America (ZOA). He was the first president of the American Jewish Congress, established at this time, and the first chairman of the Committee of Jewish Delegations, the Jewish representation at the Paris Peace Conference. In 1919 he led a delegation to President Woodrow Wilson as a result of which the president endorsed the Balfour Declaration.

In 1921, when Chaim Weizmann (q.v.) visited New York, Mack as president of the ZOA, presented him with the ZOA's conditions for supporting branches in the United States of Keren Hayesod, the fund — raising arm of the World Zionist Organization, which Weizmann was planning to establish. Mack was closely associated with Justice Louis D. Brandeis (q.v.) and the so-called Mack-

Brandeis group believed that the Jewish National Home in Palestine should be built up through investments rather than through philanthropy. They objected to combining investments with donations and felt that the Keren Hayesod should only be concerned with donations. Weizmann rejected what he called Mack's ultimatum and, at a bitter showdown at the 1921 ZOA Convention, Mack and Brandeis were defeated and resigned from the executive of the ZOA. However, Mack remained a member of the organization and at his death was a vice-president.

Mack and Brandeis then concentrated their efforts on building up investments in Palestine, and Mack was active in the Palestine Economic Corporation and many other pro-Palestine bodies. In 1930 he stressed that he saw Palestine as a national and not only a spiritual center.

Mack was a member of the Harvard Board of Overseers in which capacity he took a prominent part in opposing attempts to place a quota on the number of Jews admitted to the university (1922).

MAGNES, JUDAH LEIB (1877–1948) U.S. Reform rabbi; first chancellor of the Hebrew University of Jerusalem. He was born in San Francisco and educated at the Hebrew Union College, Cincinnati, where he was ordained as a Reform rabbi. His Zionism was unusual in the anti-Zionist college and his first student essay was entitled "Palestine — or Death" — death being assimilation. He also studied in a number of German universities, receiving his Ph.D. at Heidelberg in 1902.

Magnes's first pulpit was in Brooklyn, and to many his appearance on the rabbinical scene heralded the arrival of a new-style American-Jewish rabbinical leader, brought up in the American west, whose enthusiasms included baseball. He joined the infant American Zionist Federation and took part as an English secretary in the 1906 Zionist Congress in Basel. Influenced by the teachings of Ahad Ha'Am (q.v.), he sought to restrain the nationalistic element of the Zionist movement. In 1906 Magnes became rabbi of New York's elite Temple Emanu-El, but resigned in 1910 since he found its outlook too assimilationist. The young rabbi had a broad appeal to Zionists and immi-

Judah L. Magnes speaking at the opening of the academic year of the Hebrew University, Jerusalem, 1933. Chaim Nachman Bialik is on his right, Menachem Ussishkin, on his left.

grant radicals (for his social views). For the next twelve years he tried to create a New York democratic community structure, a *Kehilla*, that would encompass all facets of the New York Jewish community and serve as a roof organization for Jewish bodies. He won a reputation as a maverick prepared to dissent on all matters of conscience and as a communal gadfly. His popularity waned during World War I as a result of his uncompromising espousal of pacifism. However, he remained prominent in all Jewish affairs and was among the founders of the American Jewish Committee, the Joint Distribution Committee, and the New York Board of Jewish Education.

In 1923 Magnes moved to Jerusalem, where he was deeply involved in the preparations to open the Hebrew University. He served as its first chancellor, from 1925 to 1935. The university became his passion and he watched over and directed its growth and expansion, raising funds and creating its faculty, based largely on Jewish scholars from Europe (after 1933, especially from Germany). However his program and administration came under severe criticism from Albert Einstein (q.v.) and Chaim Weizmann (q.v.) and after a period of internal bitterness, he was relieved in 1935 of the post of chancellor and "promoted" to the largely nominal position of president.

The tension with Weizmann also extended to Magnes's political views. Magnes developed plans for a binational Arab-Jewish state and was severely critical of Zionist policies. Pinning his hopes on the moderate Arab leadership, he spoke of the Jewish community in Palestine becoming integrated into an Arab Near Eastern federation. He was active in the Ihud and Berit Shalom organizations, which sought a peaceful arrangement between Arabs and Jews in Palestine. He was aware that while a number of prominent Jews in Palestine (such as Martin Buber [q.v.]) supported his views, they had

no influential Arab counterparts. The moderate Arabs were cowered into silence by the radical leadership under the mufti of Jerusalem. Magnes opposed the 1937 proposal to partition Palestine.

The events in Europe in the 1930s led him for a time to abandon his faith in pacifism and he actively supported the Palestine war effort in World War II. However, during the war he led the opposition to the Biltmore Declaration, in which the Zionists for the first time came out with the demand for a Jewish state. He saw this as a declaration of war on the Arabs. Although claiming to be a loyal Zionist, he maintained that every Zionist group had the right to pursue its views as it saw fit and he lobbied the U.S. State Department to oppose the official Zionist line. Magnes fought the U.N. partition resolution of 1947, fearing that an Arab-Israel war would destroy the country and his university. A few days before the establishment of the State of Israel, he was in America trying to persuade President Harry S. Truman to change his support for the U.N. resolution. He died in New York a few months later.

N. Bentwich, *For Zion's Sake: A Biography of Judah L. Magnes*, 1954.

A. A. Goren, *Dissenter in Zion: From the writings of Judah L. Magnes*, 1982.

MAHARAL See Judah Löw ben Bezalel

MAHARIL See Mollin, Jacob

MAHLER, GUSTAV (1860–1911) Austrian composer and conductor. Mahler was born in Kalischt, Bohemia, to an Orthodox family. He grew up during a period when Austria, although tolerant toward its Jews, left no doubt as to their status as outsiders. Mahler was the second of fourteen children (only six of whom survived to maturity), and his parents' relationship was reportedly a stormy one. His emotionally stressful family life and his Jewish background seem to have had an effect on his music. Later in his life he said, "I am thrice homeless, as a native of Bohemia in Austria, as an Austrian among Germans, and as a Jew throughout all the world. Everywhere an intruder, never welcomed."

Mahler's musical talent manifested itself from an early age. As a child he was found in his grandparents' attic playing an old piano. His father encouraged his natural talent and by the age of nine Mahler was skilled enough to give music lessons to another boy. At age ten he gave his first public recital and that same year was sent to study in a high school in Prague. He continued his music lessons with a local Prague family, but when his father discovered that the boy was being mistreated there, he took him home.

At fifteen, Mahler was taken to see Julius Epstein of the Vienna Conservatory. After hearing Mahler play, Epstein declared, "He is a born musician....I cannot possibly be wrong." Mahler entered the conservatory, and concentrated on composing and learning to conduct. His genius was soon recognized by his fellow students who called him "another Schubert."

After his graduation from the conservatory in 1878, Mahler began to compose and conduct. He secured conducting appointments through the 1880s in several operatic companies in Kassel, Prague and Leipzig. His reputation grew; his performances were praised for their precision of ensemble and enthusiasm, but criticized for excessive bodily movements and unconventional tempos.

His personal life was also somewhat unconventional and emotionally tumultuous. While at Kassel, he experienced an unhappy love affair with one of the singers, Johanna Richter. In Leipzig Mahler met Carl von Weber, grandson of the great composer, and began working on the grandfather's unfinished works. In the course of this work, Mahler had an affair with Weber's wife, which inspired an intensely creative period in his composing.

In 1888 Mahler became musical director of the Budapest Opera. There he earned a reputation as an administrator as well as conductor, as he went about improving the quality of the company's performance and its profitability. However, that same year, Mahler suffered the loss of both his parents and one of his sisters, leaving him head of the rest of the family.

Mahler left Budapest to become chief conductor at the Hamburg Municipal Theater in 1891. He had begun work on his Seco d Symphony and played part of it for Hans von Bülow, then conductor of the city's symphony concerts. Bülow's admiration for Mahler's conducting ability did not extend to his composing ability, but ironically Bülow's funeral in 1894 was the impetus for Mahler's completion of the Second Symphony.

Mahler's reputation continued to grow and he appeared throughout Europe in London, Moscow,

Munich, and Budapest. In 1897 he converted to Catholicism to gain a position as Kapellmeister at the Vienna Court Opera. He soon rose to be artistic director and led the company into a golden age. In the midst of this success, he met and married nineteen-year-old Alma Schindler (daughter of painter Anton Schindler) in 1901. Their marriage was turbulent, and at one point Mahler consulted Sigmund Freud (q.v.) about his marital problems. Creatively, the period in which he was married was a fruitful experience for Mahler; he composed seven symphonies despite the demands of his work as conductor and artistic director.

In 1907 tragedy struck Mahler and his family. His five-year-old daughter died of scarlet fever and Mahler himself discovered that he had a heart ailment. He resigned from the Vienna Court Opera that year and accepted a contract with the Metropolitan Opera, New York.

He made his debut in New York on January 1, 1908. The following summer he composed *Das Lied von der Erde* ("The Song of the Earth"). In 1909 he left the Metropolitan Opera to join the New York Philharmonic. Two years later he fell seriously ill with a bacterial infection. He left for Paris to obtain treatment and then retired to a sanitarium in Vienna, where he died that year. A few months later, Bruno Walter (q.v.) paid him tribute by conducting the first performance of *Das Lied von der Erde* in Munich.

D. Cooke, *Gustav Mahler: 1860–1911*, 1980.

E. Garteberg, *Mahler: The Man and His Music*, 1978.

D. Mitchell, *Gustav Mahler: The Early Years*, 1980.

Gustav Mahler. Etching by Rudolf Hermann.

MAIMONIDES, MOSES (Moses ben Maimon; known as *Rambam* from the acronym of Rabbi Moses ben Maimon; 1135–1204). Greatest Jewish thinker of the Middle Ages; philosopher, Talmudist, and physician. He was born in Cordova, Spain, into an illustrious family; his father was a noted Talmudist as well as a mathematician and astronomer. When Maimonides was thirteen, Cordova was captured by a fanatical Islamic sect and to escape persecution the family fled, wandering for ten years in Spain, and eventually reaching Fez in Morocco (1160). At the age of sixteen, Maimonides had already written a treatise on logical terminology and in Fez he devoted himself to studies in theology and medicine. Fez was also under the rule of Islamic zealots and Maimonides had to be extremely circumspect, although allegations that he became a nominal Muslim have never been proved. The situation became so hazardous that in 1165 the family sailed for Eretz Israel, then in Christian hands. They lived for several months in Acre, visited Jerusalem and Hebron, but conditions were too oppressive for permanent settlement. The family moved on to Egypt, where Maimonides was to spend the rest of his life.

In Cairo, he went into business in precious stones with his brother David but when David was drowned — with the family fortune — in the Indian Ocean on a business trip, Maimonides abandoned commerce and earned his living as a physician. His reputation spread and he was appointed physician to the grand vizier. He has left a description of his grueling daily life, which included attending court and attending to patients, returning home to his hours of private practice, and then devoting his Sabbaths to community affairs as the recognized leader of Egyptian Jewry. He also had to find time for his studies and writing his classic comprehensive code of Jewish law, his philosophical masterpiece, and his widely acclaimed medical tractates. His death was marked by public mourning throughout the Jewish world, which regarded him as the outstanding Jew of his time. For three days both Jews and Muslims mourned in Fustat, near Cairo, where he had lived. His body was taken to the Holy Land and buried in Tiberias, where his grave has been a site of pilgrimage ever since. The tombstone reads "From Moses [of the Bible] to Moses [Maimonides], there never arose another like Moses."

His first major work was the commentary on the Mishnah, the basic rabbinic code, completed in 1168. It was written in Arabic, but most of it was translated into Hebrew during his lifetime. An introduction to the Talmud it sought to deduce the underlying principles and main legal teachings of the traditional laws. Most of the book is an exposition of Jewish law as contained in the Mishnah, but it includes three lengthy introductions of special importance; one is an essay on the transmission of the oral law from the time of Moses down to the Rabbis, which includes a lengthy excursus on prophecy; the second contains the principles of the

Traditional likeness of Maimonides with a reproduction of his signature. Woodcut.

Jewish faith, the first attempt to formulate a Jewish creed; and the third is an introduction to the sayings of the fathers, in which he expounds his system of ethics.

In preparation for his great work of codification, he wrote *The Book of the Commandments* in which he lists the 613 commandments derived by the rabbis from the Mosaic Law. His codification, completed about 1178, was called *Mishneh Torah* ("Repetition of the Law," that is, Deuteronomy), also known as *Yad Hazakah* ("Strong Hand," because the numerical value of the word "Yad" is fourteen, corresponding to the fourteen divisions of the book). This was an epoch-making composition as it was the first attempt to organize the diffuse laws of the Talmud in a logical code. It was an original synthesis, based on a clear systemization, written in a lucid Hebrew. Its scope was all-inclusive, embracing all Talmudic legislation and not only those sections which remained immediately relevant after the destruction of the Temple; he codified laws concerning sacrifices, agriculture, and the coming of the Messiah with the same attention as he devoted to laws of the synagogue and business relations. The 19th-century scholar, Heinrich Graetz (q.v.) compared the Talmud to a "Daedalian maze in which one can hardly find one's way even with the thread of Ariadne," whereas the *Mishneh Torah* was "a well-contrived ground-plan with wings, halls, apartments, and chambers through which a stranger might pass without a guide. Only a mind accustomed to think clearly and systematically and filled with a genius of order could have planned and built a structure like this." From the mass of material in his sources, Maimonides determined the final legal decision. The book came under criticism for its failure to identify the sources of these decisions but nevertheless became a standard Jewish legal classic.

His other great work, written in Arabic, was his *Guide of the Perplexed (Hebrew, Moreh Nevukhim)*, written 1185–1190, the outstanding Jewish theological-philosophical book of the Middle Ages. Through its translation in Latin, it also reached the Christian world and influenced Christian theologians. Maimonides was greatly influenced by Aristotelianism as transmitted in his time and the *Guide* is primarily an attempt to reconcile Judaism and Aristotelianism. Maimonides was essentially rational in his outlook, and where the Bible appeared to clash with reason, he sought to explain the contradiction by the use of allegory. He deals with the problems that engaged the medieval philosophers: creation, the nature of God and his relationship with the world and with man, the nature of prophecy, ethics, free will, immortality, and the end of time. He constructed a complete system of thought, embracing God and the universe in its entirety. His rationalism can be seen, for example, in his downplaying of miracles and discouragement of messianic speculation. But while usually accepting the thought of Aristotle, he was not prepared to follow him in his theory of creation based on the eternity of matter and insisted on the traditional Jewish view that God created the world out of nothing.

He also wrote a number of pastoral letters which were widely regarded. One of these, sent to the Jews of Yemen who had been swept by belief in a pseudomessiah, warns against messianic pretenders and unwarranted expectations.

Maimonides' authority was recognized by Jewish communities that turned to him for his advice and rulings. The Egyptian community formalized his leadership by giving him the title of *nagid* (leader) and the regard in which he was held was so high that this title was made hereditary and his descendants remained the leaders of Egyptian Jewry for several generations. At the same time some of his views aroused controversy in the Jewish world, and the more traditional contested his reinterpretations and rationalizations, leading to bans on the study of his works in certain places. For over a century the controversy between the Maimonists and anti-Maimonists split the Jewish world, but eventually the views of Maimonides were accepted by all.

A. Cohen, *The Teachings of Maimonides*, 1927.
D. Hartman, *Maimonides: Torah and Philosophic Quest*, 1976.
A. J. Heschel, *Maimonides*, 1982.
D. Yellin and I. Abrahams, *Maimonides*, 1903.

MALAMUD, BERNARD (1914–1986) U.S. novelist. He was born in Brooklyn and educated at New York City College and Columbia University. He was a high school teacher (at Erasmus Hall and at other New York City evening high schools) and college instructor (at Oregon State University; Bennington College, Vermont; and Harvard University), as well as a prolific American-Jewish fiction writer, some of whose works have been made into films. His novels included *The Natural* (1952), *The Assistant* (1957), *A New Life* (1961), *The Fixer* (1966), and *Dubin's Lives* (1979), and among his short story collections are *The Magic Barrel* (1958), *Idiots First* (1963), *Pictures of Fidelman* (1969), and *Rembrandt's Hat* (1973). His detailed portrayals of life in the East European shtetl and in the largely immigrant American-Jewish community of New York City can be traced to the fact that Malamud was the child of Russian Jewish immigrants. His mother's original family name — Fidelman — supplied the name of one of Malamud's artist-protagonists, Arthur Fidelman.

Strongly influenced by such masters of realistic fiction as Dostoyevsky, Malamud paints starkly realistic portraits, for example, the conditions of imprisonment suffered by Yakov Bok, a simple Jewish artisan accused of ritual Jewish murder in tsarist Russia at the beginning of the twentieth century (*The Fixer*, 1966). Malamud sometimes ventures into the realm of science fiction — as in *God's Grace*, where the only survivors of a nuclear war are a Jew, Calvin Cohn, and a chimpanzee — or fantasy — as in "The Jewbird" (in the collection *Idiots First)* which has been described as a parody

---

MAIMONIDES' THIRTEEN PRINCIPLES OF FAITH

1. The existence of God, which is perfect and sufficient unto itself and which is the cause of the existence of all other beings.
2. God's unity, which is unlike all other kinds of unity.
3. God must not be conceived in bodily terms, and the anthropomorphic expressions applied to God in scripture have to be understood in a metaphorical sense.
4. God is eternal.
5. God alone is to be worshiped and obeyed. There are no mediating powers able freely to grant man's petitions, and intermediaries must not be invoked.
6. Prophecy.
7. Moses is unsurpassed by any other prophet.
8. The entire Torah was given to Moses.
9. Moses' Torah will not be abrogated or superseded by another divine law nor will anything be added to or taken away from it.
10. God knows the actions of men.
11. God rewards those who fulfill the commandments of the Torah, and punishes those who transgress them.
12. The coming of the Messiah.
13. The resurrection of the dead.

Bernard Malamud.

of Poe's "The Raven." Nonetheless, Malamud used primarily realistic settings, going beyond those settings by means of symbolism and dream-daydream images.

While the majority of Malamud's characters are Jewish, he wanted to be recognized as an American, rather than as an American-Jewish, writer. His first novel, *The Natural*, is his only one without any Jewish characters. The book is an allegory about a baseball star who climbs to the pinnacle of success and who, through his own uncontrollable passions, suffers humiliating defeat and disaster. However, the presence of Jewish characters in a Malamud work does not necessarily signify that this particular work is exclusively — or even primarily — concerned with Jewish themes. Whereas his Pulitzer Prize-winning fourth novel, *The Fixer*, is modeled to a large extent on the sufferings of Menachem Mendel Beilis (q.v.), a Jew accused of ritual murder by the tsarist Russian authorities in 1913, the work can be seen not only as the portrayal of anti-Semitism in action, but also as a universal study of the individual struggling against the forces of injustice and cruelty, with the Jew as a mythic representation par excellence of all such individuals. The Jewish identity of Seymour Levin, the central protagonist in *A New Life*, his third novel, is suggested by the surname and alluded to in a veiled statement only toward the end of the novel; his Jewishness does not play a pivotal role in the work and he is chiefly a symbol of the struggle for academic freedom and integrity in McCarthy-era America.

Malamud often displays a flair for broad satire, as in, for example, *A New Life*, and one of his best known short stories, "Angel Levine," about a black Jewish angel who helps rescue a modern-day Job figure, a Jewish tailor named Manischewitz. Nonetheless, Malamud acknow-ledged that sadness constituted a major element in his work: "People say I write so much about misery... [but] you write about what you write best."

I. Alter, *The Good Man's Dilemma: Social Criticism in the Fiction of Bernard Malamud*, 1981.

E. G. Avery, *Rebels and Victims: The Fiction of Richard Wright and Bernard Malamud*, 1979.

S. Cohen, *Bernard Malamud and the Trial of Love*, 1974.

J. Salzberg, *Critical Essays on Bernard Malamud*, 1987.

MANASSEH BEN ISRAEL (1604–1657) Rabbi and scholar in Amsterdam; foremost advocate of Jewish resettlement in England. The son of Portuguese Marranos who had escaped from the Inquisition, he was baptized Manoel Dias Soeiro in Madeira, but renamed after his parents reached Holland. Manasseh (or Menasseh, as he spelt his name) showed early promise as a writer and preacher; he studied under Rabbi Isaac Uzziel, whom he succeeded as rabbi of the Neveh Shalom congregation at the age of eighteen. Versatile, fluent in several languages, and widely read, he became an illustrious spokesman for the Jewish faith and people, admired by fellow Jews and Christian scholars alike. He established the first

Hebrew printing press in Amsterdam (1626), which relied on new techniques and published more than seventy different works. He later headed a Talmudic college.

Although his *Thesourou dos Dinim* (1645–1647) was a guide to Jewish law for newly arrived Portuguese Marranos, practically all of the books published by Manasseh ben Israel had the educated non-Jewish reader in mind. He wrote a series of theological works in Latin (1635–1642); the monumental *Conciliador* in Spanish (1632–1651); *Piedra gloriosa* (1655), with biblical engravings by Rembrandt, who also painted and etched Manasseh's portrait; and, apart from other books, an unpublished sequel to Josephus' (q.v.) *Antiquities*. It was the first volume of his *Conciliador*, an attempt to harmonize apparently conflicting passages of scripture, that chiefly impressed the wider world. For many Christians, Manasseh ben Israel was the outstanding Jewish savant of the age: Sweden's learned Queen Christina and the Swiss Hebraist, Johannes Buxtorf II, were among those who corresponded with him; Queen Henrietta Maria, wife of England's Charles I, visited his synagogue to hear him preach.

Fame did not lessen Manasseh's awareness of Jewish communities elsewhere threatened with extinction. In 1644 he heard a statement made under oath by Antonio de Montezinos, a Marrano adventurer, relating his encounter with "Hevrews" in Ecuador who still maintained biblical practices and could recite the *Shema* (the Jewish credo). This new discovery of Israel's Ten Lost Tribes made a great impression on Manasseh ben Israel, for whom it had theological — perhaps even messianic — significance. By 1649, he was attaching further importance to the tale as "New Christians" were hounded in Portugal and Cossack massacres drove Ashkenazim westward from Poland. If there were persecuted Jews in need of a refuge, there was also a land, England, now governed by Bible-loving Puritans, where no Jewish community had existed since 1290. Quoting biblical prophecies about the dispersion and ingathering of Israel, Manasseh published *The Hope of Israel* (1650), an overtly messianic tract in Latin and Spanish which he dedicated to England's Parliament.

Thanks to the author's broad hint that no Christian millennium could take place without a Jewish return to England (*Angle-terre*, signifying "the end of the earth"), this book appealed especially to the predominant English religious movements of the time, while the general argument promoted English sympathy for homeless Jews. Oliver Cromwell's Latin secretary, John Milton, arranged for an English translation to be printed and it achieved the status of a best-seller, running to three consecutive editions. Though impressed by Manasseh's arguments and well-disposed toward victims of Catholic persecution, Cromwell had the very practical advantages of Jewish resettlement in mind, at a time when the Dutch and English were bitter commercial rivals.

Manasseh ben Israel headed a small delegation that arrived in London (Septmeber 1655) and submitted Humble Addresses to the Lord Protector in behalf of the Jewish Nation, restating the prophetic theme, as well as a petition for the "free exercise of our own Religion." Knowing that city merchants and Puritan divines had come out in opposition, the Council of State showed no enthusiasm for the admission of Jews who, it was rumored, aimed to buy Saint Paul's Cathedral and turn it into a synagogue! The Whitehall Conference summoned by Cromwell met several times (December 4–18) but proved no more helpful, apart from reaching one notable conclusion: that there was no legal impediment to a Jewish community, since the expulsion of 1290 had been a royal (not a parliamentary) decree. While hoping and waiting for a successful end to these negotiations, Manasseh published his *Vindiciae Judaeorum* (1656), a trenchant reply to the anti-Semitic bigotry of William Prynne.

It was a sudden threat to a few dozen Marranos living in London that decided the issue. Facing arrest and expropriation as "Spanish Catholic" aliens, these merchants begged for Manasseh ben Israel's signature on a petition of their own to Cromwell (March 24, 1656), acknowledging that they were in fact "Hebrews" and requesting permission to worship and bury their dead accordingly. Three months later, Council of State granted the merchants' request, although someone hacked the minuted decision out of the Council's order book after the death of Cromwell. This tacit arrangement suited the ex-Marranos perfectly, but it was a crushing blow to Manasseh ben Israel, who had expected far more of Cromwell. Convinced that his great mission had failed he returned to the Netherlands a broken man and died there shortly afterward.

Following the Restoration, Charles II's Privy Council upheld the enactment, thus allowing any Jew to settle and live in England. No special conditions were attached to Jewish citizenship, and Manasseh's "failure" therefore emerged as a historic success.

C. Roth, *A Life of Menasseh ben Israel*, 1934.
L. Wolf, *Menasseh ben Israel's Mission to Oliver Cromwell*, 1901.

MANDELSTAM, OSIP EMILYEVICH (1891–1937 or 1938)

One of the most important Russian poets of the 20th century. He was born in Warsaw, the son of a leather merchant and piano teacher, but grew up and spent most of his life in Leningrad (Saint Petersburg), which was by no means normal for Jews at the time. On graduating from school in 1907 he traveled to France, where he studied in Paris; later, he attended the Universities of Heidelberg (1909–1910) and Saint Petersburg.

Of his childhood, he wrote that he was surrounded by "the chaos of Judaism... that alien womb whence I had emerged, which I feared, about which I felt vague intimations, and which... I was always trying to escape." In about 1911 he converted to Russian Orthodoxy — perhaps little more than a formal step designed to free him from the restrictions imposed on Jews under the tsarist regime.

Mandelstam joined the poetic movement Acmeism, whose other leading figures were Nikolai Gumilyev (executed in 1921) and Anna Akhmatova, and was the author of some of the movement's programmatic articles, such as "The Dawn of Acmeism" (1913). The movement was opposed to the vagueness and mysticism of symbolism, and proposed setting Russian poetry on a new course of clarity, directness, and precision. Acmeism sought to take its place in the general cultural tradition of Western Europe. Mandelstam was fascinated by Mediterranean culture and wove many references to the themes of classical Greece into his poetry.

In 1913 he published his first collection of poems, *Kamen* ("Stone"); his second book, *Tristia* (1922) established his position as a poet of supreme importance. The tone of the poems, a quiet melancholy, contrasts with the noise of the revolution and civil war: "I have practiced leavetaking in the quiet of the night shilling/ Among the loose flowing of a woman's hair."

The book was reprinted the following year under the title *Vtoraya kniga* ("Second Book"), and was followed two years later by a volume of autobiographical prose, *Shum vremini* ("The Noise of

Osip E. Mandelstam. Portrait by Picasso.

Time"). In 1928 this was reissued in an expanded form under the title *Yegipetskaya marka* ("The Egyptian Stamp"). In the title story Mandelstam portrays an intellectual ill-adapted to the new system. In the last book published during his lifetime, *Stikhotvoreniya* ("Poems," 1928), he expresses his despair: "Your spinal cord is broken, My beautiful, pitiable century."

Much of his poetry is hard to assimilate without repeated reading, but offers great rewards to patient application.

From about 1923 Mandelstam began to find it difficult to publish his creative work. Within a few years he was effectively silenced and an object of increasing official persecution. He and his wife, Nadezhda, who knew English, French, and German far better than the poet, eked out a living a translator, but by the mid-1930s they were left without any means of support by a disapproving regime and became dependent on the charity of friends to prevent them from starvation. Aware of the fate of writers who did not support the regime, Mandelstam once commented prophetically, "Only in Russia is poetry respected — it gets people killed. Is there anywhere else where poetry is so common a motive for murder?"

Mandelstam's downfall came through a fourteen-line poem whose circulation he did not try to prevent, which was highly critical of Stalin, and mocked him as "the Kremlin mountaineer, the murderer," "the destroyer of peasants." He was first arrested in 1934, and died in mysterious circumstances in Siberia, possibly in a transit camp near Vladivostok. The exact date of his death is also unknown, but seems most likely to have been December 1938.

His later poems, known in English as the "Voronezh Notebooks" (1935–1937) were preserved by his wife, partly by being hidden in small sections with close friends, and largely through her memorizing them. She survived Stalin's terror by teaching English in a succession of provincial towns, and was finally allowed to settle in Moscow in 1964. Mandelstam's rehabilitation began in 1956, when his widow was informed that his sufferings and death had been due to a regrettable oversight. Only in 1973 was an edition of his work published in the Soviet Union, and then with a print run substantially below demand. The memoirs of his widow, Nadezhda (1899–1980) were published in English as *Hope Against Hope* (1970) and *Hope Abandoned* (1974). These works were acclaimed as a major literary achievement in themselves as well as throwing invaluable light on Mandelstam, his circle, and his period.

C. Brown, *Mandelstam*, 1973.

MANÉ-KATZ (Emanuel Katz; 1894–1962) Painter. He was born in Kremenchug in the Ukraine, where his father was a *shamash* (beadle) in a synagogue. At age sixteen, he went to Kiev and enrolled in the fine arts school. To pay his tuition, he ran a lottery that raised enough money for him to continue. Able to afford only a small alcove, he slept on a chest of drawers. Eventually, he was rescued by a relative of his mother, who gave him a monthly allowance and introduced him to the Danish consul, a Jew, who provided Mané-Katz with a place to stay in the consulate.

In 1913 his two patrons gave him money to go to Paris where he entered the Ecole des Beaux Arts. When World War I broke out, he was rejected by both the French and Russian armies because he was too small. Mané-Katz then moved to Saint Petersburg, where he received a scholarship to the modernist art academy of Countess Gazarina. The cubist tendencies of this school influenced his subsequent work. In 1917 he taught for a time in the countess's academy. When the Bolsheviks entered Kharkov, they opened an academy of art and Mané-Katz was named a professor there. The academy closed in 1920 and he decided to return to Paris.

In Paris, Waldemar George helped to organize his first exhibition of forty-one paintings in 1923. In the introduction to the catalogue, George wrote that Mané-Katz's work was always eloquent, and that he moved the viewer by his sense of style and the variety of his vocabulary. From then on, Mané-Katz's work was accepted by the Salon d'Automne regularly and he also exhibited in the Salon des Indépendents and the Salon des Tuileries.

In 1928 he made his first visit to the Middle East, returning to Palestine in 1934. Confronted by its light, his color suddenly burst into brlliant reds, oranges, and yellows. His painting *At the Wailing Wall* (1937) received a gold medal at the International Art Exhibition in Paris. Later, the artist donated it to the president of the new State of Israel.

When the Nazis occupied Paris in 1940, Mané-Katz took refuge in the United States, where he worked for Free France and was a member of France Forever. In 1945 he was one of the first artists to return to Paris from the United States.

His ties to the Paris Jewish community were close and he was interested in Jewish affairs both in France and abroad. He collected Jewish artifacts and his home was full of tablets of the Law, candlesticks, and lions of Judah. On his windows and spread over his bed were ark curtains. In 1949 the Jewish painters and sculptors in Paris organized a union called Amanoth, of which Mané-Katz was president.

France made him chevalier of the Legion of Honor in 1951 and an officer of the Legion in 1962. The French government also purchased his painting, *Place de la Concorde*, for the Paris Museum of Modern Art.

After the war, he continued to visit Palestine and, during the 1948 War of Independence, went to Tel Aviv with an exhibition of sixty paintings. In 1957 the city of Haifa invited him to live in a house and studio that they would provide for him, and thereafter he divided his time between Haifa and Paris. He died in Israel and is buried in Haifa. His home there was turned into the Mané-Katz Museum in 1977.

J. M. Aimot, *Mané-Katz*, 1933.
The Eretz-Yisrael of Mané-Katz, (Mané-Katz Museum), 1988.
The Paris of Mané-Katz, (Mané-Katz Museum), 1989.

MANNHEIM, KARL (1893–1947) Sociologist, educator, and philosopher. Born in Budapest to a well-to-do, middle-class family, he studied German and French languages and literature and philosophy, obtaining a teacher's diploma at the University of Budapest in 1916. After teaching for several years at a Budapest high school, toward the end of World War I he joined the "Sunday Circle" of Georg Lukács (q.v.). His first translations of Hegel appeared from 1911 in a progressive Hungarian periodical. Mannheim's first lecture at the Free School of Liberal Arts in 1917 was entitled "Soul and Culture."

With Max Scholer, Mannheim was the initiator of the sociology of knowledge; his doctoral thesis was entitled "The Structural Analysis of the Theory of Knowledge. After the war, he was a lecturer in philosophy at the teachers' training college of the University of Budapest, but was dismissed after the 1919 revolution. Mannheim then went to Vienna, Freiburg, and eventually to Heidelberg, where he taught philosophy and from 1926 was an assistant professor. His philosphical essays and studies in cognitive theory were published from 1920 on. During the years in Heidelberg, he explored areas of ideological synthesis, types of thought, historicity, problems of utopian philosophy, and the sociology of knowledge and culture. In 1930, he was appointed professor of sociology and economy at the University of Frankfurt. Mannheim edited the series of *Schriften zur Philosophie und Soziologie* ("Writings on Philosophy and Sociology") and during his stay in Germany wrote two of his most important early works: *Ideologie und Utopie* ("Ideology and Utopia," 1929; English translation, 1936), and *Wissensoziologie* ("Sociology of Knowledge," 1931). By this time, he was already considered one of the most important sociologists of knowledge.

When the Nazis came to power in 1933, Mannheim emigrated to England and became professor of sociology at the London School of Economics, and from 1946 held the newly created chair of sociology of education at the University of London. From about 1936, he addressed himself primarily to the "refashioning" of society and to such problems as the planning of a democracy of the masses, the formation of public opinion, and the modernization of teaching methods and their increasing importance in society.

In 1943, he founded and edited the series, *The International Library of Sociology and Social Reconstruction*, in which several of his own books were published. His ideas of the crucial role of an "intellectual elite" in the creation of a democracy "planned for freedom," were the basis of a sharp debate between Marxist and non-Marxist thinkers. In 1946 he was appointed director of the European Division of UNESCO and at the end of that year, the University of Budapest invited him to the chair of sociology which he accepted, but his untimely death prevented him from taking.

Mannheim's other major works are: *Man and Society in an Age of Reconstruction* (1940) and *Diagnosis of Our Time* (1943) and his posthumously published books, *Freedom, Power, and Democratic Planning* (1950) and *Systematic Sociology* (1958).

J. J. P. Magnet, *Sociology of Knowledge; A Critical Analysis of the Systems of Karl Mannheim and Pitirim A. Sorokin*, 1951.

MAPU, ABRAHAM (1808–1867) The father of the modern Hebrew novel. He was born in Kovno (Kaunas), Lithuania, into a poverty-stricken family. His father, a scholar, worked as a Hebrew teacher. The young Mapu was highly gifted: at the age of seven he became one of his father's most advanced students and at twelve, already considered a prodigy, left his father's class for more advanced studies. At the age of fifteen, he began to study the mystical Kabbalah with his father.

He was married at the age of seventeen, and continued to study while living at his father-in-law's home. He became influenced by Hasidic circles, to the chagrin of his parents, and even after being removed from these circles by his mother he continued to frequent the home of the kabbalist rabbi, Elijah Ragoler.

It was in this home that he first encountered a Latin translation of the book of Psalms, which he later recalled was the cornerstone of his secular education. He began to study Latin on his own, a pursuit unheard of in the society in which he was raised and lived, and from there acquired an interest in French, German, and Russian.

When his father-in-law's financial situation deteriorated, Mapu obtained a position as a tutor in a nearby village. His conditions there were even more squalid than those in which he had been brought up.

In 1832 he was appointed tutor to the children of a well-to-do merchant in the small town of Georgenberg, near Kovno. It was here that he was introduced to modern Hebrew literature and to the Haskalah movement of enlightenment, which profoundly influenced him.

A few years later he moved to Rossieny, then the center of the Haskalah movement, with his wife and children, and he lived there for seven years. He began to concentrate on Israel's ancient history and on the Hebrew language.

In 1844 he returned to Kovno to teach in the Hebrew school, remaining there for three years. His financial situation did not improve, and his wife died in 1846. The following year he moved to Vilna for another tutoring position. However, he suffered from the physical violence of his employer,

and he disliked the other enlightened scholars whom he met in the town. Therefore he accepted a teaching position in the government school in Kovno in 1848, where his days of wandering finally ended.

He remarried in 1851, and his financial situation improved slightly. This period was happier than his former years, and were also fruitful, as he became famous as a Hebrew novelist.

His first novel, *Ahavat Zion* ("The Love of Zion"), was published in 1853, although he had begun writing it over two decades earlier. Some critics claim that it had been ready for publication as early as 1844, but that Mapu, lacking in self-confidence and afraid of rejection, kept altering it.

His success with his first literary endeavor encouraged him to continue writing, and his second novel, *Ayit Tzavu'a* ("The Hypocrite"), consisted of five parts, the first of which was published in 1858, and the second and third each three years apart. An edition consisting of all five volumes was published posthumously in 1869. This novel, like the first, was greeted enthusiastically by the enlightened public, although it did not sell many copies.

A third novel, *Hozei Hezyonot* ("The Visionaries"), was sent to the censors at the same time as the first two volumes of *Ayit Tzavu'a*. However, growing opposition from his adversaries of the pietist and Hasidic movements, which had merely subjected his previous novels to delays, suppressed the publication of *Hozei Hezyonot*. The manuscript disappeared, and only a small fragment has survived.

The first part of Mapu's fourth novel, *Ashmat Shomeron* ("The Guilt of Samaria"), was published in 1865, and the second part a year later.

In addition, he published a number of textbooks, designed to improve contemporary educational methods.

His health began to deteriorate in 1860, and, when his right hand became affected with palsy, he began to write with his left hand. Despite the physical agony in his fingers he continued to write and plan further novels, which he did not have time to execute. When in late 1866 he contracted gallstones, he accepted an invitation of his brother, and planned to visit him in Paris, stopping on the way for an operation in Königsberg. However, his health declined sharply en route, and he died in Königsberg.

D. Patterson, *Abraham Mapu: The Creator of the Modern Hebrew Novel*, 1964.

MARCUS, DAVID ("MICKEY") DANIEL (1902–1948) U.S. soldier; adviser to the Israeli army during the War of Independence. He was born in New York to immigrant parents from Romania and received a Jewish and general education. Mickey, as he was affectionately called, grew up in a neighborhood where anti-Semitism was rife and he set about building up his undernourished body in order to defend himself and the honor of his family. In high school he became a good all-around athlete and also had a brilliant academic record. After eighteen months at New York City College he won an appointment to the United States Military Academy, West Point (1920). He continued to excel in athletics and in 1924 received an invitation to the Olympic tryouts. At West Point he was particularly strong in military art and leadership potential.

After graduating in 1924 Marcus studied law and remained in the army until 1927, when he entered government legal service, moving from the Treasury Department to the Attorney General's office. He was appointed Commissioner of Correction by Mayor Fiorello H. La Guardia (q.v.) of New York and in 1934 drew up the plan for the raid on the Welfare Island penitentiary when the prison was taken over by gangsters under the protection of corrupt political bosses. Marcus personally led the raid that broke underworld resistance.

In 1940 he rejoined the army with the rank of lieutenant colonel as divisional judge advocate and divisional headquarters commander. In 1942 he served as head of the Rangers' Training School in Hawaii, where he trained some 8,000 men in jungle warfare in the Pacific. In 1943 Marcus became chief of planning in the Civil Affairs Division in the War Department in Washington, where he was charged with organizing the administration of territories in Europe to be liberated or occupied, and was one of the American advisers at the "Big Three" sessions held at various locations until after the end of the war. In 1944 he volunteered to parachute into Normandy on D day, and in 1945 was appointed to the staff of the military governor in Germany. He visited the Dachau concentration camp a few days after its liberation, an experience which was to haunt him for the rest of his life. With the full approval of Generals Lucius Clay and George S. Patton, he worked to make conditions tolerable for displaced persons throughout Germany. His next appointment was head of the Nazi War Crimes Investigation Division at the Pentagon. Marcus was awarded the distinguished service medal for his service in Normandy and for his role in negotiating and drafting the surrender documents in Italy and Germany. He also received the bronze star and honorary knight commander of the British Empire. In 1947 he retired with the rank of colonel and returned to his law practice.

In 1948 Marcus acceded to the request of the Jewish Agency and the Haganah to act as military adviser to David Ben-Gurion and arrived in Palestine at the beginning of 1948 under the name of Michael Stone. He was instrumental in devising the model upon which the Israeli army was based, prepared its first military manuals, ran training courses for its commanders, and planned the strategy for the War of Independence. He was said to have been responsible for the fact that, when the Arabs invaded, Israel was ready on every front. When war broke out he actively participated in the battle for the Negev, and the attacks on Latrun, and was involved in the planning and construction of the "Burma Road" built to bring supplies to beleaguered Jerusalem. On May 28, 1948, when the Old City of Jerusalem fell he was appointed commander of the Jerusalem front, with the rank of *aluf* (brigadier general).

On June 11, 1948, during the first cease-fire, Marcus was accidentally shot by a guard in his own headquarters near Jerusalem. He was buried at West Point with full military honors, and the headstone over his grave carries the legend "A Soldier for All Humanity." Kibbutz Mishmar David in the Judean Hills, founded in 1949, was named in his honor.

T. Berkman, *Cast A Giant Shadow: The Story of Mickey Marcus, a Soldier for All Humanity*, 1967.
N. Lorch, *The Edge of the Sword; Israel's War of Independence 1947–1949*, 1968.

Colonel David Marcus was killed at 3.50 a.m. Wrapped in a blanket, he had gone outside the perimeter fence of his headquarters in Abu Ghosh. As he returned he was challenged in Hebrew by a sentry. It appears from the only witness, the sentry himself, that Marcus replied in English, or what sounded like English, and jumped over the low stone fence. The sentry claimed he fired one warning shot into the air, and when the person failed to stop, fired another shot into his chest. It was only with difficulty that the sentry was prevented from committing suicide when he discovered the identity of his victim.

N. Lorch, *The Edge of the Sword*

MARCUSE, HERBERT (1898–1979) Philosopher and social theorist. Marcuse was born in Berlin to a prosperous family and comfortable lifestyle that exposed him firsthand to those material benefits of capitalism about which he would one day have so much to say.

His family, fairly well assimilated into the German middle class, satisfied themselves with attending synagogue on the Jewish High Holy Days and sent Marcuse for weekly religious instruction before his bar mitzvah. His lack of interest was so pronounced that the rabbi assured him it was doubtful if he would ever be useful to society.

Two years into World War I, Marcuse was drafted into the army. As his extensive reading had ruined his eyesight, he spent most of the war serving in the Zeppelin Reserves in Potsdam, where the regime was fairly relaxed. Nonetheless, the war awakened him, for the first time, to political consciousness. Set on the road to radicalization, he joined the German Social Democrat party. Although at this stage he was hardly a political activist, he did participate in the abortive revolution of 1918–1919.

With the end of the war Marcuse began to study, first in Berlin and later at Freiburg University. With a comfortable stipend from home he was able to devote himself fully to the study of German literature and philosophy. Influenced at this stage by Hegel, he completed a doctoral dissertation on German literature that incorporated Hegelian dialectics. Returning to Berlin in 1922, he began a thorough study of Karl Marx (q.v.), although the interpretation of Marx in the Soviet Union troubled him. It was also at this period that he became immersed in the works of Schiller, publishing *Schiller Bibliographie* in 1925.

In 1927 the publication of Martin Heidegger's *Being and Time*, imprinted itself on Marcuse as a turning point in the history of philosophy and he returned to Freiburg for further studies. The philosophy he himself eventually evolved, of "critical theory" was a blend of Schiller, existentialism, utopianism, Marxism, and Hegelian dialectical method — which analyzed and criticized prevailing social, political, and cultural institutions.

In 1933 the specter of Nazism helped convince Marcuse to accept a position at the Frankfurt Institute for Social Research, which was itself moving its center of activity away from Germany to Geneva and the following year to New York.

In the early 1940s Marcuse accepted an invitation from Washington, where, over the next ten years he served as an intelligence analyst in various agencies of the U.S. government. He worked first on analysis of German news in the Office of War Information, and then moved to the research and analysis branch of the Office of Strategic Services Studies, where, among his major assignments were the identification of Nazi and anti-Nazi groups, and later, preparation for postwar military regulations and governance of Germany. In 1945, the agency's responsibilities were terminated and Marcuse's branch was transferred to the Department of State. There, for the next two years, while the American government slowly began to shift its policies from antifascism to anticommunism, Marcuse was occupied with the American denazification program. Marcuse himself, though not particularly pro-Soviet, tended to play down the perceived threat of communism that was pulling America toward Cold War, but he had little influence, and in 1951 he left government service to return to academic life. He was a fellow of Russian research centers at Columbia and Harvard and was appointed professor of philosophy and politics at Brandeis University in 1954. In 1965 he became a professor of philosophy at the University of California in San Diego.

Becoming increasingly radical, and eventually a hero to the new left, in all his writings Marcuse retained the idea of the fragmentation of human life in modern society.

Challenging conventional American social thought, he sought to apply a Marxian analysis to society with the hope of its eventual change. However, he rejected versions of Marxian orthodoxy

expounded by any particular nation or group. His concept of "one-dimensional man" exposes a society based on the domination of capitalism, regarding a capitalist society as repressive by nature, satisfying those material needs it generates while suppressing human needs. In this society, which is totalitarian by virtue of its economic organization, man becomes tied to the commodity market. However, western man has the potentiality to move beyond violence and anarchy to construct a revolutionary new society.

His best writings include *Reason and Revolution: Hegel and the Rise of Social Theory* (1941, 1954), *Eros and Civilization: A Philosophical Inquiry into Freud* (1955), *One-Dimensional Man: Studies in the Ideology of Advanced Industrial Society* (1964), and *An Essay on Liberation* (1969).

B. Katz, *Herbert Marcuse and the Art of Liberation: An Intellectual Biography*, 1982.

A. C. Macintyre, *Herbert Marcuse: An Exposition and a Polemic*, 1971.

M. Schoolman, *The Imaginary Witness: The Critical Theory of Herbert Marcuse*, 1980.

MARKS, SIMON, Lord (1888—1964) and **SIEFF, ISRAEL MOSES,** Lord (1889—1977 Directors of the chain store Marks & Spencer (M & S), philanthropists, and British Zionists. Simon Marks was born in Manchester, son of Michael Marks, whose market stall in Leeds developed into a series of penny bazaars and then into the multiple-store chain of M & S. He was educated at Manchester Grammar School, where he was in the same class as his lifelong friend and business partner, Israel Sieff. In 1911 he was appointed to the board of directors of M & S and made responsible for buying. After his father's death he was given increased responsibilities and in 1916 became chairman of the company, a position he held for forty-eight years. In May 1917 he was called up for military service and was posted as a gunner to the Lancashire city of Preston. After being posted back to London he was able to resume his duties as chairman. From then on he directed the company, which succeeded in combining high quality with mass-market sales in its 250 stores throughout Britain and a number of other countries.

Israel Sieff took a degree in economics at Manchester University and in 1916 was elected to the board of directors of M & S. Marks and Sieff married each other's sisters. From 1913 they worked with Chaim Weizmann (q.v.) for the Zionist cause. They were among a group of young men and women ("the Manchester Circle") who gathered round Weizmann, and in 1917 Marks was released from duty with the army to establish and direct Weizmann's headquarters in London. In 1918 Sieff was appointed secretary of the Zionist Commission, which, led by Weizmann, visited Palestine to "act as an advisory body to the British authorities in all matters relating to Jews." He was also a founder of the Anglo-Israel Association.

In 1924 Marks visited America, where he studied

*From right to left: Simon Marks, Sir Herbert Samuel, Stephen Wise and Lord Bearsted, in conference.
Washington, c.1937.*

modern methods of administration and sales. He realized the need to reeducate and retrain his staff and returned to England determined to transform M & S into a chain of "super stores" on the American model. He introduced the five-shilling price limit and set out to find new sources of supply to enable him to create a range of merchandise that could be sold within this limit. He also overcame opposition to developing contact with the manufacturers so that they would supply his stores directly.

From 1926 M & S was a public company, and Israel Sieff joined on a full-time basis, becoming vice-chairman and joint managing director. He brought a wide knowledge of the textile industry gained in his family's business. He was deeply interested in the social and economic implications of commerce, and introduced many innovations in the firm's relations with its employees, customers, and suppliers, believing that the relationship between the manufacturer and the large-scale retailer was a partnership in the common task of satisfying the needs and tastes of the customer. He supported Political and Economic Planning (PEP), an independent political and economic planning research body, and under his leadership the PEP industry group produced reports on cotton, iron and steel, coal mining, and other industries that led toward industrial reconstruction and reform of the structure of the British economic system.

Chaim Weizmann introduced Marks and Sieff to the revolutionary opportunities made possible for industry by scientific discoveries being made at the time, for example, the ability to create synthetic fibers. The directors of M & S began to exploit this field, and employed scientists and technologists who became fully integrated into the commercial organization of the business.

In 1919 Marks went to the Versailles peace conference as secretary of the Zionist delegation and held many Zionist leadership positions in Britain. In 1938 he helped found the Air Defense Cadet Corps, which became an important source of recruits for the Royal Air Force. During World War II he served as deputy chairman of the London and South East Regional Board. He was responsible for coordinating production in the area, and was adviser to the Ministry of Petroleum Warfare. He was also one of the first directors of British Overseas Airways.

During this time Sieff was invited by the Board of Trade to go to the United States to promote British exports to the dollar area. While there he founded the Marks and Spencer Import Corporation, which promoted the sale of British textiles in the United States. He also spent eighteen months in

Washington at the invitation of the U.S. government, working with the Office of Price Administration.

An extremely patriotic Briton, Marks was proud of the fact that 99 percent of his company's merchandise was made in Britain. In 1944 he received a knighthood and in 1961 was created a baron, taking the title Lord Marks of Broughton.

Although Israel Sieff preferred to work behind the scenes in the Zionist organization, he eventually became honorary president of the British Zionist Federation. He was also involved in the work of the World Jewish Congress and was chairman of its European executive. Sieff succeeded Marks as chairman of M & S on the latter's death in 1964, relinquished the office in 1967, but continued as president until his death. In his last years he devoted his time to farming and horticulture on his farm in Berkshire. He was made a life peer in 1966.

Rebecca Sieff (1890–1966), eldest daughter of Michael Marks, was born in Leeds and educated in Manchester. She married Israel Sieff and worked closely with her husband and brother in Zionist activities. In 1918 she was a founding member of the Federation of Women Zionists of Great Britain and Ireland, and in 1924 was elected the first president of the Women's International Zionist Organization (WIZO), a position she held until her death. She spent the latter part of her life in the family home in Tel Mond, Israel, where she was buried.

G. Rees, *St. Michael, A History of Marks and Spencer*, 1969.
I. Sieff, *The Memoirs of Israel Sieff*, 1960.
W. Wyatt, *Distinguished for Talent*, 1958.

MARSHALL, LOUIS (1856–1929) U.S. lawyer and Jewish community leader. Marshall was born in Syracuse, New York, the son of German-Jewish immigrants. He graduated from Columbia University Law School in 1877 and in 1894 became a partner in the law firm of Guggenheimer, Untermeyer, and Marshall, where he remained until his death.

Marshall's legal career was marked by his defense of the constitutional rights of minorities. He successfully argued before the Supreme Court against state statutes forbidding the establishment of private and parochial schools (1925) and the exclusion of black voters from primary elections. He was active in the National Association for the Advancement of Colored People (NAACP) and in 1920 defended a group of Socialists who were denied their seats in the New York State Legislature. He mediated in labor disputes, such as the 1910 International Ladies Garment Workers Union cloak-makers' strike, and fought against restrictions on immigrants, as for example, the 1907 attempt to impose a literacy test.

After the turn of the century, Marshall was the spokesman of the American-born German-Jewish elite in New York. He served as a director of the Educational Alliance, the largest and most influen-tial community center on the Lower East Side, and as chairman of the commission appointed by New York City Mayor Seth Low in 1902, whose work led to better housing for Jews and less harassment by city officials. He established the *Yiddisher Velt* newspaper that same year and was one of the founders of the American Jewish Committee in 1906. He served as chairman of the board of directors of the Jewish Theological Seminary, and as president of the influential New York Reform Temple Emanu-El. He was a founder of the Jewish Welfare Board in 1917, a director of Dropsie College in Philadelphia, and held numerous other important community positions.

Marshall was involved in various legal battles on behalf of the Jewish community. In 1911 Marshall led the successful fight to abrogate the American-Russian Commercial Treaty of 1852 because of the continuing Russian discrimination against American Jews while residents in Russia. In 1915 he unsuccessfully appealed before the Supreme Court the conviction of Leo Frank on a murder charge motivated by anti-Semitism; Frank was later lynched in Georgia. His intervention in 1922 helped prevent Harvard University from imposing a quota on Jewish students. The following year Marshall reached the peak of his leadership when he became president of the American Jewish Committee, a post that he held until his death in 1929. In that position Marshall helped found and served as president of the American Jewish Relief Committee in 1914. He guided the policies of the American Jewish Joint Distribution Committee, established that same year to relieve the suffering of Jews in the war zones. He reluctantly joined the democratic American Jewish Congress as a member of the Jewish delegation to the peace conference in 1919, where he successfully advocated provisions to protect the civil and political rights of Jews and other minorities in eastern Europe.

The campaign led by Marshall and the American Jewish Committee led to the end of Henry Ford's anti-Semitic newspaper, the *Dearborn Independent*, and Ford's formal apology to the Jews in 1927.

In 1923 Chaim Weizmann, president of the World Zionist Organization, began negotiating with Marshall to include non-Zionists in an expanded Jewish Agency that would represent World Jewry vis-à-vis mandatory Britain in matters concerning a Jewish national home in Palestine. In August 1929 the Sixteenth Zionist Congress, meeting in Zurich, finally approved the incorporation of the non-Zionists and Marshall was elected chairman of the executive of the new Jewish Agency Council.

Marshall's death, a few months later, was probably a key factor in the failure of the non-Zionists to play an active role in the rebuilding of the homeland in Palestine until many years later.

C. Reznikoff, *Louis Marshall; Champion of Liberty*, 1957.
M. Rosenstock, *Louis Marshall; Defender of Jewish Rights,* 1957.

MARTOV, JULIUS (Iulii Osipovich Zederbaum; 1873–1923) Russian revolutionary, Menshevik leader. The grandson of Alexander Zederbaum, a leading Hebrew writer of the Enlightenment school, Martov was born in Constantinople, where his father represented a Russian steamship company. Both his parents were assimilated Jews, strongly versed in European culture. In 1877 the family moved to Odessa. Julius, who suffered from a pronounced limp and fragile health, sought solace in reading. When he was only seven years old he was deeply affected by the Odessa pogrom of 1881 and always remembered the experience.

After the pogrom, his family moved to Saint Petersburg where Martov began to dream of a revolution that would create a just Russian society. Attending the University of Saint Petersburg, he became active in revolutionary student circles. In 1892 he was arrested for proclaiming extreme Jacobin views but was released after three months. Identifying himself with the radical Petersburg Union of Struggle for Emancipation of Labor, he was rearrested and sent into a two-year exile, which he spent in Vilna. There Martov urged the creation of a separate Jewish workers' organization to lead the Jewish workers to economic, civil and political emancipation. Yiddish, he felt, should be the language of the Jewish labor movement. He was thus one of the first to formulate the central idea of Bundism; that the proletariat has special national interests that necessitate organizational autonomy. His emphasis on the national aspect of the Jewish workers' movement deeply impressed those who were to become leaders of the Bund when it was founded in 1897. It was at this time that he first adopted the pseudonym Julius Martov.

Returning to Saint Petersburg in 1895, Martov joined Lenin as cofounder of the Union of Struggle for the Emancipation of the Working Class. They sought to conduct economic agitation in the shipyards and factories; however Martov was again arrested and this time exiled to Siberia (1896–1899). On his return, he reestablished contact with Lenin and helped him found the Marxist journal, *Iskra*. During the coming years, Martov was one of Lenin's closest collaborators. At this stage Martov reversed his earlier stand on the Jewish question. He now opposed the national "separatism" of the Bund, believing that this, like Zionism, obstructed the common struggle against chauvinism and anti-Semitism. He led the attack against the Bund at the Second Congress of the Russian Social Democratic Workers' party (1903), which led to the Bund's leaving the party. The absence of the Bund gave Lenin a very small majority who were called Bolsheviki (majorityites) whereas Martov's group opposing Lenin's bid for domination of the party became known as Mensheviki (minorityites). The Mensheviks advocated a broad, inclusive worker's party and opposed Lenin's scheme of a narrow party of professional revolutionaries. Martov opposed the extensive powers of control Lenin demanded and favored the western European concept of a social-democratic class party engaged in open political struggle. These differences became more apparent during the 1905 revolution.

From 1906 to 1912, Martov was in exile, mainly in Paris, where he edited the Menshevik paper, *Golos Sotsialdemokrata*. However, he continued to cooperate with the Bolsheviks on many issues. He was opposed to some of the Bolshevik terrorist tactics, but waited unil 1911 to publish an open attack in order to avoid splitting the movement.

During World War I Martov was a central figure in the pacifist movement. Returning to Saint Petersburg (Petrograd) in 1917 he advocated the establishment of a popular-front government. Martov played only a minor part in the October 1917 revolution finding himself torn between his dislike of bolshevism and the possibility of counterrevolution from the right.

Immediately after the Bolshevik revolution, Martov and the Mensheviks were forced out of the Soviet Congress by Leon Trotsky (q.v.) who cried out, "You are pitiful isolated individuals, you are bankrupts, your role is played out. Go where you belong from now on — into the dustbin of history!"

During the next three years Martov acted as the "conscience of the Revolution." He supported the struggle against the White Russians and the allies and became he leader of a semiloyal opposition that tried to make the Bolsheviks respect their own constitution and denounced Bolshevik terror. In June 1918 Martov and his colleagues were expelled from the Central Executive Committee and the Menshevik newspapers were closed down. The Menshevik party was finally outlawed in 1920. However, Lenin allowed Martov to leave Russia. He settled in Berlin leading the Mensheviks in exile, assisting the underground Menshevik remnant in Russia, and editing the *Socialist Courier*.

Martov remained a democrat in theory and

We, the few Jewish students, were confronted on all sides by a spontaneous view of ourselves as an "inferior" race rather than with anti-Semitic hatred. The others, sons of petty bourgeois Jews, carried this burden passively, attempted to survive unnoticed. I, who had been brought up in a Russified and liberal milieu, was incapable of surrendering without a struggle. Exacerbated by the whole order of school life, my sensitiveness became a disease.

Julius Martov

The "Hamlet" of democratic socialism, a man of great intellectual gifts whose failure was essentially one of will-power.

Edmund Wilson on Julius Martov

practice, who foresaw the pitfalls of the Bolshevik attempt to impose socialism by force on a reluctant society, but he had no clear alternative to offer. He was even mourned by the Bolsheviks as "their most sincere and honest opponent."
I. Getzler, *Martov: A Political Biography of a Russian Social Democrat*, 1967.
L. Trotsky, "Martov" in *Political Profiles*, 1972.

MARX BROTHERS: CHICO (Leonard; 1891–1961); **HARPO** (Adolph; 1893–1964); **GROUCHO** (Julius; 1895–1977); **GUMMO** (Milton; 1894–1977); and **ZEPPO** (Herbert; 1901–1979) U.S. stage and film comedians. The children of German immigrants, the Marx Brothers — initially Groucho and Gummo, later joined by Harpo and finally Chico — were organized by their mother, Minnie (sister of the vaudeville actor Al Shean), into a vaudeville singing act in 1909. Their natural boisterousness soon made singing take second place to comedy and by the mid-1920s they had evolved distinct characterizations. Chico was the eccentric pianist with an Italian accent, Harpo the mute red-headed harpist, and Groucho the cigar-smoking, fast-talking wisecracker with the greasepaint eyebrows and moustache. Gummo was left as straight man, replaced by Zeppo during World War I.

Fifteen years after the formation of the original singing group, the Marx Brothers became full-fledged Broadway stars in a show called *I'll Say She Is*. Their almost surreal brand of comedy delighted New York audiences in two more shows before they began making films for Paramount in 1929. Their later films (without Zeppo), made at MGM from 1935, were less anarchic, and by 1941 they had almost terminated their screen careers, although Groucho was to appear sporadically until 1968.

Chico and Harpo remained professionally active until an advanced age, while Gummo and Zeppo were for a while extremely successful talent agents. However, it was Groucho who was generally in the limelight as a solo. His quiz show, *You Bet Your Life*, ran on radio and television for over a decade, and he supplemented his performing with humorous writing, publishing several books. In the late 1960s and early 1970s there was a phenomenal upsurge of the Marx Brothers' popularity among the younger generation, with films like *Animal Crackers* (1930), *Duck Soup* (1933), and *A Night at the Opera* (1935) attaining a cult status. As the only survivor of the three Marx Brothers, Groucho was the recipient of many honors, including a special Academy Award.

Harpo, Groucho and Chico Marx in A Day at the Races.

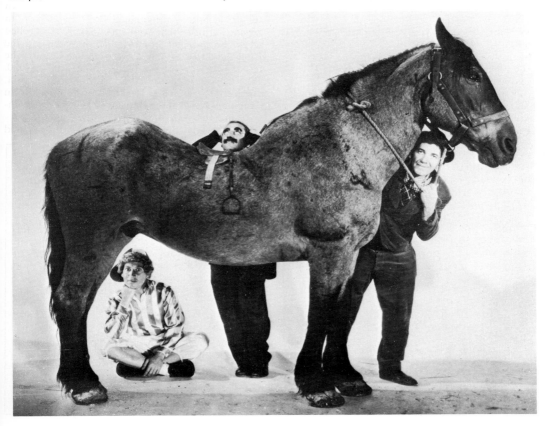

QUIPS OF GROUCHO MARX

● On being told that he could not join a swimming club because he was Jewish:
"My son's only half-Jewish. Would he be permitted to go into the water up to his knees?"

● On being blackballed at a club:
"That's just fine. I wouldn't want to belong to any club that would accept me as a member."

● As a detective:
"This murder was committed by the man next door."
"But there is no house next door."
"Then we must build one."

● As a doctor taking a pulse:
"Either you're dead or my watch has stopped."

● An assimilated Jew and a hunchback were passing a synagogue. "I used to be a Jew once," said the Jew. "Yes — and I used to be a hunchback," came the reply.

● From the moment I picked up your book until the moment I put it down, I was convulsed with laughter. Some day I intend reading it.

● Anyone can get old. All you have to do is live long enough.

● I've been around so long I knew Doris Day befor she was a virgin.

From *A Day at the Races:*

"Tell me, Dr. Hackenbush, just what was your medical background?"
"At the age of fifteen, I got a job in a drug-store filling prescriptions."
"Don't you have to be twenty-one to fill prescriptions?"
"That's for grown-ups. I filled them for children."
"Where did you get your training as a physician?"
"I took four years at Vassar."
"But that's a girls' college."
"I found that out in the third year. I'd've been there yet but I went out for the swimming team."
"And your medical experiences?"
"Unexciting — except during the flu epidemic."
"What happened them?"
"I got the flu."

J. Adamson, *Groucho, Harpo, Chico and Sometimes Zeppo*, 1973.
A. Eyles, *The Marx Brothers*, 1966.
G. Marx, *Groucho and Me*, 1959.
H. Marx (with R. Barber), *Harpo Speaks!*, 1961.
M. Marx, *Growing Up with Chico*, 1980.

MARX, KARL (1818–1883) German social, political, and ecomonic thinker. Born in Trier, Prussia, to Heinrich (originally Hirschel Halevi) and Henrietta Marx, both descendants of a long line of rabbis, he was short, stocky, and swarthy, for which he was nicknamed "Moor," a name that he used with family and close friends. He had a sharp intellect and a sharp tongue with which he tended to antagonize people, but he loved children and was adored by his daughters.

Because as a Jew his father was barred from the practice of law, he converted the entire family to Lutheranism when Karl was six years old. Marx attended a Lutheran school but later became a fervent atheist who believed that "religion is the opium of the masses." He learned French and Latin as a matter of course at school, and later taught himself Spanish, Italian, Dutch, Scandinavian languages, Russian, and English. Acceding to his father's wish that he become a lawyer, Marx studied toward a law degree at the University of Bonn, distinguishing himself primarily by writing a great deal of mediocre poetry, drinking, disturbing the peace, and fighting a duel.

Marx transferred to the University of Berlin where he soon became caught up on the Young Hegelian circle, and in 1841 was awarded a doctorate in philosophy from the University of Jena. In 1843 he married his childhood sweetheart, Jenny von Westphalen, and of their seven children, three daughters survived.

Although Marx had hoped for an academic career, he was unable to pursue this goal and turned instead to journalism, accepting a position in 1842 as editor of a liberal newspaper founded by disciples of Hegel. As a journalist he discovered that politics interested him far more than philosophy. Marx attacked the Prussian government and fought its censorship, displaying a ruthless tongue that he continued to exercise until the government finally suppressed the paper a year later. He moved to Paris, where he planned to continue his attacks on the Prussian government. It was there that he met and began his lifelong friendship with Friedrich Engels, and there that he crystallized the ideas that were to become the basis for his economic theories.

When the Prussian government pressured France to expel him in 1845, Marx moved to Brussels. A side trip from Brussels to England exposed him to working-class organizations and motivated him to begin putting socialist ideas into practice instead of on paper. He founded the German Workers' party and was active in the establishment of the Communist League. At a meeting of the League in December, 1847, Marx presented his *Communist*

Manifesto, a document drawn up by himself and Engels, defining the principles of communism.

Marx continued to be homeless. In 1848, he was expelled by the Belgian government for radicalism and moved back to Cologne to continue his journalistic work. His paper was suppressed less than a year later and he was exiled from Prussia and returned to France, but was soon expelled again and finally, settled in London as a stateless exile because Britain denied him citizenship. In London Marx worked as a journalist, writing many articles for the *New York Daily Tribune*, but he was supported primarily by Engels. Most of his energy was devoted to the promotion of communism, and in 1864 Marx helped to found the International Workingmen's Association. Political infighting, in which he too participated, led to its dissolution in 1872.

The tomb of Karl Marx in Highgate Cemetery, London.

In 1867 Marx published the first volume of *Capital (Das Kapital)*, which set out his doctrine in full. One of its most basic premises was the "materialist conception of history," which held that history is a continuous process, regulated and determined by the evolution of economic institutions. History, he believed, is a dialectical process involving thesis, antithesis, and synthesis at every stage of evolution. The evolution of communism was to be achieved by the interaction of precapitalism, which was the thesis, and capitalism, its antithesis, which would find synthesis in communism. He maintained that the working classes, the product of capitalism, would be involved in a class struggle until the proletariat was victorious and could establish a "proletarian dictatorship" that was to evolve into communism. Reversing Hegel's belief that history is determined by a universal idea that shapes institutions, he contended that institutions shape ideas.

At the age of fifty-six Marx fell ill with a liver ailment which sent him in search of treatment in resorts all over Europe. His wife's death from cancer in 1881 was a serious blow to him, as was that of his daughter two years later. He died of lung trouble in March 1883, just before his sixty-sixth birthday, and was buried in London, where his grave in Highgate Cemetery became a place of pilgrimage for communists.

Marx wrote many articles, brochures, and reports, but published only five books during his lifetime, among them the *Critique of Political Economy* and the first volume of *Capital*. The second and third volumes were published by Engels after Marx's death and consist of works written by both of them. A fourth volume was put together after Engel's death.

Karl Marx was a conscientious scholar who always looked for primary sources and spent much of his working time in London at the British Museum. Before writing *Capital* he read every available work on economic and financial theory and practice. At home he continued to work, often until four in the morning, writing and smoking so

---

FROM THE *COMMUNIST MANIFESTO*

A specter is haunting Europe — the specter of Communism...

The history of all hitherto existing society is the history of class struggles.

Freeman and slave, patrician and plebian, lord and serf, guild-master and journeyman, in a word, oppressor and oppressed, stood in constant opposition to one another, carried on an uninterrupted, now hidden, now open fight, a fight that each time ended, either in a revolutionary reconstitution of society at large, or in the common ruin of the contending classes.

much that he once said that *Capital* would not even pay for the cigars he had smoked writing it.

Marx developed a violently hostile attitude toward Jews and Judaism writing, "What is the worldly cult of the Jew? Huckstering. What is his worldly God? Money." Jews to him symbolized monetary power and capitalist rapacity and he used extreme language in describing his antagonism for them. At the same time, his own Jewish origin was a factor in his strained relations with his wife's aristocratic family.

I. Berlin, *Karl Marx: His Life and Environment*, 1963.
F. Mehring, *Karl Marx; The Story of his Life*, 1951.
R. Payne, *Marx; A Biography*, 1908.
O. Ruhle, *Karl Marx; His Life and Works*, 1929.
E. Silberner, "Was Marx an Anti-Semite?" in *Historia Judaica* 11 (1949): 3–52.

MAUROIS, ANDRÉ (originally Emile Herzog; 1885–1967). French novelist and biographer. A native of Elbeuf, he was born into a patriotic Jewish cloth manufacturing family that had left Alsace for Normandy after the Franco-Prussian War of 1870–1871. Maurois later recounted that story in his semiautobiographical novel, *Bernard Quesnay* (1926). While studying in Rouen and Caen, he was not spared the anti-Semitism engendered by the Dreyfus (q.v.) affair; and the ten years he spent working in the family business also provided material for some of his books. A turning point in his career followed the outbreak of World War I, during which Maurois served as a liaison officer with the British expeditionary force. He drew on this wartime experience for *The Silence of Colonel Bramble* (1918), a hilarious book of reportage, set in an officers' mess where French and English attitudes are subtly contrasted, that made the author famous overnight. It had a sequel in *Les discours du docteur O'Grady* (1922).

Although Maurois wrote various novels and short stories dealing with French middle-class life, he chiefly excelled as an interpreter of the Anglo-American world and as a biographer. His studies of great cultural figures, notable for their scholarship, lively description, and psychological insight, created a vogue for the *biographie romancée*. Heading the list were *Ariel, or the Life of Shelley* (1923), *Disraeli* (1927), and *Byron* (1930), followed by similar works on Dickens, Turgenev, Voltaire, and Chateaubriand. Between the two world wars, Maurois also displayed a remarkable knowledge of British culture and mentality in the stories entitled *L'Anglaise* and the popular *King Edward and His Times* (1933), *Prophets and Poets*, (1935), a volume of critical essays, and his *History of England* (1937). As with the author's later books, nearly all of these were translated into English, editions in both languages often appearing in the same year.

A member of the Académie Française from 1938, Maurois (unlike his communist brother-in-law and fellow writer, Jean-Richard Bloch) was naively prepared to accept the Vichy regime established by Marshal Petáin after the French collapse in 1940. Threatened with arrest and deportation as a Jew, however, the writer took refuge in the United States, where he taught at Princeton and continued publishing books until 1946. His output included a history of the United States. (1943–1944) and biographies of Benjamin Franklin, Dwight D. Eisenhower and George Washington.

André Maurois returned to his native land after the war and published a history of France (1947), another *Docteur O'Grady* frolic (1950), and a new series of biographical works. Apart from Cecil Rhodes (1953) and the Brownings (1955), he concentrated on French personalities, such as Alexandre Dumas, *père et fils* (1957), Napoleon, (1964) and Balzac (1965). Three outstanding examples, drawing upon the author's own research as well as unpublished documents, were *The Quest for Proust* (1949), *Lélia, or the Life of George Sand* (1952), and *Olympio, or the Life of Victor Hugo* (1954). A sixteen-volume edition of his collected works appeared in 1950–1955 and two volumes of memoirs: *I Remember, I Remember* (1942) and *Call No Man Happy* (1970). Though acknowledging himself to be a Jew, Maurois took only a marginal interest in Jewish affairs and made the converted Disraeli his one Jewish biographical subject.

G. Lemaître, *André Maurois*, 1940.
J. Suffel, *André Maurois* (French), 1963.

MAYER, LOUIS BURT (1885–1957) U.S. film executive. Born Lazar Mayer in Minsk, Russia, he was taken to Canada by his parents when still a young child. Following his father into the scrap metal business, he struck out on his own in Boston in 1904. Business problems caused him to seek a more profitable enterprise and in 1907 he invested in a small theater in Haverhill, Massachusetts, on the advice of a friend involved in film exhibition. A second theater followed in 1911 and in 1915, having branched out into film distribution, Mayer made a fortune from the New England distribution rights of D. W. Griffith's *The Birth of a Nation*. Mayer's first experience in film production came that year when he became secretary of the Metro Pictures Corporation.

Friction with the company's president caused Mayer to leave, but by 1918 he had established his own studio in Los Angeles. In 1924, the mogul Marcus Loew, who by then controlled Metro, merged it with Goldwyn Pictures and brought in Mayer to act as studio chief. Under Mayer, Metro-Goldwyn-Mayer (MGM), as the new hybrid was known, became the most prestigious of the major Hollywood studios. In addition to his stated policy of "great star, great director, great play, great cast," Mayer also took enormous personal pains that everything emanating from his studio be clean, morally uplifting, family entertainment.

Mayer's success (in 1937 he was the highest-paid man in the United States) owed much to the talent with which he surrounded himself. Many of the most highly-regarded of MGM's productions in the 1930s were the work of production head Irving Thalberg (q.v.) and the studio's standing was further bolstered by the presence of romantic idols like Greta 'Garbo, Joan Crawford, and Clark Gable. By conceding the services of the latter to his son-in-law, David O. Selznick (q.v.), Mayer once more secured distribution rights to a Civil War epic that proved an unprecedented money-maker, *Gone with the Wind*.

As the studio system waned in the late 1940s and early 1950s so did Mayer's power and he was forced to resign in 1951.

B. Crowther, *Hollywood Rajah: The Life and Times of Louis B. Mayer*, 1960.

S. Marx, *Mayer and Thalberg: The Make-Believe Saints*, 1975.

MAYER, RENÉ (1895–1972) French statesman. Born in Paris and educated at the Sorbonne, he was awarded the croix de guerre while serving in the trenches during World War I. His career began in the Conseil d'Etat (1919) and with an appointment as lecturer at the Ecole Libre des Sciences Politiques (1922–1932). In 1930 he negotiated an important agreement for coal with Germany. He soon displayed managerial abilities that led to rapid promotion, notably as administrator of Air France (1933) and of the SNCF, the French railroad system (1937). After the German invasion and the French government's collapse in 1940, however, Mayer was dismissed from public office because of the Vichy régime's anti-Jewish policy. He then joined the Resistance and escaped to Algeria, where he became a leading member of the Free French Committee for National Liberation (1943). He also became prominent in the Radical Socialist party, received various decorations, and was minister of public works and transport in the provisional government of 1944 headed by General Charles de Gaulle. In 1945–1946, he was high commissioner for German affairs.

Thereafter, Mayer served as a deputy for Constantine (Algeria) in the French National Assembly (1946–1956) and held ministerial posts in successive government coalitions. He was twice minister of finance and economic affairs (1947–1948, 1951–1952). From January to May 1953, Mayer headed the French government. An advocate of the NATO (North Atlantic Treaty Organization) alliance, which inspired him to write *Le pacte atlantique* (1950), Mayer also promoted Anglo-French relations and, after resigning the premiership, went on to chair the European Coal and Steel Authority (1955–1957). He took a keen interest in Jewish affairs, was a member of the French Consistoire Central, and from 1946 served as vice-president of the Alliance Israélite Universelle.

MEIR (c.110– c.175 CE) Early rabbinic authority; an architect of the Mishnah. Little is known about his family background, and there are hints that he was descended from proselytes and that his original name was Nehorai, the Aramaic equivalent of Me'ir ("the Enlightener"). His teachers included Rabbi Ishmael and Elisha ben Avuya (q.v.); even the latter's apostasy did not prevent Meir from continuing to hold him in unique regard. However, it was Rabbi Akiva (q.v.) whose teaching exerted the greatest influence on Meir and who was responsible for the preeminent intellectual and legal stature that Meir eventually attained.

Talmudic sources shed light on the dramatic and tragic events that punctuated the careers of Meir and his remarkably accomplished wife Beruriah. Nor was Meir destined to enjoy much tranquillity in his public life. Having taken refuge abroad from the persecutions under the Roman Emperor Hadrian, he returned to Eretz Israel and helped to reestablish the Sanhedrin at Usha in Galilee (c. 140), where he was elected that body's *hakham* (sage, or deputy president). For a number of years he taught and preached at the revived academy, also drawing on the system of Akiva to compile the collection of laws that Judah ha-Nasi (q.v.) later embodied in his Mishnah. However, when Simeon ben Gamaliel II endeavored to strengthen his authority as the new patriarch, Meir joined his colleague Nathan ha-Bavli (the president of the Sanhedrin) in attempting to have Simeon deposed. The power struggle resulted in a deadlock, but Meir himself was removed from office and severely disciplined. He then chose voluntary exile in "Asia" (an uncertain location), where he died.

This painful controversy, overshadowing his last years, in no way diminishes his importance as one of the founders of rabbinic Judaism. Where legal rulings are concerned, several hundred by Meir can be identified in the Mishnah and its supplement, the *Tosefta*. According to the Talmud, his name was deliberately omitted in many other Mishnaic passages in retaliation for his "revolt" against the patriarch. The Jewish scholarly ideal of study for its own sake appears to have originated with Meir, although he was a proficient scribe and believed in combining Torah with a suitable occupation. The educational and moral value of Torah study is emphasized in his sayings, which also castigate the ignorant.

Having lived through the Bar Kokhba (q.v.) uprising and the bloody repression that followed, Meir advocated a conciliatory approach toward the Roman authorities. Whereas many of his contemporaries opposed cultural relations with the non-Jewish world, Meir was prepared to engage in discussion with Samaritans and heathen philosophers, and he is said to have collected three-hundred "fox fables" of varied origin that were then adapted to Jewish use. Only three such tales are named in the Talmud, however, presumably because this kind of literature was disfavored. In time, Meir came to be regarded primarily as the heir to Akiva, who showed respect for his adversaries and excelled as a peacemaker. Hailed as a saintly example, he figured in popular tales and legends; moreover, it was believed that his remains had been conveyed to the Land of Israel and interred there. A pious tradition associates his burial place with that of Rabbi Meir Ba'al ha-Nes (a legendary wonder-worker) in Tiberias.

A. Blumenthal, *Rabbi Meir: Leben und Wirken eines jüdischen Weisen*, 1888.

Y. Konovitz, *Rabbi Meir* (Hebrew) 1967.

BERURIAH

Rabbi Meir's wife, Beruriah, was the only woman recognized in the Talmud as a scholar in her own right and the only woman whose views are taken into account in legal discussions. Frequent admiring mentions refer to her scholarship, intellect, and virtue. Her opinions are accepted as equal to those of other rabbinic authorities and she guided rabbinic students in their studies.

Her life was marked by a series of tragedies. Her father, Hananyah ben Teradyon, one of the outstanding sages of his time, was burned to death by the Romans. Her sister had to be rescued from a brothel to which she had been consigned by the Romans. Two of her sons died on the same day, a Sabbath, but she did not tell her husband until after Sabbath had ended. She then broke the news by asking him whether a precious object deposited with her should be returned to its owner. When Rabbi Meir replied "Of course," she took him to the room where their sons lay and quoted Job: "The Lord has given, the Lord has taken, blessed be the name of the Lord."

MEIR BEN BARUCH OF ROTHENBURG

(known by the acronym *Maharam*; c. 1215–1293). German rabbinical authority, rabbinic scholar, and liturgical poet. Born in Worms of a family of scholars and community leaders, he studied with distinguished rabbis in Würzburg, Mainz, and France. In Paris he witnessed the public burning of the Talmud near Notre Dame in 1242, writing an elegy that became incorporated in the Ashkenazic prayers for the fast of the Ninth of Ab. He settled in Rothenburg in 1246, remaining there for forty years and was recognized as the outstanding Ashkenazic rabbi of his time.

In 1286 Emperor Rudolph I confiscated the properties of many Jews, and among those who sought to flee was Meir. He was captured in Lombardy and imprisoned, perhaps for his role in encouraging the Jews to emigrate. The Jewish community tried to raise funds for his release but they did not succeed since the emperor insisted that the ransom would be regarded as the payment of taxes, which would imply recognition by the Jews that they were slaves of the emperor. Meir too would not accept payment of the ransom under such conditions, seeing it as a precedent for further blackmail. After seven years he died in prison, and only fourteen years after his death was his body released in return for a huge sum of money and buried in the Worms cemetery, where his tombstone still stands. The Jew who had paid to release his body asked for only one privilege — that of being buried next to the rabbi.

About a thousand of Meir's *responsa* (replies to legal queries), answering questions received from all parts of Europe, are extant. Scholars, rabbis, and law courts sent him queries to solve as he was regarded as the greatest authority of his generation. They deal with all practical aspects of Jewish law, and the answers are formulated clearly and logically, based on the writings of the great scholars of the past. Most deal with civil law, including fiscal matters, business problems, land and inheritance, and community organization. His approval of many customs led to their universal acceptance.

Meir also wrote comments on the Talmud. Some of these were composed in prison where he was allowed to have books and receive visits from his students. His teachings and writings were immensely influential not only in his time but in subsequent generations, both in Germany and Spain, notably through his pupil Asher ben Yehiel (q.v.), and became a permanent part of Jewish legal tradition.

I. A. Agus, *Rabbi Meir of Rothenburg*, 2 vols., 1947.

MEIR, GOLDA (1898–1978) Prime minister of Israel. Born to a poor family, she grew up in dire circumstances in her native Kiev and in Pinsk, Russia. At an early age, she watched her family defend itself against pogroms, an experience that profoundly affected her. She was taught to read and write by her elder sister, who exercised great influence on her throughout her life. In 1903 her father left to seek his fortune in America. His wife and daughters followed three years later and settled in Milwaukee.

Meir did well at school and, at age fourteen, also became involved in the local branch of Poale Zion (the Socialist Zionist movement). Hers was an elemental socialism, which included an inherent belief in a just, progressive, and equal society. Zionism represented to her the need for a Jewish state to end the anomaly of Jewish existence in the Diaspora. She made her first street-corner speech when she was fourteen and was berated by her parents, who wanted her to marry and settle down. As they refused to allow her to enter high school, she escaped from home and joined her elder sister in Denver. There she met Morris Meyerson, a poor, Russian-born sign painter. She made their marriage conditional on immigrating to Palestine and settling on a kibbutz. He reluctantly accepted and they wed in 1917.

Meir attended a teachers' training school and, for a brief period, taught immigrant children and adult education courses in Milwaukee. Most of her time she devoted to Poale Zion and to planning her move to Palestine. In 1921 she achieved her dream, arriving in Palestine and living for the next three years on Kibbutz Merhavia, where she began her public career in the Women's Workers' Council, in the Histadrut (Trade Union Federation), and on the kibbutz's executive committee. She impressed the leaders of the Labor movement with her keen mind, organizational ability, and talent to see through things quickly and reach a decision.

In 1924 Meir left the kibbutz due to her husband's ailment and moved to Jerusalem. During the next four years she lived on the verge of poverty, taking in laundry to pay the kindergarten fees for her two children. At that time she separated from her husband, but never divorced him. In 1928 she began to work as cosecretary of the Women's Workers' Council. She rose slowly in the Histadrut hierarchy and following two missions to the United States on its behalf, was elected to the Histadrut executive committee. Her roles in the Histadrut included heading its trade union section and political department, seeking work for the unemployed, and dealing with the mandatory regime over wages and benefits.

In 1930 she was one of the founders of the Socialist party, Mapai, and by then was a major force in Palestine. Meir became known as an achiever, a team worker, obedient to her superiors, eager to learn and to assume new tasks and responsibilities. From 1946 she headed the political department of the Jewish Agency and negotiated with the British mandatory regime in its final months and held secret talks with King Abdullah of Jordan. During the War of Independence she was sent to the United States, where she raised over fifty million dollars. Upon her return, David Ben-Gurion (q.v.) said, "Someday, when the history of our people will be written, it will be said that there was a Jewish woman who raised the money which made the state possible."

Meir was appointed Israel's first minister to Moscow and during her eight months in the Soviet capital, her presence ignited Soviet Jews in a rare demonstration of their true feelings. Upon her

Foreign Minister Golda Meir and Russian Ambassador to Israel, M. Bodrov Jerusalem, October 1964.

return she was elected to Israel's parliament, the Knesset (remaining a member until 1974), and joined Ben-Gurion's cabinet as minister of labor and housing. Meir was to call this period my "seven good years." She initiated comprehensive social legislation, including the National Insurance Act, and oversaw the absorption and integration of over a million immigrants. As war clouds loomed in the mid-1950s, Ben-Gurion demanded that she replace Moshe Sharett (q.v.) as foreign minister, since her views were closer to those of Ben-Gurion. She reluctantly accepted and began a ten-year career as Israel's chief international spokesman. She led Israel's diplomatic struggle to retain whatever possible from the military victory of the Sinai campaign in 1956. Meir laid the foundations for the Israeli presence in Africa and initiated extensive technical aid programs to Third World nations. She traveled extensively, representing Israel in the United Nations, defending its cause, and gaining much personal admiration.

In 1965 cancer was detected, but did not require surgery. She retired as foreign minister that year due to her illness, and also because of the split in her Mapai party and the secession of her mentor David Ben-Gurion.

A few months later she was recalled to service, this time as Mapai secretary-general. Her major task was to rebuild the shattered party in the wake of the traumatic split it had experienced with the creation of the Ben-Gurion-led Rafi party. On the eve of the 1967 Six-Day War she unsuccessfully sought to block the creation of a government of national unity and the appointment of Moshe Dayan (q.v.) as defense minister, arguing that the Israeli army would win any military test. After the war, she fulfilled a number of diplomatic missions and supported the newly created territorial status quo saying there was no urgency for Israel to make concessions prior to an Arab agreement to negotiate with Israel. She retired as party secretary in August 1968.

As early as 1967, she had been asked to consider the possibility of succeeding the ailing Levi Eshkol (q.v.) as prime minister. When he died in February 1969, she was the almost unanimous choice of the Labor party as the next prime minister. The party elders felt that her appointment would postpone a power struggle between Moshe Dayan and Yigal Allon. She reluctantly accepted the party decision and within a few days began to provide Israel with strong, assured, experienced leadership. Her foreign policy for the next five years was to pursue peace through all means. She emphasized that Israel was prepared to negotiate without prior conditions. For peace Israel would consider withdrawing from much of the territories to final, agreed, secure borders, but Israel must retain the Golan Heights, the Jordan Valley, a salient south of the Gaza Strip, a land link from Eilat to Sharm esh-Sheikh, and keep united Jerusalem as Israel's capital. She was able to retain American military and political support while resisting American schemes to force Israel to withdraw even without negotiations (the Rogers plan). Golda Meir led Israel in the 1968–1970 war of attrition and accepted the cease-fire of August 1970.

Her domestic policies were less successful. She misjudged the depth of the grievances of the poorer segments of Israeli society, mainly Sephardic Jews living in urban slums and development towns in the periphery. She had little rapport with Israel's intellectuals and writers and preached slogans that were no longer valid and meant little to a consumer-oriented society. She was unable to stem the decline of her party, even though she presided over its unification with the breakaway parties. Being a strong, charismatic leader, she did not groom a successor.

In mid-1973, against her better judgment, Meir was persuaded to continue as prime minister, a decision she later regretted. In early October 1973, she sensed that an Arab attack was impending. Despite mounting warnings, she relied on the advice of the defense minister and director of military intelligence and delayed mass mobilization of the reserves. When the Yom Kippur War broke out, she in fact became the commander-in-chief and provided much-needed military and political leadership. She could never forgive herself for not heeding her intuition and calling up the reserves earlier. Meir conducted top-level contacts with the United States, assuring the essential supply of tanks, airplanes, and other armaments. She accepted the cease-fire arranged by the United States and the Soviet Union and later conducted the negotiations with Henry Kissinger that resulted in a cease-fire and separation of forces agreements between Israel, Egypt, and Syria.

Although a commission of inquiry that investigated the army's unpreparedness before and at the outbreak of the war praised her conduct prior to and during the conflict, she was broken in spirit and body, realizing that while Israel won a major military victory, it had lost a political battle, and that the Arabs had succeeded in destroying the status quo that had reigned from 1967 to 1973. She resigned her office in April 1974. In her final days, she wrote her memoirs, *My Life* (1975), and became the elder statesman of Israel, seeking to revitalize her party, but unable to prevent its decline and stunning defeat at the hands of the Likud in the May 1977 elections. She was highly critical of the Camp David agreement negotiated by Menachem Begin and Anwar al-Sadat in September 1978.

M. Davidson, *The Golda Meir Story*, 1976.
R. Martin, *Golda Meir: The Romantic Years*, 1988.
M. Menahem, *My Mother Golda Meir*, 1983.
M. Syrkin, *A Woman of Valor*, 1969.

MEITNER, LISE (1878–1968) Austrian nuclear physicist. She was the first to calculate the enormous energy released by splitting the uranium atom and was credited with laying much of the theoretical groundwork for the atom bomb, although she neither participated directly in its creation, nor intended her discoveries to be put to such use.

Meitner's father was a Viennese doctor and she became interested in atomic physics after reading newspaper reports in 1902 that Marie and Pierre Curie had discovered radium. In 1906 she was one of the first women to receive a doctorate from the University of Vienna. Two years later she moved to Berlin to study with the quantum theorist and Nobel Prize winner, Max Planck. That same year she began her association with Otto Hahn, a Nobel Prize-winning German nuclear physicist to whom was attributed the discovery of nuclear fission. Their friendship and professional partnership lasted thirty years, during which time they achieved international fame for their work. In 1918 Meitner and Hahn discovered protactinium, chemical element number 91, which appears between thorium and uranium on the periodic table.

During World War I Meitner left her work to serve as an X-ray nurse for the Austrian army. She returned to Germany to work with Hahn after the war and the two were on the verge of discovering that the uranium atom could be split, when in 1938, because of Nazi persecution, she fled to Sweden. Nine months later Hahn announced his discovery that uranium could be split. Meanwhile, he had sent all the details of his experimentation to Meitner for her comments and analysis. She in turn named the phenomenon nuclear fission and calculated that the energy released by bombarding one uranium nucleus with a neutron was 200 million electron volts. She reported her findings to the British journal *Nature*, in January 1939. She also informed the Danish physicist Niels Bohr (q.v.) of her discovery, and he reported the results of her investigations to scientists in the United States.

When the atom bomb was created, however, it took her by complete surprise, and in an interview after the war she took pains to disassociate herself from its invention, saying, "I must stress that I myself have not in any way worked on the smashing of the atom with the idea of producing death-dealing weapons. You must not blame us scientists for the use to which war technicians have put our discoveries."

She remained in Stockholm working at the Nobel Institute and at the Atomic Energy Laboratory. In 1958 she retired and moved to Cambridge, England. In 1966 she was a corecipient of the U.S. Atomic Energy Commission's Enrico Fermi award.

MELCHETT, BARON See Mond, Alfred Moritz

MENDELE MOCHER SFORIM ("Mendele the Bookseller," nom de plume of Sholem Jacob Abramovitch, originally Broido; 1835–1917) Hebrew and Yiddish writer, known as the "grandfather of modern Yiddish literature." Born in Kapulye, Belorussia, in the province of Minsk, Abramovitch was a precocious child. He had memorized most of the Hebrew Bible by the time he was nine and was known for his quick wit and his ability as a mimic. In his teens, he was an outstanding Talmudic scholar and spent most of his time in the synagogue. His father died when he was fourteen and he left home to live at houses of study in the area. Like most students of that time, he slept on the bench where he studied and ate his meals at houses of sympathetic townspeople. When his mother remarried, to a miller, he joined her in the country. In the solitude and isolation of the mill he began to compose Hebrew verses.

Soon he resumed his studies in Kamenetz and met the Hebrew author A. B. Gottlober, who encouraged him in his writings. Abromovitch qualified as a teacher and obtained a position in a Jewish school. When his brother wrote to him complaining about his difficultes as a heder (elementary Jewish school) teacher, Abramovitch in his reply wrote an essay on the principles of modern education. One of his friends read the letter and sent it to Gottlober who forwarded it to a Hebrew journal. The published essay caused an uproar. Not only was it written in clear, simple Hebrew but it was also a carefully reasoned and logical presentation of the methods of successful teaching. Abramovitch, now only twenty-one, became greatly respected.

In 1858 he moved to Berdichev, a commercial and intellectual center, and married. His wealthy father-in-law supported the young couple and Abramovitch was able to devote himself completely to writing and communal affairs. He continued to study pedagogy and to urge teachers to reform their teaching methods. During this time he tried to write instructive fiction and published the first version of his *Parents and Children*, a social satire, in Hebrew. It was then that he realized that in order to reach the Jewish masses, he would have to write in the popular language, Yiddish. Though he wanted to give them stories in the "holy tongue," the much despised Yiddish would reach the people. He persuaded the publisher of the Hebrew journal *Hamelitz* to obtain government permission to publish a Yiddish supplement. The result was *Kol Mvasser*, which serialized his first Yiddish story, "Dos Kleyn Mentchele" ("The Hypocrite") in 1864.

The Magic Ring, Abramovitch's second work, was published the following year. Like his first work, which preached that wealth does not make one happy, this one praised the values of education. They were followed by the first versions of *Fishke the Lame* and *The Meat Tax*. The first was a sketchy tale of the Jewish poor, and the second a play that openly attacked Berdichev's city fathers. Life in Berdichev became intolerable for Abramovitch and he moved to Zhitomir in 1871. Always deeply pious, he attended rabbinical school but upon graduation was unable to find a post. He made a slim living from his writings and translations. He wrote the first version of *Di Klatche* ("The Horse") in 1873 and *The Travels and Adventures of Benjamin III* in 1878. With a family of

seven, his income remained inadequate. Luckily, Baron Horace Ginsburg, an acquaintance and admirer of his work, supported him with a small monthly stipend until he became principal of a Jewish school in Odessa. He remained there until his death.

For five years Abramovitch was unable to write; a favorite daughter died, and his only son was arrested as a political prisoner and sent to Siberia, where he lived with a Christian girl and was forced to convert in order to send his children to school. In 1884 Abramovitch returned to writing. He rewrote some of his early works, expanding them and toning down their didactic nature. He translated his Yiddish writings into Hebrew and in 1900 published a Hebrew edition of his major writings.

Abramovitch's last important work, *Shlome Reb Khaim's*, autobiographical in subject, appeared in 1899. Until the end of his life he continued to write stories and essays. He was deeply affected by the 1903 Kishinev pogrom and the 1905 massacres, but felt his home was in Russia. His seventy-fifth birthday was celebrated worldwide, especially in Odessa, where he was greeted not only by the lead-

---

FROM MENDELE MOCHER SFORIM'S *FISHKE THE LAME*

The life of the Jewish people may appear ugly externally, but it is beautiful inwardly. A strong spirit possesses them, a heavenly spirit which always blows like a wind and lifts the waves in order to wash away the filth and foulness. The thunder and lightning, the pogroms and storms, that befell them, served to cleanse them and give them new strength. The Jewish people are like the old Greek philosopher Diogenes, their heads high in the sky, fully conscious of God's greatness, and themselves living among the nations of the world, as he in his barrel, crowded in narrow quarters. Under the piles of dirt in heders, yeshivas, and synagogues glows the flame of the Torah and spreads light and warmth to all mankind. All our children, poor and rich, short and tall, study and know its content.

Want rouses him from my bed, want keeps me on my feet, want compels me to ride my horse, and want beats me in the neck and moves me from place to place. Only the first move is difficult for the Jew. Once started, he glides as if greased; he crawls even where it is not necessary, where he is not wanted; he even climbs straight walls.... A Jew lives on the go. Want compels him to run, to bustle, to act, to work; let this want be slackened the least bit and he becomes passive and inert.

ing Jewish writers and intellectuals but by the baggage porters. He was ill during the last years of his life and World War I depressed him greatly.

Mendele's writings are not novels in the modern sense. He used the technique of building a story around narration and his works are not easy for the modern reader. In *The Meat Tax* he called for the social awakening of Russian Jews. In *Di Klatche*, the horse, once a prince, talks to his mad master, and his monologues criticize the conditions of Jewish life, condemning stupidity, hypocrisy, greed, war, and brutality. *Fishke* exposes the respected Jewish institution of the poorhouse and the Jewish vagabond-beggars who populated them. *The Travels and Adventures of Benjamin III* mocked both the 12th-century traveler, Benjamin of Tudela, and the Zionist ideals of the late 1870s, a nebulous yearning of the Orthodox for the coming of the Messiah, who would return them to the Land of Israel.

Mendele was honored as the "grandfather of Yiddish literature" before he reached old age and his memory remains honored. He wrote very few works of fiction and his novels are heavily moralistic, though satirical. He was the first to record the Yiddish of the common people and to employ it in literature. His characters were drawn from Jewish life in Russia, Lithuania, and Belorussia and though he criticized them, he always showed his love.

M. Waxman, *A History of Jewish Literature*, vol. 4, 1960.

MENDELSOHN, ERIC(H)   (1887–1953) German-born architect whose work is celebrated for its organic union of form and function. He was a versatile designer of public, commercial, and private buildings. Born in the town of Allenstein (now Olsztyn, Poland), where his father was a merchant and his mother a musician, Mendelsohn aspired, at an early age, to become an architect. He trained at universities in Berlin and Munich, earning a degree in architecture in 1912.

Until the start of World War I, Mendelsohn worked on his own. It was during this period that he came to appreciate the German expressionist movement. His contact with expressionists, especially the Blaue Reiter group, had a significant influence on his work. Soon after World War I began, he enlisted in the German army and saw action on the eastern and western fronts. Architectural sketches he made during the war led him to his first major commission, the Einstein Tower, an observatory and astrophysics laboratory in Potsdam (1920–1921). The observatory was built for the further study of Einstein's theory of relativity and when Mendelsohn showed Einstein around the building, Einstein said only one word: "Organic."

Throughout the 1920s and early 1930s, Mendelsohn continued to design buildings which unified purpose and design. One of his outstanding works was the Metal Workers' Union headquarters in Berlin. Schocken department stores, which he designed for Nuremberg (1925), Stuttgart (1926),

and Chemnitz (1928), with their imaginative use of glass, exemplify his success in attaining this type of uniformity. During this time, he also designed a Jewish cemetery at Königsberg (now Kaliningrad, USSR), which was subsequently destroyed by the Nazis.

With the rise of the Nazis, Mendelsohn left Germany. In 1933, he arrived in England where he formed a partnership with Serge Chermayeff. Their most significant project together was the De La Warr Entertainment Pavilion in Bexhill in 1935, described by an English paper of the time as "the last word in modern architecture." (A British fascist newspaper deplored the award of the commission "to aliens who have found it necessary to flee their native land.")

Mendelsohn accepted many commissions in Palestine. Building in Palestine presented different problems from building in northern Europe, the greatest being the climate. Mendelsohn tackled the challenge with typical enthusiasm and success. He designed homes for Chaim Weizmann (q.v.) in Rehovot (1935–1936), and Salman Schocken in Jerusalem (1935–1936). His most important works in Palestine were the Hadassah University Medical Center in Jerusalem (1937–1938), and the government hospital in Haifa (1947–1948).

Mendelsohn emigrated to the United States in 1941, settling in San Francisco. He designed Maimonides Hospital in San Francisco (1946) and built a series of synagogues and Jewish community

Eric Mendelsohn.

centers across the United States in such cities as Saint Louis, Grand Rapids, and Saint Paul. His synagogue in Cleveland boasts a dome one hundred feet in diameter and exemplifies a form that is harmonious with its surroundings.

W. von Eckardt, *Eric Mendelsohn*, 1960.
A. Whittick, *Eric Mendelsohn*, 1940.

MENDELSSOHN-BARTHOLDY, FELIX (Jakob Ludwig Felix, 1809–1847) Composer.

He was the grandson of Moses Mendelssohn (q.v.), and the son of Abraham Mendelssohn, a distinguished banker, who said "When a boy, I was known as the son of my father; now I am known as the father of my son!" Born in Hamburg, Germany, Felix, his brother, and two sisters were brought up in a lively cosmopolitan and highly cultured environment. His mother was an excellent musician and was his first teacher. By the age of nine he was already a proficient pianist, and was soon receiving instruction from Carl Zelter, who developed his skills in harmony, composition, and violin. It was also through Zelter that the twelve-year-old boy met the great poet Goethe. There was an instant bond of mutual admiration between these two creative spirits and their relationship lasted until Goethe's death in 1832.

When he was thirteen the family home was in Berlin. Mendelssohn had already become a prolific composer with symphonies, concerti, sonatas, and vocal works to his credit. Renowned artists and musicians passed frequently through the Mendelssohn household, and provided constant stimulation for the young composer. The home became a regular meeting place for Sunday-evening concerts, which were held in the immense family dining room, and Mendelssohn was able to test out new compositions on his audiences with the help of a small private orchestra.

In 1825 Mendelssohn and his father traveled to Paris to seek the professional advice from the famous composer Luigi Cherubini. Cherubini left no doubt in Abraham Mendelssohn's mind that his son should follow his destined pathway. Father and son returned to Berlin where the following year, at age seventeen, Mendelssohn composed the overture to Shakespeare's *A Midsummer Night's Dream*. This work revealed the astonishing depth of his musical genius.

In 1827 Mendelssohn wrote his first opera, *Die Hochzeit des Camacho*, which was performed in the Berlin Opera House, but which met with limited success possibly owing to a weak libretto. He now concentrated his energies on orchestral, piano, and chamber music. He also championed the music of Bach and Handel, which was rarely performed at the time, and the rekindled interest in Bach's music, notably through conducting the first public performance of the *Saint Matthew Passion* since the composer's death nearly eighty years earlier, earning himself an international reputation throughout Europe.

In 1829, his father, who had always acted as his

Felix-Bartholdy Mendelssohn. Drawing by Dubois with an autograph of Mendelssohn.

close adviser, sent him to England. This was the first of ten journeys, during which he built strong emotional links with the countryside and people who lived there. Those influences are clear in many of his later compositions, such as the *Hebrides Overture* (1830–1832), which he wrote after visiting Fingal's Cave on the Isle of Staffa in the Hebrides.

Throughout his numerous journeys, he kept a sketch pad in which he drew pictures of places and events which captured his imagination. It was also during these travels that Mendelssohn formed a strong, lasting friendship with Queen Victoria and Prince Albert; they were themselves keen amateur musicians and when Mendelssohn completed the *Scotch Symphony* in 1842 he dedicated it to the queen.

In 1836, following the death of his father, Mendelssohn journeyed to Frankfurt, where he met and subsequently married the daughter of a Protestant clergyman. (The Mendelssohn family had been brought up as Protestants). His health had already begun to fail due to his hectic life of constant travel throughout Europe. During these years compositions flowed constantly, and in 1838 Mendelssohn began work on the Violin Concerto in E Minor. Although inundated with offers of different posts of directorship in both Prussia and Berlin, he decided to remain in Leipzig and it was there in 1843 that he fulfilled a long-cherished plan and established the great Leipzig Conservatorium.

In the meanwhile, he continued his visits abroad and finally, in 1845, he settled permanently in

Leipzig with his wife and their five children. The following year he completed the oratorio *Elijah*, which was premiered in the Birmingham Festival, England. It was received triumphantly and Prince Albert sent a message of acclaim "to the noble artist who though encompassed by the Baal worship of false art, by his genius and study has succeeded, like another Elijah, in faithfully preserving the worship of true art."

On his return to Leipzig following his great triumph, Mendelssohn's health deteriorated, and after resigning his conductorship of the orchestra there, and after the death of his favorite sister, Fanny, he too died at age thirty-eight.

H. E. Jacobs, *Felix Mendelssohn and His Times*, 1963.

E. Werner, *Mendelssohn: A New Image of the Composer and His Age*, 1963.

MENDELSSOHN, MOSES (1729–1786) Pioneer of Jewish emancipation in Germany, philosopher, Bible translator, and community leader. He was born in Dessau, Germany, the son of a humble Torah scribe. A childhood disease left him permanently disfigured by a curvature of the spine. His education was traditional and he studied with the local rabbi, David Fränkel. When Fränkel returned to his native Berlin, Mendelssohn, then aged fourteen, followed him. On his arrival, the boy had to pay the toll exacted from every Jew entering the city. Mendelssohn not only continued his religious studies with Rabbi Fränkel but also pursued a general education, studying several languages, sciences, and, in particular, philosophy. At the same time he had to earn his living and, at first, suffered many hardships. Jews without means had no right of domicile. A number of enlightened scholars were taken with his abilities and not only taught him but introduced him to learned circles. In 1750 Mendelssohn was appointed to tutor the children of an owner of a silk factory. Four years later, he became the firm's bookkeeper, and later a partner. For the rest of his life, while engaged in manifold scholarly and communal pursuits, he continued to earn his living as a merchant. However, only twenty years after his arrival in Berlin did he receive a formal residence permit.

In 1754 he was introduced — originally as a chess partner — to the liberal writer and dramatist, Gotthold Ephraim Lessing, an outstanding representative of German Enlightenment. The two became fast friends and in the same year, Lessing wrote that he foresaw in Mendelssohn "a second Spinoza." Lessing helped Mendelssohn with his German style, first publicly used in Mendelssohn's defense of Lessing's drama, *Die Juden*. This was followed by a philosophical treatise and a joint work by the two men on the English poet, Alexander Pope. Soon Mendelssohn's German was so exceptional that the king, Frederick II, inquired as to the identity of this brilliant young writer. Before long, scholars and courtiers were seeking out this "young Hebrew who wrote in German" (Mendels-

Moses Mendelssohn, on the left, playing chess with the Lutheran theologian J. C. Lavater. Looking on, Gotthold Lessing. 1866.

sohn was the first Jew to publish in German). In 1763 he married Fromet Guggenheim of Hamburg, and thanks in great measure to her abilities, their home became a salon for Jews and non-Jews. By this time, he was participating in the leading literary journals and even dared to write critically of the poetry of the King of Prussia, Frederick the Great.

In 1763, he received first prize from the Prussian Royal Academy of Sciences for a treatise on evidence in metaphysics. The unsuccessful competitors included Immanuel Kant. Following his triumph, he was accorded by the King the patent of *Schutz Jude* (a privileged Jew) and released from the harassments, including police interference, to which Jews were subjected.

He reached the heights of fame with the publication of *Phaedon*, an essay on the immortality of the soul, written in the form of a Platonic dialogue. He was lionized in German society, admired for his wisdom, and known as "the German Socrates." He was active in the learned societies which, in the absence of a university in Berlin, served as social centers for the intelligentsia. Many celebrated visitors, including royalty and great thinkers, such as Herder, sought his advice and guidance.

Until he was forty, his primary interest was the dissemination of German culture to Germans, to the rest of the world, and especially to Jews. At all times, he was a traditional and conscious Jew, ready to use his influence in the Christian world to help fellow Jews and Jewish communities in distress. In 1769, a Swiss clergyman, Johann Kaspar Lavater, a deeply emotional Christian, thought he could persuade the famous Jew to become a Christian and challenged him to prove the superiority of Judaism over Christianity. Reluctantly, Mendelssohn published a pamphlet in reply and a literary polemic ensued, which Mendelssohn — and indeed Lavater — found distasteful. One effect was that henceforward Mendelssohn devoted himself primarily to Jewish problems, especially those emerging from the challenge of Enlightenment and Emancipation. He sought to prepare the Jews in German life to enter German society. To do this he had to make them familiar with the German language (they spoke only Yiddish). With this object, he translated the Pentateuch into German, publishing it in Hebrew letters. Together with a number of like-minded scholarly colleagues, he added a

---

FROM THE WRITINGS OF MOSES MENDELSSOHN

On Judaism

Let every man who does not disturb the public welfare, who obeys the law, acts righteously toward you and his fellow men, be allowed to speak as he thinks, to pray to God after his own fashion or after that of his fathers, and to seek eternal salvation where he thinks he may find it.

We have no doctrines that are contrary to reason. We added nothing to natural religion save commandments and statutes. But the fundamental tenets of our religion rest on the foundation of reason. They are in consonance with the results of free inquiry, without any conflict or contradiction.

On Jewish-Christian Relations

It is unbecoming for one of us to openly defy the other and thereby furnish diversion to the idle, scandal to the simple and malicious exultation to the revilers of truth and virtue. Were we to analyze our aggregate stock of knowledge, we certainly shall concur in so many important truths that I venture to say few individuals of one and the same religious persuasion would more harmonize in thinking. A point here and there on which we might perhaps still divide might be adjourned for some ages longer, without detriment to the welfare of the human race. What a world of bliss we would live in did all men adopt the true principles which the best among the Christians and the best among the Jews have in common.

Hebrew commentary, reflecting the mood of the Enlightenment. This work, completed in 1783, proved a milestone in Jewish education. On his initiative, a Jewish free school was opened in Berlin.

Mendelssohn was the advocate for Jewish communities in trouble. He used his influence to avoid threatened anti-Jewish measures in Switzerland and Germany. To help the Jews of Alsace, he persuaded his friend Christian Wilhelm von Dohm to write a memorandum for submission to the French government, "On the Civil Improvement of the Jews," a pioneer plea for Jewish emancipation.

On his death, he was honored by Jews and non-Jews alike. He did not live to see the realization of Jewish Emancipation, but he was regarded as the spiritual leader in the struggle for its attainment. The trends he ushered in were not without dangers for Judaism. As Jews entered German society and culture, they were dazzled by the new opportunities and many, including Mendelssohn's own descendants (one of them, his grandson, the famous composer Felix Mendelssohn-Bartholdy [q.v.]), became Christian. Mendelssohn himself always remained an observant Jew. The nobility of his character is reflected in Lessing's play *Nathan the Wise*, in which the potrait of the hero was inspired by Mendelssohn.

His best-known work of Jewish thought was entitled *Jerusalem* (1783). In it he pleaded for the separation of church and state. Religion, he maintained, is a matter of individual spirit and conscience, and should not be subject to coercion. He affirmed that there is no contradiction between philosophical rationalism and fidelity to Judaism. Judaism is a rational religion, or rather not a revealed religion but a revealed legislation.

A. Altmann, *Moses Mendelssohn: A Biographic Study*, 1973.

E. Jospe, *Moses Mendelssohn; Selections from his Writings*, 1975.

MENDES, GRACIA (c. 1510–1569) Jewish leader in Holland, Italy, and Turkey. Beatrice de Luna was her assumed Christian name. Born to a Marrano family in Portugal, at age eighteen she married Francisco Mendes, a businessman in precious stones and a banker. When he died in 1536, leaving her with a young daughter, Gracia Mendes decided to leave Portugal, to which the Inquisition had just been extended. She moved to Antwerp, where her brother-in-law, Diogo Mendes, directed the flourishing branch of the family bank, and the two devised an underground network to get Marranos out of Spain and Portugal. The scheme enabled the refugees to complete the arduous voyage to the Balkans, where they could openly profess Judaism.

After Diogo died in 1543, she moved to Italy. There she began to practice Judaism openly and became known by her Jewish name, Gracia Nasi. Living in Ferrara, she continued to help her fellow Jews escape from Portugal, assisting them to transfer their wealth and to settle in Ferrara or

Turkey. However, intolerance again spread through Christian Europe, and former Marranos could no longer feel safe. In 1553, therefore, she took her family to Constantinople. Her arrival was an occasion for celebration by the city's Jews, as by this time she had become a legendary figure and the Ottoman authorities were eagerly welcoming wealthy Jewish newcomers. Gracia and her family took up residence in a fashionable suburb. In her princely home, some eighty paupers were given free meals each day. Charity on such a scale was made possible by Gracia's large overseas business interests with Italian cities, to which she mainly exported wool, pepper, and grain. In turn she imported cloth and textiles, and her volume of business was so great she had her own ships to transport the goods.

At the same time Dona Gracia was Constantinople's greatest patron of Jewish learning. She established a yeshiva and endowed a beautiful synagogue which for centuries was known as "the synagogue of the Señora." She financed a *bet midrash* (study center) for rabbinic study with the innovation of a rotation of its student scholars so that all the rabbis of the city could enjoy refresher courses.

She sought to utilize her financial power and influence to intervene on behalf of Jews persecuted elsewhere. Her use of financial pressure to combat anti-Semitism was an innovation and aroused controversy in the Jewish world. The setting for her most dramatic episode was the Italian port of Ancona. Promised protection by the pope, one hundred Jewish families, including Marranos, moved to Ancona, but during the Counter-Reformation their privileges were withdrawn and they were confined to a ghetto. The ex-Marranos were rounded up and after making public penance were imprisoned; those who refused to recant were strangled and burnt (1555). In reaction Gracia Mendes asked the sultan of Turkey to intervene on behalf of Anconan Jewry and organized an international Jewish boycott of the city. She urged Jews throughout the Ottoman Empire to excommunicate any Jews who continued trading with Ancona. Not all Jews supported her initiative, however, and business and rabbinical opposition to the blockade won out (with unfortunate consequences as foreseen by Gracia Mendes).

Much of her power and influence were shared with her nephew and son-in-law, Joseph Nasi (q.v.). In the last decade of her life she withdrew from public activities, leaving him to carry on her work. On her death she was mourned throughout the Jewish world as the outstanding Jewish woman of her time.

C. Roth, *The House of Nasi: Dona Gracia*, 1947.

MENDÈS-FRANCE, PIERRE (1907–1982) French statesman. Born in Paris, he distinguished himself early in life with a thesis on financial problems. He joined the Radical Socialist party when he was sixteen, and in 1932 became the youngest deputy ever elected to the National Assembly. In 1935 he became mayor of Louviers in 1938 undersecretary of state at the treasury in the government of Léon Blum (q.v.).

In World War II, he served in the air force, but after the German occupation of France in June 1940, fled to North Africa, where he was arrested for treason and sent back to France. He was imprisoned by the Vichy government at Clermont-Ferrand, but succeeded in escaping in June 1941 with the help of his wife and friends. He left behind a letter addressed to Marshal Pétain in which he wrote: "My escape is not the act of a condemned man who is running away from a punishment he deserves. It is, after using up all the legal means available to me, my last resort to proclaim once again, my refusal to submit to the lie of the judgment that has stricken me. This judgment was not a decision of justice, it is not even a judiciary error, it is a political violation.... It is not the army officer that was condemned, it was the deputy, the man of the Left, the Jew, the patriot who refuses to accept the defeat of his country. Neither the law nor my conscience compel me to obey."

He reached England in 1942, and joined the Free French Air Force. From 1943 to 1945 he participated in Charles de Gaulle's provisional government in Algeria as commissioner for finance.

In 1945 he was appointed minister of the economy, but his stringent anti-inflationary measures were opposed by other members of the government and he had to resign. The following year he was made governor of the Bank of Reconstruction and Development. In the same year he was reelected to parliament, where he made his mark with his criticisms of government policies on Indochina, Algeria, and the economy.

In 1954, following the fall of Dien Bien Phu, he was elected prime minister by a huge majority on the strength of his undertaking to end the war in Indochina in a month and to introduce economic reforms. The former promise was fulfilled at the

Pierre Mendès-France.

Geneva conference which agreed on an armistice line on the seventeenth parallel. He then formulated a plan for a European Defense Community with British participation. However his proposal to accord independence to Morocco and Tunisia was thought to have inspired the Algerian rebellion of October 1954 and early in 1955 his North African policies were rejected by parliament and he resigned the premiership.

For a few months in 1956 he was deputy premier without portfolio in Guy Mollet's government, but left over disagreements concerning North African policies. He tried to make his Radical party the key factor in the noncommunist left, but after his failure to be reelected to parliament in 1958, he resigned his leadership of the party. He returned to parliament in 1967 and the following year founded a new party, the Parti Socialiste Unifié. Thereafter he did not reattain a prominent political position, but remained a respected figure in French politics, greatly admired for his intellectual grasp. His books included *The Pursuit of Freedom* (1956) and *Modern French Republic* (1963).

He had ascetic tendencies and made a brave but unsuccessful attempt, while premier, to get his countrymen to drink milk instead of wine. He was also keenly identified Jew and Zionist, working closely with Nahum Goldmann (q.v.) on programs to solve the Arab-Israel conflict.

A. Werth, *The Twilight of France, Nineteen Thirty-Three to Nineteen Forty*, 1958.

MENDOZA, DANIEL (1764–1836) English boxing champion whose ring style revolutionized the sport. Born in Aldgate, London, he wrote in his memoirs that "I was sent, at a very early age, to a Jews' school, where I remained for some years, and was instructed in English grammar, writing, arithmetic, and... I was also instructed in the Hebrew language."

Anti-Semitic incidents led to numerous street brawls. After one outstanding performance, Mendoza was persuaded to try his hand as a professional boxer. Bare-knuckle victories over much larger opponents marked him as a coming man and earned him such names as the "Star of the East" and the "Light of Israel." The Prince of Wales (later King George IV) attended one of these contests and personally handed Mendoza his winning share of the purse.

Between 1788 and 1790 Mendoza fought three matches against Richard Humphries, the reigning title holder and public favorite. The much smaller Mendoza (five feet, seven inches, 160 pounds) defeated Humphries in two contests and was considered the champion of England, writing a popular book *The Art of Boxing*.

In 1790 a boxing writer said of Mendoza, "His blows are given with astonishing quickness, and he is allowed to strike oftener, and stop more dexterously, than any other man." Another wrote that he was "the introducer of a new, more rapid, and more elegant style of boxing."

MEMOIRS
OF
THE LIFE
OF
DANIEL MENDOZA;
CONTAINING
A FAITHFUL NARRATIVE
OF THE
VARIOUS VICISSITUDES OF HIS LIFE,
AND AN ACCOUNT OF THE
NUMEROUS CONTESTS
IN WHICH HE HAS BEEN ENGAGED, WITH OBSERVATIONS ON EACH;
COMPRISING ALSO
Genuine Anecdotes of many Distinguished Characters,
TO WHICH ARE ADDED,
OBSERVATIONS ON THE ART OF PUGILISM;
RULES
TO BE OBSERVED WITH REGARD TO TRAINING, &c.

A NEW EDITION.

London:
PRINTED FOR D. MENDOZA;
BY G. HAYDEN,
BRYDGES STREET, COVENT GARDEN.

1816.

Title page of Daniel Mendoza's memoirs.

After his victories Mendoza was received by King George III. His triumphs, both in and out of the ring, endeared him to the Jewish community. His friendship with royalty and the aristocracy helped elevate his coreligionists in the eyes of the English public.

With his earnings Mendoza opened a London boxing school. He taught the intricacies of the prize ring to the sons of the wealthy as well as to poor Jewish youngsters. In the early years of the 19th century, a number of his Jewish pupils became outstanding professional boxers.

When he took his show on the road he always billed himself as "Mendoza the Jew." Recalling his

---

MENDOZA ANNOUNCES HIS RETIREMENT FROM THE RING:

Having in the course of my life fought 33 pitched battles, most of them with antagonists far superior to me in strength and size, in nearly the whole of which I have come off victorious; being now considerably past the prime of life, and having a numerous family [he had eleven children] dependent on me for support, I trust it will be admitted it is high time for me to retire from scenes in which my life might be endangered, and the means for providing for my family entirely destroyed....

tour of the British Isles and Ireland, *The Ring* magazine said, "He was an especial favorite in Ireland... where he toured and lectured extensively, demonstrating the finer points of the boxing art as developed by him. The attentive Hibernians learned their lessons well and were to be paragons of the Mendoza school."

He lost his championship to John Jackson in 1795 in seventeen minutes. His financial difficulties began soon afterward, and troubled him the rest of his life. He spent money freely and was usually in debt. Mendoza wrote a colorful autobiography, *Memoirs* (1816).

Two descendants of his family were lawyer and statesman Rufus Isaacs (q.v.), First Marquess of Reading, and actor Peter Sellers (q.v.).

H. U. Ribalow, *Fighter from Whitechapel*, 1962.

MENKEN, ADAH ISAACS (1835–1868) U.S. actress and poet. Born Adah Theodore, also known as Dolores Adios Fuestesi, she achieved worldwide fame and notoriety for her role in *Mazeppa*, a dramatization of Byron's poem. In the final scene fo the play, she raced a horse around the theater, dressed in flesh-colored tights, that gave an illusion of nudity.

The truth of her origins are clouded by the numerous tales she spun. She claimed at different times to be the daughter of a New Orleans merchant, an Irishwoman, a Portuguese rabbinical scholar, a French settler of Louisiana, and an octoroon. Most of her biographers agree that she was born in the vicinity of New Orleans, Louisiana, around 1835.

During her teenage years, she acquired a love of poetry was sentimental and amateurish. An extremely intelligent and beautiful woman, she discovered at a yound age that she had the capacity to captivate most of the men she met. At about age eighteen, she purportedly traveled to Cuba as the mistress of an Austrian nobleman. Later, she told people that she had been an actress and dancer in Havana.

She was back in the United States by 1855, and though she had had no formal training, began looking for work as an actress. The following year, on her travels through Texas, she met and married Alexander Isaac Menken, the son of wealthy Cincinnati Jews. She permanently adopted his surname, but later changed Isaac to Isaacs.

The couple moved to Cincinnati, where the new Mrs. Menken wrote poetry (some of which had Judaism as its theme), and published poems and essays in the *Israelite*. Although it is unclear whether she was Jewish from birth of if she converted at this point, she studied Hebvrew and Judaism, and became an enthusiastic Jew. In her typically outspoken manner, she protested when Lionel Rothschild (q.v.) was denied his seat in the British House of Commons by writing an essay about the issue.

With her husband as manager, Menken resumed her search for theater work and by 1858 had secured an acting role in New Orleans. Though it soon became obvious that her acting ability was limited, she had what a later generation would call sex appeal. In an era when wearing skirts above the ankle was considered inappropriate, Menken wore flamboyant dresses, smoked cigarettes in public, and appeared on stage in sheer negligee. Despite her status as a 19th-century sex symbol, her intellect allowed her entry into the literary circles of any city in which she resided. She counted among her friends such literary greats as Walt Whitman, Algernon Charles Swinburne, Charles Dickens, Charles Reade, George Sand, and Alexandre Dumas, père.

Menken's increasingly independent behavior enraged her husband, who returned to Cincinnati and sent her a rabbinical but not a civil divorce. Believing she was legally divorced, she married the boxer John C. Heenan in 1859. Their relationship ended in a scandal after Heenan denied being her husband and the press discovered that she had never been legally divorced from her first husband. The situation made finding work a near-impossibility for Menken, who was now pregnant. She lived on the verge of poverty, usually supported by loyal friends.

After suffering a miscarriage and receiving divorces from both her husbands, she was presented with a golden opportunity: a theater director who had seen Menken's performance in a vaudeville act, suggested that she star in *Mazeppa*. The first performance was in Albany, New York, in June 1861. Audiences flocked to see the scandalous play in which it was rumored that Menken appeared nude.

For the next four years she appeared as Mazeppa in United States cities from new York to San Francisco. Most theater critics did not praise her acting ability, but one commented on what he thought made the show a sellout; "Miss Menken places the male in her audience at a disadvantage. She is so lovely that she numbs the mind, and the senses reel." Menken's third husband, the journalist Robert Henry Newell, wrote, "Adah was a symbol of Desire Awakened to every man who set eyes on her. All who saw her wanted her, immediately."

In 1864 Menken took *Mazeppa* to Victorian England, where it was an unqualified success. On a return trip to the United States in 1865 she met her fourth husband, "Captain" James Barkely. Their marriage lasted for one day; she discovered that the "Captain" was a fortune hunter and — not a military man, and he found out that the free-spending Menken did not have much left of the fortune she had earned. Pregnant and without the support of a spouse, she traveled to Paris and gave birth to a son, whose godmother was George Sand. Immediately after the birth, Menken starred in another successful run of *Mazeppa*.

In 1867 she appeared in her second stage success, *Les pirates de la savane*, an adventure story which allowed her to appear in the scanty costumes her fans enjoyed. During a rehearsal in July 1868, she collapsed. One month later, at the height of her popularity, she died. Her book of poetry, *Infelicia*, appeared posthumously and was dedicated to Charles Dickens.

B. Falk, *Naked Lady*, 1934.
A. Lesser, *Enchanting Rebel*, 1947.
P. Lewis, *Queen of the Plaza*, 1964.
W. Mankowitz, *Mazeppa: The Lifes, Loves and Legends of Adah Isaacs Menken*, 1982.

METCHNIKOFF, ELIE (1845–1916) Russian biologist and Nobel Prize winner. His mother was Jewish and his father an officer in the Imperial Guard. He studied biology at the University of Kharkov and went to Germany to complete his studies. His important advances in embryology made him famous and he was appointed professor of zoology and comparative anatomy at the University of Odessa in 1870.

From 1882 to 1886, he lived in Messina, Italy, studying marine life. These studies led him to describe the phenomenon of single-cell phagocytes, organisms that ingest and destroy foreign material, especially bacteria. Metchnikoff published his findings in an article "The Struggle of the Organism against Microbes" (1894). In 1888 he began working with Louis Pasteur in Paris and later became the deputy director, and then the director, of the Pasteur Institute, where he continued his work on phagocytosis.

In an age when the average life expectancy was low, Metchnikoff had great optimism about the possibility of prolongation of life and the prevention of premature death. His research on the prolongation of life includes the problems of old age, the causes and prevention of intestinal putrefaction and unhealthy fermentations from toxins in the bowels and the avoidance of alcohol and dangerous diets (Metchnikoff advocated a proper diet including sour milk to prolong life and avoid senility). Among other aspects of his work were somnambulism, hysteria, and the psychology of crowds.

Metchnikoff's most famous work was in the field of immunity and infectious diseases. He investigated the mechanisms of natural immunity, the use of sera in immunity, the effects of snake venoms, and the attenuation of viruses. Among the diseases Metchnikoff investigated were anthrax, tuberculosis, cholera (*Vibrio metchnikovi*, a cholera-producing organism named after him, was used for producing an anticholera vaccine), diphtheria, erysipelas, and tetanus. He also studied the effects of viral diseases such as a smallpox and rabies, despite the unknown nature of the causative viruses.

In 1908 Elie Metchnikoff received the Nobel Prize for medicine together with Paul Ehrlich (q.v.) for their works on immunity.

O. Metchnikoff, *Life of Elie Metchnikoff*, 1921.

MEYER, EUGENE (1875–1959) U.S. banker, newspaper editor, and publisher. Meyer was born in Los Angeles, graduated from Yale University in 1895, and studied banking in Europe for two years. In 1901 he founded the banking firm of Eugene Meyer, Jr., and Company, and until World War I was active in the oil, copper, and automobile industries. In 1917 he was appointed adviser to the War Industries Board and the following year was named managing director of the War Finance Corporation. In 1931 he organized the Reconstruction Finance Corporation and became its first chairman.

In 1946 President Harry S. Truman appointed Meyer as the first president of the International Bank for Reconstruction and Development (the World Bank). Under President Dwight Eisenhower he served as a member of various commissions.

In 1933 Meyer bought the bankrupt *Washington Post* at a public auction. From 1940 to 1946 he served as the paper's editor and publisher, bringing it back to financial stability and achieving a high level of influence in the Washington community.

In 1947, after the *Post* merged with the *Washington Times-Herald*, Meyer became chairman of the Board of the *Washington Post and Times-Herald*, serving in this capacity until his death. The Washington Post Company, which he headed, also owned *Newsweek* magazine and various radio stations. After Meyer's death, he was succeeded by his daughter, Katherine Graham, as publisher of the *Post*.

MEYERBEER, GIACOMO (1791—1864) German opera composer and the central musical figure in French grand opera after 1831. Born Jakob Liebmann Beer in Vogelsdorf, near Berlin, he changed his name when his grandfather promised to leave him his fortune on condition that he add Meyer to the name. His father, Jakob (Juda) Herz Beer, was a Berlin army contractor who owned sugar refineries in Berlin and northeast Italy. His mother, Amalia, the daughter of Liebmann Meyer Wulf, who became the general concessionaire of the Prussian lottery in 1794, was a contractor for both the army and the postal service, as well as being a banker.

The Meyerbeer household became, from 1800, one of the most popular meeting places for Berlin's cultural elite. Musicians and members of the court visited the house frequently. Meyerbeer began studying the piano with Franz Lauska, the piano teacher of the royal princes.

In 1810 Meyerbeer moved to Darmstadt, where he premiered his oratorio *God and Nature*. During his studies in Darmstadt, he and his fellow students wrote reviews of each other's works. Meyerbeer published his written reviews under the names Julius Billig and Philodikaois. His first operas, written while studying in Darmstadt, were successful, but the young composer took the advice of Antonio Salieri, and lightened up his musical style by introducing free-flowing Italian melodies into his somewhat heavy Germanic style. This change made Meyerbeer a household name in Italy, as he staged new operas in Venice, Turin, and Milan.

Meyerbeer moved from Italy to Paris, where his

opera *Robert le diable* premiered in 1831. Fetis wrote at the time that this new opera is not just "Meyerbeer's masterpiece; it is a work remarkable in the history of art... it incontestably places Meyerbeer at the head of the present German school and makes him chief." Within three years it was performed in seventy-seven theaters in ten countries. It was followed by *Les Huguenots* (1836), the opera that crowned the German Meyerbeer as the leading French opera composer of the time. In 1834 he was the first German musician to receive the order of chevalier of the Legion d'Honneur and was also elected a member of the French Institut.

In 1842 Meyerbeer was invited by King Frederick William IV to become the general music director in Berlin and he returned to his homeland. After six years in Berlin, however, he was dismissed from the court and returned to Paris. There he staged the premiere of *Le prophète* (1849), which was performed in its first year in forty opera houses. Meyerbeer was working on the final version of *L'Africaine*, which he had begun many years earlier, when he died in Paris. His body was returned to Berlin where the Prussian court attended the funeral services. Gioacchino Rossini wrote to the composer who composed the music for Meyerbeer's funeral: "Would it not have been better if you had died and Meyerbeer had written your funeral march!"

Meyerbeer helped Richard Wagner both artistically and financially throughout his career. Initially Wagner admired the work of the senior composer, arguing that *Robert le diable* "has a wonderful, almost sinister atmosphere.... It is deathless." But eventually Wagner criticized Meyerbeer's operas for their lack of artistic merit and Meyerbeer himself for being a Jew.

Meyerbeer was an operatic innovator who always stressed the importance of the singers in opera and who tended to choose original material for his work. He was also one of the wealthiest men in Europe and enjoyed the continuous support of the press as long as he was ready to offer monetary inducement. As the French composer, Hector Berlioz, said: "Meyerbeer had the luck to be talented, but, above all, the talent to be lucky."

E. Istel, *Meyerbeer's Way to Mastership*, 1926.
B. W. Wessling, *Meyerbeer* (German, 1984).

MICAH (8th cent. BC) Israelite prophet, who received his revelations during the reigns of Jotham, Ahaz, and Hezekiah, kings of Judah. He came from Moresheth near Gath in the southern coastal plain of the country and at least one of his prophecies was directed at this region (Micah 1:10–16). Although originally from the Kingdom of Judah, he directed his prophecies to both the northern and southern kingdoms. They were uttered in Jerusalem and he was the first prophet to foretell the future destruction of that city for its sinfulness. According to Jeremiah (q.v; 26:18–19), Micah's prophecy of the destruction of Jerusalem was only averted by the repentance of King Hezekiah.

Little is known of Micah's life. He lived at the same time as the prophet Isaiah (q.v.) and many parallels can be seen in their respective messages. Micah stressed the need for social justice and he denounced the corruption in the marketplace and the wickedness in high places. He also attacked other prophets of his day for accepting payment for their prophecies. His ultimate message was that after the destruction of the kingdom of Judah, it will be restored, more gloriously than ever, and he foresaw an era of universal peace, which God would oversee from Jerusalem (a similar message was being proclaimed by Isaiah). His ethical demands are summarized in the verse stating that what the Lord requires of man is "only to do justice, to love mercy, and to walk humbly with your God" (Micah 6:8).
A. J. Heschel, *The Prophets*, 1962.

MICHELSON, ALBERT ABRAHAM (1852–1931) Physicist; the first American scientist and the first American Jew to receive the Nobel Prize. Born in Strelno, Germany, he emigrated with his family to the United States when he was three. His parents lived in Murphy's Camp, a small mining town in the mountains of California, and sent him to school in San Francisco.

By the time Michelson had finished school, his family had moved to Nevada, and he applied for admission to the naval academy when there was a vacancy in Nevada's quota. Failing to get an appointment, he went to Washington D.C. to try for one of ten "at large" places awarded by the president. Although the ten places had been filled, President Ulysses Grant made an exception and awarded him an eleventh place.

It was at the naval academy that Michelson discovered his talent for physics, and upon graduating, after doing his duty as a midshipman for two years, he was made an instructor in physics and chemistry at the academy in Annapolis, Maryland (1875–1879). In 1877, while preparing for a lecture, he discovered an unprecedented accurate method for measuring the speed of light.

Internationally famous for this discovery by the age of twenty-six, Michelson left the naval academy in 1879 and after a year at the Nautical Almanac in Washington, went to study in Europe. While he was in Berlin he began one of his most important experiments: the attempt to measure the relative motion of earth through the ether (that was then assumed to pervade all space). In the course of these investigations he developed the interferometer, an extremely sensitive optical instrument for measuring velocity, which also made it possible to measure the diameters of the stars for the first time. Michelson's failure, in 1887, to detect the movement of the earth through the ether, led to Albert Einstein's (q.v.) theory of relativity.

Michelson was professor of physics at the Case School of Applied Science in Cleveland, Ohio (1883–1889), and at Clark University in Worcester, Massachusetts (1889–1892); from 1892 to 1929 was the first professor of physics at the University of Chicago.

In 1907 Michelson was awarded the Nobel Prize for physics. He also received numerous other awards and honorary degrees, among them the first distinguished professorship ever granted by the University of Chicago. From 1923 to 1927, he was president of the National Academy of Sciences. In 1929 he retired to Pasadena, California, where he continued to work until his death. He published *Velocity of Light* (1902), *Light Waves and Their Uses* (1903), *Studies in Optics* (1927), and a number of articles. He was also a painter and an accomplished violinist.

B. Jaffe, *Michelson and the Speed of Light*, 1960.

D. J. Kevles, *The Physicists*, 1979.

MIKHOELS, SOLOMON (1890–1948) Russian Yiddish actor. Born in Dvinsk into an Orthodox family (Vovsi) of eight children, he received a traditional Jewish education. At the age of nine he wrote and produced a Yiddish play, *Sins of Youth*, and aged twelve wrote for a periodical put out by a Zionist youth group. When, in 1905, his father went bankrupt, the family moved to Riga and he gave private lessons while still attending school. In 1915 he began studying law at Saint Petersburg University, but in 1918 gave it up to join Alexander

Solomon Mikhoels as King Lear in the Jewish State Theater production, Moscow, 1935.

Granovsky's Jewish drama studio, where he soon became adviser on Jewish tradition, literature, and drama. He took the stage name of Mikhoels.

In 1920 the studio moved to Moscow, where together with Granovsky he set up the Moscow Yiddish State Theater whose walls and sets were designed by Marc Chagall (q.v.). On the evening of the theater's premiere, a few moments before Mikhoels was due to go on stage, Chagall grabbed Mikhoels's coat "and like one possessed took up his brush and colors and painted all sorts of signs on the coat and decorated his hat with birds and animals. Despite Mikhoels's entreaties to unhand him and the urgent ringing of the bell summoning him on stage. Chagall refused to let him go until he had finished."

In 1923 Mikhoels directed his first play, *200,000*, by Shalom Aleichem (q.v.), in which he played the lead role. In 1928 the theater went on a European tour, and Mikhoels's acting in original Yiddish plays and classical dramas were acclaimed by leading European critics. On his return to Moscow, he was appointed director of the Moscow Yiddish State Theater and in 1929 he opened the Jewish Theatrical Studio to train young actors for his theater as well as for other Russian Jewish theaters.

During the Shakespeare Festival in Moscow, in 1935, Mikhoels appeared as King Lear, considered his greatest performance (partly preserved on film). His brilliant portrayal in 1938 of Tuvia in Shalom Aleichem's *Tuvia the Milkman* was his last role. On the occasion of the theater's twentieth anniversary celebrations in 1939, Mikhoels was granted the title of People's Artist of the Soviet Republic and awarded the Order of Lenin, the highest award presented to an actor in the Soviet Union. In 1941 he moved with the theater to Tashkent, Uzbekistan, and also worked with the local theater, ballet, and opera companies.

In 1942 Mikhoels was appointed chairman of the Jewish Anti-Fascist Committee in Moscow fostered by the Soviet Bureau of Information to promote information about the Soviet war effort against the Nazis through press releases and radio broadcasts to Jews in the West. In 1943, with Stalin's personal blessings, he traveled together with the Yiddish writer, Itzik Feffer, on behalf of the committee to the United States, Canada, Mexico, and England, where they were welcomed by the Jewish communities who raised nearly three million dollars for the benefit of the Russian people.

During his stay in the United States, when Mikhoels ended an address to an audience of over 50,000 with a heart-rending call to the Jews to raise their voices against the annihilation of their brethren in Europe, the crowd stormed the stage to shake his hand. Suddenly the stage crashed to the ground and Mikhoels's leg was injured; he was forced to carry out the rest of his journey in the United States on crutches. The accident left him with a permanent limp.

Mikhoels met his death in January 1948 in Minsk while on an official mission on behalf of the

State Committee for Theater Prizes. The official version attributed it to a car accident, but later evidence was produced that his assassination had been ordered by the Soviet secret police as part of Stalin's policy of liquidating Yiddish writers, actors, and artists. This was substantiated by a reference in Svetlana Stalin's book *One Year Only* to the fact that she had been present when her father had given instructions to issue the official version of an accident and that "her father saw Zionist threats everywhere."

After his death the Solomon Mikhoels Museum was founded in the Moscow Yiddish State Theater and his daughter Natalia appointed curator. The photographs, press-clippings of his roles, and stenographic records of his speeches were confiscated in 1949 by the Russian authorities as nationalist propaganda. They were later destroyed in a fire.

N. Vovsi-Mikhoels, *My Father Shlomo Mikhoels; His Life and Death as a Jewish Actor* (Hebrew), 1982.

MILHAUD, DARIUS (1892–1974) French composer. He was born in Aix-en-Provence, the son of an almond merchant and the descendant of an old Jewish family that had lived in Provence for many centuries. After taking some piano and violin lessons as a child, Milhaud entered the Paris conservatory at the age of seventeen as a violin student. During his studies he played the violin in the student orchestra and began composing in what was described as "a bold modernistic manner." Milhaud made friends with many artists who influenced him even more than did his musical colleagues. At this time he also began traveling extensively, a habit he never gave up.

As World War I broke out, Milhaud began composing regularly. He was rejected for military service because of his poor health.

In 1916 he accompanied the then diplomat and later famous poet Paul Claudel to Brazil as his secretary, when Claudel was appointed French minister in that country. In the two years he spent in Brazil Milhaud was introduced to its native music. Eventually many of its rhythms found their way to his own compositions. From the mid-1920s Milhaud devoted himself abouve everything to composition. :

Milhaud wrote over four hundred compositions which encompass almost every possible genre, from opera to chamber music, from ballet to the symphonic repertoire. Among his many innovations are what he called a miniature symphony as well as works for electronic instruments. His 1923 ballet, *La Création du monde* ("The Creation of the World"), portrays the creation myth through the eyes of Black cosmology, for which the composer used jazz and blues almost for the first time in a symphonic score.

His more important compositions include operas based on the Greek classics like *Agamemnon* and *Medée*. Milhaud created a new type of musical theater here in which his score was more than the usual incidental score composers used to provide for the theater.

Milhaud composed works that reflect his Jewish heritage, including part of a ballet titled *Moïse*, and the *Poèmes juifs*. *David*, an opera in five acts was premiered in Jerusalem in 1954 as part of a festival to honor the 3000th anniversary of King David. Milhaud himself traveled to Israel during the composition of this work in order to get the feel of the country. Other Jewish compositions include "Kaddish" for voice and organ, "Sabbath Morning Service" for baritone, chorus and organ, and Milhaud's last work, the cantata "Ani Maamin," which was written for the 1973 Israel Festival.

C. Palmer, *Milhaud*, 1976.

MINKOWSKI, HERMANN (1864–1909) German mathematician. He was born in Lithuania of German parents who returned to Germany and settled in Königsberg (now Kaliningrad, USSR) when the boy was eight.

Minkowski obtained his Ph.D. at Königsberg in 1885. He taught at the University of Bonn until 1894, then returning to Königsberg for two years, before going to the University of Zurich. In 1902 a new professorship was created for him at the University of Göttingen, where he remained until his death.

His work centered on the arithmetic of quadratic forms in *n* variables (*n*-ary forms). His most important contributions were: (1) for quadratic forms with rational coefficients, a characterization of equivalence of such forms under a linear transformation with rational coefficients, through a system of three in variants of the form; and (2) completion of the theory of reduction for positive definite *n*-ary quadratic forms with real coefficients.

His most original achievement was his geometric outlook, which he called geometry of numbers. This helped him to reach an improved understanding of the theory of continued fractions. He also examined the geometric properties of convex sets in *n*-dimensional space. Moreover, he was the first to understand the idea of hyperplane of support and proved the existence fo such hyperplane at each point of the boundary of a convex body.

In 1881 the Paris Academy of Sciences set a competition on the number of representation of an integer as a sum of five squares of an integer. The seventeen-year-old Minkowski shared the prize with one of the best-known mathematicians of the time, H. J. Smith.

In his later years, he worked in mathematical physics, participating in the development of ideas which culminated in the theory of relativity. He was the first to grasp that the consequence of Albert Einstein's (q.v.) theory of relativity was the abandonment of the traditional concept of space and time as separate identities and their replacement by a four-dimensional space-time (which became known as a Minkowski space).

His brother **Oskar Minkowski** (1858–1931) was a

physiologist and pathologist who introduced the concept that diabetes results from the suppression of a pancreatic substance (later identified as the hormone insulin).

H. Hancock, *Development of the Minkowski Geometry of Numbers,* 1939.

F. W. Lanchester, *Relativity: An Elementary Explanation of the Space-Time Relations as Established by Minkowski,* 1935.

MODIGLIANI, AMEDEO (1884–1920) Painter and sculptor. He was born in Leghorn (Livorno), Italy, to a family of small merchants. Ill health forced him to give up his general education and he concentrated on art. Leghorn had a lively artistic community and Modigliani's teacher, Gugliemo Michele, himself a student of an Italian impressionist, gave him a thorough training in the fundamentals of art and art history. Modigliani's uncle paid for his art classes, but after his death in 1905, Modigliani moved to Paris, where his mother sent him as much money as she could. He lived in cheap hotels, moving when he had no rent money, often leaving his paintings behind.

In 1906, the year Modigliani arrived in Paris, the retrial of Captain Alfred Dreyfus (q.v.) was held and anti-Semitism was rampant. Most of Modigliani's friends in Paris were Jewish artists. When he made sketches of customers in cafés to earn a few francs, Modigliani signed them, "Modigliani — Jew." Because of his poverty, he often painted on both sides of his canvases. He was greatly influenced by the work of Cezanne and he had close contacts with Picasso.

Between 1909 and 1914, Modigliani's work was mainly in sculpture, at first in wood. His wooden sculptures were made from railroad ties from the construction sites of the Paris subway. After he moved to la Cité Falguière, where Chaim Soutine and Constantin Brancusi were his neighbors, he began to work in limestone, which he found at building construction sites. Often the workers gave him stones, but if not, he went at night to take some home. On Brancusi's advice, he made a study of African sculpture.

Both wood and stone sculpture were carved — dusty work that affected his lungs. During these five years, he produced hundreds of drawings for sculptures and life drawings. He worked on drawings for a series of caryatids, but completed only two.

World War I halted Modigliani's work as a sculptor, for there was no more construction and he could never afford to buy stone. Even his small stipend stopped coming, and he sold nothing. Deprived of the means to work at sculpture, Modigliani resumed painting. He continued his sketching at cafés and would go to La Rotonde for food and drinks, often paying with his paintings. His deteriorating health, together with drink and drugs, made him irascible and often violent. He would attack his friends, including the English poet Beatrice Hastings, who lived with him. She said that he

Amedeo Modigliani. Self-portrait, 1919.

was an "enfant, sometimes terrible, but always forgiven."

He painted everybody — Beatrice Hastings more than a dozen times, and was able to get commissions, though prices were low. When he painted Jacques Lipshitz (q.v.) and his wife, he asked to be paid ten francs and brandy for each sitting.

In 1916 the Polish poet, Leopold Zborowski, became his dealer. That year and the next, Modigliani painted a series of reclining nudes, which are among his outstanding works. Zborowski arranged an exhibition at the Berthe Weill Gallery. It was Modigliani's only one-man show, and it ended before it started. The police came, removed the nudes from the gallery window, and then from the walls. Over fifty years later, the United States Postal Service forced the Guggenheim Museum to withdraw a postcard reproduction of one of these nudes from its shop. Pubic hair was still illegal.

In 1917 Modigliani met and fell in love with Jeanne Hébuterne, a nineteen-year-old art student. The following year their daughter, Jeanne, was born. She was brought up by Modigliani's sister and was to write an outstanding biography of her father. Zborowski found him a studio and models (he painted Jeanne twenty-five times) and gave him a stipend. He also sent Modigliani for two months to Nice, where he painted servants, peasants, children, and two landscapes.

In an exhibition of work by French artists in the Mansard Gallery in London arranged by Zborowski in 1919, the English author Arnold Bennett bought a painting by Modigliani — it brought the highest price in the show, substantially more that the sixty francs he sometimes received for a commission. In 1989, Sotheby's auctioned off a Modigliani portrait for over eight million dollars.

In November 1919, Modigliani began spitting blood. Legend has it that at a friend's house, he sang the Kaddish (mourners' prayer) for himself. In two months he was dead. The next day, Jeanne committed suicide by jumping out of a window on the fifth floor of her parents' house.

Modigliani's portraits are among the very best of the 20th century. He never painted a portrait without the sitter directly in front of him. Much has been written about the ovoid heads, long necks, and supposed blankness of the almond-shaped eyes. They show a natural kinship with the geometric forms of his sculpture. His work is unmistakably Modigliani, yet he caught the essence of the character of the model in every portrait.

His carvings, a series of heads — pure geometric forms — have been described, in spite of his affinity for African art, as Gothic. Here are no portraits of individuals, but universal icons of a contemplative benign humanity.

J. Modigliani, *Modigliani: Man and Myth*, 1958.
C. Roy, *Modigliani*, 1958.
A. Salman, *Modigliani; A Memoir*, 1961.
A. Werner, *Modigliani, the Sculptor*, 1962.

MOLKHO, SOLOMON (originally Diogo Pires; c. 1500–1532) Pseudomessiah, kabbalist, and martyr. Born a Portuguese New Christian (Marrano), he was the child of Jewish immigrants from Spain who had been forcibly converted in 1497. As a promising, talented young man, he became one of King Joao III's secretaries and an official in the Portuguese court of appeals. Diogo Pires might have remained a fairly obscure servant of the crown had it not been for an event that electrified the Portuguese Marrano community in 1525 — the arrival of a mysterious Jewish ambassador, David Reuveni (q.v.), who sought Christian allies for a war to wrest Jerusalem from the Turks. Alarmed by the messianic enthusiasm that his visit aroused among local conversos, Reuveni was not disposed to encourage their open reversion to Judaism. Young Diogo nevertheless unhesitatingly circumcised himself, claiming that he did so by God's command in the first of his many visions. He changed his name and, as Solomon Molkho, took the precaution of fleeing to Italy.

There he may have pursued Hebrew and religious studies before journeying east to Salonika, one of the great centers of Jewish mysticism, where he perfected his knowledge of the Kabbalah, began to view himself as the promised Messiah, and attracted many followers, including Joseph Caro (q.v.). A collection of Molkho's sermons on messianic themes (*Sefer ha-Mefo'ar* as it later became

known) was published at Salonika in 1529; legend has it that Molkho also visited the Holy Land, spending time with the kabbalists of Safed and with Reuveni in Jerusalem. It was in Italy, however, that Molkho believed his struggle for redemption had to be won. He reappeared there in 1529, preaching to large congregations and winning new followers. When some farsighted Jews treated him as an i poster, he decided to "fulfill" a Talmudic doctrine about the Messiah by adopting the guise of a beggar and sitting among diseased, crippled folk near the papal palace "at the gate of Rome" (1530). Molkho even gained a protector in the head of the Church, Pope Clement VII, to whom he predicted separate calamities that indeed took place: Rome's inundation by the Tiber River (October 8, 1530) and an earthquake in his native Portugal (January 26, 1531).

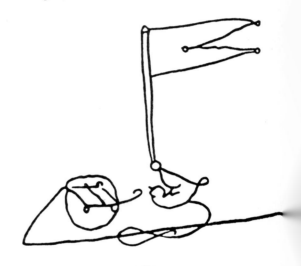

Autograph of Solomon Molkho.

Toward the end of 1530, Molkho appealed for help to the Jews of Venice, where he made an enemy of the pope's Jewish physician, Dr. Jacob Mantino, who followed him back to Rome and there denounced him as a mischievous relapsed Catholic to the Inquisition. Thanks to Pope Clement VII, however, Molkho had an amazing escape: while he was spirited away and granted shelter in the Vatican, a condemned criminal resembling him was made his substitute on the inquisitional pyre (1531). This may have led Molkho to suppose that he bore a charmed life, despite the intrigues of his various opponents. Joining forces with Reuveni in northern Italy (1532), he planned a dramatic approach to the Holy Roman Emperor, Charles V. At Regensburg (Ratisbon) in Bavaria, the Imperial Diet was considering measures to halt the Ottoman advance into central Europe; the two Jewish envoys suddenly appeared there, flying their banner and offering to raise an army of Jews and conversos for joint action against the Turks.

With Lutheranism spreading to the north and Islam to the east, however, Charles V had no time for the perilous schemes of a foreign adventurer or Marrano false messiah. Arrested and clapped in irons, they were sent for trial to Mantua, where Molkho — condemned a second time for judaizing — chose to die a martyr at the stake in December 1532.

Tales of another miraculous rescue continued to circulate years after Molkho's death, sustaining disciples from Portugal to Poland and making this new kabbalistic "saint" a forerunner of the 17th-century heresiarch, Shabbetai Tzevi (q.v.). Biographical data from the correspondence that he left were incorporated in standard Jewish martyrologies. His dramatic career also inspired a number of modern literary works, such as the play by Edmond Fleg (q.v.) *Le juif du pape* (1925) and Aharon Avraham Kabak's *Shelomo Molkho* (1928–1929), a three-volume historical novel in Hebrew.

J. H. Greenstone, *The Messiah Idea in Jewish History*, 1906, pp. 195–202.

L.W. Schwarz, *Memoirs of My People through a Thousand Years*, 1945, pp. 62–67.

MOLLIN, JACOB BEN MOSES HA-LEVI (c. 1360–1427)

A leading religious authority of 15th century German Jewry, known by the Hebrew acronym *Maharil* (Morenu Ha-Rav Yaakov ha-Levi). Born into a prestigious rabbinic family in Mainz, Jacob Mollin studied first with his father, then with noted rabbinic authorities in Vienna, where he was ordained with the additional title of scholarly distinction, *morenu*. He became the rabbi of the Mainz community upon the death of his father in 1387, and established there a yeshiva (Talmudic academy) that attracted an impressive number of disciples, many of whom later became the pivotal religious leadership of central European Jewry. As an outstanding Talmudist, Mollin was sought out by Jews throughout Europe for his halakhic decisions at an early age. He once imposed a three-day fast upon Rhineland Jewry and was instrumental in diverting disaster upon their communities by interceding with government officials to control marauding anti-Hussite crusaders. His responsa (replies to legal queries) uniquely reflected a concern for the prevailing ritual custom and life conditions of his generation and were collected and printed for the first time in Venice (1549). *Minhagei Maharil* (1556), a compilation by his student, Zalman of Saint Goar, of his sermons, commentaries, and legal pronouncements, became a revered reference, used extensively by Moses Isserles (q.v.) in his additions to the *Shulhan Arukh*, which served as the standard for Ashkenazic practice. A poet of liturgical verse *piyutim*, Mollin was also a renowned cantor whose influence on the Polish-German rite was formative and whose melodies were to be heard in the Mainz communal worship service until modern times.

G. Steiman, *Custom and Survival: A Study of the Life and Work of Rabbi Jacob Molin*, 1963.

MOLNÁR, FERENC (Neumann; 1878–1952)

Hungarian playwright, novelist and journalist. Born in Budapest of a middle-class family, he studied law at the universities of Budapest and Geneva but never practiced, choosing a career in journalism. In 1896, he joined the important daily *Budapesti Napló* and was also a permanent correspondent of a number of other journals. His popularity derived from his ability to present contemporary life in a sarcastic, witty style. He depicted the newly wealthy, rising Jewish middle class and incisively analyzed the situation of the poverty-stricken lower middle class and proletariat. During World War I, Molnar was a war correspondent, and his reports from the eastern front were published by the *New York Times*, despite the fact that Hungary fought on the side of the enemy. These articles were collected in book form, *Memoirs of a War Correspondent* (1916). His early short stories and novels realistically depict the seamy side of life beneath the glitter of Budapest society.

Molnár was a born playwright. He wrote his first play *The Lawyer*, a light social comedy, in 1902, but real success came with *The Devil* (1907), which established his reputation as one of the leading dramatists of his day. *Liliom* (1907), usually regarded as Molnár's best play, is based on his short story, *A Bedtime Story*. It was translated into many languages and gained world acclaim with its successful musical adaptation, *Carousel* by Richard Rodgers (q.v.) and Oscar Hammerstein in 1945.

Molnár produced nearly thirty more plays, among them, *The Guardsman* (1910, the basis of Oscar Straus' [q.v.] operetta *The Chocolate Soldier* and of a film with Alfred Lunt and Lynne Fontanne), *The Wolf* (1912), *The Swan* (1920), and the *Red Mill* (1923), several of which became great successes abroad and were also made into movies. They were all light comedies, often with a twist in the plot and the introduction of the supernatural, at times a little sentimental but usually ironic, with the characters recognizable types in contemporary society, speaking a sparkling and witty dialogue.

As time went by, his plays contained less and less social criticism but his short stories and novels showed him to be an outspoken critic of urban poverty. The best-known of his several novels was *The Pal Street Boys* (1907; English translation, 1927), which was published in many translations and filmed several times. It is the story of two warring gangs of boys on a vacant city lot, the playground of children who had no access to parks. Molnár's insight into the close-knit society of schoolboys, his understanding of their psychology, and the poetic qualities of the book are still enjoyed.

As the regime in Hungary became increasingly fascist, Molnár emigrated to Switzerland in the mid-1930s, and in 1940 to the United States, where he died. It was there that he wrote his autobiography, *Companion in Exile* (1950), a moving book by a man who had lost all illusions and even his cynicism.

ABOUT FERENC MOLNÁR

Many anecdotes are told about Molnár. One of the best known is connected with his habit of never rising before noon, having spent the night with his companions in their favorite coffeehouse, The New York. One day he had appear as a witness in a court case at 9:00 A.M. His friends promised to wake him up in time and accompany him to the court. When they came down to the street and Molnár saw the bustling crowds of people around him at this unaccustomed hour, he asked, "Are all these people witnesses?"

In private life, Molnár, a handsome member of café society. was a charming and witty raconteur. His first wife was the Jewish writer, Margit Vészi (1881–1961). His second wife was the non-Jewish actress Sári Fedák (1879–1955) who, after World War II, served a prison sentence for being a member of the Arrowcross (the Hungarian Nazi movement). His third wife was Lili Darvas (1902–1974), a Jewish actress who shared his exile and who won renown on stage and in films.

MONASH, JOHN (1865–1931), Australian engineer and soldier, commander of Australian forces during World War I, knighted 1918. Monash was born in Melbourne to an immigrant family that had been printers of Hebrew books in Vienna. He had his early education at a school in a small bush town, but returned to Melbourne to complete his secondary education. In 1882 he entered the University of Melbourne, pursuing diverse interests in the arts and sciences. He listened to parliamentary debates, attended trials, wrote newspaper articles, played the piano, took painting lessons, and dabbled in carpentry and conjuring. He was awarded degrees in arts, civil engineering, and law. During the course of his studies, he gained practical engineering experience in the field. One of the first major projects on which Monash was engaged was the construction of the Prince's Bridge across the Yarra River. He was also involved in a number of development projects in the state of Victoria, including the construction of Melbourne's outer circle railway.

Monash set up as a consulting engineer and patent attorney in 1894. His practice grew steadily and he became known for use of reinforced concrete and new techniques in such projects as the three-span Morell bridge in Melbourne. Monash was president of the Victorian Institute of Engineers from 1913 to 1915.

In 1883 Monash had joined the university company of the militia and was commissioned three years later. He won a gold medal in 1900 for his military articles published in the *Commonwealth Journal*. During World War I Monash led the Aus-

tralian Fourth Infantry Brigade in the ill-fated landing on Gallipoli, but when the order was given to evacuate the peninsula, he succeeded in withdrawing 45,000 men with their stores and equipment without a single casualty.

In 1916 Monash was promoted to major general and given command of the third division of the Australia and New Zealand Army Corps and fought valiantly in France. In 1918 he was given the command of the Australian Army Corps, and participated with British, Canadian, and American units in the offensive that broke the German defense lines on the Amiens front in summer 1918. He had employed for the first time the use of infantry and tanks as a unified instrument of offensive warfare. King George V visited Monash at his headquarters at Bertangles Château and personally awarded him the order of knight commander of the Bath. This was the first time in almost two centuries that a British monarch had knighted a commander in the field.

After the armistice Monash was appointed director general of the repatriation and demobilization program, initiating a program whereby soldiers awaiting demobilization were trained for civilian careers at the expense of the Australian government.

In *War Letters*, written to his wife and daughter, Monash outlined his philosophy of war and described his experiences from the moment his brigade landed in Egypt until demobilization in 1919. In *The Australian Victories in France in 1918* Monash described in precise detail the part played

Lieutenant-General John Monash (right) receives his knighthood from King George V.

by Australian troops in launching the offensive that brought about Germany's surrender.

On his return to Australia, Monash became general manager and chairman of the Victoria State Electricity Commission. Under his guidance the power resources of the state of Victoria were developed to the point of self-sufficiency, this was based on the exploitation of the brown-coal deposits in the area.

In 1931 he was made a full general, the one of the two first Australian and the first Jew to receive this rank. An equestrian statue of him was erected in Melbourne in 1950 and Monash University was opened in 1958. A cooperative village in Israel, Kefar Monash was founded in 1946 by British war veterans.

Monash took an active part in Jewish affairs and was president of the Australian Zionist Federation.

C. Edward, *John Monash*, 1970.
A. I. Smithers, *Sir John Monash*, 1973.

MOND, ALFRED MORITZ, First Baron Melchett; (1868–1930) British industrialist. He was born in the Lancashire village of Farnworth to Ludwig Mond (1839–1909), a German-Jewish scientist who patented a sulphur recovery process from alkalis and set up a factory in Liverpool for the manufacture of soda. Alfred's first language was German, as he was educated by a German governess and at a school run by a Prussian headmaster. He later went to an English public school, studied science at Cambridge and law at Edinburgh University, and practiced in London, specializing in patents law. He married Violet Goetze, a Christian, in 1892 and their children were baptized and brought up as practicing Christians, even though he never regarded himself as anything other than a Jew. In 1902, together with his brother Robert Mond (1867–1938), a chemist, he took over the management of his father's company, which had become the largest alkali works in the world. He established new enterprises in nickel and gas, created the Imperial Chemical Industries (I.C.I.) in 1926, expanding the company's enterprises to Canada, India, China, Japan, Australia, and South America.

Alfred Mond embarked on a political career in 1900 and entered parliament in 1906 as a Liberal, and apart from 1923–1924, remained there until 1928. He championed such causes as free trade and protection, prohibition, women's suffrage, reform of the House of Lords, and land reform.

With the outbreak of war in 1914, Mond was attacked in the press and labeled a "German Jewish traitor," and despite successful libel suits, the belief that Mond was a German sympathizer continued. Undaunted he turned his country estate, Melchett Court, into a military hospital, opened his London home to Belgian refugees, and subordinated his company's resources to the war effort, especially for the manufacture of explosives and the first British gas masks. Lloyd George appointed him to the Advisory Committee of Bankers and Traders the purpose of which was to keep industry alive and to prevent economic bottlenecks. He was one of the members of the Liberal group that brought the Lloyd George coalition into power and was appointed commissioner of works (1916–1921). He was responsible for the construction of the Imperial War Museum and the Cenotaph in Whitehall, London, and the War Memorial in Edinburgh. He became minister of health (1921–1922), and during his administration the School of Hygiene and Tropical Medicine was built and the Dentists' Registration Bill passed.

In 1926 Mond joined the Conservatives. He initiated the Mond-Turner conference of industrialists and the General Council of the Trades Union Congress, which prepared the way for direct relations between capital and labor in England. In 1928 he was made a peer; in the House of Lords he led the fight for the economic unity of the British Empire.

As Lord Melchett he became a passionate supporter of Zionism and was one of the first public figures to associate himself publicly with the Balfour Declaration (1917). He developed a deep personal friendship with Chaim Weizmann (q.v.), with whom he paid his first visit to Palestine in 1922. He bought a plot of land at Migdal on the shores of the Sea of Galilee, and stayed in the house he built there during his many visits. He traveled throughout Britain, the United States, and Canada, addressing public meetings on behalf of the Zionist cause, raising funds, and contributed generously himself. He was elected president of the British Zionist Federation and served as political negotiator with the British government. In 1927 he headed the Joint Palestine Survey Committee, an international commission appointed to study all aspects of Jewish settlement in Palestine, and in 1929 participated in the creation of the Jewish Agency, serving as its joint chairman (with Weizmann) until he resigned in 1930 in protest of the Passfield white paper. The agricultural settlement Tel Mond in the Sharon was established in 1929 in his honor.

Alfred Mond's writings include *Questions of Today and Tomorrow* (1912), *Why Socialism Must Fail* (1923), and *Industry and Politics* (1927).

Lord Melchett's son, **Henry Ludwig Mond**, Second Lord Melchett (1898—1949), was brought up as a Christian, but in 1933, as a reaction to the rise of Nazism he converted to Judaism, became an ardent supporter of the Maccabi movement, was elected chairman of the Jewish Agency general council in 1942 and acted as the Zionist Movement's political negotiator with the British government. In addition to his works on economics, he published *The Neighbor*, an account of Jewish persecution throughout the ages, culminating in the hope offered by Zionism.

Alfred Mond's daughter **Eva** (1895—1973), married the second marquess of Reading. Like her brother, she reverted to Judaism and was active in Zionist and general Jewish organizations, including the National Council of Women and the World Jewish Congress.

H. Bolitho, *Alfred Mond, the First Lord Melchett*, 1933.

J. Goodman, *The Mond Legacy*, 1982.

MORGENTHAU FAMILY   U.S. financiers and public servants. **Henry Morgenthau, Sr.** (1856–

Samuel Montagu, First Baron Swaythling (1832–1911), banker and philanthropist. He was born in Liverpool to Orthodox parents and remained a strict adherent to Orthodox Judaism throughout his life. Although the surname was Samuel, when he began school the officials registered him under the name of Montagu and his parents decided to change his name to Samuel Montagu. In 1847 the family moved to London and Montagu found employment in a banking institution and worked his way up to become the manager of the London branch of Monteaux, a Paris bank.

In 1853, together with his brother Edwin, Montagu established the bullion-brokerage firm of Samuel Montagu and Company. The firm entered the field of foreign exchange at the time when other banking houses were withdrawing. Montagu's house soon secured a large proportion of the exchange business, making London the chief clearing house of the international money market.

In 1885 Montagu entered Parliament as Liberal member for Whitechapel and held that seat for fifteen years. He was mainly concerned with financial matters, and was responsible for such legislation as the Weights and Measures Act (1897), which legalized the use of the metric system. He also succeeded in introducing a clause in the Finance Act of 1894 exempting from death duties bequests to public libraries, museums, and art galleries. In 1888 he became a member of the House of Commons select committee on alien immigration of persecuted Jews. He retired from Parliament in 1900.

Montagu was active in the Jewish community. In 1870 he was instrumental in founding the Jewish Workingmen's Club in Aldgate, and was the first warden of the New West End Synagogue in Bayswater. In 1887 he founded the Federation of Synagogues, and established and became president of the East London Apprenticeship Fund. He worked unremittingly on behalf of the poor of East London and was treasurer of the Jews' Temporary Shelter.

In 1875 Montagu visted Eretz Israel and helped to found a vocational school in Jerusalem. He visited Europe in 1882 to examine the situation of the Jews fleeing from Russia, and in 1886 his visit to Moscow was cut short when the government ordered "the Jew Montagu" to leave the country.

Montagu was a discriminating collector of works of art and old English silver. His collection included several notable specimens of the great importance in the history of the English goldsmith's art.

In 1894 Montagu was made a baronet and in 1907 was raised to the peerage as Baron Swaythling.

His eldest son, **Louis Samuel Montagu** (1869–1927), succeeded him to the peerage as Second Baron Swaythling. He was president of the Federation of Synagogues and like his father was anti-Zionist, declaring that Judaism was only a religion.

Edwin Samuel Montagu (1879–1924), eighth child of the family, was a sensitive child perpetually worrying about his health, haunted by a presentiment of early death.

He took an inter-science degree at University College, London, and went on to Cambridge, where he was president of the student union. After graduating in 1903 he joined a London firm of solicitors, but decided on a political career. In 1906 he was elected Liberal member of Parliament for Cambridgeshire and held the seat until 1922. He was private secretary to the chancellor of the exchequer, Herbert Asquith, and moved with him to the prime minister's office.

In 1910 Montagu began his close connection with India when he was appointed parliamentary undersecretary of state for India. His fascination with that country's problems lasted until the end of his life. He supported India's aspirations to independence and his "Report on Indian Constitutional Reforms" led to the Government of India Act of 1919, which gave that country the beginnings of self-government.

In 1915 he married Venetia Stanley, daughter of Baron Sheffield (who was romantically involved with Asquith), after she converted to Judaism. The income from his father's bequest to him was conditional upon his continuing to profess the Jewish religion and not marrying out of it.

In 1914 Montagu was appointed financial secretary to the Treasury, and was made a privy councillor in 1915 and entered the cabinet, taking up the post of minister of munitions in 1916.

From 1917 to 1922 he was secretary of state for India. As a patriotic Englishman he became a violent anti-Zionist. He wss a powerful voice in the British cabinet in opposing the 1917 Balfour Declaration, which endorsed the establishment of a Jewish national home in Palestine, being largely responsible for the modification of the original text that weakened its promises to the Zionists. He lost his seat in the 1922 parliamentary election and engaged in finance in the City of London until his death.

Ewen Edward Samuel Montagu (1901–1985), second son of Louis Samuel Montagu, studied economics and law in Cambridge. In 1924 he was called to the bar and was made a king's counsel in 1939.

His interest in boats led him to join the Royal Navy Volunteer Reserve, and in 1939 he served as naval intelligence officer at Hull. In 1941 he was posted to the naval intelligence division at the Admiralty where he ran the highly secret branch that handled counter espionage. The best-known of his several military successes was Operation Mincemeat which in 1943 involved the floating ashore in Spain of what appeared to be the body of a Royal Marine officer carrying documents indicating an imminent Allied attack on Sardinia (rather than Sicily, which was the actual target). This successful ploy was recorded in his book *The Man Who Never Was* (1953), which sold over two million copies and inspired the film of the same name (1955). He also wrote *Beyond Top Secret U* (1977), an account of what had been left out of his best-seller.

After the war, Montagu returned to law, becoming judge advocate of the fleet in 1945, a post he held till 1973. He was also appointed to a leading London judicial post as chairman of the Middlesex Quarter Sessions and acquired a formidable reputation for outspokenness on the bench.

Montagu was a devout Jew and was president of the United Synagogue from 1945 to 1962.

Lilian Helen Montagu (1874–1963) was scarcely out of her teens when she founded a club for working girls, which developed into the West Central Jewish Day Settlement. She directed this to the end of her days, uninterrupted even by the destruction of its premises by German bombardment during the World War II.

Influenced by the writings of Claude Montefiore she took up the cause of Liberal Judaism and was one of the small group that secured for it a place in England. She played a leading role in the foundation in 1902 of the Jewish Religious Union, which led to the establishment of a separate religious movement represented by the Liberal Jewish Synagogue. The first rabbi of the new synagogue was Israel I. Mattuck, under whose direction it espoused the radical version of Reform Judaism then in vogue in the United States. Lilian Montagu gave unstinting support to the rabbi, and her religious activities followed his viewpoint. She was a regular preacher at services of the Liberal synagogue and ministered to the affiliated synagogues that she promoted.

In 1926 she established the World Union for Progressive Judaism. Its headquarters were at her home, and she was its honorary secretary until her death. Its ideological basis was narrow and not attuned to the situation facing Jewry during the interwar years. Material resources were limited, and the frugality characteristic of an English social worker were not conducive to their augmentation. Through Montagu the World Union was particularly helpful to Liberal rabbis displaced by conditions in Europe. Her published writings include novels, stories, prayers, and religious pamphlets. *The Faith of a Jewish Woman* and *My Club and I* incorporate autobiographical material.

S. Aris, *The Jews in Business*, 1970.

L. Montagu, *Samuel Montagu, a Character Sketch*
H. Oxbury, *Great Britons, Twentieth-Century Lives*, 1985.

S. D. Waley, *Edwin Montagu: A Memoir of an Account of his Visits to India*, 1964.

MONTEFIORE, MOSES (1784–1885) English

Jewish leader and champion of persecuted Jewries, knighted 1837. Born in Leghorn (Livorno), Italy, during a business visit to that country from London by his parents, he belonged to a family which had gone to Italy from Spain in the 16th century. At the age of thirteen he was apprenticed to a firm of wholesale tea merchants. With the help of his affluent relatives he began a successful career on the stock exchange at the age of twenty, becoming one of the twelve Jewish brokers licensed by the city. A commanding figure, six-feet, three inches in height, Montefiore rose, with methodical application and integrity and the help of his connections, to the highest offices in the Jewish and non-Jewish world. He was one of the first Jews to join the Surrey militia in 1810 during the Napoleonic wars, rising to the rank of captain. His marriage in 1812 to Judith, daughter of Levi Barent Cohen, through which he became a brother-in-law to Nathan Mayer Rothschild (q.v.), advanced his business interests and gave him a partner who strengthened and shared his commitment to Judaism and Jews everywhere.

In 1824, at the age of forty, Montefiore retired from most of his business activities taking his wife's advice "to quit business and thank God and be content." Having no children and a considerable fortune at their disposal, the Montefiores devoted themselves to the service of others. Nevertheless he remained president of the Imperial Gas and Alliance Insurance companies, which he had founded. He pioneered the use of gaslighting in Britain and the Continent, for which he was elected a fellow of the Royal Society, the first Jew to be so honored. His last major business transaction was the successful contracting of a loan by the firm of Rothschild and Montefiore compensating the owners of freed slaves, thus enabling the British government to carry the Slave Emancipation Act into effect.

In the synagogue, Montefiore became the first member of London's Sephardic Bevis Marks congregation — which he faithfully attended Mondays, Thursdays, and Sabbaths — to be accepted before the statutory age of twenty-one in 1804. For a time he was even a member of its Lavadores, who washed the dead and prepared bodies for burial. In 1835 he was elected president of the Board of Deputies of British Jews, the representative body of British Jewry, broadening its involvement in world Jewish affairs, and holding the office for forty-four years. His strenuous opposition to the advocates of religious reform checked the growth of Reform Judaism in Anglo-Jewry.

In 1837 Montefiore became the first Jew to be elected sheriff of the City of London. When the honor was conferred, Queen Victoria noted in her diary: "Today I knighted the Sheriffs. One of them was Mr. Montefiore, a Jew, an excellent man and I was glad to be the first to do what I consider quite right." In the exercise of his office, which he demonstratively did not allow to interfere with his scrupulous observance of *kashrut* and holy days, he was distinguished for his concern for the London poor, the welfare of prisoners, and a highly unpopular abhorrence of the death penalty. He would walk five hours to a Saturday appointment, and on all his long journeys took along his own *shohet* (ritual slaughterer). His knighthood in 1837 and baronetcy in 1846 were conferred on him in recognition of his status as official spokesman of his people and champion of their rights.

Montefiore visited Eretz Israel seven times (1827, 1839, 1849, 1855, 1857, 1866, and 1874) and "Jerusalem" was emblazoned on his coat of arms. He and his wife undertook their first voyage there as a religious pilgrimage — traveling there and back on a journey lasting five months in the primitive and dangerous conditions of those times, to spend but three days in Jerusalem. As a result of what he had witnessed — both the poverty and the potentialities of the growing Jewish community — he became committed to the development of agricultural settlement. With the help of the legacy of Judah Touro, an American millionaire, Montefiore built the first modern Jewish housing project outside the walls of the cramped Old City, called Mishkenot Shaananim, together with a windmill for grinding corn, both marking the beginnings of modern Jerusalem. He obtained a *firman*, or permit, from the sultan of Turkey to rebuild Jerusalem's central Ashkenazic synagogue, the Hurvah. He sent a printing press and physician to Jerusalem and made efforts to establish a girls' vocational school.

These missions to Eretz Israel were complemented by others to champion the cause of persecuted Jews elsewhere, and to the Jewish world he appeared as their leader, always prepared to travel to distant lands on behalf of Jews in distress. Montefiore's first outstanding success was his 1840 mission to the sultan in Constantinople and to Mehemet Ali in Alexandria to combat the Passover ritual-murder accusation in the Damascus affair. He secured the release of the accused Jews and the celebrated *firman* from the sultan rebutting the infamous blood libel and promising equal treatment for the Jews of the Ottoman Empire. In 1846 and 1872 he visited, and was royally feted by the major Jewish communities in Russia, including Vilna, Riga, and Saint Petersburg, personally interceding with the tsar to abrogate discriminatory legislation and alleviate the condition of the Jews, but with very limited success. Montefiore failed in his visit to Rome to persuade the pope to restore the Mortara child, forcibly converted to Catholicism, to his parents. In 1863 he visited Morocco, and in 1867 Romania, where he was almost set upon by an anti-Semitic mob. He was generous and untiring in his contributions to Jewish and general charities. In 1865 Montefiore founded the Judith Lady Montefiore College for rabbinic scholars on their retirement, located on his private estate and synagogue at Ramsgate.

Montefiore's hundredth birthday was celebrated throughout the Jewish world. Even as far away as

Sir Moses Montefiore with the Egyptian Khedive Mehemet Ali.

Dutch-ruled Curaçao, the governor attended a special service in the synagogue, the town was illuminated with fireworks, and a full-day holiday was proclaimed on which all government bureaus were closed and all ships in the harbor flew their national flags. Two children born on that day on the island were named after him. Montefiore died in his 101st year and was buried alongside his wife in the mausoleum he had built on his estate.

M. Franklin, *Sir Moses Montefiore*, 1984.

P. Goodman, *Moses Montefiore*, 1925.

V.D. Lipman (ed.), *Sir Moses Montifiore, A Symposium*, 1982.

MORAVIA, ALBERTO (Pincherle; 1907–1990) Italian novelist, essayist, and journalist. He was born in Rome to an architect father of Venetian Jewish origin and a mother who was a Dalmatian Slav Catholic and who had the boy baptized. However, neither parent passed on a religious heritage to him. Moravia suffered a painful adolescence, contracting tuberculosis of the bone at the age of nine and passing much of his time until the age of seventeen on his back, either in a plaster cast or in traction. In an Alpine sanatorium, he read voraciously, mastering Italian and French literature.

By the time he was eighteen, he began to write his first novel, *The Age of Indifference*, which caused a sensation for its authentic attack on the selfishness and complacency of the Italian middle classes. This was followed by a stream of novels. Moravia's rejection of fascist values brought him into conflict with the Mussolini regime. In the 1930s he spent much time as a journalist reporting from various parts of the world. While in Rome in 1943 he learnt that the Gestapo was planning to arrest him for his antifascist articles and spent nine months in hiding in a remote village, sleeping in a stable and eating with the local shepherds, in company with his wife

Elsa Morante, the best-known Italian writer of her time. Moravia's experiences provided him with the background for one of his best-known novels, *Two Women*, which was made into a move starring Sofia Loren. Another novel, *The Conformist*, about an upper-class follower of Mussolini, was filmed by Bernardo Bertolucci.

After the war, Moravia was regarded as one of Europe's outstanding writers. His output was prolific; he wrote novels, stories, and criticism, served as editor of a literary review, wrote a weekly film review, and had a full literary and social life. His best-known novel was *The Woman of Rome*, whose protagonist is a tragic figure of a woman forced into a life of prostitution by the treachery of men. Sexuality is a main subject of Moravia's novels, and indeed critics found in his writings a certain repetitiveness on the subject. However, his emphasis on sex and prostitution was also seen as symbolizing a wider corruption that he was criticizing, including the worship of material and financial values by the middle classes. One succès de scandale was his book *The Two of Us*, which consisted of a dialogue between a man and his penis. He also built up a comprehensive picture of Rome in his writings, its life and inhabitants, especially the poorer and seamier sides, for example in his *Roman Tales*. His underlying pessimism was reinforced by the two world wars and by the decadence underlying people's lust for consumer goods.

Moravia was always close to communism and in 1983 he was elected a member of the European Parliament as a left-wing independent. He spoke on such causes as the environment and the rights of the Palestinians. Shortly before his death he finished his autobiography in which he wrote: "Literature must believe itself to be a surrogate for everything else, including religion." On his death, he was eulogized by Italian President Giovanni Spadolini,

---

FROM THE LONDON *TIMES* OBITUARY OF ALBERTO MORAVIA

For some time opinion on his merits was divided, especially in his own country where the candid sexuality of his writings gave public offense. As an anti-fascist he had his books vetoed personally by Mussolini and they were also put on the Vatican's (later discontinued) index of proscribed works. But after the war his international reputation grew to the extent that internal criticism of him was silenced. Sexual mores changed, nowhere more radically than in Italy, and what had seemed to be vices in Moravia's works were unanimously hailed as virtues.... In his best work, he emerges as a spirit of exceptional intelligence, perceptiveness and integrity.

---

who compared him with Boccaccio, and said, "Italian culture is in mourning."

H. S. Hughes, *Prisoner of Hope*, 1983.
L. Rebay, *Alberto Moravia*, 1970.
J. Ross and D. Freed, *The Existentialism of Alberto Moravia*, 1970.

MORGENSTERN, LINA (1830—1909) Philanthropist and writer. Born Lina Bauerlin Breslau. Germany, her desire to contribute to the betterment of society was influenced by the events of the Revolution of 1848. That same year, at age eighteen, she founded a society for the welfare of poor youth. After her marriage to Theodor Morgenstern, a manufacturer, she moved to Berlin, where she continued and expanded the scope of her work.

Morgenstern served on the board of directors of a women's society that promoted Friedrich Froebel kindergartens and helped organize the first of these. In 1860 she wrote a textbook on Froebel's methodology. From 1861 to 1866 she was president of a society that supported eight kindergartens, as well as a seminary and a nursery school. In 1866 she began to set up kitchens to feed the needy. Her kitchens served as models for other such establishments in Germany and abroad. The Berlin Housekeepers' Union, which she founded in 1873, offered education and employment services to women, such as a free employment agency and an old-age pension. Morgenstern wrote the textbooks used by the union's cooking school.

Perhaps the highlight of her long career was when she convened the first International Women's Congress in Berlin in 1896, which was attended by over eighteen-hundred delegates. She continued to be active well into her seventies, writing and working in a number of organizations. She wrote a number of books on varying topics, including children's stories, novels, biographies, and periodicals for women.

MORGENTHAU FAMILY U.S. financiers and public servants. **Henry Morgenthau, Sr.** (1856–1946), was a financier, diplomat and philanthropist. He was born in Mannheim, Germany. His father, a cigar manufacturer and exporter, took the family to the United States in 1865 and settled in New York City. On completing his elementary education, Morgenthau began working in an insurance office and then in the Bloomingdale (q.v.) department store. He studied law while teaching in a night school and graduated from Columbia Law School in 1877. Specializing in real estate law, he was president of the Central Realty Bond and Trust Company from 1899 to 1905, and until 1913 was president of the Henry Morgenthau Company. He was active not only in buying and selling properties but also as a developer, being largely responsible for the development of real estate in the Bronx.

During those years Morgenthau was active in social work as a member of the Educational Alliance, the board of Mount Sinai Hospital, and the Henry Street Settlement. Together with his wife, Morgenthau founded and financed the Bronx House Settlement for the welfare of the poor.

Having made a fortune by the time he was fifty-five, Morgenthau decided to retire from business and devote himself to politics. He supported Woodrow Wilson for president in 1912 and made his political debut as chairman of the Democratic finance committee.

In 1913, Morgenthau was appointed U.S. ambassador to Turkey and during World War I looked after the interests of Great Britain, France, Italy, Russia, Belgium, and other European countries at war with Turkey. He was particularly concerned with helping Jews in Palestine, who were suffering from shortage of food, and was also concerned with the protection of Christian missionaries and Armenians. He recorded his experiences during this period in *Ambassador Morgenthau's Story* (1918; published in England as *Secrets of the Bosphorus*).

Morgenthau was one of the incorporators of the American Red Cross and later of the International Red Cross. He was appointed vice chairman of the Near East Relief, Inc., by act of Congress, and held the post from 1919 to 1921. President Wilson appointed him in 1919 to the U.S. mission set up to investigate conditions in Poland, particularly regarding the treatment of Jews. In 1923 he was chosen by the League of Nations to be chairman of the commission that dealt with the settlement of 1,500,000 Greek refugees from Asia Minor and eastern Thrace. He recorded these experiences in his book *I Was Sent to Athens* (1930).

Morgenthau played an active role in the 1932 presidential campaign and supported Franklin D. Roosevelt's New Deal policies. He was among the first to warn against Adolf Hitler's threat to peace in Europe, predicting that Germany would rearm, contrary to the terms of the Versailles Treaty. Morgenthau continued his activities in current affairs far into his late eighties. In 1939 he demanded repeal of the embargo on arms for Spanish Loyalists, and in 1940 appealed for support for the Greek War Relief Fund.

Morgenthau opposed Zionism, regarding the movement as the "blackest error," and stated that "Zionism is the most stupendous fallacy in Jewish history... it is unsound in its econopics, fantastical in its politics and sterile in its spiritual ideals... it is a cruel playing with the hopes of a people blindly seeking their way out of age-long miseries."

His son, **Henry Morgenthau, Jr.** (1891–1967), public figure and agricultural expert, was born and educated in New York City. At age sixteen he went to the New York State College of Agriculture at Cornell, but contracted typhoid and was forced to leave. During the months spent recuperating on a Texas ranch, he developed a great love for the outdoors. His father hoped to interest him in real estate, and arranged employment on a construction job. He lived at the Henry Street Settlement, where he had charge of a boys' club. He then was

Henry Morgenthau, (left) and Adolph S. Ochs, (right) relaxing at a fairground, 1927.

employed in a private banking house and in 1912 once again entered Cornell Agricultural School, but after eight months of study left and together with his father bought a 1,700 acre farm in East Fishkill, New York, where over the years he developed ten varieties of apples as well as other fruits and vegetables.

Together with his wife, he set up a clinic in the nearby town, engaged a doctor and nurse to run it, and often helped administer the anesthetics in tonsil and adenoid operations. In 1922 Morgenthau acquired the journal *American Agriculturist*, in which he called for reforms in rural education and other services. During World War I he served as a lieutenant in the overseas transport department of the navy.

His acquaintance with Franklin D. Roosevelt began when the Morgenthaus and the Roosevelts vacationed together, and in 1928 he supported FDR in his campaign for governor of New York State. During Roosevelt's second term as governor, Morgenthau was appointed conservation commissioner, in which capacity he was active in the purchase of land for the state, reforestation, supervision of state parks, the protection of wild life, and the restocking of fish and game. He traveled up and down the country in the course of the 1932 presidential campaign, and when in 1933 Roosevelt appointed him chairman of the Farm Board, he set up the Farm Credit Administration, which provided loans to farmers.

In 1934 Morgenthau became secretary of the Treasury. He reorganized the Treasury Department and instituted monetary policies that helped bring about the stabilizatioon of the economy. He raised more money in taxes during his term of office than all the fifty-one secretaries of the Treasury who preceded him. From 1936 all U.S. currency issued bore his signature and during his career he sold over thirty billion dollars worth of government bonds.

In 1939, he violently opposed the sale of scrap iron and gasoline to Japan. He set up in the Treasury the Liaison Committee, which enabled the allies in the war against Germany to make contracts with U.S. firms for the manufacture of airplanes and munitions. This was the precursor of lend-lease. In 1943 he obtained State Department approval of a proposal by the World Jewish Congress to transfer private U.S. funds to Europe for the rescue of French and Romanian Jews. In 1945 he put forward the Morgenthau Plan, proposing the conversion of Germany into an essentially agrarian area, presenting his peace plan in *Germany Is Our Problem*. The plan came under brief consideration but was not adopted.

He played an active role in Jewish organizations such as B'nai B'rith, the Jewish Welfare Board, and the United Jewish Appeal, of which he served as chairman from 1947 to 1950 and honorary chairman from 1950 to 1953. He was also chairman of the Board of Governors of the Hebrew University (1950–1951) and of the American Financial and Development Corporation for Israel and the Israel Bond Drive (1951–1954).

J. M. Blum, *From the Morgenthau Diaries* (3 vols.), 1959–1967.
J. M. Blum, *Roosevelt and Morgenthau*, 1970.

MORGENTHAU, HANS JOACHIM (1904–1980) Political scientist.

Born in Coburg, Germany, he studied at the universities of Frankfurt and Munich. Choosing first to study philosophy because he sought answers to the "quest for the meaning of human existence," he tried later to switch to literature but was refused support from his father, who deemed it an "unprofitable occupation." He settled on studying law, a choice that, in his words, "appeared to make the least demands on special skills and emotional commitment."

From 1927 to 1930 Morgenthau practiced law in Munich. He was appointed assistant to the law faculty at the University of Frankfurt in 1931 and from that year until his departure from Germany, he served as acting president of the Frankfurt labor law court. In 1932 he went to Geneva for postgraduate work at the Graduate institute for International Studies and, when Hitler rose to power the following year, remained in Switzerland as an instructor of political science at the Institute. He moved to Spain in 1935 to teach international law at the Madrid Institute of International and Economic Studies. Two years later he emigrated to the United States, teaching at Brooklyn College (1937–1939) and the University of Kansas City (1939–1943). In 1943 he took a position at the University of Chicago where he taught international politics and directed the Center for the Study of American Foreign and Military Policy for seventeen years.

Morgenthau expounded his ideas on international politics and American foreign policy in numerous articles and books including *Politics Among Nations* (1948), which became a textbook in university courses; *In Defense of the National Interest* (1951); *Dilemmas of Politics* (1958); *The Purpose of American Politics* (1960); *Policies in the Twentieth Century* (3 vols., 1962); and *Truth and Power* (1970). His modern realist approach examines the role of power in international politics and urges adoption of realistic foreign policies. He viewed power as the chief goal in international politics and defined national interest in terms of power. Urging the United States to be more concerned with its own needs than with world opinion he said, "Never allow a weak ally to make policy decisions for you."

In a review of his book, *In Defense of the National Interest*, the *New York Times* stated, "His book is a swiftly written, eleventh-hour plea to his countrymen to throw off the four intellectual errors of post-war diplomacy: Wilsonian Utopianism, Dumbartian Legalism, Trumanian Sentimentalism, Neo-Isolationism. He urges us to analyze the national interest unemotionally in terms of power and its use."

During the 1960s Morgenthau served as a consultant to the departments of State and Defense. He gained national attention when he protested American involvement in the Vietnam conflict, stating that the risks of military participation outweighed any benefits. As chairman of the Academic Committee on Soviet Jewry, he was an outspoken critic of the Soviet Union's treatment of Jews and campaigned for the release of Soviet dissidents, including Anatoly Shcharansky. Morgenthau spoke out against the terrorist activity of the Palestine Liberation Organization (PLO) and opposed any role for the PLO in a Palestinian state.

In 1968 Morgenthau was appointed professor of political science at City College of New York and in 1974 he was named university professor of political science at the New School of Social Research where he remained for the rest of his academic career.

K. Thompson and R. J. Myers, *A Tribute to Hans Morgenthau (With an Intellectual Autobiography by Hans J. Morgenthau)*, 1977.

MOSES (c. 13th cent. BCE) Leader, lawgiver, and prophet;

key personality in the emergence of Judaism and founder of the Jewish nation. The sole source for his life is the last four books of the Pentateuch which, according to Jewish tradition, was entirely written by Moses at God's dictation.

He was born in Egypt when the Israelites were in slavery there. His parents were Jochebed and Amram of the tribe of Levi. At the time of his birth the Egyptian ruler, the Pharaoh, had decreed that every male child born to the Israelites should be drowned in the river Nile. Moses was the third child of his parents having an elder brother, Aaron (q.v.), and a sister, Miriam. To save his life, his mother concealed him among the bulrushes along the river's banks in a wicker basket, leaving Miriam on the lookout to discover his fate. There he was discovered by Pharaoh's daughter, who adopted him as her son and called him Moses (Moshe), meaning "drawn out" of the water.

Moses grew up in the Egyptian court. However, after killing an Egyptian taskmaster who was persecuting the Israelite slaves, Moses fled and found refuge in the land of Midian, where he was taken into the household of the Midianite priest, Jethro, whose daughter, Zipporah, he married and whose sheep he tended. He remained there for many years, but one day in the wilderness he experienced a theophany. God appeared to him from within a bush that burned but was not consumed by the fire. He ordered Moses to return to Egypt and lead his people to liberty. Moses reacted with reluctance, especially as he was afflicted with a stammer and did not see how he could appear as his people's spokesman; he agreed when God consented that Aaron would be responsible for the public speaking.

Moses, now aged eighty, returned to Egypt and together with his brother confronted the king. However, Pharaoh refused to release the Israelites, even for a brief visit to the desert to worship their God, and threatened to oppress them even more severely. God then afflicted the Egyptians with ten plagues, each one announced to Pharaoh by Moses and Aaron, who also performed their own miracles in an attempt to convince him to release the Israelites. Only after the tenth and most terrible plague — the killing of all the firstborn Egyptians — did Pharaoh finally relent. However, even then he changed his mind and gathered his army to pursue the Children of Israel who had reached the Red Sea on their way to the Sinai Desert (the Red Sea in Hebrew is the "Reed Sea" and for geographical reasons, it is unlikely that the Israelites had reached the modern Red Sea, but rather a body of water in western Sinai). The Israelites were saved when Moses stretched out his rod, to which magical powers were ascribed, and the sea parted to allow the Israelites to cross. When Pharaoh and his army followed the path of the Hebrews, the sea closed on the Egyptians and they were drowned. This series of events, known as the Exodus, became profoundly etched on the Jewish consciousness and remained a basic factor in the establishment of Israelite-Jewish nationhood.

After a few weeks, the Israelites, who numbered 600,000 males and their families, according to the biblical account, reached Mount Sinai, the exact location of which is unknown. Here a second traumatic event occurred. After three days of purification of the entire people, Moses ascended to the top of the mountain where God gave him the Ten Commandments inscribed on two stone tablets. Moses remained forty days on the mountain and also received the entire legislation contained in the Pentateuch ("the Mosaic Law"). According to

The finding of Moses in the Nile. From a Judeo-Persian commentary on the Book of Exodus. 1686.

Jewish tradition, he also received supplementary laws that were handed down by word of mouth (the oral law) for some fifteen centuries until codified in the Mishnah.

Moses' prolonged stay on the mountain led the people to doubt whether he would return and in their despair they forced Aaron to make for them a golden calf that they proceeded to worship. When Moses eventually came down and saw the people dancing around the idol, he broke the two tablets of the commandments in his anger. However after the people repented, he intervened with God to avert punishment for their sin and reascended the mountain to receive a second set of tablets.

Moses then conveyed instructions for building the portable sanctuary that was to house the tablets. This became the focus of Israelite ritual (eventually deposited in the Jerusalem Temple) to which the people brought their offerings, with the cult entrusted to Aaron, as high priest, and his family.

The Children of Israel remained in the desert for another forty years under Moses' leadership, mostly remaining at Kadesh Barnea. During this time, Moses was faced with a number of crises and even rebellions. His brother and sister questioned his leadership, for which they were punished; a religious revolt under Korhah challenged Moses' spiritual authority, but the rebels were punished by miraculous death; a group of representatives sent to spy out the land of Canaan brought back an overwhelmingly negative report, leading to a hostile reaction among the people, who were on the verge of relapsing into idolatry, but were again spared by Moses' intervention with God. It had been divinely decreed that none of those who left Egypt (with two exceptions) would survive to enter the Promised Land. The same fate was decreed for Moses himself and Aaron when they disobeyed a command of God to produce water from a rock by speaking to it and struck the rock instead. Both Aaron and Miriam died in the course of the journey. Moses was permitted to travel almost to the boundaries of the Promised Land. Before he died he gathered the people and delivered a massive final address (the book of Deuteronomy) in which he summarized the Sinaitic legislation and delivered his last message. When the time came for him to die, Moses, who was then 120 years old, ascended Mount Nebo for a panoramic view of the Promised Land. The Bible records that "his eyes were undimmed and his vigor unabated." He passed on the leadership to his devoted associate, Joshua (q.v.). Moses died alone and was buried by God, so that no man would know his burial place, and presumably make there a shrine. The biblical story concludes, "There has not risen a prophet in Israel like unto Moses, whom the Lord knew face to face."

Moses founded the nation and formulated its basic religious code, theologically fixed in the spirit of monotheism and grounded in the covenant between God and Israel. He was the great lawgiver of the Jewish people and also organized its judiciary. Throughout Jewish tradition, he has been regarded as its supreme figure and the rabbis wove

---

HEINRICH HEINE ON MOSES

How small Sinai appears when Moses stands on it!... There was a time when I felt little affection for Moses, probably because the Hellenic spirit predominated in me, and I could not forgive the lawmaker of the Jews his intolerance of images and of all plastic representation. I failed to see that despite his hostility to art, Moses himself was a great artist; only his artistic temperament, like that of his Egyptian fellow-countrymen, was directed solely towards the colossal and indestructible. But, unlike the Egyptians, he did not shape his works of art out of brick and granite. He built pyramids of men and carved obelisks out of human material. He took a poor shepherd tribe and transformed it into a people to defy the centuries — a great eternal, holy people, God's people, an exemplar to all other peoples, the prototype of mankind: he created Israel.

---

around him legends and stories of his wisdom. Indeed, say the rabbis, "the heavens and earth were created solely for the sake of Moses." The chain of Jewish tradition started with Moses and the Jewish belief was stated by Moses Maimonides (q.v.) in his principles of faith: "I believe with perfect faith that the prophecy of Moses our teacher, peace be on him, was true; and that he was the chief of the prophets, both those who preceded and those who followed him."

M. Buber, *Moses*, 1969.
A. Neher, *Moses and the Vocation of the Jewish People*, 1959.
M. and M. Roshwald, *Moses: Leader, Prophet, Man*, 1969.

MOSES BEN MAIMON See Maimonides, Moses

MOSES BEN NAHMAN See Nahmanides, Moses

MOSES DE LEON (c. 1240–1305) Spanish kabbalist; presumed author of the Jewish mystical classic, the *Zohar* ("Book of Splendor"). He was born in Leon, but there is no information on his early life and studies. It seems that his first interest was philosophy, but he became intrigued with mysticism. He spent years wandering through Castile and studied with a number of kabbalists. At the time, Jewish mystical works were being composed, but were published pseudepigraphically, that is, they were ascribed to an ancient authority to give them authenticity and credibility. By 1286 Moses had written such works, in both Hebrew and Aramaic; they were known as the *Midrash Ne'elam* ("The Mystical Midrash") and were to constitute the kernel of the *Zohar*.

While it was long suspected that Moses had written the *Zohar*, the most convincing scientific demonstration of his authorship (at least of the main section) came from the scholar Gershom Scholem (q.v.). Moses had pseudepigraphically attributed the *Zohar* to the 2nd-century rabbi Simeon bar Yohai (q.v.), and kabbalists accepted, and continue to accept, this ascription. According to Scholem, Moses was living in Guadalajara while he was writing the *Zohar*, remaining there until 1291, by which time its first sections had been circulated. He then continued his wanderings, eventually settling in Avila. He worked at the dissemination of the book, maintaining its antique origin. To prove this he invited another famous mystic, Isaac of Acre, to visit him to view the original manuscript, but before Isaac arrived Moses fell ill and died. After his death, his widow denied that such a manuscript existed and already some felt that Moses was in fact the author.

The *Zohar* received in some circles a sanctity second only to the Bible. It is a mystical commentary on the Pentateuch, written in Aramaic, and has been called a mixture of theosophic theology, mystical psychology, anthropology, myth, and poetry. It is a collection of writings, as a number of later additions were made to Moses de Leon's work early in the 14th century. Much of the material is presented in the form of discussions among the early rabbis but mysterious figures appear, such as the "Old Man" and the "Child," who disclose heavenly secrets. Among the problems discussed at length are the divine creation process (through a series of ten worlds) and the problem of evil (seen as a negative but powerful reality). Human action and behavior affect the upper worlds and therefore man's deeds and prayers are of cosmic significance. Many later works were based on the *Zohar* and it is still revered in many Jewish circles, especially among the Hasidim and Jews from Moslem lands. G. Scholem, *Kabbalah*, 1974.

H. Sperling and M. Simon (eds.), *The Zohar* (and English translation), 5 vols. 1931–1934.

FROM THE ZOHAR

Fear of God is the gateway of faith.

The tales of the Bible are only the outer garments of the Torah and woe to him who thinks that they are the Torah itself.

No children — then no bliss here or in the world to come.

As long as the community of Israel remains in exile, the Divine Name remains incomplete.

Love without jealousy is no true love.

MUNI, PAUL (1895–1967) U.S. actor. Muni was born Muni Weisenfreund to traveling players in Lemberg, Austria (now Lvov, USSR). He arrived in the United States with his family in 1902. When Muni was twelve, he made his stage debut in Cleveland's Yiddish theater, and after his father's death six years later, began to tour in Yiddish plays. A brief stint with the company of Jacob Kalich and Molly Picon ended prematurely in the influenza epidemic of 1918 and later that year he was spotted and signed by Maurice Schwartz for his Yiddish

Paul Muni (right) with George Raft in Scarface.

Art Theater in New York. The eight years he spent with Schwartz brought him acclaim in a variety of vehicles, notably Gogol's *Inspector General* and Romain Rolland's *Wolves*.

Muni was first exposed to the English-speaking public in 1926 in the play *We Americans*, and his next Broadway role, that of an exconvict in *Four Walls*, brought him to the attention of the Fox studios, for whom he made two unsuccessful films before returning to the stage. A third attempt to conquer the screen, the gangster classic *Scarface*, made Muni a bigger star in Hollywood than he had been on Broadway. After another stage hit with Elmer Rice's (q.v.) *Counsellor-at-Law*, he signed a long-term contract with Warner Bros. His first film under the new contract was another milestone, *I Am a Fugitive from a Chain Gang*. The only one of Muni's several Academy Award nominations to win him an Oscar was for the first of three biographical films he made under the direction of William Dieterle, *The Story of Louis Pasteur*.

Unlike most of his Hollywood contemporaries, Muni achieved stardom as a character actor, often hidden under heavy makeup, rather than by projecting a familiar personality. This was true of the other two films by Dieterle, *The Life of Emile Zola* and *Juarez*, as well as his Chinese peasant in *The Good Earth* in 1937. Muni returned frequently to the stage, particularly after his film career petered out in the mid-1940s. He achieved memorable performances in *Key Largo* and *Inherit the Wind* and moved many with his last film part in 1959, as an elderly Jewish doctor in Brooklyn in *The Last Angry Man*.

M. B. Druxman, *Paul Muni: His Life and His Films*, 1974. J. Lawrence, *Actor: The Life and Times of Paul Muni*, 1974.

MYERS, MICHAEL (1837–1950) Chief justice of New Zealand, knighted in 1922. Born in the small town of Motueka, he moved with his family in 1897 to Wellington, where he was educated at elementary school and at Wellington College. He studied law at Canterbury University College and graduated in 1896. He had a brilliant career at school and university, was admitted as a barrister and solicitor in 1897, and joined a leading Wellington law firm in which he became a partner in 1899. Myers appeared in a large number of crown cases, both criminal and civil. In 1922 he was made a king's counsel, and in 1929, after an outstanding career at the bar was appointed chief justice, holding the position for seventeen years until his retirement in 1946.

Michael Myers was a man of exceptional gifts and had a remarkable breadth of vision. In 1936 he became the first New Zealand-born judge to sit on the judicial committee of the Privy Council. He took a practical interest in international affairs and in 1945 accompanied the New Zealand prime minister to the conference of Allied Nations in San Francisco that framed the United Nations charter. At the Conference of International Jurists he took

ABOUT SIR MICHAEL MYERS

Myers had a strong sense of the dignity of his high office and took steps to increase the public standing of the Bench.

Before his time, when Parliament was opened the Chief Justice had been invited to sit on the floor of the Chamber of the Legislative Council, while the puisne Judges who were in Wellington were invited to sit in the gallery. Myers arranged that the Judgesshould attend as a contingent in robes on the floor of the Chamber. Some Judges were not enthusiastic about this procedure.... Myers, however, imported for himself the full ceremonial red robes of High Court Judge in England and attended Parliament in them, with a full-bottomed wig. Then he thought the Judges should be similarly attired.... By the appropriate transfer of wigs and robes, three Wellington Judges could attend the opening of Parliament fully attired....

Then there was Court Dress. Myers had the velvet suit with lace and ruffles, knee breeches, shoes with a buckle, and dress sword. He encouraged the style.

From Sir David Smith, *Portrait of a Profession*, **1969**

a prominent part in framing the constitution of the International Court of Justice, to which he was nominated as the New Zealand representative.

Michael Myers was a member of a prominent Jewish family and was president of the Wellington Hebrew Congregation from 1912 to 1921.

L. M. Goldman, *The History of the Jews in New Zealand*, 1958.

N

NAHMAN OF BRATSLAV (1772–1811) Hasidic rabbi; founder of the Bratslav sect. The great-grandson of the founder of Hasidism, the Baal Shem Tov (q.v.), he was born in Medzibozh and raised in a strict Hasidic atmosphere. Even as a child he made great efforts to be pious and sometimes fasted for days on end. His diligence was such that it was said he gave teachers his pocket money so that they would teach him overtime. At fourteen he married a rich man's daughter and began to prepare himself for the role of Hasidic leader. He absorbed the teachings of the Bible, the Talmud, and the Kabbalah, especially those of Isaac Luria (q.v.), but after a difficult struggle with himself, he chose a Hasidic path that differed from that of his contemporaries. He contested the view that the Hasidic leaders (the *tzaddikim*) had elevated souls, saying, "A man is never endowed with a good soul or a bad soul: everything depends on his own good deeds, everyone can elevate himself—but only by his own actions."

He left his village to move among the ordinary people and settled in the town of Medvedivsky, where he taught Hasidism to all who came and listened. He was still highly esteemed by the *tzaddikim* and this strengthened his arrogance. He claimed that the Baal Shem Tov visited him and to one rabbi he said, "I want to bless you so that in the next world you will be able to understand my everyday speeches." He realized that Hasidism was deteriorating as a result of the behavior of the *tzaddikim*, whom he regarded as unworthy of leading the movement. He felt the need to create a new direction but at the same time did not want the responsibility of destroying what existed.

The turning point in his life came with his visit to the Holy Land in 1798. He traveled anonymously and arrived in Galilee just when Napoleon was engaged in fighting the Turks in the region. He suffered great hardships and his experiences became the basis for later legends. He spent a winter in Tiberias, studying holy books and visiting the graves of famous rabbis. While wanting to remain there, he decided he had a mission to revive Hasidism and returned to eastern Europe, but said longingly, "Wherever I go, it is always to the Land of Israel."

In 1802 he settled in Bratslav, Podolia. The *tzaddikim* now strongly resented his criticism and began to attack him and combat his teachings. He in turn was completely confident of his mission, holding that the Jewish Diaspora had known only four great teachers, each of whom characterized and guided an era: Simeon bar Yohai (q.v.), Isaac Luria, the Baal Shem Tov, and himself. As for the *tzaddikim*, he said, "It was difficult for Satan to lead the world astray, so he appointed such men in high places to help him." He felt that they needed him to lead them on the right path. At the same time, he regarded himself "like Moses, the most modest of men." He did not seek quarrels with his opponents and only shook his head to show they could not understand him. They for their part persecuted his followers, refused to intermarry with them, and would not eat meat killed in their slaughterhouses.

Followers flocked to Bratslav and, unlike the other Hasidic leaders, Nahman treated them as partners in his journey to God. He regarded himself as their equal, not their master, saying, "Every one of you is a partner in my doctrine: our souls are united all the time." He taught them in many ways, writing letters, giving speeches, and relating tales and parables. These were written down and widely distributed. Especially famous were thirteen tales that he related to his followers with instructions that, after his death, they be published in the original Yiddish, and translated into Hebrew (English translation by A. J. Band, 1978). He also recorded dreams and reported them to his followers.

He stressed the importance of prayer in which man must lose himself and forget his existence. He believed that the best place to pray is in the open air, far away from others. The prayers that come from the heart, he said are superior to the set formulae. Solitude was especially recommended, for only in solitude can man become united with God. A man should therefore endeavor to be alone for an hour a day for religious meditation.

Nachman's teachings gave priority to ethical behavior in which poverty was the ideal and material benefits were disdained. At one stage, Nahman encouraged his followers to confess their sins to him. He denounced lying and any forms of cheat-

today thousands of his followers still go on pilgrimages to visit his grave in Uman.

A. Green, *Tormented Master: A Life of Rabbi Nahman of Bratslav*, 1979.

NAHMANIDES, MOSES (Moses ben Nahman, known by the acronym *Ramban*; 1194–1270) Rabbinical scholar and Bible commentator, Jewish communal leader in Spain. Born in Gerona, he was acclaimed for his Talmudic scholarship while still a youth. He became rabbi of Gerona, but his great scholarship and personality brought him recognition as the spiritual leader of all Spanish Jewry. He earned his living as a doctor and was on occasion consulted by the king, James I of Aragon. The turning point in his life came in 1263, when the king forced him to defend Judaism in a public controversy with a Jewish convert to Christianity. His opponent, Pablo Christiani, had been engaged in missionary activities among the Jews, claiming that passages in the Talmud proved the truth of Christianity.

The four-day disputation took place in Barcelona in the presence of the king, his court, and high Church dignitaries. Subsequently both an official Christian version and Nahmanides' own account were published and although these inevitably differed in many details, a comprehensive picture of the occasion emerges. The king guaranteed Nahmanides complete freedom of speech and the rabbi spoke with a frankness that offended the Church representatives. Pablo Christiani cited Talmudic legends to show that the Messiah had already appeared, that he was "human and divine," that his death atoned for mankind's sins, and that with his life and death the commandments of Judaism had lost their validity. Nahmanides countered that Talmudic legends were not meant to be taken literally and that even the Jews saw them primarily as imaginative allegories, not to be seen as true events. Therefore no christological inferences could be drawn from these texts; he went on to affirm the beliefs of Judaism and even dared to call absurd some Christian dogmas related to the nature of God. Challenging the Christian belief of Jesus as the "prince of peace," Nahmanides boldly stated "from the time of Jesus until the present the world has been filled with violence and injustice and the Christians have shed more blood than all other peoples." The Church representatives, concerned by the direction taken by the disputation and by Nahmanides' openness, pressed for its conclusion and it was broken off without any formal conclusion or summing up. According to Nahmanides, the king complimented him on his appearance saying, "I have never seen a man defend a wrong cause so well." The following week Nahmanides attended the Barcelona synagogue, where a Christian friar gave a sermon urging the Jews to convert while the king himself addressed the congregation—an unprecedented event in the Middle Ages—after which Nahmanides was allowed to reply. The king also gave Nahmanides a gift of money as a reward

---

APHORISMS OF RABBI NAHMAN OF BRATSLAV

- God is present in every action and in every thought.
- Rather a man die than lie.
- He who wishes to be a real Jew must go to the Land of Israel — despite all the obstacles and difficulties.
- When I see a poor man with his clothes in rags and his shoes torn serving God, I love him very much.
- Proper praying is like a man who wanders through a field gathering flowers: one by one, until they make a beautful bouquet. In the same way a man must gather each letter, each syllable to form them into the words of prayer.
- God is with the joyful man; he forsakes the sad man.
- Melody and song lead the heart of man to God.
- Even a criminal has his good side.
- Always be humble — but not by bowing your head, which is external humility. Real humility is internal and has its origin in wisdom.
- Honest dealing is possible only if one is not striving for wealth.
- Judge a country's prosperity by its treatment of the aged.
- Better a superstitious believer than a rationalistic unbeliever.
- Nine *tzaddikim* do not make a prayer quorum, but one common man joining them makes it whole.
- The whole world is like a very narrow bridge and the main thing is not to be afraid.
- God is present whenever a peace treaty is signed.
- The fact that Nahman, like other Hasidic leaders, had no successor, has evoked the contemporary joke: How many Bratslav Hasidim are needed to change a lamp bulb? None — because they never change the bulb.

---

ing and forbade all forms of flattery.

In his last years Nahman suffered from chronic ill health. In 1810 a great fire destroyed most of Bratslav, including his home, and he moved to Uman in the Ukraine. He assured his Hasidim that he would continue to be among them even after his death and indicated that there would therefore be no need to choose a successor. "I want always to be with you," he told them "and you will come and visit me when I am in my grave," where he wished them to talk to him as though he were alive. If they did so, he promised to bring them to heaven, even if they were sinners.

After his death his movement flourished and

and Nahmanides returned to Gerona. However, he had aroused the wrath of the Dominicans and in 1265 they instituted proceedings against him in the court of the Inquisition for blaspheming Jesus. The king proposed that he be banished for two years and that his account of the disputation be burned, but this did not satisfy the friars. Nahmanides left Spain, making his way to the Holy Land, which he reached in 1267.

The Jewish communities in Eretz Israel were in a depressed condition as a result of the Crusades and the Tatar invasion, and Nahmanides went to Jerusalem, where he found two brothers who were dyers and another ten Jews who made up a prayer quorum (*minyan*) on Sabbaths. He reorganized the community and established a synagogue, writing to his son, "We found a ruined building with a beautiful dome supported by marble columns and we took it for a synagogue as the city is ownerless and whoever wishes to take possession of some parts of the ruins may do so." For centuries it was the only synagogue in Jerusalem. He moved to Acre in 1268 to lead its community and spent his last days there.

Nahmanides is a major figure in the development of the study of the Talmud through his writings on the subject. However, he is best known for his lucid Bible commentary, written in his old age. This propounds in the first place the literal meaning of the text as well as analyses of the structure and order of the narrative This is combined with homiletical, philosphical, and mystical interpretations at the same time holding to a fundamentalist approach based on the firm belief that God dictated the entire Torah to Moses. He branches out from the text to give his own ideas on a wide variety of topics. While rejecting philosophical rationalism and insisting on the superiority of revelation over philosophy, he often utilizes philosophical ideas in his commentary. Much of his thinking is kabbalistic in origin, although he felt that mystical inquiry should be confined to the privileged few. His references to this "esoteric wisdom" are brief and elusive but they were studied and developed by later mystics, and the fact that so authoritative a figure as Nahmanides legitimated mystical think-

Personal seal of Nahmanides.

ing contributed to its subsequent central role in Jewish thought.

C. B. Chavel, *Ramban: His Life and Teachings*, 1960.
I. Twersky (ed.), *Rabbi Moses Nahmanides*, 1983.

NAMIER, LEWIS (originally Bernstein-Niemirowski; 1888–1960) British historian, Zionist, and pioneer of a revolutionary new method of studying political history that came to be known as "Namierism"; knighted 1952. Born in Wola, Okrzyska (Russian Poland), Namier came from a family that, while not entirely rejecting its Jewish he ritage, had for generations striven to integrate itself into Catholic Poland. His parents deeply aspired to enter the Polish Catholic nobility and led a fully Catholic life. Namier spent the first years of his life traveling across partitioned Poland until his parents, who were sufficiently well-established and well-known to be granted the full rights of ownership, finally acquired land in Galicia. His enforced travels familiarized him with Poland, and as a result, Namier became a strong advocate of Polish nationalism which, coupled with his Catholic upbringing, gave him a sense of belonging to Polish society. At the age of ten, however, Namier was shocked to find out about his Jewish origins. Upon being informed by his father that no one in the family could be considered a Catholic or even a Jew, Namier experienced a break with his family and his native country.

The sense of not belonging fully — either to Judaism or to Catholic Poland — was further intensifed when he encountered anti-Semitic provocations while attending Lvov University. As a result, Namier left Poland in 1906 and, after a short stay at Lausanne University and at the London School of Economics, moved to Balliol College, Oxford.

In 1914, Namier joined the British army. He

NAHMANIDES IN JERUSALEM

I am the man who saw affliction. I am banished from my table, far removed from friend and kinsman, and too long is the distance to meet again. But the loss of all else which delighted my eyes is compensated by my present joy in a day passed within your courts, O Jerusalem, where it is granted me to caress your stones, fondle your dust, and to weep over your ruins. I weep bitterly but I find joy in my heart. I rend my garments but I find solace in so doing.

served on the staff of the propaganda (1915–1917), information (1917–1918) and political intelligence (1918–1920) departments of the British Foreign Office. He attended the Versailles peace conference in the capacity of adviser on problems concerning eastern Europe.

The years following World War I were difficult. In 1920–1921 he taught at Oxford, but also tried his luck in business in Vienna. His first book, *The Structure of Politics at the Accession of George III* (1929) was widely acclaimed. Following the publication of *England in the Age of the American Revolution* (1930), he was appointed professor of modern history at Manchester University (1931), where he stayed until 1953.

An ardent Zionist, he served as political secretary of the Jewish Agency in London from 1927 to 1931, working closely with Chaim Weizmann (q.v.). However, he was never an "insider" for many of the Zionist leadership. He was never to fulfill his wish — in which he had the full support of Weizmann — to be elected a member of the Zionist Executive.

Namier's role in the Zionist movement became more active when, at the insistence of Weizmann, he was released from his university duties at Manchester to become a full-time liaison officer between the Jewish Agency and the British government offices responsible for the formulation of Britain's Palestine policy from 1938 to 1945. As the chief draftsman of the Jewish Agency, he took extreme care to redraft the policy papers in a manner and style more acceptable to both parties, and played a role in the difficult period following the Passfield white paper (1930) in keeping open the bridges between the Jewish Agency and the British government. In addition, his friendship with Professor Reginald Coupland, author of the 1937 report of the Peel Commission (which proposed a Jewish state in a partitioned Palestine), enabled Namier to be influential in the relationahip with the commission. Namier became Weizmann's political adviser as well as his spokesman. Following the publication of the anti-Zionist 1939 white paper, Namier advocated a strong Zionist stance against the British policy and criticized what he considered to be Weizmann's more passive line. Namier saw himself as a "national Jew," identifying with the Jewish nation but not its religion.

Namier's historical research was devoted to the sociopolitical structure of England in the 18th century, the 1848 revolutions, the Hapsburg monarchy, and the events leading up to World War II. In pioneering a biographical method for studying political history, Namier began what would become a major trend in the study of political science. His chief work, *The Structure of Politics at the Accession of George III* (1929) consists of a detailed examination of the composition of the House of Commons under George III. His interest lay in how politics are made by members of a governing elite. Namier was elected a member of the British Academy in 1944 and was knighted in 1952. His second wife (whom he married in church after converting to Anglicanism) was Julia de Beausobre, of Russian aristocratic origin who preferred Greek Orthodoxy. (Her suffering in Soviet prisons and concentration camps are the subject of her book, *The Woman Who Could Not Die*, 1938.)

Among Namier's works are: *Additions and Corrections to Sir John Fortescue's Edition of the Correspondence of King George III* (1957), *In the Margin of History* (1939), which contained his essay of "The Jews in the Modern World," *Conflicts* (1942), with an essay on "The Jews," *1848: The Revolution of the Intellectuals* (1946), *Europe in Decay* (1950), *Avenues of History* (1952), and *Personalities in Power* (1958). He was an editor of *History of Parliament*, for which he wrote *The House of Commons, 1745–1790* (3 vols., 1964), which included a biography of every member and a survey of their constituencies.

L. Colley, *Lewis Namier*, 1989.
J. Namier, *Lewis Namier, A Biography*, 1971.
N. Rose, *Lewis Namier and Zionism*, 1980.

NASI, GRACIA See Mendes, Gracia.

NASI, JOSEPH (c. 1524–1579) Statesman and financier. He was born a Marrano in Portugal, son of the physician to the Portuguese royal court. To escape the Inquisition, which was seeking out secret "Judaizers," he went with his aunt, Gracia Mendes (q.v.), to Antwerp in 1537. There she joined her brother-in-law, Diogo Mendes, who had established himself as a successful businessman. Nasi (or Joao Micas, as he was then known) studied at the University of Louvain and then entered the Mendes banking firm. He was responsible for the firm's foreign affairs, in connection with which he traveled throughout Europe. When his aunt departed for Italy in 1545, she left him in charge of the firm, but he was unable to save it from confiscation and he left Holland. After a period in France, he moved to Italy, but in 1554 joined his aunt in Constantinople, and married her daughter Reyna. An unfriendly observer reported, "This rogue came to Constantinople with over twenty well-dressed Spanish servants. They attend him as if he were a prince. He himself wears silk clothes lined with sable. Before him go two janissaries with staves, as mounted lackeys.... He is a large man with a trimmed black beard." He left his Marrano guise, was circumcised, and openly professed Judaism under his Jewish name, Joseph Nasi.

He worked closely with his aunt and as she aged, his responsibilities increased. He was referred to as the court Jew because of his connections with the Sultan Suleiman, and later with Suleiman's son and successor, Selim II. In appreciation of the extensive trade Nasi conducted, the Turkish rulers granted him special commercial privileges and the rank of gentleman of the royal retinue. Through his many contacts, he acquired much information and acted as confidential adviser to the sultan on foreign affairs. Nasi helped the ruler of Moldavia regain his throne and encouraged William of Orange of the Netherlands to rebel against Spanish rule. Nasi's relationship with France was less than harmonious. He had been pressing a claim of 150,000 ducats against the French crown when the Turkish authorities took his side in the dispute. They boarded French vessels in Turkish waters, seizing up to one-third of their cargo until the full sum was recovered. The French envoy to the sultan's court engineered a plot to disgrace Nasi but was unsuccessful.

Nasi was showered with honors by the court. He received a monopoly on the import of wines via the Bosphorus that was worth a fortune. In 1566 he was given the title of duke of Naxos and the Cyclades and ruled a number of Greek islands from his palace near Constantinople, which he called Belvedere.

His most satisfying reward as a Jew came in 1561 when he was given the lease of the town of Tiberias in the Holy Land, together with seven nearby villages that Nasi wished to develop as an autonomous Jewish area. He set about rebuilding the town walls, constructing homes, and developing local crafts. In particular he planted mulberry trees, which he saw as a basis for a future silk industry. Jews from Italy were invited to move to the shores of Lake Kinneret. Nasi never visited the Land of Israel and after a time his interest in the scheme waned. He retained the title of lord of Tiberias until his death, but the project failed.

With the death of Selim in 1574, Nasi's influence at the Turkish court declined and he spent the last five years of his life in retirement, concentrating on his patronage of scholarship and literature, and dispensing charity on a large scale. He supported many distinguished Jewish scholars, built up an outstanding library, and wrote a treatise attacking astrology. After his death, his widow, Reyna, continued his scholarly interests and set up a Hebrew printing press in the Belvedere Palace.
C. Roth, *House of Nasi: The Duke of Naxos*, 1948.

NATHAN, ERNESTO (1845–1921) Italian politician. Though of Italian Jewish descent, he was born in England, the Nathan and Rosselli families having established a business partnership (as well as marriage ties) in London. Their homes became well-known rendezvous for Italian political exiles such as Guiseppe Mazzini, whom young Ernesto met there even before he and his mother left England to settle in Italy (1859). His mother, Sara, was a friend and collaborator of both Mazzini and Giuseppe Garibaldi. He lived in Pisa, Florence, and Milan (1862), involved in various commercial enterprises. After living for a short time, in Sardinia, he moved to Genoa in 1865. He moved to Rome in 1871, a year after the city had been liberated from papal control and incorporated in Victor Emmanuel II's new kingdom. Entering politics, Nathan adopted Mazzini's liberal, anticlerical views and directed his republican newspaper, *Roma del Popolo*. All the time, he continued to be associated

with Mazzini after whose death Nathan worked to preserve his memory. He collected Mazzini's manuscripts and presented them to the state.

Nathan became mayor of Rome in 1907, the first Jew appointed to that office. He enjoyed great popularity and respect throughout his six-year term, noted for his financial and administrative abilities, but the fact that Catholic Rome's leading citizen happened to be a prominent freemason as well as a anticlerical led Pope Pius X to revile Nathan obliquely in 1910. During World War I, as a man of over seventy, Ernesto Nathan demonstrated his patriotism by volunteering to serve as a junior officer on the Austrian front.

NATHAN, GEORGE JEAN (1882–1958) American drama critic and playwright. Born in Fort Wayne, Indiana, he was educated at Cornell University and the University of Bologna. His career in dramatic criticism began in 1905 when his uncle, Charles Frederic Nirollinger, himself a well-known critic, got him a job as cub reporter on the *New York Herald*. During the more than fifty years of his journalist career, he concentrated mainly on the world of Broadway and contributed to such magazines as *Harper's Weekly*, the *Bohemian Magazine*, *Life*, *Vanity Fair*, and *Scribner's*, among others. From 1914 to 1923, he coedited the *Smart Set* with H. L. Mencken, and in 1924 helped him found and edit the *American Mercury*, one of the most lively and influential of American literary journals. They also wrote the satirical play *Helioglobus* together in 1920.

Nathan openly criticized the mainstream-accepted melodrama influenced by David Belasco (q.v.). In breaking with the traditional dramatic criticism of his times, he voiced an individual opinion that helped shape the taste of the American public. He was influential in the acceptance of what represented a completely new orientation in drama — that of Eugene O'Neill, Sean O'Casey, and Jean Giraudoux. By the mid-1920s he was reputed to be the most widely read and best-paid dramatic critic in the world. Known for his pungent, witty, and very lively style, Nathan lived in a cluttered hotel apartment in the heart of the New York theater district for the last fifty years of his life. "All I have to offer," he argued, "is critical opinion filtered through more than thirty years of unremitting playgoing and study of the theater and dramatic literature in the four quarters of the globe." In *The Critic and the Drama*, he states that "art is a reaching out into the ugliness of the world for vagrant beauty and the imprisoning of in a tangible dream. Criticism is simply the dream book." His philosophy of criticism is to be found in his *Autobiography of an Attitude* (1921). Altogether he reviewed over six thousand productions.
C. Frick, *Dramatic Criticism of George Jean Nathan*, 1971.

NEHEMIAH (5th cent. BCE) Jewish governor of Judah. He was the cupbearer of the Persian king, Artaxerxes I (465–425 BCE), when he received news of troubles in Judah and the destruction of the walls and gates of Jerusalem. While serving meals to the king, he found the opportunity to inform Artaxerxes of his unhappiness with the situation in Judah and requested permission to go there. The king agreed that Nehemiah should go for a limited time to rebuild Jerusalem and provided him with letters of recommendation to governors of Persian provinces beyond the Euphrates. Nehemiah traveled to Jerusalem with a military escort and took along wood for the city's reconstruction.

His first goal on arrival was to rebuild the walls of Jerusalem. He secretly inspected the ruins of the previous walls and this became known to his enemies, notably Sanballat and Tobiah, who were associated with Samaria, and even threatened to make war on him. Nehemiah convinced the local community of the need for fortifications and the work was begun. To forestall any attack instigated by Sanballat, he armed the builders, set up armed posts, and introduced an alarm system. Sanballat invited Nehemiah to a conference outside the city, but Nehemiah refused to fall into the trap and continued to supervise the construction, which was completed in fifty-two days. This achievement raised the morale of the citizens and confused his enemies.

Taking advantage of this new optimism, Nehemiah introduced religious and social reforms. These included abstention from marriages with foreigners, observance of the Sabbath, support for the Temple cult, and cancellation of debts owed to the poor. He also made arrangements for a tenth of the rural population to live in Jerusalem, as the number of its inhabitants had dropped to a dangerously low level. Nehemiah took part in the ceremony of the reading of the Pentateuch by Ezra (q.v.), was the first to sign the covenant restating Jewish religious commitment, and organized an impressive ceremony to dedicate the walls on their completion.

After twelve years Nehemiah returned to Artaxerxes but soon went back to Jerusalem where he found that the conditions had again deteriorated. Tobiah had occupied the treasury room of the Temple and was immediately expelled by Nehemiah. The priests and Levites were receiving such small payments that they had been forced to work in the fields and neglect their duties in the Temple. Nehemiah reformed the system of tithes so that the priests and Levites could devote themselves exclusively to the Temple service. Sabbath observance was being violated by merchants. He ordered that the city gates be closed throughout Sabbath and threatened with arrest anyone who traded on that day. Finding that despite his earlier ban, marriages with foreign wives had continued, he publicly cursed and beat the offenders and made them give up their foreign wives.

The story of Nehemiah can be found in his memoirs in the biblical book of Nehemiah. He was an inspiring leader, utterly devoted to his people and religion, and gifted with organizational abilities and single-minded determination.

J. M. Myers, *Ezra-Nehemiah*, 1965.

NEUMANN, JOHN (JOHANN) VON LUDWIG (1903–1957) Mathematician. After graduation from the Lutheran High School in Budapest, he studied at the universities of Budapest and Zurich, and obtained his Ph.D. in mathematics in Budapest (1927). He was assistant professor at the University of Berlin in 1927, and the University of Hamburg in 1929, and gave his first lectures as visiting professor at Princeton University in 1930. He became a full professor at the Institute of Advanced Study in Princeton in 1933. From 1954 until his death, he was a member of the U.S. Atomic Energy Commission.

Neumann started his work in mathematical logic and set theory, giving precision to this theory. His clarification of operator algebra theory was also significant. His greatest achievement in quantum theory was the mathematical foundation of the measurement theory of physical quantities. For this, he derived the definition of "pure quantum mechanical conditions." Neumann was also largely responsible for advances in the theory of games and for the development of operational research.

Neumann made a critical contribution to the development and universal acceptance of electronic computers. He elaborated the fundamental principles of the electronic computer, including the use of the binary system, program storage, instruction scheme, and automatic program modification. Fully understanding the unique importance of these machines when he built the first, the "Joniac," an enormous computer that filled a whole room, he predicted their wide use.

He took part in experiments aimed at the release of atomic energy and was awarded the Fermi Prize in 1956. Neumann edited the *Annals of Mathematics* (Princeton) and *Compositio Mathematica* (Amsterdam) and was president of the American Mathematical Society (1951–1953).

Neumann was a charming Renaissance man. He gained the great respect of scientists and had a large circle of friends. His work far exceeded the limitations of his own discipline and was a major contribution to the scientific and technological revolution of our age.

Neumann's many important published works include *Mathematische Grundlagen der Quantenmechanik* (Berlin, 1932) and *Theory of Games and Economic Behavior* with O. Morgenstern (Princeton 1944). His *Collected Works* were published in Oxford, London, and Paris (1961–1962).

S. Thomas, *Men of Space, Vol. I*, 1960.

NEUTRA, RICHARD JOSEPH (1891–1970) American architect. He claimed that his professional inclinations were rooted in his parents' home in Vienna, where he developed a taste for smooth surfaces after digging out and unhappily tasting dirt from beneath the floorboards of their living room. There, he recalled, he also began to develop his sense of height and scale when he rejected the high ceiling of that same living room in favor of the grand piano, underneath which he would play for hours.

Neutra attended the Technische Hochschule in Vienna and received his diploma in 1917. He became acquainted with a contemporary architect, Adolf Loos, and was profoundly influenced by Loos's hatred of ornament and fashion and by his fascination with American architecture. Neutra resolved to emigrate to the United States, but with the collapse of the Austro-Hungarian Empire in 1918, fled instead to Switzerland and was employed there as a landscape architect. In 1921 he moved to Berlin, where he worked in the Municipal Building Office, assisting in the resettlement of city workers in rural dwellings. In 1922 Neutra joined Erich Mendelsohn (q.v.) with whom, in 1923, he won a prize in a competition for the design of a business center in Haifa. The design was never implemented.

In 1923 Neutra finally emigrated to the United States, where he was an architect for several firms in Detroit and Chicago. He later moved to Los Angeles and opened a partnership with a fellow Viennese architect, Rudolph Schindler. In 1928 he became famous with the construction of the Health House, a unique structure perched in a ravine in Los Angeles and supported from above by steel cables suspended from its roof frame.

Neutra began to acquire an international reputation as an architect who was known for his technological advancements, and even more, for his ability to integrate buildings into their natural surroundings. He developed his own theory, called biorealism, or biological realism, which was based on his observations of the environment and which advocated the adaptation of structures to the biological realities of those who must use them. He believed that the architect must study human responses and human biochemistry rather than fashion and technical novelties. Neutra's philosophy featured in his commitment to the development of a system of providing gracious homes for increasing populations without imposing on the environment. One such project was Channel Heights in the early 1940s, a housing development in San Pedro, California, in which he managed to relieve the monotony of identical units by varying the placement of each house according to the terrain on which it was built. Another project, designed in 1925 and implemented forty years later, was his ring-plan school, combining structure and environment with its individual detached classrooms ranged around a large elliptical playground.

Neutra also designed a number of famous private homes in Southern California, and, later in his career, larger public commissions such as offices and libraries, the U.S. Embassy in Karachi, Pakistan, and the Lincoln Memorial Museum in Gettys-burg, Pennsylvania. After 1942 he collaborated with his son Dion, who continued his practice after his death. His many writings include *Survival through Design* (1954) and *Life and Human Habitat* (1956).

Richard J. Neutra, (Introduction and Notes by Rupert Spade), 1971.

E. McCoy, *Richard Neutra*, 1960.

B. Zevi, *Richard Neutra*, 1954.

NEVELSON, LOUISE (1899–1988) American sculptor. Born in Russia, she was taken to Rockland, Maine, at age six. During the 1920s she lived in New York and then went to study with Hans Hoffman in Germany, where, she said, "she recognized the cube." After her return to New York, she and Ben Shahn (q.v.) became assistants to Diego Rivera on his Rockefeller Center murals. She worked for the WPA (Works Project Administration), teaching sculpture at the Educational Alliance.

Although Nevelson worked in many mediums — clay, marble, terra cotta, black Plexiglass, and clear aluminum — she was especially associated with wooden sculpture. In the early 1940s she began to collect pieces of wood from any source — old furniture, lumberyards, dumps — to transform into "assemblages." Nevelson confined her assemblages, painted black, in black boxes during the 1950s and later assembled the boxes as units in a long wall. For exhibitions, she conceived of her sculptures as "environments" sometimes merging the individual sculptures into an environment so successfully that they seemed to lose their identity. In her home in SoHo, New York City, she painted one wall gold and began to collect and assemble gold works. She had a separate studio for black work and a third for white.

Nevelson worked for thirteen years on a series of black-painted wood pieces, which she called *Mrs. N.'s Palace*. This was intended as a permanent environment, in which the pieces were attached to a black mirror-glass base. Among the commissions she executed were: white wood sculptures for the Chapel of the Good Shepherd, Saint Peter's Lutheran Church, New York; a black wall in memory of the victims of the Holocaust in the lobby of the Federal Courthouse in Philadelphia; a fifty-five-foot wall for Temple Beth-El, Great Neck, Long Island; and outdoor monuments on Park Avenue near 92nd Street, Manhattan, at the New York World Trade Center, at Temple Israel, Boston, Massachusetts, and in a square near Wall Street, Lower Manhattan, which was named Louise Nevelson Plaza.

Many museums, including the Whitney Museum, the Museum of Modern Art, and the Jewish Museum, all in New York, purchased Nevelson's work. She represented the United States at the Venice Biennale both in 1962 and 1976. Nevelson was president of New York Artists' Equity for two years and then of National Artists' Equity. She was vice-president of the Federation of Modern Painters and Sculptors and a member of the National

Louise Nevelson

Council on the Arts and Government. Nevelson was awarded the national medal of arts in recognition of her outstanding contribution to American art.

Louise Nevelson said that she searched for a "reality that was factual, in an area where there was an unlimited source, to reach what for me would be reality." She distilled from past and current art movements the inspiration for her own work including African and pre-Columbian sculpture, architecture, and geometry. Her boxes were beautifully designed, using every conceivable geometric shape. Color and texture in her monochromatic works were created by the play of light and shade over their intricate surfaces. Later, the constructivist element in her work became more positive. The structure was no longer designed to encompass the idea, but had become the raison d'être of the idea, the material, and the techniques.

A. B. Glimcher, *Louise Nevelson*, 1976.
J. Gordon, *Louise Nevelson*, 1967.
L. Nevelson, *Dawns and Dusks*, 1976.

NEWHOUSE, SAMUEL IRVING   (1895–1979)
U.S. publisher. Born in New York City, Newhouse

went to work as soon as he had completed elementary school as an office boy for Judge Herman Lazarus. He began his career in the newspaper business at the age of sixteen, when his employer bought the *Bayonne* (New Jersey) *Times* and told him to take care of it. Newhouse studied law at night, but although he passed the bar exam he never practiced. He made the *Times* profitable, and his 25 percent of the paper's income was more than enough for him to live on.

In 1922 he purchased, in partnership with Judge Lazarus, the *Staten Island Advance*, the first of the Newhouse chain of papers. Ten years later he bought the *Long Island Press*. Afterwards, he secured the *Newark Star-Ledger* (1935), the *Long Island Star-Journal* (1938), the *Syracuse Herald-Journal*, and the Sunday *Herald-American* (1939). In 1944 he purchased the *Syracuse Post-Standard*, thus controlling both of Syracuse's daily papers. Three years later he bought both newspapers in Harrisburg, Pennsylvania, the *Patriot* and the *Evening News*.

In the 1950s Newhouse expanded his holdings to include the *Portland Oregonian* (1950), the *Jersey City Journal* (1950), the *St. Louis Globe-Democrat*

(1955) and, in what was described at the time as the largest transaction in American newspaper history, the *Birmingham News* and the *Huntsville Times*, as well as one television and three radio stations in Alabama for more than 18.5 million dollars. In 1959 he obtained a controlling interest in the Condé Nast magazines, including *Vogue, Bride's Magazine, Glamour*, and *House & Garden*, and in the Street and Smith publications *Mademoiselle, Living for Young Homemakers*, and others.

He continued to expand, and at the time of his death he controlled thirty-one newspapers with a total circulation of over three million, five radio stations, cable television with 175,000 subscribers, and numerous magazines.

The Newhouse formula for success was to cut cost stringently, stimulate advertising and circulation, and allow local editors complete autonomy. He believed that only a sound business operation would allow for truly independent editorial policy.

Newhouse contributed two million dollars to establish the Newhouse Communications Center at Syracuse University and aided in the establishment of Lincoln Center, New York City.

NEWMAN, BARNETT (1905–1970) U.S. abstract expressionist painter. Although he learned Hebrew as a child in his native New York, his immigrant family was not religious. While at high school and college he attended the Art Students League, and afterwards often worked as a substitute art teacher. His father had a thriving clothing business, and Newman, after graduation from the City College of New York (CCNY), became his partner until 1937.

Newman began to experiment in the 1940s, and produced somewhat surrealistic work based on automatic calligraphic brush-strokes. These included a series of "cosmic landscapes." In 1947, he concentrated on *The Genetic Moment*, circular (female) forms combined with long (masculine) bars, which evolved into circles and stripes. In most of his later paintings, the circles were eliminated.

His one-man shows in 1950 and 1951 did not win critical approval. Newman shunned exhibitions until 1958 when Bennington College held a retrospective of his work, which brought him many admirers among young artists looking for a new direction. He taught at the University of Saskatchewan (1959) and the University of Pennsylvania (1962–1964).

Newman was one of the artists who, with Adolph Gottlieb, William Baziotes, and Mark Rothko (q.v.), founded the short-lived school, Subject of the Artist.

Newman's paintings became large areas of flat color, divided into sections by narrow stripes of a second or third color, which he called "zips." Sometimes his stripes had ragged edges. His objective was to affect the greatest significance through the use of minimal means.

For a while he worked on tall, thin paintings, only a few inches wide. His few sculptures were similar in style, long and thin, as if he were reducing his means to the "zip" alone. An exception was *Broken Obelisk* (1967), a sculpture which he made for Rothko's chapel in Houston, Texas. When the Jewish Museum in New York held an exhibition of new ideas in synagogue architecture, Newman participated, and designed and built a synagogue model for the show.

In a brief departure from his color-field work, Newman created a series of fourteen *Stations of the Cross* in black and white, which were exhibited at the Guggenheim Museum, New York, in 1966. This series is an extension of his effort to convey deep meaning and intense feeling through a minimum of abstract shapes.

Barnett Newman saw the problems facing modern American artists as how to progress from the geometric ideas of the European abstract artists and how to liberate art from the tyranny of subject and form. He sought pure painting and communication of the aesthetic idea, and painted a series of works on the same themes.

T. S. Hess, *Barnett Newman*, 1971.
H. Rosenberg, *Barnett Newman*, 1978.

NOAH, MORDECAI MANUEL (1785–1851) American author and diplomat. Born in Philadelphia, then the capital of the United States, Noah came into contact with many of the leading scholars and statesmen of that era. His interest in the theater later expressed itself in dramatic productions that he wrote and produced. His formative years gave him the background to develop into a popular journalist, playwright, and politician.

When he was twenty-eight, Noah was appointed American consul in Tunis by President James Madison. On his way to Tunis, his ship was captured by the British, and he was interned in England. During this period he came to know the Jewish community of Great Britain and he also traveled on the European continent. Eventually reaching Tunis, he had to take diplomatic action to secure the release of a group of Americans who were being held for ransom by Berber pirates. Noah received secret instructions from Washington to pay the ransom and effect the captives' release without involving the U.S. government. However, after acting on behalf of the American government, he found that State Department refused to authorize the amount which he had expended for the ransom. A letter from the State Department, signed by James Monroe, revoked his commission and referred to the "unfavorable effect" of the "religion which you profess." After returning to the United States, he fought for rehabilitation and finally, in January 1817, the State Department indicated that it would pay the $5,216 owed to him.

After his return his political career took him to the post of sheriff, grand sachem of Tammany Hall, surveyor of the port of New York, and judge. Even the Tunisian affair did not dim his popularity

Mordecai M. Noah. Drawing c. 1820.

among American Jews. In 1818 he was chosen to deliver the main address at the dedication of the new synagogue building of Congregation Shearith Israel in New York. In this speech he expressed for the first time his hope for the restoration of the Jewish people to its own homeland. He added that "until the Jews can recover their ancient rights and dominions, and take their rank among the governments of the earth, the U.S. is their chosen country."

In 1825 Mordecai Manuel Noah announced a grandiose plan for creating a Jewish state in the United States, a temporary haven until the return to Zion. It was to be established on Grand Island in the Niagara River, opposite Buffalo, New York, and would be called "Ararat — a City of Refuge for the Jews." On September 11, arrayed in robes of black and ermine, Noah led the magnificent procession — including militia in uniform, Masons in regalia, and Indians with feathered headdresses

— for the service of dedication of Ararat (in the Episcopal church). Unfortunately, no one ever chose to settle there and Noah's plan was fiercely criticized by Jews in Europe. However, over seventy years before Theodor Herzl (q.v.), Noah had proclaimed the necessity of the establishment of a new Jewish state. His 1845 address on the restoration of the Jews to their homeland includes a map of Palestine and it became a standard document of reference for American Jews prior to the Civil War.

I. Goldberg, *Major Noah: American Jewish Pioneer*, 1937.

NORDAU, MAX (Simon Maximilian Südfeld; 1849–1923) Zionist, writer, physician. Born in Budapest, descended from a long line of Talmudic scholars and son of an Orthodox rabbi, he had a traditional Jewish education, remaining an observant Jew until the last decade of his life, when he became a follower of Darwin. Educated in Budapest, he published his first poem when he was fourteen and at sixteen was a theater critic. Nordau qualified as a physician in 1876 and opened a general practice, eventually specializing in psychiatry. He traveled widely during his student days, writing for several Budapest newspapers, chiefly the German language *Pester Lloyd*. The name Max Nordau was originally a pseudonym, which he adopted legally in 1873. In 1880 he moved to Paris, practiced medicine, married a Danish Protestant, and was correspondent for the *Pester Lloyd*, the Vienna *Neue Freie Presse*, and the *Frankfurter Zeitung*. He also wrote on contemporary political and social issues.

A trenchant critic of contemporary society and the arts, Nordau gained fame and popularity with his iconoclasic, radical, witty articles. He wrote for the theater *The War of Millions* (1882), *The Right to Love* (1894), and *The Ball* (1894). He also wrote novels: *The Sickness of the Century* (1889), *Comedy of Sentiment* (1891), *Seelenanalysen* (1892), and *Drohnenschlacht* (1898); *The Drone Must Die* (1899). His travelogues and critical essays were published in several volumes, the best known of which was *Der Sinn der Geschichte* (1909). *The Intepretation of History* (1910), *Paradoxes* (1885), and *Degeneracy* (1892–1893) brought him worldwide prominence. They were rationalist attacks on the superstitions that he saw as threatening civilized society including religion, nationalism, and racism. *Degeneracy* criticizes all forms of modernity. He proposed the establishment of a society for ethical culture that would examine works of art and publicly condemn those found to be "degenerate." *Degeneracy* was a best-seller, translated into most western languages, evoking both superlative acclaim and total repudiation. Some likened him to Heinrich Heine (q.v.) and Baruch Spinoza (q.v.); William James called the book "a pathological book on a pathological subject." George Bernard Shaw, while paying tribute to Nordau as a "vigorous and capable journalist," wrote, "he is so utterly mad on the subject of degeneracy that he finds symptoms of it in the loftiest geniuses as plainly as in the lowest jailbirds, the exception being himself, Cesare Lombroso (q.v.), Krafft-Ebbing, Goethe, Shakespeare and Beethoven." *The Conventional Lies* was forbidden in Russia and Austria and put on the Index by the Vatican. The opposition to his views culminated in his expulsion from France during World War I; he spent several years in Madrid, returning to France only after the end of hostilities.

Nordau first met Theodor Herzl (q.v.) in 1892, when both were on the staff of the *Neue Freie Presse*. There was such an instantaneous sympathy between them that Herzl wrote in his "Diary": "We were so much of one mind that I already started to think that the same ideas had led him to the same conclusions. But no, his were different. 'Anti-Semitism will force the Jews to destroy the very concept of a fatherland everywhere' he said. 'Or to create a fatherland of their own' I thought secretly to myself." Herzl consulted him while writing his *Jewish State* in 1896 and was greatly encouraged by Nordau, who became his staunchest supporter and closest life friend. When Herzl expounded his dream of Zionism, Nordau took his hand and said "You may be mad — but if you are, I am as mad as you."

Nordau's critique of contemporary society included not only the debunking of Nietzsche's theory of the superman but also of contemporary anti-Semitism and an analysis of the condition of Jews in Western society, of their pitiful efforts to seek acceptance by a society that rejected them. His drama *Dr. Kohn* (1898) illustrates this viewpoint.

Beginning with the First Zionist Congress (1897), Nordau presented a comprehensive and magisterial review of the world Jewish situation at each congress for the next ten years, insisting that the only viable solution to the Jewish question was Zionism. It was he who drafted the Basel Program, the original basic statement of the aims of Zionism. Nordau delivered these annual reviews with great verve and they were the highlight of each congress. He was an impressive figure and, in Herzl's words, "a silver-tongued orator." He foresaw the fate of European Jewry very clearly; as early as 1911, he proclaimed to the Eleventh Zionist Congress that six million European Jews were in danger of immediate extermination. The "realists" denounced this warning.

In the eyes of east European Zionists, Nordau typified the western Jew who looked upon them patronizingly. Chaim Weizmann (q.v.) described him as "a prima donna, a great speaker in the classical style," in whose development as a Zionist "the cleavage between East and West, between organic and schematic Zionism" was manifest. Nordau remained undaunted in his support of Herzl, even during the Uganda crisis. It was he who coined the phrase *Nachtasyl* ("temporary shelter") in defense of the Uganda plan.

After Herzl's untimely death in 1904, he refused the presidency of the Zionist Organization, although

Max Nordau in his study, 1897.

he presided over the 1905 congress. After 1911 he ceased to attend congresses, deprecating the direction taken by Zionism towards Chaim Weizmann's practical Zionism as against his own political Zionism.

The old and ailing Nordau welcomed the Balfour Declaration in 1917, and in 1920 when Palestine was mandated to the British, he came forward with a plan that would have made the best use of the Balfour Declaration: to settle in Palestine half a million Jews within a year, the rest of European Jewry to follow within the next ten years. Only a very few Zionists took his plan seriously.

Nordau died in Paris. In his will, he stipulated that he should be buried in Eretz Israel and his wish was carried out in 1926, when he was reburied in Tel Aviv's old cemetery.

M. Ben-Horin, *Max Nordau, Philosopher of Human Solidarity*, 1956.

Max Nordau, *Max Nordau, a Biography*, 1943.

NOSTRADAMUS (Latin surname of Michel de Nostre-Dame; 1503–1566) The most famous astrologer of all time. Despite later claims to distinguished ancestry, Nostradamus was descended from ordinary Provençal Jews. His father, Jacob (Jacques or Jaume), was the son of Abraham Solomon de Saint-Maximin, a grain dealer; his mother Reynière (Renée), was the daughter of the local tax collector. After Provence became French territory in 1482, however, there were periodical anti-Jewish riots and Louis XII forced his new unconverted subjects to choose between expulsion and baptism (1498). The edict was made final in July 1501, by which time Jaume, Renée, and their families had converted and changed their names; thereafter,

Renée's father was known as Jean de Saint-Rémy and Jaume's as Pierre (or Peyrot) de Nostre-Dame. However nominal this conversion may have been, Nostradamus himself was born in Saint-Rémy-de-Provence and raised as a Catholic, even though both of his ex-Jewish grandfathers took charge of the boy's education.

Like other converted Jews, his family still had to face prejudice and discrimination. Nostradamus's youthful interest in stargazing and the Copernican theory frightened his parents, because the Church condemned such heretical activities, and he was soon directed to a less risky career in medicine (1522). After obtaining his first medical degree at the University of Montpellier, he traveled throughout southern France, gaining practical experience and establishing his reputation as the originator of advanced, unorthodox methods to treat ailments and combat outbreaks of the plague. He received his doctor's degree in 1529 and established a lucrative medical practice, but lost his first wife and children when the plague struck their home in Agen (1536). Threatened by the Inquisition owing to some careless remark about a statue of the Virgin, Nostradamus spent the years between 1538 and 1547 wandering from place to place; he visited Italy and Sicily before returning to Provence, where he again treated plague victims, finally settling and remarrying in the town of Salon.

These tragic experiences reawakened his preoccupation with the occult. Set down as a multitude of astrological predictions, his glimpses of things to come were eventually published in a series of volumes entitled *Les prophéties de M. Michel Nostradamus*. The first edition (Lyons, 1555) comprised three groups of one hundred rhymed quatrains ("centuries") and an incomplete fourth group of fifty-three stanzas. Nostradamus mostly foretold assorted calamities, but avoided prosecution as a magician by using an obscure French style, full of cryptic expressions and anagrams, together with a deliberately confused time sequence.

Little notice might have been taken of these predictions had not one concerning Henry II's death at a royal tournament been fulfilled in 1559. This marked the beginning of Nostradamus' worldwide renown and of continual efforts to decipher his "prophecies." He was even appointed physician and counsellor in ordinary to the fourteen-year-old king, Charles IX, in 1564. The astrologer died less than two years later, but his reputation grew as more of his forecasts seemed to prove accurate and as reprints and translations of his book appeared throughout the west. Although numerous quatrains are ambiguous or incomprehensive, other predictions gave rise to astonishment as they were apparently fulfilled, including the British Parliament's execution of Charles I, Louis XVI's flight to Varennes and death under the guillotine, the Great Fire of London in 1666, the rise and fall of Napoleon, air travel and combat, the abdication of Edward VIII, and the U.S.–Soviet rapprochement. Nostradamus also predicted a leader of "Greater Germany" called "Hister" who would "cause vast bloodshed," serve no law, and was destined to unleash his "ravenous beasts" over Europe before the triumph of his opponents.

E. Cheetham, (ed.), *The Prophecies of Nostradamius*, 1973.

J. C. de Fontbrune, *Nostradamus I: Countdown to Apocalypse*, 1984.

D. P. Francis, *Nostradamus, Prophecies of Present Times?*, 1984.

J. Laver, *Nostradamus or the Future Foretold*, 1952.

O

OCHS, ADOLPH SIMON (1858–1935) U.S. newspaper publisher. Ochs was born in Cincinnati, the son of a Bavarian immigrant businessman who became a Jewish community leader and served as a volunteer rabbi for twenty-five years. The family moved to Knoxville, Tennessee, in 1865, and four years later Ochs left school at the age of eleven and began working as an office boy for the *Knoxville Chronicle*.

Adolph S. Ochs in his office.

At age fourteen, Ochs became a printer's devil at the *Knoxville Tribune* and then a compositor at the *Louisville Courier-Journal*. In 1877 he moved to Chattanooga, where he served as editor of the *Chattanooga Dispatch* until it failed. The following year he bought the failing *Chattanooga Times* with $250 that he had borrowed. He made the paper a financial success, and it soon became one of the leading journals in the South.

In 1896 Ochs bought the once prosperous, but then almost moribund *New York Times*. Fighting the then popular "yellow journalism," Ochs insisted that editorial opinion be subordinate to unbiased news. He introduced his philosophy, "All the News That's Fit to Print," to the newspaper's masthead. In 1898 he reduced the price of the paper to one

cent, which was the price of the yellow sheets, and tripled circulation. At the same time, he refused fraudulent or improper advertising and did not allow the practice, common at the time, of allowing advertisers to dictate editorial policy. With financial security assured, he expanded the paper's plants and introduced rotogravure and the book review section. In 1913 he began the *New York Times Index*, the first in the country.

Ochs retained control of the *Chattanooga Times*, and from 1901 to 1912 also published the *Philadelphia Public Ledger* and the *Philadelphia Times*. The merged papers were sold in 1913. From 1900, he was a director of the Associated Press. Ochs never held, nor sought, public office. In his later years he devoted much time to philanthropy and public causes.

G.W. Johnson, *An Honorable Titan*, 1970.
G. Talese, *The Kingdom and the Power*, 1969.

ODETS, CLIFFORD (1906–1963) U.S. playwright and scriptwriter. He was born in Philadelphia to a poor Jewish working-class family. In 1908 his family moved to the Bronx, where they eventually prospered. An amateur director and actor in his student days, he started his career as an actor, reciter of poetry, radio announcer, and sound-effects man. In 1925 he formed his own group and presented radio programs that he wrote himself. In 1926 he joined the acting company of the presitigious Theater Guild, under the auspices of which the Group Theater, directed by Harold Clurman and Lee Strasberg (q.v.), was formed in 1930 to promote plays with social orientation. Odets was invited to join the new enterprise as an actor, but soon he emerged as a playwright as well.

In the early years of the new company, Odets did not find it easy to persuade his friends at the Group Theater to produce his plays. It was his one-act, radical propaganda play *Waiting for Lefty* (January 1935) that made his name as a playwright overnight. Produced off Broadway with Group actors, the play depicted a meeting of a taxi union called to decide whether to go on strike. Before they decide, the committee members are waiting for one of their leaders, Lefty. Some of the union members are planted in the audience. Learning that Lefty was murdered, the committee members decide to vote to strike. The play excited the opening night's audience to the point of joining with the characters in the cry of "Strike!" In a scene omitted from the published version, a fired young actor is advised to read *The Communist Manifesto*. Odets, who became a spokesman for the perplexed youth of the depression years, joined the Communist party late in 1934, but left its ranks eight months later when he felt its pressures artistically stifling.

With the success of *Lefty*, which became the most exciting theatrical event of the year and was presented in 104 cities in 1935 alone, the Group presented it on Broadway, together with a companion one-acter, the hastily-written *Till the Day I Die*. The latter is an anti-Nazi play depicting the predicament of a German communist who is tortured by the Nazis to betray his comrades; he does not break, but is nevertheless marked as a traitor by the communists and can rehabilitate himself only by committing suicide. In that same year, the Group rapidly produced his formerly rejected *Awake and Sing!* (originally titled *I've Got the Blues*), and later his *Paradise Lost*. That year Odets also headed a commission to investigate the involvement of American financial interests in Cuba. The members were arrested in Havana and sent back to the United States, but the play he began to write on that experience was never completed.

Awake and Sing, which draws its title from the injunction in Isaiah 26:19, presents the poor Jewish Berger family. *Paradise Lost*, another family saga with the depression years as a background, was a failure in the theater. A similar depression-era background governs *Golden Boy* (1937), whose title character, young, ambitious Italian-American Joe Bonaparte, must choose between being a violinist or a boxer.

Odets was by far the leading playwright of the Group Theater between 1935 and 1940, when he wrote about half the Group's repertory. This included *Rocket to the Moon* (1938), a domestic, naturalist drama; *Night Music* (1940); and *Clash by Night* (1941), a conventional triangle drama where marriage collapses by lack of communication in an alienated, capitalistic world.

Odets spent many years in Hollywood. There he married in 1937 the film star Luise Rainer, but their independent careers led to their divorce four years later. In 1943 he married the actress Bette Grayson. His Hollywood years produced screenplays such as *The General Died at Dawn* (1936), *None but the Lonely Heart* (1943), and *The Sweet Smell of Success* (1957), and plays about Hollywood such as *The Big Knife* (1949), a melodrama about Charlie Castle, a movie star whose only way to retain his integrity is to commit suicide, and *The Country Girl* (1950), about life in the theater. At the time of writing this play Odets was under pressure to make a public confession before the House Un-American Activities Committee about his political involvement in the 1930s. For a time he managed to avoid such a confession, but later he gave in and

went to Washington, although he only gave names which had been given before. His confession saved the successful Hollywood screen version of *The Country Girl*. Odets' last produced play, *The Flowering Peach* (1954), is an adaptation of the story of Noah's ark told in the idiom of middle-class Jews in New York. In accounting for his making peace with the nonrevolutionary world surrounding him, Odets himself attempts, to explain his reasons for complying with HUCA. At the time of his death he was working on a musical version of *Golden Boy*.

M. J. Mendelsohn, *Clifford Odets: Humane Dramatist*, 1969.

R. B. Shuman, *Clifford Odets*, 1962.

E. Murray, *Clifford Odets: The Thirties and After*, 1968.

G. C. Weales, *Clifford Odets — Playwright*, 1971.

OFFENBACH, JACQUES (JAKOB) (1819–1880) Composer. Offenbach, the composer of more than ninety spirited operettas within twenty-five years and the man who put *opéra-bouffe* on the map, was the son of the cantor of the Cologne synagogue, who was also a modest violinist and teacher.

Offenbach's talents were evident at a very early age, and he began to take violin lessons from his father at the age of six. By eight, he was composing songs and dances, and at nine was studying the cello. It was not long before the young Offenbach, together with his sister and brother, was performing in a trio in local taverns, dance halls, and cafes.

At age fourteen, Offenbach and his older brother, Julius, were accepted by Luigi Cherubini as students at the Paris Conservatoire (despite a rule forbidding foreign entrants). Offenbach left after only a year, finding the classes dull and the discipline that Cherubini enforced on the students frustrating. He began to fend for himself in Paris, playing in the orchestra of the Opéra Comique, continuing cello lessons with the celebrated cellist, Norblin, and subseqently studying composition and orchestral arranging with the composer Fromental Halévy. He started to write the occasional dance tune for popular *café-concerts*, and in 1850 was approached by the director of the Comedie Francaise to organize and conduct a new orchestra for the princely sum of 6,000 francs a year.

However, in Offenbach's words: "During this period I often thought of the possibility, although it always seemed impossible, of founding a theater. I told myself that the Opéra Comique was no longer the home of true comic opera, that really gay, bright, spirited music — in short, the music with real life in it — was being forgotten.... I knew that the Exhibition of 1855 would bring many people into this locality. I found supporters, I gathered my librettists, and opened the Théâtre des Bouffes-Parisiens." As manager of the Bouffes-Parisiens his constant urge to create operetta could at last flourish. He poured out one operetta after another, and the audiences adored their flippant social and political satire. He was the adored enfant terrible of

Jacques Offenbach

the music theater. He established an operetta stereotype with regular appearances of the acclaimed landler, the waltz, the polka and the renowned can-can. In 1856 alone he wrote seven one-act pieces that were performed with great success. By March 1859, the latest success, *Orpheus in the Underworld*, was earning 2,250 francs an evening, and 228 performances were given before it was temporarily taken out of the repertoire. This masterpiece, together with the ambitious *Contes d'Hoffmann (Tales of Hoffmann)*, which Offenbach wrote toward the end of his life in 1879, continue to be part of standard operatic repertoire. Both the famed "Barcarolle" from *Tales of Hoffmann* and the "Can-Can" from *Orpheus in the Underworld* remain two of the world's best-known and most popular pieces of this genre.

A. Faris, *Jacques Offenbach*, 1980.
P. Gammond, *Offenbach*, 1980.
J. Harding, *Jacques Offenbach*, 1980.
S. Sitwell, *"La Vie Parisienne,"* A Tribute to *Offenbach*, 1937.

OISTRAKH, DAVID FEDOROVICH (1908–1974) Russian violinist. He was born in Odessa into a musical family. His father, a poor bookkeeper, trained the chorus of the local operatic society and played the violin. His mother was a singer and an actress. Years later Oistrakh reflected on his childhood with fondness: "I cannot think of my childhood without music. My father gave me a toy violin when I was about three and a half and I remember trying to join a party of street musi-

cians." Of his first ever audience, when he was five, Oistrakh says: "I can see myself standing in a courtyard surrounded by other children. I had some sort of music in front of me which I pretended to read but did not understand as I eagerly scratched away on that canary yellow instrument. But the notes I drew from it sounded heavenly to me at the time."

Oistrakh graduated in 1926 from the Odessa Music School in both violin and viola and a year later performed Aleksandr K. Glazunov's violin concerto in Kiev, under the baton of the composer. In 1928 he made his debut in Leningrad and then moved to Moscow, where he was appointed, six years later, to the faculty of the Moscow Conservatory. During the 1930s Oistrakh won several competitions in his homeland, but it was the first prize at the 1937 Ysaye competition in Brussels that made his name famous worldwide. During World War II he played at the front, in hospitals, in factories, and in besieged Leningrad. Only after the war did his international career flourish. In 1953 he played in Paris and in London. He made his American debut in 1955, and in New York, introduced Dimitri Shostakovich's first violin concerto, which was written for him.

Oistrakh advised many Soviet composers on technical aspects of their compositions and collaboarated with Sergei Prokofiev on arranging his flute sonata for the violin. Oistrakh taugh a large number of Soviet violinists especially his own son, Kgor (born 1931) who became a first rate violinist as well, winning awards in competitions in Budapest and Poznan.

In 1954 Oistrakh was named People's Artist of the U.S.S.R. and in 1960 he was awarded the Lenin Prize. Unlike many of his colleagues, Oistrakh never contemplated leaving his homeland for the West. "I owe the state everything. It is responsible for my upbringing and have seen to it that I have had the best musical education and training. My family is there. It would be disloyal of me to live elsewhere," he once told Yehudi Menuhin. Oistrakh died in Amsterdam during one of his extensive concert tours.

M. Campbell, *The Great Violinists*, 1981.
I. Yampolsky, *David Oistrakh* (Russian), 1964.

OLIVETTI FAMILY Italian industrialists. **Camillo Olivetti** (1868–1943), was an electrical engineer and inventor, who opened in his native town of Ivrea, a small factory that was the first to manufacture electrical measurement instruments in Italy. Continuing as an innovator, he was the first to produce typewriters in Italy, starting in 1909. At that time his product line included the Olivetti typewriter, which he had invented.

His eldest son, **Adriano Olivetti** (1901–1960), followed in his father's footsteps. After receiving a degree in industrial chemistry from the Turin polytechnic, he became an apprentice at the Olivetti Company, after which he went to the United States to study plant management and industrial methods.

After returning to Italy, he implemented a series of changes that increased production and decreased costs. In the 1930s Adriano Olivetti began to market his products internationally. In 1933 he was made managing director of the firm and after his father's retirement in 1938 became company president.

By the mid-1940s the company was making great advances. It produced eighteen business machines in six countries. By this time the Olivetti name was well-known and Olivetti products were marketed in almost every nation of the world.

The Olivettis were also known for their benevolence. The Olivetti company was interested in its employees, providing benefits ranging from camps for the children and tuition for higher education, to workers' transport systems, affordable and attractive housing, and apprentice schools.

After World War II, Adriano Olivetti extended help to more than sixty-five communities disabled by the war. He established the National Institute of Town Planning and helped to strengthen rural economies by opening small factories in outlying areas.

Both Olivettis were antifascists and anticommunists. Adriano was once quoted as saying, "Free, autonomous, let us say, Christian socialism — that is what we want." This comment reflected his belief that a healthy society must build its foundation at the community level. Communities should be autonomous and the economy decentralized. At the same time, he thought, communities should be concerned about the needs of their citizens. He wrote a number of books expounding his socioeconomic ideas.

Adriano founded more than seventy community aid centers in towns and villages. These centers promoted urbanization and included libraries and educational courses. In 1956 he was elected mayor of his hometown, Ivrea. Two years later, in 1958, he founded the Movimento di Communita, (Community Movement) based on his Community philosophy. He was elected to represent that party in parliament. However, his political career was cut short by his sudden death.

Shortly before Adriano's death, the Olivetti company purchased a controlling share of another typewriter manufacturer, Underwood, with the hope of turning it into another Olivetti success. At the time of his death the Olivetti corporation employed 25,000 workers.

Ricordo di Adriano Olivetti, 1960.

OPHÜLS, MAX   (1902–1957) French film director. Born Maximilian Oppenheimer to a military tailor in Saarbrücken, Germany, he changed his name to Ophüls when he went on the stage at age seventeen. Five years later he began what became an exceptionally prolific career as a theater director, including a period directing at Vienna's Burgtheater. Ophüls's first film work was as a dialogue director for the German UFA company in 1929; the following year he was a full-fledged film direc-

tor. In 1932 he left Germany for France, becoming a French citizen six years later. It was his last German film, *Liebelei*, (1932) that first won him serious acclaim as a director.

Liebelei, with its romantic plot set in imperial Vienna, foreshadowed his last films, on which his present-day reputation largely rests. He worked in several European countries for the rest of the 1930s, fleeing to Hollywood, after France's occupation by the Nazis. Idle for four years, Ophüls was at last given the chance to work by the director Preston Sturges. Though the producer Howard Hughes had him replaced before he had completed the project finally known as *Vendetta*, Ophüls's subsequent Hollywood period included the highly regarded *Letter From an Unknown Woman*, adapted from the story by Stefan Zweig (q.v.).

In 1950 Ophüls resumed his filmmaking activity in France with *La ronde* (1950), based, like *Liebelei*, on a work by Arthur Schnitzler (q.v.). *La ronde* and the three other films Ophüls managed to complete before his death — *Le plaisir, Madame de...*, and *Lola Montez* — have in common a basically dark view of their romantic subjects, heavily overlaid with Ophüls's fluid style of camera work. The latter had become by the 1950s an Ophüls trademark and was characterized by long and elaborately plotted shots calling for extreme mobility on the part of the camera, often from a great height. Ophüls's son Marcel, who assisted his father on *Lola Montez*, has since achieved considerable stature as a documentary director.

A. Williams, *Max Ophüls and the Cinema of Desire*, 1980.

OPPENHEIMER, ERNEST   (1880–1957) South African financier and leader of the mining industry, knighted 1921. Born in Friedberg, Germany, he was the fifth son of a cigar merchant. At age sixteen he became a junior clerk in the London diamond firm of Dunkelsbuhler and Company and was naturalized in 1901. The following year he was sent to Kimberley, South Africa, as the firm's representative.

Oppenheimer's success in Kimberley enabled him to serve as mayor from 1912 to 1915. In 1917 he founded a gold mining enterprise, the Anglo-American Corporation of South Africa Ltd., with the help of the financiers J. P. Morgan and Co. and Herbert Hoover, then a mining engineer in South Africa. In 1919 he formed Diamond Consolidated Mines of South West Africa. This was so successful that in 1929 he became chairman of the great diamond company, De Beers. In 1929 he set up the Rhodesian Anglo-American Corporation, which was instrumental in developing the copper-mining industry in northern Rhodesia (Zambia). He opened up goldfields in the Orange Free State and in 1944 created the Orange Free State Investment Trust.

Oppenheimer was knighted in 1921 and from 1924 to 1938 he represented Kimberley in the Union Parliament, supporting Prime Minister Jan Christiaan Smuts.

Sir Ernest was a generous benefactor, raising a three-million-pound-sterling loan for the creation of housing for Africans in Johannesburg and contributing to the development of medical and scientific research in South Africa and Britain. He also made a grant toward Commonwealth studies and the establishment of Queen Elizabeth House at Oxford. He was a patron of the arts and sciences and his benevolence continued after his death through the Ernest Oppenheimer Memorial Trust.

After his marriage to his second wife (his nephew's widow), who was a Catholic, he converted to Christianity.

H. Oxbury, *Great Britons, Twentieth-Century Lives*, 1985.

OPPENHEIMER, J. ROBERT (1904–1967) American physicist. Born to a wealthy liberal family in New York, he was a brilliant student, particularly in mathematics and chemistry, and by the age of eleven had amassed his own rock collection and had become the youngest member of the New York Mineralogical Society. He received a Ph.D in 1927 from the University of Göttingen with a thesis on quantum theory, only two years after having completed a B.A. degree summa cum laude from Harvard University.

After two years of postdoctoral study, he returned to the United States in 1929, with invitations to teach from almost a dozen universities. He joined the staffs of the University of California (Berkeley) and the California Institute of Technology, and moved quickly up the ranks at both institutions. At Berkeley, he built up the largest graduate and postdoctoral school of theoretical physics in the

J. Robert Oppenheimer

United States, with students so devoted that they often followed him to Cal Tech to repeat his courses there.

He also engaged in his own research in various aspects of physics, investigating among other things electron-atom collision processes, cosmic-ray showers, and quantum electrodynamics, and participating in the development of the Oppenheimer-Phillips reaction, which led to new insights into the structure of the nucleus. He simultaneously maintained his interests in other sciences and in arts and literature, and at the age of thirty learned Sanskrit in order to study Hindu scripture in the original.

In 1941 he became involved with the atomic energy program and in 1943 was appointed director of the Manhattan Project to develop the atom bomb at Los Alamos, New Mexico. Many of his former graduate students were recruited to the project. When he witnessed the first atom bomb explosion on July 16, 1945, he was so impressed that the following lines from the sacred Hindu poem, the *Bhagavad-Gita*, flashed through his mind:

If the radiance of a thousand suns
Were to burst at once into the sky,
That would be the splendor of the Mighty One

I am become Death
The destroyer of worlds.

After the war he returned to Cal Tech, and in 1947 moved to Princeton to head the Institute of Advanced Studies. He also became increasingly active on the subject of the atomic bomb, serving on various policy-making and advisory committees. From 1946 to 1952 he was chairman of the General Advisory Committee to the Atomic Energy

From Robert Oppenheimer's letter about the hydrogen bomb to James B. Conant, a fellow member of the General Advisory Committee

What concerns me is really not the technical problem. I am not sure the miserable thing will work, nor that it can be gotten to a target except by ox-cart. It seems likely to me even further to worsen the unbalance of our previous war plans. What does worry me is that this thing appears to have caught the imagination both of the Congressional and of the military people, as the answer to the problem posed by the Russian advance. It would be folly to oppose the exploration of this weapon. We have always known it had to be done; and it does have to be done.... But that we become committed to it as the way to save the country and the peace, appears to me full of dangers.

Comission, which in 1949 opposed developing a hydrogen bomb. He served for seven years on the Committee on Atomic Energy of the Research and Development Board. In 1946 he also received the presidential medal of merit. In 1953, however, his security clearance was suddenly revoked because of suggestions that he had communist sympathies and that he had opposed the hydrogen bomb for subversive reasons. Among other charges cited against him were his friendships with leftist sympathizers in the 1930s, which, though previously arousing no comment, became blown out of proportion in the inflammatory McCarthy atmosphere of the 1950s. Although cleared of the charge of treason, it was noted that he should have no access to military secrets.

Although his dismissal from the Atomic Energy Commission became a cause célèbre, especially among fellow scientists, upon retrial, he was again declared a security risk. It took ten years until, in 1963, in an attempt to clear his name, President Lyndon Johnson bestowed upon him the Atomic Energy Commission's highest honor, the $50,000 Fermi award.

He continued to head the Institute for Advanced Study in Princeton until his retirement in 1966.

J. Boskin and F. Krinsky, *The Oppenheimer Affair*, 1968.
P. Michelmore, *The Swift Years: The Robert Oppenheimer Story*, 1969.
M. Rouze, *Robert Oppenheimer: The Man and His Theories*, 1964.
P. M. Stern, *The Oppenheimer Case*, 1969.

OPPENHEIMER, JOSEPH SÜSSKIND   (1698–1738)

German financier and "court Jew," known to history as Jud Süss (Jew Süss). The son of a Heidelberg merchant and tax collector, he gained business experience in several towns, but particularly with relatives in Vienna. There Samuel Oppenheimer (1630–1703), the Hapsburg army contractor nicknamed Judenkaiser, had been cheated out of a vast fortune by the Austrian government. Joseph Oppenheimer's own rise to fame and fortune began in 1732, when Prince Carl Alexander of Württemberg gave him the post of court factor. Soon afterward, he was granted similar privileges by the landgrave of Hesse and the electors of Cologne and the Palatinate.

As Duke of Württemberg (1733–1737), Carl Alexander aimed to establish an absolutist regime financed by a mercantile economy, and for this he needed Oppenheimer's resourceful expertise. Having been made the duke's privy councillor and virtual minister of finance, Oppenheimer repaid him with loyal service, encouraging private enterprise to fill the exchequer and working hard to strengthen his master's authority. Like other court Jews, he also used his growing influence for the small Jewish community's benefit. At the same time, however, he adopted a morally questionable, apparently licentious life-style which, together with his authoritarian manner and bid for a title of

Joseph Süsskind Oppenheimer. In the medallion below, the cage in which he was executed.

nobility, created fierce resentment. While awaiting their opportunity to bring about his downfall, jealous rivals slyly fanned the flames, bewailing the fact that Protestant Württemberg was ruled by a despotic Catholic and administered by a rapacious Jew.

Immediately after the duke's sudden death, in March 1737, Oppenheimer and some other high officials were arrested and charged with offenses against the state. Jew Süss alone was convicted of mismanagement and embezzlement, deprived of all his assets, and unjustly sentenced to death. While in jail, he became a strictly observant Jew, reciting daily prayers, growing a beard, and insisting on kosher food. When all Jewish efforts to secure his ransom had failed, Oppenheimer spurned the proposal that he avoid the gallows by embracing Christianity. "A free man can decide whether to change his religion, not a prisoner," he maintained. As crowds gathered to witness the spectacle, Jew Süss defiantly met his end proclaiming the *Shema* on April 2, 1738, when he was hanged inside an iron cage suspended high above one of Stuttgart's thoroughfares. Anti-Semitic engravings and medals were produced depicting his execution.

Within the German Jewish community, Oppenheimer was honored as a martyr, the victim of political intrigue and anti-Semitic hatred. According to certain rumors, his body had been spirited away for interment in Fürth while another corpse had been substituted for the one exhibited in Stuttgart. His career was to inspire a best-selling historical novel by Lion Feuchtwanger (q.v.), which Lothar Mendes turned into a Gaumont British movie (1934). The Nazis later promoted the filming of *Jud Süss* (1940), an anti-Jewish screen version directed by Viet Harlan.

H. Pardo, *Jud Süss: Historisches und juristisches Material zum Fall Veit Harlan*, 1949.

S. Stern, *The Court Jew*, 1950.

S. Stern, *Jud Süss* (German), 1929.

ORLOFF, CHANA (1888–1968) French sculptor. Born in the Ukraine, she went with her family at sixteen to the settlement of Petah Tikva in Eretz Israel, where her father worked in the fields and she helped out as a seamstress. Six years later she moved to Paris where she studied sculpture and moved in the circles of avant-garde artists. Amedeo Modigliani (q.v.) made a drawing of her on which he wrote "Chana, daughter of Raphael." In 1913 three of her wooden sculptures were accepted by the Salon d'Automne and thereafter she exhibited regularly. In 1916 she married the poet Ary Justman, who died in the influenza epidemic shortly after World War I, leaving her with a baby son.

During the following years, Orloff received commissions for portraits of many leading Parisians and famous personalities of the art world,

Chana Orloff by Amedeo Modigliani.

The Horsewoman by Chana Orloff.

such as Pablo Picasso and Henri Matisse. In 1925 she was made a chevalier of the Legion of Honor. She also visited the United States, where exhibitions of her work were held in New York and Boston.

During the Nazi occupation of France, she continued to work on what she called her "pocket sculptures" until December 1942, when she was warned that she was due to be arrested and fled with her son to Switzerland. In her absence, her Paris studio was vandalized and much of her work stolen or destroyed. Orloff returned to Paris after the war and her series of drawings and sculptures, *Retour*, depicted the sufferings of a deportee.

In the following years, many large-scale exhibitions of her work were held, including a retrospective in the Tel Aviv Museum. She visited Israel on a number of occasions and produced public monuments in Ramat Gan and Ein Gev. She died in Tel Aviv while on a visit there.

Orloff sculpted hundreds of portraits; some of famous people such as David Ben-Gurion (q.v.) and Sholem Asch (q.v.), others tender sculptures of pregnant women, women with children, ordinary men and women, and birds. Her favored medium was wood, which she found "warm and friendly," but she worked also in stone, marble, bronze, and cement. Her work was realistic, but influenced by cubism. She said that for her the important thing was "to create a living work of art."

H. Gaurzu et al., *Chana Orloff*, 1980.

G. Talpir, *Chana Orloff* (Hebrew) 1950.

ORMANDY, EUGENE (1899–1985) American conductor, born as Jeno Blau in Budapest. Ormandy began studying the violin with his father, later recalling that his father, who wanted to be a musician but could not afford it and so became a dentist, "decided that his first son would be named after, at that time the greatest Hungarian violinist, Jeno Hubay.... I had to be a great violinist. All that was in his mind ten years before he was even married." At the age of five Ormandy was admitted to the Budapest Royal Academy, and two years later began to perform. He studied there indeed with Jeno Hubay: "My father's idea was that he was going to be my teacher and I was to have succeeded him as a performer when he died. This never happened, of course."

At seventeen Ormandy was appointed professor of violin at the academy. In 1921 he went to New York and was promised a big contract that never materialized. He found himself a job with the Capitol Theater orchestra, in 1924, where he moved from the back of the orchestra to the concertmaster's chair in less than a week. After standing in for an ailing conductor in an afternoon performance, Ormandy was summoned to the orchestra's manager and offered a job as a conductor. He refused adamantly but ended up accepting the new position only when his salary was increased by twenty-five dollars. He said that he was never interested in being a conductor.

In 1927 Ormandy became an American citizen and eventually received several conducting jobs with small ensembles. He began his long association with the Philadelphia Orchestra in the 1930 summer season, and later that year deputized for Arturo Toscanini in the major series. Those concerts led to the position of music director with the Minneapolis Symphony Orchestra, where Ormandy remained for five years, from 1931 to 1936. He returned to Philadelphia and shared two seasons

there with Leopold Stokowski before becoming sole music director in 1938. He remained at the helm of this orchestra, considered one of the finest in North America, for thirty-five years.

With the Philadelphia Orchestra Ormandy achieved many musical firsts. In 1948 he led the first symphonic concert on American television, beating Toscanini on a rival network by ninety minutes. In 1949 Ormandy made his British debut during the Philadelphia Orchestra's first transatlantic tour. In 1973 Ormandy and his orchestra were the first American symphony orchestra to perform in mainland China.

R. Chesterman, *Conductors in Conversation*, 1990.
H. Kupferberg, *Those Fabulous Philadelphians*, 1969.
H. C. Schonberg, *The Great Conductors*, 1967.

EUGENE ORMANDY ON BEING THE SUBJECT OF A BIOGRAPHY

Under no circumstances. I'm not a creator, I'm an interpreter, and I don't think an interpreter should have a biography. I have read some autobiographies of famous conductors of the past and, much as I admired the conductor, I didn't admire the autobiographer. Because it threw a certain light on the man's ego that never showed in his music, and I wanted to know him as a great musician, a great interpreter, and not some small, little details in his life which only meant something to him, but to no one else who reads it. You can imagine how many people have tried to talk me into writing my own biography or have someone write it for me. I just turn it down.

P

PALACHE, SAMUEL (died 1616) Moroccan diplomat. The Palaches were one of the most distinguished families of Spanish refugees to settle in Morocco. Samuel and his brother, Joseph, were leading advisers on the country's finances and the sultan of Morocco even entrusted them with negotiations with Philip II of Spain. On one of their visits to Spain, the brothers aroused the wrath of the Inquisition, probably for helping Marranos to leave the country and return to Judaism. They had to be hidden by the French ambassador before they escaped.

Samuel, a skilled diplomat and linguist, was appointed Moroccan ambassador to Amsterdam early in the 17th century, and helped to obtain permission for Jews to settle in the Netherlands. The first *minyan* (Jewish prayer quorum) in Amsterdam met at his home, and he is said to have built the first synagogue. As ambassador he negotiated the first treaty of alliance between a Christian state and a Muslim state — the Netherlands and Morocco — and was firmly devoted to the fight against Catholic Spain.

His problems began in 1614 when, with the permission of the sultan, he himself assumed command of a small Moroccan fleet that captured Spanish galleons, laden with gold and precious cargo, on their return from America. He took his booty to Rotterdam and returned to his ships, but later — because of a storm, had to find shelter in Plymouth harbor, in England. At that time, England and Spain were at peace and the Spanish ambassador in London had Palache arrested on charges of piracy and of abandoning Christianity to return to Judaism, and demanded the death penalty.

The Dutch Representative Assembly protested his arrest to the king of England, explaining the nature of Palache's mission and demanding his release. However, initial intervention was not strong enough and Palache remained in prison. The Spanish ambassador used his influence and expended considerable sums of money to bribe members of the aristocracy to sentence Palache to death. The Dutch ruler now sent a sharp letter demanding the release of his friend Palache, "victim of a libelous attack by the Spanish ambassa-

dor." The Dutch representative in England, addressing the nobles, said, "It is true that Palache is a Jew and therefore should not be treated differently from a dog and heaven forbid that I should support his false faith — but he is the representative and ambassador of a powerful ruler and should therefore be set free." He also told the English king that the Spanish were torturing the Protestants no less than the Jews and that they therefore shared a common cause.

When Palache was brought to trial before the King's Council, some of the nobles rose at his entrance as an expression of honor and the president of the Court seated him at his side and permitted him to keep his head covered (at that time, no Jews were permitted to live in England). Palache's successful defense was that he was a Moroccan subject, in the service of the sultan, and at war with Spain. He was acquitted, and in protest the Spanish ambassador resigned.

Palache returned to Amsterdam and, shortly after, took revenge on Spain by attacking a Spanish ship in the English Channel and capturing its cargo. His further plans to extend Islamic-Protestant cooperation to the Middle East were cut short by his death.
D. Corcos, *Zion*, 25 (122–33), 1960.

PALEY, WILLIAM S. (1901–1990) American media executive who developed the Columbia Broadcasting System. He was born in the Jewish neighborhood of Chicago's West Side to immigrants from the Ukraine. (He added the second initial at the age of twelve, but it did not stand for anything.) His father started a cigar manufacturing business and became a multimillionaire. After studying at the School of Finance at the University of Pennsylvania, William joined his father's company and was vice-president from 1922 to 1928. Having bought into Columbia (which had been founded in 1926 but was not a financial success), Paley became its president in 1928. His initial investment of some $400,000 was worth over $350 million at the time of his death.

Paley soon had some sixty radio stations that accepted network programming and had developed the system into a giant coast-to-coast network. He had an uncanny gift for recruiting talent and by the 1940s was able to spend huge sums on tempting successful performers to leave his main rival, the NBC network, and join CBS. For years CBS boasted nine or ten of the top ten shows. It was a pioneer in news coverage, of which the star was Edward R. Murrow. It also introduced a high proportion of quality broadcasting such as Saturday afternoon relays of the concerts of the New York Philharmonic.

During World War II Paley was in London where he served, with rank of colonel, as deputy chief of the Psychological Warfare Division of the Allied Command in Europe. Returning to CBS after the war, he was personally responsible for its further development. He built studios on both coasts and produced game shows, situation comedies, and westerns for a growing audience. In 1948 the company introduced the long-playing record and later also entered the world of filmmaking and publishing. At one time, it even owned the New York Yankees baseball team.

In 1983 Paley handed over the chairmanship of CBS, but when the company ran into problems in 1987, he resumed his position, although he was then eighty-six years old.

Paley had many interests outside CBS. He had considerable investment in the *International Herald-Tribune*, of which he was a cochairman. He was a trustee of many institutions and the president of the Museum of Modern Art. His own art collection — he specialized in collecting French Postimpressionists — was famous.

Paley was a close friend of Chaim Weizmann (q.v.) whom he assisted on the latter's visits to the United States. As president of the William Paley Foundation, he made large contributions to the Weizmann Institute of Science in Rehovot.

In 1979, Paley published his memoirs *As It Happened*. On his death he was characterized by the *New York Times* as "a 20th-century visionary with the ambitions of a 19th century robber baron."
S. B. Smith, *In All His Glory: The Life of William S. Paley*, 1990.

PANOFSKY, ERWIN   (1892–1968) One of the outstanding art historians of the 20th century. Panofsky was born in Hanover, Germany, where he studied the history of art. He received his doctorate from the University of Freiburg and was professor at Hamburg from 1926 to 1933. A year after the rise of the Nazis to power, he fled to the United States, where he became visiting professor of fine arts at the New York University and at Princeton University. In 1947 he was appointed to the Charles Elliot Norton professorship of poetry at Harvard.

In 1930, Panofsky had published his *Hercules at the Crossroads*; this was followed by a study of Albrecht Dürer's *Melancholia*. In the wake of these two works, Panofsky became recognized as the most prominent figure in the iconological school of art history. In addition, he showed great interest in

> Art is not a subjective expression of feeling, or the existential activity of certain individuals, but rather the realizing and objectifying settlement (or conflict), aiming at effective results, between forming power and a material to be overcome.
>
> **Erwin Panofsky.** *Der Begriff des Kunstwollens*

Netherlandish painting, discovering several frauds in works attributed to Jan Van Eyck.

In his *Meaning in the Visual Arts*, Panofsky revealed the themes and ideas inherent in the history of art, and examined them in terms of manifestations of cultural tradition. His *Renaissance and Renascences in Western Art* (1960) was a synthesis of his conception of the art history of western Europe.

Among his works are *Studies in Iconology, Humanistic Themes in the Art of the Renaissance* (1939), *The Life and Art of Albrecht Dürer* (1955), and *Gothic Architecture and Scholasticism* (1951). His wife Dora was also a distinguished art historian and the two collaborated on *Pandora's Box: The Changing Aspects of a Mythical Symbol* (1956).
M. Meiss (ed.), *Essays in Honor of Erwin Panofsky*, 2 vols, 1961.

PAPPENHEIM, BERTHA   (1859–1936) German Jewish community activist. Bertha Pappenheim was the founder and leading voice of the Jüdischer Frauenbund, a social service agency of German Jewish women that addressed the specific concerns of women of the first half of the 20th century.

She was born in Vienna to an Orthodox family. Her mother had come from Frankfurt, Germany, and Bertha and her mother returned there following her father's death. What is known of Bertha's early development comes largely from Joseph Breuer's (q.v.) famous essays in *Studie in Hysteria* (1908), compiled with Sigmund Freud (q.v.). In one essay Pappenheim is identified as "Anna O.," a case-study of hysteria — a young woman suffering from psychosomatic paralysis following the stress of nursing her father during his final illness. The care she received from Breuer ended inconclusively; his understanding of the transference that had taken place during treatment was limited.

For the next few years of Pappenheim's life, from the time her treatment under Breuer in Vienna ended until her appearance as a healthy young woman in Frankfurt in 1888, no documentation exists. Soon after her arrival in Frankfurt, she was introduced into social work, and she assisted at a soup kitchen. Her passion for social justice was aroused. She was also concerned with the status of women. Eventually, in 1904, a group of young Jewish women, which she had organized under the name Weibliche Fürsorge ("Care by Women") became the kernel of a national federa-

Bertha Pappenheim stamp issued by the West German Post Office, 1954.

tion for Jewish women, the Jüdischer Frauenbund ("Jewish Women's League").

Meanwhile, Pappenheim, who never married, had become the head of an orphanage for Jewish girls. In 1907 she founded a home for delinquent and disturbed girls and for unwed mothers. Despite the heavy organizational and communal responsibilities, Pappenheim retained other interests. She studied the past of the Jewish people in general and of her own family in particular. She was especially intrigued by her 17th-century ancestor, Glückel of Hameln (q.v.), whose memoirs she translated.

Her feminist instincts as well as her drive for society's betterment led her to active opposition of the white slave trade. Many Jews from eastern Europe were flocking westward at the turn of the century, among them a number of girls who had been caught in the hold of procurers. Pappenheim implored the rabbinic and lay Jewish leaders in both Germany and eastern Europe to speak out against the white slave trade, but her efforts were unsuccessful. Cautious members of the community thought that speaking out against procurers would publicize unsavory Jewish activities and fuel anti-Semitism.

The home at Isenburg that Pappenheim had founded and which she headed for thirty years, expanded to take in dependent children. Pappenheim brought great spirit to the children there on Sabbaths and holidays: preparing plays, presenting her own prayers, and in all ways trying to impart the meaning of Jewish observances.

Despite illness, Pappenheim continued her work with the Jüdischer Frauenbund; her involvement with the Isenburg Home; and her travels to other Jewish communities throughout Europe, the Mid-

dle East, and the United States. She learned of their condition and, when she thought appropriate, offered advice. She met with Lillian D. Wald (q.v.) and visited her settlement house. She went to see Henrietta Szold (q.v.) to convince her that Zionism and Youth Aliya would cause the break up of families. Only too late did she perceive the dangers to German Jewry.

When Hitler came to power anti-Semitic pornography posted in public contained reprints of Pappenheim's earlier expositions of Jewish connections to the white slave trade. Soon after, only weeks before her death, she called in the president of the Jüdischer Frauenbund to apologize for her earlier stance.

Shortly before she died she was forced to appear at the Gestapo offices because a feeble-minded girl in the home had spoken disparagingly of Hitler. Pappenheim lived only about two weeks after this final ordeal.

D. Edinger (ed.), *Bertha Pappenheim: Her Life and Letters*, 1968.
M. Kaplan, *The Jewish Feminist Movement in Germany*, 1979.

PARKER, DOROTHY (1893–1967) U.S. poet, author, and humorist. Born Dorothy Rothschild in West End, New Jersey (she retained the name of her husband Edwin Pond Parker after their divorce), Dorothy Parker was the daughter of a Jewish father and a Scottish mother. She began her career writing drama reviews for *Vogue* and *Vanity Fair*. She was fired from *Vanity Fair* when her review of the actress Billy Burke was considered too harsh. To protest her release, two senior-level coworkers resigned their positions at the magazine. In 1927, she reviewed books and theater for the *New Yorker* in a column signed "Constant Reader."

Parker's best-selling first book of verse, *Enough Rope*, appeared in 1926. It was followed by two other books. All three were collected in *Not So Deep as a Well* in 1936. Parker also wrote short stories, including the prize-winning "Big Blonde" (1929). Her collections of short stories include *Laments for the Living* (1930), *After Such Pleasures* (1933), and *Here Lies* (1939). In 1944 a collection of prose and verse was published in *The Portable Dorothy Parker* with an introduction by W. Somerset Maugham. Parker also collaborated on a drama in 1953 with Arnand d'Usseau, *Ladies of the Corridor*, which was successfully staged in New York.

Dorothy Parker was known as a wit among the writers who met regularly at the Round Table at the Algonquin Hotel in New York.

Her humor resulted from the combination of her social observations and her inventive mind. This combination often presented itself in appropriate phrases. For example, upon hearing that Calvin Coolidge was dead, she responded "How can they tell?"

Her wit became so famous that there was a time when everything bright or malicious said in New

York was attributed to Parker. Her personal conduct also stood out among writers and humorists. Once, to attract company she posted a sign on her office door that said "Men."

The early 1920s were a time of growing social conscience for Parker. She was arrested while demonstrating in favor of Sacco and Vanzetti. After the start of the Spanish Civil War, Parker headed the Joint Anti-Fascist Refugee Committee to raise funds for Spanish Republicans. She wrote temporarily for the Marxist publication *New Masses*. During this time period, she went to Hollywood to write screenplays and also became politically active.

Social conscience affected Parker's writing. The middle class was increasingly portrayed as vacuous and idle. In the story "Big Blonde," the main character is continually a victim of others. Parker's own insight into her sardonic wit reveals her outlook: "A humorist, I think, is just balancing on the edge of the dumps."

J. Keats, *You Might as Well Live*, 1970.

PASCIN, JULES (1885–1930) Artist. Jules Pascin was one of the large group of Jewish painters who worked in Paris in the early 20th century. He was born in Vivin, Bulgaria. His grandfather, a Sephardic Jew, changed the family name from Pinas to Pincas because it was more euphonious, he thought, to east European ears. The Pincas family moved to Bucharest. By 1901, Jules was working in his father's business. He later said that he was banished from Bucharest by his father for spending too much time at a brothel, where he sketched and painted the prostitutes. His father gave him a small allowance, and he went to Vienna, where he studied art. From there he moved to Berlin, where he sold caricatures and humorous, satirical, and grotesque drawings to the magazine *Simplicissimus*, which he signed Pascin.

In 1905 Pascin went to live in Paris. He loved the gaiety of the streets and cafés, the parties, and the liqueurs. He painted and drew constantly, sending many of his drawings to *Simplicissimus*, and exhibiting in Berlin with the Secession. He was much admired in Berlin and the art connoisseur Paul Cassirer commissioned him to illustrate a book of Heinrich Heine (q.v.), the first of a long list of books illustrated by Pascin, which included the Hebrew scriptures and *One Thousand and One Nights*. In 1913 Pascin was represented in the famous Armory Show in New York. When World War I started, Pascin, whose income was mainly derived from his sales in Germany, borrowed money from his brother and went first to Belgium and Holland, and then to the United States. He traveled through the American South, the West Indies, and Cuba, making hundreds of drawings, often recording the essence of a scene or character in seconds. His drawings have a rare freedom and delicacy of line and he often added soft and beautiful touches of color to his drawings.

By the time he returned to Paris in 1920, Pascin was a well-known painter. He worked hard and forbade visitors before 5 P.M. In the evenings he would go with groups of friends to his favorite nightspots, picking up the check for everyone.

He did his best oil paintings in these years. With his outstanding draftsmanship, combined with his delicate lovely colors, he could evoke a wide range of moods. His depictions of female nudes — sometimes seductive, sometimes erotic — are painted in fine light tones with sensitive harmonies and a sure and light touch.

In 1927 Pascin returned to the United States for a year. On his return to Paris his health deteriorated, aggravated by his life-style and heavy drinking.

In the beginning of June 1930, an exhibition of Pascin's work opened at the Galerie Georges Petit. Moïse Kisling (q.v.) was told that Pascin was in Marseilles. He went to Pascin's studio. The door was locked. With the assistance of a locksmith, Kisling opened the door and found Pascin. He had slashed his wrists and then had hanged himself on the doorknob.

Henry McBride, the art critic for the *New York Times*, wrote of Pascin: "It was due to the sweetness of his character that he excited such a great influence on his fellow painters, particularly here in America, where we are not used to so entire a devotion to the arts.... It was due to his essential integrity as an artist, I think, that he died."

J. P. Leeper, *Jules Pascin's Caribbean Sketchbook*, 1964.

A. Werner, *Pascin*, 1962.

PASTERNAK, BORIS LEONIDOVICH (1890–1960) Russian poet, novelist and Nobel Prize winner. He was born in Moscow to Leonid Ossopovich Pasternak, a noted painter, and Rosa Kaufman Pasternak a gifted pianist.

One of Boris's first memories was of Leo Tolstoy's visit to the Pasternak home in 1894 in order to hear his mother play. As a child, Pasternak, was exposed to a rich cultural life, thanks to his father's intellectual and artistic friends, including Rainer Maria Rilke, Alexander Scriabin, and Maxim Gorky. Although keenly interested in both music and philosophy, Pasternak saw his future in the field of literature. Even as a youth, he became familiar with the major literary movements and with works of contemporary literature. Rilke exerted a formative influence on the young Pasternak's poetry, which displays some of the poetic devices used by the German poet-philosopher. Shunning the collectivist thinking of the messianically oriented futurists and obscurantist symbolists, Pasternak opted for a lyrical and clear style. After breaking with the futurists, he published *My Sister Life*, a volume of pastoral and romantic poems, in 1922.

Pasternak was not only a great literary figure in Russian and world literatures: he was also a hero, especially during the 1930s, when he silenced his creative voice instead of submitting to the prevalent doctrine of social realism demanded of all artists and writers by the Stalinist regime. In the early years of that decade, Pasternak began to draw fire from party-line critics after he published a lengthy autobiographical poem, "Spectorsky." They were also disturbed by his 1932 collection of

Boris Pasternak as a child. From a sketch by his father, the artist Leonid Pasternak.

FROM PASTERNAK'S POETRY

From this general rule the boy Misha felt
The tumult of their thunder dies.
This century has come of age.
It's time to let the future happen.
 Catastrophes and revolutions
Don't clear the path to life's renewal
As do the insights, squalls and bounties
In one man's incandescent soul.

 There's ugliness in being famous.
That's not what elevates a man.
No need to institute an archive
Or dither over manuscripts.
The aim of creativity is giving.
It's not publicity or fame.

FROM *DOCTOR ZHIVAGO*

 From this general rule the boy Misha felt himself to be a bitterly unfortunate exception. Anxiety was his mainspring and no such unconcern as the rest of the world shared, relieved and ennobled him. He knew this hereditary trait in himself and watched for it with a morbid self-consciousness. It distressed and humiliated him.

 For as long as he could remember, he had never ceased to wonder how it was that a human being with arms and legs like everyone else, and with a language and way of life common to all the rest, could be so different — a being liked by so few and loved by no one. He could not understand how it was that if you were worse than other people you could not improve yourself by trying. What did it mean to be a Jew? What was the purpose of it? What was the reward or the justification of this unarmed challenge which brought nothing but grief?

poems, *Second Birth*, in which his presentation of communist achievements was not sufficiently patriotic. Pasternak stopped publishing after the appearance of his prose work, *The Last Summer*, in 1934, and declared at a meeting of the Writers' Plenum in Minsk, in 1936, that he could not force his poetry to serve the interests of any social or political system. He turned to translation from 1932 to 1942, translating Georgian poetry, as well as the poetry of Shakespeare, Raleigh, Keats, and Byron. During this period, he produced distinguished Russian translations of *Hamlet*, *Romeo and Juliet*, *Antony and Cleopatra*, and *Othello*. Despite the literary persecution, he clandestinely continued to pursue his poetic and novelistic craft and during the 1930s began working on his novel, *Doctor Zhivago*.

During World War II Pasternak was free to appear again in print and published two collections of war poems, *On Early Trains* (1943), and *Earth's Vastness* (1945). Adverse criticism by the official spokespeople of the Stalinist literary establishment led to another period of self-imposed public silence from 1945 to 1954, when a Soviet publication, *Znamya*, printed ten poems from *Doctor Zhivago*. The novel recounts the story of a Soviet physician-poet and the woman he loves against the background of four major upheavals in Russia: the Bolshevik revolution, the subsequent civil war, and the two world wars. Although the novel's manuscript was turned down by the Soviet publishing house Novy Mir because of its anti-Marxist nature, Pasternak managed to have the Italian version of the novel published in Milan in 1956.

The Soviet literary establishment moved quickly, denouncing him for treachery and expelling him from the Union of Soviet Writers. When he was awarded the Nobel Prize for literature in 1958, he was threatened with exile. With full media coverage being given to the entire affair, Pasternak declined the prize, begging Communist party chairman Nikita Khrushchev to allow him to remain in Russia. Two years later, Pasternak died in the Perdelkino writers' colony.

R. Hingley, *Pasternak*, 1983.
D. Levi, *Boris Pasternak*, 1989.
B. Pasternak, *I Remember: Sketch for an Autobiography*, 1959.
E. Pasternak, *The Tragic Years 1930–1960*, 1989.

PAUKER, ANA (1890–1960) Romanian Communist leader and deputy premier. Born Hannah Rabinsohn, she was the daughter of an Orthodox kosher butcher, received a traditional upbringing, and taught Hebrew in a Bucharest Jewish primary school. Jilted by her fiancé, she left home for Paris, where she met (and later married) a zealous communist, Marcel Pauker, who induced her to join the party in 1920. After covertly returning a Romania, she organized an underground Communist cell and began to win prominence in the Third International (Comintern). Ana Pauker was eventually arrested, however, and sentenced to a long term of imprisonment in 1936. While visiting the Soviet Union, her husband fell victim to Stalin's purge of veteran Bolsheviks; his execution, as a "Western spy," did not shake Ana's faith in the Russian dictator or Soviet justice. Following the Soviet occupation of Bessarabia (1940), she was exchanged for Romanian political detainees and welcomed by Stalin in Moscow, remaining there until 1944, when her country was invaded and occupied by the USSR.

After World War II, Pauker became one of the most powerful and effective communist leaders in Romania. She set up a coalition government, the Democratic Front, under Petru Groza (1944–1947); was secretary of the Communist party's central committee; and, following the communist takeover in 1947, served as minister of foreign affairs and first deputy prime minister in President Groza's cabinet. Only fear of an anti-Semitic backlash deterred party colleagues from electing her to the premiership, and as foreign minister she wielded vast authority. Though an avowed atheist, with no Jewish communal ties, Pauker had a warm regard for her Orthodox brother, Zalman Rabinsohn, and showed a degree of respect for Romania's chief rabbi, Moshe Rosen, who twice enlisted her aid in order to foil anti-Jewish plots. Paradoxically, it was while this dogged opponent of Zionism held office that 100,000 Romanian Jews were permitted to leave for Israel.

In June 1952, not long after the arrest of Rudolf Slansky (q.v.) in Czechoslovakia, Pauker was also arrested on various trumped-up charges. They included "right-wing deviationism," pro-Zionist activity, and the encouragement of Romanian emigration to Israel. Though expelled from the Communist party and stripped of all her government posts, she never figured in a show trial, thanks to Stalin's death and the subsequent execution of KGB chief Lavrenti Beria (who had concocted the charges). Instead, she remained under house arrest for some years after her fall from power, while her brother and other close relatives emigrated to Israel.

PEERCE, JAN (originally Jacob Pincus Perelmuth; 1904–1984) U.S. tenor. Born in New York, Peerce began his musical career as a violinist in dance bands and as a singer in several entertainment locations in New York City. In 1932 he was engaged as a singer at Radio City Music Hall. Peerce studied with several teachers, but eventually became his own teacher.

In 1938 Peerce sang in a performance of Beethoven's Ninth Symphony under Arturo Toscanini. Later that year he made his operatic stage debut as the duke of Mantua in a production of Verdi's *Rigoletto* in Philadelphia. Peerce made his Metropolitan Opera debut in 1941 as Alfredo in another Verdi opera, *La Traviata*.

Peerce remained at the Metropolitan Opera for twenty-six seasons, in which he sang 205 performances of eleven roles and at the same time performed with the leading opera companies in the United States, Germany, Russia, Austria, and the Netherlands. In 1956 Peerce became the first American since the war to sing at Moscow's Bolshoi Theater.

Aside from his numerous operatic performances, Peerce appeared regularly on television, as well as in the movies *Goodbye Columbus*, *Carnegie Hall*, and *Tonight We Sing*. He recorded not only his major operatic roles, especially with Toscanini, but also many popular songs, as well as Jewish liturgical music. On occasion, he gave cantorial recitals. Peerce made his Broadway debut in 1971 as Tevye in *Fiddler on the Roof*. He then continued to sing in variety shows and other occasions well into his seventy-sixth year.

Peerce was a true believer and always attributed

PEERCE'S ADVICE TO YOUNG SINGERS (1980)

Don't overdo on emotions. That can become forced and can cause damage. I always strove for beautiful sound. You see, I was a violinist, and that was important, because I learned what a beautiful sound should be. It was also great for phrasing. Don't look for size, look for beauty....

You must be blessed with good health, and be kind to the little things you have been given. Every morning I do bending exercises and run in place. That keeps you flexible. And watch your diet. Do everything in moderation. Most important is to be blessed with a bit of good health and a good bit of technique, which gives you an assured attitude. Age has nothing to do with your singing; the larynx is the last organ to show age. The Talmud says this too.

his successful career to God. "Being religious," he once said, "I am very thankful for the little endowment that I have, but we must have respect for our limitations. God doesn't expect us to do everything. What you do, do it with love and respect; love your fellow men, love your audience. Take care of what you have to the point of not overdoing, not going beyond your natural capacity, like singing wrong things. One should be able to sing hours and hours without fatigue. Cantorial work is a marathon and you shouldn't get tired. You become fatigued when singing because you're singing wrong."

A. Levy, *The Bluebird of Happiness: The Memoirs of Jan Peerce*, 1976.

PÉREIRE, JACOB RODRIGUES (1715–1780) French pioneeer of education for deaf-mutes. Born in Spain into a Marrano family originally from Portugal, he and his mother settled in Bordeaux, France, in 1741 after his father's death. From age nineteen he became interested in the education of deaf-mutes. He also began studying Hebrew and returned to Judaism.

In July 1746 he became the tutor of a young deaf-mute whom he followed to Caen. Although his first student was over sixteen, his progress was so striking that the prior of the Benedictine abbey of Beaumont convened a meeting at Caen to discuss the education of deaf-mutes. Pereire sent the minutes of the meeting to the physicist René-Antoine Ferchault de Réaumur, who transmitted the document to the Royal Academy of Science in Paris. Péreire's findings were reported on eleven pages of an issue of the *Mercure de France* and in his *Histoire naturelle*, Georg-Louis Leclerc de Buffon wrote a long passage about Péreire's success.

In 1749, Péreire, with his brother and sister, who assisted him in his work, as well as his student, settled in Paris, where he was presented to Louis XV. The king, the crown prince, and Madame de Pompadour became very interested in Péreire's student. One of his pupils, Marie Marois, after studying for almost twenty years, almost reached the level of normality in speech through lip-reading and called herself "the once deaf-mute." Others attempted to imitate his educational methods but were less successful. Péreire was close to the court and was the king's interpreter in Spanish and Portuguese. His protector at court was Count Saint Florentin, the queen's chancellor and minister of the royal household in charge of Protestant and Jewish affairs. The war minister, Count d'Argenson, who was also a member of the Academy of Science, sent Péreire eight-hundred livres on behalf of the king for his invention of a calculating machine, and a year later the king made the same sum an annuity. As a scientist, Péreire also worked to make sailing boats more speedy. He was elected a member of the Royal Academy of London. His fame also brought him enemies and he was the butt of anonymous letters. A communal Jewish leader, he was appointed agent of the "Portuguese nation" (i.e., the Jews of Portuguese descent) and was active in defending their rights.

Rabbi Hayim Joseph David Azulai (q.v.) of Hebron wrote in his notes that Péreire had guided him through libraries of Paris and that everywhere he went he was received with great regard. Azulai expressed his admiration for Péreire's pedagogical work with deaf-mutes, for his intelligence and for his attachment to Jewish tradition.

His grandsons, Jacob Emile and Isaac Péreire promoted his methods and perpetuated his memory. They themselves played an important role in the economic life of Paris, founding the Compagnie Transatlantique and the first railroads in France.

PERELMAN, SIDNEY JOSEPH (1904–1979) U.S. humorist. He was born in Brooklyn and brought up in Providence, Rhode Island, where his father worked "successively, but not successfully" as a machinist, a dry goods merchant, and a farmer. At first, Perelman wanted to be a cartoonist, and while studying at Brown University, he had what he called "a brief, precarious toehold as assistant art editor" of *Casements*, the campus humorous literary magazine.

In 1925, after graduating from Brown, he moved to Greenwich Village, where he began drawing cartoons for the humorous weekly, *Judge*, eventually writing prose for that magazine and a few others, including *College Humor* and *Life*. As he once said, the captions kept getting longer and longer, until they replaced the cartoons. Most of his material consisted of parodies and burlesques.

From 1934 he wrote satirical pieces for the *New Yorker*, to which he was a regular contributor for over thirty years. He is best-known for his work in that magazine, and many of the pieces were later published in collections.

His first book, *Dawn Ginsbergh's Revenge* (1929), included much of his early prose. He once recalled in an interview that the book was published without the author's name on the title page because he had been so exalted at the impending publication that, while correcting the galleys, he had completely overlooked the fact that his name was missing.

He wrote a number of books, including *Acres and Pains* (1947), a collection of humorous essays about his family life on his eighty-acre farm in Bucks County, Pennsylvania. *Westward Ha!* (1948) and *Swiss Family Perelman* (1950) are humorous reports on his two around-the-world trips. He also wrote *The Rising Gorge* (1961), *Baby, It's Cold Inside* (1970), and *Vinegar Puss* (1975).

Perelman was a serious and avid reader, and was inspired by James Joyce, T. S. Eliot, and Charles Dickens. He once said that he considered Joyce "the great comic writer of our time."

His brilliant command of language and virtuoso use of puns and wordplay made him one of the greatest 20th-century American humorists.

He began writing movie scripts in the early 1930s, and is famous for his collaboration with the Marx Brothers on the scripts for two of their early films, *Monkey Business* (1931) and *Horsefeathers* (1932). His screenplay of Jules Verne's *Around the World in Eighty Days* (1956) won the Academy Award. In 1943, he coauthored with Ogden Nash a hit musical, *One Touch of Venus* — music by Kurt Weill q.v.) — and wrote the comedy *The Beauty Part* (1962) on his own.

He was married to Laura West, the sister of novelist Nathanael West (q.v.), and collaborated with her in writing the 1933 play, *All Good Americans*. In 1970, the year his wife died, he settled in England, but later returned to the United States.

He was exasperated by continuous attempts to get him to write "something serious." After Perelman's death, the *New Yorker*'s editor, William Shawn, said of him: "He was one of the world's funniest writers. He was also one of the few remaining writers in America who devoted themselves wholly to humor. Over the years, people often put pressure on him to write something they considered serious — a novel, say — but he was never diverted from doing what he apparently was born to do, which was to write short humor pieces."
V. W. Brooks (ed.), *Writers at Work*, 1963.
N. W. Yates, *The American Humorist*, 1964.

PERETZ, ISAAC LEIB (1852–1915) Polish writer considered the founder of modern Yiddish literature. Born in Zamosc, Poland, to a traditional family, Peretz was tutored in German, Russian, and Hebrew. His father was a prosperous merchant with some liberal ideas but his religious mother prevented him from having a secular education. Peretz was essentially self-educated and in his teens began reading through the secular library of a sympathetic enlightened Jew. He also began composing verses in Hebrew, Polish, and Yiddish. At eighteen he entered into an arranged marriage. Considering herself above him, his wife persuaded him to study bookkeeping and he tried several business ventures. These, like the marriage, failed and after five years Peretz was left with their son (who eventually disassociated himself from the Jewish people) and went to Warsaw to study law.

In 1876 he returned to Zamosc, qualified for the practice of law in 1876, and remarried in 1878, this time happily. He had published some Hebrew poems in the early 1870s, but his new law practice and civic activities kept him from writing for nearly a decade. In 1886 he visited Warsaw and renewed his contacts with the Jewish literary circles. This led him to resume the writing of Hebrew poems and short stories, which were published in 1887. The following year an envious competitor denounced him to the government as a socialist and he lost the right to practice law.

In desperate financial need, Peretz turned to writing full time, now in Yiddish. Hearing that Shalom Aleichem (q.v.) was planning a Yiddish literary journal, he sent him "Monish," a frivolous, sentimental, and ironic poem that became a milestone in Yiddish literature. Peretz begged him to revise the work so that his Yiddish would be intelligible to the readers, but when the work was published, Peretz was not pleased with the revisions and — although Shalom Aleichem published more of his work — they did not become friends. Each thought little of the other's writing, Peretz being too mystical and Shalom Aleichem too common for the other's taste. Years later, when Shalom Aleichem read Peretz's *Intimate Folk Tales*, he apologized for not knowing how to appreciate his work and they were reconciled.

Peretz's financial bad luck continued and in 1890 he joined a small group under the aegis of Jan Bloch, a Warsaw philanthropist, to study the life of the Jews in small Polish towns. He visited town after town, gathering statistics and studying customs. Returning to Warsaw, Peretz gave lectures in

---

**FROM THE WRITINGS OF
S. J. PERELMAN**

● Webster's Collegiate Dictionary, which has a crew haircut, a class pipe and a yellow oilskin slicker, describes a farm as "a piece of land leased for cultivation, hence any tract devoted to agricultural purposes." I prefer my own definition. A farm is an irregular patch of nettles bounded by short-term notes, containing a fool and his wife who didn't know enough to stay in the city.

● For years I have let dentists ride roughshod over my teeth; I have been sawed, hacked, chopped, whittled, bewitched, bewildered, tattooed, and signed on again; but this is cuspid's last stand.

Hebrew, engaged in social and cultural activities, and published a collection of Yiddish short stories *Familiar Scenes*. In 1891 he published *Pictures from a Provincial Journey*, describing his findings: everything in a state of degeneracy, poverty, lethargy, and death.

In 1890 his luck turned and he accepted employment as a bookkeeper for the Jewish Civic Center, a job he kept to the end of his life. Peretz was now at his prime. Of medium height, with broad shoulders and a large head, he carried himself like an aristrocrat, impressing all who met him. He attracted a circle of both young and older writers and his home became a center for Jewish radical thought.

He was concerned for the welfare of the masses of Jews and this intense Jewishess carried over to his writings. He loved his people and sought to free them from their superstitious beliefs, meekness, and passivity. He wanted the Jews to become self-

Isaac Leib Peretz.

FROM THE WRITINGS OF I. L. PERETZ

It is about time for the intelligentsia to relegate to the old archives the question, Is Yiddish a language? Can there be a language without grammar? Can a patchwork of different languages and of different periods be called a language? ... The true intelligentsia must realize that Yiddish is a fact that came not of our volition and will not disappear overnight at our desire ... That a language is whatever means people use to communicate with one another, that four million beings who speak and understand only Yiddish are also people, and that whoever wishes to educate them must accept their language as the means.

"... Really! I tell you, everything is yours. Everything in paradise is yours. Choose! Take! Whatever you want! You will only take what is yours!"

"Really?" Bontche asks again, and now his voice is stronger, more assured.

And the judge and all the heavenly host answer, "Really! Really! Really!"

"Well then" — and Bontche smiles for the first time — "well then, what I would like, Your Excellency, is to have, every morning for breakfast, a hot roll with fresh butter."

A silence falls upon the great hall, and it is more terrible than Bontche's has ever been, and slowly the judge and the angels bend their heads in shame at this unending meekness they have created on earth.

Then the silence is shattered. The prosecutor laughs aloud, a bitter laugh.

From "Bontche the Silent"

sufficient and self-respecting. To help them to acquire the culture and status of modern Europeans he realized that he must speak to them in the one language they all understood, Yiddish, at least until they learned their country's language. At first he gave Hebrew the status of the mother tongue but later elevated Yiddish to its equal.

He greatly influenced the Jewish intellectuals in Poland and Yiddish writers everywhere. In Yiddish and Hebrew journals, he discussed topics of current interest. With both satire and irony, he attacked anti-Semitism and the shams, fanaticism, and intolerances within the Jewish community. He wrote about poverty and lack of opportunities. The religious fanaticism of the Hasidim also gained his condemnation as did the urban Jews who constantly overreached themselves to attain social status.

He also sought to achieve his goals with his fiction. In numerous stories he championed the cause of Jewish women by describing the horrors of their lives. His early short stories in the 1890s were heavily neoromantic and symbolic. Returning to his youthful infatuation with Hasidism, he uncovered the tales, legends, and anecdotes of the Hasidc communities and wrote stories of wonder-working rabbis and secret saints endowed with special powers to right wrongs and reward the just. In all these tales a man is judged by the intentions of his acts and not by his appearance. Most of all, Peretz was a poet, writing many poems expressing his social ideals and romantic inclination.

In 1899 he was arrested for attending illegal meetings and served four months in prison. His masterpiece, *The Golden Chain*, a poetic drama which expresses his idealistic insight into Jewish spirituality was published in 1907. He translated his Yiddish works into Hebrew and his Hebrew into Yiddish and dramatized many of his short stories.

He continued his activities until his death. World War I depressed him greatly and he helped many Jews who were driven out of their homes with food and shelter. He died of a heart attack and his funeral attracted the largest crowd in Warsaw's history. No mention of it appeared in the Polish press.

A. A. Roback, *I. L. Peretz, Psychologist of Literature*, 1935.

M. Samuel, *Prince of the Ghetto*, 1959.

PEVSNER, NIKOLAUS BERNHARD LEON (1902–1983) Scholar of art and architecture; knighted 1969. Born in Leipzig, he studied at German universities and worked from 1924 to 1929 as assistant keeper of the Dresden Art Gallery. He then taught for four years at the University of Göttingen. He fled Nazi Germany for England in 1934. Among other posts in England he was professor of fine art at Cambridge, from 1949 to 1955, and professor of the history of art at Birkbeck College, London, from 1959. From 1949 he was art editor of Penguin Books, editing the Penguin History of Art and the King Penguin series.

A prolific author, his books include the standard *Outline of European Architecture* (1942), *Pioneers of Modern Design: From William Morris to Walter Gropius* (1949), *Mannerism to Romanticism* (2 vols., 1968), and *Sources of Modern Art* (1962). His outstanding contribution is *Buildings of England*, a monumental 46-volume series that he edited, and many of which he wrote (1951–1974). This is a county-by-county survey of regional English architecture and was acclaimed as a major contribution to English art criticism.

Pevsner insisted that art must be considered in its context, and that the direction of creativity is deeply influenced by national and regional styles.

PHILO (Philo Judaeus or Philo of Alexandria; c. 25 BCE–50 CE) Hellenistic Jewish thinker and the first noted Jewish philosopher. Little is known of his life. He was born into one of the noblest and wealthiest Jewish families in Alexandria, then the greatest Jewish center outside the Land of Israel. He was brought up a believing Jew and also received a Greek education. His brother, Alexander, rose to be a high official of the Roman administration in Egypt, a friend of the Emperor Claudius, and one of his sons married the daughter of Agrippa, grandson of Herod. His other son, Tiberius Julius Alexander, left Judaism and was a leading figure in the Roman army, serving as procurator of Judea (46–48 CE) and prefect of Egypt under Nero. Alexander contributed gold and silver plating for the gates of the Temple in Jerusalem.

Philo rejected a worldly career and devoted himself to his studies and writings. The one incident known of his life is that, following anti-Jewish riots in Alexandria as a result of the Jews' refusal to set up a statue of the Emperor Caligula in the Jerusalem Temple, Philo was asked to head a deputation to Rome in 40 CE to appeal to Caligula to cancel his edict. Although the mission was unsuccessful, the problem was solved the following year with the assassination of Caligula and the accession of the more understanding Claudius. Philo

wrote a vivid account of the episode. He then retired from public life and devoted his remaining years to his writings.

Philo sought to synthesize Greek and Jewish thought to show that Judaism was congruent with Hellenism. In his philosophy, his object was to amalgamate Jewish doctrines based on supernatural revelation with Greek philosophical thinking. His expositions for the most part took the form of commentaries on the Bible, interpreted through the Greek allegorical tradition. The Bible, he holds, contains the truths of philosophy; the first verses of Genesis, for example, should be seen as referring to ideas and primeval matter while the heroes of the Bible are embodiments of the ethical virtues. He does not neglect the literal meaning of the text which he calls the "body," embodying the "soul" of the divine revelation. God is a transcendent being who makes himself known to man through the Logos, the divine Word, which mediates between God and man. Philo wrote in Greek and based himself on the Greek translation of the Bible (he may not have known Hebrew). He wrote different works for Jewish and non-Jewish readers. To Jews, he directed his harmonization of Platonism and Judaism, while maintaining his conviction that Judaism could answer all questions. For non-Jews, his object was to demonstrate the superiority of the Jewish scriptures.

Philo's writing reflects Alexandrian Jewish thought

FROM THE WRITINGS OF PHILO

● If a man has lost the use of his eyes, will the keen sight of his ancestors help him?

● If you see someone not taking food or drink when he should, refusing baths and oils, neglecting his clothes, sleeping on the ground, and imagining that in this way he is practicing temperance — pity his self-deception and disabuse him.

● It is the height of folly to take the arts as the standard of measurement for mankind.

● The whole heaven and the whole world is an offering dedicated to God, and He it is who has created the offering; and all God-beloved souls, citizens of the world, consecrate themselves, allowing no mortal attraction to draw them in the opposite direction, and they never grow weary of devoting and sanctifying their own imperishable life.

● Wisdom is a straight high road, and it is when the mind's course is guided along that road that it reaches the goal which is the recognition and knowledge of God. Every comrade of the flesh hates and rejects this path and seeks to corrupt it. For there are no two things so utterly opposed as knowledge and pleasure of the flesh.

and there is no evidence that he was in touch with the rabbis of Jerusalem. His works were soon forgotten among Jews and only rediscovered by them in the Renaissance period. However, he had a great influence in Christian circles, notably on the Church fathers, who were impressed by the theory of the Logos as well as by his methods of allegorization.

E. R. Goodenough, *The Politics of Philo Judaeus*, 1967.

H. A. Wolfson, *Philo: Foundations of Religious Philosophy in Judaism, Christianity, and Islam*, 2 vols., 1946.

PIATIGORSKY, GREGOR (1903–1976) Cellist. Born in Ekaterinoslav (now Dnepropetrovsk, USSR), Ukraine. Piatigorsky received his first music lessons from his father, a violinist, and began playing the cello at the age of seven. At nine Piatigorsky was accepted to the Moscow Conservatory as a scholarship student of Alfred von Glehn. In 1919 he was invited to join Moscow's leading string ensemble, the Lenin Quartet, and at the same time was appointed principal cellist of the Bolshoi Theater orchestra. In 1921 Piatigorsky left Russia for Warsaw, Leipzig, and finally Berlin, where he continued his cello studies with Julius Klengel. From 1924 to 1928 Piatigorsky was the first cellist of the Berlin Philharmonic, under Wilhelm Fürtwangler, and then left the orchestra in order to pursue his solo career. In Berlin Piatigorsky performed cello sonatas with Artur Schnabel (q.v.) and trios with Schnabel and Carl Flesch.

As a soloist in Europe Piatigorsky is most remembered for playing the cello solo in Richard Strauss's *Don Quixote* under the baton of the composer. Piatigorsky made his American debut in 1929 at Oberlin, Ohio, and later that year performed Dvorak's Cello Concerto with the New York Philharmonic to great critical acclaim. His chamber music concerts with Vladimir Horowitz (q.v.) and Milstein in the 1930s and with Jascha Heifetz (q.v.) and Arthur Rubinstein (q.v.) in the late 1940s were some of his finest musical achievements. Piatigorsky was considered the world's finest cellist after Pablo Casals, and performed regularly in concerts and recitals in all the major musical capitals of the world. He premiered several concerti that were written for him.

Piatigorsky taught at the Curtis Institute in Philadelphia and later at the University of Southern California in Los Angeles. He also performed chamber music with Heifetz and Pennario and accompanied Heifetz on his farewell tour of Israel.

One critic wrote, "Piatigorsky combined an innate flair for virtuosity with an exquisite taste in style and phrasing; technical perfection was never a goal in itself. His vibrant tone had infinite shadings and his sweeping eloquence and aristocratic grandeur created an instant rapport with his audience. He was at his best in emotional Romantic music."

Gregor Piatigorsky composed original works for the cello. He owned two magnificent Stradivarius cellos, the Batta (1714) and the Baudiot (1725).

G. Piatigorsky, *Cellist*, 1965.

PIJADE, MOSA (1890–1957) Yugoslav politician and Communist leader. A native of Belgrade, he originally studied painting abroad and then earned his livelihood as an art teacher, but was jailed in 1921, a year after joining the banned Yugoslav Communist party. During his second and much longer term of imprisonment for revolutionary agitation (1925–1939), Pijade made his name by translating Karl Marx's *Das Kapital* (q.v.) into Serbian. The German-led invasion and occupation of Yugoslavia (April 1941) transformed him into a national hero: serving under Josip Broz Tito, he became an outstanding organizer of the Communist partisans and Yugoslavia's most prominent Jewish resistance fighter.

When Tito assumed the premiership after the liberation (1945), Pijade was already one of his closest associates. Apart from safeguarding Yugoslav interests at postwar allied conferences, he helped to draft Yugoslavia's new constitution and, as president of the Serbian republic, became one of the nation's four vice presidents (with Tito as federal head of state). It was Pijade, the ranking Communist theoretician, who played a major role in distancing Yugoslavia from Moscow and the Cominform (1948), bringing it closer to the West. He also served as a key figure in the Politburo and as chairman of Yugoslavia's National Assembly, the federal parliament.

Though a veteran communist, Mosa (Moshe) Pijade retained a marked degree of Jewish consciousness and may well have facilitated Yugoslav Jewry's revival after four-fifths of the community had perished in the Holocaust. During his term in office, the American Jewish Joint Distribution Committee was permitted to help in the rebuilding of Jewish communal life; synagogues destroyed or desecrated by the Nazis were restored; Zionism and emigration to Israel could be promoted; and full diplomatic relations with Israel were maintained. When an American Jewish leader visited Belgrade in 1955, Pijade surprised him by requesting the dispatch of unleavened bread for Passover. An exhibit in Belgrade's Jewish Historical Museum is devoted to Pijade's long-standing friendship with Marshal Tito.

S. Bosilcic and D. Markovic, *Mosa Pijade*, 1960.

PIKE, LIPMAN EMANUEL (Lip; 1845–1893) U.S. baseball pioneer. When he died the *Sporting Life* of Philadelphia noted that he "could claim the unique distinction of being the first professional player, having been paid a regular salary for playing ball in 1866."

Born in New York City, he grew up in Brooklyn, then a hotbed of baseball. In 1865 Pike joined the Atlantics, the strongest team in the city of Brooklyn and the nation. The Atlantics were the champions of the National Association of Baseball

Players, a league of the best amateur teams in the country.

In an effort to strengthen their club, the Philadelphia Athletics hired Pike to play third base for them for twenty dollars a week. He was in the lineup in 1866 when the Athletics defeated the Brooklyn Atlantics for the first time in their history.

In 1870 Pike appeared in the most celebrated game of the 19th century. As a member of the Atlantics he was instrumental in the defeat of the famous Cincinnati Red Stockings — the first all-professional team — after the Reds had recorded one hundred victories over a three-year period. Before a Brooklyn crowd of 20,000, a huge throng for the time, the Atlantics won the game in the eleventh inning, 8–7.

The *Brooklyn Eagle* reported that, "In the dramatic ninth, Pike at second, reached the pinnacle of his career as a base player. Under the severest pressure, he was the central figure in retiring the entire Cincinnati side."

Between 1871 and 1881 Pike played with twelve teams in three leagues. He was player-manager in Troy, New York; Hartford, Connecticut; Cincinnati, Ohio; and Springfield, Massachusetts. As a member of the Cincinnati Reds he led the National League in home runs in 1877.

In 1893 the Philadelphia *Sporting Life* said of Pike, "He ranked high as a batsman during the sixteen consecutive seasons that he played professionally, being like all lefthanded men, a very hard hitter. It would require too much space to record all his batting feats, of which most notable was the making of six home runs — five in succession — in a game played July 16, 1866, at Philadelphia. Pike, a sure catch and a fast runner, played very well in the outfield where he brought off many remarkable catches." All this was accomplished with bare hands, as no gloves were used at the time.

In its obituary the *Brooklyn Eagle* said, "Many wealthy Hebrews and men high in political and old time baseball circles attended the funeral of Lipman E. Pike.... The Reverend Doctor Geismar, pastor of Temple Israel, conducted the services and paid fitting tribute to the exemplary life led by the deceased."

PINSKER, LEO (1821–1891) Zionist leader and thinker. Born in Tomaszów, Poland, Pinsker went to school in Odessa. He studied law at Odessa University, but, barred by anti-Semitic laws from practice, he turned to medicine and became a physician in Odessa. He firmly believed in the assimilation of Jews into Russian culture and immersed himself in activities to that end, founding and working with various magazines and societies dedicated to acquainting the Jewish population with Russian culture.

The pogroms of 1881–1882 finally convinced Pinsker that his dreams of integration were illusory and his pamphlet, *Autoemancipation: A Warning of a Russian Jew to his Brethren* (1882), was a direct result of these new sentiments. Published anonymously, the pamphlet analyzed the psychological and social roots of anti-Semitism and suggested the foundation of a Jewish national homeland. He stated that a Jewish congress should decide whether this would be in Eretz Israel or in America. Having initially believed that anti-Semitism could be dispelled either by complete assimilation or by recognition of the Jewish people as a nation in their own right, Pinsker now realized that the former was impossible and campaigned for the latter: the declaration of Jewish nationhood.

Pinsker's appeals struck home with many Jews and Hovevei Zion ("Lovers of Zion") societies all over eastern Europe received his ideas enthusiastically and made his work their manifesto. Pinsker himself joined the Hovevei Zion movement and became its leading spirit, now convinced that the Jewish home should be in Eretz Israel. In 1883 it was decided to establish a center for Jewish settlement in Palestine, and to convene a congress in conjunction with Hovevei Zion. A comittee organized at Pinsker's home, with himself as chairman, contacted existing Hovevei Zion groups and encouraged them to establish new ones. The members of these groups aimed to promote the Jewish national ideal, to revive Jewish culture and to work toward Jewish settlement in Eretz Israel. In 1884 the Hovevei Zion held its national convention in Kattowitz, then a part of Germany, because Zionism was illegal in Russia. There Pinsker was elected president of the organization. Pinsker retained the position, despite his attempts, on several occasions, to resign because of frustration over worsening relations between religious and nonreligious elements, and his own declining health. The

---

FROM PINSKER'S *AUTOEMANCIPATION*

Nations live side by side in a state of relative peace, which is based chiefly on the fundamental equality between them. But it is different with the people of Israel. This people is not counted among the nations, because since it was exiled from its land it has lacked the essential attributes of nationality, by which one nation is distinguished from another. True, we have not ceased even in the lands of our exile to be spiritually a distinct nation; but this spritual nationality, so far from giving us the status of a nation in the eyes of the other nations, is the very cause of their hatred for us as a people. Men are always terrified by a disembodied spirit, a soul wandering about with no physical covering; and terror breeds hatred.

Let Now or Never be our watchword. Woe to our descendants, woe to the memory of our Jewish contemporaries, if we let this moment pass by!

nonreligious in particular pressed him to remain out of fear that if he left the leadership might pass to the Orthodox.

The first Jewish settlements were established in Eretz Israel, but Pinsker did not live to see their eventual success. When the Turks curtailed immigration, the organization went into debt and numerous other problems arose. He lost hope in his dream of large-scale settlement in Eretz Israel and began to shift his hopes toward Maurice de Hirsch's [q.v.] activities for settling Jews in Argentina, which he thought could take the masses of emigrants, with Eretz Israel serving only as a spiritual center for the Jewish people. In 1934 his remains were buried on Mount Scopus in Jerusalem.
S. Avineri, *The Making of Modern Zionism*, 1981.
M. N. Penkower, *The Emergence of Zionist Thought*, 1986.
D. Vital, *The Origins of Zionism*, 1975.

PISSARRO, JACOB ABRAHAM CAMILLE

(1830–1903) French Impressionist painter. He was born on Saint Thomas in the Virgin Islands, where his father, Frederic, had come as executor of his uncle's estate. A year later, Frederic and his uncle's widow went to arrange for their marriage in the synagogue, but as aunt and nephew, were refused permission. However, their marriage in a private home was recognized by the Danish authorities, and eventually — after they had registered the birth of four sons at the synagogue — by the congregation.

Camille Pissarro studied art in Paris from 1841 to 1847. He returned to Saint Thomas to work in the family's general store, but after a few years left to paint in Venezuela. In 1855, he moved to Paris, never to return to the West Indies. One of his paintings was accepted for the Salon of 1859, a success that elicited financial aid from his family. Anton Melbye introduced him to J. B. C. Corot, who encouraged him and advised him, and later gave him permission to list himself in the salon catalogue as "pupil of Corot."

Before he left Saint Thomas, Pissarro had fallen in love with Julie Vellay, a servant in his parents' home. He asked his parents' consent to marry her — to protect property and inheritance rights — but his parents denied them permission.

The couple was constantly burdened with financial difficulties. In Pontoise, where they lived for over ten years, Julie had a vegetable garden and raised rabbits and chickens to sustain the family. They received some financial aid from Pissarros' mother and from Julie's family. In 1868, Pissarro took a job painting landscapes on window-shades. Painting out of doors in Pontoise, he explored the effect of the light on colors and contours.

In 1870, during the Franco-Prussian War, the couple went to England with money lent them by Pissarro's mother. There they married. When the Pissarros returned to France from England in 1871, they found that their house in Pontoise had been devastated by Prussian troops who had

Camille Pissaro in his study, 1897.

slaughtered the animals in the garden, spread paintings on the ground, and used others as aprons to protect their uniforms. The government gave Pissarro an indemnity to cover his losses during the war, but fifteen years' work had been destroyed, as well as many paintings of Claude Monet, left with Pissarro for safekeeping. Paul Cézanne and his family came to live nearby and Pissarro urged him to paint out of doors, and to paint what he observed. They often went out together searching for a "motif."

Pissarro, Monet, and Alfred Sisley organized a group to by-pass the Salon and arranged an exhibition in 1874, in which thirty artists participated, including Edgar Degas and Cézanne. A critic, reacting negatively to Monet's painting, "An Impression: The Rising Sun," gave the group the name "Impressionists." The exhibition ran for a month and admission was one franc. Costs outweighed profits, and in the end, each artist had to pay 184.50 francs. The second exhibition was somewhat more successful — each artist made a profit of three francs.

Pissarro spent days going around Paris trying to sell paintings. Pierre Auguste Renoir, as badly off, went on much the same rounds, with little luck, because, he said, everybody who could buy had already bought from "poor Pissarro with all those children." To make matters worse, a collector of Impressionist paintings was forced to auction his collection. After that, it was impossible for Pissarro to find a buyer. He earned a little money by painting ceramic tiles and fans.

At last, in 1878, he found a dealer who began to sell his paintings. Paul Gauguin, who was working in finance, also sold a few for him. Pissarro encouraged Gauguin in his artistic endeavors, and Gauguin exhibited a piece of sculpture in the fourth Impressionist exhibition. In the 1880s, Impressionist paintings began to be in demand. The critic J. K. Huysmans said that Pissarro was one of France's most remarkable and audacious painters and called him the most original landscape painter of the period.

The eighth and last Impressionist exhibition was held in 1886. The work of Pissarro and his son and pupil, Lucien — who was also a leading Impressionist painter — were among those whose work was exhibited in a special "Neo-Impressionist" room.

In 1890 the dealer Durand-Ruel took 300 paintings to the United States for a show in Madison Square Garden in New York, in which he included work by Pissarro, Paul Signac, and Georges Seurat. Pissarro's work found so many buyers that Durand-Ruel, in 1892, bought all the canvases that had not been sold when the exhibition ended. The seminal nature of his work was recognized: "Pissarro's work," wrote Georges Lecomte, "seems to preface the work of tomorrow."

Pissarro developed a recurring eye problem, and was obliged to wear a bandage over his eye for long periods. He started working indoors, staying in hotels in Paris, Rouen, and Le Havre, and painting the view from the windows. These are beautiful cityscapes, full of movement and crowds, masterful in composition.

The Alfred Dreyfus (q.v.) affair had a profound effect on Pissarro. He was overwhelmed by the injustice of the sentence and by the frenetic anti-Semitism that raged through France. His friendships with Cézanne, Armand Guillaumin, and Renoir, all anti-Dreyfusárds, were strained. Degas, contaminated by anti-Semitism, never spoke to him again.

In spite of his eye problem, in the last three years of his life Pissarro produced about 160 paintings and sold two paintings to the Louvre. He became ill, needing an operation, which was delayed due to a dispute between his two doctors. Blood poisoning ensued and Pissarro died on November 13, 1903.

Pissarro was an outstanding painter and etcher always open to new ideas. His search for basic principles led him to experiment with light and color. When Henri Matisse asked him what an Impressionist was, Pissarro replied that an Impressionist is someone who never makes the same painting twice. He was a natural teacher, and always encouraged younger artists and willingly passed on to them what he had discovered.

C. Pissarro, ed. J. Rewald, *Letters to His Son Lucien*, 1943.
J. Rewald *Pissarro*, 1963.
R. E. Shikes and P. Harper, *Pissarro: His Life and Work*, 1980.
A. Werner, *Pissarro*, 1963.

POLANYI, MICHAEL (1891–1976) Chemist, sociologist, and philosopher. His father was an engineer who built many railroads in Europe. Polanyi obtained an M.D. at the University of Budapest in 1913 and a Ph.D. in 1917. His first researches were in the field of physical chemistry, especially the chemistry of liquids and eventually the thermodynamics of absorption, on which he published his theory in 1916. The formula for the calculation of the absorption-potential bears his name.

Polanyi actively participated in the Hungarian progressive movements of the early 20th century. His articles were published in the progressive periodical *Huszadik Szazad* ("10th Century"). During World War I, he served as a medical officer and was secretary of state for health in Mihaly Karoly's government.

After the 1918–1919 revolutions, he emigrated to Germany, working first as Karlsruhe University and from 1923 to 1933 at the Kaiser Wilhelm Institute under Fritz Haber (q.v.). Here he achieved significant results in phisical chemistry, concentrating on X-ray — defractional examination of vegetable fibers and the malleable qualities of solids.

When Hitler came to power in 1933, Polanyi moved to Manchester, England, where he became professor of physical chemistry at the University. of Manchester. His book; *Atomic Reaction*, was published in London in 1932. He continued research in kinetics, polymerization, and crystal structure. At the same time, he started to take a greater interest in economics, sociology, and political issues.

In 1948 he left the chair of physical chemistry and became professor of social studies at Manchester. Joining the "Moot" group of British intellectuals cancerned with social problems, he became a close friend of two of the group's members: the sociologist Karl Mannheim (q.v.) and the poet T. S. Eliot.

Retiring from Manchester University in 1959, he became a senior research fellow at Merton College, Oxford, where he wrote his principal work *Personal Knowledge* (1958), in which he emphasizes the importance of intuitive elements of the scientific method that cannot be expressed in theorems. He was elected to the Royal Society in 1944.

His works include: *The Concept of Freedom: The Russian Experiment and After* (1940); *Full Employment and Free Trade* (1945); *Science, Faith, and Society* (1945); *Beyond Nihilism* (1966); and *Knowing and Being* (1969).

PONTE, LORENZO DA See Da Ponte, Lorenzo

POPPER, JULIUS (1857–1893) Explorer. He was born in Romania where his father headed the Jewish school in Bucharest. The only information on his early life is his own testimony. In view of his flamboyant tendency to exaggeration, this must be viewed critically. Whatever the truth concerning his early exploits — whether he was a "minyan man" in Prague or a technical engineer in Paris or New Orleans — it is known that this enigmatic character arrived in Buenos Aires in 1885.

At that time Buenos Aires was in the midst of a "gold rush fever." An expedition to Tierra del Fuego the previous year had brought back reports of gold seams embedded in alluvial formations on the beaches. Tierra del Fuego ("Land of Fire") is an archipelago at the southernmost tip of South America, separated from the mainland by the Straits of Magellan. Although discovered by Magellan in 1520, the land was left to its Indian inhabitants until the 19th century, when it was charted by the British and then, from the 1880s, settled by Europeans and Latin Americans, attracted by its sheepfarming potential and the prospect of gold.

Popper made his first expedition to Tierra del Fuego early in 1886 as the representative of a major mining company. He obtained government approval to lead the explorations in the northern part of the area, taking with him a group of men armed on the instructions of the Interior and War ministries. He was the first explorer to lead a party from Bahia Porvenir on the west of the island through the snow and brush to the Atlantic coast. His reward was the discovery of gold at Bahia San Sebastian. On his return to Buenos Aires six months later, he was the talk of the town — not a little thanks to the publicity he gave to his own adventures.

Stamp of Julius Popper.

By July 1887 he established the Gold Washers Company of the South and founded a well-organized mining establishment in San Sebastian Bay. It produced between half a pound to eleven pounds of gold daily. The greater his success the greater the threat from poachers, and he had to hire twelve armed men to protect his camp from both the local Indians and from jealous white settlers. He continued to expand his interests in the region, building several washeries, to which he gave Romanian names.

Popper's problems with the poachers continued and in 1888 he had to use force to drive a group of Chilean poachers off his land. Their retaliation by destroying his washery led to the Battle of Beta Creek, as a result of which Popper became the virtual sovereign of the northern half of the island and was known as "the dictator of Tierra del Fuego." He now issued his own gold coinage and five-dollar pieces. One side showed the inscription "Tierra del Fuego — Popper 1899" and the other "El Paramo" (the name of his camp) with a background of crossed shovel and pick. He also printed ten-cent postage stamps for mail to the mainland. In the middle of the stamp was a large "P" surrounded by the rays of the sun. In case the significance of the "P" was not apparent, the cancellation mark carried the inscription "Colonia Popper." Today these are collector's items.

However, all did not remain peaceful and his plants did not yield enough profit. He had to close the company at the end of 1889. His brother Max took over the running of the El Paramo camp and Julius Popper returned to Buenos Aires, where he established himself as an intellectual and literary figure. He was dogged by a series of lawsuits brought by creditors and was strongly criticized for his high-handed business practices. Various ambitious projects that he devised did not get off the ground. When he died the coroner's verdict was heart failure, but, according to rumor, he had been killed by one of his enemies from the south. While he was praised in local newspaper obituaries, the London *Jewish Chronicle* wrote "Foul play has been hinted at; if true, it was a fitting end to an unscrupulous adventurer."

POPPER-LYNKEUS, JOSEF (1838–1921) Austrian philosopher, inventor, and social reformer. Born in the Bohemian town of Kolin, Josef Popper studied at the Polytechnikum in Prague, which later refused him a teaching position as a Jew. In 1858 he went to Vienna to study at the Imperial Polytechnikum then at the university. Having no hope of obtaining a teaching position because of his Judaism and his unfashionable views, he took a job as a clerk in Hungary, but later returned to Vienna and became a private tutor. To supplement his earnings he attended scientific lectures and conferences, took notes in long hand, copied them over, and sold the reviews to newspapers. He later compared this type of tedious, low-paying work to the worst kind of unskilled labor.

At the age of thirty Popper invented a device to eliminate deposits from collecting in engine boilers. He and his brother, David, traveled throughout Germany and Austria to sell the invention. The work was exhausting and Popper later wrote in his autobiography, "One can hardly realize the strain involved in marketing an invention designed as an inner lining for boilers. I had always to be present when the boiler was opened for inspection after a period of use. I had to creep into the boiler while it was still hot in order to ascertain the results.... More than once I was in danger of suffocation and death from the heat." Their perseverance paid off and after inventing other devices that improved the capacity of engine boilers, surface condensers, and water-cooling apparatus, Popper was able, at the age of fifty-nine, to retire on his modest earnings.

He devoted the rest of his life to scientific, theoretical, and philosophical writing and thinking. As a scientist, Popper proved to be a visionary with a penetrating understanding of energy. As early as 1860 he was writing about flying machines, a subject that continued to interest him for the rest of his life. Two years later he realized the potential electrical energy in natural water sources and the possibility of transmitting energy. He proposed a system of transmitting energy electrically in his thesis *On the Utilization of Natural Forces* for the Austrian imperial academy of sciences in Vienna in 1862, but it was not published until 1882, after Popper witnessed the transmission of energy by French engineer Marcel Desprez at the electrical exposition in Munich. Popper was the first to develop the concept that all energy is the product of mass and level in his paper *The Fundamentals of Electrical Power Transmission* (1882). In 1884 he questioned whether the law of conservation of matter was related to the law of conservation of energy and suggested the existence of quanta of energy before Max Planck's quantum theory was ever stated.

Popper's writings on social reform dealt with the rights and obligations of the individual in society. He saw the life of the individual as the highest value and rejected the claim that a citizen must be ready to be killed when ordered, and argued for the freedom and dignity of every person — regardless of his capabilities or qualifications — within a highly organized social system. Each member of society should minimally contribute to a labor force that would be responsible for "all that physiology and hygiene show to be absolutely indispensable" and thus eliminate class enmity and related social problems. In such a state, religion in its traditional forms would be abolished because of its antagonism to humanitarianism and especially to the value of the individual. In its place, the study of the history of religions might well bring about a generation without the taint of superstition.

Popper's most popular work was a text he published under the pseudonym Lynkeus, the mythological helmsman of the Argonauts noted for his remarkable sight. *Phantasien eines Realisten*

("Fantasies of a Realist"; 1889) contains eighty stories written over a period of thirty-five years. The book went through twenty-one editions in German and was translated into several languages, but was banned in Austria for moral reasons. According to Popper, one-sixth of these stories were conceived and committed to paper from his dreams. Sigmund Freud (q.v.) expressed gratitude to Popper for the text, which formed the basis for Freud's theory of dreams. His reputation as a brilliant thinker and national figure found expression in Vienna's Rathauspark, where his bust stood until 1938, when it was destroyed by the Nazis.

Having suffered severe discrimination most of his life for maintaining his Jewish identity, Popper accused the German chancellor, Otto von Bismarck, of furthering anti-Semitism in "Fürst Bismarck und der Antisemitismus" (1886). Popper believed the answer to the Jewish question was the establishment of an independent state and although never active as a Zionist in his lifetime, he bequeathed a significant book collection to the National Library in Jerusalem.

J. Popper-Lynkeus, *Selbstbiographie*, 1917.

H. I. Wachtel, *Security for All and Free Enterprise: A Summary of the Social Philosophy of Josef Popper-Lynkeus* (introduction by Albert Einstein), 1955.

PREMINGER, OTTO (1905 or 1906–1986) U.S. film director. The Austrian-born Preminger was the son of the first Jew to be appointed chief prosecutor of the Austrian Empire. After dutifully following in his father's footsteps to the extent of obtaining a law doctorate, Preminger decided to follow his own bent for the theater and advanced as both actor and director. In 1933 Preminger succeeded Max Reinhardt (q.v.) at a Vienna theater, where he had made his professional debut in a Reinhardt production, and continued to gain prominence. Refusing to convert to Catholicism in order to become director of Vienna's State Theater, he accepted an offer from Twentieth Century-Fox's Joseph Schenck (q.v.) and left Europe in 1935.

Though he had only directed one film before going to the United States, Preminger's first, modest efforts were considered promising. A dispute with the studio head, Darryl Zanuck, sent him back to the theater, where his success as both actor and director in the play *Margin for Error* led to his return to Fox. In 1944 the thriller *Laura* consolidated his status as a major film director, but though most of his subsequent work under his contract with Fox was successful, it was eclipsed by his achievements as an independent from the early 1950s onwards.

Preminger, never known as an easy director to get along with, achieved notoriety in the 1950s, largely because of three films. *The Moon Is Blue* (1953), released by United Artists even without the standard Production Code seal of approval, broke a language barrier of sorts by using words such as

Otto Preminger directs Exodus.

"pregnant" and "virgin." Three years later, *The Man With the Golden Arm* (1956) broke another taboo by dealing explicitly with heroin addiction. At the end of the decade *Anatomy of a Murder* (1959) displayed similar frankness in its discussion of rape. Preminger's courage was also an important factor in ending the blacklist of the McCarthy era, when he insisted on crediting blacklisted screenwriter Dalton Trumbo for *Exodus*, the 1960 epic about the birth of the state of Israel. He also made the musicals *Carmen Jones* (1954) and *Porgy and Bess* (1959). Though he never totally abandoned the stage and occasionally returned to acting, Preminger's main activity remained film production and direction. Few of his efforts in these endeavors after the mid-1960s were critically highly regarded and he made his last film in 1980.

W. Frischauer, *Behind the Scenes of Otto Preminger*, 1973.

G. Pratley, *The Cinema of Otto Preminger*, 1971.

O. Preminger, *Preminger: An Autobiography*, 1977.

PREUSS, JULIUS (1861–1913) German physician and medical historian. He was born into the only Jewish family in the small German village of Gross-Schoenebeck near Potsdam, and his parents sent him to the public school in Angermunde and to the high school in Prenzlau, where he already showed himself to be a brilliant student. He studied medicine at Berlin University, qualifying in 1866 with the highest marks in the examinations set by the famous Rudolf Virchow, founder of cellular pathology and a man of uncompromising standards. Preuss' doctoral thesis was entitled "Concerning Syphilis as the Aetiology of Tabes Dorsalis

and Dementia Paralytica." Birchow complimented him as "thinking like a true physician."

Preuss practiced for a short time in his native village before settling in 1891 in Berlin, where he had a large practice. He still found time to write profusely on medical subjects and study the Talmud. Among his medical articles were "Concerning Fright in Pregnant Women" (1892) and "On the Pathology of the Tongue" (1893). Preuss is, however, best-known for his *Biblisch-talmudische Medizin*, which was preceded by several smaller articles on biblical and Talmudic subjects, the first being the *Der Arzt in Bibel und Talmud* ("The Physician in the Bible and Talmud," 1894).

Although he never attended a Jewish school as a boy, Preuss developed a deep love for the philology of ancient Hebrew as well as an exceptional grasp of Talmudic texts. His credo was "The foundation and first requirement of historical research into antiquity is philological minutiae. It was already stated by the ancient Epictetus that 'every understanding of sources begins with a study of the words.'" *Biblisch-talmudische Medizin* was acclaimed as an authoritative work, the first such study to be written by a physician and encompassing the whole range of Talmudic literature. In the introduction to the first edition (1911), Preuss, recognizing his own limitations on the subject, humbly wrote: "It is unlikely that, dealing with the subject for the first time, I should have avoided mistakes. I do not ask for the customary indulgence and I will be thankful for every notification of deficiencies and errors." The first English translation, *Julius Preuss' Biblical and Talmudic Medicine* was published by Fred Rosner in 1977. Preuss died from complications of a chest ailment. On his tombstone was incised *"rophe velo lo"*("Physician, but not for himself").

PROUST, MARCEL (1871–1922) French novelist. He was born in Paris to Adrien Proust, a physician who had rejected his father's plans that he become a priest, and Jeanne Weil, the daughter of a wealthy Jewish family from Lorraine. Although raised as a Catholic, through contact with his mother's side of the family, Marcel Proust became familiar with the traits of the French Jewish middle class that he feature in his novels. He always retained his Jewish sympathies, and was profoundly moved by the Dreyfus (q.v.) affair.

His childhood was a period of warmth and tenderness, in which he was primarily attended by his adoring mother and grandmother. The events of his childhood took place in four different settings. Through his writing they all became familiar to his readers: Paris, where he lived with his parents, and played every day in the Champs-Elysees with a group of small girls; Illiers, where the family spent their holidays; his uncle's house at Auteuil, where the family retired in periods of hot weather and which was later incorporated into Proust's presentation of Combray; and the resorts of the Channel coast to which Marcel was sent for part of each summer because of his delicate health.

Marcel Proust.

tion. The magazine, however, was short-lived. From 1892 to 1900 his health declined, with more frequent and intense asthma attacks; because they occurred primarily during the day, he developed the habit of working and socializing at night. In 1896, to the great surprise of his friends, he announced that *Les plaisirs et les jours* would soon appear. The book, a collection of poems, stories and sketches, though not up to the standard of his later work, showed promise of the writer he was to become.

Meanwhile he continued to spend his time writing letters and enjoying society life, so that even his mother, convinced as she was of her son's immense talent, despaired that he would ever do anything. He promised a novel, but did not begin it, and instead spent some years reading and translating John Ruskin, who was to have a profound influence on him.

With his mother's death in 1905, however, his childhood effectively ended, and he was able finally to begin recreating it in writing. Sometime between 1905 and 1911, the novel, *A la recherche du temps perdu* (translated to English as *A Remembrance of Things Past*), began to take shape. It was written in a room lined with cork — to keep out all sound during the day, when he slept — and filled with the vapors of his asthma medicine. *A la recherche du temps perdu* (15 volumes; 1913–1927) consisted of seven parts: *Du coté de chez Swann* (1913), *A l'ombre des jeunes filles en fleurs* (1918), *Le coté de Guermantes* (1920). *Sodome et Gomorrhe* (1921), *La prisonnière* (1923), *Albertine disparue* (originally titled *La fugitive*; 1925), and *Le temps retrouvé* (1927). Although not autobiographical, the novel is based on many of his own memories and its main themes concern time as a destroyer and memory as a preserver. One of its most memorable passages is that of the protagonist dipping a French pastry into tea, an action that reminds him of performing that same action years ago at his aunt's home, suddenly recalling the entire circumstances of his childhood to him with complete clarity.

As he became increasingly involved in his work, Proust became more and more distant from the rest of the world, locking himself in his room with his desperate obsession to "remember things past." Toward the end of his life, in 1922, he was working all night at the proofs of *La prisonnière* and literally killing himself to finish it, even to the point of refusing food in the belief that it was detrimental to the quality of his work. In October of 1922 he caught a chill that led to bronchitis and refused heating because it provoked his asthma, though he continued to revise *Albertine disparue*. This was the final blow to his health, and he died the following month.

Besides *A la recherche*, which was acclaimed as one of the great classics of 20th-century literature, he published two volumes of poetry, *Portraits de peintres* and *Les plaisirs et les jours*, as well as *Jean Santeuil* (3 volumes) and *Contre Sainte-Beuve*.

At the age of nine he suffered an attack of shortness of breath, probably caused by asthma, that left him an invalid. For this and related reasons he developed an attitude of weakness that convinced him he could do nothing unaided, and also engendered an extreme sensitivity to shades of emotion. These, together with his passion to write, his cloistered existence, and his reflective nature, all combined to help him render his subtlest impressions in language that was to delight and captivate his readers. It was to be a long time, however, before he finally began to put this genius into practice.

As a child he attended the Lycée Condorcet, where he eagerly studied literature. In 1889 he voluntarily entered the army before he was due for service, knowing that this way he would need only to serve for one year. During his service he was conspicuously undistinguished as a military man. Upon completing his service, in accordance with his father's wish that he become a diplomat, he entered the Ecole de Sciences Politiques, despite his own desire to continue studying literature and philosophy. Clearly unsuited to the profession, he eventually convinced his parents to let him study at the Sorbonne, if somewhat aimlessly. He also further developed his love for and attraction to high society, into which he soon began to make inroads by virtue of his ability to please and to be good company. His view of this society from the inside subsequently marked his writing.

His friends and family despaired of his ever making something of himself. In 1892, together with some of these friends he helped found the monthly magazine *Le Banquet*, to which each contributed ten francs a month in order to support its publica-

A. Maurois, *Proust: A Biography*, 1958.

G. D. Painter, *Marcel Proust, A Biography* (2 vols.), 1959, 1965.

R. Hayman, *Proust*, 1990.

PULITZER, JOSEPH (1847–1911) U.S. editor and publisher; a major force in setting the pattern for modern newspapers. Born in Mako, Hungary, to a Jewish father and Roman Catholic mother, Pulitzer was educated in Budapest. At the age of seventeen he obtained passage to the United States by joining the Union Army in Hamburg, Germany. He arrived in Boston in 1864, served with the Lincoln Cavalry until the following year and then moved to Saint Louis.

In 1868 Pulitzer became a reporter for the German language daily, *St. Louis Westliche Post*. As early as 1869 he was elected to the Missouri state legislature on the Republican ticket. He campaigned for Horace Greeley in the 1872 election and when his candidate lost, he joined the Democratic Party.

In 1874 Pulitzer bought the *St. Louis Staats-Zeitung* and sold the paper's Associated Press membership for enough money to enable him to study law. Two years later he was admitted to the District of Columbia bar, but never practiced.

In 1878 he purchased the bankrupt *St. Louis Dispatch* in a public auction and merged it with the *St. Louis Evening Post*. By 1880 he was sole owner of the *Post-Dispatch* which soon yielded a profit of 85,000 dollars a year.

In 1883 Pulitzer bought the *New York World* from the financier Jay Gould, and quickly made it into the country's strongest Democratic voice. His aggressive methods included news stunts, campaigns against corruption, and the use of cartoons. Two years later he was elected to the U.S. House of Representatives from New York, but resigned after a few months.

Pulitzer founded the *New York Evening World* in 1887, but his failing eyesight forced him to give up the management of the paper that same year and its editorship in 1890.

Joseph Pulitzer. Caricature by Joseph Keppler in the St. Louis Puck, 1872.

However, he resumed direct control of his papers in the 1890s in order to fight a circulation war with William Randolph Hearst's *New York Morning Journal*. Both Pulitzer and Hearst supported sensationalism and yellow journalism in the fight for readers. Their jingoism reached its peak during the Spanish-American War of 1898.

In his will, Pulitzer endowed the Columbia University School of Journalism, which opened in 1912, and the annual Pulitzer Prizes in journalism, literature, and music, which have been awarded since 1917.

G. Jeurgens, *Joseph Pulitzer and the "New York World,"* 1966.

R

RABAD See Ibn Daud, Abraham

RABI, ISIDORE ISAAC (1898–1988) U.S. physicist and Nobel Prize winner. Born to an Orthodox Jewish family in Austria-Hungary, he was taken as an infant to the United States, where his parents opened a small grocery store in Brooklyn. His parents were very concerned about both his secular and his Jewish education; when he returned from school to their rooms in the back of the store, his mother would query, "Did you ask any good questions today?"

As a youth Rabi was active in his neighborhood — organizing the local boys for discussion groups, teaching them to play chess or how to build a wireless, and always reading. Notwithstanding his traditional Jewish background and education, he was determined to become acquainted with the world beyond his neighborhood. He therefore enrolled in a mostly gentile Manual Training High School, then continued at Cornell University to major in chemistry.

Warnings that Jews had few chances in the academic world seemed self-fulfilling as he found only jobs such as analyzing mother's milk and furniture polish in one firm and computing accounts in another. Undaunted, he continued to read at the public library, and once, having attended a lecture by Albert Einstein (q.v.) at New York City College, he in turn gave a lecture on the theory of relativity to a neighborhood study group. In 1923 he returned to Cornell to do graduate work in physical chemistry.

It was at Cornell that he discovered his real bent for physics. To meet expenses he took a job teaching physics at New York, City College, and in 1927, received a doctorate from Columbia University. With a postdoctoral grant from Columbia he proceeded to Europe, where for the next two years he studied theory with Wolfgang Pauli and worked with Otto Stern on the Stern-Gerlach experiments for measuring the magnetic characteristics of atoms, work which eventually led him to a Nobel Prize. In 1929 he was offered a lectureship in Columbia University's physics department. Shifting between teaching on one hand and experimentation in nuclear physics, quantum mechanics and magnet-

ism on the other hand, he acquired a reputation in both. In 1940 he became an associate director of the radiation laboratory at the Massachusetts Institute of Technology. In 1944 he won a Nobel Prize for physics, for inventing the atomic and molecular beam magnetic resonance method for registering magnetic properties of atomic nuclei. In 1950 he became a full professor at Columbia University.

During World War II Rabi worked for the Office of Scientific Research and Development. After the war he served on advisory committees of the Defense Department and the Atomic Energy Commission and, in the early 1950s, helped to create the European Center for Nuclear Research, which brought eleven European nations together in the field of high energy physics. He was active with others, such as Enrico Fermi and J. Robert Oppenheimer (q.v.), in the advisory committee of the Atomic Energy Commission, which in the postwar years was primarily concerned with increasing the U.S. atomic arsenal. He himself, however, was concerned about finding peaceful uses for atomic energy and, when the question of a crash program for building a thermonuclear superbomb arose among the scientists, only he and Enrico Fermi among the scientists were on record as being completely opposed to the construction of the weapon.

He also worked for the Brookhaven National Laboratory for Atomic Research, the U.N. Science Committee and the Atomic Energy Agency, served as science adviser to President Dwight Eisenhower, and was on the board of governors of the Weizmann Institute in Rehovot.

D. J. Kevles, *The Physicists*, 1979.
I. I. Rabi, *Science: The Center of Culture*, 1970.

RABBENU GERSHOM See Gershom ben Judah

RABBENU TAM See Tam, Jacob ben Meir

RACHEL (c. 18th century BCE) Wife of Jacob (q.v.) and matriarch of the Jewish people. When Jacob, fleeing from the anger of his brother Esau, reached the home of his mother's family at Padan-Aram, he met Rachel at a well, where she was watering her sheep. Struck by her beauty, he fell in love with her and asked her father, Laban, for his consent to marry her. Laban agreed in return for seven years' labor for Laban. However, at the wedding, Laban substituted his elder daughter, Leah. When Jacob complained of the deceit, Laban agreed to his marrying Rachel a week later on condition that he put in another seven years' service. But these years of service "seemed unto him but a few days, for the love he had for her" (Gen. 29:20).

During the first years of their marriage, Rachel was barren, while Leah bore Jacob four children. After Rachel cried out that she would die if she had no children, she became pregnant and gave birth to Joseph (q.v.). When Jacob decided to leave Laban and return to Canaan with his family, Rachel took Laban's household gods (teraphim) concealing them in her camel cushion. When Laban came in search for them, she begged to be excused from dismounting from the camel she was riding, pretending that she was menstruating, and the idols were not discovered.

She retained her favored position in Jacob's family and when he was afraid that he and his entourage were to be attacked by Esau, he placed Rachel and Joseph in the least exposed position. As they were entering Canaan, she bore her second child, Benjamin, but died in childbirth. She was buried in Ephrath, which became identified with the entrance to Bethlehem, where a tomb, traditionally regarded as that of Rachel, is revered to this day.

In a famous passage, Jeremiah (31:15) referred to "Rachel weeping for her sons," referring to the tragic fate of the tribe of Ephraim, descended from Joseph.

N. M. Sarna, *Understanding Genesis*, 1966.

RACHEL (1821–1858) French dramatic actress. Every generation has its stars, its idols. Nineteenth-century France was no exception. She was known simply as Rachel, yet in her short lifetime she captivated audiences with her revival of the French classical tragedies. Born in Switzerland as Eliza Rachel Felix, the daughter of a peddler, her "career" began at age ten, when she sang for coins on Parisian streets in order to help feed her family.

It was there that Rachel was discovered by Etienne Choron, the singing master. He provided her with an opportunity that most would-be stars only dream of, giving her singing instruction free of charge and sponsoring her acting studies.

At age sixteen Rachel debuted at the Théâtre du Gymnase. She was popular both on and off the stage. A tragedienne at heart, she brought new life to the great classics of Racine and Corneille, performing them before nobility and aristocrats across Europe. She was both beautiful and possessed a remarkable talent.

Off stage, Rachel also possessed unquenchable passions that brought her much notoriety and made her an object of gossip. Though she never married, she was the mistress of many men, among

Portrait of Rachel.

them a nephew of Napoleon. Prince Jerome; the third son of King Louis-Philippe, the prince de Joinville; and probably the poet Alfred de Musset. Her association with another of Napoleon's relatives, his illegitimate son Count Colonna-Walewski, led to the birth of one of her two sons. In the midst of all this high living, Rachel never forgot her family. She helped her brother and four sisters launch theatrical careers of their own, and provided grand homes for her parents and siblings.

Rachel's fast and furious lifestyle soon caught up with her, taking a grave toll on her health when she became weak and consumptive. Nevertheless she continued to drive herself both professionally and socially.

A few years before her death, at a rehearsal of *Adrienne Lecouvreur*, a play written for her by Eugène Scribe and Gabriel Legouvé. Legouvé commended her on her performance, saying that she had become Adrienne, a young actress who kills herself because of thwarted love. But Rachel replied, "You are wrong... I had a sudden premonition that I, too, would die young.... And when I came to the line, 'Farewell, my triumphs of the stage! Farewell, the raptures of the art I have loved so well!' you saw me shed real tears. I was thinking that time would soon carry away all trace of my talent, and that soon there would be nothing left of her who was once Rachel."

In 1855 Rachel was invited to tour in the United States. Against her better judgment, she set sail for New York. The American tour was a failure. Although she was treated like a queen upon her arrival, Americans never got used to the style of French classical tragedy. Moreover, she became very ill and engagements were canceled. In the end she gave the final performance of her life in a small, unknown theater in Charleston, South Carolina.

In 1856 Rachel returned to France. She never acted again. Her glamorous life ended as she had foreseen — young and tragic. At her funeral, the chief rabbi of Paris delivered the eulogy in Hebrew.

J. E. Agate, *Rachel*, 1928.
M. Cost, *I, Rachel*, 1957.
B. Falk, *Rachel the Immortal*, 1936.
J. Richardson, *Rachel*, 1957.

RADAK See Kimhi, David

RADEK, KARL (originally Sobelsohn; 1885–1939?) Russian revolutionary and publicist. Karl Sobelsohn was born in the Polish town of Lemberg (today Lvov). Despite a well-grounded education in Jewish and classical sources, he rejected these at an early age in favor of revolutionary socialism and Polish nationalism. He assumed the Polish name of Radek after the revolutionary hero of a Polish novel. He joined the Polish Social Democratic party prior to World War I, and served as a publicist for the left wing of the German Social Democratic party. Noted for his pacifist opposition to the war, he attended the Zimmerwald and Kintel Pacifist congresses.

Radek settled in Switzerland, where he befriended Lenin. Upon the outbreak of the Russian Revolution in February 1917, he accompanied Lenin in the historic sealed train carriage, from Switzerland through Germany to Sweden, remaining there as representative of the Bolshevik party. He returned to Russia in the aftermath of the October revolution, and was appointed head of the central European section of the Foreign Affairs Commissariat, utilizing this position to promote the expansion of the revolution to the West.

He organized the first congress of the German Communist party in 1918 and was elected to the Communist International in 1922. He was particularly interested in promoting the revolution among the Jewish masses, lobbying fervently for the inclusion of the Poalei Zion Zionist group in the Communist International.

Radek joined the growing Trotskyite opposition to Stalin. He was briefly rector of the Sun Yat Sen University for Chinese Students in Moscow in 1926. But in 1927, he was expelled from the party and exiled to the Urals. Following his recantation in 1930, he was readmitted to the party. Radek served as editor of both *Pravda* and *Izvestia*, where he was particularly acclaimed for his articles on literature and the theater. *Portraits and Pamphlets*, a collection of his writings, was published in 1935. He was also coauthor of the initial draft of Stalin's constitution, but Stalin had never fully forgiven Radek for his earlier support for Trotsky. He was arrested in the great purges of 1936–1937; at a show trial, he was denounced as an enemy of the people, and sentenced to ten years' hard labor. Radek disappeared in 1939 and died or was apparently murdered in prison camp. Supposed witnesses to his death claimed that it was criminally rather than politically motivated.

D. Collard, *Soviet Justice and the Trial of Radek and Others*, 1939.
W. Lerner, *Karl Radek, The Last Internationalist*, 1970.

RAKOSI, MATYAS (1892–1971) Hungarian Communist politician and dictator. Leaving his native Ada (now in Yugoslavia), he moved to Budapest, where he studied and worked as a bank clerk, then joined the Socialist movement while living for a time in England. After the outbreak of World War I, Rakosi served in the Austro-Hungarian army but was captured by the Russians, spent two years in a prisoner of war camp, and secured his release when he allied himself with the Bolsheviks following the short-lived Hungarian Soviet republic of Bela Kun (q.v.). He took refuge in the USSR after the counterrevolution of August 1919, but smuggled himself back into Hungary five years later to reactivate the banned Communist party. Arrested and condemned to death, Rakosi was fortunate to have his sentence commuted to life imprisonment when prominent European intellectuals raised an outcry on his behalf.

Released from prison in 1940, Rakosi went to Moscow and stayed there until 1944, orchestrating the Hungarian Communist propaganda campaign. After the Soviet occupation of Hungary, it was Rakosi who reorganized the Workers' party; he served as deputy leader of a coalition government from which the non-Communist partners were gradually excluded and, by May 1949, had converted Hungary into a "people's democracy" subservient to Moscow. Within the next few months, even dissident leaders of the Communist national wing faced execution or imprisonment on trumped-up charges. As Hungary's prime minister from 1952 and Workers' party boss, Rakosi assumed dictatorial powers and obeyed Stalin's orders to the letter.

From his student days, Rakosi had shown no concern for the Jewish people and, after the Holocaust, he made life almost intolerable for Hungarian Jewry. Contact with the outside world — especially Israel — was prohibited; the Zionist movement was outlawed and show trials of Zionist leaders were staged; Jewish business firms became state property; and thousands were deported from Budapest and other large cities. As a faithful Stalinist, Rakosi — unlike other Politburo leaders such as Ana Pauker (q.v.) — remained in power during the anti-Jewish frenzy of 1952–1953. However, after Stalin's death, he was harshly criticized by the new Soviet leadership and, in July 1953, the more liberal Imre Nagy replaced him. Rakosi remained party secretary and was reinstated as prime minister in 1955, but the veteran dictator was compelled to resign in disgrace shortly before the outbreak of the Hungarian revolution (October 1956). This move was partly intended to placate Rakosi's anti-Stalinist archenemy, Marshal Tito. Even after the uprising had been suppressed, Rakosi was forced to remain an exile in the USSR. He was expelled from the Communist party in 1962 and it was only toward the end of his life that he succeeded in returning to Hungary.

T. Aczel and M. Meray, *The Revolt of the Mind*, 1959.

RALBAG See Levi ben Gershom

RAMBAM See Maimonides, Moses

RAMBAN See Nahmanides, Moses

RAMBERT, MARIE (1888–1982) Dance teacher, director, producer, founder of Ballet Rambert; Dame of the British Empire, 1962. In her autobiography, *Quicksilver* (a name her nurse had called her), she explains that the family name was originally Rambam and that her father was "of Jewish descent" but she does not again refer to her Jewishness. She was born in Poland and explains that her father's name was changed to Ramberg and one of his brothers took the name Rambert to avoid military service with the tsarist army — a common practice in those days. In her birth certificate she is registered as Cyvia, but changed it to Myriam which sounded better in France. In London she "took for the stage" the name of Marie Rambert. She was sent to Paris because of the disturbances of 1905. She had taken dance lessons twice a week at school but was unmoved when she was *Swan Lske*. However, when she saw Isadora Duncan, she was so wildly excited that she forced her way into her dressing room. While she was still in Paris, ostensibly to study medicine, a friend persuaded her to go with her to Geneva for a ten-day summer course at the Jacques Dalcroze School of Eurhythmics. She stayed for three years.

Rambert was by then teaching at the school and continued even when it moved to Dresden, where Sergey Diaghilev saw a class and asked Dalcroze to recommend a teacher for Vaslav Nijinsky, who was then preparing his *Rite of Spring*, with its complicated rhythms. She and Nijinsky became friends and she stayed on with the Diaghilev Company (1912–1913), developing an interest in classical ballet and taking lessons with Enrico Cecchetti. She left the Diaghilev Company to go to London, where she studied with Serafina Astafieva. In 1917 she arranged dances for a performance for the Stage Society of *Pomme d'Or*, which was later included in a C. B. Cochran review. In 1918 she married the playwright-critic Ashley Dukes.

Within two years she had established a school and by 1925 the Marie Rambert dancers were presenting recitals and staging Frederick Ashton's first ballet, *A Tragedy of Fashion*, in which she danced with Ashton. In 1930 she founded the Ballet Club, having, with her husband, acquired an old parish hall at Notting Hill Gate. It became the famous little Mercury Theatre, where Ballet Rambert (as her "club" became) and Dukes' plays were performed. Ballet Rambert is today the oldest English ballet company, though now modern in style.

Among Rambert's "discoveries" were, besides Ashton, Antony Tudor, Andree Howard, Walter Gore, Normane Morrice (for a time her codirector and later artistic director of the Royal Ballet), Frank Staff, Sally Gilmour, Pearl Argyle, and Maude Lloyd, all of whom with her encouragement became distinguished. With Rambert's cooperation Ninette de Valois founded the Camargo Society from which developed British ballet — and the Royal Ballet.

M. Rambert, Quicksilver; The Autobiography of Marie Rambert, 1972.

RANK, OTTO (1884–1939) Psychoanalyst. Born Otto Rosenfeld, in Vienna, he changed his name as a repudiation of his irresponsible and alcoholic father. (The name Rank may derive from the doctor in Ibsen's *A Doll's House*.) As a young man, he was self-taught and his extensive readings led him to the work of Sigmund Freud (q.v.). Through his family physician, Alfred Adler (q.v.), Rank was introduced to Freud at age twenty-two. Over the next twenty years he became Freud's closest and most loyal protege and virtual adopted son. Freud helped him complete a Ph.D. at the University of Vienna. Rank's creative researches did much to extend the scope of psychoanalysis to art, literature, and mythology. In this period, he edited *Imago* and the *International Journal of Psychoanalysis*, and among his books were *The Myth of the Birth of the Hero* and *The Incest Motive in Poetry and Saga*.

In 1924 he published his landmark work, *The Trauma of Birth*, in which he claimed that emotional disturbances stem from the actual experience of one's birth. This trauma needs to be worked through in therapy. Everyone subconsciously seeks to return to the primal bliss of the mother's womb. Rank focused upon the relationship between mother and infant, and in this presaged later work in psychoanalysis.

After this treatise, relations between Freud and Rank became strained and eventually were broken off because of disputes in theory and clinical application. Rivalry with other adherents of Freud, who coveted Rank's special relationship with the master, probably contributed to the rift. Such intrigue is also a possible source of unsubstantiated reports that Rank suffered from manic-depressive illness.

Rank left Vienna and eventually settled in the United States. He further developed the theory and technique of his "will therapy," emphasizing the value of creativity both in therapy and in coping with reality. Neurosis, he maintained, is a failed work of art. Analysis is rebirth in the form of the patient's reaffirmation of himself. He criticized traditional psychoanalysis as intellectual knowledge that fails to grant the unconscious emotional life its just due. Further works from Rank's later period include *Will Therapy: An Analysis of the Therapeutic Process in Terms of Relationship, Art and Artist*, and *Truth and Reality: A Life History of the Human Will*.

His first wife, Beata Tola Rank (née Mincer), was also a psychoanalyst and remained loyal to Freud after her divorce from Rank.

Rank seemed to have little affinity for Judaism, although his erudition in religion and mythology encompassed much Jewish learning, and he readily quoted sources ranging from the Bible to Rabbi Nahman of Bratslav (q.v.).

F. B. Karpf, *The Psychology and Psychotherapy of Otto Rank*, 1953.

P. Roazen, *Freud and His Followers*, 1975.

J. Taft, *Otto Rank*, 1958.

> The biblical myth of the fall has presented the human tragedy in its noblest form. Man, who advances like God in his omniscience, falls away from nature through consciousness, becomes unfortunate in that he loses his naive unity with the unconscious, with nature.
>
> **Otto Rank, *Truth and Reality***

RASHBA See Adret, Solomon ben Abraham

RASHBAM See Samuel ben Meir

RASHI (acronym of Rabbi Shelomo Yitzhaki; 1040–1105) Commentator on the Bible and the Talmud. He was born in Troyes, France, but little is known of his childhood, apart from legends. His early education was received in Worms (where the Rashi chair can be seen built into the study annex of the synagogue, although the original annex was built centuries after Rashi's death). He continued his studies in Mainz, and then returned to Troyes where he founded his own Talmudic academy. Although only about twenty-five, he was appointed the religious judge of the community and students flocked from near and far to study with him. As a judge he was unpaid, according to tradition of that time; he possibly earned his living from the vineyards that he is reported to have owned. His last years were affected by the tragic fate of the Jews in France and Germany during the First Crusade; although Troyes was untouched, many communities were destroyed. Though toward the end of his life, he had to dictate his writings, his great works had been completed. His own family — sons-in-law and grandchildren — carried on his work and

Medallion with a likeness of Rashi.

The so-called chair of Rashi at the Rashi Chapel, Worms Synagogue.

constituted the core of the *tosafists*, the main school of Talmudic study and exposition over the next two centuries.

Rashi's commentaries on the Bible and the Talmud remain standard works to this day and provide an indispensable key to their understanding. Eschewing the esoteric, polemic or mystic and minimizing the homiletic, he elucidates the text rationally, explaining the literal meaning, utilizing his profound knowledge of the sources, his understanding of the Hebrew language, and plain common sense. Often he gives the Old French equivalent for certain words and as these are written in Hebrew letters, they have provided unique evidence for students about the original pronunciation of Old French. Unlike other medieval commentaries, his explanationsof the Bible do not digress into lengthy theological, philosophical, or exegetical excursuses but concisely address themselves to explaining the unfamiliar word or the puzzling context. The text itself remains sacrosanct, but Rashi's comments have clarified many problems for Jewish students, and, through Christian scholars, influenced the classic European translations of the Bible. His commentary on the Bible was translated into Latin in the 13th century and it was the first dated Hebrew book to be printed (1475).

His commentary on the Talmud is another major achievement since the complexities of the text — both its Aramaic language and its convoluted argumentation — had threatened to close it to the masses. Indeed it was due to Rashi's commentary that the Babylonian Talmud, on which he wrote, became an open book and the accepted authority and guide, while the parallel Jerusalem Talmud, lacking such a commentary, was neglected and largely unstudied. Profoundly immersed in Jewish law, he introduces each general topic that is to be discussed and then explains, phrase by phrase, the meaning, context, and relevance of the text. He did not manage to finish the entire work and his commentary was completed by his grandson, Samuel ben Meir (q.v.). Both the Bible and the Talmud commentaries have appeared in all subsequent standard printings adjacent to the appropriate passage. Many of his interpretations were decisive in determining legal decisions.

Rashi also wrote as many *responsa*, (replies to inquiries on matters of Jewish law), and these too were accepted as authoritative. They are characterized by liberality and humility. For example, he rules that it is permissible to interrupt the grace after meals to feed one's animals, basing himself on the scriptural injunction for a man to feed his animals before himself. On one occasion he told his questioner, "I was asked this question before but I realize that my answer then was wrong and I welcome the opportunity to correct my mistake." This humility is apparent in his commentaries and, unlike the practice of other commentators, there are many places where he admits frankly that he does not understand the meaning. His two great

---

SAYINGS OF RASHI

● All the 613 commandments are included in the Decalogue.
● Any plan formulated in a hurry is foolish.
● Be sure to ask your teacher his reasons and his sources.
● Teachers learn from their students' discussions.
● A student of laws who does not understand their meaning or cannot explain their contradictions is just a basket full of books.
● Do not rebuke your fellow man so as to shame him in public.
● To obey out of love is better than to obey out of fear.

---

works were beloved by the Jewish masses and made him one of the outstanding masters of Jewish thought.

H. Heilperin, *Rashi and the Christian Scholars*, 1963.
M. Liber, *Rashi*, 1906.
C. Pearl, *Rashi*, 1988.
E. Shereshevsky, *Rashi: The Man and His World*, 1982.

RATHENAU, WALTHER (1867–1922) German statesman and industrialist. His father, Emil Rathenau (1838–1915), had been a cofounder of

Walther Rathenau.

the German Edison company, which in 1887 gave rise to the Allgemeine Elektrizitäts-Gesellschaft (AEG), a network of companies supplying Germany with electrical power and, later also, with telephone services. After training as an engineer, Walther Rathenau joined AEG's board of directors, helped to expand and diversify its activities (1899–1915), and eventually succeeded his father as the firm's president. Through his books (e.g., *Zur Kritik der Zeit*, 1912) and contributions to the press, he expressed a liberal outlook then rare among such captains of industry, with progressive declarations about state planning, social problems, and international cooperation. Religiously, however, he was a convinced assimilationist and often maintained that his German identity took precedence over his Jewishness (*Staat und Judentum*, 1911).

Following the outbreak of World War I, Rathenau saw the need for economic planning and efficiency. The German War Ministry, having accepted his arguments, placed him in charge of a special department for the supply and distribution of raw materials; he ran it successfully for almost a year, but had to retire because of his advocacy of nationalization and opposition to unrestricted U-boat warfare. The armistice and Kaiser Wilhelm's abdication made Rathenau a leading figure in the postwar Weimar Republic. Advocating a new partnership between private and public enterprise, capital and labor (*Die neue Wirtschaft*, 1918), he helped to found the German Democratic party (DDP), a middle-class group allied with the Social Democrats. He went on to serve as a negotiator at the Versailles Peace Conference (1919), became minister of reconstruction in Chancellor Josef Wirth's first cabinet (1921), and managed to secure a reduction of the war reparations payable by Germany under the Treaty of Versailles. As foreign minister in Wirth's second cabinet (1922), Rathenau devoted himself to improving Franco-German relations and, by signing the Rapallo Treaty with Soviet Russia (April 1922), aimed to strengthen economic ties with another outcast nation. The final objective of his diplomatic efforts, reversing Germany's status as an international pariah, was doomed to failure.

Instead of acknowledging the army's collapse and defeat in 1918, German revanchist circles had fostered the myth of a "stab in the back" and charged "Jewish traitors" with responsibility for the whole debacle. A primitive hatred of Jews was directed especially against "that swine Rathenau," whom ultranationalist fanatics blamed for the "humiliation" of Versailles and "creeping Communism." En route to the foreign ministry on June 24, 1922, he was murdered in cold blood by proto-Nazi terrorists, who then committed suicide. Although Chancellor Wirth fulminated against the "atmosphere of murder in Germany," a new Law for the Defense of the Republic (passed on July 18) had little effect on the Jew-baiters. Soon after the Nazis came to power, a memorial glorifying

---

FROM THE WRITINGS OF WALTHER RATHENAU

● I feel a greater sense of injury when a Bavarian rants against the Prussians than when he does so against the Jews.

● In the childhood of every German Jew there comes a moment, never to be forgotten, when he realizes that he entered this world as a second-class citizen and that no personal merit or accomplishment can deliver him from that situation.

Rathenau's assassins was unveiled in Berlin. On the thirtieth anniversary of Walther Rathenau's murder, a commemorative stamp bearing his portrait was issued by the West German government.

E. Hyams, *Killing No Murder*, 1969.
J. Joll, *Intellectuals in Politics*, 1960.
H. Kessler, *Walter Rathenau*, 1961.

RAV See Abba Arikha

RAVA (c. 285–352 CE) Babylonian rabbi, founder and head of the academy at Mahoza; the name Rava was a contracted form of Rav Abba. He was born in Mahoza, a town on the river Tigris. Together with Abbaye (q.v.), his older fellow student in the academy of Pumbedita and future rival as a preeminent teacher, Rava brought Talmudic dialectics to an impressive height. Their many statements and halakhic controversies, preserved and conceivably reworked by later generations, are a central feature of the Babylonian Talmud. Rava's gift for logical analysis enabled him to discover a host of analogies and Biblical support for numer-

---

FROM THE SAYINGS OF RAVA

● A timely quotation is like bread to the starving.
● Whoever shames someone else in public forfeits a share in the world to come.
● Longevity, children, and sustenance depend on luck, not merit.
● A man is obligated to drink so much on Purim that he can no longer tell the difference between "Cursed be Haman" and "Blessed be Mordecai."
● One does not meet trouble halfway.
● Rather allow yourself to be killed than commit murder [at a tyrant's bidding]. Is your blood redder than the other man's? Perhaps his blood is redder than yours.

ous regulations of rabbinic law. In only half a dozen cases was Abbaye's ruling rather than Rava's accepted as authoritative. When Abbaye was chosen to head the Pumbedita Academy, Rava founded a new school in Mahoza which quickly gained renown and large numbers of students. After Abbaye's death in 338, Mahoza absorbed the older academy's staff and pupils.

For Rava, the transmission and study of Torah in the broadest sense had the highest priority, and (like Abbaye) he also allied this to exemplary conduct. "Anyone whose inside does not match his outside is no true scholar," Rava declared. A teacher should be assigned no more than twenty-five pupils; fixed times were needed for study; and those attending his academy had an intensive schedule, which included not only the biannual assemblies providing "extension courses" for the general public but Sabbath afternoon lectures as well. Although God created the Torah as an antidote to man's evil inclination, Rava said, the pursuit of wisdom should not be regarded as an end in itself: it must lead one to repentance and good deeds.

Like his colleague, Abbaye, Rava was fond of using apt sayings to drive home a lesson. He emphasized respect for the feelings of other people, individual responsibility, and psychological factors determining man's behavior. The prestige which he enjoyed made him the hero of folk tales, Rava's wealth and influence at the Persian court being used generously to defend the interests of scholars and of the Jewish population as a whole.
J. Neusner, *A History of the Jews in Babylonia*, 1966–1970, vol. 4.

RAY, MAN (1890–1976) Artist whose work was in the vanguard of the American surrealist movement. He said that "in a picture, it is above all the signature that counts" and therefore adopted the name "Man Ray," instructing his family never to mention his birth name, Emanuel Radnitsky.

He was born in Philadelphia, and went to school in Brooklyn, N.Y. He studied art at the Francisco Ferrer Center and at the Art Students League. At eighteen, he was meeting avant-garde painters and writers. He soon became involved in dadaism and began doing what he called "readymades," that is, choosing a manufactured article and giving it a title that alters the viewer's conception of the article. Then he progressed to "assisted readymades;" that is, a combination of readymade with other objects. For example, he framed a photograph of an ostrich egg with a toilet seat and called it *Trompe l'oeuf*, utilizing another of his favorite devices, the pun.

Man Ray went to Paris in 1921 and his first show there was described as the first dada show of the season and the last. Dada as a movement was being supplanted by surrealism, but Man Ray was always part dada, part surrealist.

He earned his living as a photographer, becoming a favorite portraitist of the intellectual elite, and very much in demand as a fashion photographer and as an illustrator of the works of avant-garde writers. His innovations in photography included "Rayographs," an inventive and artistic use of objects, light, and photo-sensitive paper. His unique vision and iconoclastic use of the photographic techniques resulted in original photographs.

Man Ray's most famous painting is probably the eight-foot-long canvas called *A l'heure de L'observatoire—Les amoureuses*. It shows a huge pair of lips, floating in a cloudy sky over a dark landscape.

Between 1923 and 1929 Man Ray produced four short films. One of them, *The Return to Reason*, was made by scattering pins and thumbtacks on a length of film and exposing it to light. It was shown at a dada performance that ended in fistfights and the intervention of the police. He once shot a film by starting a camera, throwing it in the air, and letting it film its travels.

Man Ray left Paris just before the Nazis arrived in 1940. He settled in Los Angeles, where he did a prodigious amount of work — paintings, assemblages, photographs, etc. — and lectured and taught.

He returned to France in 1951 and there made a series of masks. He "invented" a method of painting by slapping thick layers of acrylic paint on a board, then putting another board on the paint. Pressure was applied by sitting on the top board, which, he claimed, not only was a method of expressing his feelings toward the medium, but of bringing "chance" to the creation of beauty. In the same vein, he did a series of blotting-paper pictures, framed a glass palette, *Fragile Glass*, and framed his paint-rag, *Le sans col (tel quel)*. Man Ray said that his works of art started with an idea. If the usual techniques could not realize this idea, then he explored or invented new techniques.

In a 1957 dada show, a work of Man Ray's called *Object to Be Destroyed*, was smashed to bits by a group of young artists. Man Ray rebuilt it, and renamed it *Indestructible Object*.

Man Ray's 1963 autobiography was called *Self Portrait*. He called the essay he wrote for a 1966 exhibition, "I Have Never Painted a Recent Painting." In 1972, the Musée de l'Art Moderne presented a Man Ray retrospective. The artist, aged eighty-one, came in a wheelchair and commented, "If this had only happened forty years ago I might well have been encouraged."
J. H. Martin (introd.), *Man Ray: Photographs* (with three texts by Man Ray), 1982.
R. Penrose, *Man Ray*, 1975.
A. Schwarz, *Man Ray: The Rigor of Imagination*, 1977.

RAZIEL, DAVID (1910–1941) Underground leader. Born in Russia, his family immigrated to Palestine in 1913, returned to Russia, and resettled in Tel Aviv in 1923. He studied in a yeshiva (Talmudic academy) in Jerusalem and later at the Hebrew University. During the 1929 riots he served in the Haganah (underground Jewish self-defense force) in Jerusalem. He despaired of the Haganah's policy of self-restraint and passive defense, and in 1931 joined joined a group called

Haganah B, which advocated active defense and a retaliatory policy against Arab attackers. Raziel became active in training underground fighters. He opposed the return of this group to the Haganah, and in 1937 joined the newly created Irgun Tzevai Leummi ("Irgun"), the armed underground of the right-wing Revisionist Movement in Palestine. From 1937 to 1939 he commanded its Jerusalem district. The leader of the Revisionist Movement, Vladimir Jabotinsky (q.v.), appointed him commander in chief of the Irgun in 1939. This underground claimed the right of every Jew to immigrate freely to Palestine and argued that the existence of an armed Jewish force in the country was a prerequisite for the creation of a Jewish state that would rise as a result of an armed struggle. Under his command the Irgun engaged in a series of retaliatory raids against Arab rioters, began to organize illegal immigration, and planned attacks on British facilities and installations. The British arrested him in 1939 and he was detained for a year. After his release, he was unable to prevent a split in the Irgun, which resulted in the creation of a third underground, the Fighters for the Freedom of Israel (Lehi), under Avraham Stern (q.v.), who objected to the links between the Irgun and the Revisionist Movement.

After the outbreak of World War II, the Irgun decided to suspend its anti-Arab and anti-British operations and form an anti-Nazi front for the duration of the war. Raziel volunteered for a British-sponsored mission in Iraq to fight the pro-Nazi al Khilani regime. He was killed in a bomb explosion in the Habaniyeh air base near Baghdad. His remains were reinterred in a military ceremony in Jerusalem in 1961.

J. Hirschman, *Raziel*, 1975.

D. Levine, *The Man and His Time*, 1974.

READING, MARQUESS OF See Isaacs, Rufus Daniel

REBEKAH (c. 18th century BCE) Matriarch of the Jewish people, wife of Isaac (q.v.). Her story is told in the book of Genesis (chaps. 22–27). Isaac's father, Abraham (q.v.), sent his servant to Paddan-Aram to find a bride for his son among his brother's family, lest Isaac should marry a Canaanite woman. The servant was divinely guided to the choice of Rebekah, the sign being her gracious and charitable response at the well when he requested water: "Drink, my lord...and I will also draw water for your camels." She is described in glowing terms — beautiful, a virgin, good-hearted, hospitable, and from Abraham's family. Rebekah journeyed to Canaan, with her nurse Deborah as chaperone.

Rebekah was Isaac's only wife, but, like his mother, Sarah (q.v.) and later their daughter-in-law, Rachel, she was long childless. Only twenty years after the marriage, after Isaac uttered a special prayer to God, did Rebekah become pregnant and deliver twins, Esau and Jacob (q.v.). The two sons grew up to be rivals, with Isaac favoring Esau

and Rebekah Jacob. She conspired with Jacob to obtain for him the paternal blessing for the first-born which rightfully belonged to Esau. In face of Esau's anger, she contrived Jacob's escape and his journey to her family in Paddan-Aram, where she hoped he would find a wife from among her own people (which indeed happened).

The only other story about Rebekah relates that Isaac told the king of Gerar, Abimelech, that she was his sister as he feared that the local inhabitants would desire her and would kill him to obtain Rebekah.

Although the death of Deborah, Rebekah's nurse, is mentioned in the Bible, there is no explicit notice of Rebekah's death, but it is stated that she was buried in the cave of Machpelah in Hebron.

N. M. Sarna, *Understanding Genesis*, 1966.

REICH, WILHELM (1897–1957) Psychoanalyst, one of the most original thinkers associated with the Vienna circle of Sigmund Freud (q.v.). Born in Galicia, his early interest in biology had ample opportunity to develop on his father's large farm. After fighting on the Italian front in World War I, he enrolled at the University of Vienna and completed his medical studies with distinction. By the early age of twenty-three, he was admitted to the Vienna Psychoanalytic Society, and was soon directing seminars, developing psychoanalytic theory, and introducing changes in technique. He stressed the need to conduct "character analysis," that is, a study of the fixed traits underlying neurotic conflict, instead of focusing only on symptoms. He emphasized sexual repression as a source of pathology and believed that sublimation is a harmful concession to conformity and not a productive sign of health as maintained by Freud. Orgasmic potency, as part of a full and rich loving relationship, became an indicator of emotional well-being and of progress in therapy.

Reich was an avid communist, and after moving to Berlin in 1930, founded Sexpol, an organization numbering close to 40,000 members at its peak, which promulgated communism and sexual liberation. The Freudian oedipal conflict, the source of so much discontent, could be averted according to Reich by dismantling the middle-class societal structure. He preached that communist revolution must be accompanied by a sexual revolution if one aimed for more than a stagnant bureaucratic state. Not long after he espoused these views during a lecture tour in the Soviet Union, psychoanalysis was banned there. Some see this as more than a coincidence. He also wrote a psychological and Marxist critique of fascism and its dangers, which was dismissed as alarmist and fanatical.

During the 1930s, Reich broke with both the psychoanalysts, who distrusted his theoretical innovations and reformist aspirations, and the communists, who rejected his investigations of bourgeois structure.

In 1939 he settled in the United States, where he developed his ideas further. His writing from this period includes an analysis of Jesus Christ as the incarnation of genital love. Reich stated that though he rejected all religion, his sympathies were closer to Christianity than to Judaism.

Working on a large estate in Maine, Reich developed "orgone therapy." He claimed to have discovered "biones," which are vesicles representing transitional stages between nonliving and living substance. This finding, he said, had applications for freeing libido, gathering cosmic radiation, dispersing clouds, and curing cancer. This last claim brought him into conflict with the United States Food and Drug Administration and he was sentenced to two years in prison for fraud. He died in prison after serving only several months.

Whether his last years were a period of unbridled creativity or a slow descent into insanity remains a source of controversy. Perhaps a sealed legacy that Reich left with instructions to be opened fifty years after his death will help unravel the lingering enigma of this brilliant man.

F. Alexander, S. Eisenstein, M. Grotjahn, 1966.
D. Boadella, *Wilhelm Reich: The Evolution of His Work*, 1974.
W. Briehl, "Wilhelm Reich," in *Psychoanalytic Pioneers*, 1966.
P. Roazen, *Freud and His Followers*, 1975.
C. Rycroft, *Reich*, 1971.

REIK, THEODOR (1888–1969) Psychoanalyst. His doctorate at the University of Vienna, a psychological study of Flaubert, was the first Ph.D. awarded for psychoanalytic research. From 1910, he became and remained one of Sigmund Freud's (q.v.) most faithful disciples, undergoing analysis

Theodor Reik.

- Jewish jokes start with heresies and allusions of timid aggression against the exaggerated demands made in the name of religion and will end with the abolishment of the illusion of religion.

- Suffering, consciously experienced and mastered, teaches us wisdom.

Theodor Reik

---

by Karl Abraham (q.v.) and, later, by Freud himself. At Freud's behest, he became a psychoanalyst, even though he was not a physician. This eventually led to a court case on charges of quackery. Freud's book defending lay analysis was composed on Reik's behalf.

Reik practiced in Berlin, although with the rise of the Nazis to power he relocated to The Hague. Eventually, he joined the wave of European analysts who went to the United States during the 1930s, and settled in New York City. To his dismay, he was received warily by his new colleagues, who disapproved of lay analysis, and who maintained certain doctrinal differences. Nevertheless, with time, Reik, through his writings, came to play an important role in the dissemination of psychoanalytic teaching in the United States and formed the National Psychological Association for Psychoanalysis. He became professor of clinical psychology at Adelphi University.

Reik stressed the centrality of intuition in the psychoanalytic enterprise. A systematic, rational approach to the technique of psychoanalysis is not sufficient. The analyst must be open to the subtle interplay of his unconscious with that of the patient. He expounded upon these ideas in his popular work, *Listening with the Third Ear*. He is also noted for his investigation of masochism, in *Masochism and the Modern Man*.

Reik possessed a vast knowledge of religion, and while he discarded Jewish observance early in life, many of his writings display an interest in Jewish themes. In the 1920s he wrote articles on the *Kol Nidre* prayer and on the shofar. In later years, he completed a tetralogy of psychoanalytic Old Testament exegesis, discussing Abraham and Isaac, the creation of Eve, Mount Sinai, and the origins of guilt in modern man. In *Pagan Rites in Judaism* (subtitled *From Sex Initiation, Magic, Moon-cult, Tattooing, Mutilation and Other Primitive Rituals to Family Loyalty and Solidarity*), he pointed to residues of pagan worship within Judaism even as practiced today, often recalling his Orthodox grandfather. In *Jewish Wit*, he examined the psychological undercurrents of Jewish humor, in which he found "an oscillation between masochistic self-humiliation and paranoid superiority feelings."

J. M. Natterson, "Theodor Reik," in *Psychoanalytic Pioneers*, eds. F. Alexander, S. Eisenstein, M. Grotjahn, 1966.

T. Reik, *Fragments of a Great Confession*, 1949.

P. Roazen, *Freud and his Followers*, 1966.

REILLY, SIDNEY (1874–1925?) British spy. He was born in Odessa, Russia as Sigmund Georgievich Rosenblum; little is known of his early life. It is unknown, for instance, when he arrived in England, but once there he anglicized his name by taking that of his father-in-law.

Reilly worked in Saint Petersburg as an arms dealer before and during World War I and earned large sums of money. In Saint Petersburg, he first made contact with the British Secret Service.

During World War I, Reilly, then a British agent, enlisted in the German army several times, on each occasion assuming a different identity. On one such mission, while posing as a German colonel, he attended a meeting with Kaiser Wilhelm II and generals Paul von Hindenburg and Erich Ludendorff where important war plans were discussed.

At the outset of the Russian Revolution in 1917, Reilly was stationed at Saint Petersburg, where he quickly won access to Leon Trotsky's (q.v.) office in the Foreign Ministry. He rapidly began to despise the communist government and was eager to undertake any plot which would lead to the Bolsheviks' overthrow.

On august 31, 1918, Dora Kaplan, a Russian socialist, made an attempt on Lenin's life in which the Soviet leader was seriously injured. The Russians quicly discovered that Reilly was behind the assassination attempt and he had to flee to Britain.

While in England, Reilly continued to contest communism. Politics, however, was not the only activity that occupied his time; he was also known as a womanizer. While still in Russia eight women claimed him as their legally wedded spouse and this reputation followed him to Britain.

In 1925 Reilly agreed to return to Russia to meet secretly with anti-Bolshevik groups. He reached Helsinki on September 25, but was never heard from again. Two weeks later the Russian newspaper, *Izvestia*, carried a story about the capture and death of three agents on the Russo Finnish border. It is assumed that Reilly was among those captured.

Reilly was considered one of the outstanding British spies of all times. Many legends grew up around his exploits, which have served as the basis for numerous fictional works on espionage. The life of Reilly was serialized by the BBC. Reacting to these programs, the Russians said he had been executed in November 1925, but the famous British agent Sir Robert Bruce Lockhart stated that Reilly was still alive in 1932 when he was cooperating with the Russians.

T. Bower, *The Red Web*, 1989.

R. B. Lockhart, *The Ace of Spies*, 1967.

R. B. Lockhart, *Memoirs of a British Agent*, 1935.

REINHARDT, MAX (1873–1943) Theatrical producer and director. Born Maximilian Goldmann in Baden, Austria, Max Reinhardt began his career as an actor and assistant director at the age of seventeen at the Salzburg State Theater, specializing in portraying old men. In 1894 Otto Brahm brought him to Berlin to the Deutsches Theater. In 1902 he was performing Strindberg and Wilde at the Kleines Theater and in 1903 played Luka in Gorky's *The Lower Depths*. That year he began directing and by 1904 had staged forty-two plays.

His best remembered triumph came in 1905 with his first staging of Shakespeare's *A Midsummer Night's Dream*, which made him famous throughout Germany. He employed a revolving stage that eliminated scene changes and allowed scenes to flow one into another. Karl Walser built a forest with moss, trees trailing foliage, and a pond lit from beneath for the fairies. His direction was inventive, imaginative, swift, colorful, and joyous.

In contrast, his 1908 staging of *King Lear* used angular sets. The palace was archaic and decorated with barbaric chevron design and filled with massive chairs. Reinhardt had neither style or formula. He sought to integrate the two main theatrical traditions of his time, the baroque (Vienna) and the literary and intellectual (Berlin). He chose the appropriate style for each play, be they light comedy or massive spectacles. The latter particularly attracted his attention. His 1909 *Hamlet* was performed in modern dress.

Reinhardt indirectly exerted enormous influence on the course of German and international cinema. Most of the important film directors of the

Scene from Servant of Two Masters by Carlo Goldoni, directed by Max Reinhardt.

1920s and 1930s trained under him at his theaters, including such directors as F. W. Murnau, Paul Leni, Ernst Lubitsch, Paul Wegener, William Dieterle, and Otto Preminger. Among the actors were such stars as Conrad Veidt, Emil Jannings, Luise Rainer, Marlene Dietrich, and Joseph Schildkraut.

Reinhardt succeeded Brahm as director of the Deutsches Theater in 1905, bought the theater and established an acting school to train ensemble actors. He built the Kammerspiele next door for intimate productions and modern plays. He staged over 600 productions including 22 Shakespeare plays, Greek drama, expressionist works, Molière, Shaw, Ibsen, Wilde, Synge, Strindberg, and Gilbert and Sullivan, and revived German classics. From 1915 to 1920 he presented matinee performance of new plays by young writers at the Berlin Volksbuhne. He presented *Jedermann* ("Everyman") from the medieval morality play every summer at the Salzburg Festival from 1920 until the early 1930s.

He traveled to London in 1911 and for *The Miracle* — with a cast of 2,000 — converted the Olympia Theater into a Gothic cathedral. He returned to London in 1912 with his staging of *Oedipus Rex* and spent the 1927–1928 season in New York.

When the Nazis came to power, Reinhardt lost all his theaters and left Germany. For a while he toured Europe as a guest director with various companies and in 1933 went to New York. He spent the remainder of his years producing and directing. He founded an acting school and theater workshop in Hollywood. In 1934 he produced *A Midsummer Night's Dream* at the Hollywood Bowl and a year later codirected a film version with William Dieterle. His final production was *The Eternal Road*, a biblical play by Franz Werfel (q.v.), at the Manhattan Opera House, New York, in 1937.

A man of few words, his stage philosophy was "Our standard must not be to act a play as it was acted in the days of its author. How to make a play live in our time, that is decisive for us."

G. Adler, *Max Reinhardt*, 1964.

O. M. Sayler (ed.), *Max Reinhardt and His Theater*, 1924.

REMA See Isserles, Moses

RESNICK, JUDITH A. (1949–1986) U.S. astronaut. On January 29, 1986 the U.S. space shuttle *Challenger* exploded in space with seven astronauts aboard. Judith Resnick, the second American

> "The Earth looks great."
> Cosmonaut Judith Resnick's comment radioed to earth after going into orbit on the space shuttle *Discovery*.

Judith Resnick before the launching of the Challenger.

woman to travel in space, was one of the seven who perished in the explosion. She had spent 144 hours and 57 minutes in space.

She was born in Cleveland and raised in Akron, Ohio. Her grandfather was a *shohet* (ritual slaughterer) and her family was active in the Jewish community. She received a degree in electrical engineering from Carnegie-Mellon University and a Ph.D. in electrical engineering from the University of Maryland. According to a professor at Maryland she was always the first to work in the morning, always the most industrious, and extremely computer-competent at a time when few people were.

Judith Resnick held several jobs: design engineer for RCA, biomedical engineer at the National Institutes of Health in Bethesda, Maryland, and senior systems engineer for the Xerox Corporation. In 1978, while working for Xerox, Resnick was among six women selected in a group of thirty-five space-shuttle astronaut candidates. Two of those candidates died with her in the *Challenger* explosion.

In 1984, she became the second woman to travel in space when she joined the first voyage of the space shuttle *Discovery* as a mission specialist. On that trip she was in charge of extending and retracting *Discovery*'s solar power array from the cargo bay. On the *Challenger* she was also one of three mission specialists.

REUTER, PAUL JULIUS (BARON VON; 1816–1899) News agency magnate, founder of Reuter's Telegraph Company. Born in Kassel, Germany as Israel Beer Josaphat, he changed his name to Reuter in 1844 and converted to Christianity.

In 1829 he became a clerk in his uncle's bank in Gottingen, where he met Karl Friedrich Gauss, who was experimenting with the electric telegraph.

Reuter joined a small publishing firm in Berlin in the 1840s, and after publishing a number of political pamphlets moved to Berlin in 1848. There he began translating extracts from articles and collecting commercial news and sending them to newspapers in Germany.

In 1849 he began a carrier pigeon service between Aachen, Germany, and Verviers, Belgium, the terminal points of the German, French, and Belgium telegraph lines, transmitting financial and commercial news. In 1851, Reuter moved to London. He opened a telegraph office near the London stock exchange and began to send commercial news abroad and throughout England. He soon added political news, insisting on strict objectivity and the printing of his name on each item.

In 1858 he achieved a journalistic feat by transmitting to London Napoleon III's speech fore-shadowing the Austro-French War in Italy only one hour after it was delivered. His clientele expanded and included the London *Times*.

Undersea cables helped Reuter expand to other continents. He reported on the American Civil War and was two days ahead of the competition in reporting Abraham Lincoln's assassination in 1865. By the 1870s he had extended his service to the Far East and headed the leading international news agency.

In 1857 Reuter became a British subject. In 1871 he was made a baron by the duke of Saxe-Coburg-Gotha. The title was recognized by Queen Victoria in 1891.

Reuter retired as manager of the agency in 1878 and was succeeded by his son, Baron Herbert de Reuter (1947–1915).

G. Storey, *Reuters: The Story of a Century of News Gathering*, 1951.

Paul J. Reuter's first news venture, in 1850, included a pigeon post between Aachen and Brussels. Below, the coat of arms of Baron de Reuter.

Reuter's first news venture, in 1850, included a pigeon post between Aachen and Brussels. In 1944, Reuters' pigeons brought news from the Normandy beachhead.

The coat of arms of Baron de Reuter, granted by the Duke of Saxe-Coburg-Gotha in 1871, recognised by Queen Victoria twenty years later.

REUVENI, DAVID (died c. 1535) Adventurer who inspired the pseudo-Messiah Solomon Molkho (q.v.). His real name and origin are unknown and only speculation and the "diary" ascribed to him, the authenticity of which is doubtful, refer to his early days. The first historical record dates from 1523, when he appeared in Venice. He seemed to be about forty years old and said he was commander of the army of his brother, a prince of the tribe of Reuben (hence the name "Reuveni") who ruled over the lost tribes of Reuben and Gad, and half the tribe of Manasseh in the far-off desert of Habor. Some have suggested he was an Ethiopian Jew. The following year he arrived in Rome, riding a white horse, and was received by Pope Clement VII. The Turks had just occupied Belgrade and Rhodes, and Reuveni suggested the formation of a Jewish legion and the dispatch of arms to his brother, who wanted to liberate the Holy Land. The pope gave Reuveni letters of recommendation to the kings of Portugal and Abyssinia. Notables of the Jewish community of Rhodes provided him with the means to go to Portugal, where King John III received him with great honors.

His presence in Portugal (1525–1527) aroused intense fervor among the Marranos, the crypto-Jews, who felt that he was the forerunner of the Messiah. One of them, Diego Peres, left a high position in the government, declared himself a Jew, and dedicated his time to the study of Torah. He changed his name to a Hebrew name, "Solomon Molkho," and set off for Salonika and Safed, attracted by the study of the Kabbalah there. The Portuguese authorities became worried at the extent of the messianic arousal of the Marranos, and David Reuveni had to flee Portugal for Spain and then France.

In 1529 Molkho began to teach openly in Italy. During a meeting with the pope, he predicted a flood of the Tiber River, an earthquake in Portugal, and the appearance of comets. Molcho's detractors forced him to leave Rome and he went to Venice where he was happy to find Reuveni. His

REUVENI MEETS THE POPE

I went to the apartment of the Pope who received me graciously and said "The matter is from the Lord". I said to him "My brother, King Joseph and his elders ordered me to tell you to make peace between the Emperor and the French king, for it will be well with you if you make this peace, and write for me a letter to these two kings and to King Prester John [King of Ethiopia]." The Pope answered "I cannot make peace between those two kings but if you so wish, I will write to the King of Portugal to help you. "And I answered" Whatever you wish, I will do and will pray for your welfare and good." And the Pope asked his Cardinal "Where does the ambassador [i.e., Reuveni] lodge?" and the Cardinal answered "The Jews asked him to go with them." The twelve Jews who had accompanied me on my visit to the Pope said "Let him stay with us and we will honor him for your sake." And the Pope said to them "If you honor him, I will pay all the expenses." I said to the Pope "I wish to come to see you every two days, for seeing you is as seeing God" and the Pope agreed, telling the Cardinal to accompany me every time I came to visit. So I took my leave and went with the Jews and was extremely glad.

From the "diary" of David Reuveni

various predictions came true and the pope took a strong liking to him. Molkho and Reuveni now became even more enthusiastic regarding Reuveni's dream: the conquest of the Holy Land. They tried to obtain help from the Emperor Charles V, and appeared before him in Regensburg carrying a banner inscribed with the letters MKBI (*Makabi*), which are the initial letters in Hebrew of the verse: "Who is like you O Lord, among the mighty ones?" They requested permission for the Marranos to take up arms and join the Jewish people of Arabia, and gather all the dispersed Jews to fight the Turks. In reply, Charles V had them chained and sent them back to Italy where Molkho was burned at the stake. Reuveni was imprisoned in Spain, and he probably suffered the same fate as Molcho (or was poisoned) about 1535.
E. Adler, *Jewish Travellers*, 1966.

REVEL, BERNARD (1885–1940) U.S. Orthodox rabbi, scholar, educator, and leader. Born into a rabbinic family in the Lithuanian townlet of Pren, Revel studied at the famed Telz yeshiva (Talmudic seminary) and was ordained in Kovno (Kaunas) in 1901. Having immigrated to the United States in 1906, he earned a master's degree from New York University in 1909 and a doctorate from Dropsie College in 1912. His dissertation, "Karaite Halakhah [religious law] and its Relation to Sadducean, Samaritan, and Philonian Halakhah" challenged Abraham Geiger's (q.v.) argument that the Karaites were continuing the tradition established by the Sadducees.

For a brief time, Revel worked in his father-in-law's Oklahoma oil refinery until he was called to New York in 1915 to serve as dean of the newly merged Etz Chaim Yeshiva and Rabbi Isaac Elchanan Theological Seminary. His vision of a modern Orthodox institution that would integrate American secular education with traditional Talmudic learning led to the establishment of the Talmudic Academy in 1916, the first yeshiva high school in the United States, and the founding of the Yeshiva College in 1928, later known as Yeshiva University, the first liberal arts institution under Jewish auspices. As its president, he was the first to ordain Orthodox rabbis in America. Stalwart in his convictions, and in face of the opposition of a formidable rabbinic leadership who feared that Torah study would become a secondary goal, Revel went on to establish a graduate school of advanced Jewish and cognate studies in 1937, which in 1941 became known as the Bernard Revel Graduate School. Honorary president of the Union of Orthodox Rabbis of North America and vice-president of the Jewish Academy of Arts and Sciences, he continued to devote himself to Jewish scholarship as associate editor of the Hebrew encyclopedia, *Otsar Yisrael*, as the author of rabbinic responsa and as a contributor of articles on a variety of subjects to Jewish periodicals.
S. Hoenig, *Rabbinics and Research: The Scholarship of Dr. Bernard Revel*, 1968.
A. Rakeffet-Rothkoff, *Bernard Revel: Builder of American Jewish Orthodoxy*, 1981.

RICARDO, DAVID (1772–1823) British economist. Ricardo was born in London to an Orthodox family. His father, Abraham, a recent immigrant from Holland, sent his son at the age of eleven to study in Holland for two years. Later, Ricardo described this period in his life to a friend: "We were fifteen children — my father gave me little education — he thought reading, writing and arithmetic sufficient [sic] because he doomed me to be nothing but a man of business — he sent me at eleven to Amsterdam to learn Dutch, French and Spanish — but I was so unhappy at being separated from my brothers and sisters and family that I learned nothing in two years but Dutch, which I could not help learning."

Young David must have learned something, for at age fourteen his father took him into his business in the stock market. His father had been one of the twelve "Jew Brokers" in the City of London and had earned more than a decent living. By age twenty-one, however, David Ricardo had broken away from his father and his religion; he had fallen in love with and married a Quaker woman. Eventually Ricardo joined the Unitarian Church. On his own, Ricardo proved resourceful and competent in business. He had already begun to establish a reputation on the London Stock Exchange, and this fact, coupled with the increased financial opportunities due to the wars between France and England, led to his success as a stock broker. In time, his fortune even exceeded that of his father.

Ricardo's interest in economics was piqued in 1799 when he read Adam Smith's *Wealth of Nations*. He began studying political economy, and in 1809 published a series of unsigned articles and letters in the *Morning Chronicle*, on the currency question. Due to the wars in Europe, legislation had been passed forbidding the Bank of England to redeem bank notes in gold. The bank had been increasing the supply of notes issued and the volume of lending, and the notes began to depreciate in value. The bank maintained that there was no connection between the increase in paper money and the currency's depreciation. Ricardo argued otherwise in his article. He summed up his beliefs in 1810 in a book published under his own name, *The High Price of Bullion, a Proof of the Depreciation of Banknotes*. The government charged the Bullion Committee to discuss the problem of depreciation, and their findings concurred with Ricardo's.

Through his writings and interest in economics, Ricardo became associated with James Mill (father of John Stuart Mill) and Thomas Malthus. He kept up a lively correspondence with both men and continued his studies in economics. It has been said that Ricardo shared Mill's belief in making birth control available to the working classes, but Ricardo never committed himself to that issue in writing.

Ricardo retired from the stock exchange in 1814. The following year he published his essay, *The Influence of a Low Price of Corn on the Profits of Stock*, in which he held that raising the tariff on imported grain would increase the rents charged by the landowners and decrease the profits of manufacturers. Two years later, urged on by Mill and Malthus, he wrote *Principles of Political Economy* (1817), in which he discussed the laws governing the distribution of wealth and attacked the Corn Laws, holding that profits vary inversely with wages and that wages increase or decrease according to the cost of living.

In 1819 Ricardo purchased a seat in the House of Commons, as was the practice at the time, and became a representative of Portarlington. Ricardo brought to Parliament his philosophy in economics, but it was only after his death that Parliament began to pass laws according to his ideas. "Ricardian economics" dominated Britain for more than fifty years. Some of his key ideas had to do with the finite availability of natural resources, and he developed what became known as the "iron law of wages," which stated that population growth is determined by means of subsistence: when wages are high the population will grow, creating a surplus labor force, following which wages will drop as will the standard of living and the population

growth. Britain used Ricardo's ideas to justify a policy that emphasied manufacturing and exporting finished goods and importing food.

After touring the Continent with his family in 1822 Ricardo retired from Parliament in 1823. Later that year he suffered a cerebral infection and died in his home in Gatcombe Park.

M. Blaug, *Ricardian Economics*, 1958.
S. Hollander, *The Economics of David Ricardo*, 1979.
D. Weatherall, *David Ricardo: A Biography*, 1976.

RICE, ELMER (1892–1967) U.S. playwright, producer, and director best known for his innovative, experimental plays. He was born Elmer Reizenstein in New York City, but changed his name after he began to write because Reizenstein was hard to pronounce and spell. Rice left school in the tenth grade and began to work as a clerk. While clerking in a lawyer's office by day, he completed a law degree at night, graduating cum laude in 1912. After working for a short time as a lawyer, however, he decided he wanted to become a writer. He wrote *On Trial* in 1914, and submitted it directly to a producer, who immediately accepted it. The play, which was about a murder, was unusual in that it employed for the first time on Broadway, the flashback technique that is now common in movies. *On Trial* was a success on Broadway, earning Rice 100,000 dollars, a huge sum in those days. Rice began taking drama courses at Columbia University and at the same time worked with some amateur theater groups writing plays and directing.

Rice's next success came with *The Adding Machine* (1923), an expressionist satire that explores the effect of mechanization on modern man. Mr. Zero, the antihero of the play, is replaced in his job by an adding machine. A bigoted, self-centered man, Zero is portrayed as the product of the modern world. After *The Adding Machine*, Rice wrote *Close Harmony* (or *The Lady Next Door*, 1929) with Dorothy Parker (q.v.), and *Cock Robin* (1929) with Philip Barry.

Rice's plays often served as vehicles to stage social issues. He rejected the mainstream theater that sought only to entertain and said in his autobiography, *Minority Report* (1963), that he used the theater "for discussion in emotional and dramatic terms of problems that affect the lives and happiness of millions." In his Pulitzer Prize-winning *Street Scene* (1929), Rice tells the story of tenement life in New York. The play, rejected by a number of producers until William A. Brady agreed to stage it, was directed by Rice himself. In 1947 it was turned into an opera, with music by Kurt Weill and lyrics by Langston Hughes; later it was adapted for the screen. In 1938 Rice helped to found the Playwrights' Company with Maxwell Anderson, S. N. Behrman (q.v.), and Robert E. Sherwood. For the company he directed Sherwood's *Abe Lincoln in Illinois*.

Rice was known for his activism in many social causes, a fact that did not always help him find

---

ELMER RICE'S "DECALOGUE OF PRINCIPLES"

It is better to live than to die;
to love than to hate;
to create than to destroy;
to do something than to do nothing;
to be truthful than to lie;
to question than to accept;
to be strong than to be weak;
to hope than to despair;
to venture than to fear;
to be free than to be bound.

From *Minority Report*.

---

work on Broadway. Among the issues he fought against were censorship, militarism, church-imposed morality, and resistance to political change. During the depression he was appointed New York regional director of the Federal Theater Project. He left this post when the government began to censor certain projects. As a member of the American Civil Liberties Union, Rice fought for the rights of Japanese-Americans interned during World War II. After the war, he opposed blacklisting actors accused of left-wing political connections and resigned from the Playwrights TV Theater for this reason, stating, "I have repeatedly denounced the men who sit in the Kremlin for judging artists by political standards, I do not intend to acquiesce when the same procedure is followed by political commissars who sit in the offices of advertising agencies of business corporations." In 1966 he refused a position as a consultant on drama to the Department of Health, Education, and Welfare after he was asked to sign a statement saying that he had "never been a member of a group of organizations deemed subversive."

Rice's later plays were not as successful or innovative as his earlier ones. However, *Counsellor-at-Law* (1931), the anti-Nazi *Judgment Day* (1934), *An American Landscape* (1939), and especially *Dream Girl* (1946), starring his second wife Betty Field, were notable exceptions. Rice was a prolific writer, completing more than fifty full-length plays and a number of novels, short stories, one-act plays, articles, book reviews, and movie, television, and radio scripts.

F. Durham, *Elmer Rice*, 1970.
R. Hogan, *The Independence of Elmer Rice*, 1965.
A. F. R. Palmieri, *Elmer Rice: A Playwright's Vision of America*, 1980.

RICKOVER, HYMAN G. (1900–1986) U.S. naval officer, known for supervising the development of the first atomic submarine — thus inaugurating the American nuclear-powered fleet — and for his outspoken efforts on behalf of the improvement of American education.

He was born in Makov, Russia (now Poland), where his father was a tailor. When he was still a child, the family migrated to the United States and settled in Chicago. In 1918 upon graduation from high school, Rickover entered the U.S. Naval Academy at Annapolis, Maryland.

After graduating in 1922, he served at sea for five years before returning to school to study electrical engineering in Annapolis and at Columbia University and submarine science at a submarine base in Connecticut. Subsequently he continued to serve in both land and sea posts, gradually rising through the navy hierarchy. In 1937 he received his first command post in the Philippines, and in 1939, went back to the United State to head the Electrical Section of the Bureau of Ships in Washington, where he continued to serve throughout World War II. In 1946 he was assigned to participate in the development of the atomic bomb at the Manhattan Project in Oak Ridge, Tennessee. It was there that he gained the experience that motivated his belief in, and plans for, a nuclear-powered submarine.

Fighting opposition from his superiors, he managed to obtain an assignment at the Atomic Energy Commission as head of the Naval Reactors Branch, which allowed him, in 1947, to begin working on construction of a reactor to power the nuclear submarine. His plans, which called for expenditures of more than forty million dollars, were considered risky and inordinately expensive, but he was determined and stubbornly pushed them through, alienating many government officials in the process. The submarine *Nautilus*, was launched in 1954.

When construction of *Nautilus* was well under way, he began designing a nuclear aircraft carrier and a second nuclear submarine, but controversy over his naval status prevented them from making progress. He had been passed over for promotion to admiral twice, an omission that theoretically required his retirement from the navy. However, an investigation was prompted by congressional leaders, who suspected that his superiors had deliberately failed to promote him, and he was made rear admiral in 1953.

He held influential positions in the navy for almost thirty years, but became more and more alienated from its leadership because he was so often in conflict with members of the navy establishment. He openly criticized the navy, and other aspects of American life, especially the American education system, which he compared unfavorably with its British counterpart. He loudly criticized the military-industrial complex, decrying the ties

---

Humankind will probably destroy itself and be replaced by a wiser species.

Hyman G. Rickover

---

between big business and the military, which he believed would compromise the quality of military development. With the advent of the Reagan administration, he also denounced what he considered a wasteful defense budget.

Rickover retired in 1982 but continued to be known for his difficult personality. Upon his retirement, he openly expressed regret at his role in nuclear proliferation and called for the international abolition of nuclear weapons and reactors. He established a foundation for the improvement of U.S. education. He died in Arlington, Virginia. C. Blair, *The Atomic Submarine and Admiral Rickover*, 1954.

RIF See Alfasi, Isaac

RINGELBLUM, EMANUEL (1900–1944) Historian and underground archivist during the Holocaust. Ringelblum was a native of Buczacz, Galicia. Having written his dissertation on medieval Warsaw Jewry, he received his doctorate in 1927. Ringelblum became one of the leading scholars of the YIVO Institute for Jewish Research, specializing in the history of the Jews of Warsaw. He began to work for the Joint Distribution Committee (Joint), the American Jewish welfare organization, in 1930. In October 1938 when the Germans forcibly repatriated several thousand Polish Jews to Poland, Ringelblum went to Zbaszyn near the border where they had been concentrated, as the Joint representative. His experience working with these refugees affected him deeply.

After the war broke out and the Warsaw ghetto was established, Ringelblum continued to be active in Jewish affairs. He worked for the Jewish Self-Help organization, establishing the ghetto's soup kitchens, which fed tens of thousands of ghetto residents, and advancing the welfare work of the house committees. Ringelblum was responsible for the cultural affairs section of the underground and organized an archive (known as "Oneg Shabbat," "Sabbath delight," which sought to maintain records of events as they unfolded in the ghetto. He also kept his own diary. The Oneg Shabbat archive collected information, and produced reports on the various aspects of ghetto life.

After news of the destruction of the Jews in other localities reached Warsaw, Ringelblum and his staff attempted to document the annihilation of Polish Jewry. Monographs were written on different Jewish communities, and Ringelblum considered this the most important aspect of the archive's activities. The archive staff passed on information about the deportation and murder of Polish Jews to the Polish underground, which in turn passed on the intelligence to the Polish government-in-exile in London. The data which emanated from Warsaw played a crucial role in informing the Western Allies of the fate of European Jewry. Near the end of the ghetto's existence, the archive activists hid three large metal containers, filled with the fruits of their labor. Two of the containers were found after

the war, holding the most comprehensive collection of documentary material from the Holocaust period. During the intensive mass deportation from Warsaw in the summer of 1942, Ringelblum accepted the plan for Jewish armed resistance. In March 1943, he took up an offer to leave the ghetto with his family, but at the start of the revolt on April 19, 1943, he left his sanctuary to take part in the fighting. It is not known what he went through during the fighting, but in July, he was among the Jewish inmates in the Trawniki labor camp. Dressed as a railway worker, he was liberated by members of the underground and hidden. On March 7, 1944, his hideout was discovered and he was taken to the Pawiak prison. There, he was shot to death, along with his family.

Ringelblum was the model for the main character in John Hersey's novel, *The Wall*.
J. Kermish and S. Krakowski (eds.), *E. Ringelblum on Polish–Jewish Relations during the Second World War*, 1976.
J. Sloan (ed.), *Notes from the Warsaw Ghetto: The Journal of Emanuel Ringelbum*, 1974.

ROBINSON, EDWARD G. (1893–1973) U.S. film actor. Originally named Emanual Goldenberg, Robinson was born in Bucharest, Romania, and was taken to the United States by his parents in 1902. A flair for debating and oratory at school led to a desire to make acting a profession and he became a student at the American Academy of Dramatic Art in 1911. In 1913 he made his stage debut and in the years that followed established himself as a reliable character actor, often seen in Theater Guild productions. A supporting role as a gangster in *The Racket* in 1927 showed the kind of part in which the physically unprepossessing Robinson could shine and two years later he made

Edward G. Robinson.

his first sound film, in which he was also cast as a gangster.

Little Caesar, made in 1931, became one of the early gangster classics and established Robinson as a screen star. Another notable role that made a big impression was the conscienceless tabloid editor in *Five Star Final*. At the end of the decade Robinson made a serious break with his tough screen image when he played the scientist Paul Ehrlich (q.v.) in *Dr. Ehrlich's Magic Bullet*, a role that won him acclaim. Some of his other notable roles of the 1940s were in Billy Wilder's *Double Indemnity*, Fritz Lang's (q.v.) *The Woman in the Window* and *Scarlet Street*, and another memorable gangster portrayal in John Huston's *Key Largo*.

During World War II, Robinson was active on behalf of America's war effort. He broadcast in German to Germany's anti-Nazi underground and was the first Hollywood star to appear before the troops in France after D-Day. In the late 1940s his career was clouded by blacklisting, though he testified on three occasions to the House Un-American Activities Committee that he had never been a communist. On the third occasion, in 1952, he went so far as to say that he had been duped by those organizations to which he had belonged that were later labeled communist fronts. His film career resumed, but in poorer quality vehicles than before. In the mid-1950s he had a notable stage success in the play *Middle of the Night*. Robinson was also an art connoisseur and was one of the foremost collectors of paintings in the United States.

F. Hirsch, *Edward G. Robinson*, 1975.

J. R. Parish and A. H. Marill, *The Cinema of Edward G. Robinson*, 1973.

E. G. Robinson and L. Spigelass, *All My Yesterdays*, 1973.

RODGERS, RICHARD (1902–1979) U.S. composer of musicals. His mother was a fine pianist and her husband, a doctor by profession, a good baritone. Family concerts at the Rodgers' New York apartment tended to feature numbers from the most recent musicals and operettas, and provided young Rodgers with his basic musical education. By the time he was four, he could pick out melodies at the piano, and two years later was playing with both hands. The Broadway musical fascinated the young boy who, when in his teens, spent every Saturday afternoon at a musical matinee. His favorites were those by Jerome Kern (q.v.), which he saw over and over. Rodgers would later say that "If you were at all sensitive to music, Kern had to be your idol. You had to worship Kern."

At fourteen Rodgers wrote his first song at the Wigwam summer camp in Maine. "Campfire Days" was followed with "Auto Show Girl," his first copyrighted number. His father helped him in all his musical interests and his older brother, Mortimer, presented him with his first chance to write for the theater. *One Minuet Please* was presented by the Akron Club at the Grand Ballroom of the Plaza Hotel. The fifteen-year-old Rodgers wrote all the songs, among which were "When They Rub Noses in Alaska" and "I'm a Vampire."

At seventeen Rodgers was introduced to Lorenz Milton Hart, the man with whom he would write his first musicals. The two entered Columbia University at 1919 because of its varsity show, to which they contributed their first collaboration, *Fly with Me*, a satire on undergraduate life that takes place on an island ruled by Soviets. Many musicals followed, including *A Connecticut Yankee in King Arthur's Court*, *Simple Simon*, *America's Sweetheart*, and the more famous *Babes in Arms*, *Pal Joey*, and *The Boys from Syracuse*, an adaptation of Shakespeare's *The Comedy of Errors*. After its premiere Richard Watts, Jr., of the *New York Herald Tribune* stated that "If you have been wondering all these years just what was wrong with *The Comedy of Errors*, it is now possible to tell you. It has been waiting for a score by Rodgers and Hart and direction by George Abbott."

ON RICHARD RODGERS

In the history of the American musical theatre, there has, quite simply, never been another figure to match Richard Rodgers, both in his influence in shaping the course of this form of theatrical entertainment and in the longevity of his creative powers. It is, in fact, a bit staggering to realize that if all his Broadway musicals could be presented consecutively in their original number of performances, they would run for a total of almost thirty-seven and a half years.

Stanley Green

SOME OF RICHARD RODGERS' SONGS

"Blue Room"
"Mountain Greenery"
"Thou Swell"
"With a Song in my Heart"
"Mimi"
"Isn't It Romantic?"
"Manhattan"
"The Most Beautiful Girl in the World"
"There's a Small Hotel"
"The Lady Is a Tramp"
"My Funny Valentine"
"This Can't Be Love"
"Bewitched, Bothered and Bewildered"
"Oh, What a Beautiful Morning"
"People Will Say We're in Love"
"It Might as Well be Spring"
"Some Enchanted Evening"
"There Is Nothing like a Dame"
"I'm Gonna Wash That Man Right Out of My Hair"
"My Favorite Things"

Hart died in 1943 and Rodgers, who was at his peak as a composer, looked for a new partner and found one in Oscar Hammerstein II. Their initial collaboration, *Oklahoma!*, opened a new era for the American musical. The musical broke most of the conventions of its genre. The opening number, for example, in which a simple farm woman was alone on stage, and the opening song *Oh What a Beautiful Morning*, started by the baritone off-stage, was definitely not the regular glitter spectacle musical lovers adored. But the audience and critics alike loved it. It was the first time a musical featured dances that heighten the drama and songs and story that were inseparable. More success followed with *Carousel*, in which music was again used as an integral part of the story.

Rodgers and Hammerstein's next success was *South Pacific* (1949), a musical set on an exotic island in the Pacific that tackles the subject of racism. The show ran for 1,925 performances on Broadway with the highest box office receipts (nine million dollars) of any musical to that time. It was only the second musical ever to win a Pulitzer Prize.

Their next work, *The King and I*, featured as its heroes a widowed English teacher in Bangkok and a king of Siam who really wanted to become less barbaric and more civilized. The success was once again enormous. Although there were also a few less successful efforts, *The Sound of Music* on its opening night (November 16, 1959) boasted advance ticket sales of over three million dollars, another record at the time for a Broadway musical. The story of the seven Trapp children and the love of their widowed father for their nurse, Maria, is still one of the best-loved musicals in the repertoire. Like many of Rodgers' shows it was also turned into a most successful movie.

Rodgers also wrote *All Points West* (1936), a symphonic narrative performed by Paul Whiteman and the Philadelphia Orchestra, an American folk ballet, *Ghost Town*, and some music for television and film.

D. Ewen, *Richard Rodgers*, 1972.
M. Kaye, *Richard Rodgers: A Comparative Analysis of his Songs with Hart and Hammerstein*, 1969.
D. Taylor, *Some Enchanted Evenings*, 1953.

ROMBERG, SIGMUND (1887–1951) Composer of operettas and musicals, born in Nagy Kaniza, Hungary. Romberg began early to study the violin and while in elementary school already composed his first creation, "The Red Cross March." His parents were happy with their child's musical interests but they did not want him to become a musician. He was sent to Vienna to study engineering but away from his parents' watching eyes, Romberg combined his engineering studies with composition and harmony classes with Victor Heuberger. In Vienna Romberg discovered the world of the operetta and he spent most of his evenings at theaters, savoring the works of Franz Lehar and the Strauss family.

In an attempt to persuade their son that there is more to life than music and that he should conclude his engineering degree, Romberg's parents sent him to visit England and the United States. In 1909 Romberg arrived in New York where he found a job in a pencil factory for seven dollars a week. Later he became a pianist in a small East Side café and eventually moved to a larger restaurant. He informed his parents that he had found a new home in America.

In 1914 Romberg became the staff composer for the theatrical producers J. J. and Lee Shubert. It was not an ideal position, as his creativity was never used to its full extent, but Romberg realized that this was the only way to succeed. For the Shuberts Romberg did an assortment of jobs. He added music to musicals which were imported from Europe, among them *The Blue Paradise*, and he wrote many songs for revues and spectacles. During less than two years Romberg worked on fourteen musicals, among which only *Maytime* showcased his real talent as a composer.

Eventually Romberg broke with the Shuberts and formed his own production company with Max R. Wilner. The two musicals presented by the new organization — *The Magic Melody* and *Love Birds* — were far from successful and Romberg had to return to the Shuberts. His first assignment was *Blossom Time*, an adaptation of a Viennese operetta about the life of Franz Schubert. It was admired by public and critics alike. But the next ten musicals offered Romberg no challenge whatsoever and it was only with *The Student Prince* that he once again achieved a success. *The Student Prince* had 608 performances in New York, the longest run of any of his operettas.

Eventually Romberg achieved recognition and fame and was able to work independently. *Louie the 14th*, and especially *Desert Song* and *New Moon* (with its popular line "Lover Come Back to Me"), were a few of his crowning achievements.

In the early 1930s Romberg moved to Hollywood, where he adapted his own work and wrote new scores for the screen. But even in California, Romberg did not neglect his first and prime love, writing for the theater. He once said, talking about musical trends: "I don't care what the form is. But a melody is still a melody. Nothing succeeds like a popular tune — a romantic tune. Romantic music will never die because deep at the roots of all people is the theme of love." And this theme of love is the center of all of Romberg's creations for the lyric stage.

From 1942 Romberg toured the United States with his own orchestra. In 1945 he returned to Broadway with *Up in Central Park*. Romberg died while still at work on *The Girl in Pink Tights*. This musical was produced two and half years later, when Don Walker completed the score. In 1954 the film *Deep in my Heart*, a biography of Romberg, was released.

E. Arnold, *Deep in My Heart; The Life of Sigmund Romberg*, 1949.

ROSE, BILLY (William Samuel Rosenberg; 1899–1966) U.S. impresario, producer, songwriter, and club owner. Rose began life in poverty on New York City's Lower East Side, where he was born on the kitchen table of the tenement where his family lived.

Rose began his career as a shorthand stenographer, and won many shorthand contests. Once, before a competition he broke his thumb while skating in Central Park, making it impossible for him to hold a pen. Determined to compete, he stuck his pen through a potato, held the potato in his injured hand, and won first prize. His excellence in shorthand won him a job with Bernard Baruch (q.v.), who headed the War Industries Board during World War I. Baruch later advised Rose on many of his investments.

After the war Rose traveled through the United States and on his return to New York heard that songwriters earned large amounts of money. Rose determined to become a songwriter, and after spending nine hours a day for three months studying the lyrics of hit songs of the previous thirty years, he believed he had come up with a formula for writing successful songs. He proved himself right when he wrote "Ain't Nature Grand" in 1920, earning five thousand dollars. At age twenty-four he earned over 100,000 dollars writing more songs. All told, he authored nearly four hundred songs, fifty of which were hits (including "It's Only a Paper Moon" and "Me and My Shadow").

In 1924 during the Prohibition era, he began his second career as a nightclub owner. With a combination of bootleg liquor and the patronage of gangsters and society people, his Back Stage Club earned him a small fortune. His second nightclub, the Fifth Avenue Club, catered only to the very rich and was a failure. In his subsequent nightclub venture, he decided to appeal to the middle-classes. For a price of $2.50 a couple was entitled to dinner and a show at the Casino de Paree. Rose went on to open Billy Rose's Music Hall and the Diamond Horseshoe.

During the 1930s and 1940s, Rose produced shows, his most spectacular production being *Jumbo*, a combination circus and musical show. *Jumbo* won critical acclaim, but was a financial failure. *Carmen Jones*, an all-black production of the opera *Carmen*, was more successful, running for three seasons on Broadway and becoming a movie.

It was the *Aquacade* at the 1939–1940 World Fair in New York that earned Rose his first million. The *Aquacade* was a combination water-show and musical and was the most popular attraction at the Fair, often grossing over $100,000 a week.

After World War II, Rose began writing a syndicated column that appeared in over one hundred newspapers nationwide. He began investing in real estate and art, had a "trading room" in his home, complete with ticker, telephones, and files on his investments. Rose continued investing in entertainment, purchasing the Ziegfeld Theater, which

he renamed The Billy Rose Theater, and the National Theater.

In 1965 Rose donated his sculpture collection, worth over one million dollars, to Israel. He built the Billy Rose Art Gardens in Jerusalem and placed in it over one hundred pieces, including Henry Moore's *Reclining Figure* and Rodin's *Adam*. Rose said he decided to donate the sculptures to Israel because "it is hungrier for culture than any other country in the world." On a visit to Jerusalem, he told Prime Minister David Ben-Gurion (q.v.) to melt down the sculptures for bullets in case of war. The first of his five wives was Fanny Brice (q.v.) (the story of their marriage was dramatized in the movie *Funny Lady*).

E. Conrad, *Billy Rose, Manhattan Primitive*, 1968.
P. R. Gottlieb, *The Nine Lives of Billy Rose*, 1968.

ROSE, ERNESTINE (Louise Siismondi Povtovsky; 1810–1892) Women's rights activist, influential in the passage of the first law in New York allowing married women the right to own property. She was born in Piotrkow, Poland, to an Orthodox family. It is doubtful that she was named Ernestine at birth; she probably adopted the name when she moved to England. Rose developed her feminist and humanist consciousness at an early age and said of herself that she was "a rebel at the age of five."

As she was an only child, her father, a rabbi,

Ernestine Rose.

gave her more education and freedom than was usually allowed to Orthodox girls. In the course of her education, Rose became perplexed that she was not allowed to ask deep and searching questions about the complexities of her religion and was told that "little girls must not ask questions." Once she asked her father why he fasted more than others, especially since it was detrimentally affecting his health. He replied that as a rabbi he had more obligations to God and that his devotion, which he sometimes showed by fasting, made God happy. Young Ernestine replied, "If God is pleased in making you sick and unhappy, I hate God." When she was sixteen, her mother died, leaving her some property as an inheritance. In accordance with the customs of the time, Rose's father signed a contract of marriage assigning his daughter to a man his own age. Rose rejected the contract and argued before a Polish court for her right to keep the property and remain single. She won the suit, but the following year gave most of the inheritance to her father as a demonstration of her freedom, renounced Judaism, and left Poland.

During the next few years, Rose traveled through Europe, establishing herself as a champion of human rights. In Prussia, she obtained an audience with the king to discuss a law that prohibited Jews from being in Berlin without a permit. As a matter of principle, she did not take the trouble to obtain a permit when she arrived in the city. She convinced the king to allow her to stay as long as she wished without a permit. Rose remained in Berlin for two years, earning a living from a household deodorant which she invented and sold. In Holland, Rose met a family whose mother had been jailed on a charge that she denied, leaving her husband, a sailor, with their four children. Rose drew up a petition and presented it to the king of Holland, thereby securing the woman's release.

By 1832 Rose arrived in England, where she became associated with Robert Owen, whose utopian socialist ideals she admired. With Owen and others she helped to found the Association of All Classes of All Nations (1835), whose aim was the salvation of all people by peaceful means. The following year she met William E. Rose (a non-Jew) whom she married, and they emigrated to the United States settling in New York City.

One of the leading reformers and feminists in the country in her time, Rose lectured throughout the country on women's rights, abolition of slavery, temperance, and freedom of thought. She worked for over ten years petitioning the New York State Legislature to pass a bill giving married women the right to own property. The bill was finally passed in 1848. Rose was a member of the free-thought movement and contributed to the free-thought weekly, the *Boston Investigator*. In 1843 she participated in a short-lived experimental Owenite community in Skaneateles, New York.

At the first National Woman's Rights Convention (Worcester, Massachusetts, 1850), Rose introduced a resolution calling for political, legal, and social equality with men. She worked with women's rights activists such as Susan B. Anthony and Elizabeth Cady Stanton, joining them in establishing the National Woman Suffrage Association. She maintained a hectic pace, lecturing all over the United States, receiving full emotional and financial support from her husband. However, she suffered from neuralgia and rheumatism, and ultimately Rose and her husband retired to England, where she occasionally spoke in public. In 1892 she died and was buried in Highgate Cemetery in London. Ernestine Rose never lost her Jewish identity and attacked manifestations of anti-Semitism. She referred to herself as "a child of Israel — a daughter of poor, crushed Poland, and of the downtrodden and persecuted people called the Jews."
Y. Suhl, *Ernestine P. Rose and the Battle for Human Rights*, 1959.

Excerpts from a letter Ernestine Rose wrote to Susan B. Anthony, January 9, 1899

I used my humble powers to the uttermost, and raised my voice in behalf of Human Rights in general, and the elevation of rights of woman in particular, nearly all my life. I sent the first petition to the New York Legislature to give a married woman the right to hold real estate in her own name, to which after a good deal of trouble I obtained five signatures. Some of the ladies said the gentlemen would laugh at them; others, that they had rights enough; and the men said the women had too many rights already. Woman at that time had not learned to know that she had any rights except those that man in his generosity allowed her; both have learned something since that time which they will never forget. I continued sending petitions with increased numbers of signatures until 1848–49, when the Legislature enacted the law which granted to woman the right to keep what was her own. But no sooner did it become legal than all the women said, "Oh! that is right! We ought always to have had that."

ROSENBERG, ISAAC (1890–1918) English poet and painter. Born in Bristol, he grew up in London's East End. Having left school at the age of fourteen, he worked as an apprentice with a firm of art engravers and attended art school in the evenings. He made friends with the painters Mark Gertler (q.v.) and David Bomberg and with the poet-translator Joseph Leftwich. Supported by the philanthropic efforts of a number of Jewish women, Rosenberg was able to attend the Slade School of Fine Art from 1911 to 1914. He also came into contact with W. B. Yeats and Ezra Pound, and Pound tried to get Rosenberg's poetry published.

Out of work and in poor physical and financial shape, he traveled to Cape Town, South Africa, where he stayed with his elder sister for a year.

He funded the publishing of his first pamphlet, *Night and Day*, in 1912. The second pamphlet, *Youth*, appeared in 1915, while the third and last pamphlet published a year later was a play, *Moses*.

Despite a lung disorder, Rosenberg enlisted in the British army during World War I and was subsequently stationed in France, where he wrote his "Trench Poems" and a number of versions of his play *The Unicorn*. When the Germans launched an offensive in the spring of 1918, his dawn patrol was in the direct line of German fire and he was killed. His body was never found.

Four years after his death, the first volume of his poetry was published. In 1937 his *Collected Works* were issued with a foreword by the Anglo-Jewish poet and novelist Siegfried Sassoon, who spoke of Rosenberg's "fruitful fusion between English and Hebrew culture."

When Rosenberg was nine he was sent to a Hebrew school (*heder*) but he never became interested in Judaism or Hebrew. However, he had a deep identification with his Jewish ancestry. At age sixteen, he wrote a poem called "Zion" and throughout his brief career he often was inspired by images of Zion. He wrote a moving poem "The destruction of Jerusalem by the Babylonian hordes," which concluded:

Sweet laughter charred in the flame
That clutched the cloud and the earth
While Solomon's towers crashed between,
The gird of Babylon's mirth.

In 1975, as an indication of the growing interest in his work and life, three biographies of Rosenberg appeared, while four years later, in 1979, the *Collected Poems and Other Writings* was published.

Rosenberg can be regarded as a member of the group known as the War Poets, who wrote about the World War I, and he ultimately became one of its victims. In his grim realistic non-jingoistic approach, Rosenberg — like Wilfred Owen — did not glorify war and produced poems that are quite different from those of another member of the group, Rupert Brooke, who placed considerable emphasis on the heroism that war can evoke.

Rosenberg was also an accomplished painter and an exhibition of his work was held at London's Imperial War Museum in 1990 the centenary of his birth.

J. Cohen, *Journey to the Trenches*, 1975.
J. Liddiard, *Isaac Rosenberg: The Half Used Life*, 1975.
J. Silkin, *Out of Battle*, 1972.
J. M. Wilson, *Isaac Rosenberg: Poet and Painter*, 1975.

ROSENBERG, JULIUS (1918–1953) and **ETHEL** (1915–1953) Convicted spies, whose trial and execution aroused widespread controversy. They were the first and only American civilians put to death for espionage in history of the United States. The Rosenbergs were charged with stealing the secret of the atom bomb and passing it on to the Soviet Union. Their trial and punishment received world publicity, and many books have been published on the case.

They were both brought up on the Lower East Side of New York, both were first-generation Americans, and both attended Downtown Talmud Torah. Ethel Greenglass completed high school at the age of sixteen and worked as a secretary; Julius's family was more affluent — his father had aspirations for his son to become a rabbi, but Rosenberg discovered politics. Majoring in electrical engineering at the City College of New York, he became an active member of the Young Communist League. Meanwhile Ethel had also become involved in the Communist party, and the two married after Julius's graduation. Julius Rosenberg was hired as a civilian employee of the U.S. Army Signal Corps and promoted in 1942 to the position of engineer inspector. He became chairman of the local branch of the Communist party, but in 1943 both Julius and Ethel broke off their connections with the official Communist party.

Rosenberg was fired from his job when it was discovered that he had been a member of the Communist party, but was soon able to find work at Emerson Radio Corporation. He entered into partnership with Ethel's brother, David Greenglass, and others, in a machine shop venture that failed. The Rosenberg family was not wealthy; Ethel stayed at home looking after their two sons and they lived an obscure existence until 1950.

David Greenglass, who participated in the Los Alamos atomic bomb project, confessed to having been induced to engage in espionage by Julius Rosenberg. Julius was arrested but refused to confess or to lead the authorities to other members of the alleged spy ring. The FBI files of this period show that Ethel was arrested in the hope that this would bring her husband to confess.

The Rosenbergs were charged with conspiracy

FROM ISAAC ROSENBERG'S POETRY

Break of Day in the Trenches

The darkness crumbles away -
It is the same old druid Time as ever
Only a live thing leaps at my hand -
A queer sardonic rat -
As I pull the parapet's poppy
To stick behind my ear.
Droll rat, they would shoot you if they knew
Your cosmopolitan sympathies.
Now you have touched this English hand
You will do the same to a German -
Soon, no doubt.

to commit espionage; for a conspiracy conviction, hearsay testimony is admissible and no proof is required that the conspiracy actually succeeded. During the Cold War with Russia and an era of atomic spy hysteria, the Rosenbergs were found guilty on evidence heard from David Greenglass, who cooperated with the authorities in the hope of receiving a more lenient sentense. The judge imposed the death sentence on both Julius and Ethel. Execution of an individual for conspiracy and not treason was unprecedented, but the judge and prosecution claimed that "atom spies" constituted a grave threat to national security.

The leading figures in the Rosenberg case were Jewish; Judge Irving R. Kaufman, the defense lawyer Emmanuel Bloch, and the accused. Appeal court decision of January 1952 agreed that the Rosenbergs were guilty and that it had no power to diminish a legally imposed sentence. The Rosenbergs' appeal turned into a public campaign that grew rapidly after the publication of a series of articles in the *National Guardian*, claiming that the Rosenbergs were the victims of American fascism.

After the Supreme Court refused to grant certiorari in October 1952, the *Death House Letters* were first published. These were the letters Ethel and Julius wrote to each other from their respective sections of Sing Sing prison. The Rosenberg cause became an international one. Telegrams and letters poured into the White House at the rate of over twenty thousand a week.

Fyke Farmer, a lawyer who had independenly researched the case, came to the conclusion that the Rosenbergs had been tried under the wrong law. They should have been sentenced under the Atomic Energy Act of 1946 and not the Espionage Act of 1917. Under the new statute a death penalty could only be imposed if the prosecution proved significantly that the defense had intended to injure the national defense of the United States, and only on the recommendation of the jury. The applicatons for a stay were refused, as was clemency from the president.

The Rosenbergs viewed themselves as victims of a government frame-up; the verdict in their opinion was a foregone conclusion. The date that their sentence was to be carried out was brought forward a day so as not to desecrate the Jewish Sabbath. The FBI set up quarters in the prison in the hope that the Rosenbergs would make a last-minute confession and thus stay the electrocution. Julius was taken to the electric chair first, followed by Ethel.

Even today there are two extreme schools of thought regarding the case. There are those who agree with the government version that the Rosenbergs were traitors whose theft of the "secret" atomic bomb played a significant role in ending American monopoly in nuclear weapons; and there are those who feel that the Rosenbergs could not have been important spies because they lacked the sophistication and access to highly specific scientific knowledge.

A. H. Goldstein, *The Unquiet Death of Julius and Ethel Rosenerg*, 1975.
L. Nizer, *The Implosion Conspiracy*, 1973.
R. Ronald, *The Rosenberg File: A Search for the Truth*, 1983.
J. Root, *The Betrayers*, 1963.

ROSENBLATT, JOSEPH   (Yossele; 1882–1933) Cantor and composer. Having emigrated from the Ukraine to Austria-Hungary in 1889, he first revealed his musical genius as a boy *hazzan* (cantor) touring various Hasidic communities. In 1900, he became cantor in Munkacs, a fortress of ultra-Orthodoxy, but moved a year later to Pressburg (Bratislava), where a more tolerant atmosphere prevailed and he was able to complete his musical training. His next appointment, as chief cantor of the aristocratic Deutsch-Israelitischer Synagogenverband in Hamburg (1906), gave him the opportunity to record some of his own compositions and marked an important stage in his rise to fame, if not to fortune.

With a growing family to maintain, however, the United States offered better prospects and, in June 1912, Rosenblatt moved to New York, to begin his long association with the First Hungarian Congregation (Ohab Zedek) in Harlem. Vast crowds — including non-Jewish music lovers — flocked to the services he conducted as well as to his concerts. It was after a World War I charity performance in March 1918 that Ohab Zedek's cantor made headlines, in the United States and Europe, by politely declining the Chicago Opera Association's offer to pay him the princely sum of one thousand dollars a night for singing the part of Eleazar in Halévy's *La*

Jacket of a record of Yossele Rosenblatt conducting a synagogue service.

Juive. As a staunchly observant Jew, Rosenblatt could never agree to appear in love scenes on the opera stage. This high-principled stand enhanced the cantor's reputation still further, boosting his popularity and the revenue from his concert performances.

Meanwhile, the records of Jewish liturgical music that he had been making for various American companies since 1913 sold by the tens of thousands. Mostly his own compositions, they included such perennial favorites as *Ahenu Kol Bet Yisrael, Amar Rabbi Elazar, Ke-Varakat Ro'eh Edro, Retseh Atiratam, Se'u She'arim, U-Venuhoh Yomar,* and *Ya'aleh. Kol Nidre* was recorded no less that five times, on three different labels and a single version of the Yiddish classic *Eli, Eli* (the proceeds of which were devoted to Jewish war relief) brought royalties of ten thousand dollars within the space of twelve months.

Despite his considerable earnings, "Yossele" Rosenblatt saved little, bestowing largesse on all comers at the expense of his own family and future. Worse still, he was inveigled into backing *The Light of Israel*, a shady newspaper scheme that finally collapsed, forcing the cantor into bankruptcy in 1925. Thereafter, in a long and desperate effort to repay *The Light of Israel*'s creditors, he wore himself out as a vaudeville performer, adding operatic arias and other songs to his repertoire as he traveled from one engagement to the next throughout the United States and Canada. Periodical concert tours of Europe and South America lightened the burden somewhat, and there was also an alluring offer from Warner Brothers to play the cantor's role in Hollywood's first talkie, *The Jazz Singer* (1927), a picture starring Al Jolson (q.v.), which might have restored his fortunes. However, Rosenblatt would not allow himself to be filmed, only undertaking to record nonliturgical pieces for the movie in return for one-tenth of the one-hundred-thousand dollars he had been offered.

His musical virtuosity combined with his dignified yet outgoing personality gained vast numbers of admirers. Blessed with an astonishing voice that could range over nearly three octaves, from a powerful bass to a ringing falsetto, he also wrote dozens of prayer settings for cantor and choir that have become "traditional" in the Ashkenazi synagogue. Of these, *Aheinu Kol Bet Yisra'el* and *Habet mi-Shamayim U'Re'eh* were partly a response to news of the pogroms in war-torn Russia and of Arab violence against Jews in Palestine.

As an enthusiastic Zionist, Rosenblatt did react positively to the Kol-Or Film Company's proposal that he star in *The Dream of My People*, which began production when he reached the Holy Land in April 1933. At intervals during the filming, he conducted services and gave concerts up and down the country, sang at the home of Chief Rabbi A. I. Kook (q.v.), and entranced the poet H. N. Bialik (q.v.) with his setting of *Shir ha-Ma'alot* (Psalm 126). On June 18, however, while completing work on the movie near the Dead Sea, he suffered a heart attack and died a few hours later in Jerusalem, where he was buried on the Mount of Olives.
S. Rosenblatt, *Yossele Rosenblatt: The Story of His Life*, 1954.

ROSENFELD, MORRIS (1862–1923) Pioneer of American Yiddish poetry. Born in the Lithuanian village of Boksha and reared in Warsaw and Buwalk, he enriched his traditional education by a fair knowledge of German and Polish. Acquaintance with folksongs of the *badchonim* (Yiddish jesters), with the more sophisticated lyrics of the *maskilim* (the enlightened intellectuals), and with the theatrical ditties of Abraham Goldfaden (q.v.), inspired him to compose songs from his fifteenth year.

In 1882, Rosenfeld emigrated from Russia and spent most of the next four years in London, toiling as a tailor and publishing in anarchist and socialist Yiddish periodicals his deeply felt poems of the workingmen's hard lot. In 1886 he exchanged London for New York, where for a decade he barely eked out a living in sweatshops, and where he continued to write Yiddish social lyrics of ever increasing maturity. His first two verse booklets, *Die Gloke* ("The Bell") published in 1888 and *Die Blumenkete* ("The Flower Wreath") in 1890, aroused little interest. Laboring from dawn until late at night undermined his health. Unable to break out of poverty, he gave voice to his embitterment in a satiric weekly, *Der Ashmedai*, which he coedited in 1894. Gradually his poems began to be recited at union meetings and his songs sung in tenements and cellar assemblies. His third volume of verse, *Dos Liederbuch* ("Book of Poems," 1897), contained his best poems. He characterized himself as a teardrop-millionaire who could only weep for the millions of blighted lives, enslaved men and women whose bodies and souls were broken by the unfeeling machines. He penned a poem, one of his best and most often sung, about a little boy who

Drawing of Morris Rosenfeld by Jacob Epstein, 1902.

dreams of a father whom he rarely sees during waking hours because need drives the breadwinner out of the house too early in the morning and brings him home too late at night.

After the appearance of this third poetic collection, Rosenfeld's fortune underwent a sudden change. Leo Wiener, professor of Slavic at Harvard University, discovered the talent of the poet, then still on the verge of starvation, and reviewed his book in the widely disseminated weekly, *The Nation*, wrote about him in the *Boston Transcript*, and published his poems in an English prose rendering as *Songs from the Ghetto* (1898). For American readers, the discovery of a genuine poet in the exotic Judeo-German vernacular of the immigrants, which even Jews then still deprecated as "jargon," was a sensation. The New York press soon followed with encomiums. French and German periodicals wrote about Rosenfeld, and he was translated into German. He became the first Yiddish poet to attain international vogue. Jewish contemporaries also admired him for his specific Jewish themes, his insight into the past glory and present sorrows of his people, his depicting of Jews as weary wanderers in whom a spark of hope was being fanned into a bright flame by Zionist aspirations.

After a few years of fame, his popularity waned. Adulation yielded to neglect. Poverty again assailed him. Illness plagued him. Blindness overcame him. His last years were lonely and sad.

At his death, however, thousands accompanied him to his last rest. The Yiddish playwright H. Levick wrote a play about his tragic fate. Episodes of his life formed the subject of Leon Goldenthal's novel *Toil and Triumph* (1960). His song about the candle lights that recalled Maccabean glory continued to be sung on Hanukkah evenings. Translations — such as those into English by Aaron Kramer (1955), M. I. Goldberg and Max Rosenfeld (1964), and M. J. Cohen (1979) — decade after decade, attested to his undiminished fame.

S. Liptzin, *Flowering of Yiddish Literature*, 1963.
C. A. Madison, *Yiddish Literature*, 1968.

ROSENMAN, SAMUEL IRVING (1896–1973) U.S. judge and presidential adviser. He was born in San Antonio, Texas, where his parents, immigrants from the Ukraine, ran a business until 1905, when the family moved to New York City. Rosenman received his undergraduate degree at Columbia University in 1915. The following year he entered Columbia Law School, becoming an editor of its *Law Review*. Banned from certain fraternities because he was Jewish, he later remarked, "In those days Jews were social outcasts at Columbia." In 1917 he enlisted in the army and was stationed at Camp Merritt, New Jersey. When the war ended, he arranged his continuing army duties at night so he could commute by train to Columbia during the day; he received his law degree in 1919.

Rosenman was an ambitious young lawyer who, in the days when Tammany reigned in New York,

realized that politics was the stepping-stone to success. In 1921 he received the Democratic nomination for assemblyman from the 11th district of Manhattan, a traditionally Republican district. He won a close election and held his seat until 1925, earning a reputation as a reformer. He became skilled at drafting legislation and in 1926, turning down an opportunity to run for the state senate, he accepted a more secure appointment to the Legislative Bill Drafting Commission, a nonelected position.

Rosenman began working with Franklin D. Roosevelt during Roosevelt's run for the governorship of New York in 1928. Rosenman's familiarity with state issues was invaluable to the future governor and he soon began writing Roosevelt's speeches. The two men developed a close relationship and upon Roosevelt's victory, Rosenman was offered a position as governor's counsel, in which position he played a large role drafting and advising on legislation and legal issues and writing speeches for the governor.

During the presidential election of 1932, and all subsequent elections, Rosenman worked closely with Roosevelt. He wrote the historic speech in which Roosevelt promised "a new deal for the American people," thereby coining the term *New Deal*. When he left the governor's office in 1932, Roosevelt nominated Rosenman for a judgeship in the state supreme court. His election for judge was blocked by Tammany Hall that year, but in 1933 he triumphed, remaining on the bench for ten years, and gaining a reputation as a judge who believed in and maintained judicial restraint.

While serving on the bench, Rosenman continued to advise Roosevelt. In addition to his other duties, Sammy the Rose, as the president affectionately called him, began a fifteen-year project compiling for publication the president's addresses and public papers. All thirteen volumes of *The Public Papers and Addresses of Franklin D. Roosevelt* (1938–1950) were published under his editorship. Rosenman found intensive work holding down a judgeship, editing the papers and working round the clock during election campaigns an exhilarating challenge. The grueling pace, however, finally took its toll and in 1943 he lost sight in one eye due to stress and overwork. He retired from the supreme court and became special counsel to the president, a position Roosevelt created for him.

In 1944 the president sent Rosenman to Europe with the rank of minister, to assess the nonmilitary supply needs of western Europe during the final phase of the war and in the postwar period. Rosenman relished the opportunity to become a player in international politics. While in Europe, the president summoned him to Algiers to prepare a speech on the results of the Yalta conference with Churchill and Stalin.

Rosenman was on his way back to the United States when Roosevelt died. He fully expected that the new president Harry S. Truman would dismiss him, and was surprised when Truman asked him to stay on as special counsel citing his knowlege of the state of affairs of the country and his "self-effacing zeal and patriotic devotion" that could not "yet be spared." Upon his resignation in 1946, Truman awarded Rosenman the medal of merit.

Rosenman was involved in Jewish affairs, notably in the American Jewish Committee, but did not believe in Zionism until after the tragic events of World War II convinced him it was the only salvation for Jews. He was more of an internationalist and, in 1938, advised Roosevelt not to raise the immigration quota. He believed in using private funds to create a state in Africa or South America that would serve as a haven for all refugees in the same way America did in the 17th century. However, after the war he worked for the establishment of a Jewish state and Chaim Weizmann (q.v.) addressed his first letter as president of Israel to Rosenman in tribute to his contribution.

Returning to private practice, Rosenman remained active in government affairs. Though he was happy to serve on various special committees when appointed by President Truman and by President John F. Kennedy, he declined Truman's offer to nominate him for an appointment to the U.S. court of appeals in 1951 and to the position of attorney general in 1952. He authored a book about his life with President Roosevelt, *Working with Roosevelt* (1952).

S. Hand, *Counsel and Advise*, 1979.

ROSENWALD, JULIUS (1862-1932) U.S. merchant and philanthropist. He was born in Springfield, Illinois, to family of German immigrants and worked while at school pumping a church organ, selling papers, and carrying bags for visitors to the town. At age sixteen he moved to New York and was employed in his uncle's clothing store. He opened his own retail clothing store at age twenty-one, but soon moved on to the manufacture of summer clothing. Within two years, one of the principal customers of Rosenwald and Company. was the forerunner of Sears Roebuck mailorder concern, which Rosenwald joined in 1895. After he became vice president in 1896, introducing the money-back-if-not-satisfied guarantee, the concern expanded rapidly, opening its own factories. By the time of his death, Sears Roebuck and Company mail-order catalog was distributed to over forty million addresses. In 1909 he became company president and in 1925 chairman of the board.

Rosenwald established an employees' savings and profit-sharing fund, and extensive recreation facilities for the company's employees. He was a man of modesty and attributed his wealth to luck and the efforts of those who worked with him. "I believe that success is 95 percent lunch and 5 percent ability... don't ever confuse wealth with brains.... Some very rich men who made their own fortunes have been among the stupidest men I have ever met in my life."

During World War I, Rosenwald was as a member of the Advisory Commission of the Coun-

cil of National Defense, serving as chairman of its committee on supplies. He determined that the amount of profit of any single contract for building of cantonments would be limited to 250,000 pounds sterling.

Rosenwald's success in business was overshadowed by his philanthropic activities. His gifts totaled more than fifty million dollars. He gave large sums to raise the status of American blacks, helping the Tuskegee Institute, of which he was a trustee from 1912, as well as the erection of over four thousand black schools in fourteen states. He also contributed to the establishment of sixteen YMCA and two YWCA buildings for blacks.

The Julius Rosenwald Fund, which financed these and many other charities, was founded in 1917 and by 1928 stood at twenty million dollars. A proviso stipulated that the entire principal as well as the interest be spent within twenty-five years of Rosenwald's death, as he objected to endowments in perpetuity. Inheritances extended to the third and fourth generation have proved a handicap rather than an incentive.... Coming generations can be relied upon to provide for their own needs as they arise. Among the benefactions of the fund during his lifetime were the development of medical and dental clinics for persons of moderate means, model apartments for blacks in Chicago, and the establishment of an industrial museum in Chicago. He was a trustee of the University of Chicago, to which he made a generous endowment.

Rosenwald also contributed to Jewish causes. He gave six million dollars to the American Jewish Joint Agricultural Corporation; five million dollars to Jewish relief and settlement work in Russia and Europe; half a million each to the Hebrew Union College, Cincinnati, and the Jewish Theological Seminary, New York. He headed the twenty-five-man commission that visited Europe at the end of World War I to determine the situation of Jews and was one of the founders of the Jewish Relief Committee. He was president of the Jewish Charities of Chicago, vice president of the Sinai Congregation of Chicago, and a trustee of the Baron de Hirsch Fund.

S. Birmingham, *Our Crowd*
J. Wechberg, *The Merchant Bankers*

ROSENZWEIG, FRANZ (1886-1929) German-Jewish philospher, educator, and translator. Born in Kassel to an acculturated merchant, he began to study medicine at university but moved over to philosophy, history, and classics, obtaining his doctorate at the University of Freiburg in 1912 with a thesis on Hegel and the state. Many of his relatives and friends, including his cousin Eugen Rosenstock-Huessy, had converted to Christianity and Rosenzweig seriously contemplated taking the same step. Judaism seemed to him "an empty purse" and when he discovered faith, it appeared likely that he would follow his cousin. In 1913 he decided to became a Christian, but as a Jew, not a pagan. For that he needed to become a Jew, however briefly. This meant a return to the synagogue and to achieve this he went to a small Orthodox synagogue in Berlin for High Holy Day services. The experience proved a revelation and changed his direction and his life. He reversed his decision and not only remained a Jew but devoted himself to the study of Judaism, initially with his friend, the philosopher, Hermann Cohen (q.v.). He reached the conclusion that Judaism and Christianity are both authentic manifestations of the one religious truth, an unprecendented view in Jewish theology. However, a Jew does not need to seek God; he is with God from his birth. God needs no mediation and Judaism is not a religion but a living faith.

During World War I, Rosenzweig served in a number of countries and was in the German army in the Balkans. From the trenches he conducted a lively correspondence with Rosenstock-Huessy on theological issues, eventually published as *Judaism Despite Christianity* (English, 1968). He also began to write, in the form of postcards to his mother, his magnum opus, which he completed after the war and published in 1921 under the title *The Star of Redemption* (English, 1971).

In 1920 he taught Jewish courses in Kassel and then moved to Frankfurt where he founded a new type of institute for adult Jewish education, the Freies Jüdisches Lehrhaus (Free Jewish House of Learning). Here he gathered a distinguished faculty — among them Martin Buber (q.v.), Gershom Scholem (q.v.), Ernst Simon, Erich Fromm (q.v.), Hans Kohn (q.v.) — who worked with the students in studying, translating, and publishing classic Jewish texts and examining their contemporary relevance.

From 1922 he became progressively paralyzed. Initially he was given six months to live but he survived for six yeaars, eventually communicating only by blinking his eyelid to the recitation of the alphabet. Nevertheless during this period he continued his activities, writing and editing philosophical works, translating the poetry of Judah Halevi (q.v.), and embarking with Buber on a new German translation of the Bible which reached the book of Isaiah in his lifetime. He worked on a specially built machine that helped to decipher his thoughts.

Rosenzweig was an existential philosopher. *The Star of Redemption* sees the world as consisting of three elements — man, the universe, and God, which enter a relationship through revealing themselves to one another. The three points form a triangle, which intersects with a second triangle of creation, revelation, and redemption. Their relations become historical forces, namely Judaism and Christianity — hence the star. Judaism is the fire in the star; Christianity, the rays from the star. Revelation, which is a continuing process of God, leads to redemption. Man helps to bring the universe to redemption by converting his love for God into love for his fellowman.

Rosenzweig pioneered the construction of a Jewish-Christian relation without polemic, which

INTO LIFE. (THE CONCLUSION OF *THE STAR OF REDEMPTION*)

- We Jews are eternal wanderers, deeply rooted in our body and blood. It is this rootedness in ourselves and in nothing but outselves that vouchsafes our eternity.
- Judaism is not identical with the law; it creates it. Judaism itself is not law; Judaism is — to be a Jew.
- A people's entry into universal history is marked by the moment at which it makes the Bible its own in a translation.
- To be a Jew means to be in exile.
- Jewish prayer means praying in Hebrew.
- We owe our survival to a book — the only book of antiquity that is still in living use as a scroll.
- God is not a lawgiver. But He commands.
- Asked "What does Judaism think about Jesus?" he answered "It doesn't."

Franz Rosenzweig

became the basis for the postwar dialogue. He expounded the doctine of the two covenants, which in a mysterious way are united before God. The first covenant is with the people of Israel and establishes their existence as God's people. Christianity is the Judaism of the Gentiles through which the nations of the world establish their relationship to God. The vocation of Christianity is to bring the world to God. Judaism and Christianity can recognize the other's integrity but not seek to change the other. Christianity is on its way to its goal, but Judaism has already arrived. Eventually, he felt, it would be Christianity that would change.

Rosenzweig's thought has proved very influential in postwar Jewish thinking. In a symposium conducted by *Commentary* magazine in 1965, he was credited with being the most influential modern Jewish thinker.

N. N. Glatzer, *Franz Rosenzweig: His Life and Thought*, 1961.

P. Mendes-Flohr (ed.), *The Philosophy of Franz Rosenzweig*, 1988.

S. S. Schwarzschild, *Franz Rosenzweig, 1886–1929*, 1961.

ROSH See Asher ben Jehiel

ROSS, BARNEY (1909–1967) U.S. world boxing champion and war hero. Born Barnet Rasofsky in New York City and raised in Chicago where his Orthodox immigrant parents operated a neighborhood grocery store. His family was torn apart in 1923 when his father was killed in a robbery attempt and the younger children were placed in an orphanage.

A deeply shaken Ross was quick to rebel against all his father's religious teachings. The fifteen-year-old became involved with some of Chicago's most notorious gangsters, and only an interest in boxing saved him from a life of crime. After a brilliant career in the amateur ranks, Ross became a professional fighter in 1929. Four years later he had earned enough money to reunite his family.

In 1933 he fought Tony Canzoneri in Chicago for the world lightweight title, winning a ten-round decision. Six months later he defeated Canzoneri again in a fifteen-round decision in New York City.

Weight problems persuaded him to move into the welterweight division. In 1934 and 1935 he met Jimmy McLarnin, the champion, in three bouts. Ross won the first and third contests. His initial victory over McLarnin made him the first fighter to hold the lightweight and welterweight titles simultaneously.

His boxing career ended in New York City in 1938 when Henry Armstrong gave him a terrible beating, even though Ross amazed the crowd by staying on his feet for the full fifteen rounds. His final ring record was eighty-two bouts, with twenty-four knockouts and four losses, all on decisions. He was never counted out in his ten-year career.

Describing his style Ross said, "I couldn't hit hard, but I could hit them more than they hit me. I made them fight my fight."

In 1942 the thirty-three-year-old Ross was in action again, this time as a U.S. marine in World War II. Trapped behind Japanese lines on Guadalcanal in the South Pacific, he defended his wounded comrades with rifle fire and hand grenades, killing twenty-two of the enemy. Ross's action earned him the silver star, the third highest U.S. award for valor. He came out of the encounter with shrapnel wounds and malaria. To relieve the pain he was given excessive doses of morphine by hospital personnel and was a drug addict when he was discharged from the service in 1944. Ross voluntarily surrendered himself to government officials in 1946 and was cured of his drug dependency in a federal hospital.

In later years he worked in labor-management relations, in business, and as a speaker on how to conquer narcotics addiction.

> But somehow I wasn't happy. All the years since Pa's death I had fed on bitterness and hatred, and now although I had accomplished all I had set out to do, I still found no peace. Despite Ma's assertion that Pa was looking down on me with pride, I couldn't believe it. I wouldn't admit it, even to myself, but deep down I knew the reason for this feeling. I didn't feel right — I never had felt right — since I'd thrown over the religion Pa had given me.
>
> **Barney Ross after he had won the world lightweight title in 1933.**
> **From *No Man Stands Alone*, 1957.**

Barney Ross.

His friend, Frederic P. Gehring, the Roman Catholic chaplain on Guadalcanal, said of him, "For all of his fighting heart, Barney was a gentle and devoutly religious man. His Orthodox Jewish faith was the rock that sustained him and enabled him to overcome calamities that would have crushed other men."

B. Ross and M. Abramson, *No Man Stands Alone*, 1957.

ROTHKO, MARK (1903–1970) U.S. abstract expressionist painter. Born Marcus Rothkowitz in Dvinsk, Russia, he changed his name in the early 1940s. When he was seven, he went to Portland, Oregon, with his mother and sister, to join his father and brothers. His father died soon afterwards, and Marcus worked after school for his uncle and sold newspapers to help his family. After graduation from high school, he entered Yale on a scholarship but left after two years to go to New York, where he worked at odd jobs. In January 1924 Rothko enrolled in the Art Students League. For twenty years, starting in 1929, he taught art to children in a Brooklyn synagogue school.

Rothko's early work was expressionist, and he exhibited at Alfred Stieglitz's (q.v.) Secession Gallery, as well as with the Ten, an expressionist group that opposed realism and "nationalist" art. Rothko joined the Artists' Union, which demanded government projects for artists. He worked for the

Work Projects Administration (WPA) and made a duplicate of every painting he was required to hand in.

A member of the American Artists' Congress, he left it over a resolution that he felt supported Russia's invasion of Finland and joined the Federation of Modern Painters and Sculptors, participating for many years in their group shows.

In 1943, Rothko and the painter Adolph Gottlieb wrote a letter to the *New York Times* in which they declared that "art is an adventure into an unknown world, which can be explored only by those willing to take the risks." They "favored the simple expression of the complex thought" and asserted that "the subject is crucial and only that subject matter is valid which is tragic and timeless. That is why we profess spiritual kinship with primitive and archaic art." With Gottlieb, William Baziotes, and David Hare, Rothko founded a school called Subjects of the Artist. The school folded, but the lecture programs continued at the Artists' Club.

In the 1950s, Rothko taught for three years at Brooklyn College, but was denied tenure when the other artists in the department complained about his inflexibility. In 1958 he was commissioned to paint murals for a restaurant, but when changes were made in the architecture, he refused to deliver them, giving them instead to the Tate Gallery in London. Invited to exhibit in Germany, he refused, saying that "as a Jew he had no intention of exhibiting his works in Germany, a country that had committed so many crimes against Jewry."

Rothko was a guest at the inauguration of President John F. Kennedy. In 1968 he was elected to the National Institute of Arts and Letters and in 1969 received an honorary doctorate of fine arts from Yale. Plagued by depression and by poor health, he worried about losing his creative powers, and finally committed suicide in his studio in New York.

Rothko created huge spaces of color in which floated soft-edged rectangles of glowing colors. In later years, while his canvases became larger and larger, his palette became more and more restricted and the color values darker. As one critic commented, "Rothko's concern over the years has been the reduction of his vehicle to the unique colored surface which represents nothing and suggests nothing else."

Rothko left about eight hundred paintings, 10 percent to his wife, who died six months after he did, and none to his children. The executors sold one hundred paintings to the Marlborough Gallery for $12,000 each, and gave the rest to the gallery on consignment at a commission of 50 percent. His daughter Kate, aged nineteen, suing on behalf of herself and her brother, Christopher, won a much-publicized case. She was appointed administrator in 1976, while the executors and the gallery were fined $9,250,000 to compensate for the paintings that had been sold. Four-ninths of the estate went to Kate and Christopher and the rest to the Rothko

Foundation to be distributed to the National Gallery and other museums in America and Europe.

D. Ashton, *About Rothko*, 1983.
B. Clearwater, *Mark Rothko: Works on Paper*, 1984.
P. Selz, *Mark Rothko*, 1961.

ROTHSCHILD FAMILY World-renowned bankers and philanthropists. The beginnings of the family have been traced to **Isaak Elchanan** (d. 1585) who in the 1560s acquired a house on Judengasse (the main Jewish street) in Frankfurt outside of which hung a red signboard or shield — a *rot Schild* — and his descendants took the name of the house.

Mayer Amschel Rothschild (1744–1812), founder of the house of Rothschild, attended a rabbinical school in Fürth, but after his father's death was sent to Hanover, to train in banking. He returned to Frankfurt and set up in business as a general trader, continuing to act as a money-changer. He had studied art and coins in Hanover and in Frankfurt produced an annual art catalogue of rare coins, medals, sculptures, and paintings. His wares were offered to the imperial court, and in 1769 he was appointed supplier to the principality of Hesse-Hanau.

Mayer Amschel was attracted to the radical ideas of the Enlightenment. In 1792 he attempted to found Philanthropin, a Jewish school with a modern curriculum, but the opposition within the community forced him to postpone this venture until 1804. His business prospered and by 1792 when Frankfurt was invaded by France, Mayer Amschel had become one of the wealthiest men in the city. After Frankfurt was liberated it was Rothschild who helped restore the Landgrave William's finances.

The house of Rothschild served as intermediary for Prince William and other members of royalty who bestowed honors (such as the German Order of Saint John) upon Mayer Amschel in recognition of his efficient handling of their financial affairs. In 1800 he was appointed imperial crown agent, which entitled him to bear arms, exempted him from certain taxes, and granted him freedom of movement throughout the imperial domains. The Rothschilds provided loans to Napoleon and at the same time managed the financial affairs of the exiled landgrave. They were increasingly employed in sending coded messages around Europe, conveying money in secret compartments of coaches, and concealing documents and bullion in their Frankfurt home. Mayer Amschel was instrumental in obtaining equal citizenship rights for the Jews of Frankfurt.

Mayer Amschel married in 1770 and his wife bore nineteen children of whom five boys and five girls survived. Only the sons were allowed to enter the business and all his daughters and sons-in-law were deliberately excluded — a principle followed throughout the succeeding generations of Rothschilds. In 1796 he took his two older sons **Amschel**

Mayer (1773–1855) and **Salomon Mayer** (1774–1855) into partnership and the other boys, **Nathan Mayer** (1777–1836), **Carl Mayer** (1788–1855), and **James Mayer** (1792–1868), were brought in as they reached maturity. The brothers, who became known as the "Frankfurt Five," dispersed to the capitals of Europe and within the space of two decades built up the greatest international banking syndicate in the world.

The Frankfurt House of Rothschild

Amschel Mayor took over the running of the parent bank in Frankfurt. He was conservative in his ways, led a strictly Orthodox life, dressed in the style of his ghetto ancestors. He hated traveling, partly because it made the observance of dietary laws difficult. He had a reputation for giving generously to both Jewish and non-Jewish charities. He was a firm supporter of Rabbi Samson Raphael Hirsch (q.v.), the leader of the Frankfurt Orthodox Jewish community, and he endowed a synagogue for the congregation.

In 1816 Amschel and Salomon were granted a hereditary title of nobility by the emperor of Austria in recognition of their services to the Austrian Empire. They were entitled to add "von" ("de" in France) to their names and the family's heraldic escutcheon incorporated a hand holding four arrows. (Nathan Mayer who was living in England was excluded from the honor as being "a foreign national.")

The Frankfurt bank was taken over on Amschel's death by **Mayer Carl** (1820–1886), son of Carl Mayer, but he did little to develop the parent counting house. In 1867 he was elected to the North German Reichstag, and appointed to the Prussian house of lords, the first of the only two Jews ever to be so honored.

After Mayer Carl's death his brother **Wilhelm Carl** (1828–1901) took over the Frankfurt business, which finally closed down in 1901 since there were no sons or Rothschild males to carry on the bank.

The Vienna House of Rothschild

Salomon Mayer opened the Rothschild bank in Vienna and soon developed a close relationship with Klemens von Metternich, becoming his adviser on economic policy, bringing him both new business opportunities and immense prestige. Salomon's standing was so high that Metternich banned the sale of the *Allgemeine Zeitung* for daring to criticize the Rothschilds, claiming that attacks upon the house of Rothschild reflected negatively upon the Austrian government. Salomon financed the construction of railroads to carry coal from Galicia to Vienna and in 1839, with his assistance, the Austrian Nordbahn, the first major European railway, was opened.

In 1822, all five brothers and their male descendants were raised to the rank of baron. Their coat-of-arms incorporated the Austrian eagle, a lion representing Hesse-Kassel, and a hand grasping

Baron Lionel Walter Rothschild astride a giant tortoise.

five arrows. In 1842 Salomon was made a citizen of Vienna, and his was the only Jewish family entitled to own property in the Austrian capital.

The bank in Vienna was taken over by Salomon's son **Anselm** (1803–1874). One of his greatest achievements was the establishment in 1855 of the first privately-owned credit bank in the city. Anselm acquired a fine collection of paintings by great masters and three of his children became art collectors of international repute and the fourth an accomplished musical performer and composer. His wife, Charlotte (Nathan's daughter) presided over a salon visited by artists, among them Mendelssohn, Liszt, and Rossini.

Anselm's philanthropic works included the building of over twenty schools for infants and assisting the maintenance of churches in the villages around his estates in Austria and Germany. He introduced a custom (later secured by law) whereby every Rothschild employee of twenty or more years standing would on retirement receive a pension equivalent to 101 percent of his salary.

The Vienna house of Rothschild came to an end when Anselm's grandson **Louis Nathaniel** (1882–1955) was arrested by the Nazis in 1938 and held for over a year while the Germans tried to "persuade" him to hand over the iron and coal complex at Wittkowitz to supply their munitions factories. Louis had previously persuaded the Czech and

Austrian governments to transfer ownership to a company in London, the major shareholder of which was N. M. Rothschild and Sons.

The Naples House of Rothschild

In 1821 **Carl Mayer** set up a bank in Naples. He provided loans for the Neapolitan army of "liberation," and the kingdom of Naples soon became totally dependent upon the Rothschilds for its finance. Carl remained the conservative pious Jew of the Frankfurt ghetto and did little to develop local commercial opportunities.

The Paris House of Rothschild

James settled in Paris in 1812, acting as agent for Nathan in London. After Napoleon's defeat in 1813, the Rothschilds became official bankers to the allies. They also acceded to a request to supply French gold to the English forces advancing under the Duke of Wellington.

When Napoleon returned to France in 1815 the Rothschilds once again financed the armies, and after Napoleon's defeat at Waterloo, they handled the indemnity payments.

Stocky, squat-faced, and red-haired, James was the target of the anti-Semitic attacks of the Parisian upper classes and was irritated by his exclusion from the city's fashionable salons and clubs because of his Jewish background.

In 1816 he reorganized the Paris bank as Rothschild Frères. Like the other houses, it remained a distinct business entity but regularly circulated information about its accounts and profits to the other Rothschild banks. After the Congress of Aix-la-Chapelle in 1818, James succeeded in floating a loan to the French government and helped the restored government pay off its war indemnity.

In 1824 James married Betty, daughter of Salomon, who had a salon in Paris that attracted many of the great writers, artists and musicians of the age. Chopin made his Paris debut at the Rothschilds.

James, like the other Rothschild brothers, was looked upon as the leader of the local Jewish community. He built numerous orphanages, hospitals, housing projects for the poor, sick and elderly throughout France. In 1815 he helped organize a Jewish delegation to the Congress of Vienna which was successful in obtaining a declaration granting equal citizenship to Jews living in the states represented there.

The youngest of the Frankfurt Five, James was an innovative, forceful and successful businessman and after Nathan died in 1836, it was natural for him to assume the leadership. He led the family into the era of the industrial revolution, and during the 1830s and 1840s the Rothschilds became bankers to commercial enterprises on a major scale. In the 1830s he formed a company to construct the railroad system in Paris, and in 1845 the capital for the Chemin de Fer du Nord was provided by James. Rothschild Frères also helped the Banque de France out of a severe monetary crisis by providing

large consignments of gold.

James ruled with a rod of iron and was referred to by the younger Rothschilds as "the Great Baron." He was a warm and generous person, but was subject to moods, often of violent anger, that frightened his subordinates and earned the respect of his colleagues. His main obsession was collecting almost anything of worth — paintings, antique furniture, and objets d'art.

During the Crimean War, James came to the aid of the Jewish community in Palestine by setting up the Mayer Rothschild Hospital in Jerusalem, the first modern medical institution for Jews. He also endowed a fund for the support of poor mothers and a vocational school, and set up refugee shelters.

When James died in 1868, his son **Mayer Alphonse** (1827–1905) became the head of the Paris house and in 1869 president of the board of directors of the Chemin de Fer du Nord. During the Franco-Prussian War the Rothschild bank put its carrier pigeon service at the disposal of the government. At the end of the war, the French government called on Alphonse to arrange loans for the payment of its indemnity to the Prussian government.

Alphonse was elected president of the Consistoire Central (the central organization of the French Jewish community) and was one of the major contributors to the building of the synagogue on the rue de la Victoire, opened in 1875. He supported Jewish schools, orphanages and social welfare projects.

Alphonse too was a passionate lover of art. He had impeccable taste, a wide knowledge, and the wealth to buy anything that caught his discerning eye. His house on Rue Saint-Florentin contained sculptures, antique statues, paintings by old masters (including some of Europe's rarest masterpieces), furniture, a library of rare and unusual books, and numerous objets d'art. He became a patron of contemporary artists and was elected to the French Academy. He donated works of art to over two hundred institutions throughout France.

James' youngest son **Edmond James** (1845–1934) studied archaeology and science, traveled widely, was fond of sport, and climbed the Matterhorn only shortly after it was first conquered in 1865. In 1877 he married Adelheid (daughter of Wilhelm Carl), whose Orthodox upbringing in Frankfurt had a profound effect on him.

In 1882 the first modern agricultural settlers in Palestine ran into financial difficulties. Through the intervention of the chief rabbi of France, Zadoc Kahn, Edmond acceded to the request of the settlers at Rishon Le-Zion to provide a sum of 30,000 francs to save the settlement from ruin. However, he refused the request of Rabbi Samuel Mohilever, an active member of the early Zionist movement, Hovevei Zion, to support a mass movement of Jews wishing to flee persecution in Europe, and settle in Palestine. Edmond explained that as a pragmatist he was prepared to finance an experimental settlement of Russian Jews provided that they would submit to strict supervision by his agents. He insisted that his support was to remain anonymous and reserved the right to withdraw his support if the settlers refused to obey his supervisors' instructions. He stipulated that the immigrants were to work on the land and not set up as traders and craftsmen. They were not to let or sublet their land holdings, nor were they to hire labor.

Athough Edmond envisaged large-scale settlement as a major contribution toward the solution of the Jewish problem, he realized that settlement would increasingly be opposed by the Turks. It was essential not only to establish new settlements and to consolidate the existing ones with finance, but also with agricultural and professional guidance as well. However, his supervisors had gained their expertise in France, in climatic conditions not always similar to those of Palestine, and they often antagonized the settlers with their elitist attitude, leading to revolt in several settlements.

In the course of his travels Edmond looked out for plants that would flourish on the soil of Palestine. The grapefruit grown in Israel today is a result of one of his experiments.

Because of the success of the baron's settlements, other existing settlements came under his protection and guidance. As their numbers grew, he provided houses, schools, synagogues, and free medical treatment. In 1887 Edmond first visited Palestine and laid plans for the building of a hospital to provide free treatment for malaria, yellow fever, trachoma, and other endemic diseases. He also proposed to purchase the Western Wall in Jerusalem in exchange for land that he would buy elsewhere, but was persuaded by the Sephardic rabbis to desist because of possible reprisals against the Jewish community of Jerusalem. He gave instructions for the purchase of land throughout the country for the construction of new settlements. During his second visit in 1893, Edmond visited the glass factory he had helped establish at Tantura for the manufacture of bottles for the growing wine industry. He visited the country again in 1899 and 1914 and during his last visit in 1925 was given a royal welcome by the entire Jewish community who called him "the father of Jewish settlement."

In 1900 he transferred the colonies under his aegis to the Jewish Colonization Association (JCA) set up in 1891 by Baron Maurice de Hirsch (q.v.) and the Jewish National Fund. In 1923 he created the Palestine Jewish Colonization Association (PICA) to help settle members of the free professions and provide support for numerous industrial enterprises and educational institutions in Palestine.

Despite all his good works on behalf of the Jewish community in Palestine, Edmond was not a political Zionist. In a meeting with Theodor Herzl (q.v.) in 1896, the Baron rejected the idea of a charter explaining that he did not believe that the geopolitical situation of the time would enable this, and that unorganized mass immigration of inexperienced persons and settling them on the land without proper training would be disastrous. However, in 1929 he accepted the position of honorary president of the expanded Jewish Agency.

Edmond appointed his son **James Armand Edmond** (1878–1957) as his assistant to control his Palestine ventures. James settled in England and served in the British army during World War I, going to Palestine on General Allenby's staff. He recruited volunteers for the Palestine battalion of the Jewish Legion and served as liaison officer to the 1918 Zionist Commission in Palestine. In 1924 he was appointed president for life of PICA, through which he helped to finance the Palestine Electric Corporation and other industrial enterprises in the Haifa Bay area. He was a Liberal member of Parliament from 1929 to 1945, the last M.P. to maintain the old parliamentary tradition of always attending the House of Commons in a top hat. On his death he left a bequest for the construction of Israel's parliament, the Knesset.

The London House of Rothschild

In 1798, **Nathan Mayer** set up a textile business in Manchester, and at the same time served as agent for the Frankfurt bank. This short, stout, thick-lipped, red-headed Jew with a heavy German accent was often mocked by the local traders, but was accepted by them because he always paid promptly in cash for the goods he bought. He cut production costs, sold cheaply, and delivered promptly. During the Napoleonic wars he encountered great difficulty in shipping his goods to the Continent because all the ports were closed to English ships.

Nathan expanded his business and established himself as a financier, becoming official broker to the court of Hesse-Kassel, which enabled him to launch his banking operation on a large scale, speculating heavily in gold. He opened an office in London and in 1811 sold his Manchester concern in order to devote himself completely to running the complex operation of maintaining the flow of trade across the Channel. He was heavily involved with the illicit bullion trade, using a group of Kent coast smugglers to set up a fast and efficient cross-Channel service for cargo and couriers.

By 1815 Nathan had become the principal financier to the British government, raising loans to underwrite its campaign against Napoleon. Through the other houses of Rothschild and a large network of agents and couriers, Nathan was better informed about European affairs than anyone in London. In 1820 his social standing was considerably enhanced by his appointment as Austrian consul general in London. During the 1825–1826 crisis, when 145 banks crashed in England, Nathan saved the Bank of England and the British government from disaster by providing a total of about 10 million pounds from his own stocks of gold sovereigns and by organizing shipments from other countries.

Nathan was associated with numerous philanthropic activities. He helped establish the Jews'

The Rothschild family's original house in the ghetto of Frankfurt.

1858 that Lionel was able to take his place on the Liberal benches, after he was granted permission to select the wording of the oath he wished to swear. After thirty years of working for Jewish emancipation and eleven years of struggling to be seated he was at last in Parliament. He remained there for sixteen years — without ever making a speech!

Lionel bought a country estate in Aylesbury, the first of a series of great Rothschild homes in England. By 1870 the extent of their property in the Vale of Aylesbury was so great that it was commonly known as "Rothschildshire."

The most celebrated coup in the family's history was brought off by Lionel when in 1875 he assisted his old friend Benjamin Disraeli (q.v.), then prime minister of England, to purchase the khedive of Egypt's Suez Canal shares. He arranged a loan of four million pounds sterling and netted a profit of a quarter million pounds from the commission.

In 1878 Lionel succeeded in getting the issue of Jewish rights placed on the agenda of the Congress of Berlin, and among the terms of the final agreement were the granting of full citizenship to all Jews in Romania, Bulgaria, Serbia, and Montenegro.

Lionel's son **Nathan (Nathaniel) Mayer** (1840–1915), known as Natty, succeeded Lionel as head of the London house. Together with his wife Emma, an accomplished artist and pianist, he built over four hundred modern cottages on their estate at Tring. The houses were equipped with running water and sewage systems. They kept the farms, farm buildings, and churches in good repair, providing amenities such as village halls, clubs, and schools and also operated medical, pension, and social benefit schemes.

To cope with the influx of Jews fleeing persecution in eastern Europe at the end of the 19th century, Natty established housing projects (the Rothschild Dwellings and the Nathaniel Dwellings) in the East End of London to provide maximum accommodation for minimum rent. In protest against the persecution, the Rothschilds stopped trading with the Russians, but when the tsarist regime relaxed enforcement of anti-Jewish laws, business was resumed.

In 1885 Natty was raised to the peerage, becoming the first practicing Jew to take his seat in the House of Lords.

Natty's elder son, **Lionel Walter** (1868–1937), the second baron, collected birds, butterflies, and moths from the age of five. He mounted his specimens and studied and catalogued them. By the age of thirteen his collection was so extensive that a taxidermist was employed to help him look after it. In 1899 the collection was moved to a special building at Tring and was opened to the public. It became the finest private collection of natural history specimens in the world and Walter became a famous zoologist.

Together with the curators of the museum Walter published books, articles, and monographs

Free School in London, and during the time he served as warden of the Great Synagogue drew up a scheme for alleviating the suffering among poor London Jews. During the potato famine in Ireland in the late 1840s Nathan was instrumental in setting up the British Association for the Relief of the Extreme Distress in the Remote Parishes of Ireland and Scotland to raise funds to provide food and clothing for those hard hit by the famine.

After Nathan's death his son **Lionel Nathan** (1808–1879) became the head of the London house. In addition to running the family concerns he was active in politics, and in 1847 was the first British Jew to be elected to the House of Commons as the Liberal representative of the City of London. However, he was not permitted to take his seat since he refused to swear the Christian oath required as part of the procedure of admission to the house. Public demonstrations were organized by the Board of Deputies of British Jews in support of the Jews' Disabilities Bill, and a petition containing 250,000 signatures was submitted to the government. The bill was passed by the House of Commons but was rejected by the House of Lords. Although repeatedly reelected, it was not until

based on their study of the collection. The Tring Museum periodical, *Novitates Zooligicae*, published forty volumes over a period of forty-five years. Walter's major contribution to science was his systematic zoological classification. The names of over 250 species and subspecies of plants, insects, mammals, fish, amphibians, etc., which he first recognized and catalogued bear his name.

In 1899 Walter was elected to Parliament as member for Aylesbury, but because of a speech impediment he hardly ever spoke in the House. He was an eccentric, and drove a carriage drawn by three zebras and a pony to an audience at Buckingham Palace.

Walter headed the Zionist movement in England and throughout the years of World War I had several interviews with Arthur James Balfour, the foreign secretary, advocating the idea of a Jewish home in Palestine. He held meetings with Jewish leaders and interest groups, liaised with overseas Zionist organizations, and endeavored to counteract the considerable opposition to the movement (not the least by anti-Zionist Jews), in the press and through private correspondence. The famous Balfour Declaration announcing the British government's intention to create a Jewish national home in Palestine, was addressed to him.

Nathaniel Charles (1877–1923) shared his brother's passion for natural history. He wrote *The Lepidoptera of Harrow* while still a schoolboy, and as a youth visited many remote regions around the world to collect species of butterflies. He set up a nature reserve at Ashton Wold. Charles' principal interest was fleas and his major discovery was the plague-carrying species, a rat-borne flea parasite. He wrote 150 papers on about 500 species and subspecies of fleas. In 1912 he formed the Society for the Promotion of Nature Reserves for the conservation of important natural habitats. His survey of 248 such reserves served as the basis for all future surveys.

Nathaniel Mayer Victor (1910–1990) succeeded his uncle Walter as third baron in 1937. During World War II, Victor served in the antisabotage section of British Intelligence where he invented a method for neutralizing bombs placed on ships. He was awarded the George Medal for defusing a bomb concealed in the hold of a ship.

Victor devoted much of his time to scientific research concerning the physiology of eggs and the fertilization of sperm, especially in invertebrate animals. From 1950 to 1970 he was the assistant director of research in the Department of Biology at Trinity College, Cambridge. In 1953 he was elected a fellow of the Royal Society.

In 1961 Victor accepted a consultancy with the Shell Oil Company, and became responsible for the entire research program of the Royal Dutch Shell group. From 1970 to 1974 he was head of the Central Policy Review Staff, a think tank set up by Edward Heath's Conservative government. Under Victor's direction this body produced reports on the coal industry, shipbuilding, nuclear power, and

ROTHSCHILD HUMOR

The wealth of the Rothschilds was a favorite subject of Jewish humor in eastern Europe. Here are some samples:

Two beggars visiting a cemetery in Paris see the magnificent Rothschild tomb. "Oi," says one, "the way some people live."

"If I were Rothschild, I'd be even richer than Rothschild." "How?" "I'd teach Hebrew on the side."

A beggar went to Rothschild's home to ask for a gift — and was unceremoniously ejected. When he came home, he told his wife, "Poor Rothschild is going through hard times. I looked through the window and saw that both his daughters have to play at the same piano."

Rothschild's son was suprised to see his father driving in a plain carriage whereas he himself had a beautiful carriage and magnificent horses.
"Father, why are you in such a simple carriage? Just look at mine." "That, my son, is because you have a rich father."

At a funeral of a Rothschild a large crowd goes to the cemetery and as the service is being held, a man on the edge of the multitude is crying so loudly that his sobs can be heard near and far. After the burial is over, a member of the family comes up to the man and says, "I am touched that you are so moved. But how come? After all, you aren't one of the family." "That's what I'm crying about," says the man.

Two brothers who are beggars go every week to Rothschild's home in Paris where the secretary always gives them each a coin. One week only one brother arrives and Rothschild asks him where is the other. "He died" is the answer. Rothschild expresses his sympathy. Then the secretary gives him his coin but the beggar demands, "and what about the other coin?" Rothschild intervenes. "That used to be for your brother — but you said he was dead." The beggar looks straight at Rothschild and responds, "And since when are you his heir?"

the computer industry. He also served as chairman of a Royal Commission on Gambling, whose report suggested ways in which gamblers could be protected against fraud. In 1975 he was appointed director and executive chairman of N. M. Rothschild and Sons and formed a company enabling the public to invest in biotechnical enterprises. He was a collector of manuscripts of Jonathan Swift and 18th-century first editions. Through the Rothschild Trust, Victor supported the Weizmann Institute in Rehovot and helped sponsor educational television in Israel. He also presented a golf course to Caesarea.

Victor's publications include *Fertilization* (1956), *A Classification of Living Animals* (1961), *Meditations of a Broomstick* (1977), and *Random Variables* (1984).

F. Morton, *The Rothschilds*, 1962.
C. Roth, *The Magnificent Rothschilds*, 1939.
M. Rothschild, *Dear Lord Rothschild; Birds, Butterflies & History*, 1983.
D. Wilson, *Rothschild; A Story of Wealth and Power*, 1988.

ROTHSTEIN, ARNOLD (1882–1928)

U.S. gambler, fixer, and the leading criminal mind of his time. Born in New York City, he was the prodigal son of a respected middle-class merchant. Rothstein is credited by historians with being the pioneer big businessman of American organized crime. Best known as the man who allegedly fixed the 1919 baseball World Series, Rothstein masterminded the largest gambling empire in the United States. With access to unlimited cash, he financed bootlegging and narcotics deals, bought judges and public officials, and loaned money to legitimate businesses.

Rothstein moved freely in all circles, from politicians and statesmen to bankers and bums. On his payroll at one time or another were notorious mobsters, such as Waxey Gordon, Jack "Legs" Diamond, and Frank Costello. Rothstein's wide-ranging influence earned him the title of "Czar of the Underworld." His fame was such that in 1925 he served as the inspiration for Meyer Wolfsheim, in F. Scott Fitzgerald's *The Great Gatsby*, and later for Nathan Detroit in *Guys and Dolls*.

Rothstein tutored underworld luminaries, such as Johnny Torrio, Lucky Luciano, and Meyer Lansky (q.v.), in the virtues of forming alliances independent of ethnic considerations. As he pointed out, the dollar had only one nationality and one religion — profit. Rothstein also taught these young hoodlums how to dress and behave in public. Lucky Luciano testified to Rothstein's influence on him: "He taught me how to dress, how not to wear loud things, but to have good taste. He taught me how to use knives and forks and things like that at the dinner table. If Arnold had lived a little longer, he could've made me pretty elegant. He was the best etiquette teacher a guy could ever have."

Rothstein was shot over a gambling debt in the Park Central Hotel. True to the criminal code, he refused to divulge the name of his killer before he died.

L. Katcher, *The Big Bankroll: The Life and Times of Arnold Rothstein*, 1958.

RUBINSTEIN, ANTON GRIGORYEVICH

(1829–1894) Russian pianist, composer, and educator. He was born in Vykhvatinetz, Podolia, to a family of Jewish merchants who were baptized in 1831. The family moved to Moscow, where Anton's father opened a small pencil factory and his mother gave him, and his brother Nicolai their first piano lessons. Rubinstein's only piano teacher was Alexandre Villoing in Moscow, who in 1839 took the ten-year-old pianist on a prodigy tour to Paris and eventually across the rest of Europe.

In 1844 the family settled in Berlin, but when Anton's father died, the rest of the family returned to Russia. Anton, however, spent two years in Vienna, living in great poverty, surviving by giving piano lessons. In 1848 he returned to Moscow and was taken up at once by the grand duchess Elena Pavlovna, sister-in-law of the tsar. In 1859 Rubinstein and the duchess founded the Russian Musical Society and three years later the Saint Petersburg Conservatory. It was there that Rubinstein began to establish himself as a reformer of Russian musical thought, advocating German academism and conservatism and opposing the growing national school of composition. He introduced European methods into music education and was himself the first Russian musician who was both an important composer and performer. Later, Rubinstein left the conservatory and resumed his solo career — he was compared to Liszt as one of the greatest pianists of his generation — and went on an extensive American tour in 1872–1873, with violinist Henryk Wieniawski. For 216 concerts the pianist earned an unheard of sum of 46,000 dollars. But the tour, which opened in a grand manner in New York, deteriorated as it went on far too long. Rubinstein was angry at the time and eventually commented in his autobiography: "So profound was my dissatisfaction, that when several years later I was asked to repeat my American tour, I refused point-blank."

Rubinstein was not a particularly pleasant man. He was a gambler, a womanizer, and a hard drinker who liked to do everything in a big way. During recitals he often ruined the pianos. He was also known as a sloppy pianist who lost control whenever he got excited. A colleague asserted bitterly that "Rubinstein can make any quantity of errors during his performance, and nobody is disturbed by it; but if I make a single mistake it will be noticed immediately by everyone in the audience." The music critic of London's *Musical World* commented in 1881: "Surely the passionate Rubinstein is a phenomenon — a volcanic eruption attended by fire, noises and smoke. The thing is heroic in character and proportions. We may not recognize here a pianist in the act of performing pianoforte music, but we are in the presence of an amazing display of musical impulse and inspiration which fascinate even those who do not approve." According to this critic, Rubinstein was one of those pianists "who evade criticism by the very splendor of their faults not less than by the glory of their excellences."

In 1890 Rubinstein established the Rubinstein prize, an international competition for young male musicians. There was one prize for piano playing and another for composition, and the competitions were held in Saint Petersburg, Berlin, Vienna, and Paris.

Rubinstein's compositions were well-received at the time, especially his second symphony, *The Ocean*, and his opera, *The Demon*. But even his better works show signs of haste. Once critic commented that "he has not the necessary concentration of patience for a composer."

Rubinstein is not remembered for his many compositions, which are now seldom performed. He is remembered for his reputation as a pianist, for being, in the words of Harold C. Schonberg, "a titanic figure who blasted the piano and snapped its strings, and yet who could be capable of the most intimate, sensuous playing."

His brother **Nicolai Gregoryevich Rubinstein** (1835–1881) was also a brillian pianist. He founded the Moscow Conservatory in 1864 and headed it for the rest of his life.

C. D. Bowen, *Free Artist: the Story of Anton and Nicholas Rubinstein*, 1939.

A. Hervey, *Rubinstein*, 1913.

A. Rubinstein, *Autobiography of Anton Rubinstein*, 1890.

To the Jews I am a Christian, to the Christians a Jew, to the Russians a German, to the Germans a Russian, to the classicists a Wagnerite, to the Wagnerites a reactionary. I am neither flesh nor fowl — an unfinished person.

Anton Rubinstein

RUBINSTEIN, ARTHUR (1887–1982) Pianist. Born in Lodz, to a merchant family, as soon as young Artur Rubinstein saw the piano he became attached to it. At three he was taken to Berlin and played for Joseph Joachim, who was impressed with the young prodigy. At the mature age of seven he performed in a charity concert, playing compositions by Mozart, Schubert, and Mendelssohn. He studied in Warsaw and on a return visit to Berlin played once again for Joachim. Rubinstein remained in Berlin where he continued his studies and where Joachim himself conducted his debut playing a Mozart concerti (at the age of thirteen). Recitals in Hamburg and Dresden followed and paved the way for a very busy schedule of concerts and recitals all over Europe. In 1902 Rubinstein performed with the Warsaw Symphony, conducted by Emil Mlynarski (his future father-in-law).

The young pianist was very soon able to support himself and he traveled to Paris, where he met some of the prominent musical figures of the time. In 1906 Rubinstein made his American debut as a soloist with the Philadelphia Orchestra in Carnegie Hall.

Rubinstein married Aniela Mlynarska in 1932 and after his marriage the pianist, who used to tour extensively, withdrew from the concert stage for a lengthy period in which he restudied his repertoire. At this time Rubinstein was the first pianist hero of the electrical era of recordings, his many albums advancing his career at unprecidented speed. He was an outstanding interpreter of Chopin but his other performances, such as Mozart and Beethoven and Brahms, were notable. He also favored Spanish music and 20th-century French compositions.

Rubinstein became an American citizen in 1946 and after World War II returned to perform in his native land as well as to play in the Soviet Union. But he never returned to perform in Germany. In a very revealing statement the pianist once said that there are only two countries in which he will never play, Tibet and Germany: "Tibet is too high, Ger-

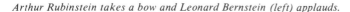

Arthur Rubinstein takes a bow and Leonard Bernstein (left) applauds.

many is too low." He played vividly into his eighties, performing, more often than not, two or even three piano concerti during the same evening. He performed regularly in Israel, where in 1974 the International Arthur Rubinstein Piano Competition was inaugurated with the pianist's warm blessing. He attended each of the competitions in his lifetime. In his last years, he went blind. He died in Geneva, where his body was cremated; the ashes were flown to Jerusalem for interment.

Rubinstein was the perfect party host, a flamboyant character who enjoyed living life very much as his two autobiographies — *My Young Years* (1973) and *My Many Years* (1980) — convey. It was still in his early days in Berlin that the young pianist discovered that there is much more to life that just music. Good food, good conversation, fancy clothes, wine, cigars, and girls were as important as his piano, and he said that he believed in "wine, women, and song" — of which 80 percent were women. In 1975 a film documentary, Artur Rubinstein, *Love of Life* was produced, capturing the essence of a pianist who was adored by all.
B. Gavoty, *Artur Rubinstein*, 1956.

RUBINSTEIN, HELENA (1870–1965) Cosmetician. Born in Cracow Poland, to a poor family with eight daughters, She began to study medicine but left in 1902 for Australia. Here she noticed that Australian women had dry skin because of the hot climate. Opening a beauty salon in Melbourne, she began to sell a cold cream made with one of her mother's Polish recipes, offered to clients along with a free consultation. The salon was an instant success.

She left Australia for Europe, settling in London in 1900. At that time, there was no beauty industry and women made their own beauty aids. After studying with top dermatologists, she started a salon in Mayfair, which was an immediate society success; her clients included Queen Alexandra. In 1912, she opened another salon in Paris, where her customers included the novelist Colette and the actresss Sarah Bernhardt (q.v.). In 1915 she went with her first husband, an American journalist, to New York, opening a salon on West Forty-ninth Street. She soon had salons all over the country, distributing her products to improve the "terrible complexion" of American women. She initiated the concept of the traveling saleswomen who sold make-up "to transform" the ordinary woman. After the World War I, she returned to Paris and was recognized as Europe's leading cosmetician, noted for her inventiveness and keen business acumen. She spent much time in her laboratories working on her products, of which there were eventually over a thousand bearing her name.

Shortly before the 1929 stock-market crash, Helena Rubenstein sold her business to Lehman Brothers for eight million dollars. The following year, she bought it back for two million dollars. Asked how she had made six million dollars so easily, she answered, "All it took was a little chutz-

> **PICASSO ON HELENA RUBINSTEIN:**
>
> She is as much a genius as I.

pah." In 1938 she married a second time, to a Russian prince, and was now known as Princess Gurieli. She tried a men's salon called House of Gurieli in New York, but it did not succeed.

After World War II she opened branches and manufacturing facilities the world over. By now the beauty industry reached out to the middle class and she enjoyed an immense personal fortune. She established homes in the United States and France and maintained famous collections of jewelry and art. She was a voracious collector of modern art and was friends with most of the leading artists of her time.

Glamorous and tempestuous, Helena Rubinstein was well known in international society and was a patron of the arts, founding the Helena Rubinstein Foundation, which gave gifts to museums, colleges, artists, and institutions for the needy. The Tel Aviv Museum benefited from her generosity when it received the Helena Rubinstein Pavilion containing her collection of miniature period rooms. She also built one of her factories in Israel.
P. O. Higgins, *Madame; an Intimate Biography of Helena Rubinstein*, 1971.
H. Rubinstein, *My Life for Beauty*, 1966.

RUBINSTEIN, IDA (1885–1960) Dancer. Born in Saint Petersburg, she was more celebrated for her beauty than for her dancing, but was nevertheless a leading member of the Diaghilev Company (1909–1911), appearing in title roles in such ballets as *Cléopâtre* and *Schéhérazade* (both choreographed by Michel Fokine). An orphan, Rubinstein was reared by an aunt, but inherited a large fortune when she came of age. This enabled her to follow a stage career that her relatives frowned on.

She studied dancing privately with Fokine — probably because, being Jewish, she was not accepted into the imperial school — and she also attended drama school. Fokine choreographed a *Salome* solo for her, which was stopped by the censors. Diaghilev saw her in this role and chose her to appear in *Cléopâtre*. This caused a sensation in Paris because at one point, Rubinstein made her entrance on a litter wrapped up like a mummy and the coverings were gradually removed to reveal her beautiful body.

Jean Cocteau said of her: "She is too beautiful, like a perfume that is too strong."

Even when she had left him, Diaghilev could not refrain from describing her as "the mysterious, extravagant, biblical Rubenstein," and Gabriele D'Annunzio said that as an artist her "whole personality breathed a mystic ardor" — but then he, like Leon Bakst (q.v.), was in love with Rubinstein.

When Rubinstein decided to form her own company (1928–1935), she commissioned music from Ravel (*Boléro, La valse)* and *Stravinsky (Le baiser de la fée*), all choreographed by Bronislava Nijinska (sister of the famous Vaslav Nijinsky). Among the other choreographers from whom she commissioned works was Léonide Massine. Among dancers in her company were David Lichine (q.v.) and Roman Jasinsky. When she retired she gave commissioned works to the Paris Opera.

Though she is remembered for her roles in ballets, Rubinstein appeared also in some plays. Her last stage performances were in Arthur Honegger's *Jeanne d'Arc au bucher* (1938) to Paul Claudel's text in Basel and in Orléans (1939).

RUMKOWSKI, MORDECHAI CHAIM (1877–1944) Chairman of the Lodz Jewish Council during World War II. Rumkowski was made chairman of the Jewish Council on October 13, 1939, and given wide powers by Hans Biebow, the German responsible for the ghetto. Biebow directed Rumkowski to set up workshops in which the ghetto's Jews would labor for the Germans; eventually Rumkowski established 120 such places. He believed that by working for the Germans the situation of the Jews would improve. Later, after the deportations had begun, Rumkowski believed that by cooperating with the Germans and making as many Jews as possible important to the German war economy, Jews would be saved.

Rumkowski earned a reputation for his organizational skill. He was diligent, but as time went on he concentrated on gaining more and more power into his own hands, and became dictatorial. When the German administration ordered the ghetto to print its own money, in lieu of Polish or German money, Rumkowski's picture adorned the bills. Later, opponents of Rumkowski were included in deportation transports.

After the establishment of the Chelmno extermination camp in December 1941, the Germans made Rumkowski take part in organizing transports from Lodz to the camp. Rumkowski strove to convince the Germans to deport fewer people, but his pleas were not answered. Some 52,000 Jews were deported from Lodz to the camp between January and May 1942. Since Rumkowski and his staff designated who would be deported, they earned much hatred among the ghetto population. During the next big deportation in September, the Germans did not employ Rumkowski. They deported over 22,000 people, using brutality. Rumkowski became more convinced that he could ameliorate the tragedy by working with the Germans. The final destruction of the ghetto began late in June 1944. In August all the workplaces and the Jewish Council were closed down. Rumkowski and his family were sent to Auschwitz, where he perished.

Because of his dictatorial mien and his policy of giving the Germans "limbs in order to save the body," the figure of Rumkowski has emerged from the Holocaust clouded in controversy. There are those who blame him for the destruction of Lodz Jewry. Others point out that in the summer of 1944 Lodz was the last large ghetto in Eastern Europe, with over 70,000 residents, and had the Soviets liberated it before the final deportations, tens of thousands of Jews would have been saved.

Rumkowski is the model for the leading character in Leslie Epstein's novel *King of the Jews* (New York, 1979).

L. Dobroszycki (ed.), *The Chronicle of the Lodz Ghetto, 1941–1944*, 1984.

RUTH (c. 12th century BCE) Woman from Moab, who was the great-grandmother of King David (q.v.). Her story is told in the biblical book of Ruth, which relates that Elimelech of Bethlehem, his wife Naomi, and their two sons, Mahlon and Chilion, moved to Moab to escape famine. In Moab the two sons married Moabite brides — Orpah and Ruth. Ten years later, after the death of Elimelech and both her sons, Naomi decided to return to Bethlehem. Both daughters-in-law wanted to accompany her but she sought to dissuade them, and Orpah agreed to remain. Ruth, however, was obdurate saying, "Ask me not to leave you or return from following you; for where you go, I will go and where you lodge, I will lodge; your people shall be my people and your God, my God; where you die, I will die and there also shall I be buried." This statement of Ruth caused her to be symbolized in Judaism as the paradigm of the righteous convert (many of whom take the name Ruth).

Back in Bethlehem, Naomi sent Ruth to the fields of Elimelech's relative, Boaz, to participate in gleaning, the right reserved to the poor of picking up the grain which falls to the earth during the barley harvest. Naomi encouraged Ruth to seek protection from Boaz as next of kin and he agreed to purchase the field, which had belonged to Elimelech, and also to marry Ruth. However, there was another (unnamed) relative who had a prior claim and his consent had to be obtained and a ceremony gone through at which this relative symbolically removed his sandal before the elders at the gate of the city. Boaz was then free to marry Ruth and their son, Obed, became the father of Jesse, whose children included David.

E. F. Campbell, Jr., *Ruth*, 1975.

S

SAADIAH BEN JOSEPH GAON (882–942) Scholar, philosopher, and community leader in Babylonia. He was born to a poor family in Upper Egypt, but nothing is known of his youth. As a young man he moved to Tiberias, then a great center for the study of the biblical text. By the time he was twenty he had completed a Hebrew dictionary and rhyming lexicon and had written a polemic against the schismatic Karaites, who rejected rabbinical Judaism. He also lived for a time in Syria but in 921/2 settled in the Babylonian town of Sura, where he taught in the academy. He engaged in a controversy with the leading scholar in Eretz Israel, Aaron ben Meir, affirming the authority of the Babylonian scholars to regulate the Jewish calendar. The issue was determined in favor of the Babylonians, which also implied recognition of the supremacy of the Babylonian over the Palestinian sages.

By 928, Saadiah was head of the academy, a position which carried the title of Gaon. Two years later he became involved in a dispute with the powerful exilarch, David ben Zakkai, the lay leader of the Babylonian community when Saadiah refused to sign a verdict given by the exilarch in a matter of probate, because he felt it was unjust. When the exilarch's son brought him papers to sign, Saadiah told him to inform his father that the Bible teaches, "You shall not respect persons in judgment." David ben Zakkai deposed Saadiah, and Saadiah issued a counterban. The dispute dragged on for six years, during which Saadiah lived in Baghdad, busying himself with study and writing. Eventually a settlement was reached and Saadiah was reinstated.

Saadiah Gaon made basic and pioneering contributions to virtually all branches of Jewish knowledge. Many of these resulted from the challenges emerging from both the Karaites and from the appeal of Greek thought in its adaptation by Arab philosophers. For the Jews of the Arabic-speaking world, Saadiah translated the Bible into Arabic for the first time, adding his own commentary. He established a new method of Bible study based on scientific and grammatical examination of the text, seeking literal meaning and only resorting to paraphrase when the text was obscure. He wanted to make the Bible available not only to Arabic-speaking Jews but to the world of Islam. Among Eastern Jews, his translation became so popular that it was read in the synagogue together with the Hebrew text of the Torah (and is still used by Yemenite Jews).

Saadiah wrote on Hebrew grammar, laid the foundations of Hebrew philology, and was a Talmudic authority whose decisions were recognized as legally binding. He also composed liturgical poems. He produced the first authoritative prayer book (*siddur*) for use by ordinary worshipers. He noted that three evils were corrupting the order of prayer: omissions, additions, and abridgments. He therefore set out to collect and arrange the prayer service in its original form, producing a logical and economical arrangement that enabled ordinary laymen to follow the service, and he also added a commentary and guide in Arabic.

His most famous theological work was *Sefer Emunot ve-Deot* (Book of Beliefs and Opinions), the first systematic exposition of Judaism and its beliefs. He explains at its outset that he felt the urge

---

SAYINGS OF SAADIAH

● The more valuable an objective, the more effort it demands.
● Reason has long since decided that God needs nothing, but that all things need him.
● Death is the means of transition to future life, which is the ultimate goal of mortal existence.
● In this world we see the godless prosper and the faithful suffer. There must be another world in which all will be recompensated in justice and righteousness.
● Any interpretation that conforms to reason must be correct.
● Distress is no excuse for disloyalty.
● We have two bases of our religion, apart from the Bible. One, which precedes it, is the foundation of reason; the other, which is later, is the source of tradition.

to guide and inspire his people in an age of moral, intellectual, and spiritual confusion. Their bewilderment is the result of the impact of many rival creeds and philosophies on his contemporaries. His answer is not to propound a particular philosophical system but to interpret Judaism in the light of reason. He endeavors to show that the basic Jewish beliefs — such as creation, the unity of God, the rational character of the Law, freedom of the will, and future life — can all be demonstrated by reason. Intellectual speculations, he holds, can only confirm the truth of Jewish beliefs; thus, from creation can be derived irrefutable proofs for the existence of God. The Torah should be seen as revealed reason and as such is meant for all mankind.

Maimonides (q.v.) said, "Were it not for Saadiah, the Torah could well have disappeared from among the Jewish people."

B. Cohen (ed.), *Saadia Anniversary Volume*, 1943.
S. T. Katz, *Saadiah Gaon*, 1980.
H. Malter, *Saadia Gaon: His Life and Works*, 1978.
A. Neuman and S. Zeitlin (eds.), *Saadia Studies*, 1943.
S. Rosenblatt, *Saadia Gaon: The Book of Beliefs and Opinions*, 1948.

SACHS, CURT (1881–1959) German musicologist and authority on musical instruments. Sachs studied piano, clarinet, music theory, and composition while attending the Französisches High School in his native Berlin. At the University of Berlin he studied music history but took his doctorate (1904) in art history, with a thesis on Verrocchio's sculpture. Sachs worked for several years as an art critic and only in 1909 embarked on musicological studies, specializing in the history of musical instruments.

After serving in the army during World War I, Sachs returned to Berlin and in 1919 was appointed director of a distinguished collection of musical instruments that he reorganized, restoring some of them so they could be played. A year later he became a professor at the Berlin National Academy of Music and was also a professor at the University of Berlin. Sachs had several posts in a variety of German museums and was invited in 1930 and in 1932 to Cairo as a consultant on Near Eastern music.

After the Nazis came to power, Sachs was deprived of all his academic titles in 1933 and had to leave his homeland. He moved to Paris to work at the Musée de l'Homme and was a visiting professor at the Sorbonne. In 1934 Sachs began a series of historical recordings, *L'anthologie sonore*, an introduction to early music that was used by students for many years. In 1937 Sachs made his home in the United States, lecturing at the Graduate School of Liberal Arts of New York University. He was also a consultant to the New York Public Library, adjunct professor at Columbia University, and for three years (1948–1950) the president of the American Musicological Society.

Sachs was one of the founders of modern organology, the science of musical instruments. He devised the classification system for instruments that gained universal acceptance and wrote the standard dictionary and a model catalogue of one of the major musical collections in the world (the Staatlichen Instrumentsammlung in Berlin). Musical instruments led Sachs to discover nonwestern cultures and their music and his studies of music in the ancient world were read through out the musical world with great interest. Sachs's fascination with the relationship between music and the other arts inspired his major study, *The Commonwealth of Art*. Among his other publications in English are *The History of Musical Instruments*, *The Rise of Music in the Ancient World: East and West*, *Our Musical Heritage*, *A World History of Dance*, and *Rhythm and Tempo: A Study in Music History*.

G. Reese and R. Brandel (eds.), *The Commonwealth of Music, in Honor of Curt Sachs*, 1965.

SACHS, NELLY LEONIE (1891–1970) German poet and Nobel Prize winner. Her father was a wealthy manufacturer in Berlin and she grew up in an affluent milieu. Sachs wrote her first poems, along with some puppet plays, at the age of seventeen. Her early work, some of which appeared in newspapers, was written primarily for her own amusement. Although her first full-length work, *Legenden und Ezrählungen* (1921), displays the strong involvement of an assimilated Jew with the concepts of the Christian intellectual world, her

Nelly Sachs receiving the Nobel Prize from King Gustav Adolf of Sweden. Stockholm, 1966.

output after 1933 reflects a strong Jewish orientation, shocked into existence by the rise of Nazism in Germany. In 1940 the intervention of the Swedish royal family and her correspondent, the writer Selma Lagerlöf, saved her from being sent to a forced-labor camp and enabled Sachs to emigrate to Sweden. There, she translated Swedish poetry into German, subsequently publishing several of her translations. Her first collection of poetry, *In the Habitations of Death*, dedicated to "my dead brothers and sisters," appeared in 1946. In her best-known poem "O die Schomsteine" ("O the Chimneys"), the body of Israel is in the smoke emitted by the chimneys of the Nazi death camps. In 1965 she was awarded the German Publishers' Peace Prize. On being awarded the 1966 Nobel Prize for literature together with the Israeli novelist and short-story writer S. Y. Agnon (q.v.), Sachs commented, "Agnon represents the State of Israel. I represent the tragedy of the Jewish people."

Much of Sachs' poetry has the Holocaust as its subject, with prominence being given to the motif of the hunter and the hunted. She combines elements of Jewish mysticism with traditions of German romanticism. Trying to convey the enigmatic horror of the Holocaust, she makes frequent use of two words: *Tod* ("Death") and *Nacht* ("Night"). Her later work looked at the relationship of the dead and the living, the fate of innocence, and the state of suffering.

Sachs wrote a number of plays, combining words, mime, and music. Her best-known play, *Eli: A Mystery Play of the Suffering of Israel* (1943), establishes a link between the murder of an eight-year-old Polish shepherd boy by a German soldier and the Jewish legend of thirty-six saints whose virtue enables the world's continued existence. She said she wrote it "under the impression of the dreadful experience of the Hitler period while smoke was still commingled with fire."

L. L. Langer, *Versions of Survival: The Holocaust and the Human Spirit*, 1982.

N. Sachs, *O the Chimneys* [selected translations], 1967.

SAINT-LÉON, ARTHUR (also known as Charles Victor and as Arthur Michel Saint-Léon); (1815 or 1821–1870). Dancer and choreographer. He was born in Paris and died there shortly after his most enduring ballet, *Coppélia* (music by Léo Delibes), was staged with great success. There was much controversy about him. C. W. Beaumont (in his *Complete Book of Ballets*) attributes to him only half of the book of *Coppélia* (with coauthor Charles Nuitter) and the choreography to Louis Mérante — but nobody else does so. Also, his appearance as a dancer has been variously described. One source said he was round-shouldered and not outstanding. Another said he was the best dancer of his time, "famous for his remarkable *ballon* and *élévation*." This may be more accurate, for he was appointed as principal dancer of *demi-caractère* in Belgium and partnered the famous ballerina Fanny Cerrito even before he married her.

His father was a ballet master in Italy and in the Württemburg ducal theater in Stuttgart. Trained by his father, Saint-Léon made his debut in Munich at the age of fourteen. He also played the violin, apparently with skill, for when he went to Russia his violin playing was included in the contract and in one of his ballets, *Le violon du diable* (1849), he played a Paganini-style solo. From 1843 when he met Cerrito, he began to choreograph extensively and his first ballet *La vivandière* was created for her in Rome. They were married in 1845, and for her debut at the Paris Opera he choreographed *La fille de marbre*. The marriage broke up in 1851, but by then they had appeared in many European cities and in London.

In 1859 Saint-Léon offered his services to the Imperial Theater in Saint Petersburg. He stayed in Russia for ten years, staging many of his own ballets in Saint Petersburg and in Moscow, sometimes under different names. He also created the first ballet on a Russian theme, *The Humpbacked Horse*. There are now other versions of this ballet, but it was Saint-Léon who first introduced a Russian subject and folk dances into ballet — for example, the czardas in *Coppélia*.

When his ballets *Goldfish* and *The Lily* failed in Russia — though he had many successes — Saint-Léon went back to Paris. He had kept in touch with the Paris Opera and had even choreographed *La source* (1866) during his Russian years. He revived *The Lily* for Paris, where it was warmly received, and he remained as choreographer and ballet-master for the Paris Opera until his death.

Among his many achievements, he wrote a book entitled *La Sténochoréographie ou l'art d'écrire promptement la danse* (1852) in which he put forward a method of dance notation. Saint-Léon was criticized as a choreographer for using tricks and gadgets to bolster the public imagination and his own lack of inspiration. Yet in this he was ahead of his time and looked forward to the era of multimedia. His wish to introduce a singing chorus in addition to the corps de ballet in *La fille de marbre*, for instance, would no longer seem remote or wild.

SAKEL, MANFRED JOSHUA (1900–1957) Austrian psychiatrist. Born in Nadvorna, Galicia, Sakel went to Vienna, where from 1936 he worked at the neuropsychiatric clinic at the University of Vienna, and specialized in the treatment of addictions. By accident, one of his patients, who was both diabetic and schizophrenic, took an overdose of insulin and went into a coma; when she recovered, her addiction to narcotics was significantly reduced.

Continuing to experiment with insulin for therapeutic purposes in the treatment of schizophrenics, Sakel discovered an 88 percent success rate in the use of the insulin coma treatment, but noticed that he had better results with younger patients. The treatment he evolved comprised four stages: (1) precoma relaxation; (2) inducement of coma; (3) recovery from coma; and (4) gradually decreasing doses of insulin as the patient's condition improved. His methods became standard procedure in the treatment of schizophrenia.

With Hitler's rise to power, Sakel decided to leave Austria, and in 1936 went to the United States, where he was invited to teach his methods in hospitals. In 1937 the First International Psychiatric Conference in Berne, Switzerland, was devoted to his treatment. His ideas did encounter some opposition, however, because of the risks of overdosing involved in inducing comas with insulin.

Sakel continued his work at the New York State Mental Health Department. He died in New York. The Sakel Foundation, established after his death, convened international congresses, in 1959 and in 1962, on biological therapy and insulin cure.

Sakel's principal works were *Epilepsy* (1958) and *Schizophrenia* (1958) both published after his death. Sakel was a strong Zionist and supporter of the Irgum Tzeva Leumi Movement.

SALANTER ISRAEL (Lipkin; 1810—1883) Lithuanian rabbi who founded the Musar (moralist) movement. He was born in a small Lithuanian town where his father served as rabbi. While still young, he married and settled in Salant, his wife's birthplace, from which he derived his name. As a child prodigy, he had delivered learned casuistic discourses before scholars when he was only ten. He became critical of the the casuistic approach, however, and soon, following his teacher's advice, concentrated on the study of Musar, (ethicoreligious literature). He decided that there is no virtue for a man as a solitary individual, but only in society. Solidarity must be the basis of all aspirations to the good. He led a small group of students and businessmen in the study of Musar. This did not suggest any new world outlook or ideal but sought the perfect service of God by banishing all selfish urges. Knowledge was not enough, however, and a new method of self-improvement was called for. He demanded regular study of ethical texts dealing with proper conduct towards one's fellow man.

From 1840 to 1847 he headed a rabbinic academy at Vilna (now Vilnius, Lithuania) and from 1849 to

---

SAYINGS OF ISRAEL SALANTER

● No sickness of the soul is worse than discouragement; man must continually renew the idea of courage in his mind.
● To be a successful businessman you must have remarkable talents; and if you have such talents, why waste them on business?
● Promote yourself, but do not demote another.
● Man is free in his imagination but bound by his reason.
● Three things can be learned from a railroad: if you are one minute late, you miss it; the slightest deflection from the rails leads to catastrophe; and a passenger without a ticket may expect punishment.
● A small coin before the eyes hides everything from sight.

1857 in Kovno (Kaunas). There he found a wide field for his talents. He sought to attract the masses by emphasizing the emotional element of religion and trained disciples to become spiritual leaders according to his ideas. In Vilna he founded an institute for the study of classical Jewish ethical literature and for its publication.

He established a conventicle for Musar study and this concept spread rapidly to other communities. The participants escaped from the outside world to spend time in self-analysis and self-improvement. The development aroused strong opposition from rabbinical leaders, who condemned the establishment of groups of "moralists."

Salanter traveled widely through Europe to found more of these groups. His most successful achievement was the Musar Talmudic academies in which, apart from the regular Talmudic studies, periods were set apart for classes in ethics. Salanter's own homilies attracted large audiences. One of the most famous episodes in his life was during a cholera epidemic, when from the pulpit he ordered his congregation to eat on the solemn Day of Atonement and himself set the example.

In 1857 he was struck by a nervous disease that caused him great suffering and afflicted him for the rest of his life. He moved to Germany in the hope of regaining his health. In 1880 he moved to Paris for two years to give spiritual leadership to the eastern European Jewish community there and returned in 1883 to Königsberg, where he died.

He left no writings, but his disciples collected and published his teachings. The Musar movement was not long-lived but proved highly influential in eastern Europe, and many of his pupils founded academies in which the teaching of ethics played a prominent role.

L. Ginzberg, *Students, Scholars, and Saints*, 1958.
K. Rosen, *Rabbi Israel Salanter and the Musar Movement*, 1943.

SALMON, ALEXANDER (1822–1866) High official in Tahiti. The son of a London banker and well-educated, he decided to settle on the island when he visited it in the late 1830s as a sailor aboard a whaler. He was not the first Jew to have settled on the island. When Captain Bligh of *Bounty* fame visited Tahiti, he encountered an escaped Jewish convict called Samuel Pollend, who lived on the island after surviving a shipwreck.

Salmon married Arii-taimai, one of the outstanding women on the island, a chieftain of the Teva clan. By this time, the Tahitians were nominal Christians, although they resented the missionaries' demands to give up dancing, tattooing, and wearing flowers in their hair.

Salmon became the chief adviser to the rulers. Under the British, the Protestants were in the ascendancy — and Salmon's wife was a Protestant. However, by 1841 the French were in charge and were attempting to impose Catholicism. Civil war threatened, and the queen of Tahiti fled on a British warship. Salmon and his chieftain wife devised a formula that persuaded the queen to return, thereby preventing bloodshed, and he persuaded the natives not to resist the French. Arii-tamaii, who was regarded as the queen's equal and had in fact refused the crown, devised the peace plan.

After the queen returned, Salmon was awarded a high place of honor in her court. He served as president of the Tahiti Chamber of Commerce and was prominent in mercantile life. He shared his wife's love for the people and in the late 1850s journeyed to Paris to try to dissuade Napoleon III from forcing Catholicism on the people. He was denied an audience with the emperor, and journeyed on to England, where in 1858 he published his letter of complaint.

Salmon and his wife had eight children. One succeeded his mother as high chief of Papara; a daughter was the wife of the last king of Tahiti, Maran Taaroa; and their son Tati was a close friend of Robert Louis Stevenson when the writer lived on the island. Arii-taimai, who published her memoirs, partly edited by Henry Adams (1901), died in 1897, aged seventy-six.

SALOME ALEXANDRA (139–67 BCE) Last effective ruler of the independent Hasmonean dynasty in the Land of Israel (76–67 BCE). The queen (known in Hebrew as Shelomzion), was the widow of both Aristobulus I and his brother Alexander Jannaeus (q.v.). She was not politically active during her husbands' reigns but became highly popular among the people.

Salome's reign was generally tranquil. Either as a result of her husband's dying request or her own initiative, she made peace with the Pharisees. They now became permanent visitors at court, and wielded enough power, according to Josephus (q.v.) to engineer the execution of King Alexander's former, apparently Sadducee, counselors. They also curtailed Sadducee influence on the country's highest legislative-judicial body, the Sanhedrin.

The most distinguished of the Pharisee sages at this time was Simeon ben Shetah (q.v.), apparently not a brother of the queen as hitherto assumed. The queen herself was a devout observer of religious traditions.

A short-lived threat appeared on the horizon with the Armenian King Tigranes' takeover of Syria. A handsome "gift" and perhaps Tigranes' need to protect his flank against Rome, saved the day for Alexandra. Her son, Aristobulus, embarked on an expedition against Damascus but scored no success. In her quietly determined manner, meanwhile, the queen greatly increased the size of her country's armed forces and won the respect of the neighboring states.

The Talmud speaks of the period of Queen Salome Alexandra and Simon ben Shetah as a period of such goodness and piety that God sent rain "in the night of every Wednesday and Sabbath, so that the grains of wheat were like kidneys, the grains of barley like olives." Alexandra's reign was additionally a period of important Pharisee legislation, one of the more striking laws being an anti-Sadducee enactment dealing with the Temple water libation ceremony. The enthusiastic Pharisaic encomium on the queen's rule is also borne out by the fact that her agile though undemonstrative diplomacy gained appreciable influence for the Jewish state throughout the region.

A. Schalit, ed., *The World History of the Jewish People*, vol. 6, 1976.

SALOMON, HAYM (1740–1785) U.S. patriot and merchant. Born in Poland, Salomon emigrated to colonial America prior to the Declaration of Independence (1776). His linguistic talents — he was proficient in German, French, Italian, Dutch, Russian, Polish, and English — as well as his financial expertise, which included friendships with key European merchants, helped him make his way in the New World. In the summer of 1776 Salomon was working as a sutler with the American forces in the area of Lake George, New York. Later that summer, after the British occupied New York City, Salomon was imprisoned as a suspected spy. His ability with languages brought him to the attention of a Russian general, who appointed him to a commissary post primarily working with the Hessian officers serving with the English troops. In 1777 Salomon — then thirty-seven — married Rachel Franks, the fifteen-year-old daughter of Moses Franks, a well-known figure in early American Jewish history.

Working with the Hessians, he induced a number of them to leave the British forces and join the colonial army. He also aided French and American prisoners to escape, assisting them with his own personal funds. When Salomon's activities became known to the British, he decided that he must escape. In 1778 he fled from New York to Philadelphia, leaving behind his wife and month-old child as well as his considerable financial resources which were confiscated by the British.

Statue of Haym Salomon in Los Angeles.

Eventually his wife and child were able to join him in Philadelphia, where he started over as a commission merchant and bill broker. The French forces in the American states chose him to sell their bills of exchange. In 1781 Robert Morris became the superintendent of finance, with the responsibility of handling the chaotic finances of the young nation. Upon recommendation from several sources, Morris chose Haym Salomon as his chief agent to sell the bills that were coming in from France, Holland, Spain, and other countries. Altnough Salomon was one of several bill brokers working for Morris, he was so highly thought of that Morris permitted Salomon to advertise himself as "Broker to the Office of Finance." In addition to assisting the American government, Salomon also loaned money to the delegates attending the Continental Congress. One of these, James Madison, later president of the United States, wrote of Salomon, "The kindness of our little friend on Front Street, near the coffee-house, is a fund which will preserve me from extremities, but I never resort to it without great mortification as he obstinately rejects all recompense."

He was a noted benefactor and contributed a quarter of the costs of building Philadelphia's Mikveh Israel synagogue. However, Salomon died penniless, and his bank account showed canceled checks for over $500,000 paid to the government treasury. His descendants petitioned Congress for a return of the money, which they maintained had helped to finance the independence of the republic. However, an examination showed that the money represented sales of securities for the U.S. government and not personal loans.

A statue of Haym Salomon with George Washington stands in the center of Chicago, while his portrait appeared on a U.S. stamp issued during the bicentennial celebrations of the Revolution, the only Jew so honored for his Revolutionary War activities.

H. Fast, *Haym Salomon; Son of Liberty*, 1945.

SALOMONS, DAVID (1797–1873) First Jewish lord mayor of London; knighted 1869. He was descended from Solomon Salomons, a leading merchant on the Royal Exchange in the 18th century, and was the son of Levi Salomons, a leading merchant and underwriter. Salomons was educated for a commercial life and in 1832 was one of the founders of the London and Westminster Bank. He began as an underwriter on his own account in 1834, being one of the few Jews to participate in the development of joint-stock banking in Britain.

In 1835 David Salomons was chosen as one of the sheriffs of London and was able to accept the position following a special act of Parliament making it possible to admit Jews to certain municipal offices by administering "such an oath as would be binding on their conscience." When he ended his term of office a silver testimonial was presented to him by the Jewish community "as an acknowledgment of his exertions in the cause of religious liberty."

However, when he was elected alderman for the ward of Aldgate, he refused to take the Christian oath, and was forced to withdraw. He continued to fight for the abolition of Jewish disabilities, but when reelected in 1844, was still unable to take office. It was only after an act of Parliament was passed the following year enabling Jews to hold municipal offices that Salomons' election as alderman in 1847 was finally recognized.

Salomons had in the meantime held other offices, being appointed high sheriff of Kent in 1839–1840, deputy lieutenant for Kent, Sussex, and Middlesex, and in 1838 the first Jewish magistrate for Kent.

In 1851 Salomons was elected to Parliament as the Liberal representative of Greenwich, but declined to take the oath "on the true faith of a Christian." However, he voted three times without having been sworn in the statutory manner. Prolonged legal proceedings followed and he was fined five hundred pounds and debarred from the house. After the parliamentary oath was amended in 1858, he was again elected for Greenwich and continued to represent that constituency until his death.

In 1855 Salomons was elected lord mayor of London and upon conclusion of his term of office he received the unique distinction of an address of congratulations signed by the leading merchants and bankers of the city.

Salomons published a number of articles on financial and monetary matters, as well as an account of the persecution of the Jews in Damascus in 1840. He was active in the Board of Deputies of British Jews and took an interest in the Westminster Jews' Free School, the Jews' Hospital, and the Society for Hebrew Literature. He was fond of art and had an excellent collection of modern paintings.

In 1869 he was created baronet, being succeeded by his nephew **David Lionel Salomons** (1851–1925), electrical engineer and pioneer of horseless carriages. He attended University College, London, and took a degree in natural sciences at Cambridge.

In 1874 he claimed to have been the first person to use electric lighting with incandescent lamps. He also made and used home-made electric carriages, took out patents on many electrical inventions, and published a number of books on the subject. He served as treasurer and vice-president of the Council of the Institution of Electrical Engineering and was one of the founders of the Royal Automobile Club and the Aéro Club de France.

A. M. Hyamson, *David Salomons*, 1939.

SALTEN, FELIX (1869–1945) Austrian novelist, journalist, dramatist, creator of Bambi. Born in Budapest as Siegmund Salzmann, he experienced a harsh childhood until he made his way to Vienna, where from 1891 he earned a meager living as feuilletonist and literary critic for various newspapers and periodicals. He associated with Jungwien, a literary circle whose most talented members were Arthur Schnitzler (q.v.) — who exerted a great influence on Salten, Hugo von Hofmannsthal and Richard Beer-Hofmann (q.v.). However, he remained a little-known literary figure until 1923. His novels, beginning with *Die Hinterblienbene* (1899), his plays, starting with the comedy *Der Gemeine* (1901), and his four books of essays before World War I did not attract many readers. He was best known as the feuilletonist and theater critic of Vienna's most influential daily, *Neue Freie Presse*, a position formerly held by his friend Theodor Herzl (q.v.).

The publication of *Bambi* (1923), the best of his animal stories, catapulted him to world fame, further enhanced by Walt Disney's adaptation of the story to the screen in 1942. *Bambi*, the tale of a deer's life in the forest, has remained a children's classic ever since and has been widely translated.

Salten's interest in Judaism and Zionism led to an extensive tour of Palestine. He recorded his observations of the pioneering Jewish settlements in *Neue Menschen auf alter Erde* ("New People on Old Land;" 1925). His visit also led him to write his only biblical novel, *Simson* ("Samson" 1928). In his innovative version of the Samson theme, Salten defends Delilah as the faithful beloved of Samson who unwittingly brings about his blinding and death. He ascribes Samson's betrayal to the Philistines as the vengeance of her jealous sister. For Salten, Samson's fate symbolized Jewish fate. Increasing anti-Semitism, culminating in the rise of Nazism, led him to pessimistic forecasts. He wrote, "Forever the rope will be about our neck, forever the brutal hand of others will drive us as though we were cattle or scum. It is an accursed blessing that we bear but still a blessing. We bear the light of the world and must hence suffer as long as darkness reigns. We bear the wisdom of the world and must hence endure ill-usage as long as stupidity prevails. We bring liberation to the world and are hence persecuted as long as there is slavery."

When the Nazis occupied Vienna, Salten was forced into exile. He found a temporary refuge in Hollywood, settling in Zurich, Switzerland, after the war.

A. K. Salten, *Bob und Baby*, 1925.

SAMSON (c. 12th cent. BCE) Israelite judge noted for his superhuman strength, whose story is related in the book of Judges, chapters 13 to 16. His father was Manoah of the tribe of Dan, whose wife was barren. Her impending pregnancy was announced by an angel, who stipulated that the son should be a Nazirite, forbidden wine and unclean food and not permitted to use a razor.

When the child grew up, he assisted his tribe in its struggle against the Philistines and "judged Israel" for twenty years, but most of his reported acts were occasioned by his passion for non-Israelite women, of whom three were crucial.

The first was an unnamed Philistine woman from Timnah whom he decided to marry. On his way to visit her, he encountered a lion, which he rent apart with his bare hands. Returning subsequently for the wedding feast, he saw that a swarm of bees had made a honeycomb in the carcass of the lion. At the wedding feast, he posed the riddle, "Out of the eater came something to eat, out of the strong came something sweet," and wagered thirty garments if the Philistines could discover the answer. They persuaded Samson's new wife to get the answer out of him by wile. Samson was so incensed that he killed thirty Philistines in Ashkelon to obtain the garments to pay the wager. Then he returned to his home to Zorah, leaving his bride, who was promptly given to his best man.

When Samson went back to claim her, her father said she had been given to another but offered her younger sister in her place. In rage, Samson caught three hundred foxes, set fire to their tails, and turned them loose in the Philistine fields which caught fire and were destroyed.

In revenge, the Philistines burned his bride and her father. Samson in return smote the Philistines, who turned to the Israelites, demanding that they hand over Samson to them. The Israelites, in fear of the Philistines, got Samson to agree to be bound and handed over. However, when the Philistines came to take him, he snapped off his bonds, and seized the jawbone of an ass, with which he killed one thousand men.

The second Philistine woman with whom he was entangled was a harlot in Gaza. The Philistines surrounded her house to trap him but Samson walked away from Gaza, carrying with him the gates of the city.

His downfall ensued from his love for a third woman, Delilah, presumably also a Philistine. She was hired by the Philistines to tempt him and, after two unsuccessful attempts, wormed out of him the secret of his strength — his unshaved locks. Then, while Samson was asleep in her lap, the Philistines cut off his hair and and had no difficulty in seizing him.

They put out his eyes and took him to Gaza where he was imprisoned and employed to grind corn at the prison mill. However, as his hair grew again, he regained his strength. At a feast in honor of their god Dagon, the Philistines decided to make fun of him, and brought him from prison. Crying, "Let me die with the Philistines," Samson took hold of the pillars on which the building rested, dislodged them, bringing down the house and perishing, along with the three thousand Philistines who were inside. The Bible notes that "the dead whom he slew at his death were more than those whom he had slain all his life."

R. G. Boling, *Judges* (Anchor Bible), 1975.
P. Carus, *The Story of Samson and Its Place in the Religious Development of Mankind*, 1907.
A. S. Palmer, *The Samson Saga and Its Place in Comparative Religion*, 1913.

SAMUEL (11th century BCE) Israelite judge and prophet whose name was given to the third book of the Prophets section of the Bible. He was the key figure in a crucial period of Israelite history: the development from a confederation of tribes to a united monarchy.

His mother, Hannah, was barren for many years. She accompanied her husband, Elkanah, who came from a leading family in Mount Ephraim, to the sanctuary in Shiloh, and there prayed for the privilege of bearing a son, vowing that he would be consecrated as a Nazirite to the service of the sanctuary. Accordingly, when Samuel was born, his mother brought him to Shiloh to be raised by the chief priest, Eli. As a boy, Samuel experienced a divine vision foretelling the destruction of Shiloh and the end of the line of Eli, which came to pass in the course of time.

Samuel's qualities of leadership and statesmanship preserved morale during those difficult days, and he became the outstanding figure among the people — a wonder-working man of God, central personality of the cult, judge, prophet, and military leader. He made his home at Ramah but visited the main centers of the cult to judge the people. He founded a school of prophets that maintained religious traditions while insisting upon moral standards among the people as a whole. However when his own sons were seen demeaning their roles as judges, the people demanded that a king be appointed to ensure national unity. Although this went against tradition, which had always regarded God as king of the Israelites, Samuel reluctantly complied with this demand and anointed Saul (q.v.) as king.

Two events soured the relationship between Saul and Samuel. The first was Saul's offering of sacrifices without waiting for Samuel; the second was his disobeying Samuel's instructions by sparing the life of the Amalekite king, Agag, after defeating him in battle. Samuel cut Agag to pieces himself, complying with the command to wipe out the Amalekites. Samuel decided to reject the line of Saul, secretly anointing David (q.v.) as his future successor. Later, when David was fleeing from Saul's anger and jealousy, Samuel gave him shelter in his Ramah home, which was where the prophet was buried after his death. (The site is traditionally identified with Nebi Samwil, overlooking northern Jerusalem.)

The Bible relates that before fighting the Philistines, Saul visited the witch of Endor. At his request she conjured up the spirit of Samuel who foretold the final defeat and death of Saul.

K. McCarter Jr., *I Samuel* (Anchor Bible), 1980.

SAMUEL (c. 180—c. 260 CE) Leading Babylonian rabbi also known by the honorific title of Mar Shemu'el ("Master Samuel"); head of the rabbinical court and academy in his birthplace, Nehardea. Together with his friend and colleague, Abba Arika (Rav, q.v.), Samuel dominated the first generation of scholars who propagated and developed the teachings of the Mishnah in Persian-ruled Mesopotamia. Their legal disputes, which recur throughout the Babylonian Talmud, provided an early basis for talmudic argumentation. Whereas Rav excelled in religious law (halakhah), Samuel was an authority on civil law and proved more versatile, although he showed much deference to his rival. However, when the Nehardea position fell vacant shortly before 220 CE, Rav's decision to give up his claim enabled Samuel to take office there, in succession to his late father, Abba bar Abba ha-Kohen. Rav thereupon established a brilliant new academy at Sura. Following Rav's death in 247, Samuel became the unchallenged spiritual leader of Babylonian Jewry.

Through cooperative effort, Samuel and Rav helped to unify public worship, expand the prayer book, and transform the Mishnah into a source of religious guidance as well as an object of study. For his part, Samuel achieved expertise not only in jurisprudence but also in medicine, astronomy, and other scientific fields. He mastered anatomy, specialized in women's ailments, taught popular remedies, and is said to have devised an ointment for eye infections that was sent to cure Judah ha-Nasi (q.v.) in Palestine. Dubbed Shemu'el Yarhina'ah ("Samuel the Astronomer"), he claimed that the paths of heaven were as familiar to him as the streets of Nehardea; he even worked out a fixed calendar of the Jewish religious year, which, unfortunately, proved too advanced for other sages of his time. An opponent of asceticism and a champion of the maltreated slave, he berated those who attributed their own defects to other people and maintained that "greatness flees from one who seeks it, yet follows one who flees from it."

Samuel's years of leadership in Nehardea partly coincided with an initial outbreak of religious persecution under the new Sasanid kings of Persia (226–241). After 241, however, Samuel managed to cultivate a warm relationship with Shapur I, whose generally tolerant policies and high regard for Samuel worked in favor of the Jews. A reflection of this modus vivendi can be seen in Samuel's classic ruling that, for all nonreligious purposes, state law — "the law of the kingdom" — is legally binding on the Jewish population (*dina de-malkhuta dina*). His other famous principle was that "the burden of proof lies on the claimant." Anxious to lay down rules of conduct governing Jewish life in the Diaspora, Samuel tightened legal procedure, by stressing, for example, the need for equity and by imposing sanctions on profiteers. He foresaw the age of messianic redemption not in supernatural events but in Israel's achievement of freedom and independence after the most vicious persecution.

B. M. Bokser, *Samuel's Commentary on the Mishna*, 1975.

D. Goodblatt, *Rabbinic Instruction in Sasanian Babylonia*, 1975.

J. Neusner, *A History of the Jews in Babylonia*, 1966–1970, vol. 2.

SAMUEL, HERBERT LOUIS, FIRST VISCOUNT (1870–1963) British statesman. Born in Liverpool, son of a wealthy banker, Samuel grew up in London, attending University College School. His upbringing was Orthodox in the conventional Anglo-Jewish mold. While an undergraduate at Balliol College, Oxford, Samuel underwent a spiritual crisis as a result of which he lost faith in Judaism. In deference to his family, however, he maintained outward observances and membership in the Jewish community. His father, who died when Samuel was a child, left him a secure income. As a result he never had to work for a living and decided at an early age to devote his life to progressive politics. While still a student he was adopted as a prospective parliamentary candidate for the Liberal party. In 1902 he was elected to the House of Commons and in 1909 he became the first Jew to serve in a British cabinet. As postmaster general from 1910 to 1914 Samuel bore the brunt of anti-Semitic attacks and false accusations of corruption in the Marconi scandal. He emerged with his reputation unblemished.

In 1914 he was president of the local goverment board, in 1915 again postmaster general, and in 1916 home secretary. In 1915 Samuel circulated to the cabinet a memorandum advocating British sponsorship of Zionism in Palestine. Behind the scenes, Samuel played a prominent role in the discussions that led to the British government's pro-Zionist Balfour Declaration of November 1917. In 1920 he was appointed first high commissioner under the British mandate in Palestine. His period of rule was marked by the severe Arab anti-Jewish riots of May 1921. Samuel responded with a policy

From right to left: Sir Herbert Samuel, Lord Balfour and Viscount Allenby, 1925.

of conciliation of Arab nationalism that alienated many of his former Zionist admirers. In the white paper policy statement of 1922, largely formulated by Samuel, the British government enunciated the criterion of economic absorptive capacity as the basis for decision making on Jewish immigration to Palestine. By the time Samuel left Palestine in 1925, peace had been restored and Jewish immigration was buoyant. The foundations of the Jewish national home in Palestine had been securely laid, but Samuel's efforts to draw the Arabs of Palestine into the political community had failed. Samuel had hoped to retire in Palestine and write philosophy books in a house on Mount Carmel. However, his successor forbade him to remain.

Back in England in 1926, he played a major role in ending the general strike. In 1931 he returned to the cabinet as home secretary in Ramsay MacDonald's National Government. As Liberal leader between 1931 and 1935 he maintained the party's independence but saw it dwindle into a small parliamentary rump. Ennobled in 1937, Samuel took the title Viscount Samuel of Mount Carmel and of Toxteth, Liverpool. He remained active in public life into old age, wrote several books on philosophy, and became a much-admired radio broadcaster. He continued to speak regularly in the House of Lords, delivering his last important speech there at the age of ninety.

Regarded as the most distinguished figure in Anglo-Jewry of his time, Samuel was active in the 1930s in work on behalf of the emigration and succor of German Jews. A strong opponent of the partition of Palestine, he nevertheless welcomed the creation of the State of Israel. Samuel called himself a meliorist. His most fundamental belief was in human rationality and capacity to improve society. Beneath a frosty exterior he concealed a fervent belief in humanitarian causes. His moderate Zionism represented a synthesis of his Englishness and his Jewishness, his liberalism and his imperialism, his political practicality and the religious sensibility that, particularly in later life, colored much of his thought. His writings include the philosophical works *Practical Ethics, Belief and Action*, and *Creature Man*.

L. Stein, *Herbert Samuel*, 1963.
B. Wasserstein, *Herbert Samuel: A Political Life*, 1991.

> The most moving ceremony that I have ever attended was on my first visit, after my arrival in Jerusalem [as British High Commissioner], to the old and spacious synagogue in the Jewish quarter of the ancient city. As it was the Sabbath I had walked over from Government House so as not to offend the Orthodox by driving; and found the surrounding streets densely thronged and the great building itself packed to the doors and to the roof.... Now, on that day, for the first time since the destruction of the Temple, they could see one of their own people governor in the Land of Israel. To them it seemed that the fulfillment of ancient prophecy might at last be at hand.... When there I read the opening words of Isaiah appointed for that day, "Comfort ye, comfort ye my people, saith your God. Speak ye comfortably to Jerusalem, and cry unto her, that her warfare is accomplished, that her iniquity is pardoned," — the emotion that I could not but feel seemed to spread throughout the vast congregation. Many wept. One could almost hear the sigh of generations.
>
> **Herbert Samuel**

SAMUEL, MARCUS, FIRST VISCOUNT BEARSTED (1853—1927) Founder fo the Shell Oil Company. Born in the East End of London, he was the tenth child of a family whose father was a "shell merchant" (from which the trade name of the oil company was taken). He attended a private Jewish school and continued his education in a Jewish boarding school in Brussels. At the age of sixteen he returned to England and began working in his father's business. He traveled to the Far East in 1873; when in India he chartered local ships to carry surplus rice from Siam to Calcutta to bring relief of the famine there. A decade later he came to the rescue when Japan's rice crops failed by importing vast quantities of rice from Rangoon.

In 1878 he founded companies in London and Japan together with his younger brother Samuel Samuel (his partner throughout his business career). He began transporting oil to the Far East from Russian wells owned by the Rothschilds [q.v.], soon cornering a sizable proportion of the oriental market. He erected tank installations and distribution depots, and built a fleet of tankers designed specifically to carry bulk oil (all the ships were given names of shells), pioneering the transport of oil through the Suez Canal.

In 1897 he established the Shell Transport and Trading Company and at the same time opened up oil fields in Borneo. As Britain's recognized expert in on liquid fuel, he advocated its use in railway engines and steamers. He was the first oilman to recognize the revolutionary implications of the invention of the motor car and also secured a license for the development of the diesel engine in Britain.

In 1901 Shell entered into a marketing alliance with Royal Dutch Petroleum to form the British-Dutch Oil Company and under Marcus Samuel's guidance built up a giant worldwide enterprise. By 1902, M. Samuel & Company had become leading merchant bankers and acted as the London bankers for the Japanese government. In 1904 the emperor of Japan conferred on Marcus Samuel the title of commander of the Rising Sun for supplying fuel to his navy during the Russo-Japanese war.

Marcus Samuel also had an active public life, sometimes to the detriment of his vast enterprises. In 1891 he was elected as an alderman in the City of London. He was sheriff of London in 1894 and chairman of the Port of London Committee in 1895. Queen Victoria conferred a knighthood on Samuel in 1898 for his services in helping free a British warship run aground at the entrance to the Suez Canal, for which he refused to accept payment. He was created a baronet in 1903 and in 1902 became the third Jew to hold the office of lord mayor of London. When planning the lord mayor's banquet he refused to invite the Romanian minister because of the persecution of Jews in that country (he refused to do business with them as well) despite strong objections from the Foreign Office, the prime minister, and even the king. His inauguration procession went through the district where he grew up and was reported as follows: "The Ghetto exceeded itself and ushered in the new Chief Magistrate with a heartiness which had never been exceeded and seldom equaled."

Samuel used his influence to alleviate the lot of the Jews in countries where they were persecuted, and a letter from the Russian ambassador assured him that steps had been taken to prevent any further massacres of Jews.

During World War I, under Samuel's leadership Shell was the principal supplier of gasoline and aviation fuel to the British forces (sold at prewar prices). A refinery to manufacture toluol, the basic element of TNT, erected in Britain and providing 80 percent of all the explosives used by the navy and army, was handed over to the ministry of munitions.

In 1921 Marcus Samuel was granted a peerage "for eminent public and national services." He took the title Lord Bearsted, the name of the parish where he established his country residence in 1895. In 1925 he was made a viscount.

Throughout his life Samuel gave generously to Jewish and non-Jewish charities (the Bearsted

Memorial Hospital in London was named for him), especially those in the city of London, and to causes related to the sea.

R. Henriques, *Marcus Samuel, First Viscount Bearsted and Founder of the "Shell" Transport and Trading Company, 1853–1927*, 1960.

SAMUEL BEN MEIR (c. 1080–1174) French

commentator on the Bible and Talmud, also known by the Hebrew acronym *Rashbam*; Tosafist. The son of Rashi's daughter, Jochebed, and Meir, one of the first Tosafists (one of a school of Talmud commentators originating in Northern France who supplemented the commentary of Rashi [q.v.]), Samuel was the older brother of the famed Rabbenu (Jacob) Tam (q.v.). Born in Ramerupt, near Troyes, he studied with his father, but more intensively with Rashi himself, who admitted to having occasionally changed his own commentary in favor of his grandson's interpretation. Samuel worked as a sheep farmer and wine grower, lived humbly and piously, devoting himself to prayer, study, and the writing of biblical and Talmudic expositions, *piyyutim* (liturgical poetry) and a Hebrew grammar (*Sefer Daikut*). His knowledge of the Latin translation of the Bible (the Vulgate) encouraged him to participate actively in disputations with Christians.

Samuel ben Meir is known for his devotion to the *peshat*, or literal understanding of the biblical text, in which he does not hesitate to express very original views. In claiming that the Torah does not require the wearing of *tefillin* (phylacteries), for example, or that a day according to the Hebrew calendar begins in the morning instead of the evening, he intended not to undermine Jewish religious law, but to clarify how the biblical and rabbinic traditions operate according to separate and distinct principles.

His most noted commentaries are on the Pentateuch, on the scrolls of Esther, Ruth, and Lamentations, and on the Talmudic tractates of *Pesahim* (chapter 10) and *Bava Batra*, which have been incorporated in every edition of the Talmud since it was first printed. He draws comprehensively from the Aramaic translation (*Targum Onkelos*), homilitic, and Talmudic sources, paying special attention to linguistic nuances in the biblical text. His explanations throw light on the realities of Jewish life in medieval Europe, providing a glimpse into the customs and language of his generation of French Jewry. He probably wrote commentaries on most books of the Bible, some of which remain in manuscript form today. His style is exacting, erudite, and lucid, tending to the verbose, and shows the unmistakable imprint of Rashi's influence.

SAMUEL HA-NAGID (993–c.1056) Statesman,

general, scholar, poet, and community leader in Muslim Spain. He was born Samuel ben Joseph ha-Levi ibn Nagdela in Cordoba. Having acquired a thorough Jewish and secular education, he began life as a humble spice dealer, rose to political grandeur, and became one of the greatest Jewish success stories of all time. After his native city fell to the Berbers (1013), Samuel fled to Malaga, where he opened another store near the residence of Abu al-Kasim ibn al-Arif, secretary to the vizier of Granada. He obligingly read and wrote letters for ibn al-Arif's uneducated servants; having marveled at the Arabic style and penmanship of these letters, and discovered the writer's identity, Ibn al-Arif gave Samuel his first appointment and recommended him to the vizier. Equally impressed, the latter availed himself of Samuel ibn Nagdela's many talents and, before the vizier died in 1020, Samuel was his chief aide and adviser.

King Habbus (1019–1038) had more loyal subjects — both Jews and fellow Berbers — within his capital, Granada, than in the rest of his Muslim kingdom. To neutralize potential rivals, Habbus entrusted Samuel with the responsibility of governing as vizier, a task that he discharged in an effective, tactful, and dignified manner. Habbus left two sons, who both claimed the throne, and Samuel was one of the very few notables who backed the older prince, a violent man who enjoyed the common people's support. In gratitude for his triumph, King Badis (1038–1073) retained his father's loyal Jewish vizier. Samuel continued to govern the kingdom wisely, but had to spend most of his remaining years at the head of Granada's armed forces, countering the attacks of Moorish enemies headed by Seville. This Andalusian campaign, which ultimateley hastened his death, involved some narrow escapes on the battlefield as well as many crucial victories — including those scored against two personal antagonists, the viziers of Almeria (1039) and Malaga (1049).

From about 1027, Samuel ibn Nagdela was honored as the *nagid* (prince or titular head) of Spanish Jewry. In Granada itself, he served as chief rabbi, founded one of the earliest Talmudic academies in western Europe, and wrote works of Jewish law. As a philanthropist, he provided for needy Jewish students at home and abroad, supplied them with biblical and rabbinic manuscripts, and even dispatched olive oil from his own estates to light the synagogues of Jerusalem. He also encouraged Hebrew poets such as Ibn Gabirol (q.v.) and, by virtue of his own religious and secu-

---

FROM THE POEMS OF SAMUEL HA-NAGID

- Rather herbs and sacks among your own
Than cake and silks where you're unknown.
- Before the wise man descends a pit,
He fixes a ladder to climb out of it.
- There are three types of companion:
Some are like food — indispensable;
Some like medicine — good occasionally;
Others like poison — to be avoided at any time.

lar verse, was an outstanding pioneer of the Spanish golden age. The poetry of Samuel ha-Nagid covers a wide range of themes and moods, from love and merriment to sad reflection and eulogy; it includes the first Hebrew war poems, written while he was on his campaigns, and exhibits great inventiveness and descriptive power. His verse collections, little known after the Middle Ages, have been published and reevaluated in modern critical editions.

His son, **Joseph ha-Nagid** (1035–1066), though in most respects a worthy and able successor, lacked his father's discretion. He finally provoked a Berber rebellion in the course of which he was executed (on December 30, 1066) and a momentous anti-Jewish bloodbath took place, the first recorded in Muslim Spain.

E. Ashtor, *The Jews of Moslem Spain (vol. 2)*, 1979.

SAPIR, EDWARD (1884–1939) U.S. anthropologist and linguist. Born in Lauenberg, Germany (now Lebork, Poland), he emigrated with his parents at the age of five to the United States, where his father, Joseph Sapir, continued in his profession of cantor. At the age of fourteen Edward won a scholarship that ranked him as "the brightest boy in New York City," enabling him to continue his schooling through to Columbia University. He studied with Franz Boas (q.v.) and graduated in anthropology in 1904. It was then that he began his field studies of American Indian languages while holding appointments at the universities of California (at Berkeley) and Pennsylvania, establishing his reputation in comparative American Indian linguistics. From 1910–1925 Sapir held the post of chief of the newly-created Division of Anthropology in the Geological Survey of the Canadian National Museum at Ottawa. In 1925 he was invited to the University of Chicago and six years later to Yale to become Sterling Professor of Anthropology and Linguistics. He was president of both the American Anthropological Association and the American Linguistic Society.

Although Sapir was noted as an expert in descriptive linguistics in a wide variety of languages, he was equally concerned with the analysis of cultural behavior and the effect of the interplay of both language and culture on the development of personality. He was a founder of formal descriptive linguistics. The versatility of Sapir's talents extended also to musical and poetry studies. Toward the end of his life he became interested in Jewish affairs, supporting the Yiddish Scientific Institute (YIVO), turning to the ethnological and linguistic study of the Talmud, and becoming appreciative of the "grand plan" that lay behind the restrictions of the orthodoxy he had rebelled against in his childhood.

His writings include *Wishram Texts* (1909), *Time Perspective in Aboriginal American Culture* (1916), *Nootka Texts* (1939), and *Language; An Introduction to the Study of Speech* (1921).
Selected Writings of Edward Sapir in Language, Culture, and Personality, 1949.

SARAH (originally Sarai; c. 19th century BCE) First of the four matriarchs of the Jewish people; wife of Abraham (q.v.). The half-sister of Abraham (Gen. 20:12), she was married to him in Mesopotamia and was his only wife. Together with her husband, she traveled from Ur of the Chaldees to Haran and from there to the land of Canaan. Her beauty was famed, and a late text, found in the Dead Sea Scrolls, gives a detailed description of her legendary beauty. On two occasions, when Abraham was afraid that foreign rulers would seek to take her for themselves and do him harm he passed her off as his sister. This occurred once in Egypt when the Pharaoh took her into his house, but the situation was saved when Pharaoh and his household were punished by plagues until Sarah

The four matriarchs (Sarah, Rebekah, Rachel and Leah). From the Amsterdam Haggadah, 1743.

● Religion is man's never-ceasing attempt to discover a road to spiritual serenity across the perplexities and dangers of daily life.
● The worlds in which different societies live are distinct worlds, not merely the same world with different labels attached. The undererstanding of a simple poem, for instance, involves not merely an understanding of the single words in their average significance, but a full comprehension of the whole life of the community as it is mirrored in the words, or as it is suggested by their overtones. Language is the most massive and inclusive art we know, a mountainous and anonymous work of unconscious generations.

Edward Sapir

was returned to Abraham (Gen. 12). A similar story is told, about Abimelech, king of Gerar, who also had his eye on Sarah (Gen. 26).

Until her old age, Sarah was barren. To provide Abraham with an heir, she gave him her Egyptian maid, Hagar, who bore Abraham a son, Ishmael. When Sarah was ninety years old, she and Abraham were informed by divine messengers that they would have a child. Sarah's reaction was one of disbelieving laughter, so that the son when he was born was called Isaac (q.v.) from the Hebrew root meaning "laugh." She now saw Ishmael as a threat to the rights of her own son and insisted — on the occasion of Isaac's weaning — that Hagar and Ishmael be driven out into the wilderness. Although Abraham took this move only unwillingly, God told him "Whatever Sarah says to you, do as she tells you, for through Isaac shall your descendants be named" (Gen. 21:12).

Sarah died in Hebron at the age of 127 and for her burial plot Abraham bought the cave of Machpelah where he and the other patriarchs and some of their wives were also subsequently buried.
N. M. Sarna, *Understanding Genesis*, 1966.

SARNOFF, DAVID (1891–1971) Pioneer of broadcasting, chairman of the Radio Corporation of America (RCA). He was born in Minsk, Belorussia, to an itinerant trader who brought his family to the United States in 1901. As a child David received grounding in Jewish education from his uncle, a rabbi, who insisted that he study two thousand words of the Talmud every day. On arrival in New York, David sold newspapers on the Lower East Side and ran errands for a butcher. He also earned extra money by singing in the synagogue choir on festivals. When he was fifteen his father died and he was left to support the family.

Sarnoff started his career as office boy at the

Commercial Cable Company. His first step to fame was on the night of April 14, 1912, when as manager of an experimental wireless station on the roof of a New York department store he monitored the *Titanic's* call for help. He quickly notified the authorities and the press, and during the next seventy-two hours monitored messages from rescue ships, noting the names of all seven hundred survivors.

By 1917 Sarnoff had become commercial manager at the Marconi Wireless and Telegraph Company of America. Combining expert technical knowledge with visionary business acumen, Sarnoff soon rose in the ranks of the company, and his innovations and bold imagination increased radio sales tremendously. RCA, which had absorbed American-Marconi, accepted his plan to make radio "a household utility in the same sense as a piano or phonograph," and began the mass production of radios as the home receiver of music.

As vice president and general manager of RCA, Sarnoff established a central broadcasting organization to feed programs to a number of interconnected radio stations, the beginning of the networks. He also acquired companies in allied industries, such as the Victor Talking Machine Company and its trademark, "His Master's Voice." His aim was to combine radio and phonograph in the same set. RCA also bought and developed Photophone and RKO. Over the years its various companies turned out products ranging from computer parts to radar sets used in tracing satellites.

In 1930 Sarnoff was elected president of RCA, but during the 1932 stock market crash the corporation nearly fell apart. However, he continued to foster research programs, including the development of television, which he had already foreseen a decade earlier. In April 1939, during the dedication ceremonies at the New York World Fair, he pioneered public television broadcasting in the United States, when he appeared before a television camera.

In 1942 Sarnoff became the board chairman and Chief Executive Officer of RCA, and under his direction the Corporation produced radar and signaling systems for the army. Sarnoff saw active duty in World War II, with the rank of colonel, serving as a communications consultant in the Pentagon and at General Dwight D. Eisenhower's headquarters in Europe. In 1944 he was promoted to the rank of brigadier general.

After the war the David Sarnoff Research Center was set up in Princeton, New Jersey, where scientists developed a compatible color television system that received black and white as well as color pictures. RCA also won the Federal Communication Commission's approval for setting its system as the standard system for color television. In 1961 Sarnoff brought RCA into the field of electronic data processing, publishing (through the acquisition of Random House), and the car rental business (through the purchase of Hertz).

In 1966 Sarnoff retired from the position of chief executive officer, but continued actively as board chairman until his death. He had dominated the electronic communications industry for over fifty years, consolidated a vast radio and TV empire with sixty-four manufacturing plants in the United States and other countries with 130,000 employees, making RCA one of the fifteen largest companies in America.

During his lifetime David Sarnoff received twenty-seven honorary college and university degrees as well as numerous awards and decorations, including the Legion of Merit.

SASSOON FAMILY Businessmen, philanthropists, and scholars originating in Baghdad, Iraq.

Its founder, **Sheikh Sasoon ben Salah** (1750–1830), headed the Baghdad Jewish community for some forty years and was the chief treasurer of the Ottoman pashas of Baghdad.

His son **David Sassoon** (1792–1864) entered his father's financial establishment. In 1828, because of revolution and oppression, he fled to Basra with his father, who died there. David Sassoon extended his business interests to Bombay where he settled in 1834. Starting on a small scale, he was soon acknowledged as the leading member of the local Jewish trading community. His firm exported, initially English textiles, to Persia and Mesopotamia and was soon the largest in India engaged in the Gulf trade. Sassoon expanded throughout most of Asia, including Indochina and southern China. A man of impressive appearance, he never abandoned the Baghdadi costume of his youth. He was an outstanding philanthropist, building fine synagogues in Bombay and Poona and supporting many institutions, Jewish scholars, and learned publications in India and elsewhere in the Far East. He remained profoundly attached to his Judaism; most of his numerous employees were Jewish and all his offices and branches were closed on Saturdays. From his two marriages he had fourteen children, including eight sons who were all involved in developing the business and carrying on their father's traditions. They moved from place to place but most of them eventually settled in London.

After David's death, the leadership of the business passed to his eldest son Sir **Abdulla** (later **Albert**) **Sassoon** (1818–1896). Like his father, he was prominent in Bombay business and philanthropy and built the first wharf on the west coast of India (the Sassoon Docks at Bombay). He developed textile manufacturing and weaving establishments and was one of the creators of India's industry. He also helped to found the Imperial Bank of Persia. In 1868 he was a member of the Bombay Legislative Council, but by 1873, when he received the freedom of the City of London, he was permanently domiciled in Britain, where the firm's activities were henceforth centered. His two brothers **Reuben Sassoon** (1835–1905) and **Arthur Sassoon** (1840–1912) were both in the close circle of Edward VII, both before and after his accession.

Another brother, **Solomon David Sassoon** (1841–1897) headed the firm in India and was responsible for its interests in Asia. An Orthodox Jew, he had a private synagogue in his home. His wife, **Flora Sassoon** (née Gabbay; 1859–1936), herself a great-granddaughter of David Sassoon, was a Hebrew scholar who was consulted on matters of Jewish law. She managed the firm in Bombay until moving to England in 1901. In England she headed a salon and delivered a discourse on a Talmudic subject at Jews' College. Whenever she traveled she took along her own ritual slaughterer and prayer quorum (*minyan*). Her son, **David Solomon Sassoon** (1880–1942) was a Hebraist and bibliophile who built up one of the greatest collections of Jewish manuscripts and wrote a history of the Jews of Baghdad. His son, **Solomon David Sassoon** (1915–1985), was an ordained rabbi who lived at Letchworth, outside London, until 1970 when he moved to Jerusalem. He published works of Talmudic scholarship. Initially he increased his father's manuscript collection, but started to disperse the collection in his later years.

One of David's eight sons, **Elias David Sassoon** (1820–1880) had an early success in China, but on returning to India felt himself stifled by the control of his brother, Albert, so he established in 1867 his own firm, E. D. Sassoon and Co., which led to bitter rivalry with the rest of the family. Elias was no less successful than his brothers and developed a gigantic worldwide company, along the same lines and traditions as the parent firm. He was succeeded by his son Sir **Jacob Elias Sassoon** (1844–1916) who built a large textile company in India, with fifteen thousand employees, and extended activities to Japan and Arabia.

Another son of David, **Sassoon David Sassoon** (1832–1867), was active in communal life in Britain. His daughter **Rachel Sassoon Beer** (1858–1927) married Frederick Arthur Beer in 1887. Beer was the proprietor of the noted Sunday newspaper, *The Observer*, and Rachel, nurturing journalistic ambitions, became its editor. Her ambition, however, went beyond editing, even when the proprietor was her husband, to owning a newspaper. In 1893 she bought the *Sunday Times*, which she edited until 1904, making her for over a decade editor of two rival newspapers.

Albert Sassoon's son, Sir **Edward Albert Sassoon** (1856–1912) married into the Rothschild (q.v.) family and became a Conservative member of Parliament. His son, Sir **Philip Albert Gustave David Sassoon** (1888–1939) was the most distinguished Sassoon politically. Educated at Eton and Oxford, he entered Parliament at age twenty-three, remaining a member until his death. He fought in World War I, when he was military private secretary to the British commander-in-chief in France, Sir Douglas Haig. In 1919 he was appointed parliamentary private secretary to the ministry of transport and from then until his death was almost continuously in government office. From 1920 to 1922 he was parliamentary private secretary to the prime minister, David Lloyd George, and was under-secretary for air from 1924 to 1929 and from 1931 to 1937. In 1937 he was appointed first commissioner of works. An outstanding art connoisseur and collector, he was a trustee of the National Gallery.

Another famous member of the family was the poet **Siegfried Lorraine Sassoon** (1886–1967), who won fame as one of the outstanding British poets of World War I, his poems relecting the ugliness of war. Entering the British army in August 1914, he won the military cross for gallantry. Shot through the neck, he was sent back to Britain, where in revulsion against the war, he issued a statement that he would no longer serve in the army. The medical board decided that his attitude was the outcome of mental strain and sent him to a home for neurasthenics at Craiglockhart, which he called Dottyville. Here he befriended the young poet Wilfred Owen, whose budding talent was spotted and nurtured by Sassoon. On recovery, he was sent back to serve in Palestine and France, now being wounded in the head and promoted to captain.

After the war, he was literary editor of the socialist newspaper, the *Daily Herald*, and then devoted himself exlusively to writing. His *Memoirs of a Fox-Hunting Man* (1928) was regarded as a minor classic and was awarded the prestigious Hawthornden prize. It conveyed the atmosphere of the English countryside and of county life. It was followed by *Memoirs of an Infantry Officer* (1930), an account of life in the trenches, and other autobiographical works.

A. Allfrey, *Edward VII and his Jewish Court*, 1991.
C. Roth, *The Sassoon Dynosty*, 1941.

SAUL (12th cent. BCE) First king of Israel. He was the son of Kish of the tribe of Benjamin, whose home was at Gibeah, identified as a short distance to the north of Jerusalem. There are three versions of the story of his election and anointment as king. According to the first, the prophet Samuel (q.v.) was told by God that he should anoint as king a man whom God had selected. The following day, Saul came to the land of Zuph in search of his father's lost asses. He is described as taller and more handsome than any other man and God identified him to Samuel as the man of whom he had spoken and Samuel duly anointed him (1 Sam. 9:1–10:1). According to the second, Samuel was approached by the elders, who demanded a king but did not propose a candidate. Samuel initially objected, seeing the proposal as compromising the kingship of God, but eventually relented and presided over Saul's election in Mizpah (1 Sam. 10). According to the third, Saul was made king by popular acclaim at Gilgal after leading an army to a victory over the Ammonites in Transjordan and rescuing the threatened city of Jabesh Gilead (1 Sam. 11).

An able and courageous soldier, Saul expanded the kingdom, making Benjamin its most important tribe. Under the command of himself and his son, Jonathan, he established a three-hundred-man standing army, the first such Israelite force. Despite the advantage of Israel's main enemy, the Philistines, in possessing iron chariots, Saul succeeded in defeating them in their first major battle, thanks largely to the courageous daring of Jonathan. The outcome was the temporary exclusion of the Philistines from the central hill country. His next victory was over the Amalekites, but on this occasion he offended Samuel by sparing the life of the Amalekite king, Agag, against the ancient commandment to exterminate all Amalekites. He also offended Samuel by offering a sacrifice before another battle, prior to Samuel's arrival. Samuel reached the conclusion that the house of Saul would have to be deposed and secretly anointed David (q.v.) as Saul's future successor. Meanwhile Saul fought not only the Philistines but also all surrounding nations, scoring a series of victories and strengthening his kingdom. He was noted as a military leader, although his killing of the Gibeonites gave him a bloodthirsty reputation. Little is known of economic developments during his reign. The organization of the kingdom was still primitive and he appointed relatives and Benjaminites, whom he could trust, to most of the key positions. He was zealous in outlawing pagan practices and promoted the religious authority of the priests.

Apart from the tension with Samuel, there was a growing rift with David, complicated by the fast friendship between David and Jonathan. David entered the court as minstrel, and played to Saul, especially during his periods of melancholia. Saul grew increasingly jealous of David as the latter's military prowess established him as a rival and potential successor. Saul made repeated efforts to kill David. Even his offer to give David the hand of his daughter Michal, if David would kill one hundred Philistines, was motivated by the hope that the challenge would lead to David's death. David succeeded, however, and became Saul's son-in-law. After David fled for his life, Saul went to great lengths in unsuccessful attempts to locate and kill him. Eventually he had to break off in order to turn his attention to the renewed threat from the Philistines. In a great battle on Mount Gilboa, the Philistines were victorious and Saul and three of this sons, including Jonathan, died — Saul either by committing suicide (1 Sam. 31:4) or, according to another account, being dispatched by an Amalekite (2 Sam. 1:5–12). His body was placed on a heathen temple in Beth Shean but was eventually rescued by the men of Jabesh Gilead who also buried his bones.

P. K. McCarter, Jr., *1 Samuel* (Anchor Bible), 1980.

SAVILLE, VICTOR (1897–1979) British film director and producer. Originally named Victor Salberg, Saville was born and educated in Birmingham. During World War I, he suffered serious injury and as a result was discharged from the army in 1916. He got a job as manager of a Coventry film theater, a position from which Saville landed a post in the features and newsreels department of Pathé

Frères. Subsequently, in partnership with Charles Wilcox, he became a film distributor in Leeds. In 1919, together with former school friend Michael Balcon (q.v.), Saville founded his own production company, Victory Motion Pictures.

Saville directed the first productions of the new company, among them its first major success, *Woman to Woman*, in 1923. In 1926 he joined Gaumont as a producer and in that capacity was responsible for a number of popular films directed by Maurice Elvey.

The following year he again formed a production company, Burlington Film Company, and two years later gained his first experience as a director of sound films while on a visit to the United States. During the 1930s, Saville directed for Gaumont-British, where his expartner, Michael Balcon, had become head of production. Among the most successful of these were several musicals starring Jessie Matthews.

In the 1930s, Saville worked with the London Film Productions of Alexander Korda (q.v.) and then signed a contract with MGM, producing two of that company's more prominent British films, *The Citadel* and *Goodbye, Mr. Chips*. From 1939 onwards he continued his association with MGM in Hollywood, still as a producer. Prestigious productions from this period include *The Mortal Storm* and *Dr. Jekyll and Mr. Hyde*. Moving to Columbia as a director, the success of *Tonight and Every Night* with Rita Hayworth led to his return to MGM, this time also as a director. During the 1950s he plied both occupations through his company, Parklane Productions. The most notable of his later efforts was Robert Aldrich's *Kiss Me Deadly*. Saville made his last film in 1962.
C. Rollins, *Victor Saville*, 1972.

SCHARY, DORE (1905–1980) U.S. film producer and writer. Born to Russian immigrant parents in Newark New Jersey, Schary shortened his first name, Isadore, to Dore when he was thirteen. His early professional years were spent as a newspaperman and stage actor, director, and writer. An unproduced play of his, *One Every Minute*, found its way to Columbia producer Walter Wanger in late 1932, and as a result Schary was in Hollywood as a screenwriter the following year. For the next five years he wrote screenplays that were produced by a number of studios. In 1938 he joined the screenwriting staff of MGM, winning an Academy Award for *Boys Town* in that year. Three years later, studio head Louis B. Mayer (q.v.) reacted to Schary's request to direct by putting him in charge of all low-budget productions.

Lassie Come Home and *Bataan* were among the films Schary produced for MGM between 1941 and 1943. From then until 1946 he was a producer for David O. Selznick's [q.v.] Vanguard Productions and supervised successes such as *I'll Be Seeing You* and *The Spiral Staircase*. After RKO's studio head Charles Koerner died, Schary accepted an offer to replace him. During his tenure at RKO,

What I needed more than luck was to acquaint myself on this new level, as head of production, with the staff of producers, directors and actors.... I started with some of the actors, the first of whom was Spencer Tracy. When he arrived for his afternoon two o'clock date he knocked on the door of my office and slowly pushed it open. Playing Uriah Heep he approached my desk rubbing his hands in a dry wash and said, "I don't know if you remember me. My name is Tracy." I love improvisations — I answered, "Of course, Samuel Tracy."

"No, no," Tracy said, "Spencer."

"Yes of course, how stupid of me to forget."

"Well, sir," Tracy added, "you may remember that I was in a play with you called *The Last Mile*." I nodded.

"Well, believe me, Mr. Schary, you can ask anyone in that play — I told all of them — just you keep your eye on that young fella who plays the reporter — one day he's going to be head of MGM." Then dropping Uriah like a dirty rag he said, "And so you are — you son of a bitch."
Dore Schary on taking over MGM

Schary was responsible for, among others. *Crossfire, The Boy with Green Hair* and *Mr. Blandings Builds His Dream House*. Returning to MGM as head of production after Howard Huges purchased RKO, Schary presided over the studio in its last days of glory, during which its musicals, in particular, reached their peak. In addition to his overall responsibility for all MGM output between 1948 and 1956, Schary also personally produced a number of films including *Bad Day at Black Rock*, *The Swan*, and *Designing Woman*.

Political machinations within MGM's parent company, Loew's Inc., cost the too-liberal Schary his position in 1956. Free to return to his early love, the theater, Schary wrote a number of plays, including *Sunrise at Campobello*, about Franklin D. Roosevelt, and *Act One*, the latter based on the autobiography of his friend, playwright and director Moss Hart (q.v.). Schary also produced screen adaptations of both plays and directed the film of *Act One*. A few years before his death he coauthored the play *Herzl* with Amos Elon. It was not well received. Dore was active in Jewish organizations, notably as chairman of the Anti-Defamation League of B'nai B'rith. In 1970 he was appointerd New York's first commissioner of cultural affairs.
D. Schary, *For Special Occasions*, 1963.
D. Schary, *Heyday*, 1979.
J. Schary Zimmer, *With a Cast of Thousands: A Hollywood Childhood*, 1963.

SCHECHTER, SOLOMON (1847–1915) Rabbinic scholar and a key figure in establishing the ideology and institutions of Conservative Judaism in the United States. Born in Romania, he went to Vienna in 1875, having acquired a wide knowledge of rabbinic Judaism. He studied at the Vienna rabbinical seminary for four years and then at the Berlin Hochschule für die Wissenschaft des Judentums, acquiring a mastery both of texts and of scientific method. In 1882, the English Jewish scholar Claude Montefiore invited Schechter to England to tutor Montefiore in rabbinic literature. During this time Schechter completed his critical edition of an early work of rabbinic ethics, *Avot of Rabbi Nathan.*

After he was appointed lecturer in rabbinic theology in 1890, he published the first of his books on rabbinic theology and on Jewish history and literature. By this time, his works were characterized by an attractive, lucid English style. While in Cambridge he became involved in the most dramatic episode of his life. Two English women informed him of some ancient Hebrew fragments they had come across in Egypt. Immediately realizing their significance, he traveled to Cairo and tracked them down in the storeroom of an old Cairo synagogue, where old manuscripts had been locked away for almost a thousand years. He managed to recover over 100,000 manuscript pages written in the Middle Ages from this Cairo *Genizah* (storeplace), which he brought back to Cambridge to study. Scholars to this day are engaged in examining this treasure, but Schechter had already identified and published some of its gems, including the original Hebrew text of the book of Ecclesiasticus (previously unknown) and the *Damascus Document*, over half a century later identified as a work of the then-unknown Qumran (Dead Sea) sect.

Solomon Schechter examining fragments of the Cairo Geniza at Cambridge University, 1897.

- There is something higher than modernity and that is eternity.
- Higher Criticism, Higher Anti-Semitism.
- Neither Scripture nor primitive Judaism, but general custom forms the real rule of Jewish practice.
- A nationality without an historical language, without a sacred literature, is a mere gypsy camp.
- Whatever the faults of the Rabbis, consistency was not one of them.

Solomon Schechter

After a short period as professor of Hebrew at London University, Schechter moved in 1902 to New York to head the Jewish Theological Seminary, the key institution of the Conservative movement, which was beginning to make its mark in the United States. Schechter reorganized the seminary along the lines of similar bodies in Europe, insisting that all rabbinic students have a university degree, attracting a faculty of world-renowned scholars, and laying the foundation for what would become one of the world's greatest Jewish libraries. He also introduced a teachers' seminary and founded the United Synagogue of America (1913), the lay arm of the Conservative movement.

In addition, Schechter was the architect of Conservative ideology. He maintained that Judaism was a living organism that changed from age to age, even while based on unchangeable teachings. The "collective conscience of Catholic Israel" (i.e., the Jewish people as an entirety) determines choice and change. The unique and holy people of Israel fosters the tradition, and not vice versa. Judaism of each age is a link in a chain, and while change can be made, it must be firmly rooted in tradition and must not endanger the overall structure. He opposed the arbitrariness of the changes introduced by Reform Judaism and its rejection of Jewish nationalism and Zionism. He himself accepted the school of cultural Zionism propounded by Ahad ha-Am (q.v.), which saw a future for the Jews in the Diaspora as well as in Zion but affirmed the return to Zion, where eventually the universal kingdom of God would be established for all mankind.

N. Bentwich, *Solomon Schechter*, 1948.
B. Mandelbaum, *The Wisdom of Solomon Schechter*, 1963.
H. Parzen, *Architects of Conservative Judaism*, 1964.

SCHENCK, JOSEPH M. (1878–1961) U.S. film producer. A native of Rybinsk, Russia, Schenck went to the United States in early childhood. He began his career as an errand boy, later progressing to ownership of drugstores in partnership with his brother Nicholas (destined to be president of Loew's/MGM for nearly thirty years). The two branched out into the area of amusement parks and in the early 1920s founded Loew's exhibition company together with Marcus Loew. Schenck married the film star Norma Talmadge in 1916, the year before he left Loew's to become an independent producer. Among the stars for whom Schenck produced were his wife, her sister Constance Talmadge, the comedian Fatty Arbuckle, and Buster Keaton, who was married to the third Talmadge sister, Natalie. It was the freedom provided by his contract with Schenck that enabled Keaton to produce his finest work between 1920 and 1928.

In 1924 Schenck was offered the position of chairman of the board of United Artists, a company five years old and in financial difficulty. Schenck attracted much new talent, including Gloria Swanson, in addition to his own stars Buster Keaton and William S. Hart. Within four years United Artists had become profitable. Following the death of its president, Hiram Abrams, Schenck assumed his position. Other important names who became associated with its during Schenck's tenure were Samuel Goldwyn (q.v.), Walt Disney, and Alexander Korda (q.v.).

In 1933, together with ex-Warner Brothers executive Darryl F. Zanuck (q.v.), Schenck founded Twentieth Century Pictures and two years later, merged the company with Fox and resigned from United Artists. Schenck, the power behind Zanuck's throne at Twentieth Century-Fox, was forced to resign as president in 1941, the year in which he served four months of a one-year prison sentence for tax offenses (for which he was later pardoned). He returned as an executive producer in 1944, finally leaving in 1952. The same year he was awarded a special Academy Award and founded his last company. This was Magna, set up with producer Michael Todd (q.v.) to exploit Todd's new widescreen process, Todd-AO.

N. Zierold, *The Moguls*, 1969.

SCHENIRER, SARAH (1883–1935) Pioneer in religious education for Orthodox Jewish girls. Born in Cracow, Poland, to a Hasidic family, she had a reputation for piety in her childhood. In her teens she worked as a seamstress, but spent her evenings studying the Bible and rabbinic texts — an exceptional activity for girls in her environment. She became concerned with the lack of education and intellectual focus among Orthodox women, which led to alienation in the family and sometimes to the temptations of non-Orthodox cultures.

During World War I she sought refuge in Vienna. There, she began to think about instituting classes in Judaism for young women. Returning to Cracow in 1917, she opened a school in her home and sent two of her assistants to open schools elsewhere. Twenty-five girls below the age of seventeen lived in Schenirer's own two-room apartment, spending months studying throughout the day under her tuition. In 1918 the ultra-Orthodox movement, Agudat Israel, adopted the program of schools for girls, whose education had been consistently ignored in such circles, and under the name Bais Yaakov ("House of Jacob") proceeded to develop a network of such institutions. In 1923 Schenirer started, on her own initiative and out of her own meager means, to train teachers for these schools, twenty of which were in operation by 1925 — some of them high schools. Sometimes she traveled to other towns to address mass meetings of women to encourage them to found schools for their daughters. In the summers she organized courses in the countryside, where girls who were training to be teachers could get out of the sweltering ghetto of Cracow and spend their time studying in the woods and meadows. By 1939 there were hundreds of Beis Yaakov schools throughout Poland.

Schenirer also founded the Bnos ("Daughters") Youth Organization for religious girls. These innovations gave unprecedented content to the life of Jewish girls and women, who thanks to the studies, comradeship, and manifold activities, were now able to live in an environment that had previously been confined to males.

Little is known of Schenirer's personal life. She divorced her first husband, who was less observant than she. Her charismatic personality attracted the love of the girls for whom she was responsible. She also had a sense of humor, expressed through stories and jokes and a cheerful personality.

Beis Yaakov schools spread to other countries, including Palestine, where teachers' training colleges were opened in Tel Aviv and Jerusalem. In Europe the work of Schenirer was almost entirely destroyed in the Holocaust, but after the war it was reestablished in the United States as well as in some of its former centers. However, the emphasis now was on the preservation of tradition rather than on finding a formula for remaking tradition with contemporary conditions as it had been during Schenirer's lifetime.

Her collected writings, translated into Hebrew from the original Yiddish, were published in Tel Aviv (1955–1960).

J. Grunfeld-Rosenbaum (Leo Jung, ed.), *Jewish Leaders, 1750–1940*, 1953.

FROM THE LAST TESTAMENT OF SARAH SCHENIRER

My dear girls, you are going out into the great world. Your task is to plant the holy seed in the souls of pure children. In a sense, the destiny of Israel of old is in your hands.

Be strong and of good courage. Don't tire. Don't slacken your efforts. You have heard of the Hassid who came to his rabbi and said joyfully, "Rabbi, I have finished the whole Talmud." "What has the Talmud taught you?" asked the rabbi, "Your learning is fine but your practical task is the main thing."

D. Weissmann (E. Koltun, ed.), *The Jewish Woman: New Perspectives*, 1976.

SCHICK, BELA (1877–1967) Pediatrician. He was born prematurely while his mother was on holiday in the Hungarian resort of Bolgar. The birth was assisted by his uncle, Dr. Sigismund Telegdi, who had a large medical practice in the region. At first it was thought that Schick would not live, but his uncle's care not only saved his life but also created a special bond between the two that was to infleunce his future career choice.

Schick's parents lived in Graz, Austria, where his father, a grain merchant, wanted him to join the family business.

During one of Schick's boyhood holiday visits to his uncle, he accompanied his uncle on a house call to a girl dying of diphteria. As a result of this visit, the young Schick determined to become a doctor against his father's wishes. Although only an average student, he discovered some old textbooks of science and anatomy in his school library and for years spent much of his spare time secretly imbibing as much knowledge as he could in preparation for university. Eventually his father relented and allowed his son to enter the small medical school in Graz.

Schick graduated in 1900, and in 1902 joined the University of Vienna faculty, where he remained until 1923. In 1918 he became assistant professor extraordinary of child diseases. His researches in Vienna concerned problems of immunity and it was he, together with his colleague Clemens von Pirquet, who first coined the term "allergy" as a clinical entity. At first he researched the problems of "serum sickness," announcing in 1908 his discovery of a test for susceptibility to diphtheria (the Schick test) which made him famous. In 1910 he made public the Schick sign for bronchial tuberculosis.

From 1923, he directed the Pediatric Department of Mount Sinai Hospital, New York, where he remained until 1942. From 1936 to 1943 he was also clinical professor of diseases of children at Columbia University and visiting professor at the Albert Einstein College of Medicine. He was chief of the Pediatric Department of Beth-El Hospital, Brooklyn, N.Y., from 1950 to 1962.

After formally retiring he remained consulting physician to a number of hospitals. Schick devoted his life to improving children's welfare. He was particularly involved with the nutrition of the newborn and feeding problems in children. M. Murray Peshkin, his friend and allergist colleague, wrote of him: "Bela Schick taught me by example that when one takes care of a chil one is taking care humanity. As aperson, as a physician, as an investigator of medical unknowns he stands in his own right as one of the giants of medicine of all time."
A. Gronowicz, *Bela Schick and the World of Children*, 1954.
I. Noble, *Physician to the Children — Dr. Bela Schick*, 1963.

SCHIFF, JACOB HENRY (1847–1920) U.S. financier, philanthropist, and community leader. He was born in Frankfurt, Germany, to a wealthy family of bankers, distinguished scholars and rabbis going back to the 14th century. He was a restless, unpredictable child, given to quick and violent bursts of anger, and as he grew older was rebellious and temperamental. He was short in stature and a great believer in physical fitness. In 1863 Jacob went to work with his father on the Frankfurt stock exchange, but two years later moved to New York, where in 1867 he formed his own brokerage firm with two other men from his hometown. When the partnership papers were ready for signature it was discovered that Jacob was not yet of legal age to sign. The partnership was later dissolved and after a brief spell as manager of the Deutsche Bank in Hamburg, Jacob returned to New York and in 1873 joined Kuhn, Loeb and Co., where he concentrated on railroad management and financing. Although a junior partner, Schiff soon dominated the field in the United States and developed contacts with European bankers on money matters concerning railroads. In 1875 when he married Therese Loeb, daughter of Solomon Loeb, he became a full partner in the firm and by 1881 was running the influential company.

Schiff, joining forces with E. H. Harriman, owner of the Illinois Central Railroad, bought the Union Pacific Railroad in 1897, and their collaboration led to the amassing of the greatest single railroad fortune in the world. In 1901 he was involved in the "Battle of the Giants" in the struggle to take over Northern Pacific, which led to a major panic on Wall Street and the British and European stock markets.

In 1904 Schiff arranged a two-hundred-million-dollar loan for the Japanese government, taking a financial risk because of his profound hatred of the anti-Semitic policies of the Russian government. He made a number of public statements at the time of the pogroms, calling the Russian government "the enemy of mankind," and urged an armed revolt against the tsar. After Japan's victory in the Russo-Japanese War, Schiff was awarded the Second Order of the Treasure, becoming the first foreigner to receive an official invitation to a meal at the imperial palace. In 1910 he was one of the leaders of a campaign to abrogate the commercial treaty with Russia because of its mistreatment of its Jews.

Schiff retained many of his Orthodox habits (he said his prayers every morning) but was affiliated with New York's Temple Emanu-El and the Reform Movement. He was active in the establishment and development of the Jewish Theological Seminary, and also supported both Yeshiva College and Hebrew Union College. He used his personal wealth and influence on behalf of Jews everywhere, and his widespread philanthropic and communal activities brought him recognition as the foremost figure of American Jewry. He was a leading supporter of the Jewish Publication Society of Amer-

Jacob Henry Schiff, seated to the right of Theodore Roosevelt (speaking) at groundbreaking ceremony of New York's Montefiore Hospital, 1900.

ica and financed its publication of the Schiff Library of Jewish Classics. Yet, he was miserly about the use of the telephone in his home and kept a little notebook on the stand beside it where each person was required to enter calls. At the end of each month he carefully compared the calls listed in the notebook with those on the bill. Schiff presented the New York YMHA with its first permanent home, complete with gymnasium, library, clubrooms, and classrooms. He introduced the "matching gift" system of philanthropy, and believed that a man's giving should be done in his lifetime, under his personal supervision. He headed Montefiore Hospital in New York and paid regular visits to the patients. He was one of the founders of the Provident Loan Society, endowed buildings at Barnard College, the Semitic Museum at Harvard University, Frankfurt University in Germany, and the Technion in Haifa. However, Schiff never permitted his name to be attached to any of these structures with the single exception of the Schiff Pavilion at the Montefiore Hospital.

Jacob Schiff was a founding member of the American Jewish Committee and in 1914 was instrumental in creating the American Jewish Relief Committee, which later became the Joint Distribution Committee. He served on the New York City Board of Education, was vice-president of the chamber of commerce, and was a member of many New York city commissions.

C. Adler, *Jacob H. Schiff; His Life and Letters*, 2 vols., 1928.

P. Arnsberg, *Jakob H. Schiff* (German), 1969.

SCHMIDT, JOSEPH (1904–1942) Romanian tenor. Born in Bavideni, Bukovina. His father, a farmer, was not interested in the arts but Schmidt's mother encouraged her son's musical aspirations. During World War I, Schmidt's family settled in Czernowitz (Cernauti), where he began to sing in the local synagogue choir. He started his concert career at the age of twenty, and also appeared as cantor in Czernowitz. Later Schmidt continued to perform as cantor at both the Leopoldstadt Synagogue in Vienna and at the Adas Yisroel Synagogue in Berlin.

Schmidt studied at the Berlin conservatory and in 1928 began his career as a radio singer. After gaining popularity in Germany, Schmidt moved to Belgium in 1933, and later to Vienna, where he had immense success. He soon rivaled Richard Tauber (q.v.) as the most popular singer of the time. A year later Schmidt visited Palestine and also performed regularly in England, France, the United States and the Far East.

In 1940, when the Germans invaded Belgium, Schmidt was saved from arrest by gentile friends. He attempted to reach America through France, but never made it. Eventually he reached Switzerland where he was interned in a refugee camp in Gyrenbad, near Zurich. There he contracted a serious throat ailment from which he died.

Schmidt was known for his great lyric expressiveness and for his rendition of light songs and operetta. His recordings were best-sellers at the time. As he was only four feet ten inches in height (he was known as the "pocket tenor" as well as "the German Caruso"), he seldom appeared in opera. His recordings and radio broadcasts, however, were very popular. He starred in his own quasi-autobiographical movie, *My Song Goes Round the World*. It was the story of a dwarf-like singer whose voice arouses the passions of women, but whose appearance results only in their pity. The premiere of the film on May 9, 1933, in Berlin, was a stunning success. Among the dignitaries was Josef Goebbels, the Reich's propaganda minister, who was reported to have said confidentially, "we should send such films abroad; they will attest to our liberal positions towards the Jews."

Today opera lovers can still enjoy Schmidt's silvery voice on compact disc featuring in some of his best loved arias.

K. and G. Ney-Nowotny, *Joseph Schmidt: das Leben und Sterben eines Unvergesslichen*, 1963.

SCHNABEL, ARTUR (1882–1951) Pianist and composer. He was born in Lipnik, Austria. When he was seven years old his family moved to Vienna, where his piano teacher, Theodor Leschetizky, told his student: "You will never be a pianist; you are a musician." Schnabel made his debut at the age of eight, and from that time concentrated on performing a rather limited repertoire. He once explained, "I am attracted only to music which I consider to be better than it could be performed. Therefore I feel that unless a piece of music presents a never-ending problem to me, it does not interest me much. For instance, Chopin's studies are perfect pieces, but I simply can't spend time on them. I believe I know these pieces; but playing a Mozart sonata, I am not so sure that I do know it, inside and out. Therefore I can spend endless time on it."

While Schnabel's Mozart recordings are considered some of his finest achievements, he was above all associated with Beethoven's music. Schnabel gave recitals of all of Beethoven's piano sonatas in Berlin and London. Arnold Schoenberg (q.v.) asserted that the magnitude of Schnabel's "creative accomplishments left technical considerations far behind. His Beethoven has incomparable style, intellectual strength and phrasing of aristocratic purity. The important thing was that even when his fingers failed him, his mind never did. Schnabel was always able to make his playing interesting. A mind came through — a logical, stimulating, sensitive mind."

Schnabel's success was acclaimed above all in Europe. His American tours were far from successful, and he never got along with his agents there. In fact, during the last eight years of his life Schnabel dispensed with the services of agents altogether. He lived in Berlin from 1900 until Hitler came to power in 1933, when he moved to Switzerland, and eventually to the United States, where he became a citizen in 1944.

In 1905 Schnabel married the contralto Therese Behr, a renowned interpreter of the songs of Schubert, Schumann and Brahms. They gave combined concerts, among which the Schubert recitals in Berlin in 1928 became legendary. Schnabel's happiest years, according to his own memoirs, were in Berlin between 1914 and 1924, a time when he made many artistic friends and also devoted some time to composition, searching for a new and highly individual musical language; his works, however, are now almost never performed. Neville Cardus described Schnabel, the composer, in the following words: "It seemed as though Wordsworth has suddenly gone off at a tangent and written like Gertrude Stein [q.v.]."

Schnabel was a short, cigar-smoking man with a big head, a stocky body and stubby fingers. He looked anything but the popular conception of a pianist. At the keyboard he was a rather unimpressive sight. Most popular pianists are necessarily showmen, and have been so since Liszt. Nearly all of the romantic pianists lifted their hands high; smoke came from their nostrils and lighting from their eyes, and their audiences screamed and carried on. But that did not apply to the new school of pianists. Schnabel never lifted his hands high, nor did he shake his head or try to see the Deity on the roof of the concert hall. Yet when he played, there was cathedral silence in the auditorium. His concerts were not circuses; they were communions. And when the audience dispersed, it was with the feeling of having been cleansed.

Arnold Schoenberg

C. Saerchinger, *Artur Schnabel*, 1957.
A. Schnabel, *My Life and Music*, 1961.
K. Wolf, *The Teaching of Artur Schnabel*, 1972.

SCHNEERSOHN FAMILY   See Shneur Zalman of Lyady.

SCHNEIDERMAN, ROSE (1882–1972) U.S. labor union organizer. Rose (Rachel) was born in the small village of Saven in Russian Poland. When she was eight years old, the family migrated to the Lower East Side of New York. Not long after, her father suddenly died; her pregnant mother could not support all her children, so she and her two brothers were temporarily placed in orphanages. By the age of thirteen, she had returned home to her mother; her formal schooling ended and she entered the working world. She was already the main support of her family.

Schneiderman's first two jobs were in stores, but within a few years she went to work in the garment industry, in a cap-making factory. Here she first encountered union workers — all male. She and a co-worker responded by recruiting the requisite number of women to have their own charter. Fired with a vision of social justice, she saw labor unions as her means of fighting her own way upward, and in her battles for minimum wages, maximum working hours, and legislation to prevent child labor, she sought to take other working women and girls with her. In this struggle she gained the support of women of means who even walked picket lines with her.

In 1906 Schneiderman helped found the National Women's Trade Union League (WTUL). From 1914 to 1917 she was a general organizer of the International Ladies Garment Workers Union. From 1918 until 1926 she served as vice president of the National WTUL; she continued as president of the New York branch of the WTUL until her retirement in 1949.

Schneiderman also worked for the Women's Suffrage Association. Following their success in winning the vote for women in 1920, the Women's party's initial efforts for an equal rights amendment began. If women had obtained the equal rights with men that these women sought, it would have meant the abrogation of the protective legislation for women that Rose Schneiderman had achieved. All the laws guaranteeing women minimum wages, maximum hours, and compensation for pregnancy would have been nullified since the laws did not apply to men. Therefore it marked a critical, paradoxical juncture for her in her quest for bettering the condition of women. She found herself defending protective legislation and thus opposing her former friends with whom she had worked in presuffrage days.

She ran for the Senate in 1920 on the Farm Labor party ticket. In 1937 Governor Herbert Lehman appointed her secretary of the New York State Department of Labor, where she worked until 1943, and she served as labor adviser to sev-

A tiny, red-haired bundle of social dynamite, Rose Schneiderman did more to upgrade the dignity and living standards of working women than any other American.

Seventy years ago, first as a department store clerk, then as a cap maker and finally as a founder of the Women's Trade Union League, she pioneered in the mission of emancipation that reached flower two decades later in the campaign for women's suffrage and the current movement for women's liberation. Franklin D. Roosevelt and his wife, Eleanor, both learned most of what they knew about unions from her — lessons that eventuated in the Wagner Act, the National Industry Recovery Act and other New Deal landmarks.

Ironically, many of the pioneer laws she helped put on the statute books to abolish the sweatshop through regulation of wages, hours and safety standards for women in industry became the target a half century later of women campaigning for the Equal Rights Amendment, who regarded all protective legislation as discriminatory. There was less paradox in that shift than appeared, however. The upward march that Rose Schneiderman did so much to start had now progressed to a point where women felt able to stand on their own feet, with walls of special protection as unwelcome as walls of prejudice. That progress is her monument.

From the obituary of Rose Schneiderman published by _The New York Times_, August 14, 1972

eral national labor and other government agencies. Her friendship with Franklin D. and Eleanor Roosevelt lasted until their deaths. She was one of their mentors in trade union matters.

H. Schneiderman and I. Carmin (ed.), _Who's Who in World Jewry_, 1955.
R. Schneiderman with L. Goldthwaite, _All For One_, 1967.

SCHNITZER, EDUARD See Emin Pasha

SCHNITZLER, ARTHUR (1862–1931) Austrian dramatist. Born in Vienna, son of a prominent Jewish laryngologist whose patients included famed actors, Schnitzler became enamored of the theater and was stimulated at an early age to write plays. Admiring his father, whom he later delineated as the title-hero of his drama _Professor Bernhardi_ (1912), he too chose medicine as his profession. After obtaining his medical degree from the University of Vienna in 1885, he engaged in the practice of psychiatry for only a few years. From 1887 to 1894 he edited the medical journal, _Internationale Klinische Rundschau_, and his own articles dealt with psychotherapy. However, he was becoming more interested in the literary analysis of the human soul. Sigmund Freud (q.v.) once stated that Schnitzler's poetic intuition led to some of the same discoveries as did his own painstaking research.

In the 1880s Schnitzler wrote poems and tales under a pseudonym, Anatol, since he did not want to jeopardize his scientific reputation. The main character in a series of playlets, which were published in 1892, Anatol is Schnitzler's symbol for youth. He may have faults but he also possesses glamor and wit. He may be unfaithful to his "sweet girls," but he also has the magic gift of genuinely falling in love again and again for the first time. The female counterpart of this philanderer is the sweet maiden, a literary type created by Schnitzler. In the _Anatol_ playlets she is treated frivolously as merely a source of adventure and pleasure. However, in Schnitzler's first full-length plays, _Marchen_ (1981), and _Liebelei_ (1895 _Dalliance_, 1896) he presents love as viewed by woman. Love then assumes more serious aspects. What may be mere flirtation for the man is shown to be laden with deepest tragedy for the woman.

As the dramatist matured, his plays centered more often on the problems and ills of married life. In the plays _Paracelsus_ (1897), _Der einsame Weg,_ (1903; _The Lonely Way_, 1904), _Zwischenspiel_ (1904; _Intermezzo_, 1915), and _Das weite Land_ (1908; _The Vast Domain_, 1923) he probes deeply into emotional sickness but offers no general solutions. He rather holds that each disturbance in the relations between human beings must be carefully studied and diagnosed before a specific remedy can be prescribed. The medicine that cures in one case may kill in another. Each human being is unique, and generalizing about human conduct is folly.

In the ten dialogues of _Reigen_ completed in 1897 (_Merry-Go-Round_, 1953) but whose publication and staging were delayed for many years because the author correctly feared misinterpretation, he depicts with sardonic humor the roundelay of sexuality. In dispassionate, melancholy conversations, he sketches the pettiness, brutality, and absurdity of the sex experience when it is purely a physical expression devoid of love. He selects his characters from all social strata and depicts each of them as equally pitiable. The play aroused an enormous scandal when first performed in Berlin in 1920, but was ultimately a tremendous success as the French film _La ronde_, as well as in British theaters of the 1980s and on television.

Schnitzler's confession of faith is contained in his autobiographic novel _Der Weg ins Freie_ 1907; _The Road to the Open_, 1913). It is the faith of an extreme skeptic who has reached the point of doubting his own doubts. Freedom and understanding loom as his ideals until he comes to realize that excessive freedom leads to a disintegration of one's personality, and that understanding, if carried too far, acts as a paralyzing force. In this novel, as well as in _Professor Bernhardi_, he also grapples with Jewish issues, primarily Zionism and assimilation. He does not minimize the difficulties

> • If a person knew at twenty how fortunate he is to be twenty, he would get a stroke because of sheer bliss.
> • Our soul is a vast panorama. There is room for so much in us at the same time: Love and treachery, faith and faithlessness, adoration of one person and longing for another, or for several others. We try to bring order into ourselves as best we can; but this order is after all something artificial. Our natural state is chaos.
> • I would not want Zionism eliminated from the world's political scene of today or from the soul economy of contemporary Jewry. As a spiritual element to elevate one's self-consciousness, as a possibility for reacting against all sorts of dark hatreds, and especially as a philanthropic action of the highest rank, Zionism will always retain its importance, even if it should some day prove to have been merely a historic episode.
>
> **Arthur Schnitzler**

of Jewish existence as a minority in each nation, but neither does he accept the Zionist solution of his friend Theodor Herzl (q.v.). Schnitzler holds that anti-Semitism will persist as long as the sense of difference remains deep-rooted between Jews and their neighbors and will operate against mass assimilation. Perhaps in a thousand years the "Jewish question" may cease to exist, but not in the immediate future. Meanwhile, it will be up to individual Jews to adjust themselves as best possible to their condition of Jewishness.

From the closing decade of the 19th century, Schnitzler was a central figure of Jungwien, the literary movement that opposed the naturalism of Berlin and Munich. This movement dominated Austrian letters until World War I. With the rise of expressionism, Schnitzler's fame waned, even though he continued with dramatic masterpieces such as *Komodie der Verfuhrung* ("A Comedy of Seduction," 1924) and *Der Gang zum Weiher* ("The Walk to the Lake," 1927). It reached its lowest ebb during the Nazi years. Since the end of World War II, his reputation rose again and his works are recognized as classics of Austrian literature.

S. Liptzin, *Arthur Schnitzler*, 1932.
H. W. Reichert and H. Salinger (eds.), *Studies in Arthur Schnitzler*, 1961.

SCHOENBERG, ARNOLD (1874–1951) Austrian composer, one of the great innovators of 20th-century music. Born into a middle-class Jewish family in Vienna, he was brought up as a Catholic, but apparently later became a Protestant. He started to play the violin at the age of eight, and almost immediately began composing. When he was fifteen, his father died, and the young Schoenberg was sent out to work. During his final school

years he taught himself to play the cello, and his friend Oskar Adler coached him in elementary harmony and aural training. Another friend, Alexander von Zemlinsky (whose sister he was later to marry), gave him advice and encouragement. Schoenberg was now the family's sole provider, and he reluctantly went to work in a small private bank. During this period, he played cello in a small orchestra conducted by Zemlinsky, and through this group his first compositions were performed.

Being self-taught, Schoenberg always remained detached from the strongly traditional Viennese musical schools. This may be why he, alone of all the composers, was able to forge a musical reconciliation between diametrically opposed musical factions: the advocators of Brahmsian traditionalism and the supporters of the Wagnerian revolution.

When he was nineteen years old, the bank for which he worked went bankrupt, and Schoenberg determined to devote himself to his music. A new musical revolution was underway, and Schoenberg almost single-handedly led the musical path of creativity in a new direction.

Verklärte Nacht ("Transfigured Night"; op. 4), written in 1903, bore strong links with the Wagnerian chromatic splendor, while its Brahmsian technical formalities are also evident. The uniquely Schoenbergian Brahms-Wagner synthesis is also displayed in the Gothic *Gurrelieder* of 1910.

Schoenberg subsequently forged a new language of musical expressionism, atonality. The years between 1903 and 1914 formed the period of free atonalism, when Schoenberg based almost all his compositions on literary texts, and during which he shared the expressionist belief that "nothing must hinder the free expression of the subjective ego." He felt compelled to use the formal organization of literary texts, because absolute freedom made it difficult to write an extended composition without any firm principle of construction.

Arnold Schoenberg. Sketch by Egon Schiele, 1917.

During this period, Schoenberg wrote Six Orchestral Songs, (op. 8), the second String Quartet (with soprano solo, op. 10), the choral *Friede auf Erden* (Op. 13), *Das Buch der hängenden Gärten* (Op. 15), *Erwartung* (Op. 17), *Die glückliche Hand* (Op. 18), *Pierrot lunaire* (Op. 21), and Four Orchestral Songs (Op. 22).

The melodrama, *Pierrot lunaire*, based on poems by Albert Giraud, employs a new Schoenbergian technique called *Sprechgesang*, combining speech and song. A period of almost ten years followed, during which Schoenberg wrote very little. During his period he was drafted into the Austrian army, and he resumed serious composition in 1923, after a long period of searching for a replacement for the classic functions of tonality and harmony. From 1923 the new methods of serial composition or dode caphony characterized his work, contrasting with his earlier free-dissonant style. In 1928 his *Variations*, (Op. 31) was the first full-scale orchestral piece composed in the new technique: like many of his future compositions, it led to a furor among contemporary theorists, composers, and critics.

From 1925 to 1933, Schoenberg taught at the Prussian Academy of Arts in Berlin. When the Nazis came to power, he sought refuge in America, and after a year in New York moved to Los Angeles, California, where he remained until his death, teaching at the University of Southern California and the University of California, Los Angeles. In 1933 he reacted to Nazism by formally adopting Judaism, and his subsequent works were influenced by his new Jewish interests. His last years in America saw major works such as *Kol Nidre*, the highly emotive *Survivor from Warsaw*, together with his Piano Concerto (Op. 42), his Violin Concerto (Op. 36), and the powerful String Trio (Op. 45), written after Schoenberg suffered a severe stroke that left him in frail health. He left a number of compositions with religious motifs unfinished: the cantata *Jacob's Ladder*, a cycle of *Modern Psalms*, and the opera *Moses und Aron*, which was successfully performed in its two-act form.

He also wrote various texts and books elucidating his teaching and composition approach, including *Structural Functions of Harmony*.

Schoenberg left his books and manuscripts to the Jewish National and University Library in Jerusalem.

R. Leibowitz, *Schoenberg and his School*, 1975.

A. L. Ringer, *Arnold Schoenberg: The Composer as Jew*, 1990.

H. H. Stuckenschmidt, *Arnold Schoenberg*, 1977.

SCHOLEM, GERSHOM GERHARD (1897–1982) Scholar of Jewish mysticism. He was born in Berlin to an assimilated family but in his youth, like many young German Jews of his background, he joined the Zionist movement. Unlike his peers, however, while still in secondary school, he also began devoting himself to the study of Judaism and Jewish sources, teaching himself Hebrew in the process.

As a Zionist, he opposed World War I because he felt it was against Jewish interests, and was expelled from school for distributing antiwar literature. Scholem studied in German universities, where he first majored in mathematics and philosophy and then changed his subject to Oriental languages. His doctoral thesis was a translation and commentary on one of the most obscure and difficult kabbalistic texts, the *Book of Bahir*. Many translations and studies on the Kabbalah followed, making Scholem a renowned authority on the Kabbalah, and the first to develop a field that had been neglected by scholars up to that time. Aside from commentary, interpretation, and analysis of kabbalistic texts, he also brought to light many unknown manuscripts, and collected a 24,000-book library of Jewish mysticism (now in the Hebrew University).

In 1922 he emigrated to Palestine, and in 1923 began to work at the Hebrew University of Jerusalem, first as a librarian, then as a lecturer and finally as a professor of Jewish mysticism and Kabbalah. This appointment allowed him to devote all his energies to the field of research that his father had once deplored as an "unprofitable pursuit."

Scholem believed that myth is central to religious tradition. He also maintained that the kabbalist movement was sparked by an underground tradition of Gnosticism among Jewish mystics. His work traced the history of Jewish mysticism from late antiquity to moderntimes, and attempted to prove that Judaism was not a monolithic tradition, but rather an interplay of conflicting forces.

Scholem's philosophy was a mixture of Zionism and anarchism. He believed that the Jews could only gain control of their existence by living in a Jewish state. This existence, however, would have to be pluralistic, rather than monolithic. His philosophy, views, and studies were represented in many writings, which fill a bibliography of 579 entries. The major works include *Major Trends in Jewish Mysticism*, *Jewish Gnosticism*, and *Sabbatai Sevi*.

- Once, in the army, I was asked if I was really the composer Arnold Schoenberg. "Someone had to be," I said, "and nobody else wanted to, so I took it on myself."
- Understanding of my music still goes on suffering from the fact that musicians do not regard me as a common-or-garden-composer who expresses his more or less good and new themes in a not entirely inadequate musical language — but as a modern dissonant 12-tone experimenter. But there's nothing I long for more intensely than to be taken for a better sort of Tchaikovsky — a *bit* better, but really, that's all. Or, if anything more, than that people should know my tunes and whistle them!

Arnold Schoenberg

D. Biale, *Gershom Scholem: Kabbalah and Counter History*, 1982.

J. Dan, *Gershom Scholem and the Mystical Dimensions in Jewish History*, 1987.

G. Scholem, *Walter Benjamin: The Story of a Friendship*, 1981.

SCHULBERG, B[enjamin] P[ercival] (1892–1957) U.S. film producer. Schulberg was born in Bridgeport, Connecticut, and attended City College of New York. His studies were interrupted by an opportunity to work for Franklin P. Adams at the *Evening Mail*. Schulberg went on to become an editor of the trade publication *Film Reports*, and this led to an acquaintance with pioneer director Edwin S. Porter, for whom he went on to work as a script editor. As the result of a takeover, Schulberg found himself working for Adolph Zukor's [q.v.] Famous Players company. As Zukor's publicist, Schulberg was credited with the successful marketing of *Queen Elizabeth*, starring Sarah Bernhardt, a film that made a fortune for Zukorg. Schulberg is also said to be responsible for terming Zukor's star Mary Pickford America's Sweetheart.

Leaving Zukor and the company (by then known as Paramount) in the late 1910s, Schulberg struck out on his own. He returned as producer in 1925, bringing with him his biggest discovery from his independent years, the IT girl, Clara Bow. By 1928 Schulberg was in charge of Paramount's West Coast production and was personally involved in the discovery of a number of the stars featured in Paramount productions of the late silent and early sound eras.

Schulberg was one of those who did not survive the major reorganization at Paramount in 1932, though he continued to release his independent productions through the company up to 1935. In that year he went to work as a producer for Columbia, where he was characterized as a has-been by the studio boss Harry Cohn (q.v.). After 1937, his remaining films were once more made as an independent producer. In 1949, six years after his last film, Schulberg was desperate enough for work as to take out an advertisement in *Variety* pleading for rehabilitation. His son is the writer Budd Schulberg, whose output includes the novel *What Makes Sammy Run?*, an unflattering portrait of a Hollywood mogul.

B. Schulberg, *Moving Pictures: Memories of a Hollywood Prince*, 1981.

SCHWARTZ, DELMORE (1913–1966) U.S. poet, author, and critic. Born in Brooklyn, he was educated in philosophy at the University of Wisconsin, New York University, and Harvard University. He achieved a reputation as a poet while still a college student. Later he served on the faculties of Harvard, Princeton, the University of Chicago, and Indiana University. At the age of twenty-six, he was awarded a Guggenheim fellowship. In 1953 he won the National Academy of Arts and Letters award.

Schwartz became an important voice in the increasingly critical examination of contemporary life that governed America in the aftermath of the depression. Having been the editor for the *Partisan Review* and poetry editor and movie critic for the *New Republic*, Schwartz gained overnight recognition with the publication of his first book, *In Dreams Begin Responsibilities* (1938). In a review of the book, Allen Tate wrote that Schwartz's poetic style was "the only genuine innovation since Ezra Pound and T. S. Eliot came upon the scene twenty-five years ago." This book includes a long philosophical poem about a young man in search of stability and coherence in a world torn between fact and fantasy, reason and emotion. The self-conscious and introspective nature of his language is expanded upon in *Shenandoah* (1941), a short play dealing with the ever-increasing absence of meaning in the life of a poet of the 1930s. In 1943 he published his most ambitious work, *Genesis, Book I*, a long introspective poem having as its central figure a young, sensitive American of Russian-Jewish origin growing up in New York City. Presenting a genuinely tragic view of life, this work deals with the struggle to develop and maintain a unique selfhood. Schwartz succeeds in interlocking theology and the mythology of his times in a very innovative manner. *The Imitation of Life* (1943), a volume of critical essays on the plight of the immigrant to the United States, was followed by *The World Is a Wedding* (1948), a collection of witty, sometimes angry, short stories about middle-class Jewish life. *Summer Knowledge* (1959), a collection of poems, was awarded the Bollingen Prize in 1960.

After resigning as visiting professor at Syracuse University in 1965, he was rarely seen even by his literary friends. Having lived in Greenwich Village for the latter part of his life, Schwartz was known as a quick and emotional person who talked so fast his words would often merge together. He died a lonely dath in amidtown New York hotel.

He was the model for Von Humboldt Flesher in Saul Bellow's novel *Humboldt's Gift*.

J. Atlas, *Delmore Schwartz: The Life of an American Poet*, 1977.

R. McDougall, *Delmore Schwartz*, 1974.

SCHWARTZ, MAURICE (1888–1960) American Yiddish actor-manager who founded the longest-lasting Yiddish theater company in America. Born in Sudilkov, Ukraine, Schwartz studied at the village *heder* as a child and was introduced to Abraham Goldfaden's (q.v.) songs by the rabbi's brother-in-law. His father was a grain merchant who left for the United States when Schwartz was eleven. He sent for his family later, but due to a mix-up in his ticket, Schwartz was stranded alone in Liverpool. He went to London, first working as a rag-picker, then became a vagrant, and saw his first theater in London. Eventually his family sent for him and he arrived in New York at age thirteen. He helped in his father's business and attended the Yiddish theater at night.

Maurice Schwartz in Yoshe Kalb, *1933.*

Schwartz became an amateur actor in 1905, appearing in Brooklyn as a sixty-year-old father in Zolatorevsky's *The Twentieth Century*, was discovered by Leo Largman and subsequently brought to a Baltimore company for two years. From there he honed his acting skills in companies in Cincinnati, Cleveland, Chicago, and Philadelphia. Even as a young man he was interested in improving the Yiddish theater, experimenting with makeup, giving lectures on naturalness in acting, and purchasing with his own money a spotlight, which was hailed as a great innovation. In Philadelphia Schwartz displayed his unique personality. He read constantly, accepted any role, understudied and played various characters, and entertained as a monologist at fraternal organizations and unions. Legend has it that his big break came when a leading man on Second Avenue fell ill and Schwartz was called in to take the part. He arrived in New York in a few hours, studied the part all afternoon, and performed the same night.

In 1910 he joined the company of actor-manager David Kessler. In order to perform he had to audition at the Hebrew Actors' Union. After failing twice, he visited Abe Cahan (q.v.), editor of the *Jewish Daily Forward* and after a demonstration of his acting ability, Cahan persuaded the union to accept Schwartz's third audition. This was in 1913; Schwartz had been acting in New York for two years.

He continued with Kessler's company taking the starring roles when Kessler was away and in 1918, after a quarrel that split the Kessler company, Schwartz took over the Irving Place Theater with Max Wilner as business partner and manager and Schwartz as director. He published a manifesto on his new theater, promising ensemble acting, rehearsals, and emphasizing its devotion to "art." He hired the best Yiddish actors — Jacob Ben-Ami, Celia Adler, Berta Gersten, Ludwig Satz, and Lazar Freed — and opened with Z. Libin's *Man and His Shadows*.

It was Jacob Ben-Ami who forced the theater to art. Ben-Ami's contract stipulated the performance of one literary play per week. Peretz Hirschbein's *A Secluded Nook* was given the traditional slow Wednesday, and, despite Schwartz's initial lack of support, the play became a success. The company went on to present a rich repertory that season, including plays by Shaw, Schiller, Wilde, and Tolstoy. Still the actors were discontented, claiming that Schwartz remained the star and such an ambitious schedule prevented fully preparing each production. At the end of the year Ben-Ami and other actors left to form the Jewish Art Theater. It failed after two years.

Schwartz went on to build the one enduring Yiddish repertory company. From 1918 to 1950 he staged over 150 productions displaying the full range of Yiddish theater. He was star, stage director, play doctor, and manager. He experimented with lighting, revolving stages, and masks and makeup, and employed such fine stage designers as Boris Aronson. He toured the United States and Canada, acted in Yiddish and Hollywood films, and, unsuccessfully, took his company to Broadway.

Schwartz was a man of contradictions. He was an egocentric actor, both a ham and a magnificent player. He was domineering and boisterous, or childlike and helpless. He was shrewd, stubborn, ambitious, passionate, and charming. He left a lasting mark, introducing the art concept in Yiddish theater and providing a laboratory that developed individuals who enriched the general American theater. The styles of production, acting, and tradition in his Yiddish Art Theater provided the inspiration and pattern for future groups in the American theater. He insisted on a high standard of Yiddish language, encouraged new talent and the repertory tradition, and created an awareness and respect for Yiddish theater among Jews and non-Jews. Schwartz closed the Yiddish Art Theater in 1950 and toured in South America and Europe. He staged a revival of his famed *Yoshe Kalb* in 1959. In 1960 he moved to Israel, hoping to set up a Yiddish theater, but died later that year.

D. S. Lifson, *The Yiddish Theater in America*, 1965.

SCHWARZ, DAVID (1845–1897) Inventor of the dirigible. Born in Hungary, he was working as a lumber merchant in Zagreb, Croatia, when he began to teach himself engineering and mechanics and to study aviation.

David Schwarz's airship.

He invented the rigid airship and became convinced that such a machine could be built from aluminum. The Austrian war minister was interested in the project but did not find the money to fund the actual flight experiments. As a result Schwarz went to Russia. There he became a government engineer, and built his first airship in 1892 with an aluminum frame and a balloon covering. It failed because the inferior material supplied for the balloon by the Russian government could not be filled with gas.

In 1892 he received a promise of funding from the German government and went to Germany where he made several improvements on the airship. The financing for the project was delayed until 1897. When in Vienna, he received news of the test flight to be held in Berlin, but in his excitement died on the spot of a heart attack.

His widow, Melanie Schwarz, was present at the ascent of the airship from Tempehof Field near Berlin, as was Count Fedirnand von Zeppelin. There they witnessed the successful rise and four-hour flight of the all-metal airship, but also its untimely demise when it crashed and was destroyed. The pilot managed to jump out in time.

Zeppelin had applied for a patent for the rigid airship in 1894–1895, and although he did not credit Schwarz at all, made use of Schwarz's method. Zeppelin bought from Schwarz's widow the plans and designs for the airship, the Zeppelin, to which he later made his own modifications.

SCHWARZBARD, SHALOM SAMUEL

(1886– 1938) Yiddish poet, assassin of the anti-Semitic Ukrainian general, Semyon Petlyura. The Bessarabian city of his birth, Izmail, had a history of anti-Jewish riots, and during the abortive 1905 revolution Schwarzbard helped to organize Jewish self-defense activity when pogroms broke out at Balta in the Ukraine. A watchmaker by trade, he displayed anarchist sympathies, and had to leave Russia in 1906, eventually settling in Paris. After the outbreak of World War I, he joined the French Foreign Legion and was awarded the croix de Guerre for heroism on the western front. Once the Bolsheviks seized power in Russia, however, Schwarzbard hurried back to the Ukraine, where

he took part in the civil war, campaigning against Anton Denikin's White Guards and Petlyura's Cossack marauders. Both were responsible for pogroms in which at least 50,000 Jews died and several times that number of children were orphaned. Schwarzbard lost many close relatives in the bloodbath, which Petlyura's Ukrainian National Army conducted with inhuman savagery (1919–1920).

Soon after his return to Paris, Schwarzbard published a volume of Yiddish poems entitled *Troymen un Virklekhkayt* ("Dreams and Reality"; 1920). He later discovered that Petlyura had transferred his Ukrainian government-in-exile from Warsaw to the French capital. Newspaper interviews and photographs enabled Schwarzbard to locate Petlyura, whom he confronted and shot to death in the Latin Quarter in 1962.

His aim was not merely to seek revenge for the Ukrainian massacres, but also to focus worldwide public attention on the atrocities committed by a national army under Petlyura's command. Following his immediate arrest, Schwarzbard faced a three-week trial in Paris (1927); his own testimony and the able defense presented by his counsel, Maître Henry Torrès, a leading Jewish advocate, made a deep impression on the court and resulted in a verdict a acquitting Schwarzbard of the murder charge. A graphic account of these events appeared in his Yiddish autobiography *Inem Loyf fun Yoren* ("Over the Years"; 1933). Schwarzbard died in Cape Town, while on a Jewish communal affairs visit to South Africa.

L. S. Dawidowicz (ed.), *The Golden Tradition: Jewish Life and Thought in Eastern Europe*, 1989, pp. 76, 448–457.

H. Torrès, *Le procès des pogromes*, 1928.

SELIGMAN, JOSEPH

(1819–1880) U.S. international banker. He was born in Baiersdorf, near Nuremberg, Germany, the first of the eleven children of the village weaver. As a child he assisted his mother in her shop selling woolen goods, and by the time he was twelve he was already operating a successful money-changing business. At age fourteen, he went to the University of Erlangen, where he proved a brilliant student, studying literature, classics, and languages. In 1837 he traveled to the United States and settled in the outpost of Mauch Chunk, Pennsylvania, where he found employment with a builder of canal boats. He branched out on his own as a peddler and was soon joined by his brothers William and James. In 1840 he opened his own store and the following year moved to Mobile, Alabama, where he opened a dry-goods store. In 1846 J. Seligman and Brothers, Merchants, opened in New York and Saint Louis.

By 1851, Joseph Seligman, together with his family (all of whom were by then in America), had enterprises scattered throughout the United States. The Seligman brothers progressed from immigrant merchants to banking. Theirs was the only commercial bank in New York to survive the panic of

1857, because Joseph Seligman kept his assets in gold and silver at home under his bed. His own rags-to-riches career and ideology was reflected in the fact that he was the first to employ Horatio Alger as tutor to his children.

During the Civil War the Seligman's acquired contracts for the manufacture of army uniforms and Joseph Seligman sold more than 200 million dollars of United States government securities in Europe. In 1865, he set up the international Seligman banking house along the lines of the house of Rothschild (q.v.). He assigned his brothers to Paris, Frankfurt, London, San Francisco, New Orleans, and New York. By 1869 the company had a working capital of over six million dollars and entered the field of railroad securities. Seligman was involved in the scandal of the Gould group (owners of the Erie Railroad), which caused gold prices to crash, but he emerged from the government investigation almost unscathed. His "railroad fever" brought him on to the boards of directors of several railroad companies which competed with each other — a fact which seemed to have escaped his notice. In the course of time Seligman made a fortune from his investments in over one hundred railroad companies. He himself seldom traveled on railroads as he considered them an unsafe means of transportation!

He believed that he had "arrived" in the world of banking when, in 1874, his bank combined with the Rothschilds to back an issue of U.S. bonds; by the end of the decade, they had a monopoly on the sale of U.S. bonds in Europe.

Under presidents Abraham Lincoln and Andrew Johnson, the Seligmans enjoyed excellent relations with the secretaries of the Treasury, and when Ulysses S. Grant became president in 1869, his secretary of state, Hamilton Fish, offered Seligman the position of secretary of the treasury. Seligman was flattered but, considering himself unable to cope with the position, he turned it down. He became involved, however, in the administration's plan to refund the public debt, stabile the currency, and build American credit abroad. Seligman also refused an offer to run on the Republican ticket for mayor of New York. In 1877 a plan he submitted to the secretary of the treasury for the refunding of the balance of the government's war debt was so successful that within two years the dollar was quoted at par for the first time since 1861.

The Saratoga affair in the summer of 1877 severely taxed Seligman's health. He had gone to spend a vacation in Saratoga Springs, New York, in his own railroad car, and was refused accommodation at the Grand Union Hotel. Run by Judge Hilton, an old business rival, the hotel refused to have Jews on its premises. The affair stirred up anti-Semitic feelings and set off a nationwide controversy.

After Joseph's death, his brother Jesse (1827–1894) became head of the firm. He not only continued Joseph's financial policy, but also contributed generously to philanthropic enterprises.

With Jesse Seligman's death, J. and W. Seligman and Company began to decline from the great international banking house it had been to a small, but prestigious investment house in New York.

S. Birmingham, *Our Crowd; The Great Jewish Families of New York*, 1967.
R. L. Muir and C. J. White, *Over the Long Term: The Story of J. & W. Seligman and Co., 1864–1964*, 1964.

SELLERS, PETER (1925–1980) British film actor. Born in Portsmouth to a theatrical family, Richard Henry Sellers was a direct descendant through his Jewish mother of the great boxer Daniel Mendoza (q.v.) At fourteen, the already stage-struck youth was allowed to go to work at a seaside theater run by an uncle in Devon, thus putting an end to his formal education. Sellers volunteered for the Royal Air Force when he was eighteen and swiftly gravitated to Ralph Reader's Gang Show, with which he toured entertaining the troops. Unable to control his gift for mimicry, he augmented these appearances with frequent and risky impersonations of officers. After World War II, Sellers gave up his difficult career as a drummer and tried to break into comedy.

After surviving six weeks at the Windmill Theater, a proving ground for comic talent, Sellers broke into radio in 1948 by the simple expedient of telephoning BBC producer Roy Speer and impersonating two radio stars who insisted that Speer audition their discovery, Sellers. In the early 1950s Sellers got together on radio with Harry Secombe and writer Spike Milligan (and, initially, Michael Bentine) to produce *The Goon Show*, an anarchic radio comedy series that ran throughout the decade and revolutionized British humor. Sellers had his

Peter Sellers.

first significant screen role in *The Ladykillers* in 1955 and by 1959, when *I'm All Right Jack* was released, had become one of Britain's most popular film actors.

By the early 1960s, Sellers was in Hollywood, where he starred in *Lolita* and *Dr. Strangelove* (in which he played three roles) for director Stanley Kubrick, and created the role of the dimwitted French Inspector Clouseau for Blake Edwards in *The Pink Panther*. In 1964 he suffered a series of massive heart attacks and almost died. Most of the films he made in the decade following his recovery were poorly received; a notable exception was *What's New, Pussycat?* A series of sequels to *The Pink Panther*, beginning in the mid-1970s, restored his standing at the box-office. His penultimate role, as Chance the gardener in *Being There*, was widely acclaimed and earned him an Academy Award nomination.

P. Evans, *Peter Sellers: The Mask Behind the Mask*, 1969.

E. Rose, (ed.), *The Book of the Goons*, 1974.

M. Sellers, *P.S. I Love You: Peter Sellers 1925–1980*, 1981.

SELZNICK, DAVID O. (1902–1965) U.S. film producer. Born in Pittsburgh, Pennsylvania, Selznick was the son of Lewis J. Selznick, a jeweler, who, when David was ten, took his first audacious steps into the film business. By the late 1910s, Selznick senior was a major force in the industry, although his unorthodox practices were anathema to most of his rivals. Both David and his brother Myron, later to be a top Hollywood agent, gained their first film experience in their father's organization. In 1923 the tide turned against Selznick's corporation, much to the satisfaction of his competitors, none of whom would extend any assistance. Lewis Selznick died in 1933, without ever having been able to effect a comeback and both his sons were to regard the success of their respective careers as a form of vengeance.

Though most doors in Hollywood closed to him after his father's fall, David Selznick's persistence resulted in a script-reading job at MGM in 1926, from which the quality of his work and his immense drive swiftly propelled him forward. He had soon risen high enough to cause friction with MGM's wunderkind, Irving Thalberg (q.v.), and left for Paramount, where the West Coast production head B. P. Schulberg (q.v.) admitted taking him on because of his sheer arrogance. He married Louis B. Mayer's [q.v.] daughter, Irene, (inspiring the quip "the son-in-law also rises"). He proposed in a memo that read: "I have been thinking of you and have decided to marry you, if you will have me. I am little middle-aged to be sure, I have a hammer-toe and I run into things. I am ex-arrogant and once I wanted to be a big-shot. I snore loudly, drink exuberantly, work excessively and my future is drawing to a close. But I am tall and Jewish and I do love you."

Selznick left Paramount for the chance to be RKO's vice president in charge of production. *A Bill of Divorcement*, *What Price Hollywood?*, and *King Kong* were among the productions that emerged from RKO under Selznick.

In 1933 Selznick's father-in-law lured him back to MGM where he stayed for three years before forming his own company, Selznick International. *Dinner at Eight*, *David Copperfield*, *A Star is Born*, and *A Tale of Two Cities* all belong to this second MGM period. The talents Selznick took under his wing as an independent included Alfred Hitchcock, Ingrid Bergman, and Jennifer Jones, who was to become his second wife. The peak of his achievements in this last phase of his career, and for many the peak of Hollywood moviemaking, was his monumental production of Margaret Mitchell's Civil War novel, *Gone With the Wind*, for which he planned every shot. In 1940 he brought Alfred Hitchcock to Hollywood to direct *Rebecca*. The very success of *Gone With the Wind* dwarfed anything he was subsequently to do and, while *Duel in the Sun* was an earnest attempt to reach similar heights, his last fifteen years were almost devoid of any actual filmmaking.

R. Behlmer, *Memo from David O. Selznick*, 1972.

R. Haver, *David O. Selznick's Hollywood*, 1980.

B. Thomas, *Selznick*, 1970.

SHABBAZI, SHALEM (1619–after 1680) Religious poet in Yemen. Little of his life is known. He came from Shabaz in the Sharab province and apparently lived in poverty as a weaver. He traveled extensively through Yemen, often visiting the homes of the affluent, and was in touch with the sages of his time and with Arab rulers and poets. In his poetry he mentions his connections with the sages of the Talmudic academy in Sana. In 1679–1680, Yemenite Jewry was exiled to Mawza, near the eastern shore of the Red Sea, and he laments his exile in his poems. Nothing is known of him after this event. One of his two sons, Shimon, was a poet and was regarded as his father's spiritual heir. Popular tradition tells of a daughter whose grave is still revered.

Shalem Shabbazi's poems reveal his familiarity with rabbinic, philosophical, and mystical sources, as well as with astronomy, astrology, and Arabic literature. He wrote in three languages: Hebrew, Aramaic, and Arabic. He apparently also had a reputation as a miracle worker, and used to cure with charms. He was buried in Ta'iz, where Jews and Arabs pray at his tomb.

His great reputation among Yemenite Jewry stemmed not only from his poetic ability, but from his ability to express his fellow Jews' tribulations and yearnings during a difficult period. His reputation was so great that various collections of poems were attributed to him even though they contained works by other poets.

More than five hundred of his poems and religious verse are known, most on the familiar themes of religious poetry, although few found their way into the liturgy. His main subject is the hope of

The traditional tomb of Shalom Shabbazi, Taiz, Yemen; revered by Jews and Muslims.

redemption. Many poems are devoted to biblical events and personalities, while others are dedicated to the Sabbath and festivals, weddings, and circumcisions. He also wrote poems on moral themes. Few of his works are on nonreligious subjects. He had a profound influence on subsequent Yemenite Jewish poetry, although he only became known to the wider Jewish public in the 19th century.
I. Zinberg, *A History of Jewish Literature*, vol. 5, 1972–1978.

SHABBETAI TZEVI (1626–1676) Jewish pseudomessiah. Born in Smyrna (Izmir) in Turkey, he was the son of a poultry merchant. A gifted child, he devoted himself to study — first of the Talmud and then of Jewish mysticism. Good looking and highly intelligent, he was ordained as a *hakham* (sage) when he was only eighteen. He began, however, to show strange symptoms, probably of manic depression, that marked his entire career. His fantasies included messianic elements which coincided with a messianic fervor among Jewish communities. Predictions that the Messiah would appear in 1648 (according to kabbalistic calculations) seemed to be confirmed by the terrible massacres that year of Polish Jewry by Cossack invaders, which were interpreted as the anticipated birthpangs of the Messiah. Shabbetai Tzevi claimed to have experienced a heavenly voice identifiying him as the redeemer. One Sabbath in the synagogue, he defiantly pronounced the tetragrammaton name of God, traditionally forbidden to all except the high priest on the Day of Atonement, and announced the cancellation of certain fast days, notably the Ninth of Av, the anniversary of the destruction of the Temples, and foretold as the birthday of the Messiah his own date of birth. The rabbis of Smyrna exiled him from the city and placed him under a ban of excommunication.

He moved to Salonika, where he symbolized his messiahship by "wedding" the Torah in a mystic marriage ceremony. The Orthodox rabbinate expelled him and he spent the next years wandering throughout Greece and Turkey, shocking the rabbinate, but also winning disciples. In Constantinople a respected kabbalist produced an ancient parchment purporting to predict the arrival of Shabbetai Tzevi as Messiah. With a growing band of followers, Shabbetai Tzevi moved to the Holy Land and, clothed in a dazzling robe, prayed at the Western Wall and at the tomb of the patriarchs in Hebron. He was even sent as an emissary to Egypt to collect funds for the support of the Jewish community in Jerusalem.

In Cairo he married a girl named Sarah (he had been married twice previously but the unions were not consummated), who had previously announced that she would be wed only to the Messiah. Of Marrano origin, she came from Poland, had been raised in a convent in Amsterdam, and had earned her living as a prostitute. At his wedding, Shabbetai Tzevi quoted the precedent of the prophet Hosea's betrothal of Gomer, and called Sarah "the bride of the Messiah." She was a striking beauty who brought added allure to his cause.

On his journey back to the Holy Land, Shabbetai Tzevi met a kabbalistic rabbi, henceforth known as Nathan of Gaza, who claimed to have experienced a vision in which Shabbetai's messiahship was revealed. Nathan now became Shabbetai's "prophet" and played a major role in further developments, first crowning Shabbetai as "King-Messiah." He also sent messengers and leaflets to many parts of the Jewish world announcing the advent of the Messiah, who would depose the sultan of Turkey and lead the Jewish exiles of the world back to the Holy Land.

Now it was the turn of the rabbis of Jerusalem to excommunicate Shabbetai (after floggings had failed to change him) and he traveled with his entourage back to Turkey, triumphantly entering Smyrna, from where he had been so ignominiously expelled fifteen years earlier. By 1665 a mass frenzy had seized the Jewish world and Jews from Holland to Yemen began to make preparations for returning to the Holy Land. Nathan of Gaza announced that he had had a further vision revealing that 1666 would be the year of redemption, when Shabbetai Tzevi would ride into Jerusalem on a lion, with a seven-headed serpent as its bridle. Shabbetai Tzevi made a public declaration of his messianic mission in a synagogue, to the accompaniment of the blowing of rams' horns. He proceeded to issue a series of antinomian decrees — turning fasts into feasts, reciting the tetragrammaton in regular services, abolishing the separation of men and women at services, and substituting his own name for that of the sultan in the prayer for the authorities. He also announced that he would now have intercourse with his wife for the first time and next morning produced the traditional "evidence" of her virginity! He then announced that he was dividing his territories into twenty-six kingdoms, to be allocated to his colleagues, each being given a biblical title, with his brother being called "King of Kings."

By now the Turkish authorities had become worried. When Shabbetai sailed to Constantinople

Shabbetai Tzevi anointed by Nathan of Gaza. From a letter of Nathan of Gaza to the Jews of Europe; 1665.

to depose the sultan he was arrested on arrival and imprisoned in a fortress in Gallipoli. With the help of bribery, he was able to hold court in his prison and continued to preach to his followers, who maintained their faith and spread stories of the miracles he was performing. It was believed that the tribulations he was suffering were only to be expected for the Messiah. The Turkish authorities were infuriated by his behavior and summoning him to the sultan's privy council offered him the choice of conversion to Islam or death; he chose the former and before the sultan, removed his Jewish hat and accepted the turban of a Muslim, and emerged from his audience as Mehmet Effendi. The sultan gave him a new wife and appointed him royal doorkeeper.

Shabbetai now tried to play a double game — maintaining his relations with the Turks (and getting some of his followers to accept Islam) while continuing to claim to the Jewish world that he was indeed the Messiah. Most of the Jewish world was shattered but many still clung to their faith in him. Their faith was derived from the mystical belief that the savior would have to plumb the depths of

evil in order to "redeem the scattered sparks" (see Isaac Luria) and save the world. The Turks eventually tired of his duplicity and banished him to a fortress in Dulcigno, Albania, where he remained in touch with his believers. He died there on the Day of Atonement, 1676.

Even his death did not bring an end to his movement. Shabbatean sects flourished for many years and one group, the Donmeh, continued to exist in Turkey until the 20th century, still believing that Shabbetai Tzevi was the Messiah who would return one day.

G. Scholem, *The Kabbalah*, 1974.

G. Scholem, *Sabbatai Sevi: The Mystical Messiah*, 1973.

SHAHN, BEN (1898–1969) U.S. artist. He was taken from his native Kovno (now Kaunas, Lithuania), to Brooklyn, New York, in 1906. At age fourteen, he was apprenticed to a lithographer and began earning his living as a commercial lithographer. He spent periods in the 1920s traveling and studying in Europe.

Shahn's first one-man show, in 1930, was the beginning of a lifelong association with the Downtown Gallery in New York. Over the years, the gallery displayed his famous series of twenty-three gouaches on the trial of Sacco and Vanzetti, his series on the persecuted labor leader, Tom Mooney, and on the *Lucky Dragon*, a Japanese fishing boat that wandered into a nuclear test zone.

He learned photography from his friend, Walker Evans, and during the Depression worked for the Farm Security Administration, taking over six thousand photographs in the southern and middle western states.

In 1932, Shahn's two mural panels on Sacco and Vanzetti were exhibited at the Museum of Modern Art in New York. His many other murals included a panel on *The Four Freedoms* at the Jamaica, Long Island, post office; one in the Department of Health, Education, and Welfare, Washington, D.C. (an assignment he won in a competition with over 350 contestants); mosaic murals for Congregation Ohab Shalom in Nashville, Tennessee, and Congregation Mishkan Israel in New Haven, Connecticut; and two mosaic murals that he made for the Israeli ship *Shalom*, which were purchased by the New Jersey State Museum when the *Shalom* went out of service.

Most of his lithographs were posters, although he worked at Fernand Morlot's atelier in Paris in 1963 and made twenty-four color lithographs inspired by Rilke in 1968. Some of his most famous works are silk-screen prints.

He loved to use Hebrew letters and designed a Hebrew alphabet that he called *The Alphabet of Creation*. His *Ecclesiastes* (1967) was handwritten and illustrated by him. In 1966, he produced a *Haggadah* with twelve illustrations and an original lithograph frontispiece.

In 1945, Shahn became the director of the graphic arts division of the Congress of Industrial

"The Welders" by Ben Shahn, 1944.

Organizations. His publications include a book about art, *The Shape of Content*, and *Love and Joy about Letters*. He won many awards, represented the United States in the Venice Biennale, designed sets for ballet and theater, taught, and lectured widely — including a stint as Charles Eliot Norton Professor of Poetry at Harvard.

He said, "I hate injustice. I guess that's about the only thing that I really do hate... and I hope I will go on hating it all my life." His work reflects his concern with justice, political freedom and the state of humanity.

He said that he preferred tempera because it was a medium that imposed clarity and control. His technique was fluid enough to encompass the austere, sorrowful gravity of his social commentary and his more humorous work. There is a strong decorative element in his work. His colors are bright, even brash, laid on with a sure, free hand in his graphics. At times, he added gold leaf to his pictures.

His work is realistic, but verges on the abstract, and he makes good use of a few favored symbols. A gallery of his painting is on display at the Vatican Museum.

K. McNulty, *The Collected Prints of Ben Shahn*, 1967.

J. D. Morse (ed.), *Ben Shahn*, 1972.

D. Pratt (ed.), *The Photographic Eye of Ben Shahn*, 1975.

J. T. Soby, *Ben Shahn: The Graphic Art*, 1963.

SHALOM ALEICHEM (1859–1916) Foremost Russian-Yiddish humorist. Born Shalom Rabinovitch in Pereyalsav, Ukraine, he grew up in Voronkov, the model for his Kaserilevke. His father was a wealthy grain and lumber merchant interested in modern Hebrew culture. During his happy early years he displayed a talent for mimicry, much to the embarrassment of his parents, and memorized the minutest details of village life.

Due to the dishonesty of a partner, his father's business failed and the family returned to Pereyaslav to operate an inn. At the age of twelve Shalom Aleichem began to read current Hebrew writings and write his own versions. In 1872 his mother died of cholera and he lived with his grandmother until his father remarried a shrewish woman whose complaints and curses provided the inspiration for his first work, an alphabetic dictionary of his step-

mother's curses. This so pleased his father that he was sent to a government school to study secular subjects.

With a surplus of curiosity, the budding writer spent much of his free time studying the numerous cantors and musicians who stayed at his father's hotel. They would form the basis of two of his early novels, *Yosele Solovye* and *Stempenu*. At the age of sixteen he fell in love with one of these cantor's daughters and courted her. When she eloped with a Russian youth, he fell sick. Upon his recovery he worked for a while as a teacher in a nearby school and then became the tutor of the daughter of Elimelech Loyev, a rich landowner. He remained there for three years, until Loyev discovered that tutor and pupil were in love. Following his dismissal he went to Kiev, lost his savings, and was deported back to Pereyaslav.

From 1880 to 1883 he worked as the government-appointed rabbi in Lubni. There he continued the Hebrew writing he had begun as a tutor and published several sketches. Hearing about the Yiddish weekly *Dos Yidishe Folksblat*, he submitted some

Page from Shalom Aleichem's autobiography.

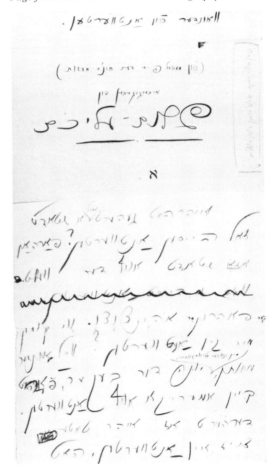

recent works in Yiddish, a daring act for an intellectual and a rabbi. In order to conceal his identity from his father and father-in-law (he had married Loyev's daughter) he adopted the pen name Shalom Aleichem (the Jewish greeting, literally "peace to you").

Entering the business world, he found that he was "...for four hours a day a wheeler-dealer on the bourse,... But from about five in the afternoon, I am Shalom Aleichem." His father-in-law's death, in 1885, made him wealthy and he devoted more of his time to writing. He published *Natasha*, his first novel, in 1884 and five more followed from 1884 to 1890, including *Sender Blank*. In 1888 he founded a literary Yiddish annual, *Di Yidische Folksbibliothek*.

This idyllic and productive period ended with bankruptcy on the stock exchange. The writer was forced to flee Russia and returned only in 1891 when his mother-in-law settled his debts. He worked as a stock and insurance broker and in 1892 published the first of his Menachem Mendel tales, "London!" The year 1893 found him once again on the Kiev stock exchange. He now wrote his first play, became the central figure in the Kiev Jewish literary scene, and discovered Zionism. By 1899 he was a regular and popular contributor to Yiddish newspapers in Saint Petersburg and Warsaw.

Shalom Aleichem left the stock exchange in 1903 to become a full-time writer. Financially he did poorly, but his works were popular and he was hailed as a Jewish folk hero. With Maxim Gorky he helped edit a Russian anthology of Yiddish writings, but censors blocked its publication.

The Kiev massacres of 1905 and the Russian revolution of that year drove him first to Switzerland and London and then to New York, where he hoped to support himself through his writings and lectures. After the failure of two of his plays, he returned to Europe in 1907. He continued to write for the stage, lectured throughout Russia and became famous for his readings and recitations. His twenty-fifth anniversary as a writer found him ill from tuberculosis and recovering in Italy. Much of the rest of his life was spent in summer resorts and spas in Italy. In bed he wrote *Motl, the Son of Peyse the Cantor* and began work on *Wandering Stars*.

His fiftieth birthday was celebrated in Jewish communities throughout the world. A committee of authors acquired the rights to his works from his various publishers and issued a collected edition with Shalom Aleichem as beneficiary, providing him with a regular income. His works began to be published in Russia and he translated some of his Yiddish works into Hebrew. He published a new series of Menachem Mendel letters, Tevya and Motl stories, and *The Bloody Jest*, an ironic novel about the relationships between Jews and Gentiles. Work was also begun on an autobiographical novel, *From the Fair*, which was published in newspaper serializations until his death.

In poor health, he continued writing and toured

- Life is a dream for the wise, a game for the fool, a comedy for the rich, a tragedy for the poor.
- Adam was the luckiest man. He had no mother-in-law.
- The rich swell up from pride, the poor from hunger.
- As a rule men love one another — from a distance.
- Little troubles are not so bad — for someone else.
- A kind word is no substitute for a piece of herring.

Yiddish superlatives

Stingy — Stingier — A pig
Hot — Hotter — A bathhouse
Clever — Cleverer — A mamzer
Certain — Certainer — What a question!
Right — More right — Of course!
Fat — Fatter — A kugel
Possible — More possible — Wat do you mean, "Not possible?"

Shalom Aleichem

Russia and Europe, returning to the United States in 1914, soon after the outbreak of World War I. There, the death of his son Misha in 1915 and news of the fate of many Jews in the war zones worsened his health. He died in 1916. Hundreds of thousands escorted his funeral and almost all the shops and factories on the Lower East Side closed on the day he was buried.

Shalom Aleichem's works have continued to be popular; they are still being published and translated — even into Chinese — and dramatic versions are still being performed. His stories tell of the Jews he observed and knew and in each of his characters he put part of himself. He took material from the small towns dear to his heart and from the large cities. He contemplated these various types of Jews with laughter. Best remembered are his tales of Kaserilevke, the small, poor shtetl (Jewish community in eastern Europe), located in an obscure corner of the world, "orphaned, dreamy, hypnotized, interested only in itself," a symbol of the small, intimate Jewish towns of eastern Europe. It is populated with characters living in isolation from the outside, requiring no worldly goods except for the satisfaction of their immediate needs; they are insignificant and conceited, poor and jolly, naive and witty. Menachem Mendel, the *Luftmensch*, the Jewish Don Quixote; Tevya, the poor dairyman, rooted in the earth, philosophizing about his existence; Reb Yosefel, the old rabbi, an idealized sage; and Motl, who is introduced as a naive child and develops into an urbanized Jew, are only some of his memorable characters.

Shalom Aleichem made himself the literary voice of his people. His Jews spoke naturally and his unique characters are authentic representations of the Ukrainian Jews at the turn of the century. He filled this world with a humor, for as he wrote in 1911, "I tell you it is an ugly and mean world and only to spite it one mustn't weep!...Only to laugh out of spite, only to laugh!"

M. Samuel, *The World of Sholom Aleichem*, 1965.
M. Waife-Goldberg, *My Father, Sholom Aleichem*, 1968.

SHAMMAI (c. 50 BCE-c. 30 CE) Sage. Nothing is known of his early and personal life except that he was a native Judean and a builder by occupation. Five pairs of scholars stood successively at the head of the exposition of the oral law between the Maccabean period and the time of Herod (q.v.), and the last of these were Hillel (q.v.) and Shammai, who succeeded Hillel's first colleague, Menahem the Essene. Hillel was the president of the Sanhedrin, and Shammai the head of the law court and vice-president.

Shammai's stringency is often contrasted with Hillel's humanity in the exposition and interpretation of Jewish law. Examples of Shammai's strictness were his ordering his young son to fast on the Day of Atonement (children under age were usually regarded as exempt from the obligation) and his decision that a person who appoints an agent to kill someone else is himself guilty of murder. Shammai's rigor stemmed from is conservative adherence to the traditional legal interpretations.

Previously no schools of disciples had emerged among the sages, but the differences between Hillel and Shammai engendered the establishment of two differing schools of legal thought and interpretation that perpetuated themselves even after the deaths of the two masters, and retained their identity until the end of the Temple period in 70 CE. The Talmud reports three hundred issues of law and observance on which the schools argued, usually reflecting the personalities of their founders.

THE TALMUD ON SHAMMAI

Our rabbis taught: A man should always be gentle like Hillel and not impatient like Shammai.... When a heathen came to Shammai and said he wanted to learn all about Judaism while he stood on one leg, Shammai repulsed him with the builder's cubit in his hand. When the heathen approached Hillel with the same question, Hillel replied, "What is hateful to you, do not to your neighbor. That is all the Torah; the rest is commentary. Now, go and study."... Three potential proselytes said, "Shammai's impatience sought to drive us from the world but Hillel's gentleness brought us under God's wings."

Talmud, *Shabbat* 30b

At first the Shammaites were more numerous and aggressive, but eventually (c. 90 CE) it was decided that the view of the school of Hillel should be accepted as authoritative.

Despite the traditional picture of Shammai as irascible, his saying, quoted in the *Ethics of the Fathers*, conveys the opposite impression; "Make your Torah study regular; say little and do much; and receive everyone with a cheerful countenance."

SHAPIRO, HARRY LIONEL (1902–1990) U.S. physical anthropologist. Born in Boston, he was one of the first Americans to receive a doctorate in physical anthropology. In 1926 he was appointed curator in the department of anthropology of the American Museum of Natural History and from 1942 was curator and chairman of the department. He was also professor of anthropology at Columbia University from 1943.

In his early years Shapiro's main concern was problems of human identity, a field that developed into forensic anthropology. His method of identifying human remains was used by the American Graves Registration Command after World War II, when he traveled widely in Europe establishing the identity of bodies of unknown soldiers. He was often called upon to help identify murder victims in New York.

He pioneered in the genetics of small and mixed populations. In 1934 he was the first to study the effects of the intermarriage of the *Bounty* mutineers and the local Tahitian women through examining their descendants on Norfolk and Pitcairn islands. Later he studied the Japanese population of Hawaii.

He was also involved in the search for the fossil remains of Peking man, which were lost in World War II during the Japanese invasion of China. The Chinese accused the American authorities of stealing the fossils before the Japanese arrived. Shapiro was involved in a gripping, but unsuccessful, attempt to discover what happened to the remains.

He published a pioneering anthropological work on the biological history of the Jewish people commissioned by UNESCO. The book, *The Jewish People* (1960), deals with the racial origins of the Jews, their changes over the ages, the effect of residence among and contact with a variety of people, and their present racial and biological status. He concluded that the Jews have contributed something of their genetic heritage to more different people than any other group and have, in return, absorbed an equal number of new genetic strains, enriching and diversifying themselves.

SHARETT, MOSHE (1894–1965) First foreign minister and second prime minister of Israel. He was born Moshe Shertok in Russia, but grew up in an Arab village near Jerusalem and graduated in the first class of the Herzliyah High School in Tel Aviv. He went to study law in Constantinople, but the university closed on the eve of World War I. Believing that Jewish citizens of Eretz Israel should become Ottoman citizens and join the Turkish army, he enlisted and served as an officer. After the war he studied at the London School of Economics, and upon his return to Eretz Israel in 1923 was appointed one of the editors of *Davar*, the newly established daily of the Trade Union Federation.

In 1931 he began his career in Zionist and Israeli diplomacy by joining the Jewish Agency's political department. In 1933 he became its head following the assassination of Chaim Arlosoroff (q.v.). In this capacity he was responsible for the foreign policy of the Jewish community in Palestine. He was noted for his moderate and cautious policy, calling for cooperation with the British Mandate. He was one of the leaders in the establishment of the Jewish Brigade in World War II. Sharett led the successful diplomatic effort in the historic United Nations General Assembly, that passed the November 29, 1947, Partition Resolution, giving the State of Israel international legitimacy.

From 1948 to 1956 he was Israel's first foreign minister, directing his energy to securing international recognition of Israel, negotiating the German reparations agreement (1952), and opening bridges to Asia. He argued that Israel must be a law-abiding nation, a decent and active member of the international community through the United Nations. While he approved a number of activist foreign policy stances, such as refusal to accept all the 1948 Palestinian refugees, he felt that peace would be achieved when the Arab world came to terms with Israel, a long-term process requiring much self-restraint and moderation on the part of Israel. He espoused a low Israeli profile and was attuned to international public opinion and U.N. pressure.

By the 1930s he had clashed with David Ben-Gurion (q.v.) over the direction of foreign policy. Ben-Gurion as prime minister led the activist camp, while Sharett was a follower of the more cautious faction associated with Chaim Weizmann (q.v.). Their differences grew in the early years of statehood, but this did not prevent Sharett from succeeding Ben-Gurion when the latter retired to work in a Negev kibbutz. His period as prime minister (1953–1955) was most difficult as he had to grapple with activist defense minister Pinchas Lavon while his colleagues continued to consult Ben-Gurion. During his premiership a group of young Jews were caught by the Egyptians and accused of sabotage. He was unable to control the Israel army under Moshe Dayan (q.v.). Lavon was forced to resign in February 1955, paving the way for the return of Ben-Gurion as defense minister. Sharett yielded the premiership to Ben-Gurion in November 1955, when their differences were irreconcilable. Ben-Gurion was planning a war against Egypt, a move vehemently opposed by Sharett. In June 1956 he was forced to resign as foreign minister. He felt that the ensuing Sinai War (October 1956) was a major hindrance on the road to peace, dooming Israel to live by its sword. From 1960 to 1965 he was chairman of the Jewish Agency executive.

He was one of the most cultured Israeli leaders, fluent in seven languages, and an excellent writer and orator. He published a number of works, including poems. His political diary appeared posthumously in five volumes and his 1953–1957 personal diaries were published in eight volumes (all in Hebrew).

W. Eytan, *Moshe Sharet 1894–1965*, 1966.
M. W. Weisgal, *An Aristocrat of the Spirit*, 1967.

SHAW, IRWIN (1913–1984) U.S. novelist, playwright, and scriptwriter. Born in New York, he attended Brooklyn College, where he was a football star. He began his career as a journalist, working for many years as a drama critic. He served in the U.S. Army during World War II and afterwards returned to Europe, where he continued to write novels, short stories, and plays. He wrote scathingly about American anti-Semitism, saying it was a factor in his twenty-five-year European exile.

His first literary successes were in the field of drama. In the 1930s he wrote screenplays, radio scripts, and stories for The *New Yorker*, among them "Girls in Their Summer Dresses." His one act antiwar play, *Bury the Dead* (1936), about a group of dead soldiers who refused to be buried, was an instant success. This was followed by six other plays, among them the comedy, *The Gentle People*, about two New Yorkers who achieve their dream of owning a boat in Florida by robbing and killing a gangster who is trying to practice extortion on them.

He was sufficiently involved in left-wing causes to be named as a communist before the House

Irwin Shaw.

Un-American Activities Committee, but by the late 1940s he was moving in another direction. He refused permission for further productions of *Bury the Dead* on the grounds that it was being used by communist groups. His war novel, *The Young Lions*, which depicted anti-Semitism in the American army, was made into a film. He made special efforts to attain a realistic understanding of his non-Jewish characters, which extended even to his portrait of a convinced Nazi. Another of his dozen novels, *The Troubled Air*, depicted the problems of radio in the McCarthy era.

From the 1950s, his commercial success grew but his literary reputation waned. His *Rich Man, Poor Man* became a megaseller after being made into a highly popular television series. He died in Davos, Switzerland, leaving a legacy of direct style and strong characterizations that was to influence a new generation of writers. At the time of his death all his novels were still in print, having sold fourteen million copies, and these and his story collections had appeared in twenty-five languages.

Shaw cooperated with the photographer Robert Capa (q.v.) on a picture book about Israel, which he visited several times.

M. Shnayerson, *Irwin Shaw: A Biography*, 1990.

SHAZAR, ZALMAN (1889–1974) Third president of the State of Israel (the name Shazar was an acronym of his original name, Shneour Zalman Rubashov). He was born in Mir, Belorussia, to a family that adhered to the Habad stream of the Hasidic movement. He received a traditional Jewish education, but left Orthodoxy to pursue a secular education, studying at the Academy of Jewish Studies in Saint Petersburg and at various universities. In 1907 he joined the Zionist Socialist Poale Zion movement and began to edit its publications. He was arrested by the tsarist authorities and, for a time, imprisoned for his Zionist activities. Shazar spent World War I in Germany editing the journal *Jüdische Rundschau* and organizing the Labor Zionist movement there.

Migrating to Palestine in 1924, he became one of the editors of the Labor daily, *Davar*, and its editor in chief, from 1944 to 1949. Shazar was a member of the executive of the Labor Federation (Histadrut) and directed its publishing company, Am Oved. A leader of the Mapai Socialist party, he participated in Zionist congresses on its behalf and fulfilled many speaking and fund-raising missions for the Histadrut and Mapai. He was elected to the executive of the elected assembly of Palestinian Jewry.

Shazar was a member of the Palestinian Jewish delegation to the 1947 United Nations General Assembly which voted the partition of Palestine. Elected to the first, second, and third Knessets (parliaments) as Mapai member, he served for two years as Israel's minister of education and culture. In 1949, during his tenure, the basic law of compulsory education was adopted. In 1951 he was nominated ambassador of Israel to the Soviet Union,

but the Soviet government rejected his nomination for reasons unknown. He headed the information division of the World Zionist Organization and between 1955 and 1960 was chairman of the executive of the Jewish Agency.

In 1963 Shazar was elected president of Israel and won another term five years later. During his presidency he traveled extensively and was official guest of the Canadian, American, Nepalese, Chilean, and other governments. In 1964 he welcomed Pope Paul VI on his one-day visit to Israel. He also sought to strengthen links between Israel and Jewish communities in the Diaspora. Fluent in six languages, at home in Jewish, German, and Russian cultures, Shazar was one of the leading orators of his generation, a noted writer and poet whose literary heritage is carefully studied for the depth of his research, style, and form. He published extensively and made original contributions to the history of the movement that followed Shabbetai Tzevi (q.v.).

His wife, **Rahel Katznelson Shazar** (1888–1975), whom he married in 1920, was herself a leader of the Labor Zionist movement, particularly its women's organizations.

E. Indelman, *President Zalman Shazar*, 1970.
S. Ish-Kishor, *Zalman Shazar; President of the People*, 1966.

> "Don't forget that you are president now, Zalman. You mustn't interfere."
>
> **Golda Meir in 1963**

SHERIRA, GAON (906–1006) Babylonian academy head (*gaon*). Sherira ben Hanina came from a noble family that claimed to trace its ancestry to King David. Appointed *gaon* of the academy of Pumbedita in 968, at the age of sixty-two, he held the position almost until his death, at the age of a hundred. He was considered the second to the last of the truly great *gaonim*, his son, Hai Gaon (q.v.), being the last.

During the period before Sherira was appointed *gaon*, the Babylonian Jewish community was in decline because of the growng infertility of the region, and the resultant emigration of both its Arab and Jewish populations. Although the Jewish communities still maintained their old traditions, and continued their studies in the academies, the academies were in poor condition. There were few financial contributions, few queries, and few students.

Sherira managed to rejuvenate his community and reverse the trend for the period that he held office, raising funds, attracting students, and maintaining correspondence with Jewish communities all over the world. Most of the responsa directed to Sherira were about questions of religious practice and interpretation of the Talmud and Mishna. The most famous case in his career stemmed from ties with one of his more distant correspondents. The Jewish community in Kairouan, in north Africa, kept in constant touch wih the academies of Babylonia, in effect creating one of the bridges across which the culture and traditions of the east reached European Jewry. At the end of the 10th century, Jacob ben Nissim from Kairouan wrote to Sherira on behalf of his fellow sages, asking him about the origins and evolution of the Mishna and the Talmud. They wished to know more about the individuals mentioned in various treatises, the dates when they were written, how academies used to be run, etc. Sherira was a prolific writer and his lengthy response, written in Aramaic, and held in great esteem as a chief source of Jewish history in the Talmudic and following periods, gives a great deal of information about the intellectual history of the Jews from 500 to 1000 CE.

When his son, Hai, joined Sherira thirty years after he had been appointed *gaon*, the volume of activity increased even more. Disciples came from all over the world, gifts of money were received, and innumerable questions were asked on matters of law. According to one source, the caliph was worried by the surge of activity and suspecting political intrigues and had Sherira and Hai arrested and throwh into prison. They were soon released, but the experience was hard on Sherira who was already a very old man, and he died shortly afterward.

On the Sabbath after his death he was accorded the great honor of a special passage being read from the book of Numbers in which Moses asked God to "set a man over the congregation who may go out before them and may go in before them, who may lead them out and who may bring them in; that the congregation of the Lord be not as sheep which have no shepherd." His followers also read the chapter in 1 Kings about David's last days and when they reached the verse: "And Solomon sat upon the throne of David his father," they substituted, "And Hai sat upon the throne of Sherira his father."

J. Neusner, *A History of the Jews in Babylonia*, Vol. 5, 1970.

SHINWELL, EMANUEL (1884–1986) British socialist politician, created life peer, 1970. Born in London to a father from Russia and mother from Holland, he left school at age eight to join his father in a seamen's outfitter's shop in Newcastle. A year later the family moved to Glasgow where he returned to school and became a voracious reader. There he lived in working class districts and received his early political education from Irish dissidents who congregated in his father's tailoring shop. At eleven he left school and ran errands for his father and a tobacco firm, and developed an active interest in sport.

At the age of seventeen, Manny, as he was affectionately called throughout his life, joined the Garment Workers' Union and was influenced by the socialist writings of Robert Blatchford and

SHINWELL
TALKING

A Conversational Biography to Celebrate his hundredth birthday

JOHN DOXAT

Quiller Press
London

Title page of Emanuel Shinwell's biography by John Doxat.

Keir Hardie. In 1903 he became a member of the Independent Labor party, traveled around Scotland and northern England addressing meetings and engaging in debates on social justice. In 1909 he was nominated to the Glasgow Trades Council as representative of the Scottish Clothing Workers Union and in this capacity took part in negotiations with the shipowners on behalf of dockers during the 1911 seamen's strike.

Shinwell took the post of secretary to the Scottish Seamen's Union and was as vice-chairman and later president of the Glasgow Trades Council, and a member of the Scottish Trade Union Congress. In 1916 he was elected to the Glasgow Town Council.

During World War I, Shinwell was not conscripted because his work of collecting seamen to man auxiliary naval vessels was considered to be a reserved occupation of national importance (he was later anonymously attacked in the press as not having served because he was a conscientious objector). In 1918 he suffered his first election defeat when he stood for Parliament as a Labour candidate, but received the highest Labour vote in any constituency in Scotland. In 1919 he was sentenced to five months imprisonment on a charge of incitement to riot during a demonstration calling for reduction of working hours in shipyards and industrial establishments.

In 1922 he entered Parliament as an Independent Labour party member, and, although inhibited by his lack of formal education, made an impressive maiden speech. He was reported in the *Daily Express* as having used mannerisms and conventions of parliamentary debate "as if he had been in the House for years instead of hours." Shinwell was appointed minister of mines in Ramsay MacDonald's socialist government in 1923, and during his tenure obtained an increase in the miners' basic wages. In the 1924 elections he was defeated, but returned in 1928. He served for eighteen months as financial secretary in the War Office, and once again as minister of mines until 1931, when he lost his seat. He returned to Parliament in 1935 (when he defeated Ramsay MacDonald) and retained his seat for the next thirty-six years.

He was extremely active during the World War II, employing two secretaries to attend to his vast correspondence — over five hundred letters a week; he wrote innumerable articles for the press and magazines and devoted his efforts to the removal of restrictions on production. His next government post was minister of fuel and power in Clement Atlee's socialist government in 1945, when he piloted the nationalization of the coal mining industry through the House of Commons. In 1947 he returned to the War Office as secretary of state, and was minister of defense in 1950–1951. Shinwell saw to the improvement in conditions of military service, including increased pay and pensions, and longer service to enable more efficient training.

In 1970, on reaching the age of eighty-five, he decided not to stand for reelection to the House of Commons. Although he had written and spoken against the upper house, he accepted membership in the House of Lords. He was most active and became chairman of the All-Party Defense Group.

Throughout his long life, Shinwell was most outspoken and loved verbal fights. He preferred the satisfaction of speaking his mind, remaining true to his ideals. In *The Daily Mirror*, the columnist Cassandra described him as "guilty of being tetchy, testy, irritable, bad-tempered, irascible, petulant, hasty, touchy, choleric, churlish and captious.... Of course, Shinwell is combative, assertive, pugnacious and intolerant and we wouldn't have it otherwise. Damn and Bless him."

Despite the Orthodox background of his family, he was not a practicing Jew. However, expressions of anti-Semitism aroused his ire and he left no doubt as to where he stood. In 1938, when Shinwell raised a question regarding foreign policy, Commander R. I. Bower, a Conservative M. P., shouted, "Go back to Poland." Shinwell crossed the floor and struck him in the face. In 1952 he had an altercation with Winston Churchill, who implied that Shinwell "put Britain's interest second to political ideology and that he owed loyalty to an idea beyond his country's frontiers." After the establishment of the State of Israel, Shinwell expressed a sense of pride in the state, especially in its courage to defend itself.

During a discussion with Harvie Watt, Churchill's parliamentary private secretary, Shinwell said that he might have some harsh things to say about Churchill regarding tank defects. Watt reacted: "Don't talk about my chief in that fashion. He is a great military expert.... what's more, a descendant of the duke of Marlborough, the greatest of our military experts."

Shinwell couldn't let that pass: "Don't talk to me about his great military ancestors. Do you know who my ancestor was? Moses. Consider the trouble he had taking the Israelites out of Egypt and across the Red Sea, and forty years in the Wilderness."

Shinwell's writings include *The Britain I Want* (1943), an outline of his proposed postwar policy; *When the Men Come Home* (1944); *Conflict without Malice* (1955); *The Labour Story* (1963); and the autobiotraphical *Lead with the Left: My First Ninety-Six Years* (1981).

Shinwell was created a life feer in 1970 and was made a freeman of London in 1980.

J. Doxat, *Shinwell Talking, A Conversational Biography to Celebrate His Hundredth Birthday)*, 1984.

SHNEOUR (SHNEUR), ZALMAN (1887–1959) pen-name of Zalkind Shneour Hebrew and Yiddish poet and novelist. Born in Shklov, Belorussia, to a Hasidic family (he was a descendant of Schneur Zalman of Lyady (q.v.), he began to write poetry at an early age. His first poem appeared in an adult journal when he was thirteen but by then he was already a frequent contributor to the children's Hebrew newspaper *Olam Katan*. Shortly after, he moved to Odessa where he was a protege of Chaim Nachman Bialik (q.v.). Two years later he went to live in Warsaw where he worked in the Tushia publishing house which brought out his first books. From 1904 he was in Vilna where he worked on a Hebrew journal in the pages of which he published many of his works, including his first novel. With his first volume of poetry in 1907, he had achieved a secure reputation in Hebrew letters.

After two years in Switzerland, he moved in 1907 to Paris where he studied and continued to write. He worked in a Yiddish newspaper to earn a living but World War I found him in Berlin studying medicine but he never graduated. From 1924 to 1941 he lived in Paris — with a brief interval in 1925 when he made an unsuccessful attempt to settle in Palestine. He escaped from France to New York in 1941 remaining there until he settled in Israel in 1951.

Frequently classed with Bialik and Saul Tschernichowsky (q.v.) as the "big three of modern Hebrew Poetry," Shneour differed in many ways from the other two. He excels in his colorful sensuality and his powerful masculinity. His secularism and humanism tend to overshadow his Jewishness and there is very little of the Zionism that motivated the other two poets. Nor does he take much interest in Jewish history concentrating very much on the present. He is full of contradictions — his Jewishness and his admiration for ancient Rome, pessimism and hedonism, are expressions of his pronounced individualism. Much of his poetry is lyrical, voicing protest, reslessness and revolution. The poet's attitude to the world and to society, he felt, should be one of struggle. His poem "Spartacus" praises the famous leader of the slave revolt and shows his inspiration in non-Jewish culture.

His writings were bilingual. Although in his youth, he swore never to write in Yiddish, he continued to produce Yiddish classics — both because of his love for the language and in order to reach a much wider audience than could be provided by Hebrew in the first decades of the century. Shneour wrote in a great variety of genres lyric poetry, dramatic epics, plays, stories, novels and memoirs. Many of his tales center on Jewish life in the Pale of Settlement. In his latter years in Israel, he adapted for the stage one of his bestl-known stories "Noah Pandre". He died while on a visit to New York but his body was brought back to Tel Aviv to be buried alongside Bialik and Tschernichowsky.
M. Waxman, *A History of Jewish Literature*, IV (281–98) 1960.

SHNEUR ZALMAN OF LYADY (1745–1813)

Founder of Habad Hasidism. Habad tradition has it that he was born on Elul 18 in Liozna, Belorussia. The same date, two generations earlier, had marked the birth of Israel Baal Shem Tov (q.v.), the father of the Hasidic movement; in the eyes of his followers, Shneur Zalman was the spiritual heir of that monumental figure. At the age of twenty, already famed as a genius in Torah study, he reached the court of Dov Ber of Mezhirech (q.v.). The depth of his knowledge greatly impressed that master, who asked him to compose a new and modernized *Shulhan Arukh* (authoritative code of Jewish law by Joseph Caro, [q.v.]). Shneur Zalman worked on the book for many years. Though most of it was lost in a fire, a portion was published posthumously, and is considered an important halakhic work.

Confronted with the vociferous opposition of traditional Jewry to the revolutionary innovations of Hasidism, Shneur Zalman traveled to Vilna in 1774, in the hope of making peace with Elijah ben Solomon, the gaon of Vilna (q.v.), head of the *Mitnaggedim*, the opponents of Hasidism. The gaon, who had led a bitter campaign against the Hasidim, refused to meet them and stepped up his persecution. Yet despite the atmosphere of enmity, Shneur Zalman's group of followers continued to grow, and in 1797, overwhelmed with questions and requests for guidance, Shneur Zalman published, anonymously, his *Likkutai Amarim* ("Collected Sayings"), retitled in the second edition as the *Tanya* ("It Is Taught").

Shneur Zalman's systematic, rational teachings,

profound and eloquently expressed, eventually earned him the respect of all circles. Yet as his influence threatened to penetrate even the hearts of his enemies, the *Mitnaggedim* made a last desperate strike against Hasidism: they informed on the Hasidim to the Russian government. Shneur Zalman was accused of treason and of founding a forbidden religious sect, arrested, and tried in 1798. He was acquitted but denounced again in 1801. He was finally released late in the same year when Alexander I became tsar. The anniversary of his release on Kislev 19 was thereafter celebrated annually as a holiday by his followers. In 1804 he settled in Lyady, Belorussia. At the disastrous end of the Franco-Russian war, he fled Russia and died en route in Piena, in the Russian interior. He was buried in Hadich, Poltava.

To Shneur Zalman, the Hasidic leader was a spiritual guide rather than a wonder worker. A dynamic spiritual leader and mystic himself, Shneur Zalman was beloved for the sensitivity he expressed in his writings and in the Hasidic melodies he composed. He founded a new stream of Hasidism founded on a more rational approach than the other emotion-laden trends. This was called Habad, an acronym of the Hebrew for "wisdom, understanding, knowledge." The *Tanya* is considered the written law of Habad Hasidism; in it, the author develops the ideal Jewish figure of the *beinoni* (average man), an image "to which every man should aspire." The *Tanya* is at once a psychological study, based on kabbalistic sources, and a theosophical inquiry, intended to arouse faith and love for God.

Shneur Zalman was succeeded as head of the Habad movement by his son, **Dov Ber Schneersohn** (1773–1827). He settled in Lubavich, Belorussia, which became the spiritual center of the Habad movement. During the period of "benevolent paternalism" of Tsar Alexander I (c. 1807), Dov Ber advocated the establishment of agricultural settlements for Jews. Men, women, and children, he felt, should learn the skills required in factories and begin to engage in working the land. In 1823 he was responsible for establishing a Habad settlement in Hebron in the Holy Land.

He was imprisoned by the Russian government in 1826 on a false charge of allotting money to the sultan of Turkey. The date of his release, Kislev 10, is still celebrated as a holiday by Habad followers.

He was known as the "Middle Rabbi" because he came between Shneur Zalman and Menahem Mendel (see below). Dov Ber wrote commentaries on the mystical classic, the Zohar, and a "Tract on Ecstasy," stressing the role of ecstasy in religious life. It was said of him that "if you cut his finger, you would find that not blood but Habad teaching runs in his veins."

His successor, **Menahem Mendel** (1789–1866), both his nephew and his son-in-law, was known after the title of this main work as *Zemah Zedek* ("Offspring of Righteousness"). He was brought up and educated by his grandfather, Shneur Zalman of Lyady. Like Dov Ber, Menahem Mendel encouraged the agricultural settlement of Jews and even bought a large tract of land where three hundred families were settled. He established a committee to assist the cantonists — young boys drafted into the tsarist army — ransoming as many as possible from the military camps. His son and successor, **Samuel** (1834–1882) endeavored to intervene at the highest government levels to stem anti-Semitic outbreaks. He was followed by his son, **Shalom Dov** (1860–1920), who went to Rostov-on-Don during World War I. He remained in the Soviet Union after the revolution, devoting himself to organizing secret centers of religious instruction. His son and successor, **Joseph Isaac** (1880–1950), established a spinning and weaving mill tha tprovided a livelihood for many Jews in Mohilev. In 1917 he founded a yeshiva (Talmudic academy) in Bukhara. Like his father, he conducted an intensified campaign for Jewish education throughout Soviet Russia and in 1927 was imprisoned and sentenced to death for "counterrevolutionary activities." The sentence was commuted to three years banishment in the Urals, but pressures by U.S. President Herbert Hoover led to his release, and he left Russia and settled im Riga. In 1934 he moved to Warsaw, where he lived through the initial horrors of World War II, but then fled to the United States, where he established his headquarters in Brooklyn. Before his death, he began to develop educational institutions in North Africa, Israel, and Australia.

Shneur Zalman's descendants perpetuated his teachings. Leadership of the Lubavicher movement has remained in the Schneersohn family, passed from father to son, until the present, when it is centered im Brooklyn, New York.

L. Jacobs, *Tract on Ecstasy of Dobh Baer of Lubavitch*, 1963.

N. Mindel, *Rabbi Schneur Zalman*, 1969.

APHORISMS OF SHNEUR ZALMAN

- Virtue flowing from reason is superior to virtue not founded on reason.
- One may not interrupt one's study of Halakhah for prayer.
- Though not itself food, salt adds flavor to dishes. The same is true of Kabbalah: though scarcely comprehensible — and tasteless — in itself, it adds flavor to the Torah.
- There are shrines in the heavenly sphere that may only be opened through song.
- Lord of the universe: I want neither Your Garden of Eden nor Your rewards in the hereafter. What I desire is You alone!
- The only way of converting darkness into light is by giving to the poor.
- Every act of kindness that God performs for man should make him feel not proud, but more humble and unworthy.

SIEFF, ISRAEL MOSES See under Marks, Simon

SIEGEL, BENJAMIN "BUGSY" (1906–1947) U.S. gangster and criminal syndicate leader. Born in New York City to middle-class parents, Siegel was the archetypal movie mobster: handsome, hotheaded, ambitious, and ruthless. At age fourteen he bossed his own criminal gang and became a feared power on New York's Lower East Side. Because of his violent fits of temper, he was called "Bugs," a nickname he hated and which no one dared call him to his face.

While still a teenager, he joined with Meyer Lansky (q.v.) to form the Bugs and Meyer Mob. The gang sold protection to night clubs, engaged in armed robbery and hijacking, and handled killings for various bootleg gangs operating in New York and New Jersey. By the time he wa twenty-one, Siegel had been arrested for hijacking, mayhem, bootlegging, bookmaking, robbery, rape, and murder of boyhood associates including Charles "Lucky" Luciano, Louis "Lepke" Buchalter (q.v.), Joe Adonis, Abner "Longy" Zwillman, and Meyer Lansky, became a founding member of the national crime syndicate.

In the 1930s, Siegel went to California to run the syndicate's West Coast operations. Suave and entertaining, Siegel hobnobbed with Hollywood celebrities includng Jean Harlow, George Raft, Clark Gable, and Cary Grant. During the war years, Siegel recognized the tremendous opportunities from legalized gambling in Nevada, and borrowed syndicate money to build a plush hotel-casino, the Flamingo, in Las Vegas. Once it was built, he tried to keep most of the profits himself. This defiance of the syndicate cost him his life. On a June evening in 1947, someone pointed a .30-caliber carbine at Siegel, as he sat in his girlfriend Virginia Hill's mansion, and pumped two bullets into his head. Siegel's oft quoted remark, "We only kill each other," proved prophetic. He was the first member of the syndicate's board of directors to be executed by his own.

D. Jennings, *We Only Kill Each Other: The Life and Bad Times of Bugsy Siegel*, 1967.

SILVA, FRANCESCO MOLDANO DE (c. 1592–1639) Marrano martyr in South America. He came from the small village of Tucuman in the north of what is now Argentina, where his father Diego Nuñez de Silva was a doctor of Portuguese origin. His skills were so renowned that he became the physician to the leading families in the town of Cordoba, some four hundred miles to the south. An office of the Inquisition had been established in Buenos Aires and its agents scoured the continent in search of Marranos (Jews converted to Christianity under pressure) whose Christianity had lapsed or who maintained Jewish practices. The Inquisition's representatives grew suspicious of Diego Nuñez and imprisoned him in Tucuman in 1601, together with his elder son, who told his jailers that his father had instructed him in the laws of Moses and rejected Christianity. The younger son, Francesco Moldano, who was nine years old at the time, had received no Jewish upbringing but was deeply impressed by his brother's declaration, which sowed for him the first seeds of religious doubt.

In 1605, Diego Nuñez was "reconciled" with the Church and received a comparatively light sentence; due to the shortage of doctors, he was released and sent to Callao (today in Peru). Here his younger son, secretly taught by his father, fervently accepted Judaism while outwardly remaining Catholic. He was greatly influenced by the second of the Ten Commandments, which forbade the worship of graven images, and saw Christianity as breaking this command. Under his father's direction, he too became a doctor and after Diego Nuñez's death in 1616, he worked as a surgeon in a hospital in Santiago de Chile. At the same time, he began to observe Jewish rituals and, when his wife was absent, secretly circumcised himself. He tried to convert his two sisters but they betrayed him to the Inquisition. They said he had fasted from time to time, put on a clean shirt on Saturdays, and had questioned the chastity of the Virgin Mary. In 1627, he was imprisoned in Lima. At his first interrogation he spoke proudly of his adherence to Judaism; the next time, he recited the Jewish morning prayers; and at the third audience he declared that Jesus preached magic and then read from his notebook the dates of all the Jewish festivals. When the 55-point accusation was read out to him, it was indicated that he would be treated mercifully if reconciled to the Church. His reaction was to accept all the accusations, and he asked his accusers to add some more, including fasting in prison on the Day of Atonement. He refused to swear on the cross and insisted on swearing in the name of the God of Israel.

Fifteen theological debates ensued in which the inquisitors tried to shake his faith and convince him of the truth of Christianity. He answered their arguments, frequently having recourse to the Bible, and maintained his Judaism. By 1634, after seven years in prison and an eighty-day fast to atone for his sins, he was so weak that he could not turn in bed. Despite his weakness, he succeeded one night in getting out of his cell but instead of making his escape from prison, he entered the dungeons of the other prisoners and actually persuaded two of them to adopt Judaism.

In 1638, the debates recommenced as the Inquisition could not tolerate his dying impenitent. He remained unyielding and presented two books that he had written on the subject while in prison. He also stated categorically that all arguments pertaining to the messianic nature of Jesus were null and void. The Inquisition then saw no alternative to executing him at an auto-da-fé at Padregal (Peru). His books were tied round his neck and to the last moment priests tried to persuade him to recant. He was burnt at the stake and his ashes cast to the winds.

SILVER, ABBA HILLEL (1893–1963) U.S. Reform rabbi and Zionist leader. Born in Sirvintos, Lithuania, he was taken to the United States in 1902. His father was a Hebrew teacher and a rabbi, and Silver grew up in an atmosphere of Jewish learning. His father also founded the first Hebrew-speaking Zionist boy's club in the United States and already as a youth, Silver represented the club at the American Zionist Convention.

Although brought up in an Orthodox environment, Silver decided to become a Reform rabbi, entering Hebrew Union College in Cincinnati. At that time, the college was strongly anti-Zionist and Silver's views were exceptional. He was ordained in 1915, when he also graduated from the University of Cincinnati. He later received doctoral degrees from both Hebrew Union College and Western Reserve University.

After serving for two years as rabbi in Wheeling, West Virginia, he was appointed rabbi of the influential Congregation Tifereth Israel (the Temple) in Cleveland, where he served from the age of twenty-four until his death. He was a noted orator and a prominent figure in Cleveland, identifying with many liberal and progressive social causes.

In 1920 he attended the London Zionist Conference, where he supported Louis D. Brandeis (q.v.) in his dispute with Chaim Weizmann (q.v.), but later he transferred his allegiance to Weizmann. However, when the British Peel Commission recommended partition of Palestine in 1937, Silver opposed Weizmann's willingness to consider the proposal as a realistic possibility. In the U.S. Jewish community, he was one of the organizers of the boycott of goods from Germany during the period of the Nazi regime.

In 1938 Silver was a founder and cochairman of the United Jewish Appeal and chairman of the Israel Palestine Appeal. During World War II, when the role of U.S. Jewry in world Jewish affairs became enhanced as a result of the destruction of European Jewry, Silver became a key figure in Zionist and world Jewish affairs. After the war had broken out, Silver, along with Stephen S. Wise (q.v.), headed the American Zionist Emergency Council. In 1941 he spoke out in favor of the establishment of a Jewish commonwealth in Palestine, ending a fiery speech by quoting the Irish leader Daniel O'Connell's "Agitate! Agitate! Agitate!" He advocated a far more activist policy than other American Zionist leaders, calling for the mobilization of public opinion and the application of political pressure to achieve Jewish statehood. He was the first Zionist leader to publicly criticize the position of President Franklin D. Roosevelt and the State Department for their views on the future of Palestine. Although other Zionists had agreed not to press the issue of Jewish statehood but to concentrate on the rescue of European Jewry, Silver spoke out at the foundation conference of the American Jewish Conference in 1943, saying, "We cannot truly rescue the Jews of Europe unless we have free immigration to Palestine and we cannot have free immigration unless our political rights are recognized."

Silver's militancy led to friction with other Zionist leaders and in 1944 he had to resign from the Emergency Council after pressing for a pro-Zionist resolution in Congress that was defeated. At the end of the war, the publication of Roosevelt's anti-Zionist stand in his correspondence with King Ibn Saud vindicated Silver's anti-Roosevelt views and he returned to the Zionist leadership in July 1945. A policy of vigorous political activism was now pursued and Silver took a leading role in the struggle for a Jewish state. He was president of the Zionist Organization of America and chairman of the American Section of the Jewish Agency. In that capacity he was the leading spokesman of the Jewish Agency in the United Nations deliberations and negotiations which culminated in the November 29, 1947, resolution that partitioned Palestine and led to the establishment of a Jewish state. When the declaration of the state was about to be questioned in the Security Council on May 14, 1948, Silver asked the Jewish leaders in Palestine to advance the time of the declaration and when the Security Council assembled he was able to announce that the state was a fait accompli.

Silver's triumph was not to last long. His dominant role was challenged by David Ben-Gurion (q.v.), who resented the extent of Diaspora control in Zionist affairs and Silver's power in the allocation of the financial resources collected in the United States, especially in view of Silver's right-wing associations (as a General Zionist and a Republican). Silver was maneuvered out of his key posts, although he continued to hold a number of lesser Zionist positions. His main activity henceforth was in the American community, in the rabbinate, and in scholarly pursuits.

His writings include *A History of Messianic Speculation in Israel* (1927), and *Where Judaism Differed* (1956) on the differences between Judaism and Christianity.

D. J. Silver (ed.), *In the Time of Harvest: Essays in Honor of Abba Hillel Silver*, 1963.

SILVERMAN, SAMUEL SYDNEY (1895–1968) Lawyer, member of British Parliament, and penal reformer. Born in Liverpool to a poor family, he earned scholarships that enabled him to attend the Liverpool Institute and then to study English literature at Liverpool University. During World War I, Silverman was conscripted for military service but registered as a conscientious objector. His pacifist beliefs were influenced by Bertrand Russell. Unable to accept any of the alternatives to military service, he went to prison. It was here that he learned firsthand the need for penal reform.

When the war was over Silverman returned to the university, where he earned prominence as a debater in the Labor Club. After completing his degree in 1921, he accepted up a post as lecturer in English at the University of Helsinki. In 1925 he returned to England and by 1927 had completed a degree in law. He began a successful career as a solicitor, defending clients from among the poor neighborhoods of his childhood in criminal cases, landlord-tenant disputes, and compensation claims. Upon moving to London he opened an office and continued his practice as the "poor man's lawyer."

Silverman entered local politics in Liverpool and in 1932 became a city councilor. He soon gained a reputation throughout the industrial north as a skilled speaker, and accepted an offer to stand for Parliament. He was elected as Labor inember for Nelson, Lancashire, retaining the seat until his death. Throughout this period he was in constant opposition to the leadership of the party, holding views to the left of the establishment, and thus remained a backbencher; he was ever offered any senior or ministerial post.

He campaigned for the abolition of capital punishment for nearly thirty years, but it was only in 1957 that he succeeded in obtaining the passage of a compromise reform act by which hanging was imposed for five categories of murder only. He wrote numerous pamphlets to promote his campaigns and published *Hanged, and Innocent* (1953), which described three cases in which the death penalty seemed to have been unjustly imposed. The passage of the Abolition of Death Penalty Bill seven years later was the climax of his prolonged fight.

Always proud of his Judaism, Silverman actively protested the activities of the Fascist leader, Sir Oswald Mosley, as well as the attacks on Jews in London and elsewhere in the 1930s. During World War II, although he usually rejected the use of force, Silverman realized that only by armed intervention would it be possible to put an end to the annihilation of Jews in Europe. In his belief, only Palestine could provide a secure refuge for the Jews of post-Holocaust Europe; he therefore openly opposed the government's policy in Palestine. Silverman constantly clashed with Foreign Secretary Ernest Bevin over both his Palestine policy and his handling of relations with the Soviet Union. Silverman campaigned against the use of nuclear weapons and was a member of the Campaign for Nuclear Disarmament.

Silverman served as chairman of the British section of the World Jewish Congress (1940–1950), a member of its World Executive Council (1950–1960) and vice-president of the Zionist Federation of Great Britain (1947–1950).

E. Hughes, *Sydney Silverman, Parliamentary Rebel*, 1969.

SIMEON BAR YOHAI (c. 100 — c. 160 CE). Rabbinical authority and mystic, an outstanding pupil of the martyred Rabbi Akiva (q.v.). There are well over three hundred references to him in the Mishnah, where he is almost invariably called Rabbi Simeon (without the patronymic). Owing to the multitude of legends woven around his personality, in Talmudic lore and in the Kabbalah, precise biographical data are hard to establish. For thirteen years, he studied under Akiva in Benei Berak, developing a reverence for his teacher as well as the intellectual independence that was to characterize his own legal methodology. Unlike Akiva and most other sages of the time, Simeon had a high opinion of himself, which may in part explain Akiva's failure to ordain him as a rabbi. Together with Rabbi Meir (q.v.), he was one of the five surviving disciples of Akiva who received ordination from Judah ben Bava during the Hadrianic persecutions that followed Bar Kokhba's (q.v.) ill-starred revolt against Rome (132–135 CE).

Having witnessed the Emperor Hadrian's systematic attempt to eradicate Judaism by prohibitive laws, torture, and wholesale execution, Simeon bar Yohai became an uncompromising Jewish nationalist. Whereas Akiva's generation had readily accepted martyrdom, Simeon believed that there were other ways of resisting oppression by preserving the Jewish heritage. Condemned to death after his outspoken attack on the Romans' anti-Jewish policies had been reported to the authorities, he went into hiding to avoid execution. Tradition relates that he and his son Eleazar found refuge in a cave near the village of Peki'in in Upper Galilee, where they spent the next thirteen years studying Torah and were sustained by mulberries, carob pods, and a spring of fresh water. Once it was safe for them to emerge under the more tolerant regime of Hadrian's successor, Antoninus Pius (138–161), Simeon may have taught at Usha, where the Sanhedrin had been relocated after its move from Yavneh. He eventually founded a school of his own at Tekoa (a Galilean village, rather than the town of that name devastated in Judea), where his students included Judah ha-Nasi (q.v.). As an acknowledged leader and spokesman of the Palestinian Jewish community, Simeon bar Yohai is thought to have undertaken a successful mission to Rome, personally persuading Antoninus to repeal a ban on circumcision and other religious observances.

Anxious to determine the meaning and purpose of the teachings which he had received, Simeon often boldly rejected the views of his predecessors when dealing with legal questions. Thanks to the ascetic way of life adopted during his prolonged sojourn in the cave, he became an admired exemplar of the Torah sage who placed study before everything else.

From the early Middle Ages, Simeon bar Yohai was thought to have written various apocalyptic or mystical compilations; and, while hidden in the Galilean cave, he was said to have authored the mystical classic, the Zohar ("The Book of Splendor"). In its present form, at least, this central work of the Kabbalah dates from the late 13th century; but Simeon's explicit belief in his own supreme merit and holiness, coupled with his reputation as a wonder-worker, may explain his frequent appearance in the Zohar and the growth of this cherished legend. From about the 16th century, his traditional grave at Meron (near Safed)

became a center of pilgrimage, especially on Iyar 18, the minor festival of Lag ba-Omer, taken as the anniversary of his death.

G. Casaril, *Rabbi Simeon bar Yochai et la Cabbale*, 1961.
Y. Konovitz, *Rabbi Shim'on ben Yohai* (Hebrew), 1966.

SAYINGS OF SIMEON BAR YOHAI

● Three people who dine together and do not exchange words of Torah are considered as though they have eaten an idolatrous sacrifice.
● Hatred upsets the social order.
● Throw yourself into a blazing furnace rather than shame a neighbor in public.
● To honor parents is even more important than to honor God.
● God is angry at him who does not leave a son to be his heir.
● It is a duty to save a woman from rape, even at the cost of the assailant's life.
● There are three crowns: the crown of Torah, the crown of Priesthood, and the crown of Royalty. The crown of a good name is superior to them all.
● It is forbidden to observe a commandment by performing a transgression.
● A liar's punishment is that he is not believed even when he tells the truth.
● Great is work, for it honors him who performs it.

SIMEON BEN GAMALIEL Name of two distinguished presidents of the Sanhedrin in the 1st-2nd centuries CE.

Simeon ben Gamaliel I was the son and successor of Gamliel I (q.v.), who officiated in the period immediately preceding the destruction of the Temple in 70 CE.

One of his best-known saying was "I have grown up among sages all my life and I have found that nothing is better than silence. What is important is not what you learn but what you do;' and too much talk leads to sin". He was an energtic leader and a number of regulations related to the Temple are attributed to him. It is said that in the celebrations of the annual Water-Drawing Festival, "he used to juggle eight lighted torches and not one fell to the ground." During the Roman siege of Jerusalem he joined the revolutionary council directing the war against Rome, but when the Zealots obtained the upper hand among the Jews in Jerusalem, he unsuccessfully opposed their ascendancy and control.

Simeon ben Gamaliel II was the son of Gamaliel II (q.v.) and father of Judah ha-Nasi (q.v.). After the failure of the Bar Kokhba (q.v.) revolt in 135 CE, he had to spend a long period in hiding to escape the Roman persecution of the sages. When the Sanhedrin was restored in Usha in Lower Galilee, he was elected its president — a tribute both to his personal qualities and his distinguished descent from Hillel (q.v.). He worked to ensure the status of the Sanhedrin and the priority of the Palestinian scholars over those in Babylonia. His opinions are frequently quoted in the early rabbinic texts — 100 times in the Mishnah where, with three exceptions, they are accepted as authoritative. He warned against imposing restrictions which the public would find difficult to sustain and insisted that local customs should be respected.

Among his dicta: "The world rests on three pillars: law, truth and peace;" "whoever makes peace in his own home is as though he made peace in all Israel;" and "it is not necessary to build monuments to the pious — their words are their monument."

SIMEON BEN LAKISH (3rd cent. CE) Talmudic sage (also known as Resh Lakish) in Eretz Israel. This distinguished scholar had most unpropitious beginnings, having engaged in his youth in brigandage and gladiatorial contests. The eminent Rabbi Johanan ben Nappaha prevailed upon him to alter his way of life; Ben Lakish studied with Johanan in Sepphoris, and married Johanan's sister. His physical strength and courage continued to manifest themselves throughout his life, but now he put highwaymen and brigands to flight for attempting to molest his scholar friends.

His courage was, however, more than surpassed by his great learning, his abiding love for his people and the Land of Israel, and his sense of compassion. His integrity was proverbial. The sage is recorded as having severely rebuked Babylonian rabbis of his day for their failure to make the Holy Land their home. Concerning his love for his people, the story is told that once, on a visit to pagan Caesarea in the company of Rabbi Abahu, the latter began to revile the entire city, which included many semi-assimilated Jews. Whereupon Rabbi Simeon put sand into his colleague's mouth saying,

"Does God then take pleasure in one who speaks ill of Israel?"

The concern he displayed for the need for respect by the scholarly for the lowly and uneducated is apparent in his homily: "Let the clusters [the scholars] pray for the leaves [the uneducated mass], for were it not for the leaves the clusters would not exist." Rabbi Simeon ben Lakish fearlessly challenged the recognized rabbinical authorities of his day, yet was equally prepared to accord them their scholarly and authoritative due. His brother-in-law, Rabbi Johanan, an outstanding scholar in his own right, eventually deferred to Rabbi Simeon's preeminence. When Johanan formed an academy in Tiberias, he was joined by Simeon and their arguments form a major element in the Palestinian Talmud. When Simeon died, Johanan went around crying, "Where are you, Bar Lakish?" until his own death.

E. Urbach, *The Sages—Their Concepts and Beliefs*, vol. 1, 1975.

SIMEON BEN SHETAH (1st cent. BCE) Sage and Pharisee leader in Eretz Israel. Simeon ben Shetah (or Shatah) was closely involved in affairs of state during the reigns of King Alexander Yannai, (q.v.) and Queen Salome Alexandra (q.v.), (103–76 BCE). It was widely believed that he was the brother of the queen, but this is now doubted.

Relations between the Hasmonean king and the Pharisee sage are depicted in the Babylonian Talmud as being bitterly acrimonious. The Jerusalem Talmud, on the other hand, closer in time and place to these individuals and events, views the disputes in a generally conciliatory light, and as being resolved with no great difficulty. In one instance, Simeon ben Shetah even insisted that the king be charged with responsibility for a murder committed by his slave.

Undisputed, however, is the niche occupied by Simeon — at one time, president (*nasi*) of the Sanhedrin — in the realm of halakhah or Jewish religious law. Perhaps under Alexander Yannai Simeon had already removed Sadducee members from this supreme legislative-judicial body. He restored the Pharisee order of the Temple service in Jerusalem, especially in the matter of the Sadducee-oriented water libation ceremony, a constant source of rancor. There is, however, the story that he ordered the execution of eighty sorceresses in Ascalon in one day, in severe contravention of Pharisaic law. In this instance, apparently, Simeon's sense of the grave danger facing the entire Jewish community prompted extreme and immediate measures.

He rebuked his colleague and chairman of the court, Rabbi Judah ben Tabbai, for overstepping the bounds of Jewish law when he ordered the execution of a witness wrongly accused of perjury. Simeon refused to annul the order for the execution of his own son even when the charge against him had been disproved, in order to teach that there should be no favoritism before the law. This

---

SAYINGS OF SIMEON BEN LAKISH

● Anger deprives a sage of his wisdom, a prophet of his vision.
● God lends a man an extra soul on the eve of the Sabbath and withdraws it at the close of he Sabbath.
● Synagogues and houses of study are Israel's fortresses.
● Great is repentance: it turns sins into incentives for rightful conduct.
● Correct yourself first; afterwards correct others.
● He who has mercy on the cruel will in the end behave cruelly to the merciful.

sad case may have led to his famous dictum: "Examine the witnesses with painstaking thoroughness, and take care lest your words be an example for others to speak falsely." Again, there is the story of his purchasing a donkey from a pagan. When his disciples found a precious gem in the donkey's sack, the rabbi ordered them to return the gem to its owner, despite their remonstrances, saying, "I purchased a donkey, not a precious stone."

To Simeon is attributed the ordinance concerning compulsory community education for all boys, regardless of social or economic status, and the increased economic protection he afforded women facing divorce.

E. Urbach, *The Sages—Their Concepts and Beliefs*, vol. 1, 1975.

SIMEON THE HASMONEAN (d. 135/4 BCE)

Second son of Mattathias the Hasmonean. He attained leadership of the Jews in Eretz Yisrael in 143–142 BCE following Judah Maccabbee [q.v.], and Jonathan. Simeon was the first of the leaders to achieve sovereign statehood for his people.

From the outset of the Hasmonean revolt in 167, Simeon and his brother Jonathan worked in close military coordination with Judah. To Simeon was allotted the task of rescuing the Jews of Galilee who were suffering at the hands of the pagan population of the region. Simeon also assisted Jonathan in his battles and in consolidating Jewish gains: and in clashes across the Jordan, as in the battle with the Seleucid general, Bacchides, from which the Jews emerged victorious. The very year that Simeon assumed the Hasmonean leadership, upon his brother Jonathan's death, the sovereignty of the Jewish state was proclaimed. This was followed by several telling political and military successes.

After fortifying Jerusalem and strengthening the defenses of the newly acquired commercially important port city of Jaffa, he succeeded in capturing the highly strategic town of Gezer in the Judean lowlands, and in finally removing the threat of the pagan-held *Akra* citadel in Jerusalem. In the year 140 BCE, in a solemn assembly of the people, Simeon was officially accorded the tripartite role of high priest, ethnarch (ruler of the area) and commander-in-chief of the Jewish armed forces. Shortly thereafter, he reconfirmed the alliance with Rome initiated by Judah, and the treaty with Sparta originally negotiated by Jonathan.

Added evidence of the new Jewish power in the region was the official recognition by the Seleucid ruler, Demetrius II, in 142. Simeon was treacherously killed in Jericho by his son-in-law Ptolemy in 135–4 in a possibly Seleucid-sponsored plot. Nevertheless, there is testimony to the true significance of his rule: the fact that he successfully contended with the powerful Seleucid monarch, Antiochus VII (Sidetes), and in the words of the First Book of Maccabees on his days in power: "He made peace in the land. And ·Israel rejoiced... and each sat under his vine and fig tree and none was left in the land to fight them."

A. Schalit, ed., *The World History of the Jewish People*, vol. 6, 1976.
S. Zeitlin, *The Rise and Fall of the Judaean State*, vol. 1, 1962.

SIROTA, GERSHON ISAAC (1874–1943)

Cantor, the first to record Jewish liturgical music (*hazzanut*) commercially. Trained in Odessa, he served as chief cantor (*hazzan*) in Vilna (1896–1905) and then, until 1927, at the Tlomacka Street (Great) Synagogue in Warsaw. He possessed a dramatic tenor robusto voice of astonishing range, with an unrivaled coloratura, and the services he conducted were religious musical events that attracted thousands of worshipers. His concert tours of major Russian Jewish communities also brought him to the notice of Tsar Nicholas II, at whose command Sirota gave annual recitals in Saint Petersburg and Moscow.

While in Vilna in 1903, he was invited to make a series of twelve phonograph disks — the earliest recordings of Jewish liturgical music. They included virtuoso interpretations of A. M. Bernstein's *Adonai, Adonai* ("The Lord, the Lord," Exod. 34:6–7) and of Isaac Schlossberg's *Retseh*, which Rimsky-Korsakov numbered "among the elect of synagogue compositions." Sirota also recorded operatic arias, Yiddish folk songs, and a memorial prayer for Max Nordau (q.v.).

Sometimes acclaimed as "the Jewish Caruso," Sirota made numerous tours of the United States between 1912 and 1938 and one of Palestine in 1935. A one-hundred-voice male choir accompanied his concert performance at the Metropolitan Opera House in New York in 1921. The Warsaw Great Synagogue, however, irritated by Sirota's frequent absences abroad on the Jewish High Holy Days, eventually chose Cantor Moshe Koussevitsky as his replacement.

Unlike other great cantors of the time, Sirota remained in eastern Europe and was trapped there after the outbreak of World War II. He is said to have been killed on April 27, 1943 (the last day of Passover), during the Warsaw Ghetto uprising against the Nazis.

SLANSKY, RUDOLF (1901–1952)

Secretary general of the Czechoslovak Communist party executed for high treason after what was known as the Slansky trial. Born Rudolf Schlesinger, Slansky rose in the ranks of the Communist party and already in 1936 was subjected to harsh criticism by the Communist International for his "opportunistic policy," and was temporarily suspended from the leadership group. In 1939, when the Nazis entered Czechoslovakia the leadership went into exile in the USSR. During the World War II period Slansky was given important assignments. He was responsible for the recruitment of party members for the Czechoslovakian army units formed in the Soviet Union and contacts with the partisan units that parachuted into Slovakia when the Slovaks rose against the Nazis in August 1944. Slansky was appointed political representative of the Czechoslovak Communist party, responsible for contacts with the Soviet partisan units to guarantee assistance to Slovak fighters and to organize partisan bands to fight behind the German lines. He himself fought in the Slovakian mountains and as a tribute for his heroism in battle many factories, quarries and other enterprises were named after him.

In 1945 Slansky was appointed secretary general of the Czechoslovak Communist party, second in command to the chairman and later president, Klement Gottwald.

He held full control of party affairs, the security services and the army. He deputized for Gottwald at party conferences and spoke in his name.

In July 1951 Slansky was awarded the highest Czechoslovak honor, the Socialism Decoration, on the occasion of his fiftieth birthday. However, Slansky became alarmed that same year while attending a top secret meeting at the Kremlin of Communist party secretaries general from eastern Europe were he was not permitted to make him report. A conception had been developing in Moscow according to which Slansky had been responsible for the appointment of unreliable and hostile people to key positions and that he may well be leading of a Trotskyist conspiracy in Czechoslovakia.

The Czechoslovakian Communist party central committee abolished the post of secretary general and Slansky was appointed first deputy prime miñister in charge of economic affairs, remaining a member of the party's political bureau.

A confession forced from Artur London, former deputy foreign minister, naming Slansky head of the conspiracy and a letter seized by security people allegedly destined for Slansky detailing arrangements for him to flee Czechoslovakia, led to Slansky's arrest on November 24, 1951. Two weeks later the party's central committee revoked his membership and removed him from all party posts.

Slansky persistently professed his innocence for nine months despite being subjected to tortuous interrogation. He was accused of leaving the naċional hero Jan Sverna to die in a snowstorm in the ountains in which they were caught during the partisan struggle against the Nazis and was also charged with plotting to speed up the death of the ailing Gottwald so as to seize his place as head of the government. In prison he was manacled and fettered to the wall. Slansky confessed to all counts and his trial, together with thirteen others (of whom ten were Jews), opened on November 20, 1952. They were accused of being "Trotskyist-Zionist-bourgeois-nationalist traitors and enemies of the Czechoslovakian people... Under the direction of Western and hostile espionage services... they set up the Anti-State and Subversive Center... designed to stamp out popular democracy in Czechoslovakia, restore the hegemony of capitalism and destroy the country's sovereignty and independence." Slansky pleaded guilty of espionage,

high treason and sabotage. He declared he had never been a true Communist and had committed many crimes against the Communists, and admitted to having collaborated with the Zionist movement, mainly through economic help for Israel to the disadvantage of Czecholsovakia. Slansky and ten others were sentenced to death, and he was executed on December 4, 1952.

A number of commissions were appointed to examine the interrogations and the trial proceedings, but it was only in 1968 that the Piller Commission found the central security services responsible for using illegal methods in preparing the political trials, extorting confessions and forged written depositions by physical and psychological coercion.

The commission's report called for the annulment of Slansky's expulsion by the party's central committee and his readmission to party membership. The Piller Report was filed away, but was smuggled out and made public in the West. The Slansky trial was called by the Czech historian Karel Kaplan "the biggest trial after the war against Communist leaders in Europe, the most political of the political trials, the cruellest and most illogical trial."

Strange are the paths of destiny: in 1990 Rudolf Slansky Junior was appointed the Czechoslovakian ambassador to the USSR.

M. Cotic, *The Prague Trial, The First Anti-Zionist Show Trial in the Communist Bloc* (1987).
K. Kaplan, *Report on the Murder of the General Secretary* (1990).
E. Lobel, *My Mind on Trial* (1976).
A. London, *The Confession* (1970).
J. Pelikan, *The Piller Report* (1970).
J. Slanska, *Report on My Husband* (1969).

SLONIMSKI, ANTONI (1895–1976) Polish poet, author, and critic. Born in Warsaw, Slonimski was the son of an assimilated Warsaw physician who converted to Christianity and the grandson of the Hebrew popular science writer and editor, Hayyim Selig Slonimski. Known as a liberal Roman Catholic, Slonimsky was part of the Polish poetic revival that took place with the reemergence of a free and independent Poland of 1918. He was the founder of *Skamander*, a Warsaw literary magazine that aimed at adapting traditional to modern forms. After the World War II, Slonimsky returned to Poland from his exile in London and chose to coexist with the communist regime, while advocating full liberalization and opposing censorship. By 1956, Slonimsky was a significant figure in the struggle for freer conditions for Polish writers.

He was sent to London as head of the Polish Cultural Institute (1949–1951) and was also a delegate to the founding congress of the United Nation's Educational, Scientific, and Cultural Organization. He was also president of both the Polish PEN Club and the very influential Polish Writers' Union, a position to which he was elected in 1958 over the Communist party candidate. This candidate later publically denounced a Slonimski poem about the space-age discoveries defiling the moon "with human pains and dreadful nightmares," as being un-Marxist. In 1972 he again defeated the Communist party candidate and he was elected to head the Congress of Polish Writers.

Slonimsky was polically active not only in the pursuit of more liberal attitudes toward writers but also in his support of Israel. In 1964 he, along with other major intellectual figures of his time, signed what was to be called the Letter of Three, protesting censorship. He identified deeply with the Jewish people and spoke out against those calling for Israel's destruction during the days preceding the 1967 Six-Day War and this issue became prevalent in his poetry of this period. After the Six-Day War, he criticized the expulsion of pro-Israel supporters from government posts, an action for which he himself came under scrutiny by the Communist party leader of the time.

He published poems, plays, and books, along with several highly regarded translations of Shakespeare into Polish.

SMOLENSKIN, PEREZ (1842–1885) Hebrew novelist, publicist, and editor. He was born in Monastyrshchina, Belorussia, to a family who had lived for generations in Smolensk, and had taken the name of the town. Because of false accusations, his father was forced to leave Smolensk and take refuge with his mother's family. He died when his son was only eleven. Smolenskin had studied with private tutors, but now was taken by an older brother to the Talmudic academy (yeshiva) at Shklov. He was an excellent student and was granted special permission to study Russian, and thus was introduced to the Haskalah (Jewish enlightenment) literature. In 1858 Smolenskin moved to the yeshiva of the Lubavich Hasidim and then to a Hasidic center at Vitebsk, where he remained until 1861. He then traveled through southern Russia, where he lectured in the Jewish agricultural settlements until he reached Odessa in 1862. He spent the next five years studying languages and teaching Hebrew.

It was at Odessa that Smolenskin made his debut in Hebrew literature with a number of articales in the journal, *Ha-Melitz*, including a scathing criticism of Meir Letteris' translation of Goethe's *Faust*. His first novel *Ha-Gemul* (or "The Jews of Warsaw at the Time of the Last Revolt"), describing the participation of Jews in the 1861–1863 Polish uprising against the Russians, appeared in 1867. During this period he also wrote the major part of his first novel *Simhat Henef* ("The Joy of the Godless").

In 1867 Smolenskin left Odessa and traveled through Romania, Germany, and Bohemia. He arrived in Vienna in 1868 and lived there until his death, working as a Hebrew teacher and author.

In 1868 Smolenskin established the Hebrew monthly *Ha-Shahar*, which was to play a vital role in the development of Hebrew literature. Almost all the talented Hebrew writers of the time contributed. It had such a tremendous influence that its readers, mainly in Russia, became known as "the generation of *Ha-Shahar* ["The Dawn"]." Each issue of the twelve volumes that appeared over a period of seventeen years contained scholarly articles, articles on religious matters, public affairs, and translations of famous works, as well as literary criticism and reviews. Smolenskin was both editor and administrator and he was "compelled to work like a slave in order to support himself and keep the journal alive; he deprived himself of sleep and enjoyed no relaxation." Together with his brother he constantly went on fund-raising tours throughout Europe.

At first Smolenskin set out to criticize the opponents of the enlightenment movement, but he later became an ardent advocate of Jewish nationalism and the Hibbat Zion movement. *Ha-Shahar* met with strong opposition from factions of the Hebrew-reading public. The enlightened opposed it because of Smolenskin's criticism of the philosophy of Moses Mendelssohn (q.v.); the Hasidim were against it because of his criticism of Orthodox Jews; the young socialists considered his nationalism reactionary.

Smolenskin's major novel *Ha-To'eh be-Darkhei ha-Hayyim* ("The Wanderer in the Paths of Life") published in serial form in *Ha-Shahar* (1868–1871), contained details of his own biography as well as a criticism of Jewish life in both eastern and western Europe. *Kevurat Hamor* ("A Donkey's Burial"; 1873) was a scathing criticism of the internal leadership of the Jewish Pale of Settlement. *Gemul ha-Yesharim* ("The Reward of the Righteous"; 1875) deals with the maltreatment of the Jews by the Poles and Russians during the 1863 revolt.

In 1874, at the request of the Alliance Israélite Universelle in Austria, Smolenskin spent three months in Romania examining the situation of the Jews there. His report advocating reforms in Jewish education set off a major controversy. It also provided the basis for his last novel *Ha-Yerusha* ("The Inheritance" published in *Ha-Shahar*, 1880–1884). This was the first Jewish sociological novel of the period. Smolenskin also wrote, under a pseudonym, the first Zionist novel in Hebrew literature, *Nekam Berit* ("Covenant of Revenge"; 1883). The novelist hero turned from assimilation to Zionism, providing a personal confession as to Smolenskin's return to his people.

Despite failing health, Smolenskin continued his work to the end, completing his last novel on his deathbed. Friends raised funds to send him to health resorts, but to no avail. In 1952 his remains were reinterred on Mount Herzl, Jerusalem.

C. H. Freundlich, *Peretz Smolenskin*, 1965.

D. Patterson, *The Hebrew Novel in Czarist Russia*, 1964.

SOFER (SCHREIBER), MOSHE (known as *Hatam Sofer* after his major work; 1762–1839) Hungarian rabbinical authority. Born in Frankfurt-

Moses Sofer (Schreiber).

on-Main, the name Sofer (scribe) denotes the occupation of his ancestors, several of whom were scribes in Frankfurt. The Hatam Sofer's first teachers were Nathan Adler and Pinhas Hurvitz in Frankfurt. His first wife was the daughter of the rabbi of Prossnitz (Moravia), and after his marriage he settled there and continued his studies. At the age of eighteen Sofer had completed studying the Talmud, its commentaries, and all relevant rabbinic literature. However, his very personal methodology developed only later. After some years of quiet contemplation, he occupied the pulpit of Dresnitz (Moravia) and in 1798 was called to the Rabbinate of Nagymarton (Mattersdorf). This was one of the "Seven Communities" in western Hungary, each small in number of congregants but flourishing under the protection and privilege of the Princes Esterhazy. In his own small community, with its centuries of tradition, Sofer began his activities. He established his first yeshiva (Talmudic academy) and introduced his own method of Talmud teaching. After the death of his first wife in 1812, he married Sarah, the daughter of the distinguished rabbi Akiva Eger of Posen. When the rabbinate of Pressburg (Bratislava) fell vacant in 1806, he was called to become chief rabbi of Hungary's largest Jewish community. By his time, he was so renowned that students came to his yeshiva from far and wide. In Pressburg, he developed the yeshiva into the world's greatest rabbinical school, which never had fewer that five-hundred pupils. While strictly adhering to rabbinic law, he also insisted on his pupils' physical fitness, compelling them to swim in the Danube. For the rest of his life, he remained in Pressburg, which, due to his fame, became a stronghold of Orthodoxy. By his second wife, he founded a dynasty of scholars.

The Hatam Sofer's unique personality left a deep impression not only on Talmudic scholarship but also on Jewish religious life in general, his decisions being regarded as relevant until this day. When the Reform movement developed from 1819, Sofer recognized the threat it meant for Orthodoxy and from the very start fought it and persecuted its adherents with all the intellecutal and spiritual force at his disposal. He fought the introduction of vernacular prayer as a threat to the unity of the Jewish people.

His strict adherence to traditional teaching inspired his followers, who unconditionally accepted his authority. Communities and scholars, even in Asia and Africa, sought his opinion and abided by his decisions.

Sofer was a modest, selfless person, of small physical stature, who signed his letters and decisions "Moshe ha-katan mi-Frankfurt" ("little Moses from Frankfurt"). The fact that many graduates of his yeshiva became leading rabbis in important communities, chiefly in western Europe, in large measure contributed to his great influence. In addition to Reform, he also opposed both Hasidism and the nascent Zionist movement, but supported the Old Jewish settlement in the Holy Land and collected funds to distribute among its members. He abstained from and even objected to the contemporary battle for emancipation, opposing Haskalah (Jewish enlightenment) which, in his view, led to assimilation, and warned against reading the works of Moses Mendelssohn (q.v.).

His pupils, Rabbi Moshe Schoenlak and M. Eisner, published part of his works in 1816. His responsa, answering queries from Jewish scholars from many parts of the world, were published in seven volumes under the title *Hatam Sofer* in 1855-1864. He also wrote short stories, poetry, and religious songs which were published in 1857. His ethical testament was published in 1863, his Bible commentary, *Torat Moshe*, in 1879-1895 an his memoirs of the Napoleonic wars and his Passover Haggadah in 1896.

His son **Avraham Shemuel Benjamin Wolf** (1815-1871), called the *Ketav Sofer*, succeeded him in the Pressburg rabbinate and yeshiva. He wrote commentaries on the Bible, Talmudic tractates, and rabbinic codes, and continued his father's struggle against the Reform movement. He was followed by his son **Simcha Bunem**, the *Shevet Sofer* (1842-1906). The last of his direct descendants to occupy the Pressburg seat, **Akiva Sofer** (1876-1959), moved to Palestine in 1940, settled in Jerusalem and reestablished there the Pressburg yeshiva, which he headed.

L. Jung, *Jewish Leaders*, 1953.

SOKOLOW, NAHUM TOBIAS (1859-1936)

Writer, journalist, Zionist leader. Sokolow was born in the small Polish town Wyszgorod, near Plotsk. His father was a well-to-do businessman but, like his father before him, he had a thorough rabbinical training and was an expert on medieval

Hebrew literature. He was also interested in secular culture. His grandfather was eager that Nahum continue the family tradition, but the gifted child, despite his deep attachment to the family, was determined to go his own way.

First, the family tradition determined that the young Sokolow should have a traditional education from which he released himself after a long struggle. He was an infant prodigy, an *illui*. The family moved to Plotsk, where Sokolov studied at the Talmudic acadamy (yeshiva) but was also exposed to the temptations beyond the walls of his closed world. Eager to learn anything and everything, he obtained dictionaries and grammar books in order to study foreign languages in secret; at the age of eight, he already was a polyglot, reading Polish, Russian, French, and German, to which he soon added English, Italian, and Spanish. He was eventually permitted to study the high school curriculum privately.

Sokolow came under the influence of both the Enlightenment and Zionist movements and early in life also showed kabbalistic interests. While the influence of German culture was superficial because Polish Jews mistrusted and disliked the Germans, Sokolow, not sharing this dislike, was to become one of the few exceptions among east European Zionists who had a wide knowledge of and admiration for German literature, and a certain respect for German civilization. However, although he lived in Germany for a long time, he never felt at home there. The Latin culture — Italy, Spain, and even France — attracted him much more.

Still in his teens, he began traveling, visiting other yeshivot and, on his return to Plotsk, he started publishing his first handwritten newpaper, *Shoshana*, in which appeared his Hebrew translations of Schiller's *The Robbers* and *Maria Stuart* and Shakespeare's *Romeo and Juliet*. He also sent Hebrew, Polish, French, and German articles to various newpapers.

Sokolow married at the age of seventeen, and at first lived in his father-in-law's house in Makow. His wife was a charming and intelligent companion, who encouraged him in all that he undertook. They wrote to each other in Polish, which remained the language mostly spoken in the Sokolow household.

Sokolow's first published article appeared in the Hebrew weekly *Ivri Anokhi* (1874) and from 1876, he became a regular contributor to the newspaper *Ha-Tzefira*; his first book, *Universal Geography*, was published in 1877 and was followed by a series of pamphlets on Judaism. He moved to Warsaw in 1880, at the beginning of the very difficult time for Jews in Russia and Poland of pogroms in Russia and growing anti-Semitism in Austria and Germany, which prompted him to write his book *The Eternal Hatred of the Eternal People*. He had to supplement his puny earnings from *Ha-Tzefira* by teaching history at the school of the Reform synagogue, and even considered entering the progressive rabbinate. From 1886, he was coeditor of *Ha-Tzefira*, which had just become a daily, and started publishing the Hebrew annual *Ha-Assif* (1885–1894), and afterwards *Sefer Ha-Shana*.

Sokolow read the *Judenstaat* of Theodor Herzl (q.v.) soon after its publication. It left him with some reservations and he launched an attack in *Ha-Tzefira's* headline "Wonderful Rumors about the Establishment of a Jewish State Originating from the Mind of a Dr. Herzl." However, when he met Herzl at the first Zionist Congress, which he attended as *Ha-Tzefira*'s correspondent, he came totally under Herzl's spell. Returning home, he gradually became the leader of Polish Zionism. He translated Herzl's novel *Altneuland* into Hebrew, giving it the title *Tel Aviv*, inspiring the name of the first Jewish city in the Holy Land. He also became a great admirer of Max Nordau (q.v.). At home, he encountered many difficulties for his Zionist activity, which was prohibited by the tsarist authorities. Gradually, he also became an orator and came into friendly contact with many prominent Jews and attracted them to the Zionist cause. From Shalom Asch (q.v.) to Ludwig Zamenhof (q.v.), the cream of Polish and Russian Jewry gathered at his house.

Loyal to Herzl, during the Uganda controversy, *Ha-Tzefira* supported Herzl because Sokolow above all wanted to preserve unity within the Zionist organization. In 1906, when *Ha-Tzefira* had to suspend publication, David Wolffsohn, Herzl's successor as president of the Zionist Organization, invited Sokolow to be general secretary. He then moved to Berlin and promptly established the Zionist Organization's Hebrew weekly *Ha-Olam* (1907). From then on to the end of his life, he devoted all his energies to the promotion of the Zionist idea. He was first elected to the Zionist Executive in 1911, and in his capacity of general secretary, he became a Jewish diplomat, traveling far and wide, and meeting most of the contemporary political leaders. Sokolow was the first Jew to have an audience with Pope Benedict XV. He first visited Palestine in 1914 and when World War I broke out, moved to London and became closely associated with Chaim Weizmann (q.v.), playing an important part in the preparations for the Balfour Declaration. With Weizmann, he was present at the Paris Peace Conference of 1919, representing the Zionists. That year also saw the publication (in English) of his monumental two-volume *History of Zionism 1600–1918*.

Sokolow was elected head of the Zionist Executive after the war, and also headed the Committee of Jewish Delegations at the Peace Conference in succession to Julian Mack (q.v.) and Louis Marshall (q.v.). He was a principal speaker at the 1920 Zionist Congress in London, which created the new Zionist fund, which Sokolow named Keren Hayesod ("Foundation Fund"), and for which he raised funds all over the world. He chaired the Twelfth Zionist Congress in Karlsbad (1921) and all congresses until his death. Succeeding Nordau, he gave the address on the Jewish situation at Congresses. In these addresses, he showed a much deeper knowledge of the Jewish condition worldwide than Nordau, which made up for the fact that he was less of an orator.

Sokolow became chairman of the enlarged Jewish Agency in 1929. The Arab riots of that time fueled the opposition within the Zionist movement to Weizmann's leadership, and the Seventeenth Congress (1931) was held in an atmosphere of crisis that resulted in Sokolow's election to the presidency in Weizmann's place. He was reelected in 1933 and when, in 1935, Weizmann again became president, Sokolow was elected honarary president of both the Zionist Organization and the Jewish Agency. He was also elected chairman of the Zionist Organization Department of Education and Culture and of the Zionist publishing house Mosad Bialik. He established the Hebrew Writers' Association. In all, he wrote over thirty books and died pen in hand in London. His and his wife's remains were reburied on Mount Herzl, Jerusalem, in 1956.

S. Kling, *Nahum Sokolow*, 1960.

SOLOMON (c. 986 — c. 930 BCE) Third king of the united Israelite monarchy; fourth son of David (q.v.) and of Bathsheba; also called Jedidiah ("Beloved of the Lord," Sam. 12:24–25). He acceded to the throne in his father's lifetime following a court intrigue. One of David's wives, Haggith, tried to have her son, Adonijah, anointed as his father's successor and enlisted powerful allies, including the army chief, Joab, and the chief priest, Abiathar. Bathsheba had the support of the prophet Nathan and the military commander Benaiah in her successful counterbid, which culminated in the anointment of Solomon, even though several of his brothers were older than he.

For a short time, Solomon was coregent with his aging father, but once he became sole ruler, on his father's death, he settled accounts with those who had opposed his accession. The Bible attributes the initiative for these killings to his father's deathbed commands; Joab was killed, Abiathar was exiled, and Adonijah too was killed once Solomon suspected that he still had designs on the throne.

Solomon could now turn to organizing his kingdom. He inherited a large region stretching from the Euphrates to Gaza and the Bible depicts his forty-year reign as a period of peace and tranquility. Both Egypt and Assyria were passing through a time of weakness, facilitating Solomon's continuing control over such a large empire.

The Bible, which offers comparatively little information on his private life, concentrates on the first half of his reign, a time of especial magnificence. It reports that he had seven hundred wives and three hundred concubines. Several of his wives were princesses of neighboring kingdoms — Moab, Ammon, Sidon, and Heth. His outstanding marital alliance was with the daughter of the Egyptian Pharaoh, who brought the town of Gezer to Solomon as her dowry. Despite the size of his harem, the Bible only mentions three of his children — his son and successor, Rehoboam, and two daughters married to provincial governors.

Solomon maintained his empire with a large army, which included not only infantry but also chariots and cavalry, especially to maintain control of the profitable trade routes that he controlled. The discovery of stalls for 450 horses in the stables at Megiddo confirms the extent of his forces. However, there are few references to military campaigns and he preferred to maintain the peace by his alliances and by settling colonies of his soldiers in strategic places. The famous visit of the queen of Sheba (in southern Arabia) was probably in the framework of trade contacts, although the Bible maintains that she came to Jerusalem to test Solomon's proverbial wisdom.

Solomon's reign was marked by an extensive building program. His best-known construction was the Temple. David had hoped to build this center of the Jewish cult and had purchased the site but was told that his hands were too bloodstained, as a man of war, and that the task would be accomplished by his son, a man of peace (the very name Solomon is connected with *shalom*, "peace"). The building took seven years, with the assistance of Solomon's ally, Hiram of Tyre, who provided workmen, timber, and gold. In return Solomon ceded considerable territory to Hiram, as well as wheat, oil, and wine. The two men also cooperated in establishing a commercial fleet operating out of the Red Sea port of Ezion-Geber. The splendor of the Temple is graphically described in the Bible (1 Kings 6–7). On its dedication Solomon uttered a moving prayer in which he praised God as the sole ruler of the universe, begged for his blessing on the people of Israel, and also requested that he hear the prayers of the non-Jews who would come to the Temple. Solomon's other major building projects in Jerusalem included his massive palace (which took thirteen years to build), a palace for Pharaoh's daughter, and shrines for his other foreign wives.

FROM KING SOLOMON'S PRAYER AT THE DEDICATION OF THE TEMPLE

Will God really dwell on earth? Even the heavens to their uttermost reaches cannot contain You, how much less this House that I have built. Yet turn, O Lord my God, to the prayer and supplication of Your servant, and hear the cry and prayer which Your servant offers before You this day. May Your eyes be open day and night toward this House, toward the place of which You said "My name shall abide there"; may You heed the prayers which your servant will offer toward this place. And when You hear the supplications which Your servant and Your people Israel offer toward this place, give heed in Your heavenly abode — give heed and pardon.

The Judgment of Solomon. From a 15th-century illuminated manuscript.

Solomon was famed for his wisdom and the Bible gives examples of his sagacity. One of the best known is the story of two women who claimed motherhood of the same child. When Solomon ruled that the solution would be to divide the child in two, one woman reacted by saying that she would renounce her claim rather than allow that to happen and Solomon immediately identified her as the true mother (1 Kings 3). Because of his reputation as a composer of proverbs, the authorship of the book of Proverbs was ascribed to him and the rabbis stated that he was the "preacher" who wrote Ecclesiastes. His womanizing reputation probably accounts for the traditional ascription to him of the authorship of the Song of Songs (also called the Song of Solomon). Apocryphal works pseudepigraphically attributed to him include the *Wisdom of Solomon* and the *Psalms of Solomon*.

Indications — especially from the second half of his reign — cast doubts on his long-term political astuteness. To maintain his expensive projects, every Israelite had to spend a third of each year in the king's service and to pay heavy taxation. This led to unrest among the people. Jeroboam of the tribe of Ephraim, one of his high officials, attempted to stir up a revolt and was unsuccessful, having to flee to Egypt. (By this time, Egypt had a new Pharaoh who was not friendly to Solomon.) The real extent of the dissatisfaction became apparent after Solomon's death when the bulk of the people (the ten tribes) refused to accept the rule of Solomon's son and successor, Rehoboam, choosing to break away and form their own kingdom Israel, in the north, under Jeroboam, leaving Rehoboam with only the rump state of Judah. Nevertheless, the prestige of Solomon among the people remained undimmed and he was the subject of many legends and to be held up as the paradigm of wisdom.

F. Thieberger, *King Solomon*, 1947.

SOUTINE, CHAIM (1893–1943) Painter. He was born in Smilovichi, Belorussia, the tenth among the eleven children of a poor Jewish tailor, who once locked Chaim in the cellar for two days because he took money to buy colored pencils. At the age of ten, he was apprenticed to a tailor, but in 1907 began working as a retoucher for a photographer in Minsk. Soutine one day asked the rabbi of his village to pose for a portrait, and the rabbi's son was so incensed that he gave Soutine a beating which sent him to hospital and cost the rabbi twenty-five rubles in damages. With this money, Soutine was able to go to Vilna to study art. There, he ate at a soup kitchen, and received some financial assistance from a doctor, whose daughter gave a benefit for Soutine, earning fifty rubles. This was enough for Soutine to go to Paris, where he enrolled at the Ecole des Beaux Arts. When World War I broke out in August 1914, Soutine obtained a residency permit. He also volunteered for the "workers' army" but was rejected because of poor health.

In Paris, Soutine lived in the Cité Falguière, where his studio adjoined that of Amedeo Modigliani (q.v.) and the two became drinking companions and close friends. Modigliani introduced Soutine to his art-dealer, the Polish poet Leopold Zborowski, who, enthusiastic about his work, gave Soutine a stipend of five francs a day. Soutine was very critical of his own paintings and destroyed many of them, but Zborowski managed to rescue some, on occasion even sending work to a restorer.

In 1922, an American collector, Albert C. Barnes, was so impressed by Soutine's work that he bought everything (more than fifty paintings) in Zborowski's possession, paying 60,000 francs. (The paintings now hang at the Barnes Foundation at Merion, near Philadelphia.) When Soutine came for his daily five francs, Zborowski increased his stipend to twenty-five francs a day. From then on, Zborowski sold Soutine's paintings regularly, for good prices.

For a while, Soutine moved frequently, but finally he took a large studio in the boulevard Saint Michel, near a slaughterhouse. Here he painted a series of paintings of carcasses of beef. Paulette Jourdain, who was his model, assisted him by going to the slaughterhouse every few days to get fresh blood to pour over the carcasses so that they would maintain their color. When inspectors from the health department came to remove the carcasses, Jourdain persuaded them to let the carcasses remain until Soutine finished his paintings, on the condition that they inject the beef with ammonia, as a deodorant.

In Montparnasse, Soutine met a German Jewish refugee, Gerda Groth, who moved into his apartment. In 1940, however, as the German army neared France, the government ordered a roundup of all German nationals and Gerda Groth was arrested and sent to an internment camp. Soutine himself received several invitations to take refuge in the United States, but refused.

He met Marie-Berthe Aurenche, the former wife of Max Ernst, in Paris. Believing that as a Jew Soutine was in danger, Aurenche took him to

Self portrait of Chaim Soutine.

friends who agreed to hide them. They remained for three months, but fearing that the concièrge would report them to the Gestapo, fled to the unoccupied zone and settled in Champigny in Touraine.

In 1943, Aurench and Soutine were living in Chinon, when Soutine began to suffer terrible pain from stomach ulcers. At the hospital in Chinon, he was told that he needed an immediate operation. Aurenche arranged for an ambulance to take them to Paris, as the operation could be performed only there. In order to avoid the police, they were forced to detour, and the trip, which should have taken five hours, took more than twenty-four. When they arrived in Paris, Soutine was operated on immediately, but died the next day. Aurenche had Soutine buried in her family plot in the Christian cemetery in Montparnasse. Space in the grave was left for her, and when, in 1960, she committed suicide, she was buried beside him. A cross is engraved on the stone slab she had placed over the grave. Among the few friends who attended Soutine's funeral were Pablo Picasso, Jean Cocteau, Max Jacob, and Gerda Groth, who had recently been released from the internment camp.

Soutine was a painter in the expressionist tradition; his turbulent paintings and bright colors conveyed his own inner tumult. His portraits are often twisted and distorted and his work is always disturbing, but he has become recognized as an outstanding representative of the school of Paris.

R. Cogniar, *Soutine*, 1977.
E. Faure, *Soutine*, 1929.
A. Forge, *Soutine*, 1965.

SPIEGEL, SAM (1901–1985) U.S. film producer. Born in Jaroslaw, Galicia, to a Zionist family, Spiegel soon began to neglect his Jewish studies to go to the movies. In the wake of pogroms, his family moved to Vienna, where he studied economics and drama. Still under his family's influence (his father had been personally acquainted with Theodor Herzl [q.v.]), he went to Palestine as a pioneer, staying there for six years before going to New York in 1927. He was heard lecturing on drama by the MGM producer Paul Bern and was hired to assist in the production of foreign-language versions of American films. Not for the first time, Spiegel was undone by his less-than-scrupulous business practices; on this occasion he was not only fired, but served several months in p ison before being deported to Poland.

A contact he made at Universal before his deportation stood him in good stead and he found work in Universal's Berlin office. His campaign on behalf of Universal's pacifist *All Quiet on the Western Front* did not endear him to the Nazis in the Reichstag and after Hitler came to power, Spiegel fled to Austria. During the 1930s he produced a number of films in Europe and reentered the United States (illegally) in 1939 from Mexico, to which he had been deported from London. He produced his first American film, *Tales of Manhattan* in 1942, using the pseudonym S. P. Eagle, a disguise he maintained until *On the Waterfront* in 1954.

From the 1950s onward, Spiegel's successes were of the spectacular variety: John Huston's *The African Queen*, Elia Kazan's *On The Waterfront*, and two epics by David Lean, *The Bridge on the River Kwai* and *Lawrence of Arabia*. Spiegel never really retired; his last film, *Betrayal*, was made three years before his death. In his later years he lived the life of a successful producer to the hilt, entertaining lavishly in the world's capitals and sporting a gigantic yacht and a priceless art collection.

His brother **Shalom Spiegel** (1899–1984) was a distinguished Jewish scholar who taught medieval Hebrew literature at New York's Jewish Theological Seminary and wrote *Hebrew Reborn* on outstanding modern Hebrew authors.

A. Sinclair, *Spiegel: The Man behind the Pictures*, 1988.

SPINOZA, BARUCH (BENEDICT DE SPINOZA; 1632–1677) Philosopher. Baruch Spinoza was born in Amsterdam, where his parents had fled from Portugal to escape the Inquisition. He received a thorough traditional Jewish education, including Hebrew language and literature, as well as study of the works of such Jewish philosophers as Moses Maimonides (q.v.), Abraham ibn Ezra (q.v.), Gershom ben Judah Me'or ha-Gola (q.v.), and Hasdai Crescas (q.v.). Although Spinoza was a brilliant student, he seemed restless and confined by this exclusively religious education. He decided to study Latin, a language that Jews associated with the hated Inquisition. He enrolled in a private school run by Francis van den Enden, an ex-Jesuit and reputed freethinker. There he became acquainted with the Greek and Roman classics, the physical sciences, and the philosophy of René Descartes.

Spinoza was instantly attracted to the rationalist approach of Descartes, so different from the traditional philosophies he had previously studied. He began to distance himself from his Jewish background and questioned the authority of Mosaic law. In 1656, Spinoza was summoned to a religious court, where he was accused of heresy; one month later, on July 27, 1656, he was publicly excommunicated. As a result Spinoza was able to develop his own philosophy without the constraints of sectarian considerations.

He moved to Ouwerkirk, a suburb of Amsterdam, and earned a meager living as an optician and tutor of philosophy, Latin, and Hebrew. At the same time he began work on his *Tractatus Theologico-Politicus*, in which he laid the groundwork for later biblical criticism.

In 1660 Spinoza left Amsterdam and settled in Rhijnsburg, near Leyden. He changed his name to Benedictus and joined a Mennonite sect known as the Collegiants. This sect lived without a clergy and held meetings (*collegia*) for prayer and religious discussions. He immersed himself in Cartesian philosophy and succeeded in preparing and publishing a geometric version of Descartes's *Principia*, which he called *Principles of the Philosophy of René Descartes*. The work was published in Latin (1663), and one year later in Dutch (1664). At the same time, Spinoza began work on his *Ethics*, using the same geometric form he had employed while writing on Descartes. He also corresponded with many people and soon felt the need to move to a larger community. Having acquired a benefactor, Johan de Witt of The Hague, who provided Spinoza with a small income, he moved to Voorburg, a suburb of The Hague.

His first two years in Voorburg were spent working on *Ethics*, in which he intended to explain his entire philosophic system. In 1665, however, he abruptly stopped work on *Ethics* and returned to *Tractatus Theologico-Politicus*. In a letter to Henry

The excommunication of Baruch Spinoza by the Amsterdam Jewish community. Painting by S. Hirszenberg.

THE THOUGHT OF SPINOZA

● As long as a man imagines a thing is impossible, so long will he be unable to do it.
● Men who are ruled by reason desire nothing for themselves which they would not wish for all humankind.
● Books which teach and speak of whatever is the highest and best are equally sacred, whatever their language and to whatever nation they may belong.
● Ceremonies do not add to blessedness.
● God is described as a lawgiver or prince and styled just, merciful etc., merely in concession to popular understanding.
● Even a cursory perusal will show us that the only respects in which the Hebrews surpassed other nations, are in their successful conduct of matters relating to government, and in their surmounting great perils solely by God's external aid; in other ways they were on a par with their fellows, and God was equally gracious to all.

***Tractatus Theologico-Politicus* 3**

Oldenburg, a Collegiant friend and member of the Royal Society of London, Spinoza explained his reason for returning to that work. He wished to refute the charges of atheism being leveled against him by showing the shortcomings of theologians turned philosophers and to defend the freedom of speech and thought from what he deemed an oppressive and tyrannical church. *Tractatus Theologico-Politicus* appeared anonymously in 1670. This rational attack on theologians and religion was immediately banned, but still managed to enjoy several printings within a few years of its initial publication.

Spinoza's reputation as a philosopher was now well established. He was offered a chair of philosophy at the University of Heidelberg but declined, preferring to stay away from large academic institutions where his freedom of thought might be threatened. He began a correspondence with Gottfried Wilhelm Leibniz, which led to their meeting in 1676.

Spinoza settled in The Hague in 1670 to be near his patron, de Witt, and lived at the boardinghouse of the artist van der Spyck. The assassination of de Witt in 1672 so enraged Spinoza that he put up placards against the "barbarians" who committed the crime. This angered his landlord, who locked Spinoza out of the boardinghouse. Spinoza began work on a Hebrew grammar, *Compendium Grammaticus Linguae Hebraeae*, but abandoned the project to complete his *Ethics*, which appeared in 1674. He soon realized that the reformed Church would prevent the book from being published, and therefore abandoned his plans to have it printed. Two years prior to his death, he began to write a political work, *Tractatus Politicus*, which he never fully completed. Spinoza long suffered from a pulmonary disease resulting from his early work at glass grinding, and this disease resulted in his death. The great philosopher of Jewish extraction who fought against the church was buried in a church in The Hague. Almost two hundred years after his death, the Israeli prime minister David Ben-Gurion (q.v.), unsuccessfully attempted to raise the excommunication against Baruch Spinoza.

Spinoza's system is a rationalistic pantheism, according to which everything known by man, mind and matter, is a manifestation of the all-embracing substance that is God. To attain supreme happiness, man has to attain knowledge of his union with the whole of nature. All individual be ngs are modifications of the one infinite substance, which has an infinite number of attributes, and is identical with God whose will is identical with the laws of nature. To know nature is to know God.

Spinoza has been seen as one of the great harbingers of modern thought and has been described as the first modern Jew.

R. McShea, *The Political Philosophy of Spinoza*, 1968.

L. Roth, *Spinoza*, 1954.

L. Strauss, *Spinoza's Critique of Religion*, 1965.

H. A. Wolfson, *Philosophy of Spinoza*, 1969.

SPIRE, ANDRE (1886–1966) French poet and Zionist leader. Born in Nancy of an old established Lorraine family, he became an auditor in the Council of State in 1894 and inspector-general at the Ministry of Agriculture from 1902 to 1925.

Originally an assimilationist, Spire was deeply shocked by the Dreyfus (q.v.) affair. He fought a duel with Edouard-Adolphe Drumont, a fierce anti-Semite, and became a supporter of self-defense organizations against pogroms in Russia. In 1911, he attended the Zionist Congress of Basel, and declared "Zionism is a symbol of life. Shame on those who deny their identity."

During World War I Spire helped to mobilize pro-Zionists in France and in 1919 represented the French Zionists at the Paris Peace Conference. He supported the stand of Chaim Weizmann (q.v.) against Sylvain Lévy, president of the Alliance Israélite Universelle, who opposed the Zionist Movement. He founded the League of the Friends of Zionism and edited its journal. During World War II Spire escaped to the United States and gave his support to the Hebrew National Liberation Movement of Hillel Kook.

In 1919 Spire published *Les Poèmes juifs* and never ceased critizing assimilation and hoping for a Jewish cultural renaissance. His essays, *Quelques Juifs et demi-Juifs*, appeared in 1928. In his poetry as in his Jewish thought, Spire passionately defended freedom. His love for justice made him inflexible at times, and this contrasted with his natural deep tolerance.

S. Burnshaw, *André Spire and his Poetry*, 1933.

STEIN, GERTRUDE (1874–1946) American writer and patron of the arts. She was born in Allegheny, Pennsylvania, into a wealthy German family, and grew up in Vienna, Paris, and later in California. She recalled that as a child, she was "an omnivorous reader, going through whole libraries, reading everything."

She studied psychology under William James at Radcliffe College between 1893 and 1897. She went on to study four years of medicine at Johns Hopkins Univesity, but did not complete the program, claiming that she was not interested in getting degrees and that examinations bored her.

After a year in London studying Elizabethan prose, she moved to Paris in 1903 with her brother, Leo Stein, a painter and art critic, and with her secretary and life-long companion, Alice B. Toklas.

Together with her brother, she began to purchase modern paintings of little-known artists, among them works of Pablo Picasso, Georges Braque, and Henri Matisse. Picasso's portrait of Stein is one of his best-known early works. In the 1920s, her Paris home was a center of artistic life, the mecca for many aspiring American writers, including Ernest Hemingway and F. Scott Fitzgerald. She coined the phrase "lost generation" for these expatriates.

With her brother's help, she studied modernist painting, and identified the art of Paul Cézanne and Picasso as most closely related to what she was attempting in writing.

Her first novel, *Three Lives* (1909), was a collection of realistic character sketches, the most famous of them being "Melanctha," a study of a black woman's unhappy love affair. Her second book, *Tender Buttons* (1914), was also a series of portraits.

Stein had a great impact on the "new writing" school, experimenting with words for their sound and rhythm. Her writing was associative, often repetitive, illogical, and at times childlike. The term "Steinese" is often used to denote her peculiar literary idiom, which was parodied and derided by many, while admired by others and considered the forerunner of the stream of consciousness genre in modern American literature. Her best-known line is: "A rose is a rose is a rose is a rose."

She expounded upon her literary theories in numerous lectures and books. "A sentence is not emotional, a paragraph is," she wrote in *How to Write* (1931). "A sentence has not really any beginning or middle or ending because each part is its part as its part," she wrote in *Narration* (1935). She avoided punctuation, claiming that it interfered with the "going on."

She wrote a number of autobiographies, the most famous of which are *The Autobiography of Alice B. Toklas* (pretending to be written by Toklas; 1933), which relates the history of her salon and her relationship with the new art, and *Everybody's Autobiography* (1937).

After her first novel, her writing grew increasingly incoherent. One critic compared it to the Chinese torture: "It never stops and it is always the same." Another wrote that most of the time her concrete meaning was "inaccessible to the reader," while even her publisher was said to have commented that he had no idea what her books were about.

Her later works were experimental plays, poems, and novels. In 1934, while on a lecture tour to the United States, her opera libretto, *Four Saints in Three Acts* (1927), was set to music by Virgil Thompson. It contained one of her more famous lines: "Pigeons on the grass alas." Stein also wrote a number of works of criticism, containing sweeping generalizations about nations. One of these in 1936 was *The Geographical History of America: The Relation of Human Nature to the Human Mind* ("In the United States there is more space where nobody is than where anybody is. That is what makes America what it is").

Stein lived in Paris until World War II, during which she was in exile with Toklas in Belignin in southern France. On the liberation of Paris, she returned there to continue her literary activities. She described her wartime experiences in two books, *Wars I Have Seen* (1945) and *Brewsie and Willie*, published a week before her death.

On her death bed in the American Hospital in Paris, Stein gathered energy to ask Toklas, "What is the answer?" When Tolkas was silent her last words were: "In that case, what is the question?"
J.B. Brinin, *The Third Rose: Gertrude Stein and her World*, 1960.
F. J. Hoffman, *Gertrude Stein*, 1961.
J. B. Mellow, *Gertrude Stein and her Company*, 1974.
A. Stewart, *Gertrude Stein and the Present*, 1967.

STEINBERG, ISAAC NAHMAN (1888–1957) Russian socialist politician, born in Dvinsk, Russia (now Daugavpils, Latvia). Throughout his life, due to the influence of an enlightened but religiously traditionalist upbringing, Steinberg remained an observant Orthodox Jew. As a newly enrolled law student at Moscow University, he became active in the Social Revolutionary party and was expelled from the university for his revolutionary activities. He continued his studies in Heidelberg, publishing his doctoral thesis, "Penal Law in the Talmud" (1910). Returning to Moscow, he embarked on a legal career. After the February revolution of 1917, he joined the left-wing Social Revolutionaries who, in alliance with the Bolsheviks, called for an end to the "imperialist war" and for peace talks with Germany. He served briefly as minister of justice in Lenin's first government (1917–1918), and it was rumored at the time that no cabinet meetings took place on Saturdays in deference to Commissar Steinberg's religious practices.

By 1923, however, Lenin had disposed of his noncommunist allies, and Steinberg had taken refuge in Berlin. There, for the next ten years, he was the leading Social Revolutionary spokesman, championing the cause of parliamentary freedom, contributing to the left-wing press in many countries, and publishing works such as *The Moral Aspect of the Revolution* (1925) and *Memoirs of a People's Commissar* (1929), which appeared in Russian, Yiddish, and German. Hitler's rise to power drove Steinberg to London in 1933, and from there he emigrated to New York a decade later.

While the Nazi menace turned many Jews into Zionists, it made Steinberg a wholehearted advocate of Jewish territorialism, that is, the search for a territory other than the Land of Israel where Jews could have an autonomous existence. When Britain's policy had virtually closed the gates of Palestine to Jewish refugees, he sought at least a temporary haven for them elsewhere, and his establishment of the Freeland League was the first step toward creating an autonomous Jewish republic far from the danger zone. The territorialist program, however, never gained international support. Steinberg advocated an autonomous Jewish settlement in Australia, but this proposition was rejected by the Australian government and his book, *Australia — The Unpromised Land*, records his bitter disappointment. In his last years, Steinberg, the onetime revolutionary, preached a kind of spiritual Zionism that would make Jerusalem "the Vilna of Israel, just as Vilna once was the Jerusalem of Lithuania."

STEINITZ, WILLIAM (1836–1900) Father of modern chess. Born in Prague to a poor Orthodox family, he was an exceptionally gifted talmudic scholar, but his interest in mathematics prevailed over his parents' wish that he continue his talmudic studies. Steinitz learned the moves of chess when he was twelve years old from a schoolmate, and by the age of twenty, when he left the city to study mathematics in Vienna, he had become the best player in Prague. He first established his reputation as a chess master of world standing in Vienna. In 1866 he won the world championship by defeating Adolf Anderssen and retained the title for twenty-eight years until he was defeated by Emanuel Lasker (q.v.) in 1894.

Steinitz's outstanding contribution to chess is his theory of the game. He formulated the principles that became the foundation of modern chess and turned the game into a science. Steinitz first began playing chess during what is called the romantic period represented by Anderssen and, at its best, by the American chess player, Paul Morphy. He created an entirely new style that reflected his scientific grasp of the principles of the game. In a book which explains the theory of Steinitz, Lasker writes that Steinitz "was a thinker worthy of a seat in the halls of a university."

Although Steinitz has become universally acknowledged as the father of modern chess, his ideas were not always understood or appreciated. His theories regarding pawn play, for example, met with general acceptance only after World War II. Lasker writes, in tribute to Steinitz, that he died "little valued by the world," and that Lasker, "who vanquished him must see to it that his great achievement, his theories, should find justice.... I must avenge the wrongs he suffered."

C. Devide (ed.), *William Steinitz: Selected Chess Games*, 1974.

R. Reti, *Masters of the Chessboard*, 1976.

STEINSCHNEIDER, MORITZ (Moses; 1816–1907) Bibliographer, Judaic scholar. Born in Prossnitz, Moravia, the son of an enlightened scholar, the boy was sent to the local non-Jewish school, which at that time was an act of provocation of the Orthodox community. As a child, Steinschneider learned music and dancing, but his father gave him a traditional education, insisting also that the boy should learn handicrafts.

At the age of thirteen, Steinschneider was sent to the yeshiva (Talmudic academy) of the local rabbi, Nehemia Trebitsch, whom he followed to Nicolsburg when Trebitsch w s appointed rabbi of the region of Moravia. From 1833 to 1836, he studied philosophy, aesthetics, pedagogy and modern languages in Prague and obtained a teacher's diploma. One of his fellow students in Prague, Abraham Benisch, subsquently editor of the London *Jewish Chronicle*, won him over to the Jewish national idea, which Steinschneider later repudiated because he considered it premature and not viable.

In 1836 he moved to Vienna where he studied history and became interested in the history of Hebrew literature and in bibliography. Prevailing Austrian legislation barring Jews prevented him from entering the Oriental Institute. He therefore continued his studies in Leipzig (1838), Berlin, and again in Prague. In 1845 he settled in Berlin and obtained a Ph.D. in Leipzig in 1851. By then, he was already a well-known scholar. Having studied Hebrew, Arabic, and Syriac, he traslated the Koran into Hebrew. By a special decree of Frederick William IV, he was granted permanent residence in Berlin in 1848, just prior to the revolution in which he was active and on which he sent reports to several newspapers.

In 1848 he also received the invitation to catalogue the Hebrew books in the Bodleian Library, Oxford, for which purpose he spent the next ten summers in Oxford, producing the three-volume (3,100 page) monumental *Catalogus librorum hebraeorum in Bibliotheca Bodleiana* (Berlin, 1852–1860). Among his over forty major works are the catalogues of the Hebrew manuscripts in the Bodleian (1857) and in the libraries of Leiden (1875), Munich (1878), and Hamburg and Berlin (1878). These catalogues not only list the items, but give a detailed description and philological analysis of each. He also published a Hebrew bibliographical journal (1858–1882); Hebrew translations of works of the Middle Ages (1893); *Arabic Literature of the Jews* (1902); and a bibliographic handbook of the literature for Hebrew linguistics (1859–1896). In addition, he wrote over four hundred articles and essays, among them all the entries on Jewish literature in Ersch and Gruber's *Encyclopä-*

die der Wissenschaften und Künste (1850), which were translated into many languages. He wrote essays on Jewish typography, on Jewish booksellers, on Italian and Arabic literature ab ut Jews, on the relationship between Judaism and the natural sciences, medicine, and mathematics, and on many other subjects.

Despite his great scholarship and international recognition, he was constrained to earn his living as a teacher (1859–1868) and from 1869 to 1883, as principal of a Jewish girls' school in Berlin. During these years, he also worked at the Prussian State Library. Much to his disgust, he was appointed to administer the Jewish oath (*more Iudaico*) in the Berlin courts, pointing out on each occasion the degrading nature of this form of oath. The title Professor was given him on his eightieth birthday and on his nintieth he was awarded the Order of the Red Eagle, third class. Steinschneider, who was considered the most erudite among-19th century Jewish scholars, was a bitter, frustrated man since, as a Jew, he was not allowed to teach at any university; he quarreled with many of his colleagues and with some in the Jewish establishment. He became a follower of the Reform movement, in his last will, demanded to be cremated. His many pupils included virtually all the contemporary students of rabbinics and Judaic scholars.

In his last years, he lived as a recluse in his Berlin apartment, where he was looked after by his faithful housekeeper, herself a bibliographer. On one occasion, he was the victim of a motorcar accident and when the ambulance took him home, he told the housekeeper, "I have been overlooked many times, but this time I was also overrun."

S. W. Baron, *Alexander Marx Jubilee Volume*, 1950.

A. Marx, *Essays in Jewish Biography*, 1947.

STERN, AVRAHAM (1907–1942) Palestine Jewish underground leader. Born in Poland, he immigrated to Palestine in 1925, graduated from the Hebrew Gymnasium (high school) in Jerusalem and later studied at the Hebrew University. A brilliant student, writer, and poet, from 1929 he devoted his life to Jewish defense. He joined the underground self-defense force, the Haganah, in 1929 but, like David Raziel (q.v.) and others, objected to its passive defense posture. He moved to Haganah B and joined the dissident underground group, the Irgun Tzevai Le'umi (Irgun) in 1937, becoming one of its commanders. After a brief stint as Irgun representative in Poland, Stern challenged Vladimir Jabotinsky (q.v.) on his policy of collaboration with the British after the outbreak of World War II. He also objected to the linkage between the Irgun, the Zionist Revisionist party and its paramilitary organization, Betar, because of his belief that the Irgun must be an independent body, free of political allegiances.

When World War II broke out, Stern opposed the mobilization of young Palestinian Jews into the British Army as long as Britain limited Jewish immigration to Palestine and did nothing to rescue

European Jewry. In January 1940, he and his associates seceded from the Irgun and formed an independent underground, which was to be called the Fighters for the Freedom of Israel (Lechi), or the Stern group. Stern sought to gain support from Fascist Italy and even Nazi Germany to help in the creation of a Jewish state. Lechi initially engaged in actions against individual British police officers and broke into banks to obtain funds. In an attempt on the life of British officers, two Jewish police officers were killed in Tel Aviv. The British authorities hunted Stern and put a price on his head. He was captured in a Tel Aviv apartment and shot by the arresting British officer. The British claimed he was shot trying to escape. Stern, whose code name was Yair, left many poems, including "Unknown Soldiers," which became the anthem of the Irgun.

STERN, LINA SOLOMONOVA (1878–1968)

Russian physiologist and biologist. Born in Orany, Lithuania, she was educated in Riga and received her M.D. from the University of Geneva, Switzerland, where she worked as an assistant in biochemistry from 1917 to 1925. In 1925 she became professor of physiology at the Second Moscow Medical Institute of Moscow University.

In 1929 Stern was appointed director and chief professor at the Physiological Scientific Research Institute, Moscow, and director of the Department of General Physiology at the All-Union Institute of Experimental Medicine. She was elected a member of the German Academy of Natural Sciences in 1932 and a member of the USSR Academy of Sciences in 1939, the first woman admitted to the latter body.

Between 1910 and 1947 Stern wrote over three hundred scientific papers on biology and physiology in Russian and German on a variety of subjects including the central nervous system, the endocrine system, sleep, catalase, oxidation ferments, oxidizing processes in animals, neurohormone regulation, the blood-brain barrier, cerebrospinal fluid, and defense mechanism and blood plexuses in the brain. She also edited *Reports of the Convention's Discussions on the Problems of the Nervous System*, (1946).

Although she had received many awards and gold medals including the Stalin medal, she was removed from all her positions during the Russian anti-Jewish purges of 1948–1949 and stripped of all her honors, being accused of "rootless cosmopolitanism." After Stalin's death she was reinstated and her honors returned to her.

Stern was described as "a lover of science and art, a tireless research worker, a highly gifted and cultivated woman of letters, a brilliant investigator, and a vivid lecturer."

S. R. Kagan, *Jewish Medicine*, 1952.

STERN, WILLIAM (1871–1938) German psychologist and philosopher, pioneer in the field of personalistic psychology, innovator of the I.Q.

(intelligence quotient). Born in Berlin, Stern was the grandson of the pedagog Sigismund Stern, one of the founders of the Reform Movement. His father being unsuccessful in business, William Stern had to take care of his ailing mother in addition to having to earn his tuition fees. He entered the University of Berlin with the intention of becoming an academician and educator, but soon turned to philosophy and psychology. During his third semester he began studying with Hermann H. Ebbinghaus, who exerted a crucial influence on Stern's training and career. Upon graduating from Berlin, he followed Ebbinghaus to Breslau, where Stern became an instructor of philosophy and psychology in 1897 and then an associate professor in 1907.

Stern's career at Breslau was seriously delayed because he was a Jew. It was quite unusual for a university lecturer to wait over ten years to be appointed associate professor. After another wait of almost ten years, Stern was offered a full professorship on condition that he convert to Christianity. Thus, in 1919, after having laid the foundation for his academic and scientific career during twenty years at Breslau, Stern felt obliged to continue at Hamburg After two decades of productivity and proliferous writing at Hamburg University and only two years after being unanimously elected as president of the German Psychologiocal Society, Stern was expelled from Hamburg University by the Nazis. Having previously held that anti-Semitism was an isolated instance of ignorant behavior, Stern exclaimed, "My Weltanschauung has collapsed" and decided to leave Germany altogether. He went first to Holland where he worked on one of his main works, *General Psychology*, which he could not publish in Germany. With a long list of important published works behind him, Stern joined the multitude of German Jewish scholars going to America. Stern was already well-known in the United States and, on a previous visit, had been awarded an honorary degree by Clark University for his contribution on the subjects of memory, testimony, and lying. He spent his last five years in the United States, where he was a professor at Duke University and lectured extensively at Harvard and other eastern colleges.

Stern was the author of many works, contributing greatly to the field of personalistic psychology in addition to the filds of differential psychology, forensic psychology, psychotehcnics, child psychology, and intelligence testing. At Breslau, he invented an instrument, the tonvariator, to study the perception of change in many sense modalities. He sought to isolate the basic elements of perception and thus get at the one-to-one relationship between stimulus and response. Stern improved on the Binet method of intelligence testing by suggesting the use of an intelligence quotient (I.Q.), which represents the child's mental age divided by his or her chronological age. This score allows for simple comparison between individuals' intelligence. He also suggested that there there is collaboration between heredity and environment so that inner and outer conditions converge in any psychological process. Known as the convergence theory, this was later incorporated and expanded upon by Gestalt theorists. His interest in child psychology had been prevalent in Hamburg, where he published several papers, including an analysis and commentary on the diaries of a young boy. He later acknowledged that it was his own diary. In the field of child psychology he was helped by his wife, Clara Joseephy (1878–1945), a child psychologist, in studying their own three children in addition to other children.

H. Kendler, *Historical Foundations of Modern Psychology*, 1987.

R. Watson, *The Great Psychologists*, 1963.

STERNBERG, JOSEPH VON (1894–1969) U.S. film director. Born Jonas Sternberg in Vienna, he was brought to the United States by his parents when he was seven. After completing his early schooling in Manhattan, he returned to Vienna to continue his education. He began his film career with a company in Fort Lee, New Jersey, where he advanced to become an editor and title-writer. Sternberg made some training films while serving with the army Signal Corps during World War I. At the end of the war he returned to the fi m industry, and graduated to scenarist and assistant director. A partnership with actor George K. Arthur resulted in *The Salvation Hunters*, an independent production which was the first film that Sternberg directed.

The Salvation Hunters was a sufficiently impressive debut to be bought for release by United Artists and Sternberg signed a contract with MGM. When this association did not fare well, Charles Chaplin hired him to direct *A Woman of the Sea*, a film that was never released. In 1926 Sternberg began directing for Paramount, gaining prominence with the gangster film *Underworld* and *The Last Command*, which starred Emil Jannings. Having directed his first sound film, *Thunderbolt*, in 1929, he went to Germany to direct *The Blue Angel*, which starred, in addition to Jannings, Marlene Dietrich, around whom most of his subsequent films until the mid-1930s revolved.

The success of his films with Dietrich (including *Shanghai Express* and *The Scarlet Empress*) gave Sternberg the freedom to indulge in visual stylistics unseen in other Hollywood films of the period (he also occasionally functioned as his own cinematographer). In 1935 he followed his mentor at Paramount, B. P. Schulberg (q.v.), to Columbia Pictures, where he filmed Dostoevsky's *Crime and Punishment* with Peter Lorre (q.v.). A lavish screen adaptation of *I, Claudius*, begun in Britain in 1937, was never completed due to a variety of setbacks. Only two of the handful of films he made during the remainder of his directorial career stand out. *The Shanghai Gesture*, from 1941, recaptured the atmosphere of his earlier work. *The Saga of Anatahan*, an intensely personal project financed by von

Sternberg himself, was made in Japan in 1953. Though appreciated by the critics, it was a financial failure. In his later years, he lectured at universities and toward the end of his life made many appearances at retrospectives of his own work.

He wrote an autobiographical work *Fun in a Chinese Laundry* (1965).

J. Baxter, *The Cinema of Josef von Sternberg*, 1971.

M. Dietrich, *Marlene*, 1971.

STIEGLITZ, ALFRED (1864–1946) U.S. photographer, considered "the father of modern photography." He was born in Hoboken, New Jersey, to a prosperous wool merchant, who took his six children to Berlin in 1881 to be educated. Stieglitz studied engineering at the Berlin Polytechnic, until he bought a camera and started studying photochemistry. In 1887 he sent twelve prints to the London amateur photographer competition and won first prize. It was the first of over 150 medals he was to win in worldwide competitions.

Stieglitz recognized photography as a new art form and soon became famous for his innovative work and experiments. In *Camera Work*, one of several magazines that he published, the quality of the photoengraving was so high that when work from his first gallery, the Photo-Secession in New York, was lost on its way to an exhibition in Brussels, the exhibition committee used reproductions from *Camera Work* instead. Photo-Secession, was dedicated to the spirit of experimentation, "seceding" from the ordinary.

In 1908 Stieglitz caused a sensation in the New York art world by exhibiting drawings by Auguste Rodin — followed by work, of such artists as Henri Matisse, Henri de Toulouse-Lautrec, Pablo Picasso, and Constantin Brancusi, and by an exhibition of African sculpture. When in 1911, Stieglitz published Rodin drawings in *Camera Work*, half of its subscribers cancelled. He also published Gertrude Stein's (q.v.) earliest work. By 1917 he was forced to suspend publication.

He was deeply committed to those American

PAUL ROSENFELD ON ALFRED STIEGLITZ IN *AMERICA AND STIEGLITZ*, 1989

Photography is an art and a technique. The fact that Stieglitz achieved his results with natural light alone attests to his status as an artist and technician. There are no tricky lighting effects in his work. He was the first to make photographs in the rain, in snow and at night. His work has been described as conforming to the real world, but the real world as never before recorded. His handling of the photographer's tool of natural light reveals depth and form, not a mere static record, but conscious perception — a work of art.

artists whose work he considered sensitive and enlightened. In a succession of famous galleries — 291, The Intimate Gallery, and An American Place — he introduced many artists: John Marin, Arthur Dove, Georgia O'Keeffe, Marsden Hartley, Max Weber, and others. In 1916 he mounted a show based on the concept of Photography as art at the Albright Museum in Buffalo, New York.

After divorcing his first wife, he married the painter, Georgia O'Keeffe. She inspired some of his most famous photographs, which Lewis Mumford said were "the exact visual equivalent of the report of the hand as it travels over the body of the beloved."

In 1924 the Royal Photographic Society of Great Britain gave Stieglitz their highest award, the Progress Medal.

Stieglitz suffered from poor health for many years, and in 1946 had a stroke at his gallery, dying a few days later.

He had donated twenty-seven photographs to the Museum of Fine Arts, Boston, and his collection of work of photographic pioneers to the Metropolitan Museum of Art, New York. After his death, O'Keeffe donated a large part of his collection of paintings and photographs to the Metropolitan and to the Art Institute of Chicago. His collection of African art and a large number of his paintings went to Fisk University and his 50,000 letters to the archives at Yale University.

D. Norman, *Alfred Stieglitz: Introduction to an American Seer*, 1960.

P. Rosenfeld, *America and Stieglitz*, 1989.

STONE, I(SIDOR) F(EINSTEIN) (1907–1989)
U.S. journalist and political critic. Born in Philadelphia of Russian-Jewish immigrant parents, Stone published his first newspaper, *The Progressive*, at the age of fourteen. An indifferent student, he studied at the University of Pennsylvania from 1924 to 1927, working at the same time as a copy editor and rewrite man for the Philadelpia *Inquirer*. From 1927 to 1932 he wrote for a number of papers in the Philadelphia area, including the Camden, New Jersey, *Courier-Post*, published by J. David Stern. He joined the Socialist party and campaigned for its candidate, Norman Thomas, in the 1928 presidential election.

In 1933 when Stern bought the New York *Post*, Stone joined the staff as editorial writer, and the same year published his first book, *The Court Disposes*, on the Supreme Court. In 1938 he became associate editor of the the *Nation* magazine and, when he left the *Post* in 1939, he became the *Nation*'s Washington editor, a post which he held until 1946.

From 1942 to 1948 Stone was a reporter and columnist for the New York liberal paper, *P.M.* He covered the illegal immigration of Jews into Palestine and the establishment of Israel. In 1948 he aided the campaign of the Progressive presidential candidate, Henry A. Wallace. When *P.M.* closed that year he worked for its successors, the New York *Star* and the *Daily Compass*, until they too closed in 1949.

Unable to find a satisfactory journalistic post, in 1953 Stone began publication of *I. F. Stone's Weekly*. Beginning with a circulation of only 5,500, the four-page newsletter eventually reached some 45,000 readers by 1968, a year after it had become *I. F. Stone's Bi-Weekly*. Its lively style and sharp criticism of bureaucracy and government actions (particularly in the Pentagon), based on the diligent reading of public documents, won praise from both his supporters and opponents, as well as from newspaper colleagues. In 1971 Stone closed the newsletter and became a contributing editor of the *New York Review of Books*, for which he had been writing articles since 1964.

Always a maverick, Stone opposed the Cold War and McCarthyism, but despite his "leftist" leanings, he frequently criticized the Soviet Union. He supported the establishment of the State of Israel, but after the 1967 Six-Day War he attacked that country's policies. He covered the Vietnam War and civil rights demonstrations.

Among his numerous books were *Underground to Palestine* (1946), *This is Israel* (1948), *The Truman Era* (1953), *The Hidden History of the Korean War* (1952), *The Haunted Fifties* (1963), *In Time of Torment* (1967), and *The Killings at Kent State* (1971). His last book, *The Trial of Socrates* (1988), was widely acclaimed as a brilliant analysis of the last days of the Greek philosopher.

STRASBERG, LEE (1901–1982) Actor, director, producer, and teacher, famous for teaching actors by using what he called "the Method." Influenced by Russian acting teacher, Constantin Stanislavsky, Straserg taught the Method because he believed it encouraged actors and actresses to use their psyches and subconsciousness in their work.

Born Israel Strassberg in Budzanow, then Austria-Hungary, he and his family emigrated to America when he was seven. He grew up in New York City on the Lower East Side and it was there that he was first exposed to the theater. His brother-in-law introduced him to the stage, giving him a small part in one of the Progressive Dramatic Club's Yiddish productions. But it was not until he was a young man that he began to think about the performing arts as a possible career.

Strasberg joined the Chrystie Street Settlement House's drama club, and during one of their productions, his acting ability was recognized by Philip Loeb, casting director of the Theater Guild. At this point Strasberg, who had a steady job as a shipping clerk and bookkeeper for a wig company, still had not considered his acting abilities seriously. By 1924, however, he had succumbed to his calling to the stage and enrolled in the Clare Tree Major School of the Theater. He later left the school to study with Richard Boleslavsky and Maria Ouspenskaya, students of Stanislavsky, at the American Laboratory Theater.

Strasberg's first professional acting appearance

was in 1925, in a play called *Processional*, produced by the Theater Guild. He eventually left acting and turned instead to directing and teaching. In 1931 he joined Harold Clurman and Cheryl Crawford to form the Group Theater company. It was there that he developed and expanded the Method. The Method consisted of a series of vocal, physical, and emotional exercises that forced the actor to delve deep into himself in order to be the character that was being portrayed. With the Group Theater, Strasberg directed Sidney Kingsley's *Men in White* and Paul Green's *The House of Connelly*, among other plays.

Strasberg left the Group Theater in 1936 to strike out on his own. He joined the Actors' Studio in 1948, one year after its founding. He quickly became the studio's guiding force; he was elected artistic director in 1951 and retained that position until his death. Through the Actors' Studio, Strasberg and the Method influenced the work of many actors and actresses, including Anne Bancroft, Al Pacino, and Maureen Stapleton.

In addition to his work at the Actors' Studio, Strasberg continued to direct Broadway and Off-Broadway productions and gave private acting classes. He founded the Lee Strasberg Theater Institutes in New York and Los Angeles. He also directed a number of productions for the Habimah Theater in Tel Aviv. In 1974 he was lured into acting, but this time in a movie, *The Godfather, Part II*. Strasberg received an Academy Award nomination in the category of best supporting actor for his role.

Three days before his death, Strasberg appeared in a production at Radio City Music Hall and on February 16, one day before he succumbed to a heart attack, he was elected to the Theatrical Hall of Fame. His daughter, Susan (born 1938) became a well-known actress and appeared in the lead role in *The Diary of Anne Frank* in 1955.

L. Strasberg, *A Dream of Passion*, 1987.

STRAUS U.S. family of merchants, diplomats, politicians and philanthropists.

Isidor Straus (1845–1912), was the eldest son of Lazarus Straus (1809–1898) who had immigrated from Bavaria to Georgia in 1852 and later established a business in New York. Isidor Straus took a law degree at Lee University. In 1863 he was sent to Europe by the Export and Import Company of Columbus as assistant to the agent purchasing steamers and supplies for the Confederate States. Returning home in 1866, he joined his father's business and in 1874, together with his brother Nathan, rented the basement of R.H. Macy and Company to sell porcelain and pottery. In 1887 they bought the whole department store. The following year the brothers established a china department in the Brooklyn store of Wechsler and Abraham and in 1893 they acquired Wechsler's share and the store became known as Abraham and Straus. Isidor Straus was the first president of the New York Crockery Board of Trade and was connected with various tariff reforms which he followed up during the period he served in Congress (1893–1895). He was the president of the Educational Alliance and served on the board of financial, charitable and philanthropic institutions.

In 1912, he and his wife died when they were passengers on the *Titanic* which went down after striking an iceberg on its maiden voyage.

Nathan Straus (1848–1931), Lazarus' second son, graduated from Packard's Business College in New York and joined the family business in 1866 as a salesman. He branched out with his brother Isidor in Macy's and Abraham and Straus. From 1889 to 1893 he was New York Park commissioner, and from 1893 was a member of the New York Forest Preserve Board, becoming president of the New York Board of Health in 1898.

In those years Nathan devoted much effort to the saving of infant life through the establishment of stations where pasteurized milk was made available. His endeavors to lower the price of milk were fought by dairymen and milk companies, and the benefit of pasteurized milk was even doubted by physicians until proof was furnished that the use of treated milk brought about a steady decrease in the rate of infant mortality. He built milk installations in cities throughout the United States and in Germany, Palestine, Cuba and the Philippines. During World War I he distributed pasteurized milk to the U.S. forces.

In 1892 Nathan Straus set up and maintained a chain of depots for the distribution of coal, bread and groceries to the poor of New York and during the winter of 1893–1894 organized a system of lodging houses for over one thousand poor. In 1909 he founded the first children's sanatorium for tuberculosis prevention at Farmingdale, New York. After the war he became the chairman of the Committee for the Defense of Jews in Poland.

Nathan was an ardent supporter of Zionism. His activities in Palestine began in 1912 with the establishment of a health department and the Pasteur Institute that served the entire population. He also maintained soup kitchens providing free meals for the poor. In 1920 he endowed health centers in Jerusalem and Tel Aviv. In 1928 he set up a half-million dollar trust fund for general work in Palestine and became the chairman of the Palestine Emergency Fund, raising over two million dollars. The city of Netanya founded in 1928 was named for him.

The youngest brother, **Oscar Solomon Straus** (1850–1926), studied at Columbia College, New York and graduated with the alumni prize awarded to "the most deserving student." In 1871 he began practicing law, but under the stress of work his health broke down and after some months' rest he gave up the profession and in 1880 joined his father and brothers in their successful mercantile ventures.

In 1887 Straus was appointed minister to Turkey where he succeeded in having sixty American schools which had been closed six years earlier, reopened for instruction. He also persuaded Sultan

From left to right. Nathan Straus, Justice Louis D. Brandeis and Rabbi Stephen S. Wise.

Abdul Hamid to allow the distribution of Bibles and other religious literature. He held this position until 1889, and was sent again to Turkey from 1897 to 1899 when he succeeded in restoring American interests and securing the rights of American missionaries serving throughout the Ottoman Empire. On his return home Straus went back to the family business.

In 1902 President Theodore Roosevelt appointed him to the Permanent Court of Arbitration at The Hague, and in 1906 secretary of commerce and labor, the first Jew to enter the American cabinet. In April 1909 he returned to Constantinople as ambassador and within a year he had obtained from the Turkish government a decision whereby all foreign religious, educational and benevolent organizations were permitted to hold landed property. In 1910 he resigned and returned home, and in 1912 unsuccessfully stood for governor of New York as the Progressive party candidate. He served on the Public Service Commission of New York State from 1915 to 1918. Straus attended the negotiation sessions of the treaty of Versailles as chairman of the League to Enforce Peace.

In 1924 Straus visited Palestine at the invitation of the British High Commissioner, Sir Herbert Samuel (q.v.) and at the request of the Federated Council of the Churches of Christ to help restore harmony among the religious sects of the Holy Land. He succeeded in obtaining a declaration in writing from the Greek Orthodox Patriarch in Jer-

usalem that he would do his best to bring about harmony among the Christian sects, the Jews and the Arabs.

During the last years of his life Straus devoted himself to research work for international peace. He was the author of several books, the first of which *The Origin of the Republican Form of Government* was published in 1885. His other writings include *Roger Williams, the Pioneer of Religious Liberty in the United States* (1896) and an autobiography *Under Four Administrations*, (1922).

Straus was chosen by the American Jewish community as one of the ten Jews who had "done the most to preserve and to further the highest ideals and traditions of America." He was among the founders of the Young Men's Hebrew Association, and in 1906 helped to found the American Jewish Committee. He was opposed to political Zionism but supported projects for the rehabilitation of Palestine. As a supporter of territorialist schemes for the settlement of persecuted Jews, Straus was one of the founders of the Baron de Hirsch (q.v.) Fund and worked to ease the plight of new immigrants to the United States. He was the first president of the American Jewish Historical Society.

Jesse Isidor Straus (1872–1936), son of Isidor, was educated in New York, took a B.A. at Harvard and graduated in law from the University of Georgia. He began his buisiness career as a clerk in the Hanover National Bank of New York, joined

Abraham and Straus and entered Macy's in 1896, becoming president of the firm in 1919.

Jesse Straus was an active Democrat and a close friend and supporter of Franklin D. Roosevelt, who, as governor of New York State, appointed Straus chairman of the New York State Temporary Relief Administration. He later became chairman of the Citizens Committee on Unemployment Relief Bond Issue. In 1933 he resigned as president of Macy's and accepted President Roosevelt's assignment as ambassador to France, being the first Jew to hold this position.

Nathan Straus' second son, **Nathan Straus Jr.** (1889–1961), graduated cum laude from Princeton University. In 1914 he purchased the humorous magazine *Puck*, which he edited until he enlisted in the U.S. navy in 1917. After the war, he continued his journalistic career.

Entering politics as a Democrat, he was elected to the New York State senate for three terms from 1921. He was appointed by President Roosevelt in 1934 as New York State administrator and in 1936 Mayor Fiorello La Guardia (q.v.) made him a member of the New York City Housing Authority. From 1837 to 1942 he was administrator of the U.S. Housing Authority in charge of the public housing program. He wrote *Seven Myths of Housing* (1943) and *Two Thirds of a Nation — A Housing Program* (1952).

In 1943 Nathan Straus Jr. purchased New York radio station WMCA and served as its president and chairman. He fought for the right of radio stations to express editorial opinions on the air. He became chairman of the Straus Broadcasting group which included station WBNY in Buffalo and Radio Press International, a taped news service.

Roger Williams Straus (1893–1957), son of Oscar Solomon Straus, studied literature and law, receiving a doctorate from Bucknell University in 1936. In 1914 he married Gladys Guggenheim, (q.v.), and entered her family's business, the American Smelting and Refining Company. He was appointed president in 1941 and chairman of the board in 1947. In 1935 he was awarded the American Society for Metals medal for the advancement of research.

During World War I Straus served as an intelligence officer on the commanding general's staff in Siberia. He was active in Republican party politics and in 1947 was appointed to the New York State Board of Regents and named its chancellor in 1956. In 1954 he served as a member of the United States delegation to the UN General Assembly. In 1928 he was a founder of the National Conference of Christians and Jews and in 1947 of the World Council of Christians and Jews.

S. Birmingham, *Our Crowd*, 1967.

N. W. Cohen, *Dual Heritage, The Public Career of Oscar S. Straus*, 1969.

G. S. Hellman (ed.), *The Oscar Straus Memorial Volume*, 1949.

STRAUS, OSCAR (1870–1954) Austrian oper-

etta composer. Straus studied privately in his native Vienna and and then moved to Berlin where he continued his studies with Max Bruch. From 1893 to 1900, following the advice of Johann Strauss Jr. to gain practical experience in the theater, Straus conducted regularly in Teplitz, Mainz, Brno, Hamburg, and Bratislava. During this time he began composing music for the stage as well as salon music. In 1901 he became the conductor of the satirical cabaret Uberbrettl in Berlin for which he wrote a few musical farces. Straus remained in Berlin until 1927 and then returned to Vienna.

After his works were banned by the Nazi regime he moved to Switzerland and France. In 1939 Straus became a French citizen but a year later he moved to the United States and lived in New York and Hollywood until 1948. He then returned to Europe and died in Bad Ischl, Austria.

Straus's name was spelled Strauss on his birth certificate. However, he deleted the second "s" in order to be distinguished from the renowned Strauss family of operetta composers.

Straus composed numerous operettas. One of his most successful was *The Chocolate Soldier*, which is based on George Bernard Shaw's *Arms and the Man.* It was premiered in Vienna in 1908 and a year later was presented in New York. Other famous works for the lyric stage include *Die lustigen Nibelungen* (1904), which is a hilarious parody of Wagner's operas *A Waltz Dream* (1907); *Love and Laughter* (1913); *Der letzte Walzer* (1920); *Walzer* (1935); and *Die Musik kommt* (1948). His

Oscar S. Straus' obituary in the New York Times, *May 4, 1926.*

OSCAR S. STRAUS DIES FROM HEART ATTACK

Diplomat and Philanthropist Passes After an Acute Illness of a Week.

FRIEND OF THE OPPRESSED

President and Members of the Cabinet Pay Tribute to Him as Peace Advocate.

A POWER IN TURKISH AFFAIRS

Funeral Services to Be Held at 10 A. M. Tomorrow at Temple Beth-El by Dr. Wise.

Oscar S. Straus, philanthropist and former diplomat and Cabinet member, died yesterday at his home, 1,010 Fifth Avenue, in his seventy-sixth year. Death was due to heart disease, the end coming as Mr. Straus breakfasted. Although he had been acutely ill for a week and had been in gradually failing health for several years, his death was unexpected. Despite the heart attacks to which he had become subject Mr. Straus, who throughout his life was exceedingly active, had continued to devote himself to research work for international peace, a task to which he had dedicated himself for years.

In recent weeks his condition had become markedly worse, although, at the advice of his physicians, he had spent the Winter in the easier climate of Florida, returning to his Fifth Avenue

OSCAR S. STRAUS
Diplomat and Philanthropist, Who Died Yesterday in His Seventy-sixth Year.

last work for the stage was *Bozena* (1952), a Slavic folk opera with huge choral scenes. Straus also composed an overture, a violin sonata, and a few other works for a variety of ensembles. He also composed music for Max Ophul's [q.v.] film *La ronde* (1950).

B. Grun, *Prince of Vienna: The Life, the Times and the Melodies of Oscar Straus*, 1955.

STRAUSS, LEVI (1829–1902) U.S. garment manufacturer. Born in Buttenheim, Germany, he was the youngest of six children. The Strauss's life was a struggle, mostly because of the restrictions placed on Jews. In 1847, two years after the father's death, they emigrated to the United States, where Levi (whose name changed from Leib upon arrival was introduced to the peddler's life in New York City. At first he sold thread, needles, thimbles, buttons, scissors, yarns, and combs. A year later he began peddling in Louisville, Kentucky, often lugging a hundred pounds of goods over the Kentucky hills. For five years he peddled his goods there, among them pants woven from light material first made in Genoa, Italy. These were "Genoese," later known as jeans. Later, this same word was used to describe Levi's pants.

In 1853 Strauss, one of many seeking his fortune in the gold country, arrived in San Francisco. Together with his brother-in-law, David Stern, he established a store. Strauss observed how dirty and torn the miners' clothes were and he came up with the idea of making a strong pair of working pants from tent canvas and wagon cover. The miners' satisfaction enabled Levi and Stern to move into a larger store named "Levi Strauss and Company." To promote business further, Strauss once again peddled his goods, this time over the treacherous terrain of the gold-rush highway. Soon he hired a salesman to do the peddling for him while he remained in the store.

By 1866 Strauss (with the help of two brothers and two brothers-in-law) was managing a wholesale and manufacturing company whose headquarters were in a four-story building on Battery Street, San Francisco, with an eastern branch in New York City. In 1873 he signed a partnership with Jacob W. Davis, a tailor from Nevada. Davis stitched the tan duck or indigo-dyed denim pants with orange thread to match the rivets on pocket openings. In addition, two V's were stitched in orange thread on the back pocket. An oilcloth with the words "a new pair FREE" was tacked to the seat of the pants guaranteeing a new pair if the original pair ripped. A leather label was stitched to the pants with the same orange thread. This singled out Levi's pants from his competitors. By 1876 company sales had reached 200,000 dollars. Levi's jeans were advertised as "excellently adapted to the use of those engaged in manual labor," increasing sales as miners, lumberjacks, cowboys, and teamsters sought them out. These jeans came to be known by the Lot Number 501.

With time Strauss relied increasingly on his

Levi Straus.

younger sister's sons until, in 1886, they were completely in charge of the day-to-day running of the business. At this point, Strauss turned to his other interests: dry-goods business, transportation, and communication (such as Strauss's unsuccessful investment in the railroad through California's Central Valley), sitting on boards of companies and corporations (e.g., the Nevada Bank, the Union Trust Company, and the San Francisco Gas Company), and real estate. In his later years, he concentrated on philanthropies (e.g., homes for

---

Strauss, a man who avoided publicity, gave a rare interview to the *San Francisco Bulletin*

I am a bachelor and I fancy on that account I need to work more, for my entire life is my business. I don't believe that a man who once forms the habit of being busy can retire and be contented. My happiness lies in my routine work. I do not think large fortunes cause happiness to their owners, for immediately those who possess them become slaves to their wealth. They must devote their lives to caring for their possessions. I don't think money brings friends to its owners. In fact, often the result is quite the contrary.

Label of Levi Strauss Co. Levi's.

the aged, for Jewish, Roman Catholic, and Protestant orphans, and university scholarship funds). When he died Strauss left 1.6 million dollars, payable in gold, to charities, friends, and relatives. To his younger sister's sons he left the business and the rest of the six million dollar estate.

E. Van Steenwyk, *Levi Strauss: The Blue Jeans Man*, 1988.

STRAUSS, LEWIS LICHTENSTEIN (1896–1974) U.S. government official, rear admiral, banker. Born in Charleston, West Virginia, to Lewis S. Strauss, president of a wholesale shoe company, he was fascinated by the field of radioactivity and dreamed of being a physicist; instead, he went to work selling shoes because he lacked the money for college. Having risen to be vice president of the company, in 1917 he joined Herbert Hoover's Belgian relief service. When Hoover was promoted to head of the U.S. Food Administration, Strauss was promoted to secretary, a position that gave him much exposure in military and official circles all over Europe.

In 1919, while in Paris, he was offered a position by the banking house Kuhn, Loeb and Company. He married Alice Hanauer, a daughter of one of the partners in 1923, and himself became a partner in 1928. He remained with the company until 1946, while developing other business connections in the leather, rubber, and transportation industries.

Activity on behalf of Jewish concerns found him serving on the executive committee of the American Jewish Committee, as treasurer to the Jewish Theological Seminary, and as chairman of the Joint Distribution Committee's relief work in Russia. He also found time for other charitable work on behalf of American children, and for such organizations as the Institute for the Crippled and the Disabled and the Foreign Service Education Foundation. His childhood interest in science was renewed when his parents' death from cancer motivated him to establish a fund for cancer research and to provide backing for work on a surge generator to produce radioactive isotopes in the treatment of cancer.

Having joined the naval reserve in 1926, he was called to active duty in 1941. Among his achievements during military service was the innovation of the Big "E" incentive program which significantly improved efficiency in navy production by awarding an "E" pennant to particularly productive plants. He also directed the development of the radar proximity fuse, which selects its own target while in flight.

In July 1945, he was promoted to commodore, and in November 1945, President Harry S. Truman appointed him rear admiral; he was one of the few reservists to attain that rank. One year later Truman appointed him to the Atomic Energy Commission, on which he served until 1950 and then again from 1953 to 1958. During his second appointment to the AEC, this time as chairman, he became known for voting against reinstating the security clearance of Robert Oppenheimer (q.v.), who had been dismissed amid a flurry of controversy.

His endorsement of the construction by Dixon-Yates of a power plant in West Memphis, Arkansas, also came under fire and the project was terminated. In 1958 President Dwight D. Eisenhower nominated him secretary of commerce, but the Senate refused to confirm him, and he left public life. He was the author of a memoir, *Men and Decisions* (1962.

STROHEIM, ERICH VON (1885–1957) Film director and actor. Few details are known about

Erich von Stroheim during the filming of Sunset Boulevard.

his early life other than that he was born Erich
Oswald Stroheim to middle-class parents in Vienna.
He apparently served for a period in the Austro-
Hungarian army, but when he went to the United
States in 1909, he created a new background for
himself according to which he sprang from aristocratic, Catholic stock and had had a distinguished
military career, a story he stuck to for the rest of his
life. He worked at various occupations, including
writing, until he first appeared on screen in 1914. In
the triple capacity of actor, military adviser, and
assistant to the director, he was on hand during the
filming of D. W. Griffith's *The Birth of a Nation*
and *Intolerance*. His Prussian looks were much in
demand in villainous roles after America's entry
into World War I and it was then that he became
known as "the man you love to hate."

Blind Husbands (1918) marked his debut as a
director and it is the only one of his films to survive
in the form Stroheim intended. Like *The Devil's
Passkey* (completed 1920, but now lost) and *Foolish Wives* (1922), it dealt with an adulterous relationship in a cynical and detailed style. With no
apparent concern for budget, Stroheim proved too
expensive for Universal, and he was replaced
before completing his film *Merry-Go-Round* in
1922. Moving to the Goldwyn studios, Stroheim
undertook a project unparalleled in its scale, a
totally faithful screen version of Frank Norris'
novel *McTeague*.

Stroheim turned *McTeague* into an epic lasting
over ten hours. Subsequent reductions proved
unacceptable to the studio, which had meanwhile
been merged with Metro and was now under the
direction of Louis B. Mayer (q.v.). Mayer turned
the film over to Irving G. Thalberg (q.v.), who had
originally fired Stroheim from Universal, and the
film was finally released, as *Greed. The Merry
Widow*, made in 1925, was successful. Away from
MGM, he took on another film too expensive for
his producer and *The Wedding March* (1928) in its
released form was not edited to Stroheim's liking.
Production of *Queen Kelly* was shut down after
Stroheim had shot little more than half of what he
intended. This fiasco left him to earn a living as a
screenwriter and actor, but in 1932 he was given a
last chance to direct at Fox.

Walking Down Broadway was finished quickly
and cheaply, but the decadent touch Stroheim had
given it shocked the Fox executives. It was partly
reshot by other directors and released as *Hello,
Sister!*

Stroheim never worked as a director again. For
the rest of his life he acted, both in America and
Europe. At least three of his roles, in Jean Renoir's
La grande illusion and in Billy Wilder's *Five Graves
to Cairo* (in which he played the German general
Erwin Rommel) and *Sunset Boulevard*, remain
classic portrayals.

T. Q. Curtis, *Von Stroheim*, 1971.
J. Finler, *Stroheim*, 1968.
R. Koszarski, *The Man You Loved to Hate: Erich
von Stroheim & Hollywood*, 1983.

SULZBERGER, ARTHUR HAYS (1891–1968)
U.S. newspaper publisher. Born in New York City,
he graduated from Columbia University in 1913
with a degree in science. From 1917 to 1919 he
served in the U.S. Army as an artillery lieutenant.
In 1917 he married Iphigene B. Ochs, the only
daughter of Adolph S. Ochs (q.v.), publisher of the
New York Times.

In 1919 Sulzberger joined the *New York Times* as
assistant to the general manager. He was given
wide-ranging training and responsibility, and when
his father-in-law died in 1935, Sulzberger was
named publisher and president of the New York
Times Company.

Under his leadership the *New York Times* circulation rose by 40 percent for its daily edition, and
its Sunday readership nearly doubled. Suzberger
expanded the services, facilities, and staff of the
paper. He extended its news coverage and analysis,
photos, and features, introducing facsimile transmission in the 1920s and 1930s. Under his supervision, the paper began to publish Los Angeles and
Paris editions with remote-control typesetting
machines. He also built up the *New York Times*-
owned radio station, WQXR, noted for its news
and music.

As president of the New York Times Company
until 1957 and its chairman from 1957 until his
death, Sulzberger also took an active part in the
operations of the *Chattanooga Times*, the Inter-
state Broadcasting Company, and the Spruce Falls
Power and Paper Company of Canada, the largest
newsprint producer in the world. From 1943 to
1952 he served as director of Associated Press, and
from 1944 to 1954 as trustee of Columbia University.

Sulzberger trained his son-in-law, Orvil Eugene
Dryfoos, to succeed him, and Dryfoos became
publisher and president in 1961. He was succeeded
by Sulzberger's son, Arthur Ochs Sulzberger.

G. Berger, *The Story of the New York Times*, 1979.
G. Talese, *The Kingdom, and the Power*, 1969.

SULZER, SALOMON (1804–1890) Austrian
cantor, composer, and reformer of synagogal
songs. He was born in Hohenems to a family of
rich manufacturers. At an early age Sulzer fell into
a river and was believed dead. His mother vowed to
devote him to a sacred career if he recovered. At
the age of sixteen Sulzer was appointed cantor at
the main synagogue in his hometown. He studied
music in Vienna, where he was the chief cantor of
the new Vienna synagogue from 1825 to 1881. His
baritone-tenor voice had admirers not only in
Vienna but also among scholars and musicians like
Franz Schubert, Robert Schumann, Giacomo
Meyerbeer (q.v.) and Franz Liszt. In 1868 Sulzer
was appointed knight of the order of Franz Joseph.

His compositions became the models upon
which congregations based their services throughout the year. He was a true reformer, who believed
that the traditional musical material of the past
should be used in a new way in order to be relevant
in the modern synagogue. Sulzer worked to improve

not only the festival services, but above all the Sabbath services. His *Schir Zion*, an anthology of music for the synagogue, was published in two separate volumes (1838–1840 and 1865–1866) aiming, according to its author, "to consider, as far as possible, the traditional tunes bequeathed to us, to cleanse the ancient and dignified type of the later accretions of tasteless embellishments, to bring them back to the original purity, and to reconstruct them in accordance with the text and with the rules of harmony." Although his music and cantorial innovations won only limited acceptance in eastern Europe, they became standard in central Europe.
A. Z. Idelsohn, *Jewish Music in its Historical Development*, 1929.

SVERDLOV, YAKOV MIKAILOVICH (originally Solomon; 1885–1919) Communist leader; first head of the Soviet Union. Yakov Solomon was born in the Russian town of Nizhnii Novgorod (present day Gorky). He established the Nizhnii Novgorod Revolutionary Committee, probably at the instigation of his brother Zinovy, adopted son of the noted Russian author Maxim Gorky. In 1909 he was sent to Moscow by the Central Committee of the Communist party with the task of reestablishing the shattered party in that city.

Sverdlov's activities soon brought him into conflict with the authorities; he was arrested and exiled, but managed to escape to Saint Petersburg where he worked with the party's faction in the Duma, the Russian parliament. Following a demonstration, he was again arrested and exiled to the remote prison camp of Maksimkinlar near the Arctic Circle, accessible by boat only twice yearly. Sverdlov made five unsuccessful attempts to escape, in the last of which he fell ill. Having been taken to medical facilities at Narya, he tried to escape in a small boat. A storm rose and Sverdlov was nearly

drowned. He was eventually picked up by a passing boat and returned to prison, where he remained until the outbreak of the revolution. While in prison he met Stalin, who was also exiled to Siberia.

Despite his lengthy exile, Sverdlov's organizational skills in the party were well remembered. Much of his rise to power was the result of his organizational ability, and Stalin once called him "an organizer to the bones of his brains." In 1912 he was coopted to the Communist Party Central Committee in absentia. After his release, he was elected secretary of the All-Russian Executive Committee and appointed the first secretary of the Central Committee of the party, making him the titular head of state of the Soviet Union (November 8, 1917).

Sverdlov was often ruthless. He used his skills in manipulating the Central Executive Committee, even barring the Mensheviks from attending meetings, to assure total control by the Bolshevik faction. He cooperated closely with Lenin and most policy decisions were made privately by the two. However, even he was unsettled by the magnitude of the order to execute the entice imperial family; when informing the Central Committee of the act, he only mentioned the execution of the tsar.

Sverdlov died suddenly on his way to a party conference in Kharkov. In his honor, the city of Yekaterinburg was renamed Sverdlovsk.
N. Levin, *Jews in the Soviet Union from 1917*, 1980.
L. Rapaport, *Stalin's War against the Jews*, 1990.
L. Shapiro, *The Communist Party of the Soviet Union*, 1970.

SVEVO, ITALO (Ettore Schmitz; 1861–1928) Italian novelist. His mother was Italian and his father German-Austrian. He was born and brought up in Trieste, to which he returned after his education in Germany. Called "the man with the split personality," Ettore Schmitz led multiple lives. He was a literary man, a lifelong bank clerk and the manager of his father-in-law's paint factory; he was born a Jew (as was his wife), but was a convinced atheist and a converted Catholic; his name and background were German, his chosen nationality Italian. He had nationalist aspirations for Trieste's union with Italy, internationalist socialist sympathies, and Austrian business interests. He adapted to life by living it as a fiction; he assumed the pseudonym Italo Svevo as he was trying to get his first novel published — *Una vita* (1892), which appeared in English as *A Life* (1962).

Most of his narrative works are about the writer who has failed. For a man who felt he that lived only that part of his life which he described, writing was a metaphysical act. Deeply influenced by Schopenhauer, he viewed writing as his sole hope for trancending an otherwise drab and unreal existence. His major work, *La coscienze di Zeno* (1923; English translation, *The Confessions of Zeno*, 1930), a "chronicle of unlived life" shows the influence and innovative adoption of Freudian theory; one of his central interests is the realm of the subconscious and dreams. In the novel, Zeno's private story suddenly intersects contemporary history; with the Great War, his farce becomes an epic truth.

James Joyce befriended Svevo in 1907, first as his English teacher and later as his critic and adviser. Their correspondence was published in 1949. Svevo's religious roots (he once called himself "no longer a Jew but still more wandering than ever") may have caused Joyce to study him as background for Leopold Bloom in *Ulysses*. Svevo never forgot his Jewish identity, though his references to his past were sometimes jocular; in 1928 he spoke of his ancestors' home as "that blessed Romania with all those anti-Semites."

Italo Svevo bared his soul to almost no one. Until as late as 1925, the writer remained invisible, hidden beneath the semblance of Ettore Schmitz. His novels, comic and tragic, fused with irony, all set in prewar Trieste, reflect his own love-hate for the bourgeoisie, whose life he chose to lead. His collective works were published in English (1962ff.). He was killed in a motor accident.

J. Gatt-Ruter, *Italo Svevo: A Double Life*, 1988.
B. Moloney, *Italo Svevo: A Critical Introduction*, 1974.

SYLVESTER, JAMES JOSEPH (1814–1897) British mathematician. With Arthur Cayley, he founded the theory of algebraic invariants; he also made important contributions to other branches of algebra including Sturn functions, canonical forms, determinants, and the theories of equations and partitions.

Sylvester was born James Joseph, sixth of the nine children of Abraham Joseph, an orthodox Jew from Liverpool. At least four of the Joseph children later assumed the name Sylvester. James was educated at Jewish schools in London until his entry to the University of London at the unprecedented young age of fourteen years. There he fell victim to Jew-baiting and was soon expelled "for taking a table knife from the refectory with the intention of sticking it into a fellow student who had incurred his displeasure."

This inauspicious event heralded a future in which Sylvester was often to pay the price of remaining loyal to his religious inheritance. At the Royal Institute in Liverpool, where he continued his education, he was taunted to the point of running away, and afterwards at Cambridge he was not awarded the degree, despite a distinguished record, because he refused to subscribe to the Thirty-nine Articles of the Church of England.

In 1838 Sylvester returned to the University of London as professor in the mathematics department that had ten years previously spurned him. A short while later, at the age of twenty-five, he was elected a fellow of the Royal Society on the strength of mathematical essays written for the *Philosophical Magazine* while he was still at Cambridge.

A luckless appointment at the University of Virginia, in 1841, triggered a break of a dozen or more years in Sylvester's association with institutions of higher learning. During this time he trained as an actuary and was later called to the bar, but all the while he maintained a prolific output of mathematical articles that were published in a variety of learned journals. He also struck up an enthusiastic and productive mathematical partnership with fellow lawyer and amateur mathematician Arthur Cayley, and the two together developed their joint masterpiece, the theory of algebraic invariants.

On his return to academic life he held chairs successively at the Royal Military Academy in

---

To a Missing Member of a family of terms in an algebraical formula

Lone and discarded one! divorced by fate,
From thy wished-for fellows — wither art flown?
Where lingerest thou in thy bereaved estate,
Like some lost star or buried meteor stone?
Thou mindst me much of that presumptuous one
Who loth, aught less than greatest, to be great,
From Heaven's immensity fell headlong down
To live forlorn, self-centered, desolate:
Or who, new Heraklid, hard exile bore,
Now buoyed by hope, now stretched on rack of fear,
Till throned Astraea, wafting to his ear
Words of dim portent through the Atlantic roar,
Bade him the sanctuary of the Muse revere
And strew with flame the dust of Isis' shore.

Having refreshed ourselves and bathed the tips of our fingers in the Pierian spring, let us turn back for a few brief moments to a light banquet of the reason, and entertain ourselves as a sort of after-course with some general reflections arising naturally out of the previous matter of my discourse.

James Joseph Sylvester

Wadwich, Johns Hopkins University in the United States (where he was the first professor of mathematics and where he founded the *American Journal of Mathematics*), and from his seventieth year, at the Oxford University (1883–1894).

Sylvester prided himself on being a man of culture and education, primarily self-taught. His mathematical works are characterized by frequent flights of poetic fancy and a bewildering array of masked literary references.

J. R. Newman, ed., *The World of Mathematics* (vol. 1), 1956–1962.

SZELL, GEORGE (1897–1970) Conductor, composer and pianist. Born in Budapest, Hungary, he studied at the Liszt Academy of Music and later in Vienna. At age eleven, he played his own Rondo for piano and orchestra with the Vienna Symphony Orchestra. From 1914 Szell regularly conducted in Berlin and was appointed musical director of the Berlin Imperial Opera in 1915. At the recommendation of Richard Strauss, the Strasbourg City Theater engaged him in 1917. After the war, from 1919 to 1922, he worked at the Prague German Theater and also in Darmstadt. Szell first conducted Bizet's *Carmen* at the Budapest Opera in 1920. In 1922 he moved to Düsseldorf and back to Berlin, where he was chief music director of the State Opera and taught at the Academy of Music until 1929. In 1930 he made his American debut with the Saint Louis Symphony Orchestra. The same year he moved to Prague where, in addition to his contract with the German Opera, he also taught at the German Academy of Music and Arts. In 1937 he became chief conductor of the Scottish Symphony Orchestra in Glasgow.

He immigrated to the United States in 1939, and on his arrival in New York, enjoyed the active support of Arturo Toscanini. He was principal conductor of the Metropolitan Opera (1942–1946), and permanent visiting conductor of the New York Philharmonic (1943–1956). The most important landmark in Szell's life was his appointment as chief musical director of the Cleveland Orchestra in 1946. It was Szell who raised this orchestra to become one of the world's finest symphony orchestras. In 1954 he toured Europe again, presenting Rolf Liebermann's two operas *Penelope* and *School of Women* at the Salzburg Festival. From 1958, he was artistic director of the New York Philharmonic and also of the Amsterdam Concertgebouw Orchestra. In 1963 he was decorated with the Order of the British Empire (CBE).

An affable person in private life, Szell was a severe, exacting perfectionist at the rostrum. He had a phenomenal memory and endless musical knowledge. He was reputed to have been able to "fingerprint" a composer, even if he had never heard his music before. A tough negotiator over fees, he incurred the dislike of managers. Szell's favorite pianist was Sir Clifford Curzon, with whom he cooperated over many years. Both being perfectionists, a love-hate relationship evolved

---

RUDOLF BING ON GEORGE SZELL

Szell, having been difficult over fees, an anecdote went round musical circles that someone had remarked to Sir Rudolf Bing, then director of the Metropolitan Opera, "Szell is his own greatest enemy," to which Bing retorted, "Not while I am alive."

---

between them, often leading to public quarrels at rehearsals. Many of the younger generation of conductors aver to have learned much from him, and one of his most successful pupils was James Levine, who was his apprentice for several years. Szell's compositions include *Variations on a Theme* (1916), *Lyrical Overture* (1920), chamber music, and piano works.

SZENES, HANNAH (1921–1944) Poet and World War II heroine. She was born in Budapest, where her father Bela Szenes was a well-known journalist and playwright. In early childhood, she heard very little about Judaism. The parents were typical assimilated, middle-class Jews, who were nonobservant. Hannah Szenes attended the local public

Hannah Szenes at Kibbutz Sedot Yam, 1939.

grade school, and from the start, was an outstanding student, excelling in composition and poetry.

At age ten, she was enrolled at the Protestant girls' high school, which had just began admitting Catholics and Jews. Although as a Jew, she had to pay three times the normal tuition fee (Catholics paid double), it never occurred to her mother to send her to the Jewish high school. At the end of the first year, when she brought home an excellent report, her mother felt encouraged to approach the principal to protest against the discrimination, and the fees were reduced to the level paid by the Catholics. Hannah was a very independent individual who, from the age of eleven, earned some money by coaching other children.

She started a diary in Hungarian at thirteen but from the age of eighteen she wrote both in Hebrew and Hungarian. The diary shows that at the age of seventeen she became involved in Zionism and started to learn Hebrew. At high school, she had as religious instructor Imre Benoschofsky, then chief rabbi of Buda, who although young was a great scholar and at that time an ardent Zionist. The rabbi's influence heightened her already burgeoning Jewish consciousness. Her school days coincided with increasing official anti-Semitism in Hungary, culminating in anti-Jewish legislation. A good Hungarian patriot in her childhood, she broke with any patriotic sentiments when at seventeen. She was elected to the office of president of the school's literary society, only to be told at the first meeting that as a Jew she could not hold office. She never again attended a meeting of the society. Her brother was not admitted to univeristy in Hungary as a Jew and left to study in France in 1938. By the time they next met in 1939, he had become an ardent Zionist and eventually moved to Palestine. Hannah joined Maccabea, the oldest Zionist student organization in Hungary, attended a Bible circle, and at the end of October 1938 wrote in her diary: "I've become a Zionist. This word stands for a tremendous number of things. To me it means, in short, that I now consciously and strongly feel I am a Jew, and am proud of it. My primary aim is to go to Palestine, to work for it. Of course this did not develop from one day to the next; it was a somewhat gradual development."

Before graduation, in March 1939, she wrote to the Girls' Agricultural School at Nahalal, Palestine, applying for a place. She arrived there in September and, in her first letter to her mother wrote: "I am in Nahalal, in Eretz. I am home.... This is where my life's ambition — I might even say my vocation — binds me; because I would like to feel that by being here I am fulfilling a mission, not just vegetating. Here almost every life is the fulfillment of a mission."

In 1941 she joined Kibbutz Sedot Yam and the Hagana (the Jewish underground paramilitary organization), eventually enlisting in the British army in 1943.

From January 1944, Szenes was trained in Egypt as a paratrooper and for service behind enemy

---

Hannah Szenes's last poem written in prison in Budapest

One — two — three...
　　eight feet long,
Two strides across, the rest is dark...
Life hangs over me like a question mark.

One — two — three...
　　maybe another week,
Or next month may still find me here,
But death, I feel, is very near.
I could have been
　　twenty-three next July;
I gambled on what mattered most,
The dice were cast. I lost.

Budapest 1944

---

lines. She was parachuted into Yugoslavia in June 1944, crossed the Hungarian border with the help of a partisan group on June 9, and was immediately captured. The Hungarian border guards sent her to Budapest where she was horribly tortured by the Gestapo and by Hungarian counterespionage. Her mother was also brought to prison but released. They were allowed to meet for a very brief time. Hannah was "tried" on October 28, and executed on November 7, 1944. Eye-witnesses, who had met her in prison, testified to her brave stance; she continued to write poetry until the end. Her remains, together with six other paratroopers who shared her fate, were brought to Israel in 1950; they are buried together in the military cemetery on Mount Herzl, Jerusalem.

Her diary and poems were first published in Hebrew in 1945 and since then translated and published in other languages including Hungarian.
M. Syrkin, *Blessed Is the Match*, 1948.

SZIGETI, JOSEPH (1892–1973) Violinist. He was born in the Transylvanian town of Sighet from which he took his family name. It was there that he started studying music with a teacher named Kohn, probably a local cantor. While still a child he studied the violin at the Liszt Academy of Budapest. Already in 1905, he gave successful concerts in Berlin and Dresden, and settled in London in 1906. During his London years (1906–1917) Szigeti became renowned also as an eminent teacher at the Berlin Conservatory (1906–1913). From 1917 to 1924, he lived in Geneva, taught at the conservatory, and gave concerts all over Europe, including the USSR, where several of his virtuoso transcripts were published. In 1927 he was offered directorship of the Moscow conservatory, but declined. He gave his first concert in America in 1925 and moved to the United States the following year.

Szigeti was among the first great violinists to play the works of 20th-century composers before their reputation had been established. These included Igor Stravinsky, Maurice Ravel, Sergey Prokofiev, Ernest Bloch, Alban Berg, Ferruccio Busoni, George Enescu and Bela Bartók, who, in 1928, dedicated to Szigeti his *First Rhapsody*. In 1939 at Carnegie Hall, New York, he played with Bartók the first two-movement version of the composer's chamber work, *Contrasts*, and in 1940, he recorded the final, three-movement trio version with Bartók and Benny Goodman (q.v.). Szigeti and Bartók together prepared a violin transcription of seven pieces from Bartok's *Four Children*, under the title *Hungarian Folk Melodies*. At the same time, Szigeti had developed an enormous repertoire of the earlier classics. Some of his recordings, such as the Mozart violin sonatas and his interpretation of the Brahms Violin Concerto, are considered gems.

In the early stages of the Cold War, Szigeti became persona non grata in the United States and was even interned, but was granted citizenship in 1951. He retired to Switzerland in 1960. He had to give up concerts at the end of the fifties but continued to teach, chiefly methodology.

Among the many honors he received was membership of the Accademia di Santa Cecilia of Rome.

Szigeti was an austere perfectionist. He was by no means one of this century's glamorous stars but arguably was one of its outstanding musicians. He had few friends and was known to treat the pianists with whom he performed rather shabbily. Gerald Moore, the noted English pianist, said of Szigeti that he regarded his colleagues at the piano — even when performing sonata duets — as employees, but Moore would nevertheless not "minimize for a moment the pleasure and benefit it was to rehearse with Szigeti; only at concerts was his lack of humanity revealed."

Szigeti's writings include *With Strings Attached (Reminiscences and Reflections*, 1947); Beethoven's *Violinwerke* (1963); and *Joseph Szigeti on the Violin*, (1969).

SZILARD, LEO (1898–1964) Physicist and biophysicist, one of the fathers of the atomic bomb. After graduating from high school in Budapest, he obtained a Ph.D. in 1922 at the University of Berlin and subsequently taught there. It was there that he first met and worked with Albert Einstein (q.v.) at the Kaiser Wilhelm Institute. With the rise of Hitler he went to England, and from 1935 to 1939 was on the staff of the Clarendon Laboratory at Oxford University. When the war broke out, he migrated to the United States, and from 1940 worked with Enrico Fermi on the theoretical problems of uranium fission at Columbia University. In 1942 he joined the Metal Laboratory in Chicago as a senior physicist, and in 1946 was appointed director of the Institute of Radiation Biology and Biophysics at the University of Chicago. From 1960

until his death, Szilard was professor at the Enrico Fermi Institute of Nuclear Studies and in February 1964 also became consultant at the California-based Salk Institute for Biological Studies.

As early as 1934 he discovered with T.A. Chalmers that in certain cases nuclear transmutation would be associated with molecular changes. Neutron irradiation of ethyliodide revealed that the radioiodine thus obtained could be recovered in the form of inorganic iodide. This process, known as the Szilard-Chalmers effect, was the basis of a number of reactions in which the nucleus, under radioactive decomposition, repelled the effect of the ejected particle as a consequence of which the molecule suffered a change in bonding, perhaps also associated with valency variation.

Szilard participated in experiments with the first nuclear reactor. With Fermi he selected graphite as a medium which enabled this first reactor to start operating at the University of Chicago on December 2, 1942.

Szilard, who had served in the Hungarian army during the last years of World War I, became a pacifist. Yet, it was he who, together with three other scientists (E. Wigner, Edward Teller, and Fermi) persuaded Einstein to sign a joint letter, dated August 2, 1939, to President Franklin D. Roosevelt in which they expressed their fear that advancing nuclear research in Nazi Germany could lead to that country's use of nuclear weapons and urged the president to promote U.S. research in the field with a view to defending democracy. They stressed that the construction of a bomb with an effect far exceeding anything known before could be envisaged. This letter secured the U.S. government's support required to start the nuclear chain reaction. Teller, Szilard, and Wigner are known as "the fathers of the atomic bomb." However, in 1945, these three joined Einstein in pleading with President Harry S. Truman not to use the bomb. After 1945 Szilard abandoned nuclear physics and worked exclusively in the fields of medicine and biochemistry.

In 1948 he organized the Council to Abolish War (Council for a Liveable World) against the arms race, in which he sought cooperation between American and Soviet scientists and politicians. For his contribution to the peaceful uses of atomic energy, he was honored with the Atoms for Peace Award of the American Academy of Sciences in 1960. He wrote satirical articles on the misuse of science published as *The Voice of the Dolphin and Other Stories* (1961).

S. R. Weartand and G. Weiss Szilard, *Leo Szilard: His Version of the Facts*, 1978.

E. P. Wigner, in National Academy of Sciences, *Biographical Memoirs*, 40 (1969).

SZOLD, HENRIETTA (1860–1945) Educator and social worker; founder of Hadassah, the Women's Zionist Organization of America, and Youth Aliyah (Youth Immigration to Palestine). The oldest of the eight daughters of Rabbi Benjamin Szold of

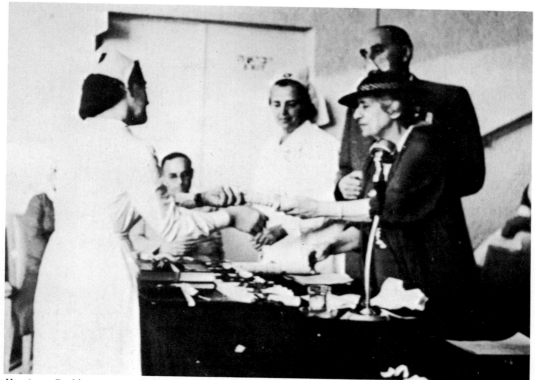

Henrietta Szold presenting diplomas to nurses in the early 1930s.

Baltimore, she was born soon after the family's arrival in the United States from Hungary. She attended the Jewish school in Baltimore, where the language of instruction was German. She began teaching in an exclusive girls' school while still young, and became involved in a number of social and civic groups in the Baltimore area, including an English night school for Russian immigrants. In managing and developing the night school, she first entered the field of fund raising. Her concern for "my Russians" became so absorbing that she wrote in a letter, "I have gone back to my early girlish longing to be a man. I am sure that if I were one I could mature plans of great benefit to them." After her father's death in 1902, she intended to gather, edit, and publish his scholarly writings. For this she felt she needed an appropriate education and so applied to the Jewish Theological Seminary in New York. They permitted her to attend (she was their first female student) on condition that she not aspire to accreditation for her work. At this time, she supported herself by working as secretary for the editorial board of the Jewish Publication Society. Her major task was editing the earliest annual editions of the *American Jewish Year Book*. In the course of time she became the outstanding figure of the JPS, which she built up and managed as well as acting as its main editor and translator.

Szold also began helping Louis Ginsburg, a professor at the seminary, with his great work, *The Legends of the Jews*. For her, this arrangement afforded more than intellectual fare. Nearly forty years old and unmarried, she felt an emotional attachment to this slightly younger man. When he returned from a holiday in Germany with a much younger wife, Szold felt betrayed. Several months of illness followed.

As she began to recover, she and her mother made their first journey to Eretz Israel in 1909; there she witnessed the misery, beauty, interest, and problems of the Holy Land. "If I were ten years younger, I would feel that my field is here," she wrote, adding, "I think Zionism a more difficult aim to realize than I ever did before ... [but] if not Zionism, then nothing — then extinction for the Jews." When she returned to the United States, she toured the country, giving speeches about Zionism. The initial women's groups she formed later became the nucleus for Hadassah.

A gift from a friend and admirer, Judge Julian Mack (q.v.), enabled Szold to devote all her time to Jewish philanthropic concerns, particularly Zionist ones. In 1915 Mack and other friends had assured her of an income for life — freeing her to volunteer her services for the good of the Jewish people. Szold resigned as secretary of the publications committee of the JPS, and took up the proofreading of their English translation of the Bible as her first piece of purely volunteer work.

Despite logging sixteen-hour days, she spoke of

the empty part of her life. "I have always held that I should have had children, many children."

In 1920 she again traveled to Palestine, intending a two-year stay to supervise the Zionist Medical Unit sent by Hadassah, and planning to be part of the International Zionist Commission, before returning to live somewhere near her sisters and increasing numbers of nieces and nephews in the United States. In fact, she was never to return to a permanent home in America; she spent the remainder of her life in Palestine.

Difficulties with the medical unit greeted her upon arrival. The resignations of forty-five doctors and a strike by seventeen student nurses tried her mettle during her first week. Within relatively short order, however, she calmed the situation. Soon there was a vast, efficiently run network of welfare stations, dispensaries, and laboratories throughout Palestine, supported by Hadassah, along with the Jerusalem Nurses' Training School, and all under Szold's aegis. This network delivered health services to both the Arab and Jewish sectors of the population, and educated them in preventative medicine in their homes and schools. In 1934 Szold proudly spoke at the cornerstone laying of the Hadassah Hospital on Mount Scopus, Jerusalem.

With the establishment of a Jewish self-governing body responsible for their internal affairs under the British Mandate, Szold was appointed as one of the three leaders of the nation in embryo. Holding the portfolio of health and education, she began working toward a women's society for public welfare work. At the time of her seventieth birthday, she took on yet more work; "I am charging myself with the task of organizing the Central Bureau for the social work being done in the whole of Palestine." The focus of her energies in this newly acquired enterprise was youth work, specifically with juvenile offenders.

The youth work was prescient, just as Hitler was gaining ascendance in Germany. When Szold went to the London Conference on the German Jewish situation in October 1933, she was in a position to pull together the "threads of an organization for settling German youngsters among the kibbutzim of Palestine." Returning to Palestine, she now held two responsible posts: the organization of social services and the immigration of the German-Jewish children. Youth Aliyah took children who were (or were soon to be) bereft of parents, uprooted them from the only culture they had known, threw them into a different part of the world, with a different language, and no nuclear family, and, instead of the urban or small-town life they had experienced, brought them into agricultural settlements. It succeeded, because of Szold's ability at management, for which her organizational skills prepared her. Despite her advancing years, her vigor scarcely waned. She sat on hot buses for hours in order to greet personally each new arrivals and escort them to their new homes.

Szold did not lack vision. During the Arab riots of the late 1930s, she took charge of accommodating over five thousand refugees from Jaffa and Hebron. She laid the blame for the massacres on the Arab agitators, the British government's even-handedness, and the Jewish community's refusal to deal with Arab-Jewish relationships. Of the last she wrote, "I believe there is a solution; and if we cannot find it, then I consider that Zionism has failed utterly."

I. Fineman, *Woman of Valor: The Life of Henrietta Szold*, 1961.

M. Lowenthal, *Henrietta Szold: Life and Letters*, 1942.

T

TAAMRAT, EMMANUEL (1898–1963) Father of modern education among the Ethiopian Jews. Born in Gondar, Ethiopia, he was the son of an Ethiopian Jew who had been converted to Christianity and he was educated at the Swedish Evangelical School in Asmara. When Jacques Faitlovich, the distinguished activist on behalf of Ethiopian Jewry, visited Asmara in 1904, he hoped to counter Christian missionary activities there. Taamrat begged to be taken to France and Faitlovich took him back to Paris. There Taamrat studied first at a Jewish school and then for twelve years at the Rabbinical College in Florence, Italy, from which he graduated with the title *maskil*.

From 1921 he spent three years in Palestine as a *halutz* (pioneer) at a kibbutz of the Ha-Shomer Ha-Tzair movement. In 1923 he returned to Ethiopia with Faitlovich and they established a teacher-training school in Addis Ababa, which combined religious and secular studies. News of its existence spread throughout Ethiopia and potential students walked hundreds of miles in the hope of enrolling. Graduates of the school were sent to the interior to open schools in Ethiopian Jewish villages. Some of the religious leaders of the Ethiopian Jewish community, however, saw this trend as a challenge to their authority and also opposed the contact with non-Jews. Some religious Jews would even wash their hands to rid themselves of the "impurity" upon coming into contact with Taamrat or his pupils.

Taamrat developed friendly relations with Emperor Haile Selassie, which often stood the Jews in good stead. The emperor, for example, on occasion agreed to intervene when local lords took Ethiopian Jews for forced labor or prevented the establishment of Jewish schools.

Taamrat's antifascist writings put him on a blacklist when Mussolini invaded Ethiopia in 1935. His school in Addis Ababa was closed and he was hunted — not as a Jew but as an antifascist. He escaped to Cairo and joined a group of Ethiopians in exile who were supporting the resistance in their home country. Many of his teachers and students were active in the resistance and the Italians reacted by obliterating a Jewish village in an air bombardment.

After Ethiopia's liberation in World War II, Taamrat returned and was asked to serve in various official capacities. He helped to establish the Ministry of Education and devoted much time to writing. He translated a work on Gandhi into Amharic and began to write a history of Ethiopia.

After the establishment of the State of Israel, he worked for the immigration of Ethiopian Jews to Israel. He asked Haile Selassie to permit the Jews to emigrate, but the emperor refused. He himself moved to Jerusalem in the capacity of counselor in the Ethiopian consulate. There he spent his last years.

TAM, JACOB BEN MEIR (known as Rabbenu Tam, i.e., "our perfect Rabbi"; c. 1100–1171) Leading rabbinical scholar of the twelfth century in France. He was born in Ramerupt, eastern France; his mother, Jochebed, was the daughter of Rashi (q.v.). As the entire family consisted of noted Talmudic scholars, his father and brothers were among his main teachers. He earned his living from viticulture and moneylending and also succeeded his father as head of the Talmudic academy in Ramerupt, which attracted scholars from many lands as well as receiving questions on matters of Jewish law from Jewish communities near and far.

In 1147, on the Feast of Weeks, French crusaders broke into Tam's home and took him to a field where they prepared to put him to death. They began by inflicting five wounds on his head, claiming that they were repaying the five wounds administered to Jesus, by attacking the leading Jew in France. A prince happened to be passing by, however, and in response to Tam's appeal, and the promise of a reward, he persuaded the crusaders to deliver their victim into his care, promising that if Tam did not become a Christian he would return the rabbi to them. Tam escaped to the nearby town of Troyes and settled there.

In Troyes, he convened rabbinical synods that enacted legislation to respond to current problems and strengthen religious observance. For example, it was decided that under pain of excommunication, disputes between Jews be settled in Jewish law courts and never referred to Christian courts. Tam also reaffirmed the ban on polygamy originally issued in the name of Rabbi Gershom Meor ha-Gola (see Gershom ben Judah).

Tam, like the rest of his family, belonged to the school of Talmudic commentators known as the Tosafists, who developed Rashi's comments on the Talmud. His own chief work was *Sefer ha-Yashar* ("Book of the Righteous"), which consists of decisions on matters of Talmudic law and new explanations of the Talmud, often based on a determination of the correct text of the Talmud. He collected and studied old manuscripts of the Talmud in order to arrive at the proper readings.

Tam was also a distinguished liturgical poet, who was influenced by the Spanish-Jewish school of poetry. When Abraham Ibn Ezra (q.v.) visited him, he was greeted by Tam in verse, to which Ibn Ezra responded in amazement, "Who has admitted the French into the temple of poetry?" Other writings by Tam dealt with Hebrew grammar and the Bible. He had many pupils and commanded universal respect. He disagreed with his grandfather concerning the order of the biblical sections placed in the *tefillin* (phylacteries) and it became a custom among pious Jews to wear two pairs of *tefillin*, one according to Rashi and one according to Rabbenu Tam.

TAUBER, RICHARD (1892–1948) Austrian tenor. Born Ernst Seiffert in Linz, he was the illegitimate son of a woman married to a provincial singer (Richard Anton Tauber) of limited means. His father, who became an able actor in Prague, helped him launch his musical career at the age of sixteen.

A fine vocalist and stylist, Tauber first made his mark in opera by singing Mozart. Tauber began his studies in the Frankfurt Conservatory and made his operatic debut as Tamino, in Mozart's *The Magic Flute*, in Chemnitz. The success of that debut led to a nine-year contract with the Dresden State Opera and then to two six-season periods with the Vienna State Opera. After the Nazi takeover of Austria, Tauber moved to London and in 1940 became a British subject. During the blitz, Tauber behaved as if London were the safest place in the world, commenting that "Hitler has stopped me singing in Germany and Austria, I'm not going to let him stop me now!" Once when Tauber was performing before a sold-out house in London, a bomb fell near the theater. The audience was about to panic when Tauber remarked, "I think that last bomb was a bit off-key." Tauber continued his recital and the audience remained to hear him.

Today Tauber is best remembered for his work in Viennese operetta, especially the compositions of Franz Lehar. He began to do operetta in 1922 when he performed in Lehar's *Frasquita*. He went on to be associated, primarily, with Lehar's *Giuditta* and *The Land of Smiles*, both written expressly for him. The Chinese prince's lush aria in this last operetta, "Dein ist mein ganzes Herz," ("You are my heart's delight") became closely associated with his name. In 1946 he appeared in a Broadway adaptation of *Land of Smiles*. When Tauber was reproached for shifting from opera to the less serious world of the operetta, he replied: "I don't sing operetta, I sing Lehar."

Tauber was also famous for his renditions of light German and Austrian songs. Later in his career he conducted operettas, composed his own (including *Old Chelsea* in 1942) and starred in movies (including *Blossom Time* in 1934). Although his somewhat stiff figure affected his stage characterizations, his pure style and musicianship ensured his success.

Tauber sang until the year before his death. His last public appearance took place in London on September 27, 1947. It was a historic event in which Tauber joined his old friends from the visiting Vienna State Opera, singing the role of Ottavio in Mozart's *Don Giovanni*.

C. Castle and D. N. Tauber, *This Was Richard Tauber*, 1971.
D. N. Tauber, *Richard Tauber*, 1949.

TEACHER OF RIGHTEOUSNESS (or Righteous Teacher; 2nd cent. BCE) Prophet and organizer of the Dead Sea community. No personal name is known and information on him is derived solely from the Dead Sea Scrolls, especially the *Zadokite Fragment* (or *Damascus Document*) and various Bible commentaries. Apparently the community had been in existence for some twenty years before his appearance, but had been leaderless. He was a priest, believed by his disciples to be endowed with the power to interpret the prophets. Although not looked upon as a messianic figure, he proclaimed the approaching end of the world and his activity indicated the imminence of the messianic age. His voice was perceived as the voice of God and salvation was promised to those "who listen to his voice."

According to the scrolls the Wicked Priest rose up to slay the Teacher of Righteousness and actually laid hands on him, but apparently (although not certainly) the Teacher was saved from his persecutor. The Wicked Priest, it is related, pursued the Teacher, "even to his place of exile" and appeared in order to confuse him on the sacred "Day of Atonement." It is known that the Dead Sea community kept a different calendar from other Jews and it would seem that on the day being observed by the Teacher as his Day of Atonement, he was confronted by the Wicked Priest, for whom this was an ordinary day and for whom the sect's calendar was heretical. The location of the place of exile is unclear: the scroll speaks of Damascus, but it is not known whether this was to be taken literally or, more probably, was a figurative name. The scrolls also speak of a conflict between the Teacher and the Man of the Lie. It is not clear whether the latter is to be identified with the Wicked Priest from outside the sect or as the leader of a breakaway group within the sect. After the confrontation, the Man of Lies got the upper hand and the Teacher and his followers went into exile, where they entered into a "new covenant." It is unknown where and when the Teacher died.

Various attempts have been made to identify the Teacher, as well as the Wicked Priest and Man of Lies, with known historical figures, but all remains obscure and it is impossible to reach conclusions on the basis of the existing texts.

F. F. Bruce, *The Teacher of Righteousness in the Qumran Texts*, 1962.

J. Carmignac, *Christ and the Teacher of Righteousness*, 1962.

TENENBAUM, MORDECHAI (originally, Tamaroff; 1916–1943) A leader of the Vilna, Warsaw, and Bialystok underground fighters during World War II. In 1938 he joined the staff of the Zionist Youth head office in Warsaw. In September 1939, Tenenbaum and his comrades left the city for Kovel and Vilna, hoping to reach Palestine. Since not enough immigration certificates were available, he obtained forged documents for many Zionist youth that allowed them to escape. Out of a sense of duty, however, Tenenbaum himself decided to remain in Vilna.

The Germans entered Vilna in late June 1941 and began murdering masses of Jews immediately. The possession of work permits saved Jews from death, and Tenenbaum provided many such false permits to Zionist youth. When there was a period of quiet, between incidents of murder, he sent word to Warsaw to tell of the atrocities that had taken place in Vilna. The leaders of the Zionist Youth Movement decided that its members in Vilna should be moved to Bialystok, where the situation was somewhat better.

On January 1, 1942, he issued a call for armed resistance at a meeting of Zionist youth. Using forged documents, he left Vilna for Grodno and Bialystok, where he organized armed undergrounds. He then returned to the Zionist Youth head office in Warsaw and at a meeting of various Jewish political groups, asserted that the murder in Vilna indicated that the Germans planned to eradicate the Jews of Europe.

He was one of the founders of the short-lived united armed underground, the Antifascist Bloc in Warsaw. From Warsaw he also visited Zionist Youth Movement branches in several ghettos, obtaining intelligence and working with resistance leaders. In July 1942, he became a founder of the Warsaw underground, the Jewish Fighting Organization. He was sent back to Bialystok in November 1942, but on his arrival discovered that the Germans had sealed off the ghetto while liquidating neighboring Jewish communities. Tenenbaum went to Grodno, but on the way was shot in the leg. After the wound had healed he entered Bialystok, where he unified the underground movement and readied them for an armed uprising. He appealed to the general Polish underground to supply weapons, and to the Western world to save the remaining Jews of Poland. He also established an underground archive and kept a diary.

February 1943 saw a large deportation of Jews from Bialystok. Tenenbaum did not launch a revolt, but instead sent messengers to the partisans in the forest. Following a lively discussion as to whether the underground should escape to the forest or fight in the ghetto and then escape, Tenenbaum's view that they first fight in Bialystok was accepted. He became the commander of a unified Bialystok underground in July.

Believing the final destruction of the Bialystok ghetto was at hand, Tenenbaum launched an armed uprising on August 16, 1943. The strong German forces surrounding the ghetto foiled his plan for breaking out of the ghetto. Tenenbaum functioned superbly during the first day of fighting, but his exact fate is unknown; he may have fallen in battle or may have committed suicide.

Jewish Resistance during the Holocaust, Yad Vashem, Jerusalem, 1971.

TERTIS, LIONEL (1876–1975) British violist. He was born in West Hartlepool, where his immigrant father was a rabbi whose singing in the synagogue attracted worshipers from near and far. As a young child Tertis loved making sounds at the unused family piano and at three he began to receive formal lessons. At thirteen he left home to earn his own living, and soon found a job playing with a small band on the pier at Southampton. His savings enabled Tertis to enroll in Trinity College of Music in London.

He studied violin at both the Leipzig Conservatory and the Royal Academy of Music in London. It was in the RAM that the principal, Alexander Mackenzie, urged Tertis to specialize in viola. Once Tertis began playing viola with several string quartets, he decided to make it his main instrument.

Tertis toured Europe and the United States as a solo violist but found it difficult to convince the public that the viola is as significant an instrument as the violin. As he wrote in his autobiography, "When I first began to play the viola as a solo instrument, prejudice and storms of abuse were my lot. The consensus of opinion then was that the viola had no right to be heard in solos, indeed the consideration of its place in the string family was of the scantiest. It was not only a despised instrument, but its cause was far from helped by the down and out violinists who usually played it." Tertis also had to create a viola repertoire. Many British composers, including Arnold Bax, Frank Bridge, Gustav Holst, and Arthur Bliss, wrote especially for Tertis. Although most of the original music composed for Tertis did not maintain a permanent place in the repertoire, it inspired the viola masterpieces written later by William Walton and Ralph Vaughan Williams.

Tertis played on a larger viola than the usual in order to achieve a rich and resonant C-string tone that avoided the characteristic nasal qualities of the viola and sounded more akin to the cello. He even codesigned a large viola and inspired instrument makers and musicians alike to adopt his idea.

Tertis retired in 1936 and spent the rest of his life teaching and encouraging interest in the viola, as well as performing on special occasions. Tertis made numerous transcriptions including the Mozart Clarinet Concerto and the Elgar Cello Concerto, and others.

His books include *Beauty of Tone in String Playing*, (1938).
L. Tertis, *My Viola and I*, 1974.

THALBERG, IRVING GRANT (1899–1936) U.S. U.S. film producer. Born in Brooklyn, Thalberg was a frail child who suffered from a rheumatic heart condition. Confined to bed for long stretches of his childhood, he became a voracious reader and acquired an appreciation of literary quality that was to become a hallmark of his work in motion pictures. Thalberg's diligence and hard work brought him to the position of assistant manager of an export company by the time he was eighteen, at which time he met Carl Laemmle (q.v.), founder of Universal Pictures. Thalberg, content with his business career, at first rejected Laemmle's job offer, but a few months later, applied for and obtained a secretarial post at Universal's New York office, without mentioning the existing offer from the firm's head.

Within a year, Thalberg had become Laemmle's secretary and was taken to California, where he swiftly exploited a chaotic situation to install himself as general manager. It was here that he first won his reputation as Hollywood's boy wonder; at the time he oversaw his first productions he was not even old enough to legally sign checks. Thalberg's respect for quality was accompanied by a demand for conformity, and mavericks, such as director Erich von Stroheim (q.v.), did not last long at Universal after Thalberg took charge. No corners were cut, however, on prestige productions like *The Hunchback of Notre Dame*.

Realizing he could do still better, Thalberg went to work as production chief for independent producer Louis B. Mayer (q.v.) in 1923 and supervised production at Metro-Goldwyn-Mayer when it was formed the following year. For the next nine years he was to a large degree responsible for the reputation of MGM as a quality studio; his personal productions included *Ben-Hur*, *The Crowd*, *Hallelujah*, *Anna Christie*, and *Private Lives*. A heart attack in 1933 put him temporarily out of action and an increasingly jealous Mayer used his absence to curtail his power. Thalberg, with only one production unit at his disposal on his return, successfully labored to reestablish himself with films like *A Night at the Opera*, *Romeo and Juliet* (starring his wife, Norma Shearer), and *The Good Earth*.

While he never took on-screen credit for any of his films (he is quoted as having said, "if you're in a position to give yourself credit, you don't need it"), Thalberg appreciated the importance of others to the filmmaking process, particularly writers. His personal involvement with each of his films was so time-consuming that even distinguished literary figures could wait for weeks until gaining an audience, giving rise to George S. Kaufman's [q.v.] quip, "On a clear day you can see Thalberg." Nonetheless, his reputation has remained awe-inspiring and F. Scott Fitzgerald wrote *The Last Tycoon* with Thalberg in mind. A year after Thalberg's death of pneumonia, aged only thirty-seven, the Academy of Motion Picture Arts and Sciences instituted a special award in his name.
B. Crowther, *The Lion's Share*, 1957.
B. Thomas, *Thalberg: Life and Legend*, 1969.

THOMASHEVSKY, BORIS (also Thomashefsky; 1868–1939) Yiddish actor, considered the founder of the Yiddish theater in America. Born in Poland, he arrived in the United States at the age of thirteen and worked as a cigarette maker in a sweat shop on the Lower East Side of New York. His fellow workers sang the folksongs and Yiddish theater tunes they loved while working. With his beautiful soprano voice, Thomashevsky sang solos.

Playbill of The Green Bill *starring Boris Thomashevsky.*

A co-worker at the factory claimed to have been part of a professional Yiddish theater family in Europe and Thomashevsky took it upon himself to bring the family to America and produce a show. In 1882 the "Famous World-Renowned Golubok Brothers" arrived from England and with the "World-Famous Singer Boris Thomashevsky" attempted a performance of Abraham Goldfaden's (q.v.) *Koldunye* at a rented theater on the Lower East Side. The theater was sold out. The police were called in to keep the crowds in order, but the leading lady had a headache and the performance failed.

A few months later, Thomashevsky reorganized the company and managed a few successful performances. The following year a company of real professionals arrived from Europe and Thomashevsky retreated to the provinces: Chicago and Philadelphia.

By the turn of the century, he was in his prime, billed on posters as "America's Darling." He was a plump young man with black curly hair, languorous eyes, and an effeminate voice. The ghetto girls thought him beautiful. They sent him flowers and presents, filled the theaters, and swooned in the aisles. His wife-to-be, Bessie, ran away from her Baltimore home to go on the stage and then marry him (she left him in 1925 to found her own theater). For several decades people worried that Thomashevsky's propensity to wear flesh-colored tights, displaying his calves, was destroying the modesty of American Jewish womanhood. It was said that when he played King Solomon, the only difference between Thomashevsky and the real king was that Solomon supported his harem, whereas Thomashevsky's harem supported him.

He favored playing young princes and romantic heroes and was described as picturesquely standing in the middle of the stage and declaiming phlegmatically. He played the works the public loved, but also tried his hand at anything he could exploit, including *Hamlet* in a literal Yiddish translation.

He tried to improve the quality of the popular theater and was always willing to try new plays and playwrights. He was the first to produce Ossip Dymov's plays in America and always produced Jacob Gordin's (q.v.) works. When all other producers refused Gordin's last play, *Dementia Americana*, he attempted its production. He sponsored new actors from abroad, among them the Schildkrauts, Jacob Ben-Ami, and the Vilna Troupe.

He continued to play romantic leads throughout the 1920s. In 1923 he brought *Three Little Business Men* and *The Jolly Tailors* to Broadway, but they failed. In 1935 he performed in the Yiddish film *Bar Mitzvah*. In the end he returned to the Yiddish stage with a play on his own life. His grandson shortened the family name and became known as the conductor, Michael Tilson Thomas.

R. D. S. Lifson, *Yiddish Theater in America*, 1965.

TODD, MICHAEL (1907–1958) U.S. impresario and producer. Born Avrom Goldbogen in Minneapolis, Minnesota, to poor Polish immigrant parents, Todd early developed his business acumen. Working at various jobs from the age of seven, Todd ended his formal education after sixth grade and at thirteen became the youngest person in the state of Illinois to hold an assistant pharmaceutical license. At fifteen, having already been assistant sales manager of a shoe store and president of a college of bricklaying, he and his brother became building contractors. By the age of eighteen, he was a millionaire. A second construction company, founded after the first had folded, gave Todd his first show business contact when it soundproofed the Columbia studio.

In the early years of the depression, Todd realized that the entertainment industry was a venture that could pay enormous dividends to those blessed with the imagination and drive that he possessed to such a staggering degree. He entered the theatrical world and began producing a variety of attractions, initially of the burlesque type and later also extending to entire musical shows, such as *The Hot Mikado* and Cole Porter's *Something for the Boys* and *Mexican Hayride*. Never satisfied with merely being a theatrical producer, Todd continued to invest in other enterprises, such as Michael Todd's Theater Cafe, an eight-thousand-seat nightclub in Chicago. He achieved a great success at the 1933 Chicago World's Fair, where he exhibited the flame dancer.

Todd's constant search for novelty caused him to become interested in the Cinerama process, in which three cameras and three projectors were employed to create an image on a huge curved screen, approximating the full field of human vision. The success of the process spurred him on to attempt a similar effect without tripling the amount of equipment used. He formed the Magna corporation to handle what was eventually named Todd-AO, a 70-mm wide-screen process. The first film made in Todd-AO was *Oklahoma!*, but the agreement arrived at with authors Richard Rodgers and Oscar Hammerstein gave them, and not Todd, control of the production. Todd devoted the last years of his life to his own Todd-AO film, *Around the World in 80 Days*, which was a tremendous success and won the Academy Award for best picture in 1956. He and his biographer Art Cohn, were killed in a plane crash. Among his wives were actresses Joan Blondell and Elizabeth Taylor.

A. Cohn, *The Nine Lives of Michael Todd*, 1959.
M. Todd, Jr., and S. McCarthy Todd, *A Valuable Property: The Life Story of Michael Todd*, 1983.

TOLLER, ERNST (1893–1939) German dramatist, poet and revolutionary. Born in Samotshin, a Prussian town with a mixed German and Polish population, and brought up in an assimilated Jewish family, he completed secondary school in the neighboring Bromberg and had begun studying law at the University of Grenoble, France, when World War I broke out. As an ultrapatriotic German, he immediately returned to his native land and volunteered for military service. He fought heroically on the Western front until he was wounded in 1916 and was discharged from the army. While resuming his studies at Munich and Heidelberg, he also agitated against the prolongation of the war. Influenced by Kurt Eisner (q.v.) and Gustav Landauer (q.v.), he participated in strikes, was imprisoned, and, upon his release, persisted in antiwar and revolutionary activities. In 1919 he rose to leadership in the short-lived Bavarian Soviet regime. After the murder of Eisner and

Police poster offering a reward for Ernst Toller's arrest in 1919.

Landauer, he was hunted as a pillar of the collapsed communist government and a price of 10,000 marks was set on his head. Apprehended in July 1919, he was sentenced to five years imprisonment.

While behind bars, he wrote the beautiful poems of *Das Schwalbenbuch* (*The Swallow-Book*, 1924) and several expressionistic plays. One of these, *Masse Mensch* (*Masses and Man*, 1923), received wide acclaim when staged in 1920. It dramatized the struggle within man's soul during a proletarian uprising between man's duty to himself and his duty to the masses. *Die Maschinenstürmer* (*The Machine-Wreckers*, 1923), staged in 1922, concentrated on the struggle between man and machine. The play culminates in the murder of the revolutionary leader because he dares to oppose riotous excesses. The leader voices Toller's own faith in a new cooperative world order. The lord of the factory and the machine-wrecking workers, however, are not won over to this idealistic faith. In *Hinkemann* (1923), Toller depicted the misery, corruption and immorality of the immediate postwar scene as it impinged upon an emasculated, proletarian character. The play aroused controversy in Germany, but was successfully produced throughout Europe and even in Yiddish by Maurice Schwartz (q.v.) in New York's Yiddish Art Theater. None of Toller's later plays experienced a similar vogue.

Upon his release from prison in 1924 he was active in many liberal causes, but no longer believed in political and social panaceas. He visited Palestine in 1925, the Soviet Union in 1926, and the United States in 1929. In 1931 and 1932 he was most attracted to Spain. In 1933 he found himself in exile from Germany when the Nazis rose to power and his books were banned and burned. He reacted by directing his last play, *Pastor Hall* (1939), against the Nazis, basing it upon the experiences of Pastor Martin Niemoeller, and by fighting with his pen and oratory against fascism. In 1939 he raised funds in New York for refugees from Republican Spain who were fleeing Franco's invading forces. When Madrid fell he was overtaken by despair and committed suicide.

Toller suffered from the duality of being born a Jew and a German. He sought to escape from his Jewishness at first, but was reconciled to it in later years. His espousal of German nationalism led to disillusionment and flight to cosmopolitanism. He once summed up his his identity: "A Jewish mother bore me, Germany nursed me, Europe educated me, the earth is my homeland, the world my fatherland."

R. Benson, *German Expressionist Drama — Ernst Toller and Georg Kaiser*, 1984.
R. Dove, *He was a German*, 1991.
M. Pittock, *Ernst Toller*, 1979.

TORRES, LUIS DE   (15th cent.) Spanish Marrano, the only Jewish-born member of Christopher Columbus's first expedition to the Indies and the first European to set foot in the New World. Little is known about Torres, apart from the fact that he was baptized only a day or two before the voyage commenced (August 3, 1492), which was also when the last unconverted Jews had been expelled from Spain. Torres was specifically appointed Columbus's interpreter because he "had been a Jew and knew Hebrew, Chaldean, and a little Arabic." This knowledge was expected to prove useful whenever the voyagers came across "Asiatic" descendants of Israel's Ten Lost Tribes.

Having already landed at San Salvador in the Bahamas, Columbus's fleet reached Cuba on October 28. There Luis de Torres went ashore again with instructions to proceed inland, either in the hope of finding gold or to bear a letter from the Spanish monarchs, Ferdinand and Isabella, to China's emperor (the Great Khan). Torres found no gold, no emperor, and no lost Israelites; since the natives whom he encountered knew none of the Old World tongues, he was forced to communicate with them in sign language, but assured Columbus that they were friendly. His report included the first account by a European of the tobacco plant's cultivation and use for smoking.

Unlike his rapacious fellow explorers, Torres was content to settle peacefully in Cuba and spend the rest of his life there. He befriended the local Arawak chief, received a grant of land on which to build a house and was given a yearly allowance

from the Spanish exchequer. A converted Jew thus became one of the pioneers of white settlement in America. He traded with the Indians, grew tobacco, and introduced tobacco smoking to Europe.
S. Wiesenthal, *Sails of Hope*, 1973.

TREBITSCH LINCOLN, IGNAZ   (1879–1943)

Adventurer. Born to an affluent Jewish family in Hungary, he was baptized in Hamburg at the age of twenty and went to Canada, where he was confirmed by the Anglican archbishop of Montreal and ordained deacon. In 1903 he moved to England and became a curate in a parish in Kent. On inheriting some money, he left the ministry ("no great loss" noted the archbishop of Canterbury) and turned to research in Europe on the land tenure system. He was adopted as Liberal parliamentary candidate at Darlington and was elected a member of Parliament in 1910. Parliament, however, was shortly dissolved and Trebitsch Lincoln did not stand for reelection because of financial problems brought on by an extravagant lifestyle. The next years were spent in doubtful oil-drilling schemes in eastern Europe.

After World War I broke out he offered his services as double agent to both England and Germany. When the British sought to arrest him as a spy he fled to the United States, where he exaggerated his unimportant spy contacts in sensational newspaper articles which gained him a reputation as a master spy. At the request of the British, he was arrested and after a period of imprisonment — which included engineered escapes and a press conference held on the run — he was extradited to England and sentenced to three years' imprisonment for treason, serving until 1919.

Trebitsch Lincoln went next to Berlin, where he became involved in right-wing intrigue. He was a leader, along with Ludendorff and others, of the five-day German revolution in March 1920, known as the Kapp putsch. While it lasted, Trebitsch Lin-

Abbot Chao Kung (Ignatus Trebitsch Lincoln), in the center, with his disciples, Vancouver, 1934.

coln was in charge of press and information. After the failure of the putsch, he continued to be prominent in the "white international," which sought to balance the "red international." He went to Hungary and received the support of its regent, Admiral Horthy, but internal quarrels led to the disintegration of the international. Trebitsch Lincoln stole its documents, which he sold to the Czech government for a handsome sum. During these years he often changed his alias but always retained the initials TL to match his linens.

The last part of his life was spent in China — one of the few places he could enter without fear of arrest. From 1922 he was involved with various Chinese warlords as adviser and arms procurer. While in Tientsin he had a mystical experience which at first attracted him to theosophy but later brought him to Buddhism. His studies of Buddhism were interrupted when news arrived that his son was to be hanged for murder in England. Trebitsch Lincoln traveled to Europe but failed to arrive in time for the execution and was not permitted to enter England.

After his return to China, he was ordained a Buddhist monk, and had twelve small stars branded on his scalp. Having unsuccessfully attempted to establish a Buddhist monastery in Europe, he awarded himself the title of abbot in Shanghai and attracted a small group of faithful followers. By this time he had assumed the Chinese name Chao Kung.

During World War II he approached the German consul general in Shanghai with a proposal that he be sent to meet Hitler, whom he was sure would immediately be aware of his supernatural powers. The consul was sufficiently impressed to forward the suggestion to Berlin but received a reply from the Nazi leader Reinhard Heydrich saying "Surely you are aware he is a Jew."

Trebitsch Lincoln spent his last months in a Shanghai YMCA, continuing to preach Buddhism. His last interview was with a Jewish newspaper in which he expounded on a plan for a settlement of Jewish refugees near Shanghai which he envisaged as "a miniature Tel Aviv."
B. Wasserstein, *The Secret Lives of Trebitsch Lincoln*, 1988.

TREPPER, LEOPOLD   (alias Leiba Domb, Jean Gilbert, Adam Mickler and others; 1904–1982)

"Conductor" of the "Red Orchestra," the Soviet anti-German intelligence and spy network during World War II.

Trepper was born into a family of shopkeepers in the small town of Novy-Targ in Galicia, southern Poland. He joined the Hashomer Hatzair youth movement and the Polish Communist party, becoming a member of the national leadership in 1920. In 1921 the Trepper family moved to Dombrova in Silesia, where he became head of Hashomer Hatzair and at the same time took part in the militant clandestine activities of the communist youth groups. Blacklisted by the police, he was unable to find work, and in 1924 moved to Palestine. After working in the malarial marshes of Hadera, he decided that the Jewish landowners were exploiting their Arab laborers and in 1925 joined the Communist party of Palestine. Faced with hostility from the Histadrut (General Federation of Labor) to its communist members, Trepper founded the Ichud movement to unite Jewish and Arab workers. The British mandatory authorities issued a decree prohibiting the Ichud movement, and in 1927 Trepper was imprisoned for several months. On his release he was appointed secretary of the Haifa branch of the Communist party, but was again arrested and expelled from Palestine in 1929.

Moving to Paris, Trepper joined the French Communist party and started a Yiddish weekly, *Der Morgen*. In 1932 a Soviet espionage network was uncovered in Paris and although Trepper was not involved, the party thought it advisable for him to leave France, and he moved to the Soviet Union.

In Moscow, Trepper was enrolled by the French section of the Comintern at the Marchlevsky University for National Minorities, where he and his wife were involved in political and revolutionary studies and presumably received their first training in espionage activity. Profoundly affected by the events in Nazi Germany, he offered his services to the Red Army Intelligence Service.

In 1937 Trepper, under the guise of a French-Canadian businessman, moved to Brussels and then to Paris, where he set up the Soviet spy network, later dubbed by the German counterintelligence as the "Red Orchestra." Members of the group managed to penetrate the highest echelons of the Luftwaffe and the German high command. A constant flow of invaluable information reached Moscow through the network of spies and radio operatives (known as "pianists") belonging to the Orchestra.

In June 1941, the Orchestra correctly informed Moscow that the German invasion of the USSR would take place the next day, at which time the Red Army could have been placed on a full state of alert. Stalin chose to ignore the warning, telling an aide that Trepper "has been intoxicated by English propaganda" and that "the war with Germany will not start before 1944...."

Trepper himself was arrested by the Gestapo in 1942. He escaped from prison a year later and resumed his activities as the head of the Orchestra and worked with the French Resistance until the Liberation.

Trepper was recalled to Moscow in January 1945. Instead of a hero's welcome, he was subjected to constant interrogation on the nature of his wartime activities and was subsequently incarcerated in the Lubyanka and other prisons, where he was to spend the next ten years. After the death of Stalin, in February 1954, following the decision of the Supreme Military Tribunal that all the charges brought against him in the past were unfounded, he was released.

The reunited Trepper family moved back to Warsaw in 1957, where Trepper hoped to participate in the revival of a Jewish communal presence in Poland. Following the virulent anti-Semitic violence of June 1967, in the wake of the Six-Day War, Trepper realized that there was no future for the Jews in post-war Poland, and he applied to leave for Israel. His request was denied repeatedly, and only in 1973 was he allowed permission to leave for Britain for essential medical treatment.

Finally, in 1974, he reached Israel. Trepper wrote his memoirs, *Le grand jeu*, which were subsequently published in English, Hebrew and other languages. He died in Jerusalem.

G. Perrault, *The Red Orchestra*, 1969.

TRILLING, LIONEL (1905–1975) U.S. literary critic, passionately concerned with intellectual, social, and cultural issues.

Trilling was born in New York City, studied at Columbia University, and subsequently taught there for over four decades. He joined the English department in 1931, some seven years before receiving his doctorate, and rose to the rank of full professor in 1948, becoming the first Jew in the department to be granted tenure. Although Trilling did not found a school of thought or a theory of literary criticism, he was, nevertheless, "a figure of extraordinary influence."

His best known works are brief essays: *The Liberal Imagination* (1950), *The Opposing Self* (1955), and *Beyond Culture* (1965). He contributed frequently to *Partisan Review* and the *Kenyon Review*.

With his direct and engaged style, Trilling combined in his critical writings insightful analysis of individual work and authors with a dedication to the continuation and development of liberalism in the political as well as in the literary arena.

He viewed Freudian psychology as an effective tool for literary analysis. As he notes in *Freud and Literature*, Freudian psychology's depiction of "human nature ...is exactly the stuff upon which the poet has always exercised his art"; thus, "criticism has derived from the Freudian system much that is of great value, most notably the licence and the injunction to read the work of literature with a lively sense of its latent and ambiguous meanings, as if it were, as indeed it is, a being no less alive and contradictory than the man who created it."

Despite his commitment to the vision of a liberal culture and society, Trilling never lost sight of his first and foremost responsibility to his own discipline — literature and literary criticism — and to his students. While recognizing that students should be encouraged to read literary works, he argues that criticism should not be regarded as an interfering medium; on the contrary, criticism's role is to facilitate that direct contact with literature.

In his academic and creative pursuits, Trilling considered himself part of the general American literary scene, rather than a "Jewish author and critic." In 1944, he wrote in a Jewish journal, *Contemporary Jewish Record*, that he did not think of

TRILLING ON WORDSWORTH AND THE MISHNAH

In speaking of Wordsworth a recollection of boyhood cannot be amiss — my intimacy with *Pirkei Aboth* ("Sayings of the Fathers," a tractate in the Mishnah) comes from my having read it many times in boyhood. It certainly is not the kind of book a boy is easily drawn to read, and certainly I did not read it out of piety. On the contrary, indeed: for when I was supposed to be reading my prayers — very long, and in the Hebrew language, which I never mastered — I spent the required time and made it seem that I was doing my duty by reading the English translation of the *Pirkei Aboth* which, although it is not a devotional work, had long ago been thought of as an aid to devotion and included in the prayer book. It was more attractive to me than psalms, meditations, and supplications; it seemed more humane, and the Fathers had a curious substantiality. Just where they lived I did not know, nor just when, and certainly the rule of my life they recommended had a very quaint difference from the life I knew, or, indeed from any life that I wanted to know. Yet they were real, their way of life had the charm of coherence. And when I went back to them, I could entertain the notion that my early illicit intimacy with them had had its part in preparing the way for my responsiveness to Wordsworth, that between the Rabbis and Wordsworth an affinity existed.

himself as a Jewish writer. "I do not have it in mind to serve by my writing any Jewish purpose. I should resent it if a critic of my work were to discover in it either faults or virtues which he called Jewish." Yet, he cannot be accused of denying his Jewish identity for, in an essay appearing in one of his major collections of critical pieces, "Wordsworth and the Rabbis," Trilling speaks freely of his Jewish background and utilizes that background in his work, for example in explicating Wordsworth's poetry.

W. M. Chace, *Lionel Trilling: Criticism and Politics*, 1980.

N. A. Scott, *Three American Moralists: Mailer, Bellow, Trilling*, 1973.

TROTSKY, LEON (Lev Davidovich Bronstein; 1879–1940) Russian revolutionary. Born to a wealthy Jewish farmer in the village of Yanovka near Bobrinetz in southern Ukraine, at the age of nine he was sent to school in Odessa. An excellent pupil, he was involved in revolutionary groups while still a student, and became interested in Marxism. He was arrested in 1898, and was in prison for two years (he had a jailer called Trotsky,

whose name he was later to assume). Tried in 1900, he was sentenced to four years of exile above the Arctic Circle in Siberia. Escaping in 1902, he made his way to London, where he joined Lenin in editing the Social Democratic journal, *Iskra*. He moved to Geneva the following year when the journal's offices were transferred there.

After the split in the Russian Social Democratic Labor party in 1903, Trotsky for a time supported the Mensheviks and then wavered between the Mensheviks and the Bolsheviks. When disturbances broke out in Russia in 1905, he hastened back and took a leading role in the revolutionary workers council (the Soviet) in Saint Petersburg. Arrested the following year, he was again sentenced to exile in Siberia but escaped en route and made his way to Vienna, where he lived as a journalist, writing especially on revolutionary theory. During the early years of World War I he was in Paris but was ordered out of the country when the paper he was editing was banned. He reached New York in January 1917, but a few weeks later word arrived of uprisings in Russia and he rushed back to cooperate with Lenin. Jailed briefly by the Kerensky government, Trotsky was elected to the Central Committee of the Bolshevik party while still in prison, and on release was appointed president of the Petrograd soviet.

Trotsky was one of the chief organizers of the October revolution, which brought the Bolsheviks to power, and directed the armed uprising. After its success, he was appointed commissar for foreign affairs (after turning down Lenin's offer to head the new government or be commissar for home affairs on the grounds that in these posts his Jewish origin could prove a hindrance). Sent to Brest-

TROTSKY'S TESTAMENT

For forty-three years of my conscious life I have remained a revolutionist; for forty-two of them I have fought under the banner of Marxism. If I had to begin all over again I would of course try to avoid this or that mistake, but the main course of my life would remain unchanged. I shall die a proletarian revolutionist, a Marxist, a dialectical materialist, and, consequently, an irreconcilable atheist. My faith in the communist future of mankind is not less ardent, indeed it is firmer today, than it was in the days of my youth.

Natasha has just come up to the window from the courtyard and opened it wider so that the air may enter more freely into my room. I can see the bright green strip of grass beneath the wall, and the clear blue sky above the wall, and sunlight everywhere. Life is beautiful. Let the future generations cleanse it of all evil, oppression, and violence and enjoy it to the full.

Workers! This Is Not Our War!
It Is A War for Boss Profits!
Join Hands in Independent
Labor Action Against the War!

LABOR ACTION

In This Issue —
LIFE OF TROTSKY
Pages 2 and 4

AUGUST 26, 1940 — ORGAN OF THE WORKERS PARTY, SECTION OF THE FOURTH INTERNATIONAL — THREE CENTS

STALIN HAS MURDERED OUR COMRADE TROTSKY

Leon Trotsky has fallen. Our comrade, the great leader of the world revolution is dead. He was murdered at the dictate of Joseph Stalin.

Jacques Dreschd who wielded the axe that struck Trotsky is beyond any doubt a GPU agent. The last possible doubt was removed by the murderer's statement to the police that he had acted as he did because Trotsky had wanted him to commit acts of sabotage in Russia. So vile a lie could be mouthed only by the GPU.

Assigned the task of murdering Trotsky in the event that other attempts failed, Dreschd wormed his way into the household, pretending to be a "friend." The GPU gave him time, time to engratiate himself, time to pretend that he had been "won over" to Trotsky's views.

The Stalinists, trying to cover the trail that can lead only to themselves, will claim that Jacques Dreschd or Monard or Jackson was a "follower" of Trotsky, that he acted in disillusionment. So too they dared accuse Trotsky of himself organizing the May murder attempt. But Jacques Dreschd was not a follower of Trotsky. Jacques Dreschd was a follower, and an employee, of Stalin who has levelled the muzzle of his murder machine at the man whose very life was a challenge to the Kremlin tyrant.

One by one, that murder machine has struck down those closest to Trotsky, trying more desperately each time to strike at Trotsky himself.

There was Blumkin, loyal soldier of the Russian revolution. Stalin murdered him in 1929.

There was Erwin Wolff, secretary to Trotsky, who was kidnapped and brought to Russia in 1936 by the GPU. Stalin murdered him.

There was Ignace Reiss who was found dead in Switzerland in 1937 after he had severed his connections with the reactionary GPU. Stalin murdered him.

There was Rudolph Klement, secretary to Trotsky, whose mutilated body was found in the Seine River in 1938. Stalin murdered him.

There was Sheldon Harte, bodyguard to Trotsky, who was spirited away from Trotsky's Coyoacan home when the GPU's May attack failed. Stalin murdered him.

There were the sons and daughters and countless friends of Leon Trotsky. Each of them, directly or indirectly, fell prey to Kremlin gangsterism. Only two years ago, Leon Sedov, Trotsky's son and close collaborator, suddenly died in Paris under mysterious circumstances. Stalin murdered Sedov. Stalin murdered them all.

Trotsky alive was an indomitable threat to the rotten regime of revolutionary betrayal that Stalin has foisted with knout and bullet upon the Russian masses. Each in his turn, the leaders of the glorious revolution of 1917, that liberated one-sixth of the earth until Stalin again enslaved it, have met death at the decree of Stalin. Only Trotsky, organizer of the Red Army, co-worker of Lenin, remained alive—a living challenge, epitomizing the spirit of socialism and of revolution. And now he is dead—murdered.

For twelve years, ever since he was driven by Stalin from the land whose rebellious forces he led to victory in 1917, Trotsky was the target of the GPU murder machine. They hounded him from country to country, striking at his friends and collaborators. And, finally, in Mexico, they laid fine plans for the dirty business of his assassination. George Mink, a notorious GPU agent, was in Mexico for the express purpose of organizing the murder. Last May they staged an armed assault on Trotsky's home which failed in its aim only by the merest accident.

But they had reckoned with that possibility.

(Continued on page 2)

Farewell, Leon Trotsky---

Our leader, teacher and comrade, Leon Trotsky is dead. Thus an historical epoch is ended. Lenin's co-worker and co-thinker, the leader of the October insurrection and the organizer of the once glorious Red Army is the last of the Old Bolsheviks.

Leon Trotsky is the victim of Cain Stalin, the gravedigger of the Russian Revolution, the assassin of brave revolutionists. For almost twelve years the Kremlin oligarchy has sought to take the life of Trotsky, but each time he foiled. The unspeakable GPU acting through its hireling, Van Den Dreschd finally succeeded. Gaining the confidence of our warm-hearted and genial Leon Trotsky, pretending to be a disciple of our great comrade, this scoundrel in the pay of the GPU struck down the lion of October in a brutal attack. But Joseph Stalin is the real assassin—as real as if his own hand had struck the treacherous blow.

Stalin mortally feared the man whom he had driven into exile, whose comrades he murdered, whose family he destroyed. Stalin mortally feared that the deep dissatisfaction in the Soviet Union would grow to revolutionary proportions and turn to Leon Trotsky for guidance and leadership in the overthrow of his regime of terror. Stalin mortally feared that the world working class, unfettered by the treacherous teachings of the usurpers would turn to Trotsky and the Fourth International for leadership in the struggle against reaction and for world socialism.

Stalin's hands drip with the blood of a host of fighters for proletarian emancipation. But if he thought to wipe out the revolution, he has struck in vain! If Trotsky is no more, he has left an imperishable heritage. In the period of the degeneration of the Russian Revolution, in the triumph of reactionary Stalinism, his voice and his pen remained alive to explain and to teach a new generation of young revolutionaries to fight against the decaying order of capitalism and for the new socialist society of universal freedom for the masses of our planet.

To our brave, sorrowing comrade Natalia Ivanovna, lifelong companion of Lev Davidovitch, we extend our most heartfelt sympathy in this dreadful hour. You have been the comrade-in-arms of our L.D. for many decades and you have been our beloved comrade for many years. Your great devotion to your comrade and companion under the most perilous and trying conditions of the Russian revolutionary movement, in the gigantic events of the October insurrection and through the period of Stalinist degeneration and reaction, is a glorious lesson in revolutionary devotion and comradely sacrifice. Dear Natalia Ivanovna, you are not alone! Thousands stand with you in this dark and bitter hour, sworn to carry on.

Leon Trotsky, the greatest disciple of Marx, Engels and Lenin, is no more. But he lives in his heroic deeds, in his great teachings! The Kremlin Borgia has finally succeeded in his villainous deed. But let him not think that thereby he has broken the living spirit of Trotsky. There are thousands now, there will be millions of avengers who will avenge his death. They will not only avenge the murder of our dear Leon Trotsky. They will avenge the murder of the hundreds and thousands whom Stalin has destroyed in his counter-revolutionary savages. They will march onward in the spirit of revolutionary Marxism, in the spirit of Lenin and Trotsky.

A new generation of revolutionaries is emerging. They will grow up in the spirit of Bolshevik courage and devotion to carry on until the victory of socialism. Under the banner of the Fourth International, founded by Leon Trotsky, the new movement will triumph. By his teachings, by his devotion and by his peerless courage in the face of the greatest dangers, the Fourth International will be nourished. Rising upon the edifice of the epoch of Lenin and Trotsky, it will sweep away the rubbish of the old order and give birth to the new movement of Socialist emancipation.

Farewell Leon Trotsky!

Hail the Fourth International!

Hail the liberating world revolution!

NATIONAL COMMITTEE, WORKERS PARTY
NATIONAL COUNCIL, YOUNG PEOPLES SOCIALIST LEAGUE! (4th International)

Left: A recent picture of Leon Trotsky taken in Mexico.
Below: Trotsky with several of his collaborators during the Russian Revolution.

AS THE LEADER OF THE RED ARMY

NATALIA TROTSKY
MEXICO D F

OUR HEARTS ARE TORN WITH GRIEF OVER THE LOSS WHICH IS IRREPARABLY YOURS AND IRREPARABLY THAT OF INTERNATIONAL PROLETARIAN MOVEMENT. THE CAPTAIN OF THE WORLD ARMY OF REVOLUTION HAS FALLEN AT THE HANDS OF THE COWARDLY ASSASSIN IN THE KREMLIN. OUR FLAG IS DIPPED AT THE OPEN GRAVE OF THE IMMORTAL LEON TROTSKY. OUR DEEPEST SYMPATHY AND LOVE IS WITH YOU IN YOUR HOUR OF SORROW. LONG LIVE THE FOURTH INTERNATIONAL. LONG LIVE THE LIBERATING TRIUMPH OF THE WORKING CLASS.

WORKERS PARTY
SHACHTMAN, SECRETARY

The front page of Labor Action, *edited in New York. August 26, 1940.*

Litovsk, he signed a humiliating treaty of peace with the Germans at Lenin's insistence.

He was next appointed commissar for military affairs in 1918, with the formidable task of preparing the new republic to fight the combined threat of foreign military intervention as well as the internal antirevolutionary armies. He efficiently organized the Red Army and steered it to victory.

In the following years, he came into frequent conflict with another close lieutenant of Lenin, Joseph Stalin. After Lenin's death in 1924, Stalin maneuvered Trotsky out of a central role while he himself eventually became sole ruler. Trotsky continued to advocate world revolution; Stalin's policy was to concentrate on establishing "socialism in one country." In 1927 Trotsky was removed from the party, the following year exiled to Turkestan, and in 1929 expelled from the USSR.

Trotsky first lived for four years on an island near Istanbul, then in France and Norway, and finally, in 1936 found refuge in Mexico. He continued to attack Stalin and Stalinism until eventually Stalin organized his assassination by a Spanish communist, who killed Trotsky with an ice pick in 1940. Even after his death, "Trotskyism" and "Trotskyite" parties continued to exist in many countries.

I. Deutscher, *The Prophet Armed: Trotsky 1879–1921*, 1954.

I. Deutscher, *The Prophet Unarmed: Trotsky 1921–1929*, 1959.

I. Deutscher, *The Prophet Outcast: Trotsky 1929–1940*, 1963.

B. D. Wolfe, *Three Who Made a Revolution*, 2nd ed., 1960.

F. Wyndham and D. King, *Trotsky: A Documentary*, 1972.

TRUMPELDOR, JOSEPH (1880–1920) Pioneer, soldier, Zionist. Born in Pyatigorsk, northern

Zionist Newssheet published by Joseph Trumpeldor, for Russian Jewish soldiers taken prisoner by the Japanese

Caucasus, Russia, he learned about loyalty first hand from his father and was concerned that his children learn similar values. Joseph's education in traditional Judaism, on the other hand, was minimal: he spent half a year in a Jewish elementary school at the age of seven.

Barred from attending high school by anti-Semitic laws, Trumpeldor studied dentistry. In his early twenties, he founded a Zionist group in his hometown. At the same time he became attracted to the Tolstoyan movement and its ideal of the collective commune. Under its influence he adopted his own modest and simple lifestyle and developed his ideal of Zionist agricultural communes in Eretz Israel. In 1902, he was drafted into the Russian army, distinguished himself as an exemplary foot soldier in the Russo-Japanese war, which broke out in 1904.

Naively believing that by excellent soldiering he could dispel anti-Semitic attitudes, Trumpeldor was disappointed many times. He remained loyal, nonetheless, to the army, and even after losing an arm, requested to serve again. Posted to East Siberia, he was promoted to the rank of noncommissioned officer and received several decorations for his service.

After the surrender of Port Arthur in 1904, Trumpeldor spent some time in a Japanese prisoner-of-war camp, where he organized a Zionist group for immigration to Eretz Israel. When he was released and returned to Russia, he began to study law in Saint Petersburg. On his vacations he would go to the Tolstoy commune and engage in rural and manual labor. By the time he had finished his studies, he had formulated a plan for emigrating to Eretz Israel and for founding a network of agricultural socialist settlements there.

In 1911 he founded a group that he hoped would implement that plan; he arrived in Eretz Israel in 1912 with six other members of the group. Their attempt at a commune failed and they soon disbanded.

When Turkey joined forces with Germany during World War I, those Jews of Palestine who held foreign citizenship were forced to choose between Turkish citizenship or expulsion. Trumpeldor, refusing the former, was expelled to Alexandria, where he first met Vladmir Jabotinsky (q.v.), who suggested to him the establishment of a Jewish force in the British army to fight the Turks. Having enlisted one hundred men in the plan, they approached the British, who agreed only to let the volunteers serve as mule skinners. Jabotinsky was outraged and abandoned the plan, but Trumpeldor, pressed on. The Zion Mule Corps served bravely in Gallipoli, earning the respect of their superiors for performing their duties even under heavy fire.

Despite the excellent reports, the Mule Corps was disbanded once Gallipoli was evacuated, and failing to have the decision revoked, when the Russian Revolution broke out, Trumpeldor decided that his place was there. His efforts to form a

Jewish fighting force were at first accepted by the Russian government, but then rejected when a peace treaty with Germany was signed in 1918. Meanwhile he had also organized a Jewish self-defense force and was arrested and thrown into prison for these activities. Upon his release he became active in the Zionist Halutz (pioneer) movement. In 1919 he was sent to Palestine as a representative of the movement, to pave the way for a group of settlers who intended to emigrate. Deeply disturbed by splits in the camps of the labor leaders, he became involved in an effort to convince them to form a single and central organization. In the midst of this activity, word reached him of a crisis in Upper Galilee, and he was once again called upon to assist in the defense of the Jewish settlements there. He had planned to remain in Galilee for only a few days and return to his duties with his movement, but a survey of the situation convinced him to remain and take command of Tel Hai on January 1, 1920. On March 1 of that year, armed Arabs attacked Tel Hai, and during negotiations between the Jewish and Arab leaders, Trumpeldor was wounded during an exchange of fire. Toward evening he died, reportedly with the words, "Never mind, it is good to die for our country," on his lips.

After his death his story became an inspiration for pioneering youth groups, particularly the right wing Betar (Berit Trumpeldor, "Trumpeldor Covenant") movement.

P. Lipovetzky, *Joseph Trumpeldor*, 1953.

TSCHERNICHOWSKY, SAUL (1875–1943)
Hebrew poet. Saul Tschernichowsky was born in the village of Michaelovka, in the southern Ukraine, near Crimea. In view of his deep affection for his birthplace, it could be argued that many of the landscapes in his poetry are, in fact, transplantations of Michaelovka and the surrounding countryside.

Unlike other Hebrew writers, his childhood memories were not of misery and fear but of blue skies and the joy of freedom. His native tongue was Russian. When he was nine, two Hebrew teachers arrived in the village and began to instill in the children a love for Hebrew language and literature and for the ancestral Jewish homeland in Eretz Israel.

Displaying his interest in language and in translation even as a boy, Tschernichowsky compiled a Russian-Hebrew dictionary. This love for precision in language and for crossing linguistic borders would later be expressed in his wide-ranging translation activities and in his generation of terminology for the *Dictionary of Medicine and Allied Sciences*, published in Jerusalem in 1934 (together with Dr. A. M. Masie).

From 1890 to 1892, he attended the privately run High School of Commerce in Odessa, where his interests were channeled toward Hebrew language and literature, as Odessa was then a major center of the Hebrew renaissance that was sweeping through

part of the Jewish nation during the late 19th century. Here he learned English, French, German, and later Greek, Latin, and Italian, devouring their literatures voraciously. His life in Odessa was also marked by a series of romantic love affairs, which found expression in a series of love lyrics. Tschernichowsky's early friendship with the scholar and critic Jacob Klausner was an important event in the young poet's life, since Klausner sent two of Tschernichowsky's poems to Hebrew editors: "Be-Halomi" ("In My Dream"), which was subsequently published in the Baltimore-based American-Hebrew periodical *Ha-Pisgah*, and "Massat Nafshi" ("My Ideal"), which would see light in the Cracow journal *Ha-Sharon*. Klausner influenced Tschernichowsky to write only in Hebrew and to abandon any thoughts of becoming a Russian poet.

Tschernichowsky's first published volume of poems, *Visions and Melodies*, appeared in Warsaw in 1898. It was received quite caustically by the critic J. H. Ravnitsky, who took the young Tschernichowsky to task for an allegedly poor Hebrew and for an absence of striking motifs and who felt that the poems were, in fact, not originals at all, but "merely" translations. Ravnitsky later regretted his vicious attack and published a large volume of Tschernichowsky's poems a decade and a half later, in 1914.

Tschernichowsky was a physician by profession, receiving medical degrees from the universities of Heidelberg and Kiev and serving in several communities, including rural districts and the city of Saint Petersburg. In September 1914, soon after

FROM SAUL TSCHERNICHOWSKY'S POETRY

In memory of those fallen in the Ukraine
● There are many like him here, without epitaph, without a mound.
The ox pulling a plow stumbles on him,
The peasant behind the plow swears at him furiously,
And his clearing will be the shelter of the locust.

● In all the world, three precious crowns there be —
Of strength, of Torah, and of beauty are the three.
● Death is where love is not
● Let the time be dark with hatred,
I believe in years beyond
Love at last shall bend the peoples
In an everlasting band.
● The God of might, who conquered Canaan in a whirlwind,
Then bound to him with straps of their tefillin.
● Blessed are the unimportant, as much as the important.

World War I had broken out, he was conscripted and became a medical officer in the Russian army, serving in a hospital in Minsk. For his work at the hospital and on the battlefield, he was awarded a decoration by the Russian government.

Between 1917 and 1919 Tschernichowsky was vice-president of the Russian Red Cross's Sanitary and Statistical Branch. During this period, he translated into Hebrew an anatomy textbook intended for use by the students of the yet-to-be-established Hebrew University of Jerusalem.

In 1922 he moved to Germany and in 1931, Tschernichowsky took up residence in Tel Aviv and was later joined by his wife, of Russian aristocratic background, and his daughter. Although many of his poems deal with biblical themes — Saul is a major figure in his poetry — Tschernichowsky also wrote about rural Jewish life in Russia and about events in contemporary Jewish history, such as the pogroms launched against the Jews of the Ukraine in the wake of World War I. His poetry displays a wealth of genres and metrical experimentations. One critic, Eisig Silberschlag, claims that Tschernichowsky "was as much the father of the Hebrew idyll as Theocritus was the father of the Greek idyll." In addition to a play, *Bar Kokhba*, and several short stories, he wrote poems for children.

He had an abiding interest in Greek literature and thought: Tschernichowsky believed that beauty must take precedence over strength and even over knowledge. His inclination toward secularism became almost a pagan worship of beauty, which sounded a new, and for many a shocking, note in Hebrew literature. His love for Greek culture can be seen in his translations of several Greek classics, such as the *Iliad*, the *Odyssey*, and Plato's *Symposium*. In addition, he translated works from other languages, among them Latin, French, German, English, Serbian, Georgian, Persian, and Icelandic; they include Molière's *Le malade imaginaire*, Goethe's *Reineke Fuchs*, Longfellow's *Evangeline*, and Shakespeare's *Twelfth Night* and *Macbeth*.
E. Silberschlag, *Saul Tschernichowsky: Poet of Revolt*, 1968.

TUCHMAN, BARBARA (1912–1989) U.S. historian; daughter of Maurice Wertheim, the international banker, publisher, and philanthropist, who was president of the American Jewish Committee.

World War I became a reality for her at a very young age while en route with her parents to Constantinople in 1914, on a visit to her grandfather, Henry Morgenthau, Sr., then U.S. ambassador to Turkey. From their Italian ship the family saw an exchange of gunfire between a British warship and two German naval vessels. Many years later the incident featured in *The Guns of August*, her bestseller about World War I.

Her interest in history began with children's history books and continued throughout her college years at Radcliffe College, where she studied history and literature. She was determined to see the

> • I belong to the "How" school rather than the "Why." I am a seeker of the small facts, not the big Explanations; a narrator, not a philosopher.
> • If a man is a writer, everybody tiptoes around past the locked door of the breadwinner. But if you're an ordinary female housewife, people say, "This is just something Barbara wanted to do; it's not professional."
>
> **Barbara Tuchman**

world, and after graduating from Radcliffe, accompanied her grandfather to the World Economic Conference in London. She began to work as a research assistant for the Institute of Pacific Relations in New York, and was sent to its Tokyo branch to help produce an economic handbook of the Pacific area.

Upon her return to New York she began working for the *Nation*, which her father had bought to save it from bankruptcy. Initially clipping newspaper articles, she was soon writing and editing them herself, and in 1937 was sent to Spain to report on the Spanish Civil War.

From Spain she traveled around Europe, working for a while in London as a magazine writer as well as at her own book, *The Lost British Policy*, on British policy toward Spain. She continued working as a journalist when she returned home in 1938.

With the specter of Hitler looming, her husband, Dr. Reginald Tuchman, preferred not to bring children into the world, but as she wrote, "The tyranny of men not being quite as total as today's feminists would have us believe," their first daughter was born nine months later. Two more daughters followed after the war, but she continued to write while raising her family. From 1943 to 1945 she worked for the U.S. Office of War Information. Her second book, *Bible and Sword* (1956), was on relations between Britain and Zionism and expressed her sympathy for the Zionist cause.

The Zimmerman Telegram, appearing two years later, was about the repercussions of a message (intercepted and publicized by the British) which had been sent from Germany to a German diplomat in Mexico, proposing that Mexico reconquer certain territories in the southwestern United States.

Her subsequent book was the Pulitzer Prize-winning *The Guns of August*, an ambitious sketch of the prelude to and first thirty days of World War I, which she described as "the chasm between our world and a world that died forever." She researched her subject thoroughly, driving around the battlefields in a rented Renault sedan, and taking notes on index cards which she carried around in her purse. Notwithstanding its military subject, the book's emphasis on human qualities gave it a popular appeal, and it was made into a documentary film in 1964.

Other books she wrote included *The Proud*

Tower, on the pre-World War I years, including a section on the Dreyfus (q.v.) affair; *Stilwell and the American Experience in China, 1911–45*; *Notes from Asia*; and *The March of Folly*, which covered several historical crises from the fall of Troy to Vietnam.

She preferred history to fiction because she believed that it offered a greater challenge and responsibility to the writer. She adhered to the school that held that historians should try to write history as it actually occurred, although she admitted that this was an unattainable goal. Her idea of heaven was the National Archives and the manuscript division of the Library of Congress. Although she was at times accused of omissions, misinterpretations, and oversimplification, for the most part, critics praised her for her intelligence, clarity and consummate narrative skill. Her last books — *A Distant Mirror: The Calamitous 14th Century* and *The First Salute* — were best-sellers.

TUCKER, RICHARD (1913–1975) American tenor and cantor. Born Reuben Ticker in Brooklyn, New York, he sang as a child in a synagogue choir and then studied voice with Paul Althouse. He began singing on radio and was *hazzan* at Temple Adath Israel, Brooklyn, before turning to opera. Tucker's operatic debut was as Alfredo in Verdi's *La Traviata* with the Salmaggi Opera Company in New York in 1943. He continued to officiate at the Brooklyn Jewish Center until 1967.

In 1945 he made his Metropolitan Opera (New York) debut as Enzo in *La Gioconda*. This was the first of his 499 performances in New York and 225 on tour with the company in the course of thirty seasons, singing above all the Italian and some French repertoire. His most frequent roles at the Metropolitan were Rodolpho in Puccini's *La Bohème*, and Don José in Bizet's *Carmen*. At his twenty-fifth anniversary gala at the Metropolitan Tucker was partnered by famous opera stars Joan Sutherland, Renata Tebaldi, and Leontyne Price.

Tucker especially enjoyed singing the role of the Jewish father Eleazar in *La Juive* by the French composer Fromental, Halévy. Tucker sang the role in concert in New York in 1964 and on the stage in New Orleans (1973) and Barcelona (1974), toward the end of his career.

In 1947 Tucker made his European debut at the Verona Arena, Italy, once again singing Enzo, in a production of *La Gioconda* that also marked the Italian debut of Maria Callas in the title role. Tucker continued singing in the major opera houses of the world, including Covent Garden, London, La Scala, Milan, and the Colon, Buenos Aires. In 1973 Tucker made his last Israeli tour, performing the role of the gypsy Manrico in Verdi's *Il Trovatore* with the Israel Philharmonic Orchestra, under the baton of Zubin Mehta. He is remembered as a tenor with a vibrant sound, relentless intensity of projection, and musical perfectionism.

Tucker was always a very generous colleague.

However, when the young Italian tenor Franco Corelli arrived at the Metropolitan, Tucker was somewhat taken aback by the attention his new colleague/rival was receiving. When Corelli approached Tucker for assistance with a particular aria, Tucker allegedly replied: "To sing it right, you have to be Jewish." Tucker never lost his love for cantoral music, occasionally officiating and making records of *hazzanut*.

Tucker died suddenly in Kalamazoo, Michigan, while on a concert tour. Tucker is the only singer whose funeral took place on the stage of the Metropolitan opera. He was the brother-in-law of American tenor Jan Peerce (q.v.).
J. A. Drake, *Richard Tucker*, 1984.

TUCKER, SOPHIE   (1884–1966) U.S. entertainer. Known as "the last of the red-hot mamas," Sophie Abuza was born in a peasant home somewhere in Russian Poland. Her mother was en route, with her two-year-old son, to join her husband in America.

Sophie spent the first eight years of her life in Boston. The family (now with four children) then moved to Hartford, Connecticut, where her parents opened a restaurant and rooming house, serving kosher meals for twenty-five and fifty cents. The young Sophie would rise before dawn to prepare lunches for the workers. To ward off the cold, she had to pad her dress with newspapers. Before the school day began, she would scrape the frost off salami, peel vegetables, run errands, and do the housework. This grueling experience was to stand her in good stead in later years on the hard road to stardom. From the show people who frequented the restaurant, Sophie developed a passion for the stage. Dubbed in school "the girl with personality," and being possessed of a powerful voice and a good ear, she was called upon to lead the singing. Before long she was winning prizes at outdoor concerts and entertaining at the restaurant, belting out tearjerkers for tips.

Shortly after receiving her high school diploma, she married Louis Tuck and was soon a mother. When she realized that her husband was content to live off her family while earning a pittance, she insisted on a separation, which was unthinkable at the time in Orthodox circles. For her it was a case of bitter history repeating itself, her father having gambled away much of her mother's hard-earned money. She vowed she would earn enough to extricate her parents from the restaurant business, buy them a home, put her younger brother through law school, give her son a fine education, and provide her sister Anna (in whose care she left her son) with a splendid wedding. She also swore to return to Hartford one day in triumph. All these ambitions were eventually fulfilled. (She even arranged for Cantor Joseph Rosenblatt [q.v.] to officiate at Anna's nuptials.)

Sophie Tucker left for New York with one hundred dollars in her pocket. From dingy lodgings she made the rounds of Tin Pan Alley in search of openings. Desperate at the lack of results, she coaxed her way into her first job, singing for her supper at the Cafe Monopol, and changing her surname to the more felicitous Tucker.

Considered "too big and ugly" for the stage as a white singer, she appeared for some time in black-face. In 1909 she did a short stint in the Ziegfeld Follies between slots all over the United States in burlesque shows. The turning point in her career came in 1914, when she was a sensation at the Palace Theater in New York. She was accompanied at the piano by Frank Westphal, who was to become her second husband, although she had sworn — wisely, it transpired — never to marry into the "profession." A third marriage, to Al Lackey many years later, fared better.

Her sixty-two-year career embraced burlesque, vaudeville, night-club circuits (in England, Holland, Austria, and France, as well as the United States), Hollywood movies (including *Broadway Melody* and *Follow the Boys*), and Broadway musicals. In 1938 she played in the long-running musical, *Leave It to Me*, scored by Cole Porter. That same year she became president of the American Federation of Actors.

It was Sophie Tucker who introduced jazz to Britain. She was a phenomenal success there and was invited back many times. Members of the nobility were among her closest friends, and she was held in respect and affection by the royal family. One of the highlights of her career was a royal command performance. At the request of the lord mayor of London, she organized and performed at a concert in aid of the King George V Memorial Fund. (It turned out to be an emotion-laden event, coinciding as it did with the announcement of Edward VIII's abdication.)

Even when she had reached the top of the ladder, she remained proud of her Jewishness, returning home whenever possible to celebrate the Jewish festivals. Wherever she happened to be, she would observe family *yahrzeits* (memorial days) and visited Israel in her later years.

She worked into her 78th year, retaining her inimitable brassy style and naturalness. She immortalized "My Yiddishe Mama" and "Some of These Days," which became her signature tune.
S. Tucker (in collaboration with D. Giles), *Some of These Days*, 1945.

TUWIM, JULIAN (1894–1953) Polish poet. Born in Lodz to an assimilated family who had emigrated from Lithuania, he was educated in a Russian high school, and his first poems, written as a student, were in Russian.

It was while he was studying at the University of Warsaw, that he began to be known as a successful Polish poet. He published a futurist manifesto that was much discussed. Soon he was contributing regularly to the Polish monthly, *Skamander*, which featured the best young Polish poets of the day. As he began to publish more frequently, he was recognized as an innovator and as one of the leaders of the Polish modernist movement in poetry.

Tuwin wrote poems (including children's poems), satires, and musical comedies. His love of the Polish language also led him to research Polish folklore and idiom and to translate French poets, such as Arthur Rimbaud, and Russian poets, such as Aleksandr Pushkin, into Polish. For a time he was literary manager of the Polish theater in Warsaw, for which he adapted many plays. He also served as the chairman of the Association of Polish Poets.

Initially, he modeled himself on Walt Whitman. Tuwim's poems were youthful, enthusiastic, and optimistic. At a later stage, however, he adopted a more refined style that demonstrated a skilled mastery of language while reflecting a more cynical view of life in Poland, particularly of the unjust sufferings of the ordinary man. Later still, as his anger grew, he became even more openly critical of the Polish regime, which he berated for oppressing and exploiting the poor.

Tuwim did not hide his Jewish origins but did not identify greatly with his background. He was chairman of the Friends of the Hebrew University in Warsaw and a member of the Jewish Committee for Israel-Polish Friendship. As an exile during the years of World War II, he often spoke out against the suffering of European Jewry.

In September 1939, he escaped from Nazi-occupied Warsaw to Romania, from Romania to France, and from France to Brazil. In Rio de Janeiro, in 1940, he began to write a lengthy poem about his childhood, "Flowers of Poland," which was completed four years later in New York (published in 1949). During the same period he also published *We Polish Jews* about his dual nature as a Pole and as a Jew.

Immediately after the end of World War II, Tuwim returned to Poland where he was welcomed by the new Polish regime. There he adopted a Jewish orphan and Holocaust survivor. Once more he found himself at the center of the literary and cultural life of Poland, and a collection of his poems, published in 1949 won him a state prize. He did not publish many new works, but was involved instead in compiling an anthology of revolutionary poetry by lesser-known poets of the 19th century. When Tuwim died, the Polish government gave him a state funeral.

Many of his works were published in Poland including *Words Bathed in Song* (1926), which portrayed the emptiness of urban life, and *Locomotive* (1938), poems for children. His poems have been translated into many languages and collections of his poems have appeared in Czech, Hungarian, Chinese, Russian, and Hebrew.
H. Schwartz and A. Rudolph (eds.), *Voices Within the Ark: The Modern Jewish Poets*, 1980.

TZARA, TRISTAN (born Sami Rosenstein; 1896–1963) Romanian and French poet; a founder of dadaism. Born in Moinesti, Romania, Tzara's works were renowned both in his native land and later in his adopted country, France. The nascent symbolist style of his poems in Romanian, which

late prophet, Tzara proclaimed the collapse of traditional humanism and the birth of a "new man." The dada man has no depth; he is stripped of accursed memory, his language is destroyed. Tzara insists that spontaneity is man's only hope of truth: "Thought comes to be in the mouth." Some collections of this period are *Vingt-cinq* (1918) and *Cinéma, Calendriers du coeur abstrait* (1920).

As the avant-garde turned to surrealism, Tzara joined forces with that group. His writing became more contained and sober, and in 1931 he published *L'homme approximatif* and his revolutionary essay, "Sur la situation de la poésie." In 1935 he broke with the surrealist group and joined the Communist party. Pursued by the Vichy regime, he continued to write clandestinely and was active in the French underground during World War II.

Among his later works are: *Où boivent les loups* (1932), *L'antitête* (essys, 1933), *Le coeur à gaz* (1946), *La fuite* (a drama, 1947), *La face intérieure* (1953), and *Parler seul* (1950). Many contemporary artists and friends of Tzara illustrated his writings, including Henri Matisse, Georges Braque, Fernand Léger, Wassily Kandinsky, and Pablo Picasso.

R. Lacôte and G. Haldas, *Tristan Tzara*, 1952.
F. Picabia, *Seven Dada Manifestos and Lampisteries*, 1977.
M. Tison-Braun, *Tristan Tzara inventeur de l'homme nouveau*, 1957.

Tristan Tzara. Drawing by Fernand Léger, 1948.

first appeared in 1912, was a presentiment of the avant-garde literary movement he was to found. He greatly influenced an entire generation of Romanian poets.

Hans Arp recounts that "Dada was born on the lips of Tristan Tzara at six P.M. on February 8th, 1916, in a Zurich café." In search of a name for their visions of literary and artistic iconoclasm, the twenty-year-old opened a dictionary at random and discovered the completely irrelevant word "dada." The dada revolt, "halfway between despair and utopia," was obsessed with the meaning of life, and chose the most provocative means to make itself heard. Considered dada's most articu-

Art, when time was in its infancy, was prayer. Wood and stone were truth. In man I see the moon, plants, stars, metal, fish. ... The hand is strong, great. The mouth contains the power of darkness, invisible matter, goodness, fear, wisdom, creation, fire.

Tristan Tzara

U

ULLSTEIN Family of German publishers. **Leopold Ullstein** (1826—1899) founded the newspaper empire that bore his name. Born in Fürth, Bavaria, Leopold left his father's paper business at the age of twenty-two and went to Berlin. In 1877 he bought the failing *Neues Berliner Tageblatt*, changed its name to *Deutsche Union*, and later merged it with the *Berliner Allgemeiner Zeitung* and the *Berliner Bürgerpost*. The new paper reached a circulation of 40,000 and made its owner one of the largest publishers in Germany. It reflected Leopold's progressive political views.

Ullstein's five sons all entered the family business. **Hans** (1859–1935) was its legal adviser; **Louis** (1863–1933) headed the firm after his father's death; **Franz** (1868–1945) was editorial director and the guiding force behind the company; **Rudolf** (1873–1964) was the company's technical director; and **Hermann** (1875–1943) was manager of the firm's magazine and book departments.

In 1898 the three eldest sons founded the *Berliner Morgenpost*, which became the largest German daily, with a circulation of 600,000. They also managed the *Berliner Zeitung am Mittag*, the first daily to be sold by street vendors rather than by subscription. They owned numerous other newspapers, picture and news services, radio stations, and movie studios. From 1894 they published the *Berliner Illustrierte Zeitung*, a magazine with a circulation of two million, and numerous other magazines in a variety of fields.

The Nazis forced the family to sell the publishing empire at a fraction of its value. After World War II the Americans rebuilt the Ullstein factory in West Berlin and appointed Rudolph as chairman. By 1957 the Ullstein-owned *Berliner Zeitung* and *Morgenpost* had the largest circulation in West Berlin. However, in 1960, controlling interest in the firm was sold to Axel Springer and the family's role in the business ended.

H. Ullstein, *The Rise and Fall of the House of Ullstein*, 1943.

USSISHKIN, ABRAHAM MENAHEM MENDEL

(1863–1941) Zionist leader. He was born in Dubrovno in the Mogilev district, Russia, to a Hasidic family, who gave him an Orthodox education. In 1871 the family moved to Moscow where he received a secular education. He continued to study of Hebrew and avidly read the works of the writers of the Haskalah (Jewish Enlightenment) movement. Shocked by the Russian pogroms against the Jews, Ussishkin became involved in the creation of the Moscow branch of the early Zionist movement Hoveve Zion. In 1882 he entered the Technological Institute in Moscow where he founded a Jewish students' society.

In 1884 he was one of the founders of the Moscow student Zionist group, the Bene Zion society, and in 1887 was elected as a delegate to the Hoveve Zion conference held at Druzkeniki. It was here that he was revealed as one of the outstanding younger leaders of the movement.

Ussishkin joined the Bene Moshe society founded by Ahad Ha-Am (q.v.) in 1889, with the aim of ensuring personal dedication to the spiritual renaissance of the Jewish people as preparation for settlement in Eretz Israel. He visited Eretz Israel for the first time in 1891.

Ussishkin settled in Yekaterinoslav (later Dnepropetrovsk) where he soon became one of the leaders of Russian Zionists. He advocated the establishment of a mass movement that would unite the Jews of eastern and western Europe and pave the way for settlement in Eretz Israel.

In 1896 Ussishkin first met Theodor Herzl (q.v.) in Vienna and accepted Herzl's offer to help organize the first Zionist congress. He was elected its Hebrew secretary and took part in the debates. Upon his return to Russia, Ussishkin plunged into Zionist activity. At the second Zionist Congress (1898) he was elected to the Zionist General Council of which he remained a member for the rest of his life. He was active in the dissemination of Hebrew literature and was energetic in supporting the publication of Hebrew periodicals in eastern Europe.

In 1903, with Herzl's blessing, Ussishkin went to Eretz Israel on behalf of the Geulah company founded by Russian Zionists to purchase land to be parceled out and sold to settlers. He organized a three-day conference in Zikhron Ya'akov attended by seventy representatives of the Jewish settlements at which he advocated the organization of the Jewish community in the country. Despite the enthusiastic report he delivered on his return to Russia, there was no practical outcome to this conference. However, a meeting of sixty teachers that he organized in Zikhron Ya'akov succeeded in establishing the Hebrew Teachers' Association.

On his return to Europe, Ussishkin discovered that the sixth Zionist congress had passed a resolution to send a commission to Uganda to examine the British government's offer to establish an autonomous Jewish colony there. He decided to fight this decision and sent to the congress delegates an open letter expressing his strong objection to the resolution. Angered by this attack, Herzl penned a strong reply castigating Ussishkin for publicly criticizing a resolution taken by the body of which he was a member. Undaunted, Ussishkin convened a conference of an anti-Uganda faction called Zionists for Zion and successfully led the struggle for the abandonment of this scheme at the seventh Zionist congress. In 1904 he published *Our Program* in which he formulated his plan for pragmatic Zionism — a synthesis of political and practical Zionism. He pointed out that the Jewish peo-

ple must prepare itself to be able to set up an independent political, cultural and economic center. He proposed the establishment of a Jewish labor brigade that would send unmarried Jews to Palestine to serve for three years in agricultural work. This would be considered as their military service on behalf of the Jewish people.

In 1919 Ussishkin attended the Paris Peace Conference which he addressed in Hebrew, the first time the language was used at an international conference. Later that year, Ussishkin settled in Palestine where he was appointed head of the Zionist commission which led the struggle of the Jewish community to establish the national home.

Ussishkin's major contribution to the practical development of Palestine was made during the years 1923–1941 when he was chairman of the Jewish National Fund. In this capacity he was instrumental in raising funds throughout the Jewish world to purchase and develop large tracts of land throughout Palestine.

J. Goldstein, *Russian Zionism. The Formative Years*, (Hebrew) 1991.
D. Vital, *Zionism. The Formative Years*, 1982.

V

VAMBERY, ARMINIUS (1832–1918) Hungarian traveler and orientalist. He was born Hermann Vamberger in Saint Georghen, Hungary (now Juf pri Bratislava, Czechoslovakia), to poor Orthodox parents. Soon after his birth, his father, a Talmud scholar, died in a cholera epidemic.

After Vambery's mother remarried, the family moved to Dun Szerdahely (now Dunjaska Streda, Czechoslovakia). He was congenitally lame and all his life he walked with a pronounced limp. In the few years that he was allowed the luxury of school, he proved to be a willing and able student. His talent for languages was early apparent and by age eight he could read and translate Hebrew and read and write Hungarian and German. Due to the poverty of his family, he was forced to leave school at age twelve to become an apprentice dressmaker. He soon left that position to become a tutor to an innkeeper's son, a boy his own age. When he earned enough money for an education, his mother enrolled him in Latin classes at a Catholic school. Although she was an Orthodox Jew, she believed her son needed a more practical education than a Jewish school could offer. Vambery, having to rely on the charity of the Jewish community for his room and board, suffered rejection from many of the Jews who were suspicious of a Jewish boy studying heretical subjects in the Catholic school.

He continued his studies at the Benedictine College at Pressburg (Bratislava) and later enrolled in a Protestant school because of its more liberal attitude toward Jews, supporting himself as a tutor of languages. Apart from Latin, he began to study several other languages on his own, including French, Italian, Czech, Turkish, Russian, and Arabic and soon began think of traveling to the East.

In 1854, with help from his friend Baron Joseph Eotvos, he was able to realize his dream and set off for Constantinople. There he maintained himself as a tutor of European languages, eventually obtaining work in the houses of prominent Turkish officials, including Husain Da'im Pasha (who named him "Rashid," the brave), and later became the private secretary to the statesman, Mehmed Fuad Pasha. His Turkish improved rapidly and he began to translate the works of Turkish historians into Hungarian. His work in this field brought him to the attention of the Hungarian Academy of Sciences, who made him a corresponding member and awarded him money for an expedition into Central Asia to study the relationship between Hungarian and the languages spoken there.

He had now acquired a knowledge of Persian and other Oriental (Near Eastern and Central Asian) languages and had studied in the *Medresseh* (Islamic college) in Constantinople, claiming to be the first European to have done so. Though he never officially converted, he had an excellent knowledge of the practices of Islam and in outward appearance was able to pass for an authentic Turkish effendi, though he later wrote in his memoirs, "My adopted Turkdom, my pseudo-Oriental character, were all confined to external things, in my inmost being I was filled through and through with the spirit of the West." In March 1862, with enough money to take him to Teheran, he hired an Armenian muleteer and set off on his adventure. By the time he was ready to leave Teheran to continue his journey, he had assumed the guise of a Sunni dervish from Baghdad by the name of Rashid Effendi. Joining a caravan of pilgrims returning from Meshed he traveled through Armenia, Persia, and Turkestan, returning to Constantinople in 1864. Though tested time and again, he was able to maintain his disguise and thereby gained access to places that were prohibited to Europeans. He was not allowed to take any notes in the presence of his fellow travelers, but the memory of his experiences were sufficiently vivid to allow him to write a book about them, *Travels in Central Asia* (1864), that won him instant fame and popularity, especially with the British. The British had more than just a passing interest in his observations, because of their struggle with the Russians for control of Central Asia and Vambery, who had pro-British sympathies, proved a valuable source of information to them.

He returned to Hungary in 1865 and after becoming a Protestant, was appointed professor of Oriental languages at the University of Budapest. He continued to write articles and books on Oriental history, politics, language, and culture, including *Wanderings and Adventures in Persia* (1867),

> I have met one of the most interesting of men in this limping, seventy-year-old Hungarian Jew who doesn't know whether he is more Turk than Englishman, writes books in German, speaks twelve languages with equal mastery, and has professed five religions, in two of which he has served as a priest. With an intimate knowledge of so many religions he naturally had to become an atheist. He told me 1,001 tales of the Orient and of his intimacy with the Sultan. He told me he was a secret agent of Turkey and of England and that the professorship in Hungary was merely window-dressing after the long torment he had suffered in a society hostile to Jews. He told me, "I don't want any money; I am a rich man. I can't eat gold beefsteaks. If I help you, its for the Zionist cause."
>
> He kept telling me incidents from his life. Through Disraeli he became an agent for England. In Turkey he began as a singer in a coffee house; eighteen months later he was the Grand Vizier's confidant. He eats at the Sultan's table — on intimate terms, with his fingers from the bowl — but he cannot get the idea of poison out of his mind. And a hundred other things, equally picturesque."
>
> **From the Diaries of Theodor Herzl.**

Manners in Oriental Countries (1976), and *Western Culture in Eastern Lands* (1906). In 1885 he wrote his autobiography in English. He served as an adviser to Britain on Indian and Asiatic policy and came into contact with many of the elite of British society, including Edward VII (then prince of Wales). Though he considered himself a free thinker, Vambery was a supporter of Zionism in its early stages and introduced Theodor Herzl (q.v.) to the Sultan Abdul-Hamid in 1901, and after Herzl's death, his successor, David Wolfsohn, continued to consult Vambery on Zionist political problems. He retired from the University of Budapest in 1905, but continued to write.
L. Adler and R. Dalby, *The Dervish of Windsor Castle*, 1979.

VARNHAGEN, RAHEL (1771–1833) The most influential of the Berlin salon hostesses. She was born Rahel Levin to a wealthy Jewish family, and died the wife of the Prussian diplomat and author, Karl August Varnhagen von Ense. For over a generation, interrupted only by the Napoleonic occupation of Berlin after 1806, her salons were a pleasant and informal meeting place for aristorcrats and scholars, men of enlightenment and romanticists, statesmen of the Holy Alliance and radicals of *Jungdeutschland*. A word from her made or unmade reputations. In her circle, Goethe, whom she met in Carlsbad in 1795, found his greatest understanding and most ardent admirers before he was generally acknowledged to be Germany's supreme literary genius. A "Rahel" cult developed during her lifetime and she is still considered the most brilliant Jewish woman of the era. Heinrich Heine (q.v.), who met literary celebrities at her salon, was stimulated by her to publish his first collection of poems in 1821. He referred to her as the most gifted woman of the universe. Thomas Carlyle introduced her to English readers.

Her Jewish origin was a source of embarrassment to her. Judeo-German (western Yiddish) was still spoken in her Orthodox parents' home (in her early years, Rahel wrote letters to her family in Yiddish). The surge of the Enlightenment, ushered in by Moses Mendelssohn (q.v.), led her to feel ashamed of her background and she yearned to escape from it. After the death of her father in 1790, the Jewishness of the family waned. Her brother Ludwig, a dramatist, was baptized a decade later and exchanged his Jewish-sounding name Levin for Robert. She, too, had no objection to baptism, but refrained from it because she was financially dependent upon her mother. After her mother's death in 1809, she also assumed the name of Robert. Count Karl von Finkenstein, to whom she was engaged in 1795, broke off the engagement after four years because his aristocratic Prussian family objected to his alliance with a Jew. She was next engaged to the secretary of the Spanish legation to Prussia, Don Raphael d'Urquijo, but this engagement was also broken off after a few years. In 1814 she finally married and underwent conversion to Protestantism. She was then forty-three and her husband, Karl August Varnhagen von Ense, was barely thirty years old.

Her early dissatisfaction with her Jewish origin

Rahel Varnhagen, 1817.

gave way at the end of her life to a happy acceptance of her ancestry. Five days before her death she wrote: "That which for so long a period of my life seemed my greatest disgrace, my bitterest pain, namely to have been born a Jewess, I would not now dispense with at any price."

H. Arendt, *Rahel Varnhagen: The Life of a Jewess*, 1957.

E. Key, *Rahel Varnhagen*, 1913.

S. Liptzin, *Germany's Stepchildren*, 1944.

VEKSLER, VLADIMIR IOSIFOVICH (1907–1966) Soviet nuclear physicist best known for his work on the theory of particle accelerators — machines for the acceleration of particles to the very high energies at which they can split the atomic nucleus ("smash" the atom) or interact with each other to form exotic new particles.

Veksler was born in Zhitomir in the Ukraine. After first working as an apparatus assembler in a factory, Veksler moved to Moscow and, in 1931, gained the diploma of electrical engineering. His early research was in the field of X-rays. In 1936 he was appointed to the Lebedev Institute of Physics in Moscow where, initially, he studied cosmic rays (naturally occurring high-energy particles). He participated in expeditions to the Pamir Mountains of Central Asia, and there discovered a new type of interaction between high-energy particles and atomic nuclei.

In 1944 Veksler made his great contribution to science with his proposal of the principle of phase stability, a discovery that initiated the postwar growth of a new and far more powerful generation of particle accelerators — synchrotons. The essential feature of the principle was its ability to sidestep limitations inherent in the then-conventional accelerators — cyclotrons — when particles reached such high speeds that considerations of Einstein's theory of relativity became significant.

In a remarkable case of scientific parallelism, E. M. McMillan of the University of California independently and simultaneously arrived at the same conclusions and his name is frequently coupled with Veksler's. The two soon recognized what had happened and, aware of their mutual good faith, they avoided a dispute over priority and became, and remained, good friends.

Following this discovery, Veksler devoted himself to accelerator research and, until his death, the largest Soviet accelerators were designed and constructed under his direction. In 1959 he was awarded the Lenin and State prizes for his contribution to Soviet accelerator research.

In 1956 when the Joint Institute for Nuclear Research was established in Dubna as a cooperative venture of the communist-bloc countries, Veksler was invited to become director of its high-energy laboratory. He became active in international cooperation in nuclear research, speaking out publicly in praise of U.S. scientists even when East-West tension was high. His services were recognized abroad with the award, in 1963, of the U.S.

Atoms for Peace Prize (jointly with McMillan). In his acceptance address Veksler expressed his belief that "the time has already come when not only in the cosmos but also in our physics here on earth the collaboration of our countries for the penetration into the depths of the microworld will be particularly fruitful."

VILNA GAON See Elijah ben Solomon Zalman

VISHNIAC, ROMAN (1897–1990) Photographer. Born into a wealthy Jewish family in Saint Petersburg, he early developed a passion for the living world and at the age of seven photographed the leg of a cockroach through the eyepiece of a microscope. He obtained a doctorate in zoology at Moscow University and later took a government course in medicine designed to ease the shortage of doctors during World War I. After the Russian Revolution Vishniac lived in Latvia and then in Berlin, where he continued his work in microphotography.

When the University of Berlin, under Nazi rule, refused to grant him his doctorate in art, he began an eight-year journey through the Jewish communities of Poland, Lithuania, Latvia, Hungary, Czechoslovakia, and Germany, recording their lives. He did not know it, but this was to be the last opportunity for capturing the everyday life of east European Jewry. Vishniac later referred to his feeling of foreboding: "I felt that the world was about to be cast into the shadow of Nazism and that the outcome could be the annihilation of a people who had no spokesman to record their plight." He portrayed the everyday life with an eye for the domestic and the religious, ranging from family prayer to bagel-making to the haunting images of yeshiva students. He often participated in the experience, hauling buckets of water across a mile of cobbled street and then up three flights of stairs, before photographing a water carrier in Lublin. In Germany he sometimes even dressed in Nazi uniform so as to be able to record historic moments with his hidden camera — the 1933 SA book burning in front of the Reichstag or the orgy of plunder and destruction on Kristallnacht.

After the Nazis invaded Poland Vishniac escaped to France and was interned for a time in a concentration camp before escaping to the United States with as many negatives as he could stitch in his clothes. Of the 16,000 negatives he had taken, only 2,000 survived, hidden in a French farmhouse throughout the war.

He reached New York in December 1940, and at first earned his living as a portrait photographer, but soon his microphotography was recognized and subjects such as "Frost on Leaves" and "The forty-two Blue Eyes of the Scallop" attracted attention. Eventually he became a professor of humanities at the Pratt Institute, Brooklyn.

Vishniac's books of Jewish life in pre-war Europe won acclaim, notably *Polish Jews* (1947), *Life of the Six Millions* (1969), and *A Vanished World* (1983). A major exhibition of his historical and scientific work was shown in New York in 1971. Throughout his life he was reluctant to describe his prewar technical achievement, without miniature or disguised cameras (one of his problems was the reluctance of religious Jews to be photographed). He often used a Leica and a Rolliflex in natural light and made great efforts to win the confidence of his subjects.

His micrographs of minute living organisms have been extensively shown in museums and medical schools. Among his specialities were cytoplasmic circulation in microscopic algae as related to photosynthesis and the formation of thrombosis in blood vessels. He also pioneered in moving microphotography.

VISSER, LODEWIJK ERNST (1871–1942)
Dutch jurist and communal leader. The son of an old Dutch Jewish family, Visser was born in Amsersfoort. Educated as a lawyer, he was prevented from fulfilling his ambition to become a diplomat because he was Jewish. Visser was appointed general prosecutor in Amsterdam and judge of the district court in 1903. In 1915 he was named as a judge of the High Court of Holland and in 1939 he became president of the High Court. As an authority on commercial law, Visser helped draft the 1928 Dutch company law. He was vice-chairman of the Royal Commission on Civil Legislation and a member of the Netherlands Privy Council.

Visser helped Jewish refugees from eastern Europe at the end of World War I and was one of the founders of the Jewish Aid Committee for German Jews in 1933. For many years he was chairman of the executive of the Keren Hayesod in Holland.

In May 1940, on the day the Germans invaded Holland, he appeared in the High Court in his full regalia and opened the session with a speech in which he condemned the "treacherous attack." In November 1940, he, like all other Jewish state officials, was dismissed. He objected to and refused to accept the identity cards, marked with the letter J,

that the Germans issued to the Jews, lodging a protest to both the German and Dutch authorities. A symbol of Jewish resistance, he tried to help Jews who had been arrested by the Nazis and was part of the general resistance, contributing regularly to the resistance newspaper, *Het Parool*. He strongly opposed the Jewish Council for its collaboration and wrote to its president: "It is possible that in the end the occupier will have his way with us but it is our duty as Dutchmen and as Jews to do everything we can to thwart him and to prevent anything that might smooth his path."

After the Nazis desecrated the synagogue in The Hague, Visser, who had become president of the community although not a practicing Jew, walked to synagogue on the Sabbath through the streets of The Hague wearing his Sabbath clothes and carrying his prayer book and prayer shawl.

On February 14, 1942, he was notified by the president of the Jewish Council that if he did not cease his anti-German activities, he would be sent to a concentration camp. Visser wrote in reply: "I have taken note of what you say and am quite overcome by the humiliation which you, who are well aware of the historical importance of these measures, have brought about." Three days later Visser died. His wife and son perished in concentration camps. The square in front of the Sephardic synagogue in Amsterdam was named after him in 1968.

J. A. Polak, *Leven en werken van mr. L. E. Visser*, 1974.

VITAL, HAYYIM (1542–1620) Mystic. He was
the subject of many legends and was regarded as a wonder-worker to whom many turned to exorcize evil spirits. He was probably born in Safed, in Eretz Israel, where his father was a scribe. He attended Talmudic academies in Safed and in 1564 began to study Kabbalah, initially according to the system

Allegoric picture from The Tree of Life *by Hayyim Vital. From an 18th-century manuscript.*

From Visser's speech at a meeting to protest the Nuremburg Laws, 1935

For many centuries, our ancestors suffered repression and violence, as have no other men, for the sake of what they considered was their ultimate blessing. Throughout, they preserved their integrity, their pride, their honor. With heads held high, they stood firm, no matter what storms were raging around them. And why could they do this? Because deep in their hearts they were convinced of the truth of the Latin injunction *Spernere se sperni*, their despisers to despise. Those who can do so are safe from calumny.

of Moses Cordovero (q.v.). He was also interested in other esoteric subjects and spent two years studying alchemy. The turning point in his life was the arrival in Safed of Isaac Luria (q.v.). During the two years Luria spent there before his death, Vital was his main disciple. After Luria's death it was Vital who organized Luria's teachings in written form and developed them according to his own interpretation. He did all he could to prevent other disciples of Luria from producing their own versions of his teachings and he gathered a circle who accepted his authority. In 1575, twelve of Luria's disciples signed a pledge to study Lurianic Kabbalah only with Vital and not to prompt him to reveal more than he thought proper.

In 1577 Vital moved to Jerusalem, where he served as rabbi and head of an academy until 1585. He then returned to Safed for six years. During this period, he had a serious illness, and while he lay unconscious, certain scholars bribed his brother to allow them to copy six hundred pages of Vital's manuscripts, which they proceeded to circulate. From 1592, Vital lived mainly in Jerusalem, but frequently visited Safed, and from 1598 until his death he lived in Damascus. From 1604, he suffered from poor eyesight and at times was blind. While in Damascus, he assembled autobiographical material, including his dreams. He was convinced that the spirit of the Messiah, son of Joseph, had passed from Luria to himself.

Vital wrote prolifically; many of his works were on Talmudic subjects, but few survive. His *Etz haHayyim* ("Tree of Life") is accepted as the basic work on the teachings of Luria.

G. Scholem, *Kabbalah*, 1974.

VOGEL, JULIUS (1835–1899) Prime minister of New Zealand; knighted 1875. Born in the East End of London, after the death of his parents Julius spent most of his childhood at the home of his West Indian grandfather, a wealthy merchant. Because of his delicate health, he was educated at home until age thirteen and then attended London University School. At sixteen Vogel went to work in the London office of his grandfather's firm, but, as his interests turned to the Australian gold fields, he studied at the Royal School of Mines, where he gained a certificate in smelting and assaying.

In 1852 Vogel went to Australia, where he set up business as an assayer, but in 1854 his firm was dissolved. Vogel then began a career in journalism and wrote for and edited several Victorian newspapers. His interest in local politics led him to bid for a seat in the Victoria legislative assembly, but after being defeated he moved to New Zealand and settled in the South Island city of Otago in 1861.

He turned completely to journalism and founded the *Otago Daily Times*, New Zealand's first daily, which he edited until 1868, turning it into one of the country's leading newspapers.

Vogel was elected to the Otago provincial council in 1863, and soon was at the forefront of agitation for the political separation of the South Island from the North Island. Toward the end of 1866 he became provincial treasurer and in September of the same year was elected unopposed to the central government. The first Jew in the House of Representatives, he objected to religion being taught in schools. His main concern in the national assembly was to uphold the interests of the provinces and gold fields. He was invited by William Fox to join his cabinet as colonial treasurer. To procure the funds to open the country to settlement, Vogel negotiated loans with the British government for the construction of roads and railways.

Vogel was to become notorious for his travels and for his good living, as his ample figure plainly showed. He was well-known for his tremendous appetite and for the quantities he could drink. His expansive nature was also seen in his love of gambling. He was short, stocky, and unprepossessing in looks, his squarish face adorned with a long black beard. Vogel was a forceful speaker and had an insatiable capacity for work. Although he easily won friends, he also acquired many foes, some of whom called him "Jew-lius Rex."

He was prime minister (1873–1875), and also held the offices of postmaster-general, commissioner of customs, and telegraph commissioner for most of the period up to 1876, and for a short time was also minister of immigration.

From 1876 to 1881 he was agent-general in London. During this period he came under fire from the government in New Zealand when he stood, unsuccessfully, for the Conservative party in the 1880 British elections and became involved in a scandal regarding his role in the New Zealand Agricultural Company, which sold land to prospective immigrants.

Vogel was back in New Zealand in 1884, and again became colonial treasurer in the government, but in spite of his financial wizardry was unable to stave off depression, and in 1887 the government was ousted.

Vogel instituted a public works and immigration scheme and the government life insurance bill, which enabled settlers to take out insurance locally. He arranged for a steamer link with Great Britain via San Francisco. He was a strong supporter of women's franchise, but this was introduced only in 1893. Vogel also continually pressed Britain to annex some of the Pacific islands, including Samoa, which was needed as a coaling station for trading and security, but the Colonial Office refused to accede to his request. He was considered to have been New Zealand's first outstanding politician and statesman, a man of vision far ahead of his times.

Vogel left for England in 1888, never to return. He spent the last eleven years of his life writing and making speeches, suffering from increasing ill health and poverty. His writings included *Great Britain and Her Colonies* (1865) and *New Zealand and the South-Sea Islands* (1878). Later in life he wrote a prophetic novel *2000 A.D. or Woman's Destiny*.

W. Gisborn, *New Zealand Rulers and Statesmen from 1840–1879*, 1897.
R. M. Burdon, *The Life and Times of Sir Julius Vogel*, 1948
R. Dalziel, *Sir Julius Vogel*, 1968.
L. M. Goldman, *The History of the Jews in New Zealand*, 1960.

VOLTERRA, VITO   (1860–1940) Italian mathematician. Born in Ancona to an ancient Italian Jewish family, he spent much of his youth in Florence. A precocious child, at the age of thirteen he was working on ballistic problems; after reading Jules Verne's novel *From the Earth to the Moon* he worked out the trajectory of a gun's projectile in the combined gravitational field of the earth and the moon; forty years later he was to demonstrate the veracity of his childhood solution in a course of lectures at the Sorbonne.

As his family had little money, they urged him to follow a commercial career, but he succeeded in pursuing his interest in the sciences. The physicist Antonio Roiti nominated him an assistant in the physics laboratory at the Univeristy of Florence even before Volterra was enrolled as a student. By the age of twenty-three he had already become a full professor of mechanics at the University of Pisa. He moved to Turin and then to the chair of mathematical physics at the University of Rome in 1900.

When he was twenty-seven he published a paper on linear differential equations, followed by a second part five years later. These two papers lay at the core of his career. He now had a worldwide reputation and was a member of academies in many parts of the world from Leningrad to Washington. He was a very popular figure in Rome, where he was a senator from 1905 and president of the prestigious Academia del Lincei. His apartment on the Appian Way was the meeting place for leading figures from many fields of life.

Volterra became politically involved on a number of occasions. In World War I he spoke out for Italy's entering the war on the side of the Allies and spoke later against the Socialist 1917 initiative to make a separate peace. At aged fifty-five, he enlisted as an officer in the army engineering corps, joining its air branch. He also founded and directed the Italian Office of War Inventions and was the first to suggest the use of helium instead of the more volatile hydrogen in balloons.

A pronounced antifascist, he was a principal signator of the "Intellectuals' Declaration" against fascism. Together with Benedetto Croce, he headed a group in the Senate that consistently voted against Mussolini. In 1931, following his refusal to take the oath of allegiance to the Fascist party, Volterra was expelled from his chair and was forced to resign from all the scientific academies in Italy. Most of his remaining years he spent lecturing abroad.

Volterra's major contributions were in the fields of higher analysis, mathematical physics, integral equations, celestial mechanics, calculus of variations, mathematical theory of elasticity, and mathematical biometrics. His solution of the type of integral equations with variable limits bears his name. He received many honors, being a lifetime member of the Royal Society and the French Institute and was made an honorary knight by the king of England.

G. Corbellini, *Vito Volterra nel centenario della sua nascita*, 1960.
Academia Nazionale dei Lincei, *Vito Volterra nel i centenario della nascita*, 1960.

VORONOFF, SERGE   (1866–1951) Physiologist. Born in Voronege, Russia, he settled in Paris in 1884 and graduated from the Paris medical school in 1893. Specializing in surgery, he was appointed chief surgeon at the auxiliary hospital, Paris, in 1914, with a special interest in bone and tissue grafting. He was made director of the biological laboratory at the Ecole des Hautes Etudes. In 1917 Voronoff was appointed director of the experimental laboratory in surgery at the Collège de France in Nice.

Among his successes in tissue grafting, he demonstrated the possibility of increased weight and wool yield in sheep by gland grafting. His reputation was mainly the result of his experiments in endocrine gland transplantation. He attempted to cure thyroid deficiency by transplanting higher primate thyroid glands into humans and in a similar manner tried to increase the human life span (which he thought could be brought up to 140) by transplanting primate sex hormone glands (popularly known as "monkey gland treatment").

Voronoff was a prolific author. Among his most notable works are: *Hysteria* (1895); *Treatise on Human Grafting* (1916); *Testicular Grafting* (1923); *Animal Grafting* (1925); *Studies on Senility and Rejuvenation by Grafting* (1926); *The Conquest of Life* (1928); *From Cretin to Genius* (1941).

Voronoff was forced to flee from France when the Germans invaded during World War II. He escaped to Portugal and later settled in the United States.

WAKSMAN, SELMAN ABRAHAM (1888–1973) Biochemist, discoverer of streptomycin, and Nobel Prize winner. He was born in Priluka, in the Ukraine, into a religious family. Even as a child he was impressed with Jewish hygienic practices that he observed in his home, where his father taught him Bible and Talmud. He received a primitive secular education. Living in a farming community he took an early interest in the soil. At the age of nine, he watched his sister suffocate from diphtheria at a time when a new antitoxin against the disease had been discovered in Europe but was not available in the Ukraine. This tragedy sparked his ambition ιo save other children struck with the disease.

At the age of twenty-two, he went with his family to the United States, where he chose to study microbiology and began to research in 1914. In 1918 he received his Ph.D. from the University of California. Most of his career was spent at Rutgers University, New Brunswick, New Jersey, where he was professor of soil microbiology from 1929 to 1940, professor of microbiology from 1940, and head of the Institute of Microbiology from 1949. His research led to the separation of microorganisms into "good" (helpful, beneficial) and "bad" (pathogenic, disease-producing) forms.

The events and casualties of World War II encouraged the search for new antibacterial substances. Waksman applied himself to this task and coined the term "antibiotic" as "a substance produced by one organism which kills other microorganisms." In 1943 he discovered streptomycin from a strain of fungus, *Streptomyces griseus*. The new drug was found to be highly effective against a large number of bacteria, including tuberculosis, and because of its wide application streptomycin was classed as a "broad spectrum" antibiotic. In the course of his research, Waksman developed many methods for the isolation and purification of antibiotics as well as for the cultivation of microorganisms. He also isolated and developed neomycin and other antibiotics used for the treatment of various infectious diseases.

Waksman received many international and academic honors, including the Nobel Prize for medicine and physiology in 1952.

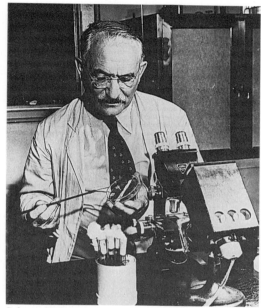

Selman Waksman at work in the 1950s.

His books included *Principles of Soil Microbiology* (1927), which became a standard work on the subject, *The Conquest of Tuberculosis* (1964), and an autobiography, *My Life with the Microbes* (1954), which he summarized as "the story of the life of an immigrant boy who went from the steppes of the Ukraine to the New World in search of a better education and better opportunities to do what he wanted with his life.... I tried my best."
S. A. Waksman, *My Life with the Microbes*, 1954.

WALD, LILLIAN D. (1867–1940) Pioneer of public health nursing, who established Henry Street Settlement house in New York. Although born into a comfortable, assimilated family of German Jewish origin in Cincinnati, Ohio, she devoted her life to the eastern European immigrants crowded into New York's Lower East Side.

Traumatized by the death of an older brother, and in quest of direction for her life, she was intrigued by the first nurse she ever met — a woman who came to tend her married sister. She applied to and was accepted by a school of nursing in New York City. Although this was not a usual career for young ladies of her social milieu, her family consented.

Within a few months of graduation from nursing school, Wald faced the trials of impoverished, disease-stricken new immigrants in their overcrowded tenements. For her work, she gained the support and encouragement of Jacob Schiff (q.v.), the noted financier and philanthropist, and his mother-in-law, Betty Solomon Loeb. Wald, with her friend and co-worker, Mary Brewster, sought out potential recipients of nursing care in their tenements. To that end they chose to live among those whom they would serve.

In searching for a suitable apartment, the young nurses discovered the College Settlement House, founded to bring together the forerunners of modern social work with their clients in the clients' own neighborhood.

Wald's vision had these components: that treatment of the patient include nutrition, sanitation, and dealing with unwholesome aspects of his environment; that the nurses not be sent by one of the existing charities and that there be a fee of ten cents per visit to maintain the immigrant's self-respect; that the nurses be headed and administered by the nurses themselves.

The house on Henry Street, purchased for Wald and her nurses by Jacob Schiff, became a settlement house in 1893 as well as the headquarters of the Visiting Nurse Service. Wald continued, with her growing staff, to knock on her neighbors' doors, dispensing free advice on prevention of illness and tending any stricken member of the household. She also joined social active organizations. She turned the backyard of the Henry Street house into the first children's playground in the area and in 1898 helped form the Outdoor Recreation League, public parks and playgrounds being at that time an enlightened, reformist issue. Wald also established the first convalescent home for women, children, and workers, and helped establish the first special education classes.

Wald initiated public school nursing; her staff visited the classrooms to examine the health of every school-age child. She spoke out for school lunches, and in 1909 President Theodore Roosevelt asked her to arrange a conference on the care of dependent children.

Wald believed that mutual efforts of the privileged and the impoverished could alleviate the sorrows arising from society's inequities. Her progressive approach (decidedly nonconfrontational) was in tune with that of labor organizer Rose Schneiderman (q.v.). The Henry Street house lent its space for activities of Schneiderman's Women's Trade Union League.

Wald and Schiff both desired the immigrant's Americanization. But whereas Schiff wanted them to hold fast to their Jewish identity, Wald found

---

LILLIAN WALD ON HER JEWISH IDENTITY

When approached by an editor for an autobiographical statement, Wald said: "All my work has been non-sectarian and my interests are entirely non-sectarian. I am, therefore, not sure that I properly belong in your book since the title suggests work done by women as Jews."

Jewish identity inconsequential, if not actually a threat, to the Americanization process. Certain outward signs of observance reflected in personal appearance distressed her. "Habits consistent with the conventions of other countries, though varying from our own, often mark as 'alien' and 'queer' people who might otherwise prove to be sympathetic." She convinced many Orthodox married women to discard their wigs. However, she valued for their charm other traditions such as the *sukkah*, and even used them to foster mutual respect between the immigrant and his American-born children.

Her financial backers questioned her suffragette stance, the ultimate confrontation arising during World War I. At first her political views were like Woodrow Wilson's, who greeted her personally in 1914. However, when her pacifism continued unabated when the United States entered the war in April 1917 (she was president of the American Union against Militarism at the time), many withheld funding from her settlement house and her Visiting Nurse Service. Despite her political views, Wald let her settlement house — which had by then expanded to three buildings — be incorporated in the war effort. At her suggestion, one of her nurses became director of the U.S. Army School for Nursing.

In 1923 Wald's mother died, and a few months later she lost her most ardent supporter, Schiff. She suffered a heart attack, and remained troubled by poor health until her death in 1940. She wrote *The House on Henry Street* (1915) and *Windows on Henry Street* (1934).

R. Duffus, *Lillian Wald*, 1938.
S. Rogow, *The Nurse in Blue*, 1966.
B. Siegel, *Lillian Wald of Henry Street*, 1983.

WALLACE, IRVING (born Wallenchinsky; 1916–1990) Popular U.S. novelist whose thirty-four books sold almost 200 million copies. Born in Chicago, to immigrants from Russia, he grew up and was educated in Kenosha, Wisconsin. He studied at the Williams Institute, Berkeley, and Los Angeles City College before embarking on a career as journalist and magazine writer. He had sold his first article, "The Horse Laugh" to *Horse and Jockey Magazine*, while still at school. He ghostwrote articles for Hollywood celebrities and contributed biographies of stars to film magazines. During World War II he served in the film unit of the U.S. Army Air Unit and after the war wrote a number of film scripts. He then turned to writing books, his first being *The Fabulous Originals* (1953), which told the stories of the real people behind famous works of fiction.

When he subsequently began to write novels, he worked with the formula: "Start from a one-line topical idea from the newspapers: evolve a gripping plot to dramatize it. Draw up a detailed outline — a blueprint — and then develop it as readably as possible." He first hit the jackpot with *The Chapman Report* (1960), inspired by the Kinsey Report, about a group of women in Los Angeles whose sex lives are being studied (made into a film with Jane Fonda). He followed this with *The Prize* (1962), a romance-thriller about the Nobel Prize, the leading character of which was based on William Faulkner (played by Paul Newman in the film adaptation). The book offended the Swedes and was banned from sale in Sweden. In 1964, in the middle of the civil rights movement, he wrote *The Man*, in which a black man is elected President of the U.S. *The Word* (1972) exploited the idea of a new gospel written by the brother of Jesus. *The Fan Club* (1974) had obsessed fans kidnapping their movie sex symbol. *The Second Lady* (1980) depicted the wife of the U.S. president being abducted by the Soviets while still on a state visit to Moscow and replaced by a Russian undercover agent. *The Miracle* (1984) postulated the discovery of the diary of Saint Bernadette. The novels all mingled romance, intrigue, social problems, and sex and were noted for a technically accomplished style that ensured that each was a best-seller.

Wallace also produced an ingenious and successful series of works of intriguing facts, coauthored with his son David, who retained the name Wallechinsky. These included three volumes of *The People's Almanac*, three volumes of *The Book of Lists*, and *The Intimate Sex Lives of Famous People*, which was described as compulsive reading, even for those who would not admit it.

WALTER, BRUNO (1876–1962) Conductor. Born Bruno Walter Schlesinger in Berlin, at the age of eight he entered the Stern Conservatory in Berlin, making his public debut as a pianist the following year. When he was thirteen he realized that conducting was his main interest, and four years later became opera coach at the Municipal Opera of Cologne, where he also conducted occasionally. A year later Gustav Mahler (q.v.) engaged Walter as his assistant conductor at the Hamburg Stadttheater. It was Mahler who advised Walter to drop his original family name, Schlesinger. In 1896 Walter was the second conductor in Breslau as well as the principal conductor in Pressburg. In 1898 Walter conducted for a season at Riga.

In 1900 Walter was invited to be a conductor for five years at the Berlin Opera. Walter accepted but broke his contract a year later when Mahler invited him to be his assistant at the Vienna Opera. Walter remained in Vienna for many years, establishing himself as a leading opera conductor.

In 1923 Walter returned to Germany, this time to Munich, where he led legendary performances of Mozart operas. He conducted many orchestras in Europe, establishing the Bruno Walter Concerts with the Berlin Philharmonic (1921–1933) and conducting in the Salzburg summer festival.

He made his English debut in 1909 and in 1932 made his first appearance in the United States with the New York Philharmonic, which he then began to conduct on a regular basis as an associate to Toscanini.

When the Nazis came to power in 1933, Walter could not continue to conduct in Germany and led concerts in Amsterdam and Salzburg. In 1936 he became the director of the Vienna Opera, but this position was terminated two years later with the Anschluss. He moved with his family to France and when war broke out traveled to America, making his home in California.

Walter is still considered one of the finest interpreters of Mahler's music. He himself composed two symphonies, chamber music, and songs and published several books including *Gustav Mahler*

IRVING WALLACE'S LIST OF CELEBRATED JEWS
(From *The People's Almanac*, Vol. 2)

Felix Mendelssohn — Sarah Bernhardt — Sigmund Freud — Henri Bergson — Emma Goldman — Helena Rubinstein — Andre Citroen — Albert Einstein — Amedeo Modigliani — Niels Bohr — Al Jolson — Marc Chagall — Theda Bara — Dorothy Parker — Edward G. Robinson — Groucho Marx — Benny Leonard — Walter Winchell — George Gershwin — Meyer Lansky — J. Robert Oppenheimer — Jonas Salk — Boris Spassky — Bob Dylan — Mark Spitz

---

If individual taste or personal emotional participation are ruthlessly suppressed, the result will be a sort of emotional impoverishment of the performance. The conductor should strive to encourage every sign of emotional participation in the orchestra; he should explore and employ to the fullest degree the capacities of his collaborators; he should excite their interests, advance their musical talents; in short, he should exert a beneficial influence on them. In this way the orchestra will not be a subjugated, that is, artistically inhibited, mass of people and the conductor will have at his disposal an instrument which his soul pours forth.

Bruno Walter

(1936 in German; English translation, 1936), and his autobiography, *Theme and Variations* (1946).

A. Holde, *Bruno Walter* (German), 1960.
H. C. Schonberg, *The Great Conductors*, 1968.
D. Wooldridge, *Conductor's World*, 1968.

WARBURG, FELIX MORITZ (1871–1937) U.S. financier and philanthropist. His family derived from bankers believed to have originated in Italy and from Simon von Cassel, a pawnbroker and money dealer who settled, in 1559, in Warburg, Germany, from which the family later took its name. Felix was one of the seven children of Moritz Warburg, who ran the banking firm of M. M. Warburg and Co., which had been founded in Hamburg in 1789 and existed in Germany until 1938, when it was confiscated by the Nazis. He was also the official leader of the Jewish community of Hamburg. Felix grew into a strikingly handsome youth, with a happy face, dark hair, black eyes, and a mustache. He loved beautiful women, clothes, books, music, paintings, horses, sailboats, and motorcars. He was nicknamed "Fizzie" for his vibrant personality and for the Vichy Clestin "fizzy water" he loved to drink.

At the age of sixteen he left school and was sent to Frankfurt to work with the Oppenheims, his mother's family, in their precious stones business.

He married Frieda Schiff, daughter of the Amer-ican financier, Jacob Schiff (q.v.), who gave him a position with his firm, Kuhn, Loeb and Co. in New York, in 1895. He became a partner and later a senior partner of the company and was involved in the financial aspects of the industrial development of North America. He enjoyed an international reputation as a financier, philanthropist, and a champion of social causes.

One of the earliest social enterprises with which he was associated was Lillian Wald's (q.v.) Henry Street Settlement, which helped provide open-air playgrounds for children in crowded tenement districts of the city. He later participated in the establishment of the Playground Association and initiated the visits of nurses to the ailing poor of the Lower East Side. He was also associated with the Educational Alliance, the main purpose of which was to assist the absorption of immigrants in the United States.

In 1902 Warburg was appointed a commissioner of the New York Board of Education, and, during the many years that he held the position, introduced reforms in the public school system, special classes for the mentally retarded, and the appointment of trained nurses to schools. He was also involved in the organization of the first children's court in New York, was instrumental in passing of a probation bill enabling the courts to deal with juvenile delinquency, and in 1907 was appointed

Felix W. Warburg (front center) at foundation meeting of the American Jewish Joint Distribution Committee, 1914. Far left, Louis Marshall.

the first state probation commissioner. His activity in the field of health included from the establishment of a babies' hospital and a tuberculosis preventorium for children. He became vice-president of the Neurological Institute, the first hospital in the United States devoted exclusively to the prevention, treatment, and study of nervous diseases. He was also a director of the Solomon and Betty Loeb Home for Convalescents and the White Plains Hospital.

Warburg's interest in education and the arts led him to join the board of the American Museum of Natural History, and to become a trustee of such institutions as Teachers College at Columbia University, Hebrew Union College, and the Jewish Education Association, as well as a director of the Jewish Theological Seminary of America. He was involved in the development of the Juilliard School of Music and the New York Philharmonic Symphony Orchestra, and took part in the establishment of the Fogg Museum of Art at Harvard University. In 1914 he became the chairman of the newly-established American Jewish Joint Distribution Committee, a position he held until 1932. During World War I he directed the census of food supplies of New York City. In 1917 he was the prime mover in the formation of the Federation for the Support of Jewish Philanthropic Societies of New York; he was elected its president and remained so for twenty years.

Although Warburg was not a political Zionist and consistently opposed the idea of a Jewish state in Palestine, he was directly involved in furthering the country's development through his support of the Palestine Economic Corporation and was one of the founders and patrons of the Hebrew University of Jerusalem. In 1929 he became cofounder, with Louis Marshall (q.v.), of the Jewish Agency, and chairman of its administration committee, but resigned in 1931 to protest against the British restriction of Jewish immigration. In 1933 he assumed leadership of the campaign to raise money in aid of the oppressed Jews in Hitler's Germany. In 1937 he publicly protested the British plan for the partition of Palestine.

Warburg found time to indulge his passion for the arts and for recreation. He had a full Stradivarius string quartet and an extensive collection of etchings, paintings, tapestries, and sculptures. His former New York home on Fifth Avenue is now the Jewish Museum.

S. Birmingham, *Our Crowd; the Great Jewish Families of New York*, 1967.

S. M. Stroock, *In Memoriam Felix Warburg*, 1937.

J. A. Wechberg, *The Merchant Bankers*, 1966.

WARNER BROTHERS: HARRY (1881– 1958), **ALBERT**(1884–1967), **SAM**(1888–1927) and **JACK** (1892–1978) U.S. film executives. The children of Polish immigrants, the four Warner brothers were part of a large family of whom few survived to adulthood. Most began careers as salesmen but switched to motion pictures when Sam's enthusi-

Harry Warner, actor Fernand Gravet and his wife, c. 1936.

asm convinced them to invest in a projector and print of Edwin Porter's *The Great Train Robbery*. Their first theater was called the Bijou and occupied a vacant store, making do with chairs borrowed from an undertaker. Success was followed by expansion into distribution and, in 1912, into production. The films made by the Warners were undistinguished until a timely breakthrough, *My Four Years in Germany*, captured the mood of a nation entering the war in 1917.

Warner Brothers remained a minor operation for most of the 1920s with the dog Rin Tin Tin as its major asset. Duties among the brothers were split in a manner suitable to their temperaments, with Albert and Harry in charge of distribution and finance, respectively, while the flamboyant Jack oversaw West Coast production. Sam, whose vision had first pushed his brothery into the industry, died tragically the day before the family's greatest triumph, which he had largely engineered. This was the premiere of *The Jazz Singer*, the part-talking film that in 1927 sounded the death knell of the silent cinema.

In the 1930s the Warners became known for their backstage musicals and their hard-hitting films dealing with social evils, particularly gangsterism. Major stars of the studio included Paul Muni (q.v.), James Cagney, Bette Davis, and Humphrey Bogart, and additional players and studio facilities were acquired when First National was taken over at the onset of the decade. During World War II, Jack, as a colonel in the Air Force, set up an Army Air Force motion picture unit. In the mid-1950s, the surviving brothers parted with most of their interest in the company, but Jack continued energetically as a producer, with musicals such as *My Fair Lady*, *Camelot*, and *1776* to his credit.

R. Behlmer, *Inside Warner Bros. (1935–1951)*, 1986.

J. L. Warner with D. Jennings, *Bibliography: My First Hundred Years in Hollywood*, 1964.

WASSERMANN, AUGUST VON (1866–1925) German bacteriologist who discovered a blood serum test for syphilis. Born in Bamberg, Germany, he took his medical degree at the University of Strasbourg in 1888 and was then appointed assistant to Robert Koch at the Koch Institute of Infectious Diseases in Berlin (1890–1906). In 1891, in collaboration with another scientist, Wassermann reported on the toxins of diphtheria and became famous after publishing a paper on immunity and toxin fixation in 1892. His reputation was enhanced in 1898 by a further paper on tetanus toxin in which he showed its affinity to nervous tissue. This work led to the development of biological methods of differentiating animal albumins. The precipitin reaction he produced became important in medicolegal applications. He also developed innoculations against cholera and typhoid.

He received the titular rank of professor in 1898 and was appointed professor at the University of Berlin in 1903. In 1906 Wassermann announced his development of a serodiagnostic test for syphilis (the Wassermann test) following Jules Bordet and Octave Gengou's discovery of complement fixation. Blood or spinal fluid producing a positive reaction indicates the existence of antibodies formed as a result of infection with syphilis. Wassermann also proved that tabes dorsalis and progressive paralysis were late results of syphilis. This achievement revolutionized the diagnosis, control, and treatment of syphilis.

In 1907 he became director of therapeutic and serum research at the University of Berlin. From 1913 he directed the department of experimental therapy at the Kaiser Wilhelm Institute of Experimental Therapy, at Dahlem, Germany. He was responsible for discovering diagnostic tests for tuberculosis.

Wassermann's main genius as a brilliant scientific worker was to adapt and develop the research of others into practical use. He wrote over sixty scientific papers on serology and immunology and published a book *Immune Sera, Haemolysins, Cytotoxins and Precipitins* in 1904 (translated into English). Together with the German bacteriologist Wilhelm Kolle, he published the six-volume *Handbook of Pathological Microorganisms* (1903–1909). W. Bullock, *History of Bacteriology*, 1960. S. R. Kagan, *Jewish Medicine*, 1952.

WASSERMANN, JAKOB (1873–1934) German novelist. Born in Fürth, northern Bavaria, Wassermann had an unhappy youth. He was alienated from his father, an unsuccessful manufacturer, and despised by his step-mother. Sent to Vienna to serve as an apprentice in his uncle's business, he ran away. He experienced anti-Semitism when he was drafted into the German army and when he sought employment. He knew the pangs of hunger and of extreme loneliness. On the edge of an abyss, he found work in the satirical periodical *Simplizissimus*. When he showed his own fictional writings to his superior, the minor novelist Ernst von Wolzogen, he was encouraged to continue in this genre and was helped to publish *Die Juden von Zirndorf* (1897), a novel on Jewish life, past and present, in his native Franconia.

A decade passed, however, before Wassermann gained popular recognition with his novel *Caspar Hauser* (1909), which castigated the inertia of the human heart. In this narrative about a mysterious foundling, regarded by some as a prince and by others as a charlatan, the author set out to show how human beings, the most brutal and selfish as well as the most refined and sensitive, are utterly blind and helpless when confronted with the phenomenon of innocence; how they defile the tender, dreamy, divine qualities of Caspar's makeup, and end by murdering him.

The apex of Wassermann's creativity was attained in *Christian Wahnschaffe* (1919), his first American bestseller under the title *The World's Illusion* (1921; translated by Ludwig Lewisohn). It was a prose epic about European civilization edging toward the brink of war. The title-hero, scion of an industrial baron, arrives at the recognition that he is a pillar of an unjust and immoral economic and social system. He cannot justify his profiteering from such a system. At the end, he renounces his flirtations, disposes of his wealth, turns his back upon his parasitical past, descends to the slums, nurses a harlot, fraternizes with a murderer, and serves his fellow-men as the humblest of the humble. The novelist continued to portray moral decay, material greed, and the sick souls that needed readjustment, throughout the 1920s.

Wassermann suffered from the duality of being both German and Jewish. His autobiography,

August von Wassermann. Etching by B. Feigl.

Mein Weg als Deutscher und Jude (1921; *My Life as
German and as Jew*, 1933) symbolizes in its title his
desire to affirm both components of his personality. He opposed Theodor Herzl's (q.v.) Zionism.
He maintained, even after the Balfour Declaration
of 1917, that Jews were a sum of individuals but
not a nationality or a people united by common
characteristics. Jews therefore did not need a state
of their own. He granted that he might be driven
from his central European home by insane anti-
Semitic agitation, but insisted that even in exile he
would remain a German. As for the ingathering of
Jews on a common soil he asked, how could
anyone expect German Jews, who had for centuries imbibed German culture, to form a happy
union with other Jews with whom they had had
little in common for at least half a millennium. He
refused to accept the alternatives of German or
Jew. He emphasized that he had succeeded in forging both into a higher synthesis.

Wassermann's intense suffering, because of the
strained relationship between Germans and Jews,
led his friends to warn him against succumbing to
persecution-mania. His fellow-novelist, Thomas
Mann, assured him that Germany was the land
least suited for the growth of anti-Semitism.

The Nazi victory of 1933 doomed Wassermann's
hopes of a German-Jewish symbiosis. His dream
of assimilation turned into a nightmare.
J. C. Blankenagel, *The Writings of Jacob Wassermann*, 1942.
S. Liptzin, *Germany's Stepchildren*, 1944.

WEILL, KURT (JULIAN) (1900–1950) Composer. Born in Dessau, Germany, Weill was the
son of the chief cantor at his hometown's synagogue. His father was himself a composer and all
four Weill children had a good musical background. Kurt began to compose at the age of
twelve, and by the time he was fifteen showed
considerable potential. His father took him to
Albert Bing, then the Kappelmeister of the Court
Opera in Dessau. Bing was so impressed by the
boy's talents that he took him on as a pupil and
worked with him for three years, providing the
young Weill with a second home and later work as
répétiteur at the Court Opera.

Following a short period in 1918 at the Hochschule fur Musik in Berlin where he took composition with Engelbert Humperdinck, he returned to
Dessau, where he took a post as conductor of a new

Kurt Weill.

municipal opera company in Lüdenscheid. He
remained in that capacity until 1920, when he
joined Ferruccio Busoni's master class for promising young composers at the Prussian Academy of
Arts. He studied counterpoint with Busoni's
assistant, Philipp Jarnach, who was more truly
Weill's teacher than Busoni; Weill dedicated his
Sinfonia Sacra, op. 6, to him. The early 1920s were
a period of enormous creative output for Weill. He
met and collaborated with the leading expressionist playwright of the day, Georg Kaiser.

His journeys together with his wife, singer Lotte
Lenya (1898–1981), whom he had married in 1926,
took him to Paris, where he underwent a period of
unsuccessful receptions of his new works, including *The Seven Deadly Sins*, which he had always
considered to be one of his best scores. The Nazis
condemned his work as decadent, and Weill left for
New York in 1935 to supervise musical preparations for the premiere of *Der Weg der Verheissung*,
a vast piece of music-theater written together with
Franz Werfel (q.v.) and Max Reinhardt (q.v.). The
production was postponed becouse of insufficient
funding. Meanwhile Weill found work with the
Group Theater, collaborating with playwright
Paul Green on an antiwar musical play, *Johnny
Johnson;* this was staged in New York in November
1936 and two months later followed the long-
awaited premiere of the Broadway version of *Der
Weg der Verheissung*, now known as *The Eternal
Road*. This play portrayed a group of Jews brought

together in a synagogue by fear of a pogrom, whose faith is restored by a rabbi reading stories from the Bible. Both productions proved unsuccessful and did not attract the regular Broadway audiences. Nevertheless, Weill felt that he had begun to establish roots in the United States. For the next thirteen years, he devoted all his energies to Hollywood and the Broadway stage, producing operettas and musicals. These included *Lady in the Dark* (with Moss Hart [q.v.] and Ira Gershwin, 1941); *One Touch of Venus* (with Ogden Nash and S. J. Perelman [q.v.], 1943), and, more seriously, *Street Scene* (1947) and *Lost in the Storm* (1947). Two of his songs have retained their popularity — "September Song" from *Knickerbocker Holiday* and "Mack the Knife" from *The Threepenny Opera*. In 1948 he wrote the music for *A Flag Is Born*, a pageant by Ben Hecht (q.v.), to celebrate the establishment of the State of Israel. Weill also wrote a violin concerto and two symphonies.

By the age of twenty-eight, he had composed — in collaboration with Bertold Brecht — the operas *Die Dreigroscheroper* ("Threepenny Opera," 1928, the *Mahagonny Songspiel* (1927), and *Augstieg und Fall der Stadt Mahagonny* ("The Rise and Fall of the City of Mahagonny," 1930). These Brecht-Weill pieces continue to hold the stage today, and through them the creation of the "number" opera concept in the context of a meaningful musical play, combined with popular cabaret and jazz music inspired by Austro-German tradition, emerged as a new art form of popular musical theater and opera — *Gebrauchtmusik*, "musical theater of social consciousness."

K. H. Kowalke (ed.), *A New Orpheus: Essays on Kurt Weill*, 1986.

S. Ronald, *The Days Grow Short, The Life and Music of Kurt Weill*, 1980.

WEININGER, OTTO (1880–1903) Austrian psychologist and philosopher. Born in Vienna of a middle-class Jewish family, he graduated from the University of Vienna in 1902. His doctoral dissertation became the basis for his only major work, *Sex and Character*. On the day of his graduation he converted to Protestantism, not because of conviction but because of his hatred of the Judaism into which he had been born. When his book appeared a year later, it might have attracted less attention if not for his sensational suicide. His aphorisms and essays appeared posthumously under the title *About the Last Things* (1918).

Weininger's *Sex and Character* may be divided into scientific, philosophic, and anti-Semitic sections. The scientific part deals with the effect of sex on character. He projects the existence of male and female substances in every human being. The pure male and the pure female are theoretical concepts. All human beings contain both substances but in different proportions. A man is a person in whom maleness predominates; a woman is a person in whom femaleness is dominant.

In his philosophic section Weininger postulates Maleness and Femaleness as Platonic ideas. Masculinity and Femininity are opposite poles, positive and negative, but attracting each other even as do electrical charges. The former is Being; the latter non-Being. Woman is nothing but man's projection of his own sexuality. Every man creates for himself a woman in whom he embodies his own guilt, his lower self.

In the final, anti-Semitic section, Weininger stands under the influence of Houston Stewart Chamberlain, the British-German philosopher of Nordic or Aryan superiority. Weininger equates Aryanism and Christianity with Masculinity and Judaism with Femininity. The former is Being, the latter non-Being.

Zionism is, in Weininger's opinion, the negation of Judaism, for it seeks to ennoble what cannot be ennobled. Judaism stands for world dispersion of Jews while Zionism stands for their ingathering. Before Zionism can succeed, the Jew must first war against his inner nature and free himself from Jewishness. Jesus was the only Jew to overcome Judaism. But perhaps another savior is at hand who will liberate the world from the guilt of womanhood and the sin of Judaism. Weininger saw himself as this liberator.

After his death his book went through thirty editions and was translated into various languages, including Hebrew. Its startling ideas penetrated Nazi ideology. His Jewish disciple, Arthur Trebitch, saw in him a martyr who found in death the only way of destroying the Jewish heritage in his personality. The philosopher Theodor Lessing viewed Weininger as a major symbol of Jewish self-hatred. On the other hand, the historian Oswald Spengler saw him as one of the three saints produced by Judaism in modern times, comparable to Baruch Spinoza (q.v.) and the Baal Shem Tov (q.v.). Weininger's story was dramatized in the play *Soul of a Jew* by the Israeli playwright, Yehoshua Sobol.

D. Abrahamsen, *The Mind and Death of a Genius*, 1946.

WEISS, PETER (1916–1982) German playwright, novelist, and film producer. He was born in Nowawes, near Berlin, to a prosperous textile manufacturer, a Czech Jew converted to Christianity, and a Swiss mother. Assuming his father's Czech nationality and raised like his mother as a Lutheran, the child spent his youth in Berlin and Bremen. In 1934, after the advent of the Nazis, the family emigrated first to London, where young Weiss studied photography at the London Polytechnic, and two years later to Prague, where he studied at the Academy of Art and spent what he describes as two years without hope. In 1938 Weiss left for Switzerland, and in 1939 arrived in Sweden, where he was to spend a great part of his life. He married Gunilla Palmstierna, who designed the costumes for his plays. His writing, however, was mainly in German.

His experience of exile, rootlessness, and alienation left a significant impression on his life and work. His first artistic endeavor was as a painter, and in 1941 he held a first exhibition of his works in Stockholm. But his apocalyptic, visionary depiction of the immobile moment did not satisfy his creative energies. He turned to filmmaking, and in the fifties produced experimental surrealistic and documentary movies, including a full-length feature like *The Mirage* (1958), "a poem of a day in the city," a Kafkaesque account of a starving man's attempts to find a way to exist. His interest in films produced also theoretical work, like his essay "Avantgarde Film" (Swedish, 1950; German, 1955).

His first written works were two small collections of verse in Swedish (1946, 1947). He went on to record his spiritual autobiography in a series of narrative works. The motif of rootlessness and wandering is notable also in the fragmented prose piece *Das Gespräch der drei Gehenden* ("The Talk of the Three Walkers," 1962).

Weiss' turn to the theater was, in a sense, a dialectical synthesis of his abstract cinematic works and his interest in living human beings. His first dramatic piece was the one-acter *Der Turm* ("The Tower," 1948), first performed in Stockholm. *Nacht mit Gästen* ("Night with Guests") was his first play to be produced on the German stage (Schiller Theater, Berlin, 1963).

It was his next play, produced in the same theater the following year, that brought Weiss his international fame. *Marat/Sade*, or as its full name translates, *The Persecution and Assassination of Marat as Performed by the Inmates of the Asylum at Charenton under the Direction of the Marquis de Sade*, was received in Germany (and then in Britain and France) as the direct successor of Brecht's political theater. Weiss employs the basic framework of historical events to construct his own fictional drama, in which Sade, interned in Charenton, engages in an imaginary philosophical and political debate with Marat, whose murder by Charlotte Corday he enacts with his fellow inmates. Imagination and radical individualism encounter socialism and revolution, while Sade directs his frenzied cast, including Marat, who sits constantly in his bath to ease the pains of his psychosomatic skin disease. *Marat/Sade* was Weiss's most prominent success and was filmed in English. His following play, *Die Ermittlung* ("The Investigation," 1965), though opening simultaneously in seventeen theaters throughout Europe, never achieved the same popularity. Based on the Auschwitz trial in Frankfurt-am-Main in 1964, it is a lengthy piece of documentary theater, a shocking dramatic oratory on inhumanity.

Reverting, like the work of many German writers of his age, to Marxism, Weiss's drama points to a linkage between evils of the past and present political concerns. Thus his subsequent plays deal with the historical developments leading toward current events such as the Angolan and Mozambiquan situations in the political musical *Gesang vom lusitanischen Popanz* ("Song of the Lusitanian Bogey," 1967), or *Viet Nam Diskurs* ("Vietnam Discourse," 1968).

Weiss' two last major plays were *Trotzki im Exil* ("Trotsky in Exile," 1970), an epic drama on Trotsky's lifelong political career, and *Hölderlin* (1971), which portrayed the German Romantic poet as a revolutionary hero. "Every word I write is political," was Weiss's summing up of his writing. I. Hilton, *Peter Weiss: A Search for Affinities*, 1970. P. Weiss, *Leavetaking and Vanishing Point*, 1968.

WEISZ, VICTOR (VIcky; 1913–1966) Cartoonist. Born in Berlin of Hungarian parentage, he went to art school in Berlin and started his career as a cartoonist when only sixteen, working for the *12 Uhr Blatte*. In 1928 he published his first anti-Hitler cartoon and moved from Germany to England in 1935 after Hitler came to power. When he arrived he knew of only three British politicians: Neville Chamberlain, Winston Churchill, and Stanley Baldwin. By 1941 he was sufficiently well up in British politics to become the cartoonist of the *News Chronicle*. He had an English sense of fun and was steeped in the works of Lewis Carroll and A. A. Milne, as well as in the policies of left-wing socialism, with which he was deeply sympathetic. Although readers sometimes accused him of being acidic, he was not unkind. His quick mind and fertile imagination enabled him to react speedily to political events. Refugees and starving children were often featured in his work.

Weisz left the *News Chronicle* in 1949 when it refused to publish his cartoon about Kenya and joined the *Daily Mirror*. In 1958 the press magnate Lord Beaverbrook persuaded him to move to the London paper, the *Evening Standard*, guaranteeing him freedom of expression. Here he often featured "Supermac," the transformation of Prime Minister Harold Macmillan into a political superman who eventually sprouted wings. From 1954 he also contributed regularly to the left-wing weekly, *New Statesman and Nation*.

A lifelong socialist, Weisz never joined the Labor party so as to preserve his freedom of expression. He himself said that his best work was done in opposition to the government.

Weisz' paintings were exhibited in London galleries. Much of his work was collected, in *Let Cowards Flinch, Meet the Russians, How to be a Celebrity*, and *Vicky's World*. R. Davies and L. Ottway, *Vicky*, 1990

WEIZMANN, CHAIM (1874–1952) Zionist statesman, the first president of the State of Israel, and chemist. Born in Motol, near Pinsk, Russia, he received both a Jewish and secular education, excelling in the study of science. As a youth he became active in the local Zionist group and taught Hebrew. Attracted to the natural sciences, he studied chemistry in various universities in Germany and later in Switzerland. In both countries he forged close friendships with the leading Russian and German Zionists and deepened his involvement in the nascent Zionist movement. He obtained his doctorate from Freiburg University in chemistry in 1899 and began to publish scientific papers and work on inventions in this field. In 1901 he married Vera Chatzman and moved to Geneva.

He attended his first Zionist Congress in 1898 and soon became one of the leaders of the Democratic Faction, which sought to inject into Zionism Jewish traditions, culture, and heritage, in addition to the focus on diplomatic and organizational work favored by Theodor Herzl (q.v.). As early as in 1902 he became interested in a project to establish a university for Jews, which eventually became the Hebrew University. In 1903 he was one of the vocal opponents of the Uganda Plan supported by Herzl and helped defeat it.

In 1903 he secured a teaching position in chemistry at Manchester University and for the next few years concentrated on his scientific work as well as on building the Zionist movement in Britain. In 1906 he became senior lecturer. In Manchester he converted to Zionism a number of young Jews who were to become outstanding figures in the Anglo-Jewish community and who remained his ardent

Dr. Chaim Weizmann (right) with Lord Balfour. Palestine, 1925.

First known letter of Chaim Weizmann, written in 1885 at the age of ten to his teacher.

How lofty and elevated the idea which inspired our brethren the sons of Israel to establish the Lovers of Zion Society. Because by this we can rescue our exiled, oppressed brethren who are scattered in all corners of the world and have one place where to put up their tents, and all will attack us and the Jew is a burden on all the nations and on all the Kings of Europe in general and on the King of Russia in particular, and this may become the *beginning of redemption*. Therefore we must support this esteemed society and we must also thank all the supporters of this society and all who have rallied beneath the flag of this society. We must also thank the two patriots who are *Moshe Montefiore and Rothschild*. In conclusion we must support this society which understands what lies before it and sees the evil threatening us, therefore the obligation rests upon us to establish a place to shich we can flee for help. Since in America, where enlightenment prevails, we will be beaten. And in all the countries of Africa in general and the State of Morocco in particular we will be beaten and we will not be pitied. Let us carry our banner *to Zion and return to our first mother upon whose knees we were born.* For why should we look to the Kings of Europe for compassion that they should take pity upon us and give us a resting-place? In vain! All have decided: *The Jew must die,* but England will nevertheless have mercy upon us. In conclusion to Zion! — Jews — to Zion! let us go.

---

supporters. Through them he met the editor of the *Manchester Guardian,* C. P. Scott and also came to know Arthur James Balfour, then a member of the British cabinet. At the eighth Zionist Congress in the Hague (1907), Weizmann coined the phrase Synthetic Zionism for the fusion of political and practical Zionism, calling for diplomatic efforts to win Jewish nationhood and the settlement of Eretz Israel by Jews coupled with cultural activities. In that year he made his first visit to Eretz Israel, which convinced him of the need to intensify settlement there.

After World War I broke out, Weizmann moved to London, where his scientific research made important contributions to the Allied war effort. At the same time he engaged in intensive diplomatic activity and lobbying and was the chief architect of the Balfour Declaration. In that Declaration (November 2, 1918) the British government declared its intention of establishing a Jewish National Home in Palestine. In 1918, when Palestine had been conquered from the Turks by the British army, Weizmann headed the Zionist Commission sent there to coordinate activities with the British military authorities. In July 1918 he laid the cornerstone for the Hebrew University in Jerusalem. Later he was one of the heads of the Zionist delegation to the Versailles peace conference and also negotiated an agreement with the

Arab leader Emir Feisal concerning Jewish settlement in Palestine. The Zionist effort was crowned when Palestine was awarded to Britian as a League of Nations mandate with the Balfour Declaration written into the mandate. Weizmann was now closely cooperating with Britain, a country he admired and in whose government he placed trust.

To create the national homeland he was instrumental in establishing Keren Hayesod ("The Foundation Fund") as the fundraising arm of the World Zionist Organization. At a Zionist conference in London (July 1920), Weizmann was elected as president of the Organization and served in that capacity until 1931 and again from 1935 to 1946. During the 1920s he traveled extensively on fund-raising missions; his main work centered on expanding the base of the Zionist movement to include non-Zionist Jews, whose financial support was crucial. In 1929 he presided over the founding of the Jewish Agency, which brought together Zionists and non-Zionists and was the representative body of the World Zionist Organization. His policy of close cooperation with the British received a blow when, in 1930, after the 1929 Arab riots in Palestine, that government issued a white paper that for the first time linked Jewish immigration to Palestine with the absorptive capacity of the country. Weizmann resigned and the policy was rescinded. A year later he was not reelected as president of the WZO as a protest against his overtly pro-British policies.

Between 1931 and 1935 he continued to travel on fund-raising missions and focused his attention on the establishment of the Daniel Sieff Institute in Rehovot, Palestine, which was the nucleus for the future Weizmann Institute of Science. When clouds gathered over Europe, he was recalled to the presidency of the Zionist movement and concentrated his diplomacy on the rescue of Jews from Nazi Germany. In 1937, he supported the plan of the British Royal Commission to partition Palestine and create a Jewish state. However, his pro-British line crashed with the publication of the May 1939 white paper, which limited Jewish immigration to Palestine, banned the sale of land to Jews, and doomed the Jewish community to the status of permanent minority in Palestine.

During World War II he worked on the creation of a Jewish Brigade in the Allied forces (achieved in 1944) and was one of the fathers of the May 1942 Biltmore Program, which called for the establishment of an independent Jewish commonwealth at the end of the war. His son Michael was lost in action while serving in the Royal Air Force. At the end of the war, the newly elected Labor government of Britain sought to appease the Arabs at the expense of the Jews, ignoring the Holocaust. It resisted American efforts to have at least 100,000 survivors admitted to Palestine. Despite his disappointment, Weizmann rejected David Ben-Gurion's (q.v.) activist line of military resistance, fearing it would doom the Jews of Palestine to British repression and later Arab onslaught.

In 1946 he was not elected as president of the World Zionist Organization, but even while out of office, his reputation and charisma as the elder statesman of Zionism was such that he was enlisted in the diplomatic battles that preceded the United

Postcard showing the synagogue of Pinsk from Chaim Weizmann to his fiancée; 12 April 1904.

Nations partition decision of November 1947. Aged, ill, and half blind, he was able to persuade President Harry S. Truman to support partition and to include the entire Negev in the area of the future Jewish state. His dream came true when Israel was proclaimed on May 14, 1948. Ben-Gurion insisted that Weizmann become the president of the Provisional Council and he moved to full-time residence in his home in Rehovot. In February 1949 he was elected as the first president of the State of Israel. By then he was too ill to have any meaningful impact on the state and to leave his imprint on its formative years. He died in Rehovot and was buried on the grounds of the Weizmann Institute, which had been officially dedicated in 1949.

A towering, majestic figure, he led his people for almost three decades of tireless and often thankless struggle to achieve independence. He was the supreme Zionist leader, with a worldwide reputation. A man of vision and a realist, he played a key role in Jewish history in the 20th century. While he had many political opponents, no one doubted his moral stature, his integrity, and his exalted position in the ranks of the Zionist movement and the Jewish nation.

He wrote an autobiography, *Trial and Error* (1949), as did his wife, *The Impossible Takes Longer* (1967). His letters were published in twenty-three volumes under the general editorship of his friend, Meyer Weisgal (1969–1980),

N. Rose, *Chaim Weizmann: A Biography*, 1987.

Y. Reinharz, *Chaim Weizmann: The Making of a Jewish Leader*, 1985.

WERFEL, FRANZ (1890–1945) Austrian poet, dramatist, and novelist. Born in Prague to a prosperous glove manufacturer, he revolted against entering upon the business career planned for him by his father, and found more congenial employment as a reader for a Leipzig publisher. Coming into contact with the pioneers of German expressionism, he followed this new literary trend in his early poems and found himself catapulted into the front rank of the expressionistic poets with his first volume, *Der Weltfreund* (1911). The title is symbolic. He is the friend of the entire world, which is divinely created and divinely inspired. He eschews skepticism and sophistication and revels in religious exultation. *Der Gerichtstag* (1919) contains his poems of World War I and its aftermath, poems of death, rebirth, doom, and salvation. *Beschwörungen* (1923) is a collection of the poems of the post-war years, when expressionism reached its crest. His passion for Verdi led him to translate some of the musician's operas and to write *Verdi: A Novel about Opera* (1924). With the collapse and dismemberment of the Austro-Hungarian Empire, he opted for Vienna as his permanent home, where he lived with and eventually married Alma Mahler, the widow of Gustav Mahler (q.v.). Her life with the gentle poet is portrayed in her autobiography, *And the Bridge Is Love* (1958). She had strong anti-Semitic tendencies and her condition for marrying Werfel in 1929 was that he leave the Jewish community. As he could never bring himself to embrace Catholicism, to which she was drawn, she arranged for him to be "baptized by desire" after death.

Drama now replaced poetry as his principal literary medium. He had experimented with drama on the eve of the war when he adapted Euripides' pacifist drama, *Trojan Women*, as *Die Troerinnen* (1915), a tragedy of war as experienced by the conquered and enslaved. His magical trilogy, *Spiegelmensch* (1920), was acclaimed as an expressionist masterpiece. It was followed by the plays *Bockgesang* (1921) and *Juarez und Maximilian* (1924), which also introduced him to American theatergoers. His religious dramas, *Paulus unter den Juden* (1926) and *Das Reich Gottes in Böhmen*, were less successful.

With the waning of expressionism and the resurgence of realism, Werfel followed the newest trend and gained in clarity. He turned to history for his most fruitful themes and to the novel as his preferred literary medium. In his prose epic, *The Forty Days of Musa Dagh* (1933), he agonized with the Armenians in their desperate and ultimately hopeless struggle against the Turkish hordes. After Hitler's rise to power, he wrote the text for the spectacle, *Der Weg der Verheissung* (1936), which Max Reinhardt (q.v.) staged in New York as *The Eternal Road*. It espoused the cause of the medieval Jews who had to submit to exile because of their adherence to their faith. He was then unaware that two years later, with the Nazi takeover of Austria, he himself would suffer exile because of his Jewish origin. He initially sought refuge in France but, after the fall of France to Nazi invaders, succeeded in escaping to the United States at the end of 1940. His sojourn in France inspired him to write his novel, *The Song of Bernadette* (1941). It idealized Catholicism, to which he felt attracted, but which his sense of kinship with his imperiled coreligionists prevented him from embracing. This novel won him a worldwide audience, especially when it was made into a film, and sold 400,000 copies. Its success enabled him to stave off the penury that assailed most exiled writers.

Settling comfortably in Beverly Hills, California, he was able to devote his last years to completing his grandiose prose epic *Star of the Unborn*

- No man can be wise against his own wishful thinking.
- The Jews historically are impetuous. They are effervescent and rush along precipitously.
- Religion is the everlasting dialogue between man and God. Art is its soliloquy.

Franz Werfel

(1946). It has been labeled an anti-Utopia. Taking place in an incredibly remote future, it gives voice to Werfel's reflections on eternal problems for which there is no final answer short of eternity, but with which he wrestled throughout his life. He also had success with his play, *Jacobowsky and the Colonel* (1944), which was made into a film with Danny Kaye (q.v.). His novel on the prophet Jeremiah, *Hearken unto the Voice*, contains insights into Jewish history.

L. B. Foltin (ed.), *Franz Werfel, 1890–1945*, 1972.
P. S. Jungk, *A Life Torn by History*, 1990.
L. B. Steiman, *Franz Werfel: The Faith of an Exile*, 1985.
L. Zahn, *Franz Werfel*, 1960.

WERTHEIMER, MAX   (1880–1943) Founder of Gestalt psychology. Born in Prague, Wertheimer grew up in an intellectual and artistic home; his father taught and directed a business school and wrote a successful novel. Wertheimer was stimulated by his father's interest in the study of methods of instruction and was also encouraged to pursue his multiple intellectual endeavors. As a young child, Wertheimer demonstrated a talent in mathematics, philosophy, literature, and most importantly music. He took music lessons and composed symphonies and chamber music. His training in music was to permeate his psychological thinking, as he illustrated many of his ideas with examples from music.

After studying law for two years, he turned to philosophy. He attended Prague, Berlin, and Wurzburg universities, and received his Ph.D in philosophy from Wurzburg, where he studied under the influential Oswald Külpe, in 1910, he began lecturing at Frankfurt. While a doctorate student, Wertheimer was intrigued by the problem of how to transform his holistic notions of psychology into a concrete experimental design. While traveling on a train, he realized that he could tackle his question by studying the phenomenon whereby a series of still images give the impression of movement. Moved by this idea, he got off the train in Frankfurt and rushed to buy a toy stroboscope, a device that produces this effect, one that he later described as the phi phenomenon. After contacting a former professor at the Frankfurt Psychological Institute, Wertheimer was offered a laboratory and the assistance of two postdoctoral students, Wolfgang Köhler and Kurt Koffka, in order to pursue his studies. This marked the beginning of what would develop into the paradigm-breaking Gestalt theory.

After receiving his doctorate, Wertheimer concentrated on several areas of psychological study, including the perceptual ability of children suffering from reading disorders, the psychology of music, and the thinking patterns of people of various cultures. During World War I, Wertheimer served as a captain in the German army and investigated the process of sound localization. Following the war, he went to Berlin University and founded as well as edited the first twenty volumes of the *Psychologische Forschung*. Although he was an extremely successful and prestigious lecturer and researcher, he was not offered a professorship until 1929, when the University of Frankfurt gave him an appointment. With the rise of Hitler to power, however, Wertheimer grew increasingly disillusioned with the course the German nation was beginning to take and in 1934 joined the first group of Jewish refugee scholars who were to set up the faculty of the New School for Social Research in New York.

By approaching an old problem in a drastically different way, Wertheimer developed a completely new approach in psychology. Arguing that perception is more that a summative combination of individual sensations, as he proved with his description of the phi phenomenon, Wertheimer contradicted an atomistic notion of perception. He concluded that in the case of the phi phenomenon, for example, brain processes organize static sensations into an overall apparent movement — the whole being greater than the sum of its parts. He maintained that perception is the product of the organization of individual sensations. Having identified several principles by which parts are organized into the whole, Wertheimer extended Gestalt theory to issues of logic, aesthetics, and art.

H. Kendler, *Historical Foundations of Modern Psychology*, 1987.
R. I. Watson, *The Great Psychologists*, 1963.

WEST, NATHANAEL   (1903–1940) U.S. writer. Born Nathan Weinstein in New York to Jewish immigrants from Russia, he was a thin, awkward, quiet child child who showed no academic distinction at school. His passions were baseball and reading and he reportedly trained his bull terrier to bite anyone who came into his room when he was reading.

He first attended Tufts University, but left after two months because of academic difficulty. On being accepted to Brown University the following year, however, West suddenly became a serious student, and even managed to finish his studies in under three years. There, his passion for reading continued; he studied literature, philosophy, and history, and was known for having the college's biggest private library at the time.

After graduating, West spent two years in Paris, after which he returned to New York and began working as assistant manager in various hotels. Being on night duty gave him plenty of time for reading.

West spent a good part of his life trying to escape his Jewish identity. He avoided Jewish women; at college he shunned organized Jewish activities and vainly hoped for acceptance to the non-Jewish fraternities; and on the publication of his first novel, *The Dream Life of Balso Snell*, changed his name to the less Jewish-sounding West.

Nathanael West was a lonely man who gained little satisfaction from his personal life until his marriage in 1940. The marriage and his life ended tragically the same year, when both he and his wife were killed in a car accident on their way home from a hunting trip in Mexico.

West published four novels but received no critical acclaim in his own lifetime. Rejected and disillusioned as a writer, he turned to script writing, at which he was more successful. This gave him a larger income and the chance to live in greater comfort. Since his death, his reputation as a novelist has improved to the point that he has been called one of the most important writers of the 1930s. A parodist who had a clear and ruthless vision of the world he wrote about, his four novels represent a grim and frightening existence.

His two best-known novels are *Miss Lonelyhearts* and *The Day of the Locust.* The former tells of a newspaper columnist for the lovelorn whose misguided attempts to help end in tragedy. The latter centers on misfits on the fringe of Hollywood society and reaches a violent climax of apocalyptic proportions.

S. E. Hyman, *Nathanael West*, 1962.
R. Reid, *The Fiction of Nathanael West*, 1967.

WIENER, NORBERT (1894–1964) U.S. mathematician, best known as the founder of cybernetics, a name he coined himself from the Greek word for "helmsman" to refer to the science concerned with finding common principles in the function of automatic machines and the human nervous system. Wiener was born in Columbia, Missouri, to a family of Jewish immigrants. His father, Leo Wiener, was a distinguished linguist, who wrote a standard history of Yiddish literature. Arriving in the United States in 1882, he taught Slavic studies at Harvard, being appointed a professor in 1911.

Norbert Wiener grew up in an academic environment. Having been under the tutelage of his father during a significant part of his childhood, Wiener recalls (in his autobiography, *Ex-Prodigy: My Childhood*) that his "father's way of teaching was scarcely conducive to peace of mind." His father's discipline and extremely demanding nature would often result in the young Wiener's feelings of humiliation and even terror. Although he was treated as slow and unintelligent by his impatient father, Wiener showed signs of genius at a very early age. Considered a child prodigy, he read incessantly and by age four was studying scientific books and by seven he had read the most important natural science works of his time, among them Darwin. He entered high school at age nine, attended Tufts University at eleven, graduated at fourteen, and received his Ph.D. degree from Harvard University at eighteen.

Despite his father's early career as a Yiddish scholar, he never disclosed to his son that they were Jewish. The secret of the family's Jewish orgin was maintained by his father's silence on the one hand and by his mother's extremely prejudicial attitude toward all members of other groups on the other. The discovery of his Jewish origin came quite by accident in his teens when a friend of his father's casually inquired about rumors that the Wiener family had as an ancestor the Jewish philosopher Maimonides (q.v.).

Like his father, Wiener was a natural linguist and spoke thirteen languages. He studied at Cornell, Columbia, and Cambridge universities, was a Guggenheim Memorial Foundation fellow at the universities of Göttingen, Germany, and Copenhagen, Denmark, lectured at the National Tsing Hua University in China, and was a Fulbright scholar at the Collège de France. He began to teach in the department of mathematics at the Massachusetts Institute of Technology in 1919 and was appointed professor in 1932. After forty years of teaching, Wiener was appointed institute professor, a distinguished academic position that at that time was held by only four other MIT scholars.

Wiener's main contribution to mathematics is the development of a mathematical approach that, by employing certain terms that reflect the randomness and irregularity of the physical world, attempts to arrive at some harmony. A civilian researcher during World War II, Wiener further developed his ideas into important work on such electronic inventions as gunfire control, antiaircraft predictors, radar systems, and increased speeds in computation.

Among his works were extensive professional texts and mathematical articles including the epoch-making *Cybernetics* (1948), *The Human Use of Human Beings* (1954), and a semi-autobiographical science fiction novel called *The Tempest*. His last work was a booklet called "God and Golem Inc." Shortly before his death President Lyndon B. Johnson presented him with the national medal of science, citing him for "marvelously versatile contributions, profoundly original, ranging within pure and applied mathematics, and penetrating boldly into engineering and biological sciences."

N. Wiener, *Ex-Prodigy: My Childhood*, 1953.
N. Wiener, *I Am a Mathematician*, 1956.

WIENIAWSKI, HENRYK (HENRY) (1835–1880) Polish violinist and composer. He was born in Lublin where his father was an army surgeon. His mother was a talented pianist who, on the advice of her pianist-composer brother, Edouard Wolff, took her young child to Paris, where he entered the conservatory at the age of eight. Three years later Wieniawski graduated with first prize in violin, the first young boy to graduate with distinction from the Paris Conservatory.

Wieniawski made his debut in Paris in 1848, and two months later performed his first concert in Saint Petersburg. After touring extensively in Europe, he returned to the Paris Conservatory in 1849 to study composition. Once again he graduated with the top prize.

Wieniawski continued his travels, often accompanied by his brother Joseph at the piano, and in 1860 was appointed as solo violinist to the tsar in Saint Petersburg. There the exceptional violinist

larly today, including his two violin concerti, *Legende, Souvenir de Moscou,* and *Le Carnaval russe.* He owned two exquisite violins, but had to sell both to pay gambling debts.

L. Auer, *My Long Life in Music,* 1923.
W. Duleba, *Henryk Wieniawski,* 1967.

WILLSTAETTER, RICHARD (1872–1942) German chemist and Nobel Prize winner. Born in Karlsruhe, Germany, he studied chemistry and began working under Friedrich Bayer at the University of Munich, where he obtained his doctorate in 1894 for work in the structure of cocaine, and became associate professor of chemistry in 1902. From 1905 he was professor of chemistry at the Technische Hochschule (technical institute) in

Henryk Wieniawski with his brother, Joseph

taught at the new Saint Petersburg Conservatory for six years and played the viola with the Ernst String Quartet.

In 1872 Wieniawski embarked on an extensive two-year American tour, initially with pianist Anton Rubinstein (q.v.). The two performed 256 concerts in 239 days and received 200 dollars per concert. After Rubinstein returned to Europe, Wieniawski performed one more year all over the United States.

Back in Europe Wieniawski continued to tour extensively, even after suffering a heart attack during a concert in Berlin in 1878, while playing his second violin concerto. As Wieniawski was carried off the stage in the middle of the performance, the famous violinist Joseph Joachim (q.v.), who was in the audience, rushed backstage. A few minutes later Joachim came on stage with his friend's violin announcing: "Although I cannot play my friend's wonderful concerto, I shall play Bach's Chaconne." As Joachim concluded his playing, a somewhat recovered Wieniawski returned to the stage to embrace his colleague. Wieniawski spent his last few years in Moscow where he died at the age of forty-four.

Wieniawski was as accomplished a composer as he was a violinist. Among his twenty-two compositions for the violin many are still performed regu-

> ## WILLSTAETTER LEAVES THE UNIVERSITY
>
> At a meeting of the Munich University senate, a discussion had arisen about the appointment of a mineralogist. A candidate was proposed, a front-rank mineralogist by the name of Goldschmidt. As soon as the name was mentioned a murmur arose in the meeting and someone remarked, "Weider ein Jude." ("Another Jew.") Without saying a word Willstaetter rose, collected his papers and left the room. He never crossed the threshold of the university again, this despite the repeated entreaties of his colleagues and of the Bavarian government, who felt that he was too valuable a man to lose, that his withdrawal was a severe blow to the prestige of the university.
>
> It was a tragedy for Willstaetter to be deprived of the laboratory but he found a place in the Munich Academy of Science. Not that he entered that place either! He directed the work from outside and he would be on the telephone with his assistant for one to two hours every day. Although his reputation was immense, he was modest, unassuming and retiring in character; he often reminded me of the old-time venerable type of great Jewish Rabbi.
>
> He came to Palestine to the opening of the Sieff Institute (in 1934). I was not the only one to plead with him to stay with us... but he was not to be moved. His last word on the subject was, "I know that Germany has gone mad, but if a mother falls ill, it is not a reason for her children to leave her. My home is Germany, my university — in spite of what has happened — is Munich. I must return."
>
> **Chaim Weizmann in *Trial and Error***

Zurich, Switzerland, until 1912, when he became professor of chemistry at the Kaiser Wilhelm Institute for Chemistry in Berlin-Dahlem.

During World War I he did work on the development of gas masks for which he was awarded the civilian iron cross. In 1915 he succeeded Bayer at the University of Munich, where he worked until 1924 directing the State Chemistry Laboratory.

Willstaetter worked on fundamental research in organic and inorganic chemistry. He emphasized the chemical nature of enzymes (biological catalysts) and did much research on plant alkaloids, blood, and plant pigments. Among his most important achievements was the description of the relationship of the green plant pigment chlorophyll and carbon dioxide synthesis to plant respiration and the production of free oxygen by living plants. He also demonstrated that the structure of the red blood cell pigment heme was essentially the same as that of green chlorophyll, the difference being that the chlorophyll molecule had a magnesium ion at its center while heme contained a ferrous ion. For his work on the structure and function of chlorophyll he was awarded the Nobel Prize for chemistry in 1915.

Willstaetter's other researches were concerned with different plant pigments such as carotenes, anthocyanins, atropine, and cocaine. He also developed a general anesthetic. In 1928 he published *Researches on Enzymes* and was the author of numerous papers and articles on chemistry and physiology.

In 1924 he resigned his chair at the University of Munich in protest against its anti-Semitic policy of not appointing Jews to university positions. He continued his work privately but retained the title of professor emeritus. Willstaetter continued to work as an industrial consultant, devoting himself to writing and lecturing. In 1939 he was ordered to leave Germany by the Gestapo and settled in Lucarno, Switzerland.

E. Farber (ed.), *Great Chemists,* 1961.

WINCHELL, WALTER (1897–1972) U.S. journalist, radio columnist, and gossip columnist. Winchell was a vaudeville performer for twelve years before he became a journalist. At the age of twelve he sang in a trio with George Jessel. He served in the U.S. Navy during World War I. In 1920 Winchell began contributing gossip material to *Billboard* and the *Vaudeville News.* The latter

Walter Winchell.

gave him his own column in 1922. Two years later Winchell's "On Broadway" column moved to the New York *Evening Graphic* and then to the New York *Daily Mirror* in 1929, where the popular and widely syndicated column appeared until 1963. His weekly radio program, which always opened with the words "Good evening, Mr. and Mrs. America and all the ships at sea," began in 1932 and ran for more than twenty years.

Winchell's show business and political gossip, although often inaccurate, was extremely popular. His sensational disclosures and rapid-fire delivery of opinionated news appealed to millions of listeners. As a molder of public opinion, his sources were legion, and his acquaintances included top politicians, show people, and even gangsters.

He supported President Franklin D. Roosevelt and the New Deal. After World War II, with the onset of the Cold War, Winchell's philosophy turned right and anticommunist. He became a sharp critic of President Harry S. Truman and a supporter of the communist-hunting Senator Joseph McCarthy.

Winchell's original slang idiom was widely imitated and became a part of the English language of the time.

In 1946 he founded the Damon Runyon Cancer Fund, in memory of his close friend, and over the next quarter of a century he raised more than thirty million dollars for cancer research. He retired to California in 1965.

H. Weiner, *Let's Go to Press: A Biography of Walter Winchell,* 1955.

- Hollywood: a place where they shoot too many films and not enough actors.
- It's a sure sign of summer when the chair gets up when you do.
- Money sometimes makes fools of important persons, but also makes important persons of fools.

Walter Winchell

WISE, ISAAC MAYER

WISE, ISAAC MAYER (1814–1900) U.S. Reform rabbi; leading architect of Reform Judaism in America in the 19th century. He studied in Bohemia, where he was born, and after receiving rabbinical ordination, officiated in the town of Radnitz. Finding the political atmosphere of Bohemia and the rigidity of his Orthodox congregation too oppressive, he moved to the United States in 1846. He was appointed rabbi of Congregation Beth El in Albany, New York, where he introduced various reforms such as family pews, a mixed choir, and the confirmation ceremony. However, after he had declared that he did not believe in a personal Messiah or bodily resurrection, he was forcibly removed from the pulpit in 1850. His supporters then left Beth El and organized a separate congregation, Anshe Emeth, the third Reform synagogue in the United States. In 1854 he left for B'nai Jeshurun in Cincinnati, which offered him greater scope and influence. This was originally an Orthodox congregation, but Wise introduced a series of reforms including the abolition of second days of festivals and bare headed worship. He remained there for forty-six years.

In his first year in Cincinnati, Wise founded the Anglo-Jewish weekly, *The Israelite* (later the *American Israelite*), which pioneered Jewish journalism in English in the United States. He also founded a German weekly, *Die Deborah*. At all times, he wrote extensively and in 1854 published the first of his two-part *The History of the Israelitish Nation.* He also wrote on theology, poetry, and liturgy. His prayer book, *Minhag America* (1856), a revision of the traditional prayer book, was intended to provide a liturgy that could be accepted by all American Jews. Its innovations (omission of prayers for the return to Zion and the rebuilding of the Temple) were rejected by the Orthodox, but the book was widely used by Reform congregations.

Wise was largely responsible for the establishment of the main Reform institutions in the United States. He took a leading role in the founding of the Union of American Hebrew Congregations in 1873. When the Reform Rabbinical Seminar, Hebrew Union College, opened in Cincinnati in 1875, Wise was elected its first president, holding office until his death and placing it on a strong foundation. It took him longer to realize another objective — the creation of an organization of Reform rabbis, but this was achieved in 1889 with the formation of the Central Conference of American Rabbis, of which Wise was also president until his death.

Wise was less extreme than some of his Reform colleagues and his attempts to conciliate the Orthodox did not win the approval of many of them. He accepted the Pentateuch as the source of authoritative law but regarded only the Decalogue as binding, the remainder subject to reinterpretation as the composition of Moses but not divine revelation. Rabbinic legislation similarly was not binding and could be changed. He stressed the universal ethical basis of Judaism and its influence on the constitution and mores of the United States. "Legalism," he concluded, "is not Judaism. Judaism is the fear of the Lord and the love of man in harmony with the dictates of reason."

J. G. Heller, *Isaac M. Wise*, 1965.
I. Knox, *Rabbi in America: The Story of Isaac M. Wise*, 1957.

WISE, STEPHEN SAMUEL

WISE, STEPHEN SAMUEL (1874–1949) U.S. Reform rabbi, Jewish and Zionist leader, and civic activist. Born in Budapest, he was the son of Rabbi Aaron Weisz and Sibine Farkashazi-Fischer, daughter of Moritz Farkashazi-Fischer, founder of the world-famous Herend porcelain factory. When Aaron Weisz emigrated to the United States in 1875, he adopted the American spelling of his name, Wise, and was appointed rabbi of the congregation of Rodeph Scholom in New York City.

Stephen Wise's early years were spent in New York, where he entered City College at fifteen and received instruction in rabbinic subjects from his father and noted scholars. In 1891, he entered Columbia University, attained distinction as a Greek and Latin scholar, and graduated with honors in 1892. Wise spent the next year in Vienna and Oxford, and having been ordained by Vienna's chief rabbi, Adoph Jellinek, was installed as assistant rabbi and then rabbi at the Conservative Temple B'nai Jeshurun (Madison Avenue, New York).

Four events that occurred during his ministry at B'nai Jeshurun deeply influenced Wise's future life: His father died suddenly and, at twenty-three, he became obliged to provide for his family. The Dreyfus (q.v.) affair in France and the pogroms in tsarist Russia convinced him of the need to end Jewish powerlessness. The appearance of Theodor Herzl (q.v.) on the Jewish scene prompted him, together with others, to found the Zionist Federation of New York in 1897. And in 1898, when he attended the second Zionist Congress, Herzl appointed him American secretary of the Zionist Movement.

Wise traveled to the West Coast in 1899 on a speaking tour for Zionism and was invited by Temple Beth Israel of Portland, Oregon, to become its rabbi.

During his Portland years, Wise completed a translation of the book of Judges (1917) and obtained a Ph.D. from Columbia University. He also accepted the unpaid post of commissioner of child labor in Oregon. In 1906, he left for New York, where the following year he founded the Free Synagogue (now the Stephen Wise Free Synagogue) based on freedom of speech from the pulpit and free seating without payment of dues. His political career began with the establishment of the Free Synagogue's Social Service Division (1908) and the founding of the National Association for the Advancement of Colored People with the Rev. John Hayes Holmes, Jane Addams, and others (1909). With Holmes and Frank Oliver Hall, he started nonsectarian services and forums on "Religion and the Social Problem" (1910). He played an important role in Woodrow Wilson's election campaign (1912), visited Eretz Israel for the first time (1913), and with Louis D. Brandeis (q.v.) created the Provisional Executive Committee for General Zionist Affairs (1914). In 1915, Wise became active in the American Union against Militarism and the League to Enforce Peace. With Brandeis and Julian W. Mack (q.v.) he founded the American Jewish Congress (AJC) in 1915. It was after a visit from Wise that President Wilson wrote to him an endorsement of the Balfour Declaration (1918). Wise was vice president of the Zionist Organization of America (ZOA; 1918–1920) and advocated both the Zionist and Armenian causes at the Versailles peace conference. In the immediate postwar years, Wise was involved in fighting monopolies, in establishing the American Civil Liberties Union, and in planning and founding the Reform rabbinical seminary, the Jewish Institute of Religion (1922).

He coauthored *The Great Betrayal* (1930), indicting the British government for its failure to implement the promises made in the Balfour Declaration.

Wise was also deeply involved in New York City politics. With his friend John Hayes Holmes he headed the New York City Affairs Committee and, exposing the corruption in New York City, and demanded that Franklin D. Roosevelt, then governor of New York, force the removal of James J. Walker as mayor of New York City (1932). Although a convinced Democrat, Wise fell out with Roosevelt around this time. With the rise of Hitler to power, Wise assumed the role of leader in the fight against the Nazis, mobilizing Jews and non-Jews alike, and initiated the formation of the World Jewish Congress. From 1933 to 1935, he led the American Jewish Congress not only in organizing the boycott against Nazi Germany but also the boycott of the 1936 Olympics in Berlin.

Wise was reconciled with Roosevelt in 1936, and participated actively in the campaign for Roosevelt's reelection. He also served a second term as president of the ZOA (1936–1938). He went to London in 1939 to participate in the Saint James's Conference of Jews and Arabs and led the protest against the British white paper restricting Jewish immigration to Palestine. As a member of the President's Advisory Committee on Political Refugees, Wise was instrumental in obtaining immigration permits for a large number of Jews and non-Jews threatened by the Nazis. At the outbreak of war in Europe in September 1939, he used his position to draw attention to the Jewish refugee problem and urged the emigation of European Jews both to the United States and to Palestine. He was in the forefront of the struggle against American isolationists, especially the American First movement.

Upon receiving information of the final solution in August 1942, Wise was the first to release this information to the public. By this time, the United States was at war and he had become a close friend of both President and Mrs. Roosevelt. He made almost daily calls on the White House and the State Department, demanding a joint declaration of the Allies threatening Hitler and his accomplices with severe retribution for the crimes perpetrated on the Jews of Europe. He also demanded permission from the Treasury for the transmission of funds to Europe to be used for the rescue and relief of persecuted Jews. The Allied Declaration came on December 17, 1942, and the from the Treasury permit on December 23, 1943.

Meanwhile, Wise energetically led the activities of the American Zionist Emergency Council, the short-lived American Jewish Conference, the American Jewish Congress, and the World Jewish Congress. In 1944, he presided over the WJC's War Emergency Conference at Atlantic City, New Jersey. With the end of the war in sight, the conference presented a plan for the punishment of war crimes and crimes against humanity, restitution and indemnification by Germany, the reconstruction and rehabilitiation of European Jewry, and the establishment of a Jewish state in Palestine. In 1945 Wise participated in the London World Zionist Conference and visited the displaced persons' camps in liberated Europe. What he saw there more than ever convinced him of the need to establish a Jewish State and in his testimony before the Anglo-American Commission of Enquiry in 1946, he eloquently pleaded for it. Although the British refused him a visa to visit Palestine, he supported the American loan to the United Kingdom, demonstrating his respect for the British, who had fought the Nazis alone. In 1946 he was appointed a member of the President's Commission on Higher Education. In 1947 he pressed for a policy of quiet diplomacy the adoption of the U.N. partition plan, which led him into sharp conflict with Abba Hillel Silver (q.v.).

In 1948, he brought about the merger of the Jewish Institute of Religion with Hebrew Union College, and presided over the Second Plenary Assembly of the WJC in Montreux, which reelected him president. His memorable address at the opening session was his swansong. He finished his memoirs, *Challenging Years* (1949), shortly before his death.

J. W. Polier and J. W. Wise, *The Personal Letters of Stephen S. Wise*, 1956.
M. Urovsky, *A Voice that Spoke for Justice: The Life and Times of S. Wise*, 1982.
C. H. Voss, *Rabbi and Minister: The Friendship of Stephen S. Wise and John Haynes Holmes*, 1964.
C. H. Voss, *S. Wise, Servant of the People*, 1969.

Y

YADIN, YIGAEL (1917–1984) Israeli soldier, archaeologist, and politician. Born in Jerusalem, the son of a noted archaeologist, Eliezer Sukenik, Yadin at age fifteen, joined the underground defense organization, the Haganah. He served in various command and training capacities, rising to chief of operations. He simultaneously studied archaeology in Jerusalem.

During Israel's War of Independence (1947–1949), owing to the prolonged illness of the army chief of staff, Yadin was acting chief of staff and in that capacity advised David Ben-Gurion (q.v.) to proclaim Israel's independence against the military odds, saying the chances for victory were fifty-fifty.

He relied on the morale of the Jews and their fledgling army. His knowledge of archaeology stood him well when the Israel army outflanked the Egyptian army in the Negev using an ancient Roman road. After leading the Israeli delegation to the armistice negotiations with Egypt, he was appointed chief of staff (1949–1952). In those three years, Yadin laid the foundations for the modern Israeli army, designed its reservist system, subordinated the navy, air force, and armored corps to a single general staff, instituted the standing army, and built the army's support system. He resigned following arguments with Ben-Gurion, who demanded a massive cut in the defense budget. Yadin

Yigael Yadin in a Judean Desert cave, examining finds from the Bar Kokhba period.

remained a protégé of Ben-Gurion, who saw in him a political heir, and both worked (unsuccessfully) for a reform in Israel's electoral system.

From 1952 Yadin was professor of archaeology at the Hebrew University, training scores of gifted archaeologists, and excavating the ancient city of Hazor and the ancient desert fortress of Masada. He also discovered relics in the Judean desert caves and was connected with the purchase by Israel of the Dead Sea Scrolls, whose significance was first understood by his father in 1947. In 1967 Yadin was called to serve as military adviser to Levi Eshkol (q.v.) and following the 1973 Yom Kippur War, served on the Agranat Commission of Inquiry, which investigated Israel's lack of military preparedness on the eve of the war.

As the Labor party's fortunes declined, he created, in 1976, a new political body, the Democratic party, which joined with another reformist group, Shinui, to become the Democratic Movement for Change. It called for electoral reforms and concentration on Israel's social and economic problems in addition to administrative reforms. It attracted many intellectuals, civil servants, and the better-off Ashkenazic segment of the population who despaired of Labor but would not vote Likud. In the May 1977 elections, Yadin's party won fifteen seats, an unprecedented feat for a new, small party in Israel. After hedging for a while, his party joined the first government of Menahem Begin, and Yadin became deputy prime minister responsible mainly for the implementation of social projects. Yadin's party had limited influence on Begin's foreign policy. It disintegrated in 1980, and Yadin, despondent over his inability to push electoral reform, retired from politics and returned to his first love, archaeology.

Yadin was a brilliant archaeologist, with a gift for popularization in his lectures and books, and for catching the public's imagination. He published major works on the Dead Sea Scrolls and claimed to have identified documents signed by Bar Kokhba (q.v.) and the lots used by the last defenders of Masada, including Eleazar ben Jair (q.v.), to decide the order of their suicide. His best-known books include *The Message of the Scrolls* (1957), *Masada* (1965), and *Bar Kokhba* (1971).

YANNAI (JANNAEUS), ALEXANDER (c. 126–76 BCE) Hasmonean ruler, the first to assume the kingly title in addition to the already traditional high priesthood. He was the third son of John Hyrcanus (q.v.) and was held in low esteem by his father and brothers. During the brief reign of his brother Aristobulus (104–103), he was imprisoned, but when his brother died, he was released; he married Salome Alexandra (q.v.), his brother's widow, and acceded to the throne. In his twenty-seven year reign in the Land of Israel (103–76 BCE) he expanded the country's borders to what is today northernmost Galilee and a huge chunk of territory east of the Jordan River. With the exception of Ascalon, the largely pagan-populated Mediterranean coast also came under Jewish control.

All these achievements, however, were not without their severe vicissitudes. Alexander's entire rule was one of almost unending turbulence, much of it on the domestic scene. Josephus (q.v.) tells of violent clashes between Alexander and the Pharisee spiritual leaders — who felt themselves threatened by his growing ties with the Sadducees — and the dire punishment he meted out to them for their alleged participation in a civil war against him. These stories are now considered to be tendentious. By the same token, certain perjorative references in the Dead Sea Scrolls, previously considered to be barbs aimed at Alexander Yannai, have recently also been seriously questioned. The Jerusalem Talmud, at any rate, historically closer to the Alexander and his period, views the king in a favorable light.

Alexander's political, military, and even domestic maneuverings were conducted against the backdrop of two declining but still troublesome empires — the Ptolemies of Egypt and the Seleucid House in Syria — on the one hand and the already great superpower, Rome, on the other. He also had serious clashes with the Nabateans of Transjordan, very likely for control of the trade routes that cut through the area.

An illustrative incident in his stormy career relates to the Ptolemaic queen, the famous Cleopatra, and her plan at one point to subjugate the Land of Israel to Egyptian rule. One of the queen's leading generals, the Jew Hananiah, warned her of the dire repercussions of such a step, saying, "the evil step against Jannaeus will turn all us Jews into your enemies." Cleopatra desisted.

The king's deathbed request of his wife, Salome Alexandra, was to see that peace prevailed between the royal court and the Pharisees, "as they had the confidence of the mass of the people." He left a land with borders unequaled since the days of King David.

J. Efron, *Simon ben Shatah and King Jannaeus, In Memory of Gedaliahu Alon, Essays, etc.* (Hebrew), 1970.
A. Schalit (ed.), *The World History of the Jewish People*, vol. 6 1976.
S. Zeitlin, *The Rise and Fall of the Judean State*, vol. 1 1962.

YEZIERSKA, ANZIA (1883?–1970) U.S. author of short stories and novels who often used the dense immigrant milieu of New York for her scenery and a Yiddishized English dialogue for reporting direct speech. Several versions of Yezierska's life have been published and she herself gave out variant accounts. Born in a Polish village, she arrived in America with her family sometime during her adolescence. Though she hungered to learn, she was forced to work in sweatshops and a laundry on the Lower East Side, the setting of most of her early writing. She worked her way through college, married, and had one child. *Red Ribbon on* a *White Horse* (1950), called an autobiography by her publisher (though Yezierska's daughter labeled it fiction), is dedicated to her daughter, but the book itself makes no mention of husband or child, skipping over that part of her life. Indeed she left her husband and child to concentrate on her writing.

She successfully sold her first collection of short stories, *Hungry Hearts*, to Hollywood in 1920 (it was produced by Samuel Goldwyn [q.v.] in 1922) and her story *Salome of the Tenements* (1922) was filmed by Jesse Lasky (q.v.). After this taste of glamor, Yezierska returned, dejected, to New York, where she continued to produce fictional works during the 1920s and early 1930s. Then a dry spell ensued, in literary as well as economic terms, until her autobiographical book, written in a contemplative mood on the edge of old age. Following its publication her works had a slight revival and she managed to bring out stories and articles until her death.

In the fiction of Yezierska's youth, anger was aimed in all directions. The one consistent object of hostility was the social worker. These bourgeois women, calling themselves "friendly visitors," came from German Jewish families that had become Americanized decades before. They lived in comfortable Upper West Side homes from which they periodically descended upon the Lower East Side to dispense "scientific charity" (conceived as a rational method of apportioning alms) to their newly arrived, unfortunate east European sisters and brothers.

A YEZIERSKA FRAGMENT

As the children were scurrying about for hammers and iron lasts with which to crack their nuts, the basement door creaked. Unannounced, a woman entered — the "friendly visitor" of the charities. Her look of awful amazement swept the group of merrymakers.

"Mr. Shmendrik! — Hannah Breineh!" Indignation seethed in her voice. "What's this? A feast — a birthday?... I came to make my monthly visit — evidently I'm not needed."

Shmendrik faced the accusing eyes of the "friendly visitor." "Holiday eating..."

"Oh — I'm glad you're so prosperous." Before any one had presence of mind enough to explain things, the door had clanked. The "friendly visitor" had vanished.

"Pfui!" Hannah Breineh snatched up her glass and drained its contents. "What will she do now? Will we get no more dry bread from the charities because once we ate cake?"

"What for did she come?" asked Sophie.

"To see that we don't overeat ourselves!" returned Hannah Breineh.

From "My Own People," in *Hungry Hearts*

On many occasions the targets of Yezierska's wit and sarcasm shifted: frequently the older generation, the foreign born and bred, and the religious were the objects of her scorn. *The Bread Givers* (1925), an autobiographical novel of her early years, was subtitled "A Struggle between a Father of the Old World and a Daughter of the New," and she clearly delineated the tension between the two, with all sympathy lying on the daughter's side. By the time she wrote *Red Ribbon on a White Horse*, however, her attitude had mellowed. The title comes from one of her father's favorite quotations, "Poverty is an ornament on a Jew like a red ribbon on a white horse."

For all its seriousness, there is also much laughter, often bitter, in Yezierska's writing. Her dramatic tones shed light on the vivacity of many immigrant women of her generation. She drew well the polarities in the world that they faced and illuminated some basic truths, if not all the facts, of her time.

A. Kessler-Harris (ed.), *The Open Cage: An Anzia Yezierska Collection*, 1979.

YOSE BEN YOSE (5th-6th century) Hebrew liturgical poet. The name of Yose ben Yose alone emerges from the earliest anonymous period of *piyyut* (Hebrew liturgical poetry). His pure, simple, and elegant Hebrew suggests his home was in Eretz Israel, which was in fact the birthplace of the oldest form of *piyyut*. Some scholars, however, claim he was Babylonian, as his works were disseminated very early in that country; others, that he was Spanish or European. As for his time, stylistic elements of his works indicate he probably lived in the 5th or 6th century. His poems are usually unrhymed and devoid of the literary embellishments that characterize later medieval *piyut*.

Almost nothing is really known about Yose ben Yose, and his figure is thus obscured in legend. He was sometimes called "the orphan," either because he bore the same name as his father, or as a title of honor in the sense of unique or esteemed. Saadia Gaon (q.v.) recognized him as the most prominent among the illustrious poets of antiquity. Others referred to him as "high priest," perhaps believing he lived in the times of the Temple, and some even identify him, anachronistically, with the Talmudic rabbi Yose ben Yose. However, allusions to later rabbinic literature are woven throughout his works, and this places him solidly at the end of the Talmudic period, when Talmudic traditions began to enter liturgical poetry. Compositions attributed to Yose ben Yose form part of the New Year (Rosh Hashanah) and Day of Atonement (Yom Kippur) prayers, and are preserved in the rituals of German, French and Italian communities. He frequently speaks of divine manifestation in Jewish history, recalling episodes in which God was seen as having intervened.

YULEE, DAVID LEVY (1810—1886) U.S. public figure. The son of Moses Elias Levy (q.v.), he was

David Levy Yulee.

the first senator from Florida and the first Jew to be a member of the United States Senate.

David Yulee, first known as David Levy, was born on the island of Saint Thomas in the Caribbean, and was taken to the United States by his father as a boy to be educated in Norfolk, Virginia. When David was seventeen, for some unknown reason, Moses Levy stopped paying for his son's upkeep. For some time David worked on one of his father's plantations and then studied law in a private office. He was admitted to the bar in 1832, and soon entered politics, "without blare or trumpets" (as his grandson stated), after he became clerk of the territorial legislature. In 1838 he was one of the delegates to the convention that produced decided the constitution of Florida, and in 1841 ran as the Democratic candidate for the office of territorial delegate to Congress. He fought vigorously for Florida's admission to the Union. His efforts were crowned with success, and in 1845 he became the state's first senator. He married the daughter of the former governor of Kentucky, Charles Anderson Wycliffe, who was known as the Wycliffe Madonna

for her beauty. It was at this time that he added Yulee to his name, first as Levy Yulee and later signing just D. L. Yulee. He was defeated in the next election in 1850 but was elected again in 1854.

Yulee made many friends in Virginia and in Washington but he also had opponents who tried to end his political career by contesting the legality of his and his father's American citizenship. For many years he was to be harassed by this question, which was brought before a Congress commission of inquiry. It was argued that David Levy's father was not a resident of Florida on July 17, 1821, when American sovereignty over Florida was declared, and that he had come to Saint Augustine a few days after "the changing of the flag."

Because of his radical views, David Levy Yulee was termed a "firebrand." He was fiercely disliked by John Quincy Adams, who wrote in his diary on June 21, 1841, "Levy is said to be a Jew and what will be, if true, a far more formidable disqualification is that he has a dash of African blood in him, which *sub rosa* is the case of more than one member of the house." On other occasions, he mentions him as "the alien Jew delegate from Florida" and "the contemptible little Jew." On the other hand, Yulee was commended by his colleagues for his "diligence and acuteness." On one occasion, a senator seeing a high pile of books and and papers on his desk, said, "I move, Mr. President, that we save time by giving the senator from Florida whatever he wants. We know he is going to get it."

In contrast to his father, David Levy Yulee fought against the abolition of slavery, probably because of the influence of his childhood in Virginia. He was also opposed to the abolition of flogging in the Navy, believing that this would undermine efficiency.

Yulee devoted his time to the development of his state. He planned an extensive railroad system across Florida which crossed the state from the Gulf of Mexico to the Atlantic, and was utilized for the commerce of New York and the Mississipi Valley.

In 1861 he was the first senator to announce the secession of a Southern state. He then served in the Southern Congress. After the defeat of the South, Yulee was appointed to go to Washington to have Florida reinstated in the Union. Before reaching Washington, he was arrested in Georgia and sent as a prisoner to Fort Pulaski near Savannah. After his release a year later, thanks to the intercession of General Ulysses S. Grant, he took no active part in politics but devoted his time to rebuilding the ruined railroad system of Florida of which he was president. He retired and settled in Washington.

Yulee completely lost touch with Judaism, and although he never formally converted, he went to church and his children were raised as Christians.

On the Gulf coast, a tract of land was named Levy County to honor the senator from Florida.
C. Wycliffe Yulee, "Senator Yulee." *Publications of the Florida Historical Society*, 2, Nos. 1 & 2 (1909).

Z

ZACUTO, ABRAHAM (1452–c.1515) Astronomer, mathematician, and historian. Born in Castile, he attended the University of Salamanca, where he studied astronomy and astrology. The bishop of Salamanca greatly admired the young scholar, encouraging him to write on astronomy. Zacuto remained at the bishop's court until the bishop died in 1480, leaving instructions in his will to bind all Zacuto's writings in a single volume to be deposited in the cathedral library. Zacuto then found a new patron in the person of the grand master of the order of the knights of Alcantara, moving to Gata (Caceres province). Here he wrote works on the influence of the stars and on eclipses of the sun and moon.

When the Jews of Spain were expelled from the country in 1492, Zacuto took refuge in Portugal, where he served as court astronomer to the king, Joao II, and to his successor, Manuel IV, writing quadrennial ˌables of solar declination. Zacuto played a major role in preparing Vasco da Gama for his historic voyage to India. The king consulted Zacuto on the position of the stars and Zacuto forecast that the expedition would succeed and that much of India would fall under Portuguese rule. Vasco da Gama met with Zacuto before setting out and received from him the astronomical tables and charts that Zacuto had prepared for the voyage. Zacuto also instructed the sailors in the use of his improved astrolabe.

In 1497, the king of Portugal ruled that all Jews had to convert to Christianity and Zacuto had once again to flee — this time to North Africa. Along the way he was twice taken prisoner, but after a hazardous journey reached Tunis. There he wrote *Sefer Yuhasin* ("Book of Genealogies"), a lucid account of the history of Jewish tradition with detailed information on the rabbis of the Mishnah and Talmud. The main section covers the period from Ezra to the final redaction of the Talmud but Zacuto then decided to continue the history down to his own times and append an outline of the history of the world since creation. The book contains considerable information on the individual scholars.

Little is known of his later years. In 1513 he was in Jerusalem, where he wrote an almanac in Hebrew and in 1515 he was in Damascus.

For another twenty years, all solar navigation tables in Portugal were based on his reckonings and made a great contribution to the great Spanish and Portuguese voyages of discovery. Columbus used Zacuto's tables and it was reported that on one occasion they saved him from death. In the knowledge that Zacuto had shown the imminence of an eclipse, Columbus told natives who were threatening him that he would take the light from them. (The story was later utilized by Mark Twain in *A Connecticut Yankee at the Court of King Arthur*.) Among his astronomic achievements were the production of the first astrolabe of copper (previously they had been made of wood), increased precision in reckoning the position of the sun, and improved tables (which he wrote in Spanish and Hebrew) to determine latitudes and work out the dates of eclipses.

ZAMENHOF, LUDOVIC LAZARUS (1859–1917) Polish physician and philologist, creator of the Esperanto language. He was born in Bialystok. His father was a Hebrew scholar and teacher of languages. A sickly, frail child, Zamenhof was educated at the Realschule until 1873 when the family moved to Warsaw, and he was admitted to the Philological Gymnasium (high school). At age fifteen, Zamenhof made his first attempt to create a new international language (he already had a good knowledge of French, German, Polish, Hebrew, and Yiddish) and, by the time he was nineteen, had invented a language he was convinced could be learned, written, and spoken.

Zamenhof studied medicine, first in Moscow and then in Warsaw. Simultaneously he continued to develop his language, constantly testing it by translation and writing verse. Because of the oppressive regime in Poland at the time, he was compelled to carry on this work in the utmost secrecy. Outraged at the pogroms of 1881, he turned to Zionism, and in 1882 became a founding member of the early Zionist movement, the Lovers of Zion, a member of its executive committee, and wrote for the Hebrew periodical *Ha-Sefira*. At about this time he began work on a Yiddish grammar. Zamenhof also toyed with the idea of founding a Jewish state in the Mississippi area of the United States and published articles to this end.

After graduating in 1885, he began to work as a general practitioner in the Lithuanian town of Veiseyai, and his compassionate attitude toward his patients gained him the reputation of "the good doctor." However, he decided that general practice did not suit his temperament and he turned to ophthalmology, ministering particularly to the poorer classes without charge.

In 1887 Zamenhof published *Lingvo Internacia* under the pseudonym of "Doktoro Esperanto" ("Dr. Hopeful"), hence the name of the new language. It had nine hundred root words and a grammar with sixteen rules. The English translation, *Dr. Esperanto's International Language*, appeared in 1889. Zamenhof edited *La Esperantisto*, the first Esperanto magazine, published by the World Esperanto Club until 1895.

In 1893, Zamenhof founded the League of Esperantists, and in 1905 the first Universal Esperanto Congress convened in Boulogne, France, with 688 participants from 20 countries. Zamenhof delivered the opening address with his characteristic humility, pointing out that the movement's purpose was to spread the use of a neutral language which would "give people of different nations the possibility of understanding one another."

Esperanto clubs were established throughout Europe and in 1901 in North America. Zamenhof translated into Esperanto most of the books of the

Tomb of Ludwik Zamenhof in the Warsaw Jewish cemetery.

**FROM ZAMENHOF'S FIRST
PUBLISHED VERSION OF PSALM 121
IN ESPERANTO**

Al vi mi levas miajn okulojn, al la montoj;
de kei venas al mi helpo.
Mia helpo venas de Dio,
Kiu kreis la cielon kaj la teron.
Li ne lasos vian piedon falpusigi;
via gardanto ne dormetas.
Jen ne dormetas kaj ne dormas
la gardanto de Izraelo.

English:
I will lift mine eyes unto the mountains:
From whence shall my help come?
My help cometh from the Lord,
Who made heaven and earth.
He will not suffer thy foot to be moved;
He that keepeth thee will not slumber.
Behold, He that keepeth Israel
Doth neither slumber nor sleep.

Bible from Hebrew, and many classics from a number of languages.

In 1901 Zamenhof published anonymously a pamphlet in which he proposed "Hillelism" (later called *Homaranismo*, "Humanism") as a world religion that would reconcile all religions to promote tolerance and respect. He believed that by constant interrelationship on the basis of a neutral language (Esperanto), and neutral religious principles and customs human beings would eventually fuse into one neutral human people. The proposal encountered bitter opposition from the Christian Church and rabbis and even from supporters of Esperanto.

In 1908, Zamenhof became honorary president of the Universala Esperanto-Asocio, a position he held until 1912 when he renounced his leadership of the movement. Zamenhof aged prematurely due to ill health, overwork, and the strain of constant quarrels and attempts to undermine the movement.

When Ludovic Zamenhof died, he was eulogized by H. G. Wells as "one of the finest specimens of that international idealism which is the natural gift of Jewry to mankind." Statues were erected in his honor in Poland, in Warsaw (1928) and Bialystok (1934), and streets were named in his honor in Warsaw (1937) and in Tel Aviv.

M. Boulton, *Zamenhof, Creator of Esperanto*, 1960.
I. Lapenna, *Dr. L. L. Zamenhof's Greatness*, 1959.
E. Privat, *The Life of Zamenhof*, 1931.

ZANGWILL, ISRAEL (1864–1926) English author and Jewish public figure. Born to an extremely poor family in London, Zangwill first encountered the dual worlds of his existence in the persons of his traditional father, who peddled in order to support a large family, and his mother, who yearned for the ways of the non-Jewish world. A man who loved the values of the Jewish past, yet who wanted to escape from the ghetto, Israel Zangwill's entire life was influenced by the paradox. He was proud of his Jewishness; he loved England as much as any other Briton. He admired Jesus, Saint Francis, the Baal Shem Tov (q.v.), and Shabbetai Tzevi (q.v.).

Raised in Bristol, Zangwill spent seven years studying and teaching at the Jews' Free School in London's East End. During that period he wrote his first book, *Motza Kleis* ("Matzoh Balls"), about market days in London's Jewish East End, but did not publish it because of objections on the part of the school's authorities. He later resigned from his position at the school because of further attempts to limit what he considered his freedom. Financially destitute, he wrote *The Premier and the Painter* (1888), which was a complete failure, and for the next few years worked as an editor of the comic paper *Ariel*.

In 1891 he wrote two humorous books, *The Bachelor's Club* and *The Old Maid's Club*, which suddenly launched him on the road to success. He had also published an article entitled "Judaism" in the *Jewish Quarterly Review*, which had attracted the attention of the Jewish Publication Society of America. They subsequently asked Zangwill to write a "Jewish novel" for them. Zangwill had kept notebooks with observations on every aspect of Jewish life which went into the writing of this and later ghetto novels. Thus *Children of the Ghetto* (1892), inspired by the story of his own family, was born; it became an instant success.

Numerous books and short stories followed. *The King of the Schnorrers* (1894) dealt amusingly with London Jewry in the 18th century. *Dreamers of the Ghetto* (1898), *Ghetto Tragedies* (1893) and *Ghetto Comedies* (1907) continued the trend of ghetto writing. There were also many novels on non-Jewish subjects. *The Master* (1895) relates the story of a simple disadvantaged boy who becomes a successful and sought-after artist. It was followed by *The Mantle of Elijah* (1900) and *Jinny the Carrier* (1919). Zangwill also published several collections, among them *Without Prejudice* (1896), of essays on widely varied subjects, *The Grey Wig*, consisting of stories and novelettes, and *Blind Children*, a book of religious and moral poems. His plays, including *The War God* (1911), *The Cockpit* (1921), and *The Forcing House* (1922), were vehicles for expressing his political beliefs, but were generally less successful. However, *The Melting Pot* (1909), the title of which was applied to the entire process of U.S. immigrant acculturation, had a long run on Broadway.

Zangwill was also extremely active in public affairs, including women's issues and pacifism. In 1895 he met Theodor Herzl (q.v.), who interested him in Zionism. Deeply impressed, Zangwill helped Herzl in his first address to a London audience and became an extremely active follower, joining a pilgrimage to Eretz Israel in 1897 and attending the First Zionist Congress. When at the Sixth Zionist Congress in 1903, however, Herzl's proposal to accept the British offer of an area of Uganda (now in Kenya) as a Jewish homeland met with opposition, Zangwill was incensed. After Herzl's death in 1905, he seceded from the Seventh Zionist Congress to head the Jewish Territorial Organization, whose aim was to found a Jewish home of refuge wherever territory could be found. He sought many such solutions, all unsuccessfully. After the Balfour Declaration of 1917, he temporarily readopted Zionist ideals, but problems in Palestine restrengthened his commitment to territorial views.

Zangwill also dreamed of a fusion of Judaism and Christianity. Two plays, *The Next Religion* (1912) and *Plaster Saints* (1915), dealt with the themes of international brotherhood and love, but were not well received. The *Voice of Jerusalem*, a collection of essays published in 1920, reflected a return to belief in the traditions of his forefathers.

J. Leftwich, *Israel Zangwill*, 1957.

M. Wohlgelehrnter, *Israel Zangwill: A Study*, 1964.

ZHITLOWSKY, CHAIM (1865–1943) Yiddish philosopher and writer, theoretician of "Diaspora Nationalism." Born in Vitebsk, Russia, he spent the early years of his life in an affluent Hasidic home, almost completely cut off from alien influences. In 1879, age fourteen, he began his high school education, but two years later, considering himself a "socialist, revolutionary cosmopolitan," he left Vitebsk and moved to Tula in central Russia, only to return in 1883.

His next move was to Saint Petersburg, where in 1887 he published his historical and philosophic study, *Thoughts on the Historic Destiny of Judaism* (Russian), in which he examined the contrast between the moral superiority of the Jewish people in ancient times and what he claimed was its degeneration in modern times. This study came under attack by the historian, Simon Dubnow (q.v.), and the Jewish press accused him of being a Jewish anti-Semite and heretic. In 1888 Zhitlowsky left Russia for Berlin, Zurich, and Bern, where he completed his Ph.D. In Switzerland he was recognized as the leader of a group of Russian students who remained loyal to the Narodniki (intellectual socialist) ideology. In 1892 he published his essay, "A Jew to the Jews," a mixture of Jewish nationalism and agrarian Narodniki socialism.

Zhitlowsky became interested in Zionism, but he considered the strong connection the movement had with Orthodox Jews and the central role played by the rabbis and lay leaders of the community as having a negative effect on the movement, and in the course of time he became fanatically opposed to it.

In 1893 he was one of the founding members of the Russian party of Socialist-Revolutionaries in exile and coeditor of its journal. Zhitlowsky was severely shocked by the Kishinev pogroms (1903) and this brought him closer to the movement of Jewish territorialism, which sought territories for autonomous Jewish settlement.

In 1904 he went to the United States and was coeditor of the territorialist socialist publication *Dos Folk*. In a series of lectures on "Jews and Man," he gave his first systematic exposition of the essence of Jewish nationality, describing three main aspects of direction of the Jewish people toward physical labor — especially agriculture; integration with European culture; and the creation of a Yiddish culture. He stressed the fact that language was the basis upon which the cultural life of a people was constructed. The national language of the Jewish people must be Yiddish and this, rather than religion, should serve as its framework.

After a short stay in Europe, during which he was elected to the Second Russian Duma and served as chairman of the Czernowitz Yiddish Conference in 1908, Zhitlowsky returned to New York to edit the Yiddish monthly *Dos Naye Lebn* (1908–1913). In 1909 and 1910 he was active in the establishment of the first radical national school in New York. He joined the Arbeiter Ring ("Workman's Circle") with the object of furthering the cause of Jewish education in Yiddish among workers. In 1914 he spent two months in Palestine, but the opposition he encountered to Yiddish caused him to leave the country and strengthened his opposition to Zionism. However, he subsequently changed this negative attitude and advocated a policy of maximalist Zionism. Zhitlowsky joined the Labor Zionist Poalei Zion movement in 1917 and campaigned for the recruitment of volunteers to the Jewish Legion in World War I. After the 1929 riots in Palestine he reached the conclusion that Zionism was no longer valid, and during the last years of his life expressed his support of the Stalinist regime.

Zhitlowsky's publications include a two-volume work *Die Filosofye, Vos Zi Iz un Vi Zi Hot Zikh Antvikelt* ("The Development of Philosophy," 1910) and *Gezamlte Shriftn* (1912–1919), his collected writings, in ten volumes.

ZINOVIEV, GRIGORI YEVSEYEVICH (1883–1936) Russian communist leader, one of the triumvirate that ruled the Soviet Union after Lenin's death, and first chairman of the Comintern (Communist International). Zinoviev was born Radomyslski in Kirovograd (then Yelizavetgrad) to a family of Jewish bourgeoisie. He joined the Russian Social Democratic party in Switzerland in 1901, and its Bolshevik wing in 1903. He played an active role in the 1905 Saint Petersburg uprising, and was a delegate to the party's congress in Stockholm in 1906. Zinoviev was exiled in 1908, and became one of Lenin's closest collaborators, editing various Bolshevik newspapers and journals, and being elected to the party's central committee in 1912. He and Lenin wrote *Against the Tide*, criticizing World War I and the Social Democratic leaders who supported it.

In April 1917, after the collapse of the tsarist regime, Zinoviev and Lenin traveled in a sealed train across Europe to Russia. Together they went into hiding after the July uprising against the provisional government. In October Zinoviev split with Lenin on the question of the seizure of power, believing that a Bolshevik coup in Russia at that time would lead to foreign intervention and a counterrevolutionary peasant uprising. After the revolution he was opposed to the formation of a one-party government. Nonetheless, he remained a member of the party's central committee, became chairman of the Leningrad (then Petrograd) soviet and party, and in 1922 was appointed to the Politburo.

In 1919 he was made head of the Comintern, founded to promote worldwide communist revolution. In 1924 Zinoviev's name was linked to a letter written to a leader of the British Communist party giving instructions for subversive work to be carried out in the country. The letter was leaked to the British press on the eve of a general election and was used to discredit Labor's policy of improved relations with Soviet Russia. Subsequent research has thrown considerable doubt on the authenticity of the document.

Following Lenin's death in January 1924, Zinoviev joined with Stalin and Kamenev (q.v.) to form the triumvirate that drove Trotsky (q.v.) into political isolation and ruled the country. In 1925 he and Kamenev became leaders of the "new opposition," which argued, similarly to Trotsky, that socialism could not be created in Russia without the support of proletarian revolutions in the West because the country was so economically and culturally backward. This belief contrasted with Stalin's call for the creation of "socialism in one country."

In November 1927 Zinoviev joined with Trotsky in a last bid for political survival by organizing demonstrations in Moscow and Leningrad during celebrations to mark the tenth anniversary of the Revolution. A week later, together with Trotsky, Zinoviev was expelled by the party. In January 1928 he was exiled to Siberia.

In 1936, during Stalin's purges, Zinoviev, along with other former political leaders, was arrested and charged with plotting to overthrow Stalin's government. After public "admissions of guilt," they were all executed.

L. Chester, *The Zinoviev Letter*, 1967.

ZUCKERMAN, YITZHAK (Antek; 1915–1981) A leader of the Zydowska Organizacja Bojowa (ZOB; Jewish Fighting Organization) in Warsaw during World War II. A native of Vilna, Zuckerman became a general secretary of the Dror-he-Halutz Zionist youth movement in 1938, moving to its main offices in Warsaw. Soon after the Germans invaded Poland on September 1, 1939, Zuckerman fled east. In the areas which the Soviet Union annexed, he organized underground Zionist youth cells. In April 1940 he went back to the German-occupied area of Poland to foster clandestine Zionist activities. At this time he and Zivia Lubetkin (q.v.) established a close relationship, and later married.

During the intensive deportations from Warsaw in the summer of 1942, Zuckerman called for the use of force against the Germans. Around the same time, he became a founder and leader of the ZOB. Sent to Cracow on a ZOB mission in December 1942, he was wounded in the leg and barely managed to get back to Warsaw. On January 18, 1943, Zuckerman led an armed clash with the Germans during a deportation round-up. Afterward, in preparation for a larger uprising, he was made commander of one of the three areas into which the ghetto was divided. Just before the revolt of April 19, 1943, began, he was ordered to leave the ghetto and represent the ZOB in "Aryan" Warsaw. During the uprising he tried to obtain weapons for the rebels. As the revolt was suppressed, he formed a team to rescue fighters by way of the sewer system.

When the Polish uprising broke out in Warsaw in August 1944, Zuckerman led a group of Jewish fighters. Upon his liberation in January 1945, Zuckerman and his wife became involved in the Beriha, the movement which tried to bring Jews out of eastern Europe and into Palestine. He went to Palestine in 1947 and was one of the founders of the Ghetto Fighters' Kibbutz and its museum.

Z. Lubetkin, *In the Days of Destruction and Revolt*, 1981.

ZUKOR, ADOLPH (1873–1976) U.S. film executive. Born in Ricse, Hungary, Zukor immigrated to the United States in 1888. Starting off by sweeping floors, he saved and studied until he had become the junior partner in a furrier's establishment. Initial interest in motion pictures coincided with a brief partnership with another furrier, Marcus Loew, who was also destined to found an entertainment empire. In 1903 the two first invested in the penny arcades of the day and this prosperous enterprise gave birth to the Loew Company, of which Zukor was treasurer. Zukor's daring in importing Sarah Bernhardt's [q.v.] feature-length *Queen Elizabeth* in 1912 led to the foundation, in partnership with Daniel Frohman, of Famous Players in Famous Plays.

With Mary Pickford as his major star, Zukor expanded his business rapidly, merging with Jesse L. Lasky's [q.v.] company in 1916 and shortly thereafter taking over the Paramount distribution company. Paramount gave its name to the new giant, the most powerful studio of the time. Zukor, in addition to having backed the winning side in the legal battle between the independents and the monopolistic but doomed Motion Picture Patents Company, went on to pioneer and improve subsequently standard industry practices such as block-booking, that guaranteed sale of lesser studio product to exhibitors eager to screen the cream of the crop.

Zukor consolidated his position further by taking over the Barney Balaban (q.v.) and Katz theater chain, thereby establishing himself as a force in every area of the industry. Paramount was, however, badly hit by the depression, and although

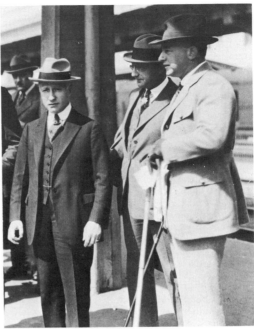

Adolph Zukor (left) with Jesse Lasky and Cecil B. De Mille.

Zukor survived the reorganization of the early 1930s, his new post as chairman of the board represented a loss of control, which he was partially to regain in 1936 when Barney Balaban was installed as company president. Zukor's remarkable longevity was more than biological; he was the only founder of a major studio to remain its titular head for well over half a century and almost to the end of his life, he continued to attend Paramount board meetings. His hundredth birthday in 1973 was the occasion for a major Hollywood celebration; Zukor commented "If I had known I was going to live this long, I would have taken better care of myself."

W. Urwin, *The House that Shadows Built*, 1928.
A. Zukor with D. Kramer, *The Public Is Never Wrong*, 1953.

ZUNZ, LEOPOLD (1794–1886) Scholar; one of the pioneers of scientific Jewish studies. He was born in Detmold, in the Rhine province of Germany, to a poor family. Orphaned at an early age, he was raised at an institution for poor Jewish children in Wolfenbüttel, where the major subject taught was Talmud. He showed his liberal inclinations early by secretly studying Hebrew grammar with a fellow-pupil, Marcus Jost, who was to become a noted historian. His outstanding abilities brought him to the local high school and to the University of Berlin, where he received training in methodical, scientific research. His doctorate, from the University of Halle, was a survey of rabbinic literature, classified by period.

His first employment was as a lay preacher for Reform congregations. In 1819 he was a cofounder of the Society for Jewish Culture and Science, whose aim was to master Jewish literature and organize it according to world literary standards. The ambitious project (one of its members was Heinrich Heine [q.v.]) only lasted a few years but it paved the way for more successful developments. In 1823 Zunz became editor of the *Zeitschrift für die Wissenschaft des Judentums* ("Journal for Jewish Science"), an outstanding journal of Jewish studies. He himself published many important studies in its pages including a biography of Rashi (q.v.).

One of the Reform temples at which Zunz had preached in German had been closed by the king of Prussia on the grounds that prayer and preaching in the vernacular were contrary to Jewish tradition. To prove the inaccuracy of this view, Zunz published one of his greatest works, *Sermons of the Jews* (1832), which demonstrated the antiquity not only of preaching itself but of preaching in the vernacular. When another royal order in 1836 forbade Jews to take German first names, Zunz wrote another study to show that Jews had always used foreign names.

From 1825 to 1829 he headed a Sunday school. After a period as rabbi in the Prague Reform Synagogue, he was appointed director of the Berlin Jewish Teachers' Seminary in 1840. He modified his earlier views on Reform Judaism, maintaining that traditional rituals and customs that were being rejected by the Reform must be retained as they give Judaism its distinctiveness.

Zunz pioneered in his scientific studies of Jewish history and literature. He wrote many studies, shaping the methodology and research tools that were to guide future Jewish scholarship, and was known as "father of Jewish studies in the 19th century." One of his works on Jewish sacred poetry covered a millennium and identified 6,000 poems and over 1,000 poets. He tutored a group of outstanding students who carried on and expanded his work.

S. Schechter, *Studies in Judaism*, third series, 1924.
L. Wallach, *Liberty and Letters: The Thoughts of Leopold Zunz*, 1959.

ZWEIG, ARNOLD (1887–1968) German novelist, playwright, and essayist. Born in Glogau, Lower Silesia, he completed his university education in the same year that his first volume of stories (*The Klopfer Family*, 1911) appeared. It attracted less attention than his *Claudia* (1912), but gave an early indication of the author's lifelong interest in Jewish themes and issues. Zweig was to publish many volumes of fiction, drama, and critical essays, all marked by an elegant style, descriptive power, psychological penetration, and a fine sense of irony. His prize-winning drama, *Ritualmord in Ungarn* ("Ritual Murder in Hungary," 1914), was concerned with the Tisza-Eszlár bloodlibel case of 1882.

Having seen action on the western front in Serbia during World War I, Zweig became an ardent pacifist. His social and political views found expression in a long series of novels and short stories, two outstanding examples being *The Case of Sergeant Grischa* (1927) and *Education before Verdun* (1935). A scathing attack on Prussian militarism and wartime miscarriage of justice, *Grischa* was acclaimed the best novel of its kind so far in German and became an international best-seller.

As a freelance writer in Berlin (1923–1933), Zweig witnessed the growth of Nazism, which made him — unlike most other German Jewish literary figures of the 1920s — an active Zionist. He foresaw Palestine's emergence as a dynamic center of Jewish national and cultural renewal, and served for a time as editor of the German Zionist Federation's biweekly, *Jüdische Rundschau*. In the course of a decade he wrote *Die Umkehr* ("Return of the Apostate," 1925), a play ironically surveying a converted Jew's preferment in the Church; *Caliban* (1927), essays dealing with anti-Semitism; and *De Vriendt Goes Home* (1932), a novel based on the life and death of Jacob Israel de Haan (q.v.).

Immediately upon Hitler's appointment as chancellor in 1933, Zweig left for Palestine and settled in Haifa. Over the next fifteen years, he wrote many more works in German. *Bilanz der deutschen Judenheit* ("Insulted and Exiled," 1934) comprised essays on the German Jewish tragedy; *Bonaparte in Jaffa* (1939) was a historical drama; and *The Axe of Wandsbeck* (1947), a novel that gave rise to a motion picture, evoked the horrors of the Third Reich. Meanwhile, however, Zweig's Labor Zionism had been shattered by Arab-Jewish conflict in Palestine, and he now felt drawn toward communism.

In October 1948 Arnold Zweig made his "return journey" to East Berlin, where the communist GDR authorities gave him a triumphal reception. He later served as president of the East German Academy of Arts (1950–1953) and was awarded the Lenin Peace Prize in 1958. His subsequent writing, however, had only limited impact. Zweig's attitude toward Zionism and Israel seems to have undergone a further change in his last years. After the Six-Day War of 1967, he refused to toe the party line when asked to join other East German intellectuals in signing an anti-Israel declaration.

G. Salamon, *Arnold Zweig*, 1975.

ZWEIG, STEFAN (1881–1942) Austrian poet, dramatist, narrator, essayist, and biographer. Born in Vienna, the son of a wealthy industrialist, he was able to devote his entire life to literature. Theodor Herzl (q.v.), feuilletonist of Vienna's *Neue Freie Presse*, discovered the talent of the nineteen-year-old Zweig, accepted his first sketches for publication, and tried, in vain, to win him to the Zionist cause. When he was twenty, Zweig's first slender volume of poems, *Silberne Saite* (1901) appeared. Until his mid-thirties, he remained under the influence of "Young Vienna," the impressionistic literary circle that rose to prominence in the *fin-de-siècle* decade, whose most gifted members were Arthur Schnitzler (q.v.), Hugo von Hofmannsthal, and Richard Beer-Hofmann (q.v.).

After obtaining his doctorate in Romance literature, he traveled through various European countries and came primarily under French influence. While in the circle of the Belgian poet, Emile Verhaeren, he met Europe's literary elite, translated Verhaeren's poems into German, and published his biography in 1910.

Extending his travels to other continents, he became more cosmopolitan in his outlook. Not wanting to confine himself to Austrian or Jewish nationalism, he spoke of himself as a "Good European" and, during World War I, joined Romain Rolland and Henri Barbusse in advocating pacifism. His main contribution was his antiwar tragedy *Jeremias* (1917), staged in Zurich in 1918. Its title-hero, is the Hebrew prophet Jeremiah, reviled when he preached nonresistance rather than armed revolt against the Babylonian overlords. However, he became the great comforter of his people after the failure of the revolt.

In 1919 Zweig settled in Salzburg and entered upon his happiest and most productive years. His efforts to bring to German readers a better understanding of their French neighbors were continued in his biographies of Romain Rolland, Stendhal, Joseph Fouché, and Marie Antoinette. He also wrote biographies of Mary, queen of Scots, Magellan, and Amerigo Vespucci.

In the 1920s, three volumes of biographic essays were completed, each volume containing a triad of figures with some common denominators (Balzac, Dickens, and Dostoievsky; Hölderlin, Kleist, and Nietzsche; Casanova, Stendhal, and Tolstoy), all nine of whom he regarded as intellectual architects of the world. He appraised their achievements

Stephan Zweig stamp issued by Austria, November 1981.

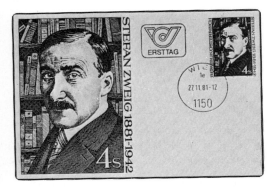

> ● The eternal secret of all great art, indeed of every mortal achievement is concentration.
> ● Nine-tenths of what the world celebrated as Viennese culture at the turn of the century was promoted and created by Viennese Jewry.
> ● History has not time to be just. She keeps her eyes fixed on the victorious and leaves the vanquished in the shadows.
>
> **Stefan Zweig**

sympathetically even though they represented diverse peoples, cultures, and generations. In the biographic volume, *Erasmus of Rotterdam* (1934), his own identification with the views of the Renaissance humanist emerges. His novel, *Beware of Pity* (1939), is a moving psychological study of a crippled girl. Like his story, *Letters to an Unknown Woman*, and several others of his works, it was made into a film.

Zweig's mature narratives, included in *Angst* (1920), *Amok* (1922), and *Conflicts* (1926), as well as the historical miniatures of *The Tide of Fortune* (1927), heightened his popularity. His rewriting of Ben Jonson's *Volpone* (1926) was a theatrical success in New York no less than on European stages.

In 1933 Zweig's humanistic ideal was trampled by Nazi totalitarianism. When the Nazi deluge also overran Austria in 1938, he found himself a refugee. For several years England welcomed him, then the United States, and finally Brazil. In his last years he was assailed by depression and pessimism. He tried to find his way back to ancestral roots and immersed himself in Jewish themes. His sad affirmation of Jewishness found expression in the novelette *The Buried Candelabrum* (1934), about the fate of the Temple candelabrum when taken into exile, and in his autobiography *The World of Yesterday*, completed in 1942, when the Nazi avalanche reached its crest. Despair then overtook him and led to his suicide in Petropolis, near Rio de Janeiro.

Zweig left a rich heritage as a writer of short stories that touched on abnormal psychic states, as a sensitive critic whose essays on literary masters showed profound insight and exceptional tolerance of their failings, as a biographer who restored to life legendary figures, as a humanitarian, and as a pacifist, a citizen of the world, and a liberal of international repute.

H. Arens, *Stefan Zweig*, 1950.

D. A. Prater, *European of Yesterday; A Biography of Stefan Zweig*, 1972.

J. Romain, *Stefan Zweig; Great European*, 1941.

ACKNOWLEDGMENTS

The Publishers have attempted to observe the legal requirements with respect to copyright. However, in view of the large number of illustrations included in this volume, the Publishers wish to apologize in advance for any involuntary omission or error and invite persons or bodies concerned to write to the Publishers.

p.9 The British Library; p.13 Royal Library, Copenhagen; p.14 Diaspora Museum; p.17 Courtesy G.Wigoder; p.19 Photo Reportagebild, Stockholm; p.20 CZA; p.21 British Museum; p.25 Courtesy John Rylands University Library, University of Manchester; p.25 Central Zionist Archives, Jerusalem; pp.26,29 JNUL Schwadron collection; pp.30,31 Central Zionist Archives, Jerusalem; p.32 Courtesy YIVO, New York; pp.33,35 Diaspora Museum; p.37 JNUL Schawdron collection; p.39 From "Isaac Babel, The Lonely Years" by N.Babel, Farrar and Strauss, 1964; p.40 Courtesy Leo Baeck Institute, Jerusalem; p.42 Dr. Leron collection; pp.46,47 Wingate Institute for Physical Education and sport; p.48 Governement Press Office, Jerusalem; p.51 The Jewish Chronicle, London; p.53 CZA; p.55 Government Press Office; p.60 H.Tryster collection; p.62 Photo Schweig; p.61 Central Zionist Archives, Jerusalem; pp.63,67 Diaspora Museum; p.64 Freudenberg collection, New York; p.66 Diaspora Museum/Photo Mary Black; p.68 GPO; p.70 Central Zionist Archives, Jerusalem; p.76 Press Service, French Embassy, New York; p.78 Copenhagen University; p.81 JNUL Schawdron collection; p.82,84 Diaspora Museum/Photo Sweeny, Dublin; p.85 Central Zionist Archives, Jerusalem; p.88 Government Press Office; p.91 H.Tryster collection; p.92 Photo New York Times; p.93 Israel Museum Jerusalem/Photo IMJ; p.95 Government Press Office; pp.98,107 Diaspora Museum; p.101 Government Press Office; p.112 Museum for Music and Ethnography Haifa; p.114 Government Press Office; p.121 Central Zionist Archives; pp.123,126 Diaspora Museum; p.125 Copyright SPADEM 1990; p.127 JNUL Schwadron collection; p.129 National Film Archive, London/Courtesy H.Tryster; p.132 Israel Museum Jerusalem/Photo Hillel Burger; p.133 JNUL Schwadron collection; p.137 Diaspora Museum; p.138 Government Press Office; p.139 JNUL Schwadron collection; p.144 Leo Baeck Institute, New York; p.146 JNUL Schwadron collection; p.149 AAFF/AFS, Amsterdam; p.153 Gleystone Press Agency Ltd. London; p.159 Israel Museum Jerusalem/Photo IMJ-D.Harris; p.160 National Film Archive London/Courtesy H.Tryster; p.164 Diaspora Museum/G.D.Hacket, New York; p.169 Sun Magazine; p.170 JNUL Schawdron collection; p.177 American Jewish Archives, Cincinnati; p.178 New York Public Library, Otto F.Hess collection; p.183 Jewish Publication Society, Philadelphia; p.183 UPI; p.186 Guggenheim Brothers; p.187 Bibliotheque Nationale, Paris; p.189 Jerusalem Post; p.195 Heinrich Heine Institute, Dusseldorf; pp.199,200 CZA; p.207 Israel Museum Jerusalem/Photo IMJ-D.Harris; p.209 Diaspora Museum; p.214 From "Houdini The Man Who Walked Through Walls" by W.L.Gresham, London 1960; p.215 Courtesy Cinematheque Jerusalem/Photo D.Harris; p.216 Israel Museum Jerusalem; p.217 Diaspora Museum; p.222 Israel Museum Jerusalem collections/Photo IMJ-D.Harris; p.229 YIVO, New York; p.231 Wolfson Museum Hechal Shlomo, Jerusalem/Photo D.Harris; p.235 Diaspora Museum; p.239 Warner Brothers Inc/Courtesy H.Tryster; p.243 Vatican Library; p.245 Library of the Jewish Theological Seminary, New York; pp.249,250 Diaspora Museum; p.252 JNUL Schwadron collection; p.259 Governement Press Office; p.259 Courtesy H.Tryster; p.267 Central Zionist Archives, Jerusalem; p.269 YIVO; p.270 National Film Archive, London/H.Tryster collection; p.272 Governement Press Office; pp.275, 281,282 Diaspora Museum; p.278 National Film Archive, London/Courtesy H.Tryster; p.283 From "Landowska on Music" by Denise Restout (Stein and Day New York, 1969); p.285 H.Tryster collection; p.287 Lasker-Schuler Archives, Jerusalem; p.289 JNUL Schwadron collection; p.295 Wingate Institute for Physical Education and Sport; p.296 H.Tryster collection; p.300 American Jewish Archives, Cincinnati; p.304 Diaspora Museum; p.309 H.Tryster collection; p.310 Courtesy G.Wigoder; pp.314,318 Diaspora Museum; p.317, From "Dissenter in Zion" by Arthur A.Goren, Harvard University Press 1982; pp.319,323 JNUL Schwadron collection; p.321 American Jewish Archives, Cincinnati; p.328 Diaspora Museum; p.331 H.Tryster collection; p.333 Courtesy G.Wigoder; p.337 GPO; pp.340,341 Diaspora Museum; p.342 Zentralbibliotek, Zurich; p.344 Diaspora Museum; p.349 Central Archives for the History of the Jewish People, Hebrew University; p.352 JNUL Schwadron collection; p.354 From "Famous Jewish Lives" by John R.Gilbert, Hamlyn, 1970; p.358 From "Sir Moses Montefiore" by A.Blond, Muller Blond and White, London, 1984; p.362 Israel Museum Jerusalem/Photo IMJ- Hiller Burger; p.364 National Film Archive, London/H.Tryster collection; p.368 Israel Museum Jerusalem/Photo IMJ D.Harris; p.373 Pace Gallery, New York/Photo G.Calamari; p.375 American Jewish Historical Society, Waltham, Mass; p.376 Central Zionist Archives, Jerusalem; pp.380,384 Diaspora Museum, Tel Aviv; pp.382,385 JNUL Schwadron collection; p.386 Courtesy Tel Aviv Museum and Madan A. Tamir, Paris; p.386 Copyright SPADEM 1991; p.390 From "Boris Pasternak" by Peter Levi, Hutchinson Pub. 1990; p.394 YIVO, New York; p.398 Diaspora Museum, Tel Aviv; p.402 Steven Spielberg Jewish Film Archives, Hebrew Univesity; p.404 Library of Congress, Washington; p.406 JNUL Schwadron collection; p.409 The Judaic Heritage Society, New York; pp.410,415 Diaspora Museum, Tel Aviv; p.416 NASA; p.421 H.Tryster collection; p.423 Schlesinger Library, Radcliff College, Cambridge, Mass.; p.427 Courtesy Gabriel Sivan; p.428 From "The Spirit of the Ghetto" by S.H.Hapgood, Cambridge, Mass. 1967; p.432 Wingate Institue for Physical Education and Sport; p.434 From "Dear Lord Rothschild" by Miriam Rothschild, Balaban Publishers, 1983; p.440 Governement Press Office; p.444 Photo Reportagebild, Stockholm; p.451 Central Zionist Archivles Jerusalem; p.459 Jewish Theological Seminary; p.462 Montefiore Medical Center, New York; p.465 JNUL Schwadron collection; p.469 National Air and Space Museum, Washington; p.470 H.Tryster collection; p.472 Diaspora Museum, Tel Aviv; p. 473 Teddy Kollek collection/Photo D.Harris; p.474 Museum of Modern Art, New York; p.474 Central Zionist Archives Jerusalem; p.491 From "Shinwell Talking" by J.Doxat, Quiller Press; p.492,495 Israel Museum Jerusalem/Photo IMJ D.Harris; pp.496,597 Diaspora Museum, Tel Aviv; p.505 JNUL Schwadron collection; pp.507, 518 American Jewish Archives, Cincinnati; pp.508,511 H.Tryster collection p.512 Governement Press Office; p.515 Ministry of Health, Jerusalem; p.521 "From the Secret Lives of Trebitsch Lincoln" by B. Wassertein, Yale University 1988; p.525 Central Zionist Archives; p.530 From "Tristan Tzara" G.Haldas and R.Lacote, 1952; p.529 American Jewish Archive Cincinnati; p.536 Wolfson Museum Hechal Shlomo; pp.542,545 Diaspora Museum Tel Aviv; p.543 Tryster collection; p.544 Leo Baeck Institue New York; p.548 Central Zionist Archives; p.549 From "The Letters and Papers of Chaim Weizmann" Oxford University Press 1972; p.553 JNUL Schwadron collection; p.554 UPI New York; pp.557,572 Courtesy G.Wigoder; p.560 National Archive Washington/Photo Diaspora Museum; p.565 H.Tryster collection.

Typesetting: Yael Kaplan Typesetting Ltd.; *Printing:* E. Lewin-Epstein Ltd.; *Binding:* Peli Printing Works Ltd.; *Printing coordinator:* Avinoam Gat